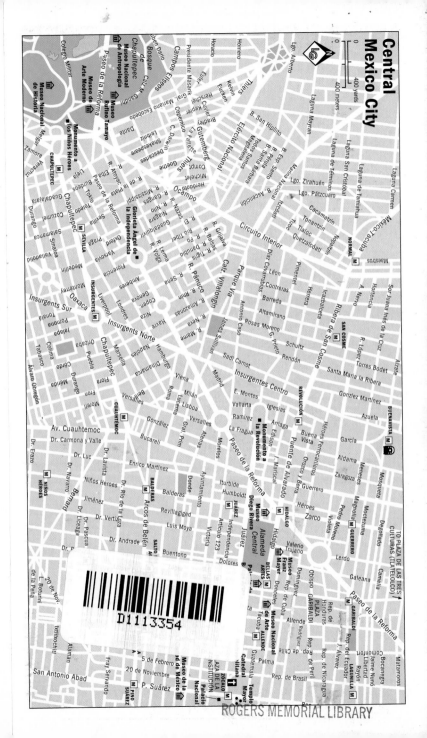

Central Mexico City

Mexico City Metro

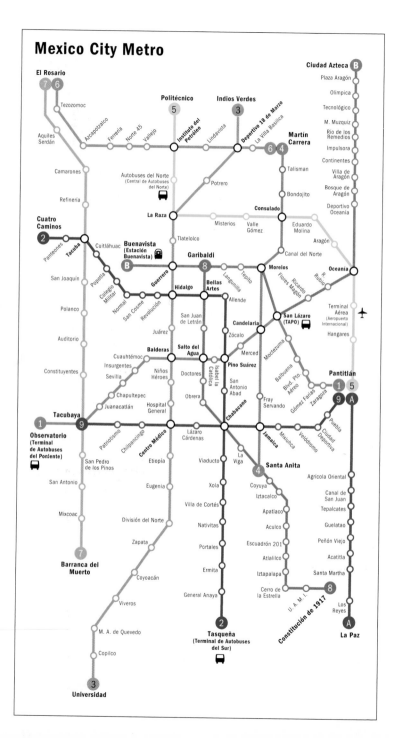

ROGERS MEMORIAL LIBRARY

LET'S GO

■ THE RESOURCE FOR THE INDEPENDENT TRAVELER

"The guides are aimed not only at young budget travelers but at the indepedent traveler; a sort of streetwise cookbook for traveling alone."

—The New York Times

"Unbeatable; good sight-seeing advice; up-to-date info on restaurants, hotels, and inns; a commitment to money-saving travel; and a wry style that brightens nearly every page."

—The Washington Post

"Lighthearted and sophisticated, informative and fun to read. [Let's Go] helps the novice traveler navigate like a knowledgeable old hand."

—Atlanta Journal-Constitution

"A world-wise traveling companion—always ready with friendly advice and helpful hints, all sprinkled with a bit of wit."

—The Philadelphia Inquirer

■ THE BEST TRAVEL BARGAINS IN YOUR PRICE RANGE

"All the dirt, dirt cheap."

—People

"Anything you need to know about budget traveling is detailed in this book."

—The Chicago Sun-Times

"Let's Go follows the creed that you don't have to toss your life's savings to the wind to travel—unless you want to."

—The Salt Lake Tribune

■ REAL ADVICE FOR REAL EXPERIENCES

"The writers seem to have experienced every rooster-packed bus and lunar-surfaced mattress about which they write."

—The New York Times

"A guide should tell you what to expect from a destination. Here Let's Go shines."

—The Chicago Tribune

"[Let's Go's] devoted updaters really walk the walk (and thumb the ride, and trek the trail). Learn how to fish, haggle, find work—anywhere."

—Food & Wine

LET'S GO PUBLICATIONS

TRAVEL GUIDES

Alaska 1st edition **NEW TITLE**
Australia 2004
Austria & Switzerland 2004
Brazil 1st edition **NEW TITLE**
Britain & Ireland 2004
California 2004
Central America 8th edition
Chile 1st edition
China 4th edition
Costa Rica 1st edition
Eastern Europe 2004
Egypt 2nd edition
Europe 2004
France 2004
Germany 2004
Greece 2004
Hawaii 2004
India & Nepal 8th edition
Ireland 2004
Israel 4th edition
Italy 2004
Japan 1st edition **NEW TITLE**
Mexico 20th edition
Middle East 4th edition
New Zealand 6th edition
Pacific Northwest 1st edition **NEW TITLE**
Peru, Ecuador & Bolivia 3rd edition
Puerto Rico 1st edition **NEW TITLE**
South Africa 5th edition
Southeast Asia 8th edition
Southwest USA 3rd edition
Spain & Portugal 2004
Thailand 1st edition
Turkey 5th edition
USA 2004
Western Europe 2004

CITY GUIDES

Amsterdam 3rd edition
Barcelona 3rd edition
Boston 4th edition
London 2004
New York City 2004
Paris 2004
Rome 12th edition
San Francisco 4th edition
Washington, D.C. 13th editio

MAP GUIDES

Amsterdam
Berlin
Boston
Chicago
Dublin
Florence
Hong Kong
London
Los Angeles
Madrid
New Orleans
New York City
Paris
Prague
Rome
San Francisco
Seattle
Sydney
Venice
Washington, D.C.

COMING SOON:
Road Trip USA

LET'S GO

MEXICO

ANTHONY GABRIELE EDITOR
ALEJANDRO MARES ASSOCIATE EDITOR
R. KANG-XING JIN ASSOCIATE EDITOR

RESEARCHER-WRITERS
LEANNA BOYCHENKO
PETER R. BRYCE
HUNTER ANTHONY MAATS
EMILY MATCHAR
NORA BRENNAN MORRISON
FRANCISCO A. ROBLES
JULIE DIMOND ROSENBERG
JON STAINSBY

EVAN HUDSON MAP EDITOR
SARAH ROBINSON MANAGING EDITOR

ST. MARTIN'S PRESS  NEW YORK

Maps by David Lindroth copyright © 2004 by St. Martin's Press.

Distributed outside the USA and Canada by Macmillan.

ISBN: 0-312-32008-6

First edition
10 9 8 7 6 5 4 3 2 1

Let's Go: Mexico is written by Let's Go Publications, 67 Mount Auburn Street, Cambridge, MA 02138, USA.

CONTENTS

RESEARCHER-WRITERS

Leanna Boychenko
Mexico City

The loveliest *güera* ever to steal the hearts of Mexico's capital—all the men said so—swept us away with a big smile and an expansive vocabulary. Though their comparative statures would suggest otherwise, el D.F. was no match for this intrepid R-W; she outdid herself with each successive batch of copy, and played mother to a house full of cats. And she *still* found the time to send us some fine literature from the road; her Classics professors would be proud.

Peter R. Bryce
Gulf Coast

Peter attacked Mexico like a true ninja: in and out before anyone knew it happened. The man with the dulcet tones found a second home in Xalapa, but thankfully for us, he pushed onward, sending back stacks upon stacks of delightful features and conscientiously written copy. Returning to our office as a proofer, Peter's attention to detail was invaluable; during breaks, he delighted with tales of Xalapa and sips of Papantla's oh-so-smooth vanilla liqueur.

Hunter Anthony Maats
Northwest Mexico

This famed veteran researcher barely had time to fly back from Italy before heading to Northwest Mexico. Our very own Nancy Drew, Hunter stuck his nose everywhere it didn't belong, and discovered the secret of Mexico in the process. That secret? *Pozole.* Unsurprisingly, our Saudi-French-Dutchman was right at home in Mexico. And if we ever thought his talents ended with writing, we recant: as many Mexicans could attest, he's mastered chemistry, too.

Emily Matchar
Southern Pacific Coast and Chiapas

The girl with the wry smile turned down our offer of a machete and headed to Chiapas armed with her rapier wit instead. She proved her ninja status by handling two thefts with grace and the occasional expletive, and this take-no-prisoners attitude made for a great read. It seems that Mexico itself wasn't enough for her: this Advocate writer kept us all continually amazed at her adventures with balloon hats, volcano skiing, and certain enemy islands.

Nora Brennan Morrison
Northeast Mexico

The most talented of veteran globe-trotters, Nora took time from her world tour to grace us with four weeks of unadulterated copy bliss. With unmatched enthusiasm and impeccable punctuation, this American historian hit the northeast where it hurt, delivering the dirt on everything from the *Frontera Violenta* to Monterrey's underground electronica scene. In the end, she rocked her route like *Norteño*, and made us all wish we had her just a little bit longer.

Francisco A. Robles
Central Mexico, Pacific Coast

An avid boxer, Francisco used his ingenuity and inner toughness to tear through his copy after nearly being KO'd by a disastrous injury amid a whirling maelstrom midway through his route. Undeterred, Frisco made full use of his Mexican heritage and sent back copy reflecting his unique perspective. We could always count on his concise, no-nonsense writing to bring a smile to our faces.

Julie Dimond Rosenberg
Yucatán

We're not in Dixie anymore. Hailing from Atlanta, Julie eagerly plunged into one of Mexico's most varied routes. The Cancún Killer flew into the spring break capital of the world and, after giving it what for, took her anthropology book learning to the next level, braving storms and spotty transportation to explore the mysteries of the Yucatán Maya. In the end, her excitement yielded the most new coverage, as she relentlessly pursued rising ecotourism opportunities.

Jon Stainsby
Baja California

Navigating fearlessly through all manner of Baja's suspect carriageways, Jon made short shrift of the sand-swept tarmac, shredding the occasional rental car on the way. The peninsula charmed even this discriminating British gentleman, who can now add its sand-traps and border police to his storied travel résumé, which includes a teaching residency in Cuba. Horn in hand, Jon was always quite the source of witty, comprehensive copy—nary a detail escaped his keen eye.

CONTRIBUTING WRITERS

Isaac Campos is a Ph.D. candidate at Harvard University in Latin American history, with a focus on Mexico. He is writing a dissertation on Mexican social and cultural history during the Porfiriato and has been funded for research on the rise of prohibitionist ideas on drugs in Mexico.

Derek Glanz was the editor of *Let's Go: Spain & Portugal 1998*. He is now a freelance baseball writer contributing regularly to St. Louis Cardinals' *Gameday Magazine*. He has written for *Baseball America* and *Baseball Weekly* and appeared as a guest analyst on ESPN Radio and Colombia's Telecartagena.

ACKNOWLEDGMENTS

LET'S GO

ANTHONY: Dan Howe, Karol Rudy, and Mary Bob Straub—so many important things wouldn't have been possible without you. Jandro and KX, thank you, not just for incredible work and companionship every step of the way, but for the humor without which I would have been lost. Sarah, oh Sarah, the Hong Kong Phooey to my Ho Chi Minh, my gratitude is almost inexpressible. You are brilliant, irrepressible, a bit off, and overwhelmingly supportive; you are my ideal ninja, Sarah. Evansonic, my dark half, you give my life direction; thanks for all your toil. To all the amazing folks on the right, these books would be nothing without you.
Megan, thanks for taking a chance on me, and for saving my sanity on the telephone. J, you saved more than my sanity, and I never thanked you enough.
My grateful appreciation to the cast of 3 Leonard, to my friends and my family, and to Bruce from Pucallpa. To M.

ALEJANDRO: David, Jane, Gabriel, and the rest of the family, without whom I wouldn't be here for reasons too numerous to elaborate. Kate, you've been at the heart of so much that I've done in the last two years. All the 10men—Zoe, Alex, Sab, Soph, Nat, HJ, Als, Samuel, and LiLi. Anthony, who took me in with Titus and only needed two years to trust me with responsibility; KX, juggler of blocks and books; Evan, your work inspired my own. Scrobs, you're amazing for endless proofing and for being so understanding through the Nintendo incident. Those I haven't seen in a while—let's do lunch.

KANG-XING: A and J, my beloved bookmates, thank you for making this summer absolutely incredible and for the introduction to the wonders of obsolete technology. Sarah, your optimism and smile always brighten my day. And of course, no book would be complete without marvelous Evan. Thanks to my amazing podmates across the Atlantic, Catherine and Katie. Grandmaster Matt, thanks for the always-welcome entertainment. Mark, Jen, Ali, Jim, Jess, friends, and parents, thanks for the support.

EVAN: AKA, a.k.a. Anthony, Kang-Xing, and Alejandro, each of you is the man; together, you are the men. Thanks for the lessons in Kung Fu, football, and accent placements in farmacia. Sarah, Marathon Woman, I still owe you one.

Editor: Anthony Gabriele
Associate Editors: Alejandro Mares, R. Kang-Xing Jin
Managing Editor: Sarah Robinson
Map Editor: Evan Hudson
Typesetter: Chris Clayton

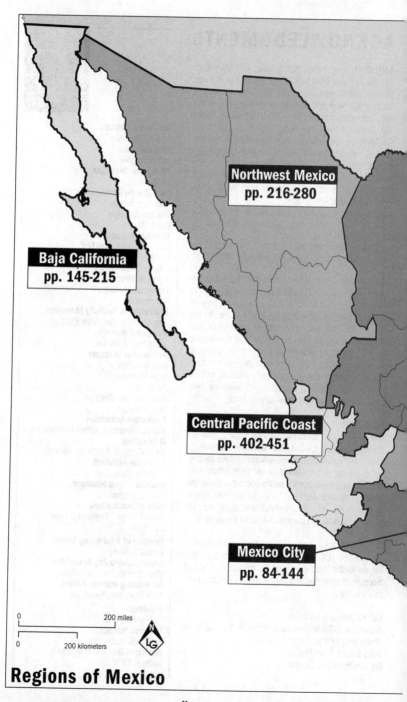

Northwest Mexico
pp. 216-280

Baja California
pp. 145-215

Central Pacific Coast
pp. 402-451

Mexico City
pp. 84-144

0   200 miles

0   200 kilometers

N

LG

Regions of Mexico

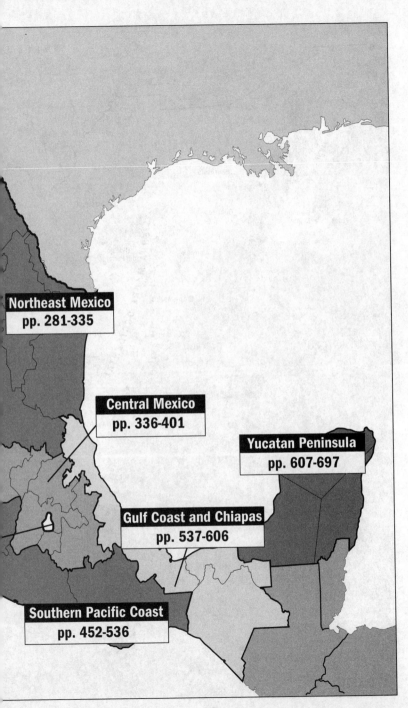

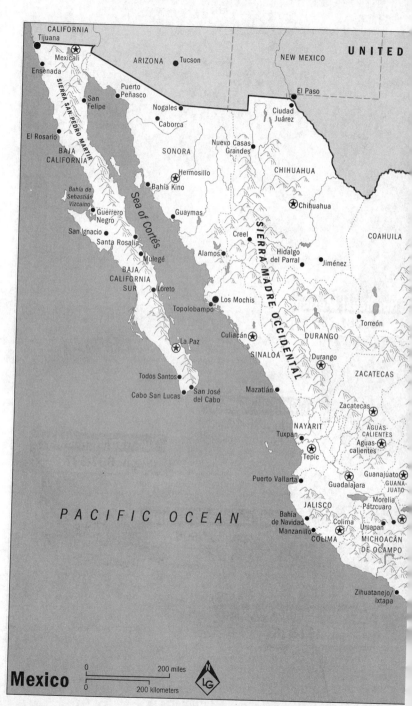

Mexico

0   200 miles

0   200 kilometers

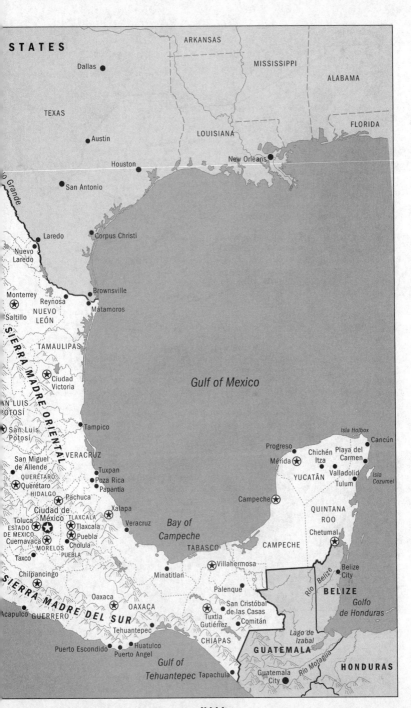

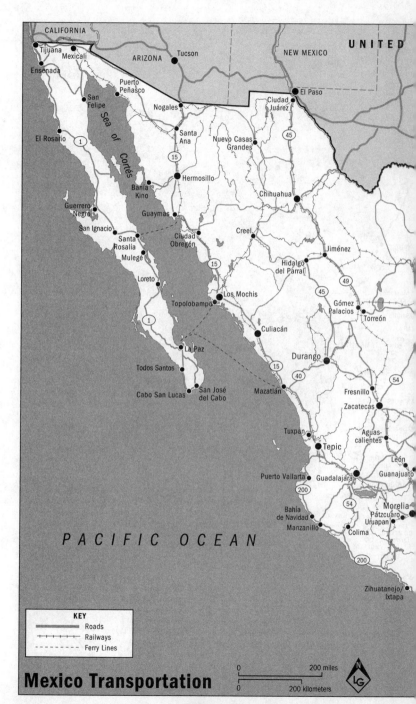

Mexico Transportation

KEY
Roads
Railways
Ferry Lines

0   200 miles
0   200 kilometers

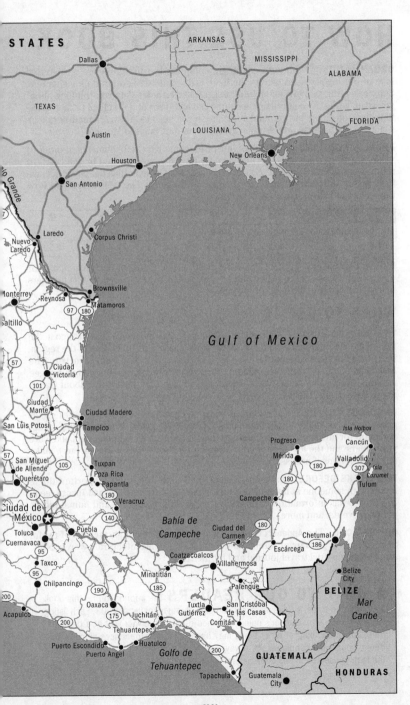

HOW TO USE THIS BOOK

ORGANIZATION. The book's coverage, comprised of the diligence, sweat, and love of our eight researchers in the field, is divided by region into nine chapters. Supplementing this invaluable info, **Suggested Itineraries** gets you thinking about your trip, while the cultural crash course **Life and Times** and practical primer **Essentials** give you all the background information you need to know. **Alternatives to Tourism** jump-starts those interested in giving something back to Mexico.

PRICE RANGES AND RANKINGS. Our researchers list establishments in order of value, starting with the best. Our absolute favorites are denoted by the Let's Go thumbs-up (👍). Since the best value does not always mean the cheapest price, we have incorporated a system of price ranges in the guide. The table below lists how prices fall within each bracket.

MEXICO	❶	❷	❸	❹	❺
ACCOMMODATIONS	< 100 pesos	100-149	150-199	200-249	> 249
FOOD	< 15	15-24	25-39	40-59	> 59

PHONE CODES AND TELEPHONE NUMBERS. Area codes for each region appear opposite the name of the region and are denoted by the ☎ symbol. Phone numbers in text are also preceded by the ☎ symbol.

WHEN TO USE IT

TWO MONTHS BEFORE. Alternatives to Tourism might give you a reason to go in the first place, and the first chapter, **Discover Mexico**, contains highlights of the region, including **Suggested Itineraries** (see p. 4) that can help you plan your trip. The **Essentials** (see p. 7) section contains practical information on planning a budget, making reservations, renewing a passport, and has other useful tips about traveling in Mexico specifically.

ONE MONTH BEFORE. Take care of insurance, and write down a list of emergency numbers and hotlines. Make a list of packing essentials (see **Packing**, p. 22) and shop for anything you are missing. Read through the coverage and make sure you understand the logistics of your itinerary (catching trains, ferries, etc.). Make any reservations if necessary.

TWO WEEKS BEFORE. Leave an itinerary and a photocopy of important documents with someone at home. Take some time to peruse the **Life and Times** (see p. 57), which has information on Mexico's history, culture, flora and fauna, recent political events, and more.

ON THE ROAD. The **Appendix** contains handy **conversions**, a **phrasebook** of useful Spanish, and a **glossary** of foreign and technical (e.g. architectural) words. Now, arm yourself with a travel journal and hit the road.

A NOTE TO OUR READERS The information for this book was gathered by *Let's Go* researchers from May through August of 2003. Each listing is based on one researcher's opinion, formed during his or her visit at a particular time. Those traveling at other times may have different experiences since prices, dates, hours, and conditions are always subject to change. You are urged to check the facts presented in this book beforehand to avoid inconvenience and surprises.

ABOUT LET'S GO

GUIDES FOR THE INDEPENDENT TRAVELER

Budget travel is more than a vacation. At *Let's Go*, we see every trip as the chance of a lifetime. If your dream is to grab a knapsack and a machete and forge through the jungles of Brazil, we can take you there. Or, if you'd rather enjoy the Riviera sun at a beachside cafe, we'll set you a table. If you know what you're doing, you can have any experience you want—whether it's camping among lions or sampling Tuscan desserts—without maxing out your credit card. We'll show you just how far your coins can go, and prove that the greatest limitation on your adventure is not your wallet, but your imagination. That said, we understand that you may want the occasional indulgence after a week of hostels and kebab stands, so we've added "Big Splurges" to let you know which establishments are worth those extra euros, as well as price ranges to help you quickly determine whether an accommo-dation or restaurant will break the bank. While we may have diversified, our emphasis will always be on finding the best values for your budget, giving you all the info you need to spend six days in London or six months in Tasmania.

BEYOND THE TOURIST EXPERIENCE

We write for travelers who know there's more to a vacation than riding double-deckers with tourists. Our researchers give you the heads-up on both world-renowned and lesser-known attractions, on the best local eats and the hottest nightclub beats. In our travels, we talk to everybody; we provide a snapshot of real life in the places you visit with our sidebars on topics like regional cuisine, local festivals, and hot political issues. We've opened our pages to respected writers and scholars to show you their take on a given destination, and turned to lifelong resi-dents to learn the little things that make their city worth calling home. And we've even given you Alternatives to Tourism—ideas for how to give back to local com-munities through responsible travel and volunteering.

OVER FORTY YEARS OF WISDOM

When we started, way back in 1960, Let's Go consisted of a small group of well-traveled friends who compiled their budget travel tips into a 20-page packet for students on charter flights to Europe. Since then, we've expanded to suit all kinds of travelers, now publishing guides to six continents, including our newest guides: *Let's Go: Japan* and *Let's Go: Brazil*. Our guides are still annually researched and written entirely by students on shoe-string budgets, adventurous travelers who know that train strikes, stolen luggage, food poisoning, and marriage propos-als are all part of a day's work. Even as you read this, work on next year's editions is well underway. Whether you're reading one of our new titles, like *Let's Go: Puerto Rico* or *Let's Go Adventure Guide: Alaska*, or our original best-seller, *Let's Go: Europe*, you'll find the same spirit of adventure that has made *Let's Go* the guide of choice for travelers the world over since 1960.

GETTING IN TOUCH

The best discoveries are often those you make yourself; on the road, when you find something worth sharing, please drop us a line. We're Let's Go Publications, 67 Mt. Auburn St., Cambridge, MA 02138, USA (feedback@letsgo.com).

For more info, visit our website: www.letsgo.com.

PRICE RANGES >> MEXICO

Our researchers list establishments in order of value, starting with the best; our favorites are denoted by the Let's Go thumbs-up (👍). Since the best value is not always the cheapest price, we have incorporated a system of price ranges for quick reference. Our price ranges are based on a rough expectation of what you will spend. For **accommodations,** we base our price range on the cheapest price for which a single traveler can stay for one night. For **restaurants** and other dining establishments, we estimate the average amount that you will spend in that restaurant. The table below tells you what you will *typically* find in Mexico at the corresponding price range; keep in mind that a particularly expensive ice cream stand may still only be marked a ❶.

ACCOMMODATIONS	RANGE	WHAT YOU'RE *LIKELY* TO FIND
❶	under 100 pesos	Camping; mostly dorm rooms, such as HI or other hostels or university rooms. Expect bunk beds and a communal bath; you may have to provide or rent towels and sheets.
❷	100-149 pesos	Upper-end hostels or small hotels. You may have a private bathroom, or there may be a sink in your room and communal shower in the hall.
❸	150-199 pesos	A small room with a private bath. Should have decent amenities, such as a phone or TV. Breakfast may be included in the price of the room.
❹	200-249 pesos	Similar to ❸, but may have more amenities or be in a more touristed area.
❺	250 pesos and above	Large hotels or upscale chains. If it's a ❺ and it doesn't have the perks you want, you've paid too much.
FOOD	**RANGE**	**WHAT YOU'RE *LIKELY* TO FIND**
❶	under 15 pesos	Mostly street-corner stands, *taquerías*, or fast-food joints. Rarely ever a sit-down meal.
❷	15-24 pesos	Sandwiches, appetizers at a bar, or cheap entrees. You may have the option of sitting down or getting take-out.
❸	25-39 pesos	Mid-priced entrees, possibly coming with an appetizer. Tip will bump you up a bit, since you'll probably have a waiter or waitress.
❹	40-59 pesos	A somewhat fancy restaurant or a steakhouse. Either way, you'll have a special knife. Few restaurants in this range have a dress code, but some may look down on t-shirt and jeans.
❺	60 pesos and above	Classy establishments with wine lists. Slacks and dress shirts may be expected.

DISCOVER MEXICO

In every way, Mexico is a country of extremes. Along the coasts, steamy jungles teeming with rare flora and fauna give way to pristine, white-sand beaches. In the north and Baja, dry deserts form some of the most inhospitable places on Earth. In the country's fertile center, the massive twin snow-capped peaks of Popocatépetl and Ixtaccíhuatl punctuate the capital's skyline. These geographic extremes are fitting—they mirror the variety in Mexico's people. Mexico City bombards the senses with the sort of overload that can only come from the largest metropolis in the world. But Mexico's most modern city is also one of its most ancient; built on the ruins of the Aztec capital, el D.F. epitomizes the uniquely Mexican mix of past and present. Not far away are sleepy *pueblos* where modern comforts are as scarce as residents, who cling steadfastly to their traditional lands and languages.

Perhaps most noticeable are the economic contrasts in this, one of the world's most unequal countries. World-favmous beach resorts are the playgrounds of the rich, but walk a few blocks—if at all—off the touristed path to see *campesinos*, street vendors, and homeless children living in abject poverty. Despite these contradictions, Mexicans share an intensely proud identity, one born in a radical revolution, solidified by struggle against an overbearing northern neighbor, and now finding its place in a new era of democracy.

When in Mexico, you will assuredly come across legacies of the colonial and *indígena* pasts in architecture, religion, dress, and local economy; but to truly experience what Mexico is today, you will need to understand the peculiar combination of these two traditions that has created a *mestizo* nation.

WHEN TO GO

Mexico's lush jungles, golden beaches, and textured highlands entice visitors year-round. Temperatures fluctuate widely throughout the country. Winters tend to be mild while summers vary from warm to excruciatingly hot: **temperatures** in both the arid north and the moist Gulf regions soar to the neighborhood of 50°C (122°F), while high altitude regions such as the Valley of Mexico and the Oaxaca Valley remain spring-like in any month. Rainfall, like temperature, varies greatly between the temperate north and the tropical south. While it seldom rains in the deserted northern border states, rain falls abundantly in the humid south and the Gulf Coast, sometimes exceeding 15cm per month. The **rainy season** lasts from May to November, during which the south receives an average of two to three hours of rain every afternoon. The best time to hit the beach is during the dry season (November-May), when afternoons are sunny, evenings balmy, and nights relatively mosquito-free.

The **peak tourist season** (high season) encompasses December, *Semana Santa* (the week before Easter), and mid-summer. The waning weeks of March and early part of April, the traditional US spring break, also see resort towns like Mazatlán, Cabo San Lucas, and Cancún fill with boozing college students. Central Mexico and spots on the so-called *gringo* trail see the most tourist traffic during mid- to late summer, when throngs of Spanish-language students hit both the books and the trendy cafes, seeking "Spanish immersion." If you travel to Mexico during any of these times, expect to pay slightly higher prices at hotels and restaurants.

DISCOVER

THINGS TO DO

Mexico has no end of attractions. From climbing age-old Maya temples to haggling for silver trinkets in colonial open-air markets to diving near coral reefs to dancing the *merengue* with margarita in hand, visitors head to each region for its individual cultural allure. See the **Highlights of the Region** section at the beginning of each chapter for specific regional attractions.

THE GREAT CIVILIZATIONS

A journey through Mexico is like a whirlwind tour through time. The ancient Olmecs—famous for their colossal carved heads—were the first to call Mexico home, settling the villages of **San Lorenzo** (see p. 567), **La Venta** (see p. 572), and **Tres Zapotes** (see p. 563) in the humid Gulf Coast around 1000 BC. Centuries later, a mighty empire rose in the Valley of Mexico at **Teotihuacán** (see p. 138). Its ruins were so impressive that even the Aztecs thought the city had been built by the gods. Farther south, the Zapotec capital **Monte Albán** (see p. 513) rivaled Teotihuacán from a stately hillside position overlooking the verdant Oaxaca Valley. To the east, in the lowland jungles of the Yucatán Peninsula, the Classic Maya built grand cities such as **Palenque** (see p. 597), which continue to dazzle visitors with their distinct architecture and lush settings. Returning to central Mexico, admire the Tlaxcalans who drew the breathtaking murals at **Cacaxtla** (see p. 383), and the Totonacs who carved the Pyramid of Niches at **El Tajín** (see p. 550). After the fall of the Classic civilizations, Post-Classic powers like **Tula** (see p. 361), the birthplace of the feathered-serpent deity Quetzalcóatl, and **Mitla** (see p. 511), whose intricate carvings and religious architecture are second to none, advanced Mesoamerican civilization. Head to the Yucatán for a rendezvous with the warring Post-Classic Maya trio of **Chichén Itzá** (see p. 641), **Mayapán** (see p. 635), and **Uxmal** (see p. 631). Finally, witness the last stand of Pre-Hispanic Mexico in the Aztec capital of **Tenochtitlán** (in modern-day Mexico City; see p. 109).

SAND AND SURF

Mexico's infinite stretches of sparkling golden and white beaches will please even the most discriminating beach-goer. Those desiring an audience like to strut their stuff in front of millions of other bronzed bodies in **Cancún** (see p. 655). If the glam tourist scene isn't your style, ramble down the turquoise coast toward **Tulum** (see p. 684), and cavort amidst the beachside ruins. The splendid shores of **Isla Mujeres** (see p. 664) offer a quiet respite from the insanity, as do **Isla Cozumel** (see p. 677), where coral is king and scuba is queen, and **Isla Holbox** (see p. 669), quiet keeper of the most splendid sunsets in the Western Hemisphere. The Southern Pacific Coast harbors golden sands in the surfing towns of **Puerto Escondido** (see p. 527), **Puerto Ángel** (see p. 522), and **Zipolite** (see p. 524), which beckon with formidable waves and scantily-clad beach bums. Farther up the coast sprawls the grand old dame of beach resorts, **Acapulco** (see p. 490), complete with men in tiny briefs leaping from high cliffs. The stately duo of **Ixtapa** and **Zihuatanejo** (see p. 482) host tons of sun-worshippers, as do always popular **Puerto Vallarta** (see p. 426) and **Mazatlán** (see p. 269); **San Blas** (see p. 403) welcomes more hard core surfers. Bolder beachgoers might want to stray off the beaten track and head north to some of the most overlooked—and most spectacular—beaches in the country. Discover **San Felipe** (see p. 170), on the calm Sea of Cortés, or bask beneath the stars on beautiful **Bahía de la Concepción** (see p. 188), one of the most pristine beaches in the world. For those who like things shaken—not stirred—no trip to Baja California would be complete without a quick jaunt down the peninsula to rocking **Cabo San Lucas** (see p. 205).

COLONIAL LEGACIES

The influence of Mexico's colorful history has left its imprint on the national architecture. If it could speak, each brick in each church in each city could tell stories of treason, murder, and conquest. The best place to begin a historical exploration is, of course, **Mexico City** (see p. 84), the sprawling megalopolis with a population (25 million and counting) about that of a medium-sized country. Check out the stately **Palacio Nacional** (see p. 109), home to Spanish viceroys and Mexican presidents, and stop by **Coyoacán** (see p. 132), where Hernán Cortés established his government and tortured the Aztec Emperor Cuauhtémoc. Heading out of el D.F., visit **Cuernavaca** (see p. 368), former home of Cortés and current home of untold numbers of international students, and **Taxco** (see p. 477), the colonial silver town whose winding streets recall visions of Spain. Skip south to the faded limestone streets of **Oaxaca** (see p. 497), birthplace of the nation's first indigenous president, Benito Juárez. Swing by **Mérida** (see p. 617), a large Maya center the Spanish converted into a modern city. Frolic with mummies in **Guanajuato** (see p. 336), and don't miss artsy **San Miguel de Allende** (see p. 344) or its friendly neighbor, **Dolores Hidalgo** (see p. 350), where Father Hidalgo sounded the *Grito de Dolores* (the electrifying speech calling for Mexican Independence). Relax in **San Luis Potosí** (see p. 322), the nation's wealthy silver and gold capital, before coming back down through steamy **Veracruz** (see p. 551), the first city founded by the Spanish, Mexico's main port, and the site of numerous foreign invasions. Farther inland is **Tlaxcala** (see p. 376), the city-state that collaborated with Cortés to defeat the Aztecs. Neighboring **Puebla** (see p. 385) epitomizes colonial Mexico, its order and rigidity exhibited in gridded streets and cobblestone walkways.

■ LET'S GO PICKS

BEST WAY TO WARM YOURSELF UP: On a distillery tour in **Tequila** (p. 424), where 3 free shots x 16 factories will definitely bring on a flush.

BEST MOUNTAINTOP VIEW: The dazzling vista of the calm turquoise Sea of Cortés, the frothy deep-blue Pacific, and the rugged Baja peninsula from Picacho del Diablo (3086m) in **Parque Nacional Sierra San Pedro Martír** (p. 175).

BEST PLACE TO REVEL IN DRUNKEN, LOUD, OBNOXIOUS AMERICANISM: Wearing a sombrero and downing a beer while having a photo taken atop a donkey painted like a zebra in **Tijuana** (p. 149).

BEST PLACE TO BE AWED BY NATURE'S SUPREME BEAUTY: The annual meeting of more than 20 million monarch butterflies from at their winter sanctuary of **El Rosario** (p. 176).

BEST PLACE TO LOSE YOURSELF IN THE CROWD: Amid the 25 million residents of big, bad **Mexico City** (p. 84).

BEST DRIED UP DEAD PEOPLE: The 122 naturally mummified residents of **Guanajuato**'s (p. 336) infamous Museo de las Momias, and their sugary, *sombrero*-wearing miniatures sold outside.

BEST ONLY-IN-MEXICO ICE CREAM FLAVORS: *Chicharrón* (pork rind), *elote* (corn meal), *aguacate* (avocado), and *cerveza* (beer).

BEST PLACE TO TAKE A VERY LONG NAP: On the long, isolated and unbelievably soft sands of Playa los Algodones in **San Carlos** (p. 236).

BEST TIME TO BREAK OUT THE SHORT SHORTS: Hurling yourself off a 35m cliff while emulating the famous, half-naked **Acapulco** (p. 490) cliff divers.

BEST PLACE TO OBSERVE WILD ANIMALS IN THEIR NATURAL HABITAT: Spy on the *bronzus americanus* romping in the **Cancún** (p. 655), **Mazatlán** (p. 269), and **Cabo San Lucas** (p. 205) ecosystems.

BEST PLACE TO ADMIRE REALLY LARGE HEADS: At Parque-Museo La Venta in **Villahermosa** (p. 568), where 33 gigantic Olmec sculptures collected from throughout the Gulf Coast stare at you along a winding jungle path.

BEST THIGH-MASTER SUBSTITUTE: Climbing the massive Pyramid of the Sun in the ancient and sophisticated city of **Teotihuacán** (p. 138).

DISCOVER

SUGGESTED ITINERARIES

SEA OF CORTÉS

YUCATÁN & CHIAPAS

SEA OF CORTES (4 WEEKS) Get going on the raucous shores of **Puerto Peñasco** (see p. 222). Calm down in tranquil **Bahía Kino** (see p. 232) and groove with transvestites in **Guaymas** (see p. 233). Catch a ferry from **Los Mochis** (see p. 265) to **La Paz** (see p. 195), the capital of Baja California Sur. Swing down to **San José del Cabo** for a quick rest before partying with José's brother, **Cabo San Lucas** (see p. 205) and his spring-breaking chums. Say hello to the artsy expats of **Todos Santos** (see p. 202) and stroll along the *malecón* in **Loreto** (see p. 190). Soak up some rays on the beaches of pristine **Bahía de la Concepción** (see p. 188) before visiting pretty **Mulegé** (see p. 186). Cool off in **San Ignacio** (see p. 183), and marvel at the sunsets in **Bahía de los Ángeles** (see p. 177). Then pack up the 4x4 and enjoy amazing views from **Parque Nacional Sierra San Pedro Mártir** (see p. 175). Improve your tan on the endless beach of **San Felipe** (see p. 170), and sleep lakeside at **Parque Nacional Constitución** (see p. 165) before rejoining *gringos* in **Ensenada** (see p. 159) and **Rosarito** (see p. 157), home of *Titanic*. Finally, share stories of your spectacular trip with drunken tourists in bawdy **Tijuana** (see p. 149).

YUCATAN AND CHIAPAS (3 WEEKS) Kick things off with some alcohol-drenched nights in **Cancún** (see p. 655), and recover on the peaceful shores of **Isla Mujeres** (see p. 664). Back on the peninsula, don't miss the cavernous *cenotes* of **Valladolid** (see p. 647) on your way to the ruins of **Chichén Itzá** (see p. 641). Sit back and people-watch in busy **Mérida** (see p. 617). Traverse the **Ruta Puuc** (see p. 630) and dance in plazas within the walls of **Campeche** (see p. 609). Venturing south into the Chiapan jungle, crest the soaring temples of **Palenque** (see p. 595). Head west to the sprawling capital **Tuxtla Gutiérrez** (see p. 578), home of one of the best zoos in Latin American and a base from which to explore the green walls of the **Sumidero Canyon** (see p. 582). Expose yourself to indigenous culture in **San Cristóbal de las Casas** (see p. 583). Back on the Yucatán Peninsula, dally in **Chetumal** (see p. 691) and peruse its world-class museum, while mesmerizing **Tulum** (see p. 684) beckons. Toast the trip in lively **Playa del Carmen** (see p. 671) before returning to crazy **Cancún**.

CENTRAL MEXICO (2 WEEKS) Begin your journey in action-packed **D.F.** (see p. 84), but don't dally too long. Travel east to

CENTRAL MEXICO

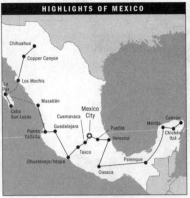

HIGHLIGHTS OF MEXICO

DISCOVER

peaceful **Tlaxcala** (see p. 376) before moving on to bustling **Puebla** (see p. 385), with its immense cathedral and colonial streets. Relive old memories at Cortés's palace in **Cuernavaca** (see p. 368), before practicing your haggling skills in **Taxco** (see p. 477). Cool yourself down and enjoy the bronzed bodies in sunny **Acapulco** (see p. 490), pause in more innocent **Barra de Potosí** (see p. 488), and continue up the coast to the energetic beachside duo of **Zihuatanejo** and **Ixtapa** (see p. 482). Head back inland to the stately colonial city of **Morelia** (see p. 466), and kick back with backpacking language students in revived **Guanajuato** (see p. 336) before chatting it up with retired North American expatriates in **San Miguel de Allende** (see p. 344). Finally, wrap it all up with a few more days in **la capital.**

BEST OF MEXICO (4 WEEKS) Start your trip in **Chihuahua** (see p. 247). Ride the thrilling train through the **Copper Canyon** (see p. 260) and into **Los Mochis** (see p.

265). Hop on a ferry for a quick trip to **La Paz** (see p. 195) and skip down the coast to rocking **Cabo San Lucas** (see p. 205) before heading back across the Sea of Cortés to the golden sands of **Mazatlán** (see p. 269) and **Puerto Vallarta** (see p. 426). After relaxing a moment, take off for busy **Guadalajara** (see p. 410), and continue to **Zihuatanejo** and **Ixtapa** (see p. 482). Shop till you drop in **Taxco** (see p. 477) and practice your Spanish in **Cuernavaca** (see p. 368). Stay for a couple of days in cosmopolitan **Mexico City** (see p. 84) before hitting equally sophisticated **Puebla** (see p. 385). **Veracruz** (see p. 551), Mexico's steamy port, is next, and stately **Oaxaca** (see p. 497) will cool you off. Heading to the peninsula, stop by **Palenque** (see p. 595) en route to colonial **Mérida** (see p. 617). Finally, swing through **Chichén Itzá** (see p. 641) before engaging in some **Cancún** (see p. 655) mischief.

Avg. Temp. (lo/hi), Precipitation	January			April			July			October		
	°C	°F	mm	°C	°F	mm	°C	°F	mm	°C	°F	mm
Acapulco	22/31	72/88	1	25/32	77/90	0	25/33	77/91	27	24/32	75/90	18
Cancún	19/28	66/82	110	22/31	72/88	35	25/32	77/90	110	23/31	73/88	220
Guadalajara	7/23	45/73	15	14/31	57/88	8	15/26	59/79	257	10/25	50/77	54
La Paz	13/23	55/73	23	17/33	63/91	1	23/36	73/97	32	17/29	63/84	28
Mérida	18/28	64/82	60	21/34	70/93	148	23/33	73/91	122	19/29	66/84	269
Mexico City	6/22	43/72	8	13/27	5/81	19	13/24	55/75	129	9/23	48/73	44
Monterrey	9/20	48/68	18	20/31	68/88	29	22/34	72/93	62	12/23	54/73	78
Oaxaca	8/28	46/82	3	15/32	59/90	26	15/28	59/82	88	10/28	50/82	44
San Cristóbal	5/20	41/68	2	9/22	48/72	30	10/22	50/72	160	7/20	45/68	150
Tijuana	6/20	41/68	49	12/23	54/73	20	16/27	61/81	1	10/23	50/73	13

ESSENTIALS

FACTS FOR THE TRAVELER

ENTRANCE REQUIREMENTS

Passport (p. 8). Recommended for citizens of the US and Canada. Required for citizens of Australia, Ireland, New Zealand, South Africa, the UK, and most other countries.

Visa (p. 9). Visas are not required for citizens of the US, Canada, and most EU countries. Citizens of countries in Eastern Europe, Africa, and Asia need visas, as do individuals entering the country for work or extended study.

Inoculations (p. 18). None required, but some are recommended for travelers to more rural and humid parts of the country.

Driving License and Permit (p. 9). All foreign licenses are accepted. Insurance is recommended. A **Vehicle Permit** (p. 11) is required to bring an automobile more than 22km over the US-Mexico border.

EMBASSIES AND CONSULATES

MEXICAN SERVICES ABROAD

Embassies: Australia, 14 Perth Ave., Yarralumla, Canberra 2600 ACT (☎02 6273 3905; fax 6273 1190; www.embassyofmexicoinaustralia.org); **Canada,** 45 O'Connor St. #1500, KIP 1A4 Ottawa, ON (☎613-233-8988; fax 235-9123; www.embamexican.com); **UK,** 42 Hertford St., London W1 J7JR (☎020 7499 8586; fax 7495 4035; www.embamex.co.uk); **US,** 1911 Pennsylvania Ave. NW, Washington, D.C. 20006 (☎202-728-1600; fax 728-1766).

Consulates: Australia, 58 Godfry Terrace, Erindale, SA 5066 (☎08 8331 3764; fax 8332 7443); **Canada,** 2055 Peel St. #1000, H3A 1V4 Montreal, QC (☎514-288-2502; fax 288-8287; www.consulmex.qc.ca); **UK,** 8 Halkin St., London SW1 X7DW (☎020 7235 6393; fax 7235 5480; www.mexicanconsulate.org.uk); **US,** 2827 16th St. NW, Washington, D.C. 20009 (☎202-736-1000; fax 234-4498).

TOURISM OFFICES

Chicago: 300 N. Michigan Ave., 4th floor, Chicago, IL 60601 (☎312-606-9252; fax 606-9012).

Houston: 1010 Fomdren St., Houston, TX 77096 (☎713-772-2581; fax 772-6058).

London: Wakefield House, 41 Trinity Square, London EC3N 4DJ (☎020 7488 9392; fax 7265 0704).

Los Angeles: 2401 W. 6th St., 5th floor, Los Angeles, CA 90057 (☎213-351-2075; fax 351-2074).

Miami: 1200 NW 78th Ave. #203, Miami, FL 33126 (☎305-718-4091; fax 718-4098).

Montreal: 1 Place Ville Marie, #1931, Montreal, QC H3B 2B5 (☎514-871-1052; fax 871-3825).

New York City: 21 E. 63rd St., 3rd floor, New York, NY 10021 (☎212-821-0314; fax 821-0367).

Toronto: 2 Bloor St. W #1502, Toronto, ON M4W 3E2 (☎416-925-2753; fax 925-6061).

Vancouver (and Northwest US): 999 W. Hastings #1610, Vancouver, BC V6C 2W2 (☎604-669-2845; fax 669-3498).

CONSULAR SERVICES IN MEXICO

EMBASSIES

Canada: Schiller 529, Col. Polanco, 11580 México, D.F. (☎5724 7900; fax 5724 7980; www.dfait-maeci.gc.ca/mexico-city).

UK: Río Lerma 71, Colonia Cuauhtémoc, 06500 México, D.F. (☎5207 2089; fax 5207 7672; www.embajadabritanica.com.mx).

US: Paseo de la Reforma 305, Colonia Cuauhtémoc, 06500 México, D.F. (☎5080 2000; fax 5525 5040; www.usembassy-mexico.gov).

US CONSULATES

Ciudad Juárez: López Mateos 924 Nte. (☎656 611 3000; fax 616 9056).

Guadalajara: Progreso 175 (☎33 3825 2700; fax 826 6549).

Hermosillo: Monterrey, 141 Poniente (☎662 217 2375; fax 217 2578).

Matamoros: Primera 2002 y Azaleas (☎868 812 4402; fax 812 2171).

Mérida: Paseo Montejo 453 (☎999 925 5011; fax 925 6219).

Monterrey: Constitución 411, Poniente 64000 (☎81 8345 2120).

Nogales: San José s/n, Fracc. Álamos (☎631 313 4820; fax 313 4652).

Nuevo Laredo: Calle Allende 3330, Col. Jardín (☎867 714 0512; fax 714 7984).

Tijuana: Tapachula #96, Colonia Hipódromo (☎644 622 7400; fax 681 8592).

DOCUMENTS AND FORMALITIES

PASSPORTS

REQUIREMENTS. Citizens of Australia, Ireland, New Zealand, South Africa, the UK, and most EU countries need valid passports to enter Mexico and to re-enter their own country. Mexico does not allow entrance if the holder's passport expires in fewer than six months; returning home with an expired passport is illegal and may result in a fine. It is recommended that citizens of the US and Canada carry a valid passport, but proof of citizenship (such as an official birth certificate, naturalization certificate, consular report of birth abroad, or a certificate of citizenship) and a photo ID will also be accepted. A passport, however, carries much more authority than does a birth certificate, makes returning home by air easier, and is mandatory for anyone traveling from Mexico to Central America.

SAFETY. Be sure to photocopy the page of your passport with your photo, passport number, and other identifying information, as well as any visas, travel insurance policies, plane tickets, and traveler's check serial numbers. Carry one set of copies in a safe place, apart from the originals, and leave another set at home. Consulates also recommend that you carry an expired passport or an official copy of your birth certificate in a part of your baggage separate from other documents.

LOST PASSPORTS. If you lose your passport, immediately notify the local police and the nearest embassy or consulate of your home government. To expedite its replacement, you will need to know all information previously recorded and show

ID and proof of citizenship. In some cases, a replacement may take weeks to process, and it may be valid only for a limited time. Any visas stamped in your old passport will be irretrievably lost. In an emergency, ask for immediate temporary traveling papers that will permit you to re-enter your home country. Your passport is a public document belonging to your nation's government. You may have to surrender it to a foreign government official, but if you don't get it back in a reasonable amount of time, inform the nearest mission of your home country.

NEW PASSPORTS. Citizens of Australia, Canada, Ireland, New Zealand, the UK, and the US can apply for a passport at the nearest post office, passport office, or court of law. Citizens of South Africa can apply for a passport at any Home Affairs office. A new passport or renewal application must be filed well in advance of the departure date, although most passport offices offer rush services (for a very steep fee). Citizens living abroad who need a passport or renewal services should contact the nearest consular service of their home country.

OTHER FORMS OF IDENTIFICATION

When you travel, always carry two or more forms of identification on your person, including at least one photo ID; a passport combined with a driver's license or birth certificate is usually adequate. Many establishments, especially banks, may require several IDs in order to cash traveler's checks. Never carry all your forms of ID together; split them up in case of theft or loss, and keep photocopies of them in your luggage and at home.

TEACHER, STUDENT & YOUTH IDENTIFICATION. The **International Student Identity Card (ISIC),** the most widely accepted form of student ID, provides discounts on sights, accommodations, food, and transport. The ISIC is preferable to an institution-specific card (such as a university ID) because it is more likely to be recognized and honored abroad. All cardholders have access to a 24hr. emergency helpline for medical, legal, and financial emergencies (in North America call ☎877-370-ISIC, elsewhere call US collect ☎+1 715-345-0505), and US cardholders are also eligible for insurance benefits (see Insurance, p. 22). Applicants must be degree-seeking students of a secondary or post-secondary school and must be of at least 12 years of age. Because of the proliferation of fake ISICs, some services (particularly airlines) require additional proof of student identity.

The **International Teacher Identity Card (ITIC)** offers teachers the same insurance coverage as well as similar but limited discounts. To receive an ITIC, you must prove that you're employed at a recognized educational establishment for at least 18 hours per week. For travelers who are 25 years old or under but are not students, the **International Youth Travel Card (IYTC)** also offers many of the same benefits as the ISIC. Similarly, the **International Student Exchange ID Card (ISE)** provides discounts, medical benefits, and the ability to purchase student airfares.

Each of these identity cards costs US$22 or equivalent. ISIC and ITIC cards are valid for roughly 1½ academic years; IYTC cards are valid for one year from the date of issue. Many student travel agencies (see p. 30) issue the cards; for a listing of issuing agencies, or for more information, contact the **International Student Travel Confederation,** Herengracht 479, 1017 BS Amsterdam, Netherlands (☎ +31 20 421 28 00; fax 421 28 10; www.istc.org)

VISAS AND PERMITS

Unless you're a North American tourist visiting for fewer than six months, it's a good idea to check with the nearest Mexican consulate or embassy for exact entry requirements. Checking beforehand is particularly important for those seeking to enter for human rights purposes; the political uprisings in Chiapas have made many Mexicans sensitive to meddling foreigners, and many have been detained, expelled, or deported for violating their tourist visa status or allegedly interfering in the country's internal politics. Also note that children traveling into Mexico may have to present special papers (see **Travelers with Children**, p. 41).

TOURIST CARDS (FOLLETO DE MIGRACIÓN TURÍSTICA)

All persons, regardless of nationality, must carry a **tourist card** (**FMT**, Folleto de Migración Turística) in addition to proof of citizenship. Most tourist cards are good for up to 180 days; some, however, are only good for 30 days or less. If you need to leave and re-enter the country during your trip, make sure your tourist card will enable you to do so; you might have to ask for a multiple-entry permit. US and Canadian citizens don't need the tourist card if they are staying in the country for less than seventy-two hours or intend to stay within the 22km US-Mexico border zone. If you are traveling into the country by plane, the US$19 tourist card fee is included in the airline ticket price, and the tourist card will be given to you to fill out during your flight. If driving into Mexico, you will be charged the fee at your point of entry. You can avoid any delays by obtaining a card from a Mexican consulate or tourist office before you leave (see **Embassies and Consulates**, p. 7).

 DON'T LEAVE HOME WITHOUT IT. Because you may be asked to present your tourist card when leaving the country, you must keep it for the duration of your trip. Keep it in a safe place along with your other valuables, and make a copy just in case.

TOURIST VISAS

Tourist visas are **not necessary** for citizens of Australia, Canada, New Zealand, the UK, the US, and most EU and Latin American countries for stays of up to 180 days; the tourist card is sufficient. Individuals with Eastern European, Asian, African, or Middle Eastern citizenship must procure a tourist visa from the nearest Mexican consulate; in order to do so, a valid passport, a valid I-94 form, three passport photographs, proof of economic solvency, and evidence of a round-trip ticket are necessary. A consular fee of US$37 may also be charged, depending on nationality.

BUSINESS VISAS

Under the North American Free Trade Agreement (NAFTA), US and Canadian citizens can enter Mexico to conduct business for up to 30 days with an **FMN permit** (free). To do so, travelers must present a letter from their company or firm stating the purpose of the trip and how expenses will be covered, as well as a valid passport. Travelers planning on staying longer than 30 days will have to apply for an **FM3 permit** (consular fee of US$161), which is good for up to one year.

STUDENT VISAS

Students interested in studying in Mexico for longer than 180 days must obtain a student visa from their nearest Mexican consulate. In order to do so, they must submit the acceptance letter from the school they wish to attend, several photographs, and a statement proving economic solvency. Those studying under a specific program must also submit a letter from the sponsoring organization. The consular fee depends on nationality and procedure; citizens of some nationalities might have to pay a US$99 fee. Note that students planning on studying for less than six months may enter the country with a normal tourist visa or tourist card.

RETIREMENT VISAS

Seeking a temperate climate and favorable exchange rates, many foreigners have chosen Mexico as their place of retirement. Those whose retirement income comes from abroad may apply for a non-immigrant visa, or **FM3 permit** (US$99), at the nearest consular office, and present a valid passport, several photographs, proof of economic solvency, and other documents. The FM3 visa will be good for between 30 days and 1 year, whereupon retirees must go to an immigration office in Mexico, prove solvency, and receive another stamp on their FM3 visa, which must be renewed every couple of years. After 10 years, status changes to **FM2** status, non-immigrant resident.

CUSTOMS

ENTERING MEXICO

BY CAR

Crossing into Mexico by land can be as uneventful or as complicated as the border guards want it to be. You may be waved into the country or directed to the immigration office to procure a tourist card (FMT) if you don't have one already. Make sure all papers are in order before proceeding; if there is anything amiss when you reach an immigration checkpoint 22km into the interior, you'll have to turn back.

If you plan on driving into Mexico, you will need to obtain a **vehicle permit** at the border or at the Banjercito website at https://www.banjercito.com.mx/iitv/index_en.htm. Permits are US$22 when you pay with a valid debit or credit card. Those without credit cards will have to provide a cash deposit or bond worth US$200-$400, depending on the make of the car. Your deposit will be repaid in full when you return across the border, but paying the minimal fee by credit card is strongly advised. To extend a permit beyond its original expiration date and to avoid confiscation, contact the temporary importation department of Mexican customs. The maximum length granted to tourists is six months. A permit is valid only for the person to whom it was issued unless another driver is approved by the federal registry. Violation of this law can result in confiscation of the vehicle or heavy fines. In order to get a permit, you will need an original copy and a photocopy of several documents: a state vehicle registration certificate and vehicle title, a tourist entry form (FME, FMT, FM6, FM3), and a valid driver's license accompanied by either a passport or a birth certificate. If leasing a vehicle, you must provide the contract in your name (also in duplicate). **Vehicle permits are not needed if you do not plan to travel more than 22km past the border.** Furthermore, only legitimate drivers may purchase car-ferry tickets. Regulations change frequently; for updated information, contact a consulate or check the Banjercito website.

BY AIR

Entering Mexico by air is somewhat easier. Dash out of your plane as fast as possible to beat the rush to *aduana* (customs). Beware that agents randomly examine luggage using a press-your-luck light system—and it turns out 'small arms' still count as 'arms'.

Mexican regulations limit the value of goods brought into Mexico by US citizens arriving by air or sea to US$300 per person and by land to $50 per person. Amounts exceeding the duty-free limit are subject to a 32.8% tax.

ESSENTIALS

LEAVING MEXICO

Upon returning home, you must declare all articles acquired abroad and pay a duty on the value of those articles that exceed the allowance established by your country's customs service. To establish the value when you return home, keep receipts for items purchased abroad.

It's a very bad idea to take illegal drugs out of Mexico. If you have questions, call the **Mexican Embassy** in the US (☎202-728-1669) or contact your specific embassy or consulate. In the north, especially along the Pacific coast, expect to be stopped repeatedly by burly, humorless troopers looking for contraband. That innocent-looking hitchhiker you were kind enough to pick up may be a drug peddler with a stash of illegal substances. If the police catch it in your car, the drug possession charges will extend to you, and your car may be confiscated. If you carry **prescription drugs** while you travel, it is vital to have a copy of the prescriptions themselves and a note from a doctor, both readily accessible at country borders.

Note that when entering the US, you may be hassled by immigration officers if you are a minority or resident alien of the US, or simply have a Latino surname.

MONEY

If you stay in cheap hotels, diet rigorously, and avoid sights and attractions, expect to spend US$10-15 per person per day. A less stingy (but substantially happier) traveler, depending on his or her level of extravagance, might expect to spend about US$20-35 traveling in less touristed areas and about US$35-50 near the US border or in resort areas. Prices for hotels start at about US$7 per night for a single at rock bottom. A basic sit-down meal will cost around US$3. For information about pricing in *Let's Go: Mexico 2004*, refer to p. xvi.

CURRENCY AND EXCHANGE

The currency chart below is based on August 2003 exchange rates between local currency and Australian dollars (AUS$), Canadian dollars (CDN$), Irish pounds (IR£), New Zealand dollars (NZ$), South African Rand (ZAR), British pounds (UK£), US dollars (US$), and European Union euros (EUR€). Check the currency converter on financial websites such as www.bloomberg.com and www.xe.com or a large newspaper for the latest exchange rates.

CURRENCY	
AUS$1 = 7.04 PESOS	1 PESO = AUS$0.14
CDN$1 = 7.71 PESOS	1 PESO = CDN$0.13
IR£1 = 15.17 PESOS	1 PESO = IR£0.07
NZ$ = 6.29 PESOS	1 PESO = NZ$0.16
ZAR$1 = 1.47 PESOS	1 PESO = ZAR$0.68
US$1 = 10.73 PESOS	1 PESO = US$0.09
UK£1 = 17.05 PESOS	1 PESO = UK£0.06
EUR€1 = 11.95 PESOS	1 PESO = EUR€0.08

International Currency Express (☎888-278-6628) delivers foreign currency or traveler's checks 2nd-day at competitive exchange rates for a US$12 fee.

Changing money in Mexico is easy in all but the most rural areas, where banks might be scarce or have limited hours. The more money you change at a time, the less you will lose to commission. Also keep in mind that while all banks exchange dollars for pesos, some might not accept other currencies; foreign travelers of all nationalities would be wise to keep some US dollars on hand. **Casas de Cambio** (currency exchange booths) may offer better exchange rates than banks and are usually open as long as the stores near which they do business. In most towns, the exchange rates at hotels, restaurants, and airports are extremely unfavorable; avoid them unless it's an emergency.

TRAVELER'S CHECKS

Traveler's checks are one of the safest means of carrying funds in Mexico. Travel agencies and banks sell them for a small commission. Each agency provides refunds if your checks are lost or stolen, and many provide additional services, such as toll-free refund hotlines abroad, emergency message services, and stolen credit card assistance.

While traveling, keep check receipts and a record of which checks you've cashed separate from the checks themselves. Also leave a list of check numbers with someone at home. Never countersign checks until you're ready to cash them, and always bring your passport with you to cash them.

Exchanging traveler's checks in Mexico is fairly easy. Remember however, that some places (especially in northern Mexico) are accustomed to US Dollars and will accept no substitute. It might also be difficult to exchange traveler's checks in the more rural parts of Mexico and other less touristed areas. Finally, it's probably best to buy most of your checks in small denominations (US$20) to minimize your losses at times when you can't avoid a bad exchange rate. Purchase checks in US dollars; many *casas de cambio* refuse to change other currencies.

American Express: Checks available with commission at select banks, at all AmEx offices, and online (www.americanexpress.com; US residents only). American Express cardholders can also purchase checks by phone (☎888-269-6669). AAA offers commission-free checks to its members. Checks available in US, Australian, British, Canadian, Japanese, and Euro currencies. *Cheques for Two* can be signed by either of 2 people traveling together. For more information contact AmEx's service centers: In the US and Canada ☎800-221-7282; in the UK ☎0800 587 6023; in Australia ☎800 68 80 22; in New Zealand 0508 555 358; elsewhere US collect ☎+1 801-964-6665.

Visa: Checks available (generally with commission) at banks worldwide. To find the nearest issuing location, call Visa's service centers: In the US ☎800-227-6811; in the UK ☎0800 51 58 84; elsewhere UK collect ☎+44 020 7937 8091. Checks available in US, British, Canadian, Japanese, and Euro currencies.

Travelex/Thomas Cook: In the US and Canada call ☎800-287-7362; in the UK call ☎0800 62 21 01; elsewhere call UK collect ☎+44 1733 31 89 50.

CREDIT CARDS

Credit cards are accepted by all but the smallest Mexican businesses. **Visa** (US ☎800-336-8472) and **MasterCard** (US ☎800-307-7309) are the most readily accepted. **American Express** (US ☎800-843-2273) is also accepted. AMEX holders may cash personal checks at AmEx offices abroad, access an emergency medical and legal assistance hotline (24hr.; in North America call ☎800-554-2639, elsewhere call US collect ☎+1 715-343-7977), and enjoy American Express Travel Service benefits. All major cards can be used to get **cash advances,** which allow you to withdraw pesos from networked banks and ATMs throughout Mexico. Credit card companies get the wholesale exchange rate, which is generally 5% better than the retail rate used by banks and other currency exchange establishments. Transaction fees and sky-high interest rates for all credit card advances (up to US$10 per advance, plus 2-3% extra on foreign transactions after conversion), tend to make credit cards a more costly way of withdrawing cash than ATMs or traveler's checks. To be eligible for an advance, you'll need to get a Personal Identification Number (PIN) from your credit card company.

ESSENTIALS

ESSENTIALS

ATM (CASH) CARDS

Cash cards—popularly called ATM cards—are widespread in Mexico. Depending on the system that your home bank uses, you can most likely access your personal bank account from abroad. ATMs get the same wholesale exchange rate as credit cards, but there is often a limit on the amount of money you can withdraw per day (around US$500). There is typically also a surcharge of US$1-5 per withdrawal. Be sure to memorize your PIN in numeric form since machines often don't have letters on their keys. Also, if your PIN is longer than four digits, ask your bank whether you need a new number.

The two major international money networks are **Cirrus** (to locate ATMs US ☎ 800-424-7787 or www.mastercard.com) and **Visa/PLUS** (to locate ATMs US ☎ 800-843-7587 or www.visa.com). **Visa TravelMoney** is a system allowing you to access money from any ATM on the Visa/PLUS network. You deposit an amount before you travel (plus a small administration fee) and can then withdraw up to that sum. TravelMoney cards are available at Travelex/Interpayment locations worldwide, and through AAA. **American Express Express Cash** allows AmEx cardholders to withdraw money from American Express ATMs worldwide. To enroll, US cardholders may call ☎ 800-227-4669.

GETTING MONEY FROM HOME

The cheapest way to receive money in Mexico is to have it sent through a large commercial bank to associated banks in Mexico. The sender must either have an account with the bank or bring in cash or a money order. If the sender can supply the bank with exact information on the recipient's passport number and the Mexican bank address, the cabled money should arrive in one to three days; otherwise, there will be significant delays. Other options are listed below.

WIRING MONEY. It is possible to arrange a bank money transfer, which means asking a bank back home to wire money to a bank in Mexico. This is the cheapest way to transfer cash, but it's also the slowest, usually taking several days or more. Note that some banks may only release your funds in local currency, potentially sticking you with a poor exchange rate; inquire about this in advance. Money transfer services like Western Union are faster and more convenient than bank transfers—but are also much pricier. **Western Union** has many locations worldwide. To find one, visit www.westernunion.com, or call a Western Union office: in the US, ☎ 800-325-6000; in Canada, ☎ 800-235-0000; in the UK, ☎ 0800 83 38 33; in Australia, ☎ 800 501 500; in New Zealand, ☎ 800 27 0000; in South Africa, ☎ 0860 100031; in Mexico, ☎ 5546 7361.

FEDERAL EXPRESS. Some people choose to send cash abroad via **FedEx** to avoid transmission fees and taxes. While FedEx is reasonably reliable, note that this method is illegal. In the US and Canada, FedEx can be reached by calling ☎ 800-463-3339; in the UK, ☎ 0800 12 38 00; in Ireland, ☎ 800 535 800; in Australia, ☎ 13 26 10; in New Zealand, ☎ 0800 733 339; and in South Africa, ☎ 011 923 8000.

US STATE DEPARTMENT (US CITIZENS ONLY). In dire emergencies only, the US State Department will forward money during normal business hours to the nearest consular office, which will then disburse it, according to instructions, for a US$15 fee. If you wish to use this service, you must contact the Overseas Citizens Service division of the US State Department (☎ 202-647-5225; nights, Sundays, and holidays ☎ 202-647-4000).

TIPPING AND BARGAINING

Ah, the age-old question: To tip or not to tip? In Mexico, it can be hard to know what to do. Overly eager tipping can be offensive (never, for example, throw a couple of pesos at someone you just asked for directions), but many people make their livings assisting tourists in exchange for tips. In general, anyone who offers a service and then awkwardly waits around afterward is expecting a tip. In a restaurant, waiters are tipped based on the quality of service; **good service deserves at least 15%.** Cab drivers are generally not tipped, as they do not run on meters. Regardless of the quality of service, never leave without saying *gracias*.

In Mexico, skillful bargaining separates the savvy budget traveler from the timid tourist. If you're unsure whether bargaining is appropriate, observe the locals and follow their lead. When hailing a cab, settle the price of the ride beforehand, lest you get pegged as a tourist and are charged exorbitantly.

 KNOW WHEN TO WALK AWAY, KNOW WHEN TO RUN. Buying quality crafts sometimes requires special knowledge. When buying **turquoise,** ask the vendor to put the rocks to the "lighter test." Plastic or synthetic material will quickly melt under the flame. When buying **silver,** look for a stamp with the number **.925** on the underside. This stamp indicates that the silver is sterling (i.e. it is at least 925 parts per 1000 pure). If there's no number, the piece might be inferior silver—silver-plated or silver *alpaca* (nickel silver).

SAFETY AND SECURITY

Mexico as a whole is relatively safe; however, in some areas, and especially in big cities, crime is a serious concern. While most is of the petty and annoying variety—pickpocketings, purse-snatchings, etc.—violent and brutal attacks on tourists are reportedly on the rise. Exercise caution; common-sense precautions and heightened attention can help you avoid dangerous situations.

PERSONAL SAFETY

EXPLORING. To avoid unwanted attention, try to blend in as much as possible. Respecting local customs (in many cases, dressing more conservatively) may placate would-be hecklers. Familiarize yourself with your surroundings before setting out, and carry yourself with confidence. Check your map in shops and restaurants rather than on the street. If you are traveling alone, be sure someone at home knows your itinerary, and never admit that you're by yourself. When walking at night, stick to busy, well-lit streets and avoid dark alleyways.

For more info on safety for specific groups of travelers, see p. 36.

DRIVING & TRANSPORTATION. Mexican highways, especially free *(libre)* roads, are fairly dangerous. Travelers have been kidnapped, assaulted, and/or robbed on these roads. The US State Department recommends traveling only on toll *(cuota)* roads, which are somewhat safer, and riding in **first-class buses.** If you plan on spending time driving, consider bringing **spare parts and gas.** A cellular phone will also be useful. Try to restrict all travel to daylight hours. **Sleeping in your car** is one of the most dangerous (and often illegal) ways to get your rest. When traveling in large cities, beware **taxicab crime.** Passengers are assaulted and robbed with alarming frequency. In general, and especially in Mexico City, avoid taking street cabs; instead, call the radio taxi (See p. 94). Ask for the cab's license plate and the driver's name.

For info on the perils of **hitchhiking,** see p. 35. For specific info on transportation safety, see p. 35.

TERRORISM. There are several insurgent groups operating in Chiapas, Guerrero, and Oaxaca, the most prominent of which are the Zapatistas, the Popular Revolutionary Army, and the Insurgent People's Revolutionary Army. While these groups are not heavily active, they have initiated violent uprisings in the recent past. In addition, the Zapatistas have occasionally been hostile towards foreigners. The box below on **travel advisories** lists offices and webpages that give the most updated list of your home country's government's advisories about travel.

> **TRAVEL ADVISORIES.** The following government offices provide travel information and advisories by telephone, by fax, or via the web:
>
> **Australian Department of Foreign Affairs and Trade:** ☎ 1300 555 135; faxback service 02 6261 1299; www.dfat.gov.au.
> **Canadian Department of Foreign Affairs and International Trade (DFAIT):** In Canada and the US call ☎ 800-267-8376, elsewhere call US ☎ 613-944-4000; www.dfait-maeci.gc.ca. Their free booklet, *Bon Voyage, But...*, and other travel publications are available online.
> **New Zealand Ministry of Foreign Affairs:** ☎ 04 439 8000; fax 439 8532; www.mft.govt.nz/travel/index.html.
> **United Kingdom Foreign and Commonwealth Office:** ☎ 020 7008 0232; fax 7008 0155; www.fco.gov.uk.
> **US Department of State:** ☎ 202-647-5225, faxback service 647-3000; http://travel.state.gov. For *A Safe Trip Abroad,* call ☎ 512-1800.

FINANCIAL SECURITY

PROTECTING YOUR VALUABLES. To prevent theft, don't keep all your valuables (money, important documents) in one place. **Photocopies** of important documents allow you to recover them in case they are lost or pilfered. Bring one copy separate from the documents and leave another at home. Carry as little money as possible, keep some aside to use in an emergency, and never count your money in public. **Don't put a wallet with money in your back pocket.** If you carry a purse, buy a sturdy one with a secure clasp, and carry it crosswise on the side away from the street and with the clasp against you. Secure packs with small combination **padlocks** that slip through the two zippers. A **money belt,** a nylon, zippered pouch with a belt that sits inside the waist of your pants or skirt, combines convenience and security; you can buy one at most camping supply stores. A **neck pouch** is equally safe, but refrain from pulling it out in public. Avoid keeping anything precious in a fanny-pack (even if it's worn on your stomach); your valuables will be highly visible and easy to steal. **Be cautious when using ATMs—** the US State Department advises travelers to avoid highly visible, street-side ATMs and to restrict transactions to business hours.

ACCOMMODATIONS & TRANSPORTATION. Never leave your belongings unattended; crime occurs in even the most demure-looking hostel or hotel. Bring your own **padlock** for hostel lockers, and don't ever store valuables in any locker.

Be particularly careful on **buses** and **trains;** horror stories abound about determined thieves who wait for travelers to fall asleep. Carry your backpack in front of you where you can see it. When traveling with others, sleep in alternate shifts. When alone, use good judgement in selecting a train compartment: never stay in an empty one, and use a lock to secure your pack to the luggage rack. Try to sleep on top bunks with your luggage stored above you (if not in bed with you), and keep important documents and other valuables on your person. If traveling by **car,** don't leave valuables (such as radios or luggage) in it while you are away.

DRUGS & ALCOHOL

DRUGS. Contrary to international opinion, **Mexico rigorously prosecutes drug cases.** A minimum jail sentence awaits anyone found guilty of possessing any illegal drug, and Mexican law does not distinguish between marijuana and other narcotics. Even if you aren't convicted, getting arrested and tried will be long and incredibly unpleasant. The Mexican judicial process assumes you are guilty until proven innocent, and it is not uncommon to be detained for a year before a verdict is reached. Foreigners and suspected drug traffickers are never released on bail. Ignorance of Mexican law is no excuse, and a flimsy "I didn't know it was illegal" won't get you out of jail. If you are arrested, there is little your embassy can do other than inform your relatives and bring care packages to you in jail. (For information on how to address those packages, see **Keeping in Touch,** p. 27.) Travelers should also exercise caution with **prescription drugs.** The US State Department cautions against bringing large amounts of prescription drugs into the country. Mexican police can arrest you if they feel that your drugs are being abused or exceed the amount needed for personal use. It may be helpful to bring a doctor's letter certifying the drugs' legitimacy. It is also not advisable to buy large amounts of prescription drugs in Mexico—foreigners have been arrested even though they bought drugs legally. Counterfeit drugs are also prevalent, and depending on your home country, importing large amounts of prescription drugs may be illegal.

ALCOHOL. Mexicans are fed up with foreigners who cross the border for nights of debauchery, so avoid public drunkenness—it is against the law and could land you in jail. Drinking to excess is unsafe for other reasons. The US State Department warns of tourists—almost always traveling alone—at nightclubs or bars who have been drugged or intoxicated and then robbed, abducted, or raped.

OTHER AREAS OF CONCERN

There are certain areas of the country where special care is advised.

MEXICO CITY. Mexico City, like most bloated metropolitan areas, has more than its share of crime; in fact, it has the highest crime rate in the country. But before you cancel your visit to *el D.F.*, keep in mind that most crimes against tourists fall under the category of **petty street crime**—muggings, pickpocketings, and purse-snatchings. Although the government has prided itself on reducing crime in the city, visitors to the capital should still exercise extreme caution, particularly on public transportation.

CIUDAD JUÁREZ. Because of its position along the US border, the narcotics trade has flourished in Ciudad Juárez. Many foreigners involved in the trade have been kidnapped or murdered. The US State Department urges special caution for those visiting the "entertainment" district west of Av. Juárez.

CANCÚN. Cancún, an international tourist mecca, has drawn pickpockets and petty thieves from all over the country. Muggings, purse-snatchings, and hotel-room burglaries are on the rise. Use common sense and protect your valuables. A relatively new phenomenon are the sexual assaults and rapes that occur in the early morning hours in the Zona Hotelera. Intoxicated clubbers are separated from friends and then attacked. Such assaults, while few and far between, are on the rise. There have also been reports of increased police harassment and abuse.

CHIAPAS. Recent Zapatista activity has meant that tourists need to be especially careful when traveling in Chiapas. While the Mexican government has brought much of the area under control, armed rebels are occasionally active in the highlands north of San Cristóbal de las Casas, Ocosingo, and in the jungles east of Comitán. These rebels have in the past been openly hostile toward foreigners.

GUERRERO AND OAXACA. Due to political unrest in the rural parts of these states, visitors might encounter roadblocks and increased military presence. If your bus or car is pulled over, be prepared to show ID. There is no evidence, however, that the insurgent groups, the Popular Revolutionary Army and the Insurgent People's Revolutionary Army, have targeted tourists.

BEACHES. Crime has infested even the most beautiful and pristine parts of the country, and tourists have not escaped attack. As tempting as it sounds, stay away from hidden or secluded beaches, unless they are known to be especially safe. If you are going to the beach, it's a good idea to go during the afternoon or during weekends, when families and visitors are more numerous and beaches are less empty. Several US citizens have been killed while frolicking alone on beaches; some of these attacks happened during the morning hours. Exercise caution.

HEALTH

Before you can say "pass the jalapeños," a long-anticipated vacation can turn into an unpleasant study of the wonders of the Mexican health care system. While you can't foresee everything, some careful preparation can minimize trips to the clinic.

BEFORE YOU GO

In your **passport,** write the names of any people you wish to have contacted in case of a medical emergency and list any allergies or medical conditions of which doctors should be aware. If you take prescription medicines, carry up-to-date, legible prescriptions or a statement from your doctor stating the medication's trade name, manufacturer, chemical name, and dosage. While traveling, be sure to keep all medication with you in your carry-on luggage.

IMMUNIZATIONS AND PRECAUTIONS

Visitors to Mexico do not need to carry vaccination certificates unless they are entering from South America or Africa, in which case proof of vaccination for yellow fever may be required. Despite Mexico's lax attitude toward inoculations, all travelers over two years of age should have their standard vaccines up to date and should consult a doctor for any additional recommended inoculations.

 INOCULATION REQUIREMENTS. Mexico does not require visitors to carry vaccination certificates, nor does it require specific vaccinations for entry. It is advisable, however, to consult your doctor four to six weeks before departure. In addition to **booster shots for measles and tetanus,** consider the following vaccines and prescriptions:

Malaria Tablets: Chloroquinine is recommended for those traveling in rural and coastal areas in the southern half of the country.
Hepatitis A: Vaccine or immune globulin (IG).
Hepatitis B: Recommended for those planning long stays, those who might be exposed to blood, or those who plan on being sexually active.
Rabies: Recommended for those who might have contact with animals.
Typhoid Fever: Recommended for those traveling to rural areas only.

USEFUL ORGANIZATIONS AND PUBLICATIONS

The US **Centers for Disease Control and Prevention** (**CDC;** ☎877-FYI-TRIP; tollfree fax 888-232-3299; www.cdc.gov/travel) maintains an international travelers' hotline and an informative website. The CDC's comprehensive booklet *Health Information for International Travel*, an annual rundown of disease, immunization, and general health advice, is free online or US$30 via the Public Health Foundation (☎877-252-1200). Consult the appropriate government agency of your home country for consular information sheets on health, entry requirements, and other issues (see the listings in the box on **Travel Advisories,** p. 16). For quick information on health and other travel warnings, call the **Overseas Citizens Services** (☎202-647-5225), or contact a passport agency, embassy, or consulate abroad. US citizens can send a self-addressed, stamped envelope to the Overseas Citizens Services, Bureau of Consular Affairs, #4811, US Department of State, Washington, D.C. 20520. For information on medical evacuation services and travel insurance firms, see the US government's website at http://travel.state.gov/medical.html or the **British Foreign and Commonwealth Office** (www.fco.gov.uk).

For detailed information on travel health, including a country-by-country overview of diseases, try the *International Travel Health Guide*, by Stuart Rose, MD (US$25; www.travmed.com). For general health info, contact the **American Red Cross** (☎800-564-1234; www.redcross.org).

MEDICAL ASSISTANCE ON THE ROAD

The quality of medical care in Mexico often varies directly with the size of the city or town. The same applies to the availability of English-speaking medical practitioners. Medical care in Mexico City is first-class, while care in more rural areas can be spotty and limited. Along with the town clinic or Red Cross, local pharmacies can be invaluable sources of medical help. Most pharmacists are knowledgeable about mild illnesses—particularly those that plague tourists—and can recommend shots or medicines. Wherever possible, *Let's Go* lists pharmacies open for extended hours.

If you are concerned about being able to access medical support while traveling, there are special support services you may employ. The *MedPass* from **GlobalCare, Inc.,** 6875 Shiloh Rd. East, Alpharetta, GA 30005, USA (☎800-860-1111; fax 678-341-1800; www.globalems.com), provides 24hr. international medical assistance, support, and medical evacuation resources. The **International Association for Medical Assistance to Travelers** (**IAMAT;** US ☎716-754-4883, Canada ☎519-836-0102; www.cybermall.co.nz/NZ/IAMAT) has free membership, lists English-speaking doctors worldwide, and offers detailed info on immunization requirements and sanitation. If your regular **insurance** policy does not cover travel abroad, you may wish to purchase additional coverage (see p. 22).

ONCE IN MEXICO

ENVIRONMENTAL HAZARDS

Heat exhaustion and dehydration: Heat exhaustion, characterized by dehydration and salt deficiency, can lead to fatigue, headaches, and wooziness. Avoid it by drinking plenty of fluids, staying away from salty foods (e.g. crackers), and eschewing dehydrating beverages (e.g. alcohol, coffee, tea, and caffeinated soda). Continuous heat stress can eventually lead to heatstroke, characterized by a rising body temperature, severe headache, and cessation of sweating. Victims should be cooled off with wet towels and taken to a doctor. The risk of heat exhaustion is greatest in Baja California and northern Mexico, where the combination of heat and dryness can result in rapid water loss.

Sunburn: Nowhere in Mexico are you safe from sunburn, though the risk increases as you travel toward the equator and up in altitude. If you get sunburned, drink more fluids than usual and apply an aloe-based lotion.

Air Pollution: In 1999, Mexico City earned the distinction of having the worst air in the world for children. It's not too great for adults, either. Fortunately, many of the possible effects—wheezing, tightness in the chest, bronchitis—tend to reverse themselves once exposure stops. Unfortunately, long-term exposure can result in serious problems such as lung cancer and heart disease. To protect yourself, heed daily pollution warnings. Pollution is usually worst during the winter and in the early morning hours.

Altitude Sickness: Many places in mountainous Mexico, including Mexico City, are high enough for altitude sickness to be a concern. Symptoms may include headaches, dizziness, and sleep disruption. To minimize possible effects, avoid rapid increases in elevation, and allow your body a couple of days to adjust to a new elevation before exerting yourself. Note that alcohol is more potent and UV rays stronger at high elevations.

INSECT-BORNE DISEASES

Many diseases are transmitted by insects, primarily mosquitoes, fleas, ticks, and lice. Be aware of insects in wet or forested areas, and while hiking, camping, or climbing around ruins. **Mosquitoes** are most active from dusk to dawn and are rampant along coastal areas. Use insect repellents that have a 30-35% concentration of DEET (5-10% is recommended for children). Wear long pants and long sleeves (fabric need not be thick or warm; tropic-weight cottons can keep you comfortable in the heat) and consider buying a **mosquito net** for travel in rural (especially coastal or humid) regions. Natural repellents can be useful supplements: taking vitamin B-12 pills regularly can eventually make you smelly to insects, as can garlic pills. Calamine lotion or topical cortisones (like Cortaid) may stop insect bites from itching, as can a bath with a ½ cup of baking soda or oatmeal.

Malaria: Malaria is transmitted by *Anopheles* mosquitoes that bite at night. The incubation period varies from six days to as long as months. Early symptoms include fever, chills, aches, and fatigue, followed by high fever and sweating, and sometimes vomiting and diarrhea. See a doctor for any flu-like sickness that occurs after travel in a risk area. Left untreated, malaria can cause anemia, kidney failure, coma, and death. If you are visiting coastal or rural areas of Campeche, Chiapas, Guerrero, Michoacán, Nayarit, Oaxaca, Quintana Roo, Sinaloa, Tabasco, or Yucatán, consider getting a prescription for **Chloroquine.** Chloroquine may have side effects such as nausea, headache, and vomiting; consult your doctor. Antimalarial drugs are not recommended for travelers to the major resort areas on the Pacific and Gulf coasts or to the northern parts of the country.

Other insect-borne diseases: Filariasis is a roundworm infestation transmitted by mosquitoes. Infection causes enlargement of extremities and has no vaccine. **Leishmaniasis** is a parasite transmitted by sand flies. Common symptoms are fever, weakness, and swelling of the spleen. There is a treatment, but no vaccine. **CHAGAS disease (American trypanomiasis)** is another common parasite transmitted by the cone-nose and kissing bugs, which infest mud, adobe, and thatch. Its symptoms are fever, heart disease, and, later on, an enlarged intestine. There is no vaccine and limited treatment. All three diseases are rare and limited to the tropical areas of Chiapas and the Yucatán.

FOOD- AND WATER-BORNE DISEASES

The biggest health threats in Mexico are food and water. **Traveler's diarrhea,** known in Mexico as *turista,* often lasts two or three days. Symptoms include cramps, nausea, vomiting, chills, and fever. Scientifically speaking, *turista* is a temporary reaction to bacteria in new food ingredients. In plain speak, *turista* will blow your bowels inside out. **Watch what you drink and eat.**

Dirty water is enemy number one. Never drink water straight from the tap or from dubious sources, such as water fountains. Don't brush your teeth with tap water, don't rinse your toothbrush under the faucet, and don't keep your mouth open in the shower. Be suspicious of the most clever disguise of impure water—the treacherous ice cube. **Drink only purified, bottled water (agua embotellada).** If you must purify your own water, bring it to a rolling boil (simmering isn't enough) and let it boil for about 30min., or treat it with **iodine drops or tablets.**

If impure water is enemy number one, poorly-cooked food is enemy number two. Stay away from those tasty-looking salads; eating uncooked vegetables (including lettuce and coleslaw) is a quick way to get *turista*. Other culprits include raw shellfish, unpasteurized milk and dairy products, and sauces containing raw eggs. Peel fruits and vegetables before eating them. Beware food from markets or street vendors that may have been "washed" in dirty water or fried in rancid oil. Juices, peeled fruits, and exposed coconut slices are all risky. Also beware frozen treats; they may have been made with bad water.

 THE GOLDEN RULE IN MEXICO. Beware food and water. Drink only bottled water *(agua embotellada)* or purified water *(agua purificada).* Eat food that has been boiled, peeled, or cooked. Otherwise, forget it. Remember: a careful tourist is a diarrhea-free tourist.

If you have the misfortune of developing *turista*, try quick-energy, non-sugary foods with protein and carbohydrates to keep your strength up. Good things to eat are tortillas and salted crackers. Perhaps the most dangerous side effect of *turista* is dehydration and loss of electrolytes; drink lots of (pure) water with ½ tsp. of sugar or honey and a pinch of salt, uncaffeinated soft drinks, and bottled juices. If you develop a high fever or your symptoms don't go away after four to five days, consult a doctor; it might be more than just *turista*. More serious diseases with *turista*-like symptoms (diarrhea, nausea, and cramps) include:

Hepatitis A: The symptoms of this viral liver infection acquired primarily through contaminated water include fatigue, fever, loss of appetite, nausea, dark urine, jaundice, vomiting, aches, and light stools. Risks are highest in rural areas, lower in cities. Ask your doctor about the vaccine (Havrix or Vaqta) or an immune globulin injection (IG; formerly called gamma globulin).

Typhoid Fever: Caused by the salmonella bacterium, typhoid is most common in villages and rural areas in Mexico. While primarily transmitted through contaminated food and water, it may also be acquired by direct contact with an infected person. Early symptoms include fever, headache, fatigue, loss of appetite, constipation, and sometimes a rash on the abdomen or chest. Antibiotics are available, but a vaccination (70-90% effective) is recommended.

AIDS, HIV, & STDS

For detailed information on **Acquired Immune Deficiency Syndrome (AIDS)** in Mexico, call the **US Centers for Disease Control's** 24hr. hotline at ☎ 800-342-2437, or contact the **Joint United Nations Programme on HIV/AIDS (UNAIDS),** 20, ave. Appia, CH-1211 Geneva 27, Switzerland (☎ 22 791 3666; fax 791 4187). Mexico does not screen tourists for HIV/AIDs. For more information, contact the Mexican consulate.

WOMEN'S HEALTH

Women traveling in unsanitary conditions are vulnerable to **urinary tract** and **bladder infections,** common and very uncomfortable bacterial conditions that cause a burning sensation and painful (sometimes frequent) urination. **Vaginal yeast infections** may flare up in hot and humid climates. Wearing loosely fitting trousers or a skirt and cotton underwear will help.

While **maxi pads** are plentiful in Mexican pharmacies and supermarkets, **tampons** are harder to come by and, if available at all, come only in regular sizes. It might be wise to bring a supply along, especially if you are traveling to smaller cities. Contraceptive devices are also hard to find, with the exception of condoms, which are found in most large pharmacies.

Abortion remains illegal in Mexico. Women considering an abortion should contact the **International Planned Parenthood Federation (IPPF)**, Regent's College, Inner Circle, Regent's Park, London NW1 4NS, UK (☎ 020 7487 7900; fax 7487 7950; www.ippf.org), for more information.

E S S E N T I A L S

INSURANCE

Travel insurance generally covers four basic areas: medical/health problems, property loss, trip cancellation/interruption, and emergency evacuation. Although your regular insurance policies may extend to travel-related accidents, you should consider purchasing travel insurance if the cost of potential trip cancellation/interruption or emergency medical evacuation is greater than you can absorb. Prices for travel insurance purchased separately generally run about US$50 per week for full coverage, while trip cancellation/interruption may be purchased separately at a rate of about US$5.50 per US$100 of coverage.

Medical insurance (especially university policies) often covers costs incurred abroad; check with your provider. **US Medicare** covers travel to Mexico. **Canadians** are protected by their home province's health insurance plan for up to 90 days after leaving the country; check with the provincial Ministry of Health or Health Plan Headquarters for details. **Homeowners' insurance** (or your family's coverage) often covers theft during travel and loss of travel documents (passport, plane ticket, railpass, etc.) up to US$500.

ISIC and its cousin, **ITIC** (see p. 9), provide basic insurance benefits, including US$100 per day of in-hospital sickness for up to 60 days, US$3000 of accident-related medical reimbursement, and US$25,000 for emergency medical transport. Cardholders have access to a toll-free 24hr. helpline (run by the insurance provider **TravelGuard**) for medical, legal, and financial emergencies overseas (US and Canada ☎ 877-370-4742, elsewhere call US collect +1 715-345-0505). **American Express** (US ☎ 800-528-4800) grants most cardholders automatic car rental insurance (collision and theft, but not liability) and ground travel accident coverage of US$100,000 on flight purchases made with the card.

INSURANCE PROVIDERS. STA (see p. 30) offer a range of plans that can supplement your basic coverage. Other private insurance providers in the **US and Canada** include: **Access America** (☎ 800-284-8300); **Berkely Group/Carefree Travel Insurance** (☎ 800-323-3149; www.berkely.com); **Globalcare Travel Insurance** (☎ 800-821-2488; www.globalcare-cocco.com); and **Travel Assistance International** (☎ 800-821-2828; www.europ-assistance.com). Providers in the **UK** include **Columbus Direct** (☎ 020 7375 0011). In **Australia,** try **AFTA** (☎ 02 9264 3299).

PACKING

LUGGAGE. Unless you plan on spending most of your time in one location, a sturdy **internal frame backpack** is recommended. Shop carefully for a pack; if the fit isn't perfect your life on the road could be very miserable. Remember that packs may be strapped atop buses or otherwise exposed to the elements, so bring along a waterproof pack cover or trash bags. A smaller **daypack** will be helpful for carrying around daily necessities, such as bottled water and your copy of *Let's Go*.

CLOTHING. Mexican culture values neat and clean appearances, and visitors are recommended to do likewise, especially when dealing with officials at border crossings or military roadblocks. Shorts are rarely worn outside of beach towns and touristy ruins, and bathing suits are only appropriate on the beach.

Regardless of the season, those headed to into the great outdoors should bring a waterproof **rain jacket,** sturdy shoes or **hiking boots,** and **thick socks.** Cotton socks are not recommended as they tend to soak up and retain moisture. **Flip-flops** or waterproof sandals are crucial for scuzzy hotel showers and beach areas, and hiking sandals should be enough for any adventure in the hot, dry northwest. Keep the intense sun out of your eyes with a wide-brimmed **hat** or **sunglasses.** Those headed to the highlands or to mountainous national parks should pack a wool sweater or medium-weight fleece for the chilly nights.

TOILETRIES. Basic toiletries are easy to find in most of Mexico, but those traveling in more rural areas should pack a supply of more specialized products. **Contact lens** wearers, especially, may want to bring along extra pairs and plenty of saline solution, as well as glasses and a prescription in case an emergency replacement is needed. **Sunscreen** is essential, and those traveling in coastal areas or through the southern jungles will want a lot of **insect repellent.**

ELECTRIC CURRENT. Appliances in Mexico use the same voltage and plugs as the rest of North America (110V, parallel plugs). Those with European appliances (220V) should visit a hardware store for an **adapter** (which changes the shape of the plug) and a **converter** (which changes the voltage). Do not make the mistake of using only an adapter, unless appliance instructions explicitly state otherwise).

OTHER USEFUL ITEMS. Many travelers like to store their essentials in a **money belt** and **padlock** their packs. A **sleepsack**—basically a full-size sheet folded over and sewn together—and a pillowcase can be useful in lower-end accommodations, which sometimes have dirty sheets. A small absorbent **towel** or chamois will also come in handy when you tire of scratchy budget hotel towels. Definitely bring a **flashlight** if you are planning to camp or drive. Other handy items include: a **mosquito net,** a **water bottle,** a **travel alarm clock, earplugs** (hostels and hotels can be noisy inside and out); **toilet paper,** a **needle and thread** or duct tape for tears, a **clothes line,** a pocket **calculator,** resealable **plastic bags** (for damp clothes, spillable toiletries, a cockroach collection, etc.), and **laundry soap.**

ACCOMMODATIONS

HOSTELS

A HOSTELER'S BILL OF RIGHTS. There are certain standard features that we do not include in our hostel listings. Unless we state otherwise, you can expect that every hostel has no lockout, no curfew, a kitchen, free hot showers, some system of secure luggage storage, and no key deposit.

The few hostels that exist in Mexico are youth-oriented, dorm-style accommodations, often having large, single-sex rooms with bunk beds. Many have kitchens, laundry facilities, and storage areas, though they may inconvenience their patrons with curfews and daytime "lock-out" hours. Perhaps most importantly, Mexican hostels tend to be run-down and far from town. Although a bit cheaper than hotels—around US$5-6 per person—the money you save usually doesn't make up for the inconvenience. For more information about Mexican hostels, contact the **Red Mexicana de Alojamiento para Jóvenes** (☎5518 1726; www.hostellingmexico.com) or the **Asociación Mexicana de Albergues Juveniles, A.C.** (☎5564 0333; www.hostels.com.mx), both of which are hostelling organizations affiliated with Hostelling International.

BOOKING HOSTELS ONLINE One of the cheapest and easiest ways to ensure a bed for a night is by reserving online. Our website features the **Hostelworld** booking engine; access it at **www.letsgo.com/resources/accommodations.** Hostelworld offers bargain accommodations everywhere from Argentina to Zimbabwe with no added commission.

HOTELS

Bargain-seekers will not be disappointed with Mexico's selection of hotels. Although some (particularly in resort towns) are among the world's most overpriced, the majority of Mexican accommodations are affordable and convenient. Usually located within a block or two of a city's *zócalo*, the cheapest hotels (about US$7-10 per night) rarely provide amenities such as air conditioning, though they usually have hot water and private bathrooms. Higher priced hotels (about US$20 per night) are often located in the same district but are much better equipped, with telephones and the occasional television. Before accepting a room, ask to see it, and always find out whether the price includes any complimentary meals and if there are any extra surcharges before you pay.

All hotels, from luxury resorts in Cancún to rent-by-the-hour joints in Tijuana, are controlled by the government's **Secretaria de Turismo (SECTUR).** This ensures that hotels of similar quality charge similar prices; you should always ask to see an up-to-date **official tariff sheet** if you doubt the quoted price. Many hotels post their official tariffs somewhere near the reception area. Although hotel prices are regulated, proprietors are not prohibited from charging *less* than the official rate. A little bargaining can work wonders, especially if you stay several days.

ESSENTIALS

 PLAN AHEAD, WAY AHEAD. Reservations are almost always necessary during Christmas, *Semana Santa* (the week before Easter), and local festivals. At most other times, even during the summer season, you need not worry much about having to reserve rooms in budget hotels.

CAMPING

Travelers accustomed to clean and well-maintained campgrounds may be in for a few surprises. By and large, Mexican national parks exist only in theory. The "protected lands" are often indistinguishable from the surrounding countryside or city and may be dirty, unappealing, and overrun with amorous teenagers. Privately owned **trailer parks** are relatively common on major routes—look for signs with a picture of a trailer, or the words *parque de trailer, campamento,* or *remolques*. These places often allow campers to pitch tents or sling up a hammock.

 UNDER THE STARS. While all beaches in Mexico are public, not all of them are safe for camping. Hotel security in glitzy resort areas have a reputation for being unkind to beach campers. There have also been more serious reports of beachside robberies, rapes, and assaults. It's a good idea to check in with the local tourist office or police department to see whether camping is safe or permitted. Use common sense: don't camp on very secluded beaches or beaches near unsafe urban areas.

For those budget-minded individuals traveling along the coast, the hammock is the way to go. Most beach towns in Mexico are dotted with **palapas** (palm-tree huts). For a small fee, open-air restaurants double as places to hang your hat and hammock when the sun sets. At beaches and some inland towns frequented by backpackers, **cabañas** (cabins, usually simple thatch-roof huts) are common. For the truly hard-core, camping on the beach can sometimes be an option. Lax permit laws and beach accessibility—every meter of beach in Mexico is public property—offer campers oodles of options.

USEFUL PUBLICATIONS AND WEB RESOURCES

BOOKS

Backpacking in Mexico, Tim Burford. Bradt Publishing ($17).

Traveler's Guide to Camping Mexico's Baja, Mike and Terri Church. Rolling Home Press ($13).

Mexico: A Hiker's Guide to Mexico's Natural History, Jim Conrad. Mountaineers Books ($17).

Mexico's Copper Canyon Country, John Fayhee. Johnson Books ($17).

For topographical maps of Mexico, write or visit the **Instituto Nacional de Estadísticas, Geografía e Informática (INEGI),** Calle Patriotismo 711, Torre A, Del. Benito Juárez, Col. San Juan Mixcoac, México, D.F. ☎5278 1035. Available online at **Global Perspectives** (www.global-perspectives.com) and **Omnimap** (www.omnimap.com).

KEEPING IN TOUCH

BY MAIL

SENDING MAIL HOME FROM MEXICO

Mexican mail service is painfully slow. **Airmail** from major cities in Mexico to the US and Canada takes anywhere from two weeks to one month; to Australia or New Zealand, one month; to the UK or Ireland, three weeks to one month; to South Africa, one to two months. Add another one or two weeks for mail sent from more rural areas. Mexican mailboxes are notorious for being infrequently picked up, but the bright plastic orange boxes labeled *Express* that have popped up around Mexico City and other large cities are quite reliable and are picked up every morning. Anything important, however, should be sent *registrado* (registered mail) or taken directly to the post office, at the very least. To speed service, it's a good idea to write Spanish abbreviations or names for countries (i.e., EE.UU. for the US). Also write "por avión" on all postcards and letters; though method of travel is determined by the type of stamp, it's a good backup.

Packages cannot weigh more than 25kg. Keep in mind that all packages are opened and inspected by customs at border crossings; closing boxes with string, not tape, is recommended. Sometimes you may have to provide certain information: your tourist card data, contents, value, and nature of the package ("Gift" works best), and your address and return address.

Mexpost promises 2-day delivery out of state; it also works with Express Mail internationally to deliver mail quickly and reliably. Three days is the official Mexpost delivery time to major cities internationally, but expect a week for delivery, more if the destination lies outside of the city proper. Packages have a 20kg maximum. Mexpost offices are usually found next to regular post offices, but if not, the post office staff can usually give you directions to the nearest Mexpost office.

SENDING MAIL TO MEXICO

Mark envelopes "air mail" or "por avión" to avoid having letters sent by sea or land. Additionally, **Federal Express** (US and Canada, ☎ 800-247-4747; Australia, ☎ 13 26 10; Ireland, ☎ 1800 535 800; New Zealand, ☎ 0800 733339; UK, ☎ 0800 123 800) handles express mail from those countries to Mexico. Note that Federal Express will not deliver to post offices in Mexico, only to businesses and residences.

RECEIVING MAIL IN MEXICO

There are several ways to arrange pick-up of letters sent to you by friends and relatives while you are abroad.

General Delivery: Mail can be sent to Mexico through **Poste Restante** (the international phrase for General Delivery; **Lista de Correos** in Spanish) to almost any city or town with a post office. Mail sent via *Poste Restante* will go to a special desk in the central post office, unless you specify a post office by street address or postal code. Letters should be marked *Favor de retener hasta la llegada* (Please hold until arrival); they will be held up to 15 days. It's probably not a good idea to send valuable items to a city's *Lista de Correos*.

American Express: AmEx's travel offices throughout the world offer a free **Client Letter Service** (mail held up to 30 days; forwarding on request) for cardholders who contact them in advance. Address the letter in the way shown above. Some offices will offer these services to non-cardholders (especially AmEx Traveler's Cheque holders). *Let's Go*

WITH LOVE, FROM ME TO YOU. Address *Poste Restante* letters to:
Scrobstacle VON MITTENSON (name)
Lista de Correos
Ortiz Rubio 40 (street address for post office, or leave it blank)
Tecate (city), Baja California (state), 21400 (postal code)
MEXICO

lists AmEx office locations for most large cities in **Practical Information** sections; for a complete list, call ☎800-346-3607.

Packages sent via Express Mail International, FedEx, UPS, or other express services might be held at a different office (often Mexpost, see below). It's a good idea not to send anything particularly valuable via any sort of mail to Mexico.

BY TELEPHONE

CALLING HOME FROM MEXICO

The **LADATEL phones** that have popped up all over the country have revolutionized the way Mexico calls. To operate one, you'll need a colorful **pre-paid phone card,** available at most *papelerías* (stationery stores) or *tiendas de abarrotes* (general stores)—look for the "De venta aquí LADATEL" signs posted in store windows. Cards come in 30-, 50-, and 100-peso increments. Once you are armed with your precious LADATEL phone card, calling will be a snap.

INTERNATIONAL CALLS WITH A CALLING CARD. A calling card is probably the cheapest way to make international calls from Mexico. To use a calling card from Mexico, contact the operator for your service provider by dialing the appropriate toll-free Mexico access number. If your provider does not have a Mexico-specific access code, you should inquire beforehand as to the correct dialing procedures.

AT&T: ☎01 800 288 2872 (using LADATEL phones) or 001 800 462 4240.

Sprint: ☎001 800 877 8000.

MCI WorldPhone Direct: ☎001 800 674 7000.

DIRECT INTERNATIONAL CALLS. To call directly, insert your LADATEL card, dial 00 (to get an international line), the country code of the place you are calling, the area code, and the phone number. You can then chat quickly (and nervously) while the seconds tick away, as it can be very expensive to make direct international calls. At 5 pesos per minute, calling the US is only somewhat pricey. Dial ☎**87 on a LADATEL phone for toll-free assistance, or go to http://www.telmex.com.mx/internos/deviaje/tladatel.htm for information on calling costs.

CALLING COLLECT. If you speak Spanish and can't reach the international operator, dial 07 for the national operator, who will connect you (sometimes even a local operator can help). The term for a collect call is a *llamada por cobrar.* Calling from hotels is usually faster but beware of exorbitant surcharges. Remember, however, that there can be a fee of 1-5 pesos for collect calls that are not accepted.

CALLING MEXICO FROM HOME

To call Mexico from home, first dial the **international access code** of your home country. International access codes include: Australia 0011 (fax 0015), Ireland 00, New Zealand 00, South Africa 09, UK 00, US 011. Country codes and city codes are sometimes listed with a zero in front (e.g., 033), but after dialing the international access code, drop successive zeros (with an access code of 011, e.g., 011 33). Then,

AREA CODES The entire Mexican telephone system has been revamped and reorganized in the last two years. Before, numbers were listed as five or six digits accompanied by a two- or three-digit city code. Now, all local numbers are **seven digits** (with the exception of those in Mexico City, Guadalajara, and Monterrey, which are **eight**). Area codes are three digits (two where local numbers are eight digits) and are only used when calling to a different area code. The area code is always preceded by the national access code, 01. To call from Oaxaca to Guadalajara, therefore, dial 01 + 33 + 8-digit local number. All area codes can be found on the telmex website at www.telmex.com/internos/clavesLADA/list100.html. Note that numbers starting with 01 800 or 800 in *Let's Go: Mexico* are toll-free.

dial 52 (Mexico's country code). Finally, dial the area code (across from the city or town name) and local number. (This step will add up to ten digits.)

EMAIL AND INTERNET

With many Mexican businesses, language schools, and individuals now online, the Internet and the electronic communication it offers provide a cheap and accessible alternative to pricey phone calls and slow postal service. Cybercafes, included in the **Practical Information** of most town listings, are the most prominent form of Internet access in Mexico. These cafes can even be found in some of the smaller Mexican towns; expect to pay US$1-8 per hour for access. For lists of additional cybercafes in Mexico, check out www.netcafes.com.

Some, but not all, Internet providers offer telnet, Internet Relay Chat (IRC, pronounced "eerk" in Spanish), and instant messenger (IM) programs such as America Online Instant Messenger or ICQ. All Internet providers maintain some sort of World Wide Web access, be it via Netscape or Internet Explorer. Take www.mail2web.com up on its promise "From any computer, anywhere in the world," or use a free **web-based email account** (such as Hotmail or Yahoo!).

GETTING THERE

BY PLANE

When it comes to airfare, a little effort can save you a bundle. The keys are to hunt around, to be flexible, and to ask persistently about discounts. Students, seniors, and those under 26 should never have to pay full price for a ticket.

DETAILS AND TIPS

Timing: The most expensive time to travel is between mid-June and August. Midweek (M-Th morning) round-trip flights run US$30-70 cheaper than weekend flights but may be more crowded and less likely to permit frequent-flier upgrades. Traveling with an "open return" ticket can be pricier than fixing a return date when buying the ticket.

Route: Round-trip flights are by far the cheapest; "open-jaw" (arriving and departing from different cities) tickets tend to be pricier. Patching 1-way flights together is the most expensive way to travel.

Round-the-World (RTW): If Mexico is only 1 stop on a more extensive globe-hop, consider an RTW ticket. Tickets usually include at least 4 stops and are valid for about a year; prices range US$1200-5000. Try **Northwest Airlines/KLM** (US ☎ 800-447-4747; www.nwa.com) or **Star Alliance** (www.staralliance.com), a consortium of 13 airlines including United Airlines (US ☎800-241-6522) and, recently, US Airways (US ☎800-245-4882).

Gateway Cities: Flights between capitals and regional or tourist hubs will offer the cheapest fares. The cheapest gateway cities in Mexico are typically Mexico City, Guadalajara, and Cancún.

Fares: The cheapest round-trip fares to Mexico City from New York usually range from US$300-400; from London US$1000-1200; from Los Angeles US$250-350; from Sydney US$2100-2300; from Cancún US$220-350; from Monterrey US$300-350.

Taxes: Add US$110 in taxes on plane tickets to Mexico. Taxes average US$90.

BUDGET AND STUDENT TRAVEL AGENCIES

While knowledgeable agents specializing in flights to Mexico can make your life easy and help you save, they may not spend the time to find you the lowest possible fare. Students and under-26ers holding **ISIC and IYTC cards** (see p. 9), respectively, qualify for big discounts from student travel agencies. Most flights from budget agencies are on major airlines, but in peak season some may sell seats on less reliable chartered aircraft.

usit world (www.usitworld.com). Over 50 **usit campus** branches in the UK, including 52 Grosvenor Gardens, **London** SW1W 0AG (☎0870 240 10 10); **Manchester** (☎0161 273 1880); and **Edinburgh** (☎0131 668 3303). Nearly 20 **usit NOW** offices in Ireland, including 19-21 Aston Quay, O'Connell Bridge, **Dublin** 2 (☎01 602 1600), and **Belfast** (☎02 890 327 111). Offices also in Athens, Auckland, Brussels, Frankfurt, Johannesburg, Lisbon, Luxembourg, Madrid, Paris, Sofia, and Warsaw.

CTS Travel, 30 Rathbone Place, **London** W1T 1GQ (☎0207-290-0630; www.ctstravel.co.uk). A CTS card, £15 and available to everyone, is good at venues around London, with limited use at locations around the world.

STA Travel (www.sta-travel.com). This long-established travel organization has been serving youth and students since 1949. It recently combined with **Council Travel** to form a network of over 450 branches worldwide, with countless US offices (in cities such as Atlanta; Boston; Chicago; L.A.; New York; San Francisco; Seattle; and Washington, D.C.) and 67 in the UK (including several in London).

Travel CUTS (Canadian Universities Travel Services, Limited), 187 College St., **Toronto,** ON M5T 1P7 (☎416-979-2406; www.travelcuts.com). The Canadian Federation of Students runs the 60 offices across Canada; 9 locations in the US are concentrated in California but include the northwest and northeast. Also in the UK with 2 locations in **London,** including 295-A Regent St., London W1R 7YA (☎0207-255-1944).

COMMERCIAL AIRLINES

Most major international airlines travel in and out of Mexico City. Popular Mexican carriers include **Aeroméxico** (☎800-237-6639; www.aeromexico.com), which flies to practically every Mexican city with an airport, and **Mexicana** (☎800-531-7921; www.mexicana.com), North America's oldest airline, which flies to most major US and European cities.

Taking **standby flights** requires considerable flexibility in arrival and departure dates and cities. Companies dealing in standby flights sell vouchers rather than tickets, along with the promise to get you to your destination (or near your destination) within a certain window of time (typically 1-5 days). **Air-Tech** (☎212-219-7200, www.airtech.com), out of New York City, boasts a 94% success rate—"as long as the traveler is sufficiently flexible."

Another cheap option is to buy from **ticket consolidators**, or **"bucket shops,"** companies that buy unsold tickets in bulk from commercial airlines and sell them at discounted rates. The best place to look is in the Sunday travel section of any major newspaper (such as *The New York Times*), where many bucket shops advertise dirt cheap flights to popular Mexican destinations such as Acapulco and Cancún. Not all bucket shops are reliable, so insist on a receipt that gives full details of restrictions, refunds, and tickets, and pay by credit card (in spite of the 2-5% fee) so you can stop payment if you never receive your tickets. For more info, see www.travel-library.com/air-travel/consolidators.html or pick up Kelly Monaghan's *Air Travel's Bargain Basement* (Intrepid Traveler. Out of print, but available through Amazon.com for under $8).

BY BUS OR TRAIN

Greyhound (☎800-229-9424 or 402-330-8552 for Discovery Pass holders outside the US and Canada; www.greyhound.com) serves many US-Mexico border towns, including El Paso and Brownsville, Texas, as well as Tijuana. Schedule information is available at any Greyhound terminal, on the web page, or by calling the 800 number. Smaller lines serve other destinations. Buses tend not to cross the border, but at each of these stops you can pick up Mexican bus lines (among them Estrella de Oro, Estrella Blanca, ADO, and Transportes Del Norte) on the other side. Guatemalan bus lines operate at Guatemala-Mexico border towns, including Talismán and La Mesilla. Buses usually stop just short of the border, and you can walk across to Mexico and pick up a local bus to the nearest town. Buses also operate between Chetumal (see p. 691) and the capital of Belize, Belize City.

If you travel by train, your options are limited to the US-Mexico border. You can take **Amtrak** (☎800-872-7245; www.amtrak.com) to El Paso, walk across the border to Ciudad Juárez, and continue on with other forms of transportation. Amtrak also serves San Diego and San Antonio, where you can catch a bus to the border towns.

GETTING AROUND MEXICO

BY BUS

Mexico's bus system never ceases to astound, amaze, and mystify. From most large cities, it is possible to get almost anywhere in the republic, and companies like **Autotransportes del Oriente (ADO)**, **Estrella Blanca**, and **Estrella de Oro** run cheaply and efficiently—as efficiently as is possible in Mexico, that is. Several types of bus services exist. Executive service, called **servicio ejecutivo**, is fairly rare but provides royal treatment: plush reclining seats, sandwiches and soda, sometimes too frigid A/C, and movies galore. Less fancy are **primera clase** (1st-class) buses, which usually feature ridiculously bad movies and A/C. **Segunda clase** (2nd-class) buses are lower in quality, usually converted school buses or some variation thereof. They may be overcrowded and uncomfortable, but the surest difference is drivers' willingness to pick up people along the road; together with less direct routes, such travel may be and painfully slow. Buses are categorized as either *local* or *de paso*. **Locales** originate at the station from which you leave. **De paso** (in passing) buses originate elsewhere and pass through your station. Because they depend on the seating availability when the bus arrives, tickets are not available in advance. Be on the watch for when tickets do go on sale: they do not stay in the station long and may fill quickly.

BY CAR

Driving in Mexico can be hazardous to your health. The maximum speed on Mexican routes is 100km per hour (62mph) unless otherwise posted, but, like most other traffic signs and regulations, it is often ignored. Mexicans tend to be a rowdy bunch on the road. It's not unusual to hear drivers exchange such greetings as *"¡Baboso!"* (Drooling fool!), *"¡Eh, stúpido!"* (Hey, stupid!), and, of course, the ubiquitous *"¿Dónde aprendiste a manajar, menso?"* (Where did you learn how to drive, dumbass?). With enough practice, you'll be able to curse with the best Mexican driver. It's also not unusual for Mexican drivers to overuse their car horns; drive down any busy street, and you'll be serenaded by a harmonious chorus of honks. In such a climate, it's best to drive defensively. Please be careful.

Driving norms aside, it's a good idea to avoid driving during the rainy season (May-October), when road conditions deteriorate. If you are planning on driving extensively between cities, check with local authorities or with your nearest consulate for updates on potential danger. In general, it is a good idea to avoid less secure freeways *(libres)* in favor of toll *(cuota)* roads. Also avoid driving at night, when chances of hijacks and other criminal acts are higher. While on the road, you may be stopped by the military or other law enforcement for a search of your car and its contents. Be as cooperative as possible; they will usually just open your trunk, look around your car, and wave you through. For information about driving a car into Mexico and obtaining a **vehicle permit,** see **Entering Mexico By Car,** p. 11.

 FILL 'ER UP. Petroleos Mexicanos, more commonly, **PEMEX,** the national oil company, sells two types of unleaded gas: **Magna** (regular) and **Premium** (plus). Prices vary by region, but in most of the country gas is a little more than in the United States. PEMEX usually only accepts cash and checks.

If you're unlucky enough to break down on a major toll road between 8am and 8pm, pull completely off the road, raise the hood, stay with your car, and wait for the **Ángeles Verdes** (Green Angels) to come to the rescue. If you have access to a phone, call ☎818 340 2113. These green-and-white emergency trucks, dispatched by radio and staffed by almost a thousand mechanics, are equipped for performing common repair jobs, towing, changing tires, and addressing minor medical problems. Your green saviors may take a while to show up, but the service (except for parts, gas, and oil) is free. Tipping is optional but a good idea. These guardian angels will assist you anywhere but in Mexico City, where you can contact the **Asociación Nacional Automovilística (ANA;** ☎5292 1970).

Some credit cards cover standard **insurance.** If you rent, lease, or borrow a car, you will need a **green card,** or **International Insurance Certificate,** to prove that you have liability insurance. You can obtain it through the car rental agency; most include coverage in their prices. If you lease a car, ask the dealer for a green card. Some travel agents offer the card, and it may also be available at border crossings. Even if your auto insurance applies internationally, you will still need a green card to certify this to foreign officials. If you have a collision abroad, the accident will show up on your domestic records if you report it to your insurance company. Be aware that you may be taken into police custody until liability is worked out. Rental agencies may require you to purchase theft insurance in countries that they consider to have a high risk of auto theft. Ask your rental agency about rules applying specifically to Mexico.

BY TRAIN

The Mexican railroads are all owned by the government, with most lines operating under the name of **Ferrocarriles Nacionales de México** (National Railways of Mexico, FFNN). Passenger trains have always been inefficient and had limited reach, but with recent cuts, they are frequently not even an option anymore. Other than the spectacular ride through the **Copper Canyon** (**Los Mochis-Creel;** see p. 260) you probably won't want to rely on trains unless you crave a leisurely crawl through the countryside.

BY PLANE

Flying within Mexican borders is a method of transportation usually overlooked by budget travelers. That said, time is money. As a general rule, whenever busing will take you longer than 36hr., consider flying; chances are it will cost about the same or be only marginally more expensive, but save you many, many hours. If you are considering traveling by plane, visit one of the ubiquitous travel agencies that lurk on main streets; agents will be more than happy to help you find cheap, last-minute fares. If you are a student or a senior citizen, say so and ask about the possibility of standby seats. You can also check with Mexican airlines directly (see **Commercial Airlines,** p. 30).

BY THUMB

Mexicans who pick up tourists, especially in rural areas, are often friendly, generous and well-meaning; in fact, people who *don't* pick you up may give you an apologetic look. Unfortunately, it's not all fun and games. Depending on where you are, getting hit by passing vehicles may be your greatest danger. Women should never hitchhike, even when traveling in groups. Hitchhikers should size up the driver and find out where the car is going before getting in; this will also give you an opportunity to smell any alcohol that may be on the driver's breath. Think twice if a driver opens the door quickly and offers to drive anywhere. Some bandit-ridden routes are particularly dangerous for hitchhikers (see **Traveling by Car,** p. 36). If you do decide to accept a ride, exercise caution and make sure you will be able to make a quick exit. For example, do not sit in the middle, and try to keep all of your belongings easily accessible. If you have trouble getting out for any reason, affecting the pose of someone on the verge of vomiting has been known to work.

 THUMBS DOWN. *Let's Go* urges you to consider the risks before you hitchhike. We do not recommend hitchhiking as a safe means of transportation.

SAFETY WHILE GETTING AROUND

BY BUS

While bus travel is one of the safest ways to get around in Mexico, travelers should still exercise caution. Mexican highways have a reputation for being unsafe, and hijackings of buses, while uncommon, do occur. **To minimize risk, take first-class buses rather than second-class buses.** First-class buses are more likely to take toll (*cuota*) roads instead of free (*libre*) highways, which have more reports of hijacking and incidents of crime. It is also a good idea to arrange your travel schedule so that any lengthy intercity bus travel is done **during daylight hours,** when there is a lower chance of crime. Once on a bus—be it a local or intercity bus—keep your wits about you: rumors abound about determined thieves who wait for travelers to fall asleep, though pickpocketing is more likely. Carry your backpack in front of you where you can see it, or store it in the underside of the bus. Traveling with a companion is always safest. In certain areas of the country, buses may be pulled over and boarded by humorless armed federal officials *(federales)* looking for drugs or illegal aliens. In such a situation, be quiet and cooperative.

BY CAR

Those who choose to drive on Mexican highways should be extremely careful, as both highjackings and reckless driving are real dangers. **Whenever possible, drive during daylight hours and with others.** Once again, be sure to check ahead with local authorities and others (e.g. rental agencies, as they will be keen to get their cars back in good condition) for warnings about dangerous highways. Keep valuables out of sight, in your trunk if you can, and park your vehicle in a garage or well-traveled area. **Sleeping in your car** may often be illegal, it can also be extremely dangerous. If you must sleep in your car, do so as close to a police station or a 24hr. service station as possible.

Driving is unsafe for other reasons. Road conditions in Mexico are highly variable. The expensive *cuota* roads are not only the safest, but they provide the smoothest ride and the best road conditions. Free highways and local roads might have poor (or nonexistent) shoulders, few gas stations, and roaming animals. If you plan on spending a lot of time on the road, you may want to bring spare parts.

BY FOOT

To avoid unwanted attention, try not to stand out. Respecting local customs—in many cases, dressing more conservatively and avoiding obvious tourist paraphernalia, including shorts outside beach areas—may divert attention, and looking like you know (or actually knowing) what you're doing can go a long way toward blending in. It helps to familiarize yourself with your surroundings. When walking at night, stick to busy, well-lit streets and avoid dark alleyways and large, deserted areas. Look for children playing, women walking in the open, and other signs of an active community. You may want to carry a **whistle** or another noise-making device to scare off attackers and to attract attention. Memorize the emergency number of the city or area. If you are traveling alone, be sure that someone at home knows your itinerary, and **never admit that you're traveling alone.** Whenever possible, *Let's Go: Mexico* lists unsafe areas, but it still helps to ask about safety at tourist offices or at hotel reception desks. For more information on safety for **Women Travelers,** see below.

SPECIFIC CONCERNS

WOMEN TRAVELERS

Mexican women seldom travel without the company of men, and to find foreign women doing so is often surprising and draws attention. Moreover, Mexican men are notorious for their exorbitant *machismo*, a brand of Latin American chauvinism that translates into whistles, catcalls, and stares. Persistent men will insist on joining you and "showing you the sights." If you're fair-skinned or have light-colored hair, *"güera, güera"* will follow you everywhere; if not, expect to hear the typical come-on, *"¿Adónde vas, mamacita?"* (Where are you going, babe?). The best answer to this unwanted attention is to offer no answer at all. Ignore it and avoid making eye contact. *Machismo* is usually more annoying than dangerous, but in real emergencies yell for help or otherwise draw attention to yourself and the situation. It might be a good idea to wear a **whistle.** Be aware, however, that many police officers and uniformed officials are the biggest *machistas* of all; don't consider yourself safe from harassment just because men in uniform are nearby. **Local elderly women** or **nuns,** who may be able to help, and often discourage Casanovas simply by being there.

Your awareness of Mexican social standards and dress codes may help to minimize unwanted attention. Mexican women seldom wear shorts, short skirts, tank tops, or halter tops. In many regions, to do so may draw harassment or stares. Shorts and tank tops are appropriate only in beach and resort areas or in towns with a high number of foreign students and tourists. Even though locals may be more tolerant of travelers, more traditional areas of the country generally require quite conservative dress; bring a long skirt to wear in churches or in places like Chiapas, where locals are very religious. If you are traveling with a male friend, it may help to pose as a couple; this will make it easier to share rooms and will also chill the blood of Mexican Romeos. Wearing a **wedding ring** on your left hand or a **crucifix** around your neck may help discourage unwanted attention, as can talking loudly and frequently about your muscular boyfriend *(novio muy fuerte)* or easily-angered husband *(esposo muy facilmente enojado);* some savvy women even carry pictures of these "boyfriends" and "husbands," gladly displaying them to prospective suitors. Most importantly, act deliberately in potentially dangerous situations. Feigning confidence can deter potential harassers.

OLDER TRAVELERS AND RETIREES

Mexico's temperate climate, natural and historical attractions, and favorable exchange rates lure older travelers and retirees. Thriving and tight-knit expatriate communities have popped up all over the country—in the center (San Miguel de Allende, Guadalajara, and Xalapa), north (San Carlos and Todos Santos), and south (Oaxaca, Puerto Escondido, and the breathtaking turquoise coast of Quintana Roo). For information on retiring in Mexico, see **Retirement Visas,** p. 11. Senior citizens just looking to travel in the country will be pleasantly surprised: Mexican culture fosters respect of one's elders, which may carry over to tourists; seniors often receive among the best service and treatment. Don't be surprised if young people embarrass you by insisting you take their seat on the *metro* or on the bus. In addition to preferential treatment, seniors are eligible for a range of discounts, from transportation tickets to museums to accommodations. If you don't see a senior citizen price listed, ask and you may be rewarded. Many seniors also travel to Mexico to take advantage of the country's excellent language schools, many of which offer special discounts and programs for senior citizens (see **Studying Abroad,** p. 50).

Elderhostel, 11 Ave. de Lafayette, Boston, MA, USA 02115 (☎877-426-8056; www.elderhostel.org), or P.O. Box 4488 Station A, Toronto, ON M5W 4H1 for Canada. A non-profit organization that organizes 1- to 3-week "educational adventures" in Mexico on varied subjects for those 55 and over. Prices range $1200-3000.

The Mature Traveler, P.O. Box 1543, Wildomar, CA, USA 92595 (☎909-461-9598, www.thematuretraveler.com). A monthly newsletter that includes deals, discounts, and travel packages for travelers 50 and over. Subscription US$30.

FURTHER READING

Living Well In Mexico: How to Relocate, Retire, and Increase Your Standard of Living, Ken Luboff. Avalon Travel Publishing ($16).

Choose Mexico for Retirement, John Howells and Don Merwin. Globe Pequot Press ($15).

No Problem! Worldwise Tips for Mature Adventurers, Janice Kenyon. Orca Book Publishers ($16).

How Mexico's son made it big in the big leagues

As he gradually entered his windup his eyes rolled skyward (toward the heavens, some said) and his long skinny right leg reached high into the air until it momentarily concealed his soft paunch; then he'd close his eyes as his momentum shifted toward home plate and re-open them before delivering a devastating fastball, change-up, curveball, or that trademark screwball (the "scroogie"). The lollipop-figured 20-year-old rookie with shaggy dark hair flowing from his Dodger Blue cap indeed looked like he was from the Mexican hinterlands of Etchohuaquila, Mexico, and like his screwball, appeared nothing like what the major leagues had seen before. But neither he nor that trademark pitch were any kind of gimmick—the incredible success of Fernando Valenzuela to start his career, his unathletic physique, and refreshingly true-to-his-roots personality launched Fernandomania, a pivotal moment in sports history in Mexico and the US.

After a spring-training injury to pitcher Jerry Reuss in 1981, L.A. manager Tommy Lasorda named Valenzuela his Opening Day starter. As a 19-year-old the previous season, he had made just a handful of relief appearances. But in the opener at Dodger Stadium against the Houston Astros, Fernando threw a complete-game, five-hit shutout to win, 2-0. He proceeded to toss seven straight complete-games, of which five were shutouts and all were victories. His stats after seven games: 7-0, 0.29 ERA, 7 starts, 7 CG, 5 shutouts, 63 IP, 40 H, 2 R, 2 ER, 0 HR, 16 BB, 61 K. He was also hitting .318.

By the time the Dodgers arrived in New York for a series against the Mets, Fernandomania was born. Valenzuela, still speaking to the press through an interpreter, his friend the Spanish-language broadcaster Jaime Jarrin, began convening with the media at pre-series press conferences—like Bonds and McGwire during their home-run record seasons—because the throng had swelled to such a degree. Etchohuaquila, too, was receiving this media frenzy. For the game with the Mets alone, the number of Venezuelan radio stations carrying the Dodgers' broadcasts was increased from 20 to 40, and the number of Mexican stations from three to 17. The Mets were averaging 11,358 fans per night

till then, but drew 39,848 to see Valenzu Fernando's outings drew Latino fans i Dodger Stadium in droves that summer— weekday starts routinely drew 50,000 fans. May he had been invited to the White Hous lunch with the new president, Ronald Reag and Mexican President Jose Lopez Portillo. Fernandomania lasted all the way through World Series, which the Dodgers took in se games, with the young Mexican as their a Valenzuela also became the first pitcher eve win Rookie of the Year and the Cy Young Aw in the same season. In 25 starts during strike-shorted campaign, he finished 13-7 wi 2.48 ERA, good for second in the league in w and seventh in ERA, although he did lead league in innings (192.1) and strikeouts (180)

The Fernando phenomenon had a deep lasting cross-border influence. From the st Fernando's image was carefully managed to project stereotypical images of Mexicans or inos in the United States. To ensure this, he often accompanied by Mike Brito, the Cub born Dodgers scout who signed him; Jarrin; his agent and best friend, Antonio de Mar who also represented Hollywood celebriti but who henceforth devoted himself to Valen ela. On his own, Valenzuela projected a cha ing innocence; to Mexicans and Latinos he lovingly known as "El Torito." In 1985, when was getting miserable run support, a repor asked him to recall the last time the Dodg scored six runs for him. By this time he was getting over his discomfort speaking Engl publicly. Deadpan as ever, he replied: "T gave me five in San Diego and one in San Fr cisco. That adds up to six." Sports Illustra reported that Valenzuela had already turr down $200,000 in endorsements early in rookie year. He always accepted Mexican de first; his charitable involvements were comm De Marco turned down cerveza deals, taco a and anything prototypically Mexican. cringed when Fernando cracked open a b during a postgame interview.

According to *Los Angeles Times* wri Patrick J. McDonnell, although Valenzuela's c fidantes tried not to convey a Mexican caricat to mainstream American audiences, Valenzu himself did not conceal two of his favorite p s—beer and television. For Mexicans in L.A., y of whom concealed their ethnicity to avoid udice, Fernando's stardom was a liberating He humbly claimed his first post-stardom l was to purchase a home for his family. ando furthermore had a unique crossover eal. As a baseball star—rather than a soccer er—Fernando was admired by Mexicans in homeland, Mexican Americans, Mexican igrants, and Anglo-Americans alike. When Dodgers won the World Series in '81, they had tations in Mexico. They added 28 stations e. When Valenzuela was let go by the Dodg-n 1991, the stations maintained their Dodger He was also the first media-crazed "mania" wing imported athletes in the US, like base-'s Hideo Nomo and Ichiro Suzuki of Japan, basketball's Yao Ming of China. The "cool to thnic" trend may have started with Fernando, es McDonnell.

Fernando's mid- to late-1990s twilight, San go Padres co-owner Larry Lucchino would the lefty as much for the potential marketing p as for whatever he had left in his pitching . Lucchino sought to beam more games into xico and draw more fans into the stadium n across the border, particularly Baja. After signing Valenzuela before the 1996 season, the Padres opened a ticket and merchandise store in Tijuana's Plaza Rio mall. Successful promotions with a Tijuana grocery store chain prompted the Padres to develop game packages that include transportation from Mexico and admission to the game. Valenzuela had more in that arm than many expected, too. When the first ever regular season major-league baseball game was played outside the US or Canada, in Monterrey, Mexico, Valenzuela was the Padres' starting—and win-ning—pitcher. He said he had never been so ner-vous since that Opening Day start back in 1991. Since that monumental game, Major League Baseball has played regular season games in Puerto Rico and Japan, and is considering full-time franchises in Latin America.

After his numerous comebacks and stints back in the Mexican leagues during the nineties, Valen-zuela retired after the 1997 season, having tallied 173 career wins and a 3.54 career ERA. Although El Toro himself never appeared upset, many were affected by the Dodgers' decision to release Valenzuela in 1991, but in 2003 Valenzuela returned to Dodgers baseball, joining Jarrin in the Spanish-language broadcasting booth.

Derek Glanz was the editor of Let's Go: Spain & Portugal 1998. *He is now a freelance baseball writer contributing regularly to* St. Louis Cardinals' Gameday Magazine. *He has written for* Baseball America *and* Baseball Weekly *and appeared as a guest analyst on ESPN Radio and Colombia's Tele-cartagena.*

ESSENTIALS

BISEXUAL, GAY, AND LESBIAN TRAVELERS

Mexico's conservative and Catholic traditions makes homosexuality frowned upon at best, violently despised at worst. Intolerance is especially rampant in more rural areas of the country, where displays of affection may attract violence. More urban areas are generally more accepting of homosexuality; there are fledgling gay-rights movements in Mexico City and Monterrey and a thriving community in Puerto Vallarta. However, the best rule of thumb is to avoid public displays of affection at least until you know you are in a safe and accepting environment, such as one afforded by gay-friendly clubs and establishments (of which there are many). Whenever possible, *Let's Go: Mexico* lists gay and lesbian establishments; the best way to find out about the many others that we do not list is to consult organizations, mail-order bookstores, and publishers that offer materials addressing gay and lesbian concerns.

International Gay and Lesbian Travel Association, 4331 N. Federal Hwy. #304, Fort Lauderdale, FL, USA 33308 (toll-free ☎ 1-800-448-8550; fax 776--3303; www.iglta.org). An organization of over 1200 companies serving gay and lesbian travelers worldwide. New offices in Rozelle, Australia (☎ 61-2-9818-6669) and Munich, Germany (☎ 49-89-9542-0248).

International Lesbian and Gay Association (ILGA), 81 rue Marché-au-Charbon, B 1000 Brussels, Belgium (☎/fax +32 2 502 2471; www.ilga.org). Not a travel service; provides political information, such as homosexuality laws of individual countries.

WEBSITES

Aquí Estamos: www.aquiestamos.com. Chat, personals, and an online guide (still under construction) to over 30 Mexican cities.

Gay México: www.gaymexico.com.mx. All-purpose information.

Out and About: www.planetout.com. This international site includes a travel section with gay/lesbian listings for food, accommodations, nightlife, etc. for cities in Mexico.

Ser Gay: www.sergay.com.mx. A Mexico City-based site with chat forums and event listings for around the country, as well as news stories.

FURTHER READING

Spartacus International Gay Guide. Bruno Gmunder Verlag (US$33).

Damron Men's Travel Guide, Damron Accommodations, and *Damron Women's Traveller,* among others. Damron Travel Guides ($17-23). For more info, call ☎ 800-462-6654 or visit www.damron.com.

A Man's Guide to Mexico and Central America. Señor Córdova ($19).

TRAVELERS WITH DISABILITIES

Mexico is increasingly accessible to travelers with disabilities, noticeably in popular resorts like Cancún and Cabo San Lucas. Northern cities closer to the US, such as Monterrey and Saltillo, also tend to be more wheelchair-friendly. Generally, the more you are willing to spend, the less difficult it is to find accessible facilities. Keep in mind, however, that most public and long-distance modes of transportation and most of the non-luxury hotels don't accommodate wheelchairs. Public bathrooms are almost all inaccessible, as are many ruins, parks, historic buildings, and museums. Still, with some advance planning, an affordable Mexican vacation is possible. Those with disabilities should inform airlines and hotels when making arrangements for travel, as some preparation time may be needed. For links to websites with information on travel planning, try www.makoa.org/travel.htm.

USEFUL ORGANIZATIONS

Mobility International USA (MIUSA), P.O. Box 10767, Eugene, OR, USA 97440 (voice and TTY ☎541-343-1284; www.miusa.org). This non-profit sells a variety of internationally-oriented publications, including *A World of Options: A Guide to International Educational Exchange, Community Service, and Travel for People with Disabilities* (US$35).

Society for Accessible Travel and Hospitality (SATH), 347 Fifth Ave., #610, New York, NY, USA 10016 (☎212-447-7284; www.sath.org). An advocacy group that publishes free online travel information and the travel magazine *OPEN WORLD* ($13 per year, free for members). Annual membership $45, students and seniors $30.

TOUR AGENCIES

Directions Unlimited, 123 Green Ln., Bedford Hills, NY 10507 (☎800-533-5343). Books individual and group vacations for the physically disabled; not an info service.

Search Beyond Adventures, (☎800-800-9979; www.searchbeyond.com). Offers packages for people with disabilities, ages 17 and up.

MINORITY TRAVELERS

Nearly all of the Mexican population is white, Indian, or a combination of the two. This means that many travelers are bound to stick out, particularly when traveling in rural or less touristed parts of the country. In general, the whiter your skin, the better treatment you'll receive. (Unfortunately, light-skinned travelers are also viewed as wealthier and therefore are more likely to be the targets of crime.) Travelers of African or Asian ancestry will likely attract attention. Asians may find themselves called *chinos*, while African-Americans are often called *morenos* or *negros*. None of these words are meant to be offensive; they are simply descriptive terms. In many rural areas, non-Spanish speakers may be viewed as a threat.

TRAVELERS WITH CHILDREN

Though Mexico is an extremely child-friendly destination, traveling with children requires little more than a bit of planning and a lot of extra patience. When deciding where to stay, for example, consider staying in more moderately priced establishments, as many budget accommodations are not child-friendly. It's also a good idea to call ahead to make sure your hotel welcomes children. As far as food is concerned, simple and tasty *taquitos*, quesadillas, and *sopas de fideo* (yummy noodle soups) are universally appealing. Unless your child has a particularly adventurous palate, stay away from the *salsa picante*. Finally, be very careful with food and water safety. Always give children plenty of bottled water to drink (especially if it's hot out), and take them to a doctor if they develop severe diarrhea (though a touch of it might not be unexpected). When traveling by car between cities, make sure that your car has a seat for young children (if it doesn't, request one from your rental company). Also keep in mind that many Mexican highways—particularly those connecting Mexico City to the coasts—are hilly and windy and have a tendency to make children carsick.

 BABY ON BOARD. In Mexico, children traveling by themselves or with only one parent must carry a parental consent form that has been signed, in the presence of a notary public, by the parent not traveling. If the one parent is deceased, then a death certificate or court order is required. These rules are meant to curb the numbers of parents who try to flee with their children across international borders. Although the rules are seldom enforced, some travelers have been turned away at the border for not providing proper documentation for their accompanying children.

Although Mexico City has many things to fascinate children, parts of the city may also prove to be the least child-friendly places in Mexico: the big-city noise, congestion, and pollution tend to affect children more than adults. If you are staying in *el D.F.* with children, keep them indoors when pollution is at its heaviest—generally in early mornings during the winter. Stay alert for updates of the pollution index (*Indice Metropolitana de Calidad del Aire*, or IMECA), which is frequently broadcast on radio and television. Outside of the capital, Mexico is extremely child-friendly. This is particularly true of the coastal regions, which offer children miles of golden beaches upon which to frolic and build sand castle after sand castle. Remember to slather on the sunscreen—though Mexico is kind to children, the Mexican sun can be harsh.

FURTHER READING

Let's Go Traveling in Mexico, Robin Rector Krupp. An illustrated journey through Mexico with the mythical Quetzalcóatl as guide. Ideal for children ages 4-8 years old. No relation to our favorite *Let's Go.* William Morrow & Company ($17).

Backpacking with Babies and Small Children, Goldie Silverman. Wilderness Press ($10).

How to Take Great Trips with Your Kids, Sanford and Joan Portnoy. Harvard Common Press ($10).

Tropical Family Vacations: In the Caribbean, Hawaii, South Florida, and Mexico, Laura Sutherland. Griffin Trade Paperback ($17).

Have Kid, Will Travel: 101 Survival Strategies for Vacationing With Babies and Young Children, Claire and Lucille Tristram. Andrews and McMeel ($9).

Adventuring with Children: An Inspirational Guide to World Travel and the Outdoors, Nan Jeffrey. Avalon House Publishing ($15).

DIETARY CONCERNS

Vegetarians are rare in Mexico, and vegans are almost unheard of. Expect incredulous stares in many places—sometimes from concerned patrons at nearby tables as well as waiters. If pressed, allergies or illness ("I have *turista;* I will vomit on you if I eat lots of meat") make better alibis. With that said, the carnivorous nature of Mexicans can make it difficult for **vegetarian tourists,** as almost all meals are prepared using animal products. Some popular vegetarian dishes available in most restaurants include quesadillas (melted cheese wrapped in tortillas), *chilaquiles* (strips of fried tortillas baked in tomato sauce with cheese and fresh cream), *molletes* (french bread smothered with refried beans and cheese), *tortas de queso,* and *frijoles* (beans). Be aware that nearly all flour tortillas and many types of beans are prepared with *manteca* (lard). **Vegan tourists** will have a harder go at it and may have to subsist on the old standbys of corn tortillas and rice. It's a good idea to bring high-calorie protein snacks (such as granola bars and peanuts) to maintain your energy. Wherever possible, *Let's Go: Mexico* includes vegetarian dining options. For **more information on vegetarianism abroad** contact the **North American Vegetarian Society,** P.O. Box 72, Dolgeville, NY 13329 (☎518-568-7970; www.navs-online.org).

Despite the increasing number of Jews in Mexico (especially in Mexico City), keeping **kosher** can be difficult. Many large supermarkets sell kosher foods, but travelers will have less luck in restaurants and smaller towns. Those who keep kosher should contact synagogues for information on kosher restaurants. Your own synagogue or college Hillel should have access to lists of Jewish institutions across Mexico. Another good resource is the *Jewish Travel Guide 2003,* by Michael Zaidner (Vallentine Mitchell, $18).

OTHER RESOURCES

Let's Go tries to cover all aspects of budget travel, but we can't put *everything* in our guides. Listed below are books and websites that can serve as jumping-off points for your own research.

TRAVEL PUBLISHERS & BOOKSTORES

Hippocrene Books, Inc., 171 Madison Ave., New York, NY 10016, USA (☎718-454-2366; www.hippocrenebooks.com). Publishes foreign language dictionaries and language learning guides, as well as cookbooks and other helpful guides.

Stanfords, 12-14 Long Acre, Covent Garden, London WC2E 9LP, UK (☎020 7836 1321). This is Stanfords' flagship store, established in 1901, and it houses the company's "complete range of maps, books, and travel related goods."

Rand McNally, P.O. Box 7600, Chicago, IL 60680, USA (☎847-329-8100; www.randmcnally.com), publishes road atlases.

Adventurous Traveler Bookstore, P.O. Box 2221, Williston, VT 05495, USA (www.adventuroustraveler.com).

Travel Books & Language Center, Inc., 4437 Wisconsin Ave. NW, Washington, D.C. 20016, USA (☎800-220-2665; www.bookweb.org/bookstore/travelbks/). Over 60,000 titles from around the world.

THE WORLD WIDE WEB

Almost every aspect of budget travel (except, of course, experience) is accessible on the Internet; in less than 10min. at the keyboard, you can make a reservation at a hotel in the Yucatán, get advice on travel hotspots from travelers who have just returned from Baja California, or find out how much a bus from Ciudad Juárez to Guadalajara costs. Listed here are some budget travel sites to start off your surfing.

THE ART OF BUDGET TRAVEL

How to See the World: www.artoftravel.com. 25 chapters of travel tips available at no cost and covering preparation at home as well as challenges on the road, including cheap flights, self-defense, and opening yourself to local cultures.

Rec. Travel Library: www.travel-library.com. Includes personal travelogues and great links for general information.

Lycos: http://travel.lycos.com/destinations/. A wealth of information is available on cities and regions in Mexico, including general introductions and links to history, news, and local tourism sites.

INFORMATION ON MEXICO

Mexico Connect: www.mexconnect.com. An e-resource that includes a myriad of articles on culture, destinations, and food (among other things) in Mexico. The pay site, www.mexconnected.com ($30), houses the full version of most articles, though the free site can access some complete texts in archives.

CIA World Factbook: www.odci.gov/cia/publications/factbook/index.html. Tons of vital statistics on Mexican geography, government, economy, and people.

Foreign Language for Travelers: www.travlang.com. Navigate the pop-up windows to free online translating dictionaries and lists of phrases in Spanish.

ESSENTIALS

ESSENTIALS

MyTravelGuide: www.mytravelguide.com. Country overviews, with everything from history to transportation to live web-cam coverage of Mexico.

Geographia: www.geographia.com. Highlights, culture, and people of Mexico.

Atevo Travel: www.atevo.com/guides/destinations. Detailed introductions, travel tips, practical day-to-day info, and suggested itineraries.

PlanetRider: www.planetrider.com/. A subjective list of links to the "best" websites covering attractions of Mexico, most readily of the Yucatán Peninsula.

Mexico Reference Desk: www.lanic.utexas.edu/la/Mexico. An abundance of links to Mexico-related sites, covering academics, popular culture, travel, and current issues.

Microsoft Expedia: www.msn.expedia.com. This mega-site has everything you need to make travel plans—compare flight fares, look at maps, and book reservations.

US State Department Consular Information Sheet for Mexico: http://travel.state.gov/mexico.html. The word from above on travel safety and recommended precautions.

Yahoo! Mexico Links: www.yahoo.com/regional/countries/mexico. Well-indexed and searchable database of thousands of links related to Mexico.

Zapatista Web Page: www.ezln.org. Provides up-to-the-minute information in Spanish and frequently English about Mexico's most prominent rebel group.

WWW.LETSGO.COM OOur website, www.letsgo.com, now includes introductory chapters from all our guides and a wealth of information on a monthly featured destination. As always, our website also has info about our books, a travel forum buzzing with stories and tips, and additional links that will help you make the most of a trip to Mexico.

ALTERNATIVES TO TOURISM

When we started out in 1961, about 1.7 million people were traveling internationally each year; in 2002, nearly 700 million trips were made; and there may be up to a billion by 2010. The dramatic rise in tourism has created an interdependence between the economy, environment, and culture of many destinations and the tourists they host. Tourism to Mexico has exploded, rising from 82 million to over 100 million tourists per year—tourists who spend over US\$8 billion annually.

Two rising trends in sustainable travel are ecotourism and community-based tourism. **Ecotourism** focuses on the conservation of natural habitats, using them to build up the economy without exploitation or overdevelopment. **Community-based tourism** aims to channel tourist pesos into the local economy by emphasizing tours and programs that are run by members of the host community. Since the mid-1990s, Mexico has made public commitments to promoting ecotourism.

Those looking to **volunteer** have many options, from working with physicians to speaking against drug abuse to collecting seeds of native jungle trees, either on an infrequent basis or as the main component of your trip. Later in this section, we recommend organizations that can help you find the opportunities that best suit your interests, whether you're looking to pitch in for a day or a year.

Studying at a college or language program is another option. The use of natural resources is often minimal, and the benefits of learning in a new environment are substantial; some students manage to get college credit in the process. As in volunteer programs, students will stay largely in a small region of the country and have more direct interaction with the destination's local community, but with less responsibility and community involvement.

For those who seek more active involvement, Earthwatch International, Operation Crossroads Africa, and Habitat for Humanity offer fulfilling volunteer opportunities all over the world. For more on volunteering, studying, and working in Mexico and beyond, consult Let's Go's alternatives to tourism website, **www.beyondtourism.com**.

FIND THE PATH. To read more on specific organizations that are working to better their communities, look for our **Giving Back** features throughout the book. See **Heroes in a Halfshell** (p. 407) and **Seeking Sunnier Skies** (p. 586).

VOLUNTEERING

Mexico, while rich in culture, history, and religion, faces significant challenges regarding rural development, education, public health, and the environment. Its fabulous natural wealth has spurred much of the country's development, but has also created one of the most unequal distributions of wealth in the world. For some, volunteering will be one of the most fulfilling experiences in life; in Mexico it will not only put you in touch with humanity at its most needful, it will add to the thrill of traveling in a new place. Volunteering is one way of not only seeing foreign places and people, but engaging with them to experience another culture. The

A NEW PHILOSOPHY OF TRAVEL

We at *Let's Go* have watched the growth of the 'ignorant tourist' stereotype with dismay, knowing that the majority of travelers care passionately about the state of the communities and environments they explore—but also knowing that even conscientious tourists can inadvertently damage natural wonders, rich cultures, and impoverished communities. We believe the philosophy of **sustainable travel** is among the most important travel tips we could impart to our readers, to help guide fellow backpackers and on-the-road philanthropists. By staying aware of the needs and troubles of local communities, today's travelers can be a powerful force in preserving and restoring this fragile world.

Working against the negative consequences of irresponsible tourism is much simpler than it might seem; it is often self-awareness, rather than self-sacrifice, that makes the biggest difference. Simply by trying to spend responsibly and conserve local resources, all travelers can positively impact the places they visit. Let's Go has partnered with **BEST (Business Enterprises for Sustainable Travel;** see www.sustainabletravel.org), which recognizes businesses that operate based on the principles of sustainable travel. Below, they provide advice on how ordinary visitors can practice this philosophy in their daily travels, no matter where they are.

TIPS FOR CIVIC TRAVEL: HOW TO MAKE A DIFFERENCE

Travel by train when feasible. Rail travel typically requires only half the energy per passenger mile that planes do.

Use public mass transportation whenever possible; outside of cities, take advantage of group taxis or vans. Bicycles are an attractive way of seeing a community firsthand. And enjoy walking—purchase good maps of your destination and ask about on-foot touring opportunities.

When renting a car, ask whether fuel-efficient vehicles are available. Honda and Toyota produce cars that use hybrid engines powered by electricity and gasoline, thus reducing emissions of carbon dioxide.

Reduce, reuse, recycle—use electronic tickets, recycle papers and bottles wherever possible, and avoid using containers made of styrofoam. Refillable water bottles and rechargable batteries both efficiently conserve expendable resources.

Be thoughtful in your purchases. Take care not to buy souvenir objects made from trees in old-growth or endangered forests, such as teak, or items made from endangered species, like ivory or tortoise-shell jewelry. Ask whether products are made from renewable resources.

Buy from local enterprises, such as street vendors. In developing countries and low-income neighborhoods, many people depend on the "informal economy" to make a living.

Be an on-the-road-philanthropist. If you are inspired by the natural environment of a destination or enriched by its culture, join in preserving their integrity by making a charitable contribution to a local organization.

Spread the word. Upon your return home, tell friends and colleagues about places to visit that will benefit greatly from their tourist dollars, and reward sustainable enterprises by recommending their services. Travelers can not only introduce friends to particular vendors but also to local causes and charities that they might choose to support when they travel.

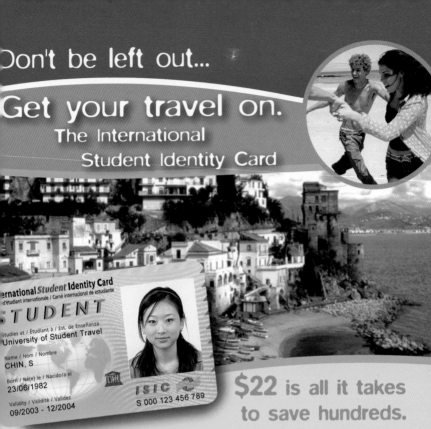

enough already...
Get a room.

Book your next hotel with the people who know what you want.

Before handing your money over to any volunteer or study abroad program, make sure you know exactly what you're getting into. It's a good idea to get the name of **previous participants** and ask them about their experience, as some programs sound much better on paper than they are in reality. The questions below are a good place to start:

-Will you be the only person in the program? If not, what are the other partici-pants like? How old are they? How much will you be interacting with them?

-Is room and board included? If so, what is the arrangement? Will you be expected to share a room? A bathroom? What are the meals like? Do they accommodate any dietary restrictions?

-Is transportation included? Are there any additional expenses?

-How much free time will you have? Will you be able to travel around Mexico?

-What kind of safety network is set up? Will you still be covered by your home insurance? Does the program have an emergency plan?

ALTERNATIVES TO TOURISM

options for volunteering in Mexico are nearly endless given the natural and social diversity of the country. Do be aware that—particularly in rural areas—volunteer-ing will likely mean giving up basic comforts (hot water, waffles for breakfast) and may involve greater risks than other travel, whether due to disease, snakes, scorpi-ons, or simply less accessible health care. It is easy to minimize these risks, how-ever, by doing some background research on the organization you're working with and the region to which you're traveling, and preparing accordingly.

Many volunteer services charge a fee for participation. These costs can be sur-prisingly hefty (although they frequently cover airfare and most, if not all, living expenses); remember that willingness to pay a fee will open up many more oppor-tunities. Most people choose to go through a parent organization that takes care of logistical details and frequently provides a group environment. There are two main types of organizations—religious and non-sectarian—although there are rarely restrictions on participation for either. You can sometimes avoid high application fees by contacting the individual work camps directly, or save even more money by seeking out local volunteer opportunities after arriving in Mexico. Different programs are geared toward different ages and levels of experience, so make sure that you are not taking on too much or too little. The more informed and realistic your expectations, the more enjoyable the program will be.

CONSERVATION

The quest for sustainable development is a hot topic in Mexico. On the one hand, exploitation of Mexico's abundant natural resources has been important to growth throughout the country's history; on the other, reliance on non-renewable resources results in widespread environmental degradation. Moreover, the Mexi-can government recognizes that the irresponsible use of resources inhibits growth. In Mexico some of the relevant concerns are disappearing southern rain-forests in Chiapas and the Yucatán Peninsula, destruction of marine habitats in coastal areas, soil erosion in the northern highlands, and chronically dangerous levels of air pollution in large urban areas. Below are listed some resources to get you started tracking down information and opportunities for action.

American Friends Service Committee, 1501 Cherry St., Philadelphia, PA 19102, USA (US☎215-241-7000; www.afsc.org). This Quaker organization has offered summer projects in Mexico continuously since 1939. The current program focuses on community projects for youth to engage indigenous communities in Xilitla, Querétaro on ecological, political, and economic issues.

Centro Ecológico Akumal (CEA), Apartado Postal 2, Akumal, Quintana Roo 77760 (☎984 875 9095; www.ceakumal.org). Founded in 1993, CEA engages in research and direct action, including turtle and reef monitoring, and teaching. Length of stay negotiable.

Earthwatch, 3 Clocktower Pl., Suite #100, Box 75, Maynard, MA 01754, USA (US☎800-776-0188; www.earthwatch.org). Arranges 1-3 week programs promoting ecological conservation; engages volunteers (no special skills needed) in field research. Programs average US$1600.

Environmental Education and Ecological Action Center, AC (CEDUAM), Cerrada del Ferrocarril, 3 Col. El Mirador, Calpulalpan, Tlax. 90200 (www.prodigyweb.net.mx/cedu-amcal/). Teaches soil and water conservation techniques to peasant farmers in a drive for environmentally sustainable development. Stays range from 3 days (US$25) to over three months (cost can be arranged).

ESPWA (HOPE), P.O. Box 2071, Rouseau, Commonwealth of Dominica (US☎767-449-0322; www.espwa.org). Embracing environmental, community/public health, and archaeological concerns, Espwa offers a variety of volunteer opportunities for US$390-$450 (airfare not included).

Intercultural Center for the Study of Oceans and Deserts (CEDO), Apartado Postal #53, Puerto Peñasco, Sonora 83550 (US☎520-320-5473; www.cedointercul-tural.org). Also with an office in Tucson, AZ, this conservation organization engages in both research and educational programs. 13-month internships available for those 21+. "Eco-adventures" range US$10-85 (see p. 226).

SOCIAL SERVICE

While environmentally-sustainable development focuses on balancing protection of resources with growth, skewed income distribution has produced serious imbalances in wealth that growth alone cannot solve. Rural areas in particular suffer from lack of access to health care and education—as well as military occupation in some of the poorest indigenous areas, a legacy of the past authoritarian regime; urban areas face housing shortages, lack of sanitation, domestic violence, and growing numbers of street children. Poverty overruns the urban-rural distinction, though, and these and other problems can be found throughout the country. Organizations in Mexico are very active in pursuing social and economic justice.

Amigos de las Americas, 5618 Star Lane, Houston, TX 77057, USA (US☎800-231-7796; www.amigoslink.org). Sends high school and college students in groups of 2-3 to work in rural Latin American communities for 4-8 weeks. Program themes include public health and environmental education. Two years (or equivalent) Spanish instruction required. Costs average US$3500, including airfare and insurance.

Casa Alianza, SJO 1039, P.O. Box 025216, Miami, FL 33102, USA (www.casa-alianza.org). The Latin American branch of the Christian, New York-based Covenant House. Focus on the rehabilitation and defense of street children—including attempts to reunite them with their families. Commitments 6 months to a year working with kids, shorter options available within the organization. Housing is US$120 per month.

Child Family Health International, 953 Mission St., Suite 220, San Francisco, CA 94103, USA (US☎415-957-9000; www.cfhi.org). Sends pre-med undergraduate and medical students to work with physicians in the developing world. Focus is more on working with communities and existing, local organizations, plus learning about health care distribution, rather than actually providing medical assistance. Program fees are around US$1500, but don't include airfare.

Global Exchange, 2017 Mission #303, San Francisco, CA 94110, USA (US☎415-255-7296 ext. 239; www.globalexchange.org/countries/mexico). Mexico campaigns focus on challenges of inequality and military occupation in indigenous regions surviving democratic transition. Aims to put activists in contact with Mexican grass roots movements. Also offers "Reality Tours" on local life and politics. Tours cost US$500-1100.

Habitat for Humanity International, 121 Habitat St., Americus, GA 31709, USA (☎ 229-924-6935; www.habitat.org, www.habitatmexico.org in Spanish). 1-3 week stays in Mexico for building houses in a host community. Costs range US$1200-2500.

Visions in Action, 2710 Ontario Rd. NW, Washington, D.C. 20009, USA (US☎ 202-625-7402; www.visionsinaction.org). Non-religious, apolitical organization aiming at promoting social and economic justice through grass roots approaches. 6- to 12-month (and some 3- to 7-week) programs link volunteers with local NGOs, research institutes, health clinics, media, etc., aiming at educational experiences. Must have college degree, Spanish proficiency. US$4000-6000, airfare not included.

Volunteers for Peace, 1034 Tiffany Rd., Belmont, VT 05730, USA (US☎ 802-259-2759; www.vfp.org). Arranges placement in work camps in Mexico, mostly for adults (18+). Commitment 3 months to 2 years. Registration fee (usually includes room and board) US$200. Lists substantial links to other volunteer service organizations.

TEACHING ENGLISH

Teaching jobs abroad are rarely well paid, although some elite private American schools can pay somewhat competitive salaries. Volunteering as a teacher in lieu of getting paid is also a popular option; even in those cases, teachers often get some sort of a daily stipend to help with living expenses. In almost all cases, you must have at least a bachelor's degree to be a full-fledged teacher, although college undergraduates can often get summer positions teaching or tutoring.

Many schools require teachers to have a **Teaching English as a Foreign Language (TEFL)** certificate. Not having a certificate does not necessarily exclude you from finding a job, but certified teachers often find higher paying jobs. Native English speakers working in private schools are most often hired for English-immersion classrooms where no Spanish is spoken. Those volunteering or teaching in public, poorer schools are more likely to be working in both English and Spanish. Placement agencies or university fellowship programs are the best resources for finding teaching jobs in Mexico. The alternative is to make contacts directly with schools or just to try your luck once you get there. If you are going to try the latter, the best time of the year is several weeks before the start of the school year. The following organizations are extremely helpful in placing teachers in Mexico.

International Schools Services (ISS), 15 Roszel Rd., Box 5910, Princeton, NJ 08543-5910, USA (☎ 609-452-0990; fax 609-452-2690; www.iss.edu). Hires teachers for more than 200 overseas schools; candidates should have experience teaching or with international affairs, 2-year commitment expected.

Amity Institute, Amity Volunteer Teachers Abroad Program, 3065 Rosecrans Place, Suite 104, San Diego, CA 92110, USA (☎ 619-222-7000; fax 617-222-7016; www.amity.org). Offers both full-year and semester-long positions. US$25-50 processing fee and US$500 placement fee.

Office of Overseas Schools, US Department of State, Room H328, SA-1, Washington, D.C. 20522, USA (☎ 202-261-8200; fax 261-8224; www.state.gov/m/a/os/). Keeps a comprehensive list of schools abroad and agencies that arrange placement for Americans to teach abroad.

Teaching English in Mexico: http://www.mexconnect.com/mex_/travel/dadams/daenglishinmexico1.html. A detailed four-part article on ESL teaching in Mexico, including resources for finding a job.

ALTERNATIVES TO TOURISM

GENERAL RESOURCES AND OTHER

AmeriSpan, P.O. Box 58129, Philadelphia, PA 19102, USA (US☎215-751-1100, toll-free US☎800-879-6640; www.amerispan.com). Internships and placements all over Mexico in the fields of education, public health, the environment, ESL, and social work.

Archaeological Institute of America, 656 Beacon St., Boston, MA 02215, USA (US☎617-353-9361; www.archaeological.org). The *Archaeological Fieldwork Opportunities Bulletin,* available on the organization's website, lists field sites throughout Mexico. An online forum invites students to discuss experiences and offer advice.

Elderhostel, Inc., 11 Avenue de Lafayette, Boston, MA 02111, USA (US ☎877-426-8056; www.elderhostel.org). Sends travelers age 55 and over around the world on educational adventures. Costs average US$200 per day plus airfare.

Idealist.org. A comprehensive search-engine with job and volunteer opportunities domestically and internationally. You can specify searches by area of interest as well by region.

STUDYING ABROAD

Study abroad programs range from basic language and culture courses to college-level classes, often for credit. In order to choose a program that best fits your needs, you will want to research before making your decision.

In programs that have large groups of students who speak the same language, there is a trade-off. You may feel more comfortable in the community, but you will not have the same opportunity to practice a foreign language or to befriend other international students. For accommodations, dorm life provides a better opportunity to mingle with fellow students, but there is less of a chance to experience the local scene. If you live with a family, there is a potential to build lifelong friendships with natives and to experience day-to-day life in more depth, but conditions can vary greatly from family to family.

Some American schools still require students to pay them for credits obtained elsewhere. Most university-level study-abroad programs are meant as language and culture enrichment opportunities, and therefore are conducted in Spanish. Still, many programs do offer classes in English and beginner- and lower-level language courses. Those relatively fluent in Spanish, on the other hand, may find it cheaper to enroll directly in a university abroad, although getting college credit may be more difficult. A good resource for finding programs that cater to your particular interests is www.studyabroad.com, which has links to various semester abroad programs based on a variety of criteria, including desired location and focus of study. The following is a list of organizations that can help place students in university programs abroad, or have their own branch in Mexico.

VISA INFORMATION

Staying longer than 180 days? Get a student visa from your nearest Mexican consulate. You must submit an acceptance letter from the school you wish to attend, several photographs, and a statement proving economic solvency. The fee depends on nationality, but can be up to US$99.

AMERICAN PROGRAMS

Central College Abroad, Office of International Education, 812 University, Pella, IA 50219, USA (US☎641-628-5284, toll-free US☎800-831-3629; www.central.edu/abroad). Offers internships, as well as semester- and year-long programs in Mérida. US$25 application fee.

Council on International Educational Exchange (CIEE), 633 3rd Ave., 20th floor, New York, NY 10017, USA (toll-free US☎ 800-407-8839; www.ciee.org/study) sponsors volunteer programs in Mexico, as well as a summer educational program in Guanajuato.

School for International Training, College Semester Abroad, Admissions, Kipling Rd., P.O. Box 676, Brattleboro, VT 05302, USA (US☎ 802-257-7751, toll-free US☎ 800-336-1616; www.sit.edu). Semester- and year-long programs in Mexico run US$10,600-13,700. Also runs the **Experiment in International Living** (toll-free US☎ 800-345-2929; www.usexperiment.org), 3- to 5-week summer programs that offer high school students cross-cultural homestays, community service, ecological adventure, and language training in Mexico and cost US$1900-5000.

Augsburg College Center for Global Education, 2211 Riverside Ave., Minneapolis, MN 55454, USA (toll-free US☎ 800-299-8889; www.augsburg.edu/global/). Semester-long programs based in Cuernavaca focus on issues of gender, human rights, and ecology.

Arcadia University for Education Abroad, 450 S. Easton Rd., Glenside, PA 19038, USA (US☎ 866-927-2234; www.arcadia.edu/cea). Operates programs in Guadalajara. Costs range from US$2300 (summer) to US$14,120 (full-year).

International Association for the Exchange of Students for Technical Experience (IAESTE), 10400 Little Patuxent Pkwy. Suite 250, Columbia, MD 21044-3519, USA (US☎ 410-997-2200; www.aipt.org). 8- to 12-week programs in Mexico for college students who have completed 2 years of technical study. US$75 application fee.

International Student Exchange Program, 1616 P St. NW, Suite 150, Washington, D.C. 20036, USA (US☎ 202-667-8027; www.isep.org). Places students in one of seven Mexican universities for anywhere from one semester to two years.

ALTERNATIVES
TO TOURISM

AFS, 71 W. 23rd St., 17th fl., New York, NY 10010, USA (US☎212-807-8686; www.afs.org). In the AFS exchange program, high school students live with a host family in a community and attend a summer semester.

UNIVERSITIES IN MEXICO

Applications to Mexican universities are usually due in early spring and require a transcript and a copy of your passport or birth certificate.

Universidad Nacional Autónoma de México (UNAM), Apdo. 70-391, Ciudad Universitaria, México, D.F. 04510 (☎5622 2470; www.cepe.unam.mx), is the largest public university in Mexico, with over 100,000 students. It operates the **Centro de Enseñanza para Extranjeros (CEPE),** which provides semester, intensive, and super-intensive programs in Spanish, art, history, and literature. The school also runs a campus in Taxco.

Universidad de las Americas (UDLA), Santa Catarina Mártir, Cholula, Puebla 72820 (☎222 229 2000; http://info.pue.udlap.mx), is a private university that has the distinction of being the only Mexican university accredited in the US. Their extensive international education program is well established.

Tecnológico de Monterrey, Av. Eugenio Garza Sada 2501 Sur, Monterrey, Nuevo León 64849 (☎81 8328 4065; http://dri.sistema.itesm.mx/dial/proyectos/sim/). One of the most prestigious private universities in Mexico, focusing on science, math, and engineering. Eight campuses across the country each host their own international program.

Universidad Iberoamericana, Paseo de la Reforma No. 880, Col. Lomas de Santa Fe, Deleg. Alvaro Obregón, 01210 México, D.F. (☎5950 4000; www.uia.mx), or Ibero for short, is a private university that offers semesters abroad, summer programs, and intensive Spanish instruction. Its main campus is in Mexico City, but there are satellite campuses.

LANGUAGE SCHOOLS

Unlike American universities, language schools are frequently independently run organizations or divisions of foreign universities that rarely offer college credit. Language schools are a good alternative to university study if you desire a deeper focus on the language or a slightly less rigorous course load. These programs are also good for younger high school students and older adults that might not feel comfortable with older students in a university program. Language schools in Mexico are concentrated in colonial cities, such as Cuernavaca, Puebla, and Oaxaca. Visitors to these cities can easily obtain information directly from the schools. Programs generally cost anywhere from $100 to $500, depending on duration and whether the school is foreign or Mexican-owned. Some good programs include:

Language Immersion Institute, 75 South Manheim Blvd., SUNY-New Paltz, New Paltz, NY 12561-2499, USA (US☎845-257-3500; www.newpaltz.edu/lii). 2-week summer language courses and some overseas courses in Spanish. Program fees are around US$1000 for a 2-week course.

The Center for Bilingual Multicultural Studies, San Jerónimo 304, Col. San Jerónimo, Cuernavaca, Morelos 62179 (☎777 317 1087; www.bilingual-center.com). Intensive classes starting at US$200 per week. Offers semester-long language study and special language programs for executives, teachers, and other businesspeople.

Instituto Falcon, Callejón de la Mora 158, Guanajuato, 36000 (☎473 731 1084; fax 731 0745; www.institutofalcon.com). Offers a 16-week program in Mexican culture and Spanish language for US$595. Regular classes US$65-120 per week. Dorms and homestays US$8.50-23 per day.

Instituto Habla Hispana, Calzada de la Luz 25, Apdo. 689, San Miguel de Allende, Guanajuato, C.P. 37700 (☎415 152 0713; fax 152 1535; www.mexicospanish.com). Intensive month-long Spanish courses starting at US$100 per week.

Spanish Institute of Puebla, 504 15 Pte., Puebla, Puebla 72420 (☎222 240 8692; www.sipuebla.com). US$1695 for four weeks of intensive classes.

WORKING

The Mexican government is wary of giving up precious jobs to foreigners when many Mexicans are either unemployed or underemployed. Mexico generally restricts foreign employment to jobs requiring skills not readily available in the country. Teaching English (see p. 49) is the most commonly available job. If you want to work in Mexico, you must secure a work visa (see **Business Visas,** p. 10).

LONG-TERM WORK

If you're planning on spending a substantial amount of time (more than three months) working in Mexico, searching for a job in advance is often the way to go. International placement agencies are generally the easiest way to find employment abroad, especially for teaching English. **Internships,** usually for college students, are a good way to segue into working abroad, although they are often unpaid or poorly paid (many say the experience, however, is well worth it). Be wary of advertisements or companies that claim the ability to get you a job abroad for a fee—often the same listings are available online or in newspapers.

SHORT-TERM WORK

Seasonal jobs are available in the tourism and hospitality industries. Upscale resort hotels often have a demand for English-speaking foreigners. A variety of positions are typically available, including concierges, bartender, waiter, lifeguard, and receptionist, as well as some managerial positions. Unfortunately, there are not many online databases for these jobs—it is probably easier to contact the prospective employers directly.

Omni Hotels Employment: www.omni.hospitalityonline.com. Omni Hotels has two locations in Mexico, and their employment page is updated frequently.

Ritz Carlton: www.ritzcarlton.com/corporate/employment/default.asp. The Ritz's searchable employment page has listings for its hotel in Cancún.

Cruise Job Finder: www.cruisejobfinder.com/members/resorts/listings/resorts_mexico.php. Lists Mexican resorts with seasonal employment information.

Intern Abroad: www.internabroad.com/Mexico.cfm. A site with searchable internship listings. Most are unpaid.

FOR FURTHER READING ON ALTERNATIVES TO TOURISM

Alternatives to the Peace Corps: A Directory of Third World and U.S. Volunteer Opportunities, by Joan Powell. Food First Books, 2000 (US$10).

How to Get a Job in Europe, by Sanborn and Matherly. Surrey Books, 1999 ($US22).

How to Live Your Dream of Volunteering Overseas, by Collins, DeZerega, and Heckscher. Penguin Books, 2002 (US$17).

International Directory of Voluntary Work, by Whetter and Pybus. Peterson's Guides and Vacation Work, 2000 (US$16).

International Jobs, by Kocher and Segal. Perseus Books, 1999 (US$18).

Work Abroad: The Complete Guide to Finding a Job Overseas, by Hubbs, Griffith, and Nolting. Transitions Abroad Publishing, 2000 ($16).

Work Your Way Around the World, by Susan Griffith. Worldview Publishing Services, 2001 (US$18).

LIFE AND TIMES

LAND

Mexico curves from north to south, maximizing coast and topographic variance to form two million square kilometers of the world's most diverse landscape. The combination of parched scrub-brush deserts, jungle rainforests, soaring volcanoes, temperate valleys, low coastal lagoons, and red canyons make Mexico one of the most physically and ecologically striking countries in the world.

GEOGRAPHY AND GEOLOGY

Mexico is situated along the eastern extremity of the "Ring of Fire," the region of tectonic activity encircling the Pacific Ocean. Over the millennia, these geologic forces have shaped Mexico into a land of crags, valleys, and high mountain chains.

BAJA CALIFORNIA AND THE NORTH

Northern Mexico is low, arid, and hot. The *noreste* (northeast) is drier than the *noroeste* (northwest), whose seasonally overflowing rivers have carved the region into deep canyons. The treasure of the region is the **Barranca del Cobre** (Copper Canyon) where five canyons converge to form a geological wonder that covers an area four times the size of Arizona's Grand Canyon.

The long and narrow **Baja Peninsula** stretches 1330km south from California, dividing the **Sea of Cortés** from the Pacific Ocean. A series of mountains runs the length of the rocky and scalding peninsula, sloping gently to the eastern shore, and cutting sharply on the west to create a craggy coast and miles of pristine beaches.

THE CENTER

Two lofty mountain ranges, the **Sierra Madre Occidental** to the west and the **Sierra Madre Oriental** to the east, cut a V-shape through the heart of the country. Between the ranges lies the **Altiplano**, a network of highlands stretching from the US to the **Isthmus of Tehuantepec**, near the Guatemalan border. The hospitable southern Altiplano, which includes the Valley of Mexico, is home to Mexico City and more than half of Mexico's population. The region south of Mexico City at the base of the V, the **Cordillera Neovolcánica,** is the most volcanic in Mexico. Though many of these volcanoes have been dormant since the 1800s, **Popocatépetl** erupted in 1994, spewing ash over Puebla. Farther south are the **Southern Highlands,** a series of mountains, plateaus, and valleys in the states of Guerrero and Oaxaca.

The lands directly to the east and west of the area bounded by the Sierra Madres are far less mountainous than the interior. Bordering the Sea of Cortés, the **Pacific Coastal Lowland,** west of the Madre Occidental, is a dry, relatively flat region of *mesas*. Along the eastern coast of Mexico, past the Madre Oriental, is the much wetter **Gulf Coastal Plain.** This swampy land runs from the US border to the Isthmus of Tehuantepec. Northeast of the isthmus is the **Tabasco Plain,** and southeast are the **Chiapas Highlands,** an area of high mountains surrounding a large rift valley.

THE YUCATÁN PENINSULA

Northeast of the Highlands juts the **Yucatán Peninsula,** an extremely flat region. The northern part of the peninsula is much drier than the southern part, and the porous limestone soil absorbs moisture before it can consolidate into rivers.

Pockmarking the limestone are caverns and **cenotes,** natural wells that were often part of Maya cities or ceremonial centers. These *cenotes* provide the only source of fresh water on the Yucatán. Some scientists believe the unusually high density of *cenotes* in the Yucatán is the result of the same **meteor impact** that may have killed the dinosaurs 65 million years ago. In the 1940s, an oil company drilling in the Yucatán uncovered evidence of what is now known as the **Chicxulub Crater.** A gigantic bowl 180km across and more than 200km deep, buried half on land and half under the Gulf of Mexico, the crater and its surrounding ring of caves support the hypothesis of a link between meteor impact and the formation of *cenotes.*

CLIMATE, FLORA & FAUNA

Mexico's climate ranges from desert to rainforest. Most of the country has two main seasons: wet (May-Aug.) and dry (Sept.-Apr.). Hurricanes and tropical storms sometimes stir up along the southern coasts in August and September, while the north remains mostly dry. In part due to its varied climate, Mexico is one of the most biologically diverse countries in the world and has many unique specimens—it is estimated that Mexico possesses 10% of the world's land species diversity.

Pollution, deforestation, and erosion are serious **environmental issues** in Mexico. Mexico City is infamous for its poor air quality; while reforms have improved the situation, Mexico City's air quality still reaches unhealthy levels far too often. Logging and deforestation have endangered many of Mexico's species and have also contributed to land erosion, which causes water pollution and loss of arable land.

BAJA CALIFORNIA AND THE NORTH

Baja California is generally dusty, bone-dry, and oppressively hot. Annual rainfall is generally less than 25cm, and summer temperatures may exceed 43°C (110°F). Though days in Baja are the hottest in all of Mexico, the setting of the scalding sun precedes surprisingly chilly nights.

The Sonoran and Chihuahuan deserts meet in the north of Mexico, and, together with the Mojave and Great Basin deserts in the US, comprise one of the world's largest desert regions. Over 250 kinds of cactus populate the **Chihuahan Desert.** Not to be outdone, the **Sonoran Desert** is the only place where one can find the huge **cardón cactus** that dominates the barren landscape and the unique **boojum tree,** a columnar succulent that can reach heights of over 15m.

Baja California and the northern Pacific Coast are home to many large **aquatic mammals.** Those who yearn to swim with the dolphins will finally get their chance, while those who prefer to save the whales can treat themselves to an eyeful of over 15 different species. Several companies offer **ecotourism** whale-watching packages. If your tastes run to the exotic and slightly erotic, Baja California offers ample opportunity to view the mating of elephant seals. The seals frolic up and down the coast, but **Bahía de Sebastián Vizcaíno,** near Guerrero Negro (see p. 179), is the best place to view the dirty deed. The beach is on the border of Mexico's largest biosphere reserve, **la Reserva de la Biosfera el Vizcaíno.**

THE CENTER AND SOUTH

The central and southern climate varies greatly, mainly due to fluctuations in altitude. As you get higher, temperatures get lower. Both the Sierra Madre Occidental and Oriental receive rainfall year round. At lower elevations (300-1000m) the mountainside is covered in deciduous forest. Trees and flowering plants such as orchids and bromeliads flourish during the summer, but most trees lose their leaves during the winter. As the altitude increases (1000-2000m), the forests become coniferous, dominated by pines, junipers, and evergreen oaks. Above the treeline (4000-5000m), snow covers the ground year round. Between the two mountain ranges, the Altiplano is covered in grassland, punctuated by scrub brush and prickly-pear cactus. Many large mammals make their homes in the highlands, among them foxes, mountain lions, and coyotes.

The states of **Tabasco** and **Campeche**, southwest of the Yucatán Peninsula, contain the only true **rainforests** in Mexico. These rainforests are composed of several interlocking ecosystems—each level, from ground to canopy, supports a community of distinct species. Anteaters, tapirs (floppy-snouted, odd-toed beasties), and monkeys abound, along with an endless variety of birds, lizards, frogs, and insects. At higher elevations, the rainforests give way to **cloud forests.** Here, moisture from standing clouds continually surrounds the forest. Home to the Zapatista rebels, the **Selva Lacandona** is Mexico's largest tropical forest. Despite some conservation efforts, **logging** is a serious problem for Mexico's rainforests. Swamps and marshlands, each supporting their own abundant array of plant and animal life, compose the remainder of the Gulf Coast. Mangrove trees densely line the sweltering shore, as fresh water mixes with salt in the region's many river deltas.

HISTORY

Over the last 10,000 years, Mexico has seen the rise and fall of mighty empires, the pain of foreign conquest, three tumultuous revolutions, and the struggle to rebuild in the era of modern capitalism.

PRE-HISPANIC SOCIETIES

Archaeologists generally categorize Mexican Pre-Hispanic societies into five historical periods: **Pre-Agricultural** (or Paleoindian, 40,000-8000 BC), **Archaic** (8000-2000 BC), **Formative** (or Pre-Classic, 2000 BC-AD 200), **Classic** (200-900), and **Post-Classic** (or Historical, 900-1521). Relatively little is known about pre-Formative, hunter-gatherer societies.

THE FORMATIVE PERIOD

The development of agriculture gave rise to the great empires of Mesoamerica. Society during the Formative (or Pre-Classic) Period depended on maize and linked agricultural fertility to religion. **The Olmecs** flourished in the warm, humid area that today comprises the states of Veracruz (see p. 538) and Tabasco (see p. 568), growing out of **San Lorenzo** (see p. 567) around 1700 BC. By 1350 BC, the Olmecs had developed large scale public works and a recognizable artistic style marked by the famous stone heads, as well as delicate jade figurines and masks. The **hieroglyphic writing** and **long count calendar** systems also survived the Olmecs, as their derivatives featured prominently in Maya civilization. Around 900 BC, the settlements at **La Venta** (see p. 572), southeast of San Lorenzo, and **Tres Zapotes** (see p. 563) replaced the dwindling

1750-1350 BC: Olmecs establish Mesoamerica's first large-scale settlements and have a distinctive artistic style.

600 BC: La Venta declines, taking the Olmecs with it.

500-100 BC: Monte Albán becomes *the* place to be for the Zapotecs. By AD 700 the dream is over.

AD 100-900: The Maya are on top of their game. Arts, sciences flourish as had rarely been seen in the world.

AD 200-900: Classic Period. Good times.

500: Teotihuacán is the largest and mightiest Classic center.

power base at San Lorenzo. These, too, suddenly declined by 600 BC, ending the Olmec golden age.

THE CLASSIC PERIOD

Between AD 250 and 900 the great Mesoamerican empires returned. **Teotihuacán** (see p. 138) was likely the most powerful; the name ("Place of the Gods" in Náhuatl) was given by Aztecs, who were awestruck by the site centuries later. By around 200 BC, Teotihuacán had an advanced urban design with a complex road system anchored by ceremonial plazas and massive pyramids. Around these lived the world's sixth largest population— 125,000 people in AD 400. Evidence of trade as far south as Guatemala confirms the extensive reach of Teotihuacán's influence. Meanwhile, the Zapotec empire in the Oaxaca Valley centered on **Monte Albán** (see p. 513). Settled between 500 and 100 BC, it rapidly grew into an imperial capital; neighboring rivals, such as the Mixtec at **Mitla** (see p. 511), may have been responsible for the city's decline between AD 400 and 700.

The **Classic Maya** civilization was unique for its lack of a single, centralized capital. Instead, **Palenque** (see p. 597), **Tikal,** and **Copán,** stood out among various regional capitals in the Yucatán and Central America. The Classic Maya are best known for their broad cultural achievements, embracing engineering, mathematics, art, architecture, and astronomy. They could predict the movement of celestial bodies with sophisticated precision, permitting a sophisticated calendar, and were the first in the world to understand the mathematical concept of zero; their famous temples are now among the most popular ruins in Latin America. However, they had warlike achievements to match, probably including human sacrifice, and internal revolts likely triggered the demise of the Maya around 900.

THE POST-CLASSIC PERIOD

800-1100: The Toltecs have their fifteen minutes and then some in Tula.

900: The demise of the Classic Maya signals the Post-Classic Period.

987: A prophecy from light-skinned Topiltzin-Quetzalcóatl sets the stage for fatal confusion.

1050-1450: The Post-Classic Maya set themselves up in the Yucatán.

The demise of the Classic civilizations was complete by 900 and the Post-Classic Period lasted until the Spanish conquest. These later civilizations established great military empires, but suffered lesser artistic and technological innovation.

The Toltecs, originally known as the **Chichimeca** or the **Toltec-Chichimeca,** grew out of settlements today in Zacatecas and Hidalgo in central Mexico. The greatest Toltec leader, **Ce Acatl Topiltzin** (later called **Topiltzín-Quetzalcóatl**) founded the capital **Tula** (see p. 360) in 968. At his exile in 987, he vowed to return in the next year of Ce Acatl, the year of **One Reed** (that year, 1519, prophetically did coincide with a royal arrival— the beginning of the Spanish invasion under Cortés). The Toltec empire thrived into the 1100s, when drought and famine ravaged their civilization.

In contrast to earlier Maya sprawl, the Post-Classic Maya settled almost exclusively in the Yucatán Peninsula around *cenotes,* or sinkholes, the peninsula's only source of fresh water. Unlike the Classic Maya, Post-Classic Maya art drew from many cultures, particularly the Toltecs. Three major city-states, **Chichén Itzá** (see p. 641), **Mayapán** (see p.

635), and **Uxmal** (see p. 631) together formed the **Mayapán League,** long dominated by Chichén Itzá. After the brief prominence of Mayapán, its collapse in 1441 marked the end of a centralized Maya civilization.

THE AZTECS (THE MEXICA)

The Aztecs, then known as the **Mexica,** arrived in the fertile **Valley of Anáhuac** (the Valley of Mexico today) in the 13th century. In the early 14th century, under **Itzcóatl,** they established their capital, **Tenochtitlán** (modern-day Mexico City; see p. 84), from which they ruled over central Mexico. Cresting at over five million people, this final Pre-Hispanic empire was also the largest. The Aztec system depended on tribute (goods, land, and sacrificial victims) from subdued townships.

1200-1521: The Aztecs spread their tough love across Mesoamerica.

AZTEC SOCIETY. Tenochtitlán was at one point the largest city in the world, and among the most magnificent: it was superior in cleanliness, urban planning, and architecture. The imperial hierarchy became increasingly regimented and complex as the empire grew. The royal family and nobles occupied the highest level of Aztec society, followed closely by the warriors—distinction on the battlefield was one of the few ways males could enter the nobility. **Pochteca** (traders), who linked all of Mesoamerica, were next in line, followed by the common class of farmers, laborers, and artisans. Women were active in religion, agriculture, and politics as a result of greater rights than those enjoyed by their European counterparts.

1350: Tenochtitlán, the Aztec capital, is a model of urban planning.

The religion of the Aztecs reflected their militarism. They believed in cyclical time: the earth and sun had been recreated four times, and it was during the present time, that of the fifth sun, that the earth would finally be destroyed. To stave off apocalypse, the Aztecs appeased their patron god, Huitzilopochtli, through human sacrifice, culminating in the offering of a human heart. Such ceremonies took place in Tenochtitlán's main temple, the **Templo Mayor** (see p. 110).

1441: A blood bath heralds the end of Maya empire again.

Among the most famous of the Aztec pantheon are the rain god **Tlaloc** and the feathered serpent **Quetzalcóatl.**

CONQUEST & COLONIZATION

The arrival of the Europeans in the 16th century radically changed the course of Mexican history, as a new hybrid of native and Spanish cultures began to emerge.

1492: Columbus sails the ocean blue.

ENTER CORTÉS

In the early 16th century, the governor of Cuba, **Diego Velázquez,** launched numerous expeditions to search for slaves and gold; **Hernán Cortés** was responsible for investigating rumors of a mighty mainland empire. In 1519, Cortés landed on the island of **Cozumel** (see p. 677). There he met and brought along a Spaniard and former prisoner of the Maya, **Jerónimo de Aguilar,** who spoke fluent Maya.

1519: A light-skinned king returns?

As Cortés worked his way up the Gulf Coast, he took a war prize: 20 maidens, including **Malintzin (Doña Marina** to the Span-

LIFE AND TIMES

ish and, later, traitorous **la Malinche** to Mexicans), an enslaved Aztec who would become his mistress and advisor. Using his two interpreters (Náhuatl to Maya by la Malinche, Maya to Spanish by Aguilar), Cortés was able to overcome the language barrier. Further up the coast, Cortés traveled to the Totonac capital of **Zempoala** (see p. 557) and eastward to **Tlaxcala** (see p. 376), persuading both to join him against their enemy, the Aztecs. Cortés then attacked his hosts in **Cholula** (see p. 395), massacring 6000 Aztec allies in the **Cholula Massacre.**

The Aztec emperor **Moctezuma II** (popularly known in the US as Montezuma) nervously awaited Cortés's arrival: rumors abounded that the light-skinned Quetzalcóatl had returned. The initially peaceful meeting of the two leaders quickly soured when the Spaniards took Moctezuma hostage. The Aztecs drove Cortés from Tenochtitlán on July 1, 1520, a night known to the Spanish as **la Noche Triste (Sad Night).** Nevertheless, Cortés quickly regrouped and the Aztecs—weakened by plagues and famine and overwhelmed by the foreign guns and steel—were unable to overcome the Spanish. On August 13, 1521, the Aztecs, and their new emperor **Cuauhtémoc,** were finally defeated at **Tlatelolco.**

1521: The former Aztec empire has a new king across the sea.

THE COLONIAL PERIOD

Because the Aztec empire had controlled much of central Mexico, the Spanish were able to control most of the area immediately by superimposing colonial administration on existing imperial structures. *Conquistadores* came in droves to rein in the rest of Mesoamerica, chasing the **Northern Mystery**—cities of gold. **Francisco Vázquez de Coronado** and **Juan Rodríguez de Cabrillo** were two who pursued the myth as far north as Kansas and California; however, their search proved futile.

1521-1600: The former Aztec empire is rapidly bereft of former Aztec subjects as disease, religion, and landlords all prove adept at killing the indigenous population.

THE PLAGUES OF MESOAMERICA. Disease proved to be a powerful ally of the advancing Spaniards. European sicknesses became plagues that killed millions. **Smallpox, typhoid,** and **dysentery** were some of the most important factors in the Spanish conquest, opening fertile land by wiping out whole villages.

THE ENCOMIENDA SYSTEM. When it turned out that gold was not lying around waiting to be picked off the ground, the *conquistadores* turned to the exploitation of land and labor. Villages had to send a quota of laborers to Spanish farms, called **encomiendas;** in return, the **encomendero** was responsible for Christianizing and educating his workers. With little regulation of the system (and few Spaniards who cared), abuse was rampant.

THE RELIGIOUS CONQUEST. As soon as the Spaniards took Tenochtitlán, they razed the Aztecs' central temple and built a cathedral—now Mexico's **National Cathedral** (see p. 110)—with the rubble. Across the new territory, missionaries spread Catholicism, which became interwoven with traditional practices, creating the religious fusion that persists today in many rural areas.

RACE AND CLASS. Spaniards attempted to align racial and class boundaries. **Peninsulares,** whites born in Spain, were at the top of the social hierarchy, while **criollos,** Spaniards born in Mexico, were excluded from high positions in the Church and government. Spain tried to segregate them from the **indígenas** (or **indios**), but this was impossible, and, within a few generations, a huge new racial group had emerged—**mestizos,** children of mixed Spanish and *indígena* parentage. Together with **mulatos,** of African descent, they formed a motley class of "common people."

1550-1821: Under Spanish colonial administration, a new people is born, paving the way for the idea of Mexico.

A COUNTRY IS BORN

THE TUMULTUOUS FIRST CENTURY

"My children: a new dispensation comes to us today. Will you receive it? Will you free yourselves? Will you recover the lands stolen three hundred years ago from your forefathers by the hated Spaniards? Will you not defend your religion and your rights as true patriots? Long live our Lady of Guadalupe! Death to bad government!"
—Miguel Hidalgo, *El Grito de Dolores*

Sept. 16, 1810: The *Grito de Dolores* initiates the independence struggle. **Revolution #1.**

LIFE AND TIMES

INDEPENDENCE

Rebellion first coalesced around **Father Miguel Hidalgo y Costilla,** a rebellious priest from the small parish of **Dolores** (see p. 350) who, with fellow priest **Ignacio Allende** and others, formed a "literary club," which soon turned its thoughts from literature to revolution. The arrest of Allende galvanized the others. On the morning of **September 16, 1810,** Hidalgo summoned parishioners to church with loud bells, and there delivered an electrifying call to arms—**el Grito de Dolores (The Cry of Dolores)**—to end Spanish rule, to promote the equality of races, and to demand a redistribution of the land. **Mexican Independence Day** commemorates this beginning.

Hidalgo's army quickly grew and blitzed through several cities before a Spanish ambush in March 1811 captured Hidalgo in the desert town of Monclova in Coahuila. Though Hidalgo was promptly tried and executed for treason and heresy, the quest for independence had begun: another parish priest, **José María Morelos y Pavón,** rose to lead the independence movement. He had early success, capturing Oaxaca, Orizaba, and Acapulco before being captured and executed, too.

VICTORY. Following the Hidalgo and Morelos movements were other guerilla heroes such as **Vicente Guerrero** and **Guadalupe Victoria.** Meanwhile, in Spain, pressure on **King Ferdinand VII** led to the reaffirmation of the Spanish Constitution of 1812, which promoted popular sovereignty and other liberal ideals. This new radicalism plus the rural rebels led many Mexican conservatives and clergy to mobilize for independence as the best way to preserve conservative government.

1812-1820: The results are in: Mexicans have had enough of Spain. Liberals and conservatives still hate each other, though.

The most important convert was **Agustín de Iturbide**, a *criollo* who had led Spanish troops against Hidalgo. In 1820, Iturbide turned his thousands of soldiers to the independence cause. Together with his former foe Guerrero, he issued the **Plan de Iguala** on February 24, 1821, calling for three guarantees: an independent constitutional monarchy, Roman Catholicism as the state religion, and equality before the law. The **Ejército de las Tres Garantías** (the **Army of the Three Guarantees**) drew support particularly from conservative *criollos* and forced the new Spanish general, **Juan de O'Donoju,** to formalize the Plan de Iguala through the **Treaty of Córdoba.**

1822: In celebration of independence, Iturbide names himself emperor, dances.

CHALLENGES FOR THE NEW NATION

Iturbide successfully "convinced" the national congress to coronate him Emperor of Mexico on July 21, 1822. The victory was bittersweet, as a decade of war had left the economy in shambles and Iturbide dispelled the uncooperative national congress on October 31, 1822. **Antonio López de Santa Anna** made his entrance on the national stage, launching a rebellion a month later, with the support of many independence leaders for the anti-imperialist **Plan de Casa Mata;** Iturbide abdicated in February 1823, preferring European exile.

1823: Celebration over: Santa Anna and others send Iturbide into exile.

Santa Anna was to be the dominant personality of Mexican politics for the country's first decades. Alternately liberal and conservative, he was primarily interested in possessing power rather than exercising it responsibly. His abilities as an organizer helped him constantly reinvent himself, and his several military successes helped him overcome repeated political failures: he gained and lost control of Mexico as president or dictator eleven times from 1833 to 1855. His chaotic personal career matched the instability that stagnated Mexico's development during Santa Anna's life (over the same period, Mexico had thirty-six different leaders).

1832: Santa Anna follows up his presidential victory by disappearing—then overthrows his own vice president.

In 1832, Santa Anna overwhelmingly won the presidency, riding his popularity for defeating a Spanish attempt at reconquest. Bored, he left the capital in the charge of the vice president, **Valentín Gómez Farías,** a liberal who pursued anti-Church reforms to break its links with the state. Santa Anna returned, allied with the conservatives against his own government, and created a centralized military state. Debt problems led to French intervention in Veracruz, dubbed the **Pastry War** in honor of a French pastry chef whose wares were seized by rioting Mexican troops. Victory and a personal wound bolstered Santa Anna's image.

1838: French mistakenly attempt to fry Mexico in the Pastry War. Santa Anna's leg becomes famous.

> **ALL HAIL MY LEG.** During the Pastry War, Santa Anna's left leg was severely wounded and eventually had to be amputated. Not a man to take a lost limb lightly, Santa Anna had his leg transported to Mexico City where, after an elaborate procession and a formal entombment in an urn atop a pillar, the decayed limb was serenaded and applauded by cabinet members and diplomats.

LIFE AND TIMES

The **Texas secession** temporarily damaged that image. US citizens had settled in the northern Mexican province of Texas throughout the early 1800s. When they outnumbered Mexicans, the government became concerned. When independence movements mobilized against restrictive immigration laws, Santa Anna responded with 6000 troops. In February of 1836, his troops overwhelmed Texan rebels at the **Alamo** and killed all 150 defenders. "Remember the Alamo!" became a rallying call under **Samuel Houston** and the Texans won their independence after capturing Santa Anna and his army on April 21, 1836.

1836: Texas takes its ball and goes home.

WAR WITH THE STATES

The United States had long coveted the Lone Star Republic, but Congress did not annex it until 1845. Mexico, which had never officially recognized Texas, was enraged. War began in May 1846, as the US wanted to set the border back to the Río Bravo (known to the US as the Rio Grande). US troops moved quickly through the northern half of the country, but the most dangerous attack was launched by general **Winfield Scott** who, at the head of 10,000 men, landed on March 9, 1847 in Veracruz. After a brutal bombardment and sack of the city that killed twice as many Mexican civilians as soldiers, the victorious army continued toward Mexico City. Despite valiant, street-by-street fighting, the Mexicans were overwhelmed and by September 7, only the **Castle of Chapultepec** (see p. 118) remained unvanquished. The young cadets defending the castle were revered throughout Mexico for their bravery; a monument at the castle remembers the six teenagers who leaped to their deaths rather than surrender.

1845: The United States annexes Texas against Mexico's wishes. The only solution is war, which starts the following year.

1847: Gen. Scott invades at Veracruz and is fortunate that war crimes tribunals won't start for 100 years.

On February 2, 1848 the **Treaty of Guadalupe Hidalgo** ended the war by accepting a Río Bravo border and relinquishing California and New Mexico for a paltry US$19 million (less than one year's budget). This spurred a virulent *yanquifobia* (fear and hatred of the Yankees) and led Santa Anna to resign in shame. Back again five years later, though, he agreed to the **Gadsen Purchase** selling Arizona and southern New Mexico, before a final exile in 1855.

1848: The Treaty of Guadalupe Hidalgo ends the war. Mexico is displeased with the terms.

1853: Manifest Destiny triumphs: after the Gadsen Purchase, the US possesses half of Mexico.

REFORM

The Reform Era paved the way for modern Mexico. However, this was hardly a time of peace and prosperity, as the country was bitterly divided between liberal reformers and conservatives, including supporters of the Catholic Church.

Liberals such as **Melchor Ocampo, Santos Degollado, Guillermo Prieto,** and **Benito Juárez** rallied around the **Plan de Ayutla** and rebel leader **Juan Álvarez** against Santa Anna. New liberal reforms began with the **Ley Juárez,** which abolished clergy and military privileges, while the new **Constitution of 1857** formally established Mexico as a representative democracy and republican nation with greater rights and liberties. Conflict with frightened conservatives in 1858 touched off Mexico's bloodiest revolt to date, known as the **War of the Reform.** Although the liberals repelled the conservatives by 1860, default on debts prompted another foreign intervention.

1855: Juárez (the first indigenous president) and the Liberals overthrow Santa Anna for a final time.

1857: The new constitution firmly establishes Mexico's liberal state. **Revolution #2.**

LIFE AND TIMES

CRAZY CARLOTA The wife of Emperor Maximilian, Carlota, has gone down in Mexican history as a woman a few bolts short of a tool kit. In 1867, with the knowledge that her husband's regime was about to topple, Carlota left Mexico to appeal directly to Napoleon III. Her pleas were ignored, and, guilt-ridden and depressed, the 26-year-old Carlota really lost it. Convinced that Napoleon was trying to poison her, she tied up chickens in her room and refused to eat anything but the eggs they laid or drink anything but water fetched directly from the Trevi Fountain in Rome. Institutionalized soon thereafter, Carlota survived to the ripe old age of 86 and outlived nearly every other person involved in the French Intervention.

1862: France invades. Mexico wins a big victory on May 5, but France prevails.

1863-1867: Maximilian is emperor with French help. His lack of support in Mexico is his downfall.

1867: Juárez and the Liberals return.

Although the British and Spanish participated, imperial ambitions led the French to dominate the conflict. **Cinco de Mayo** celebrates a Mexican victory in 1862, but the French eventually forced the Juárez government to surrender on May 31, 1863, while conservatives rejoiced in his defeat. Napoleon III chose the Austrian archduke **Ferdinand Maximilian** as emperor. Unfortunately for him, his left-leaning, anti-Catholic policies quickly alienated conservatives and he surrendered on May 15, 1867 to be executed, after French troops withdrew. Juárez returned triumphantly with a program for greater social equity: for the first time, education was free and compulsory. He died shortly after another electoral victory in 1871, to be succeeded by fellow liberal **Sebastián Lerdo de Tejada.** On November 16, 1876, General **Porfirio Díaz,** loser in the 1871 election, led a successful coup that established what would be a 30-year rule.

THE PORFIRIATO

1876-1910: The Mexican economy prospers under the Díaz dictatorship, but privileges and most of Mexico's wealth are concentrated in a small group.

Porfirio Díaz was Mexico's second truly dominant leader, but he was very different from Santa Anna. He brought stability to the country for the first time, and the economy flourished during the **Porfiriato** or the **Pax Porfiriana.** One of the most important developments was the new railroad system, but institutional and bureaucratic reform also contributed tremendously to the period of growth. However, these benefits were concentrated in a relatively small social group, dominated by his advisors (the **científicos**) and large foreign investors. Land concentration was one of the most visible effects, and many also resented Díaz's dictatorial rule, which was enforced by Díaz's personal army corps, the **rurales,** who blanketed and oppressed the countryside. Díaz's cronies controlled much of local politics, while *indígenas* suffered the most.

A NEW CENTURY

THE REVOLUTION

1911: Madero runs for president on a no-re-election platform. After his arrest, Madero calls for revolution. **Revolution #3.**

Widespread discontent allowed **Francisco Madero,** a wealthy *hacienda* owner from Coahuila, to run on an anti-re-election platform. Madero was soon imprisoned after openly criticizing

Díaz, but after Madero fled to Texas he called for revolution through the October 5, 1910 **Plan de San Luis Potosí**. Discontent was rampant and so was preparation. Two days earlier, a Puebla leader named **Aquiles Serdán** was discovered accumulating ammunition; Díaz made him and his family early martyrs in the Revolution. **Emiliano Zapata, Pascual Orozco**, and **Pancho Villa** supported revolution with guerilla tactics in both south and north. After the fall of Ciudad Juárez (see p. 240) on May 10, 1911, Díaz accepted defeat and resigned four days later.

1911-1917: Fighting of the Mexican Revolution rages on.

1911: Díaz resigns, Madero becomes president.

REVOLUTIONARY GOVERNMENTS

The 1911 election brought in Madero and his vice president, **José María Pino Suárez**. The government tried to improve education, infrastructure, and labor regulation, but it failed to fundamentally challenge the social structure, instead favoring the bourgeoisie excluded by Díaz. Hostile politicians further inhibited the government's effectiveness, and the radical Zapata, from Morelos, set off a string of revolts with his **Plan of Ayala**, which rejected the Madero presidency. It was machinations in the capital that eventually toppled the government, however. For ten days in 1913 in Mexico City, known as the **Decena Trágica**, federal general **Victoriano Huerta** fought against rebels with ties to Díaz. On the 10th day, however, US ambassador **Henry Lane Wilson** (who would come to represent for the Mexican imagination the self-interested, interventionist United States) helped engineer a betrayal and Huerta suddenly switched sides in the **Pact of the Embassy**. He arrested Madero and Suárez and immediately had them shot; Huerta assumed the presidency that day.

1913: Gen. Huerta betrays his president at the end of the *Decena Trágica*. US involvement creates much resentment.

Henry Lane Wilson had supported Huerta as a man who would reestablish the order of the Díaz era that had been so favorable to US economic interests. Despite Huerta's strong hand, his cruelty and intolerance unified the rebel opposition, led by Villa, **Álvaro Obregón**, and **Venustiano Carranza**, in the **Plan de Guadalupe**. Zapata continued to fight too, seeking the distribution of land to *indígenas*. The US eventually undermined the dictator with an invasion in Veracruz following a diplomatic faux pas involving US sailors, and Huerta resigned under pressure on July 8, 1914.

1913-1914: Villa, Obregón, and Carranza unite against Huerta. Zapata continues fighting independently.

VILLA, ZAPATA, AND THE CONSTITUTIONALISTS. The forces of Villa and Zapata met for the only time in the capital at the end of 1914, but their failure to articulate a national program created an opportunity for the **constitucionalistas** (Constitutionalists) of Carranza. After Huerta resigned, Villa, Zapata, Obregón, and Carranza all vied for control; yet once Obregón cast his lot with Carranza and defeated Villa at the **Battle of Celaya**, Villa and Zapata were isolated in the north and south. The remarkably liberal **Constitution of 1917**, which set out the world's most progressive labor rights and declared that private ownership of land was a privilege, not a right, helped create a national consensus in favor of Carranza, who won the 1917 elections. Villa, angered by US recognition of the latest incarnation of government, raided Columbus, New Mexico, spurring a

December, 1914: Villa and Zapata meet in the capital but do not formulate a national program.

1916-1917: Gen. Pershing invades Mexico with thousands of troops, yet fails to find Villa.

LIFE AND TIMES

1917: A new constitution is born and Carranza is made president. Villa and Zapata marginalized.

1919: Carranza betrays Zapata and kills him.

1920: Carranza dies and Obregón becomes president.

1924: The presidency passes to Calles.

1928: Obregón is assassinated, *Maximato* begins.

1929: A new party, the PNR, begins a 71-year rule of Mexico.

1934: Cárdenas presidency begins; end of *Maximato*.

1936: Former president Calles unceremoniously exiled.

1940: The Revolutionary Period ends with the Cárdenas presidency.

rash invasion under General **John Pershing** that was wildly unsuccessful in hunting down Villa, while more effective in insulting the newly recognized government.

THE SONORAN DYNASTY. Meanwhile, Carranza eliminated one rival by assassinating Zapata, who had arranged to surrender. Carranza's failure to implement the radical provisions of the constitution, however, helped to alienate Obregón, who allied with fellow Sonorans **Adolfo de la Huerta** and **Plutarco Elías Calles,** under the **Plan de Agua Prieta.** As Carranza attempted to flee, he was killed by one of his own guards, paving the way for the **Sonoran Dynasty,** which began with Obregón's election in 1920. Through 1928, successive governments worked to implement the constitution. However, this group was as divided as any since Díaz. Ideologically, Obregón favored peasants while Calles tied himself to labor, and power struggles were behind both the de la Huerta revolt, when, in 1924, Calles was chosen to succeed Obregón, and the Obregón assassination, when, in 1928, he tried to circumvent prohibitions on re-election. Calles recognized the need for a conflict-limiting mechanism and, to that end, founded the **Partido Nacional Revolucionario (PNR)** in 1929. This party and its two descendants would rule Mexico for 71 years. The period from 1929 to 1934 became known as the **Maximato** as Calles, the **Jefe Máximo** (Highest Chief), was the increasingly conservative power behind three presidents.

LÁZARO CÁRDENAS. The 1934 elections ushered in the most revered figure in the Revolutionary period, Lázaro Cárdenas. He refused to be another puppet president, causing a conflict that culminated in the 1936 exile of Calles. Cárdenas took full advantage of the new *sexenio* (six-year presidency) to undertake drastic land reform, distributing 44 million acres—twice as many as all of his predecessors combined—to thousands of Indians. He also was responsible for linking popular organizations to the state by recreating the party as the **Partido de la Revolución Mexicana (PRM)** in 1940. His single most famous (and most universally popular) action was the nationalization of the oil industry, consolidating it as **Petróleos Mexicanos (PEMEX),** in response to defiance from foreign companies.

THE "PERFECT DICTATORSHIP"

Peruvian novelist Mario Vargas Llosa coined this term for the one-party state that was unique among Latin American states for its combination of political stability and stunning economic growth in the post-war era, on par with the most dynamic in East Asia. Although Cárdenas was the one person most responsible for fulfilling the radical promise of the Revolution, it was his integration of popular organizations and the state through the party that permitted the social control necessary for a capital-intensive industrialization project. Despite the exorbitant power of individual presidents, the Mexican system became known for pendular shifts between leftist and rightist presidents, which helped keep the system inclusive.

THE POST-WAR "MEXICAN MIRACLE"...

In 1946 the new president, **Miguel Alemán**, restructured the PRM, bestowing it with its present name, the **Partido Revolucionario Institucional (PRI)**. Alemán was both the first civilian president since the Revolution and the most conservative. He encouraged capital accumulation and violently broke the vigorously independent national unions. His modernization drive also instilled him with a passion for public works. He built dams and hydroelectric plants, and completed Mexico's section of the Pan-American highway. He also oversaw the completion of the modern campus of the **Universidad Autónoma Nacional de México,** (**UNAM;** see p. 127), a marvel of modern and architecture. Not until his successor, Adolfo Ruiz Cortines, though, did the Revolution finally bring women the right to vote.

President **Gustavo Díaz Ordaz** oversaw troubled times. In the summer of 1968, amidst dissatisfaction with a corrupt and unresponsive government, rioting broke out in the capital, most prominently at the UNAM. Standoffs between students and the military reached crisis levels in **Tlatelolco Plaza** (or **Plaza de las Tres Culturas;** see p. 120), where police killed an estimated 400 peaceful demonstrators and jailed another 2000 just 10 days before the 1968 Olympics were to open in Mexico City. The 1970 election of the Minister of the Interior, **Luis Echeverría,** whose role in the massacre is still unknown, did little to relieve the dissatisfaction many Mexicans felt. After an aggressively populist presidency, inflation skyrocketed and foreign debt brought the miracle to a close.

...AND HARD TIMES

After a brief period of plenty under José López Portillo came to a halt when oil prices dipped, Mexico stumbled with the rest of Latin America into the International Monetary Fund (IMF)-led **Lost Decade** of the 1980s, which reversed decades-long gains in the standard of living. Under **Miguel de la Madrid**, president from 1982 to 1988, the PRI faced its first serious political crisis. Perhaps the biggest blow was the **1985 Mexico City earthquake,** which registered an 8 on the Richter scale, killed thousands; its aftermath, and the rubble of earthquake-safe D.F., starkly revealed corruption and incompetence in government.

PRI REVIVAL. Despite the PRI's serious loss of respectability, its candidate, the Harvard-educated **Carlos Salinas de Gortari,** won the widely-contested 1988 election when a mysterious, week-long computer crash was alleged by political opponents to have reversed an approaching victory for **Cuauhtémoc Cárdenas,** son of Lázaro and head of the leftist PRI spin-off, the **Partido de la Revolución Democrática (PRD).**

DASHED HOPES. Although hopes were high for the PRI's 1994 candidate, Salinas protégé **Luis Donaldo Colosio,** the

---

1946: The party gets its current name, the PRI.

1950-1970: The "miracle" period, when Mexican growth well outperforms the US economy.

1968: Police kill an estimated 400 student protestors in the Tlatelolco Massacre.

1976: Growing deficits lead Mexico to accept an IMF economic stabilization plan.

1978-1981: Oil discoveries launch hopes of a new golden age in Mexico.

1982-1988: The debt crisis causes dramatic economic... crisis.

1985: Aftermath of a massive earthquake in Mexico City awakens mistrust of ineffective government.

1988: Salinas "elected."

1992: NAFTA.

LIFE AND TIMES

1994: Year of the Disasters. Zapatistas revolt on New Year's, presidential candidate Colosio assassinated, and the year closes with the worst peso crisis since 1982.

house of cards eventually came crashing down. The Salinas reforms left many behind, and on January 1, 1994—the day NAFTA went into effect—the **Ejército Zapatista de Liberación Nacional (EZLN)**, or the **Zapatista National Liberation Army**, captured the city of San Cristóbal de las Casas (see p. 583) and held it in a 12-day siege. Over 9000 Maya peasants followed the eloquent masked guerilla **Subcomandante Marcos** (revealed to be Rafael Sebastián Guillén Vicente, a university-educated Marxist). The Zapatistas called for a complete government overhaul, extensive land reform, social justice for *indígenas*, and fair elections. Months of negotiations followed, until the Bishop of Chiapas, **Samuel Ruiz**, eventually mediated a tenuous compromise.

During the tense period of negotiations, in March 1994, Colosio was assassinated at a rally in Tijuana under mysterious circumstances. Salinas turned to a weaker candidate, Budget Minister **Ernesto Zedillo Ponce de Léon**, who had never held an elected office. However, there was nothing any candidate could do with the **devaluation crisis** that exploded within a month of Zedillo taking office. Amidst crisis, Salinas had postponed devaluation that would have slowed the economy, instead allowing pressures to accumulate to dangerous levels. After a US$20 billion bailout, interest rates soared and inflation accelerated, nearly collapsing the banking system. Moreover, within a year revelations of corruption, extreme even for Mexico, implicated many in Salinas's inner circle, ruining Salinas's legacy. Most notorious was his brother, **Raúl Salinas de Gortari**, who murdered his former brother-in-law and had lucrative ties with drug cartels.

1994: Zedillo elected. Continues economic reform, accelerates political reform.

1997: PRI loses control of the lower house of congress and Cuauhtémoc Cárdenas, from the rival PRD, becomes mayor of Mexico City.

LIFE AND TIMES

REFORM AND CHANGE

Zedillo secured his place in history not by resurrecting the system, but by securing fundamental change. Economically, he steered the reformist course of Salinas, but he matched this with meaningful political reform. His attacks on corruption earned him US endorsement as a "partner in the war on drugs" and he distanced himself from the PRI, allowing a landslide victory by Cuauhtémoc Cárdenas in the Mexico City mayoral race and permitting the PRI loss of congressional majority in the lower house for the first time. He formally ended the **dedazo**, the president's traditional right to name the next PRI presidential candidate (and therefore his successor) and ushered in the democratic transition by personally announcing the victory of opposition candidate **Vicente Fox** on national television, ahead of the official results.

2000: Zedillo shuns the *dedazo* and Vicente Fox, from the PAN, wins the presidential election.

TODAY

The momentous reforms enacted by the Zedillo administration foreshadowed the end of the PRI's reign. "A Crowning Defeat—Mexico as the Victor," cried *The New York Times* on July 4, 2000, one day after opposition candidate **Vicente**

Fox Quesada soundly defeated the slick PRI candidate **Francisco Labastida Ochoa.** The tall, outgoing Fox, a former Coca-Cola executive and governor of Guanajuato state, ran as a candidate of the conservative **Partido de Accion Nacional (PAN)** on a platform of free trade, advocating increased wages and foreign investments, reduction of bureaucracy, elimination of corruption, revival of agrarian land reform, and a return of the country to its Catholic roots. Declared by many international observers to be the cleanest Mexican election ever, the campaign was hard-fought with mud-slinging galore; Fox questioned his opponent's virility while Labastida ridiculed Fox's divorced status. When the dust settled, Fox emerged as the surprising victor, and the humbled PRI was finally removed from power.

Fox at the helm, Mexico entered the 21st century with a sluggish economy and a growing land shortage, forcing many to emigrate north and feeding the fires of the EZLN and other reform movements. Though many of his campaign promises—police reform and more employment opportunities among them—have gotten bogged down in the first half of his presidency, Mexico under Fox has experienced many breakthroughs in the international theatre. Soon after gaining a seat on the United Nations Security Council, Mexico enjoyed Council presidency in April 2003, and Fox has been the first to allow human rights observers into the country. On the southern front, Fox honored the agreement of San Andres Larrainzar, ordering national troops out of Zapatista-heavy Chiapas; in August 2001, the accords, which included guarantees to ensure justice for *indígenas*, became law. The midterm elections of July 2003 found the public showing a lack of support for Fox, handing more than 20 new Chamber of Deputies seats to the PRI and making the next three years a challenge in cooperation.

PEOPLE

Mexico's heterogeneity is grounded in history. The Spanish conquest gave rise to the nation's largest ethnic group, **mestizos**—persons of mixed indigenous and European blood—who now comprise 60% of the population. Today, **criollos**—light-skinned Mexicans of pure European descent—make up around 9% of the population and concentrate in urban areas and the north. **Indígenas**—sometimes referred to by the politically incorrect appellation **Indios**—comprise 30% of the population and to this day make up the majority in rural areas, particularly in the southern half of the country.

Mexico's official language is *castellano* (Spanish), spoken smoothly and without the lisp that characterizes speakers from Spain. Many people, mostly *indígenas*, still speak some form of a native language, and many villages still bear names in these tongues. In the Valley of Mexico, one can often hear the Aztec language, **Náhuatl;** in the Yucatán Peninsula and Chiapas, **Maya** is frequently spoken in villages and markets; **Zapotec** is still spoken in the Oaxaca Valley. The 50 traditional languages, spoken by over 100,000 people in the country, are just one link to Mexico's storied cultural past.

RELIGION

Although religion is never explicitly mentioned in the constitution, Mexico's Catholic consciousness permeates the country and unites the population. Walk around village streets, and you'll pass wooden crosses and roadside shrines dedicated to the Virgin Mary. Ride in a Mexico City taxi cab, and you might see a rosary hanging from the rearview mirror. Shop in a supermarket, and you'll see polychrome candles depicting Christ and the saints. Step inside a parish church and discover dozens of devout Mexicans, crossing themselves and whispering. With around 90% of the population Catholic, Mexico is a country devoted to its faith. This faith, however, has fused with native traditions and created a distinct flavor of Catholicism. The best example of this syncretism is the **Virgin of Guadalupe** (see p. 121), the dark-skinned apparition of the Virgin Mary that prompted the conversion of thousands of Indians in the 16th century. Moreover, recent years have seen a developing interest in native faiths, perhaps prompted by new archaeological research and a new embrace of Mexican indigenous identity. Aztec symbols have become synonymous with nationalism and Mexican pride. The famous Aztec **Sun Stone,** for example, adorns everything from belt buckles to soccer jerseys. Recent years have also seen the increasing presence of Protestantism. Although only about 6% of the population is Protestant, the numbers are on the rise, perhaps thanks to missionary activity. Other faiths, while not as well represented in Mexico as in the rest of the world, are increasing in numbers, particularly Judaism and Pentecostalism.

CULTURE

CUSTOMS & ETIQUETTE

RESPECT. Mexicans almost always use proper terms of address when speaking to one another. As in other countries, professional and academic titles convey respectability. Those who have earned a college degree may be addressed as *licenciado* or *licenciada*, and those with doctorates as *doctor* or *doctora*. When introducing yourself to anyone new, a simple *señor, señora,* or *señorita* (for young or unmarried women) is always appropriate.

I THOUGHT WE SAID 5 O'CLOCK. Outside of the business world, Mexico is notorious for its lack of commitment to any sort of fixed schedule. The legendary Mexican ambivalence toward promptness seems even more exaggerated when compared to the frenetic pace of life in many Western countries. This phenomenon stems not from a national inconsiderateness but from a more relaxed and easygoing attitude toward time and its pressures. So, if you find yourself tapping your foot and staring at the clock expectantly while awaiting the arrival of a Mexican friend, it may be more comfortable to pull up a chair.

GRINGO LOVE. Originally reserved for those of European descent, the term *gringo* has recently welcomed all English-speaking visitors to share in its splendor. Americans may sometimes find themselves labelled more specifically as *yanquis,* and minority travelers will have to put up with racial epithets, but the *gringo* community embraces all. The traditional negative connotation that accompanied the term in its early days has all but disappeared, and expatriate residents of Mexico have even taken to referring to themselves as *gringos.*

FOOD & DRINK

Leave your preconceived notions of what constitutes "real Mexican food" at home and prepare your taste buds for a culinary adventure. With some dedication (and at times, a little courage) the pleasures of Mexican cuisine can be yours.

THE STAPLES

Although regional and local cuisine varies widely, **tortillas** are popular throughout the country. This millennia-old staple is a flat, round, thin pancake made from either *harina* (wheat flour) or *maíz* (corn flour). In the north, flour tortillas are the norm while corn rules the south. *Arroz* (rice) and *frijoles* (beans) round out the triumvirate of Mexican staples. **Rice** is usually yellow Spanish or white Mexican rice and prepared with oil, tomato sauce, onions, and garlic. **Beans** can range from a thick paste to soupy "baked" beans. Expect to see this trio of staples accompany nearly every breakfast, lunch, and dinner.

DESAYUNO (BREAKFAST)

Breakfast can range from a simple snack to a grand feast, rivaling the midday meal. Eggs are the mainstay of most Mexican breakfasts and are prepared in any and all conceivable ways and often served with *café con leche* (coffee with milk) and *pan dulce* (sweetened bread). *Huevos revueltos* (scrambled eggs) are usually prepared with *jamón* (ham), *tocino* (bacon), *machaca* (dried, shredded beef), or *nopales* (cactus). *Huevos rancheros* (fried eggs served on corn tortillas and covered with a chunky tomato salsa), *huevos albañil* (scrambled eggs cooked in a spicy sauce), *huevos motuleños* (eggs served on a fried corn tortilla, topped with green sauce and sour cream), *huevos ahogados* (eggs cooked in simmering red sauce), and *huevos borrachos* (fried eggs cooked in beer and served with beans) are other common ways in which eggs are prepared. In more expensive restaurants omelettes are offered with any of the common meats plus *camarones* (shrimp) or *langosta* (lobster). To round out your *desayuno*, leave room for the tortillas and *frijoles*.

COMIDA (MIDDAY MEAL)

Mexicans eat their biggest meal of the day—*la comida*—between 2 and 4pm. Both children and parents come home for an hour or two, eat, and relax afterwards, perhaps indulging in a little *siesta*. Restaurants often offer *comida corrida* (sometimes called *la comida* or *el menú*), which is a fixed price meal including soup, salad, tea or *agua fresca*, a *plato fuerte* (main dish), and sometimes a dessert.

SOPA

One of the most popular *caldos* (warm soups) is *sopa de tortilla* (or *sopa Azteca*), a chicken-broth soup with strips of fried tortilla, chunks of avocado, and *chipotle* peppers. Other favorites are *caldo tlalpeno*, a smoky blend of chicken broth and vegetables, and *sopa de mariscos*, which features fish and shellfish. Mexico's strong national pride is evident in **pozole,** a chunky soup with red, white, or green broth. Served with *tostadas* (fried tortillas) and lime wedges, *pozole* is made with large hominy kernels, radishes, lettuce, and meat—usually pork.

PLATO FUERTE

The main dish of any *comida* will usually feature some sort of meat platter (usually beef in the interior or fish along the coasts) with sides of *frijoles*, tortillas, and *arroz*. *Platillos* vary throughout the republic, and many regions produce specialties that have earned renown worldwide.

CENA (SUPPER)

Mexicans tend to snack lightly around 9 or 10pm. Dominating nearly every Mexican menu, *antojitos* (little cravings) are equivalent to a large snack or a small meal. Tacos consist of grilled pieces of meat folded in a warm tortilla and topped with a row of condiments. Burritos, which are especially popular in northern Mexico, are thin, rolled tortillas filled with meat, beans, and cooked vegetables. *Enchiladas* are rolled corn tortillas filled with meat or cheese and baked in sauce. Quesadillas are flat tortillas with cheese melted between them; *quesadillas sincronizadas* (sometimes called *gringas*) are filled with ham or gyro-style pork. *Tostadas* resemble flat, open tacos topped with raw vegetables. *Chimichangas* are essentially burritos but are deep-fried and have a rich crunchy shell. *Flautas* are similar to *chimichangas* but are rolled thin (like a cigar) before being deep-fried.

DULCES (SWEETS)

Mexicans have an incurable sweet tooth. Beyond the ubiquitous chocolates and pastries on store shelves, traditional desserts include *flan*, a vanilla custard served over burnt sugar, *nieve* (ice cream), and *arroz con leche* (rice pudding). Puebla, the country's candy capital, is full of sweet shops selling *dulces de leche* (milk sweets) and *camotes* (candied sweet potatoes). Morelia and Michoacán specialize in *ates*, sticky sweet blocks of ground and candied fruit concentrate. San Cristóbal de las Casas and parts of Chiapas are renowned for their *cajetas* (fruit pastes) as well as coconut candies and cookies, while the Yucatán boasts yummy pumpkin marzipan.

BEBIDAS (DRINKS)

BEER AND LIQUOR

Along with tortillas, beans, and rice, *cerveza* (beer) might as well be the fourth national staple. It is impossible to drive through any Mexican town without coming across numerous Tecate and Corona billboards, painted buildings, and roadside beer stands proudly selling their products. Popular beers in Mexico (listed roughly in order of quality) are **Bohemia** (a world-class lager), **Negra Modelo** (a fine dark beer), **Dos Equis** (a light, smooth lager), **Pacífico, Modelo, Carta Blanca, Superior, Corona Extra,** and **Sol** (watery and light). Mexicans share their love for bargain beer with the world, demonstrated by the Mexican-made Corona Extra's status as a leading export and international chart topper in Canada, Australia, New Zealand, France, Italy, Spain, and many European markets.

Tequila is the king of Mexican liquor. A more refined version of *mezcal*, tequila is distilled from the maguey cactus, a large, sprawling plant often seen along Mexican highways. **Herradura, Tres Generaciones, Hornitos,** and **Cuervo 1800** are among the more famous, expensive, and quality brands of tequila. **Mezcal,** coarser than tequila, is sometimes served with the worm native to the plant—upon downing the shot, you are expected to ingest the worm. If you get a chance to sample **pulque,** the fermented juice of the maguey, don't hesitate—it was the sacred drink of the Aztec nobility. **Ron** (rum), while originally manufactured in the Caribbean, enjoys incredible popularity in Mexico and is manufactured in parts of the Valley of Mexico. Coffee-flavored **Kahlúa** is Mexico's most exported liqueur, but well-made **piña coladas** (pineapple juice, cream of coconut, and light rum), or **cocos locos** (coconut milk and tequila served in a coconut) are just as tasty.

THE ARTS

VISUAL ARTS

Mexican art is generally classified into three periods: **Indigenous** (6000 BC to AD 1525), **Colonial** (1525-1810), and **Modern** (1810-present). Art created before the Spanish invasion is studied by archaeologists; for the most part, no written commentary on artistic expression exists from the time before the Conquest. With the arrival of the Spanish, Mexican art changed dramatically and has continued to do so throughout the Modern period.

LIFE AND TIMES

THE PRE-HISPANIC ERA

Much of the art and architecture from this period has provided the basis for understanding early Mexican history (see **Pre-Hispanic Societies,** p. 59). Some aspects of Pre-Hispanic styles were prevalent across Mexico. The use of **stone** is perhaps one of the most noticeable. The Olmecs shaped basalt into the colossal heads for which they are famous. The Maya used limestone and sandstone all over their cities as building blocks for palaces and temples, stelae (upright stone monuments often inscribed with glyphs and reliefs), and altars. Cities such as Teotihuacán, Tula, and Tenochtitlán exhibit the continued use of monumental stone architecture in their buildings, carved reliefs, and statuary.

On a smaller scale, some of the most impressive pieces of Pre-Hispanic art would fit in the palm of your hand. **Carved jade** and **ceramic figurines** are plentiful from the very beginnings of Mexican culture through the Colonial period. Maya gods and nobility are often depicted adorned with massive headdresses replete with lengthy feathers, necklaces of egg-sized beads, and gold and copper bracelets to match the enormous bangles hanging from their earlobes. Most of the information gained from art such as monuments or carvings pertains only to elite society; much less material has been recovered from the other classes of these cultures.

Besides buildings and monuments, another form of creative expression employed by Pre-Hispanic peoples was narrative depiction. **Murals** such as those covering the walls at the Maya site of Bonampak reveal scenes of warfare, sacrifice, and celebration. **Frescoes** on interior walls of buildings at Teotihuacán depict, among other subjects, paradise scenes, floral arrangements, religious rituals, and athletic events. Scenes painted onto the **pottery** of these cultures depict mythological stories. Other reliefs and objects reveal calendrical events and dates—the famous **Aztec Stone of the Sun** is a prime example. This prophetic calender measures nearly 4m in diameter. Within its concentric rings are contained the four symbols of previous suns—rain, jaguar, wind, and fire—the plagues responsible for the destruction of earlier populations. The Aztecs believed that they were living in the period of the fifth sun, and they expected to be obliterated by an earthquake—the symbol for which also ominously appears on the stone.

THE ARCHITECTURE OF NEW SPAIN

Not surprisingly, the first examples of **colonial art** were created specifically to facilitate religious indoctrination of the *indígenas.* Churches were often constructed on top of pre-existing temples and pyramids. Volcanic stone, plentiful in most areas, was the main building material. Colonial architecture, recalling **Romanesque** and **Gothic** traditions, incorporates huge buttresses, arches, and crenelations (indented or embattled moldings). An early architectural development was the open chapel *(capilla abierta),* a group of arches enclosing an atrium.

Monasteries and churches under the direction of **Franciscan, Dominican,** and **Augustinian** missionaries were built according to limitations of climate and geography. The Franciscan style tended to be functional and economic, while the Dominican style was more ascetic and harsh. Augustinian style was the most free-spirited and grandiose, and architects indulged in gratuitous, excessive decoration whenever possible. Remarkable Augustinian buildings include the **Monastery of St. Augustín of Acolman** near Mexico City and the **Monastery of Actopán** in Hidalgo.

A BLOSSOMING OF THE BAROQUE

The steady growth and spread of the Catholic Church throughout the 17th and 18th centuries necessitated the construction of cathedrals, parochial chapels, and convents. Moreover, this period brought the Baroque style to New Spain. Luxurious **Baroque** facades, teeming with dynamic images of angels and saints, aimed to produce a feeling of awe and respect in the hearts of the recently converted *indígenas*. The narratives set in stone could be understood even by *los analfabetos* (illiterate people) and easily committed to memory. A look at the cathedrals of Zacatecas and Chihuahua reveals the degree of artistry that Baroque ideals encouraged. Baroque painting found its quintessential expression in the works of **Alonso López de Herrera** and **Baltazar de Echave Orio** (the elder).

Sumptuousness, frivolity, and ornamentation became more prevalent in the works of the late 18th-century artists and builders who couldn't get too much of a good thing. During this time, the **Churrigueresque** style was born and **Mexican High Baroque** was carried to the extreme. A hallmark of this style is the intricately decorated *estípites* (pilasters), often installed merely for looks, not support.

20TH CENTURY ART

As the Revolution reduced their land to shambles, Mexican artists began to reject European models in their work, instead developing a national style that reflected native Latin American culture. After the Revolution, Mexican artists found themselves under the rule of a new government, intent on building the concept of Mexico as a nation, and eager to use nationalist art to do so. **José Vasconcelos,** the Minister of Public Education, developed a program that commissioned *muralistas* to create their art on the walls of hospitals, colleges, schools, and ministries, and sent artists into the countryside to teach and participate in rural life.

The Mexican **mural,** unequivocally nationalistic in its current form, dates back to the early days of the Conquest when Catholic evangelists, who could not communicate with the *indígenas,* used allegorical murals to teach them the rudiments of Christian iconography. **Diego Rivera,** the most renowned of the *muralistas,* based his artwork on political themes—land reform, Marxism, and the marginalization of *indígena* life. Rivera used stylized realism to portray the dress, action, and expression of the Mexican people, and natural realism (complete with ugly faces, knotted brows, and angry stances) to represent Spaniards and other oppressors of the *indígenas.* His innovative blend of Mexican history and culture reached a wide audience and embroiled him in international controversy.

Though Rivera is credited as the first to forge the path for *muralistas,* two other artists were vital in defining the art form and achieved national recognition: **David Álfaro Siqueiros,** who brought new materials and dramatic revolutionary themes to his murals; and **José Clemente Orozco,** whose dark, angular shapes captured the brooding nature of his works' racial themes. Murals were also adopted by other artists, including Cubism-influenced **Rufino Tamayo.**

Not all 20th-century Mexican artists have exchanged the traditional canvas for walls. **Juan Soriano,** by combining vanguard and traditional Mexican art, forged a name for himself as a painter and sculptor. Due in part to her incredible talent and **Hayden Herrera's** landmark biography, **Frida Kahlo** (1907-54) surpasses many Mexican artists in worldwide recognition. Kahlo's paintings and self-portraits are icons of pain, forcing the viewer to confront the artist's self-obsession in its most violent and extreme manifestations. **Manuel Álvarez Bravo,** Mexico's master photographer, brought the art of the lens to the fore. Still photographer on Sergei Eisenstein's unfinished *¡Qué Viva México!,* Álvarez Bravo exhibited at New York's Julien Levy Gallery with Henri Cartier-Bresson and Walker Evans and continues to advance a new Mexican style of photography.

LITERATURE

PRE-HISPANIC WRITING

As far as linguists and archaeologists have been able to tell, two languages were dominant in Mexico before the arrival of the Spanish: **Náhuatl** and **Maya.** The earliest examples of writing are thought to be the glyphs inscribed at **San José Mogote** and **Monte Albán,** Oaxaca—two sites containing reliefs perhaps dating back to 600 BC. The destructiveness of the Conquest, particularly in its initial years, and the imposition of the Spanish language resulted in the loss of valuable information relating to *indígena* language. Considered a dangerous affront to Christian teachings, Maya and Aztec **codices** (unbound "books" or manuscripts) were fed to the flames. But due to the foresight of some indigenous leaders and a handful of missionaries, a number of Maya and Aztec codices did survive. Other historical works such as the **Books of Chilam Balam** and the **Annals of the Cakchiquel** cover a range of topics. They are not exclusively historical works, but are instead narrative and poetic, laden with symbolism and metaphor. **Rabinal Achi,** the story of a sacrificed warrior, is considered to be the only surviving example of Pre-Hispanic drama.

COLONIAL LITERATURE

Surrounded by a new world, the Spanish were eager to send news home about the land they had conquered and the Mexican way of life. These letters home, among them Cortés's *Cartas de Relación* (Letters of Relation), were mainly crown- and church-flattering documents detailing the exhaustive ongoing efforts to educate and Christianize *indígenas*. Other chronicles, such as the *Nuevo Mundo y Conquista* (New World and Conquest), by **Francisco de Terrazas,** and *Grandeza Mexicana* (Mexican Grandeur), by **Bernardo de Balbuena,** were written in rhyme in order to take the edge off the monotonous stream of facts.

Although historical documents dominated output throughout much of the 16th and 17th centuries, poets also found their place in Mexican literary culture. **Sor Juana Inés de la Cruz** (1648-1695), a *criolla* of illegitimate birth who joined a convent in order to pursue an education, became a master lyricist known for her wit, as well as an intellectual favorite of Mexico City. Her most famous works are *Respuesta a Sor Filotea* (Response to Sor Filotea) and *Hombres Necios* (Injudicious Men), poems renowned for their passion and portrayal of a feminist sensibility ahead of its time.

STRUGGLING FOR A LITERARY IDENTITY

By the end of the 18th century, the struggle for independence became the singular social fact from which many Mexican texts emerged. In 1816, **José Fernández de Lizardi,** a prominent Mexican journalist, wrote the first Latin American novel: *El Periquillo Sarniento* (The Itching Parrot), a satirical tale indicative of Mexican society's displeasure with the status quo and the social restlessness of the times. Many novels used historical themes to mask sweeping indictments of the military and clergy. Novelists sought to define Mexico's national identity, glorifying strength, secularism, progress, and education. Whereas European Romanticism was an aesthetic challenge to Neoclassicism, Mexican Romanticism was an artistic response to the country's political and social realities. Shortly after the heyday of the Romantic novel came popular novels of manners, most notably *El Fistol del Diablo* by **Manuel Payno** and *Juanita Sousa* and *Antón Pérez* by **Manuel Sánchez Mármol.**

Literature during the **Porfiriato** (1876-1911) abandoned Romanticism for realism, and most writers expressed little sympathy for the poor. A Modernist trend and aesthetic movement, *modernismo*, also developed at the end of the 19th century, emphasizing language and imagery and replacing didactic social themes with psychological topics. *Modernismo* reshaped Spanish literature under the direction of figures like **Manuel Gutierrez Nájera.** Both poet and journalist, Nájera founded *Revista Azul*, a literary periodical, and established himself as a precursor of Modernism in his elegant works of poetry and prose. Also at the center of the Modernist movement was **Amado Nervo,** the famed "monk of poetry." Nervo abandoned his

LIFE AND TIMES

studies for the priesthood in order to pursue his writing and ultimately produced several collections of his
introspective and often mystical poetry, such as
Serinidad and *Elevación.*

20TH-CENTURY GLOBAL PERSPECTIVES

Mexican literature in the Post-Revolutionary era is
marked by a frustrated desire to forge a national
tradition on the vestiges of pre-colonial culture.
Works produced immediately after the Revolution
centered predominantly around social themes, particularly the plight of Mexico's *indígenas.* **Mariano
Azuela,** who joined **Pancho Villa**'s forces in 1915,
relays a first-hand account of the military exploitation of the *indígenas* in *Los de Abajo* (The Underdogs). Similar works such as *El Indio* by **Gregorio
López y Fuentes** reinstated the novel as a vehicle of
social reform. **Octavio Paz,** the first Mexican writer
to win a Nobel Prize, draws on Marxism, Romanticism, and post-Modernism to explore the making
and unmaking of a national archetype in such
works as *El Laberinto de la Soledad* (The Labyrinth of Solitude). Paz concerns himself with myths
and legends in an effort to come to terms with Spanish cultural dominance. The 1960s saw the advent of
Magical Realism in Spanish-American literature, a
literary movement that blends the ordinary and
common with fantasy and wonder, resulting in texts
that portray a dreamlike and distorted reality. At
the forefront of this movement in Mexico stood **Carlos Fuentes,** an acclaimed contemporary novelist
whose many works include *La Región Más Transparente* and *La Muerte de Artemio Cruz* (The
Death of Artemio Cruz).

Of late, the work of female writers, such as Hollywood darling **Laura Esquivel** *(Like Water for Chocolate)*, has been well received both nationally and
internationally. **Elena Poniatowska,** the author of
Tinísima—a novel recounting the life of photographer **Tina Modotti**, has made a name for herself in the
world of Latin American writers. In the past three
decades, a new literary movement has emerged from
Mexico—the **Chicano movement.** Chicano literature
describes the experiences of Latinos who come to
the US and must overcome numerous barriers to
adapt to the new culture. Many Chicano authors are
rapidly gaining respect in the international community. **Sandra Cisneros**'s *House on Mango Street*—a
novel narrated by an 11-year-old girl who talks about
her life on both sides of the Mexican border—has
made Cisneros one of the most recognized Chicana
authors today. Other Chicano writers such as **Américo
Paredes** have used their literary status to put traditional Mexican folklore into written form. In *With*

His Pistol in His Hands, Paredes immortalized the tale of **Gregorio Cortez,** a Mexican who was persecuted by the US judicial system for shooting a sheriff in self-defense. The poetry of **Gary Soto** has garnered critical acclaim; though American by birth, Soto writes about the Mexican-American experience, focusing on his Fresno boyhood.

MUSIC

Every aspect of Mexican life is filled with music. A constant melody permeates restaurants, public events, and street corners where people gather around local *guitarristas*. To understand Mexican music is to understand the soul of the nation.

FOLK MUSIC

On bus rides, in local bars, and on the street, you will hear three major types of traditional Mexican music:

CORRIDOS. *Corridos*, usually sung by guitar-plucking troubadours, remain truest to their folk origins. Grown out of oral storytelling, *corridos* recount the epic deeds of famous, infamous, and occasionally fictional figures from Mexico's past. A *corridista* may additionally function as a walking newspaper, singing songs about the latest natural disaster, political scandal, or any other decisive event.

RANCHERAS. Born in a fit of nationalistic fervor following the 1911 Revolution, **rancheras** were originally conceived as "songs of the people," dealing with matters of work, love, and land. Once performed with marimba and flute, *rancheras* are now backed by the guitar and trumpets of *mariachi* bands. The songs are characterized by a passionate, sincere singing style, with final notes dragged out. Like American country western music, today's *rancheras* are sentimental songs about down-and-out towns, faithful dogs, and love gone wrong. **Norteños** are a type of *ranchera* based in the northwest and strongly influenced by polka. Popular *norteño* bands such as **Los Tigres del Norte** kick it accordion style, and have attracted a number of fans on both sides of the border.

MARIACHI. The black-and-red-clad men with bells and capes—the same ones that appear in tequila ads around the world—are **mariachis.** The most famous of Mexican musical styles, *mariachi* is lively and light-hearted, with strong guitar and energetic horn sections. Wandering *mariachis* strike up in front of restaurants and play at traditional *fiestas*. The world-famous tradition of women being serenaded by a group of *mariachis* in Mexican garb is an almost obligatory supplement to a romantic

6. El Gran Cenote. (p. 613) As you watch butterflies flit over the placid surface of this mini-paradise you may forget why you ever were anywhere else. But take the plunge anyway—the snorkeling is even better.

5. Cenote Zací. (p. 580) In the heart of Valladolid, Zací is not just a *cenote;* tropical gardens and stunning rock formations, as well as a nearby zoo, make it *the* weekend spot.

4. Cenote Dzitnup. (p. 580) A swimming hole in a cavern, this chill underground pool played host to ancient Maya. Morning finds a stream of light cascading from the circular hole above.

3. Sacred Cenote. (p. 575) Chichén Itzá's most important religious symbol, this *cenote* harbored the rain god Chac, who swallowed the over 30,000 sacrificial remains that have been recovered in its depths.

2. Xel-Ha. (p. 615) 184 hectares of jungles, caves, and coves, Xel-Ha is an interactive aquarium between Tulum and Cobá that is guaranteed to amaze. Swim with the dolphins or gape in awe at sea turtle nests, but know that you're one of roughly 1600 people who enter this park daily.

1. Cenote Dos Ojos. (616) The longest and most extensive set of underwater caverns in the world words may not do Dos Ojos justice. Filled with astounding rock formations from its time as a dry cave system, Dos Ojos plays home to swordfish and other peaceful marine life as well as stupefying plant life unlike anything you've ever seen. At 33,855m long, this *cenote* could fill an entire Mexican vacation—just remember to occasionally come up for air.

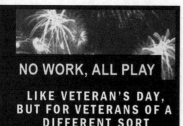

NO WORK, ALL PLAY

LIKE VETERAN'S DAY, BUT FOR VETERANS OF A DIFFERENT SORT

So. They've nearly turned you into roadkill more times than you care to remember, and you're sure you've paid their "special" tourist rates more often than not. On August 12, however, forget your bitter memories, remember the good times, and join in celebrating **El Día del Taxista,** the country-wide holiday honoring taxi drivers all over Mexico.

The day typically begins with a special 8am mass; although many cab drivers keep little *santos* (figurines of the saints) in a place of honor on the dashboard, they appreciate the priests' blessing of the cabs at the end of mass, which guarantees their safe travels for the next year (well, safe by some standards). Drivers then decorate their radiator grills, stringing them with flowers before the cabs pass proudly through the city streets—hopefully a little more slowly than usual, but you can certainly expect the same deft musical touch from their horns. Later in the day, taxi drivers celebrate amongst themselves, and you'll have an even harder time than usual finding a driver on the unusually barren streets. If you do manage to flag down a taxi, be prepared to thank the driver profusely and offer a hefty *propina* (tip)—it is, after all, the day of the cabbie.

evening. Traditional *mariachi* music may deal with one or several of the following topics: being very drunk, loving a woman, being abandoned by a woman, wanting to get drunk, needing a woman, pondering the fidelity of one's horse, loving one's gun, and marveling at one's own stupefying virility. In their more somber (and sober) moments, *mariachis* have also been known to sing of death, politics, and revolutionary history.

OTHER MUSIC

Mexican music along the east-central coast and continuing into the Yucatán carries a strong dose of Afro-Caribbean **rhumba.** In Veracruz and Quintana Roo, drum-laden bands often strike up irresistible beats in the sea breeze and evening twilight of central plazas. The style has inspired countless **marimba** bands, whose popularized music can be found blasting in markets throughout the republic. Imported from Columbia, **cumbia** has joined **salsa** as the dance music of choice across central and southern Mexico, inspiring young and old alike to cut loose with **merengue** dance steps.

Mexico was not immune to the Latin explosion of the late twentieth century, and several Mexican and Mexican-American singers rocketed to stardom. Tejana **Selena** Quintanilla Perez won several Grammys before being tragically killed after a dispute with an employee. **Paulina Rubio** and **Thalía** have each pushed from actress to diva, and both are gaining worshippers north of the border as well.

Mexico also knows how to rock. The latest alternative groups like **El Nudo** and **Caifanes** provide stiff competition to Spanish and American bands. Travelers from up north will still feel at home, though, as American pop and hip-hop is ubiquitous in bars and *discotecas.* Striving to Mexicanize imports (and exports), Mexican artists often take American pieces and make them their own by altering lyrics or adding Latin beats.

FILM & TELEVISION

Film came to Mexico before *Titanic,* before even *First Knight*—the industry is a century old and a vital part of Mexican culture. With the Revolution came a slew of documentaries, notably those of **the Alva brothers,** Salvador, Guillermo, Eduardo, and Carlos. In 1931, Russian filmmaker (and former bolshevik) **Sergei Eisenstein** began lensing *¡Qué Viva México!,* an unfinished scrutiny of the Mexican landscape that was innovative in its social critique. The 1940s ushered in the golden age of Mexican cinema, launching with **Emilio "El Indio"**

Fernández's *Maria Candelaría* (1943)—a Cannes honoree—and **Luis Buñuel**'s *Los Olvidados* (1950), a grisly portrait of the Mexico City *barrio*. Buñuel filmed a number of satires in Mexico over the next ten years, and in 1960 cinema hit a new high with **Roberto Gavalín**'s *Macario*, a film about a starving woodcutter who strikes a deal with Death and gets the gift of healing. *Macario* was the first Mexican film to receive an Oscar nomination. American film explored Mexico heavily during these middle years as well, with dozens of famous features—especially Westerns, and especially the Westerns of John Wayne—filming in Mexico, and in 1996 US-based Fox Studios built the first American studio in Mexico (see p. 159).

In addition to a burgeoning direct-to-video market, the 1990s brought both advances in Mexican-made film and increased cross-over with Hollywood. For example, **María Novaro** received critical acclaim for 1991's *Danzón*, about a Mexico City telephone operator who journeys to Veracruz to find ballroom dance and also love, while Texan **Robert Rodriguez** gathered a shoestring budget to film 1992's *El Mariachi*. **Laura Esquivel**'s seminal novel, *Como Agua para Chocolate*, became a 1992 feature that was the highest-grossing foreign film in the US, and at the turn of the century, Mexican film cemented its place in American culture with two art-house heavies: **Alejandro González Iñarritu**'s *Amores perros* (2000) and **Alfonso Cuarón**'s *Y tu mamá también* (2001).

Mexican television can, for the most part, be broken down into four different categories: *telenovelas* (soap operas), comedic variety shows, *noticias* (news shows), and imported American TV. Of these, *telenovelas* are second to none and occupy huge chunks of mid-afternoon airtime. Though sitcoms are not terribly popular, Mexico loves its variety shows, featuring sketch comedy intermixed with musical numbers and audience participation contests; long-running variety show *Chespirito* is so popular its characters have become cultural icons—and proved the inspiration of Bumblebee Man on *The Simpsons*. News and current events shows are popular in the late evenings, and *fútbol* matches dominate airwaves at all hours, especially during the World Cup. The rest of Mexican television is generally American shows poorly dubbed in Spanish.

SPORTS

Although more commonly associated with Spain, **bullfighting**—the epic combat between man and large male cow—is Mexico's national sport. During the summer months, matadors and their entourages perform in packed bullrings across the country, including Mexico City's **Plaza México,** the largest bullring in the world.

While bullfighting is popular, Mexico's heart belongs to **fútbol** (soccer). Any unused patch of dirt, grass, or concrete is likely to be swarming with young boys, and the occasional brave girl, playing a rowdy pick-up game. (For your safety, it's best not to take sides, as games can get quite vicious.) In addition to informal street games, Mexico has a popular professional football league with at least one team in each major city. Guadalajara, for example, has arch-enemy teams—Las Chivas and Atlas—complete with rival fan bases. At the international level, the entire country cheers and jeers the **Mexican National Team,** the gang of green-clad flashy young men who always seem to be the underdogs, and life comes to a standstill during important *fútbol* matches. Mexico played host to the World Cup in 1970 and 1986, and hosts other important matches in the **Olympic Stadium** and the enormous **Estadio Azteca,** both in Mexico City.

Other sports coexist to a lesser degree with these two monoliths. Mexico has had its fair share of world **boxing** champions in the lighter weight divisions, and there have been some notable Mexican **marathon runners** in past years. **Baseball** is starting to attract players and spectators at all levels. Finally, no discussion can be complete without mention of Mexico's illustrious history in the Olympic event of **race walking,** one of the only sports in which Mexico has medaled.

HOLIDAYS & FESTIVALS

Mexico loves to celebrate its rich history, and nearly every month boasts a national holiday. In addition to these official *fiestas,* cities and towns across the country host smaller-scale but still lively events to honor patron saints or local traditions. Further information about these frequent celebrations can be found in individual city listings. Additionally, in this country that is, well, religious about its Catholicism, Sundays are always special. "Daily" schedules frequently assume "of course not Sundays."

Most Mexican businesses close to observe national holidays, and hotels and sights flood with vacationing families. Advance reservations are absolutely necessary when planning travel during *Semana Santa* and the Christmas holidays. Dates listed below are for 2004, and official holidays are in **bold.**

DATE	NAME	DESCRIPTION
1 January	**Año Nuevo**	**New Year's Day**
6 January	Día de los Reyes	Mexicans have traditionally honored the historic journey of the Three Wise Men by giving and receiving gifts on this day (rather than on Christmas).
17 January	Día de San Antonio de Abad	Feast of the Blessing of the Animals
2 February	Día de la Candelaria	Candlemas commemorates Mary's purification 40 days after the birth of Jesus.
5 February	**Día de la Constitución**	**Constitution Day**
24 February	**Día de la Bandera**	**Flag Day**
18-24 February	Carnaval	A spectacular week-long festival of indulgences before the 40-day abstinence of Lent. The liveliest celebrations take place in coastal cities such as Mazatlán.
21 March	**Día del Nacimiento de Benito Juárez**	**Birthday of Benito Juárez, 1806**
5-11 April	Semana Santa	Mexico's most popular holiday is marked by colorful processions re-enacting the resurrection of Christ and highways clogged with vacationing families.
1 May	**Día del Trabajo**	**Labor Day**
5 May	**Cinco de Mayo**	**Anniversary of the Battle of Puebla, 1862**
10 May	Día de las Madres	Mother's Day
15-16 August	Feast of the Assumption	Churches are carpeted with flowers to celebrate the feast day of the Blessed Virgin Mary.
1 September	Informe Presidencial	Presidential State of the Union Address
16 September	**Día de la Independencia**	**Anniversary of the Cry of Dolores, 1810**
12 October	**Día de la Raza**	**Columbus Day**
1-2 November	Día de Todos Santos and Día de los Muertos	Families honor the souls of their ancestors, who are thought to return to earth on this day, by visiting cemeteries and creating shrines laden with offerings.
20 November	**Día de la Revolución**	**Anniversary of the Revolution, 1910**
12 December	Día de Nuestra Señora de Guadalupe	Feast day of Mexico's patron saint.
16-24 December	Posadas	Candlelit processions that celebrate the voyage of Mary and Joseph to Bethlehem.
24-25 December	**Nochebuena and Navidad**	**Christmas Eve and Christmas Day**

LIFE AND TIMES

ADDITIONAL RESOURCES

GENERAL

The Labyrinth of Solitude, by Octavio Paz (1950). The classic social critique by Mexico's most acclaimed author.

Mexican Slang: A Guide, by Linton Robinson (1982). Accurate and hilarious.

Mexico: A Higher Vision, by Michael Calderwood (1996). Carlos Fuentes provides an introduction to Mexico in this stunning collection of large format aerial photographs.

Dancing Alone in Mexico, by Ron Butler (2000). The author's solo wanderings throughout the country come alive in a series of intelligent and entertaining vignettes.

On Mexican Time, by Tony Cohan (2001). A chronicle of 15 years in the life of the author, who moved from busy Los Angeles to peaceful San Miguel de Allende.

HISTORY

Mexico: From the Olmecs to the Aztecs, by Michael D. Coe (1994). This engaging and current text chronicles the history and society of major Pre-Hispanic civilizations.

The Course of Mexican History, by Michael C. Meyer et al. (1998). Absolutely the most comprehensive and easy-to-read survey of Mexican history from the ancient civilizations to the politics of the PRI.

POLITICS

¡Basta! Land and the Zapatista Rebellion, by George Allen Collier (1999). Comprehensively studies the reasons and catalysts for the 1994 Zapatista uprising in Chiapas.

Bordering on Chaos: Mexico's Roller Coaster Journey to Prosperity, by Andres Oppenheimer (1998). Examines the collapse of the peso and subsequent economic ups and downs in the aftermath of the political controversy surrounding former president Carlos Salinas de Gortari.

Distant Neighbors: A Portrait of the Mexicans, by Alan Riding (1989). An American perspective on the politics and society of modern Mexico.

FICTION

Pedro Páramo, by Juan Rulfo (1955). A haunting tale of life and death set in rural Mexico; Rulfo's masterpiece (and only novel).

Terra Nostra, by Carlos Fuentes (1975). A work of historical fiction dealing with Spain and Latin America, written by one of Mexico's most prominent novelists.

Like Water for Chocolate, by Laura Esquivel (1990). A Mexican love story that earned international acclaim. The film based on the novel was nominated for a Golden Globe.

FILM

Y Tu Mama También, directed by Oscar Cuarón (2002). A story of adolescence and the sexual awakening of two Mexican teenagers as they travel through their country. The widely-acclaimed film is notable for its honest portrayal of Mexican life, albeit with some strong political undercurrents.

El Mariachi, directed by Robert Rodriguez (1992). The acclaimed director's Sundance Award-winning first film, shot on a US$7000 budget, is a fast-paced action flick centered around a case of mistaken identity.

Amores Perros, directed by Alejandro Iñárritu (2000). A widely awarded film centered around the three parties involved in a Mexico City car accident.

MEXICO CITY

Welcome to the biggest city in the world. With between 17 and 30 million people, depending on the count—one quarter of Mexico's entire population—it will seem "biggest" in every possible way. If you're lucky enough to fly into the city at night, the sea of lights below will greet you as it seems to stretch to the ends of the earth. Once you're standing in the middle of the city, you'll think you were right about how far those lights reached. In the city, Mexicans refer to the megalopolis as **el D.F.** (deh-EFF-ay, short for **Distrito Federal**), but to the rest of the country, it is simply **México,** a testament to its immense size and importance.

Over the years Mexico City has faced myriad disasters of the natural world: flooding, sinking, earthquakes, and the ominous shadow of an explosive volcano. It has also faced man-made problems such as pollution, crime, over-crowding, revolution, and war. All of these things, however, have combined to produce the culturally and historically rich city it is today. Where else can you find ancient pyramids alongside eight-lane highways? Catholics going back to the pyramids to celebrate their indigenous pagan roots? Palm trees and cacti growing alongside deciduous trees? The paradoxes are endless, but somehow in this gigantic metropolis of 350 *colonias* (neighborhoods), filled with the awe of tourists and the love of patriotic *chilangos* (D.F. natives), it all seems to make sense.

HIGHLIGHTS OF MEXICO CITY

MOURN for Frida Kahlo at her former home while perusing the remnants of her shattered life in the **Museo Estudio Diego Rivera y Frida Kahlo** (p. 126).

LOSE yourself in the **Bosque de Chapultepec** (p. 118), the largest urban park in the Americas—it's got everything from panda bears to free concerts to the **Museo Nacional de Antropología** (p. 116), Mexico's biggest and best museum.

RULE over a kingdom of dance floors in the flashy and glamorous **Zona Rosa** (p. 131).

KNEEL with the devout in the **Basílica de Guadalupe** (p. 121).

PICNIC beneath shady poplars in pretty **Parque Alameda Central** (p. 112), before enjoying a dazzling show of **Ballet Folklórico** in the **Palacio de Bellas Artes** (p. 112).

HIT the road; many of Mexico City's most fabulous attractions lie outside the city itself. Check out our **daytrips** (p. 144), including the nearby pyramids at **Teotihuacán** (p. 138), the most visited ruins in all of Mexico. Or, get a workout and climb out of the pollution on a ▓ **mountain bike** tour of the Valley of Mexico's mountains (p. 95).

A BRIEF HISTORY

Cities like this just don't happen. Centuries upon centuries of intentions and chance crafted and shaped Mexico City into the biggest, baddest city in the world.

ORIGINS 101: FACT AND FICTION

The history of the Valley of Mexico begins with the arrival of the **Mexica** (mee-SHI-ka, later known as the **Aztecs**) in the 13th century AD. According to legend, the Aztecs were guided by Huitzilopochtli, their god of war, who told his chosen people to settle where they discovered an eagle with a serpent in its beak, perched on a cactus. Lo and behold, the Aztecs saw this sight at **Lake Texcoco.** Initially shunned by neighboring tribes as barbarous and uncouth, the Aztecs slowly rose to power through trading and strategic alliances (as well as the occasional backstabbing). At its height in the 15th century, the central Aztec city, **Tenochtitlán**, sat at the center of an empire that dominated the Valley and was a wonder to behold.

THE COLONIAL ERA

When **Hernán Cortés** arrived in Tenochtitlán in 1521, the gleaming city spread before him for miles, laid out in an inconceivably meticulous manner. Impressed, the Spaniard reacted in the only way he knew—he conquered it. After the fall of Tenochtitlán, the triumphant conquistador busied himself with transforming the Aztec city into a capital for his new empire. Spaniards razed Aztec temples and used the rubble to build new *palacios* and cathedrals, including those now in the *zócalo;* they drained the grids of Aztec canals and replaced them with roads— some form the backbone of the city's modern infrastructure. Despite all the energy that went into recasting the great city, however, beginning in 1629 a five-year flood of the Valley of Mexico nearly wiped it off the map. Most of the city was under water, its rooftops like rafts adrift on the ocean; all but 400 Spaniards abandoned the city. Under engineer Enrico Martínez, the drainage project Desagüe General revived the city and Spanish viceroys once again came and went as the city, the new empire's bureaucratic center, thrived under Spanish control. By the time of Independence, Mexico City was Latin America's cultural capital; consecration as a bishopric as early as 1533 made it the spiritual capital as well. The 18th century especially was a time of great construction and renovation; a new aqueduct linked the city to reservoirs in Chapultepec, and the giant underground lake was finally drained, opening more of the Valley for settlement.

INDEPENDENT MEXICO

Mexico City just happened to be smack in the middle of the country and it is no wonder that the huge, important city was often the goal of both revolutionary and foreign armies. Independence brought half a century of instability: no sooner had the *Grito de Dolores* (see p. 63) left Hidalgo's lips than construction and sanitation fell by the wayside and the city became booty, traded back and forth between the Mexican people and US soldiers (in 1847), French interventionists (in 1863), and revolutionary armies (in 1821, 1867, and 1876). Not until the dictatorship of Porfirio Díaz did the city regain some stability. Construction resumed and the turn of the century ushered in new building projects, such as the magnificent Palacio de Bellas Artes. Countless immigrants sought work and housing, and by the mid-1930s, over one million people identified themselves as *chilangos*.

THE MODERN CITY

The wartime economic boom of the 1940s and 1950s gave way to stagnation and frustration by the late 1960s, and Mexico, along with the rest of the world, fell upon desperate times. Emblematic of social controversies were the popular protests of 1968, when, prior to the Olympics, innocent protestors were gunned down in places like UNAM and Tlatelolco. Yet the city continued to grow. Within a span of 50 years, the capital's population soared—from one million in 1930 to eight million in 1980. City planning abruptly halted under the stress of millions of domestic immigrants arriving in search of work, which paved the way for growing shantytowns and slums that still line the roads to the capital. And when it rains, it pours. With the economy in shambles in the Lost Decade of the 1980s, a mighty earthquake sent both buildings and spirits tumbling to the ground. The June 1985 eruption of Popocatépetl was another powerful reminder of the city's precarious position atop a highly active geological area. To add insult to injury, the 80s and 90s saw air quality in the city deteriorate to dangerous levels; the city renowned

Central Mexico City

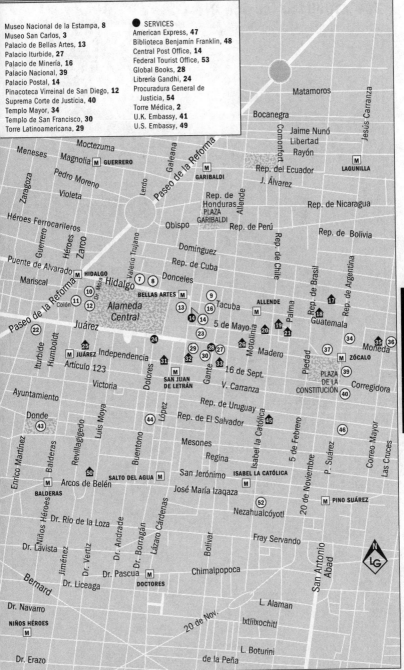

Museo Nacional de la Estampa, **8**
Museo San Carlos, **3**
Palacio de Bellas Artes, **13**
Palacio Iturbide, **27**
Palacio de Minería, **16**
Palacio Nacional, **39**
Palacio Postal, **14**
Pinacoteca Virreinal de San Diego, **12**
Suprema Corte de Justicia, **40**
Templo Mayor, **34**
Templo de San Francisco, **30**
Torre Latinoamericana, **29**

● SERVICES
American Express, **47**
Biblioteca Benjamín Franklin, **48**
Central Post Office, **14**
Federal Tourist Office, **53**
Global Books, **28**
Librería Gandhi, **24**
Procuradura General de
   Justicia, **54**
Torre Médica, **2**
U.K. Embassy, **41**
U.S. Embassy, **49**

MEXICO CITY

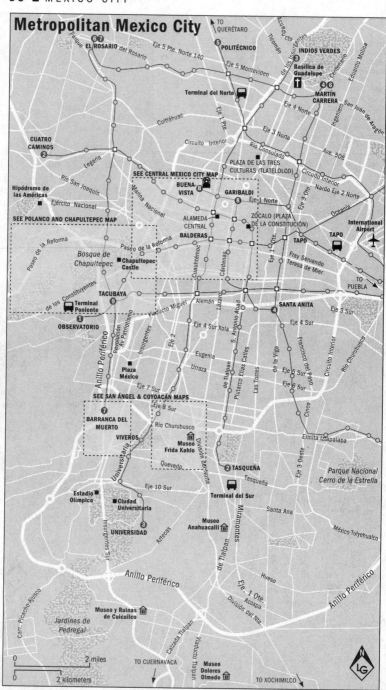

Metropolitan Mexico City

TO QUERÉTARO

⑥⑦ EL ROSARIO Parque del Rosario

⑤ POLITÉCNICO

Eje 5 Pte. Norte 140

Eje 5 Montevideo

③ INDIOS VERDES

Acueducto de los Insurgentes

Ticomán

Basílica de Guadalupe

④⑥ MARTÍN CARRERA

Centenario

Eduardo Molina

Eje 1 Pte.

Cuitláhuac

Terminal del Norte

Eje 4 Norte

Ingeniero San Juan de Aragón

Eje 3 Norte

CUATRO CAMINOS ②

Legaria

Circuito Interior

Río Consulado

Ave. 506

Río San Joaquín

Hipódromo de las Américas ■

Ejército Nacional ■

Marina Nacional

SEE CENTRAL MEXICO CITY MAP

BUENA VISTA ⑧

PLAZA DE LAS TRES CULTURAS (TLATELOLCO)

Circuito Interior

Nardo Eje 2 Norte

Eje 3 Ote.

GARIBALDI

Eje 1 Norte

⑧

Oceanía

International Airport

SEE POLANCO AND CHAPULTEPEC MAP

ALAMEDA CENTRAL

ZÓCALO (PLAZA DE LA CONSTITUCIÓN)

Paseo de la Reforma

Paseo de la Reforma

BALDERAS

TAPO

TAPO

Bosque de Chapultepec

Chapultepec Castle

Cuauhtémoc

Cárdenas

Eje 1 Ote.

Fray Servando Teresa de Mier

TO PUEBLA

de los Constituyentes

TACUBAYA ⑨

Alemán

Lázaro

SANTA ANITA ④

Eje 3 Sur

Terminal Poniente

Viaducto Miguel

Eje 4 Sur Xola

Eje 4 Sur

OBSERVATORIO ①

Revolución

Patriotismo

Insurgentes

Eje 2

S. Antonio Abad

Eugenia

Francisco del paso

Circuito Interior

Río Churubusco

Anillo Periférico

Plaza México ■

Urraza

de Tlalpan

Plutarco Elías Calles

Las Torres

de la Viga

Eje 5 Sur

Eje 6 Sur

Cinco

Eje 7 Sur

SEE SAN ÁNGEL & COYOACÁN MAPS

Eje 8 Sur

Ermita Iztapalapa

BARRANCA DEL MUERTO ⑦

Río Churubusco

Museo Frida Kahlo

VIVEROS

División del Norte

Quevedo

② TASQUEÑA

Tasqueña

Parque Nacional Cerro de la Estrella

Universitaria

Eje 10 Sur

Terminal del Sur

Estadio Olímpico ■

■ Ciudad Universitaria

Museo Anahuacalli

Santa Ana

México-Tulyehualco

③ UNIVERSIDAD

Aztecas

de Tlalpan

Insurgentes Sur

Anillo Periférico

Anillo Periférico

Jardines de Pedregal

Carr. Picacho-Ajusco

Anillo Periférico

Hueso

Museo y Ruinas de Cuicuilco

Calzada Tlalpan

Viaducto Tlalpan

División del Nte.

Acoxpa

Eje 1 Ote.

0 ___ 2 miles
0 ___ 2 kilometers

TO CUERNAVACA

Museo Dolores Olmedo

TO XOCHIMILCO

N

for its cleanliness and breathable air had become one of the world's most polluted. The resumption of economic growth in the 1990s was a silver lining that promised better days. The creation of a governor of Mexico in 1998 brought newfound hope to the millions who call the city home, and the subsequent election of progressive **Cuauhtémoc Cárdenas** raised the hopes of many *chilangos*. Optimism has begun to bear fruit: most notably, crime has dissipated from notorious levels during severe recession. The city has also pursued new approaches to fighting pollution, using educational campaigns and strict controls. Perhaps most importantly, Mexico City has gained confidence in its complicated identity. The clearing of the Templo Mayor in the early 80s kindled indigenous pride, and the city today is a dizzying mix of old and new, foreign and native. Although cynical and street-wise, most *chilangos* are head over heels in love with their city. Huitzilopochtli, wherever he is, is no doubt smiling upon his beloved nomads.

■ INTERCITY TRANSPORTATION

All roads lead to Mexico City. Buses, trains, and planes from every town in the republic haul passengers through the smoggy hyperactivity of the city's many temples of transport—the constantly expanding Benito Juárez International Airport, four crowded bus stations, and a network of freeways. Fortunately, airports and stations have information booths, sometimes with English-speaking personnel; official zone-rated taxi service; and nearby Metro stations.

BY AIR

Benito Juárez International Airport (☎5571 3295) lies 6.5km east of the *zócalo*, the formal city center. **Blvd. Capitán Juan Sarabio** heads northeast to the airport from **Blvd. Puerto Aéreo**, one of the major roads circling the city.

GETTING TO AND FROM THE AIRPORT

Transportation into the city is uncomplicated. The Metro (see **By Metro**, p. 93) is the cheapest route to the city. The airport metro station, **Terminal Aérea**, Line 5, at Sarabio and Puerto Aéreo, is just outside Sala A. Signs will point the way. Large bags are officially prohibited, but if you avoid rush hour (6-10am and 6-9pm) and can maneuver through the turnstile, a backpack should not pose too much of a problem. Special fixed-rate airport **taxis** (☎5784 4811 or 5571 3600), or *transporte terrestre*, also run into the city. Ticket windows by the exits to both arrival gates sell fare-tickets, whose price depend on the zone of your destination. Expect to pay 120-150 pesos to reach hotels in central Mexico City. Give the ticket to one of the cabs waiting outside while avoiding uniformed "taxi supervisors"—porters who will expect a tip for taking your bags to the cabs.

 GET OFF HERE. If traveling to the airport by Metro, **do not get off** at the Aeropuerto stop on Line 1 (also known as Blvd. Aeropuerto). The correct stop is **Terminal Aérea**, on Line 5.

FLIGHT INFORMATION

Flight Info Hotline and General Information: ☎5571 3600 or 5762 6773. Specify domestic or international flights.

Terminals: Sala A: All Aeroméxico, baby. **Sala B:** Mexicana, Aeromar, and AeroCalifornia. **Sala C:** Aerolíneas Internacionales and AVIACSA. **Sala D:** ALLEGRO, TAESA, and charter flights. **Sala E:** International arrivals. **Sala F1:** Aeroméxico (international flights), America West, Avianca, Continental, Delta, Ecuatoriana, Lan Chile, and LAB. **Sala F2:** Air

France, Aviateca, British Airways, Canadian, Copa, Cubana, ETA, JAL, KLM, Malaysia, Miami Air, Northwest, and Grupo Taca. **Sala F3:** Air Canada, American Airlines, Argentinian Airlines, Iberia, Lufthansa, TWA, and United Airlines.

Domestic Carriers: Prices are similar from airline to airline, but flight schedules and prices do change frequently. Ask about *tarifas promocionales,* which may save you up to 50%. **AeroCalifornia,** Sala B (☎5207 1392), tends to be the most competitive. Open daily 7am-7pm. **Aeroméxico,** Sala A (☎5726 0234; reservations hotline 5133 4050 or 800 021 4050). Open daily 4:30am-2am. At Paseo de la Reforma 445 (☎5514 9736), at Mississippi. Open M-Sa 9am-8:15pm. Also at Reforma 80 (☎5566 1078), at Versailles. Open M-Sa 9am-6:15pm. **Mexicana,** Sala C. Open daily 5am-1am. Office at Reforma 312 (☎5511 3579, ext. 4508), at Amberes in the Zona Rosa, and at other offices throughout the city. Open M-F 9am-5:45pm.

International Carriers: Air Canada, Reforma 389-14 (☎5208 1883). **Air France,** Edgar Allen Poe 90 (☎5627 6060), in Col. Polanco. Open M-F 9am-2pm and 3-6pm. **American** (☎5209 1400), Sala F and Reforma 314. Open M-F 9am-6pm, Sa 9am-8:30pm. **British Airways,** Balmes 8, Mez. office #6 (☎5387 0300), in Col. Polanco. Open M-F 9am-5:30pm, Sa 9am-1pm. **Continental** (☎5283 5500 or 800 900 5000), between Salas D and E. Open M-F 7am-7pm, Sa-Su 7am-6pm. **Delta,** Sala F (☎5279 0909) and Reforma 381 (☎5202 1608). Open daily 6am-6pm. **Lufthansa,** Las Palmas 239 (☎5230 0000), Col. Lomas de Chapultepec. Open M-F 9am-6pm. At the airport (☎5571 2702). Open daily 2:30-9:30pm. **TWA,** Sala F (☎5627 0222 or 800 007 8000). **United,** Sala F (☎5627 0222 or 800 003 0777) and Hamburgo 213 (☎5627 0222). Open daily 9am-noon and 3-5pm.

AIRPORT SERVICES

Tourist Office: in Sala A (☎5786 9002), with the yellow signs. Hotel reservations available. Open daily 8am-8pm. Information kiosks in Salas A and F have flight info.

Buses: Airport bus service allows direct access to nearby towns from just outside Sala D. Ticket booth in front of parked buses. Buses go to: **Cuernavaca** (21 per day 6:30am-11pm, 80 pesos); **Pachuca** (15 per day 7:15am-9:15pm, 100 pesos); **Puebla** (42 per day 6am-12:30am, 100 pesos); **Querétaro** (14 per day 8:30am-9:15pm, 160 pesos).

Currency Exchange: Banks exchange currency and traveler's checks in almost every *sala.* **ATMs** are in Sala A, directly under Sala B, and in Salas E and F. *Casas de cambio* have rates comparable to what you'll find throughout the city. Open daily 6am-9pm.

Car Rental: in Sala E. Companies offer similar rates. Open until about 10:30pm.

Luggage Storage: corner of Sala A and in Sala E. 50 pesos per bag per day. Open 24hr.

Police: ☎5599 0053, upstairs from Sala C. Also in Sala E1 (☎5599 0044).

Pharmacy: in Sala C. Open daily 6am-10pm. Also in Sala F. Open daily 6am-11pm.

Medical Assistance: upstairs from Sala C; follow the Red Cross signs.

Fax: between Salas D and E. Open 24hr.

Internet: Axon Cyber Cafe, in Sala E (☎5786 9372). Fast connection 1 peso per min. Web kiosks scattered around the airport operate on LADATEL phone cards.

Post Office: in Sala A. Open M-F 8am-7pm, Sa 9am-5pm. **Postal Code:** 15620.

BY TRAIN

Mexico City no longer has passenger train service to or from other cities.

BY BUS

Mexico City's four main bus stations correspond to the cardinal directions and serve corresponding areas of the country. The Metro serves all the stations, which also have 24hr. fixed rate taxi service. Buy your ticket inside to avoid being ripped off. *Peseros (colectivos)* also serve the four stations. Bus prices change frequently, and listings are not comprehensive.

Central de Autobuses del Norte (North Station): Baja California, northern Veracruz, Jalisco, and all of northern Mexico.

Terminal Central de Autobuses del Sur (Tasqueña; South Station): Guerrero, Morelos, and Oaxaca.

Terminal de Autobuses de Pasajeros de Oriente (TAPO; East Station): Puebla, southern Veracruz, Oaxaca, Chiapas, and the Yucatán Peninsula.

Terminal de Autobuses del Poniente (West Station): Estado de México and Michoacán.

CENTRAL DE AUTOBUSES DEL NORTE

The vast Central de Autobuses del Norte (☎5587 1552), commonly known as Cien Metros or México Norte, is on Cien Metros at **M: Autobuses del Norte** (Line 5). Services include: **hotel reservations** (open daily 7am-9pm), **tourist information** booth (open daily 9am-7pm), and **casa de cambio** (open daily 11am-6pm), all near the entrance. There are **ATMs** and a **pharmacy** (all open 24hr.). At least one Sendetel office has **Internet.** (15 pesos per hr. Open daily 6am-10pm.) From the **taxi stand,** rides to the *zócalo* or Revolución are 65 pesos.

ADO (☎5133 2424) goes to: **Oaxaca** (6hr., midnight, 314 pesos); **Papantla** (5hr., 7 per day 9:30am-12:30am, 137 pesos); **Puebla** (2hr., every 30min. 4am-10pm, 77 pesos); **Tuxpan** (6hr., 3 per day 12:30pm-11:45pm, 200 pesos); **Veracruz** (7hr.; 9am, 11:30pm; 269 pesos); **Villahermosa** (10hr., 10pm, 541 pesos); **Xalapa** (5hr.; 3pm, 12:15am; 147 pesos).

Élite (☎5729 0707). The name says it all. Posh service to: **Hermosillo** (30hr., every hr. 5:30am-1:15pm, 795 pesos); **Puerto Vallarta** (14hr., 3 per day 5-11:45pm, 600 pesos); **San Luis Potosí** (7hr., every hr., 236 pesos).

Estrella Blanca/Futura (☎5729 0707) motors to: **Acapulco** (5hr., every 1½hr. 6am-11:30pm, 230 pesos); **Aguascalientes** (6hr., every hr. 7:30am-12:30am, 300 pesos); **Chihuahua** (18hr., every hr. 8:50am-11:30pm, 837 pesos); **Durango** (12hr., 6 per day 5:30am-11:45pm, 515 pesos); **Matamoros** (14hr., 5 per day 2:15-10:30pm, 586 pesos); **Monterrey** (12hr., every hr. 7am-midnight, 530 pesos); **Tampico** (9½hr., every 2hr., 262 pesos); **Zacatecas** (7hr., every hr., 362 pesos).

Flecha Amarilla (☎5587 5222) runs to: **Guadalajara** (9hr., every hr., 300 pesos); **Guanajuato** (6½hr., 4 per day 11:45am-7:40pm, 187 pesos); **Morelia** (5hr., 16 per day, 145 pesos); **Querétaro** (3½hr., every 15min. 4:50am-12:20am, 120 pesos); **San Miguel de Allende** (4½hr.; 7:10, 11:15am, 5:40pm; 126 pesos).

TERMINAL DE AUTOBUSES DE PASAJEROS DE ORIENTE (TAPO)

Follow the indoor walkway from **M: San Lázaro** (Line 1) to General Ignacio Zaragoza 200 (☎5762 5977). Services include **ATMs** and **pharmacy. Police** booths are scattered throughout. **Taxi** ticket booths are near the Metro entrance (to the *zócalo* 65 pesos, to Monumento a la Revolución 70 pesos).

ADO (☎5542 7192) sends buses to: **Cancún** (23hr., 3 per day 9am-1:30pm, 931 pesos); **Córdoba** (4½hr., 5 per day 10am-8:10pm, 203 pesos); **Mérida** (19hr.; 11am, noon; 831 pesos); **Oaxaca** (6hr., 8 per day 9:30am-12:15am, 314 pesos); **Palenque** (12hr.; 4, 6pm; 485 pesos); **Veracruz** (5hr., 17 per day 8am-12:15am, 269 pesos); **Villahermosa** (10½hr., 5 per day 10am-9:30pm, 541 pesos); **Xalapa** (4½hr., 10 per day 8am-midnight, 189 pesos).

Autobuses Cristóbal Colón (☎5133 2433) travels to: **Oaxaca** (6hr., 5 per day 12:30-11:30pm, 246 pesos); **San Cristóbal de las Casas** (18hr.; 2:30, 5:30, 7:30pm; 502

pesos); **Tonalá** (13hr.; 5 per day noon-10pm; 449 pesos); **Tuxtla Gutiérrez** (15hr.; 3, 8pm; 578 pesos).

Autobuses Unidos (AU; ☎5133 2424) goes to: **Córdoba** (5hr., 21 per day, 145 pesos); **Oaxaca** (9hr., 11 per day, 198 pesos); **San Andrés Tuxtla** (8hr.; noon, 9pm; 247 pesos); **Veracruz** (5hr., every hr. 7am-11pm, 175 pesos); **Xalapa** (5hr., 20 per day, 131 pesos).

Estrella Roja (☎5542 9220) goes to **Puebla** (2hr., 60 pesos).

UNO (☎5522 1111) rolls to: **Oaxaca** (6hr., 6 per day 8:30am-11:45pm, 435 pesos); **Veracruz** (5½hr., 9 per day 8:15am-midnight, 335 pesos); **Villahermosa** (10hr., 4 per day 8-11:30pm, 748 pesos); **Xalapa** (4½hr., 6 per day 9am-midnight, 263 pesos).

TERMINAL DE AUTOBUSES DEL PONIENTE

Follow signs from **M: Observatorio** (Line 1) to Central Camionero Pte., Av. Sur 122 (☎5271 4519); a vendor-lined bridge leads to the terminal. From the terminal to the Metro, walk up the staircase and turn left. The station is built in the shape of a "V" with the most important services at the vertex. Services include: **pharmacy** (open daily 7am-10pm), **Telecomm fax** (open M-F 8am-7pm, Sa-Su 9am-4pm), and **Western Union.** Buy **taxi** tickets from the authorized stand (to the *zócalo* 80 pesos, to the Monumento a la Revolución 70 pesos).

Autobuses del Occidente (☎5271 0106) goes to: **Guadalajara** (12hr., 4 per day 1:15am-6:10pm, 263 pesos); **Manzanillo** (16hr., 4 per day 7:10am-9:40pm, 410 pesos); **Morelia** (6hr., every hr. 6:15am-4:15pm, 146 pesos).

Caminante drives to **Toluca** (1hr., every 5min. 5:50am-10:30pm, 33 pesos).

Élite (☎5271 0578) travels to **Chihuahua** (20hr., 2:30pm, 832 pesos); **Morelia** (4hr.; 10:30am, 3:30pm; 170 pesos).

ETN (☎5273 0305) motors to: **Guadalajara** (7hr., 7 per day, 480 pesos); **Morelia** (4hr., 34 per day, 240 pesos); **Toluca** (1hr., every 30min., 40 pesos); **Uruapan** (5½hr., 8 per day, 320 pesos).

Pegasso Plus (☎5277 7761) sends buses to: **Morelia** (4hr., 36 per day, 185 pesos); **Pátzcuaro** (5hr., 10 per day 6:30am-midnight, 205 pesos).

Servicios Coordinados goes to **Morelia** (5½hr., 11 per day 9:30am-11pm, 146 pesos).

CENTRAL DE AUTOBUSES DEL SUR (TASQUEÑA)

To get to the Tasqueña terminal, Tasqueña 1320 (☎5689 9745), exit **M: Tasqueña** from the "Central" exit on the upper level, then go down a staircase on your left. The terminal is across the market, yellow fence, and row of trees. Services include: mini-**travel agency** for hotel reservations in select cities (open Su-F 9am-9pm, Sa 9am-3pm), **Telecomm** with cash wire transfer (☎5549 8015; open M-F 8am-7:30pm, Sa-Su 9am-4:30pm), and a **pharmacy** (☎5689 0883; open 24hr.). Cabs are at the **taxi** stand (to the *zócalo* 65 pesos, to the Monumento a la Revolución 75 pesos).

ADO, Cristóbal Colón (☎5544 2414) and **Estrella Roja** (☎5549 8749) go to: **Oaxaca** (6hr., 3 per day 1-11:30pm, 314 pesos); **Puebla** (3hr., every hr. 6:30am-9:30pm, 77 pesos); and places on the **Gulf Coast** and **Yucatán.**

Estrella de Oro (☎5549 8520) serves: **Acapulco** (5hr., 17 per day, 260 pesos); **Cuernavaca** (1½hr.; 6:40, 8:40pm; 52 pesos); **Ixtapa/Zihuatanejo** (9hr., 4 per day 8:20am-11:20pm, 340 pesos); **Taxco** (2hr., 6 per day 7:40am-8:10pm, 82 pesos).

Futura and **Turistar** (☎5628 5739) leave for: **Acapulco** (5hr., 38 per day, 230 pesos); **Ixtapa/Zihuatanejo** (9hr., every 30min., 359 pesos); **Taxco** (2hr., every hr. 7am-10pm, 86 pesos).

Pullman de Morelos (☎5549 3505) goes to: **Cuernavaca** (1¼hr., every 15min. 5:30am-midnight, 47 pesos); **Tepoztlán** (1hr., every 30min. 6:30am-9pm, 45 pesos).

BY CAR

Few car-related experiences can match the shock of driving into Mexico City, the heart of the nation's highway arteries. Traffic keeps the city crawling from 9 to 11am and 3 to 7pm. Don't expect anyone to drive defensively—*chilangos* in a hurry dismiss stoplights as optional (see **Getting Around By Car,** p. 95). Major roads into the district change names as they intersect with the **Circuito Interior,** the route that rings the city. **Mex. 57,** from Querétaro and Tepoztlán, becomes **Manuel Ávila Camacho** just outside the Circuito. **Mex. 15,** from Toluca, turns into **Reforma** as it enters the city. **Mex. 95,** from Cuernavaca and Acapulco, becomes **Insurgentes,** which enters the city from the south side. **Mex. 150,** from Puebla and Texcoco, becomes **Ignacio Zaragoza** on the city's east side. **Mex. 85,** from Pachuca, Teotihua-cán, and Texcoco, also becomes **Insurgentes** at the northern city limits.

GETTING AROUND

BY METRO

The Metro never ceases to amaze. Fare is cheap, crowds are enormous, the ride is smooth and efficient, the service extensive, and the stations immaculate. Built in the late 1960s, the Metro now transports five million people per day, making the equivalent of two and a half trips around the world.

WOMEN AND CHILDREN FIRST

Sexual harassment on the Metro is one of the most common complaints among female visitors to the city; women and girls of all ages are subject to mistreat-ment, including being shouldered aside. In response, the Metro management has reserved the first two cars of each train for women and children before 10am at the busiest stations; at a few, the cars are also separate for the evening rush hour. Look for signs saying "Mujeres y Niños," or "Damas." Unfor-tunately, men do enter the cars at unguarded stations, and this plan fails to address problems outside rush hour. Still, the front two cars are always a good bet, as they tend to be less crowded and contain more women anyway. Addi-tionally some women only wear loose-fitting slacks or jeans on the Metro, and many tie a sweater around their waists. Traveling with a man may also help. Despite all your precautions, it may be impossible to completely avoid unwanted attention and sometimes even the horrible experience of being groped. Do not hesitate to call attention to the offender with a loud *"¿No tiene vergüenza?"* (Don't you have any shame?) or, *"¡Déjame!"* (Leave me alone!).

Metro tickets (2 pesos, including transfers) are sold in *taquillas* (ticket booths) at every station. Directions are given in terms of the station at either end of a given line, and each of the two *andenes* (platforms) has signs indicating the terminus toward which trains are heading. For example, if you are on Line 3 between Indios Verdes and Universidad, you can go either "Dirección Indios Verdes" or "Dirección Universidad." During rush hour (M-F 7:30-9:30am, 2-4pm, and 6-9pm) commuters pack the cars like sardines, and getting on and off is a daunting—and sometimes unsuccessful—experience. (Trains run M-F 5am-12:30am, Sa-Su 6am-12:30am.)

Theft on the Metro is rampant yet avoidable. To avoid hassles, it's a good idea to carry bags in front of you or on your lap. The safest place in a crowded car is with your back to the wall and your belongings in front of you. Remember that rear pockets are easy to pick, front pockets are safer, and empty pockets are best. Because of overcrowding, large bags or suitcases are sometimes not allowed on the Metro. If you are intent on carrying a big pack, travel early or after 10:30pm.

Most transfer stations have information booths with Metro maps, also available at the tourist office. Also helpful is **COVITUR** (Comisión de Vialidad y Transporte Urbano del D.F.; Public Relations), Felicia 67 (☎5709 8036), outside M: Salto de Agua (Lines 1, 8). Nearly all stations have guards and security offices; all must have a *jefe de la estación* (chief of station) in a marked office to deal with questions, complaints, and panic attacks. The **Oficina de Objetos Extraviados,** in M: Candelaria (Lines 1, 4), handles lost belongings. (☎5542 5397. Open M-F 9am-8pm.)

EL METROPOLITÁN

Some Metro stops are sights in their own right; nearly every transfer station boasts some kind of exhibit, from elementary school drawings of the subway system to a re-creation of a London theater. Some notable stops are:

Pino Suárez, Lines 1, 2: a small Aztec building at mid-transfer.

La Raza, Lines 3, 5: Túnel de la Ciencia (science tunnel). Marvel at nifty fractals, glow under a black-lit map of the constellations, or visit the science museum. Open M-Sa 10am-6pm.

Zócalo, Line 2: models of the *zócalo* as it has appeared throughout history.

Bellas Artes, Lines 2, 8: Aztec statuettes, replicas from the Templo Mayor.

BY BUS

Peseros, autobuses, trolebuses—the variety of buses makes getting around more convenient rather than complicated. *Peseros* (more affectionately known as *micros*) date back to the time when riding the green-and-white minibuses cost only one old peso, which is equivalent to about US$0.01 today. Although not quite the steal they once were, *peseros* are still extremely affordable and—though crowded—excellent ways to make short, direct trips around town. *Autobuses* are the big long buses like those in Anglo/European countries. They run on the most popular *pesero* routes, though less often. Fare is 2-5 pesos depending on destination, and all destinations cost 5 pesos 11pm-6am. Destinations are posted on the front window. If you are unsure, ask the driver: *"¿Se va a...?"* ("Are you going to...?"). *Trolebuses* (electric buses or "trackless trolleys") are even rarer than *autobuses*, and charge 2 pesos for the smoothest ride in town.

In 1997, a great effort was made to establish set bus stops; look for the nifty stainless steel bus shelters or a little blue sign with a picture of a *pesero*. Failing that, the nearest big intersection is probably a designated stop. Note that you must hail buses even from designated stops. Most *peseros* will slow down for anyone with an arm out, even in the middle of a block. To get off, ring the bell (if there is one) or simply shout loudly *"¡La parada, por favor!"* (The stop, please!).

Most *peseros* run until midnight, but major routes—on Reforma, between Chapultepec and San Ángel, and along Insurgentes—run 24hr. Other frequented *pesero* routes are M: Hidalgo to Ciudad Universitaria (via Reforma, Bucareli, and Cuauhtémoc); La Villa to Chapultepec (via Reforma); Reforma to Auditorio (via Reforma and Juárez); *zócalo* to Chapultepec (via 5 de Mayo and Reforma); San Ángel to Izazaga (via 5 de Mayo and Reforma); Bolívar to Ciudad Universitaria/ Coyoacán (via Bolívar in *centro*); San Ángel to M: Insurgentes (via Av. de la Paz and Insurgentes Sur); and M: Chapultepec to San Ángel, La Merced, and airport.

BY TAXI

Due to increased hijackings, robberies, and rapes in the 1990s, the US State Department issued a warning against hailing cabs off the street—including those delicious lime-green Volkswagen bugs. If traveling by taxi, call a **sitio taxi** (radio taxi). Late at night when buses no longer run, they're worth the cost (about twice as much as regular taxis). Ask your hotel or check the yellow pages for the best rates; if it comes to it, an overpriced cab recommended by a night club or restaurant is better than nothing. Despite their names, *sitio* cab companies often don't operate *sitios* (stands). If you can't locate a *sitio* number or a hotel cab, try **Servi-taxi** (☎5271 2560). To get to the airport in a pinch, call **Transporte Terrestre al Aeropuerto** (☎5571 9106). Convenient taxi stands at the bus station and airport will give you a fixed rate. It's appropriate to tip in any taxi. If you insist on using cruising *(libre)* cabs, make sure that the picture on the displayed badge matches the driver's face—if it doesn't, or if there isn't one, don't get in. You may want to note the licence plate number and driver's name, and avoid riding alone. Alternatively, chat up a cab driver and get his or her number so that you will have a reliable taxi you can call without having to face the high fares of a *sitio*. Finally, be aware that four-door taxis have easier escape routes than the two-door VW Bugs.

BY BIKE

Sick of city pollution and crowds? At ▨**Advent Mexico Mountain Biking,** Periférico Sur 2930, Local 14, 2nd fl., expert guide Pedro Saad and associates lead travelers on 1- to 15-day all-inclusive English-language mountain bike tours of the volcanoes, mountains, forests, and towns (including Taxco and Cuernavaca) surrounding Mexico City. Tours are also available for destinations farther afield, such as Chihuahua. A new package includes guided tours of D.F.'s cultural and historical sites, followed by a trip through neighboring mountains. (☎5681 4714; fax 5681 4574; www.advent.com.mx. From US$85 per day; inquire about student discounts. Reservations recommended one month in advance.)

BY CAR

Driving is the most complicated and least economical way to get around, not to mention the easiest way to get lost. The city's drivers are notoriously reckless and aggressive, roads are over-trafficked and confusing, divider lines are frequently absent, pedestrians pounce on any sign of hesitation, and stop signs are planted midstream. Red lights are so routinely defied that police officers often direct traffic. If your car breaks down, call the **Asociación Nacional Automovilística** (**ANA;** ☎5292 1970 through 77) for assistance. Wait beside your car with the hood raised.

 AND ON THE SEVENTH DAY... All vehicles, even those of non-Mexican registration, are subject to Mexico City's strict anti-smog regulations. Restrictions apply Monday-Friday 5am-10pm, and penalties for violations are stiff. Every vehicle must "rest" one day per week and stay off the streets. The last digit of the license plate determines the day. Note that some cars manufactured after 1995 may be exempt from the limitations.
Monday: 5/6. **Tuesday:** 7/8. **Wednesday:** 3/4. **Thursday:** 1/2. **Friday:** 9/0.

Parking within the city is seldom a problem; garages are everywhere (4-8 pesos per hr.). Be wary of valet parking; cars sometimes wind up with the wrong person. Street parking is difficult to find, and vandalism is common. Police will put an *inmobilizador* on your wheels if you park illegally; alternatively, they'll just tow your car. If you return to an empty space, locate the nearest police depot (not station) to find out whether your vehicle has been towed—or stolen. If anything is missing from your car and you suspect that the police tampered with it, call the English-speaking **LOCATEL** (☎5658 1111).

Car rental rates are exorbitant, driving is a hassle, and the entire process is draining. Still interested? To rent a car you must have a valid driver's license (from any

THE LOCAL LEGEND

THE FOUNDING OF MEXICO

Sure, everyone knows the story behind the Mexican flag: green symbolizes the independence movement, white is for the purity of the Catholic faith, and red honors the blood of the national heroes. Yet, while the central feature of the flag, an eagle with a serpent in its mouth perched atop a cactus, is universally familiar, the tale behind that picture is less known.

Way back when, the Aztecs were looking for a place to build their empire, and so consulted the gods on the matter. Huitzilopochtli, god of creation, the sun, and war, sent out a vision in reply. In this vision, an eagle with a serpent in its mouth was on top of a cactus. The Aztecs were supposed to find this vision and build their empire in that very spot.

The image was a powerful one. Eagles were taken to represent the sun, Huitzilopochtli himself, and serpents were associated with the god Quetzalcóatl. This land was to be a blessed one.

After years of wandering, the Aztecs finally happened upon the vision: an eagle with a snake in its mouth, atop a cactus...on a tiny island...in the middle of huge Lake Texcoco. Oops.

Yet the Aztecs were true to their gods. They worked hard to drain and fill in the land around the island to build their empire, Tenochtitlan, or "place of the cactus". And look what happened.

country), a passport or tourist card, and be at least 25 years old. Prices for rentals at different agencies tend to be similarly high: a small VW or Nissan with unlimited kilometers, insurance, and tax (known as IVA) costs about 350-450 pesos per day or 3000-3500 pesos per week. Most agencies have offices at the airport or in the Zona Rosa: **Avis,** at the airport (☎5588 8888 or 800 70 777; open daily 7am-11pm) and at Reforma 308 (☎5533 1336; open M-F 7am-10:30pm); **Budget,** at the airport (☎5271 4322; open 24hr.) and at Hamburgo 68; **Dollar,** at the airport (☎5207 3838) and at Chapultepec 322 (open daily 7am-8pm); **Hertz,** at the airport (☎5592 2867; open daily 7am-10:30pm).

■ ORIENTATION

Mexico City extends outward from the *centro* roughly 20km to the south, 10km to the north, 10km to the west, and 8km to the east, though there is much debate about where the city actually begins and ends. Few tourists venture past the Bosque de Chapultepec to the west, La Basílica de Guadalupe to the north, the airport to the east, or San Ángel and the UNAM to the south; this roughly corresponds to the extent of Metro coverage. A rectangular series of routes (the **Circuito Interior**) and a thorough system of thoroughfares **(Ejes Viales)** help to make cross-city travel manageable. Of these, the **Eje Central,** commonly known as **Lázaro Cárdenas,** is the central north-south route. At a more local level, the city is difficult to know well; even most *chilangos* don't have it all down pat. What's more, many different neighborhoods use the same street names—more than 300 streets are named for Benito Juárez. Still, it is only a matter of cardinal directions and good ol' trial and error before you've mastered the basics of this megalopolis. The most important thing is to know the name of the **colonia** (neighborhood). Mexico City has over 350 such *colonias;* **Col. Polanco, Zona Rosa, Col. Roma,** and **Col. Juárez** are some of the most touristed. Disregard street numbers, and orient yourself using nearby monuments, museums, *glorietas* (traffic circles), cathedrals, and skyscrapers. Street names tend to be themed regionally. Streets in the Zona Rosa are named after European cities, those directly across Reforma bear the names of large rivers of the world, and those in Polanco honor famous philosophers. If you are insane enough to drive around the city, a good map of the outer routes is essential. **Guía Roji Ciudad de México** (110 pesos), a comprehensive street atlas, is a valuable aid for anyone planning to stay in the city for some time. You can also pick up its little sibling, the abridged *mini-Guía Roji* (60 pesos).

CIRCUITO INTERIOR AND EJES VIALES

Aside from the large thoroughfares—Insurgentes, Reforma, Chapultepec, and Miguel Alemán—the majority of traffic is routed through the Circuito Interior and via the system of *Ejes Viales* (axis roads) that run north-south or east-west, making a grid of faster roads laid over the city. *Eje* numbers increase heading away from the *zócalo*. Heavy traffic inhibits fast travel along the *Ejes* and Circuito.

CITY CENTER

As huge as Mexico City is, most areas of interest to visitors lie within easy reach of the city center. Many attractions are on or just off **Paseo de la Reforma,** the broad concourse that runs southwest-northeast, or **Insurgentes,** which cuts north-south through the city. These two main arteries intersect at **Glorieta Cuauhtémoc.** From Bosque de Chapultepec, Reforma proceeds northeast, punctuated by *glorietas* (traffic circles), each with a monument in the center. Some of the more famous ones, in southwest-to-northeast order, include: Glorieta Ángel de la Independencia, Glorieta Cuauhtémoc, and Glorieta Cristóbal Colón.

Accommodations and food listings for Mexico City are divided according to the areas of most interest to visitors. Moving northeast on Reforma from Chapultepec, the **Zona Rosa** is followed by the area **near the Monumento a la Revolución,** the **Alameda,** and, east of the Alameda, the **Centro Histórico.**

CENTRO HISTÓRICO. The *centro histórico* contains the *zócalo*, the largest number of historic sights and museums, extensive budget accommodations, and lively, inexpensive restaurants. The area is bounded by Cárdenas to the west, El Salvador to the south, Pino Suárez to the east, and Rep. de Perú to the north. **Metro: Allende** (Line 2) for accommodations and the Alameda; **Zócalo** (Line 2) for the center of the city; **Isabel la Católica** (Line 2); and **Pino Suárez** (Lines 1, 2) for sites to the south.

THE ALAMEDA. The Alameda, the central city park and its surroundings, contains many great museums, cheap hotels, and a few restaurants. It is right next door to the *centro histórico*. The area is bounded by Eje 1 Pte. (known as Rosales, Guerrero, and Bucareli) to the west, Arcos de Belén to the south, Lázaro Cárdenas to the east, and Pensador Mexicano to the north. **Plaza Garibaldi** is approximately ½km northeast of the Alameda. **Metro: Hidalgo** (Lines 2, 3); **Bellas Artes** (Lines 2, 8) for the park, Palacio de Bellas Artes, Plaza Garibaldi, and the post office; and **San Juan de Letrán** (Line 8), close to most food and accommodations.

NEAR THE MONUMENTO A LA REVOLUCIÓN. The area around Monumento a la Revolución—**Col. Buenavista** and **Col. Tabacalera,** on the north and south sides of Puente de Alvarado, respectively—contains perhaps the greatest number of inexpensive hotels and eateries, though considerably fewer glitzy attractions than other neighborhoods. It is bounded by Insurgentes Centro to the west, Reforma to the south and east, and Mosqueta to the north. **Metro: Revolución** (Line 2).

ZONA ROSA. The capital's most touristy commercial district, home to some of the country's most active nightlife, is contained by Reforma to the north and west, Chapultepec to the south, and Insurgentes to the east. A few of the area's listings lie just east of Insurgentes, and a string of clubs leaks south past Chapultepec along Insurgentes Sur. The **Bosque de Chapultepec** sits just west of the Zona Rosa. The mostly residential Colonia Roma lies south of the Zona along Insurgentes; cheaper, laid-back versions of the Zona's entertainment, restaurants, and accommodations spill into here. **Metro: Insurgentes** (Line 1), right in the middle of the action; and **Sevilla** (Line 1), toward the Ángel de la Independencia.

AWAY FROM THE CENTER

THE NORTHERN DISTRICTS. Approximately 3km north of the *zócalo* is the district of **Tlatelolco** (**M: Tlatelolco,** Line 3), famous for its pyramid and Plaza de las Tres Culturas. Approximately 4km farther north lies **La Villa Basílica** (**M: La Villa Basílica,** Line 6), home to the Basílica de Guadalupe.

THE SOUTHERN DISTRICTS. Several major southern districts are strung along Insurgentes Sur, 10-15km southwest of the *zócalo*. Roughly from southwest to northeast are **Ciudad Universitaria** (**M: Universidad,** Line 3), the suburb **San Ángel** (**M: M. A. Quevedo,** Line 3), and posh **Coyoacán** (**M: Coyoacán,** Line 3). Approximately 20km southeast of the *zócalo* is **Xochimilco** (**M: Tasqueña,** Line 2)—with its canals, the Venice of Mexico City.

SAFETY AND HEALTH

Like most bloated metropolitan areas, Mexico City has a fair amount of crime. Before you cancel your visit to D.F., however, keep in mind that most crimes perpetrated against tourists fall under the category of petty street crime—pick-pocketings, purse-snatchings, and muggings. A community of con artists concentrates in highly touristed areas, sending teary-eyed children armed with sob stories to extract funds from altruistic tourists. Shake your head, avoid eye contact, and walk to a more crowded area. Some tourists find that crimes are also committed by men in uniform. Just because someone is dressed as a figure of authority doesn't mean he won't rob you blind. Foreigners are particularly vulnerable near obvious tourist spots, such as the Zona Rosa and the *zócalo*. In general, the downtown area, where most sights and accommodations are located, tends to be safer, but the back streets near Buenavista and the Alameda are significantly less so.

That said, violent crime against tourists is a continuing problem. To avoid becoming the next victim, stay away from untouristed streets and areas, particularly at night or when traveling alone. Refrain from ostentatious displays of wealth: never display your cash, and use ATMs in well-lit places, preferably at a bank during banking hours. Obvious marks of the vulnerable *extranjero* include shorts, baseball caps, waistpacks, and cameras. Speaking in Spanish makes would-be attackers less likely to bother you. Never follow a vendor or shoeshiner out of public view. Car hijackings are a serious danger, especially at night—lock your doors and keep your windows rolled up. For more information about general safety, see **Safety and Security,** p. 15.

Women generally face a higher risk of attack. The famous Mexican *machismo* usually involves insistent stares, provocative smiles, whistling, cat-calling, and vulgar propositions. Light-colored hair or skin are lightening rods for unwanted attention. These displays are usually more annoying than dangerous, and it's best to ignore them. To avoid unwanted attention, dress conservatively and try not to wear shorts, tank tops, or short skirts. For more advice, see **Women Travelers,** p. 36.

WHEN THE RAIN COMES... If you visit the capital during the summer, keep a light poncho or umbrella handy. The rainy season (May-Oct.) brings daily 1-2hr. rain storms in the late afternoon or early evening. Otherwise, sunny and moderate weather prevails year-round.

Travellers to Mexico City should also consider protective measures against pollution. The city once known as *la región más transparente del aire* (the region with the clearest air) is now the most polluted in the world, and its layer of smog can cause problems for contact lens-wearers, those with allergies, the elderly, and small children. Travelers may want to bring eye drops or throat spray, and asthmatics would be wise to bring along an extra inhaler. Pollution is particularly bad during the winter, due to "thermal inversion," a phenomenon that occurs when warm air passing above the city traps the colder, polluted air in the Valley of Mexico. The summer rainy season, on the other hand, does wonders for air cleanliness, and from May to October the air is quite breathable. Newspapers and news programs often provide daily pollution indices.

🔀 PRACTICAL INFORMATION

TOURIST SERVICES

City Tourist Office: Infotur, Amberes 54 (☎5525 9380), at Londres in the Zona Rosa, M: Insurgentes (Line 1), with info booths around town. Helpful staff speaks English. Excellent city and Metro maps available on request. Lists hotels and restaurants grouped by region and price range, as well as upcoming events. Open daily 9am-7pm.

Tourist Card (FMT) Info: Secretaría de Gobernación, Dirección General de Servicios Migratorios, Homero 1832 (☎5626 7200), in Col. Palanco. Take the Metro to Chapultepec, and take a "Migración" *pesero* to the last stop to extend your FMT or clear up immigration problems. Arrive early to avoid long lines. Open M-F 9am-12:30pm.

Embassies: Visa processing can take up to 24hr. If you find yourself in an emergency after hours, call anyway—recorded messages provide important information.

Australia, Rubén Darío 55 (☎5531 5225; www.dfat.gov.au/missions/countries/mx.html), at Campos Eliseos in Col. Polanco. M: Auditorio (Line 7). Open M-Th 8:30am-5:15pm, F 8:30am-2:15pm.

Belize, Bernardo de Galvez 215 (☎5520 1274; www.belize.gov.bz/diplomats.html), in Col. Lomas de Chapultepec. M: Observatorio (Line 1). Open M-F 9am-5pm.

Canada, Schiller 529 (☎5724 7900; www.canada.org.mx), in Col. Polanco. M: Polanco or Auditorio (Line 7). Open M-F 8:45am-5:15pm.

Costa Rica, Río Po 113 (☎5525 7764), between Río Lerma and Río Pánuco, behind the US Embassy. Open M-F 9am-5pm.

European Union, Reforma 1675 (☎5540 3345; www.delmex.cec.eu.int), in Col. Lomas de Chapultepec. M: Auditorio (Line 7). Open M-Th 7:30am-3pm, F 7:30am-1pm.

Guatemala, Explanada 1025 (☎5540 7520), in Col. Lomas de Chapultepec. M: Auditorio (Line 7). Open M-F 9am-1:30pm.

Honduras, Alfonso Reyes 220 (☎5211 5747; emhonmex@mail.internet.com.mx), between Saltillo and Ometusco in Col. Condesa. Open M-F 10am-2pm.

New Zealand, Lagrange 103, 10th fl. (☎5283 9460; kiwimexico@compuserve.com.mx). M: Polanco (Line 7). Open M-Th 8:30am-2pm and 3-5:30pm, F 8:30am-2pm.

UK, Río Lerma 71 (☎5207 2089; www.embajadabritanica.com.mx), M: Sevilla (Line 1). Open M-F 8:30am-3:30pm. Operators available 24hr.

US, Reforma 305 (☎5080 2000), at Glorieta Ángel de la Independencia. Open M-F 9am-5pm. Operators available 24hr.

FINANCIAL SERVICES

Currency Exchange: Exchange rates in the city are generally pretty good. Banks offer one exchange rate and usually charge commission. *Casas de cambio* keep longer hours, give better exchange rates, exchange non-US currencies, and sometimes stay open Su. Among those found in the *centro*, along Reforma, and in the Zona Rosa: **Casa de Cambio Tíber,** on Río Tíber at Papaloapan, one block from the Ángel (☎5514 2760; open M-F 8:30am-5pm, Sa 8:30am-2pm); **Casa de Cambio Plus,** Juárez 38, on the south side of the Alameda (☎5510 8953; open M-F 9am-4pm, Sa 10am-2pm); **Casa de Cambio Catorce,** Reforma 51, 4th fl., near the Monumento a la Revolución/Buenavista and the Glorieta de Colón (open M-F 9am-4pm). Hotels often exchange currency too, but they offer the worst deals.

ATMs: Lost or stolen cards can be reported 24hr. (☎5227 2777). **Citibank,** Reforma 390 (☎5258 3200 or 5227 2727), can also help in an emergency.

American Express: Reforma 350 (☎5207 7282 or 5208 6004), in the Torre del Ángel, at Lancaster and the Glorieta del Ángel, in the Zona Rosa. Cashes personal and traveler's checks and accepts customers' mail and money wires. Report lost credit cards and lost traveler's checks to either office. Open M-F 9am-6pm, Sa 9am-1pm.

LOCAL SERVICES

English Bookstores: Global Books, Gante 4-A (☎5510 9362; www.global-book.com.mx), off Madero. English text books as well as dictionaries and reading material. Open M-Sa 10am-7pm. **Pórtico de la Ciudad de México,** Central 124 (☎5510 9683), at Carranza. English and Spanish books on Mexican history and archaeological sites. Open M-F 10am-7pm, Sa 10am-5pm. Also popular is **Librería Gandhi** (☎5510 4231), on Juárez along the Alameda. Open Su 11am-8pm, M-Sa 10am-9pm. Another at M: M.A. de Quevedo 128 (☎5661 0911) in San Ángel.

English-Language Library: Biblioteca Benjamín Franklin, Londres 16 (☎5080 2000, ext. 4089; www.usembassy-mexico.gov/biblioteca.htm), at Berlín, 2 blocks southeast of the Cuauhtémoc monument. Books, newspapers, and periodicals. You must be 18 years old to enter. Open M-F 10am-6pm.

Cultural and Arts Info: Palacio Nacional de Bellas Artes (☎5521 9251, ext. 152 and 159), Juárez and Eje Central. Open Su 9am-7pm, M-Sa 11am-7pm. Check *Tiempo Libre* for city-wide listings.

Gay, Lesbian, and Bisexual Information: Perhaps the best way to find out what's going on in the gay community is through the grapevine. *Tiempo Libre* and the smaller *Ser Gay* (available in gay clubs) provide a little info on gay social and political events along with the nightlife listings. *Ser Gay's* (www.sergay.com.mx) website contains a wealth of information on gay rights issues, gay-friendly businesses, and medical professionals. **Colectivo Sol** has info on upcoming political and social events. Write to: Apdo. 13-320, Av. México 13, D.F. 03500. **LesVoz** (☎5399 6019; www.lesvoz.org.mx), the literary and political journal for feminist lesbian and bisexual women, tries to be a springboard for community development. Open M-Th 9am-1pm.

Women's Advocacy: Organización Nacional Pro-Derechos Humanos de las Mujeres y las Lesbianas (☎5399 6019; proml@laneta.apc.org), gives free legal advice and support to women in cases of sexual discrimination or harassment. Open M-Th 8am-1pm.

LOCATEL: (☎5658 1111). The city's official hotline for missing persons and cars.

Supermarkets: Higher prices than *mercados*, but lower than corner stores. Most are far from the *centro*, at residential Metro stops. **Mega,** on the way to Tlatelolco from M: Tlatelolco (Line 3). Take the González exit, turn right on González, and walk 3 blocks; it's at the intersection with Cárdenas. Open daily 8am-10pm. **Superama,** Río Sena and Balsas, in the Zona Rosa, directly outside M: Polanco (Line 7). Open daily 8am-9pm.

Information: ☎040.

EMERGENCY

Emergency: ☎060 or 080.

Police: Secretaría de Seguridada Pública (☎5242 5100; ext. 5010, 5266, and 5418). **Protección Civil** (☎5683 1154 or 5683 1142).

Tourist Police: Seguridad y Información Turística (☎5535 4021), the tourist unit of the metropolitan police, often patrolling the Zona Rosa. English spoken. **Patrullas de Auxilio Turístico** (☎5250 8221 or 5250 0123), is an auto service for tourists that deals primarily with accidents, break-downs, and thefts. Little English spoken. **Procuradura General de Justicia,** Florencia 20 (☎5625 7692 or 061), in the Zona Rosa, is a department of justice catering especially to tourists. File reports on anything—minor robberies, major abuses of power, lost or stolen tourist cards. Some English spoken. Open 24hr.

Emergency Shelter: Casa de Asistencia Social (☎5744 8128 for women, 5530 4762 for men), on Calle Santanita in Col. Viaducto Pietá, near the treasury building.

Rape Crisis: Hospital de Traumatología de Balbuena, Cecilio Robelo 103 (☎5552 1602 or 5764 0339), M: Moctezuma (Line 1). Or dial ☎060.

Legal Advice: Supervisión General de Servicios a la Comunidad, Fray Servando 32 (☎5625 7208 or 5625 7184), M: Isabel la Católica (Line 1). South of the *centro* on José María Izagaza, 2 blocks south of the Metro stop. Call if you are the victim of a robbery or accident and need legal advice. Little English spoken. Open daily 9am-9pm.

Sexually Transmitted Disease and Innoculation Information: Secretaría de Salud, Benjamín Gil 14 (☎5277 6311), in Col. Condesa. M: Juanacatlán (Line 1). Open M-F 8am-7pm, Sa 9am-2pm.

AIDS Hotline: TELSIDA/CONASIDA, Florencia 8 Calzada de Tlalpan, 2nd fl. (☎5207 4143 or 5207 4077), at Col. Torielo Guerra. From M: General Anaya (Line 2) take a *micro* headed for "Zona de Hospitales." General help center. AIDS tests, prevention info available. Open M-F 9am-9:30pm.

Red Cross: Ejército Nacional 1032 (☎5557 5757), in Col. Polanco.

Pharmacies: Small *farmacias* abound on almost every street corner. In addition, all **Sanborn's** and supermarkets have well-stocked pharmacies.

Medical Care: The **US Embassy** (see p. 99) has a list of doctors' addresses and phone numbers. In an emergency, ask for the nearest **IMSS** (Social Security) clinic; there is usually one in each *colonia*.

Dirección General de Servicios Médicos (☎5518 5100) has information on all city hospitals. Open M-F 9am-5pm.

American British Cowdray (ABC) Hospital, Calle Sur 136 (☎5230 8000; for emergencies call 5230 8161), at Observatorio Col. Expensive but trustworthy. No foreign health plans. Major credit cards accepted. Open 24hr.

Torre Médica, José María Iglesias 21 (☎5705 2577 or 5705 1820), at Mariscal, has a few doctors who speak English. M: Revolución (Line 2).

COMMUNICATIONS

It is easy to find **fax** services in Mexico City, and **Internet terminals** abound in corner stores and improvised cybercafes.

Courier Services: UPS, Reforma 404 (☎5228 7900. Open M-F 8am-8pm). **Federal Express,** Reforma 308, in Col. Juárez near the Glorieta Ángel de Independencia. (☎5551 0996. Open M-F 8am-7pm, Sa 9am-1:30pm.)

Central Post Office: (☎5521 7394). On Lázaro Cárdenas at Tacuba, across from the Palacio de Bellas Artes. Open for stamps and *lista de correos* (window 3) Su 9am-noon, M-F 8am-6pm, Sa 9am-4pm. **Mexpost** inside. Open M-F 9am-4pm, Sa 9am-2pm. Postal museum upstairs with turn-of-the-century mailboxes and other old-school gear. Open Su 8am-4pm, M-F 8am-10pm, Sa 8am-8pm. **Postal Code:** 06002.

MEXICO CITY PUBLICATIONS

Tiempo Libre: The best resource for getting down and dirty in the city. Available at most corner newsstands. Covers movies, galleries, restaurants, performances, museums, and most cultural events. Every Th. 7 pesos. www.tiempolibre.com.mx

El M (the Metro): An informative and professional newspaper featuring both national and international news. Available at most Metro stops. Pick one up early—they tend to go fast. Free.

La Jornada: A top national paper, with news and event listings. 6 pesos.

Ser Gay: Available at most gay bars. Contains a complete listing of gay and lesbian nightlife options.

⌐ ACCOMMODATIONS

Mexico City offers over 1000 hotels; rooms abound in the *centro histórico* and near the Alameda Central. The best budget bargains are near the Monumento a la Revolución on Plaza de la República. Avoid the filthier sections around the Alameda and anywhere that makes you feel uncomfortable. Beware of any hotel marked "Hotel Garage," where clientele enter rooms directly from the garage for illicit rendezvous. Rooms for 100-150 pesos for one bed and 150-200 pesos for two beds should be clean and have carpeting, a TV, and a telephone. Some budget hotels charge according to the number of beds, not per person, and beds tend to be large enough for two. If you don't mind snuggling (or need an excuse), sharing a bed can save major pesos. Finally, always ask to look at a room before you accept it; this is easier to do after check-out time (noon-3pm).

The shabby neighborhoods by the four bus stations generally offer expensive rooms. If you arrive late at night, it is not safe to walk even the few blocks to your hotel. Both the **TAPO** and **Poniente** stations are in especially unsafe neighborhoods. If you arrive at either, take the Metro or a taxi to safer accommodations.

CENTRO HISTÓRICO

The accommodations in the *centro histórico* come in all shapes and sizes: busy hostels filled with international youth, tranquil hotels in historic buildings, and ritzier modernized hotels. Best of all, you're right in the *centro* of things, with many of the city's most spectacular sights within walking distance. Although the quiet of the streets at night is a huge change from the bustle of the day, nighttime activity is on the rise, and the government has been improving safety conditions at night as well as cleaning up the city. **Metro: Zócalo** (Line 2). Also **Isabel la Católica** (Line 1), **Bellas Artes** (Lines 2, 8), and **Allende** (Line 2).

■ **Hostel Catedral (HI),** Guatemala 4 (☎5518 1726 or 5518 1065; www.hostelcate-dral.com), behind the cathedral. The place to be for young internationals. Guests snack at the bar in the spacious lobby or surf the web (20 pesos per hr.). Shared kitchen, washing machine (20 pesos), pool table, and lockers (padlocks 20 pesos). Bulletin boards display ads for work, apartments, language lessons, and parties. Simple and clean dorms 120 pesos, 100 pesos for members; doubles 240 pesos. ❷

■ **Hostal Moneda,** Moneda 8 (☎5522 5821 or 800 221 7265; www.hostal-moneda.com.mx), between the Palacio Nacional and the Templo Mayor. Big kitchen, washing machine and dryer (35 pesos), Internet, elevator, TV room, lockers, rooftop bar and cafe, and a friendly, international vibe. Breakfast included. 5- and 6-bed dorms 100 pesos; 3- and 4-bed dorms 110 pesos; singles 180 pesos; doubles 480 pesos. ❷

Hotel Rioja, 5 de Mayo 45 (☎5521 8333, 5521 8273, or 5518 3852), three blocks from the *zócalo.* Clean, comfortable, cool, and in a great location. Singles 130-140 pesos, with windows 150-160 pesos; doubles 160-230/170-260 pesos. ❷

Hotel Isabel, Isabel la Católica 63 (☎5518 1213 or 5518 1214; http://come.to/mex-hotels), between Salvador and Uruguay. Old-Mexico atmosphere, atrium and outer courtyard, elevator, and large rooms with TV, phone, and safe. Many rooms have skyline views. Singles 115 pesos, with bath 180 pesos; doubles 130/230 pesos. Triples, quads, and quints, all with bath, 300/380/450 pesos. ❷

Hotel Juárez, 1a Callejón de 5 de Mayo 17 (☎5512 6929, 5512 0568, or 5518 4718), in an alley between Isabel la Católica and Palma. Hidden sign. Comfortable, quiet rooms with gleaming bathrooms, TV, and phone—but only half have windows. Singles 150 pesos; doubles 200 pesos; each additional person 50 pesos, four person max. ❸

Hotel Principal, Bolívar 29 (☎5521 1333, 5521 2032, or 5512 4382; www.hotelprin-cipal.com.mx), between 16 de Septiembre and Madero. Large, bright atrium and eleva-tor. Rooms are well-kept and tidy. Those without bath lack TV and phone; singles 100 pesos. Rooms with bath include TV and phone, though many have no windows; 1-5 peo-ple per room, prices range from 185-450 pesos. ❷

Hotel Catedral, Donceles 95 (☎5518 5232 or 5512 8581; www.hotelcatedral.com), behind the cathedral. Luxury hotel. Elegant bar and restaurant, rooftop terrace, eleva-tors, rooms with phone, cable TV, bath, and balconies. Singles 340-410 pesos; doubles for 2-4 people 485-585 pesos; triples 635 pesos; each additional person 70 pesos. ❺

Hotel Ritz, Madero 30 (☎5518 1340). Newly renovated and with excellent service and attention. This hotel may not be related to the famous chain, but it will certainly take good care of you. Rooms are huge and all have large windows with views of the city. 2 breakfasts included; doubles 550 pesos. ❺

Hotel Washington, 5 de Mayo 54 (☎5512 3502, 5521 1143, or 5518 4929). All rooms have bath, telephone, and complimentary bottled water. Singles 160-180 pesos; doubles 210-250 pesos. ❸

THE ALAMEDA

There may be more and better offerings in the *centro*, but that does not mean that there is nowhere to stay in the Alameda. The area is really being cleaned up, but as with most places in D.F., remember to be careful at night. **Metro: Balderas** (Line 1), **Salto del Agua** (Line 8), and **San Juan de Letrán** (Line 8).

Hotel Avenida, Eje Lázaro Cárdenas 38 (☎5518 1007, 5518 1008, or 5518 1009), right down the street from Bellas Artes and the Torre Latinoamericana. The entrance looks dingy, but inside it is clean and secure. On a busy street, so safe at night, if a little noisy. Great central location. Singles 170-180 pesos; doubles 220-270 pesos. ❸

MEXICO CITY

Hotel Manolo I, Moya 111 (☎5521 3739, 5521 7709, or 5521 7749), near Arcos de Belén. A little out of the way, but definitely a good choice. The hotel is a burst of color off dingy streets. Elevator, clean rooms with king-size bed, phone, TV, and large bath. All rooms (2 person max.) 190 pesos. ❸

Hotel Calvin, José Azueta 33 (☎5521 7952 or 5521 1361; fax 5512 4828), on the corner of Independencia. Just 50 meters from the Alameda Central with room service, TV, and telephone in each room. Singles 150-160 pesos; doubles 230-250 pesos, with jacuzzi 250 pesos; jacuzzi suites 330 pesos. ❸

Hotel Marlowe, Independencia 17 (☎5521 9540; www.hotelmarlowe.com). This ritzy hotel is right by the Alameda. Singles 339-394 pesos; doubles 433 pesos; triples 494-566 pesos. 90 pesos for each additional person. ❺

NEAR THE MONUMENTO A LA REVOLUCIÓN

Hotels near the Monumento a la Revolución are quieter than their counterparts in the *centro* or the Alameda. It is easy to find a cheap, nice room and, although the area itself does not offer much to do, the location—right between the Alameda and the Zona Rosa—is tops. **Metro: Revolución** (Line 2).

◪ **Casa de los Amigos,** Mariscal 132 (☎5705 0521 or 5705 0646). Once the home of painter José Clemente Orozco, the Casa now houses backpackers, grad students, and eco-warriors from all over the world. The 4-day minimum stay seeks to promote involvement and understanding. Library, lounge, kitchen, and laundry. Quiet hours 10pm-8am. No drugs or alcohol. If you're not a volunteer in one of the Casa's community service projects (or at the Casa itself) they ask that you not stay for more than 3 weeks, unless you're studying in Mexico. Breakfast 20 pesos. Dorms 80 pesos; singles 100-200 pesos; doubles 180-250 pesos. ❶

Hotel Oxford, Mariscal 67 (☎5566 0500), next to the small park behind the Museo San Carlos. Large, comfortable rooms have TV, phone, and views of the park. At night, the adjoining bar attracts a lively local crowd. Singles 100 pesos; doubles 150 pesos; rooms with king-sized bed 130 pesos. 50 pesos for each additional person. ❷

Hotel Ibiza, Arriaga 22 (☎5566 8155), between Edison and Mariscal. Has an elevator and rooms with small bath, phone, and TV. Singles 130 pesos; doubles 160 pesos. ❷

NEAR THE ZONA ROSA

The few budget rooms in the glamour district should be reserved far in advance.

Hostal las Dos Fridas, Hamburgo 301 (☎5286 3849 or 5286 3857; www.2fridashostel.com), between Toledo and Burdeos; turn right on Toledo as you exit M: Sevilla (Line 1), then go left on Hamburgo. Shared luxuries include cable TV, VCR, washer/dryer (40 pesos per load), kitchen, and Internet (10 pesos per 30min.). No drugs or alcohol; smoking only in central hall. Shared rooms 120 pesos; singles 250 pesos; doubles 340 pesos. Breakfast included. 5% ISIC discount. ❷

Hotel Saratoga, Álvaro Obregón 38 (☎5147 8233), M: Insurgentes (Line 1). Not actually in the Zona Rosa, but in Roma, about a 15min. walk from the action. Compact but comfortable rooms with cable TV, phone, clean private bath, and room service from the adjoining restaurant. Singles 200 pesos; doubles 280 pesos. ❹

Hostel Home (HI), Tabasco 303 (☎5511 1683; www.hostelhome.com.mx), between Valladolid and Medellín. From M: Insurgentes, take Insurgentes Sur and turn right on Tabasco; from M: Sevilla, walk down Salamanca and turn left on Tabasco. 10min. walk from the Zona Rosa. Shared TV room and kitchen, plus 6- and 8-bed bunk rooms. 80 pesos, 70 pesos for HI members. ❶

▣ FOOD

Options for meals fall into six basic categories: very cheap (and sometimes risky) vendor stalls scattered about the streets; fast, inexpensive, and generally safe *taquerías*; slightly more formal *cafeterías*; more pricey and decorous Mexican restaurants; locally popular US-style eateries; and expensive international fare. In addition, US fast-food chains mass-produce predictable fare for the timid palate. **VIPs** and **Sanborn's**, popular with middle-class Mexicans, run hundreds of restaurants throughout the capital. Vegetarians will have more to eat here than anywhere else in Mexico; the bright orange chain **Super Soya** has soy versions of all your Mexican and US fast-food favorites. For fresh produce and meats, try **La Merced** (see p. 135), the mother of all markets.

15 PESOS AND UNDER (❶)	
El Tigre (107)	A
El Jarocoho (108)	CO
La Finca Café Solo Dios (108)	SA

16-25 PESOS (❷)	
Café el Popular (105)	CH
▨ La Especial de París (106)	R
Super Cocina los Arcos (106)	R
▨ Saint Moritz (107)	ZR
Vegetariano (107)	CH
VegeTaco (108)	CO
La Mora (108)	SA

26-40 PESOS (❸)	
Restaurantes Vegetarianos del Centro (105)	CH
Los Alcatraces (105)	CH
Comedor Vegetariano (106)	CH
▨ El Moro (106)	A

26-40 PESOS (❸), CONT'D	
Centro Naturista (106)	A
El Mesón de la Huerta (107)	ZR
Las Fuentes (107)	ZR

41-60 PESOS (❹)	
▨ Café Tacuba (105)	CH
▨ Fonda Santa Anita (106)	A
Oriental (106)	A
Vegetariano Yug (107)	ZR
Coffee House (107)	ZR
Los Murales (107)	ZR
▨ El Kioskito (107)	CH
El Guarache (108)	CO
Café el Pernaso (108)	CO

OVER 60 PESOS (❺)	
Rinconada (106)	CH
Café del Bosque (107)	CH

CENTRO HISTÓRICO

The *centro*'s restaurants serve traditional Mexican food. Locals offset throngs of tourists, keeping prices lower than in Zona Rosa but not as low as near Revolución. After the Zona Rosa, this is the best place for vegetarian fare. **Metro: Zócalo** (Line 2), **Bellas Artes** (Lines 2, 8), **Allende** (Line 2), and **Isabel la Católica** (Line 1).

▨ **Café Tacuba,** Tacuba 28 (☎ 5518 4950), a block from Bellas Artes. Vaulted ceiling, stained glass, *azulejo* tiles—the gorgeous interior complements this restaurant's storied history (numerous wedding feasts including Diego Rivera's; Anthony Quinn movie buffs may recognize it as well) and well-prepared Mexican dishes. Menu in English and Spanish. *Antojitos* 22-69 pesos, entrees 54-198 pesos. Open daily 8am-11:30pm. ❹

Restaurantes Vegetarianos del Centro, Madero 56 (☎ 5521 6880), upstairs, 1½ blocks from the *zócalo*. Another at Mata 13 (☎ 5510 0113), between 5 de Mayo and Madero. Three locations lie to the south and in Colonia Roma. This all-vegetarian restaurant's large menu has meatless takes on traditional Mexcan dishes. Salads 40-60 pesos, other dishes around 30 pesos. Open daily 8am-8pm. ❸

Café El Popular, 5 de Mayo 52, (☎ 5518 6081) close to the *zócalo*. This small cafe is not only popular, but inexpensive and always open. *Comida corrida* 33 pesos, other options 11-46 pesos. Open 24 hr. ❷

Los Alcatraces, Madero 42 (☎ 5521 0807), between Isabel La Católica and Motolinía. This cafe is one of few with outside seating, which is in an old church courtyard. A pleasant, peaceful escape. Breakfast 25-40 pesos. *Comida corrida* 35 or 45 pesos. ❸

Rinconada, Rinconada de Jesus 13 (☎5542 6809 or 5542 3245), across the street from the Museo de la Ciudad de México. In the courtyard of a beautiful stone building built in 1535 and restored in 1969, this oasis provides a welcome respite from the heat and the busy *zócalo*. Specials 50-105 pesos. The friendly staff will help transform some dishes into meatless fare. Open M-Sa 12-7pm. ⑤

Comedor Vegetariano, Motolinía 31 (☎5512 6515), upstairs, between Madero and 6 de Septiembre. Five-course *comida corrida*-only menu (35 pesos, 32 pesos for seniors) features a changing selection of original vegetarian variations on Mexican staples. Staff is friendly and helpful. Open daily 1-6pm. ❸

THE ALAMEDA

Restaurants are not as abundant as in the *centro*, but there are a few gems. For Chinese, go down to Dolores and Independencia. Some restaurants there have better vegetarian options, and some have better deals. The **Parque Alameda,** Juárez 75, next door to the Sheraton Centro Histórico, is a shopping center that has several restaurants as well. **Metro: Hidalgo** (Line 2), **Bellas Artes** (Lines 2 and 8), **Juárez** (Line 3), and **San Juan de Letrán** (Line 8).

▨ **Fonda Santa Anita,** Humboldt 48 (☎5518 4609 or 5518 5723). M: Juárez (Line 3). Walk down Balderas away from the Alameda. Head right on Artículo 120, turn right on Humboldt, and continue half a block. The restaurant has represented Mexico in five World's Fairs and has incredible versions of old favorites from all over the country. At least one vegetarian option every day. Go between 2-4pm and be serenaded with traditional Mexican songs on the harp and guitar. *Comida corrida* 45 pesos, specials 65 pesos. Open daily 10am-7pm. ❹

▨ **El Moro,** Cárdenas 42 (☎5512 0896 or 5518 4580). M: San Juan de Letrán (Line 3). Indulge in Mexican tradition and finish your night with conversation over chocolate and *churros*. Delicious chocolate available in *mexicano* (light), *español* (thick and sweet), *francés* (medium thickness and sweetness), and *especial* (slightly bitter). Each cup comes with 4 freshly-made cinnamon-sugary pastry strips (30-33 pesos). Open 24hr. ❸

Centro Naturista, Dolores 10 (☎5512 0190), between Juárez and Independencia behind a new age store. Locals and tourists pack this place before 3pm, when the food is freshest. *Comida corrida* with 1, 2, or 3 *guisados* (dishes; 28, 31, and 35 pesos). Vegetarian variations of traditional Mexican dishes. The café de trigo (wheat coffee) might not be for everyone. ❸

Oriental (☎5521 3099), at Dolores and Independencia, with other Chinese options; the myriad restauraunt advertisers will point the way. The prices here are slightly lower (*comida corrida* 45 pesos) and there's a huge bronze Buddha at the entrance. Open daily 10am-11pm. ❹

NEAR THE MONUMENTO A LA REVOLUCIÓN

Without many affluent residents or big tourist draws, this area lacks the snazzy international cuisine of other areas. Instead, homey cafes, *torterías*, and *taquerías* dominate the scene. For hearty portions and low prices, this is the spot. **Metro: Revolución** (Line 2).

▨ **La Especial de París,** Insurgentes Centro 117 (☎5703 2316). This *nievería* (ice cream place) has been in the same family since it started scooping frozen wonders in 1921. 100% natural ingredients, from *malteadas* (milkshakes; 24 pesos) to the delicious crepes (22-25 pesos). Double scoop 22 pesos, triple scoop 30 pesos, quadruple scoop 36 pesos. Open daily 11am-9pm. ❷

Super Cocina los Arcos, Ignacio Mariscal at Iglesias. Delicious food and quick service recommend this small cafeteria. *Comida corrida* 17 pesos. Most dishes 12-30 pesos. Open M-Sa 7am-10pm. ❷

El Tigre, at Mariscal and Iglesias, is home of the formidable *Super Torta Gigante*. The friendly guys behind the counter will make you a big, big *torta* (13 pesos), such as the *española*, with ham, *chorizo* (spicy sausage), and cheese; or the *milchory*, with *chorizo*, cheese, and *milanesa* (breaded steak). Open daily 8:30am-10pm. ❶

ZONA ROSA

A hipster scene, good coffee, and great vegetarian cuisine—all less expensive than expected. Rock-bottom-cheap cafeterias and *taquerías* cater to the budget-conscious. **Metro: Insurgentes** (Line 1) and **Sevilla** (Line 1).

▥ **Saint Moritz,** Genova 44, in an alleyway, next to Java Chat. Cheap, basic lunch in a clean, spartan cafeteria. *Comida corrida* 20 pesos. Open M-Sa 1-4:30pm. ❷

El Mesón de la Huerta, Río Pánuco 137 (☎5511 4891), between Río Ebro and Río Guadalquivir. Cheerful, bright-yellow decor and solid vegetarian cuisine attract crowds of office workers, especially 12:30-3pm, when the lunch buffet (50 pesos) is tastiest. Open M-F 8:30am-noon (breakfast 25 pesos) and 12:30-6pm (buffet only). ❸

Vegetariano Yug, Varsovia 3 (☎5533 3296 or 5525 5330; www.yug.com.mx), between Reforma and Dresde, with a cafeteria in the Roma neighborhood. Tasteful decor and creative, "international" vegetable dishes. *Comida corrida* 42-49 pesos. Lunch buffet upstairs 53 pesos (1-5pm). Open Su 1-8pm, M-F 7am-10:15pm, Sa 8:30am-8pm. ❹

Coffee House, Londres 102 (☎5525 4034), between Niza and Génova. In a city where most restaurants serve instant coffee, a real latte (19 pesos) can be a life-saver. Good sandwiches (37-54 pesos; includes a meatless option), pastries (14-34 pesos), and people-watching (free). Open daily 8am-9pm. ❹

Las Fuentes, Río Pánuco 127 (☎5207 6414 or 5525 7095) at Río Tíber, 3 blocks from the Ángel de Independencia. Relaxing atmosphere, great variety of vegetarian dishes, and a fab brew that garnered praise from the Mexican Institute of Coffee. Breakfast 48 pesos, *comida corrida* 79 pesos, a la carte 20-45 pesos. Open daily 8am-6pm. ❸

Los Murales, Liverpool 152 (☎5726 9911, ask for the restaurant), at Amberes, on the ground floor of the Hotel Century. Veggie buffet (69 pesos, M-F 1:30-5pm), sandwiches (48-61 pesos), and other dishes (50-135 pesos). Menu in English and Spanish. Open daily 7am-11pm. ❹

NEAR CHAPULTEPEC

Inside the Bosque de Chapultepec, sidewalk stands offer an enormous variety of snacks, but these are always risky for a foreign stomach. The small restaurants cluttered around **M: Chapultepec** (Line 1) are a safer alternative. For the ritzier tastes, get *antojitos* in beautiful Colonia Polanco, north of the Museo de Antropología and accessible by **M: Polanco** and **M: Auditorio** (both Line 7).

▥ **El Kioskito** (☎5553 3055; kioskito@mexico.com), on Chapultepec at the corner with Sonora, serves succulent entrees (50-60 pesos) in a classy, relaxed atmosphere with a tiled fountain and old city photos. You can also eat at the adjoining taco counter (6-7 pesos each). Open daily 8am-9pm. ❹

Vegetariano, Veracruz 3 (☎5286 8827), at Acapulco, facing M: Chapultepec. One of the few places offering both meat and vegetarian dishes—the staff is happy to point out what's what. Try the soup. *Comida corrida* 26 pesos. Open daily 10am-8pm. ❷

Café del Bosque, at Chapultepec Margen Oriente del Lago Menor, the second section of the park (☎5515 4652 or 5516 4214; www.cafedelbosque.com.mx). Eat, drink, and be merry as you watch the majestic swans (well, large white geese) in the lake that borders this classy steak house. The only restaurant in the lower-key second section of the park. Pasta 55 pesos, steaks 125-299 pesos. ❺

MEXICO CITY

COYOACÁN

If you crave great coffee, cheesecake, or pesto, spend an afternoon in one of the outdoor cafes or *taquerías* that line the cobbled streets of Coyoacán. For excellent, inexpensive meals, try the **indoor food market** on Hijuera, just south of Plaza Hidalgo. Heavily frequented by locals, these tiny restaurants serve home-cooked food at delicious prices. (Open M-Sa 9am-9pm.) **Metro: Coyoacán** (Line 3).

El Guarache (☎ 5554 4506), by the Jardín Centenario. Bask in the beauty of the nearby coyote fountain from a *jardín*-side table at this classy cafe. *Comida corrida* (M-F only) 40 pesos, entrees 50-70 pesos, *antojitos* 22-45 pesos. Open daily 9am-10pm. ❹

El Jarocho (☎ 5554 5418), on Allende and Cuauhtémoc. Follow the smell of freshly ground coffee to this legendary place. Straight from Veracruz, Jarocho has been serving some of the city's best java since 1953. Cappuccino, mocha, and hot chocolate 6-8 pesos each. Open daily 7am-midnight. ❶

VegeTaco, Carrillo Puerto 65 (☎ 5659 7517 or 5658 9311), past the other taco joints. Create a meal of vegetarian tacos (6 pesos each) or enjoy a combination *platillo* (33-59 pesos) from a wooden stool at the counter. Open daily 10am-8pm. ❷

Café el Parnaso, Carrillo Puerto 2 (☎ 5554 2225 or 5658 3195). A celebrated book and record store with an outdoor cafe, all on the edge of the Jardín Centerario. Though the food is a bit pricey, the people-watching and eavesdropping are unbeatable. Pastries 18-35 pesos, coffee 12-24 pesos. Open Su-Th 8am-midnight, F-Sa 8am-late. ❹

SAN ÁNGEL

Though some restaurants here are too hip (and too expensive) for their own good, quite a few homey establishments sell solid, reasonably priced food. Great lunch deals can be found in the very stylish Plaza Jacinto. **Metro: M. A. Quevedo** (Line 3).

La Mora, Madero 2 (☎ 5616 2080). Quaint views of the plaza from the upstairs dining room pair with traditional Mexican *comida corrida* (30 pesos). Open daily 8am-6pm. ❸

La Finca Café Solo Dios (☎ 5550 3302), on Madero right off Plaza San Jacinto. This hole-in-the-wall coffee stand only serves 100% Mexican-grown beans from Chiapas. Delicious hot mocha, espresso, and chocolate 8-14 pesos. Kilos of Chiapan coffee beans start at 60 pesos. Open daily 8:30am-8:30pm. ❶

◎ SIGHTS

Overflowing with history, culture, and entertainment, Mexico City truly has something for everyone. It is impossible to see everything, and on even the longest trip there always seems to be somewhere else to go. Most museums are closed on Mondays and are free on Sundays. Often students and teachers with a current ID can get in free or for a reduced fee; unfortunately, most archaeological sites and some major museums only offer these discounts to Mexican nationals. There is often a fee for those who wish to carry cameras or video cameras.

CENTRO HISTÓRICO

*To reach the centro histórico by Metro, take Line 2 to **M: Zócalo**. The station's exit is on the east side of the square, in front of Palacio Nacional. Catedral Metropolitana lies to the north, the Federal District offices to the south, and the Suprema Corte de Justicia (Supreme Court) to the southeast. Some sights south of the zócalo can be better accessed by **M: Isabel La Católica** (Line 1) or **M: Pino Suárez** (Line 2).*

Mexico City spans thousands of kilometers and thousands of years, but all comes together in the *centro*. On the city's main plaza, known as the **zócalo**, the Aztec **Templo Mayor,** the **Catedral Metropolitana,** and **Palacio Nacional** sit serenely side by side. The architecture fits the eclecticism of the people: there are street vendors hawking everything from hand-woven bags to batteries, AK-47-sporting soldiers, ever-present political protestors, homeless people, and hordes of picture-snapping tourists. The tourist masses don't even begin to compare to the number of Mexicans who pass through or work in this center of centers everyday. With so much culture and life, this is a great place to start your visit to Mexico City.

■ THE ZÓCALO

Officially known as Plaza de la Constitución, the *zócalo* is the principal square of Mexico City. Now surrounded by imposing colonial monuments, the plaza was once the nucleus of Tenochtitlán, the Aztec island-capital and the center of the entire Aztec empire. Southwest of the Templo Mayor—the Aztecs' principal place of worship (*Teocalli* in Náhuatl)—was the Aztec marketplace and major square. The space was rebuilt and renamed several times, becoming Plaza de la Constitución in 1812. Legend goes that the dictator Santa Anna ordered that a monument to Mexican independence be constructed in the center of the square. Only the monument's *zócalo* (pedestal) was in place when the project was abandoned. The citizens of Mexico City began to refer to the square as the *zócalo*, a term which has since become the generic name for the central plazas that mark most cities and towns in Mexico.

PALACIO NACIONAL. Stretching the entire length of the enormous *zócalo*, the Palacio Nacional occupies the spot of Moctezuma's palace; some of the ruins of the palace are on display inside, near the entrance of the Recinto de Homenaje a Benito Juárez. After Tenochtitlán fell in 1521, the King of Spain granted the land to Cortés, who constructed his own home here using stones from the original palace. In 1562, the King bought back the house from Martín Cortés, the illegitimate son of the *conquistador*, to build a palace for the royal viceroys. It was destroyed by a riotous mob in 1692 and rebuilt a year later with the same stones. In the 1930s, the building was restored and a third story added under the direction of architect Augusto Petriccioli. Today the *palacio* houses the headquarters of the president's administration and other federal bureaucracies. Stern security guards will keep you from going into the courtyard to the right of the entrance, where the most important executive business is conducted.

Over the *palacio* entrance is the **Bell of Dolores,** came to the capital in 1896 from the village of Dolores Hidalgo (see p. 350). Miguel Hidalgo rang this bell on the morning of September 16, 1810, summoning Mexicans to fight for independence. Every year on the 16th the bell is rung again as the president repeats Hidalgo's inspiring *Grito de Dolores* to a *zócalo* packed with enthusiastic lookers-on.

The *palacio's* biggest attractions are the **Diego Rivera murals** in the main staircase and along the western and northern walls. Rivera spent the years from 1929 to 1951 sketching and painting the frescoes *Mexico Through the Centuries*. The mural is divided into eight smaller scenes, each of which depicts an event in the social history of Mexico. On the east side of the *palacio's* second floor (turn left at the entrance) is the recently renovated and expanded **Museo del Recinto de Homenaje,** dedicated to revered Mexican president Benito Juárez. The museum occupies the room in which Juárez died and displays a collection of his personal artifacts, described in Spanish. Also interesting is the **Museo del Recinto Parlamentario,** on the second floor of the central courtyard, which displays political artifacts as well as the recently restored room where the constitutional congress met and where the parliament was housed from 1829 to 1872.

Don't leave the *palacio* without visiting the pleasant **gardens** at the back of the palace, straight ahead from the entrance. Immaculate landscaping highlights flowers and cacti from all over Mexico. *(On the east side of the zócalo. Open daily 9am-5pm.*

Free. Trade your ID for a turista badge at the entrance. Guided tour usually available M-F 10am-4pm, 60-70 pesos. Museo del Recinto de Homenaje and Museo del Recinto Parlamentario open Tu-F 9am-5pm, Sa-Su 10am-5pm. Free.)

■**CATEDRAL METROPOLITANA.** The first cathedral built in New Spain was the **Catedral Metropolitana.** The area was originally part of the main Aztec temple, but it was quickly replaced by a cathedral, begun by Cortés in 1524 and completed in 1532 by the famous bishop Juan de Zumárraga. In 1626, the cathedral was demolished and rebuilt. Construction projects continued off and on through the years until the building was finally completed in 1813.

The cathedral has a series of altars and *capillas* (chapels) throughout the interior. The **Altar de Perdón** (Altar of Forgiveness) and **Altar de los Reyes** (Altar of Kings) are decadently covered in gold and offset with beautiful paintings, including Juan Correa's murals of dragon-slaying and prophet-hailing on the sacristy walls. Lifelike statues of saints and important church figures can be found throughout the cathedral; the choir gallery and chapels honoring the Virgin of Guadalupe are worth a good look. Mass takes place almost hourly on weekends; at these times visitors are only allowed in the front of the cathedral and should take extra care to show respect and be silent.

The cathedral was built on especially soft soil, and sank lopsidedly into the ground at an even faster rate than the rest of Mexico City. Several years of work completed at the end of 2000 have ensured the building's integrity, secured by high-tension wires and green girders running the width of the ceiling, but the reconstruction is not finished. Note that unauthorized individuals will often try to sell tours outside the entrance, though volunteers guide free tours in Spanish and English (Sa 10:30am-1:30pm). Tours of the *coro* and *sacristia mayor* (chorus and primary sacristy; M-F 11am-2pm and 4-7pm, Sa 11am-1pm and 4-7pm), which are the most sacred areas of the cathedral, as well as tours of the *campanaria* (bell tower; M-Sa 8am-6pm, Su 9:30am-6pm), are available for 10 pesos, with a four person minimum. There are informative plaques inside for each of the altars, but they are all in Spanish. *(On the left side of the zócalo when facing the Palacio Nacional. ☎5510 0440, ext. 101. Information desk open daily 8am-4pm. No flash photography. Free.)*

■**TEMPLO MAYOR.** When Cortés defeated the Aztecs in 1521, one of the first things he did was to destroy the Aztec's main center of worship, the *Teocalli*. He took stones from the plaza and its main temple (the Templo Mayor) to build his magnificent cathedral across the street. The temple and surrounding plaza were eventually paved over and almost forgotten until 1978, when workers unearthed it while laying wires and piping for the Metro. From 1978-1982, the site was extensively excavated, revealing layers of pyramids and artifacts. Today, a catwalk leads through the outdoor ruins, which include the remnants of several pyramids and colonial structures. The tour makes for a surreal escape from the throbbing *zócalo*. One of the big highlights is the Great Pyramid, which houses the remains of a twin temple, dedicated to Tlaloc (god of rain) and Huitzilopochtli (god of war and patron of the Aztec), and a *chaac mol*. Legend has it that the temple sits on the exact spot where the Aztecs discovered Huitzilopochtli's predicted eagle perched on a cactus eating a snake.

At the back of the site, the **Museo del Templo Mayor** takes you on a tour through Aztec civilization. The museum is divided into eight rooms that are meant to imitate the layout of the original temple, and the artifacts found in the excavation are accompanied not only by dry museum inscriptions but also excerpts from the ancient Aztec texts that describe them (both in Spanish). The greatest treasure of the museum is the flat, round sculpture of **Coyolxauhqui,** goddess of the moon and mother of Huitzilopochtli. An English audio guide is worth every *centavo* if you don't read Spanish, but the Spanish version only repeats the detailed written information. *(On the corner of Seminario and República de Guatemala, between the cathedral and the Palacio Nacional. ☎5542 4943. Open Tu-Su 9am-5pm. 37 pesos; bring exact change. Audio guides in Spanish or English, 30 pesos.)*

SUPREMA CORTE DE JUSTICIA. Although some come for the bookstore full of thick Mexican law manuals, most visitors head to the Supreme Court to see the murals. The four murals painted by José Clemente Orozco in the 1940s cover the second-floor walls of the court, which was built in 1929 where the southern half of Moctezuma's royal palace once stood. The huge, patriotic murals depict death, destruction, anger, fear, and above all, strength. There are also murals by Andrés Sánchez Flores, in addition to newer additions by Hector Cruz García in honor of the millenium. *(On the corner of Pino Suárez and Corregidora. ☎5522 1500. M-F 8am-4:30pm. Bring an ID to leave at the entrance. Free.)*

MUSEO NACIONAL DE LAS CULTURAS. Originally built in 1731 by Spanish architect Juan Peinado to house the *Real Casa de la Moneda* (royal mint), the building was turned into an anthropology museum by order of Emperor Maximilian in 1865. In 1964, the vast collection of Pre-Hispanic artifacts was moved to Chapultepec and the museum was redesigned to promote understanding of different world cultures. The exhibits are colorful and well put together. This is a great place to introduce children to different cultures and their art. Near the entrance is a mural by Rufino Taymayo. *(Moneda 13, just behind the Palacio Nacional. ☎5521 1490, ext. 226. Open Tu-Su 9:30am-5:45pm. Free.)*

SOUTH OF THE ZÓCALO

MUSEO DE LA CHARRERÍA. As you pass through the rooms of this old monastery from 1589, plaques in Spanish, English, and French tell you about the lifestyles of the *charros*, Mexican cowboys, and the development of *charrería* (forerunner to the rodeo), Mexico's national sport. Spurs, saddles, and traditional costumes abound. The *Museo* is a fun place for kids as long as they aren't too disappointed that there are no horses. It also houses the Mexican Federation of Charrería. *(At Izagaza and Isabel la Católica, by M: Isabel la Católica (Line 1). Open M-F 11am-5pm. Free.)*

MUSEO DE LA CIUDAD DE MÉXICO. This museum, once the home of some distant cousins of Cortés, is still searching for its place in Mexico City's vast constellation of museums. With only a small permanent collection, the museum hosts a variety of different exhibits. The bookstore sells excellent information on the city and the rest of Mexico. *(Pino Suárez 30, 3 blocks south of the zócalo. ☎5542 0083. Open Tu-Su 10am-6pm. Free.)*

NO WORK, ALL PLAY

COWSPORTS

Although anyone who has tuned in to a soccer game in Mexico would think otherwise, the national sport of Mexico is, in fact, the *charrería*.

Colonial owners and servants found the day-to-day work of contending with undomesticated livestock grueling and discouraging. To make the experience a little more enjoyable, *charros*, or Mexican horsemen, adapted the equestrian contests brought by sixteenth-century *conquistadores*, incorporating a series of practices and techniques into everyday work which gave the process a little flair. Soon every festival featured contests for the *charros*, and even *corridas*, or bullfights, included the burgeoning *charrería* as filler entertainment.

This is no rodeo. The *charrería* is a ten-event trial in horsemanship and cattle wrangling. Difficult tasks focus on the bull: roping it, flipping it, even riding it. Perhaps none of the events is quite so trying as the final event, known as *el paso de la muerte*—literally, the passage of death—in which the rider must jump from a tame horse onto a wild mare and stay on her until she slows down.

Surprisingly, *charrería* is a team sport, with only one person per team competing in all events. Women compete in only one event: the *escaramuza*, or skirmish, in which eight women make synchronized patterns while riding horses, to the strains of music.

THE ALAMEDA

The Alameda is serviced by 4 Metro stations: **M: Bellas Artes** *(Lines 2, 8), at Hidalgo and Eje Lázaro Cárdenas;* **M: San Juan de Letrán** *(Line 8), a block from the Torre Latinoamericana;* **M: Juárez** *(Line 3), on Balderas 1 block from the park; and, in a less safe area,* **M: Hidalgo** *(Lines 2 and 3) at Hidalgo and Paseo de la Reforma.*

The museums, libraries, and historical buildings clustered around the Alameda are worthy of any cultural capital, and you'll face some tough time-budgeting decisions vis-à-vis the attractions and astounding sights in the *centro histórico*, Chapultepec, and elsewhere. Still, serious shoppers cannot afford to miss the best crafts market in the city, **La Ciudadela**. Chess addicts will be happy to find Mexico City's most popular chess park in the **Plaza de la Solidaridad**, on the steps near the Museo Mural (vendors usually rent sets). Best of all, the Alameda has been cleaned up, and emergency call buttons help make it much safer now.

ALAMEDA CENTRAL

Today's downtown was originally an Aztec marketplace and later the site where heretics were burned during the Inquisition. Don Luis de Velasco II created the park in 1592 for the recreation of the city's elite. Enlarged in 1769 to its current size, the park was repaired after the 1985 earthquake. The park takes its name from its rows of shady *álamos* (poplars). Vendors, lovers, and ornately sculpted fountains give the tranquil park just the right dose of activity.

At the center of the Alameda's southern side is the **Monumento a Juárez,** a semi-circular marble monument constructed in 1910 to honor the beloved president on the 100th anniversary of Mexican Independence. A somber-faced Benito Juárez, accompanied by the Angel of Independence and Lady Liberty, sits on a central pedestal among 12 doric columns. On July 19 of each year, a civic ceremony commemorates the anniversary of Juárez's death.

EAST OF THE ALAMEDA CENTRAL

■**PALACIO DE BELLAS ARTES.** The construction of this gorgeous Art Nouveau palace began in 1904 under the direction of the Italian architect Adamo Boari. However, work stopped nine years later due to the Revolution. In 1916, after completing only the building's exterior, Boari went back to Italy. Construction resumed in 1932, and the building was finally inaugurated in 1934. Architecture aside, most tourists come here to see the middle two floors, which are covered by the work of the most celebrated Mexican muralists of the 20th century. The best-known is a mural on the third floor by Diego Rivera. John D. Rockefeller commissioned Rivera to paint a mural depicting "Man at Crossroads, Looking with Hope and High Vision to the Choosing of a New and Better Future" for New York City's Rockefeller Center. However, Rivera was dismissed from the project when overseers discovered the Soviet flag and a portrait of Lenin in the foreground. The Mexican government asked Rivera to recreate the work here: the 1934 result was **"El Hombre, Controlador del Universo."** A Marxist vision of revolution, it shows a white man at the controls of a massive industrial apparatus. Not only did he keep the portrait of Lenin, but he added a degrading picture of Rockefeller.

Elsewhere on the third floor are murals by Roberto Montenegro, José Clemente Orozco, and David Álfaro Siqueiros, plus more by Diego Rivera. Descriptions of all the murals are written in Spanish on plaques. The second floor holds two Tamayo murals, as well as a temporary exhibit. On the top floor is the **Museo Nacional de Arquitectura** (☎5510 2853 ext. 203, 204, 217, and 300), showcasing temporary exhibits on the city's architecture.

The amazing ■**Ballet Folklórico de México** performs regional dances here as well. Their exciting and vivacious performances combine *indígena* dancing with more formal aspects of traditional ballet. Many concerts, mostly orchestral works, also occur here. Attending a Bellas Artes performance is the only way to see the **Tiffany crystal curtain,** which weighs 21,228kg and depicts the volcanoes Popocatépetl and Ixtaccíhuatl. The **ticket office** sells tickets for these and other performances throughout the city. An **information booth,** up the stairs next to the ticket booth, has information on these performances. Travel agencies snatch up many tickets during Christmas, *Semana Santa,* and the summer; check first at Bellas Artes, then try along Reforma or in the Zona Rosa. *(Juárez and Eje Central, by the park. ☎5512 2593 or 5521 9251 ext. 152, 153, and 154. Open Tu-Su 10am-6pm. Ticket booth open Su 10am-7pm, M-Sa 11am-7pm; information booth open daily 9am-9pm. 30 pesos for murals and art exhibits on the upper floors; children under 12, students, and teachers free. Dance performances and concerts at various times throughout the week. No children under 5, no shorts or sport clothing. Tickets 100-400 pesos depending on the event and seating. Some English spoken.)*

◼ MUSEO NACIONAL DE ARTE. Opened in 1982 and thoroughly renovated and expanded in 2000, the museum houses the city's (and perhaps the world's) most comprehensive collection of Mexican fine arts. Paintings and sculptures dating from 1550 through 1954 are organized chronologically and carefully explained in Spanish. A number of *salas de orientación* have fun hands-on multimedia displays on how art is made, displayed, and interpreted. The elegant building was originally built during the Porfiriato to house the Secretary of Communications. The architect, Silvio Conti, took particular care with the central staircase; its Baroque handrails were crafted by artists in Florence. In front of the museum is the famous equestrian statue of Carlos IV of Spain, El Caballito, sculpted by Manuel Tolsá. A plaque explains, "Mexico preserves it as a monument of art"—and not in honor of the king. *(Tacuba 8, half a block from Bellas Artes. ☎5130 3460. Open Tu-Su 10:30am-5:30pm. Free tours at noon and 2pm. 30 pesos; students, teachers, children under 13, and those with disabilities free; Su free.)*

CASA DE LOS AZULEJOS. Built in the 1500s and originally called the Blue Palace, over the next century the exterior and much of the interior were covered with gorgeous (and expensive) *azulejos* (blue and white tiles). According to legend, the son of the Count of Orizaba ordered the redecoration in order to impress his father, who had told him he'd never amount to much. The Sanborn's restaurant chain now occupies the building, and the dining area, in the courtyard, is a great place to eat. You can view the interior for free from the upstairs balcony by ascending the staircase in the main dining room or taking the elevator in the gift shop; don't miss the Orozco mural by the staircase. *(Madero 4, the only tile-covered building in the* centro. *Sanborn's ☎5512 1331. Open daily 7am-1am.)*

THE MURALISTS. During World War I, a new artistic movement flourished, continuing into the 1960s and earning acclaim worldwide. The movement was dominated by three men: **Diego Rivera, José Clemente Orozco,** and **David Alfaro Siqueiros.** Though each had a distinct technique, they shared common aspirations, embracing the new spirit of nationalism and populism encouraged by the Constitution of 1917. They worked during the time of liberation just after the suffocating regime of Porfirio Díaz and received government commissions to decorate public buildings with themes that glorified the Revolution and Pre-Hispanic history of Mexico. The principal messages of the murals were easily understood by any Mexican: that Europeans had strangled the art of Mexico. The artists returned to *indígena* themes, shunning the elaborate decorations of colonialism and exaltations of the church. With their grand scope of expression, the murals soon became the silent voice of the Mexican people.

TORRE LATINOAMERICANA. At 182m and 44 stories high, the Torre is one of the tallest buildings in the city. The tower's top-floor observatory commands a startling view of the sprawling city. At night, the view is positively sexy, with city lights sparkling for miles in every direction. Completed in 1956, this was Mexico City's first quake-resistant building taller than 40 stories. In 1957, the tower successfully survived a minor earthquake. The *torre* repeated its performance in the far more devastating quake of 1985, swaying rather than breaking apart. *(Lázaro Cárdenas and Madero. Observatory open daily 9:30am-10pm. 40 pesos, children 30 pesos.)*

TEMPLO DE SAN FRANCISCO. Built in 1525, only four years after the fall of Tenochtitlán, the temple was the first church in the Americas. Soon after construction ended, Cortés himself visited the vast Franciscan complex, which included several churches, a school, and a hospital. In 1838, the church hosted the funeral of Emperor Iturbide. After extensive remodeling in 1716, only the temple and the *capilla* (chapel) remain. *(Madero 7, near the Torre Latinoamericana. Office open M-F 9am-1pm and 5-7pm, Sa 9am-1pm.)*

PALACIO ITURBIDE. Built in 1780, the grand *palacio* is best known as the home of Mexico's short-lived first Emperor, Agustín Iturbide. The Fomento Cultural Banamex, with its beautiful temporary exhibits on Mexican history, now occupies the building. *(Madero 17, between Bolívar and Gante. ☎ 5225 0247. Open daily 10am-7pm. Closed for renovations at press; scheduled to reopen for 2004. Free.)*

WEST OF THE ALAMEDA CENTRAL

▧ MUSEO MURAL DIEGO RIVERA. Also known as Museo de la Alameda, this fascinating building holds Diego Rivera's 1947 masterpiece, **"Sueño de una Tarde Dominical en la Alameda Central"** (Sunday Afternoon Dream in the Alameda Central). The key points out, in English and Spanish, the famous figures woven into the work: Frida Kahlo, Antonio de Santa Anna, and Hernán Cortés (with his hand covered in blood), among others. Exhibits on Rivera's life and the cultural climate in which he lived, including a chart listing all of his works and their locations, inhabit the walls. One exhibit explains the attack on the painting by 100 university students the morning of June 4, 1948. Ignacio Ramírez was originally depicted holding up the words "God does not exist," an excerpt from a speech he had given in 1836; students blotted out "does not exist," leaving just "God." Rivera eventually allowed the phrase to be left out when the mural was repaired. Upstairs, where you can get a great view of the mural, is a modern art exhibit. *(Colón and Balderas, facing the park at the end of the Alameda farthest away from Bellas Artes. ☎ 5512 0759. Open Tu-Su 10am-6pm. 10 pesos, students free; Su free.)*

CENTRO CULTURAL JOSÉ MARTÍ. The poet José Martí, a Cuban independence leader in the late 19th century, warned against foreign imperialism and dreamed of a united and free Latin America, led by Mexico. A rainbow-colored mural commemorates his poetry, while a tally sheet in the corner of the mural records Spanish, British, French, and US interventions in Latin America from 1800 to 1969: the grand total is a staggering 784. Temporary exhibits on Cuba share the space. Movies, concerts, plays, and other cultural events take place in the adjoining theater. *(Dr. Mora 2. ☎ 5521 2115; www.cultura.df.gob.mx. Open M-F 9am-9pm, Sa 10am-7pm. Free.)*

PINACOTECA VIRREINAL DE SAN DIEGO. Constructed as a church between 1591 and 1621, the building now holds unique exhibits of contemporary multimedia art. *(Dr. Mora 7, next to Centro Cultural José Martí. ☎ 5512 2079. Open Tu-Su 9am-5pm. 15 pesos, students and teachers 7.5 pesos; Su free.)*

ALONG AVENIDA HIDALGO

■ MUSEO FRANZ MAYER. In the small, sunken Plaza de Santa Veracruz, the restored Hospital de San Juan de Dios houses a beautiful international collection of applied arts: furniture, textiles, ceramics, tiles, and church ornaments, especially from the *virreinal* (colonial or viceroyal) period. A section with paintings expands the meaning of "applied art." Fliers in English explain parts of the collection (2 pesos each). The upstairs library specializes in the arts and rare books. Although anyone can enter it, only researchers with credentials can use the books. The courtyard cafe alone is worth the price of admission. *(Hidalgo 45. ☎ 5518 2266; museo@franzmeyer.org.mx. Museum open Tu and Th-Su 10am-5pm; W 10am-7pm. Library open Tu-F. Admission to everything 20 pesos, students 10 pesos, adults over 70 and children under 12 free; Tu free. Guided tours 10 pesos per person. Entrance to just the cafe and library 5 pesos.)*

MUSEO NACIONAL DE LA ESTAMPA. The museum once held the National Institute of Fine Arts' graphic arts and engraving collection but now has only temporary exhibits of engravings by famous artists, both Mexican and international. Highlights have included the work of José Guadalupe Posada, Mexico's foremost engraver and printmaker. His woodcuts depict skeletons dancing, singing, and cavorting in ridiculous costumes—a graphic indictment of the Porfiriato's excesses. *(Hidalgo 39, next to the Museo Franz Mayer. ☎ 5521 2244 or 5510 4905. Open Tu-Su 10am-6pm. 10 pesos, students and teachers free; Su free.)*

PALACIO POSTAL (LA QUINTA CASA DE CORREOS). Architect Adamo Boari, of Bellas Artes fame, designed the beautiful central post office in 1907, combining the Spanish Gothic and Art Nouveau styles. It was restored between 1996 and 2000. The Museo Postal is less impressive, with artifacts and history of that amazing phenomenon known as the *Servicio Postal Mexicano*. *(Tacuba 1, on the corner of Tacuba and Lázaro Cárdenas. ☎ 5510 2999. Open Tu-F 10am-5:30, Sa-Su 10am-4pm. Free tours Tu-F noon and 4pm, minimum 10 people. Free. Bring an ID to leave at the desk.)*

PALACIO DE MINERÍA. This masterpiece of Neoclassical architecture is worth visiting just for the beautiful rooms. The museum, **Museo Manuel Tolsá,** has a diverse collection of art, mainly sculpture, plus an exhibit on meteorites. *(Tacuba 5, across from the Museo Nacional de Arte. ☎ 5623 2982 or 5623 2981, www.palaciomineria.unam.mx. Museum open Tu-Su 10am-6pm. Building tours Sa-Su 11am and 1pm, 25 pesos. Museum entrance 10 pesos; 50% student discount for tours and entrance.)*

NEAR THE MONUMENTO A LA REVOLUCIÓN

*To get to the Monumento a la Revolución, take **M: Revolución** (Line 2).*

MONUMENTO A LA REVOLUCIÓN/MUSEO NACIONAL DE LA REVOLUCIÓN. In the early 1900s, president Porfirio Díaz planned this site as the seat of Congress, but progress halted as Revolutionary fighting paralyzed the city streets. Between 1932 and 1938, architect Carlos Obregón Sanacilia changed the plans slightly, and made a monument to the overthrow of Díaz and his congress. In each of the four supporting columns lies the body of one of Mexico's Revolutionary heroes: Francisco Madero, Plutarca Elías Calles, Lázaro Cárdenas, and Francisco Villa. The museum, which is under the monument, takes you through 81 years in the history of Mexico (1857-1938) and features Revolutionary artifacts including military uniforms, guns, civilian clothing, and old pesos. Sunday is the only day you can climb to the top of the monument. *(At Plaza de la República. ☎ 5546 2115. Museum open Tu-Su 9am-5pm. 12 pesos, students and children 6 pesos; Su free. Call ahead to arrange a tour.)*

MUSEO DEL CHOPO. The modern, relatively tourist-free Chopo (as it's commonly called) displays the works of rising Mexican artists in every medium. Every mid-June to mid-July for 12 years running, the museum has proudly hosted a show of gay and lesbian photography, sculpture, and painting. The unusual building was built in France and rebuilt at this spot in 1910. A small cafeteria in front serves coffee (9-20 pesos) and snacks (1-20 pesos). *(Dr. Enrique González Martínez 10. Off Puente de Alvarado/San Cosme. Open Tu-Su 10am-2pm and 3-7pm. 6 pesos, students 3 pesos, children until 10 free; Tu free. Free guided tours; call ahead ☎ 5546 8490.)*

MUSEO SAN CARLOS. The museum is in the old **Palacio Buenavista,** constructed from the end of the 18th century through the beginning of the 19th century by architect Manuel Tolsa for the Count of Buenavista. The building served as temporary residence for Santa Anna and later belonged to Emperor Maximilian. Housing the former collection of the Academy San Carlos (founded by the King of Spain in 1783) its impressive holdings include European art spanning the 14th to the 19th centuries. The museum features excellent work by minor artists, as well as heavyweights such as Rubens. Temporary exhibits often highlight themes in post-Renaissance European art. *(At the corner of Puente de Alvarado and Ramos Arizpe. ☎ 5566 8522. Open Su-M and W-Sa 10am-6pm. 25 pesos, students and teachers 12.5 pesos; M free.)*

BOSQUE DE CHAPULTEPEC

*The park is divided into three sections. To reach the first, take the Metro to **M: Auditorio** (Line 7), by the Auditorio Nacional and the zoo, or **M: Chapultepec** (Line 1), at the other end of the section and closer to the Niños Héroes monument and most museums. Alternatively, take any pesero on Reforma to Auditorio or Chapultepec. For the second section, get off at **M: Constituyentes** (Line 7) and walk towards the blue-tiled building (Museo del Niño). Alternatively, take a "La Feria" pesero from M: Chapultepec. For the third, by the water parks, take an "El Rollo" pesero from M: Constituyentes.*

Mexico City has to do everything a little bigger and better, and the D.F.'s major park and recreational area is no exception. The Chapultepec area is home to a slew of fabulous museums, myriad hiking paths, and balloon vendors. A bike is the best way of seeing the whole park (rentals near the corner of Reforma and Gandhi, by the anthropology museum), though the private boats are the most relaxing. The liveliest time to visit is on Sunday, when families flock to open-air concerts and take advantage of free admission to the zoo and museums.

■ **THE PARK.** Chapultepec Park is an adventure in itself. It covers 2100 acres and is the oldest and biggest urban park in the Americas since the Aztec emperor Moctezuma established it in the 15th century as a recreational area full of streams and aqueducts. It is beautiful and peaceful, huge and confusing, frustrating and rewarding, all at the same time. The three sections make it more manageable.

The first section is the busiest with the most museums, sights, and people. Chapultepec Castle, the zoo, and Mexico's most famous museum, the **Museo Nacional de Antropología,** are all here (as well as much, much more). The second section has fewer tourists and more locals, and is generally less busy. Children's attractions are concentrated here, plus there are great fountains and statues including Xochipili (one of the finest statues of the Nahuatl culture), Diego Rivera's Tlaloc, and Mito del Agua, in addition to reproductions of the giant Olmec heads and a bronze statue of George Washington. The third section has the fewest attractions but features the water parks El Rollo and Atlantis. It is also the least safe, with hardly any security guards. *(Park open daily 5am-4:30pm.)*

SECTION ONE

■ **MUSEO NACIONAL DE ANTROPOLOGÍA.** To visit all 23 halls in this huge museum, be prepared to walk five kilometers. Besides holding Mexico's most impressive archaeological and ethnographic treasures, this museum is the biggest

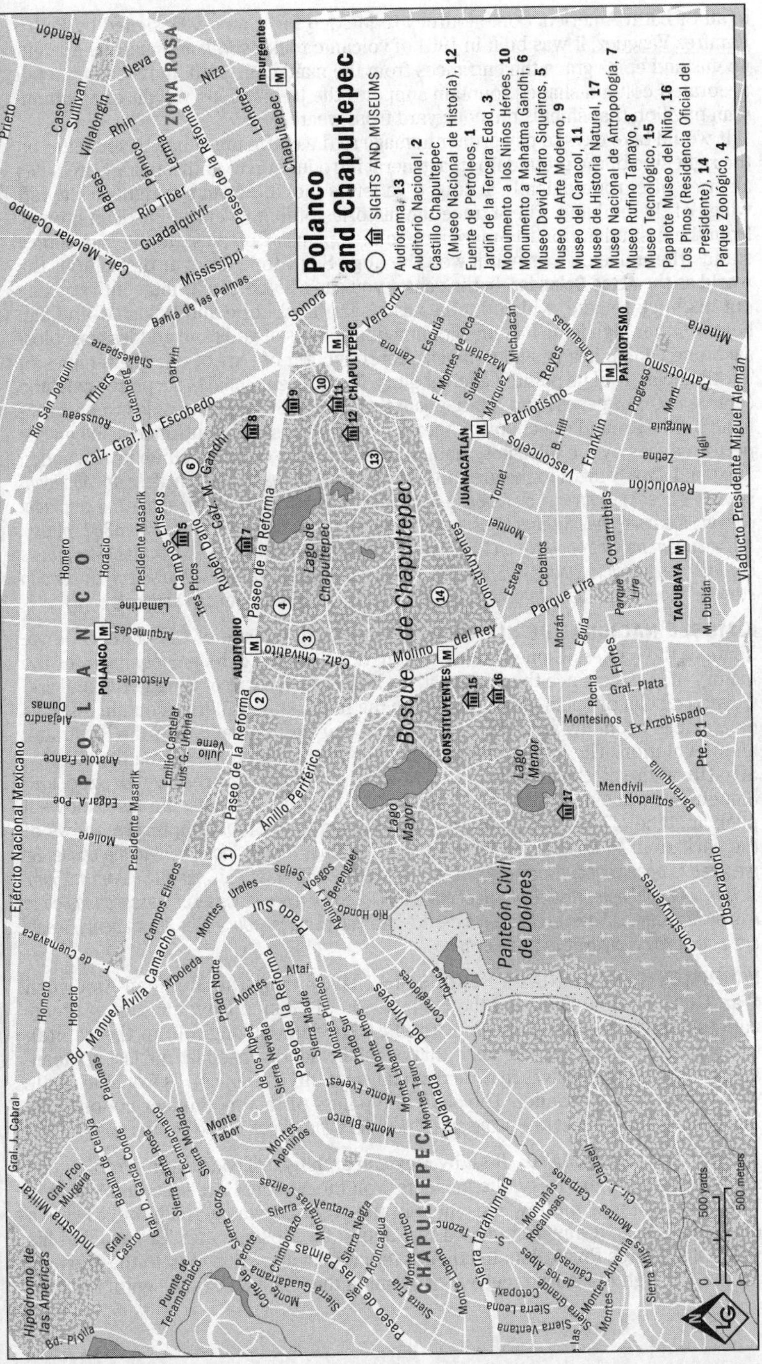

Polanco and Chapultepec
SIGHTS AND MUSEUMS
Audiorama, 13
Auditorio Nacional, 2
Castillo Chapultepec (Museo Nacional de Historia), 12
Fuente de Petróleos, 1
Jardín de la Tercera Edad, 3
Monumento a los Niños Héroes, 10
Monumento a Mahatma Gandhi, 6
Museo David Álfaro Siqueiros, 5
Museo de Arte Moderno, 9
Museo del Caracol, 11
Museo de Historia Natural, 17
Museo Nacional de Antropología, 7
Museo Rufino Tamayo, 8
Museo Tecnológico, 15
Papalote Museo del Niño, 16
Los Pinos (Residencia Oficial del Presidente), 14
Parque Zoológico, 4
POLANCO
ZONA ROSA
CHAPULTEPEC
Bosque de Chapultepec
Lago de Chapultepec
Lago Mayor
Lago Menor
Panteón Civil de Dolores
Paseo de la Reforma
Anillo Periférico
Calz. Gral. M. Escobedo
Calz. M. Gandhi
Calz. Melchor Ocampo
Viaducto Presidente Miguel Alemán
Constituyentes
Bd. Manuel Ávila Camacho
Ejército Nacional Mexicano
Hipódromo de las Américas
POLANCO
AUDITORIO
CHAPULTEPEC
JUANACATLÁN
CONSTITUYENTES
TACUBAYA
PATRIOTISMO
Insurgentes
500 yards
500 meters

in all of Latin America. Some journey to Mexico for it alone. Designed by Pedro Ramírez Vázquez, it was built in 1964 of volcanic rock, wood, and marble. Ancient poems and epics grace the entrances from the main courtyard. In its center, a tall decorated column-shaped fountain supports the tremendous weight of an aluminum pavilion that shields the courtyard from weather.

It would take days to pay proper homage to the entire museum. As you enter on the right side of the ground floor, a general introduction to anthropology precedes a series of chronologically arranged galleries moving from the right to the left wings of the building. These trace the histories of many central Mexican groups, from the first migration to America up to the Spanish Conquest. In the **Sala México** stands the museum's crown jewel, the huge Sun Stone, known throughout the world as the **Aztec Calendar.** In the center you can see the god Xiuhtecuhtli sticking out his huge tongue, which doubles as a sacrificial knife and holds two human hearts. Other highlights include monumental statues of gods and goddesses, colossal stone Olmec heads, and a life-size reproduction of part of one the temples of Teotihuacán in all its painted ancient glory. The museum also has a pricey **cafeteria** (entrees 60-113 pesos) and a large **bookshop** that sells English guides to archaeological sites around the country. Across from the museum's entrance, you can see performances by the **voladores,** who, in true Totonac tradition, climb up a wooden mast and slowly swirl to the ground. (Paseo de la Reforma and Gandhi. Take an "Auditorio" pesero (2 pesos) southwest on Reforma and signal the driver to let you off at the 2nd stop after entering the park. The museum is just east down Reforma. ☎ 5553 6386 or 5553 6381; http://sunsite.unam.mx/antropol/. Open Tu-Su 9am-7pm. Call ahead for a free tour, available for groups of five or more. Audio guides in Spanish 50 pesos, in English 60 pesos. The voladores perform every half hour from 10am-4pm. Museum 37 pesos, discounts for Mexican nationals only.)

▨ MUSEO NACIONAL DE HISTORIA. Housed in the Castle of Chapultepec, once home of the hapless Emperor Maximilian, this museum exhaustively narrates the history of Mexico since the Conquest. An immense portrait of King Ferdinand and Queen Isabella of Spain greets visitors in the first room. Galleries contain displays on Mexican economy and society during the War for Independence, the Porfiriato, and Revolution. The upper level exhibits Mexican art and dress from the viceroyalty through the 20th century. Some of the always impressive Orozco and Siqueiros murals decorate the interior. Admission to the museum also allows a peek at some of the castle's interior and access to the most impressive views of the park area. (Walk up the hill directly behind the Niños Héroes monument to the castle. Be prepared to open your bag for the guard. ☎ 5241 3114 or 5241 3115. Open Tu-Su 9am-4:15pm. Tickets sold until 4pm. Historical part of museum closed for renovations as of press; scheduled to reopen for 2004. 37 pesos, children under 13, disabled persons, adults over 30, students, teachers, and nearly everything in creation free.)

MONUMENTO A LOS NIÑOS HÉROES. In 1847, during the Mexican-American War, Gen. Winfield Scott led the US invasion of Mexico City; military academy cadets eventually had to protect the last Mexican stronghold in the capital, Chapultepec Castle. Legend has it that as the invaders closed in, the last six teenagers wrapped themselves in a Mexican flag and threw themselves from the castle wall rather than surrender. The six white pillars of this monument honor those boy heroes. (On the east side of the park, follow the signs or look for the gigantic white pillars.)

MUSEO RUFINO TAMAYO. Built by Mexican architects Teodor González de León and Abraham Zabludovsky, the museum won the National Architecture Award in 1981 and is one of the few museums in the city that was actually built to be a museum. The government donated the land in the Bosque after Tamayo and his wife, Olga Flores Rivas, donated their international arts collection to the Mexican people. Though his work received criticism in the first half of the century for not being sufficiently nationalistic, his abstract style is now universally respected. The permanent collection consists of Tamayo's work, as well as works by Willem de Kooning, Fernando Botero, and surrealists Joan Miró and Max Ernst—in Tamayo's words, "the most relevant examples of international art of our time." First-rate temporary exhibits grace the walls as well. (*Down the street from the Museo Nacional de Antropología–walking away from the Auditorio–on the corner of Reforma and Gandhi. Walk straight into the woods as you leave the main entrance of the museum: Tamayo is 100m straight ahead. From M: Chapultepec, take the 1st right onto Gandhi. After a 5min. walk, the museum is to the left through trees. ☎5286 6519; info@museotamayo.org. Open Tu-Su 10am-6pm. Permanent collection closed; set to reopen in 2004. 15 pesos; Su free.*)

MUSEO DE ARTE MODERNO. This museum houses a fine collection of paintings, including works by Rivera, Siqueiros, Orozco, and Kahlo, with excellent temporary exhibits as well, often showcasing up-and-coming Mexican artists. It also features a cafe and an outdoor sculpture garden with benches and views of the park. (*On Reforma and Gandhi, opposite the Museo de Antropología. ☎5553 6233. Open Tu-Su 10am-6pm. 15 pesos; students, teachers, and children under 10 free; Su free.*)

MUSEO DEL CARACOL (GALERÍA DE HISTORIA). Officially Museo Galería de la Lucha del Pueblo Mexicano por su Libertad (Museum of the Struggle of the Mexican People for Liberty), the museum is more commonly known as Museo del Caracol (Museum of the Snail) because of its spiral design. It contains 12 halls dedicated to independent Mexico's history: the downward spiral begins with Hidalgo's *Grito de Dolores* and ends with the establishment of democracy. The exhibitions consist mainly of lifelike mini-dioramas and lots of text (all in Spanish). The staircase leads to a beautiful, round, sky-lit hall that holds a handwritten copy of the Constitution of 1917. (*On the road to the castle, turn right at the sign just before the castle itself. ☎5241 3144. Open Tu-Su 9am-4:15pm. 32 pesos, under 13, over 60, students, teachers, and disabled persons free; Su free.*)

MUSEO SALA DE ARTE PÚBLICO DAVID ÁLFARO SIQUEIROS. Famed muralist, Revolutionary soldier, republican, fanatical Stalinist, anti-fascist, and would-be Trotsky assassin David Álfaro Siqueiros donated his house and studio to the people of Mexico 25 days before his death in January 1974; the walls are covered with his murals. Also on display are the photos he used for his models, showing the development from idea to art. Temporary exhibits exalt rising artists. (*Tres Picos 29, at Hegel, just outside the park. Walk uphill from the Museo Nacional de Antropología to Rubén Darío. On the left, Tres Picos forks–follow it for one block and the museum is on the right. ☎5203 5888 or 5531 3394; www.salasiqueiros.arte.com. Call to arrange a guided tour. Open Tu-Su 10am-6pm. 10 pesos.*)

PARQUE ZOOLÓGICO DE CHAPULTEPEC. Lions and tigers and bears—oh my! Add to that the zoo's prized possession, pandas! This excellent zoo has very informative signs (in Spanish) about the life and habitat of each type of animal, including the status of some endangered species. (*Accessible from the entrance on Reforma, east of Calzada Chivatitio. From the M: Auditorio, head away from the National Auditorium. ☎5553 6263. Open Tu-Su 9am-4:30pm. Free.*)

OTHER SIGHTS. The **Auditorio Nacional**, at *M: Auditorio*, is *the* concert venue in Mexico City: the hottest music groups in the world come here to play. (☎5280 9250; www.auditorio.com.mx.) **Los Pinos** (☎5267 8000), beyond the guard booth at Chivatito and Molino del Rey, is the presidential residence. To see the varied works of art inside, you'd better call for an appointment. At the heart of that crazy place called Chapultepec is the **Lago de Chapultepec.** Rent rowboats for a romantic experience of the park's oddly green water. (*Rentals available daily 7:30am-4pm. 20 pesos per hr. Bring a picture ID.*) For an organic connection with Pre-Hispanic Mexico, seek out **El Sargento,**

between Audiorama and the Fuente de la Templanza, a 700-year-old Ahuehuete tree that is over 40m tall and 12.5m in circumference. On the way up to the castle, stop at the **Casa de los Espejos,** where you can be tall and skinny, short and fat, or just sort of crooked looking, depending on which of its sixteen mirrors you face.

SECTION TWO

■ **LA FERIA.** The highlight of this awesome theme park is certainly Montaña Rusa, one of the last wooden roller coasters on the continent, but there is tons more to see and do, such as the aquatic show starring Beluga whales. *(☎5230 2131 or 5230 2121; www.feriachapultepec.com.mx. Open M-Th 10am-6pm, F 10am-7pm, Sa-Su 10am-9pm. Entrance 10 pesos, buy tokens inside for rides; beluga show 10 pesos.)*

"PAPALOTE" MUSEO DEL NIÑO. This children's museum features more than 400 interactive exhibits. It is a great place for kids, and it also has the only IMAX theatre in Mexico City. *(The big blue-tiled building. ☎5237 1777; www.papalote.org.mx. Open M-F 9am-1pm and 2-6pm, Sa-Su 10am-2pm, additional hrs. Th 7-11pm. 60 pesos, children 2-11 and over 60 50 pesos.)*

MUSEO TECNOLÓGICO. Another good experience for kids, the large yard in front of the museum holds a planetarium, a model solar-powered house, and a real helicopter—plus models of trains, electrical plants, and much more. Inside are exhibits on engines, cars, ships, and more, and an Internet room. *(Next to Papalote. ☎5229 4000, ext. 90266 and 90267. Open daily 9am-5pm. Free. Only "experienced users" allowed in the Internet room.)*

MUSEO DE HISTORIA NATURAL. Opened in 1964, this museum has educational exhibits on the universe, evolution, humanity, the origin of life, and other natural-historic themes. *(Follow the signs toward what appear to be circus tents. ☎5515 6882 or 5515 6304. Open Tu-Su 10am-5pm. 17.5 pesos, students and teachers 9 pesos; Tu free.)*

TREN ESCÉNICO. Grab your kids or your honey and hold on tight. This nine-minute ride on a miniature train takes you slowly around the second section of the park. The long tunnel at the end might be scary for young children. *(Down the hill from the Museo de Historia Natural. ☎5515 1790. Open W-Su 10am-4:30pm. 5 pesos.)*

SECTION THREE

PARQUE MARINO ATLANTIS. Performances feature dolphins, sea lions, trained birds, and, somehow, cowboys. Pet and feed the dolphins (20 pesos). Also present are rides and a marine museum. Best of all, on weekends visitors can swim with the dolphins and sea lions. *(☎5271 8618, 5273 3176, or 5277 1682; www.parqueatlantis.com.mx. Open Sa-Su and holidays 10am-7pm. Dolphin feeding 3:30pm, only the first 20 people allowed. Up to 8 people at a time over 6 years old may swim with dolphins and sea lions between 9:30am and 2pm.)*

PARQUE ACUÁTICO EL ROLLO. Fun waterslides are one of the highlights of this attraction. *(☎5515 1385. Open Sa-Su and holidays 10am-6pm. A measuring stick outside will let you know if you can get in free (under 0.9m), pay 50 pesos (between 0.9m and 1.2m), or pay the full 85 pesos.)*

TLATELOLCO

Go to **M: Tlatelolco** *(Line 3), and take the González exit. Turn right on González, walk 3 blocks east to Cárdenas, then turn right and walk up 1 block. The plaza is on the left.*

Archaeological work has shown that the city of Tlatelolco ("Mound of Sand" in Náhuatl) existed long before the great Aztec capital of Tenochtitlán. By 1473, the Tlatelolco king, Moquíhuix, had built his city into a busy trading center coveted by the Aztec ruler, Axayácatl. Tension mounted over territorial boundaries, and soon the Aztecs geared up for attack. The Aztec war machine was too powerful for Moquíhuix, and Tlatelolco was absorbed into the huge empire.

PLAZA DE LAS TRES CULTURAS. Tlatelolco's central square, at the corner of Lázaro Cárdenas and Ricardo Flores Magón, 13 blocks north of the Palacio de Bellas Artes, recognizes the three cultures that have occupied it: Aztec, colonial Spanish, and modern Mexican. Today, the three cultures are represented by ancient ruins, a colonial church, and the surrounding modern buildings. A plaque in the southwest corner of the plaza explains: "On August 13, 1521, heroically defended by Cuauhtémoc, Tlatelolco fell to Hernán Cortés. It was neither a triumph nor a defeat, but the painful birth of the *mestizo* city that is the Mexico of today." That battle marked the last serious armed resistance to the conquest. More than 400 years later, the plaza witnessed another bloody event, for which it is most famous: the Tlatelolco Massacre of October 2, 1968.

PIRÁMIDE DE TLATELOLCO. In the plaza, parts of the Pyramid of Tlatelolco (also known as the **Templo Mayor**) and its ceremonial square remain dutifully well-kept. Enter on Cárdenas at the far side of the plaza. At the time of the conquest, the base of the pyramid extended from Insurgentes to the Iglesia de Santiago. The pyramid was second in importance only to the great Teocalli, and its summit reached nearly as high as the skyscraper just to the south (the Relaciones Exteriores building). During the Spanish blockade of Tenochtitlán, the Aztecs heaved freshly sacrificed bodies of Cortés's forces down the temple steps, within sight of the *conquistadores* camped to the west at Tacuba. Nearby is the **Templo Calendárico "M,"** an M-shaped building used by the Aztecs to keep time. Scores of skeletons were discovered near its base. A male and female pair that were found facing each other have been dubbed "The Lovers of Tlatelolco." *(Open daily 8am-6pm. Free.)*

IGLESIA DE SANTIAGO. On the east side of the plaza is the simple, fortress-like church erected in 1609. The stonework and plain masonry of the church were designed to fit in with the surrounding ruins and their stonework, in contrast to other sights where colonial construction obliterated pre-existing structures.

LA VILLA BASÍLICA

M: La Villa Basílica (Line 6). Pass the vendor stands and turn right on Calzada de Guadalupe; the Basílica will be directly in front of you.

THE LOCAL LEGEND

THE DARK VIRGIN

The Virgin of Guadalupe, patron saint of Mexico, is an embodiment of the religious hybrid that characterizes the nation. In December 1531, ten short years after the Aztec empire fell at the hands of the Spanish, *indígena* peasant Juan Diego had a vision of the Virgin at Tepeyac, a hill just northwest of Mexico City. When Diego told the Franciscan bishop of his vision, the clergyman was doubtful. Juan Diego returned to the hill and had another vision; this time the Virgin told him that on the hill he would find, in the middle of winter, a great variety of roses that he should gather and bring to the bishop as proof. Juan Diego gathered the roses in his cloak, and when he let them fall at the feet of the bishop, an image of the Virgin remained emblazoned on the cactus-cloth cloak, or *tilma*.

After news of the miracle spread, a temple was erected in her honor. In 1541, an historian wrote that 9 million *indígenas* had converted, and many say the miracle of Guadalupe was responsible. The Virgin of Guadalupe's prominence arose from her ability to unite native beliefs with the Catholic tradition; her dark skin and knowledge of Náhuatl reassured many *indígenas* that Catholicism looked kindly upon them as well as upon the light-skinned Spaniards. Not only did the Pope choose her sanctuary as his first trip outside Rome, but in 1990 Juan Diego was beatified.

Ever since the legend of Juan Diego, Our Lady of Guadalupe has been the patron saint of Mexico, an icon of the nation's religious culture. The famous cloak is now housed in the Basílica de Guadalupe, north of the city center.

LA BASÍLICA DE GUADALUPE. Designed by the respected Pedro Ramírez Vásquez and finished in 1975, the new *basílica* is an immense, aggressively modern structure. Nonetheless, it is deeply tied into tradition and is the place of the Pope's mass during his visit in 2002 to oversee Juan Diego's canonization. Although the flags from different cultures inside of the Basílica make it feel more like the United Nations than a church, thousands flock daily to observe the Virgin's miraculous likeness emblazoned in Juan Diego's robe. Visitors crowd around the central altar and impressive organ to step onto the Basílica's moving sidewalk—it allows for easier (and faster) viewing of Diego's holy cloak. A focal point is the gold Byzantine script, "*¿Aquí no estoy yo que soy tu madre?*" ("Am I not here, I who am your mother?"), across the top of the edifice. *(Open daily 5am-9pm.)*

MUSEO DE LA BASÍLICA DE GUADALUPE. Next to the new *basílica* is the old one, built at the end of the 17th century and remodeled in the 1880s. Religious services and quiet prayers still occur, amid gawking visitors and a gift shop. The primary function of the old *basílica* is to house the **Museo de la Basílica de Guadalupe,** whose entrance is at the back left side as you face the *basílica* entrance. Colonial religious paintings and portraits comprise most of the collection, although they pale in comparison to the emotional collection of *ex-votos* in the entryway. *(Plaza Hidalgo 1, in the Villa de Guadalupe. ☎5781 6810. Open Tu-Su 10am-6pm. 5 pesos, children under 12 free.)*

TEPEYAC HILL. Behind the *basílica*, winding steps lead up the side of a small hill, past small fountains, crowds of pilgrims, and beautiful flower beds. A small chapel sits on top of the hill, at the very spot Juan Diego indicated as the site of the apparition of the Virgin. Murals inside depict the revelation. From the steps beside the church, you can absorb a panoramic view of the city framed by the hillsides and distant mountains. Descending the other side of the hill, in the Jardín de Ofrendas past the spouting gargoyles, statues of Juan Diego and a group of *indígenas* kneel before a gleaming Virgin.

TEMPLO DEL POCITO. Perhaps the most beautiful of all the buildings, this little round chapel, built between 1777 and 1791, has a golden altar inside, and blue and white tiles outside, decorating the dome of the temple.

COYOACÁN

*To reach Coyoacán from downtown, take the Metro to **M: Coyoacán** (Line 3).*

The Toltecs founded **Coyoacán** (Place of the Skinny Coyotes, in Náhuatl) between the 10th and 12th centuries. Cortés later established the seat of the colonial government in Coyoacán and, after the fall of Tlatelolco, he tortured the Aztec leader Cuauhtémoc here in hopes that he would reveal the hiding place of the legendary Aztec treasure. Well-maintained and peaceful today, Coyoacán merits a visit for its museums, or simply for a stroll in beautiful **Plaza Hidalgo,** neighboring **Jardín Centenario,** or nearby **Placita de la Conchita.** The neighborhood centers around Plaza Hidalgo, which is bounded by the cathedral and the **Casa de Cortés.** Calle Carrillo Puerto splits the two parks, running north-south just west of the church. Obtain **tourist information** (☎5659 2256, ext. 181; open daily 9am-8pm) in the Casa de Cortés, the big red building north of the plaza. The office gives free tours of the area in Spanish (Sa every hr. 8am-noon).

■MUSEO FRIDA KAHLO. Works by Rivera, Orozco, Duchamp, and Klee hang in this restored colonial house, the birthplace and home of surrealist painter Frida

MEXICO CITY

San Ángel

FOOD
La Finca Café Solo Dios, **4**
La Mora, **2**

★ **NIGHTLIFE**
La Cantina San Ángel, **3**
La Planta de Luz, **5**
New Orleans, **1**

Francia
Margaritas
Hortensia
Camelia
Insurgentes Sur
Ponce
Río San Ángel
Revolución
San Carlos
Altavista
Reforma
Jardín
Frontera
San Jacinto

TO MUSEO ESTUDIO DIEGO RIVERA Y FRIDA KAHLO

Vito Alessio Robles
Atenil
Sosa
TO COYOACÁN (50m)
Universidad
Quevedo
MIGUEL ÁNGEL DE QUEVEDO Ⓜ

Parque de la Bombilla
Monumento Álvaro Obregón
Camino al Desierto de los Leones
La Paz
Madero
Amargura
Reina
Río Magdalena

Museo Carrillo Gil 🏛
Museo del Carmen 🏛
Centro Cultural San Ángel 🏛 ★3
Casa de Risco 🏛
PLAZA CARMEN
★2
★4
PL. SAN JACINTO
Bazar del Sábado
Insurgentes Sur
Revolución
Museo Soumaya 🏛 5
Jardín del Arte
PLAZA LORETA

TO CIUDAD UNIVERSITARIA (300m)

0   250 yards
0   250 meters

Coyoacán

FOOD
Café el Parnaso, **7**
El Guarache, **8**
El Jarocho, **6**
VegeTaco, **9**

San Pedro
Londres
Morelos
San Pedro
Gómez Farías
Berlín
Abasolo
Xicoténcatl
Malintzin
Cuauhtémoc
Moctezuma
Fernández Leal
Ayua
África
PL. LA CONCHITA
Quevedo
Higuera
Hidalgo
Carrillo Puerto
Tres Cruces
Carranza
Sosa
Pino
Zaragoza
Torresco
Valenzuela
Melchor Ocampo

Cineteca Nacional 🎬
Cuauhtémoc
Centenario
Aldama
Guerrero
París
Domínguez
Madrid
Viena
Mina
México
Bruselas
Matamoros

Ⓜ COYOACÁN

Viveros de Coyoacán

Universidad

Museo León Trotsky 🏛
Museo Frida Kahlo 🏛
Allende
Aguayo
Centenario

Mercado ■
PL. HIDALGO
Jardín Centenario
★ El Hijo del Cuervo
Casa de Cortés 6
Museo Nacional de las Culturas Populares 🏛
TO CONVENTO
Iglesia de San Juan Bautista 🕆 7
★3
9
0   250 yards
0   250 meters

TO SAN ÁNGEL (50m)

Kahlo (1907-1954). Kahlo's disturbing work and traumatic life story have gained international fame since her death, and she is today regarded as one of Mexico's greatest artists. At 18, Kahlo was impaled by a post during a trolley accident, breaking her spine, rendering her infertile, and confining her to a wheelchair for much of her life. Married twice to the celebrated muralist (and philanderer) Diego Rivera, Kahlo was notorious for her numerous affairs with both men and women, most famously with Leon Trotsky—whom she later plotted to kill. Some of Kahlo's early and late work, as well as portraits of her painted by other artists, fill the first two rooms. The third room holds work by other contemporary artists including Diego Rivera. The rest of the museum is a walk-through of the house as it was when Frida and Diego lived there. Read the excerpts of her diary and letters posted on the walls that intimately describe childhood dreams, Rivera's adultery, and the inspiration that fueled her work. Kahlo's ashes are in a jar in the back of the studio, beneath her desk mask. The house is blue, which Kahlo believed would ward off bad spirits, and fronts a gorgeous courtyard, a green sanctuary decorated with Pre-Hispanic artifacts from Rivera's collection. Explanatory labels are sparse, so you may want to bring this guide in with you. (Londres 247. ☎ 5554 5999. Open Tu-Su 10am-6pm. 30 pesos, 20 pesos with student ID. Guided tours in Spanish.)

MUSEO CASA DE LEÓN TROTSKY. After Stalin expelled León Trotsky from the USSR in 1927, he wandered in exile until Mexico's president Lázaro Cárdenas granted him political asylum at the suggestion of Trotsky's friends, muralist Diego Rivera and painter Frida Kahlo. Trotsky arrived in 1937 with his wife, and Diego Rivera and Frida Kahlo lent them their house, Casa Azul (now the Museo Frida Kahlo, above), for a while. Eventually, they relocated to this house on Churubusco. Though bunny rabbits now nibble peacefully in the gardens, bullet holes riddle the interior walls, relics of an attack on Trotsky by the muralist David Álfaro Siqueiros on May 24, 1940. Siqueiros and a group of men wildy sprayed the inside of the house with machine-gun fire, wounding Trotsky's grandson in the foot, and barely missing Trotsky and his wife. Fearing further violence, this self-proclaimed "man of the people," living in a posh house in a posh suburb, installed bullet-proof bathroom doors and hired a team of bodyguards. Despite precautions, Trotsky was eventually assassinated by a Spanish communist posing as a friend-of-a-friend, who buried an ice pick in his skull. (☎ 5658 8732. Open Tu-Su 10am-5pm. 20 pesos, students 10 pesos.)

CASA DE CORTÉS. Contrary to popular belief, the Casa, built in the 1750s, never housed Cortés's administration. Instead, the present-day municipal building honors the past by displaying murals by local artist Diego Rosales, a student of Rivera's. The murals depict scenes from the Conquest and relay information about Coyoacán. (On the north side of the plaza. ☎ 5659 2256, ext. 181. Open daily 9am-8pm.)

IGLESIA DE SAN JUAN BAUTISTA. The church, between Plaza Hidalgo and Jardín Centenario, was begun in 1560 and rebuilt between 1798 and 1804. The interior is elaborately decorated with gold and bronze, and the roof supports five beautifully painted frescoes, depicting scenes from the New Testament. (Open M 5:30am-7:30pm, Tu-Sa 5:30am-8:30pm.)

MUSEO NACIONAL DE LAS CULTURAS POPULARES. The MNCP houses temporary exhibits about contemporary indigenous culture in Mexico. Learn about agriculture, crafts, and art by indigenous children. The Museo also distributes information on events in Coyoacán and the concerts that are held in the courtyard. (On Hidalgo by the Plaza Hidalgo, 2 blocks east of Plaza Hidalgo. ☎ 5554 8610. Open Tu-Th 10am-6pm, F-Su 10am-8pm. Free.)

CONVENTO DE NUESTRA SEÑORA DE LOS ÁNGELES DE CHURUBUSCO. The convent was built on the site of a pyramid dedicated to the Aztec war god Huitzilo-pochtli, all traces of which vanished after the convent was rebuilt in 1676. On August 20, 1847, 800 citizen-soldiers, led by generals Manuel Rincón and Pedro Anaya, defended the building against 8000 US invaders, surrendering only when the last cartridge had been spent. Today, bullet holes still mark the front wall, where two cannons used in the defense are kept as memorials. Inside is the **Museo Nacional de las Intervenciones.** Artifacts and an extensive written narrative in Spanish tell the sordid history of the attacks on Mexico's sovereignty perpetrated by the Spanish, French, British, and US governments from the late 18th century to 1917. You have to pass through the museum to reach the **Acervo Artístico de Churubusco,** several rooms of Mexican religious art from the 17th and 18th centuries. *(20 de Agosto and General Anaya. From Coyoacán, walk 4 blocks down Hidalgo and then follow Anaya as it branches left; follow this street 4 blocks. M: General Anaya (Line 2), is only 2 blocks east of the convent along 20 de Agosto. The "Gen. Anaya" pesero (2 pesos) goes from Plaza Hidalgo to the museum; take the "Sto. Domingo" back. ☎ 5604 0699. Museum open Tu-Su 9am-6pm. 32 pesos; Su free.)*

MUSEO ANAHUACALLI. Designed by Diego Rivera with Aztec and Maya architectural motifs, the formidable stone building is an exhibit in and of itself. The interior exhibits Rivera's huge collection of Pre-Hispanic art. Built atop a hill, Anahuacalli commands an excellent view of the area, including nearby Azteca Stadium. *(Calle Museo 150. To reach the museum from Plaza Hidalgo or Churubusco, take a "Huipulco" or "Huayamilpa" pesero south and get off at Calle Museo—keep an eye out, the stop is not immediately visible. Turn right onto Calle Museo and you'll soon be there. ☎ 5617 4310. Open Tu-Su 10am-6pm. 30 pesos, students and teachers 20 pesos, children under 6 free.)*

VIVEROS DE COYOACÁN. Wander among rows of skinny saplings and frolicking Mexican squirrels in this botanical garden paradise, whose tranquility is enforced by rules prohibiting bicycles, balls, dogs, cameras, and food—though jogging, strolling, dancing, and PDA are welcome. *(Enter on México, between Madrid and Melchor Ocampo, between M: Coyoacán and Plaza Hidalgo. Open daily 6am-5:30pm. Free.)*

SAN ÁNGEL

*To reach San Ángel, 10km south of the centro along Insurgentes, take the Metro to **M: M. A. Quevedo** (Line 3). Head west on Quevedo, away from the big Santo Domingo bakery, for 3 blocks; when it forks, take a left onto La Paz, and continue along the Parque de la Bombilla. The Metro is a bit of a walk; for a more direct route, buses traveling Insurgentes with a "San Ángel" sign in the windshield will take you straight to the heart of the neighborhood. To get back from San Ángel to points as far north as Buenavista station, take a bus with an "Indios Verdes" sign.*

Near Coyoacán is another well-heeled (if is less bohemian) neighborhood, San Ángel. Though as much in the city as anywhere else, great museums and beautiful colonial buildings on narrow cobblestone streets are a refreshing change of pace.

PARQUE DE LA BOMBILLA. The centerpiece of this park is the **Monumento al General Álvaro Obregón,** which honors one of the Revolutionaries who united against Victoriano Huerta, the militaristic dictator who executed Francisco Madero and seized power in 1913. The main statue accurately depicts Obregón, who lost an arm during the Revolution. A separate statue of the severed limb stands on the lower level of the monument. In 1920, Obregón became the first president of the post-Revolutionary era, but he later died, assassinated by a religious fanatic. The inscription on the sunken lower level reads, "I die blessing the Revolution."

MUSEO DEL CARMEN. Expropriated under the Reform Laws of 1857, this former Carmelite convent was abandoned in 1861 and restored in the 20th century to house a museum of art and history. The collection of colonial art has crucifixes galore, but few labels or explanatory texts. Some of the upstairs rooms have been restored to look as they did when the building was a convent; note the flat wooden beds and oh-so-comfy log pillows. Downstairs is the crypt, where the mummies are displayed. The identities of the eerily preserved bodies are a mystery—they were discovered in 1916 by invading Zapatistas, who thought the crypt held treasures. The adjoining church, the **Iglesia del Carmen,** was designed and built from 1615 to 1626 by Fray Andrés de San Miguel of the Carmelite order; beautiful *azulejos* adorn the inner walls, and the golden altar is stunning. *(At Revolución and Monasterio.* ☎ *5550 1848. Open Tu-Su 10am-4:45pm. 30 pesos, children, students, and teachers free; Su free. Iglesia del Carmen open daily 6:30am-9pm.)*

CASA DE RISCO. This well-preserved 17th-century house contains an important collection of well-labeled 14th- to 19th-century art. The inner courtyard has an amazing fountain made of pieces of *talavera* tile (called *riscos*), plates, cups, and other bits of porcelain from China, Mexico, and Europe. Upstairs, in the last room, are three small paintings by Mexico's landscape master, José María Velasco (1840-1912). A variety of European portraits, religious paintings, and furnishings form the heart of the collection. The ground floor hosts temporary exhibits of contemporary art. *(Plaza San Jacinto 15.* ☎ *5550 9286. Open Tu-Su 10am-5pm. Free.)*

MUSEO DE ARTE CARRILLO GIL. Inside the dull grey building is one of the capital's most interesting collections of art. It includes works by the big three muralists—Siqueiros, Orozco, and Rivera—but only their paintings on canvas, not the famed murals. Siqueiros's renowned **Caín en los Estados Unidos** (*Cain in the United States*, 1947) depicts the lynching of a black man by a crowd of monstrous whites. The Rivera paintings date from his early years and show heavily influence from Picasso. Other 20th-century artists are also represented. The top two floors house rotating exhibits. *(Revolución 1608.* ☎ *5550 3983. Open Tu-Su 10am-6pm. Free.)*

MUSEO ESTUDIO DIEGO RIVERA Y FRIDA KAHLO. These two buildings were the home of Mexican art's royal couple, Diego Rivera and Frida Kahlo, from 1934-40. Rivera lived in the pink one until his death in 1957, and his wife Frida stayed in the blue house until returning to her home in Coyoacán in the early 1940s. Juan O'Gorman designed the two giant blocks, which were among the first houses built in the functionalist style that inspired the public housing blocks later popularized all over the Americas and Europe. The museum shows a small collection of Rivera's work and photographs, as well as displays on the artists' lives. On the top floor of the Rivera house, you can see where and how he worked—his leftover paints are still lying around. *(At Altavista and Diego Rivera, 5 blocks up Altavista from Revolución. Look for the pink and blue pair, with a cactus fence.* ☎ *5550 1518. Open Tu-Su 10am-6pm. 10 pesos; Su free.)*

MUSEO SOUMAYA. This museum's pride and joy is its vast collection of Rodin sculpture, promoted as the third most important in the world. On a national level, there is a collection of Mexican portraits from the 18th and 19th centuries, colonial Mexican art, and paintings by Tamayo. *(In Plaza Loreto, a small shopping mall, at Revolución and Río Magdalena.* ☎ *5616 3731 or 5616 3761; www.soumaya.com.mx. Open Su-M and Th-Sa 10:30am-6:30pm, W 10:30am-8:30pm. 10 pesos, students 5 pesos; Su-M free.)*

OTHER SIGHTS. Across the street from the Iglesia del Carmen is the **Centro Cultural,** which borders lovely **Plaza del Carmen.** Besides hosting changing art exhibits and plays, it's a good source of information on local happenings, especially at the numerous small performance venues. *(*☎ *5616 1254. Open Su 10am-7pm, M-Sa 10am-8pm.)* One block up Madero is **Plaza San Jacinto,** at San Francisco and Juárez, which fills on Saturdays with shoppers scoping out pricey arts and crafts at the **Bazar del Sábado** (see p. 135). One block past Casa de Risco on Juárez lies the beautiful **Iglesia de San Jacinto**, a 16th-century church with a magnificent golden altar and a peaceful courtyard. *(Open daily 8am-8pm.)*

CIUDAD UNIVERSITARIA (CU)

*www.unam.mx. The sheer size of UNAM makes it difficult to navigate by foot. Luckily, **M: Universidad** (Line 3), lets you off (salidas D and E) by the free shuttle service (go right at the bottom of the stairs). Shuttles are limited and irregular over summer vacation (July 22-Aug. 15), but still available to all campus areas. Always expect to wait. There are 3 principal routes. Route #1 will take you to the green and lively heart of the campus—Jardín Central, to the far north of the station. Walk toward the big mosaic-covered building that is the library, away from Insurgentes. Alternatively, if you have a good sense of direction, a few pesos, and are willing to walk a bit, buses on Insurgentes run to the edge of driveways leading to both the Jardín Central and the Centro Cultural Universitario. In an emergency, call **university security** (press the button on any security phone throughout campus).*

The **Universidad Nacional Autónoma de México** (National Autonomous University of Mexico), or **UNAM,** is the largest university in Latin America, with a staggering enrollment of over 100,000. Immediately after the new colonial regime was established, the religious orders that arrived in Mexico built elementary and secondary schools to indoctrinate new converts and to educate young settlers from Spain. The original university, the University of Mexico, was established in 1553 in the building at the corner of Moneda and Seminario, just off the *zócalo*. Modern UNAM was brought into existence by president Justo Sierra at the turn of the century. The Ciudad Universitaria campus was dedicated in 1952, one of the greatest achievements of President Miguel Alemán. Designed by famous architects like Félix Candela and Juan O'Gorman, the campus boasts 26km of paved roads, 430,000 square meters of greenery, and four million planted trees.

CENTRO CULTURAL UNIVERSITARIO (CCU). Films, plays, concerts, and temporary art shows abound in UNAM's modern, beautifully maintained facilities. A big booth in the center of the complex has tons of fliers with information about what is going on at the CCU and all over the city. Most events of interest to tourists take place in the Centro Cultural Universitario (CCU—not to be confused with CU), Insurgentes Sur 3000. This large, modern complex houses the **Teatro Juan Ruiz de Alarcón,** the **Foro Sor Juana Inés de la Cruz** (☎5665 6583; *ticket booth open Su 10am-1:30pm and 4:30-6:30pm, Tu-F 10am-2pm and 5-8pm, Sa 10am-1:30pm and 4:30-7:30pm; tickets 100 pesos, students 50 pesos),* **Sala Miguel Covarrubias, Sala Carlos Chavez,** the artsy movie theaters **Sala José Revueltas** (☎5622 7021) and **Sala Julio Bracho** (☎5665 2850; *both 30 pesos, students 15 pesos),* and **Sala Netzahualcóyotl** (☎5665 0709 or 5622 7125; *60-150 pesos, 50% student discount),* which regularly hosts big-name concerts and music festivals. Also at the CCU is the **Azul y Oro Cafe** (open daily 9am-10pm, *comida corrida* 30-35 pesos) and a bookstore. *(Take Line 3 of the UNAM shuttle. Cafe open daily 9am-10pm; comida corrida 30-35 pesos.)*

LIBRARY. A huge mosaic by Juan O'Gorman wraps around the university library, to the left of the Jardín Central. You could spend hours gazing and trying to interpret the busy mosaic, which depicts Aztecs, eagles, the Olympic rings, a constellation wheel, and a huge atom, among other things. Across the grass from the library is the **Museo Universitario de Ciencias y Artes** (MUCA), which features large temporary exhibits. Opposite the museum entrance is the university's **administrative building,** graced by a 3-D Siqueiros mosaic on the south wall that shows students studying at desks supported by society. *(Library ☎5622 1659. Open daily 8:30am-9:30pm. Museo de Ciencias ☎5622 0273 or 5622 0206. Open Sept.-June M-F 10am-7pm, Sa 10am-6pm. Free. Guided tours daily 11am-5pm, min. 5 people.)*

MEXICO CITY

ESTADIO OLÍMPICO. The stadium, built in the 1950s, was designed to resemble a volcano with a huge crater, and real hardened lava coats the ground upon which it is built. The impressive mosaic over the entrance to the stadium was created by Diego Rivera using large colored rocks. It depicts eagles, a little boy holding an eaglet between a man and a woman, and a man and a woman holding two torches, a symbol of the 1968 Olympics, which were held here. Today, the stadium is home to UNAM's popular professional *fútbol*-playing **Pumas**; you'll see their navy blue and gold logo everywhere around campus. *(On the opposite side of Insurgentes Sur from the Jardín Central; cross via the footbridge. ☎ 5622 0495.)*

ESPACIO ESCULTÓRICO. Just outside the CCU, this impressive collection of large sculptures dates from the 1980s. The largest is *Las Serpientes del Pedregal*, by Federico Silva (1986), a long snake crafted from uneven blocks of stone several meters high and separated by narrow spaces. The Espacio Escultórico should only be visited during the day—its secluded location makes it dangerous in the dark.

UNIVERSUM (MUSEO DE LAS CIENCIAS). This natural science museum is filled with educational exhibits aimed toward kids, but is fun for adults too. All instructions are in Spanish. A cafeteria with sandwiches (12-25 pesos) is located in the museum. *(In the giant peach-colored building down the hill from the CCU. www.universum.unam.mx. Open M-F 9am-6pm, Sa-Su and holidays 10am-6pm; ticket booth closes at 5pm. 30 pesos, children and students 25 pesos.)*

CUICUILCO ARCHAEOLOGICAL ZONE. A bit south of the CCU is the archaeological zone of Cuicuilco (Place of the Many-Colored Jasper). The centerpiece, **El Gran Basamento,** was built between 800 and 150 BC. The area served as a ceremonial center with a population of around 20,000, making it the largest central settlement in Mesoamerica before the rise of Teotihuacán in the early Classic Period. Measuring 110m in diameter and 25m in height, the pyramid was built in at least 8 different stages and terminates with altars at its summit. The area was abandoned near the end of the Pre-Classic Period, when the tiny volcano of **Xitle** erupted around AD 100, coating 8 sq. km of surrounding land in a thick layer of lava. On a clear day, the summit affords a faint view of Xitle to the south and the much larger Popocatépetl to the east. A small museum displays artifacts found at the site, including a tomb, with lengthy descriptions in Spanish of the site and the civilization. Also on display is Camarena's painting "La Erupción de Xitle." *(On the southeast corner at the intersection of Insurgentes Sur and Anillo Periférico, south of Ciudad Universitaria. From M: Universidad (Line 3), exit on the side away from campus (salidas A, B, and C), toward the small outdoor market, and take any "Cuicuilco" or "Villa Olímpica" pesero (2 pesos) to the entrance on the west side of Insurgentes Sur, just beyond the Periférico, the big highway overpass. A sign, "Parque Ecológico Cuicuilco," marks the entrance to the site. Peseros will let you off on the other side of Insurgentes, next to the Villa Olímpica housing and business development. To return, take any "CU Metro" pesero. ☎ 5606 9758. Open daily 9am-5pm. Free. Free guided tours in Spanish M-F 9am-1:30pm.)*

XOCHIMILCO

M: Tasqueña (Line 2). Ride the tren ligero (trolleybus; 1.5 pesos; follow the "correspondencia" signs) in the "Embarcadero" direction. For the gardens, get off at the "Xochimilco" stop. For the museum, get off at the "La Noria" stop.

In Xochimilco ("so-she-MIL-co"; Place of the Flower Growing), there are two things to do. The first is what everyone does: cruise the **floating gardens** of Xochimilco in a hand-poled *chalupa*. The second is far less known. Beyond the gardens a gorgeous museum, the **Museo Dolores Olmedo,** houses an impressive Rivera collection and the largest Kahlo collection in Mexico.

■ **THE FLOATING GARDENS.** The floating gardens of Xochimilco were not for pleasure, but were essential elements of the Aztec agricultural system. Settled in the Pre-Classic times, it was only under the rule of Axayácatl that the city became an Aztec territory. In the Aztec's brilliantly conceived system, *chinampas* (artificial islands) were made by piling soil and mud onto floating rafts. These rafts were held firm by wooden stakes until the crops planted on top sprouted roots, reaching through the base of the canals. They became fertile islands, supporting several crops per year. Though polluted today, the canals still bear the waterborne greenery planted centuries ago.

Multicolored **chalupa** boats crowd the maze of canals, ferrying passengers past a floating market of food, flowers, and music. Families, young people, and couples lounge and listen to the *mariachis* and *marimba* players while downing goodies and booze from the floating taco stands and bars. Prices have now been standardized, but still, beware: vendors might try to rip you off. Private boats come in two sizes; the larger is 160 pesos per hr. and the smaller 140 pesos per hr. The price is for the boat and not per person. A shared boat is much cheaper, with a one-way trip at 10 pesos, and a round-trip at 20 pesos (available only weekends and holidays). *Mariachis* go at 70 pesos a song and all the other musicians for less than that. Beers are a good deal at 10-15 pesos each.

Xochimilco also offers two enormous land-bound **markets,** one with the usual food and household items, the other filled with live plants and animals. To reach the marketplace from the trolley bus, turn left on any street within three blocks of the station as you walk away from it, then walk until you reach the market. *(At the "Xochimilco" stop on the tren ligero, numerous "Embarcadero" signs and white-shirted boat owners will direct you. Peseros below the station can also take you; ask to stop at "un embarcadero.")*

■ **MUSEO DOLORES OLMEDO.** As a young woman, the beautiful Dolores Olmedo Patiño mingled with Mexico's elite. This museum, once her estate, features the art collection she amassed throughout her life. As the long-time lover of Diego Rivera, she is the subject of many of his paintings. The collection holds 144 of these canvases, including a series of 25 sunsets painted from Olmedo's Acapulco home in 1956, the year before Rivera's death. Perhaps even more impressive, the 25 paintings by Frida Kahlo, much of whose work is held abroad or in private collections, make this the best Kahlo collection in all of Mexico. Temporary exhibits support lesser-known but excellent work by current Mexican artists. Take a brief stroll on the museum grounds to appreciate its gorgeously landscaped lawns; peacocks strut around the mansion and boldly approach visitors. *(Av. México 5843. From the "La Noria" stop on the tren ligero, exit to the left, turn left at the corner, turn left again at the next corner, and walk straight. It will be across the street ahead of you. ☎ 5555 1221 or 5555 0891; www.museodoloresolmedo.com. Open Tu-Su 10am-6pm. 30 pesos, students and teachers 15 pesos, children under 6 free; Su free.)*

🎵 🎭 ENTERTAINMENT AND NIGHTLIFE

Whether you want to dance, drink, talk, sing, listen, or watch, you will find your kind of place in *D.F.* Clubs offer salsa, rock, electronic pop, and everything in between—but there are also laid-back bars, theaters, cinemas, and wild *cantinas*. The options, like the city, are almost limitless.

Cover charges are a necessary evil of the capital's night life. At *discotecas* (dance clubs) they range from 50-200 pesos for men. Women are often admitted free before a certain hour (usually 11pm or midnight) or at half-price. Unfortunately, after this time you will still have to buy drinks—rarely will you be lucky enough to find a *barra libre*. If drink prices are not listed, ask to avoid exorbitant *gringo* prices. *Bebidas nacionales* (Mexican-made drinks, from Kahlúa to *sangría*) are considerably cheaper than imported ones.

FROM THE ROAD

A NIGHT ON THE PUEBLO

You've spent endless hours conjugating verbs and rolling your "r"s, but you still don't fit in. What you need is something that no 7th-grade Spanish teacher could (or would) teach—a brief review of all the slang necessary for a night out on the town. Luckily, Let's Go has compiled a list of the basics. Incorporate these into your vocab, and watch as your *gabacho* (gringo) status fades away.

The night begins when you greet your friends, "*¿Qué onda?*", *¿Qué tal?*", or "*¿Qué pasa?*" (What's up?), and head out *al antro* (to the disco). Once there, don't be a *codo* (tightwad)—grab a *chupe* (drink) or a *chela* (beer) and comment on how *chido* or *padre* (cool) the place is—*fresas* (snobs) prefer the phrase *de pelos*. Of course, keep your eyes peeled for *papacitos* (studs) and *mamacitas*—women that are *buenísima* (very fine). Perhaps you'll *echarle perros* or *flores* (compliment or flatter him/her), *ligar* (hook up), and—if you are *cachondo* (horny)—maybe you'll *ajar* (make out/get down with) a fellow discotechie. The next day, if you're not too *crudo* (hung over), swap stories of the previous night with your friends. If they're telling tales, bring them back in line with a "*¡No mames, buey!*" (Get off it!/Don't kid me, man!). As you relate your own night, let everyone know how *alumbrado* (lit up/drunk) you were.

> **! SOME BACKSEAT DRIVING.** Taxis run all night and are the safest way to get from bar to disco to breakfast to hotel, but—especially after dark—avoid flagging cabs off the street. Remember to get the number of a *sitio* taxi company from your hotel or hostel before you leave, or ask any respectable-looking bartender, bouncer, or waiter to call one for you. See p. 94 for more info.

The hours, prices, and coolness of entertainment establishments sometimes change faster than even an annually updated book can track. In the summer of 2001, night life-seekers were stopped in their tracks by mysterious green seals, reading *CLAU-SURADO* (SHUT DOWN), placed over the doors of dozens of the city's bars and clubs. The seals explained that the city government had closed the establishments indefinitely, "for violations of the regulatory statutes in effect." Some establishments reopened within a few weeks, but the future of most is still unclear. The Zona Rosa, the Centro Histórico, and the city's gay nightlife were the hardest hit. For the most current information, consult the publications *Tiempo Libre* (7 pesos) and *Ser Gay* (for gay entertainment; free), or ask locals.

Women venturing out alone will likely be approached by men offering drinks, dances, and much more. In light of Mexico City's sometimes staggering crime statistics, both men and women should go out with friends.

CENTRO HISTÓRICO

Although the *centro* is known for being quiet at night, the emerging nightlife now offers both tourists and locals some great places to go. **Metro: Zócalo** (Line 2), **Bellas Artes** (Lines 2 and 8), **Allende** (Line 2), and **Isabel la Católica** (Line 1).

La Gioconda, Filomena Mata 18-E (☎5518 7823) between Madero and 5 de Mayo. Sit back with your cup of coffee (12 pesos), beer (20-32 pesos), or tequila (40-60 pesos) and relax in this friendly, bright cafe/bar. Attracts Mexicans and international clientele of all ages. A blues band plays every Saturday from 9pm-midnight. Great atmosphere and friendly staff. Baguettes, pasta, and soup during the day. Open daily 1pm-midnight.

La Casa Del Sol, 5 de Febrero 28 (☎1054 6840), upstairs. Restaurant, bar, and dance club: this place has something for everybody. Live music and karaoke. A 2-for-1 happy hour (daily 4-5pm and 8-9pm). A TV to watch your favorite soccer team (México, of course!).

Beers start at 20 pesos. Open M-Th 10am-9pm, F-Sa 10am-4am.

Salon Baraimas, Filomena Mata 7 (☎5510 4488), between Tacuba and 5 de Mayo. Not only is this a good place to dance salsa, it is also a good place to learn the salsa (40 pesos per class). Beer 30 pesos. Cover 45 pesos. Open Th-Sa 9pm-3:30am.

Insomnio, Madero 39 (☎3093 8714), upstairs. Doubles as a *discoteca* and a concert hall. Depending on the event, entrance prices vary. Beers 20-25 pesos, hard alcohol 35-85 pesos. Open daily 9pm-4am. Call for event information.

NEAR THE MONUMENTO A LA REVOLUCIÓN

True *chilangos* fill the inexpensive bars scattered around the monument's flood-lit dome. The darkened streets are not particularly safe—it's best to visit these places with a group of friends. Sadly, the sweeps in the summer of 2001 cut short this area's budding club life. Nevertheless, **Bar Milan,** Milan 18, all by itself between the monument and Reforma, is emerging as a place for young beautiful people to be seen—in t-shirt and jeans or in designer evening wear. You can dance during the week, but the shoulder-to-shoulder crowd on weekend nights only leaves enough room to sip 25-peso bottles of domestic beer and shout "conversation." (☎5592 0031. No cover. Open Tu-Sa 9pm-3am.) **Bar Rasta,** at the intersection of Reforma and Insurgentes, a 15min. walk from either the Revolución or Insurgentes stations, hosts a young, gregarious crowd grooving to reggae, hip-hop, and other pop tunes behind a huge, Disney-esque facade. (Domestic open bar. Cover men 180 pesos, women 30 pesos. Open daily 9pm-5am.) **Metro: Revolución** (Line 2).

ZONA ROSA

Home to some of the republic's fanciest discos and highest cover charges, on weekend nights the Zona Rosa can feel like the center of the universe. Clubs come and go, but a few very commercial chains have had the muscle to stay. Exemplars are US-sports-bar-themed **Yarda's** and **Freedom,** which attract the young and moneyed set. At these and other Zona clubs, you're guaranteed a comfortable environment, large crowds, and no flack from bouncers. Mixed among these mainstream establishments are also strip clubs, in which hang a very different atmosphere. The high covers at most clubs makes club-hopping prohibitive. Sidewalk recruiters will likely try to lure in groups, especially those with high female-to-male ratios; hold out and you might get a deal. Dress codes

THE LOCAL LEGEND

CANTINFLAS

While walking down a bus[y] street, you're confronted by a ma[n] in a jumpsuit holding a small box. "I can make those really shine sir," he says, looking at your feet. "But they're sneakers," you say. " have something especially fo[r] sneakers," he replies. "But bought them yesterday!" you pro test. "I have something especiall[y] for new sneakers!" he answers. S[o] you submit to a sneaker-shine overwhelmed by this man's unlim ited optimism and a strange fee ing you've seen him before.

And indeed, you have, in [a] way: it's the spirit of Cantinfla[s] (1911-1993), the most famou[s] Mexican comedian of all time beloved by millions throughou[t] the Americas. Born Mario Moreno the actor played essentially th[e] same character in all of his films a down-and-out man trying to ge[t] by using good humor and sly fast talk, a part played by Mexicans i[n] real life then and today. In one o[f] his most famous films, *El bolerc de Raquel* (1956), Cantinflas por trays a Mexico City *bolero* (shoe shine man) getting the better o[f] *gringo* tourists, rich locals, an[d] the police, and using his earning[s] to support an adopted son Today, a statue of Cantinflas stands in front of Hospita[l] Obregón (Obregón 123) in Colo nia Roma. A quotation by th[e] actor inscribed on the base sum marizes his life well: "Man's com mitment to life is to be happy an[d] to make others happy."

are relaxed, but sneakers are never a good idea. After a wild night, hop in an all-night *pesero* on Reforma or Insurgentes Sur (5 pesos). **Metro: Insurgentes** (Line 1) and **Sevilla** (Line 1).

Cantina las Bohemias, Londres 142 (☎5207 4384), at Amberes. Small, cozy, and best of all, populated with *mariachis*. A great escape. Beer 20 pesos, tequila 40-75 pesos. *Antojitos* 30-70 pesos, entrees 80-160 pesos. Open M-Sa 1pm-1am.

Cielo Rojo, Genova 70 (☎5525 5493). A huge menu of mixed drinks, live salsa music, and a dance floor make this a great place to be. Beer 25 pesos.

Escándalo, Florencia 32 (☎5525 7426). For all the salsa and merengue lovers out there. Live music. Beer 25 pesos. Cover 90 pesos. Open Th-Sa 8am-4am.

Melodika, Florencia 52 (☎5208 0198), between Londres and Liverpool. Enormous menus of mixed drinks (100 pesos) and songs make this karaoke bar a fun (if pricey) place to start the night. Cover 40 pesos. Open M-Sa 8pm-3am.

Yarda's, Niza 40 (☎5512 2108). Early in the evening, US and Canadian pro sports dominate the big screen. Later, disco lights bring the all-ages crowd to its feet. If you don't like the song but need some Yarda's in your life, run across the street to the other location. Domestic beer 25 pesos. No cover. Open M-Sa 7pm-4am; doors close at 2am.

Taberna Kloster, Genova 17 (☎5514 7992) Live rock from the 60s, 70s, 80s, and 90s. Beer 27 pesos, mixed drinks 37-58 pesos. No cover. Open W-Sa 6pm-3am.

Freedom, Copenhague 25 (☎5207 8456), at Hamburgo. Three floors of throbbing pop (but no dance floor) and no cover may lure you despite sometimes rude staff and always cheesy decor. Live music W, Th, Sa. Beer 26-33 pesos, mixed drinks 37-78 pesos. Open daily 1pm-2am.

■ PLAZA GARIBALDI

Plaza Garibaldi flaunts some of Mexico City's gaudiest and most amusing nightlife. By 5pm, wandering *mariachis* and roving *ranchero* bands begin to play for negotiable prices. Fifty pesos for a three-song set (10 pesos for solo performers) is a good deal. Tourists, locals, prostitutes, musicians, vendors, children—anybody and everybody mingles here, enjoying the alcoholic offerings of the plaza. The big nightclubs surrounding the plaza aggressively lure crowds. Though they advertise no cover, per-drink prices are astoundingly high. Your best bet is to find a table at one of the open-air cafes, where you can order cheap beers (12 pesos) or try *pulque*, an alcoholic drink made from the maguey cactus (14-70 pesos per liter, available straight or with special flavors). If you're hungry, don't miss the **Mercado de Alimentos San Camilito ❶**, on the northwest corner of the plaza. This indoor market contains tons of small, inexpensive eateries. Most will feed you quite well for around 30 pesos. Exercise caution and especially avoid wandering beyond the plaza to the back streets, which are considerably less charming. The best time to visit Garibaldi is in the evening, between 8pm and midnight on Friday or Saturday.

The plaza is at the intersection of Lázaro Cárdenas (Eje Central) and Rep. de Honduras, north of the Alameda. **Metro:** get off at **Bellas Artes** (Lines 2, 8) and walk three blocks away from the Palacio de Bellas Artes on Cárdenas; Garibaldi will be on your right. **Garibaldi** (Line 8) plants you three blocks away from the plaza. Exit to your left and walk towards the Palacio de Bellas Artes or the zócalo.

COYOACÁN

Plaza Hidalgo, Coyoacán's historic heart, is the place to be. The biggest crowds form on weekend evenings, drawn to free performances by comedians, mimes, and musicians. The buildings nearby often host plays and other performances. Inquire at Casa de Cortés before 8pm for showtimes. **Cineteca Nacional,** México-Coyoacán 389, next to the footbridge, screens classic films and recent flops.

Check *D.F.*'s daily, *La Jornada,* for information on shows. (☎5688 5926 or 5688 8864. Open M-Sa; showtimes vary.)

Many restaurants host live music, but clubs in the area are sparse: by midnight things quiet down a lot. One nightlife option is **El Hijo del Cuervo,** on the north side of Jardín Centenario, where a diverse crowd listens to live rock and Latin music. (☎5658 7824. Open daily 1pm-3am; music starts at 9pm.) **Metro: Coyoacán** (Line 3).

COLONIA ROMA

Next to the Zona Rosa, this tranquil residential neighborhood has become a great destination for less commercialized, more relaxed nightlife. An increasing number of gay clubs and bars are also opening here. Unfortunately, there's no single nightlife cluster; you'll need to know where you're headed before coming. *Tiempo Libre* and *Ser Gay* have especially good listings for this area. **Café-Bar Las Hormigas,** upstairs in Casa del Poeta, Álvaro Obregón 73, has live music and spoken word performances in its intimate bar. On the alcoholic side, Las Hormigas offers domestic beer for 18 pesos and free *botanas* many nights. Expect to pay a modest cover for some of the weekend musical acts. Call before you go or pick up a schedule. (☎5533 5456. Open M-F 11am-10pm, Sa 6-10pm.) **Metro: Insurgentes** (Line 1).

NEAR THE WORLD TRADE CENTER

Lining Insurgentes near the World Trade Center skyscraper are a bunch of themed nightlife hotspots. Although not the most authentic entertainment in the capital, these places are fun and less expensive than their counterparts in the Zona Rosa and *centro histórico.* The area also has a share of semi-sleazy strip clubs—in which male performers dance for groups of screaming women. Take any "San Ángel" bus on Insurgentes from points north or from Buenavista. If you're coming from San Ángel or Ciudad Universitaria, board an "Indios Verdes" bus.

- 🏯 **La Cantina de los Remedios,** Insurgentes Sur 744 (☎5687 1037). The vast bar will blow you away. 2-for-1 drinks 6-10pm (domestic beer 26 pesos, cocktails 33 pesos). Live music nightly, usually *mariachi* but also *son* and rock. Also serves food: *botanas* 30-70 pesos, main dishes 50-130 pesos. No cover. Open M-Sa 1:30pm-midnight.

- 🏯 **Polyforum Siqueiros,** Insurgentes Sur 701 (☎5536 4520), at Filadelfia. An entire building constructed to display the audacious murals of David Alfaro Siqueiros. Different multimedia shows on the man appear here—call for schedule. By night, patrons enjoy a theater, restaurant, piano bar (open 7pm-3am), and disco (open F-Sa 10pm-3am).

- **Congo,** Insurgentes 810 (☎5543 0309). Live *merengue* and salsa every night, live rock F-Sa, and strippers on Th—includes performers from neighboring Chippendale's. F-Sa cover 100 pesos; no cover 9-11pm. Open Th-Sa 9pm-5:30am.

- **Liverpool Pub,** Insurgentes 858 (☎5523 2732). Come listen to The Beatles *a la mexicana.* Stop by Th-Sa at 1:30am to rock with a cover band that looks and sounds just like those famous Brits. Other bands play other live music from the 60s and 70s. Open W-Sa 8:30pm-3am. Cover 90 pesos.

SAN ÁNGEL

The many upscale bars along Insurgentes and Revolución cater to an executive crowd, who often arrive clad in business suits. Cover charges here are low or nonexistent. Although there are no real dance clubs—besides a couple of strip joints on Insurgentes—there's plenty of activity, even on a Wednesday night. Jazz bars abound, and several small venues host classical concerts and plays. Check in at **Centro Cultural San Ángel** (☎5616 1254 or 5616 2097), the big yellow building at Revolución and Madero, before 8pm to find out what's on. Take a "San Ángel" bus on Insurgentes to get here from points as far north as Buenavista station.

New Orleans, Revolución 1655 (☎5550 1908). The self-proclaimed "Cathedral of Jazz in Mexico" features live jazz amidst wood paneling. See *Tiempo Libre* for show info. Cover 35 pesos, F-Sa 50 pesos. Open daily 5pm-midnight; music usually starts at 8pm.

La Cantina San Ángel, Insurgentes Sur 2146 (☎5661 2292). This upscale bar plays loud pop and rock to entertain the pretty young people filling the small tables. Beer 32 pesos. Domestic rum 30-40 pesos. Open daily 1pm-4am.

La Planta de Luz (☎5616 4761), in Plaza Loreto at Revolución and Río Magdalena. Features a changing roster of live music, comedy, and drama. Cover for shows. Su noon or 6:30pm, M and W-F shows start at 8:30, 9, or 10pm; call ahead about performances. Cover ranges from 100 to 250 pesos, depending on the event.

GAY AND LESBIAN ENTERTAINMENT

The capital presents a full range of social and cultural activities for gays and lesbians, and an active, fledgling gay rights movement has made its presence known. General tolerance of homosexuality is still very low, and although not illegal, public displays of affection by gay and lesbian couples on the street or on the Metro are sure tickets to harassment, especially by the police. Gay men will have a much easier time finding bars and discos, although more and more venues have begun to welcome lesbians. The free pamphlet *Ser Gay* is a great source of information, with listings for gay entertainment, art events, clubs, and bars in the city. Copies are available at all the clubs listed below. For exclusively lesbian activities, contact one of several Mexico City lesbian groups (see p. 100). In June, Mexico's gay pride month, a massive number of parties, rallies, art exhibits, marches, and *fiestas* occur throughout the city. Gay-friendly clubs and restaurants are usually marked with a recognizable rainbow flag.

■ **El Celo,** Londres 104 (☎5514 4309), in the Zona Rosa. This laid-back bar/club draws one of the city's hippest crowds, with gays and lesbians crowding its floors to get down to techno and pop. In the afternoons it is a gay-friendly cafe. Beers 20 pesos. No cover, but 2 drink minimum. Open Th-Sa 4pm-4am.

■ **Butterflies,** Izazaga 9 (☎5761 1861), between Cárdenas and Bolívar, near M: Salto del Agua (Lines 1, 8). This unmarked, cavernous dance club fills on weekend nights with a mixed crowd. Great drag shows, irresistibly danceable rock, techno, *salsa* and *merengue*, and an extremely relaxed atmosphere make this one of the most fun clubs in the city for anyone. Snack bar in the back. Domestic beer 25 pesos. Cover F-Sa 60 pesos (includes 2 drinks). Open Tu-Su 9pm-4am.

Praga 40, Praga 40 (☎5208 5280). This laid-back bar is a good alternative to the high-energy clubs that predominate. Beer 20-25 pesos. During the day it is a cafe (*comida corrida* varies, but is usually around 40 pesos).

La Cantina del Vaquero, Algeciras 26 (☎5598 2195), in Col. Insurgentes, near Parque Hundido, between M: Mixcoac (Line 7) and M: Zapata (Line 3). The first openly gay *cantina* in Mexico has been a favorite for over 25 years. Working-class gay men still flock to the bar to watch XXX videos, sample the darkroom, or simply grab a beer and chat. Videos screened daily 5-11pm. 35-peso cover includes 2 beers. Open daily 5pm-late.

Living, Orizaba 164 (☎5584 7403; www.living.com.mx), in Col. Roma. Pop and electronic music fill this classy club. Beer 28 pesos. Open F-Sa 7pm-4am. Cover 120 pesos.

Cabaré-tito, Londres 117 (☎5207 2554), under a stained-glass awning, in the Zona Rosa. A busy disco full of young people, both gay and lesbian. Domestic beer 25 pesos, tequila 35-50 pesos. Tu-Su stage shows (usually drag, strippers on Su) start at 10:30pm. Cover for shows. Call for weekly program. Open daily 1pm-4am.

El Taller, Florencia 37A (☎5533 4984), underground in the Zona Rosa next to El Almacén. A well-known blue-collar hangout. Throbbing music, construction-site decorations, and dark, private alcoves create an intense, men-only pick-up scene. Private barroom attracts an older crowd. Open daily 8pm-4am.

El Almacén, Florencia 37 (☎5207 0727). Mediterranean food and pop dance music. Although mostly men, lesbians are welcome. Open daily 5pm-4am. Cover 80 pesos.

⬛ SHOPPING

While most Mexican cities rely on one large, central market, Mexico City seems to have one on every corner. Each *colonia* has its own market, and downtown markets rival the size of small cities. Markets are all relatively cheap, but vary widely in quality and content. Shopping throughout the *centro* and the Alameda proceeds thematically: there is a wedding dress street, a lighting fixtures street, a lingerie street, a windowpane street, even a military surplus street.

Mercado de la Ciudadela, 2 blocks north of M: Balderas (Lines 1, 3), off Balderas. Nonstop tourist traffic flows through the capital's biggest and best *artesanía* market, where traditional clothing is also available at low prices. Open daily 8am-7pm.

San Juan Artesanías, Plaza el Buen Tono, 4 blocks south of Alameda Central, 2 blocks west of Lázaro Cárdenas. From M: Salto de Agua (Lines 1, 8), walk 4 blocks up López and make a left on Ayuntamiento. 3 floors of *artesanía* from all over Mexico, ranging from standard tourist items to exquisite handmade treasures. Prices similar to La Ciudadela, but comparison shopping always helps. Fewer tourists wander here, which gives you more bargaining power. Open Su 9am-4pm, M-Sa 9am-7pm.

La Merced, Circunvalación at Anaya, east of the *zócalo*. M: Merced (Line 1). Not just a market but a way of life. The largest market in the Americas has an enormous selection of fresh produce from all over the country and maybe more raw meat than your nose can handle—all at rock-bottom prices. The nearby **Mercado de Dulces** (Candy Market) will make you feel like the proverbial kid in a candy store. Between the two lies the **Mercado de Flores** (Flower Market). All 3 markets open daily 8am-7pm.

The Zócalo, along Corregidora, the street between the Palacio Nacional and the Supreme Court, is the unofficial "market" and subject of much controversy through the years. Vendors clog the street with stands, their brightly colored umbrellas stretching as far as the eye can see. The government has long been trying to drive out these non-rent-paying shopkeeps, but to no avail. The persistent vendors have some of the best prices in town on sundries, clothing, toys, CDs, and electronics. If you don't mind insanely crowded streets, come here for your non-*artesanía* needs.

FONART, Patriotismo 691 (☎5563 4060), also at Juárez 89 (☎5521 0171). A national project to protect and market traditional crafts sells *artesanía* from all over the country: giant tapestries, rugs, silver jewelry, pottery, and colorful embroidery. Regulated prices are not quite as low as those in the markets, but crowds and haggling are eliminated. Open Su 10am-7pm, M-Sa 9am-8pm.

Sonora, Teresa de Mier and Cabañ, 2 blocks south of La Merced. This unique market attracts those who enjoy witchcraft, medicinal teas and spices, figurines, and ceremonial images. Search no further for lucky cows' feet, shrunken heads, eagle claws, black salt, and powdered skull (for the domination of one's enemies). Also sells more mundane goods, like household wares, toys, and pets—a very sad sight. Beware, this is a prime spot for pickpockets. Open daily 8am-7pm.

Bazar del Sabado, Plaza San Jacinto, in the center of San Ángel. Overflowing onto the plaza, this market tends to be pricey and touristy, but is one of the few to which contemporary artists bring their work. One of San Ángel's biggest draws. Open Sa 9am-6pm.

🏅 SPORTS

Whether consumed by their passion for bullfighting, *fútbol* (soccer), *béisbol* (baseball), or horse racing, Mexican fans share an almost religious devotion to *deportes* (sports). If sweaty discos and endless museums have you craving a change of pace, follow the sports-loving crowds and prepare yourself for a rip-roarin' rowdy good time. *¡Ándale!*

GOOOOOOOOOOOOOAAAAAAAAAAAAAL! Although *charrería* may be the official national sport of Mexico, *fútbol* is by far the most popular. Those interested in the phenomenon are in luck—matches take place year-round. The Winter League runs July-Dec. and the Summer League Jan.-May. In addition, countless minor and amateur *fútbol* leagues play throughout the year. Every fourth June, the World Cup takes Mexico by storm—even gas and water delivery stops as soccer fans throughout the country pack bars and restaurants to watch the games. Whenever Mexico scores a goal, the entire nation shakes in unison as the word "GOL!" rings from every bar, boulevard, business, and bus.

■ **Estadio Azteca,** Calz. de Tlalpan 3465 (☎5617 8080 or 5617 1516; www.esmas.com/estadioazteca). Take a *pesero* or *tren ligero* (trolley bus) from M: Tasqueña (Line 2). Proud home of the *Águilas de America* (American Eagles), Mexico's largest stadium packs in 100,000-person crowds for popular *fútbol* matches. Good luck getting tickets; start with Ticketmaster (☎5325 9000; www.ticketmaster.com.mx). Season runs Oct.-July. Tickets 50-1200 pesos. If you can't get tickets, but still want to see the stadium, there are guided tours Su-W and F-Sa (5 per day 10am-5pm) and Th (4 and 5pm). 10 pesos, children under 5 free.

■ **Plaza México** (☎5611 4413), M: San Antonio (Line 7) on Insurgentes Sur, is Mexico's principal bullring, seating 40,000 fans. July-Nov. professional fights; Nov.-Feb. *novillada* (novice) fights. Tickets run 40-2225 pesos, depending on proximity to the ring and the *sombra* (shade) or *sol* (sun). Next door is the very big and very blue **Estadio Azul** (www.cruz-azul.com.mx), home of Mexico City's professional *fútbol* team Cruz Azul. Bullfights take place Su 4pm.

El Foro del Sol, in the Ciudad Deportiva, M: Ciudad Deportiva (Line 9). This "sports city" complex contains volleyball courts, a boxing ring, an ice-skating rink, many soccer fields, and other assorted facilities. The *Foro*, at the center of the complex, hosts the home games of Mexico City's 2 professional baseball teams, the *Diablos Rojos* (Red Devils) and the *Tigres* (Tigers). Sparks fly when the teams face each other, and local papers have dubbed the matchup the *Guerra Civil* (Civil War). Tickets (10-80 pesos) are easy to come by and can be purchased at the gate.

Hipódromo de las Américas (www.hipodromo.com.mx), M: Tacubaya (Lines 1, 7, 9). This compound houses a horse track and hosts *jai alai* matches, an extremely fast game a bit like raquetball (see p. 406). Though some may not call it a sport, *lucha libre*, Mexico's version of professional wrestling, takes over the *hipódromo* every F night. Mexico City's main *jai alai* venue, the famous **Frontón México,** facing the north side of the Monumento a la Revolución, was closed as of this writing.

🏛 DAYTRIPS FROM MEXICO CITY

Even those who've fallen deeply in love with Mexico City need some time away to maintain a healthy relationship. Fortunately, the capital's great location makes for easy and painless escape. From small towns to not-so-small towns, from ruins to volcanoes, all of the following places make convenient daytrips.

Near Mexico City

0   20 kilometers

0   20 miles

TO ATLACOMULCO AND QUERÉTARO

TO IXTAPAN DE LA SAL

Parque Nacional Nevado de Toluca

TO ZITÁCUARO, VALLE DE BRAVO

Tenancingo

Joquicingo

Malinalco

Tenancingo

Metepec

Mexicaltzingo

Toluca

Xonacatlán

MEXICO

TO XOCHICALCO

Cuernavaca

Parque Nacional Lagunas de Zempoala

Parque Nacional Desierto de los Leones

NAUCALPAN

Tepotzotlán

TO TULA

TLALNEPANTLA

Parque Nacional El Tepozteco

MORELOS

Tepoztlán

TO CUAUTLA

FEDERAL DISTRICT

Mexico City

CD. NEZAHUALCÓYOTL

Chalco

Ozumba

Amecameca

Tlalmanalco

Parque Nacional Ixta Popo

Tlamacas

San N. de los Ranchos

PUEBLA

Huejotzingo

Cholula

Puebla

TO VERACRUZ

Acolman

Tepexpan

Teotihuacán

San Martín de las Pirámides

TO PACHUCA

MEXICO

Parque Nacional Zoquiapan

HIDALGO

Nanacamilpa

Texmelucan

Calpulalpan

Apan

Santa Rosa

Tlaxcala

Tenancingo

Cacaxtla

Hueyotipan

MEXICO CITY

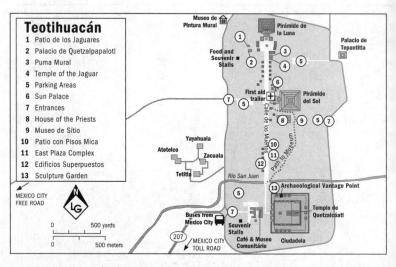

Teotihuacán
1 Patio de los Jaguares
2 Palacio de Quetzalpapalotl
3 Puma Mural
4 Temple of the Jaguar
5 Parking Areas
6 Sun Palace
7 Entrances
8 House of the Priests
9 Museo de Sítio
10 Patio con Pisos Mica
11 East Plaza Complex
12 Edificios Superpuestos
13 Sculpture Garden

TEOTIHUACÁN

Direct bus service from Mexico City is available via Autobuses Teotihuacán (1hr., every 15min. 7am-3pm, 25 pesos), in the Terminal de Autobuses del Norte (☎ 5587 0501) at Sala 8. Buy your tickets for the "Pirámides" bus. The last bus back to Mexico City leaves from the Puerta 1 at 6pm. There are 5 entrances to the site. Buses drop visitors off by Puerta 1, the main entrance. Puerta 5, the easternmost entrance, is by the Pirámide del Sol. Free guided tours for groups of 5 or more can be arranged at the administration building by Puerta 1 (southwest corner). Site open daily 7am-6pm. 37 pesos, children under 13 free. Free parking. At some entrances, booths sell guided tours; opt for the free ones.

The massive ruins at Teotihuacán present a perplexing mystery: nobody is quite sure who the Teotihuacanos were. They may have been the Olmeca-Xicalanca, a Mixtec-speaking group, or, as another theory argues, a Totonac tribe. They were most likely a Pre-Toltec or Pre-Aztec, Náhuatl- or Mixtec-speaking people. The area was settled in the late Pre-Classic period, around 100 BC. Teotihuacán was meticulously planned and split into quadrants, with the Calle de Los Muertos and a now lost road forming the axes of the city. The city sprawled over an area of 20 sq. km, and controlled the entire Valley of Mexico, with evidence of trade and influence extending as far south as the Maya city of Tikal in Guatemala. The Pirámide del Sol, one of the largest pyramids in the world, was built in the late Pre-Classic period, while the newer Pirámide de la Luna was built during the Classic period. At its height (AD 150-250), Teotihuacán accommodated a population of nearly 200,000, making it the sixth-largest city in the world.

Sometime around AD 700, Teotihuacán began to weaken. While the reasons for its downfall are far from certain, many speculate that the city eventually collapsed under its own weight, having grown so large and crowded that it could no longer produce enough food to properly support its inhabitants. As if that weren't enough, overcrowding seems to have led to new buildings built atop old ones, setting the stage for a tremendous fire, marked today by layers of blackened stone, around AD 800. By AD 850, few residents remained in the enormous urban complex. When the Aztecs founded Tenochtitlán in the 14th century, Teotihuacán, 50km northeast of their capital, lay abandoned. The Aztecs were so impressed by the size and scope of the buildings that they adopted the areas as ceremonial grounds, believing its huge structures to be built by gods and those buried there to be of some superhuman order. They christened the area Teotihuacán, meaning "Place Where Men Become Gods"; in fact, all of the names of the buildings are those given by Aztecs. When the Spaniards destroyed Tenochtitlán in the 16th century, they were almost certainly unaware of the pyramid's existence, and this fortunate oversight allowed the site to remain astonishingly intact. Porfirio Díaz initiated extensive excavation in 1906 as part of a project to emphasize Mexico's cultural wealth for the 1910 celebration of 100 years of Mexican independence; little did he know how soon his own regime would join Teotihuacán in the annals of Mexican history.

CALLE DE LOS MUERTOS (STREET OF THE DEAD).

The ceremonial center, a 13 sq. km expanse, was built along a 4km stretch now called Calle de los Muertos, so named because the Aztecs believed ancient kings had been buried alongside it. The northern limit of the street is the Pirámide de la Luna, while the southern boundary remains little explored. The main structure, the Pirámide del Sol, lies to the east, aligned with the point on the horizon where the sun sets at the summer solstice. An east-west thoroughfare of equal length and importance is believed to have bisected the Calle at some point in front of the Ciudadela. Along the sides of the Calle are the Patio con Pisos de Mica, the Viking complex, and the West Plaza and East Plaza Complexes. Farther down is the Puma Mural and Puma Complex.

CIUDADELA (CITADEL).

At the southern end of the site is the expansive Ciudadela, where priests and government officials once lived. The large plaza was so named because of its resemblance to a military complex, though it actually functioned as royal residences. On the northern end of the Ciudadela lie four small pyramids. The top of the second one is an "Archaeological Vantage Point," which gives a wonderful view of the two nearby pyramids.

TEMPLO DE QUETZALCÓATL.

At the center of the Ciudadela is the Templo de Quetzalcóatl, 50m wide at its base and dedicated to the serpent god. This pyramid was obstructed by another, later pyramid, which actually served to preserve the shape of the older one; restoration removed part of the new pyramid to provide access to the old. Lining the main staircase, enormous carvings of the plumed serpent Quetzalcóatl pop out from the stone flowers. Along the outer surface, images of Quetzalcóatl alternate with those of the rain god Tlaloc, easily identifiable by his google-eyes and fangs. The still-visible red

ATHENS 2004

PLAY BALL!

The great ball courts found at Chichén Itzá and other Maya cities were constructed for a game called **ulama,** in which two contending teams of seven players each endeavored to keep a heavy rubber ball (3-5kg, six inches in diameter) in constant motion using only their hips, knees, shoulders, and elbows. In this exhausting game, players scored by knocking the ball through small stone rings placed high on the I shaped court's side walls.

For the Maya, the game was more than an idle pastime: playing it invoked the very creation of the heavens themselves. Twin gods Hunhunahpo and Seven Hunahpo were players whose racket on the court angered the lords of the underworld, resulting in the brothers' deaths. Hun's sons, Hero Twins Hunahpo and Xbalanke, avenged their father's demise, defeating Lords One and Seven Death despite the underworld's home court advantage. Rewarded for their honor, the Twins became the sun and moon.

Petty humans played the game as both symbol of the battle between good and evil and an important rite to keep the celestial bodies in motion, with the ball as sun and moon and the court as earth. The game also served as gory ceremony; it is unclear whether winning teams or losing teams were decapitated, but is certain that heads rolled, with winners profiting from deification.

paint that originally decorated these sculptures was made by collecting *nopales* (broad, flat cactus leaves) into which tiny bugs had burrowed, carving out the colorful critters, and smashing them.

EDIFICIOS SUPERPUESTOS. Continuing north along Calle de los Muertos, you will cross what was once the San Juan river. On the west side of the street are the remains of two temples, the Edificios Superpuestos, that were built in two phases (AD 200-400 and AD 400-750) atop older, partially demolished temples. The older buildings were filled in to clear the way for construction—again, unintentionally preserving the temples, which can now be viewed with the aid of metal catwalks.

PIRÁMIDE DEL SOL (PYRAMID OF THE SUN). Farther north and east towers the Pirámide del Sol, the single most massive structure in the ceremonial area. The biggest American pyramid of its time, at 222m by 225m, it is now second in size only to the pyramid at Cholula, and its volume is over one million cubic yards—dimensions comparable to those of Cheops in Egypt. It was begun sometime in the late Pre-Classic era, around 100 BC, and completed just before the zenith of Teotihuacano civilization, around AD 150. The inside of the pyramid is filled with rubble and brick, and there is evidence that it was built over the remains of another pyramid, perhaps originally of equal size. It turns out that 16th-century historical chronicles suggesting that the Pirámide was dedicated to the deity of the sun may have been off-base; modern evidence makes it seem more likely that it was dedicated to Tlaloc, the god of heavenly water. The evidence? The discovery of a 10ft. wide moat that once surrounded the pyramid, child burials at the pyramid's corners (offerings to Tlaloc), and a cave deep beneath the pyramid with the double symbolism of a life-giving womb and the entrance to the realm of the dead. At over 60m in height, the pyramids afford a breathtaking view of the surrounding valley. Smokers and slowpokes: don't quit. A railing helps you up the steepest stretch, and the platforms of the multi-tiered pyramid make convenient rest stops. Don't get discouraged as small children and dogs race past you.

MUSEO DE SITIO. To the right of the Pirámide del Sol stands the Museo de Sitio. Exhibits show the culture and stages of Teotihuacán, partly with displays of artifacts and graves. In one room, a transparent floor allows you to walk over a model of the ancient layout of the site. All of the pieces in the museum are replicas; the originals are at the Museo Nacional de Antropología in Mexico City (see p. 116).

PALACIO DE QUETZALPAPALOTL (PALACE OF THE QUETZAL BUTTERFLY). Between the Pirámide del Sol and the Pirámide de la Luna on the west side of the street is the Palacio de Quetzalpapalotl. This columned palace, next to the ceremonial space, kept its royal residents far from low-income and student housing. The gorgeous inner patio features colored frescoes and bird glyphs, which, though faded, have survived years of decay and retain much of their intricate detail. On the columns are images of plumed butterflies, which give the Palacio its name.

PATIO DE LOS JAGUARES. Behind the palace and through the short maze of an entrance stands the Patio de los Jaguares and the now-subterranean **Templo de las Conchas Emplumadas** (Temple of the Feathered Seashells). The patio features several murals of jaguars, symbolizing an ancient creator god that the Olmecs adopted. The Templo has some beautifully preserved frescoes sporting parrots and a four-petaled flower that symbolizes the cardinal directions.

PIRÁMIDE DE LA LUNA (PYRAMID OF THE MOON). At the northern end of Calle de los Muertos is the stunning **Pirámide de la Luna.** This pyramid, too, has links to water: a sculpture of **Chalchiutlicue,** the revered Aztec water goddess, was discovered here. The pyramid was built later than the Pirámide del Sol, most likely during Teotihuacán's height around AD 300. The base measures 150m by 130m and the pyramid is 42m high. The hike up this pyramid is steeper than the Pirámide del Sol, but it is also shorter and less crowded.

PALACIO DE TEPANTITLA. On the northeast side of the Pirámide del Sol near Puerta 4 sits the **Palacio de Tepantitla,** which has some of the best-preserved frescoes in Teotihuacán, still showing a full range of colors. Priests with elaborate headdresses and representations of Tlaloc exist pictorially within the Teotihuacano ideal of a butterfly-filled paradise.

DESIERTO DE LOS LEONES

Set off from San Ángel. There is only direct service to the Convent on the weekends. During the rest of the week, take a bus to Santa Rosa (3.5 pesos) and then take a taxi (40 pesos) up to the Convent. Make sure you get a phone number to call for a return trip. To return to the city on the weekend, colectivos to San Ángel or M: Tacubaya leave from the entrance approximately every hr., last bus 5pm. Park open daily 6am-5pm. Convent open Tu-Su 10am-5pm. 10 pesos. Free tours Sa-Su 11am-3pm.

Just outside the city, the Desierto de Los Leones (Desert of the Lions) offers solace and clean air among millions of pines. Hundreds of paths wind through the woods, perfect for hiking, picnicking, walking, or jogging. At the heart of the park sits the pristine **Convento Santo Desierto,** for which the park is named. Like all Barefoot Carmelite convents, this was purposefully built in a desolate area to facilitate the extreme self-abnegation practiced by its sisters. The lions who lived in this desert-like region were not those of African glory, but pumas. The Convent was originally built between 1606 and 1611 and, exactly 100 years later, an earthquake demolished it. The reconstruction finished in 1723, but from 1780 to 1801, the sisters abandoned it for another convent in the Nixcongo mountains, due to weather conditions. Wander through the immense corridors to catch a glimpse of a bedroom as it was left in 1801. Bring a flashlight or buy a candle (5 pesos) to descend into the basements. It is completely dark underneath the Convent, and the winding passages are not for the claustrophobic.

On Saturdays and Sundays from noon-3pm, the church hosts free (with admission) **theatre,** ranging from passion plays to the more avant-garde work of Federico García Lorca. Shows change weekly. The **cafeteria** serves decent but expensive food (*comida corrida* 130 pesos). Another food option is at **El León Dorado** restaurant, just outside the Convent, which serves delicious *conejo* (rabbit) and *trucha* (trout) specialties. (Open daily 8am-9pm.) Even less expensive is **Restaurante Letty,** which serves eggs (20 pesos), soups (30 pesos), meats (30-40 pesos) and more. (Open daily 8am-10pm.)

POPOCATÉPETL AND IXTACCÍHUATL

*From TAPO, several bus lines go to **Amecameca**, the best jumping-off point for Ixtaccíhuatl. Volcanos has the most frequent service (1½hr., every 30min. 5:30am-10pm, 18 pesos). Taxis in front of Hotel San Carlos on the Amecameca plaza can take you to the La Joya trailhead. Prices are high: a one-way taxi costs 300 pesos, and no return taxi is guaranteed. If you decide to visit Ixtaccíhuatl via **San Rafael**, catch a pesero going to Tlalmanalco (5am-7pm, 3.5 pesos) and get off in front of La Fábrica, a printing press (ask the driver to point it out). From there, another pesero (4.5 pesos) will take you to the San Rafael trailhead. To return to Mexico City, take a Volcanos bus or any bus labeled Metro San Lázaro (the TAPO station). They stop along the plaza in Amecameca or on the road labeled "Mexico" in Tlalmanalco (every 30min. 6am-8pm). From Cuernavaca, you'll want to take Estrella Roja to **Cuautla** (every 15 min. 6am-10pm), then walk to the Cristóbal Colón station. Go right on Ing. Mongoy as you exit the station, walk 1 block and turn left* *on 5 de Mayo; the station is half a block ahead on your left. Catch a Volcanos bus to* **Amecameca** *(1hr., every 15min. 5am-7pm, 8 pesos). Buses return to Cuernavaca from Cuautla (1½hr., every 15min. 5am-7pm, 14 pesos).*

Overlooking Morelos and Puebla are two snow-capped volcanoes, Popocatépetl (5452m) and Ixtaccíhuatl (5282m), the second- and third-largest peaks in the country. Aztec legend has it that the warrior Popocatépetl ("Smoking Mountain" in Náhuatl) loved Ixtaccíhuatl ("Sleeping Woman"), the emperor's daughter. Once, when Popocatépetl went off to battle, Ixtaccíhuatl came to believe that he had been killed, and she subsequently died of grief. When Popo (as he has come to be known—hardly surprising, given his hard-to-pronounce name) learned of his lover's death, he built the two great mountains. On the northern one he placed her body (which you can see by looking at Ixtaccíhuatl from afar, with a little imagination), and on the southern one he stood vigil with a torch. Locals pay their respects to the supine, death-pale Ixtaccíhuatl on the mountain's snowy summit. The passage between the two is called *Paso de Cortés* because it is the route the Spanish conqueror took to the valley of Tenochtitlán.

Due to its volatile status, Popocatépetl has been closed to hikers since 1994; regular explosions have continued to the time of writing, and approaching within 12km of the crater is not recommended. Signs pointing to *Rutas de Evacuación* (escape routes) in all nearby towns are reminders of the omnipresent danger. Parts of Ixtaccíhuatl can be explored on easy daytrips, but only seriously seasoned or those with a tour group should attempt the peak. Federación Mexicana de Alpinismo, all Mexican officials, and *Let's Go* strongly recommend against making even a daytrip when the **Socorro Alpino** (Alpine Assistance ☎5531 1401) is not nearby. Should you have an accident or **medical emergency** in the mountains, do your best to reach Danton Valle Negrete, Socorro Alpino's medical director in Mexico City (☎5740 6782; beeper 227 7979, code 553 1773). No season is free from rapid weather change; always bring both warm clothes and rain gear. By taking all the right precautions, you can have a superb adventure hiking the volcano. The Socorro Alpino is at **Paraje la Joya trailhead** every weekend to provide guidance. Although Ixtaccíhuatl is most easily reached from San Rafael via Tlalmanalco, a safe hike is well worth the extra pesos it takes to get to La Joya via Amecameca. Arrangements can be made with Socorro Alpino from Mexico City or at the trailhead on weekends. If you are planning a longer or non-weekend trip, be certain to register with Socorro Alpino before you go.

MALINALCO

Take a 2nd-class bus to Xalapa, which passes through Malinalco, from Terminal Poniente (1-2hr. depending on stops, 25 pesos). To avoid overpaying and to make sure the driver remembers to stop, tell both the ticket-seller and the bus driver your destination. From Cuernavaca's Estrella Blanca station, take a bus to Santa Marta (25 pesos), then one to Chalma (10 pesos), and finally a taxi (shared 6 pesos, private 36 pesos) to Malinalco. To get to the ruins from the zócalo, follow the blue pyramid signs along Guerrero and go straight. Take a left on Melgar, a right at the next street (the museum is here), and another right at the blue sign that appears to lead into someone's driveway. From there, it is a long walk up a lot of stairs. Malinalco's helpful **tourist office** *is in the white municipal building in the park next to the zócalo. (☎7147 0111. Open M-Sa 9am-3pm.) Site open Tu-Su 9am-5:30pm. 32 pesos; students, teachers, adults over 60, and children free.*

Malinalco is a small, peaceful town with one huge attraction: one of the best preserved Aztec temples in the country. **El Cuauhcalli**, or the **Templo de la Iniciación**, was cut whole from a nearby mountain and, along with pyramids in India, Jordan, and Egypt, is one of only four monolithic pyramids in the world. The Aztecs conquered Malinalco between 1469 and 1481, and emperor Ahuizotl oversaw the pyramid's construction in 1501. Every year on March 21, hundreds of people pour into

Malinalco to witness the temple's dazzling effect on the spring equinox, when a ray of light shines through the doorway and reveals the image of an eagle on the floor.

The ruins are believed to have been the sacred ground for the rituals that transformed an Aztec youth into a tiger or eagle warrior. On the open circular stone platform past the main temple, prisoners were bound to a pole with only their arms free and made to wrestle the recently initiated warriors. If the prisoner won consecutive bouts with two *águila* and two *tigre* warriors, followed by a wild-card lefty, he won his freedom. Defeat, on the other hand, had more unpleasant consequences; the small rectangular basin in front of the entrance to the pyramid would hold the prisoner's blood after his ritual sacrifice. Behind the pyramid, the bodies of the sacrificed were burned to ashes on the oval bed of rock. Inside the pyramid, all of the statues, rooms, and facades were originally painted a brilliant crimson. Around the pyramid are various dwellings and a *temascal*, an ancient sauna. The museum, **Museo Universitario de Dr. Luis Mario Schneider,** has artifacts from the site and exhibits on Malinalco's traditions. (☎ 7147 1288. Open Tu-Su 9am-6pm. 10 pesos.)

MEXICO CITY

OTHER DAYTRIPS FROM MEXICO CITY

Cuernavaca: This lovely colonial-town-turned-chic-upperclass-getaway overflows with expats and language schools. The gaggle of *gringos* and high prices come part and parcel with Cuernavaca's lush greenery, luxurious living, and trendy nightlife. (Morelos; 85km; see p. 368.)

Grutas de Cacahuamilpa: An underground wonderland of huge rock formations, some over 85m high. Guides point out formations that look like the Virgin Mary, people making out, and pretty much everything in between. (Guerrero; 130km; see p. 481.)

Ixtapan de la Sal: Although most people visit peaceful Ixtapan for the water-parks, spas, and resorts, the little city holds a charm far beyond all that commercialism. The lovely central plaza and Mediterranean-style church are filled with townspeople and good will. (Estado de México; 117km; see p. 364.)

Pachuca: An important silver mining and processing center since the 16th century, Pachuca offers invigorating mountain air, friendly inhabitants, and possibly the most beautiful *zócalo* in Mexico. (Hidalgo; 90km; see p. 358.)

Puebla: Legend has it that Puebla's gridded streets were laid by angels who streaked across the land to shape this elegant city. Modern sophistication complements the city's rich past. (Puebla; 120km; see p. 385.)

Taxco: Silver, silver, silver, all amazingly beautiful and inexpensive. Picturesque Taxco sits way up in the hills, and its pink stone Catedral de Santa Prisca ranks among the loveliest in the republic. (Guerrero; 180km; see p. 477.)

Tepoztlán: Surrounded by towering cliffs, this cobbled *indígena* village preserves an ancient feel and the Náhuatl tongue. Bring plenty of spirit (and bottled water and sunscreen) if you're scaling the town's steep pyramid. (Morelos; 70km; see p. 375.)

Tlaxcala: Known for its calm, colonial Tlaxcala enchants the eye with pretty *talavera* and an abundance of museums and art galleries. Sit in one of the quiet parks and take a breather from the capital (Tlaxcala; 85km; p. 376).

Tula: The archaeological site at Tula houses the ruins that once formed the capital of the Toltec civilization. Set in a hilly semi-desert landscape, the ruins are famous for their 10m tall stone warrior statues, known as the Atlantes. (Hidalgo; 65km; see p. 360.)

Valle De Bravo: Wealthy *chilangos* go play in the beautiful town of Valle de Bravo, where the lake may be man-made, but the white stucco houses, cobblestone streets, and blossoming bougainvillea are irresistible. Grab a picnic basket and loll around the hills. (Estado de México; 140km; see p. 362.)

Xochicalco: Ceremonial center, fortress, and trading post in one, Xochicalco is the most impressive archaeological site in the state. The only sounds to be heard among the rolling green hills are the buzzings of swarms of dragonflies. Budding photographers will be in ecstasy here. (Morelos; 120km; see p. 374.)

BAJA CALIFORNIA

Cradled by the warm, tranquil Sea of Cortés on the east and the cold, raging Pacific Ocean on the west, the peninsula of Baja California claims one of the most spectacular and diverse landscapes in the world. Sparse expanses of sandy deserts give way to barren mountains jutting into cloudless sky. The high-altitude national parks of northern Baja California are home to seemingly out-of-place evergreens and snow during the winter months. And then, of course, there's the unbelievably blue-green water surrounding Baja California's miles of uninhabited shore. Its waters flow past coral reefs, circle rocky storybook coves, and lap at thousands of miles of white sandy shores lining both coasts. Called *"el otro México"* (the other Mexico), Baja California is neither here nor there, not at all California, yet nothing like mainland Mexico. Permanently settled by the Franciscans and Jesuits in the 1600s, its small Jesuit missions are a contrast to mainland Mexico's massive Maya and Zapotec temples. The peninsula's tradition of carefully blending wildness and tranquility, domesticity and simplicity, are epitomized by the Jesuit legacy in sleepy towns like San Ignacio.

Until relatively recently, the only way to reach Baja California's rugged desert terrain was by plane or boat. However, with the completion of the Transpeninsular Highway (Mex. 1) in 1973, and the addition of better toll roads and ferry service, Baja has become a popular vacation spot among Californians, Arizonans, and Mexicans. Vacationers range from hardy campers to families that reside in the peninsula's many RV parks. Large resort hotels and condominium complexes are rapidly developing to accommodate human torrents to the south. Cabo San Lucas, the mega-resort haven on the southern tip, now has almost as little integrity and authenticity as Tijuana, the bawdy border wasteland of **Baja California** state wedged in the hilly crevices of the peninsula's northern extreme. The honest Mexican city of La Paz, the capital of **Baja California Sur,** is a southern beacon of beauty for resort-weary port-seekers. But it is Baja's southern midsection—from the tranquility of Mulegé to the palm-laden oasis town of San Ignacio to the thousands of undisturbed beaches beneath sheer cliffs—that is most pristine and mysterious. Most of Baja California is still somewhat of an undiscovered country, prime for the hearty budget traveler to explore.

HIGHLIGHTS OF BAJA CALIFORNIA

DISCOVER the secluded and beautiful beaches of **Bahía de la Concepción** (p. 188), 48km of turquoise water, powdery sand, bubbly springs, and abundant marine life.

SLEEP under a million stars in **San Ignacio** (p. 183), a tiny leafy Northern Baja oasis with a remarkable **mission** (see p. 184).

HIKE through the amazing **Parque Nacional Sierra San Pedro Mártir** (p. 175), home to mountains, valleys, waterfalls, and Mexico's **National Observatory.**

STROLL down the gulf side boardwalk of breezy, beautiful **La Paz** (p. 195), the good-natured capital of Baja Sur and a favorite Mexican vacation destination.

DROP IN on artsy expatriates in the friendly town of **Todos Santos** (p. 202), and then catch the perfect wave at one of the area's pristine surfing beaches.

GETTING AROUND

BY CAR

Driving in Baja is far from easy. Highways often degrade into pothole-ridden, rotting pavement, making speeds in excess of 80km per hr. dangerous. Livestock on the highways and a general lack of guardrails make night driving impossible—if this warning doesn't convince you, check out the huge number of roadside shrines to the deceased. Furthermore, the intense heat pummels cars, and repair service can be hard to find. Still, a car is the only way to get close to the more beautiful and secluded areas of Baja, and the ride is probably one of the most beautiful in Mexico. Though the proposition might make your mother cringe, driving in Baja is reasonably secure if you stay slow, never drive at night, and keep your tank full. If you need roadside assistance, the **Ángeles Verdes** (Green Angels) pass along Mex. 1 twice per day. Unleaded gas may be lacking along this highway, so don't pass a **PEMEX station** without filling up. If you are driving in from the US, obtain a **vehicle permit**, which is required south of San Felipe on the Sea of Cortés side and Ensenada on the Pacific side. If you will be driving in Baja for more than 72 hours, show the vehicle's title and proof of registration for a free permit at the border. For more information on driving in Mexico see **Getting Around: By Car**, p. 34.

BY BUS

If you plan to navigate the peninsula by bus, note that almost all buses between Ensenada and La Paz are *de paso* (in passing), which means that buses pass through cities, rather than originate and terminate in them. It is therefore impossible to reserve seats in advance. You'll have to leave at inconvenient times, fight to procure a ticket, and then probably stand the whole way. A much better idea is to buy a reserved seat in Tijuana, Ensenada, La Paz, or Los Cabos, and traverse the peninsula in one trip. Getting around by bus, while certainly possible, will try your patience (for more info, see **Getting Around: By Bus**, p. 33). Some swear by **hitching**—PEMEX stations are thick with rides. *Let's Go* does not recommend hitchhiking, as it is unpredictable and potentially hazardous. (For more information on the evils of hitchhiking, see **Getting Around: By Thumb**, p. 35.)

BY SEA

Ferry service was instituted in the mid-1960s as a means of supplying Baja California with food and supplies. There are three different ferry routes: **Santa Rosalía to Guaymas** (10-11hr.), **La Paz to Topolobampo/Los Mochis** (5hr.), and **La Paz to Mazatlán** (17hr.). The La Paz to Topolobampo/Los Mochis route provides direct access to the train from Los Mochis through the **Copper Canyon.** Ferry tickets are generally expensive, even for *turista*-class berths (two-person cabins with sink); bathrooms and showers are down the hall. It's extremely difficult to find tickets for *turista* and *cabina* class, and *especial* berths are only two per ferry. This leaves the bottom-of-the-line *salón* ticket, entitling you to a seat in a large room with few communal baths. If you find yourself traveling *salón*-class at night, ditch your seat and stake out a spot on the floor or outside on the deck. Storage is available, but your belongings will be inaccessible until arrival. For those who plan to take their car aboard a ferry, make reservations a month in advance—passenger vehicles may take up only the space left over by the top-priority commercial vehicles. For further ferry information, contact a **Sematur** office, listed in the **Practical Information** sections of the cities from which the ferry departs. Beware: By the time you finish reading this page prices will have risen dramatically and schedules altered drastically—both favorite practices of Sematur.

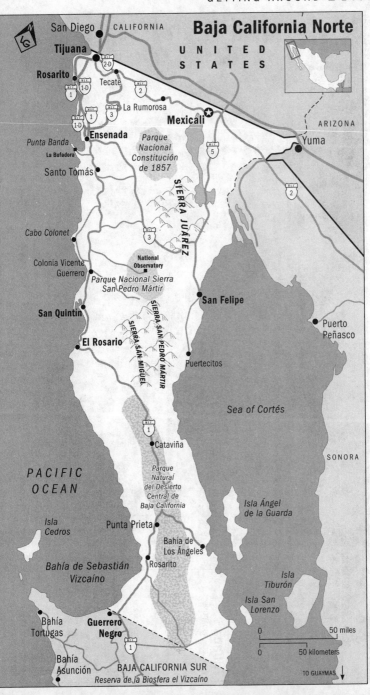

Baja California Norte

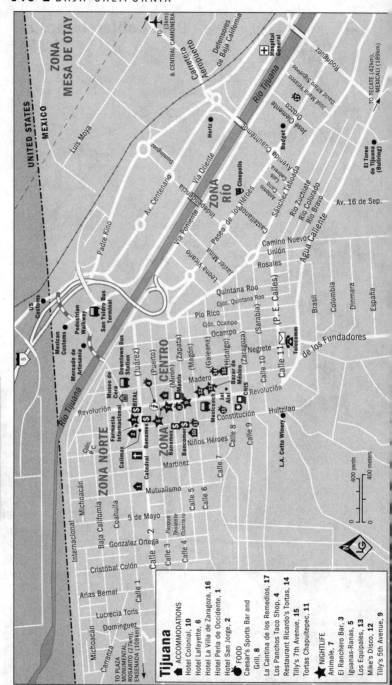

Tijuana

♠ ACCOMMODATIONS
Hotel Colonial, **10**
Hotel Lafayette, **6**
Hotel La Villa de Zaragoza, **16**
Hotel Peña de Occidente, **1**
Hotel San Jorge, **2**

🍴 FOOD
Caesar's Sports Bar and
Grill, **8**
La Cantina de los Remedios, **17**
Los Panchos Taco Shop, **4**
Restaurant Ricardo's Tortas, **14**
Tilly's 7th Avenue, **15**
Tortas Chapultepec, **11**

★ NIGHTLIFE
Animale, **7**
El Ranchero Bar, **3**
Iguanas-Ranas, **5**
Los Equipales, **13**
Mike's Disco, **12**
Tilly's 5th Avenue, **9**

BAJA CALIFORNIA

NORTHERN BAJA CALIFORNIA

TIJUANA ☎ 664

In the shadow of swollen, sulfur-spewing factories lies the most notorious specimen of border subculture: Tijuana (pop. 2 million). It's hard to say whether it's the city's strange charm, its cheap booze, or its sprawling, unapologetic hedonism that attracts 30 million visitors to Tijuana each year. Border traffic counts strange bedfellows in tourists, businessmen, migrant workers, and their families alike. In the wake of the Mexican-American War, modest Rancho Tía Juana found itself on the new border between US Alta California and Mexican Baja California. At first, the town grew slowly, but Prohibition brought it opportunities to serve the vices of its northern neighbors, a set of industries that has become deeply ingrained in "TJ." In recent years, city officials have made an effort to clean up, virtually eliminating sex shops and prostitution from the town center. Today, TJ has become a fun day out for the family, with street hawkers pushing hollow boasts of debauchery on cheap t-shirts, the chance to have a photograph taken with a painted donkey, and hats bearing lewd slogans. This is not to say that the city has lost its dirty luster: catering to the US thirst for illicit substances is a fabulous source of wealth for some in Tijuana, one of the largest ports of entry for illegal drugs. As an introduction to Mexican culture, TJ's about as unrepresentative as they come.

▐ TRANSPORTATION

CROSSING THE BORDER At the world's largest border crossing, northbound lanes often have backups of more than 150 cars. The best time to cross is during weekday mornings. The southbound ride is almost always smoother, but weekends can be rough in both directions. If you're crossing into Tijuana for a day or so, it's easier to leave your car in a lot on the US side and walk across the border. Remember that a tourist card (US$20) is needed if you plan to travel farther south than Ensenada. Regardless of which way you are crossing, bring proper ID—ideally a driver's license or passport—and leave your bushels of fruit, truckloads of livestock, stashes of drugs, and armory of weapons behind.

INTERCITY TRANSPORTATION

From San Ysidro: Take the red Mexicoach bus (☎619-428-9517 in the US) from its terminal at Border Station Parking. It stops in the middle of Revolución. (Every 20-30min., 9am-9pm, US$2.) Alternatively, follow the signs to the *centro* on foot; head for the tall arch at the top of Revolución (15min. walk). If you can't wait, take a taxi (US$5).

From San Diego: Grab a trolley on the blue line and ride to the border. (25min. from downtown, approx. US$2.50.) From there, follow the instructions for San Ysidro above.

From Mexicali: If you drive in from Mexicali on Mex. 2, get on to Mex. 2D, the toll road, and follow the "Aeropuerto" signs west. The airport road turns into Cuauhtémoc and crosses the river before running into Agua Caliente and eventually Revolución.

From Rosarito: Homeward-bound beachgoers on Mex. 1 arrive on 16 de Septiembre, head north until the intersection with Agua Caliente and turn left to reach the *centro*. Those who choose scenic 1D drive in on Calle 2A, which continues east to Revolución.

By bus: Tijuana has 3 main bus stations, all in different parts of the city. To make things difficult, there is also a separate Mexicoach station.

Downtown Station: The most convenient station, located just a block away from the top of Revolución. **Élite** (☎688 1979) buses stop here 1hr. before embarking from the Central Camionera for **Mexico City** (46hr., every hr. 7am-8pm, 1186 pesos) via **Hermosillo** (12 hr., 387 pesos) and **Guadalajara** (34hr., 909 pesos). **Greyhound** (☎688 1979) also picks up passengers downtown before leaving the *Central* for **Los Angeles** (3hr., every hr. 6am-1am, US$20) and connecting to other North American cities. **Suburbaja** (☎688 0082) sends buses to: **Tecate** (1¾hr., every 20min., 31 pesos); **Ensenada** (3¾hr., every 3hr.); and **Mexicali** (2½hr., every 30min., 104 pesos).

San Ysidro Terminal: Near the main border crossing and just a short walk from the city center (see directions from San Ysidro above). **Estrellas del Pacífico** (☎624 9614 or 624 1455) runs to **Guadalajara** (32 hr., 11 per day 9am-10:30pm, 909 pesos) via **Hermosillo** (12hr., 387 pesos), **Mazatlán** (26hr., 690 pesos), **Mexicali** (2½hr., 154 pesos), **Los Mochis** (19hr., 531 pesos), and **Obregón** (17hr., 507 pesos).

Central Camionera: Near the airport. **Autotransportes de Baja California** (☎621 2424 ext. 1214) runs to: **Ensenada** (1½hr., 32 per day 6am-midnight, 80-89 pesos); **La Paz** (22hr., 4 per day 8am-9pm, 980 pesos) via **Loreto** (17hr., 705 pesos), **San Ignacio** (13hr., 530 pesos), and **Santa Rosalía** (15hr., 569 pesos); **Mexicali** (3hr., every 30min. 5:30am-9pm, 121-182 pesos); **Puerto Peñasco** (8hr.; daily 5:30, 10:30am, 4:30pm; 309 pesos); and **San Felipe** (6hr., 4 per day 8:30am-3:30pm, 25 pesos). Station accessible only by overpriced taxi (US$12-15) or by local bus (30min., 5.5 pesos). To find one of these buses at the terminal, go out of the main exit, turn left, and walk to the end of the building. The buses marked "Centro/Buena Vista" should be waiting. These will let you off on Calle 3 and Constitución, 1 block west of Revolución. 2 blocks away, at Calle 1 and Constitución, is the place to catch the bus back to the Central; it also stops opposite the San Ysidro terminal near the border.

Mexicoach Station: On Revolución between Calles 6 and 7. **Mexicoach** (☎685 1470; www.mexicoach.com) buses depart for the **San Ysidro border crossing** (30 min., every 20-30min. 8am-9pm, US$2). They will also take you to **Rosarito** (1hr., every 2hr. 9am-7pm, US$5; *colectivos* are much cheaper), and on to **Foxploration** (see p.159) for an extra dollar.

LOCAL TRANSPORTATION

Traveling within the city, traditional **yellow cabs,** which prey almost exclusively on tourists, charge absurd rates; set a price before getting in. White and orange **taxis libres** are likely to offer slightly better value. Much cheaper **communal cabs,** otherwise known as *colectivos* or route taxis, are an option popular with many locals and go almost anywhere in the city for 10-20 pesos. Operating as buses, they run circuits of the routes painted above the rear tires and on the windshield, where you'll also see the standard fares written out. Most originate on or around Madero or Constitución between Calle 1 and Calle 5. They go to: **Parque Morelos** (5.5 pesos, orange and grey, originating on Calle 4 and Madero); **Rosarito** (10 pesos, yellow and white, originating on Madero around Calle 3); **El Toreo** (5 pesos, red, originating on Calle 4 between Constitución and Revolución); and the **Zona Río** (5 pesos, originating on Calle 3 between Constitución and Revolución), among other destinations. At night, you may prefer to travel by cab in the *centro*.

✦ ▮ ORIENTATION AND PRACTICAL INFORMATION

For the vast majority of visitors, Tijuana simply *is* **Avenida Revolución,** and most tourists never set foot beyond it. If they were to venture onto some of the *calles* which cross it (numbered from north to south) or the *avenidas* which parallel it (Constitución is nearest to the west, Madero to the east) they would be exploring the **Zona Centro.** This reaches its northern limit at the prominent steel arch, where Revolución intersects with Calle Primera and the diagonal street which leads over the river to the border crossing. Between Calle Primera and the border to the west of the river is the **Zona Norte,** the most notorious area for drug-smuggling, prostitution, and border-running—**not a safe place to go.** East of the Zona Centro is the **Zona Río,** whose main street is **Paseo de los Héroes;** it's here that some of Tijuana's most exciting recent developments, such as the Centro Cultural, are to be found.

TOURIST, FINANCIAL, AND LOCAL SERVICES

Tourist Office: (☎685 2210), in the small free-standing booth on the corner of Revolución and Calle 3. Friendly English-speaking staff armed with good maps. Open M-Th 10am-4pm, F-Su 10am-7pm. **Branches** in the Mexicoach station and at the border crossing.

Customs Office: (☎683 1390) at the border on the Mexican side, after crossing the San Ysidro bridge. Open 24hr.

Consulates: Canada, Gérman Gedovius 10411-101 (☎684 0461 or 800 706 2900 for after-hours emergency assistance), in the Zona Río. Open M-F 9am-1pm. **UK,** Salinas 1500 (☎681 8402 or 681 5320 for after-hours emergency assistance), in Col. Aviación, La Mesa. Open M-F 9am-5pm. **US,** Tapachula Sur 96 (☎622 7400 or 681 8016), in Col. Hipódromo, adjacent to the racetrack southeast of town. In an emergency, call the San Diego office (☎619-692-2154) and leave a message and phone number; an officer will respond. Open M-F 8am-4pm.

Currency Exchange: Banks along Constitución exchange money and traveler's checks at the same rates. **Banamex,** Constitución at Calle 4, has shorter lines (☎688 0021; open M-F 8:30am-4:30pm) than more central **BITAL,** Revolución 129 at Calle 2 (☎688 1914; open M-F 8am-7pm, Sa 8am-3pm). Both have 24hr. **ATMs.** *Casas de cambio* offer better rates but may charge commission and refuse to exchange traveler's checks.

Supermarket: Calimax (☎633 7988), Calle 2 at Constitución. Open daily 6am-midnight.

Car Rental: @West Rent a Car, 3045 Rosecrans St. #215, just north of downtown San Diego. (☎619-223-2343; www.atwestrentacar.com. Open daily 8am-8pm.) Before driving into Mexico from the US, get **car insurance** for US$5 per day in San Ysidro. Many drive-through insurance companies have offices just before the border at Sycamore and Primero. **Budget,** Paseo de los Héroes 77, next to the Hotel Camino Real (☎634 3303; open M-F 8am-7pm, Sa-8am-4pm), and **Hertz,** Av. Centenario (☎607 3949; open M-Sa 8am-6pm), offer similar rates and a wide variety of vehicles.

EMERGENCY AND COMMUNICATIONS

Emergency: ☎060.

Police: (☎685 6557), Constitución at Calle 8. English spoken. Specialized tourist assistance (☎688 0555).

Red Cross: (☎621 7787; emergency 066), Gamboa at Silvestre, across from Price Club. Some English spoken.

IN RECENT NEWS

BIG TROUBLE IN LITTLE TJ

Police in Tijuana have been trying to cut crime for as long as anyone can remember, and are keen to promote the border town as a safe tourist haven. Recently, however, they have been forced to acknowledge what they must always have known: much of the city's crime is committed by precisely those tourists they're trying keep safe. In an attempt to curb the problem, the city has published a booklet, "Know Your Rights in Tijuana," which is freely available. While the majority of the common offenses listed therein are the predictable border-town cocktail of drugs- and weapons-smuggling, the less flashy listings provides a startling insight into the holiday pastimes of your fellow tourists. These include: using costumes or disguises which cause a public nuisance; creating excessive noise with cars or musical equipment; being undressed in public; satisfying physiological needs on the street; drag racing on public streets or roads; lighting or exploding fireworks.

Of course, Tijuana's tourist industry will continue to thrive on a three-year difference between Mexican and American law. But while the city may be duty free, it's not without firm laws of its own. Next time you're arrested for taking a "pit stop" in the middle of a noisy drag race, having just stepped out of your gorilla outfit, don't say you weren't warned.

Pharmacy: Everywhere in the Zona Centro. For 24hr. service go to **Farmacia Internacional** (☎685 2790), on the corner of Constitución and Calle 2.

Hospital: Hospital General, Centenario 10851 (☎684 0237 or 684 0922), in the Zona Río. **IMSS** (☎629 6342), Agua Caliente and Francisco Zarabia. Both have 24hr. emergency service.

Fax: Telecomm (☎684 7902; fax 684 7750), to the right of the post office, in the same building on Negrete. Open M-F 7am-7pm, Sa-Su 7am-3:30pm.

Internet Access: Matrix Internet Place, Revolución and Calle 5 (☎688 2273; open 8am-1:30am; 10 pesos per 30min., 15 pesos per hr.), and at **CNIS** at Revolución between Calles 8 and 9 (☎688 3840; open 24 hr.; 15 pesos per hr.).

Post Office: (☎684 7950), on Negrete at Calle 11 (Elías Calles). Open M-F 8am-5pm, Sa 9am-1pm. **Postal Code:** 22000.

▛ ACCOMMODATIONS

As a general rule, hotels in Tijuana become less reputable the farther north you go. Avoid any in the Zona Norte. While crowded during the day, even the Zona Centro can be unsettling at night, especially between Revolución and Constitución close to the Zona Norte; it's advisable to take a cab if you need to cross this area then. The city's hotel rooms can be roachy—ask to see them before paying—but the following establishments should keep you free of any uninvited guests.

Hotel Colonial, Calle 6a 1812 (☎688 1620), between Constitución and Niños Héroes, in a quieter, residential neighborhood away from Revolución. Large, very clean, comfortable rooms have A/C and private baths. Singles and doubles 260 pesos. ❺

Hotel Perla de Occidente, Mutualismo 758 (☎685 1358), between Calles 1a and 2a, 4 blocks from the bedlam of Revolución. Private baths, cozy beds, fans on request. Singles 150 pesos; doubles 300 pesos. ❸

Hotel Lafayette, Revolución 325 (☎685 3940 or 685 3339), between Calles 3a and 4a. Remarkably quiet for being in the middle of Revolución's chaos; you may still find that your bed throbs to the beat coming from Iguanas Ranas across the road. Large rooms have color TV, phone, fans, and private baths. Singles 220 pesos; doubles 290 pesos. ❹

Hotel San Jorge, Constitución 706 (☎685 8540 or 685 2601), at Calle 1a. A respectable hotel on the edge of the lurid Zona Norte. Spartan rooms with bad lighting and private baths, fan, TV, phone, and room service. Singles 240 pesos; doubles 280 pesos. ❹

Hotel La Villa de Zaragoza, Madero 1120 (☎685 1832), between Calles 7a and 8a. Spacious rooms with TV, phone, and king-sized beds. Laundry, room service, and 24hr. security. Singles from 393 pesos; doubles 474 pesos (excluding tax). ❺

▐ FOOD

Like most things in Tijuana, restaurants are often loud and in-your-face; promoters try to drag tourists into the overpriced restaurants lining **Revolución**. Sometimes, however, paying a couple of extra bucks can reap delicious rewards. For cheap, fast food, **taco stands ❶** in the *centro* sell several tacos or a *torta* for 10 pesos.

▨ **La Cantina de los Remedios,** Diego Rivera 19 (☎634 3065), in the Zona Río. Bursting with local memorabilia, competing *mariachis*, a huge range of *tequilas*, and a big crowd. Authentic Mexican cuisine extending well beyond the usual (from 75 pesos). A treat well worth the price. Open Su 1-10pm, M-Th 1pm-midnight, F-Sa 1pm-2am. ❺

Restaurant Ricardo's Tortas (☎685 4031), at Madero and Calle 7. This diner is deservedly popular among both locals and *gringos,* serving some of the best *tortas* in town

(25-40 pesos). Try the *super especial*, with ham, *carne asada*, cheese, avocado, tomato, and mayo. Fills growling tummies 24hr. ❸

Tilly's 7th Avenue, on Revolución and Calle 7. Uncommonly good Mexican dishes served up in a refreshingly airy space with Tecate on tap. Delicious combination dishes US$7.50. Also a good place for a drink, with happy hour 4-7pm (beer US$1). ❺

Tortas Chapultepec (☎685 1412), at Constitución and Calle 6. A local favorite which turns out tasty *tortas* and breakfasts (35-50 pesos). Open daily 8am-10pm. ❹

Caesar's Sports Bar and Grill, Revolución between Calles 4 and 5. One of the definitive experiences of a visit to Tijuana surely has to be a visit to the place claiming to be the birthplace of the Caesar salad. You can still have the genuine article lovingly made for you at your table (US$6.50)—it might just be the best you ever taste. Open 9am-late. ❺

Los Panchos Taco Shop (☎685 7277), Revolución at Calle 3. A handy pitstop for hungry (and raucous) clubbers. Juicy burritos generously filled with meat US$3-4. Open Su-Th 8am-midnight, F-Sa 8am-2am. ❷

◉ SIGHTS

Many of the most entertaining sights in town are, of course, right on Revolución, but if you want to avoid becoming one of them, fear not; while the so-called "attractions" of the main tourist drag have a tendency to mind-numbing predictability, Tijuana's cultural assets and parks counter its one-dimensional image. Pay them a visit and you'll go home with a less impressive collection of straw hats but also with a more balanced sense of the city's present-day life.

Tijuana is not known for its architecture, but two buildings do catch the eye. The distinctive **Frontón Palacio**, on Revolución and Calle 7, was finished in 1947 after 21 years of complications as the home of *jai alai*. The complications continue, and the sport has not been played there for years; only the betting shop remains in use. The **Catedral de Nuestra Señora de Guadalupe**, at Calle 2 and Niños Héroes, features a large chandelier and a giant image of the Virgin.

▨ CENTRO CULTURAL TIJUANA (CECUT). Po. de los Héroes is punctuated by a series of monuments, but its most visually striking feature is probably Tijuana's cultural center. The main attraction for visitors is the superb **Museo de las Californias,** where a collection of artifacts and models with bilingual commentaries traces the history of the peninsula from its earliest inhabitants through the Spanish conquest to the Mexican-American War and the 20th century. It's all attractively presented and (unlike the city outside) makes for the best possible introduction to the peninsula's cultural heritage. CECUT also hosts temporary science and art exhibitions and showcases Tijuana's current cultural vitality with dance performances, concerts, and opera in the **Sala de Espectáculos.** The spherical building contains **Cine Omnimax,** where films incorporating the usual aerial shots of epic landscapes are shown on a vast 180-degree screen every hour in the afternoon; foreign films and children's flicks show in a separate theater. If you'd rather be out in the sun, there's also the charming **Jardín Caracol,** a garden with reproductions of pre-Columbian sculptures, where there are occasional interpretative tours and live dance performances. *(CECUT ☎687 9633. Museum open daily 10am-7pm. 20 pesos, students and children 12 pesos. Cine Omnimax tickets 40 pesos, students and children 20 pesos.)*

MUSEO DE CERA. If you want to visit a museum in Tijuana without losing sight of Revolución's tackiness, make a bee-line for the wax museum. Eighty-six life-size figures await you, organized into the realms of Mexican History, International Politics, Stage and Screen, and Horror. Memorable combinations (there are several) include President Vicente Fox and Fidel Castro towering over Mother Theresa and Mahatma Gandhi. *(Calle 1 and Madero. ☎688 2478. Open daily 10am-7pm. 15 pesos.)*

PARQUE MORELOS. This sprawling state-run park is close to the highway but offers pleasant walks, rides, an open-air theater, and a small zoo. *(Blvd. de los Insurgentes 26000. Take an orange-and-grey communal cab for 5 pesos from Calle 4 and Madero.* ☎625 2470. Open Tu-Su 9am-5pm. 5 pesos, children 2 pesos; parking 10 pesos.)*

L.A. CETTO WINERY. Established in 1926 by Italian immigrants, the family-run winery maintains its vineyards in the Valle de Guadalupe, northeast of Ensenada. Rather underwhelming tours are offered; the real draw is the chance to sample and purchase the products. *(Cañón Johnson 2108. ☎685 3031. Tours M-F 10am-6:30pm, Sa 10am-5pm; avoid coming during lunch hour around 1-2pm. US$2 including tasting.)*

🎵 🎭 ENTERTAINMENT AND NIGHTLIFE

In the 1920s, Prohibition drove US citizens south of the border to revel in the forbidden nectars of cacti, grapes, and hops. The flow of Americans thirsty for booze remains unstopped, with many continuing to take advantage of foreign laws (drinking at 18) to circumvent US prohibitions. Stroll down Revolución after dusk and you'll be bombarded with music, lights, and club promoters (of both the strip and dance varieties) hawking overpriced "two-for-one" margaritas. The chaotic mix of pop, reggae, rap, and Latin hits spun by DJs sets the tone for all of Revolución: the throbbing music is often all that can be heard within a three-block radius of the street. Those who prefer laid-back nights of chat are in the wrong place.

Animale, Revolución at Calle 4a. The biggest, glitziest, and loudest hedonistic haven of them all. 2 drinks for US$5. Watch out—the similarly named Animale Continental next door is an altogether more "adult" experience. Open daily 10am-4am.

Iguanas-Ranas (☎685 1422), Revolución at Calle 3a. A sublimely wacky (and tacky) world of life-size plaster clowns, balloons, and kitschy US pop culture paraphernalia. Where else do you get the opportunity to pound beers (US$3) in an authentic yellow school bus perched high above Revolución? Packed on weekends with US and Mexican 20-somethings. Open M-Th 10am-2am, F-Su 10am-5am.

Tilly's 5th Avenue (☎685 9015), at Revolución and Calle 5a. A small club by Tijuana standards, Tilly's attracts customers with an intimate dance floor and a dance-happy staff that mingles with customers. Open M-Th 10:30am-2am, F-Sa 10:30am-5am.

GAY AND LESBIAN NIGHTLIFE

Clubs catering to gays and lesbians cluster in the southern part of the *centro* around Calle 6a and 7a or down the hill to the north of Calle 1a. **El Ranchero Bar,** in front of the fountain in Plaza Santa Cecilia, is a popular spot. Rainbow-colored parrots and palm trees decorate the long, dimly lit bar where a mellow mixed crowd drinks 10-peso beers. (☎685 2800. Open 24hr.)

CULTURAL

Tijuana's primary cultural draw is its Centro Cultural (see p.153). In addition, several theaters screen first-run films. **Cinepolis,** in the Plaza del Río mall facing the Centro Cultural, is closest to the *centro*. (☎684 0401. Open daily 2pm-midnight. 32-45 pesos.) Nearby **Cinepolis VIP** offers a smaller selection of the same films with bigger seats and better facilities (57 pesos). Blue-and-white buses (5 pesos) on Calle 2a at Constitución can take you to the Centro Cultural and the cinema.

SPORTS

If you're in town on the right Sunday, you can watch the graceful and savage battle of man versus bull in one of Tijuana's two bullrings. **El Toreo de Tijuana,** southeast of town just off of Agua Caliente, hosts the first round of fights (alternate Su, May-July). Catch a bus on Calle 2a west of Revolución. The seaside **Plaza Monumental** hosts the second round (Aug.-Oct.). Mexicoach sends buses (US$4 round-trip) on fight days. Alternatively, take the blue-and-white local buses (5 pesos) on Calle 3a at Constitución all the way down Calle 2a. Tickets to both rings go on sale at the gate (☎ 685 1510 or 685 1219) or at the Mexicoach office (☎ 685 1470) on Revolución between Calles 6a and 7a the Wednesday before a fight (95-400 pesos).

SHOPPING

As soon as tourists cross the footbridge from the US, they're bombarded with vendors peddling everything a *gringo* could possibly desire. The gaudy shopping scene continues most of the way up Revolución, as far as the intersection with Calle 7a. Other spots for assorted tourist-oriented wares are the **Mercado de Artesanía**, on Calle 1a under the pedestrian footbridge, and the vendors on **Plaza Santa Cecilia**, near the arches on Revolución. Bargaining is a must, as quoted prices can be over twice the bottom line. For a good selection of marginally higher-quality *artesanías* and less hassle, visit the **Bazar de México** on Revolución at Calle 7a.

TECATE   ☎ 665

Tecate (pop. 100,000) provides a peaceful respite from the frenzy of Tijuana. Best known as the birthplace of Mexico's unofficial national beer, this friendly border town prides itself not just on the vats of sudsy goodness that emerge each day from its brewery, but also on its small-town camaraderie and the safety of its streets. There's no getting around it: instead of being blanketed by smog and pollution, Tecate's cool mountain air carries the pleasant smell of barley and hops. There's no huge list of things to do here, but that gives you all the more reason to sit back and relax with a *cerveza* in the town in which it was first brewed.

▐ TRANSPORTATION. Catch **buses** one block east of the park on Juárez at Rodríguez. **Autotransportes de Baja California** (☎ 554 1221) sends buses to: **Ensenada** and the **Valle de Guadalupe** (2hr.; 10 per day 6:30am-7pm; 67 pesos, 92 pesos luxury); **Mexicali** (2hr.; every hr. 6:30am-6:30pm, and 7pm; 96 pesos, 110 pesos luxury); **Tijuana** (1¾hr., every 20 to 30min. 5am-9pm, 31 pesos); **Puerto Peñasco** (3 per day); **Santa Rosalía** and **Rosario** (2:30pm); and **La Paz** (7pm). **Transportes Norte de Sonora** (☎ 654 2343) offers cushy *de paso* buses every hr. beginning at 7:45am to: **Mexicali** (2hr., 99 pesos); **Sonoita** (5hr., 290 pesos); **Guaymas** (14hr., 400 pesos); **Hermosillo** (12hr., 340 pesos); **Mazatlán** (26hr., 618 pesos); **Guadalajara** (36hr., 800 pesos). They also go to **Nogales** (12hr., 5pm, 436 pesos); **Ciudad Juárez** (20hr., 7:30pm, 700 pesos) and **Mexico City** (44hr., 7 per day, 1120 pesos).

▐ ▐ ORIENTATION AND PRACTICAL INFORMATION. Tecate lies 42km east of Tijuana on **Mex. 2.** Driving in from Mexicali or Tijuana, the main street, **Juárez,** intersects Cárdenas at the northwest corner of Parque Hidalgo, the center of social and commercial activity. East-west streets parallel **México,** which runs along the border fence; continuing south, they are: Madero, Revolución, Reforma, Juárez, Libertad, and Hidalgo. Streets named for early 20th-century presidents run north-south perpendicular to Juárez and the border. Starting from the east, they are: Portes Gil, Rodríguez, Ortiz Rubio, Cárdenas, Elías Calles, Obregón, de la Huerta, Carranza, and Aldrete.

Pretty but somewhat useless maps are available from the English-speaking staff at the **tourist office,** Libertad 1305, facing Parque Hidalgo. (☎ 654 1095. Open M-F 8am-8pm, Sa-Su 9am-1pm.) **Bancomer,** on the corner of Cárdenas and Juárez, exchanges traveler's checks and has a 24hr. **ATM.** (☎ 554 1350. Open M-F 8:30am-4pm, Sa 10am-2pm.) **Banamex,** at Juárez and Obregón, has more of the same. (☎ 654 1188. Open M-F 9am-4pm.) Big, yellow **Calimax,** on Juárez between Carranza and

Aldrete, sells groceries and more. (☎554 0039. Open daily 7am-10pm.) The **police** are at Paseo Morelos 1978. Walk east on Juárez out of town; it will become Mex. 2. The station is at the traffic circle, a 10min. walk from the *parque*. (☎655 1091. English spoken.) Other services include: **emergency** ☎060; **Red Cross,** Juárez 411 (☎654 1313, emergency 066; some English spoken); **Farmacia Roma,** on the corner of Juárez and Aldrete (☎554 1818; open 7am-midnight) and a 24hr. branch at the Plaza de los Encinos mall (☎654 2193); the **IMSS Centro de Salud,** south of town at Juárez and Gil (☎654 5803; some English spoken); **Lavamática,** on a side-street off Juárez, opposite the large branch of ElecZion (open daily 8am-8pm; small wash 12 pesos, large wash 25 pesos, dry 9 pesos); **Telecomm,** next door to the post office (☎554 1375; open M-F 8am-2pm, Sa 8-11am); **Café Internet de Rivera,** one block south of Parque Hidalgo, on Hidalgo near Ortiz Rubio, inside a small complex of shops (open daily 9am-9pm; 15 pesos per hr.). The **post office,** Ortiz Rubio 147, is two blocks north of Juárez. (☎554 1245. Open M-F 8am-3pm; some services cease 1hr. before closing time.) **Postal code:** 21400.

⌂🛏 ACCOMMODATIONS AND FOOD. Tecate has several budget hotels scattered throughout the city. A friendly welcome compensates for a lack of luxury at the family-run, old-fashioned **Hotel Frontera ❹,** Madero 131, in a residential neighborhood between Obregón and Elías Calles. (☎654 1342. US$5 key deposit. Rooms with sink US$22, with private bath US$30.) Very central **Hotel Tecate ❹,** on Libertad at Cárdenas around the corner from the tourist office, has simple and clean but dark rooms with private baths and fans. (☎554 1116. Singles and doubles 200 pesos, with TV 275 pesos.) **Motel Paraíso ❸,** Aldrete 83, one block north of Juárez and four blocks from Parque Hidalgo, has clean, spartan rooms. Some are dark and feel like jail cells, while others get plenty of light from big windows. (☎654 1716. Singles 180 pesos; doubles 250 pesos; each additional person 55 pesos.)

Taquerías ❶ lining Obregón and Juárez, east of the park, serve Tecate's cheapest food, with tacos and burritos starting at 5 pesos. **Restaurant Jardín Tecate ❸,** next to the tourist office on the southern end of Parque Hidalgo, has outdoor tables right on the square. Enjoy breakfasts, Mexican classics like *burritos de machaca* (dried shredded beef) or a huge club sandwich (35-50 pesos) under the shady trees. (☎654 3453. Open daily 8am-10pm.) You'll feel right at home in the cozy dining room/kitchen of family-run **La Escondida ❸,** the yellow building on Libertad between Ortiz Rubio and Rodríguez (on the right as you walk from Parque Hidalgo). Vegetarians will enjoy the *ensalada de aguacate* (30 pesos), a huge bowl of veggies, olives, and lots of avocado. (☎654 2164. Open M-Sa 8:30am-6pm.) For food at all hours, **Restaurant el Mesón ❹,** on the corner of Ortiz Rubio and Revolución a couple of blocks from the border, offers a range of Mexican dishes (US$6 and below), beers (US$2), and wines as you look out over Tecate from the balcony. It also hosts live music on Friday nights. (☎654 5383. Open 24hr.)

🎭🎵 SIGHTS AND ENTERTAINMENT. The town's biggest building, the **Tecate Brewery,** on Hidalgo at Obregón, looms over everything, literally and figuratively, in Tecate and attracts thousands of beer-loving visitors throughout the year. Opened in 1944, the brewery, officially known as the Cervecería Cuauhtémoc Moctezuma, now pumps out 39 million liters of pleasure each month. You can sample it for yourself—on the house—at the **🍺Jardín Cerveza Tecate,** a courtyard just outside where every visitor gets one free drink. (Open M-F noon-4pm, Sa-Su noon-2pm.) Should you become a convert to the local brew, the souvenir stall next to the bar will help you become a walking advertisement for Tecate or one of the company's seven other beers: Bohemia, Carta Blanca, Dos Equis, Indio, Sol, Superior, and the Christmas-time-only Noche Buena. (Open M-F 10am-5pm, Sa-Su 10am-2pm.) You can also go on a free tour of the brewery. (☎654 9478 or 654 9490. Tours are officially at noon and 3pm on weekdays, but really are available any time the Jardín is open; still, it's best to call ahead. No shorts or sandals may be worn inside.)

Other than hanging out in the Jardín, Tecate offers little in the way of entertainment. One way to spend your evening would be to go and watch Tecate's **baseball** team, sponsored by the brewery and called the Cerveceros. The team attracts a small but devoted following, whose enthusiasm might just be connected to the fact that as the home score goes up, the price of beer in the stands goes down. (Season June-Aug. 30-60 pesos; children 14 and under 10 pesos.)

ROSARITO ☎ 661

Rosarito (pop. 120,000) has many selling points, as its tourist promoters have discovered during the city's transformation from elite hideaway to all-out *gringo*-magnet, but none of them counts more than its proximity to the US border. Baja's youngest city is just 28km from San Diego, and this distance seems to shrink every year as Californian weekenders flock in. The city remains a popular Hollywood filming site, and Fox Studios Baja, the famed *Titanic* water tank, lies 2km south of town. Few enterprises here are not geared towards tourists, and the two most widely accepted languages are English and the American dollar. If you're looking for the "real Baja," then this is probably not the place to come, but if the creeping Americanization doesn't bother you, the beaches and clubs are yours to enjoy.

🖪 **TRANSPORTATION.** To get to Rosarito from **Tijuana,** grab a yellow-and-white *taxi de ruta* (30min., 9 pesos) from Madero near Calle 3. The same vehicles congregate in front of the Rosarito Beach hotel for the return journey; you can also flag them down along northbound Juárez, which is also the easiest way of getting from one end of Rosarito to the other. If you have money to waste, **Mexicoach** also runs to **Tijuana** (US$5) from the Rosarito Beach Hotel and also serves **Foxploration** (see p.159) on request. Just behind where the taxis wait is the **ABC bus terminal** (☎613 1151). Buses run to **Ensenada** (1¼hr., 4 per day, 53 pesos); ask the station to call Tijuana for pick-up by the next Ensenada service. There are also buses to **La Paz** (24hr.; 12:30, 6:30pm; 882 pesos) and **Mexicali** (6 hr., 3pm, 142 pesos).

🔳🔽 **ORIENTATION AND PRACTICAL INFORMATION.** Rosarito lies 27km south of Tijuana. **Mex. 1** runs straight through Rosarito, becoming the city's main drag, **Juárez,** before continuing south. Coming from the toll road, the first Rosarito exit takes you to the north end of Juárez, which, with its non-sequential street numbers and persistent lack of street signs, can be befuddling. Virtually all the businesses in town are on Juárez, with most facilities concentrated at the southern end, between the PEMEX at the corner of Avenida Cipres and the Rosarito Beach Hotel. On weekends, hordes of SUV-driving visitors clog up Juárez, progress becomes painfully slow, and parking spaces are hard to come by.

The **COTUCO tourist office** is in the Oceana Plaza. (☎612 0396; emergency 134. Open M-F 9am-6pm, Sa 10am-2pm.) The **SECTUR tourist office** recently relocated, inconveniently, to the very southern end of town. (☎612 0200. Open M-F 8am-8pm, Sa-Su 9am-1pm.) **Banamex,** on Juárez at Ortiz Rubio, exchanges cash and checks and has a 24hr. **ATM.** (☎612 1556. Open M-F 9am-4pm, Sa 10am-2pm.) If you want to change money outside these hours, visit a *casa de cambio* on Juárez and pay commission; most visitors just stick with dollars, however. For groceries, try the **Calimax,** at Cárdenas and Juárez, before Hotel Quinta del Mar heading south on Juárez. (☎612 0060. Open daily 7am-midnight.) Other services include: **laundry** at **Lavamática,** on Juárez near Acacias (open daily 9am-9pm; 40 pesos for wash and dry); **Internet access** at **El Tunel.com,** Juárez 208 near Cárdenas, upstairs in the yellow building with the arcade (☎612 5061; 20 pesos per hr.; open M-F 9am-10pm, Sa-Su

ON THE MENU

LOBSTER, PUERTO NUEVO STYLE

Baja is almost as full of places to enjoy fresh lobster as it is of lobster-colored beachgoers, but for the true connoisseur, there's always been one place that, ahem, blows the competition out of the water. Baja oldsters fondly remember Puerto Nuevo as a tiny fishing village where locals used to free-dive off the rocks into waters thick with some of the best lobster in the world, which was then served up in no-frills huts along the shore. Those huts have long since been replaced by two mariachi-strewn blocks packed solid with restaurants—around 35 in all, though most of them are owned by just two families. To the first-timer the choice may seem overwhelming, but rest assured that, wherever you dine, the menu will always be pretty much the same. Although the chefs will often agree to boil or grill the lobster to suit picky northerners, real Puerto Nuevo lobster is invariably cut in half lengthwise and then deep-fried in lard, and served with the ubiquitous rice, beans and tortillas. The level of competition brings the price of this cholesterol feast down to around US$12-14 in all but the swankiest restaurants. Bear in mind, though, that while the chefs now run to a year-round tourist timetable, the lobster don't; if you visit out of season, your authentic Puerto Nuevo lobster may well arrive via the deep freeze.

10am-10pm); the **post office** on Juárez, near Acacias (☎612 1355; open M-F 8am-3pm, Sa 8am-noon); and the pharmacy **Farmacia Roma,** set back from Juárez at Roble (☎612 3500; open 24hr.). In case of **emergency,** call ☎060, or contact the **police** (☎613 0612 or 613 3411), at Juárez and Acacias next to the post office, or the **Red Cross** (☎613 1120, emergency 066), on Juárez at Ortiz Rubio, around the corner from the police; some English spoken at both. **Postal code:** 22710.

🏠☐ ACCOMMODATIONS AND FOOD. Most budget hotels in Rosarito are cramped or situated on the outskirts of town. Prices soar during spring break, holidays, and summer weekends. Probably the pick of the "budget" options is cheery **Hotel el Portal de Rosarito ❺,** at Juárez and Via de las Olas, with TVs, A/C, large rooms, and parking spaces. (☎612 0050. Singles US$27; doubles US$33.) **Hotel Palmas Quintero ❹** is a well-kept secret, tucked away on Privada Guadalupe Victoria 26, three blocks inland from Hotel Quinta del Mar. To find it, drive up Cárdenas until it turns into a dirt road, continue for one block, and turn left; the hotel is ahead and to the right. Large rooms have cable TV and clean baths. (☎612 1359. Su-Th singles US$20; doubles US$40. F-Sa US$25/US$50.) Out of the way but close to the beach is **Motel Marsella's ❹,** where the rooms are spotless and come with TV, fan, and bath (☎612 0468. Su-Th singles US$22; doubles US$35. F-Sa US$35/US$45). **Alamo Campground ❷,** Calle Alamo 15, less than a block from the beach, has RV space and six clean beds for rent in a dorm with one widescreen TV. (☎613 1179. Bunks US$10 in winter, US$15 in summer. RV space from US$25.)

With tons of pricey restaurants serving international cuisine, Rosarito's culinary scene caters mostly to tourists who consider US$10 cheap. Nevertheless, searching yields quality budget eateries with simple, yummy fare. **🍴La Flor de Michoacán ❺,** Juárez 291, at the north end of town, is a carnivore's paradise that has been in business for more than half a century. Huge *órdenes de carnitas* (60 pesos) come as either "solid" or "mixed" pork—solid comprises typical cuts, while mixed includes tongues, stomachs, and all sorts of good stuff. Those with big appetites can order by the kilogram. The decor features entertaining porcine memorabilia. (☎612 1858. 240 pesos per kg. Open Su-Tu and Th-Sa 9am-10pm. Also a branch on Juárez at Encinas, which has a broader menu but less quirky ambience.) Enjoy the best tacos in town at **Macho Taco ❸,** Juárez 60, across from Hotel Festival Plaza. The special combo—two tacos, rice, beans, and a soda (US$3)—can't be beat. (Attached to the nightclub of the same name. ☎613 0630. Open daily 10am-2am.)

SIGHTS AND ENTERTAINMENT. Rosarito entices with fancy resorts, beautiful shores, and wild nightlife. Spanning the coast two blocks west of Juárez, **Rosarito Beach** has soft sand and gently rolling surf. If you want to delve deeper, the **Museo de Historia Wa Kuatay**, on Juárez next to the Rosarito Beach Hotel, showcases local folk art and history. (☎613 0687. Open W-Su 9am-5pm. Admission and informative tours from curator Pedro Arias free; donations welcome.) Rosarito has a proud tradition of hosting vacationing movie stars, but it has recently taken on new importance in the form of **Fox Studios Baja** and the attached **Foxploration** tourist park, 2km south of Rosarito. Fox's blockbuster flick *Titanic* was filmed here, and the site remains the world's premier locale to film on water. Following the film, Fox decided to open part of the site as a tourist park. Unfortunately, with a lack of foresight worthy of the original designers of the *Titanic* herself, the studio has dismantled its main attraction—the ship is no longer there. As a result, a visit to Foxploration feels a bit like sitting through a series of trailers without the feature presentation. (A 10min. drive on Mex. 1 south of Rosarito. Mexicoach's Tijuana-Rosarito buses continue to Foxploration (every 2hr. 9am-5pm, US$1) on request—you have to tell the driver in advance when you want to be picked up. Foxploration ☎614 9444; www.foxploration.com. Open Su-M, Th-Sa 9am-5pm.)

Rosarito's nightlife revolves around Hotel Festival Plaza, which has a number of bars and clubs of its own. The mega-clubs on the streets behind the hotel are packed with drunken revelers on weekend and summer nights. **Iggy's** is a behemoth of a nightspot with its own pool, foam party, ATVs on the beach, and even bungee jumps from an onsite crane; don't puke upside down. The three bars offer all-you-can-drink cocktails, as well as food. (☎612 0537. Cover approx. US$10. Open 8pm-3am, later on weekends.) **Papas and Beer,** a multilevel party palace which can accommodate up to 7000 guests on busy nights, includes a great beach volleyball court and, most importantly, a mechanical bull. (☎612 0444. Drinks US$1.50-7. Open Su-Th 11am-3am, F-Sa to 4am.) If all these bells and whistles aren't quite your thing, **Tequila Safari,** on Juárez between Roble and Encino, is a good place for cheap drinks, with happy hour from 5-7pm (all drinks ½-price), and US$10 buckets of six beers. They also have pool tables, a DJ, and groovy safari-themed upholstery. (☎612 0202. M-Th noon-10pm, F-Su noon-2am.)

ENSENADA ☎646

Nestled in the beautiful Bahía de Todos Santos, Ensenada (pop. 370,000) still retains some of the salty atmosphere of a fishing harbor. These days, though, the biggest catch of the day is likely to be the tourist crowd coming off one of the cruise liners that regularly pay the town a visit. The beautifully restored central stretch of Calle Mateos can feel a little claustrophobic on weekends, but that simply provides all the more reason to discover the city's real draw as a comfortable and friendly base from which to explore the dramatic surrounding landscapes.

CREEPY CREATURE FEATURES "Scorpions?! But this isn't the jungle," you gasp. Tough break. These pests (*alacranes* in Spanish) frequent Baja, especially mid-peninsula. Unless allergic, you won't encounter a slow, painful death—these aren't the fatal buggers found in Asia and Africa—but if stung, expect intense pain for a few days. Ice eases discomfort; locals swear by garlic. The critters like dark, warm, damp places, so shake your shoes and clothing before you put them on. If you wake up to a scorpion crawling on you, don't try to squash it—it will sting. Instead, give it a flick from the side and watch it fly far, far away.

BAJA CALIFORNIA

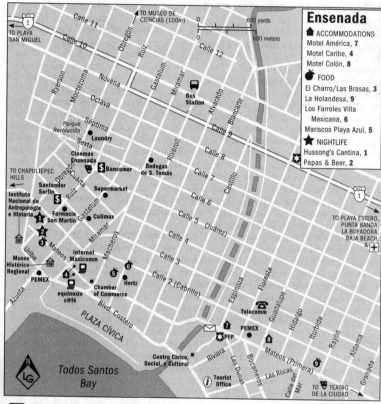

Ensenada

🏠 ACCOMMODATIONS
Motel América, **7**
Motel Caribe, **4**
Motel Colón, **8**

🍖 FOOD
El Charro/Las Brasas, **3**
La Holandesa, **9**
Los Farroles Villa
   Mexicana, **6**
Mariscos Playa Azul, **5**

⭐ NIGHTLIFE
Hussong's Cantina, **1**
Papas & Beer, **2**

🖥 TRANSPORTATION

Ensenada is 108km south of Tijuana on **Mex. 1D.** The 1½hr. drive offers an almost continuous view of the Pacific, and the last 20min. stretch on the Ensenada *cuota* is especially breathtaking—if traveling by bus, grab a seat on the right-hand side (car toll 21 pesos). Car drivers might like to stop to admire the view from the *mirador* just beyond Bajamar. The less scenic **libre, Mex. 1**, is a poorly maintained highway that parallels the *cuota* until La Misión, then cuts inland for the remaining 40km. Drive only during the day—there are no streetlights, but plenty of curves.

   Buses from Tijuana arrive at the **Central de Autobuses,** at Calle 11 and Riveroll. To get to the *centro*, turn right as you come out of the station, walk south 10 blocks, and you'll be at Mateos (also called Primera), the main tourist drag. **Transportes Norte de Sonora** (☎ 178 6770) travels to **Los Mochis** (22hr., 5 per day 11:30am-8:30pm, 550 pesos) via **Guaymas** (16hr., 436 pesos). Luxury **Élite** buses also go to Los Mochis (22hr.; 10am, 6, 7:15pm; 650 pesos). **Autotransportes de Baja California** (☎ 178 6680) runs buses at 10am, 2, 7, 8, 9:30, and 11pm to: **Guerrero Negro** (8hr., 355 pesos); **Mulegé** (11½hr., 541 pesos); **San Ignacio** (9hr., 439 pesos); **Santa Rosalía** (12hr., 479 pesos). All except the 7 and 9:30pm buses also go to **La Paz** (20hr., 822 pesos) and **Loreto** (16hr., 568 pesos). Additional buses to **Mexicali** (4hr., 8 per day 5:30am-8pm, 206 pesos); **San Felipe** (4hr.; 8am, 6pm; 178 pesos); **Puerto Peñasco** (11hr.; 8am,

2pm; 383 pesos); **Tecate** (2hr., every 3hr. 7:15am-7:15pm, 67 pesos); and **Tijuana** (1½hr., every 30min. 5am-11pm, 90 pesos). **Transportes Brisas** (☎178 3888), Calle 4 771, near Macheros, runs buses to small towns nearby.

🔲 🛈 ORIENTATION AND PRACTICAL INFORMATION

Mateos, the main tourist drag, is also known as **Primera** (Calle 1). Numbered *calles,* including **Juárez** (Calle 5), run east-west, approximately parallel to Mateos. Alphabetized *avenidas* run north-south, starting with Alvarado and moving east. Street signs are nonexistent more than one block from Mateos. If you're driving, follow signs to downtown Ensenada or "Centro"; these will lead you to **Costero,** which runs along the harbor one block south of Mateos. Local *urbanos* (☎178 2594) leave from Calle 2 at Macheros (5.5 pesos for most destinations in the city). After sundown, exercise caution in the poorly-lit area near the shore and in the region bounded by Miramar, Macheros, Mateos, and Calle 4.

Tourist Office, Costero 540 (☎172 3022; fax 172 3081), at Azueta. Friendly, English-speaking staff doles out maps and pamphlets. Open M-F 8am-8pm, Sa-Su 9am-1pm. The **Chamber of Commerce,** Mateos 693, 2nd fl. (☎178 2322), at Macheros, is closer to the center of town but less tourist-friendly. Open M-F 8:30am-2pm and 4-6:30pm.

Currency Exchange: The main tourist area lacks banks. The closest is **Santander Serfín** (☎174 0009) at Ruíz and Calle 3. Open M-F 9am-5pm, Sa 10am-3pm. Others cluster around Ruíz and Juárez, including **Bancomer** (☎178 1801). Open M-F 9am-4pm, Sa 10am-2pm. Both change dollars and travelers checks and have 24hr. **ATMs.**

Supermarket: Calimax (☎178 3397), Gastelum at Calle 3. Open daily 7am-11pm.

Laundry: Lavandería Lavadero, Obregón 674 (☎178 2737), between Calles 6 and 7, facing Parque Revolución. Small loads 21 pesos, large loads 42 pesos, drying 5 pesos. Open Su 8am-8pm, M-Sa 7am-8pm.

Luggage Storage: In the main station. 5 pesos per hr.

Car Rental: Hertz (☎178 2982; fax 178 3776), Calle 2 at Riveroll. Cars from 560 pesos per day with free mileage (not including tax and insurance). Open M-F 8am-2pm and 4-6pm, Sa 8am-2pm.

Emergency: ☎060.

Police: (☎176 4343), Calle 9 at Espinoza. Some English spoken. The **Policía Federal Preventativa,** Mateos 1360 near the post office (☎176 1311), deal with road traffic and may be a useful source of information on roads in the surrounding countryside.

Red Cross: (☎174 4545, emergency 066), on Clark at Flores. Some English spoken.

Farmacia: San Martín (☎178 3530), at Ruíz and Calle 3. Open 24hr.

Hospital: Hospital General (☎176 7800), on the Transpeninsular at km 111.

Fax: Telecomm (☎177 0545), on Floresta at Calle 3. Open M-F 8am-6pm, Sa 8-11am.

Internet: Café Internet MaxiComm (☎175 7011), on Mateos between Miramar and Macheros, upstairs. 15 pesos per 30min., 20 pesos per hr. Open M-F 9am-9pm, Sa-Su 9am-8pm. Alternatively, friendly **equinoxio c@fé** (☎174 0455) on Costero charges 20 pesos per hr. and serves coffee. Open Su-M 9am-10pm, Tu-Sa 8am-10pm.

Post Office: (☎176 1088), on Mateos at Espinoza. Open M-F 8am-6pm, Sa 9am-1pm. **Postal Code:** 22800.

🏠 ACCOMMODATIONS

Ensenada may be an upmarket destination, but plenty of budget motels exist, particularly at the eastern end of Mateos away from the main shopping district.

BAJA CALIFORNIA

ON THE MENU

FORGET THE TEQUILA PASS THE PULQUE!

You may well be, um, intimately acquainted with the *maguey* cactus (aka agave)—or, more likely, the tequila and mezcal it produces. What Mr. Cuervo never told you is that when its sap (called *agua miel*, or honey water) is fermented instead of distilled, *maguey* yields the wondrous drink of the Aztecs: pulque.

Pulque is thought to have originated over 2000 years ago. Legend has it that it was discovered by the goddess Mayahuel; associated with virility and fertility, it was used as an aphrodisiac and given to the sick as a medicine.

The supreme god of pulque is Ometotchtli, also known as Two Rabbit, who was said to have 400 sons. There are other pulque gods, who together are known as Centzon Totochtin, or 400 Rabbit, representing the 400 stages of inebriation—try to count them all.

To make, harvest the *agua miel* from 12-year-old maguey—a good plant produces about a gallon a day for up to a year. The *agua* is transported by hand to a fermenting house, or *tinacol*, a sacred area women are not allowed to enter where men must remove their hats. (In the old days, pulque producers were not even allowed to have contact with women.)

To drink pulque the right way, pour some onto the floor first as an offering to the gods, then let the gooey, milky liquid take you back to the Aztecs.

Motel América (☎176 1333), Mateos at Espinoza. Huge rooms with overhead fans, baths, and cable TV; some have kitchens. Singles US$24; doubles US$32-36. ❹

Motel Caribe, Mateos 627/8 (☎178 3481). Occupies 2 buildings in the lively center of town. Rooms in the main building are huge and carpeted, and have cable TV, fans, and baths, while those across the street are more modest and cheaper. Singles US$15-20; doubles US$25. Rates rise US$5 on weekends. ❸

Motel Colón (☎176 1910), Guadalupe between Mateos and Calle 2. Large, slightly worn-looking rooms with cable TV, fans, big baths; some with kitchenettes. Singles US$24; doubles US$30-45. ❹

🍴 FOOD

Most restaurants on Mateos have outdoor seating and sky-high prices, but a few affordable eateries populate even these digs; your options increase as you move farther out. For the best deals, visit the fish market on the waterfront, west of the huge flag, where **loncherías** ❶ serve delicious fish tacos for under US$1 apiece.

Mariscos Playa Azul (☎174 0622), Riveroll between Mateos and Calle 2. One of the cheapest seafood restaurants in town, with no compromise on quality. Main dishes around 50-60 pesos. Open daily 10am-10pm. ❹

La Holandesa (☎177 1965), Mateos and Rayón. Tasty breakfasts in a homey setting. Shrimp omelettes 50 pesos. Open Su 8am-5pm, M-F 7am-10pm, Sa 8am-10pm. ❹

Los Farroles Villa Mexicana, Riveroll and Calle 2. Quick, tasty, and cheap *tortas* (25 pesos) are served at the outdoor counter. Open daily 7am-4pm. ❷

El Charro (☎178 2114), on Mateos between Ruíz and Gastelum. A budget oasis in the heart of the tourist district. Simple but effective: enjoy a ½ chicken rotisserie grilled before your eyes (49 pesos). Open Su-Th 10am-11pm, F-Sa 10am-11pm. Smaller **Las Brasas,** next door, offers the same menu but keeps more erratic hours. ❷

👁 SIGHTS

A cosmopolitan dream by Baja California Norte standards, Ensenada has enough museums and other cultural attractions to pleasantly fill a couple of days.

RIVIERA DEL PACÍFICO. The lovely Moorish buildings and perfectly maintained gardens of this huge complex once housed a world-famous casino. Today, kids and adults alike paint, sing, and rehearse plays within the center's walls. You're welcome to stroll around the building's elegant interior imagining yourself as one of the beautiful people who flocked here in its heyday and stop for a drink at the original **Andaluz Bar**, or the **coffee shop**. The building also hosts temporary exhibitions in the **Galería de Arte de la Ciudad**. The permanent display of the **Museo de Historia** charts the history of the region in a gallery made to look like a cave system. *(On Costero, 1 block from the tourist office. ☎176 4310; www.ensenadahoy.com/riviera. Open daily 8am-8pm. Free. Andaluz Bar open Su-Tu and Th-F 4pm-midnight, W and Sa 9am-midnight. Coffee shop open daily 9am-9pm. Galería open M-F 8am-7pm, Sa 10am-4pm. Museo de Historia ☎177 0594; open M-F 9am-5pm, Sa-Su 10am-5pm; 7 pesos, children under 12 5 pesos.)*

BODEGAS DE SANTO TOMÁS. The mild, dry climate of Baja's northern coast has made it Mexico's prime grape-growing area. These *bodegas*, the oldest in Mexico, have produced wine since 1888. Today, Santo Tomás distills over 500,000 cases of wine each year. Tours show the traditional techniques as practiced today and conclude with a tasting complete with breads and cheeses. The winery also sponsors a small art gallery across the road, with temporary exhibits that include photography. *(Miramar 666, at Calle 7. ☎178 3333. Tours daily 10, 11am, noon, 1, 3pm. Tours US$5 with tasting of 5 wines, US$10 with a wider selection.)*

MUSEO DE CIENCIAS. The young and friendly staff will show you around basic exhibits on geology and natural history, and their application to the peninsula. The highlight is the large "Noah's Ark" boat outside that houses photographs and information on endangered species in Baja. *(Obregón 1463, at Calle 14, a 15min. walk from Mateos. ☎178 7192. Open M-F 9am-5pm, Sa 10am-3pm. 16 pesos, children 14 pesos.)*

CHAPULTEPEC HILLS. The hills offer a stunning view of the bay and the city from a ritzy residential neighborhood northwest of town. *(To reach the top, follow Calle 2 up the steep hill; turn right to look out over the town, left for the harbor. 15-20min.)*

🎵 ENTERTAINMENT

Mateos is packed with popular restaurant/bar/disco establishments, which stuff tourists with overpriced food during the day and overpriced booze at night. To escape the chaos, head towards the pool halls on Calle 2a, which are perpetually packed with locals. No trip to Ensenada would be complete without a pilgrimage to ◾**Hussong's Cantina**, Ruiz 113, the most famous bar in Baja and possibly Mexico. A venerable watering hole which first opened in 1892, Hussong's maintains a semblance of Mexican flavor with dusty floors and deer heads on the walls. (☎178 3210. Beer 20 pesos, margaritas 27 pesos. Open daily 10am-1am.) If you tire of *mariachis*, cross the street to **Papas and Beer**, an ultra-modern bar/dance party. Packed with college students, Papas is loud, rowdy, and serves up good 40-peso margaritas. (☎174 0145. Open M-W noon-midnight, Th-Su noon-3am. Live music F-Sa, in-house DJ otherwise. On Sa the party spills outside onto the rooftop terrace. Cover US$5 F-Sa.)

Those looking to stay sober can kick back at **Cinemas Ensenada**, on Juárez at Ruiz, which screens recent American hits, mostly avoiding the sin of dubbing. (☎178 8679. Shows daily 4-10pm. 25 pesos.) The **Teatro de la Ciudad** (☎178 3100), a black-and-white striped building out to the east of town on Diamante near Mateos, hosts visiting companies from around Mexico and abroad.

🎭 DAYTRIPS FROM ENSENADA

Ensenada is an excellent base for exploring sights in Baja California. Unfortunately, you'll need wheels, ideally with four-wheel-drive, to reach many of them. Tijuana and San Diego have the best rental rates (see **Tijuana: Car Rental**, p. 151).

BAHÍA DE TODOS SANTOS

Ensenada's own shoreline is devoted to shipping rather than sunbathing, but following the steady stream of daytrippers southwest along the Punta Banda Peninsula will bring you to a series of beautiful beaches and lovely ocean views.

PLAYA ESTERO. Packed with volleyball courts, banana boats, and *gringos*, Playa Estero is a pleasant, if not secluded, place to pass time. The area can get muddy during low tides, when sea lions come ashore—keep your eyes out. Access is available through the **Estero Beach Resort**, which houses the **Estero Beach Museum**, an impressive display of Olmec, Aztec, and Maya art. *(Take a right at the "Estero Beach" sign on Mex. 1 heading south. Free parking in the first hotel lot. Alternatively, catch a bus marked "Aeropuerto," "Zorrillo," "Maneadero," or "Chapultepec" from Pl. Cívica. Estero Beach Resort ☎ 177 5520. Museum open Su-M and W-Sa 9am-5pm. Free. Beach open daily 8am-5pm.)*

PLAYA EL FARO. Playa el Faro, 10km south of town, is similarly rife with volleyball courts and *gringos*, but has slightly better sand and allows camping on the beach. Horse rentals are available nearby. Signs warn swimmers about strong offshore currents. *(☎ 177 4620. Camp space, parking, and bathroom privileges US$7 per car. Full RV hookup US$12.)*

PLAYA SAN MIGUEL. Out to the north of the city, this rocky beach isn't of any use to sun worshippers or swimmers, but the large waves breaking off shore attract plenty of surfer dudes. *(Drive west on Calle 10, which joins Mex 1D; continue as far as the toll gate. Don't go through the gate, but make a U-turn and then turn right onto the cobbled road marked "Playa San Miguel." Alternatively, catch a "San Miguel" bus departing Gastelum at Costero (6.5 pesos) and flag down your return. 24hr. parking, with camping facilities including hookup and baths with hot water is US$10. All-day surfing until 8pm costs US$6. Prices drop if you stay for a few days. Campsite ☎ 174 7948.)*

PUNTA BANDA

Take a right onto the Transpeninsular Highway off Mateos at the south end of town, and head past exits for the airport, military base, and Playa Estero. After 20min., take a right on Mex. 23 at the "La Bufadora" sign. This road goes the length of the Punta Banda peninsula. By public transport, take a yellow microbús from Ensenada to the town of Maneadero (7 pesos) and get a connecting "Nativos" bus to La Bufadora (3 pesos). The driver will let you off anywhere along Mex. 23; return trip not assured.

Punta Banda, the peninsula at the southern end of Bahía de Todos Santos, boasts better hiking and more secluded beaches than the north. The mountains near the tip of the peninsula are laced with beautiful, solitary trails, and many other parts of the peninsula are equally breathtaking and warrant exploration. The following sights are listed in order from mainland to peninsular tip.

BAJA BEACH. Clean, soft, and uncrowded sands are buffeted by small waves and provide some of the best swimming in the area. The rolling hills provide a pleasant backdrop for sunbathing and relaxing. Horses are often available for rent. *(By car, bear right at the 1st fork after turning onto the Punta Banda road. Follow the signs saying "Horses for rent" and "Aguacaliente" that lead to the beach. Be careful: the loose sand can trap cars.)*

THE TOWN OF PUNTA BANDA. The town is little more than a roadside **Minimart**, some fruit stands, and a tiny **post office.** You can camp or park an RV at **Villarino ❶**, adjacent to the plaza, which has modern bathroom facilities and full hookups. *(Minimart open Su 7am-8pm, M-Sa 6am-8pm. Post office open M-F 8am-3pm. Villarino ☎ 154 2045; fax 154 2044. 65 pesos, children 45 pesos; hookup 50 pesos. Call for reservations.)*

CERRO DE LA PUNTA. Punta Banda offers several little-known hiking trails which are perhaps best entered from Cerro de la Punta, under the radio tower on the road to La Bufadora near the end of the peninsula. The ascent to the top provides sweeping views of the surrounding area; alternatively, you can descend to the shoreline to a number of beautifully secluded rocky coves, where you can be alone with the Pacific. Opportunities for swimming and cliffside picnics abound. Most of the trails are unmarked footpaths and rocky dirt roads, but be sure to stick to them; trail blazing will damage surrounding flora. (*Turn right up a long driveway at the "Cerro de la Punta" sign. You'll see a small clearing and a house on the cliffs. Parking 10 pesos.*)

LA BUFADORA. The Pacific coast's largest geyser is one of Ensenada's biggest attractions. Once you've reached the end of the dramatically curving road and peninsula, there's no mistaking the route to the blow hole, lined with trinket stalls and *churros* stands. You can get decent seafood and enjoy a more placid ocean view in one of the nearby restaurants. The cause of all this commercialization is a natural cave through which seawater is forced by the ebbing waves, causing the spray to burst up to 40m into the air, accompanied by dramatic snorts. (*Parking US$1-2.*)

PARQUE NACIONAL CONSTITUCIÓN DE 1857

Follow Mex. 3 from Juárez east toward San Felipe and Ojos Negros (ignore the sign just outside Ensenada for Calle Ojos Negros). At the military checkpoint, stay on Mex. 3 toward San Felipe. Around km 58, turn left onto a marked dirt road leading into the park. Then turn right onto the paved road in Ojos Negros which turns to dirt; after 6km you'll pass through a town, followed 3.5km later by a cattlegrid. Ignore the sideroads. Another 3.5km on, the road forks twice in quick succession; take the right fork both times, cross another cattlegrid, and pass a small community on your left, ignoring a fork to the right. 4km later a sign points to the park, 24km away; take the left fork here and again 3km later. After 14km take the marked left fork toward the park. From here, the road leads straight to the park entrance. The road is usually passable (with caution) by a passenger car, but be sure to inquire in Ensenada about current conditions before venturing into the wilderness, and to fill your tank before leaving.

Situated 1650m above sea level, the 5009-hectare **Parque Nacional Constitución** is unlike anyplace else in Baja. Here a long and at times grueling desert drive gradually winds its way into a thick coniferous forest high up in the mountains, an enchanting landscape of deep greens and isolated ranches. The focal point of the park is Laguna Hanson, a small lake frequented by grazing cows, with a number of small campsites dotted along its perimeter. The annual rainfall here is low, and the lagoon may well be dry if you come in summer; locals say that the best time to visit is the winter, when the peaks and trees may be covered with snow, which melts to replenish the lake. The towering pines and granite boulder mountains are enticing but guarded by foreboding "*Zona Restringida*" (Restricted Area) signs. Nevertheless, a few excellent hiking trails are accessible. The *Aventura en el bosque* (Adventure in the woods) is a 2km loop beginning west of Laguna Hanson, which opens out onto views of the forest. Signs along the trail describe various plants and animals in the park, including coyotes, rattlesnakes, and pumas that "occasionally attack humans." If planning on camping in the park, bring warm clothes and a good sleeping bag—temperatures drop dramatically at night.

MEXICALI   ☎ 686

Mexicali (pop. 1.2 million) celebrated its centennial year in 2003 with festivals, exhibitions, and even a concert in the desert by Luciano Pavarotti. The city seems suffused with a spirit of optimism, with town officials emphasizing its agricultural and industrial dynamism, its cultural sophistication and diversity, and its beauty as an urban center. This positive outlook and sense of opportunity has been characteristic of Baja California's capital throughout its history; Mexicali was first popu-

BAJA CALIFORNIA

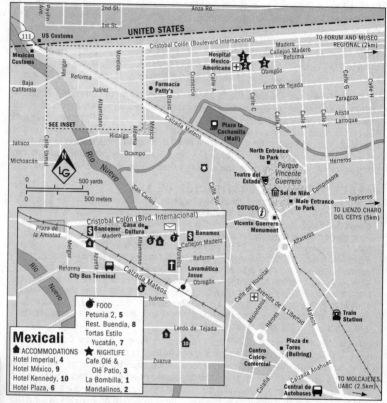

Mexicali

ACCOMMODATIONS
Hotel Imperial, **4**
Hotel México, **9**
Hotel Kennedy, **10**
Hotel Plaza, **6**

FOOD
Petunia 2, **5**
Rest. Buendía, **8**
Tortas Estilo
 Yucatán, **7**

NIGHTLIFE
Cafe Olé &
 Olé Patio, **3**
La Bombilla, **1**
Mandalinos, **2**

lated by laborers from the Colorado River Land Company, and many of its first residents were Chinese immigrants who came in search of a new working environment and whose vibrant culture continues to form a major part of Mexicali's identity today. Unfortunately, La Chinesca also shows Mexicali's other face, that of the run-down border town grappling with poverty, crime, prostitution, and drugs. The area's social problems form an uneasy contrast with the leafy boulevards, beautifully maintained parks, and fine museums that represent the best that Mexicali has to offer the visitor, who may well leave sharing some of the locals' optimism.

▐▘ TRANSPORTATION

To get to the **Central de Autobuses** (☎557 2415), take any bus headed south (away from the *frontera*) on López Mateos (every 10min., 4.5 pesos) to its intersection with Independencia, two blocks beyond the big Plaza de Toros on your right. Turn back to your right, almost as if to double back, and walk a block along Independencia. The station is on the left. To get to the **border** from the bus station, cross the footbridge just outside the station and hop on the local bus marked "Centro" (every 10 min. 5am-11pm, 4.5 pesos). When the bus goes around the rotary and starts heading the other way on López Mateos, it's time to get off. The border is five blocks farther along López Mateos. **Autotransportes de Baja California** (☎557

2440) goes to: **Ensenada** (4hr., 6 per day, 206 pesos); **Puerto Peñasco** (5hr., 4 per day, 215 pesos); **San Felipe** (2½hr., 5 per day, 130 pesos); **Tijuana** (2½hr., every 30min. 6am-9pm; service alternates between luxury, 182 pesos, and standard, 154 pesos). Some buses stop in **Tecate** (2hr., 96 pesos). **Élite** (☎557 2450) motors east to **Ciudad Juárez** (16hr., 3 per day, 629 pesos); **Guaymas** (13hr., every hr., 367 pesos); **Hermosillo** (10hr., every hr., 315 pesos); **Nogales** (10hr., 3 per day, 296 pesos); and **Los Mochis** (12hr., every hr., 461 pesos). Greyhound's partner **Golden State** (☎553 6169) can take you to **Los Angeles, CA** (4½hr., 7 per day, US$36) via **Coachella, Colton,** and **Onteria;** and **Phoenix, AZ** (5hr., 3 per day, US$38) via **Yuma** and **Tucson.**

✦ 🛈 ORIENTATION AND PRACTICAL INFORMATION

Mexicali stands on the US border 189km inland from Tijuana, just south of Calexico and California's Imperial Valley. The city's streets really shouldn't be difficult to navigate, but somehow it's easy to lose your bearings and end up walking in entirely the wrong direction. If you drive across the border you'll end up on **Mateos,** the main boulevard in the *centro*, which heads southeast through **La Chinesca** (Chinatown), past the enormous Plaza la Cachanilla mall to the civic center. From there it continues past the Central de Autobuses and the ritzy clubs and restaurants of the **Zona Hotelera** before leaving town, where it becomes Mex. 2. The university district, home to the Universidad Autonoma de Baja California, is east of La Chinesca close to the border, which is also where you'll find the city's liveliest nightlife. The Río Nuevo cuts through the western part of the city, spreading its unmistakable odor wherever it goes.

Tourist Office: Comité de Turismo y Convenciones (☎557 2376 or 557 2561; fax 552 5877), the adobe-colored building on Mateos facing the Vicente Guerrero Monument and park, 3km south of the border. Take any bus headed away from the border on Mateos, and get off at the rotary after Plaza Cachanilla. Loads of brochures, knowledgeable English-speaking staff, and huge, detailed street maps. Open M-F 8am-7pm. For **tourist cards,** visit the Mexican customs office in the immigration office at the border. There is also a SECTUR **state tourism office** (☎654 1095) on Benito Juárez and Montejano, which carries information about Mexicali state. Open daily 8am-8pm.

Currency Exchange: *Casas de cambio* line Madero, and banks occupy corners in La Chinesca. **Banamex** (☎551 6030), at Morelos and Madero, changes currency and has a 24hr. **ATM.** Open M-F 9am-5pm. So does **Bancomer** (☎553 4610), closer to the border on Madero at Azueta. Open M-F 8:30am-4pm. Branches also at the Plaza la Cachanilla mall.

Car Rental: Colorado (☎564 6080 or 564 3333), Sierra at Marmoleros Sur, near the state tourism office. Basic rates starting at US$60 per day. Open daily 8am-8pm. **Optima,** Sierra 901 (☎568 2919), next to the Siesta Inn, starts at US$64 per day. Open Su 8am-1pm, M-Sa 8am-8pm.

Luggage Storage: In the bus station, to the right as you enter the station. 5 pesos per hr.

Laundry: Lavamática Josue, Obregón and Morelos. Wash 15 pesos, dry 15 pesos. Bring your own detergent. Open M-Sa 9am-8pm.

Emergency: ☎060, or call the tourist office at 078.

Police: (☎060) at Calle Sur and Mateos. Some English spoken.

Red Cross: Cárdenas 1492 (☎552 9275), Quinta and Durango. Some English spoken.

Pharmacy: Farmacia Patty's, México 305 (☎554 1406), south of Obregón. Open 24hr.

Hospital: Hospital Mexico-Americano (☎552 2300), Reforma at Calle B, in a district full of clinics and other medical services. Some English spoken.

Fax: Telecomm (☎552 2002), next to the post office. Open M-F 7am-6:15pm, Sa-Su 8am-3pm.

Internet Access: La Zona Internet and Games Club (☎552 4008), Plaza Cachanilla, on the right close to entrance 5, offers a fast connection and a range of games. 38 pesos per hr. **Fax** also available. Open daily 10am-9pm.

Post Office: Madero 491 (☎552 2508), at Morelos. Open M-F 8:30am-6:30pm, Sa 9am-1pm. **Postal Code:** 21100.

ACCOMMODATIONS

La Chinesca overflows with budget lodgings, some respectable, others stretching the definition of the word "hotel." Ask to see a room before you pay—it may be unworthy of your money. Hotels on Madero close to Mateos dig deeper into your wallet but tend to be cleaner and safer, especially for women traveling alone.

Hotel México, Lerdo 476 (☎554 0669), at Morelos. Clean, cheerful pink rooms with TV and super-cold A/C surround the central gated parking lot. The office doubles as a grocery store. Free parking. Singles and doubles 250 pesos. ❺

Hotel Kennedy, Morelos 415 (☎554 9062), between Lerdo and Zuazua. Large, dim rooms in a characterless building, spiced up by garish carpets. TV, A/C, and phone make it better. Doubles 210-260 pesos, each additional person 100 pesos. ❹

Hotel Plaza, Madero 366 (☎552 9757), between Altamirano and Morelos. The Plaza puts distance between you and bustling La Chinesca with beautiful tiled floors, soft beds, A/C, TV, phone, and spacious baths. Singles 290 pesos; doubles 540 pesos. ❺

Hotel Imperial, Madero 222 (☎553 6790; fax 552 2901). Big, comfortable beds, A/C, TV, phone, and baths. Rooms with one double bed 330 pesos; doubles 540 pesos. ❺

FOOD

Mexicali has more Chinese restaurants per capita than any other city in Mexico, and not surprisingly, most of these restaurants are concentrated in La Chinesca. Restaurants offering lunchtime specialties and veggie combinations line Juárez and Lerdo south of Mateos. For even cheaper fare, head to the food court in **Plaza la Cachanilla ❷**, where huge combination plates of 3 or 4 items cost less than 25 pesos. If soy sauce isn't your thing, you can chow down on hearty *tortas de carne asada* (15 pesos) at **sandwich stands ❶** on Madero and Reforma west of Mateos.

Petunia 2 (☎552 6951), Madero between Altamirano and Morelos. Petunia dishes out tasty and strictly Mexican *tortas* (25-30 pesos), tacos (8-10 pesos), and large burritos (40-50 pesos) at a friendly, colorful outdoor counter with bar-style seating and a private parking lot. Fruit juices are also good. Open daily 7am-9pm. ❸

Restaurant Buendía, Altamirano 263 (☎552 6925). Specializes in Chinese cuisine—but chefs will always whip up some *antojitos*. Large plate of beef with broccoli, fried rice, egg roll, and fried chicken 32 pesos; veggie combo 32 pesos. Open daily 7am-9pm. ❸

Tortas Estilo Yucatán (☎552 3152), at Morelos and Madero. Huge, filling *tortas* (35 pesos) cooked on the griddle at the front and served in a chaotic but friendly atmosphere. Accepts take-out orders. Open daily 8am-9pm. ❸

SIGHTS

Mexicali's pollution problems mean visitors to the city might not realize how spectacular its geographical setting is: the mountains to the west are only dimly visible, thanks to the ever-present urban smog. Nevertheless, the tree-lined boulevards that run through the university district offer plenty of respite for the eye, and there are several places within the city limits where it's possible to escape the fumes and relax. Mexicali's parks are among its most attractive features and, along with its extensive museums, testify to the city's prosperity and pride.

A major attraction for kids and grown-ups alike, Mexicali's **Bosque y Zoológico** is on Alvarado between San Marcos and Cárdenas in the southwestern part of town. To get there, hop on a southbound black and white "Sta. Isabel" bus at the stop on Juárez, near Mateos. Get off when you see the Bosque's entrance. If you're driving, head south on Azueta over the Río Nuevo. The road becomes Uxmal south of the river; turn left on Independencia, then right on Victoria. Admire birds in the aviary, pedal paddle boats on the lake, or pity the lions, tigers, and llamas sweating it out in the sun. The grounds contain carousels, sports facilities and playground equipment, a small water park (15 pesos per hr.), and a mini train. It's also home to the **Museo de Historia Natural,** which charts the history of life on Earth with a special focus on Baja and includes a complete whale skeleton. (☎556 6861. Open daily 9am-4pm; between Easter and Oct. open until 7pm. 15 pesos, children 6 pesos.)

Take it easy and mingle with young lovers and families enjoying the jungle gyms, picnic spots, and grassy lawns at **Parque Vicente Guerrero,** off Mateos right next door to the mall. (☎554 5563. Open Tu-Sa 8am-10pm.) Just next to the park on Mateos is the large pavilion of **Sol de Niño,** an excellent modern interactive museum with over 150 hands-on exhibitions that will keep children amused for hours. The captions to the exhibits are in Spanish and English, and the team of young, enthusiastic guides will be only too happy to strap you into a large machine that will repeatedly turn you upside down in the name of science. There's also a building-top walkway providing views of the city. (☎554 9494 or 553 8383. Open Tu-Th 8am-5pm, F 8am-7pm, Sa-Su 10am-8pm. May be overrun with marauding schoolchildren during the week. 42 pesos, children 3-12 36 pesos.) Closer to the border on Madero between Azueta and Altamirano is **Parque Niños Héroes de Chapultepec,** a small grassy park full of trees and ice cream vendors.

The bright orange **Catedral de la Virgen de Guadalupe** is part of La Parroquía de Mexicali, founded in 1918 by Padre Juan Rossi after he discovered that no official church existed and the sacraments were being administered out of a tiny shack. (Open Su 7am-6pm, M-Sa 7am-9pm.)

In a pleasant district on Reforma at Calle L, the Universidad Autónoma de Baja California (UABC) maintains two museums that are well worth a visit. Together they comprise the **UABC Museo Universitario.** The **Sala de Historia** presents a concise history of the Baja region. Next door, a larger section presents **temporary exhibitions** relating to the life and history of Mexicali. (☎552 5715 or 554 1977. Call for current programs. Both museums open M-F 9am-6pm, Sa-Su 10am-4pm. Sala de Historia free. Temporary exhibits 12 pesos.)

🎵 📷 ENTERTAINMENT AND NIGHTLIFE

Unless you're looking for strip clubs, most entertainment options in Mexicali lie in the eastern part of town, away from the tawdriness of La Chinesca. Public buses stop running at 11pm, so you'll have to call it an early night or take a cab. Relatively close to the border are **Cafe Olé** and **Olé Patio** at Reforma 1150, between Calles C and D. The Cafe is a bar and restaurant that draws a slightly older, more sedate crowd. Patio is the Cafe's younger, wilder brother. Offering music in a large open air venue with thatched roof bars, Patio is the place to see and be seen for Mexicali's *jovenes.* (☎568 3111. Open M-Tu 5:30pm-midnight, W-Th 5:30pm-2am, F-Sa 5:30pm-3am. F-Su Patio cover 40 pesos.) One block away, **Mandalinos,** Reforma 1070, is a classy Italian restaurant by day (pasta dishes 80-90 pesos) and a hopping bar by night. Mandalino's offers live music free of cover (Th-Sa), but they'll make you pay with drinks—beers are around US$3 and margaritas nearer US$5. (☎553 6477. Open M-F until midnight, Sa-Su 7pm-2am.) Directly across the street, **La Bombilla** recently opened on spacious, stylish premises and presents live music every night. (Open Su-Th 1pm-1am, F-Sa 1pm-7am.)

The huge **Plaza de Toros Calafia** (☎557 1417 or 557 3864), on Calafia at Independencia, hosts regularly scheduled bullfights and other events. To get there, go to the *centro* stops at Mateos and Reforma and get on a blue-and-white "Centro Cívico" bus headed away from the border (10min., 4.5 pesos). Tickets for the bullfights range from 100-400 pesos, but almost all seats offer a great view, and the plaza holds up to 10,000. (Season Feb.-May, Sept.-Nov.) **Lienzo Charro del Cetys,** at Cetys and Ordente, hosts rodeos in the winter and spring. Check with the tourist office for schedules.

Mexicali boasts two major theaters and a very active **Casa de la Cultura,** on Madero and Altamirano. Hundreds of people, from grade school students to senior citizens, flock to this beautiful Neoclassical building to study sculpture, drawing, painting, theater, dance, and English. The Casa holds rotating displays of student art and presents plays, concerts, and dance shows. For information on public events, call Marco Antonio. (☎552 9630. Open M-F 9am-9pm. Free.) **UABC,** the university, also presents cultural and theatrical performances in its theater and has artistic displays in the **Galeria Universitaria** and **Sala de Arte** on campus. (☎566 4276 for more information.) If you're looking for a major play, symphony, or musical, visit **Teatro del Estado,** on Mateos at the northern end of Parque Vincente Guerrero. (☎554 8401. Shows 170-200 pesos.)

SAN FELIPE   ☎686

Nestled between the desert, the *sierra*, and the Sea of Cortés, and far from the Transpeninsular, San Felipe's tranquil bay isn't a place anyone just passes through. With its beautiful beach, gently teased by warm gulf waters, the town has an unhurried, untroubled quality that has persuaded a growing number of North Americans to come here for good, taking as their unofficial slogan, "No bad days in San Felipe." Admittedly, the tempo quickens on weekends, when more casual visitors drive into town and the bars and souvenir vendors go into overdrive—and the spell may be broken forever if the Mexican government ever completes its plan to continue the Mexicali road south beyond San Felipe and Puertecitos to link up with Mex. 1. Many locals would welcome such a development as a boon to the town's economy, but come here during the week and you'll find an expat community that could hardly be more content with the way things are.

⌐ TRANSPORTATION

The bus station is at the intersection of Mar Caribe and Mediterraneo. To walk downtown (15min.), turn left upon leaving the station, walk along Mar Caribe, and turn right onto Manzanillo. **Autotransportes de Baja California** (☎577 1516) departs from San Felipe to: **Ensenada** (3½hr., 8am and 6pm, 178 pesos); **Mexicali** (2½hr., 5 per day 6am-8pm, 130 pesos); **Tijuana** (5½hr., 5 per day 6am-5pm, 284 pesos).

✳ ⓘ ORIENTATION AND PRACTICAL INFORMATION

San Felipe is 190km south of Mexicali at the end of dip-plagued Mex. 5. This road connects with Mex. 3 from Ensenada, a route whose mountainous sections involve several sharp and poorly signed bends. Los Arcos (a tall, white double arch) marks the entrance to town. **Chetumal** continues straight from the arch toward the sea and is one of the east-west *calles* named after Mexican ports. Perpendicular to these are the north-south *avenidas*, including the beachfront **Malecón,** and behind it **Mar de Cortés,** on which hotels, restaurants and curio shops are clustered.

Tourist Office: Mar de Cortés 300 (☎577 1865 or 577 1155), at Manzanillo. English spoken. Open M-F 8am-8pm, Sa-Su 9am-1pm. For a US perspective, direct questions to Linda at the **People's Gallery,** 2 blocks south of the tourist office on the opposite side of Mar de Cortés. Open mid-Sept. to mid-June daily 9am-4pm. The most useful info source for travelers is the town's website (www.sanfelipe.com.mx).

Currency Exchange: Bancomer (☎/fax 577 1090), Mar de Cortés Nte. at Acapulco, is the only bank in town. It exchanges cash and traveler's checks and has a 24hr. **ATM.** Open M-F 8:30am-4pm.

Laundry: The Washtub (☎577 2001), right next to The Net on Mar de Cortés. Self-service US$2, drop-off US$4.50. Open Sept.-June M-F 8am-4pm, Sa 8am-2pm; July-Aug. M-Tu and F 8am-4pm, Sa 8am-2pm.

Emergency: ☎060.

Police: (☎577 1134), on Isla de los Cedros at Mar Negro. Some English spoken. A more central branch (☎577 1203) is next to the tourist office.

Red Cross: (☎577 1544, emergency 066), Mar Bermejo and Peñasco. English spoken.

Pharmacy: Farmacia Regina, Av. Chetumal 228 (☎577 1258). Open daily in summer 8am-midnight, in winter 8am-10pm. A **24hr. pharmacy** at the Saint James Infirmary.

Medical Assistance: Saint James Infirmary, Mar Negro 1285 (☎577 0117). English spoken.

Fax: Copicentro (☎577 1402; fax 577 1466), on Chetumal. Open daily 8am-9pm.

Internet Access: The Net (☎577 1600), next to the People's Gallery on Mar de Cortés. US$2.50 for first 15min., US$5 per hr. Open Oct.-May M-Sa 8am-4pm; June-Sept. M-F 8am-1pm, Sa 9am-1pm. Ask about additional evening hours. More affordable but less reliable facilities at **Thrifty Ice Cream.** 15 pesos per hr. Open daily 9am-10pm.

Post Office: Mar Blanco 187 (☎577 1330), at Ensenada. Open M-F 8am-3pm. To send letters through US mail, visit **Yetmail** (☎577 1225) on Mar de Cortés; they sell US stamps and take mailbags to the border. Open M-F 8am-3pm. **Postal Code:** 21850.

⌐ ACCOMMODATIONS & CAMPING

Many visitors to San Felipe resolve the issue of accommodation by simply buying a house, so it comes as no surprise that budget lodgings are limited. Most are located on Mar de Cortés and Mar Báltico near the beach. Generally, the smaller the hotel, the lower the price. If you can't afford to sleep in a bed, there are enough RV parks to provide secure alternatives; tourist officials warn against camping on the federally owned *playas*. For a bargain, try renting a room in a private home (look for signs that say *"se rentan cuartos"*).

Carmencita's (☎577 1831), a very friendly 4-room guest house across from Motel Chapala. Nothing on the building announces the name of the establishment; there's just a sign on the street offering rooms for rent. Powerful A/C, mini-fridges, *agua purificada*, spacious baths, and a limited choice of cable TV. Singles and doubles 300 pesos; 250 pesos per night for stays of 4 or more days. ❺

Motel Aragón Hermanos, Chetumal 293 (☎577 2490), on the left entering town, just past Mar Bermejo. Very pleasant and very large rooms with bath and TV; a 5-minute walk from the beach. Singles 300 pesos; doubles 400 pesos. 50 pesos extra F-Sa. ❺

La Posada de Don Jesús Mini Motel, Mar Báltico 186 (☎577 0685 or 560 9576). If you don't have your own trailer, try renting one at La Posada. Each comes equipped with kitchenette, electricity, and a small bath. Trailers for two people US$25. ❺

Casey's Beach Cabins (☎577 1431; www.sanfelipe.tv), on Mar y Sol, a private road 2 blocks past Campo San Felipe to the left off Mar de Cortés. Among the best deals in town if you're traveling with 2 or more people. Modern condos have 2 bedrooms, kitchenette, A/C, and satellite TV with a mind-blowing 155+ channels. Pristine location on a quiet stretch of beach south of the noisy public beach. Check in between 3 and 7pm to avoid incurring an extra charge. Condos from US$65 per night, up to 10 people. ❺

Ruben's (☎577 2021), toward the end of Golfo de California in Playa Norte. At the end of Mar de Cortés, walk around the edge of the baseball stadium and turn left onto Golfo de California; it's about a 10min. walk from the center of town. The best-known RV park. Beachfront and other spaces are topped with cool 2-story, open-air bungalows that look like *palapa* tree-forts. Each spot easily accommodates carloads of folks with sleeping bags. Hook-ups include electricity, hot water, and sewer connections. On-site restaurant and bar. Office open daily 7am-7pm. 2 people in summer Su-Th US$15, F-Sa US$20; in winter US$12; each additional person US$2. ❷

Campo San Felipe (☎577 1012), Mar de Cortés, just south of Manzanillo. Fabulous beachfront location close to the center of town. Thatched roofs over each fully loaded trailer spot. Spaces US$15-20; each additional person US$2, children under 6 free. ❸

🔲 FOOD

Mar de Cortés is crammed with restaurants and expat coffee shops advertising air-conditioned relief, while **taquerías** ❶ on the *malecón* offer shrimp, fish, or *carne asada* tacos (8-10 pesos). Look out for the seafood specials at ▨**Restaurant el Club** ❹, on the Malecón at Acapulco; huge plates of delicious steamed clams are served up for 40 pesos. Try breakfast (around 45 pesos) on the terrace overlooking the bay. (☎577 1175. Open daily 7am-10:30pm.)

🔲🔲 SIGHTS AND BEACHES

Each year, more than 250,000 people come to San Felipe to swim in the warm, tranquil, invitingly blue waters of the **Sea of Cortés.** The beach in town follows the Malecón and gets very crowded on weekends. South of town, away from the rumbling of shrimping boats and jet skis, clearer water and peaceful beaches provide a better setting for snorkeling. The southern beaches are also a seashell collector's paradise; low tides reveal perfect sand dollars and thousands of colorful shells. There's rarely a shortage of people riding **banana boats** (20min., 80 pesos). Landlubbers can rent ATVs from **Motos Carrillo's** directly outside Campo San Felipe. (☎577 2453. US$25-35 per hour depending on size. Check out the diagrams of the vehicles' spare parts, with prices attached, before you embark.)

Take time to visit the **Capilla de la Virgen de Guadalupe,** a shrine to the Virgin at the top of a small hill north of the town center, accessible via the narrow footbridge from the end of Mar de Cortés. Breathtaking views of the town, the sparkling blue bay, and the surrounding hills await you at the end of a short climb. If the views entice you to get out and explore more of the dramatic scenery just beyond San Felipe, you'll find few more enchanting desert landscapes than the **Valle de los Gigantes.** This hidden valley at the foot of the Sierra San Pedro Mártir is home to the world's largest strand of huge *cardón* cacti, one of which represented Mexico at the 1992 World's Fair in Seville, Spain. To reach the valley, drive up Chetumal away from the sea, but at the rotunda turn left toward the south rather than continuing onto Mex. 5 towards Mexicali. Where the airport road leaves the main highway, take a left fork. After about 20km, take the small dirt road on the right marked with a sign proclaiming, "*Sahuaro, Valle de*

Los Gigantes." Local ranchers don't mind letting visitors in as long as you remember to close the fence behind you (or you'll let the cows out); you may be charged a small entrance fee (around 20 pesos) if one of them happens to be on duty. Passenger vehicles with partially deflated tires should be able to navigate the sandy terrain as far as the small *palapa*, where you should park, though there is a small risk of getting stuck. In the valley, towering *cardón* (many nearly 15m tall), thorny orange-tipped *ocotillo*, bearded *abuelo*, and easily-provoked jumping *cholla* cacti shelter a small community of cows, roadrunners, jackrabbits, coyotes, and other desert dwellers. Local activists are campaigning for designation of the Valle as a national reserve in order to protect the gnarly 200-year-old *cardón*.

If you want to explore the San Felipe region but don't have your own transport, **Casey Hamlin,** on Mar y Sol, two blocks south of Campo San Felipe in town, offers tours of the area in air-conditioned SUVs. Groups of 4-8 can visit El Valle de los Gigantes (3½hr., US$25 per person), Puertecitos (7hr., US$55), nearby waterfalls (7hr., US$50), and a petrified forest (4hr., US$35). (☎577 1431; www.sanfelipe.tv. Trips include food. Reserve in advance. Office open daily 8am-8pm. Kayak rental US$20 for 1st hr., US$15 each additional hr.)

ENTERTAINMENT

San Felipe courts tourists with beautiful beaches and an enormous variety of venues to get tipsy. **Rockodile,** on the Malecón at Acapulco, attracts a young crowd with a central volleyball/basketball/soccer court, outdoor terrace, and loud pop music. The relatively low-key daytime crowd gets shoved out at night by a super-sweaty dance party. On busy nights, you may be lucky enough to encounter a *fiesta de espuma,* or foam party. Try the obscenely-named, electric-blue, king-sized beverage (US$4). (☎577 1219. Sa cover US$3. Open Th-Su 11am-3am.) A block down the Malecón lies **Beach Comber,** Rockodile's marginally less rowdy cousin. By day a sports bar (complete with mellow beer-sipping tourists), the bar changes into a raucous dance party at night, with karaoke on Thursdays and Sundays. (Happy hour with 2-for-1 drinks M-Th 4pm-6pm. Open M-W 5pm-1am, Th-Su 11am-3am.) Seasoned veterans nurse drinks at **Bar Miramar,** at the north end of the Malecón. The oldest bar in San Felipe may look like a 60s *cantina,* but the patrons (many of them expat regulars) come for an escape from the debauchery and glitz. Play a round of pool on the open-air patio overlooking the sea. (☎577 1192. Beer 20 pesos, margaritas 25 pesos. Open daily 10am-3am.)

VALLE DE SAN QUINTÍN ☎616

On the lonely mid-Pacific coast of northern Baja, the unassuming San Quintín Valley is the lifeblood of Baja California agriculture. Enclosed by huge barren mountains to the east and the Pacific Ocean to the west, nearly every square inch of land here earns its keep as cropland. The closest thing the region has to an urban center is a collection of services strung out along Mex. 1, more or less divided into three discrete towns: **San Quintín, Lázaro Cárdenas** (distinct from the other Lázaro Cárdenas, 100km to the northeast), and **El Eje del Papaloto.** The few tourists who visit usually come for superb fishing and surfing in and around the bay to the west. They may not look like much, and most travelers simply fill their tanks and stomachs before moving swiftly on, but the sleepy towns of the San Quintín Valley are friendly and cool, making them a great rest stop for trips, especially for travelers about to launch themselves into nearby **Parque Nacional Sierra San Pedro Mártir.**

⚏🖉 TRANSPORTATION AND PRACTICAL INFORMATION. The one **bus terminal** that serves the area is at the southern end of Cárdenas, on the right hand side of Mex. 1 from the north. However, public transport within the Valle is limited, and it is virtually impossible to travel from here to any of the nearby points of interest except in your own transportation.

All three towns huddle around Mex. 1. Streets off the highway lack street signs and common-use names, and addresses are designated by distance from Ensenada. Beaches are all located to the west of the highway, accessible by small dirt roads. Coming from the north, San Quintín is the first town, Cárdenas (as it is known in the region) is next, and Eje rounds out the trio.

Directions to all the following locations are given for travelers driving north to south. All places are on Mex. 1 unless otherwise stated. The Valle de San Quintín **tourist office,** with its friendly English-speaking staff, comes well before the towns themselves on the right at km 178 in Col. Vicente Guerrero—look for signs. (☎ 166 2728. Open M-F 9am-4pm, Sa-Su 9am-3pm.) To exchange currency or traveler's checks, or for 24hr. **ATMs,** head to **BITAL** in Cárdenas behind the PEMEX station, on the square to the right of the highway (☎ 165 2101 or 165 2125; open M-F 8am-7pm, Sa 8am-5:30pm), or **Bancomer** just before on the opposite side of the Transpeninsular (open M-F 8:30am-4pm). These are the **last banks before Guerrero Negro.** Other services include: **police,** in San Quintín at km 190, off a side street to the left by the PEMEX station (☎ 165 3295, emergency 060; some English spoken); **Farmacia San José** in Cárdenas, at km 192.5 (☎ 166 8125; open daily 8am-midnight); the **hospital IMSS,** at km 193.5 in San Quintín (☎ 165 2222), some English spoken; **Internet** cafes dotting Mex. 1 in Cárdenas, including **Internet Milenio** on the left at km 192.5 (☎ 166 8000; 10 pesos per hr.; open daily 8am-7pm) and **Network,** upstairs two doors before Bancomer on the left (☎ 165 3984; open daily 8am-10pm; English spoken); laundry in the **Lavamática Osearin** on the left at km 192.5 (☎ 165 3737; open daily 8am-9pm; wash 15 pesos, dry 15 pesos); and the **post office,** towards the end of Cárdenas on the right (open M-F 8am-3pm); **fax** service next door at **Telecomm** (☎ 165 2269; open M-F 8am-2pm, Sa 8am-11am). **Postal code:** 22930.

⚏🖰 ACCOMMODATIONS AND FOOD. Hotel rooms tend to be clean, modern, and reasonably priced. Drivers will be grateful for the ultra-firm orthopedic beds at the **Motel Chávez ❹,** just before the bridge at the end of San Quintín on the right. The clean rooms with A/C are also equipped with baths and satellite TV. (☎ 165 2005. Singles 205 pesos, doubles 270 pesos; be sure to pay these prices rather than the inflated dollar rates.) Don't be fooled by the ramshackle exterior of **Motel Uruapan ❸,** at km 190 in San Quintín. Inside, large sparkling rooms come with fans, baths, and white tile floors. (☎ 165 2108. Singles 200 pesos, doubles 250 pesos.) **Taquerías ❶** line both sides of Mex. 1 and serve excellent *tacos de pescado* or *carne asada* (approx. 10 pesos); fresh local clams claim a spot on every menu. **Asadero el Alazán ❹,** near Motel Chávez in San Quintín, is plastered with pictures of John Wayne and other Marlboro-man types, who would presumably enjoy the meaty menu, including broiled beef (360 pesos, serves 4). More modest appetites can get *carne asada* for 65 pesos. (☎ 156 8114. Open daily 8am-1am.)

◎🗗 SIGHTS AND ENTERTAINMENT. Tourists who stop in San Quintín for more than a night have come for the area's great fishing. The nearby stretch of protected bays (**Bahía San Quintín, Bahía Falsa,** and **Bahía Santa María**) host dizzying numbers of cabrilla, corvina, rock cod, sea bass, and halibut year-round. In July and August, the open water beyond the bays supports healthy populations of tuna (albercore, yellow, and bluefin) and sometimes marlin and other sailfish. Many *pangas* around the Old Mill Hotel, at the southern end of Cárdenas, offer fishing tours. Most speak English well enough to show you the fish, but only if you show them the money. **Don Eddie's Landing** is right next to the Old Mill, and offers summer daytrips for bottom fishing (US$280-300 for groups up to 4) and tuna fishing (US$320-360). Rates include bait, radio, a depth finder, and the services of a captain; there are also accommodations starting at US$45 for a double room, which can be combined with trips in package deals. (☎162 3143; www.doneddies.com.)

San Quintín boasts exceptional **surfing** with little competition for amazing waves. To get to most surfing spots, you'll need 4WD and a good map from the tourist office. The best surf is accessible at offshore breaks only by boat. Capt. Kelly Catian of **El Capitán Sportfishing,** about half a mile short of the Old Mill Hotel, transports eager surfers on his fancy fishing cruiser. (☎162 1716. Surfing US$250 per day for groups of up to 5. Sport fishing and spear fishing both US$360 per day for groups of up to 4.) Kelly can provide equipment, or you can bring your own.

Those in desperate search of spirits can visit **Bar Romo,** on Mex. 1 in Cárdenas, next to the motel of the same name. *Mariachis* and local singers croon into the wee hours. (☎165 2396. Open 8am-2am.) In San Quintín, grab a chilly beer (18 pesos) or margarita (25 pesos) and join in the karaoke at the touristy **Restaurant Bar San Quintín** (☎165 2376), on Mex. 1 next to Hotel Chavez.

■ PARQUE NACIONAL SIERRA SAN PEDRO MÁRTIR

The road leading to the park branches off Mex. 1, 51km north of San Quintín at San Telmo de Abajo, a small village between Camalu and Colonet, and runs east of the highway for 100km. The ride to the entrance is approximately 2½hr., starting on a paved road and continuing on a fairly well marked dirt road (closed during heavy rainfall). This access road becomes the main road inside the park, passing through Vallecitos and ending at the closed observatory gates. Passenger vehicles should be able to manage the route, though long sections of it make for heavy going. Camping 10 pesos per day; if no one is at the ranger station, set up camp and someone will come to collect your money. Campfires are strictly limited to certain areas. Be sure to buy a map of the park before you start your trip, since the maps distributed at the entrance are poor. Direct inquiries to the park's main office in Mexicali, ☎686 554 4404.

Most travelers bypass breathtaking Parque Nacional Sierra de San Pedro Mártir, making it one of the least visited of Mexico's national parks. Such neglect seems essential to the lonely spirit of the area. The somber peaks of the Sierra de San Pedro Mártir are visible from San Felipe and San Quintín as a distant presence. Those few intrepid souls who venture up here to the area around the Vallecitos plateau discover a world apart from the surrounding desert, in which comparatively high levels of precipitation sustain verdant forests of pine and juniper. Here puma and eagles make their home alongside a plentiful population of deer, and ice-cold streams support an endemic population of Nelson rainbow trout.

The jagged double peak of **Picacho del Diablo** (also known as **Cerro de la Encantada** or **La Providencia**), is the Baja peninsula's highest point and its greatest challenge to mountaineers, and should be attempted only by experienced climbers or those with a reliable guide. Allow 2-3 days to hike to the base from the main road, climb to the summit, and return to your car. Everyone attempting the climb must register at the ranger station. Hikers not brave, skilled, or deluded enough to attempt Picacho del Diablo can take in the view at **Mirador el Altar,** an awesome lookout 2880m above sea level. On a clear day, it's sometimes possible to see as far as the Pacific coast to the west and the Sea of Cortés to the east. The 2½hr. trail there is a steep double track strewn with loose rocks; look for signs from the main road just east of Vallecitos. An alternative, shorter route from the gates of the Observatorio Nacional is also possible, though it is virtually unmarked.

In 1967, the Mexican government took advantage of the park's secluded location by choosing it as the site for the **Observatorio Nacional.** The largest of the

BAJA CALIFORNIA

THE HIDDEN DEAL

CAVES OF CATAVIÑA

Visiting most of Baja's cave painting sites involves setting aside a full day and obtaining permits, transport, and a registered guide. If you can't afford to spend this much time and money but would still like to get a sense of Baja's remarkable rock art heritage, one site is within easy reach of the Transpeninsular and can be visited for free.

The paintings are close to Cataviña (pop. 120), 124km southeast of El Rosario. Near km176 on Mex. 1, about 4km north of Cataviña, a dirt track close to a small wooden shack leaves the highway (on the right from the south). Take this track to a clearing where you can park, and look away from the main road, across a depression in the land: 500m away, a small beige INAH sign should be visible on the opposite slope, which is unfortunately covered in more contemporary forms of painting. The sign marks a rock outcropping that you can crouch or crawl under. The best position for observing the images is lying flat on your back. The circles, spirals, and what appear to be images of the planets are most easily seen with the aid of a flashlight.

If you're unable to find the paintings, the locals of Cataviña can direct you, although they may not be entirely accurate. Some of them may be willing to act as free guides to the site. There's also a hotel or two in Cataviña and a PEMEX station open 4-8pm.

observatory's three gigantic telescopes boasts a lens diameter of 2.12m. Friendly scientists are usually willing to lead free daytime tours, but it's essential to arrange them in advance by calling the observatory's Ensenada headquarters (☎646 174 4580, ext. 301 or 312). The road to the observatory is clearly signed from Vallecitos; park at the gate and walk along the dirt road to the right, passing the workshops. Register at the observatory's office, the large building on the left. The smaller buildings up ahead are the astronomers' private rooms. You should avoid making excess noise around the camp, since the researchers are usually asleep during the day.

EL ROSARIO

El Rosario is little more than a bend in the road perched at the point in which the Transpeninsular turns its back on the west coast and embarks on its journey across Baja's rugged interior. Hardcore Baja enthusiasts pause here and enjoy a final taste of civilization before setting off into true back country Baja—the Desierto Central and beyond. Most importantly, El Rosario is where you'll find **the last PEMEX station for nearly 100 miles,** as well as one of the Transpeninsular's most famous culinary filling stations, just 50m down the hill: the legendary **Mama Espinoza's Place ❺**. Since 1930, Mama Espinoza herself has stuffed generations of Baja trekkers with her famous lobster burritos (US$12.50). (☎165 8770. Open daily 6am-10pm.) It would be pretty much unthinkable to eat anywhere else in El Rosario, but if you are feeling stingy, try **Baja's Best Cafe ❶**, around the corner and about 150m to the left. The tacos (10 pesos) are decent and cheap. (Open 7am-3pm.) If you're too gorged to move on, **Motel El Rosario ❸**, next door to Mama Espinoza, will put you up in a basic room with powerful fan, adequate bath, and cable TV. The only problem may be the noise caused by the PEMEX next door. (☎166 8850. Singles 195 pesos; doubles 230 pesos.) Mama Espinoza also has rooms and is slightly farther from the pumps. (Singles 250 pesos; doubles 350 pesos.) Other services include the **police** (☎165 8858, some English spoken), the **Centro de Salud** (close to the corner, no English spoken), a small **pharmacy** at the **Supermercado San José** (☎165 8838; open 7:30am-10:30pm), **fax** at Papelería Mickey (☎165 8864; open 8am-8pm), and **Internet** access at the cafe next door (20 pesos per hr.; open 8am-8pm). **Autotransportes de Baja California** stops at El Rosario's **bus terminal** (☎165 8889) on its way between **Tijuana** and **La Paz**.

BAHÍA DE LOS ÁNGELES ☎ 667

After mile upon mile of rugged mountains, desert, and dust, the glistening sapphire ocean of heavenly Bahía de los Ángeles (pop. 720) is one of Baja's most enchanting sights. The sheltered coves and offshore islands of isolated Bahía (as it is known to locals) are a tiny paradise for a wide array of marine species and for visitors who cherish the peace and simplicity of one of the real jewels of the Sea of Cortés.

■ ⑦ **ORIENTATION AND PRACTICAL INFORMATION.** A very bumpy paved road leads from Mex. 1 to Bahía de los Ángeles, approximately 1hr. from the Guerrero Negro junction. The access road becomes the town's main drag. Your best bet for tourist information is probably **Carolina Shepard Espinoza,** curator of the **Museo de Naturaleza y Cultura** behind the town square. Carolina has spent three decades in the area and also speaks English. Although Banamex reportedly has plans to open an ATM, at present the closest banks are in Guerrero Negro, and all local business is conducted in cash—**bring all the money you will need with you.** Within town, many establishments can be reached by phone through the local *caseta* (☎ 124 9101). The **police** are at the Delegación Municipal on the square (emergency ☎ 060; via *caseta* ☎ 124 9101), and speak little English, though potential interpreters are rarely far away. **24hr. medical assistance** is available just behind the police station at **ISE Salud.** (Open M-F 8:30am-2pm and 4-6:30pm, Sa-Su 9am-1pm.) **Isla** is not just a restaurant, but also sells **groceries** and has a small **pharmacy.** It also has an **Internet** cafe and is one of the few places where you can make long-distance **phone calls.** (Open 6am-10pm. Internet 25 pesos per hr.)

⑦ ⚑ **ACCOMMODATIONS AND FOOD.** If you've got a tent, camping is the cheapest way to stay in Bahía. The best sites are at ▨**Campo Archelón ❶,** a friendly campground right on the water. Cool stone-walled *palapas* and rustic *cabañas* for up to eight people come with the use of clean bathrooms and hot showers. (*Palapas* US$8 for two people, US$3 per additional person; *cabañas* US$25-35.) Just down the road is **Daggett's Campground ❶,** an orderly village of stick *palapa* huts, spacious rooms, RVs, spotless bathrooms, and hot showers. (Via *caseta* ☎ 124 9101; www.campdaggetts.com. *Palapas* US$4 per person; rooms US$30 per couple, US$5 per additional person.) To get to the campgrounds, follow the signs down the dirt track off the main road just before the beginning of town. Those looking for an affordable roof will appreciate **Casa Díaz ❹,** at the far edge of town where the road curves. Rooms have baths but no A/C. In summer, the coolest option may be to sleep in one of the cots on the porch, where offshore breezes provide some relief. (Singles US$20; doubles US$25.) Park your RV at **Guillermo's ❶,** which also has good rooms for large groups. (RV parking US$4 per person. No hookup. Doubles US$45. Each additional person US$10, with a max. of 10.)

Because of its isolated location, food in Bahía isn't cheap. Your best bet is to grill up your catch of the day. If the fish just aren't biting, head to ▨**Restaurante las Hamacas ❹,** in front of the hotel of the same name. The simple, trophy-adorned dining room is cooled by fans and ice-cold *cerveza.* (Warm, buttery *pescado al mojo de ajo* 50 pesos, beer 14 pesos. Open 7am-9pm.) The rooftop patio at **Restaurante Isla ❹,** across from Las Hamacas, is a great place to linger over yummy fish tacos (45 pesos) or delicious breakfasts while gazing at the bay. (Theoretically open daily 6am-9pm.) For something quicker and cheaper, the fish tacos at **Taquería Carreta ❶,** next to Las Hamacas, have an excellent local reputation.

◎◪ **SIGHTS AND SAND.** Small and undeveloped Bahía de los Ángeles has had a surprisingly rich history. Originally inhabited by the **Cochimi,** an indigenous group prevalent in central Baja, the town was later used as a major mining center for copper, silver, and gold, and subsequently served as the center of Baja's sea turtle industry until the business was outlawed. All of these phases are represented in the excellent **Museo de Historia y Cultura,** a small building behind the police office, surrounded by a 54ft. whale skeleton. In addition to newspaper articles on the area and a re-creation of a rancher's house, the museum has extensive shell and fossil displays, information on the area's natural history, and a Baja-focused bookstore. (Open daily Nov.-May 9am-noon and 3-5pm; June-Oct. 9am-noon and 2-4pm. Free, but donations gratefully accepted.)

The turtle population around Bahía has been recovering slowly but surely since the ban on their capture, and the friendly folks at the **Sea Turtle Project,** part of Campo Archelón, have had a lot to do with the recovery. The project studies the physiology and ecology of the turtles in the bay—mostly black turtles, but also loggerheads and hawksbills. Their recent satellite tracking of turtle migration revealed that the animals swim from Mexico as far as Japan to lay their eggs. The rehabilitation area provides a chance to get up close and personal with injured turtles (though not *too* personal—they do bite). (The project is signposted on the dirt road toward Daggett's. Open from early morning to evening. Free, but donations gratefully received.) Antonio Resendiz, the lead scientist, also conducts **boat trips** for interpretative tours of the marine ecosystem, fishing, snorkeling, or diving (from US$120, up to 6 people).

Bahía's widely touted **fishing** is excellent year-round, and a constant stream of *gringos* passes through the town. Expect to hook corvina, yellowtail, dorado, grouper, and halibut from late spring to summer and roosterfish, sailfish, cabrilla, and sierra in winter. Triggerfish swallow bait year-round. Smart fishermen bring their own equipment, as rentals are both expensive and rare. Guides, on the other hand, are everywhere. The turtle project recommends hiring guides affiliated with **Grupo Marino,** which is committed to sustainable practices in the bay. Ask at Campo Archelón, or contact **Joel's fishing tours,** opposite the museum in town.

There is also **sea kayaking** for the experienced, but winds in the bay can pick up without warning, and a few kayakers are lost to the ocean each year. Daggett's Campground rents kayaks. (US$5 per hr., lessons offered.) **Diving** has gained popularity, though the currents provide a major challenge for all but the most experienced. You won't see as many colorful fish as on the cape, but the warm water makes the depths worth a look. **Mauro Rossini,** who lives in the two-story house next to Campo Archelón, leads certified divers on tours of the bay. If you can't find him, ask at the Sea Turtle Project. Daggett's also takes divers out in its *pangas.* Fill your tanks (US$7) or get equipment at **Larry and Raquel's,** next door.

One of the most memorable features of the landscape around Bahía is the series of offshore islands, whose colors gradually shift as the light conditions change and are home to a host of rare wildlife. Information on visiting and camping on the islands is available from the office of **Las Islas del Golfo de California,** on the main street through town near the park. (Open M-F 8am-2pm and 4-6pm. Sa-Su, ask around town for licensed guides.)

The beaches in town are not exactly sandy, but broken shells give way to fine, gold-grey sand farther north, along the **Punta la Gringa** peninsula. To get to la Gringa, follow signs to Daggett's along the dirt road at the edge of town. Instead of turning right into Daggett's, stay straight for 12km. The series of small roads leading off the road to the water are usually passable in a passenger car, but flooding can turn them into gooey mud.

BAJA CALIFORNIA SUR

GUERRERO NEGRO   ☎ 615

For most of the year, Guerrero Negro's (pop. 10,000) biggest attractions are the salt plant and two PEMEX gas stations. Yet this town leads an unlikely double life as a launching pad for some of Baja's most exciting ecotourist activities in the Reserva de la Biosfera El Vizcaíno, whose headquarters are here. The town receives by far its greatest influx of visitors in January, when nearby Scammon's Lagoon, Laguna Ojo de Liebre, fills with playful grey whales. Once the whales move on, so do the tourists, and for most people Guerrero returns to being a place to fill up on gas, enjoy a salty breeze or two, and blaze along to the next town.

> **IN THE ZONE** Baja California Sur is one hour ahead of Baja Norte, so be sure to set your clock forward when you arrive in Guerrero Negro.

TRANSPORTATION. The **Autotransportes de Baja California terminal** (☎ 157 0611), on Zapata, is near the town entrance on the left. ABC sends buses north (6 per day midnight, 7, 8:30am, 7:30, 8:30, 10pm) to: **Tijuana** (12hr., 452 pesos) via **El Rosario** (4hr., 192 pesos), **Lázaro Cárdenas/San Quintín** (5hr., 244 pesos), and **Ensenada** (7hr., 365 pesos); and south to: **La Paz** (10hr., 5 per day 6am-midnight, 499 pesos); **Mulegé** (4hr., 5 per day, 192 pesos); **Santa Rosalía** (3hr., 7 per day, 139 pesos); and points in between. A single bus to **Mexicali** departs at noon (15hr., 622 pesos). Yellow **minivans** run frequently on Zapata to both ends of town and residential neighborhoods (8am-6pm, 7 pesos).

ORIENTATION AND PRACTICAL INFORMATION. Guerrero Negro lies along a 3km strip west of the Transpeninsular Highway, with most businesses on **Zapata,** a straight road which eventually curves toward the salt plant. A large orange water tank in the middle of the straight section of road serves as a useful reference point. The town has no official tourist office, but **Mario's Tours and Restaurant,** at km 217.3 on the Transpeninsular, has free **information** and advice. (☎ 157 1940. Open 7am-11pm.) **Banamex,** on Zapata in front of the salt plant, exchanges currency and has **ATMs.** (☎ 157 0555. Open M-F 9am-4pm.) Travelers continuing south should use this opportunity to stock up on cash, as this is the **last bank until Santa Rosalía.** Other services include: **laundry** at **Lavamax,** two blocks off Zapata just beyond the water tank; **police,** in the Delegación Municipal, before the salt plant on the left (☎ 157 0022; little English spoken); **Farmacia San Martín,** the big yellow building on the left of Zapata going into town, close to the bend in the road, with **fax** machine (☎ 157 1211; faxes 16 pesos per min.; open Su 10am-5:30pm, M-Sa 8am-10pm); **IMSS** on Zapata at Tabasco, past PEMEX (☎ 157 0433; little English spoken). **Internet** access at **Compu-Servicios,** on the street off Zapata one block before Hotel Malarrimo, on the right coming into town. (☎ 157 1337. 20 pesos per hr. Open Su 11am-8pm, M-Sa 9am-10pm.) The **post office** is one block off Baja California, beyond the end of Zapata, two blocks past the church and left onto a dirt road just before the basketball courts. (☎ 157 0344. Open M-F 8am-3pm.) **Postal code:** 23940.

ACCOMMODATIONS AND FOOD. Guerrero Negro has a healthy supply of good budget accommodations, though during whale season, rooms are at a premium and reservations are a good idea. If you have a tent and don't mind roughing it without water supplies, you can sleep for free at **Mario's ❶,** just north of the turn-

BAJA CALIFORNIA

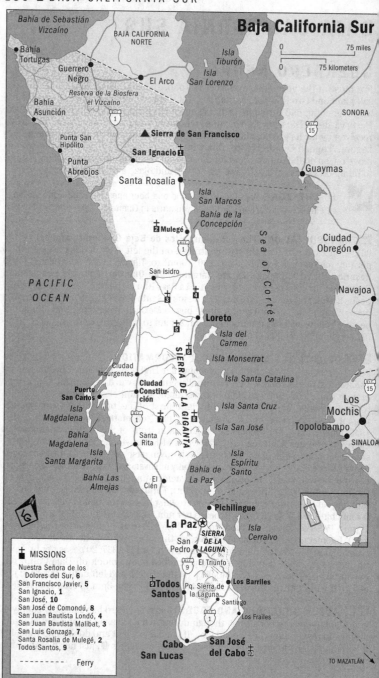

Baja California Sur

Bahía de Sebastián Vizcaíno

BAJA CALIFORNIA NORTE

Bahía Tortugas

Guerrero Negro

El Arco

Isla Tiburón

Isla San Lorenzo

SONORA

Bahía Asunción

Reserva de la Biosfera el Vizcaíno

Punta San Hipólito

Punta Abreojos

▲ Sierra de San Francisco

San Ignacio

Santa Rosalía

Guaymas

Isla San Marcos

Bahía de la Concepción

Mulegé

San Isidro

PACIFIC OCEAN

Ciudad Obregón

Sea of Cortés

Loreto

Isla del Carmen

Isla Monserrat

Ciudad Insurgentes

SIERRA DE LA GIGANTA

Isla Santa Catalina

Navajoa

Puerto San Carlos

Ciudad Constitución

Isla Magdalena

Isla Santa Cruz

Los Mochis

Bahía Magdalena

Santa Rita

Isla San José

Topolobampo

SINALOA

Isla Santa Margarita

Bahía Las Almejas

El Cién

Isla Espíritu Santo

Bahía de La Paz

Pichilingue

La Paz

Isla Cerralvo

San Pedro

SIERRA DE LA LAGUNA

El Triunfo

Los Barriles

Todos Santos

Pq. Sierra de la Laguna

Santiago

Los Frailes

Cabo San Lucas

San José del Cabo

TO MAZATLÁN

✝ MISSIONS

Nuestra Señora de los Dolores del Sur, **6**
San Francisco Javier, **5**
San Ignacio, **1**
San José, **10**
San José de Comondú, **8**
San Juan Bautista Londó, **4**
San Juan Bautista Malibat, **3**
San Luis Gonzaga, **7**
Santa Rosalia de Mulegé, **2**
Todos Santos, **9**

- - - - - - - - Ferry

0   75 miles
0   75 kilometers

ing for Guerrero Negro on the Transpeninsular. In town, friendly and quiet **Motel Las Ballenas ❸**, one block from Zapata behind Motel el Morro, offers cheap, comfortable rooms with small baths, fans, and cute whale-shaped wall fixtures. (☎157 0116. Singles 180 pesos; doubles 215 pesos.) The paint job at **Motel Brisa Salma ❸**, on Zapata four blocks beyond the water tank, may hurt your eyes, but you should sleep soundly in the knowledge that the motel has left your budget intact. Tidy rooms have TV and fans. (Singles 160 pesos; doubles 200 pesos.) Street-side **stands ❶** offer the city's cheapest, and perhaps best, food. **Asadero Viva Mexico ❶**, on Zapata, two blocks beyond the water tank, is a *taquería* with outdoor counter seating and indoor tables. (*Carne asada* tacos 7 pesos. Open daily 2pm-1am.) **Cocina Económica Edith ❷**, on Tabasco, off Zapata next to the IMSS, has a family atmosphere. (Tasty *tortas* 20-25 pesos. Open daily 7am-10pm.)

◪ SIGHTS. In addition to serving as a base for trips into the Biosfera el Vizcaíno, Guerrero is home to the largest open-evaporation **salt refinery** in the world. If you're in town during the summer when the whales and most of the birds have deserted the area, consider taking a tour. The tour goes through an eerie landscape of vast lagoons, and the mountains of salt look oddly like snow, a disconcerting sight in the blistering heat.

▣ DAYTRIP FROM GUERRERO NEGRO

RESERVA DE LA BIOSFERA EL VIZCAÍNO

*The best source of information on the reserve is its **main office** (☎157 1777 or 157 0177), on Marcelo Rubio in Guerrero Negro, five blocks farther into town from the water tank and two blocks off to the right. The staff there can offer advice on expeditions into the Biosfera, though these are generally most easily organized through one of the local tour companies. **Eco-Tours Malarrimo**, on Zapata, on the right as you come into town, leads a range of tours within the reserve. For all of their tours it is advisable to make reservations at least one day in advance. (☎/fax 157 0100. Office open M-Sa 8am-5pm.) If you have a particular interest in seeing something that is not covered by the regular tours, such as the more remote **mission sites** or a particular bird, animal, or plant species, contact Malarrimo one or two months in advance to discuss the organization of a special trip. While some sights in the Biosfera can be visited in a day, others will take more time.*

Guerrero Negro is the gateway to the stunning **Reserva de la Biosfera el Vizcaíno,** which is the largest nature reserve in Latin America and contains many of southern Baja's most extraordinary natural and archaeological treasures. The reserve encompasses the band of the Baja peninsula from the 28th parallel down to the Sierra de San Francisco, bounded by the Tres Vírgenes volcanic area in the east and the entire Vizcaíno peninsula to the west; it also contains the marine areas on either side. All in all, it totals over 2.5 million hectares. Within this sparsely populated region, a number of conservation projects are working to save some of North America's most endangered species. Developing ecotourism is one facet of these projects, and several of the most fascinating sites are open to visitors. Most parts of the reserve are most easily reached from Guerrero Negro in the north, although for some it is better to travel via San Ignacio (see p. 183) in the south.

WHALE WATCHING. Most visitors to Guerrero Negro use it as a base for trips to the **Laguna Ojo de Liebre,** 10km away, where from mid-December to early April more than 50% of the world's grey whale population is born. Malarrimo runs popular whale-watching trips. You can also drive yourself. The road to the Laguna is 10km south on Mex. 1—watch for a sign with a whale on it. Follow the sandy bumps for 24km until you reach the Laguna's new visitor center, where parking is

US$3. The whales are shy and sensitive, so private boats are prohibited during mating season (Dec.-Apr.). Trained local fishermen can give you a closer look. *(Malarrimo trips 4hr.; 8 and 11am; US$45, children under 11 US$35. Includes transportation, bilingual guide, and a light lunch. Other trips are typically 1½hr.; US$15, children US$10.)*

BIRD-WATCHING. The salt flats to the west of Guerrero Negro are a bird-watcher's mecca, with 120 species of migratory birds visiting between October and March. Malarrimo leads regular tours in these months to see a huge range of hawks, kestrels, falcons, terns, bitterns, pelicans, grebes, ospreys, and more.

CAVE PAINTINGS. Malarrimo uses Guerrero Negro as a base for one- and three-day trips into the Sierra de San Francisco to see Cochimi cave paintings. Five hundred paintings, probably more than 10,000 years old, are contained within a 12 sq. km area. Anthropologists are unsure who created these paintings or why, but unassuming central Baja boasts more rock art than more famous sites in Spain and France. Most of the paintings are found high (around 10m) above ground, leading local Cochimi to believe a race of giants made them. *(Trips cost US$90 per person for one day and US$150 per person for 3 days, though costs go down as the size of the tour group increases. Make reservations at least one day in advance, if not earlier.)*

VIZCAÍNO PENÍNSULA. Guerrero Negro is also a convenient base from which to set out for the Vizcaíno Península, a remote area which is home to one of the Bio-sphere's most important conservation projects. To get there, drive 70km southeast on the Transpeninsular to the town of Vizcaíno, and turn right towards Bahía Tor-tugas and Bahía Asunción. The main road into the peninsula is in reasonable con-dition, though sometimes sand dunes drift onto it and cause difficulties.

DESERT PRONGHORN RESERVE. Sixty kilometers from Vizcaíno, a dirt road peels off to the left towards Bahía Asunción. Another turn to the left about 4km along this road leads to the **Campamento del Berrendo,** a protective reserve for the *berrendo* or **desert pronghorn,** one of North America's most endangered species and one of the most fascinating members of the desert population. These remark-able, beautiful creatures are able to survive the region's intense heat without drinking water by ingesting moisture from the plants in their diet. Moving at speeds up to 100km per hr., they are also the second-fastest animals in the world, and the fastest on the continent. This hasn't stopped the pronghorn from being brought to the edge of extinction by hunting, however, and it is estimated that the current population in the wild numbers just 200. The government is committed to saving the species and has outlawed hunting and established the conservation camp in the Biosphere. Here just over 100 pronghorns are kept in large fenced cor-rals. The staff at the camp are usually happy to let visitors have a rare close-up peek at the animals. *(Ask at the reserve's main office in Guerrero Negro before making a visit.)*

BAHÍA ASUNCIÓN. Past the turn for the pronghorn camp, the road eventually reaches the coast at Bahía Asunción, an isolated fishing community that is sometimes visited by American sport fishermen. The village looks out onto a small collection of offshore islands, which are home to a large and noisy **sea lion colony.** Manuel "El Loco" Arce, who lives near the fishing cooperative building at the far side of the bay, is one of a number of locals happy to take enthusiasts out on his boat to watch the lions swimming, fighting, playing, and basking in the sun. The Biosphere staff in Guerrero Negro can help you orga-nize a visit. Should you get stuck in Bahía Asunción, it does have one small hotel, **Los Hermanos ❸,** which charges 180 pesos for a room and has a restau-rant. There is also an unmarked PEMEX station across the road where you can fill up before heading back to the Transpeninsular. *(Sea lion trips around US$60.)*

SAN IGNACIO ☎ 615

From a distance, San Ignacio (pop. 2000) appears as a cruel illusion—leafy palms, flowering bushes, and broad swaths of lush green appear magically in the blistering desert. Go ahead and pinch yourself—you're not dreaming. The area around San Ignacio is blessed with the most plentiful underground supply of freshwater in Baja California Sur. Of late, it's been pumped up to form a murky lake, which is used for swimming and irrigating local orchards. A prime point of departure for cave painting and whale-watching tours, and a delightful place to sample small-town Baja life, the town, with its intimate atmosphere, nighttime starscapes, and historic mission, has seduced many a traveler.

E TRANSPORTATION. Buses pick up and drop off at the sheltered bench next to the PEMEX 2km outside San Ignacio on Mex. 1. Trek north along C. Luyando, or grab a **taxi** at the *zócalo* (25 pesos). *De paso* buses head north to **Tijuana** (14hr., 7 per day 2am-8pm, 530 pesos) via **Guerrero Negro** (3hr., 90 pesos) and **Ensenada** (13hr., 435 pesos); and south to **La Paz** (8hr., 6 per day 7:30am-11pm, 383 pesos) via **Santa Rosalía** (1hr., 52 pesos); **Mulegé** (2hr., 102 pesos); **Loreto** (3hr., 174 pesos).

⚎ 🛈 ORIENTATION AND PRACTICAL INFORMATION. San Ignacio lies 142km southeast of Guerrero Negro on Mex. 1. A winding road canopied by swaying date palms leads south from the highway and becomes **Luyando** at the *zócalo*. Most activity revolves around the tranquil *zócalo*, bordered by Luyando to the west, **Morelos** to the east, **Juárez** to the north, and **Hidalgo** to the south.

There is no official tourist office, but for an informative chat visit **Jorge Antonio Fischer,** the owner of the mini-mart next to Restaurant Chalita on Hidalgo at the *zócalo.* (☎154 0150. Open daily 8am-8pm.) He also leads whale expeditions and tours to the cave paintings (see **Sights,** below). **Nuevos Almacenes Meza,** on the corner of Juárez and Luyando, facing the *zócalo*, sells general goods. (☎154 0122. Open Su 8am-noon, M-Sa 8am-noon and 2-7pm.) Other services include: **police** (☎154 0147), in the Delegación Municipal on Ocampo and Zaragoza, a 5-10min. walk out to the southeast of the *zócalo*; **pharmacy** at **Boticas Ceseña,** Madero 24A, one block back from Juárez (☎154 0076; open Su 9am-1pm, M-Sa 9am-1pm and 3-8pm). To reach the **Centro de Salud,** walk down Hidalgo away from the Mission and turn right on Cipris, a tiny dirt road; when you reach the auto parts shop, turn right, then left just past the tin-roofed warehouse. Continue straight for two blocks; it's the white building set back from the road on the right side and surrounded by flowers. (Open M-F 8am-2:30pm and for emergencies.) **Mail** can be sent from the small post office next to the Delegación Municipal.

🛏 ACCOMMODATIONS. San Ignacio's few hotels don't come cheap, and reservations are necessary during *Semana Santa* and *El Día de San Ignacio* (July 31). Just outside town on the entry road, **Ignacio Springs ❸** is a Canadian-run bed and breakfast with a twist: guests stay in large, luxurious *yurts* (tents) close to the lagoon, where you can fish, bird-watch, and have free use of the owners' kayaks. (☎154 0333; www.ignaciosprings.com. 450-550 pesos for 1-2 people; smaller *yurt* 200 pesos for 1 person. Each additional person 100 pesos. Breakfast included.) Perhaps the nicest place to stay in the town itself is the former **Casa Lerée ❺,** also known as **Casa Elvira,** one block from the corner of Juárez and Morelos. This gorgeous adobe house is a local institution, and its front room hosts a small gallery of works by local artists and historic photographs of San Ignacio. The two comfortable rooms in the beautiful back garden share a bathroom, and one is equipped with a kitchenette. (☎154 0158. Rooms US$35 each.) You can also stay at **Restaurant Chalita ❸**, Hidalgo 9, on the *zócalo*, with three rooms in the back garden, each with two beds, fan, and bath with hot water. (☎154 0082. Doubles 180 pesos.) If you'd prefer a more conventional budget hotel, **Hotel Posada ❹**, a 5min. walk down Cipris from Hidalgo, has clean rooms with baths, fans, and nifty colorful windows in a family atmosphere. (☎154 0313. Singles and doubles 250 pesos.) Campers should try **El Padrino RV Park ❶**, 500m from the *zócalo* on the road connecting San Ignacio to the highway. Phone ahead—the camp sometimes closes during the summer. There is a restaurant, and the owners also run tours to cave-painting and whale-watching sites. Some rooms with A/C and hot water are being added. (☎154 0089. Full hookup for two people 80 pesos. Electricity 40 pesos extra. Each additional person 20 pesos. Camping 40 pesos per person, cars 100 pesos. Singles 200 pesos; doubles 350 pesos. Room prices include breakfast.)

🍴 **FOOD.** San Ignacio's small selection of delectable, affordable restaurants is within a stone's throw of the *zócalo*. Seafood receives top billing on most menus. Eat out on the terrace or in a thatched hut at **Restaurant-Bar Rene's ❸**, just outside the *zócalo*, on Hidalgo. The menu's seafood (from 70 pesos) is limited by the day's catch, but it will be deliciously fresh and cooked to perfection. (Open daily 8am-10pm.) **Restaurant Chalita ❸**, on Hidalgo at the *zócalo*, is a family kitchen that provides a truly authentic family taste of contemporary Mexican family life. Just don't be surprised if this means your *antojitos* (30-40 pesos) are prepared with the assistance of the family microwave. (☎154 0082. Open daily 8am-10pm.)

📷🎭 **SIGHTS AND ENTERTAINMENT.** After nearly three centuries, the architectural focus of San Ignacio is still the **Mission of San Ignacio,** on the west side of the *zócalo*. The mission was founded in 1728 by Jesuit missionary Juan Bautista Luyando. The construction of the mission proved a logistical nightmare; wood had to be hauled from the Guadalupe mission in the Sierras, furniture brought from Mulegé on a four-day mule ride through the desert, and paintings carried by boat from the mainland. Its walls, over 9m thick, are made from blocks of volcanic rock. (Mass Su 11am.) The **Mission Museum,** next door, is a great source of information on the cave paintings around San Ignacio, with captions in Spanish only. There's even a huge faux cave painting for those who can't make it into the Sierra. (☎154 0222. Open May-Oct. M-Sa 8am-3pm; Nov.-Apr. daily 8am-5pm. Free.)

For extra fun, hit town during the week-long celebration of **El Día de San Ignacio,** beginning on July 28, which celebrates the day of the town's patron saint (July 31) and coincides with the harvest celebration (July 30). San Ignacio blossoms into a huge *fiesta* complete with singing, dancing, horse races, fireworks, and food.

San Ignacio lies at the southern end of the **Reserva de la Biosfera el Vizcaíno** (see p. 181) and makes a good base from which to visit some of the reserve's sights. The **painted caves** (see p. 182), 75km out of town in the Sierra de San Francisco mountains, are San Ignacio's main tourist draw. All cave trips from San Ignacio require quick approval from the INAH office next to the mission. (☎154 0222. Open May-Oct. M-Sa 8am-3pm; Nov.-Apr. daily 8am-5pm.) Guides are available all over town to take you to any of the sites in the Sierra. Most popular are **Cueva el Ratón,** a short hike from a parking area, and **Cueva la Pintada,** the most spectacular site. Oscar and Dagoberto Fischer of **Hotel Posada** (☎154 0313), or their relative Jorge at the mini-mart on the *zócalo*, will bring you to any of the sites (US$120 for 1-5 people or US$25 per person for groups of 6 or more). For a more professional tour, contact **Eco-tour Malarrimo** in Guerrero Negro (US$90-150 per person; see p. 181).

San Ignacio has also become a popular launch point for whale-watching trips. **Laguna de San Ignacio** fills with literally tons of grey whales from January to March, offering visitors a great chance to get up close and personal with the animals—whales in San Ignacio have a reputation for being especially friendly. The Fischers take tours (8am-3pm, US$55 per person including lunch), as do **El Padrino RV Park** (☎ 154 0089; 4-6hr. tour US$120).

East of San Ignacio is the area of the Biosfera el Vizcaíno dominated by the **Tres Vírgenes volcano.** The reward of the two-day hike to the summit is the possibility of being able to view both the Sea of Cortés and the Pacific. The best source of guidance for this trip is the Biosphere's **Campamento Borrego Cimarrón** (☎ 155 4241), located at km 31 on the Transpeninsular Highway southeast of San Ignacio. To reach the camp, take the left turn off Mex. 1 marked "Campo Geotermaleléctrico las 3 Vírgenes"; about a kilometer in from the turn, a short, steep dirt road on the left leads up to the camp. The camp serves as the base for conservation efforts relating to the endangered *borrego* (big-horn) sheep. The friendly rangers at the camp are able to lead day-long guided trips to observe these rare animals if you call ahead. They also have small *cabañas* and camping spaces next to their camp for people who wish to explore the area.

SANTA ROSALÍA   ☎ 615

The violence of the Baja peninsula's geological past is rarely more evident than in the dramatic landscape around Santa Rosalía (pop. 10,500), a town which owes its existence to the 1868 discovery of rich deposits of copper here. Soon afterwards, a French mining company settled this steep-sided valley, giving the land at the top of the slopes to wealthier, higher-ranking officials and accommodating the poorer classes below. Though the mines closed in 1986, the town retains relics of its industrial past, and its wealth of surviving French colonial architecture, unique in the peninsula, makes Santa Rosalía an intriguing stop.

▐ TRANSPORTATION. Buses depart from the **ABC/Aguila station** (☎ 152 1408), in the same building as the ferry office. Buses travel north to **Tijuana** (15hr.; 3, 5am, 5, 6:30pm; 586 pesos) via **San Ignacio** (1hr., 52 pesos); **Guerrero Negro** (3½hr., 139 pesos); **El Rosario** (9hr., 331 pesos); **San Quintín** (9½hr., 376 pesos); **Ensenada** (13½hr., 493 pesos). In addition, a 4am bus goes to San Ignacio and Guerrero Negro only, while a 9pm bus goes on from Tijuana to **Mexicali** (731 pesos). Heading south, buses go to **La Paz** (8hr., 6 per day 9am-midnight, 342 pesos) via **Mulegé** (1hr., 74 pesos); **Loreto** (3hr., 134 pesos); **Ciudad Constitución** (4½hr., 238 pesos).

From Santa Rosalía, you can catch the **ferry** connecting Baja California to **Guaymas** on the mainland (10-11hr.; Su, Tu, F 10pm; 410 pesos, round-trip 780 pesos; ages 3-11 half-price). The boat leaves from the **Baja Ferries** terminal on Mex. 1, just south of downtown. (☎ 152 2200. Open daily 9am-2pm and 5-8pm.) Purchase 1 month in advance, since demand can be high, although in summer a week may suffice. Those traveling with cars must purchase tickets in advance (2000 pesos for a standard passenger car) and show a tourist card, registration, and a vehicle permit (get one at the border or at La Paz—they don't have them in Santa Rosalía). To get downtown from the ferry or bus station, turn right as you leave the ferry compound and walk along the main road to the old train engine.

▐▐ ORIENTATION AND PRACTICAL INFORMATION. Santa Rosalía lies 555km north of La Paz. Almost all services are on the two main streets, **Obregón** and **Constitución,** which run east-west. Crossing these, named and numbered streets run north-south. Attractive **Mesa Francesa** lies up the hill via **Alta Mirano,** which runs parallel to and north of Obregón before it starts winding its way to the top; pedestrians can also get there by ascending the dilapidated steps nearby.

Banamex, on Obregón and Calle 5, changes traveler's checks and has a 24hr. **ATM.** (☎ 152 0984. Open M-F 9am-3pm.) Other services include: **police** (☎ 152 0651), at Carranza and Plaza; **pharmacy** in the **Farmacia Mini-Super** on Obregón near the church (☎ 152 2850; open daily 8am-midnight); **General Hospital** (☎ 152 0789 or 152 1336), at Costeau opposite the museum in Mesa Francesa, some English spoken; **Red Cross** (☎ 152 0640, emergency ☎ 065), on Calle 2 and Carranza, right off Constitución, little English spoken. There is a **Telecomm** on Constitucíon, across from the post office. (☎ 152 2122. Open M-F 8am-7pm, Sa 8am-11:30am.) The **post office** is on Constitución, between Calle 2 and Altamirano. (☎ 152 0344. Open M-F 8am-3pm.) **Internet Vision,** on Obregón near Banamex, provides access. (20 pesos per hr. Open daily 10am-10pm.) **Postal code:** 23920.

▮◨ ACCOMMODATIONS AND FOOD. For those looking to relive Santa Rosalía's French past, there's really only one place to go: the **Hotel Francés ❺**, at the far end of Costeau on the Mesa Francesa. This was where the El Boleo company accommodated the unmarried members of its French staff. The hotel may have seen better days, but the furnishings and wood paneling hint at its past splendor. (☎ 152 2052. Rooms with weak A/C 448 pesos; ask for one with a sea view.) Among more affordable options down in the center of town, the standout is probably **Hotel Olvera ❹**, Calle Plaza 14, three blocks from shore on Constitución, right of the foot bridge. (☎ 152 0267. Singles 200 pesos; doubles 300 pesos.) **RV Park Las Palmas ❷**, a few kilometers south of town, has full hookups, laundry, and a restaurant, but closes for much of the boiling-hot summer. (2 people US$10.) Wherever you stay in Santa Rosalía, you'll thank yourself for paying the extra few pesos for A/C.

Constitución is lined with cheap and good *taquerías*. The town's best-known eatery is another French legacy: ▧**El Boleo Bakery ❶**, on Obregón at Calle 4, has locals lining up each morning to buy its fabulous French bread, *pan dulce*, and other goodies, all from about 3 pesos. (☎ 152 0310. Open Su 9am-1pm, M-Sa 8am-9:30pm.) For a heavier meal, head to **Terco's Pollito ❹**, at Obregón and Playa, where A/C offers relief from the heat. (Both 50 pesos. ☎ 152 0075. Open daily 8am-11pm.)

◪ SIGHTS. The wooden houses, general stores, and saloons in Santa Rosalía recall the town's mining-boom days, and make for good wandering territory. A good place to start is up on the Mesa Francesa, where you can retrace the daily promenade of the El Boleo administrative workforce from the **Hotel Francés** to their former office, which is now the **Museo Histórico Minero de Santa Rosalía.** The museum preserves the offices as if the mines were still working, giving the impression that the employees have just stepped out for lunch. (☎ 152 2929. Open M-Sa 9am-2pm. Free.) From just outside the museum you can take in a fine view of the town below, which contains startling specimens of 19th-century French architecture, including the many-windowed **Palacio Municipal,** on Plaza Juárez between Carranza and Constitución, and **El Boleo Bakery,** on Constitución, all with pure colors, simple forms, and modern use of glass and steel. The pre-fabricated, white, cast-iron **Iglesia Santa Bárbara,** at Obregón and Calle 1, designed for a mission in Africa by none other than Gustave Eiffel, was never picked up by the company that had commissioned it. French mining moguls spotted the church at the 1889 Exhibition Universale de Paris and decided Santa Rosalía couldn't do without it.

MULEGÉ
☎ 615

Mulegé (pop. 3000) has long been a favorite stop for travelers, and many see no need to continue any further south. It's apparent why: with its thick forest of glossy palms ushering the Río Mulegé into the Sea of Cortés, so close to the glistening beaches and cobalt sea of **Bahía de la Concepción,** this desert oasis has all the elements of a tropical paradise and offers rewards to divers, fishers, and even archaeologists. Yet so far, the influence of outsiders hasn't quite spelled the death of Mulegé's own distinct character. Set back from the shoreline, the narrow streets of this small mission town remain friendly but introverted, retaining their own pace of life while visitors rush out to seize the region's many opportunities.

TRANSPORTATION. The **Igriega bus station** is a sheltered blue bench at the turn-off to Mulegé from Mex. 1. All buses are *de paso*. Tickets and bus info are available at the restaurant overlooking the bench (☎153 0388). Northbound buses leave to **Tijuana** (16hr.; 3, 4am, 4, 5, 8pm; 643 pesos) via **Santa Rosalía** (1hr., 74 pesos); **San Ignacio** (2hr., 105 pesos); **El Rosario** (10hr., 388 pesos); **Lázaro Cárdenas/San Quintín** (11hr., 436 pesos); **Ensenada** (14½hr., 557 pesos). The 8pm goes on to **Mexicali** (19½hr., 788 pesos) via **Tecate** (17hr., 684 pesos). Southbound buses go to **La Paz** (6hr.; 10:30, 11am, noon, 9, 10:30pm; 309 pesos) via **Loreto** (2hr., 81 pesos) and **Ciudad Constitución** (3½hr., 174 pesos). Arrive 30min. early for all buses.

ORIENTATION AND PRACTICAL INFORMATION. With its compact bundle of steep, narrow streets, Mulegé is a fun town to explore on foot. Coming from the north, the road into town peels off to the left from the Transpeninsular and then forks again. To the left is **Moctezuma**, while to the right is **Martínez**; if you're driving, one-way traffic will force you onto the latter. Both streets are crossed a block further in by **Zaragoza**. Martínez continues east and converges with **Madero**, which follows the north bank of the Mulegé River for about 3km, ending at the town beach, **Playa de Mulegé**. The *zócalo* is on Madero at Zaragoza, one block west of the intersection with Martínez.

Mulegé has no official tourist office or banks—**obtain all the cash you will need here in Santa Rosalía or Loreto**—but the town has plenty of other tourist services. **Hotel las Casitas,** Madero 50 (☎153 0019), has tourist info, including free maps. Ask for Javier—besides leading tours, he has info on beaches, camping, and fishing. Other services include: **Lavamática Claudia,** on Zaragoza just downhill from Hotel Terrazas (☎153 0057; wash 17 pesos, dry 6 pesos; open daily 8am-7pm); **police** (☎153 0049), in the old Pinatel de Educación building on Martínez, next to the PEMEX station; **Red Cross** (☎153 0110), 20m past the turn-off into town on the left side of Mex. 1 (coming from the north); **Farmacia Moderna** at Madero on the plaza (☎153 0042; open daily 8am-1pm and 3-10pm); **Centro de Salud B (ISSTE),** Madero 28 (☎153 0298; English spoken). **Video Mulegé** (☎/fax 153 0401), on Zaragoza at Martínez, one block north of plaza, offers **fax** service. (Open 10am-1pm and 4-10pm.) The **post office** is in the same building as the police. (☎153 0205. Open M-F 8am-3pm.) **Internet access** is available across the road from Restaurant Equipales on Moctezuma. (20 pesos per hr. Open daily 9:30am-8pm). **Postal code:** 23900.

ACCOMMODATIONS AND FOOD. You can sip a free morning coffee on a terrace overlooking the town at the **Hotel Terrazas ❺,** uphill on Zaragoza. Rooms are large and clean, and come with A/C and bath (☎153 0009. Singles 300 pesos, doubles 350 pesos). If funds are running low, **Casa de Huéspedes Manuelita ❷,** on Moctezuma, next to Restaurant los Equipales, has basic, small rooms with baths and A/C. (☎153 0175. Singles 120 pesos; doubles 150 pesos. Campers can use baths and showers for 15 pesos.) **Orchard RV Park ❶** occupies a stretch of the Río Mulegé's south bank, accessible via a dirt road from km 133 on Mex. 1. The immaculate park boasts great palm-shaded spots. (☎153 0109. Tent sites US$5, full hookup US$16. Paddleboats and canoes US$3.50 per hr.)

For something informal and delicious, **Taquería Doney ❶** is across from Hotel Mulegé, past the bus station coming into town. Locals cram indoor tables and outdoor stools, wolfing down delectable nine-peso steak tacos. (☎153 0095. Open Su-M and W-Sa 8am-10pm.) **El Candil Restaurant ❺,** on Zaragoza near Martínez, mellows out evenings. Some shellfish can be pricey, but you can get very tasty dishes here for around 60 pesos. Service can be slow. (☎153 0454. Open daily 7am-10pm.)

BAJA CALIFORNIA

◙ ♫ SIGHTS AND ENTERTAINMENT. Mulegé is a great spot for exploration of cave paintings at nearby **La Trinidad** and **Cuevas San Borjita**. **Salvador Castro** at Hotel las Casitas leads hiking tours to the caves. Trips (5-6hr.; 8am in summer, 9am in winter) include stops at nearby *ranchos* and lectures on native plants and wildlife, in addition to transportation, *ranchero* lunch, and the necessary permits. (☎ 153 0232. Tours 400 pesos per person, less if party is bigger than 5.) If you want to bring a camera, you'll need a permit from the INAH office. (Guides can obtain this for you; permits 40 pesos for cameras, 250 pesos for camcorders.) Mulegé offers great sport-fishing, mostly confined to outside the Bahía de la Concepción. Talk to Javier at **Hotel las Casitas**. (☎ 153 0019. Trips US$120 for 1-3 people.)

Eighteenth-century **Misión Santa Rosalía de Mulegé** sits on a hill west of town. Walk down Zaragoza away from the *zócalo*, go under the bridge, and turn right on the shaded lane. Don't miss the views from the *mirador* behind the mission.

The **Museo Comunitario Mulegé** is housed in the town's old prison at the top of the hill. The building was once known as the "prison without doors" for its policy of allowing inmates out into the town during the day; they would be summoned back at 6pm by the blowing of a conch shell, a ceremony which visitors are invited to recreate at the entrance. Exhibits include artifacts of the indigenous Cochimí, displays of local marine life, and a piece of a spaceship that fell to earth on a *rancho* near Mulegé. (Open M-F 8am-2:30pm, Sa 9am-1pm. 10 pesos.)

The seas and river around Mulegé offer a great variety of activities. To explore the river, rent a canoe or paddleboat from **Orchard RV Park**. (☎ 153 0300. Canoes and paddleboats US$3.50 per hr.) For snorkeling or diving tours of Mulegé or the Bahía, head to **Cortez Explorers,** Montezuma 75A, the only dive shop in town. Experienced Swiss divers will take you to Punta la Concepción or the Santa Inéz Islands, another great dive spot. (☎ 153 0500. Dive tours US$80 with full equipment, US$70 with two tanks and weight belt, or US$60 if you bring your own. Snorkeling tours US$35 with full equipment, US$30 without. You can also rent a package of a bicycle, snorkeling mask, and fins for US$20 per day. It's essential to make reservations at least 1 day in advance. Open M-Sa 10am-1pm and 4-7pm.)

BAHÍA DE LA CONCEPCIÓN

The Baja peninsula's coastline is so endless and often so beautiful that you can end up taking its beaches for granted; but even long-term residents adopt a hushed, almost reverential tone of voice when they mention Bahía de la Concepción. Rocky outcroppings, shimmering sands, hills studded with palms and cacti, and unearthly blue water combine to form a 48km stretch of mesmerizingly beautiful coastal landscapes, while the distant outline of the bay's opposite shore lends a tantalizing sense of the unknown. Look more closely at the serene waters and you'll find that they contain a rich variety of marine life, the delight of divers and snorkelers. Only at Christmas and Easter is the tranquility disturbed by serious tourist traffic; for much of the rest of the year, you might just find that there's almost no one else around to break the spell.

BEASTS OF THE BEACH During summer months, stingrays mate close to shore, hidden from view underneath the sand. So as not to interrupt and get stung, shuffle your feet as you walk into the water. If they nab you, find the hottest water you can stand, immerse the stung area, and wait out the pain. Or, locals swear finding a *garumbillo* ("old man") cactus, cutting a chunk and squeezing a few drops of juice onto the sting will get rid of the pain in seconds. But be sure to cut off all the cactus spines first, or you'll have even more pain on your hands. For serious stings, seek medical attention.

▣ TRANSPORTATION

Visiting Bahía de la Concepción without a car is difficult, since there are no regular buses. It may be possible to negotiate a fee for drivers of southbound intercity buses from Mulegé to drop you off, but the walk from the highway to the shore is sometimes long. This approach also leaves the problem of the return journey unresolved. If at all possible, consider renting a car for a day in Loreto.

◪ BEACHES

The Bahía is completely sheltered and calm as a lake, so don't expect great waves. Camping is safe, but stick to well-populated beaches and always be on guard. Those traveling alone should head to larger camping complexes like EcoMundo on Playa la Posada. (**Palapas ❶**, found on most beaches, 20-60 pesos.) The beaches below are listed from north to south.

PLAYA LOS NARANJOS. This is the closest of the bay's beaches to Mulegé, and has decent, no-frills facilities for camping. You can pitch your tent under a *palapa* (60 pesos), and bungalows with water supply cost 150 pesos for two people or 200 pesos for four. *(3km down a signed dirt road at km 119.)*

PLAYA PUNTA ARENA. Despite Punta Arena's proximity to Mulegé, most campers are deterred by the hard-packed sand, making it a quiet place for breathtakingly scenic beach walks. There are some private beach huts but no *palapas* for temporary visitors. Spending the day here will cost you 20 pesos and camping overnight 40 pesos. *(Take the turn signed for Playa los Naranjos and Punta Sueños at km 119 and then the first fork to the right.)*

PLAYA SANTISPAC. The immensely popular Santispac draws crowds with its convenient location, right off Mex. 1 close to Mulegé. The beach's broad expanse can feel a little like a parking lot—the hard-packed sand behind the motor homes is rougher than asphalt—but you'll soon forget this as you get closer to the softer sand near the warm water. Day parking is 30 pesos, camping 60 pesos. **Ana's Restaurant ❶**, on the northern end of the beach, has firewood, a bakery, and showers (25 pesos, strict 8min. limit. Open daily 7am-10pm.) For food, head to **Ray's Place ❺**, one of the bay's best restaurants, with shady outdoor tables and delicious seafood. (Catch of the day 85 pesos, seafood combo for two 175 pesos. Open Tu-Sa 2-8pm.) *(Playa Santispac is just off the highway near km 114.)*

PLAYA LA POSADA/PLAYA LA ESCONDIDA. Most of Playa la Posada is dominated by an RV/beach home village, but just to the south is **EcoMundo ❸**, a camping village for nature lovers. Huge, well-kept *palapas* are equipped with hammocks, fans, and lights, and the encampment prides itself on its sustainable living practices. After a day of kayaking, unwind at the "Thirst Aid Station"—Jimmy Buffet himself couldn't imagine a better place to sip a *cerveza*. (☎ 153 0409. Open 8am-4pm. *Palapas* US$12-20, showers US$1, tent camping US$8, kayak rentals US$20-25 per day.) The bumpy dirt road next to EcoMundo leads to **Playa la Escondida,** a beautiful beach with *palapas* (60 pesos), water, and rudimentary toilet facilities.

PLAYA EL BURRO. El Burro's soft sands and quiet atmosphere have enticed many Americans to set up semi-permanent homes, but there's still room for campers and sunbathers. The beach has few facilities, but a small restaurant/bar lies on Mex. 1 at the turnoff. Camping is 70 pesos per day. *(Near Mex. 1 at km 109.)*

PLAYA EL COYOTE. One of the less attractive beaches in Bahía, El Coyote is still one of the most popular. Rocky sand and dirty outhouses litter the area, but better sands and *palapas* await on the southern end. *(A short dirt road off Mex. 1 at km 108.)*

PLAYA REQUESÓN. The Bahía's best sands are here, amid some of the area's most spectacular landscapes. Adventurous souls sometimes camp on the sand bar, but the rising tide may leave you and your gear soaking wet. Day parking 20 pesos; camping 40 pesos. *(On a short dirt road at km 92; also accessible from Playa la Perla.)*

PLAYA LA PERLA. La Perla is a thin, heavenly strip of sand tucked between two rocky outcroppings. Excellent *palapas* make the lonely beach a perfect place to achieve zen-like tranquility. Check out the neighboring rock formations outlined in white paint by University of Tijuana students. *(Close to the road at km 91.)*

LORETO

☎613

Despite the spectacular rugged mountains on the horizon, it is hard to imagine what a wild, inhospitable place Loreto must have been in 1697, when the Jesuits landed and established it as the first capital of the Californias. Even a hundred years later, the area proved itself resistant to attempts at civilization—it had to be abandoned following a catastrophic hurricane, and lay empty for decades. The recent restoration of the town center, however, has banished all sense of threat, and the cobblestone streets around the *zócalo* are now spotlessly clean, surrounded by impeccably manicured trees. Right now, the town is indisputably beautiful—though it remains to be seen if Loreto's tranquility and historic character will endure as the Mexican government seeks to use the attractions of the Sea of Cortés to turn Loreto and its surroundings into the next mega-resort.

Loreto map

ACCOMMODATIONS
Hotel Junípero, 3
Motel Brenda, 6
Motel Salviaterra, 7
El Moro RV Park, 1

FOOD
Café Olé, 2
McLulu's, 4
ML y Qué Rico, 5

▌ TRANSPORTATION

Autotransportes Águila buses stop by the bus terminal on Salvatierra two blocks west of Allende, near the highway, about 1km from Madero. (☎135 0767. Ticket office open 7am-11:30pm.) To get to the *centro* from the bus station, walk down Salvatierra (15min.) or indulge in a taxi (30 pesos). There are seven northbound buses every day. The 2:30 and 5pm buses terminate at **Santa Rosalía** (4hr., 134 pesos); the 2am goes on to **Guerrero Negro** (7½hr., 275 pesos) via **San Ignacio** (5hr., 180 pesos); the 1, 3am, and 3pm buses go on to **Tijuana** (17hr., 726 pesos); the 6:15pm continues to **Mexicali** (20hr., 869 pesos). Southbound buses go to **La Paz** (5hr., 6 per day 8am-12:30am, 210 pesos).

■ ? ORIENTATION AND PRACTICAL INFORMATION

Loreto is easy to navigate, with the mission tower and the shoreline serving as useful reference points. The **mission** site is just to the south of the **zócalo,** the town's quiet center; the road connecting these two places is **Salvatierra,** which runs north to the seafront **malecón** and south to the highway. Parallel to Salvatierra to the east is **Hidalgo;** these two roads carry the heaviest concentration of services. They converge at the point where they are both crossed by **Independencia;** locals refer to this important intersection as "Los Cuatro Altos."

A **tourist info center** in the **Palacio Municipal,** on Madero at the *zócalo*, offers maps, brochures, and an English-speaking staff. (☎ 135 0411. Open M-F 8am-3pm.) The only bank, **Bancomer,** on Madero across from the *zócalo*, changes dollars and checks and has a 24hr. **ATM.** (☎ 135 0315. Open M-F 9am-3:30pm.) **Budget,** on Hidalgo a block from the water, rents cars with unlimited mileage for US$55 per day, including insurance. (☎ 135 1090. Open Su 8am-3pm, M-Sa 8am-1pm and 3-6pm.) The **supermarket El Pescador** is on Salvatierra and Independencia. (☎ 135 0060. Open daily 7:30am-10:30pm.) Other services include: **police** (☎ 135 0035); **Red Cross** (☎ 135 1111), on Salvatierra at Deportiva, some English spoken; **Centro de Salud** (☎ 135 0039), on Salvatierra, one block from the bus terminal, English spoken; **fax** at **Telecomm,** next to the post office (☎ 135 0387; open M-F 8am-2pm, Sa 8-11am); **Internet C@fé,** on Madero next to Café Olé (☎ 135 0084; 30 pesos per 30min.; open M-F 9am-2pm and 4-7pm, Sa 10am-1:30pm); the **post office,** on Salvatierra and Deportiva, behind the Red Cross (☎ 135 0647; open M-F 8am-3pm). Every night, a different **pharmacy** is open 24hr. Check the door of **Farmacia Flores,** on Salvatierra, between Ayuntamiento and Independencia, for the schedule. (☎ 135 0321. Open 8am-10pm.) **Postal code:** 23880.

▮ ACCOMMODATIONS

Loreto caters to a fairly affluent crowd; good cheap rooms can be tough to find. But fear not—a bit of searching rewards the diligent.

Hotel Junípero (☎ 135 0122), on Hidalgo between Pino Suárez and Misioneros, in front of the mission. Perhaps the best location in town, with some rooms looking onto the mission. Rooms come with TV and private bath and are large—too large, in fact, for the underpowered A/C. Singles 300 pesos; doubles 360 pesos. ❺

Motel Brenda (☎ 135 0707), on Juárez near Marquez de León. Immaculate rooms with powerful A/C and TV. Free parking. Singles 220 pesos; doubles 250 pesos. ❹

Motel Salvatierra (☎ 135 0021), on Salvatierra, across from PEMEX and near the bus station. Small, bare, yellow rooms with loud but effective A/C and tiny private baths. The busy road out front can be noisy in the morning with drivers filling their tanks. Singles 200 pesos; doubles 220 pesos. ❹

El Moro RV Park, Robles 8 (☎/fax 135 0542), a couple of blocks inland off Salvatierra. A big parking lot with minimal shade, but friendly staff. Pitch a tent anywhere. Office open daily 7am-midnight. Trailer US$12; camping US$5 for one, US$8 for two. ❶

▐ FOOD

Loreto has plenty of restaurant options, but most of them are tailored toward tourists and are overpriced. There are also a few *taquerías*, where you have a chance of sampling local flavors for more local prices.

Mexico Lindo y Qué Rico (☎ 135 1175), on Hidalgo just past the intersection with Salvatierra. A loyal clientele comes here for the covered patio's lively atmosphere, the friendly service, and the tasty specialties: cholesterol lovers should gorge themselves on the *alambres* (a mixture of beef, cheese, peppers, onion, and bacon; 50 pesos). Open daily 8am-11pm. ❹

McLulu's, on Hidalgo between Independencia and Militar. Don't let the name deceive you; you won't find any chain food here, just friendly cooks and perhaps the largest selection of taco fillings in Baja—8 different types at last count, including *machaca*, *carne con chile*, and *chorizo*, as well as familiar classics such as *carne asada*, fish, and shrimp (8-10 pesos). Open daily 10am-8pm. ❶

Café Olé, Madero 14 (☎ 135 0496), just off the *zócalo*. The local breakfast spot. Tourists and locals alike lounge at outdoor tables, chatting over *chilaquiles con huevos*, *huevos rancheros*, and the ubiquitous hot cakes (all around 30 pesos). Order at the bar. Open Su 7am-2pm, M-Sa 7am-10pm. ❸

🎥 🎵 SIGHTS AND ENTERTAINMENT

With its blissful sea views, Loreto's *malecón* is a popular place to take an evening stroll or pause for thought on one of the many benches looking out over the waves. The **public beach,** at the south end of the *malecón*, has fine grey sand but slightly murky water. FONATUR, the Mexican tourist promotion group, has long known that the best beaches around here are at **Nopoló**, 7km south of town, and the development of resort hotels and golf courses is beginning to transform the landscape. Nevertheless, the beaches are open to the public, and the snorkeling is excellent.

Three desert islands and a few rocky points jut from the water like sentinels guarding the port of Loreto. **Isla del Carmen,** the largest island in the Sea of Cortés, is home to several animal and plant species unique to the island, including a species of gigantic barrel cacti. Unfortunately, access to the privately-owned island has been seriously restricted. Nearby **Isla Coronado** is easier to access, and its wide white sand beaches host a herd of friendly sea lions. To learn more about the ecology of Loreto's bay, a National Marine Park, pay a visit to the tiny natural history museum maintained by the **Grupo Ecologista Antares** next to Restaurant Mexico Lindo y Qué Rico on Hidalgo. (☎ 135 0086; antaresgea@prodigy.net.mx. Open M-F 9am-4pm, Sa 9am-1pm.) In addition to monitoring the activities of fishermen and sailors in the bay, GEA offers a number of opportunities for ecotourism, including boat trips to observe the birds, whales, and dolphins that visit the bay and islands (5-6hr.; approx. US$200 for up to 5 people). **Las Parras Tours,** Madero 16 (☎ 135 1010; www.lasparrastours.com), next to Café Olé, takes small groups on boat trips around Isla Coronado. The 4-5hr. trip (US$35; min. 2 people) includes plenty of time to snorkel (equipment rentable) or relax on the beautiful beach. Las Parras also offers diving trips (US$70-80 for a ½-day trip, equipment rental extra), mountain bike rentals (US$5 per hr.), kayak rentals (singles US$5 per hr., doubles US$7.50 per hr.), and trips to sites like the mission and village of San Javier (6hr.; US$59, extra US$20 for optional 3hr. mule ride; min. 3 people). **Arturo's Sports Fishing Fleet** (☎ 135 0766), on Hidalgo half a block from the beach, offers fishing trips. If you prefer to go it alone, sizable red snapper and grouper hide among the large rocks at the end on the left side of the pier, toward the north end of the *malecón*.

With so many offshore delights, Loreto's historical attractions are beginning to feel like a sideshow. Still, the recently restored **Misión de Nuestra Señora de Loreto** is an essential stop for anyone interested in the Baja's Jesuit history; as the plaque above the door proclaims, this is the mother of all California missions. The church was consecrated in 1697, made permanent in 1699, and enlarged to its present form by 1752. It echoes the simple lines and plain walls of early Renaissance churches, with semicircular stone arches in perfect proportion to the height of the whitewashed nave. (Mass daily 7pm, also Su 11:30am.) Next door in the monastic complex, the **Museo de las Misiones** tells the story of the Jesuits' activities in Baja; the displays are almost all in Spanish, but there are also sculptures, paintings and other artifacts. (☎135 0005. Open Tu-Su 9am-1pm and 1:45-6pm. 28 pesos.)

Loreto is not the place to go for rip-roaring nightlife, but **Mike's Bar,** on Hidalgo a few blocks from the water, does its best with live rock music in the evenings. (☎135 1126. Beer 20 pesos. Open daily 10am-10pm.)

CIUDAD CONSTITUCIÓN ☎613

Few foreigners find reason to stop in the transportation hub of Ciudad Constitución (pop. 35,000) except to fill up on gas and grab a bite to eat, but if you do linger you'll find a busy town and a local population pleased that you've decided to pay them a visit. **Autotransportes Águila** (☎132 0376), at Suárez and Juárez, goes south to **La Paz** (3hr., 15 per day 1am-6pm, 115 pesos). The 7:30am and the 3pm buses go on to **San José del Cabo** (235 pesos) via **Todos Santos** (175 pesos) and **Cabo San Lucas** (224 pesos). For those going north, there are *de paso* buses (9 per day 11:45am-12:45am). The 4:15 and 8:45pm terminate at **Loreto** (2hr., 100 pesos); the 11:45am and the 2:45pm go on to **Santa Rosalía** (238 pesos) via **Mulegé** (174 pesos); the 11:45pm goes as far as **Guerrero Negro** (371 pesos); the 12:45pm, 10:45pm, and 12:45am go to **Tijuana** (818 pesos) via **Ensenada** (731 pesos); the 3:45pm goes on to **Mexicali** (963 pesos). There are also buses to **Puerto San Carlos** (1hr., 10:45am and 5:15pm, 30 pesos). From the bus station, walk two blocks across the palm-shaded plaza to the corner of Olachea, the main street. There's a **Bancomer** on the corner of Olachea, level with the bus station (open 8:30am-4pm) and a **Banamex** a few blocks farther north, at Olachea and Francisco Mina close to the PEMEX station (open 9am-4pm); both have 24hr. **ATMs.** The **police** station (☎132 1112) is on Olachea, opposite the turn-off for Puerto San Carlos. The **Red Cross** (☎132 1111) is five blocks off Olachea at Ramírez and Degollado; follow the sign from Olachea just before the southern end of town. **IMSS** (☎132 0388) is located at Olachea and Independencia, close to the turning for the Red Cross. Little English is spoken at any of these places. **Farmacia San Martín** is on Olachea at Suárez and has a list of local pharmacies that rotate overnight duties. (☎132 0124. Open Su 9am-4pm and 6-10pm, M-F 8am-10:30pm, Sa 9am-2pm and 4:30-10:30pm.) Pick up groceries at **Supermercado el Mar,** at Olachea and Morelos. (☎132 1021. Open daily 7am-10pm.)

On Olachea at Hidalgo, two blocks away from the plaza, is olive-colored **Hotel Conchita ❸.** Rooms vary in size and are furnished practically, with TV and A/C. (Singles 170 pesos; doubles from 230 pesos.) On the other side of Hidalgo on Olachea, **Taquería Karen ❶** serves up delicious meat tacos (8 pesos; open 24hr.).

PUERTO SAN CARLOS ☎613

Every year at whale-watching time, tiny Puerto San Carlos (pop. 3000) undergoes a magical transformation. Beginning in November, hotels dust off their bedposts, tent encampments blossom, and local pilots commandeer every available fishing boat to transport tourists to see the thousands of grey whales that migrate from the Bering Sea through the Pacific to Bahías Magdalena and Almejas. During peak mating season (mid-Jan. to mid-Mar.), the lovestruck creatures wow crowds with aquatic acrobatics. When they leave in April, the town once again becomes a sleepy village of boarded-up restaurants and nearly vacant sand roads.

▐ **TRANSPORTATION.** Puerto San Carlos is at the end of Mex. 22 and accessible by car and bus. **Autotransportes Águila** (☎136 0453) has a tiny terminal on La Paz and Morelos, with only two daily buses at 7:30am and 1:45pm. Both go to **Ciudad Constitución** (1hr., 30 pesos) and **La Paz** (3½hr., 146 pesos). The 1:45pm then goes on to **Cabo San Lucas** (6½hr., 235 pesos) and **San José del Cabo** (7hr., 255 pesos).

▣ ▨ ORIENTATION AND PRACTICAL INFORMATION. Coming from Ciudad Constitución (the only way to Puerto San Carlos), Mex. 22 curves around the town to the docks; a dirt track leads down to the left and becomes **La Paz,** the only (albeit unevenly) paved street in town, where most services are located. All other streets here are sandy tracks that can easily trap the unwary driver; take great care when parking at the side of the road. Street signs are at best sun-bleached to the point of illegibility and at worst non-existent. The new, well-marked **tourist office** near the docks is theoretically open during the whale season. If the office is closed, the friendly staff at the **Hotel Alcatraz** (☎ 136 0017), on La Paz, have limited English but plenty of information. The one thing nobody can direct you to in San Carlos is a **bank**—there are **no ATMs, casas de cambios, or credit card connections** in town, so you'll have to bring enough cash from the banks in Ciudad Constitución (see p. 193). The **police** are located at La Paz and Callejón Baja California on the park. (☎ 136 0396. No English spoken.) On the opposite side of the park is the **Farmacia Novedades del Puerto.** (Open daily 8am-1pm and 4-8pm.) The **IMSS** is at La Paz and México. (☎ 136 0211. No English spoken.) Near the park is the **post office,** on La Paz between México and Juárez. (Open M-F 8am-3pm.) **Internet** access is available at **Computime,** on the northern edge of town. (☎ 136 0002. Open daily 9am-1pm and 3-10pm.) **Postal code:** 23740.

▨▣ ACCOMMODATIONS AND FOOD. Finding budget rooms isn't easy. This town has only 100 rooms among its few hotels, and come whale-watching season they are at a premium. The best value in town is hidden away at **Motel las Brisas ❷.** From the bus station, take a right onto La Paz, then make a right and a quick left on Madero; the hotel will be on your left. Rooms are basic but clean and have fans and private baths, but (despite the name) no sea breezes. (☎ 136 0498. Singles 135 pesos; doubles 160 pesos.) For a taste of the sea, try **Hotel Palmar ❹,** on Acapulco and Puerto Vallarta. Rooms have private bath, TV, fan, and mosquito nets. (☎ 136 0035. Singles 225 pesos; doubles 275 pesos.) **Nancy's RV park ❷** (☎ 136 0195; www.hideoutrv.com), near the port, offers parking/camping spots for 75 pesos, and full hookups for 125 pesos, with discounts available for stays longer than three days. They are also building bungalows for up to 4 people. **Camping ❶** on the barrier islands is free, but only accessible by boat; be sure to bring insect repellent.

Dining in San Carlos is homey: a string of restaurant/living rooms along La Paz and Morelos allow you to meet locals while enjoying fresh delicacies from the sea. **Tortas Lore ❷,** a friendly family-run place on La Paz next to the post office, serves up big meat or fish *tortas* (15 pesos). It's also a good place for morning egg dishes (20-25 pesos). (Open Su 9am-1pm, M-Sa 8am-6pm.) **Lonchería la Pasadita ❸,** on La Paz and México, is a town favorite, the epitome of informal dining, with concrete floors and counter seating as well as outdoor tables. Platters of *pollo con mole* or grilled fish and generous *tortas* cost 30-35 pesos, while the prices for fresh shellfish are somewhat higher. (☎ 136 0129. Open daily 7am-9pm.) **Mariscos los Arcos ❹,** on La Paz near IMSS, is known for its seafood, which can be sampled in all its variety for just 50 pesos in a huge tentacular bowl of soup. (☎ 136 0347. Open daily 8am-10pm.) If you're not quite this hungry, **Don Blas ❶,** the wooden stall on the corner of the park close to the police station, makes what are reputedly the tastiest beef tacos in town for 9-10 pesos. (Open after dark Su-M and W-Sa.)

◙◪ SIGHTS AND BEACHES. Both **Bahía Magdalena** and **Bahía Almeja** lie just south of Puerto San Carlos and are home to some of the best whale-watching in the world. Grey whales migrate south from feeding grounds in Alaska to visit Baja California every winter. The warm, shallow waters of Bahía Magdalena make it one of the most important calving areas, and hundreds of whales stop over here in November and December for this purpose. Fertile soon after calving, the whales spend their days from January to March mating and dazzling tourists in the bay. Veterans also insist that the warm climate here makes San Carlos a more comfortable place than Guerrero Negro for visitors during the winter.

Lying at the intersection of temperate and tropical currents, Bahía Magdalena and the ocean just beyond it is rich in both temperate and tropical species of fish, shellfish, and birds, making it a worthwhile visit even in whale-less summer months. The **barrier islands** appear to be mostly sand and dunes, but extensive mangroves, intertidal sand and mud flats, and sea grass beds make these ecosystems as biologically diverse as the bay itself. Among the animals calling the islands home are two colonies of sea lions. Dolphins also swim in the bay. The **Center for Coastal Studies**, affiliated with Boston University, is just east of town at Punta Palapa. Visitors can embark on their own more informal investigations by taking eco-tours by boat with local agencies. **Viajes Mar y Arena** (☎136 0070) has an office on Mex. 22 near the tourist office and can also be contacted at the Administración Portuario Integral by the docks. Their boat trips can be tailored to focus on whales (seasonally), dolphins, birds, or the islands (approx 3 hr.; 250 pesos per person for 6-10 people). Independent exploration of the islands is possible if you make transportation arrangements with local fishermen at Punta Palapa, though it is essential to arrange in advance to be picked up afterwards. Boats for up to five people are also rented out (500 pesos per hr.) by **Hotel Alcatraz**, which also has sea kayaks available for 36 pesos per day. (☎136 0017. Office open daily 7am-10pm.)

Although the use of gill nets has severely damaged the fish population within the bay, anglers who go farther out into the water from September to December are rewarded with some of the best fishing in the world; the waters here are regularly used for attempts at catching record-breaking quantities of marlin. Viajes Mar y Arena or the Hotel Alcatraz will happily organize a fishing trip, as will **Mag Bay Tours** (☎136 0004); costs for groups of up to 6 people are around US$40 per hour, US$120 per half day, or US$200 per day. Mag Bay also runs a **surf encampment** from July through December; be warned that it's not possible to just turn up and arrange a trip here, since bookings are taken up to three years in advance and prices start at US$1150 per week. Independent surfers will find it difficult to join in the fun, since the Mag Bay encampment has virtually the only facilities in the area.

LA PAZ   ☎612

John Steinbeck's novella *The Pearl* depicted La Paz (pop. 200,000) as a tiny, unworldly treasure chest whose way of life was irreversibly corrupted by the forces of commerce and greed. Since then, the tiny village has grown into Baja California Sur's biggest city and a major commercial center, but this is no reason to assume that Steinbeck has been proven entirely right. Although the traditional pearl industry was wiped out several decades ago by a disease afflicting the local oyster population, La Paz has retained a friendly, even small-town atmosphere, and is by far the most engaging of the peninsula's major cities. Even in the blistering heat of one of the most sweltering parts of the country, the steep streets invite exploration. And, at the end of the day, gentle sea breezes seem to draw the whole town out onto the seafront *malecón*—the only place in Baja where you can join Mexican families, skateboarders, glammed-up teens, and scruffy backpackers to watch the sun set over the Sea of Cortés.

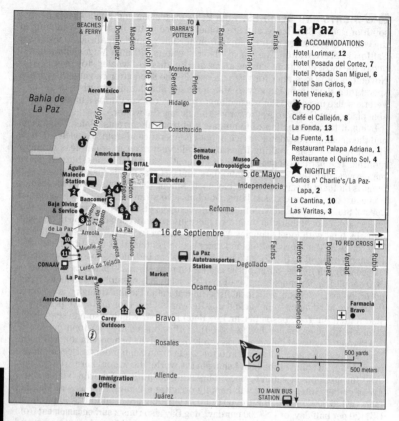

La Paz

▲ ACCOMMODATIONS
Hotel Lorimar, **12**
Hotel Posada del Cortez, **7**
Hotel Posada San Miguel, **6**
Hotel San Carlos, **9**
Hotel Yeneka, **5**

● FOOD
Café el Callejón, **8**
La Fonda, **13**
La Fuente, **11**
Restaurant Palapa Adriana, **1**
Restaurante el Quinto Sol, **4**

★ NIGHTLIFE
Carlos n' Charlie's/La Paz-Lapa, **2**
La Cantina, **10**
Las Varitas, **3**

⊏ TRANSPORTATION

As the capital and largest city of Baja California Sur, La Paz is also the region's main transportation hub. In addition, it's possible to reach the Mexican mainland via the ferry connecting La Paz to Mazatlán and Los Mochis. The **municipal bus system** serves the city irregularly (every 30-45min. 6am-10pm, 4 pesos). Flag down buses anywhere, or wait by the main stop on Revolución and Degollado, next to the market. The city center is easily navigable on foot.

Airport: West of La Paz, easily accessible by taxi (120 pesos). The airport is served by **Aeroméxico** (☎ 122 0091), on Obregón between Hidalgo and Morelos. Open Su 9am-5:30pm, M-Sa 9am-7:30pm. Also an **office** (☎ 124 6367) at the airport. Open daily 7am-8pm. **AeroCalifornia** (☎ 125 1023), on Obregón between Ocampo and Bravo. Open M-F 8am-8:30pm, Sa-Su 8am-8pm.

Buses: La Paz has 3 bus stations.

Main station: On Jalisco and Independencia, about 25 blocks southeast of downtown. Open for tickets daily 6am-9:30pm. 2 municipal buses, "Central Camionera" and "Urbano," head to the terminal; catch them near the public market at Degollado and Revolución. **Taxis** 30 pesos. **Águila Autotransportes** (☎ 122 4270, ext. 112, 113, or 114) runs the main *de paso* route along Mex. 1. Buses (15 per day 7am-10pm) go to **Ciudad Constitución** (3hr., 115 pesos). Of these,

HAVING A WHALE OF A TIME! In 1970 the grey whale, long preyed upon by Pacific coast whalers, was thought to be extinct. Today, with an estimated total population of up to 25,000, the species has become a poster child for the effectiveness of wildlife preservation laws. Their breeding grounds along the coast of Baja California Sur are among the most important protected coastlines in North America. The entire world population of grey whales gives birth and mates in three sections of Baja California's coast: the lagoons of Ojo de Liebre, the lagoons of San Ignacio, and Bahía Magdalena. The whales are generally friendly, curious, and playful, and although it's illegal for boats to go closer than 30m from the whales, or for passengers to touch them, some of them may come closer to welcome you to their habitat. Watch for the following kinds of behavior:

Fluking: Before beginning a deep dive, a whale will arch its back above water and display its tail.

Breaching: A whale will jump out of the water, flip over, and enter the water nose-first. They often slap the water with their flukes (tails) on reentry.

Blowing: As a whale exhales, it will often "spit" water droplets into the air.

Feeding: Although whales generally fast during the winter months, they have occasionally been observed eating in the bay late in the season. They will scoop up a large mouthful of sediment from the bottom of the bay and, lying on one side, let the mud and water filter through a series of baleen plates, which trap small crustaceans and edible particles.

Spyhopping: A whale will pop its head out of the water, fix an enormous eye on whatever strikes its fancy, and stare for minutes on end, like a submarine periscope. They often pivot to survey the area before slipping back into the water.

the 9, 10am, noon, 1:30, 6, 9, and 10pm go on to **Santa Rosalía** (8hr., 342 pesos) via **Loreto** (5hr., 209 pesos) and **Mulegé** (7hr., 289 pesos). The 9pm goes on to **San Ignacio** (9hr., 394 pesos). The 10am, 1, 8, and 10pm buses continue to **Tijuana** (22hr., 935 pesos) via **San Quintín** (15hr., 729 pesos) and **Ensenada** (18hr., 847 pesos). Buses head south to **Cabo San Lucas** (2½hr., 9 per day 7am-8pm, 108 pesos) via **Todos Santos** (1hr., 60 pesos).

La Paz Autotransportes: On Degollado at Prieto, sends buses south to **San José del Cabo** (3hr., 90 pesos) via **Todos Santos** (1½hr., 8 per day 6:45am-7:45pm, 50 pesos) and **Cabo San Lucas** (2½hr., 86 pesos).

Águila Malecón: (☎ 122 7898), on Independencia at Obregón, sends buses south to the cape along two different routes. The faster "Vía Corta" buses (7 per day 7:30am-7:30pm) go to **Cabo San Lucas** (2½hr., 108 pesos) and **San José del Cabo** (3hr., 119 pesos) via **Todos Santos** (1½hr., 60 pesos). The longer "Vía Larga" service (5 per day 10am-5:30pm), is only really useful for destinations on the east cape, stopping at **Los Barriles** (2hr., 60 pesos) and **Santiago** (2½hr., 80 pesos); it takes 3½hr. to reach San José del Cabo and 4hr. to reach Cabo San Lucas (both 108 pesos). The same station has buses to nearby beaches: **Playas el Caimancito** and **El Coromuel** (10min., 5 pesos), **Palmira, Tesoro,** and **Pichilingue** (25min., 15 pesos), and **Playas Balandras** and **Tecolote** (35min.; noon, 2, 5pm; 25 pesos). The last bus back to La Paz leaves Tecolote at 5:30pm and Pichilingue 7:30pm; be sure to confirm schedules with the driver.

Ferries: Ferries leave from the suburb of **Pichilingue** for the mainland. **Águila** buses run between the dock and the downtown **Águila Malecón** terminal on Obregón, between Independencia and 5 de Mayo. Taxis from the dock to downtown cost 100 pesos. Ferries to **Mazatlán** are operated by **Sematur** (☎ 125 8899), and tickets can be purchased from their office, on 5 de Mayo at Prieto. Open M-F 8am-6pm, Sa-Su 8am-noon. Dock office open daily 8am-10pm. Ferries go to Mazatlán (17hr.; daily 3pm; 660-1126 pesos, from 2020 pesos per vehicle). **Bajaferries** (☎ 125 7444 ext. 121), runs to **Topolobampo** (5hr.; M-F 4pm, Sa 11pm; 580 pesos, under age 12 290 pesos, cars 870 pesos), a suburb of **Los Mochis.** Tickets available either at the docks or at the **Águila Malecón** bus terminal. To get a vehicle on either ferry, you will need certification

BAJA CALIFORNIA

of ownership of the car or rental in your name, a major credit card, your driver's license, your passport, and a tourist card. For a permit, these documents and a fee of US$22 should be taken to **Banjército,** at the ferry stop in Pichilingue (☎ 122 1116; open daily 9am-2pm), or to **AAA** in the US. Whether or not you have a car, you will need a **tourist card (FMT)** if you entered Mexico via Baja California and are bound for the mainland (see p. 198). Clear all paperwork before purchasing the ticket; otherwise, Sematur may deny you a spot whether or not you have reservations.

TICKET TO RIDE. Getting a ferry ticket isn't as easy as it seems—it requires persistence and determination. To secure a ticket, make reservations several days in advance. Go to the ticket office first thing after arriving into town, preferably right after it opens, and get the ticket in hand as soon as possible. During holidays, competition for tickets is fierce. *Clase salón* (3rd class) is cheapest, and usually most in demand. In addition, Sematur has a reputation for raising prices without prior announcement.

■ PRACTICAL INFORMATION

TOURIST, FINANCIAL, AND LOCAL SERVICES

Tourist Office: (☎ 122 5939), Obregón between Bravo and Rosales, in the small park. Excellent maps and information from helpful English-speaking staff. Weekends and evenings staffed by the tourist police. Open M 8am-8pm, Tu-Th 8am-10pm, F 8am-midnight, Sa-Su noon-midnight.

Tourist Police: Fabulous folks easily recognized by their starched white uniforms and big grins. Their job is "protection and orientation," but they will also give recommendations about hiking, beaches, hotels, restaurants, and barbers.

Immigration Office: Servicios Migratorios, Obregón 2140 (☎ 125 3493; fax 122 0429), between Juárez and Allende. You must stop here to obtain a tourist card (205 pesos) if you entered Mexico via Baja California and are bound for the mainland, and haven't already obtained one elsewhere. Open M-F 9am-6pm. After hours, visit the **airport post** (☎ 124 6349). Open M-F 8am-8pm, Sa 9am-3pm. Guards at the airport can assist you 7am-11pm.

Currency Exchange: Banks line 16 de Septiembre within a few blocks of the bay. **Bancomer** (☎ 125 4248), on 16 de Septiembre, ½ block from the waterfront, is open for exchange M-F 8:30am-4pm. **BITAL** (☎ 122 4644, 122 0809, or 122 9303), on 5 de Mayo, at Madero. Open for exchange M-F 8am-7pm, Sa 8am-3pm. Both banks have 24hr. **ATMs** and exchange traveler's checks and foreign currencies.

American Express: (☎ 122 8666, fax 125 3939), 5 de Mayo at Domínguez. Open Su 9am-1pm, M-F 8am-8pm, Sa 9am-7pm.

Laundry: La Paz Lava, Mutualismo 260 (☎ 122 3112), on Ocampo a block down from Mijares. Small load wash or dry 15 pesos, large load wash or dry 30 pesos; full service small load 48 pesos, large load 85 pesos. Open daily 8am-9:30pm.

Luggage Storage: At the main bus station. 4 pesos per hr.

Car Rental: Hertz (☎ 122 0919), on Obregón between Allende and Juárez. From 638 pesos per day. Open Su 8am-2pm, M-F 8am-7pm, Sa 8am-4pm.

EMERGENCY AND COMMUNICATIONS

Emergency: ☎ 066.

Police: (☎ 122 1399; emergency 060), on Colima at México. Little English spoken.

Red Cross: Reforma 1091 (☎ 122 1222), between Católica and Ortega. English-speaking staff Sa-Su.

Pharmacy: Farmacia Bravo (☎ 122 6933), Bravo at Verdad, opposite the hospital. Open 24hr.

Hospital: Salvatierra (☎ 122 1496 or 122 1497), on Bravo at Verdad, between Domínguez and the Oncological Institute. Some English spoken.

Fax: Telecomm (☎ 125 9071; fax 125 0809), upstairs from the post office. Open Su 8-11:30am, M-Sa 8am-7:30pm.

Internet: At the **CONAAV store** (☎ 122 4009) on Obregón at Muelle. 15 pesos per hr. Open daily 9am-10pm. Alternatively, use the machines at **Cafe El Callejón** (see **Food,** below). 9 pesos per hr.

Post Office: (☎ 122 0388), on Revolución at Constitución. Open M-F 8am-3pm, Sa 9am-1pm. **Postal Code:** 23000.

ACCOMMODATIONS

La Paz has a number of affordable, basic rooms, but few of them offer much in the way of comfort. The heat makes air-conditioning a priority.

Hotel Lorimar, Bravo 110 (☎/fax 125 3822), between Madero and Mutualismo. Half of this family-run hotel has been renovated. Newer rooms are freshly painted, with new baths. Old singles 200 pesos; old doubles 270 pesos. New singles and doubles 360 pesos; new triples 415 pesos; each additional person 50 pesos. ❺

Hotel Yeneka, Madero 1520 (☎ 125 4688), between 16 de Septiembre and Independencia. Backpacker-hangout decor—whale skeletons and a stuffed monkey driving a bright blue Model-T Ford decorate the lush courtyard. Very firm beds in clean rooms. Laundry, fax, bike rentals, and restaurant. Reservations recommended. Prices per person. One person 219 pesos; two people 285 pesos; three people 364 pesos. ❹

Hotel Posada del Cortez, 16 de Septiembre 202 (☎/fax 122 8240), between Madero and Domínguez. A good budget offering, whose pleasant, airy, and spacious rooms come with TV and fan. Singles 150 pesos; doubles 200 pesos; triples 255 pesos. ❸

Hotel San Carlos (☎ 122 0444), on 16 de Septiembre between Revolución de 1910 and Serdán. A wide range of room types available: depending on your budget, you could treat yourself to a room with A/C, TV, and a balcony facing out onto the street, or subsist in a bare inner chamber with a bed and a bath. Singles 150-250 pesos; doubles 225-340 pesos; triples 300-430 pesos. TV 20 pesos extra. ❸

Hotel Posada San Miguel, Domínguez 1510 (☎ 125 8888), off 16 de Septiembre. Photographs, painted tiles, and wrought-iron scrollwork recall La Paz's early days. Too bad there's little charm in the spartan rooms, which have fans, large, comfortable beds, and bath. Singles 112 pesos; doubles 132 pesos; triples 153 pesos. TV 20 pesos extra. ❷

FOOD

On the waterfront you'll find decor, menus, and prices geared toward peso-spewing tourists. Move inland a few blocks and watch prices plunge. Seafood meals are generally fresh and *tacos de pescado* delicious (and cheap). Grab fruits, veggies, and fresh fish at the **public market,** at Degollado and Revolución, where you can also join locals eating *tortas* and *antojitos* from a cluster of competing stalls in a large shed. La Paz loves its ice cream and *paletas;* Revolución alone has five **La Michoacana** ❶ ice cream shops. **La Fuente** ❶, on the *malecón,* serves up a wide variety of flavors—including cactus—and is a required evening stop for huge crowds of local teenagers.

La Fonda (☎ 125 4700), Revolución and Bravo. Undiscovered by tourists, La Fonda serves good, cheap food in the *centro*. *Comida corrida* or delectable *pescado a la plancha* 30 pesos. Open daily 7am-10pm. ❸

Restaurant Palapa Adriana (☎ 122 8329), on the beach off Obregón at Constitución. Practically in the water, with unmatched sunset views. Red snapper 76 pesos, specials around 50 pesos. *Pollo con mole* 40 pesos. Open M-F 8am-10pm, Sa-Su 1-9pm. ❹

Restaurante el Quinto Sol (☎ 122 1692), on Domínguez at Independencia. One of the few strictly vegetarian joints in Baja California, the menu includes excellent *licuados* (20 pesos) and a tasty veggie combo (40 pesos). A good place for breakfast if you've finally tired of endless *huevos rancheros*—here you can find muesli and yogurt instead. Open Su 8am-4pm, M-Sa 7:20am-10pm. ❹

Café el Callejón (☎ 125 2928), on de La Paz just off Obregón. Be serenaded by guitar-wielding musicians as you enjoy the salty air and munch on traditional Mexican dishes. Generous *antojitos* (21-38 pesos) draw a big crowd. Open Tu-Su 9am-1am. ❸

👁 SIGHTS

The **Museo Regional de Antropología e Historia,** at 5 de Mayo and Altamirano, has four floors of fascinating, well kept exhibits on the history of the southern peninsula from Pre-Hispanic to modern times, and hosts occasional temporary exhibits. All descriptions are in Spanish. (☎ 122 0162; fax 125 6424. Open daily 9am-6pm. Free.) Fans of handicrafts will appreciate **Ibarra's Pottery,** opposite Colegio Anáhuac near the corner of Guillermo Prieto and República. Artisans will gladly show you around, though their English ranges from limited to nonexistent. Be aware that, although you are welcome to take pictures of the potters at work, the finished designs are copyrighted and should not be photographed. Coffee mugs (120-260 pesos) and plates (from 60 pesos) are on sale. (☎ 122 0404. Open M-Sa 8am-4pm; closed Sa in summer.)

🏖 BEACHES

The beaches of La Paz snuggle into small coves, between cactus-studded hills and calm, transparent water. This is prime windsurfing territory. Be careful—lifeguards make appearances only on weekends and at popular beaches. Some of the smaller beaches along the *malecón* have fine sand for sunbathers, but don't expect cleanliness or tranquility—the city's main road runs 20ft. from the water.

NEAR PLAYA TECOLOTE. The best and most popular beach is **Playa Tecolote** (Owl Beach), 25km northeast of town on Mex. 1. A quiet extension of the Sea of Cortés laps against this gorgeous stretch of gleaming white sand near tall mountains. Tecolote is terrific for **camping ❶.** Spots on the east side of the beach, along the road to the more secluded but rockier **Playa el Coyote,** come equipped with a stone barbecue pit. The road to El Coyote itself is only passable by high clearance vehicles with 4WD. **Actividades Aquática,** on Tecolote, rents snorkeling gear (50 pesos for 2-3hr.) and organizes trips to **Isla Espíritu Santo** (350 pesos per person, including snorkeling gear, insurance, and a permit to enter the island; 4 person min.) Actividades is run by the Hotel Miramar. (☎ 122 1607. Office open 10am-5pm.) **Playa Balandra,** just south of Tecolote, is the answer for those looking to escape from the latter's restaurants and crowds. A stunning ring of white sand surrounds the shallow cove. Snorkeling at Balandra is excellent. **Palapa Azul** (☎ 125 2596) rents snorkeling gear (60-90 pesos per day) and kayaks (singles 60 pesos per hr., 250 pesos per day; doubles 100 pesos/300 pesos), and runs boat trips to nearby islands, with snorkeling gear included (300 pesos per person). A short scramble along the shore beyond the right-hand end of the beach leads to some intriguing and impressive rock formations. *(Take an Autotransportes Águila bus from the mini-station on Obregón and Independencia. 45min., noon and 2pm, 20 pesos; return bus at 5:30pm.)*

NEAR PLAYA PICHILINGUE. Beaches near Playa Pichilingue are out of walking distance from the city center, but within a 30min. bus ride. From the stop at the ferry dock, an additional 500m walk leads to **Playa Pichilingue,** a favorite among teens, who splash in the shallow waters and rent small rowboats (50 pesos per hr.) from **Restaurant Playa Pichilingue** (☎ 122 4565). The bus route loops, passing many beaches near the city. Although **Playa el Coromuel** is closest to La Paz, it's the last bus stop. The powdery sands are often dirty and packed with raucous partiers, but small rock outcroppings at the north end of the beach hide a relatively tranquil stretch. **Playa Caimancito,** a little past Coromuel, is cleaner and more scenic, but just as busy. Most beaches between La Paz and Tecolote have *palapa* shelters and some kind of food and drink available. *(Take the "Pichilingue" bus up the coast. Up to 30min., every hr., 15 pesos. You'll see the beaches from the bus before you reach them, so if you like what you see, let the driver know.)*

DIVING AND SNORKELING. The fun doesn't stop at the shoreline—magnificent offshore opportunities await snorkelers and certified divers. North of La Paz is **Salvatierra Wreck,** a dive spot where a 91m ferry boat sank in 1976. Decked with sponges and sea fans, the wreck attracts hordes of colorful fish, but strong currents may deter inexperienced divers. Also popular is the huge **Cerralvo Island,** east of La Paz, which promises reefs, large fish, giant pacific mantas, and untouched wilderness. **Isla Espíritu Santo** has hidden caves, pristine beaches, good diving reefs, and excellent snorkeling; the shallow reef at **Bahía San Gabriel** here is appropriate for both snorkeling and diving. Due to strong currents, fluctuating weather conditions, and inaccessibility, diving in the La Paz area requires guides, but unguided snorkeling is possible if you stay close to shore and check conditions before heading out. **Baja Diving and Service,** Obregón 1665, between 16 de Septiembre and Callejón La Paz, organizes daily scuba and snorkeling trips to nearby reefs, wrecks, and islands. (☎ 122 1826; fax 122 8644. Trips leave at 7am and return between 3 and 5pm. Scuba trips 920 pesos per day, US$20 extra includes equipment; snorkeling trips 450 pesos per person per day. All include lunch; diving trips include 2-3 tanks. Office open daily 8am-1pm and 4-8pm.) They also rent kayaks (singles US$18 half day, US$30 full day; doubles US$30/US$50) for exploring the calm waters of Bahía de la Paz. **Carey Outdoors,** at Topete and Legaspi close to the *malecón,* runs dive trips to the islands (☎ 123 2333. Office open daily 10am-6pm). For excellent, easily accessible snorkeling, head to **San Juan de la Costa** just past Centenario, 13km north of La Paz on the Transpeninsular. Nearby on the same road is the beachcomber's paradise of **El Comitán,** with sand and mud flats where the tides deposit shells, amethyst, and other semi-precious stones.

◪ NIGHTLIFE

There are few more enjoyable things to do in the evening in La Paz (or perhaps in all Baja) than strolling the *malecón,* but if you decide to forego its waterfront delights, the city also has plenty of other nightspots. Guys, let her get this one—women are often charged less for drinks.

Las Varitas (☎ 125 2025), Independencia and Domínguez. A large stage and live bands dominate one side of the club, and a young crowd packs the multi-level platforms. The central dance floor never seems to have enough room—dancers gradually take over tabletops. Lively and fun, even on weeknights. Open Tu-Su 10pm-3am. F-Sa cover 30 pesos; free entry and drinks for women F 9-11pm.

La Cantina, at Obregón and Muelle, across from the dock. A pool hall occupies the front (pool 30 pesos per hr.); a loud disco dance party breaks it down in back. 2-for-1 drinks 7-9pm. Open Tu-Th 7pm-midnight, F-Su 7pm-3am.

Carlos n' Charlie's/La Paz-Lapa (☎ 122 9290), Obregón and 16 de Septiembre. Savor huge margaritas (38 pesos), or go buck-wild at the outdoor booze and rockfest. US and Mexican teens get down to everything from hard rock to rap to house under giant palm trees. Tu ladies' night 9-11pm (free drinks and no cover). Cover 30 pesos other nights. Restaurant open daily; club open Tu and F 9pm-3am, Sa 10pm-4am.

TODOS SANTOS   ☎ 612

Plenty of visitors to Baja end up staying for good. Nowhere is this easier to understand than in laid-back Todos Santos (pop. 4000), ensconced in rolling hills close to spectacular beaches on the lonely Pacific coast. A retreat for a community of ex-pat artists, the town is gradually filling with galleries, gourmet restaurants, and classy shops—yet so far this gentrification has been limited to the central streets, and the rest of Todos Santos retains the flavor of small-town Mexican life, from the popular daily *siesta* to the abundance of excellent *taquerías*. It's partly this juxtaposition that makes it such a delightful place to visit.

▄ TRANSPORTATION

The **bus stop** (☎ 145 0170) is in front of Pilar's Taco Stand, on the corner of Zaragoza and Colegio Militar. Buy tickets inside from Pilar, or from the driver. *De paso* buses run north to **La Paz** (1hr., 10 per day 6:45am-8pm, 60 pesos) and south to **San José del Cabo** (1½hr., 8 per day 8am-9pm, 75 pesos) via **Cabo San Lucas** (1hr., 70 pesos). Arriving buses may drop you off near Degollado and Militar, where the Transpeninsular Highway turns to head toward Los Cabos from La Paz.

✳ ⚡ ORIENTATION AND PRACTICAL INFORMATION

Most services are located in the *centro*. **Legaspi** begins next to the church and runs north-south through town, paralleling **Centenario** on the other side of the church. Next come the two main streets, **Juárez** and **Militar,** which continue south to the *parque* and bus station. Be sure to grab the monthly *Calendario de Todos Santos*, which is available for free (try El Tecolote Libros) and has a useful map.

There is no tourist office, but **El Tecolote Libros,** on Juárez and Hidalgo, sells English magazines, maps, and a comprehensive book on the town, written by the proprietor. (☎ 145 0295. Open June-July and Nov. M-Sa 9am-5pm; Aug.-Oct. M-F 9am-5pm; Dec.-May daily 9am-5pm.) **Banorte,** on the corner of Obregón and Juárez, the only bank in town, exchanges currency and traveler's checks and has a 24hr. **ATM.** (☎ 145 0056. Open M-F 9am-2pm.) **Mercado Guluarte** is at Morelos between Militar and Juárez. (☎ 145 0006. Open Su 8am-2pm, M-Sa 8am-9pm.) Buy fruit at the **markets** on Degollado and Juárez. The **police** station is in the Delegación Municipal complex at the plaza. (☎ 145 0365. No English spoken.) Other services include: the **hospital,** on Juárez at Degollado (☎ 145 0095; office open M-F 8am-2:30pm; English spoken); **Red Cross,** at Obregón and Huerto (☎ 145 0618; no English spoken); **Tienda ISSTE pharmacy,** on Juárez between Morelos and Zaragoza (☎ 145 0244; open 8am-8pm); **Lavandería Cris,** at the corner of Militar and León (☎ 145 0442; open daily 9am-2pm and 4-7pm; full-service 45 pesos); **Internet** at **Los Adobes,** on Hidalgo (☎ 145 0203; open Su 10am-5pm, M-Sa 9am-9pm); the **post office** on Militar at León (☎ 145 0330; open M-F 8am-3pm). **Postal code:** 23300.

▪ ACCOMMODATIONS AND CAMPING

The best way to sleep on the cheap is to camp. Todos Santos has plenty of gorgeous beaches, rolling hills, and pot-smoking, boogie-boarding bodies. Closer to town, **El Litro RV park ❶** offers full hookup (110 pesos) and spots under shady *palapas* (80 pesos), with discounts for stays of a week or more. The site has two hot showers and claims to have the cleanest bathrooms in Baja. Find it by following the signs from the PEMEX. For those who prefer a roof, ▪**Motel Guluarte ❸**, on Juárez at Morelos, has clean, cozy rooms, fans or A/C, refrigerators, and TV. (☎ 145 0006. Singles 170 pesos; doubles 250 pesos.) Cozy **Hotel Misión del Pilar ❹**, at the corner of Militar and Hidalgo, has comfortable, attractive rooms with bath, TV, and A/C, arranged around an adobe courtyard. (☎ 145 0114. Rooms 200 pesos.) Surfers should check out **Pescadero Surf Camp ❶**, south of Todos Santos on Mex. 9 near km 64. The camp is run by enthusiastic Americans, and offers a sweet pool with a swim-up *palapa* bar. Accommodations vary from *cabañas* to camping spots under *palapas*. Advance reservations of one or two weeks recommended; for US holidays, book up to six months in advance. (☎ 130 3032; www.pescaderosurf.com. Camping US$7; tent rental US$2 per night; *cabañas* US$35 per person.)

▪ FOOD

Loncherías ❶ line Militar near the bus station (tacos 10-14 pesos). For the best meat tacos in town, take a short walk to **Tacos Chilakos ❶**, on Juárez near Tecolote Libros. (Open daily 8:30am-9pm.) Locals are understandably addicted to **Barajas Tacos ❶**, an outdoor stand on Degollado and Cuauhtémoc, uphill from the PEMEX, that has the only late-night bites around. By day the cook serves up succulent *carnitas*; after 6pm, the soul of a lively taco stand takes over. (Open Su-M, W-Sa 8am-midnight.) **Cafe Brown's ❶**, around the back of Hotel Misión del Pilar, does excellent value breakfasts. (Open daily 7am-3pm.)

▪ ART GALLERIES

Modern art lovers are sure to be wowed by the galleries. The best place to get an overview of the scene is the **Galería de Todos Santos,** on Legaspi and Topete, where Michael Cope displays his own work alongside that of fellow ex-pats, visiting artists, and local people. (☎ 145 0500. Open June-Sept. M-Sa 11am-1pm and 2-4pm; Oct.-May M-Sa 10am-1pm and 2-5pm.) A branch of the gallery dedicated solely to abstract art recently opened on Centenario at Hidalgo. Meanwhile, at the **Charles Stewart Gallery and Studio,** on Obregón at Centenario, you can see how it all began. Charles Stewart arrived from Taos, New Mexico in 1983, and in the two decades that he has spent here his work has ranged from realistic landscapes to densely symbolic, mystical tableaux. (☎ 145 0265. Usually open M-Sa 10am-4pm.) **Galería Logan,** at Juárez and Morelos, is devoted to the exotic landscapes and bold, swirling colors of Todos Santos resident Jill Logan. (☎ 145 0151. Open M-Sa 11am-5pm; closed from Labor Day until Oct. 1st.) Catherine Wall's work, on display at **Galería Wall** (☎ 145 0527), is notable for its engagement with contemporary Mexican life.

▪ BEACHES

Todos Santos is surrounded by some of the region's most unspoiled beaches. Unfortunately, **powerful currents make many unsafe for swimming.** If you find yourself swept out to sea, do not thrash toward shore—instead, swim parallel to the beach for a few hundred meters, and then calmly swim for land. The isolation of these beaches may be unsettling; always bring a friend and return to town before dark. Romantic **La Posa** can be found by following the small blue-and-white signs to the Hotel Posada la Posa, either behind the PEMEX and over the hill or along Topete, off Juárez. **Vicious undercurrents and waves make La Posa unsuitable for swimming,** but there are few better places for solitary beach walks. Unfortunately a barbed wire fence was recently erected across the path to the beach, so you should probably get to La Posa via **Punta Lobos.** To reach Punta Lobos, the stomping ground of the local sea lion population, turn left onto Degollado as you walk away from town. Roughly six blocks later, the city ends as the road becomes Mex. 19. Around km 54, turn right and follow the road until you come to the beach, near the lighthouse.

A safer place for swimmers is **Playa de las Palmas (Playa San Pedrito).** To get there, drive 5km south from town on the highway, and turn right when you see the white Campo Experimental buildings on the left. Travel another 2½km, past faded signs and over vicious speed bumps, into an area thick with palm trees. Park at the locked gate (vehicles are prohibited on the beach, as is camping and fire), and follow the palm grove down to the secluded beach. The serene and deserted shore, with rocky slopes rising up on either side, is excellent for swimming and body surfing (as long as you stay close), and the fine sand is some of the best in the area.

A quiet and lovely surfing beach by the highway is **Playa San Pedrito,** 8km south of town. Turn at the sign for San Pedrito RV Park, where you can camp. (☎108 4316. Day parking 20 pesos; camping 30 pesos per person; full hookup 150 pesos; *cabañas* with A/C 45 pesos.) It's easy to find a sunbathing spot; head south for the best sands. Again, strong waves and currents endanger swimmers.

Playa los Cerritos, a popular family beach, lies approximately 14km south of Todos Santos. Look for a turn on the right side of the highway around km 65. The current is tamer here than elsewhere, but the waves are just as big—potentially dangerous for weak swimmers who stray too close to the rocks, but great for surfing, especially from November through March. Although relatively well-populated, the endless sands are not crowded. A small shop on the beach rents out surf boards (100 pesos per day) and boogie boards (50 pesos per day); the owner also offers 1hr. lessons and a day's board rental (350 pesos) and rents out tents (50 pesos per night). A more extensive range of equipment is available at **Pescadero Surf Camp** (see p. 203). All boards are less than a year old. (Surfboards US$15 per day; boogie boards US$7 per day. 1hr. surfing lesson US$35, includes day's board rental.) A skateboarding facility is being developed nearby.

▶ DAYTRIPS FROM TODOS SANTOS

SIERRA DE LA LAGUNA

To get to the trailhead, drive south out of Todos Santos. After passing km 53, you will see the turn-off on the left at the top of a small hill, directing you towards Rancho la Burrera. Drive down this dirt road (preferably with 4WD) through a fenced-off cattle ranch and bear right at the 1st unmarked major fork in the road. Follow signs for 40min. until you reach a locked gate and the end of the road. There is a small dirt lot in which to park your car.

Sierra de la Laguna, the mountain range that lines the cape, is visible from virtually any beach around Los Cabos and Todos Santos. The dark rain clouds hovering above the mountains are responsible for some of the most exotic flora and fauna in Baja California. The climate of the mountains is completely different from the surrounding coastal areas and can, in the winter, drop below freezing. **La Laguna,** the Sierra's most popular hiking destination, is a meadow of about four sq. km perched at an altitude of 1700m amid the rocky peaks of **Picacho la Laguna** and **Cerro las Casitas,** the range's tallest points. Once a lake, erosion from excessive rainfall destroyed the laguna's edges in the late 19th century, transforming La Laguna into a grassy meadow. The climb to the meadow is a grueling 8hr., with steep inclines toward the top. Successful hikers are rewarded with many beautiful vistas and rest-stops along the way, one of which (3hr. into the hike) offers a view of the entire width of the peninsula. The trail is well marked, with several campsites along the way and at La Laguna as well. If you want to hire the services of a local guide, ask around in Todos Santos or get in touch with one of the ranches. At **Rancho el Salado** (☎ 108 4412), accessible by bearing left at the first major fork in the road to the trailhead, Martín will accompany you and give you the use of a mule for 2000 pesos. Daniel at **Rancho las Piedritas** (☎ 105 7517), farther along the road and just 4km short of the gate, offers a similar deal.

LOS CABOS

At the end of the long, lonely drive from the US border, you might be forgiven for thinking that the Transpeninsular Highway would peter out at some remote outpost with barely any connection to the rest of civilization. Instead, it swoops down into huge malls and hotels. The cape region is a far cry from the sleepy getaway that many Baja veterans remember from the old days, and gets further every year as the coastline fills with more resorts, clubs, and golf courses. Yet even though Los Cabos are crammed with *gringos* year-round, it's still possible to escape the crowds and enjoy the southern coast's stunning natural beauty—spectacular rock formations, unique underwater sandfalls, surf that rivals that of Hawaii, and, of course, glistening white beaches, which are arguably the most beautiful in Baja.

CABO SAN LUCAS   ☎ 624

The copper-tinted cliffs and craggy rock arch that stand at Baja's southern tip, where the Sea of Cortés meets the Pacific, are the most famous images of Cabo San Lucas (pop. 50,000). What the postcards don't show is that it's difficult to see those natural wonders without high-rise malls, the glitzy marina, and acres of naked *gringo* flesh getting in the way. Cabo is the ultimate resort, and probably the most expensive place in Mexico. As tourists pour money into its restaurants and clubs, the town can't help but prosper. Nevertheless, Cabo has remained a friendly town, particularly if you move beyond the commercialized *centro*. Cabo's pleasures merit the occasional splurge, and even budget travelers can delight in fabulous fish tacos, gloriously tacky nightlife, and the nonstop flow of margaritas.

▐ TRANSPORTATION

Local **Subur Cabos** buses run to San José del Cabo (30min., every 15min., 16 pesos). Hop on the bus at the stop on Cárdenas between Vicario and Mendoza. **Águila** (☎ 143 7880) is north of town, by the PEMEX station and Hotel Oasis—follow signs to Todos Santos; the bus station is right after you get on the highway. To get into town from the bus stop, take a local yellow bus (4 pesos) to Blvd. Marina. "Vía Corta" **buses** go to **La Paz** (2½hr., 11 per day 5:45am-7:45pm, 108 pesos) via **Todos Santos** (1hr., 50 pesos). "Vía Larga" services (7:15, 10:30am, 1:15, 5:15pm) take 4hr. to reach La Paz, but go via **San José del Cabo** (30min., 20 pesos). Buses to the ferry terminal at Pichilingue (3hr., 130 pesos) leave daily at 7:40 and 9:45am, and on Saturdays at 6pm. One *de paso* bus per day leaves at 4:30pm and heads north to **Tijuana** (26½hr., 1043 pesos) via **La Paz** (3hr., 108 pesos), **Ciudad Constitución** (6hr., 224 pesos), **Loreto** (8½hr., 317 pesos), **Mulegé** (10½hr., 398 pesos), **Santa Rosalía** (11½hr., 450 pesos), **San Ignacio** (12½hr., 503 pesos), **Guerrero Negro** (14½hr., 607 pesos), **San Quintín** (19hr., 834 pesos), **Ensenada** (23hr., 955 pesos).

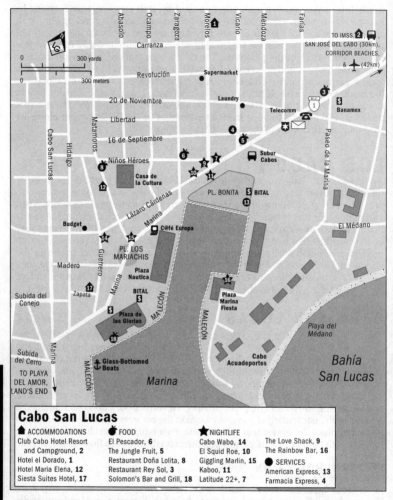

Cabo San Lucas

⌂ ACCOMMODATIONS
Club Cabo Hotel Resort
  and Campground, **2**
Hotel el Dorado, **1**
Hotel Maria Elena, **12**
Siesta Suites Hotel, **17**

🍎 FOOD
El Pescador, **6**
The Jungle Fruit, **5**
Restaurant Doña Lolita, **8**
Restaurant Rey Sol, **3**
Solomon's Bar and Grill, **18**

★ NIGHTLIFE
Cabo Wabo, **14**
El Squid Roe, **10**
Giggling Marlin, **15**
Kaboo, **11**
Latitude 22+, **7**

The Love Shack, **9**
The Rainbow Bar, **16**
● SERVICES
American Express, **13**
Farmacia Express, **4**

✈ 🛈 ORIENTATION AND PRACTICAL INFORMATION

Restaurants, bars, and most tourist services concentrate on **Cárdenas,** between Morelos and the western edge of town, and along **Boulevard Marina.** Plazas are concrete malls or tight conglomerations of shops, and follow the curve of the marina.

> **Tourist Information:** No official offices. Cabo's "Tourist Info" booths are simply a cover for time-share hawkers. Car rental agencies have better maps (and often better advice).

> **Currency Exchange:** Many hotels and restaurants prefer US dollars and exchange them at 10 pesos per US$1 regardless of the going rate. **BITAL,** in Plaza Bonita (☎ 143 3888), has a 24hr. **ATM** and exchanges traveler's checks and foreign currencies. Open M-F 8am-7pm, Sa 8am-3pm. Another branch down the side of Plaza de las Glorias (☎ 143 4186) has the same hours.

American Express: (☎ 143 5766), in Plaza Bonita. Open M-F 9am-6pm, Sa 9am-1pm.

Supermarket: Bimbo/Almacenes Grupo Castro (☎ 143 0566), Morelos at Revolución. Open daily 7:30am-11pm.

Car Rental: Budget (☎ 143 4190), on Cárdenas between Guerrero and Hidalgo. Economy cars from US$48 per day. Open daily 8am-10pm.

Laundry: Lavandería San Lucas, Vicario and 20 de Noviembre. Open daily 8am-10pm.

Police: (☎ 143 3977), on Cárdenas, 2 blocks north of Morelos. No English spoken.

Red Cross: (☎ 143 3300), at km 121 on the *carretera* to Todos Santos, near the PEMEX. Some English spoken.

Pharmacy: Farmacia Express (☎ 143 9333), Vicario and 16 de Septiembre. Open 24hr.

Hospital: IMSS (☎ 143 1444 or 143 1445), uphill from the bus station, near the Red Cross and PEMEX. No English spoken.

Faxes: Telecomm (☎ 143 1968; fax 143 0231), next to the post office. Open Su 8am-11am, M-F 8am-7:30pm, Sa 8am-3pm.

Internet Access: C@fé Europa, on Blvd. Marina in Plaza Nautica. 1 peso per min. Open Su 9am-9pm, M-Sa 9am-10pm.

Post Office: (☎ 143 0048) on Cárdenas, next to the police station. Open M-F 9am-4pm, Sa 9am-noon. **Postal Code:** 23451.

ACCOMMODATIONS

Resorts dominate Cabo San Lucas, and even the cheapest hotels will take a bite out of your wallet. During the winter high season, call ahead and be prepared to shell out 25% more than during the slower summer months. Most hotels base rates on US dollars and not pesos.

Hotel Maria Elena (☎ 143 3296), on Matamoros between Cárdenas and Niños Héroes. Sparkling rooms have A/C and cable TV, and there's a laundromat on the ground floor. Singles 357 pesos; doubles 400 pesos. ❺

Hotel el Dorado (☎ 143 2810), on Morelos near Carranza. Gigantic tiled rooms are spotless and simply furnished, with modern A/C, fan, clean bath, TV, and cute finishing touches such as heart-shaped head-boards. A big swimming pool for grown-ups and a separate little one for the kiddies. Singles 350 pesos; doubles 450 pesos. ❺

Siesta Suites Hotel (☎ 143 2773, US 602-331-1354; siesta@cabonet.net.mx), on Zapata near Guerrero. Smart, well-maintained American place offering comfortable suites with kitchens (complete with utensils) and a separate bedroom off a living/eating area. Suites for two people US$45, with A/C US$56. Each additional person US$10. ❺

Club Cabo Hotel Resort and Campground (☎ 143 3348). Head out Cárdenas to the intersection with Mex. 19; continue to the beach and Hotel Cascadas, and turn left down a dirt road. Cabo is about 1km down on the left. A tidy one-acre campground. Ping-pong, hammock area, jacuzzi, trampoline, and pool. Most of the 15 sites are shaded. A short walk to the beach. US$8 per person for full hookup or tent site, US$10 if you're on your own. Also has 10 suites, fully equipped with kitchen, A/C, and satellite TV. Singles US$45; doubles US$55. *Cabañas* US$15 per person, min. 4 people. ❶

FOOD

Fancy *palapa*-shaded waterfront meals are not for the budget traveler; for better deals, head inland along Morelos and its side streets or to the abundant *taquerías*.

Restaurant Doña Lolita, at Niños Héroes and Matamoros, is a tiny open-air shack filled with chattering locals. The open barbecue fills your eyes and nose with charcoal prior to delighting your taste buds. The wall is adorned with a blackboard listing the day's specials, along with the axe for chopping the wood and keeping the fire going long into the evening. Suitably fiery *fajitas* 60 pesos. Open Su 8am-4pm, M-Sa 8am-midnight. ❸

Restaurant Rey Sol (☎ 143 1117), on Cárdenas near Vicario. A loud and purely local restaurant. Tasty food served with a smile. Fabulous Acapulco-style *ceviche* or *enchiladas* 50 pesos. Open daily 6am-10pm. ❹

Solomon's Bar and Grill (☎ 143 3050), in Plaza de las Glorias, on the marina. Comfortable wicker divans overlook the marina. Relatively cheap tacos 15-20 pesos. Your catch grilled for a small fee. Margaritas 25 pesos, beer 15 pesos. Unfortunately, there's a constant parade of souvenir-sellers and *mariachis*. Open daily 7:30am-10pm. ❷

El Pescador (☎ 144 3586), on Niños Héroes and Zaragoza. This local favorite provides hungry diners with tasty and reasonable seafood dishes, from fabulous *ceviches* (50-65 pesos) to a whole crab for 90 pesos. Open daily 10am-10pm. ❺

The Jungle Fruit (☎ 105 0977), at the corner of Cárdenas and Vicario. The Fruit offers refreshment from the blistering heat with deliciously fresh and generous fruit juices and smoothies. Open 24hr.; claims to be closed only during hurricanes. ❷

👁 📷 SIGHTS AND BEACHES

Cabo bills itself as the "marlin capital of the world," and many tourists visit to reel in their share of the millions of huge fish caught each year. Prices for fishing trips are astronomical—nearly all exceed US$200 per day (anglers on a tighter budget should check out **Money for Nothing,** below). Nearly all daytime activity in Cabo San Lucas takes place in the pristine waters off the coast. Many head toward the beautiful **Los Cabos Corridor** (see p. 210), linking San Lucas and San José, but there are plenty of beaches right in Cabo. **Playa del Médano,** the best for swimming, reaches east from the marina. The waters here resemble an aquatic zoo, featuring exotic species of parasailers, roaring jet skis, and motorboats full of lobster-red, beer-guzzling vacationers. The very professional **Cabo Acuadeportes,** in front of Hotel Hacienda, rents a variety of water equipment. (☎ 143 0117. Open daily 9am-5pm. 2hr. snorkeling tours US$25, includes equipment and guide. 2hr. diving tours US$25; 1-tank US$43, 2-tank US$71; prices do not include equipment. Also offers kayak (US$10 per hr.) and sailboat (US$20 per hr.) rentals. Parasailing US$30.) A fabulous array of tropical fish swim between colorful, waving sea fans, rewarding those who venture underwater with nonstop entertainment. Divers should ask about trips to the **sandfalls,** in a deep canyon off Playa del Amor, where spilling sands flow into sublime underground rivers that tumble straight down for miles.

The famous Arch Rock of Cabo San Lucas, known as **El Arco** or **Land's End,** is only a short boat ride from the marina. Here the tranquil Sea of Cortés meets the rough Pacific. The rocks around the arch are home to about 40 sea lions who like to hang out and sun themselves. To get there, walk through Plaza las Glorias Hotel to the docks at the far right of the marina. Eager, English-speaking boat captains will be happy to take you on a **glass-bottom boat** ride to El Arco and back (45min.; US$8-10; some hotels offer discounts or free rides).

These boats also stop at **Playa del Amor** (yes, that's the Beach of Bump and Grind), a good swimming beach next to El Arco. Disembark and head back later on a different boat for no additional charge; it's 25 pesos if you switch companies. The beach is far from isolated, but the area is free of souvenir vendors. Where there's love, there's **Playa del Divorcio** (Beach of Divorce). Quiet and beautiful, it lies opposite Amor on the Pacific side. **Dangerous currents and fierce undertow make swimming unsafe.** The rocky area just before Playa del Amor is a protected national park and underwater wonderland. **Snorkeling** is the best way to explore the stony recesses packed with coral, urchins, tropical fish, moray eels, stingrays, and

MONEY FOR NOTHING. The only sharks lurking around the stunning cape are the time-share vendors. Anyone who looks over 28 and in possession of a major credit card will be greeted by a constant cacophony of "Can I help you?" or "¡Hola, amigo!" The savvy budget traveler knows no greater glory than turning the tables on those trying to take advantage of his hard-saved cash: if you have a free afternoon, hawkers will happily give you a day's free car rental, take you golfing, or pay for your pricey fishing trip and follow it with dinner. All you have to do is "listen," ears shut, eyes open, mouth pleasantly grinning, and head nodding. The standard pitch? They ask only US$15,000 for part ownership at an exclusive time-share resort. Just remember not to blow your cover until you've eaten your fill.

octopi. Bring your own gear or rent equipment from a nearby vendor (boat tour and snorkeling package around US$15). The avid snorkeler will also appreciate **Playa Santa María** and the reef at **Playa del Chileno**, both on the highway between Cabo San Lucas and San José del Cabo (see **The Corridor**, p. 210).

▣ NIGHTLIFE

In Cabo San Lucas, those who play hard pay hard. However, most clubs only charge cover on certain nights or when a particularly good band is playing. *Chicas*, this town is for you: ladies' nights rotate, so drinks are always free somewhere. Clubs and bars concentrate on **Cárdenas** and **Boulevard Marina**, which become a huge laser-lit party ground by night, winding down at 3 or 4am.

▧ **El Squid Roe** (☎ 143 0655), on Cárdenas at Zaragoza. Love it or hate it, you can't fail to notice the airplane whirling above this carnival calling itself a bar. Everyone comes here, and most end up reveling in the madhouse pick-up scene, conga lines, vats of tequila, and short-skirted, shot-peddling girls dancing on any and all surfaces. Beer 45 pesos, mixed drinks around 40 pesos. Food available until 11pm. Open daily noon-4am.

The Love Shack (☎ 143 5010), on Morelos off Cárdenas, around the corner from Squid Roe. A scaled-down, more intimate version of Cabo's mega-clubs. One small room with a tiny dance floor, pool table, and well-stocked jukebox. Happy hour (3 margaritas for the price of 1; other drinks 2-for-1) M for the duration of the soccer match. US$1 tequila shots Tu night. Ladies drink free W 9pm-11pm. Open daily 11am-3am.

Giggling Marlin (☎ 143 1182), across Matamoros from Plaza de los Mariachis. The main event, enjoyed every night from 8pm, involves the chance to discover the origin of the club's name by being hung upside down like a prize fish. Beer 35 pesos, other drinks 40-45 pesos. Open daily 9am-1am.

Cabo Wabo (☎ 143 1188), on Guerrero near Cárdenas. Live rock (Th-Su), very occasionally featuring Van-Halen-member-cum-club-owner Sammy Hagar. Beer 30 pesos, *waborita* (house margarita) 40 pesos. Open daily 7pm-2am.

Kaboo (☎ 143 8700), on Cárdenas opposite the end of Morelos. The *palapa* interior and the "authentic" wood carvings try to capture some Mexican ambience, which is shattered just as soon as the party gets going. Come before 9pm for cheap drinks (by Cabo standards, at least—US$2 for a beer, US$8 for a bucket of 6). Ladies pay no cover Tu.

Latitude 22+ (☎ 143 1516), on Cárdenas. If dancing and silly games aren't your thing, head for this mainstay of Cabo's bar scene. Beer 20 pesos. Open daily 8am-11pm.

The Rainbow Bar, on the water by the Marina Fiesta hotel. A mixed crowd frequents Cabo's only gay bar. No wild shows or crazy antics, just friendly atmosphere. A small space with room for dancing and a patio overlooking the quiet end of the marina. Beer 25 pesos. 2-for-1 drinks all night Th and Su. Open Su-Th 8pm-3am, F-Sa 8:30am-4am.

▶ DAYTRIPS FROM LOS CABOS

THE CORRIDOR

The easiest way to get to your oasis of choice is to drive there. For those without wheels, "Subur Cabos" buses, which run between San José del Cabo and Cabo San Lucas, will leave you at any of the listed beaches (8-15 pesos). To get back, flag down a passing bus.

Amazing beaches dot the 30km stretch of coast between Cabo San Lucas and San José del Cabo. Unfortunately, development is creeping in from both sides. The most pristine, undeveloped beaches are those in the middle. The calmest waters and best swimming areas are those closest to Cabo San Lucas. All of the beaches listed below are accessible from the highway; many lie at the end of winding, roads, but all are reachable in passenger vehicles if you don't try to drive across the beach itself. Access roads to some are identified by blue-and-white palm tree signs or small road signs with the name of the beach. A few are marked simply by dirt roads, and closer to San José it becomes increasingly difficult to locate specific beaches unless you're traveling by bus and can ask the driver for the right stop. The following beaches are listed in geographical order, starting at Cabo San Lucas and moving east along the corridor to San José del Cabo.

PLAYA BARCO VARADO (SHIPWRECK BEACH). Not recommended for swimmers, Barco Varado is a scuba-diving paradise. A sunken tuna boat lies 27m below the water's surface. The slightly pebbly sands are rarely crowded. *(Take the turnoff to the Cabo del Sol complex immediately before km 10; the guards should let you through the gate. Follow the road downhill and turn right, and continue as far as the Sheraton Hacienda. A paved road immediately beyond the hotel leads to a small parking area.)*

PLAYA TWIN DOLPHIN. Crashing waves and jagged outcroppings shelter a quiet, secluded, and rocky beach. Swimming not advised. *(Follow the rough sandy road immediately next to the gated entrance to the Twin Dolphin resort at km 11.5. Open daily 6am-8pm.)*

PLAYA SANTA MARIA. A cove protects the clear waters of this small beach from harsh waves, and swimming is safe year-round. Some of Cabo's best snorkeling can be found here, and if you forgot to bring gear you can rent it from **Servicios Taide** on the beach. (Full snorkeling gear 120 pesos per day; boogie board 50 pesos per day; kayak for two people 200 pesos per hr.; shade umbrella 80-100 pesos per day. Open daily 9am-5pm.) The sand may be slightly coarse, but the spectacular hills on either side of the cove are worth a look. *(Just past Playa Twin Dolphin at km 12. Parking lot open 7am-7pm; supervised parking is free, though tips are appreciated.)*

PLAYA CHILENO. A popular swimming spot, Chileno has free public showers and a small dock. Kayaks (US$10-15 per hr.), snorkel gear (US$12 per day), and diving packages are available for rent from **Cabo Acuadeportes** at the right side of the beach. (Open daily 9am-5pm.) The beach is popular with local families as well as tourists, and heavy traffic sometimes dirties the sugary sands. *(At km 14.)*

PLAYA EL TULE. The long, rocky shore is unsuitable for swimming, but surfers fight for waves. You won't find any facilities. *(Leave the road via a sandy track just before Puente del Tule, at around km 15. If you don't have 4WD, park close to the bridge, since the sand rapidly becomes treacherously thick and the tracks are hard to see.)*

PLAYA BUENOS AIRES. Like the neighboring beaches of **Canta Mar, Costa Brava, El Zalate, San Carlos,** and **El Mirador** (all between km 16 and km 20), Playa Buenos Aires is currently under development. However, heavy construction has not yet shut down the beach, and visitors can still enjoy the rough waves and long, empty shore. *(Accessible by a crude sand and dirt road from km 22, which is difficult to spot.)*

PLAYA PALMILLA. Smooth, gentle waves, great swimming and nice shady *pala-pas* attract lots of families and weekenders. If you get thirsty, you can pop into nearby Restaurant/Bar Pepe's. *(From km 26, drive into the Hotel Palmilla complex and turn right down the cushy access road. Follow signs to the beach and Pepe's for about 1½km.)*

PLAYA ACAPULQUITO. Big waves and soft sand make this a popular beach with surfers, swimmers, and sunbathers alike. *(Look for cars parked along the highway at km 27, just before the Acapulquito Scenic Overlook. Walk down a steep dirt path, through the huge underground pipe, and between the condominiums to the beach.)*

PLAYA COSTA AZUL. The last beach before San José del Cabo, Costa Azul is the best surfing beach in all of Los Cabos. The water is usually filled with expert surfers riding the waves. Those who want to display their skills can rent a board (US$15 per day), while wannabes can learn the basics (US$20 per hr.) at **Zipper's**, on the beach, to the left of the parking area. *(At km 28. Zipper's open daily 9am-5pm.)*

SAN JOSÉ DEL CABO ☎ 624

If Los Cabos were brothers, José would be the one their mother loved more. Unlike his hard-partying, bad-boy younger brother Lucas, José would be better-looking, charming, sincere, and polite, but still fun. Unfortunately, José would also suffer from a congenital disease that made him sweatier than his brother, and therefore less popular. Thanks to the humidity syndrome, San José del Cabo remains tranquil, collected, and peacefully Mexican, a haven from the Resortville that dominates the rest of the cape. Budget travelers will find San José cheaper than San Lucas, although prices are still much higher than on the mainland.

▐ TRANSPORTATION

The **Águila/ABC bus station** (☎ 142 1100) is on González, two blocks from the highway. To get to town, go left from the station, and walk 8-10min. down González to Morelos. Turn left, walk six blocks, and make a right on Zaragoza towards the *zócalo*. Águila and ABC run to: **La Paz** (3hr.; 6, 7, 9, 10am, noon, 1:15, 3, 4, 5, 7pm; 119 pesos) via **Cabo San Lucas** (30min., 20 pesos) and **Todos Santos** (1½hr., 66 pesos). Of these, the 10am continues to **Ciudad Constitución** (235 pesos) and **Loreto** (328 pesos), while the 4pm goes on to **Tijuana** (1055 pesos) via **Mulegé** (409 pesos), **Santa Rosalia** (460 pesos), **San Ignacio** (514 pesos), **Guerrero Negro** (618 pesos), **San Quintín** (845 pesos), **Ensenada** (966 pesos). There are additional services to **La Paz** via the **east cape** at 8, 11:15am, 2, and 6pm, which stop at **Santiago** (35 pesos) and **Los Barriles** (45 pesos). **Subur Cabos** buses depart from a stop on the highway 50m uphill from Doblado. To get to the *centro* from the stop, walk six blocks down Doblado and go left one block on Morelos. Buses run to **Cabo San Lucas**, stopping at most corridor beaches (30min., every 15min., 16 pesos).

▐ PRACTICAL INFORMATION

Bank: Banamex (☎ 142 3184) on Mijares, 2 blocks south of the *zócalo*, has a 24hr. **ATM,** and exchanges currency and checks. Open M-F 8:30am-4:30pm, Sa 9am-2pm.

Rental Car: Thrifty Rent-A-Car (☎ 142 4151), on Mijares at Juárez. Rent VW jalopies with insurance and unlimited km for US$45 per day. Open daily 8am-1pm and 3-6pm.

Laundry: Cabomatic (☎ 142 2933), 5 blocks south of the *zócalo* on Mijares. Wash and dry 14 pesos each; full-service 53 pesos. Open Su 9am-5pm, M-Sa 7:30am-7pm.

Emergency: ☎ 060.

San José del Cabo

⬆ ACCOMMODATIONS
Hotel Ceci, **5**
Hotel Diana, **4**
Hotel Youth Hostel Nuevo
San José, **1**
Trailer Park Brisa del Mar, **10**

🍎 FOOD
Cafetería Rosy, **3**
El Descanso, **7**
Taquería Erika, **8**

⭐ NIGHTLIFE
Excala, **9**
Señor Baco, **2**
Shooters, **6**

Police: (☎ 142 0361), west of town on Mex. 1 near km 33, across from the huge Tecate Agencia. Little English spoken.

Red Cross: (☎ 142 2188, emergency 142 0316 or 065), on Mijares in the same complex as the post office. Little English spoken.

Hospital: Centro de Salud, Doblado 39 (☎ 142 0241). Little English spoken. Open daily 8am-8pm. For 24hr. assistance, head to **IMSS** (☎ 142 1681), on Coronado and Hidalgo. Little English spoken.

Pharmacy: Farmacia la Moderna (☎ 142 0050), on Zaragoza between Degollado and Guerrero. All-night pharmacies rotate; check the list on the door. Open Su 9am-1pm, M-Sa 9am-9pm.

Internet Access: Trazzo Digital (☎ 142 1220), on Zaragoza between Morelos and Hidalgo. 25 pesos per 30min. Printing, scanning, other services. Open M-Sa 8am-9pm.

Fax: Telecomm (☎ 142 0906), next to the post office. Open M-F 8am-7pm, Sa-Su 8am-11am.

Post Office: (☎ 142 0911) on Mijares and González, several blocks toward the beach on the right-hand side. Open M-F 8am-6pm, Sa 9am-1pm. **Postal Code:** 23401.

ACCOMMODATIONS

Thanks to ever-encroaching development, room prices in San José del Cabo are rising. Compared to Cabo San Lucas, however, San José del Cabo is still a virtual heaven for budget accommodations, most of which are on or near Zaragoza.

Hotel Diana (☎ 142 0490), on Zaragoza near the *centro*. Friendly staff keep the Diana spotless and pleasant. Bright woven bedspreads add color to clean and tidy but bland rooms, each with small bath, satellite TV, and A/C. Singles and doubles 300 pesos. ❺

Hotel Ceci, Zaragoza 22, 1½ blocks from Mijares. Basic rooms with comfortable beds. Small singles and doubles 200 pesos, with A/C and big cable TV 250 pesos; triples with A/C 280 pesos. ❸

Hotel Youth Hostel Nuevo San José (☎ 142 1705), on Obregón and Guerrero. The rooms here come with absolutely no frills, and many of them have open windows on central hallways. Still, it's one of the only budget options. Downstairs rooms with cable TV 200 pesos; upstairs, possibly quieter rooms with no TV 150 pesos. ❸

Trailer Park Brisa del Mar (☎ 142 3999), near km 29 off the highway to San Lucas. Offers sweet beachfront *palapas*, sparkling bathrooms and showers, a good-sized pool, and a restaurant/bar. Beachfront hookup US$25 (US$5 more in the winter), back row spots US$18.50; tents US$10. All prices for double occupancy. ❷

FOOD

The influx of fancy tourist eateries has left few options between taco and filet mignon. A healthy suspicion of restaurants with menus printed in flawless English will save you money.

Cafetería Rosy, on Zaragoza and Green. The food is exquisite for the price, the service is spectacularly friendly, and a good bowl of soup and unlimited lemonade come with your meal. Delectable *bistec pipian* (45 pesos). Open M-Sa 8am-5pm. ❹

Taquería Erika (☎ 142 3928), on Doblado near Mex. 1. No place in the *centro* offers fare as superb or as inexpensive as the tacos, quesadillas, baked potatoes, and other *antojitos* served at Erika's. Tacos 9-10 pesos. Open daily 9am-5am. ❶

El Descanso, Castro near the *mercado*. Tasty and piping hot *barbacoa* (stringy meat soup) and *menudo* (stomach stew) from huge black vats on the fire (30-40 pesos). Just don't be too curious about which part of what animal you're eating. Open 24hr. ❸

SIGHTS AND BEACHES

A 20min. walk down Mijares leads to good, uncrowded beaches. Hurry—even as you read this, new resorts are popping up. Long, empty **Playa California** is great for sunbathing, but like many beaches in the area, undertow makes swimming unwise. To get to the best **surfing,** flag down a local bus on Mex. 1 (every 15min.) where it meets Doblado, and ask to be dropped at **Costa Azul** or **Playa de Palmilla** (see **The Corridor,** p. 210). **Killer Hook Surf Shop** (☎ 142 2430), on Juárez three blocks from Mijares, has the latest surf conditions. (Open Su 10am-5pm, M-Sa 10am-8:30pm.) For more solitude, head 4-5km down Juárez to **Pueblo la Playa** and bear right at the fork before town. *Pangeros* will take tourists **fishing** (5-6hr., approx. US$180 for 3 people). Tuna and dorado are plentiful near shore, and you can catch marlin farther out. Info booths along Mijares are more than happy to "inform" you about the fishing and **snorkeling** trips that they sell along with timeshares. Trip prices are often not bad and perhaps even worth the sales pitch. Just outside town, at km 31 on Mex. 1 in the Plaza las Palmas mall opposite the San José exit, **Baja Salvaje** (☎/fax 142 5300; www.bajasalvaje.com) offers high-end gear rentals, tours, and classes for diving, kayaking, surfing, and even rock climbing.

Misión Estero de las Palmas de San José del Cabo, on Hidalgo between Obregón and Zaragoza, is one of the most noticeable structures in town. Founded in 1730, the mission could never quite find enough indigenous people to convert. Locals revolted in 1734, and a vivid mosaic above the mission's entrance depicts them dragging Father Nicolás Tamaral to be burned alive. The huge yellow-and-white building which now stands on the square is a later replacement, and is imposing from the outside but a bit of a let-down inside. Nature-lovers should visit the **Estero de San José,** which is home to over 200 species of birds. A pleasant, shaded path meanders among huge palm trees and chirping birds, ending on Blvd. Mijares, near the post office. Find the entrance by heading away from the town center on Mijares and turning right; the estuary is at the end of the road on the left, near the Hotel Presidente. One good way to see the estuary is on horseback with the English-speaking guides of **Hacienda Vieja,** in the large field on Mijares opposite Juárez (1-2hr.; US$36 per hr. for one person, US$60 for two). If you're here on the right weekend, you might be lucky enough to catch one of their monthly demonstrations of *charrería.* (☎144 5144; cell 044 624 869 0808. Open daily 8-11am and 4-7:30pm.) Alternatively, contact Mike at **La Playita Tours** (☎140 6470; www.bajaturtles.org), attached to the hotel of the same name in Pueblo la Playa. Mike is engaged in an effort to protect sea turtles from poachers and allows visitors to join him on his nightly patrols in search of turtle eggs, which he takes to be incubated and hatched. He also runs daytime nature walks on the beach and through the estuary and can arrange walks in the surrounding desert or rental of ATVs, kayaks, or horses. Rental prices fluctuate; walks cost US$25 per person.

▓ NIGHTLIFE

San José del Cabo can't compete with wild Lucas, but a good time isn't hard to find—just kick back, relax, and don't expect conga lines or table dancing. The newest and most sophisticated arrival on the night-time scene is the Canadian-owned **Shooters,** above the Tulip Tree restaurant just off Mijares at Doblado. The roof terrace is probably the closest you'll find to somewhere to chill out in San José's tropical heat, and the prices should help you keep your cool; you can get two drinks for the price of one every day before 6pm, and there are different special offers every night. (☎146 9900. Live music F-Sa. Open M-F noon-midnight, Sa-Su noon-2am.) **Excala** has pool tables and karaoke every night; the two-for-one offers on beer (Wednesday night) and rum (Thursday night) may increase your confidence but will erode your ability in both. (☎142 5155. Open Su 11am-3am, M-Tu 11am-2am, W-Sa 11am-4am.) **Señor Baco,** on Zaragoza at Guerrero, is an upstairs dance club which also has pool tables and seats overlooking the street below. Beers cost US$2; margaritas are US$3. (Open daily 8pm-midnight or later.)

▓ DAYTRIPS FROM SAN JOSÉ DEL CABO

LOS BARRILES

Águila Malecón "Vía Larga" buses from La Paz to San José del Cabo and Cabo San Lucas stop (5 per day 10am-5:30pm) in Los Barriles (2hr., 60 pesos) and Santiago (2½hr., 80 pesos). Los Barriles and Santiago are also accessible by bus from San José del Cabo.

Aficionados insist that windsurfing at the small town of Los Barriles, where brisk breezes can carry you for several kilometers along the inside of Bahía de Palmas, is the best in Baja. Unsurprisingly, this is creating a *gringo* stronghold on one of the most isolated stretches of the east cape's mountainous coastline. The most popular dive spots are near **Cabo Pulmo** and **Los Frailes,** south of Los Barriles, and separated by secluded beaches and coves. Off Cabo Pulmo, eight fingers of a living coral reef—thought to be 25,000 years old and one of only three in North America—host hundreds of species of fish, crustaceans, and other critters.

Most rooms are in all-inclusive resorts, but camping on the town's vast stretch of beach is free and safe north of the PEMEX station. **Martín Verdugo's Beach Resort Motel ❷** (☎ 141 0054), a block before the laundromat, is a tidy and extensive campground/hotel/restaurant. Full RV hookups (US$13) and tent sites (US$11) include *palapa* shelter, baths, electricity, and pool access. **Little Martín ❹** (no relation), off the *entrada principal* past the little mall, rents basic and not always clean rooms with washing machines and kitchenettes. Most have A/C. (230 pesos; reduced rates for longer stays.) Budget meals are found exclusively at **Tío Pablo's Bar and Grill ❹**, which specializes in massive, tasty burgers (US$6-7). There are also vegetarian dishes. (☎ 141 0330. Open daily 11am-10pm.) **Police** can be found in the **Delegacion Municipal** (☎ 141 0525), and **IMSS** is at the *entrada principal* and 20 de Noviembre (☎ 141 0322; open M-F 8am-2pm and 4-7pm; little English spoken).

SANTIAGO

Santiago is accessible via the same buses that go to Los Barriles (see above), although buses may drop visitors around 2km outside of town.

Little Santiago (pop. 4500) is the prime access point for the nearby **hotsprings** in **Chorro.** Sulfur pools await aching feet, and in high season, the springs are diverted into more luxurious tubs. Follow the main road toward Palomar's Restaurant until it ends, turn right, and continue past the town's zoo for 7km until you arrive in the town of **Agua Caliente.** Bear right at the Casa de Salud and follow this road, keeping to the right at the forks. After 5km, the road ends, and the sulfur smell indicates your arrival. Depending on rainfall levels, you may have to hike upstream for about 40min. to find larger pools; the tranquility and beauty is worth the effort.

NORTHWEST MEXICO

Northwest Mexico is home to raucous border towns, calm fishing villages, vast expanses of desert, and gentle beaches along the alluring Sea of Cortés. For many, the area serves as an introduction to Mexico—full of nights of debauchery, rounds of tequila shots, oversized straw sombreros, and blistering heat. In the midst of all this madness, many tourists overlook the rows of shantytowns and miles of industrial wasteland that consume a large part of the cities. Things calm down considerably as you venture farther south. The grime and frenetic madness of Ciudad Juárez and Nogales, Mexico's brawny border towns, give way to bustling markets, colonial mansions, and a surreal cactus-studded landscape. In some towns, things slow to a virtual standstill—you can hear the flies buzz and the wind whistle through the desert, and you can see *vaqueros* clad in tight jeans swaggering about. You may want to bring a pair of cowboy boots and a sombrero of your own—the rugged terrain requires a lot of stamina, and the *noroeste* sun is merciless.

The Sierra Madre Occidental rips through the heart of Northwest Mexico, creating natural wonders that are overlooked by tourists eager to get to points farther south. To the east of the mountains, the desert and frequent sandstorms give even the larger cities in **Chihuahua** the feel of dusty frontier. Along the coast, in the states of **Sonora** and **Sinaloa,** a blend of commercial ports, quiet fishing villages, and sprawling beaches overlooks the Sea of Cortés. The condominiums, time-shares, and resort hotels looming over the glistening sands mark the presence of US and Canadian expats who have discovered the area's elegant beaches. Land-locked **Durango,** traversed by the Sierra Madres, thrives on mining and is known for its Old West ruggedness. But the most stunning sight in the *noroeste* is the **Barranca del Cobre (Copper Canyon),** a spectacular series of deep gorges and unusual rock formations in Chihuahua brimming with tropical vegetation, all cut through by the Río Urique far below. The caves in the area are home to the reclusive Tarahumara Indians. When it comes to the Northwest, those who look past the border towns and into the region's heartland and coasts will reap the rewards.

HIGHLIGHTS OF NORTHWEST MEXICO

EXPLORE one of Mexico's best-kept secrets, the **Barranca del Cobre** (Copper Canyon; p. 260), and take in some of the most awe-inspiring vistas in the world.

NAP on the beaches of **Bahía Kino** (p. 232), a pair of tiny laid-back fishing towns which share a seemingly endless stretch of palm-lined coast.

TASTE a slice of **Mennonite** life—and their yummy homemade cheese—at one of their many *campos* near the town of **Cuauhtémoc** (p. 252).

SADDLE UP in dusty **Durango** (p. 275), whose rugged surroundings have appeared onscreen in more than 200 classic Western films.

ROLL AROUND in the unbelievably soft sands of **Playa Los Algodones** (Cotton Beach) in seaside **San Carlos** (p. 236).

BRONZE your body and show off your newest bikini on the golden shores of the sumptuous beachside resort of **Mazatlán** (p. 269).

SONORA

NOGALES ☎ 631

There's a restless energy to Nogales (pop. 350,000), which can be both absorbing and unsettling. Walk toward the border during the day and you can feel the tension increase as the streets become awash with gaudy souvenir shops all vying for the daytripper's dollar. The *primer cuadro* welcomes many each day, only to see the vast majority move off in a matter of hours or even minutes. It's hard to imagine

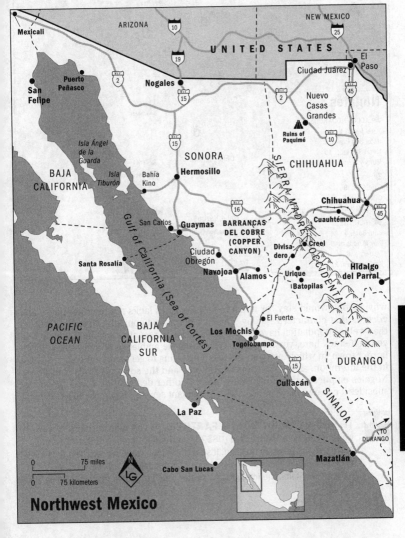

Northwest Mexico

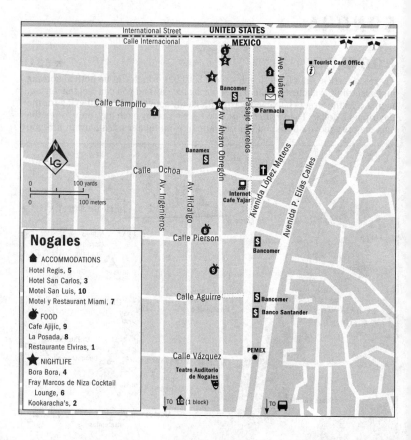

Nogales

🏠 ACCOMMODATIONS
Hotel Regis, **5**
Hotel San Carlos, **3**
Motel San Luis, **10**
Motel y Restaurant Miami, **7**

🍴 FOOD
Cafe Ajijic, **9**
La Posada, **8**
Restaurante Elviras, **1**

⭐ NIGHTLIFE
Bora Bora, **4**
Fray Marcos de Niza Cocktail
    Lounge, **6**
Kookaracha's, **2**

why anyone would stay for much longer; Nogales lacks the pleasant parks and *zócalos* that characterize many Mexican cities, and competition for dollars and the swelling population have raised crime levels in recent years. But if you do find yourself stuck here, you'll be able to soak up the ambience of a classic Mexican border town, in which everyone seems to be trying to get to somewhere else. Late in the afternoon, as the daytrippers go home and the souvenir stalls shut down, Nogales empties eerily. For those without another destination, when the energy subsides it can be a place imbued with a poignant sense of having been left behind.

IF YOU PLAN ON GOING FARTHER. If you plan to travel beyond Nogales, obtain a **tourist card** (US$20; see **Tourist Cards,** p. 10) at the border and have your passport on hand. It's much simpler to get the card here than far-ther south. After you walk across the border through the arched crossing com-plex, turn right into the **immigration center,** the last door in the first building on the right.

TRANSPORTATION

The sleek, modern **bus terminal** (☎313 1603, 313 5401, or 313 1703) is on Carretera Internacional, 4.5km south of the town center, with a fast food outlet, pharmacy (7am-11pm), luggage storage (5 pesos per hour), and call center with fax, copy and Internet facilities (20 pesos per hour). Next to the pharmacy is the **taxi** kiosk (60 pesos to the center of town). If you're not in a hurry, white buses marked "Central Camionera" do the journey (4 pesos). They go from a plaza at the end of the block—from the bus station, cross the main road, turn left and walk to the junction; downtown Nogales is the last stop. This service stops around 7pm. For the return journey, buses line up along López Mateos between Campillo and Ochoa; if in doubt, ask for the bus to "el Central." You can also catch it at any of the blue stops along López Mateos, which merges with Obregón on its way south.

Buses leave the main station for: **Mexico City** (34hr., 7 per day, 1160 pesos); **Puerto Peñasco** (7hr., 4pm, 225 pesos); **Tijuana** (12hr.; 10am, 1, 7, 8:30pm; 385 pesos) via **San Luis** (8hr.) and **Mexicali** (9hr.); and **Guadalajara** (26hr., 10 per day, 841 pesos) via **Hermosillo** (4hr.), **Obregón** (8hr.), **Los Mochis** (11hr.), **Culiacán** (15hr.), **Mazatlán** (18hr.), and **Tepic** (22hr.). The last route down the west coast of Sonora is also well served by a number of carriers operating from stations just up the road towards Nogales, such as **Estrellas de Pacífico, Tufesa** (which offers discounts of 25% to students and 50% to those over 60 and children 2-8) and **TBA** (which also offers a 3pm service to **Puerto Peñasco**; 5hr.). You can stock up on provisions for the journey at **Oxxo,** a 24-hour supermarket next to TBA.

If you're heading north into Arizona, Greyhound's partner **Crucero** has buses to **Tucson** (1 hr., 8 per day, US$8), though you'll probably find it more convenient to walk across the border, where a Greyhound terminal has departures on the same route. (midnight, 3:45, 4:45, 7:15, 8:45am, 1:30, 5:30, 7:45pm.)

ORIENTATION AND PRACTICAL INFORMATION

Nogales stretches up into chaotic hillside *barrios*, but the grid of the small *primer cuadro* area, where tourists are likely to spend most of their time, is fairly easy to navigate. **Calle Internacional** is the first of the streets running east to west, parallel to the corrugated iron fence which marks the frontier. If you come across the border on foot, you'll find yourself walking from north to south on **Pesquiera;** west of this, **Juárez** (home to the main concentration of budget hotels), **Morelos** (a narrow alley for pedestrians and stallholders only), **Obregón** (the main tourist drag), **Hidalgo,** and **Ingenieros** are all also perpendicular to the border. If you come from Arizona by car, you'll be on **López Mateos,** which runs at an oblique angle to the north-south avenues and cuts into the grid, merging with Juárez, Morelos, and, eventually, Obregón. Shadowing López Mateos to the east is **Elías Calles,** the northbound road. These two major thoroughfares eventually reach the main bus terminal on the southern edge of town. **The tourist office cautions that the *barrios* on both sides of the *primer cuadro* are unsafe and should be given a wide berth.**

Tourist Office: (☎312 0666) next to the immigration center, to your left walking in from the US. The staff is helpful and friendly, albeit somewhat surprised if you express any interest in Nogales itself. Basic maps available. Open daily 9am-5pm.

Currency Exchange: The *primer cuadro* contains a number of **banks** and **Casas de Cambio,** most of which line López Mateos and Obregón. **Banamex** (☎312 0780 or 312 5505) is on Ochoa between Hidalgo and Obregón. Open M-F 9am-4pm. All exchange dollars and traveler's checks and have 24hr. **ATMs.**

Luggage Storage: At the bus terminal. 5 pesos per hr.

Emergency: ☎060.

Police: (☎312 0104 or 312 1104) at González and Leal. Some English spoken.

Red Cross: (☎312 5808) at Elías Calles and Providencia. Open 24hr.

Medical Assistance: Hospital Básico (☎313 0794), about 3km south of the border on Obregón. English spoken. Open 24hr.

Pharmacy: Comercial 3 en 1 Farmacia, Campillo 73 (☎312 5503), on the corner with Morelos. Doubles as a liquor store. Open 24hr.

Fax: Telecomm, above the post office, or the communications booth in the central bus station.

Internet: Yajar, upstairs on the corner of Morelos and Ochoa. (20 pesos per hr. Printers also available.) **Amigos en Red,** López Mateos 258, is more expensive (30 pesos per hr.), but has cheaper weekend rates. (☎312 3978. Open M-F 9am-9pm, Sa-Su 11am-8pm.) There's also Internet access at the bus station (20 pesos per hour).

Post Office: Juárez 52 (☎312 1247). Open M-F 8am-5:30pm. **Telecomm** in the same building. **Postal Code:** 84001.

▶ ACCOMMODATIONS

Nogales's position on the border guarantees it more visitors than might otherwise be expected, and at times its accommodation facilities can be stretched. The high demand has raised the quality of what's available; unfortunately, it has also raised prices. The most obvious concentration of "budget" hotels is near the border crossing on Juárez; options further afield may have more vacancies.

Motel y Restaurant Miami (☎312 5450 or 312 5470), Ingenieros at Campillo. From the border crossing, turn left onto Campillo, cross Juárez, and walk another four short blocks. Friendly place offering large rooms with clean bath, TV, telephone, and overly enthusiastic A/C. Restaurant attached. The rooms on the upper floors have views out over the town to the border fence and beyond. Singles 300 pesos; doubles 320 pesos. 50 pesos for each additional person. 100 pesos deposit for key and TV remote. ❺

Hotel Regis (☎312 5181, 312 5580, or 312 5509), between Internacional and Campillo. Clean rooms with A/C, phone, and TV. Sink into the comfy leather couches in the lobby. Reservations necessary. Singles 375 pesos; doubles 400 pesos. MC/V. ❺

Hotel San Carlos, Juárez 22 (☎312 1346 or 312 1409; fax 312 1557), between Internacional and Campillo. Spacious, clean rooms have A/C, cable TV, high-pressure showers, and phones. Mingle with the ever-present locals watching TV in the lobby. Reservations recommended. Singles 250 pesos; doubles 290 pesos. MC/V. ❺

Motel San Luis, (☎312 4170, 312 4219, or 312 4035; fax 312 4060), on the corner of González and Ingenieros. Clearly signposted from Elías Calles and Obregón. Arranged around a central courtyard opening onto C. Flores, this motel offers rooms similar to the lodgings crowded along Juárez in a less-touristed part of town. Singles 320 pesos; doubles 355 pesos. MC/V. ❺

▶ FOOD

Nogales is home to several high-priced restaurants catering to daytrippers from the US. If tourist pricing is driving you crazy, you could do as the locals do and head for the **plaza** on López Mateos at Ochoa, where vendors entice your tastebuds with an array of fruits and *tortas* for rock-bottom prices. For a truly economical meal, look no further than the tiny makeshift counters a few steps off of Obregón, where local families offer up excellent traditional *antojitos* (5-20 pesos).

Restaurante Elviras, Obregón 1 (☎312 4743). Elviras is a curiously alluring place: a peaceful courtyard just a few yards from a major international border and right next to a club which shatters the tranquility from 8pm onwards. There's also lots of space inside, where the decor and low neon lighting stay just the right side of kitsch. The menu includes traditional Mexican dishes, steak, and seafood specialities, including the tasty, award-winning *pescado elvira*. Almost exclusively tourist clientele, with prices to match. Entrees US$9-15. Open daily 9am-11pm. MC/V. ❺

La Posada Restaurante, Pierson 116 (☎312 0439), west of Obregón. Bustling, family-run place, with the father figure Rodolfo sternly presiding over proceedings and greeting the (predominantly male) local regulars who come here for the hearty breakfasts. The dining room is colorfully decorated with Mexican art and handicrafts. Omelettes and egg dishes 25-40 pesos. Open daily 7:30am-10pm. ❸

Cafe Ajijíc, Obregón 182 (☎312 5074). The terrace features tiled tables, a picturesque fountain, and live musicians belting out popular Mexican tunes. Less memorable for the food than for the huge, tantalizing selection of coffees (15-22 pesos). Entrees 50-60 pesos. Open daily 8am-midnight. English spoken. MC/V. ❹

El Marcos Bar and Grill (☎313 8082 or 313 8092), on Boulevard El Greco up the hill from the cluster of smaller bus stations on the edge of town. If the bus timetable leaves you with hours to kill and a stomach to fill, El Marcos provides a chance to treat yourself rather than settle for the mediocre snacks at the main terminal. Appetizers are around US$6, while the mouth-watering selection of steaks averages US$13.50. ❺

🔊 NIGHTLIFE AND ENTERTAINMENT

Despite the rather half-hearted attempts of the tourist bureau to pass off the statue of Juárez, the industrial park, and even the border crossing itself as attractions, there isn't much in the way of museums or other cultural excitement to entice you in Nogales. Most of the Arizonans who come over for the day do so in search of bargain prices on pharmaceuticals and Mexican trinkets, either in the crowded area around Obregón, Campillo, and Morelos, or in a more genteel, air-conditioned setting like the El Greco building on the corner of Obregón and Pierson. Merchandise is priced in anticipation of haggling, so confidence and knowledge of the goods can get you great deals. Shops farther from the border on Obregón are less exclusively aimed at the tourist crowd.

If earthenware curios don't set your heart aflame, **Cinemas Gemelos,** Obregón 368 (☎312 5002), between González and Torres (not to be confused with the chain store of the same name further up Obregón), shows recent American films dubbed or subtitled in Spanish (40 pesos). For those seeking a bit of culture, the spacious modern **Teatro Auditorio de Nogales,** Obregón 286 (☎312 4180), between Vázquez and González, seats just under 1000 and stages theatre, music, dance, and other events. Call or visit for showtimes and prices; the calendar is posted on the door.

If Tequila is a must, Nogales's nightlife may have something to offer. Right after lunch, the bars on Obregón open their doors to a mix of locals and tourists, and by 10pm on Friday or Saturday, walking through the crowds is nearly impossible.

Kookaracha's, Obregón 1 (☎312 4773). Dance the night away and down tequila shots (US$2), or just chill with a *cerveza* (US$2) on the balcony overlooking the border and the fountain in the Roach's techno-colored courtyard. For open bar, go on W, when the cover charge is US$15. Open W and F-Sa 9pm-3am.

Bora Bora, Obregón 38, a large, dingy room between Campillo and Internacional offers live music nightly after 9pm. Enjoy 1 free drink on Sundays; beer and mixed drinks are 10 pesos. Open W-Su noon-3am.

Fray Marcos de Niza Cocktail Lounge (☎312 1112), at Obregón and Campillo. If all you're looking for is a chance to drown your sorrows as you mull over the fallout of US-Mexican trade relations, Fray Marcos may fit the bill. Alternatively you can just sit back on the comfy leather couches and watch baseball on the big-screen TV. Beer US$2. Open daily 11am-1am.

PUERTO PEÑASCO   ☎638

Puerto Peñasco (pop. 40,000) is home to incredible stretches of rocky coastline interspersed with spotless sandy beaches. It's also become home to a large community of US retirees and a favorite getaway for thousands of spring break revellers and weekenders. Once a launching pad for shrimp boats, the town dried up when overfishing decimated the shrimp population in the Sea of Cortés, and it now depends heavily on tourism. Nor does the trend show any sign of abating; with the creation of huge new timeshare developments and a major golf course, Puerto Peñasco—or "Rocky Point," as it has been renamed by its regular visitors—looks set to become increasingly prosperous and exclusive in the next few years. Despite the throngs of Americans, the magnificent Sea of Cortés, the swaying palms, and the pristine beaches make for a beautiful—if not exactly tranquil—retreat, particularly during the week, when the hotels empty and the place can start to feel like the last great Arizonan ghost town. It's also an attractive base from which to launch an expedition into the mysterious wilderness of the Pinacate National Biosphere Reserve.

▐ TRANSPORTATION

Puerto Peñasco's main interstate bus terminal is on Constitución, one block away from its intersection with Juárez and a short walk from budget lodgings on Calle 13 and Playa Hermosa. To get to the accommodations, turn right as you leave the bus station and follow the road until you reach a large crossroads with a Santander Serfin bank; turn right onto Calle 13. **Autotransportes de Baja California** (☎383 1999) goes to: **Ensenada** (10hr., 368 pesos); **La Paz** (34 hr., 1261 pesos); **Mexicali** (5hr., 198 pesos); **Tecate** (6hr., 287 pesos); and **Tijuana** (8hr., 309 pesos). All buses are *de paso* and there are only four departures per day (1am, 8:30am, 1pm, 5pm). The 1am bus (whose prices are slightly higher) goes as far as Tijuana (via Mexicali and Tecate), the 8:30am heads to every destination listed above, the 1pm goes to Ensenada (via Mexicali and Tecate) and the 5pm goes only to Mexicali.

For travel within Sonora, you need to go several blocks farther out along Juárez to its intersection with Calle 24; turn right and walk another block. There **Transportes Norte de Sonora** (☎383 3640) can transport you to **Hermosillo** (7hr., 4 per day, 130 pesos) and **Nogales** (5 hr., 1:30am). Next door is **Transporte Mota's Place** (☎383 3640), which offers service to Phoenix (4hr., 5 per day, US$40).

✳❓ ORIENTATION AND PRACTICAL INFORMATION

Puerto Peñasco is a small town, but it can end up feeling large since its visitor attractions are surprisingly (and exhaustingly) spread out. The oldest and most labyrinthine area of town is also the smallest: the **Old Port,** crowded onto the small hook of land in Peñasco's southwest corner. On the other side of the harbor is the most concentrated tourist drag, **Calle 13,** leading out towards **Playa Hermosa.** To the north and east of Calle 13 is the gridded main body of the town and the area

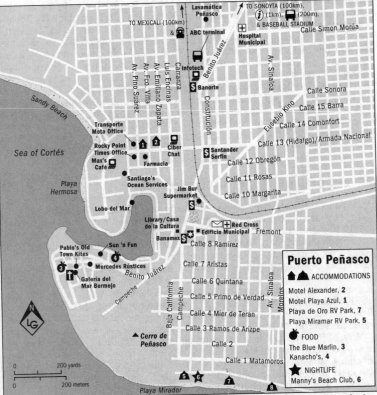

least frequented by foreigners. Farther along the coast to the east, the exclusive enclave of **Las Conchas** continues to grow. Tying most of these loose ends together is **Benito Juárez**, which enters at the northeast from Sonoyta, cuts across the residential area's grid, crosses Calle 13, and passes through a town center of sorts at the intersection with **Fremont**. South of here the road splits: the branch called **Campeche** drops down towards the RV parks near **Playa Miramar**, while Juárez swings round to the west and loops back on itself to lasso the Old Port, briefly becoming the seafront *malecón* in the process.

Unfortunately, the **tourist office**, Juárez 320, is on the edge of town least frequented by tourists, just beyond Juárez's intersection with Calle 32. (☎383 6122. Not always open during its stated hours M-F 9am-2pm and 3-5pm.) You'd be much better off dropping into a hotel or bar to pick up a free copy of *The Rocky Point Times* or *Join Us*; most of these tourist guides contain decent maps. **Bancomer,** on Juárez and Estrella, exchanges currency and traveler's checks. (☎383 2430. Open M-F 8:30am-4pm, Sa 10am-2pm.) **Banamex,** on Juárez just south of Fremont, provides the same services. (☎383 2582. Open M-F 8:30am-4:30pm.) Both have 24hr. **ATMs.** The **police** are at Fremont and Juárez (☎383 2110. Little English spoken.), and the **Red Cross** (☎383 2266) is at Fremont and Chiapas. The **Hospital Municipal** is on Morúa and Juárez. (☎383 2110. Little English spoken.) A 24hr. **pharmacy** is on Calle 13 across the road from the Hotel Playa Azúl. Stock up on snacks and bottled water at **Supermarket Jim Bur,** on Juárez in the Jim Bur Plaza. (☎383 2561. Open Su 8am-4pm, M-Sa 8am-9pm.) For laundry, locate **Lavamática Peñasco,** on Constitución across from Hotel Paraíso del Desierto. (☎383 6170. Open Su 9am-2pm, M-Sa 8am-7pm. 50 pesos per load.) Peñasco has several Internet cafes, including **Ciber Chat** on Luis Encinas, one block away from Calle 13; (Open Su-Th 9am-11pm, F-Sa 9am-3am. 10 pesos per hour.) and **Max's Cafe,** opposite Hotel Plaza Las Glorias. (☎383 1011. Open daily 8am-3pm. Internet use free for customers eating at Max's.) The *Rocky Point Times* office, on Pino Suárez just off Calle 13, has a **book exchange** and free **drop-off US mail service.** (☎383 6325. Mailbags go to the post office in Lukeville, Arizona on W.) If you prefer the Mexican postal system, the **post office** is hidden around a corner on Chiapas, off Fremont two blocks east of Juárez. (☎383 2350. Open M-F 8am-3pm.) A **fax** service is available in the same building. (☎383 2782. Open M-F 8am-2:30pm, Sa 8am-11:30pm.) **Postal code:** 83550.

ACCOMMODATIONS AND CAMPING

As expensive resorts, condos and time-shares take Puerto Peñasco upscale, budget rooms are becoming a rare commodity. To make things worse, rates rise US$10-15 during spring break. The cheapest way to spend the night is to camp in a trailer park around Playa Miramar. **Playa Miramar RV Park ❷,** at the southern end of Campeche, rents scenic spots year-round with cable TV, full hookup, and spectacular views. Washers, dryers, and showers are available. (☎383 2587. 1-2 people US$14, each additional person US$2; weekly US$85; beachfront spaces slightly higher.) Along the same stretch of beach is **Playa de Oro ❸.** (☎383 2668; 1-2 people US$17, beachfront US$20). Camping is permitted northwest of the Playa Boruta Resort on Sandy Beach all the way down to La Choya. Camping at trailer parks is safer; sleeping on the beach is not recommended unless you're with a large group.

Most of Peñasco's budget hotels are on or around Calle 13, which makes this area a good base for your stay. Unfortunately, fellow travelers have the same idea, so choose somewhere slightly set back from the action. A good option is **Motel Alexander ❺,** Emiliano Zapata 89, just off Calle 13 three blocks from the railway crossing. This small motel offers just the right combination of convenience and seclusion. Arranged around a courtyard, the rooms offer A/C, TV, and hot and cold water in the private bathrooms. (☎383 3749. Singles US$30, additional person US$45; suites US$60.) **Motel Playa Azul ❻,** Calle 13 and Suárez, is about two blocks from Playa Hermosa and offers nicely furnished, clean rooms with cable TV, generous A/C, free bottled water, and private baths. (☎383 6296. Singles US$25; doubles US$35; prices rise US$5 on weekends.)

FOOD

As you might expect from a resort town, Puerto Peñasco has no shortage of tourist-oriented restaurants selling middle-of-the-road *burritos* and *enchiladas,* or of more informal stalls doing the same at lower prices and greater risk to your stomach. There are plenty of these along Calle 13, along with some acceptable Chinese food, but the real draw in Puerto Peñasco is the seafood, at its freshest and most delicious in the Old Port. **Kanacho's ❺,** Recinto Portuario and C. Lauro Contreras Ojeda, is a family restaurant serving succulent fresh seafood dishes with a Mexican twist. The restaurant is off to the right as you head towards the Old Port on Juárez, opposite Sun-n-Fun. (cell ☎383 867798. Open M, W-Su 9am-6pm. Entrees 70-120 pesos.) A slightly cheaper option renowned for its fish tacos is **The Blue Marlin ❹,** in the Old Port half a block back from *malecón.* (☎383 3614. Open daily 9:30am-5:30pm. Tacos US$6 each.)

◎ ☞ SIGHTS AND BEACHES

Most people—and it's a *lot* of people in high season—come to Puerto Peñasco for the beaches and their warm, turquoise water. **Sandy Beach** and **Playa Hermosa** are the best choices for swimming; both have curio shops, restaurants, and hotels galore. To reach Sandy Beach, head north on Encinas or Juárez until the intersection with Camino a Bahía Choya, 2km north of Fremont. Turn left and follow the souvenir shops and bars until you see signs that say "To Sandy Beach." To get to Playa Hermosa, turn right on Calle 13 when heading south on Juárez; the beach is straight ahead five or six blocks down, but you'll have to veer right around the wall of luxury hotels. The beaches around **Miramar** and **Las Conchas,** at the southern end of town, are less crowded but also rockier, rougher, and less suited to swimming. To reach Playa Miramar, head south on Juárez, and take a left onto Campeche near the Benito Juárez monument. Continue uphill for three blocks; Playa Miramar is straight ahead. To reach Playa Las Conchas, head south on Juárez, turn left on Fremont after Bancomer, take a right onto Camino a las Conchas, and follow the rock-slab road for 3km. **Jeff and Audrey Reeco,** who operate out of La Galería de Mariano and the adjoining yard, across the street from Thrifty Ice Cream on Victor Estrella/C. 1 de Julio in the Old Port, rent sea kayaks (single US$35 per day; double US$45) and boogie boards (US$10 per day). Multi-day and group discounts can be negotiated. (☎383 6209 or 383 2007; www.rockypointgangas.com. Open 9:30am-6pm.) **Sun n' Fun,** a very friendly and respected American-run dive shop on Juárez at the entrance to the Old Port, will charter boats for various excursions if enough people are interested. (☎383 5450. Open Su 8am-5pm, M-Th 8am-6pm, F-Sa 8am-7pm.) The shop offers fishing trips (½-day or full day all-inclusive, US$35-70), whale-watching (3hr., US$30, in season), sunset cruises (2hr., US$25), and guided dives. (5hr., US$50.) You can also talk directly to some of the boat companies which do such trips regularly, such as **Lobo del Mar** (☎383 2802) or **Santiago's Ocean Services** (☎383 5834), both a couple blocks behind Keno's on Calle 13.

A pleasant time can also be had wandering around the **Old Port,** which heaves with tourists on weekends but is much more genteel during the week. It's not exactly the quaint fishing village it once was, but it's still the most intriguing part of town. The **Malecón** is undergoing extensive renovations but should eventually provide a lovely promenade with fabulous views over the Sea of Cortés. Much of the other side of the road is occupied by generic souvenir shops, but there are some more idiosyncratic options for browsing further away from the *gringo* crowd. **Galería del Mar Bermejo,** Av. Estevan Pivac 11, tucked behind the church, offers Mata Ortiz Pottery by named artists, paintings, and books about Mexican art. (☎383 3488. Open M-Tu and Th-Su 9:30am-5pm.) Farther up the hill and across the street is **Pablo's Old Town Kites,** and around the corner at the intersection of Circunvalación and Alcantar is **Mercedes Rústicos,** where giant metal sculptures poke their heads out onto the sidewalk.

♫ ENTERTAINMENT

Nightlife in Puerto Peñasco goes from bustling to boring. Calle 13, Campeche, and the *malecón* all host a ridiculous number of bars, pool halls, *discotecas*, and some raunchier establishments, most of which are full and lively during spring break and on weekends. During the week, you may have to settle for exchanging fishing stories with US retirees. Manny's Beach Club, Playa Mirador, is a favorite among the spring break crowd for chilling by day or partying by night. (☎383 3605. Open daily 7am-11pm, F-Sa until 3am. Karaoke Th-Su nights. Margaritas US$3, beers US$2.25; no cover.)

THE LOCAL LEGEND

LOST IN SPACE

Faced with Pinacate's strange and mysterious landscapes, many visitors find themselves reaching for comparisons to otherworldly locales, such as the moon. While such a comparison might seem fanciful, they are not the only ones to have made it: NASA clearly detected a parallel, and in 1970 the crew of Apollo 14 was sent here on an exercise designed to accustom them to a landscape alien to anything they might have encountered before. Astronauts tested their skills in the Molina Crater. Apparently, the crew couldn't resist the temptation to leave their mark; staff members can show you a photograph of some graffiti, scratched on a rock in the desert by the crew.

The reserve has always caused people to think of worlds beyond Earth, and there have even been UFO sightings in the area. Regular visitors to the park insist that on some nights it is possible to see lights hovering on the horizon to the north and to hear mysterious noises from the same direction. The probable explanation? A training exercise by another American crew: the US Air Force maintains a base in the Arizona desert, and their exercises are sometimes visible and audible from Pinacate.

You can see photographs of astronauts Edgar Mitchell and Alan Shepard during training at Pinacate by following the links to the Apollo 14 mission at www.apolloarchive.com.

If you don't like the club scene, you could go to the other end of town and catch the Tiburones, Peñasco's **baseball** team, in action. The stadium is on your right as you go up Juárez away from the town center, at 25th street. (Season runs Apr.-Aug. or Sept. Games F-Su 8pm. Tickets 30 pesos.)

⚡ DAYTRIPS FROM PUERTO PEÑASCO

MARINE BIOLOGY CENTERS (CETMAR AND CEDO)

*Two research centers are located just outside of Puerto Peñasco. The **Center for Technological Sea Studies (CETMAR)** is 4km from the center of town on the Las Conchas road. (☎382 0010. Open daily 10am-5pm. Adults US$3, children US$1.) The **Intercultural Center for the Study of Deserts and Oceans (CEDO)**, is 3km farther down the road. (☎382 0113; www.cedointercultural.org. Visitor center and gift shop open Su 10am-2pm, M-Sa 9am-5pm. Free.) Both are difficult to visit without a car. Taxis run from Puerto Peñasco to CETMAR (30 pesos) and CEDO (up to 100 pesos).*

CETMAR operates a small aquarium consisting of a single room with a series of somewhat dirty open tanks. Some visitors may be distressed by the cramped conditions in which the aquarium keeps exhibits such as the large sea turtles and the sea lions at the back, which visitors are allowed to feed. There are also open pools on the floor, from which the curator may fish out dripping invertebrates for your viewing pleasure. For better or for worse, CETMAR provides a rare opportunity to see these creatures and a great many smaller species such as crabs, shrimp, sea horses, snails, and sea urchins, in close quarters.

CEDO gives free guided tours of its wet lab and has a 55ft. whale skeleton standing outside. CEDO has served for over 20 years as a research station in this fascinating and vulnerable bioregion and also engages in a full program of educational activities. The center is currently still developing its visitor center, which was uniquely constructed using only sand, cement, and recycled materials. In the meantime, tourists can enjoy the small botanical garden and informative talks on local marine life. (Tu 2pm and Sa 4pm. In English.) However, the main attraction is CEDO's exciting ⚑**Eco-Adventures** program, which organizes spectacular, expertly-guided nature excursions to neighboring sites. (Offered during spring and fall. Reservations required. Excursions US$15-85.) If you have your own transport, you can detour to the Morúa Estuary, which is home to one of Puerto Peñasco's best-kept secrets: a small **oyster farm** where you can enjoy delicious *ceviche* and oysters so fresh that you have to remember to tip the seawater out of them before eating.

EL PINACATE

Guides are necessary. For information about tours, ask at the tourist office or call CEDO's Eco-Adventures. (☎ 382 0113. Tours available in spring and fall. See above listing.) If you do decide to go it alone, 4WD high-clearance vehicles with partially deflated tires are a must, as are tons of water, a shovel, a spare tire, a compass, and firewood. Camping is permitted, although spaces are limited and reservations are not taken. The ideal time to visit is Nov.-Mar., when temperatures range 15 to 32°C, as opposed to summer months, when the daytime temperatures can often exceed 47°C. Free, but donations accepted.

Forty-eight kilometers north of Puerto Peñasco on Mex. 8 lies the El Pinacate volcanic preserve, one of the largest and most spectacular biospheres in the world. Created in June 1993 to limit rock excavation and protect endangered species, El Pinacate encompasses more than four million acres and extends from the Sea of Cortés to the Arizona border, where it becomes the Cabeza Prieta National Wildlife Refuge and the Organ Pipe National Monument. Within this space, the landscape ranges from vast dunes to nine huge craters, the most spectacular of which, El Elegante, is 1600m across and 250m deep. The visitor's lasting memory, however, is likely to be the awesome emptiness and almost lunar strangeness of the volcanic desert, strewn with ash and pock-marked with around 400 cinder cones.

Visitors are required to register at the Visitors' Center, which is the group of orange-roofed buildings on the left of Mex. 8 coming from Puerto Peñasco. The knowledgeable staff will be able to offer you advice for your visit, maps of the reserve, printed interpretative guides to the major trails, and safety information regarding natural hazards. There are also videos and exhibits.

HERMOSILLO ☎ 662

Once an indigenous settlement named Pitic (meaning "where two rivers meet"), Hermosillo gained its modern name in 1828 as a tribute to General José María González Hermosillo, the man credited with bringing the Revolutionary spirit to Sonora. A sprawling metropolitan center of commerce and education, the capital of Sonora state entices visitors with imposing government palaces, beautiful murals, huge manicured parks, a glorious cathedral, and an ecological research center and zoo. Not all of Hermosillo (pop. 1,000,000) is, however, so alluring. The crowded,

THE LOCAL LEGEND

IN THE DESERT

While welcoming visitors to come and see the Pinacate Biosphere, the reserve's staff rarely shies from stressing the dangers of making a trip without adequate equipment—principally meaning a suitable vehicle and plentiful supplies of water and food. Their warnings are not heeded by all, but those who choose not to follow their advice are not all devil-may-care adventurers.

The Pinacate area has famously held great significance for the people of the Tohono O'odham Nation, and according to an ancient ritual, adolescent boys, guided by shamans, would cross the barren expanse, surviving only on water retained in natural rock tanks. Exhausted by this formidable journey, they were then made to run across the beaches. The accompanying light-headed semi-consciousness was taken as a sign of spiritual nirvana. If they completed the rite successfully, the men were allowed to marry. Those who passed out from exhaustion were left to die. To this day, members of the Tohono O'odham Nation cross the desert on foot from their own reserve in Arizona to bathe in the waters of the Sea of Cortés, which they believe to be sacred and have healing properties. Their practices are still, however, shrouded in mystery, since all who are not members of the Nation are excluded from the park while these rituals are taking place.

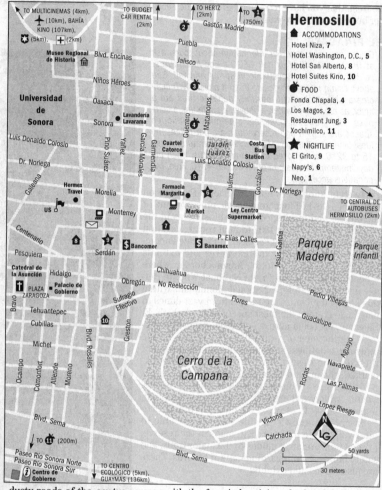

Hermosillo

🏠 ACCOMMODATIONS
Hotel Niza, **7**
Hotel Washington, D.C., **5**
Hotel San Alberto, **8**
Hotel Suites Kino, **10**

🍴 FOOD
Fonda Chapala, **4**
Los Magos, **2**
Restaurant Jung, **3**
Xochimilco, **11**

⭐ NIGHTLIFE
El Grito, **9**
Napy's, **6**
Neo, **1**

dusty roads of the *centro* scream with the frenzied activity of urban life, and, by sundown, little more than garbage lines the streets. Many visitors breeze through on their way to the more glamorous towns and beaches to the south, giving Hermosillo only a passing glance. Although parts of the city can be unsavory, those who choose to spend a day are in for a pleasant surprise.

⬛ TRANSPORTATION

Airport: (☎261 0008), 10km west of town on Transversal toward Bahía Kino. To get there, take a small red bus from the bus station (4 pesos) or catch a taxi (70 pesos). **Aeroméxico** (☎218 0612) goes to: **Guadalajara** (2hr., 4 per day); **Mexico City** (2½hr., 8 per day); **Tijuana** (1hr., 2 per day). **Aero California** (☎260 2555) will take you to **La Paz** (1hr., 1 per day) or **Los Angeles, CA** (1½hr., 1 per day).

NORTHWEST MEXICO

Buses: 2km east of the city center on Encinas. To get from the station to town, catch a "Centro" bus (every 10min. 5am-8pm, 4 pesos). To take a **taxi**, you must pre-pay by purchasing a *boleto* for your destination. Prices vary by destination, but a trip to the *centro* comes in at around 40 pesos. One of the two receipts is for the driver. To get back to the station from the *centro*, wait for a bus at Elías Calles and Matamoros, across from Óptica Morfín. **Transportes Norte de Sonora** (☎213 0610) goes to: **Chihuahua** (12hr., 591 pesos); **Ciudad Juárez** (11hr., 6:30pm, 530 pesos); **Mazatlán** (12hr., 443 pesos); **Mexico City** (31hr., 1045 pesos). **Élite** (☎213 4050) sends buses every hr. to nearby cities including: **Caborca** (4hr., 46 pesos); **Guaymas** (2hr., 96 pesos); **Nogales** (3½hr., 179 pesos).

■ ? ORIENTATION AND PRACTICAL INFORMATION

Hermosillo lies 271km south of the border on **Mex. 15,** the main highway connecting the western US and central Mexico. Most of the activity in Hermosillo occurs inside the *centro*, the area bordered by **Rosales** on the west, **Juárez** on the east, **Serdán** on the south, and **Encinas** on the north.

TOURIST AND FINANCIAL SERVICES

Tourist Office: (☎800 716 2555; US 800-476-6672), on the 3rd fl. of **Centro de Gobierno** at Cultura and Comonfort. Walk south on Rosales over the highway, turn right, and walk 1 block west to the big pink building on the right. Open M-F 8am-3pm.

Banks: Banks line Encinas and Serdán. **Banamex** (☎214 7615), on Serdán at Matamoros, has a 24hr. **ATM.** Open M-F 8:30am-4:30pm, Sa 9am-3:30pm.

American Express: Hermex Travel (☎213 9371), on Rosales at Monterrey. Open M-F 8:30am-1pm and 3-6:30pm, Sa 9am-1pm.

LOCAL SERVICES

Supermarket: Ley Centro (☎217 3294), Juárez at Morelia. Open daily 6:30am-10pm.

Laundry: Lavandería Lavarama (☎217 5501), on Sonora at Yañez. Wash 22 pesos per 3.5kg, dry 16 pesos. Open Su 8am-2pm, M-Sa 8am-8pm.

Car Rental: Budget (☎214 3033), Garmendia 46 and Tamaulipas. Open M-F 8am-6pm, Sa-Su 8am-3pm. **Hertz** (☎212 1695), Rodríguez and Guerrero. Open M-F 8am-6pm, Sa-Su 8am-3pm.

EMERGENCY AND COMMUNICATIONS

Emergency: ☎080 or 066.

Police: (☎218 5564), at Periférico Nte. and Solidaridad. Some English spoken.

Tourist helpline: ☎800 903 9200.

Consulates: US (☎217 2382 or 24hr. 217 2375), on Monterrey between Galeana and Rosales. Open M-F 9am-4pm.

Red Cross: (☎065 or 214 0010), on Encinas at 14 de Abril. English-speaking staff on hand 9am-5pm.

Pharmacy: Farmacia Margarita, Morelia 93 (☎213 1590), at Guerrero. Open 24hr.

Hospital: (☎259 2590 or 259 2523), on Transversal at Reyes. English spoken.

Fax: Telecomm (☎217 2150), in the same building as the post office on the Rosales side. Open Su 9am-12:30pm, M-F 8am-7pm, Sa 8:30am-4pm.

Internet Access: C@fe Internet, Morelia 109C (☎213 1368), between Garmendia and Guerrero. Offers an excellent connection for 10 pesos per hr. Open M-Sa 9am-9pm. **Suministros Computacionales VETA,** Monterrey 86 (☎212 7987 or 213 5987; fax 213 1091), between Pino Suárez and Rosales. 15 pesos per hr. Open M-Sa 9am-6pm.

Post Office: (☎212 0011), on Elías Calles at Rosales. Open M-F 9am-3pm, Sa 9am-1pm. **Postal Code:** 83000.

ACCOMMODATIONS

In Hermosillo, low prices tend to come at the expense of cleanliness, with one notable exception.

▨ **Hotel Washington, D.C.,** Dr. Noriega 68 Pte. (☎213 1183), between Matamoros and Guerrero. Almost too good to be true, the D.C. boasts comfortable beds, sparkling rooms, warm showers, A/C, English-language advice, free coffee, a communal refrigerator, ironing board, and microwave. Room with queen sized bed 160 pesos; room with 2 single beds 175 pesos; 20 pesos for each additional person. ❸

Hotel Suites Kino, Suárez 151 Sur (☎800 711 5460, 213 3131, or 213 3183; www.hotelsuiteskino.com). A step above budget. Hang out with business travelers around the pool table and restaurant/bar. All rooms have cable TV, powerful A/C, phone, and nice bathrooms. Free parking and swimming pool. Reservations recommended. Singles from 300 pesos; doubles from 395 pesos. ❺

Hotel San Alberto (☎213 1840), at Rosales and Serdán. From the corner, walk up the length of the dark brown hotel building and turn left into the parking lot. An oasis complete with A/C, rustic furniture, magazines, TV, and phone. Free parking and swimming pool. Singles 324 pesos; doubles 344 pesos. ❺

Hotel Niza, Elías Calles 66 (☎217 2028), between Guerrero and Garmendia. Rooms have A/C, TV, and comfortable beds (but uncomfortably dim lights). Private baths are small and not always the cleanest, but Niza's central location makes it a decent choice for those just looking for a place to sleep. A lobby restaurant serves *menú del día* (21 pesos). Singles 150 pesos; doubles 200 pesos. ❸

FOOD

Like most major cities, Hermosillo offers a wide range of dining options, the best of which feature local specialties like *carne asada* and that most Sonoran of dishes, *cabrito* (baby goat—no kidding). On the sweeter side of things, Hermosillans delight in *coyotas*, or cookies filled with molasses. For cheap refueling, head for the **taco and torta places** ❶ around Serdán and Guerrero, where *taquitos* and quesadillas cost 7-8 pesos and *comida corrida* goes for 15-20 pesos. If you feel brave, the food counters lining **Mercado Municipal** on Elías Calles, between Matamoros and Guerrero, cook up tasty and very cheap *antojitos*. Most are sufficiently sanitary, but avoid eating any uncooked vegetables. If you're bored of burritos, consider **Fook Lam Moon** ❹, Rosales 91, which offers a wide selection of Chinese dishes. (42-69 pesos. ☎212 7717. Open M-Sa noon-11:30pm.)

Xochimilco, Obregón 51 (☎250 4089 or 250 4052; restaurantxochimilco.tripod.com). Walk down Rosales and, after crossing the highway, turn right. Continue past the long green school building and turn left; the restaurant is 400m ahead on the right. "If you come to Hermosillo and don't eat at Xochimilco then you might as well never have come at all," proclaims the restaurant's motto. This may seem a little brash, but only to those who haven't eaten there. Specializing in every variety of Sonoran *carne asada*, Xochimilco has been setting the standard since 1949. If you've got a hearty appetite, try the *paquete Xochimilco* (230 pesos for 2 people). Open daily noon-9pm. MC/V. ❺

Los Magos, Madrid 32 (☎213 9199). If you like to eat kids, this is the place for you. Los Magos claims to be *la casa del cabrito en Hermosillo,* and despite its hokey, saloon-themed decor, the locals seem to agree. If you don't favor the cloven-hoofed, you can find a whole array of *carnes asadas,* including the sublime *arracheras* (102 pesos) or the *filete miñón con cebollitas* (130 pesos). Kid parts go for 42-136 pesos. Open M-Sa 12-9pm. ❺

Fonda Chapala (☎212 3992), on Guerrero between Sonora and Oaxaca. Mexican oldies blare while middle-aged men drown their sorrows in 40 oz. bottles of Tecate. Chicken, fish, or meat comes fried to crispy perfection and served with french fries, *frijoles,* tortillas, salad, and a drink (42 pesos). Open Su 8am-2pm, M-Sa 8am-10pm. ❹

Restaurant Jung, Niños Héroes 75 (☎213 2881), at Encinas. Attached to a health-food store, this restaurant serves as the perfect retreat for vegetarians who feel like they've been missing out. Relax to the strains of ambient music as you enjoy vegetarian versions of all your Mexican favorites. Noteworthy is the 75-peso all-you-can-eat breakfast buffet, featuring everything from *burritos de hongos* to hotcakes. Open Su 9am-5pm, M-Sa 7:30am-8pm. ❺

🔲 🎵 SIGHTS AND ENTERTAINMENT

Hermosillo's two architectural wonders grace opposite sides of the tree-lined Plaza Zaragoza. On the far side of the plaza lie the cross-capped yellow spires of the **Catedral de la Asunción,** while the grey-and-white **Palacio de Gobierno** towers nearer to the center of town. A chapel has stood on the site of the Catedral since 1777, but the current cathedral was only completed in 1908. The main attraction of the Palacio, from which the state of Sonora is governed, is a series of murals commissioned in the 1980s depicting key periods in Sonora's history.

On Rosales just before Encinas, a long staircase to the right leads to the **Museo Regional de Historia.** The museum has two main rooms, containing an examination of Sonora's pre-history (including two perfectly preserved mummies recovered in Yécora) and an exhibit on Sonora's intense 19th century—a period of social, political, and economic change. (Open M-Sa 9am-1pm. Free.) **Cuartel Catorce** is a rough structure with walls of brown brick on Guerrero and Colosio. The room in the back of the colonnaded inner courtyard once housed the army's cavalry. (☎217 1241. Open M-F 8am-3pm.)

As a university town, Hermosillo has a vibrant and youthful nightlife. Shoot pool, watch sports, or surf the Internet at **La Biblioteca,** on Rosales at Dr. Noriega. (☎212 4750. Beer 18 pesos, tequila 25 pesos. Internet from 15 pesos per hr. and a game of pool from 25 pesos. Open M-Sa 10am-2am.) If local music is of more interest, **El Grito,** Suárez 72, will offer you all the *Norteño* you can handle. (☎217 5337. Open daily 10am-2pm.) **Napy's,** Matamoros 109, between Dr. Noriega and Morelia, offers more of a club scene. After 9pm, food service stops, the speakers are pumped to maximum volume as couples hit the dance floor, and friends cheer them on with pitchers of Tecate. (50 pesos. ☎213 2870. F-Sa live salsa. Open daily 10am-2am.) If you feel like dancing but country of any kind leaves you cold, then **Neo,** Juárez 49, between Veracruz and Tamaulipas, is a fairly classic disco. (☎210 1689. Open Th-Su 9pm-2am.) The more sedentary will appreciate the **Multicinemas,** Encinas 227, a 5min. bus ride from the center of town. (☎214 0970. Open daily 3-9pm. 38 pesos.)

▶ NEAR HERMOSILLO

CENTRO ECOLÓGICO DE SONORA

Take a Ruta 6 or 11 bus from the Guerrero and Dr. Noriega stop (20min., 4 pesos). ☎250 1225. Open Tu-Su 8am-6pm; winter Tu-Su 8am-5pm. 20 pesos, children 4-12 and students 10 pesos.

More than your token neighborhood **zoo**, the Centro is host to an impressive array of animal life, a mini-aquarium (complete with outdoor sea lions), hundreds of plant species, and groundbreaking biological research. A clearly marked walkway dotted with water fountains, shady benches, restrooms, and a wading pool guides visitors through the exhibits and affords a spectacular view of Hermosillo and its surrounding mountains. The most spectacular feature of Centro Ecológico is its incredible collection of cacti—over 340 species are labeled and displayed throughout the animal exhibits and just outside the main pavilion. Keep your eyes peeled for the rare and beautiful *cina* and *biznaga*, from which candy is made, and the *maguey bacanora*, the fanned-out, spiked cactus that is the source of all those tequilas you've been downing. Children delight at clowns and animated films in the air-conditioned **movie theater** (Sa-Su 11am-4pm; free).

BAHÍA KINO ☎ 662

Bahía Kino, a 20km stretch of glistening sand, brilliant blue water, and radiant sun, is comprised of a pair of beach towns on the beautiful Sea of Cortés. **Kino Viejo**, a dusty, quiet fishing village, lies down the road from **Kino Nuevo**, a 4km strip of posh secluded homes and condos. Diving, fishing, and sailing entertain the more adventurous traveler, while soft, sandy beaches and gentle waves beckon those looking to relax. As weekend daytrippers from Hermosillo will tell you, Kino provides an ideal escape from raucous urban desert to *palapa*-shaded tranquility. Soothing breezes, warm waters, and vast expanses of sand make the rickety ride from the city more than worthwhile.

🚍 **TRANSPORTATION.** Bahía Kino is 107km west of Hermosillo, at the end of a dusty two-lane highway. **Buses** in Hermosillo leave from the old blue and red-striped **Costa Expresso** station on Sonora between Jesús García and González, near Jardín Juárez (2hr., 12 per day 5:30am-6:30pm, 46 pesos). The bus stops in **Kino Viejo** before going on to **Kino Nuevo**. Look for water on your left and get off where you'd like. Early birds can make it a daytrip—get an early bus from Hermosillo and sleep (if you can) during the ride. Missing the 6:30pm bus back to Hermosillo means spending the night in Kino. To get from one Kino to the other or back to Hermosillo, flag down the bus (every hr., 5 pesos) on Nuevo's only road, **Mar de Cortés**, or on **Blvd. Kino** in Kino Viejo. If you choose to walk the few kilometers between towns, be sure to keep plenty of water and sun protection on hand. Hitching may be a popular mode of transportation in Kino, but *Let's Go* discourages it.

🛈 **PRACTICAL INFORMATION.** In case of an **emergency**, call ☎ 080 or contact the **police** at Santa Catalina and Mar de Cortés (☎ 242 0047) in Viejo or at Blvd. Kino and Cruz in Nuevo (☎ 242 0032. Some English spoken). If it's just information you're after, stop by the **tourist office** in Kino Nuevo next to the police station. (☎ 242 0447. Open Th-Su 9am-5pm.) **Farmacia San Francisco**, at Blvd. Kino and Topolobambo in Viejo, serves the needs of both towns. (☎ 242 0230. Open daily 9am-1pm and 2-9pm.) A **Red Cross** is located at Blvd. Kino and Manzanillo in Viejo, near the post office and police station. There is no phone, but it can be contacted via the emergency number. For English-speaking **medical attention**, call Dr. José Luis (☎ 242 0395). **Long-distance phones** are available at the clothing shop at Blvd. Kino and Tampico in Kino Viejo; **LADATELs** dot Mar de Cortés in Nuevo and can be found across from the *farmacia* in Viejo. There is a **post office** next to the police in Viejo. (Open M-F 9am-3pm.) Kino Bay RV Park (see below) offers **Internet access** for 20 pesos per 30min. **Public bathrooms** can be found in Nuevo toward the beginning of the beach in front of La Palapa Restaurant. In Viejo, they are available at the **Centro de Salud** at Tampico and Blvd. Kino; bring your own toilet paper. In an emergency, your best bet might be to look for the American-run **Club Deportivo** (☎242 0321); turn right at the Super Kino Bay minimart toward the end of Mar de Cortés. It's just past the Prescott College Ecological and Research Center on Cadiz. Knock on the door; although officially open only to members, the friendly expatriate community takes good care of visitors.

▛▟ **ACCOMMODATIONS AND FOOD.** Safe and comfortable lodgings are plentiful on the beachfront—find a free *palapa* and set up camp. For those who prefer mattresses to sand, Kino's version of "budget" awaits at **Hotel Posada del Mar** ❺, on Mar de Cortés at the beginning of Kino Nuevo. The price of a room includes A/C, baths, and use of the pool. (☎242 0155. Singles 360 pesos; each additional person 70 pesos.) If you've got big wheels, you're in luck—more than 10 RV parks offer beachfront hook-ups. **Kino Bay RV Park** ❸, at the end of Kino Nuevo, is the largest in the area with a bilingual staff and over 200 full hook-ups. (☎242 0216; www.kinobayrv.com. US$18 per day.) **Islandía Marina** ❶ is right on the beach in Viejo. Take Blvd. Kino and follow the road to the end. It has one of the better locations and also rents cabins complete with four beds, a refrigerator, a kitchen, a bathroom, and two powerful fans. (☎242 0081. Quads 360 pesos; each additional person 60 pesos.)

Restaurants in Kino tend to be expensive; for a meal that's as economical as you want it to be, do as the *hermosillanos* do and pack a lunch to enjoy under a beach *palapa*. If brown-bagging doesn't cut it, **Jorge's Restaurant** ❸, at Mar de Cortés and Alicante toward the end of Kino Nuevo, offers all the *mariscos* your heart might desire. The *camarones empanizados* (70 pesos) are one of the house specialties. (☎242 0049. Open daily 9am-10pm.) **Restaurante la Palapa** ❸, toward the beginning of Nuevo's beach, cooks up fresh *pescado* any way you like it (55 pesos). Homesick *gringos* will like the juicy *hamburguesas* (30 pesos). Relax under the *palapa*-covered balcony and watch the sunset. (☎242 0210. Open daily 8am-8pm.)

◧◪ **SIGHTS AND BEACHES.** Kino's **beaches** are all peacefully deserted early in the week, but weekends bring crowds. Fortunately, the masses in Kino are nothing compared to the masses at other beach towns, and it is possible to find an unoccupied and garbage-free *palapa*. *Gringos* with homes in Kino tend to populate the beaches in winter, making for some long, lonely stretches of sand during the summer months. In general, beaches are better in Kino Nuevo. To rent **diving** equipment or hire a guide, call **Carlos Montes** (☎260 8901 or 269 2896) or find him at Islandía Marina on weekends. **Fishing** trips can be arranged with **Ernesto Hínojosa** (☎242 0320), or ask a local fisherman if you can come along for a ride.

For non-beach entertainment, **Museo de los Seris,** on Mar de Cortés at Progreso near the end of Kino Nuevo, offers an air-conditioned refuge and teaches you about the Seris, an indigenous fishing tribe. (Open W-Su 9am-4pm. 3 pesos, children 2 pesos.) The Seris also offer eco-tours of nearby **Isla del Tiburon,** a protected nature reserve and the largest island in Mexico. Tours can be arranged by phoning their office in Kino Viejo. (☎242 0557 or 242 0556.)

GUAYMAS ☎622

Nobody is quite sure what "Guaymas" means—the two most popular suggestions are "to shoot arrows at the head" and "tree toad." These seem fitting for a city that has long been tugged in completely different directions. Founded in the 18th century as a Jesuit mission, the town of San José de Laguna de San José de Guaymas teetered on the verge of destruction by local Seri Indians. Thanks to expansive

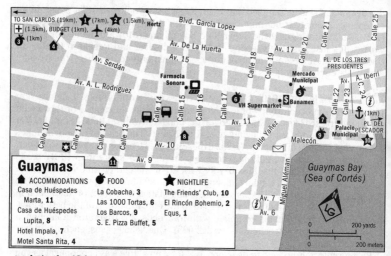

trade in the 19th century, it became clear the harbor city would survive, even if most of its name didn't. Modern Guaymas is still conflicted; at once northwest Mexico's busiest port and a luxury tourist destination, Guaymas is a vigorous city full of unexpected opportunities and extreme hospitality 10min. away from San Carlos's beachside haven.

▐ TRANSPORTATION

Airport: To reach the airport, catch a "San José" bus along Serdán (10min., every hr., 4 pesos). **Aeroméxico** (☎222 0123), Serdán at Calle 16, flies to: **La Paz** (1½hr., Sa-Su 4:20pm); **Los Angeles** (2hr.; Th, Su 9:25am); **Mexico City** (3½hr., via **La Paz**); **Phoenix, Arizona** (1½hr., Sa-Su 10:55am). Office open M-F 8:30am-6pm, Sa 9am-2pm.

Buses: Buses arrive at Calle 14. To get to the main street, Serdán, turn left if you're coming out of the Transportes del Norte station, and turn right if you're coming out of the Transportes del Pacífico or the Transportes Baldomero Corral stations. **Transportes del Pacífico** (☎222 1271) buses leave every 45min. for: **Guadalajara** (20hr., 763 pesos); **Hermosillo** (1½hr., 46 pesos); **Los Mochis** (5hr., 205 pesos); **Mazatlán** (12hr., 579 pesos); **Mexicali** (12hr., 582 pesos); **Nogales** (6hr., 209 pesos); **Puerto Peñasco** (9hr., 310 pesos); **Tepic** (18hr., 740 pesos); **Tijuana** (13hr., 729 pesos). **Transportes Norte de Sonora** (☎222 1271) offers similar service. Across the street, **Transportes Baldomero Corral** can take you to **Navojoa** (4hr., every hr., 72 pesos).

Ferries: (☎222 8406). Ferries leave from a small dock on Serdán, about 2km east of the *centro*. To get to the dock, take any local bus headed east on Serdán and ask the driver to let you off at the ferry. A blue and white "Sematur Transboradores" sign will be on your right. Ferries go to **Santa Rosalía** (7hr.; M, Th, Sa 10am; 540 pesos, children ages 3-11 270 pesos, under 3 free. 10% discount for seniors over 60).

✦ ▐ ORIENTATION AND PRACTICAL INFORMATION

Guaymas is 407km south of Nogales on **Mex. 15**. The *centro* is the area surrounding the chaotic main strip, **Serdán,** beginning at **Calle 10** and ending at **Calle 29**.

Running perpendicular to Serdán are Calle 1, Calle 2, Calle 3, etc. The waterfront begins at **Calle 20,** two blocks south of Serdán at **Av. 11** (the *malecón*), and Serdán itself continues along the sea after **Calle 24. Women should avoid walking alone more than two blocks south of Serdán or east of Calle 25 after dark.**

Tourist Office: (☎224 4114), Av. 6 and Calle 19. There is also an air-conditioned booth (☎222 4400) at Av. Serdán between Calle 24 and Calle 25. Open daily 9am-6pm.

Currency Exchange: Banamex (☎224 1870), Serdán at Calle 20. Exchanges currency and traveler's checks and has 24hr. **ATMs.** Open M-F 8:30am-4:30pm.

Luggage Storage: Lockers are available at the Transportes Norte de Sonora bus terminal. 12 pesos for the 1st 8hr., 5 pesos each additional hr. Open 24hr.

Car Rental: Hertz, Calzada García López 625 (☎222 3028). Open M-F 8am-6pm, Sa-Su 8am-3pm. **Budget** (☎222 5500), Serdán and Calle 4. Open M-F 8am-6pm, Sa-Su 8am-3pm.

Market: VH Supermarket (☎224 1949), on Serdán between Calles 19 and 20. Open Su 7am-8:30pm, M-Sa 7am-11:30pm.

Police: (☎224 0104 or 224 0105), on Calle 11 at Av. 9. Some English spoken.

Red Cross: (☎222 5555 or 224 0876), on México 15, about 1.5km north of the *centro* at km 1980. Also has **ambulances.**

Pharmacy: Farmacia Sonora (☎222 1100), Serdán at Calle 15. Open 24hr. **Pabellón Guadalupe** (☎222 0485), Av. 6 at Calle 11. Some English spoken. Open 24hr.

Fax: Telecomm (☎222 0292), next to the post office. Open M-F 8am-7:30pm, Sa-Su 9am-noon.

Internet Access: OmniRed, on Serdán between Calle 15 and Calle 16. 10 pesos per hr. Open daily 9am-11pm.

Post Office: (☎222 0757), Av. 10 between Calle 19 and 20, next to the pink Luis G. Davila School. Open M-F 9am-3pm, Sa 9am-1pm. **Postal Code:** 85400.

ACCOMMODATIONS

Heat and humidity conspire to create the perfect micro-climate for the proliferation of roaches, fleas, gnats, and other vermin, making otherwise adequate budget hotels somewhat uncomfortable. It may be worth your while to pay for A/C, cleanliness, and frequent fumigation.

Motel Santa Rita, Serdán 590 (☎224 1919), at Calle 9. Large, sparkling-clean rooms with A/C, TV, and phone. A good pick for a quiet, bug-free night of shut-eye. Has a huge parking lot. Singles 300 pesos; doubles 400 pesos; triples 500 pesos. ❹

Casa de Huéspedes Marta (☎222 8332), Av. 9 and Calle 13. Clean and tidy rooms with bathrooms, fans, and parking at superb prices. Singles 90 pesos; doubles with A/C 100 pesos. TV with cable 50 pesos. ❶

Casa de Huéspedes Lupita, 125 Calle 15 (☎222 1945), 2 blocks south of Serdán. Tidy, small rooms come equipped with fans, and an *agua purificada* dispenser awaits downstairs in the office. Singles 80 pesos, with bath 110 pesos, with A/C 160 pesos; doubles with bath, cable TV and A/C 200 pesos. ❶

Hotel Impala, 40 Calle 21 (☎224 0922 or 224 0923), 1 block south of Serdán. A/C, telephones, and cable TV make the "death by peach" color scheme and tawdry lobby more palatable. Singles 200 pesos; doubles 250 pesos; triples 300 pesos. ❹

FOOD

Seafood is Guaymas's specialty. Local favorites include *cahuama* (manta ray steaks), and *ostiones* (oysters) in a garlic and chile sauce. Unfortunately, if you want to sample these local delicacies, you will pay dearly. For those on a tighter budget, **Mercado Municipal,** on Calle 20 one block from Serdán, sells fresh produce, and an abundance of *comida corrida* joints dots Serdán.

Restaurant Bar Los Barcos (☎222 7650), Malecón between Calle 21 and Calle 22. Los Barcos offers the very finest in seafood. Savor Mexican surf and turf (165 pesos) and *camarones empanizados* (122 pesos). Open daily 10am-8pm. ❺

La Cobacha, Carretera Internacional km 1982 (☎221 2270), just outside Guaymas on the road to San Carlos. With a reputation as one of Guaymas's best seafood restaurants, La Cobacha will delight with an array of *mariscos* for 160 pesos or less. Open daily 10am-10pm. ❺

Las 1000 Tortas, Serdán 188, between Calles 17 and 18. Not just for *torta*-lovers. Serves up delicious *burritos de machaca* (3 for 33 pesos), *bistec ranchero* (40 pesos), and quesadillas (3 for 33 pesos). Open daily 8am-11pm. ❸

S. E. Pizza Buffet (☎222 2446), Serdán at Calle 20. Disney images and framed posters of American cars and athletes decorate the walls. Satisfy your appetite with the all-you-can-eat buffet of pizza, spaghetti, and salad (28 pesos). Open daily 11am-11pm. ❷

◪ ▣ BEACHES AND ENTERTAINMENT

Guaymas's **beaches,** popular with both tourists and locals and accessible via a short bus ride from Serdán, are located to the north in **San Carlos** (see p. 236) and **Miramar** (10min., 7am-10:30pm, 9 pesos). The nicer (but smaller) beaches in Miramar are back along the bus route in front of the fancy villas. Also in Miramar, Perlas del Mar de Cortéz cultivates pearls aplenty, and offers free tours of the facilities every hr. M-F 9am-3pm, Sa 9am-11pm.

Guaymas has its share of bars, but travelers hunting for more than a bottle of Pacífico find their entertainment on the road to San Carlos. **El Rincón Bohemio,** Carretera Internacional km 1982, is far more understated than Hotel Flamingos, in which it resides. (☎221 3161. Live music Th-Sa 9pm-2am.) For a more up-to-date version of cool, backpackers ride down the Carretera to **Equs;** besides being the hottest disco around, Equs is also a sushi bar. (☎221 3032. Disco open daily 9pm-2am.) For those who prefer a quieter evening, **The Friends' Club,** Av. Rodríguez at Calle Abelardo, offers pool for 20 pesos per hr. (☎222 0053. Open daily 6pm-2am.) If even stickwork is too much exertion, **Cinema Plus,** on Calle 18 three blocks south of Serdán, has two screens for a low 34 pesos. (Open M-F until 9 pm.)

SAN CARLOS   ☎622

Thirty-five years ago, San Carlos (pop. 2500) was just a dusty road in the desert north of Guaymas; now, condos, hotels, and malls sprout like wildflowers to accommodate the growing tourist influx. San Carlos greets visitors with a lush country club, Sonora's only five-star hotel, and the largest, shallowest artificial shipwreck in the world. With a population that swells to 8000 come winter, when sunseeking American and Canadian retirees return to their pastel-colored beachfront homes, San Carlos knows exactly how to pamper its guests.

E TRANSPORTATION. White striped **buses** come from downtown **Guaymas** and run down the main road to the **Marina Real** and **Plaza Las Glorias,** but don't make it all the way to the El Mirador Escénico or Playa Los Algodones. (Approx. every 10min. 7am-10:30pm; to Guaymas 9 pesos, within San Carlos 5 pesos.)

■ 7 ORIENTATION AND PRACTICAL INFORMATION. The main road in San Carlos, **Manlio F. Beltrones,** runs east-west. Most shops, restaurants, and accommodations lie on Beltrones between Hacienda Tetakawi Hotel and Trailer Park to the east and the small road to Plaza Las Glorias to the west. The **tourist office** is in **Hacienda Tours,** on Beltrones just before El Mar Diving Center. (☎ 226 1314. Open M-F 9am-5pm, Sa 9am-2pm.) **Banamex,** on Beltrones next to the PEMEX station, exchanges dollars and traveler's checks and has a 24hr. **ATM.** (☎ 226 1240. Open M-F 8:30am-4:30pm.) Like everything else in San Carlos, **Internet** doesn't come cheap; the most reasonably-priced connection is above Gary's dive shop, Beltrones km10, at 50 pesos per hr. (☎ 226 0049. Open daily 7am-8pm.) Buy your groceries at the **San Carlos Super Mercado,** in front of the church at the end of the road to Plaza Las Glorias. (☎ 226 0043. Open daily 7am-9pm.) **Lavandería Automática,** next to Piccolo Restaurant, offers full- or self-service and hand-washing. (☎ 226 0013. Wash 18 pesos, dry 22 pesos. Open daily 9am-5pm.) In case of **emergency,** call **Rescate,** which is funded entirely by donations from San Carlos residents. (☎ 226 0101. English spoken.) The **police** station is up the hill on the road to Plaza Las Glorias. (☎ 226 1400. English spoken.) **Farmacia Bahía San Carlos** is located across the street from Motel Creston. (☎ 226 0097. Open M-Sa 8am-7pm.) The **post office** (☎ 226 0506) is next to Ana María's Beauty Shop. **Postal code:** 85504.

■ ACCOMMODATIONS AND FOOD. San Carlos is full of hotels, none of which suit budget travelers. For those wise enough to pack a tent or an RV, **El Mirador RV Park ❸,** on the road to El Mirador Escénico, provides full hookups in RV paradise—scenic views, a glistening pool, abundant free modem access, many table games, plentiful pristine showers, and two new tennis courts. (US$15 per day, US$120 per week.) **Hacienda Tetakawi ❷,** on Beltrones km 8.5 at the beginning of the main strip, has full hookups and tent spaces. (☎ 226 0220 or 226 0248. RV hookups US$20 per day, US$130 per week; tent space 1-2 people US$10, each additional person US$3.) **Motel Creston ❺,** across the street from Jax Snax, and an easy walk to the beach, is the cheapest hotel you'll find. Sparkling rooms have two beds, A/C, and bath. The patio faces a clean pool. (☎ 226 0020. Doubles 450 pesos; each additional person 50 pesos.)

While most restaurants are on the expensive side, a few places here and there cater to the budget traveler. Peso-pinchers can satisfy cravings with *burritos de carne asada* or fresh *almejas* (clams) eaten raw with salsa, *limón*, or chocolate from vendors toward the western end of Beltrones. Local expatriates enjoy starting the day with breakfast (44 pesos) and fabulous malts (25 pesos) at **Jax Snax ❸** (☎ 226 0270), on Beltrones. Expats and locals alike swear by **Blackie's ❺,** on Beltrones past the Motel Creston. The menu changes daily but always features great steaks and seafood. The Ribeye (145 pesos) is one of the house specialties. (Open Tu-Su noon-11pm. MC/V.) **Mamacita's Cafe ❸,** also on Beltrones, serves "healthy food." (☎ 229 5021. Salads 25-40 pesos, juices 10-15 pesos, big fruit and yogurt plates 35 pesos. Open M-Sa 7am-2pm.)

■ SIGHTS AND BEACHES. A colorful array of marine flora and fauna make their home in the Sea of Cortés, attracting divers eager to catch a glimpse of the underwater brilliance and fishermen eager to catch dinner. Near the town is **San Pedro Nolasco Island,** a popular dive site where sea lions and marine birds coexist

NORTHWEST MEXICO

in harmony. The state of Sonora recently spent a large sum of money to sink a 120 ft. tuna boat and 300 ft. passenger liner to create an artificial reef for scuba divers. **El Mar Diving Center,** off Beltrones, rents scuba gear and sea kayaks (US$30) and leads guided dives (US$75 per person for two people, US$65 for three people or more for an 8hr. trip to the island). El Mar also rents bikes (US $15) for those who prefer *terra firma.* (☎226 0404. Open Mar.-Oct. daily 7am-6:30pm; Nov.-Feb. M and W-Su 7:30am-5:30pm. AmEx/MC/V.) If fishing is your thing, the US-run **Surface Time,** 1 Edificio Villa Marina near the Plaza de las Glorias, gives you the chance to charter a boat and will arrange licenses and equipment for you. Bottom fishing costs US$50 per hr. for four hrs., and trolling costs US$80 per hr. for 6 hrs. (Full range of diving services available. One-tank local or night dive US$40 per person with four persons. ☎226 1888 or 480-897-2300 from the US; surfacetime@cox.net. Open daily 7am-7pm.). To go it alone, pick up a license (58 pesos per day) at the **Secretaria de Pesca** on Beltrones just before the turn-off to Plaza Las Glorias. (Open 9am-3pm.) It's illegal to fish without one.

Playa San Francisco, which extends parallel to the freeway from Guaymas, is the most easily accessible beach. The sands are rocky, but the water is pleasant. If you have access to a car, **El Mirador Escénico,** a vista atop a steep road, affords views of Tetakawi and the secluded coves of **Playa Piedras Pintas.** A dirt road near the gate to Costa Del Mar about 8km past the end of the bus route leads to ◪**Playa Los Algodones** (Cotton Beach), so named because the soft sand is often compared to cotton. Taxis can take you on a tour of the area, including El Mirador, Piedras Pintas, and Los Algodones. (200 pesos per 1½hr.)

ALAMOS ☎647

The sleepy town of Alamos (pop. 8000), in the scenic foothills of the Sierra Madre Occidental, is a rambling collection of handsome colonial *haciendas.* Founded in 1531, Alamos was relatively ignored until silver was discovered there in 1683. For nearly a hundred years, Alamos produced more silver than any area in the world, but when the silver veins ran dry at the turn of the century, the former boomtown shrank to ghost-town proportions. Over the last 50 years, however, wealthy Americans and Canadians have taken an interest in the town, particularly in the rambling mansions left behind by the silver tycoons. Thanks to their funds, Alamos has returned to its glory days—the refurbished *haciendas* and cobblestone streets give the city a bygone feel unlike any other in northwest Mexico.

⛟ TRANSPORTATION. To reach Alamos by bus, you must change **buses** in **Navojoa,** 53km southwest of Alamos. From the **Transportes Norte de Sonora** and **Élite** bus stations in Navojoa, stand at the corner of Allende and Ferrocarril, looking down Ferrocarril as you face the bus stations. Walk one block to the **Transportes del Pacífico** station and turn left (toward the center of town) onto Guerrero. Three blocks along Guerrero is the **TBC** bus station at Blvd. No Reelección, where you can catch a bus to **Alamos** (1hr., every hr. 6am-6:30pm, 40 pesos). From the other stations, ask directions for buses to Alamos. The return trip from Alamos starts from the station at Plaza Alameda.

⛏⚑ ORIENTATION AND PRACTICAL INFORMATION. Small and compact, Alamos is easily explored on foot. As you come into town on **Madero,** you'll reach a fork in the road at the bronze statue of Benito Juárez; the left branch leads to **Plaza Alameda,** the commercial center (where the bus stops), and the right branch to **Plaza de Armas** in the historic district. A small alley known as **Callejón del Beso** connects Plaza de Armas with the market behind Plaza Alameda. The cathedral south of Plaza de Armas marks the entrance to **Barrio la Colorada,** where the expats have concentrated their *hacienda*-restoring efforts.

The Alamos **tourist office,** Juárez 6, under Hotel los Portales on the west side of the Plaza de Armas, has maps and historical information. (☎428 0450. Open M-F 10am-3pm.) **Banorte,** on Madero before the fork in the road, offers currency exchange. (☎428 0357. Open M-F 9am-2pm.) A 24hr. **ATM** is next door. If you're hungry for some English-language reading, feast your eyes on **Los Amigos,** Victoria at Obregón. (☎428 1014; www.losalamosmexico.com/losamigos. Carrot cake 10 pesos. Upscale rooms May-Sept. 400-500 pesos, Oct.-Apr. 600 pesos.) **SuperTito's,** at the fork of Madero, operates as a **pharmacy, grocery store,** and liquor store. (☎428 0512. Open daily 7:30am-10:30pm.) The **police** station (☎428 0209), just off Plaza de Armas on Comercia, has some English-speaking staff. Farther from the center, on Madero is **Hospital Básico** (☎428 0025 or 428 0026). For **Internet** access, try **Compulmages** on Morelos 39. Walk down Callejón de Beso from the Plaza de Armas, continue straight one block, and turn right on Morelos. (☎428 0270. 10 pesos per hr. Open daily 8am-10pm.) The **post office** is located in the Palacio Municipal. (Open M-F 8am-3pm.) **Postal code:** 85763.

⚑ ACCOMMODATIONS. Unless you re-discover silver on your way into town, you'll probably have to pass on the *hacienda* hotels. Luckily for budget travelers, there is *one* bargain option left in the *centro*. **Hotel Enrique ❷,** next to Hotel los Portales on Juárez, on the west side of the Plaza de Armas, has rooms in reasonable condition, with fans and slightly sagging beds, in a beautiful old building. (Singles without bath 100 pesos; doubles without bath 150 pesos. Separate bathrooms 50 pesos.) **Hotel Dolisa ❺,** Madero 72, offers *agua purificada,* A/C, and baths in every room. (Singles and doubles 300 pesos; each additional person 80 pesos.) Just up the road, **Motel Somar ❺,** Madero 110, has clean rooms in good repair. (☎428 0195. Singles and doubles 300 pesos, with A/C 340 pesos.)

❑ FOOD. For chow on the cheap, check out taco stands like **Taquería Blanquita ❶** in the Mercado Municipal by Plaza Alameda. (Open daily 7am-10:30pm.) For a view of the Plaza de Armas and the distant foothills, eat under the arches at **Restaurant Las Palmeras ❸,** Cárdenas 9, northeast of the Plaza de Armas. (☎428 0065. Breakfast 25-40 pesos, *antojitos* 20-35 pesos. Open daily 7am-10pm.) To work up an appetite before dinner, hike to **Restaurant el Mirador ❸,** on the hill overlooking Alamos. (Sonoran *chimichangas,* or flour tortilla tacos, 26 pesos; hamburgers 26 pesos; *enchiladas mexicanas* 38 pesos. Open Su-M and W-Sa 3-10pm.)

◪ SIGHTS. The best reason to visit Alamos is to glimpse the glory days of the *hacienda.* One of the grandest homes in town was constructed in 1720 and refinished in the 19th century, when it became the home of José María Almada, owner of one of the world's richest silver mines. **Hotel los Portales** now occupies most of the building, including Don Almada's foyer and courtyard. Other impressive restored homes can be found around the cathedral, including **Casa de los Tesoros** (a former convent), **Hotel la Mansión, Casa Encantada,** and **Las Delicias.** For 10 pesos you can tour the incredibly swanky **Hacienda de los Santos,** a series of colonial homes that have been turned into a five-star hotel. Tours start daily at 1pm from the main entrance on the corner of Molina and Gutiérrez.

The town's cathedral, **La Parroquia de la Purísima Concepción,** was completed in 1786 and occupies a commanding position on Plaza de Armas. The town jail and the Mirador offer excellent views. To get to the jail, walk along Madero west of the center of town and follow the signs. **Museo Costumbrista,** the yellow and white building across from Las Palmeras in the Plaza de Armas, has exhibits of Alamos's history. (☎ 428 0053. Open July-Aug. W-Su 9am-6pm; Sept.-June W-Su 9am-3pm. 10 pesos, students and children 5 pesos.) **Museo Casa de María Félix**, at Galeana 41, in the Barrio la Colorada, occupies the birthplace of Mexico's much-idolized screen queen, who hails from Alamos. (☎ 428 0929. 10 pesos.)

CHIHUAHUA

CIUDAD JUÁREZ   ☎ 656

Long before Juárez became Mexico's 4th-largest city, it established its name and its fame from the notorious exiles to whom it had played host. Originally known, along with El Paso, Texas, as the Paso del Norte, Juárez got its modern name in 1860 when President **Benito Juárez** fled here to escape the French intervention and seek US aid in the overthrow of Emperor Maximilian (see **History**, p. 66). The city was later occupied by Pancho Villa several times during the Mexican Revolution. Today, the exiles come from the North, fleeing the tyranny of American prices for a few hours at a time—the city has carved itself a niche, offering cheaper alternatives for services that range from dentistry to the, more exotic and less legal.

 CROSSING THE BORDER. The easiest way to cross the border is to walk. From the train station in El Paso, head out the main entrance and walk two blocks until you reach the bus station. Walk past the buses and turn right; after four blocks, turn right onto Santa Fe St. The Santa Fe St. Bridge, which serves as the main border crossing, is about 6 blocks away. There is a parallel bridge that comes off Stanton Ave. and it is possible to cross at either, staying to the right-hand side of the bridge following the pedestrian traffic. There is a US$0.25 fee to cross. If you are planning to venture more than 22km into Mexico's interior, you need a **tourist card,** available at the Mexican immigration office, directly to your right as you cross the Stanton Ave. Bridge. If **driving** into or out of Mexico, note that vehicles are charged US$1.25 each way and may require a permit. Furthermore, you can expect a wait of up to an hour. See p. 11 for more information on border crossings.

◼✳◗ ORIENTATION AND TRANSPORTATION

Besides being confusing, Old Juárez can be dangerous, and **tourists are advised not to go west of Avenida Juárez.** Furthermore, **it's best to go out during the day and stick to major, crowded streets.**

Street numbers start in the 800s near the two border bridges and descend to zero at **16 de Septiembre,** where **Avenida Juárez** (the main street) ends. To the east lies the **ProNaf Center,** a safe, tax-free area organized by the government to showcase the glory of Mexico. The ProNaf is a little far to get to by foot, but **taxi** drivers are friendly and serve as unofficial tour guides. Be sure to agree on a price beforehand, and don't pay more than 70 pesos to get from Old Juárez to ProNaf.

Most buses leave from near the intersection of **V. Guerrero** and **Francisco Villa;** ask the driver whether your bus will take you to your destination. To reach ProNaf and the Río Grande Mall, catch the "Juárez/Aeropuerto" bus heading east from Av. Juárez on 16 de Septiembre. To get from the central bus terminal to downtown, walk out the door to the left of where you entered and up the parking lot to the

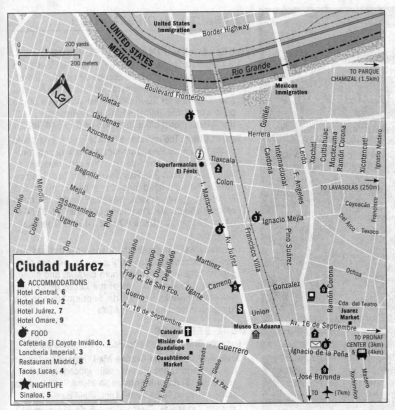

Ciudad Juárez

🏠 ACCOMMODATIONS
Hotel Central, 6
Hotel del Río, 2
Hotel Juárez, 7
Hotel Omare, 9

🍖 FOOD
Cafetería El Coyote Inválido, 1
Lonchería Imperial, 3
Restaurant Madrid, 8
Tacos Lucas, 4

⭐ NIGHTLIFE
Sinaloa, 5

main road. Do not cross, but wait for an old converted school bus labeled "Ruta 1A" or "Ruta 6," both of which go to Av. Juárez. Again, ask the driver if he or she is going to Av. Juárez, as Ruta 6 will take you to the shantytowns on the outskirts of town if you travel in the wrong direction.

Airport: (☎ 633 0734), about 17km out on Mex. 45 *(Carretera Panorámica)*. Catch the "Juárez/Aeropuerto" bus near the train tracks on Francisco Villa (3.5 pesos). **Aeroméxico** (☎ 613 8719 or 613 8089) flies to **Chihuahua, Mexico City, Monterrey,** and a few nearby US locations.

Buses: Central Camionera, Blvd. Oscar Flores 4010 (☎ 613 2083), north of the ProNaf Center. To get there, take the "Ómnibus de México" bus from the El Paso terminal to Juárez (US$5), or cram into a bus with "Central Camionera" or "Futuras" written on the front window from the area around F. Villa and V. Guerrero (4-5 pesos). Regardless of destination, you must go through customs before you pass through to the boarding area. **Chihuahuenses** (☎ 629 2229), **Estrella Blanca** (☎ 629 2229), **Ómnibus de México** (☎ 610 7297), and others offer service to: **Chihuahua** (7hr., every hr., 230 pesos); **Guadalajara** (24hr., 8 per day, 977 pesos); **Hermosillo** (10hr., 5 per day, 539 pesos); **Mazatlán** (24hr., 12:45pm, 793 pesos); **Mexico City** (26hr., 6 per day, 1150 pesos); **Dallas** (US$62); **El Paso** (50min., every hr., US$5); **Los Angeles** (US$50).

IN RECENT NEWS

PROMISED LAND

It is estimated that there are over 5 million unregistered Mexican citizens living in the US, most taking the risk of crossing the border to work in low-paying jobs that many Americans would be unwilling to take.

The border between the US and Mexico has always been heavily patrolled, and the heavy vigilance has only increased in the wake of September 11th. The border is now being patrolled by some 10,000 US agents. This increased security has forced immigrants to cross farther from population centers, increasing the risk of death by dehydration and exposure. In addition, it also increases the risk that the people-smugglers, known as *polleros*, or chicken farmers, will abandon their cargo in the desert.

With over 200 such immigrants dying every year, presidents Vicente Fox and George W. Bush have both pledged to make efforts to protect immigrants and create safer ways for them to work in the United States. On the table are measures such as registration for migrant workers and a greater number of work visas being made available for low-skill jobs. For now, however, the attention of US foreign policy makers has shifted elsewhere, leaving the US-Mexican border issue sidelined and the death toll still on the rise. According to the *Tucson Citizen*, immigrant deaths were at near-record levels in 2003.

⚡ PRACTICAL INFORMATION

TOURIST AND FINANCIAL SERVICES

US Consulate: López Mateos Nte. 924 (☎613 4048 or 613 4050), at Hermanos Escobar. From Av. Juárez, turn left on 16 de Septiembre, right on López Mateos, and then walk for 20-30min; a taxi should be 60-70 pesos. Open M-F 8am-4:45pm. In an emergency, call the El Paso tourist office in the US (☎915-544-0062).

Tourist Office: The main tourist office is on the east side of the Chamizal Park; Tarahumara natives sell traditional handicrafts outside. The city also features an information booth 3 blocks down Juárez from the border on the right-hand side that provides maps and English-language advice. However, unlike the main office, its hours are often theoretical. (☎611 3174 or 611 1767; in the US ☎800-221-0660. Open daily 9am-4pm.)

Currency Exchange: Both pesos and dollars are accepted throughout Juárez. Pesos can give the competitive edge when driving a hard bargain, and money is easily exchanged at any of the *casas de cambio* downtown. Banks line 16 de Septiembre and Av. Juárez, and most have 24hr. **ATMs.**

LOCAL SERVICES

Luggage Storage: At the bus station. 3 pesos per hr.

Supermarket: The **Río Grande Mall,** Ruta 8 by bus at Guerrero and López Mateos, sells groceries, clothes, and more. **Soriana Market,** also along Ruta 8, sells groceries. Open Tu-Sa 7am-11pm, Su-M 8am-11pm.

Laundry: Lavasolas, Tlaxcala and 5 de Mayo (☎612 5461). 12 other locations in town. Washers 8-9 pesos, dryers 6 pesos. Open Su 8am-4pm, M-Sa 9am-9pm.

EMERGENCY AND COMMUNICATIONS

Emergency: ☎060.

Police: Oro and 16 de Septiembre (☎615 1551), near Juárez. English spoken. You can also contact the **Federal Highway Police** (☎647 8000, 647 8016 or 647 8017), or **tourist security** (800 903 92 00).

Red Cross: In the ProNaf Center (☎616 5806; fax 616 5089), next to the OK Corral. English spoken. Open 24hr.

Pharmacy: Pharmacies abound along Juárez, but for late-night needs, try **Superfarmacias El Fénix** (☎615 8057), at Av. Juárez and Tlaxcala. Open 24hr.

Hospital: **Hospital Latinoamericano,** 250 N. López Mateos (☎616 1467 or 616 1415; fax 616 1375), in the ProNaf area. English spoken. Open 24hr. Take bus Ruta 8A.

Fax: Secrefax (☎615 1510 or 615 2049; fax 615 1611), on Juárez near the Santa Fe St. Bridge, partially obscured under a white awning. Open 24hr.

Telephones: LADATEL phones are plentiful on Av. Juárez and 16 de Septiembre.

Internet: Instituto America England, Av. Lerdo 206 Nte. (☎614 2706, 614 9084, or 614 0455). Besides the chance to brush up on your English, America England offers Internet service at 15 pesos per hr. In the ProNaf area try **Interclick,** Paseo Triunfo de la República 4407-3 (☎616 0906). 20 pesos per hr. Open daily 10am-10pm.

Post Office: Lerdo at Ignacio Peña. Open M-F 8am-5pm, Sa 9am-1pm. **Postal Code:** 32000.

ACCOMMODATIONS

The most reasonable selections are found on Av. Juárez and Av. Lerdo. As with traveling, remember that staying west of Av. Juárez is not to be advised.

Hotel del Río, Juárez 488 Nte. (☎615 5525). Pricey, but if you need to crash in Juárez, this is the place to do it. Clean, white rooms, vigilant staff, and good A/C distinguish this hotel from its neighbors, as does the "No Guests in Rooms" sign in the front desk window. Singles 280 pesos; doubles 330 pesos. ❺

Hotel Central, Corona 151 Nte. (☎615 0117), 1½ blocks up from 16 de Septiembre. Caters to a loyal crowd of Mexicans who return frequently to Juárez on business. The hotel has been recently renovated and offers A/C in all rooms. The congenial family atmosphere is keen. Singles 96 pesos, with TV 111 pesos; doubles 130 pesos; triples 132 pesos. ❶

Hotel Omare, 12 Corona 213 Sur (☎612 0618), 2 blocks south of 16 de Septiembre on the right. The rooms upstairs are clean and painted in eye-poppingly bright colors. Singles and doubles 120 pesos. ❷

Hotel Juárez, Lerdo 143 Nte. (☎615 0298, 615 0358, or 615 0418), at Mejía. Simple, safe, and convenient. All rooms have TV and A/C. For each floor you ascend, prices descend about 10 pesos. Singles start at 130 pesos; doubles 165 pesos. ❷

FOOD

Eateries in Ciudad Juárez vary from tourist traps in the **ProNaf** area to roadside shacks and open-pit grills. For cheap eats, head to the open-air *mercado* behind the cathedral, where taco stands abound. Vegetarians be warned: tacos are made with everything but the squeal.

Cafetería El Coyote Inválido, Juárez 615 (☎614 2727). El Coyote is the place to dilute the tequila during a night of revelry on Calle Juárez. Open all night, this authentic holdover from the 1950s may have updated its premises to include high-power A/C, but its food remains utterly traditional. Burritos 25 pesos; hamburgers 35 pesos; Mexican plates 40 pesos. Open 24hr. ❸

Lonchería Imperial, Mejía 170 Ote. (☎125 0432), 1½ blocks off Juárez. Homey little diner where you can sit at the counter and watch your food being grilled while sipping a cup of fresh-brewed coffee. *Comida corrida* 35 pesos. Open M-Sa 8am-7pm. ❸

Restaurant Madrid, Plaza Continental building (☎612 4214), on Ignacio de la Peña between Corona and Lerdo. Offers calm, air-conditioned dining off the main street. Cheap Mexican breakfast (20-25 pesos) served all day in addition to the usual Juárez fare and the occasional Spanish dish. ❷

Tacos Lucas, Av. Juárez and Mejía (☎612 5531). A good place to sit and watch Juárez stumble by. Burritos go for around 25 pesos. Open daily 8am-3pm. ❸

◙ SIGHTS

The Siberia of Mexico, Juárez historically functioned as a place of escape and exile. By the 20th century, it began to assume a similar role for US citizens fleeing everything from Prohibition to divorce laws. For a pocketable tour guide and a bit of Juárez history, grab a "Downtown Historic Walking Tour Juárez" pamphlet from the tourist office info booth, or just keep an eye out for the placards that lay out the suggested route.

Down Av. Juárez is the Victorian **Aduana Fronteriza**, or customs house, finished in 1889 as the official point of entry for import goods. In 1911, Porifirio Díaz signed away his dictatorship here, granting the Revolutionaries victory after a bloody battle. Today the Aduana Fronteriza is open as the **Museo Ex-Aduana de Ciudad Juárez**, which plays host to a range of exhibitions of varying relevance to the region.-(☎612 4707. Open Tu-Su 10am-5pm. Free.)

Turn right at the customs house and down 16 de Septiembre to Mariscal to find a bust and commemorative plaque in honor of the city's most famous exile, namesake **Benito Juárez**, who hid here during the French coup under Maximilian in 1865-66. After a right turn at the end of Av. Juárez, at the far end of the plaza lies the thoroughly modern **Catedral**, and next to it the white adobe **Misión de Guadalupe**, built in 1662. (Both the Catedral and the mission are open daily 6:30am-10pm.)

The **Museo de Arte e Historia**, at the **ProNaf Center**, exhibits Mexican art of the past and present. (☎616 7414. Open Tu-Su 10am-6pm. Admission 10 pesos, students free.) To escape from the clamor and commotion of downtown Ciudad Juárez, head to **Parque Chamizal**, down Av. Presidencia east of the Stanton Bridge. The **Museo Arqueológico**, Av. Pellicer in Parque Chamizal, houses plastic facsimiles of Pre-Hispanic sculptures as well as prehistoric fossils, rocks, and bones. (☎611 1048 or 613 6983. Open Su 11am-5pm, Tu-Sa 9am-5pm. Free.)

♫ ENTERTAINMENT

On weekends, *gringos* swarm downtown Juárez in a 24hr. quest for fun, fights, and *fiestas*. Every establishment along Av. Juárez that isn't selling Viagra or pulling teeth is likely to be a restaurant or a bar. Although these watering holes are easiest to get to, the best nightlife is found in the ProNaf area on Mejía. Take the "Juárez/Aeropuerto" or Ruta 8 bus (3 pesos) or a cab (60-70 pesos) to get there.

Vertigo, Mejía and Montes de Oca (☎611 0030). The resident DJ spins "pure house" Th (cover US$3), "Spanish" F (US$2), and "Top 40" Sa (US$4). Inexpensive beers (US$1) will keep you dancing and dizzy all night. Open W-Su til 1 or 2am.

Charmucas, Mejía and Franklin (☎616 8937). Home to a slightly older. Beer 15 pesos. From M-W you can challenge the talented house pool team to a game.

Dalí, Mejía 3118 (☎611 4898). A pseudo-intellectual nightlife escape for sophisticates-in-training. Surrealist posters, quiet music, and a variety of coffee drinks (with and without alcohol, 28 and 25 pesos, respectively) promote conversation and completely un-Juárez ambience. Open daily 5pm-1am.

Sinaloa, Juárez 142. If you must party downtown, this is the place to do it. Cowboys sit at a long bar looking sultry whilst their women-folk get down on the large dance floor. *Cumbia* and *Norteño* bands play on alternate nights. Beer 15 pesos, tequila 15-18 pesos. Open M-Th till 1:30am, F-Sa till 2:30am.

Once you are sufficiently partied-out, remember that Juárez offers more than just bars and clubs. If you enjoy bullfights, you can find them at **Plaza Monumental de Toros** (☎613 1656), Paseo Triunfo de la República at López Mateos. They usually occur at 5:30pm on Sundays from April to September. **Lienzo Charro** (☎627 0555), on Charro off República, also hosts bullfights and a *charreada* (rodeo) on Sunday afternoons during the summer. Prices range from 70 pesos for seats in the sun to 95 pesos for nice seats in the shade. At the western edge of town, **Galgódromo** (also known as the Juárez Racetrack; ☎625 5394) rises from Vicente Guerrero. Dogs run Wednesday through Sunday at 7:30pm, with a Sunday matinee at 2:30pm.

NUEVO CASAS GRANDES (NCG)   ☎636

Nuevo Casas Grandes (pop. 80,000) belongs to a time when cowboys ruled the land. A quiet town in the expansive Chihuahuan desert, NCG arose at the beginning of this century after a group of pioneering families from the old Casas Grandes decided to move to the newly constructed railroad station. Nuevo Casas Grandes is still an agricultural center and a good place to pick up *vaquero* (Mexican cowboy) garb. Travelers use the city as a base for exploring **Casas Grandes;** the ruins of **Paquimé,** Casas Grande's Zuñi namesake and one of the most important cities in Pre-Hispanic northern Mexico; and the pottery-making town of **Mata Ortiz.**

◀▐▌ ORIENTATION AND TRANSPORTATION.

Nuevo Casas Grandes is most easily reached by bus. To get from the bus stations, on **Obregón** and **16 de Septiembre,** to the center of town, walk one block down 16 de Septiembre to **Constitución,** which runs along the railroad tracks that form the backbone of the city. Constitución, along with **Calle Juárez** (one block over), **5 de Mayo,** and 16 de Septiembre form the grid that is the city center. **Taxis** loiter near the corner of 16 de Septiembre and Constitución.

Estrella Blanca and **Ómnibus de México** (☎694 0780) run buses to: **Chihuahua** (4hr., every hr., 180 pesos); **Ciudad Juárez** (3½hr., every hr., 141 pesos); **Cuáuhtémoc** (6½hr., 3 per day, 160 pesos); **Hermosillo** (8-10hr., 6 per day, 456 pesos); **Monterrey** (16hr., 6 per day, 675 pesos); **Tijuana** (16hr., 3 per day, 767 pesos).

▐ PRACTICAL INFORMATION.

The tourist office is no longer, but the receptionists at all the hotels listed are experienced in helping travelers. Change money at **Casa de Cambio California,** Constitución 207, at 5 de Mayo. (☎694 3232 or 694 4545. Open M-F 9am-2pm and 3:30-7pm, Sa 9am-2pm and 3:30-6pm.) Banks line 5 de Mayo, and most have 24hr. **ATMs. Police** are located on Blanco and Obregón. (☎694 0973. No English spoken.) **Red Cross** (☎694 2020) is housed on Carranza at Constitución. **LADATELs** can be found throughout the town. Do laundry at **Lavasolas Susy** (☎694 5003) on Madera between Madero and Obregón. **Internet** access is available at **La Playa,** Juárez 105, 1½ blocks up from the church on the right. (☎694 1212. Open M-Sa 10am-8pm. 20 pesos per hr.) The **post office** is at 16 de Septiembre and Madero (☎694 2016. Open M-F 9am-4pm). **Postal code:** 31700.

▐▐ ACCOMMODATIONS AND FOOD.

Nuevo Casas Grandes's numerous hotels and restaurants cluster on Constitución and Juárez between 5 de Mayo and Urueta. The only budget accommodation, **Hotel Juárez ❶,** Obregón 110, is an easy 36 ft. stumble down Obregón from the bus station. It is cheap for a reason—the stuffy and windowless rooms lend the feeling of incarceration. Mario, the owner, speaks flawless English and is a great source of information about the region. The lobby is a late-night hangout for travelers and locals, and a good place to restock your supply of stories and dirty jokes. (☎ 694 0233. Singles 100 pesos; doubles 110 pesos.) For something more sterile, head to **Hotel California ❺**, Constitución 209, whose spacious white stucco rooms have A/C and satellite TV. (☎ 694 1110 or 694 2214; fax 694 0834. Singles 290-325 pesos; doubles 340-380 pesos.) Nicer still is the **Hotel Piñon ❺**, Juárez 605, complete with adjoining bar and swimming pool, whose rooms have A/C and TV. The front desk staff has good advice for visiting the surrounding areas. (☎ 694 0655 or 694 0166. Singles 340 pesos; doubles 410 pesos.)

NCG's restaurants combine American diner decor with classic *Norteño* cuisine. **Restaurante Constantino ❹**, on Juárez at Minerva, has been a family business for over fifty years, serving all the Mexican specialties the heart may desire. Try the chicken tacos (31 pesos) or steaks (70-80 pesos), the house specialty. (☎ 694 1005. Open daily 7am-midnight.) Still more steaks can be found just up Juárez at **Denni's Restaurant ❺**, Juárez 412 (☎ 694 1075), where the ranching set comes to drink coffee and read the paper. Chow down on a big breakfast (35 pesos) or any kind of drippy red meat you can imagine (55-145 pesos). **Taqueria Rosas ❷**, 5 de Mayo 831 (☎ 624 1160), may look like another impromptu taco stand, but it's actually a link in a highly successful chain. *Hamburguesas*, quesadillas, tacos, and more can all be had for 15-25 pesos. (Open daily 9am-3am.) Vegetarians can escape to **Dinno's Pizzas ❸**, Mexico 1196. Before devouring an individual pizza (30 pesos), check with the staff to make sure it is meat-free. *Norteños* have a hereditary desire to put a little animal in everything. (☎ 692 0840. Open daily 7am-11:30pm.)

ENTERTAINMENT. Although there is a small movie theater at Constitución and Minerva, **Cinema Vaviedades** (☎ 669 3535), the main activity in NCG seems to be drinking one's troubles away. **El Badito Pub** (☎ 694 6553), at Juárez and Prado, is a good place to do this. The big pickup trucks parked outside may be intimidating, but the interior has a clean-cut western friendliness. Enjoy live romantic music on weekends. Wet your gullet with beer for 18 pesos, tequila for 20 pesos and up. Of course, they also serve steaks—something's got to fuel all that *machismo*. While the *banditos* succumb to "romantic" music, the real men (and women) head to the bars on Juárez, including the bars at **Hotel Piñon, Hotel Paquimé,** and especially **Hotel Hacienda.** Practice your swagger before walking into that last one. If the wild west is making your saddle sore, dance it off at **Camelot,** the *discoteca* in NCG, located all the way down Juárez at the entrance to town. Here, a Latin dance mix plays for a young crowd. (Open weekends only, 9pm-1 or 2am.)

NEAR NUEVO CASAS GRANDES

Surrounding Nuevo Casas Grandes are many points of archaeological interest, including the **Cueva de Olla** (55km southwest), the **Arroyo de los Monos** (35km southeast), and **Mata Ortiz** (40km south). About 254km southeast of NCG is **Madera,** from which the **Cuarenta Casas** site can be reached (54km north). See below.

PAQUIMÉ (CASAS GRANDES)

*Paquimé is an easy 10min. walk from the town of Casas Grandes. From NCG, catch a bus labeled "Pueblo" from the intersection of Constitución and 16 de Septiembre (10min., 1-2 per hr., 4.8 pesos). Get off at the main plaza of Casas Grandes and walk back in the direction the bus just came on Constitución. This road rounds a few bends before arriving at Paquimé. ☎ 692 4140. Ruins and attached **Museo de las Culturas del Norte** open Tu-Su 10am-5pm. 37 pesos.*

The huge network of earthen walls rising out of the desert plain just beyond Casas Grandes make up part of what is reputedly northern Mexico's most significant pre-Columbian site. Built by a people culturally related to the Anasazi of the American Southwest, Paquimé is an 11th- to 14th-century city that thrived on mining and corn. A sophisticated system of aqueducts and channels carried precious rainfall from the distant mountains and made it possible to farm the arid valley. Minerals were traded for shells from the coast and brightly feathered macaws from the south, which were kept in bird-size adobe houses and later used in religious ceremonies. Paquimé has filled its museum with an amazing collection of artifacts found on-site, including exquisite pottery, with explanations in Spanish and English. The museum also houses extensive scale recreations of the city to help explain the partially eroded site.

If you are traveling by car or have a generous budget, there are many areas around NCG worth visiting. A bus leaves daily around 4pm from the corner of Constitución and 16 de Septiembre for **Mata Ortiz,** a town famous for its revival Paquimé-style pottery. Be sure to ask around locally for the most accurate departure time, as it varies. The beautiful town is home to artists who have followed in the footsteps of **Juan Quezada,** who recreated the Navajo-looking Paquimé style. Despite the town's attractions, be forewarned that hotels in the area are expensive. On the way to Mata Ortiz, the dirt road passes **Colonia Juárez,** 23km southwest of NCG, which was founded by Mormons escaping the 19th-century prosecution of polygamy in the US. Nineteenth-century buildings and apple-growing **Mennonite colonists** abound here. Discover more archeological sites at **Arroyo de los Monos** (35km south), which has ancient cave paintings, and **Cueva de la Olla** (55km southwest), which is a series of adobe structures built into a cave. Although Colonia Juárez can be reached by staying on the "Pueblo" bus past Paquimé, most sites are inaccessible without a car; it is best to hire a guide who has a truck. Mauricio Guzmán, bartender at Hotel Piñon (☎ 694 0166), runs tours for US$60-70 that include Mata Ortiz, San Dijo, Colonia Juárez, and Paquimé. Arrange tours a day or two in advance.

CHIHUAHUA ☎ 614

The capital of Mexico's largest state, Chihuahua (pop. 800,000) is a historically rich outpost in the northern desert. The city has seen its share of bloody conflict in the almost 300 years since its founding in 1709. It was here in 1811 that Miguel Hidalgo's quest for independence ended in his execution, and here that Pancho Villa established his Revolutionary headquarters during the Porfiriato. Revolutionary skirmishes aside, modern-day Chihuahua is a peace-loving city with a bustling downtown and pastoral surroundings. A major transportation hub for the northwest, Chihuahua's culture has been shaped by a diverse array of influences, from Mennonites to backpackers bound for the Copper Canyon to the indigenous Tarahumara who arrive on market days to sell their crafts.

▉ TRANSPORTATION

Airport: (☎ 420 0676), 14km from town. The "Aeropuerto" bus stops near Niños Héroes and Independencia; look for the sign. **AeroCalifornia** (☎ 437 1022), **Aeroméxico** (☎ 415 6303 or 416 1171), and **Continental** (☎ 411 8787).

Buses: From the **bus station,** a municipal bus (3 pesos) will take you to the cathedral. Taxis cost 40 pesos. **Ómnibus de México** (☎ 420 1580) sends luxurious buses to: **Aguascalientes** (7 per day, 602 pesos); **Casas Grandes** (6 per day, 180 pesos); **Cuauhtémoc** (7 per day, 63 pesos); **Durango** (9 per day, 379 pesos); **Guadalajara** (3 per day, 754 pesos); **Mexico City** (6 per day, 936 pesos); **Monterrey** (4 per day, 520 pesos); **Torreón** (314 pesos); **Zacatecas** (484 pesos). **Estrella Blanca** (☎ 429 0240) has a slightly older fleet that chugs to nearly all the same locations. **Rápidos Cuauhté-moc** (☎ 410 5208) runs to **Cuauhtémoc** (1½hr., every 30min. 5am-noon, 75 pesos).

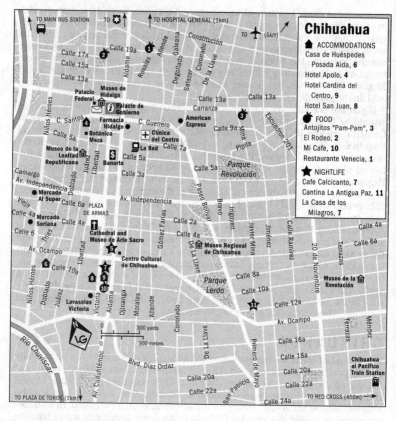

Chihuahua

🔺 ACCOMMODATIONS
Casa de Huéspedes
   Posada Aida, **6**
Hotel Apolo, **4**
Hotel Cardina del
   Centro, **9**
Hotel San Juan, **8**

🍎 FOOD
Antojitos "Pam-Pam", **3**
El Rodeo, **2**
Mi Cafe, **10**
Restaurante Venecia, **1**

⭐ NIGHTLIFE
Cafe Calcicanto, **7**
Cantina La Antigua Paz, **11**
La Casa de los
   Milagros, **7**

Autotransportes Rápidas Relicias (☎ 120 0751) goes to **Hidalgo de Parral** (12 pesos).

Trains: The **Chihuahua al Pacífico** train station, Méndez at Calle 24, is south of the center off Ocampo and 2 blocks from 20 de Noviembre. To shorten the 20min. walk in, hop on one of the public buses (3.5 pesos) that run up and down Ocampo to Libertad. The station is popular with backpackers for its daily trip between Chihuahua and **Los Mochis**, which cuts through the breathtaking **Barranca del Cobre** (13hr., 7am, 500 pesos for the second-class train). The train stops at various points along the way, including **Creel, Divisadero, Posada Barraces, Bahuichivo, Temoris,** and **El Fuerte.** A 2nd station, **Estación Central de los FFNN**, features the nighttime Division del Norte train, with service between **Ciudad Juárez** and **Mexico City.**

➹🛈 ORIENTATION AND PRACTICAL INFORMATION

Don't let the sheer size of Chihuahua intimidate you—most sights are within walking distance of the cathedral. With the exception of Victoria, streets in Chihuahua are poorly lit and may be dangerous at night. Avoid walking alone.

Tourist Office: (☎410 1077; fax 416 0032), on Aldama between Carranza and Guerrero, in the Palacio del Gobierno. Helpful staff and tourist guides. Open M-F 8:30am-6pm, Sa-Su 10am-5pm.

Currency Exchange: *Casas de cambio* cluster along Victoria. **Banorte,** Victoria 104 (☎410 1593). Open M-F 9am-3pm. **Hotel San Francisco** (☎416 7550), down the street, has 24hr. exchange. **ATMs** crowd the streets near the cathedrals.

Car Rental: Alamo, Borunda 2500 (☎416 5031) before Revolución. **Avis** (airport ☎420 1919, *centro* 414 1919). **Hertz,** Revolución 514 (☎416 6473), at Santos.

Emergency: ☎060.

Police: Homero 540 (☎481 1900), across from the Ford plant. No English spoken.

Red Cross: (☎411 9500), Calle 24 and Revolución. No English spoken.

Pharmacy: Farmacia Hidalgo (☎410 6508), at Guerrero and Aldama.

Hospital: Hospital General (☎415 9000), Av. Rosales and Calle 33a. **Clínica del Centro,** Ojinaga 816 (☎416 0022).

Internet: La Red, Ojinaga 511-B (☎415 5615). 15 pesos per hr. Open Su noon-9pm, M-Sa 9am-9pm.

Laundry: Lavasolas Victoria, Victoria 1009, south of the hotel San Juan. 45 pesos for wash and dry. Open M-Sa 8am-9pm.

Post Office: (☎437 1200), on Libertad in the Palacio Federal. Open M-F 8am-7pm, Sa 9am-1pm. **Postal Code:** 31000.

ACCOMMODATIONS

Budget hotels in Chihuahua resemble the city itself—charm smiling through grit. Cheap hotels of questionable moral fiber can be found around the market, uphill from Niños Héroes before Ocampo. American chains dot the roads into town.

Hotel Apolo, Av. Juárez 907 (☎416 1100, 416 1101, or 416 1102; www.hapolo.com), just before Guerrero. If you feel like treating yourself, then this is the place to do it. The lobby comes complete with painted reliefs and moldings that very much set the tone for the place. All rooms come with bath, A/C, cable TV, and telephone. Singles 420 pesos; doubles 450 pesos; triples 500 pesos; quads 550 pesos. ❺

Casa de Huéspedes Posada Aida, 106 Calle 10 (☎415 3830), between Niños Héroes and Juárez. Should be listed as the last stop for the *Barranca* train. Backpackers love it, and with its courtyard garden and clean, simple rooms it's easy to see why. Aida herself cooks breakfast for those who ask. Singles 80 pesos; doubles 100 pesos. ❶

Hotel San Juan, Victoria 823 (☎410 0036). A 1930s gem, with a beautiful tile courtyard and great views from the 3rd fl. Most rooms have A/C, and the hotel is connected to a popular *cantina* and a small restaurant. Internet access is 10 pesos per hr. TV 10 pesos, plus a 100-peso deposit. Towel deposit 10 pesos. Singles 95 pesos; doubles 105 pesos. ❶

Hotel Cardina del Centro, Victoria 818 (☎415 1832), opposite the Hotel San Juan. Clean rooms come with fan and cable TV and overlook a small courtyard where birds gently twitter. A little island of tranquility in the heart of the city. Singles 160 pesos; doubles 180 pesos. ❸

FOOD

Chihuahua's eateries favor function over form, with an abundance of cheap, hearty meals served at the city's many 1960s style diners. Good meals can be found

ARE YOU CALLING ME A BITCH?

The chances are that the first time you heard the word "chihua-hua" was in relation to the small dog that has become somewhat of a Mexican icon—or, at least, a Tex-Mex icon, right alongside the toll-ing bell and running for borders. Strangely enough, though the ori-gins of *canis americanus* are unknown, the dog is almost cer-ainly not from the Mexican state of Chihuahua.

Theories regarding the dog's origin are varied and plentiful. Some speculate that hairless dogs of China and the Middle East were brought across Asia to Central America somewhere between 700 BC and AD 500. Others posit that the world's smallest dog is descended from tiny mutts brought over from the Philippines in the 18th century by Jesuit priests. However, ruins from Toltec and Aztec times suggest the dogs were not only extant during that era but were, in fact, revered; Aztec folklore seems to have main-tained that the sins of the master could be transferred to her Chi-huahua, helping ensure safe pas-sage to the world beyond.

Whatever their origin, the asso-ciation of name with dog has become so strong that the adjec-tive *chihuahueño*, once used to describe all things Chihuahuan, is no longer suitable, leaving the vis-tor with the far less pronounce-able *chihuahuenses*. It's also best to avoid the phrase *Yo quiero*.

in the small *cantinas*, where bands serenade drunken, rowdy men. **Women should avoid entering cantinas alone.** Stands line the *mercado* north of Calle 69 and Ángel Trias, as well as the pedestrian blocks of Libertad north of Independencia. Plates in Chihuahua run the gamut, including *antojitos mexi-canos, mariscos* and *carne asadas*. Vegetarians find refuge at **Nutry Vida ❺**, Aldama 137, which serves a variety of vegetarian *comidas corridas* for 38 pesos M-F 12:30-4:30pm.

El Rodeo, Libertad 1705 (☎416 3080), on Libertad just past Calle 15a. The rich, heavy, dark-wood interior is much like the cuisine of traditionally Chihuahuan *carne asada*. The *arrachera chihuahua especial* (95 pesos) is delightful, but don't tease: the *filete cabreria* (85 pesos) is why you came. Open daily noon-8pm. ❺

Restaurante y Cafetería Venecia, Rosales 1901 (☎416 5934), just past Calle 19a. The Venecia serves a full range of *antojitos* and *carnes* and seems to always be bustling. *Burritos deshebradas* 15 pesos, *chuleta de puerco* 53 pesos. Open daily 7:30am-10pm. ❹

Antojitos "Pam-Pam," Carranza 1204-A (☎410 5147), at Calle 11. Follow Carranza as it branches off to the right from the Palacio del Gobierno. Locals come to this small vintage diner to read the paper, chat, and eat cheap, good food. *Tostadas* 30 pesos, *tortas* 18 pesos. Open daily from 8:30am-11pm. ❸

Mi Cafe, Victoria 1000 (☎410 1238), at Calle 10, just south of Hotel San Juan. Generous portions and friendly staff. Breakfast 40-85 pesos, chicken burritos 18 pesos. ❶

🔍 SIGHTS

After you buy your cowboy hat and boots, an even more eye-opening shopping experience awaits at **Botánica Meza,** Juárez 523, which sells a wide selec-tion of herbs, talismans, *milagros*, magic powders, and charms to a serious clientele of *curanderas* (tra-ditional healers) and the occasional witch. Even if you think it's moonshine, don't say so—*botánica* is not a good place to make enemies. (Open M-Sa 9am-2pm and 3pm-8pm, hpurs less predictable Su.)

🏛 **MUSEO DE LA REVOLUCIÓN.** Also known as **Quinta Luz,** this 50-room mansion was the home of Villa's (legal) widow, Luz Corral, who lived here, maintained the museum, and led tours until her death in 1981. Items on display include Villa's per-sonal effects, photographs, and the Revolutionary's gun collection. The star of the show is the bullet-rid-den Dodge in which the unsuspecting Villa was assassinated. *(Calle 10a 3010. Walk 1.5km south on Ocampo, turn left on 20 de Noviembre, and go 2 blocks to Calle 10 and Méndez. The museum is in the large off-pink building to the left. ☎ 416 2958. Open Su 10am-4pm, Tu-Sa 9am-1pm and 3-7pm. 10 pesos, children 5 pesos.)*

▓ QUINTA GAMEROS CENTRO CULTURAL UNIVERSITARIO (MUSEO REGIONAL DE CHIHUAHUA). One of the more stunning mansions in Mexico, this building is a prime example of the French Art Nouveau style. Mining engineer Manuel Gameros, the aristocrat who contracted the building (1907-1911), never had a chance to live here before the Revolution drove him to Texas. The house was seized by Revolutionaries, and at one point served as Pancho Villa's barracks and Venustasio Carranza's home. Upstairs is an impressive collection of modern Mexican art, while the downstairs houses rotating exhibits. Don't miss the extravagant lily-pond bathroom or elaborate wooden dining room. *(On the corner of Calle 4 and Paseo Bolívar, a 10min. walk from the cathedral. ☎ 416 6684. Open Tu-Su 11am-2pm and 4-7pm. 22 pesos, children 12 pesos; W half-price.)*

PALACIO FEDERAL AND POST OFFICE. Constructed on the foundation of a much older Jesuit College that comprised the center of Spanish colonial Chihuahua, this Neoclassical building was finished in 1910. Walk down the stairs and to the back of the building to find the **▓ Calabozo de Miguel Hidalgo**, visible as a small entrance several steps below street level. Here you can visit the building's 17th-century foundation, where Revolutionary priest **Miguel Hidalgo** was held until his execution by the Spanish government in 1811. The chilling museum displays his writings, crucifix, and the wall of his jail cell on which he scrawled a few parting words to his captors with a piece of charcoal. *(The entrance to the Calabozo is on Juárez. ☎ 429 3300, ext. 1056. Open W-Su 9am-6pm. 5 pesos, children and students 2 pesos.)*

PALACIO DE GOBIERNO. A 19th-century testament to Chihuahuan history, the palace holds Aarón Piña Mora murals, with flames marking the spots of Hidalgo's and Allende's executions, and a nude statue of Emiliano Zapata, whose modesty is maintained by a well-placed rifle. *(At the center of Chihuahua on Aldama and Victoria. Open daily 8am-7pm.)*

MUSEO DE LA LEALTAD REPUBLICANA CASA DE JUÁREZ. An appropriately sober museum chronicles the years the Mexican government spent in exile during the Maximilian-Hapsburg reign. Spanish writings by Benito Juárez and timelines elaborate the renovated rooms of Juárez's Chihuahuan home, where he lived from 1864 to 1866, when the Republican government was restored. *(On Juárez between Independencia and Carranza in a rose building marked Museo de Casa Juárez. Open Tu-Su 9am-7pm. 5 pesos, children 2 pesos.)*

CATHEDRAL. Due to Apache raids and the unpredictable nature of mining money, it took 100 years to construct Chihuahua's **Nuestra Señora de Regla y San Francisco de Asís.** Finally finished in 1826, it was well worth the wait. The beautiful Churrigueresque facade features the apostles and a humongous pipe-organ. In the southeast corner is the small **Museo de Arte Sacro**, housing pastoral 18th-century religious paintings and a chair on which the Pope sat during his 1990 visit. *(Entrance to the museum is on Victoria. Open M-F 10am-2pm and 4-6pm. 20 pesos, students 12 pesos.)*

♫ ENTERTAINMENT

In Chihuahua, plenty of folks just home from the range like to cut loose in the many *cantinas* surrounding the market southwest of the cathedral. The darkened taverns are saturated with enough tequila and heartbroken accordion riffs to soften even the most leathery *vaquero*.

Two blocks east but worlds away, sophisticates young and old enjoy coffee, wine, and pastries at **Cafe Calcicanto,** Aldama 411, across from the Casa de Cultura. Live "romantic" and Bolivian music fills the open-air courtyard. (After 9pm on weekends, *tortas* 25 pesos, beer 16 pesos, tequila 25 pesos and up. ☎410 4452. Open Su-Th 4pm-midnight, F-Sa 4pm-2am.) Beautiful people rub elbows at **La Casa de los Milagros,** 1½ blocks south of the cathedral on Victoria. An impressive selection of beer (18 pesos) and wine are served in the tiled courtyard to the sounds of live guitar music. (☎437 0693. Open Su-Th 5pm-midnight, F-Sa 5pm-1am.)

Blissfully free of the aforementioned pretense is the **Cantina La Antigua Paz,** Calle 12a 2201, which offers all the usual *machismo* in a 90-year-old setting, complete with heavy wood bar, inspiring reliefs, and old newspaper clippings. (Beer 15 pesos. ☎410 1466. Open daily 10am-midnight.) For those more interested in grabbing the bull by its horns, the **Expogan** is held at the exit to Cuauhtémoc in the first week of October, Chihuahua's very own regional cattle show featuring rodeo, *palenque,* horse races, and fascinating agro-industrial exhibits. Chihuahua also sports its very own **Plaza de Toros,** Reforma 2001. *Corridas* occur in the summer, but only intermittently—inquire at the tourist office for more details. Tickets go for around 200 pesos in the shade and 150 pesos in the sun.

If all this is too intense, escape to the movie theater on Santos and Pablado, or **Cinema 2001** on Guerrero 618 at Escorza. (☎416 5000. 20 pesos.)

▶ DAYTRIPS FROM CHIHUAHUA

CUAUHTÉMOC

Cuauhtémoc lies halfway between Creel and Chihuahua, a 1½hr. bus ride from each. From Chihuahua, both Ómnibus de México (☎582 1201), at Morelos and Calle 7a, and Estrella Blanca (☎429 0240), at Allende and Calle 9a, run regular service to Cuauhtémoc for about 65 pesos. The new tourist office, in the Plaza Principal on Morelos between Melgar and Suárez, offers general advice and will organize outings to local restaurants for groups of 5 or more. (☎581 3488. Open daily 10am-2pm and M-Sa 4-7pm.)

Cuauhtémoc is both a modern center for agricultural production and supply station for the extremely traditional societies of the Mennonites and the Tarahumara. Residents don't look when they pass the oddly dressed Germanic Mennonites on the street, but instead busily occupy themselves with their own cowboy boots and souped-up lowriders.

For visitors passing through Cuauhtémoc on their way to or from **La Barranca,** the Mennonites and their tidy *campos* in the surrounding valley are the city's main attraction. Founded in the 15th century, this German pacifist religious group moved from Europe to Russia to Canada trying to escape persecution and forced military service. After the British government impressed Mennonites into WWI, many migrated to Mexico with the stipulation that they would not fight any wars. Since the 1920s, they have become the most important agricultural producers in the state and enjoy traditional agrarian lifestyles in numbered *campos.*

To see the famous Mennonite cheese in production, your best bet is to head to **Lacteos de Noreste de Chihuahua,** at km 26 along Carretera Cuauhtémoc-Álvaro, a modern factory using traditional techniques. (☎578 6140 or 578 6144. Cheese about 50 pesos per kg. Open M-Sa 9am-5pm.) The **Museo de los Mennonitas,** near the entrance to Campo 21, features displays on all aspects of Mennonite life, from agriculture to the home, and has a series of English-language videos on the history of the Mennonites and their experiences coming to and being in Mexico. (Open M-Sa 9am-5pm. 20 pesos, children 12-18 10 pesos.)

Most *campos* are reachable by **Ómnibus de México** buses, which will stop along the freeway about 1km from the camp's houses. (7 per day; 5:30am-9pm; 27 pesos to Campos 26, 15, 21, and 101.) The station is on Calle 7a at Morelos.

The best way to see these sights is with a guide, and they don't come any better than ▉**John Friesen,** a member of the Mennonite church who used to live in the communities near Cuauhtémoc. His half-day tour incorporates the above-mentioned sites, traditional churches and schools, and even a trip to a Mennonite household where you can buy **fantastic homemade cookies** (3 pesos each). He gives tours in English, Spanish, and German. (☎044 625 594 7057, 581 3488 or 582 1322. Tours can also be booked through the tourist office. A half-day tour will cost around 210 pesos per person, though discounts are available for larger groups.)

In celebration of its cultural diversity, Cuauhtémoc holds the annual **Festival de las Tres Culturas** in the first two weeks in May. 2004 will hold the 11th such festival, which promises some 90 separate events featuring nearly 2000 participants.

If you want to go native but aren't sure which group is for you, Cuauhtémoc has many cheap places to stay while you think it over. Sleeping at **Hotel Cuauhtémoc ❶,** Morelos 306 between Calles 3 and 5, is a bit like lying in a swimming pool—though very blue and a little claustrophobic, the price helps keep things afloat. (☎852 0006. Singles 95 pesos; doubles 105 pesos. Cable TV 25 pesos extra.) One step up is **Hotel San Francisco ❶,** around the corner on Calle 3. (☎582 3152. Free breakfast 8-9:30am. Singles 115 pesos; doubles 135 pesos. Cable TV 10 pesos extra.)

Late risers can eat at **El Den,** across from the *zócalo*, which has real coffee, breakfast, reasonably priced dinner fare, and a tranquil ambience that refreshes you after the frenzy of Cuauhtémoc's streets. (☎582 3843. Open daily 7am-10:30pm.) 24hr. no-frills convenience is available at **Cafe de la Esquina ❶,** around the corner on Varezcoello.

HIDALGO DEL PARRAL ☎627

For the first 300 years of its history, Parral was as close as Mexico ever came to living the legend of *El Dorado*. In 1640, when silver from local mines began pouring into Spain, the king himself dubbed Parral "The Silver Capital of the World." So it was until the mines became unprofitable in the 1950s. Locals remained unabashed by this turn of fate, simply dropping the silver bit to rename Hidalgo "Capital of the World." Today they continue to act the part. Proud and unaccommodating, residents can be as difficult to navigate as the city's winding streets, but efforts to do so will be rewarded. The mining days left behind a trove of beautiful buildings dating from the 17th century to the 1970s. Local disregard for timetables and technology distinguish Parral from the more developed north.

TRANSPORTATION. To go downtown from the bus station, exit left out of the front door and walk two blocks down Pedro de Sille. Turn left onto Independencia and follow it as it careens downhill to the *centro*. A 20-25 peso taxi ride can replace the 15min. walk.

Estrella Blanca (☎523 0075) runs buses to: **Chihuahua** (4hr., 7 per day, 121 pesos); **Ciudad Juárez** (7hr., 8 per day, 348 pesos); **Guadalajara** (1 per day, 615 pesos); **Mexico City** (20hr., 3:30pm, 829 pesos).

ORIENTATION AND PRACTICAL INFORMATION. Parral's center consists of a compact, confusing tangle of streets. It helps to get a map (20 pesos) at a **papelería** or the **Museo de Pancho Villa.** In general, you're never too far from the city center if you're near the river. Taxis can be hailed at **Plaza Principal,** and buses to the outskirts stop along **Mercaderes,** which parallels the river.

The 9 to 5 is unheard of in Parral. This city takes *siesta* seriously. Everything but the *cantinas* and restaurants closes from 1-3:30pm, and they won't help you, even if you beg. Parral has no official tourist office, but the staff of history freaks at the **Museo de Pancho Villa** will be happy to point out sights.

The **Red Cross** (☎523 4700) is at Balderas and Chapultepec; alternatively the **Hospital de Jesús** (☎522 0027 and 522 0064) resides at Cintrón and Zaragoza. For non-medical emergencies the **police** (☎523 0575) are at Independencia and Lozoya. Parral has many competing **casas de cambio,** and the most centrally located **ATM** is **Banamex's** on Mercaderes just before Ojinaga. The **pharmacy** is located next to El Camino Market on the corner of Madrazo and Independencia. (☎523 0663. Open daily 8am-midnight.) For your grocery needs, try the **supermarket El Camino** (☎523 0663), on Independencia just outside downtown, next to Hotel Margarita's. The **post office** is on the corner of Rago and Libertad, a few blocks from the Cathedral. (Open M-F 8am-3pm.) **Postal code: 33800.**

ⅡⅭ ACCOMMODATIONS AND FOOD. Parral is home to what may very well be the cheapest hotel in northwestern Mexico. **Hotel Zaragoza ❶,** Zaragoza 115, a 10min. walk up Calle Rangel Baisma from the *centro,* has polyester sheets, styrofoam pillows, and a communal bathroom with an odor all its own. While this may not be endearing, the prices are. (☎522 6590. Singles 56 pesos; doubles 72 pesos. 25 pesos for each additional person.)

Those with standards should avoid Zaragoza and stay in one of the slightly pricier hotels in the *centro.* The most central budget option is **Hotel Chihuahua ❷,** Colón #1 (☎522 1513). To get there from Plaza Baca, walk on Mercaderes heading back toward the center, but turn left on Garcia. Keep left on Garcia until Colón. The hotel is kitty-corner from Club Viet-Nam. Clean rooms with good ventilation and showers like fire hydrants. (Singles 130 pesos; doubles 180 pesos. Cable TV 20 pesos extra.) At **Restaurante el Aseradero ❸,** on the left side of Independencia after Primavera going toward the *centro,* watch your food cook over a wood fire. Chow on good chicken, beef, and *cabrito* for 35-45 pesos. (Open daily 10am-10pm.)

◙ ♫ SIGHTS AND ENTERTAINMENT. Parral's mining days may be over, but the city has just begun to capitalize on the history left behind. A good place to get a sense of Parral's former wealth is the **Palacio Álvaro.** Constructed from 1899-1903 by a man so wealthy he once offered to pay off Mexico's entire national debt, the building has just been extensively restored and decked out with all its original furniture. Look for two windows to the left of the main entrance—through the one on the right, Don Pedro Álvaro paid the miners every eighth day (the building's decorative molding has a caricature of one of their agonized, overworked faces), while through the holes in the bar of the other, he gave money to the sick and farmers whose crops had failed. It is said that a young Pancho Villa once came to the window with a wounded leg, and seeing his promise, Don Álvaro took him in and had his leg treated by a personal physician. The two became fast friends: Álvaro eventually gave Villa the building to the left of Catedral Guadalupe and Villa invaded Texas to rescue Álvaro's son from an American jail, where he was being held for manslaughter. (Calle Riva Palacio. ☎522 0290. Open daily 10am-6pm. 10 pesos, children 7 pesos.)

Villa spent the last years of his life on Mercaderes across the river until assassins perforated him and his car with 150 bullets. Right next to the scene of the crime is the **Museo de Francisco Villa,** which indulges his cult-like followers with a downstairs shrine and an upstairs exhibit focusing on Villa's martyrdom, complete with pictures of his gory end. (☎525 3292. Open Tu-Su 9am-1pm and 3-7pm. 5 pesos, children 3 pesos.)

The violence of the city's mining history is slightly less evident, though a visit to the **Templo de la Virgen de Fátima** gives a sense of the local devotion to the patron saint of miners. The walls are constructed from thousands of small glittering chunks of local ore, and the square pews replicate those in the mine's underground shrines. Many of the city's other churches are also elaborately decorated. The oldest is the **Templo de San José,** which was finished in 1684. The latter Templo houses a small collection of religious art in the form of the **Museo de Arte Sacro.** (Open W-Su 9am-1pm and 3-7pm. 5 pesos, children 2 pesos.)

Outside of the usual *cantinas*, the good times roll at **J. Quísseme,** a lounge and dance club on Independencia near the bus station. Things start hopping after 10pm. (Beer 25 pesos. Cover 30 pesos. Open Th-F 8pm-1am, Sa 9pm-2am.) The **Lone Star** club, by the stadium, is another local favorite. (Open W-Sa 9pm-3am.) You can take in a **bullfight** two weekends each summer, usually in mid-July and late August. To get to the stadium, follow the noise; walk a few blocks left of Independencia, and turn left near Pedro de Lille as you leave town. And of course, there's always **Mega Cinema** (☎523 3060), at Independencia and Constitución.

silver baron and Pancho's longtime friend, found out about the robbery, he had Pancho's body moved from lot 632 in the Panteón de Los Dolores to lot 10. Unfortunately, this left Don Alvarado in a bit of a bind, as he had to find a John Doe to take the place where Pancho Villa was buried. Two years later, a young woman who was terminally ill with cancer made her way to the US for treatment. On the way, she had a turn for the worse and died with only the money she was going to use to pay for her treatment. At this point, the men who had helped Don Alvarado move Pancho's body contacted him and told him that they had, at last, found a replacement body, but that it was of a young woman. Don Alvarado decided they couldn't wait any longer, and so they placed her body in lot 632 where Pancho's was supposed to be.

Many years later, when the Mexican government came to collect the remains, they found buttons from a dress along with a pelvis, a femur, and a few other bones. Apparently, when the chief medical examiner was handed the pelvis, he assumed they were playing a joke on him, as the pelvis was that of a woman who was no more than 35 years of age.

All told, maybe it's for the best, according to the Villa historians. After all, a woman who would have gone to an unmarked grave mistakenly receives thousands of visitors every year. And, perhaps most importantly, Francisco "Pancho" Villa is still in Hidalgo del Parral where he belongs.

For more information on the sites mentioned above, see **Hidalgo del Parral,** p. 253.

CREEL

☎ 635

A western boom town whose railway drags in tourists rather than gold, Creel's high altitude and dramatic, rocky surroundings help it stay cool and collected in the midst of backpacker bombardment. While the steady flow of foreign visitors has turned the main street into a row of hotels, restaurants, and gift shops, it hasn't diluted the town's rugged ambience. Frigid winter temperatures, a hospital and school for indigenous Tarahumara children, and the town's position as a base for the local lumber industries help keep things real. Creel is the most popular base for excursions into the Sierra, and its incongruous mix of budget travelers, *indígenas*, and small-business entrepreneurs make it a worthy stop in its own right.

▐ TRANSPORTATION

Creel is one of the few towns in the Copper Canyon accessible both by bus and train and a good starting point for trips into the Copper Canyon.

Trains: CHEPE trains (☎ 456 0015) leave daily for **Chihuahua** (1st class 6hr., 2pm, 463 pesos; 2nd class 6hr., 5pm, 227 pesos), and **Los Mochis** through the Copper Canyon (1st class 10hr., 11:30am, 557 pesos; 2nd class 11hr., 1pm, 275 pesos). You can get off along the way to avoid paying full price. Tickets aren't sold in advance from the Creel station, so scramble on quickly when the train pulls up and elbow for a seat.

Buses: The **Estrella Blanca** station (☎ 456 0073) is a small white-and-green building uphill across the tracks from town. Buses to **Chihuahua** (5hr., 9 per day 7am-5:30pm, 166 pesos) pass through **Cuauhtémoc** (4hr., 108 pesos). To travel to **Hidalgo de Parral,** take a bus to **Guachochi** (noon and 5:30pm, 70 pesos) and transfer to **Parral.** Buses also go to **Ciudad Juárez** (8:30am, 395 pesos). Buses to **Batopilas** (6hr.; M, W, F 9:30am, Tu, Th, Sa 7:30am; 160 pesos) leave across from Hotel los Piños. Tickets are available from Hotel los Piños, Café Creel, and on the bus. Service is highly contingent upon weather and road conditions.

❋ ▐ ORIENTATION AND PRACTICAL INFORMATION

The railroad tracks function as a rough compass: toward Chihuahua is north and toward Los Mochis is south. The *zócalo* is the best place from which to get your bearings. The main street, **Mateos,** runs parallel to the trains on the opposite side of the *zócalo* and is the only street near the *zócalo* that extends any distance. Practically everything listed is south of the train station on Mateos, or on **Batista** and **Flores** which branch off Mateos to the east. **Villa** parallels the tracks on the opposite side of Mateos.

Tourist Information: ▧ **Café Creel,** Mateos 9 (cafecreel@yahoo.com), next to Casa Margarita. Café Creel—run by three American ex-pats—describes itself as the weirdest little shop in Creel, and without a doubt most certainly is. Besides offering free English-language tourist advice, Café Creel doubles as a doggie orphanage, English-language book store, coffee bar, soup kitchen, and guide-booking agency. Whether you want free martial arts lessons or just a free map, Café Creel has it all. Open daily 6am-8pm, though hours are very flexible. People with allergies or aversions to dogs should try the **Artesanías Misión** (☎ 456 0097), on the plaza near the train tracks. Juanita has a profound knowledge of the area and is supremely helpful. Sells maps and Tarahumaran books and crafts. Proceeds are donated to the Tarahumaran Children's Hospital Fund. English spoken. Open Su 9:30am-1pm, M-Sa 9:30am-1pm and 3-6pm.

Currency Exchange: Banco Serfín, Plaza 201 (☎ 456 0250), diagonally across the plaza from the train station, has a 24hr. **ATM.** Exchanges US dollars M-F 9am-1:30pm. Open M-F 9am-3pm.

Market: Comercial de Creel, Mateos 55. Open M-Sa 9am-8pm.

Bike Rental: Bike rental is available across town, but no one beats Café Creel's 50 pesos per day.

Police: (☎456 0450), in the Presidencia Seccional, on the south side of the *zócalo*.

Pharmacy: Farmacia Rodríguez, Mateos 43 (☎456 0052). Open Su 10am-1pm, M-Sa 9am-2pm and 3-8pm.

Medical Services: Clínica Santa Teresita (☎456 0105), on Parroquia, at the end of the street, 2 blocks from Mateos. Little English spoken. Open M-F 10am-1pm and 3-5pm, Sa 10am-1pm.

Fax: Papelería de Todo, Mateos 30 (☎/fax 456 0122). Open Su 9am-2pm, M-Sa 9am-8:30pm.

Internet: Compu Center, Mateos 33 (☎456 0345). 10 pesos per 30 minutes. Open daily 8:30am-10pm.

Post Office: (☎456 0258), in the Presidencia Seccional, on the south side of the *zócalo*. Open M-F 9am-3pm. **Postal Code:** 33200.

▐ ACCOMMODATIONS AND CAMPING

Due to Creel's popularity with Canyon-seeking tourists, a large number of establishments compete for tourist pesos. The result: budget rooms are plentiful and prices may be negotiable during low season. Many accommodations are within a couple of blocks of the *zócalo*. For the adventurous, the **Villa Mexicana** campground offers safe and affordable camping, as does the area around **Lake Arareco.**

Margarita's Casa de Huéspedes, Mateos 11 (☎456 0045). This hostel is always filled with travelers, as Margarita's staff is often waiting at the train station to lead new arrivals to the hostel. Although the hostel is only partially finished, the parts that are look wonderful. Breakfast and dinner included. Laundry 40 pesos. Bicycle rental 80 pesos per day. Horse rental 50 pesos per hr. Dorms 70 pesos, or 50 pesos for a cot; singles 200 pesos; doubles 250 pesos. ❶

Casa de Huéspedes Perez, Flores 257 (☎456 0391). From the train station, head down to the main plaza and turn right on Mateos. Make a left at the "Cafe Luli" sign, walk down the street, cross the green bridge, and walk directly uphill to the first house. The comfortably rustic accommodations are located behind the family's house. Prices and arrangements are negotiable, but always include heaters, meticulously clean baths, and the tremendous hospitality of Luli and her family. Kitchen and laundry facilities available. English language tours offered by Luli's sons. Dorm-style housing 80 pesos. Private rooms from 100 pesos. ❶

Hotel Los Valles (☎456 0092), on Batista just off Mateos. The hotel is less than 2 years old and is therefore in immaculate shape. All rooms come with heater, private bath, and satellite TV. The hotel restaurant, located at Mateos 37 and open daily 7am-11pm, is notably good as well. Singles 200 pesos; doubles 300 pesos. ❹

Hotel la Posada de Creel (☎456 0142), across the train tracks from the *zócalo* and to the left, is a cheap option for nice private rooms. Spacious rooms with wood paneling have gas heating and 24hr. hot water. Singles 70 pesos, with private bath 150 pesos; doubles with private bath 180 pesos. ❶

Hotel la Villa Mexicana (☎/fax 456 0665 or 456 0666; www.vmcoppercanyon.com), on Mateos. From the train station, cross the *zócalo* and turn right on Mateos; Villa Mexicana is on the left after about 1.5km. Log cabins, RV hookups, and camping spots are clustered around a main clubhouse. Tent camping 50 pesos; full RV hookups with electricity and plumbing 200 pesos per day; 4-person cabins 1250 pesos during *Semana Santa*, Jul.-Aug., and Dec., 600 pesos the rest of the year. ❶

🔾 FOOD

The vast majority of restaurants in Creel are remarkably similar; that said, they're usually pretty good.

El Caballo Bayo, Mateos 23 (☎456 0136). Using a secret technique that he won't even tell his family, Julio, the owner and chef, prepares probably about the best steak you've ever tasted (rib-eye 100 pesos), served in a wood-paneled den decorated with the hats and caps he trades for beer. Open Tu-Su 12:30pm-11:30pm. ❺

Tío Molcas, Mateos 35 (☎456 0033). The cheerful banter of the waitresses entertains customers during commercial breaks. Filling beef dishes 46 pesos, fried chicken 37 pesos, burritos 13 pesos. Open daily 8am-11pm. ❸

Cafetería Gaby, Mateos 50 (look for the "Cafe Combate" illustration). Offers a full range of Mexican treats (burritos and *tortas* 12 pesos) and occasionally great combo meals for 30 pesos. If confused by the door, just pull the string. Open daily 7am-10pm. ❶

👁 🎵 SIGHTS AND ENTERTAINMENT

Tourists come to Creel to visit the breathtaking Copper Canyon, which lies south of the town. To explore the surroundings, you'll need a car, a tour guide, or a brave heart and strong legs (see **Barranca del Cobre,** p. 260). Still, the town has some sights closer to home. **Museo Creel Tarahumara,** on Ferrocarril 17, in the old railroad station across from the *zócalo,* displays local and Tarahumara arts, crafts, and an assortment of historical relics. (☎456 0080. Open Su 9am-1pm, Tu-F 9am-1pm and 3-6pm, Sa 9am-6pm. 10 pesos, students 7 pesos, under 12 5 pesos.) Prehistoric relics and hallmarks of the region's mining past can be found at **El Museo de Paleontogía,** near the beginning of Mateos; follow the signs that say "Museo." (Open daily 9am-1pm and 3-6pm. 10 pesos.)

While most establishments in Creel close before 9pm, a few stay open late. Tourists roam the streets and people strum guitars until midnight. At night, **Laylo's Lounge and Bar,** Mateos 25, inside El Caballo Bayo restaurant, is a local *cantina* with a touch of class. The comfy lounge chairs and charming decor outdo most watering holes. (☎456 0136. Beer 15 pesos. Open Tu-Su 6pm-2am.) **Tío Molcas,** Mateos 35, at Caro, also breaks *cantina* stereotypes with its relaxed atmosphere. (Open daily 11am-1am.) A happening place for foreigners is the bar at **Margarita's Plaza Mexicana.** Turn left on Batista heading away from the *zócalo,* and then right into the hotel courtyard. (Beer 15 pesos, comes with a free shot during happy hour, 7-10pm. Open daily 6:30-11:30pm.) After hours, most people stumble out to **Los Parados del Don Pancho,** the chipboard booth on Mateos next to Laylo's. Fernando, who used to keep bar at Laylo's, chats with tourists in English while his wife prepares food their simple palates can't appreciate. (Burritos 10 pesos. Open daily noon-1am.)

🔁 DAYTRIPS FROM CREEL

The rocky, alpine valleys surrounding Creel shelter plenty of worthwhile sights, and are one of the few areas in the Barranca where it is safe to explore without navigational equipment or a guide. Most sights are en route to **Laguna Arareco.** To get to the Laguna "trailhead" from town, take Mateos past the Villa Mexicana and continue straight, even after the road turns to dust. When the road forks, take the

TOURS

One of the safest and surest ways to get to the surrounding Copper Canyon sights is with a tour. In practice, the cost is about the same as doing it on your own, but with a lot less waiting. Day tours should be arranged a day in advance, while overnight treks must be planned 2-3 days in advance. Band together with as many other interested travelers as possible to keep costs down. Most tours head to **Aguas Termales de Rekowata, El Divisadero, La Bufa, Basihuare, Río Urique, Basaseachi Falls,** and sometimes **Batopilas.** Most companies also run tours to **Lago de Arareko, Cueva de Sabastián, Valle de las Ranas,** and **Valle de los Hongos,** but these destinations are all easy day hikes from Creel.

Eco-Paseos "El Aventurero": A super-friendly English-speaking guide organizes tours with quality horses for small groups (2-7 people). A wide variety of tours, from 2 hours (120 pesos) to ten days (about 1000 pesos per day), with tents and sleeping bag included on longer tours. An 8hr. tour to Rekowata hot springs costs 480 pesos. Visit the stables just past the Pueblo Viejo off Mateos. (☎456 0557 or 456 0550; cell 594 9436; elaventurero@hotmail.com. For more information, see Casey at Café Creel (see p. 256) and ask to book a tour with the cowboy.)

Excursiones en Caballo El Menchu: El Menchu's guide speaks English, Spanish, some Tarahumara, and a little German. A good group if you're interested in any sort of eco-tourism, with expeditions specializing in flora, fauna, and birdwatching. Offers trips by horse, by bike, by foot, and combination hiking and bus transport. Specializes in large groups (12-16 people) and offers flexible prices: a 3-day trip to Batopilas for 10-15 people, including all the major sites, will cost 350 pesos per person. (☎456 0079 or book through Café Creel.)

Umarike Tours: Arturo, who speaks English with a Welsh accent, leads tours by mountain bike and also offers rock climbing. Umarike has an excellent website with links to all the pages in town. (☎456 0248; www.umarike.com.)

Casa Perez: The Perez brothers run tours from their family's hotel, on Flores 257 off Mateos. Trips to Rekowata (100 pesos), Cusárare (180 pesos), and Batopilas (340 pesos). Make arrangements at the hotel (☎456 0391).

Casa Margarita: Margarita offers reasonably-priced van tours to all the standard Canyon locations with sack lunches included for larger groups. The most popular tour is down into the Canyon to the hot springs in the Río de Rekowata (8hr., 100 pesos); a trip to Batopilas costs 350 pesos. General guide services 100 pesos per day (not including transportation). Visit either the Casa de Huéspedes Margarita or Margarita's Plaza Mexicana (☎456 0045) to arrange a tour.

Tarahumara Tours: Tarahumara Tours is actually a union of sorts for numerous tour guides; as such, prices may vary per guide, but most excursions cost 2500 pesos for 4-6 people per night. Many guides will approach you directly, but tours can also be booked through their booth on the *zócalo.* (☎456 0184. Open daily 9am-4pm.)

Villa Mexicana Campground: A fleet of cute yellow minivans conveys you to the usual array of destinations. Trips to Basaseachi or Batopilas with a minimum of 6 people cost 500 pesos. Call or visit the campground (see p.257).

NORTHWEST MEXICO

left path uphill past the graveyard until you reach the gate, where you'll have to pay 15 pesos for admission and a rough map of the area. This is a good place to ask more specific instructions to your destination. The first sight on the way to the Laguna is **San Ignacio Mission,** which stands in a valley surrounded by Tarahumara farms. Though the mission was constructed by Jesuits in 1744, San Ignacio's Sunday mass is celebrated in Raramuri, the native language of the Tarahumara. After the mission, the trail passes through **Valle de los Hongos,** whose strange rock formations are said to resemble mushrooms. The map at the entrance also locates nearby **Valle de las Ranas** (Valley of the Frogs) and **Valle de las Chichis** (Valley of the Breasts). A more ambitious 9km walk out of Creel is the **Valle de las Monjas** (Valley of the Nuns). Ask at the trailhead for directions.

About 7km southeast of the "trailhead" lies the man-made **Laguna Arareco,** 3km long and 8 acres in area. The lake's cold water is not ideal for swimming—to take a dip, head to the nearby **Recowata Hot Springs** (admission 10 pesos). Despite minor concrete additions, the hot springs maintain their natural feel and 35°C temperature. The round-trip hike to Laguna Arareco from Creel takes at least 6hr., though it would be wise to factor in extra time for getting lost.

BARRANCAS DEL COBRE

Fast becoming the most popular travel destination in northern Mexico, rumors of the Copper Canyon's tremendous size, remoteness, and beauty have lured thousands of backpackers north from the well-trodden Maya Riviera. Also known as the **Sierra Tarahumara,** the **Copper Canyon** is actually just one of six huge, interlocking canyons that traverse the Sierra Madre Occidental, covering an area four times the size of the United States's Grand Canyon and encompassing micro climates ranging from tropical rainforest (in the Canyon's depths) to rocky Alpine heights that resemble California's Sierra Nevada.

Though there can be no doubt about the Canyon's stunning natural beauty, travelers often find that visits to the Sierra are by turns rewarding and terribly frustrating. While the **Chihuahua al Pacífico (Chepe)** train that winds through the canyons en route to the coast makes passengers long to get out and hike through the spectacular sights passing by their windows, actually doing so often proves very difficult. The area lacks trails, transportation, adequate topographical maps, administrative infrastructure, and even decent roads, so hiking much of the canyon requires extremely advanced outdoorsmanship or the aid of a knowledgeable and dedicated guide. Infrastructure problems are exacerbated by the fact that most people visit during the rainy season (July-Aug.), when storms routinely wash out the roads and the train tracks, stranding visitors for days on end. In the end most resort to being shuttled to the sights by a Creel-based tour company. Anyone interested in hiking extensively in the canyons should plan carefully, allow extra time for complications, and be prepared to pay dearly for a guide.

Those who spend the time will be amply rewarded. The Sierra's back country is laced with a uniquely picturesque human history visible in the traditions of the indigenous Tarahumara people and the beautiful colonial missions that tend to pop up unexpectedly in the rugged landscape.

BASASEACHI

Basaseachi lies west of Creel on Mex. 16, which runs between Hermosillo and Chihuahua. To reach Basaseachi from Creel, take Mex. 127 north 45km, and then Mex. 16 110km west. Otherwise take a tour or a bus. The latter will probably only cost about 50 pesos less and entail a considerable amount of waiting and walking. From Chihuahua (5hr., 2 per day, 212 pesos) or Cuauhtémoc (3½hr., 2 per day, 178 pesos), take one of Estrella Blanca's buses to Hermosillo. From Creel, take a bus towards Chihuahua and get off at San Pedro, where Mex. 16 meets Mex. 127. The 7am and noon buses (1hr., 75 pesos)

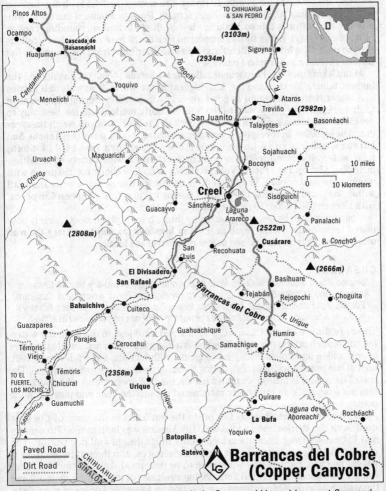

will get you to San Pedro in time to catch the Basaseachi-bound buses at 9am and 2:30pm (3hr., 100 pesos). Either way, you'll have to wait an hour or more. The last bus leaves Basaseachi at 5pm.

With water cascading from a height of 311m, Basaseachi (Raramuri for "place of the cascade" or "place of the coyotes") is located in the Basaseachi National Park. and during the rainy season (July to September) becomes Mexico's largest watefall. Tucked into a corner of Canyon Candameña, the falls don't get many visitors, but those who do make the trip are rewarded with scenery from a postcard photographer's wildest dreams. The falls can be reached either from the town of Basaseachi or from the military checkpoint about 6km before the town. From the military checkpoint it's only 6km, as opposed to the 12km from the Las Estrellas junction in town where the bus stops. Either way, the road is paved almost all the way and the entrance fee is only 10 pesos. The way to the falls is clearly marked with signs reading "C. Basaseachi" and actually leads to a natural *ventana* (window), which affords a breathtaking view of the falls and surrounding canyon (45min. each way). Adventurous spirits can trek to the base of the falls by following the path. The hike is difficult and takes another hour from the *ventana*, but the end reveals a sub-tropical paradise.

About 4km from the Basaseachi falls, **Piedra Bolada** (453m) is considered the highest falls in Mexico and the 12th-highest in the world. The waterfall carries less water than Basaseachi and is only really impressive during rainy season (July to September). The way to the falls is poorly marked and the best way to get there is to hire a guide either as far back as Creel or once you reach Basaseachi. About 800m before you reach the *ventana*, you'll pass the **Rancho San Lorenzo**, which runs Lobo Turismo de Aventura (☎614 414 6046; lobo_waterfallsadventure@yahoo.com.mx), offering a wide variety of activities, including 5 hr. tours to Piedra Volada on foot or on horseback for 250 pesos with a minimum of 6 people. They also offer camping, cabins, and a restaurant, all within the park. (Camping 100 pesos; 4 person cabin without kitchen 526 pesos, with kitchen 650 pesos; 10 person cabin 1111 pesos.)

Along the way to Basaseachi, you'll pass through some of the most sparsely populated areas of the Sierra Tarahumara. **San Juanito is the only town along the road with gasoline, reliable phones, and decent restaurants and hotels.**

CUSÁRARE

Situated 25km southeast of Creel. Most guides offer single- or two-day trips to Cusárare. Alternatively, Estrella Blanca runs buses to Hidalgo del Parral which pass Cusárare (20min., 2 per day, 18 pesos). The last bus leaves Cusárare at 6pm. A 15-peso ticket will grant you admission to the mission and the waterfall and can be purchased at either.

There are three exits for Cusárare. The first and third lead to the Cusárare waterfall and branch off to your right. The first is a fairly hilly, 3km path, while the other is only 1.9km and considerably more gentle. Although the waterfall is only 98ft. high, it can reach a width of 85ft. during the rainy season (July to September). The rest of the year it is little more than a trickle, but that doesn't stop school kids and tourists from walking the poorly maintained path to the base and playing in the pools.

The second exit which branches off to the left leads to the town of Cusárare itself, with the **Mission** and its museum. The Mission was built in the 17th century and features strong Tarahumara elements in its design and decoration. The wooden slat floor is where locals sit during services, and the loft in the back is where the choir gathers. The walls used to be decorated with paintings by Mexican greats such as Correa and Salzedo, but centuries of guano took their toll and the walls had to undergo extensive restoration by a team of European specialists. The results are remarkable and are now being housed in the custom-built bat-free **Museo de Loyola** located next door. (Open Tu-Su 9am-6pm.)

BATOPILAS   ☎649

68km south of Creel on Mex. 23 is the turn-off for Batopilas. From here, the road turns to dirt and is wide enough for only one car, with canyon pressing close on both sides. The road looks extremely perilous and it can be especially so during rainy season (Jul.-Sept.), when rain often washes out sections of the road. Travelers are generally advised to hire a professional driver or to take the bus, which is very safe. That said, if you can pluck up the courage to look out the window, the drive down the 86km switchback dirt road affords some of the best views in Copper Canyon. The bus leaves across the street from the Los

Piños hotel in Creel. (5-6 hours; M, W, F 9:30am, Tu, Th, Sa 7am; 160 pesos.) The return bus leaves from in front of the church in Batopilas in time to get travelers to Creel before any of the Chepe trains pass through (5-6 hours; M-Sa 5am; 160 pesos). Tickets are available at Hotel Los Piños, Café Creel, and on the bus.

Batopilas (pop. 1150) was founded in 1708 by Pedro de la Cruz and quickly gained prominence as the center for mining operations throughout the canyon system. The mule trains loaded with silver that flowed out of Batopilas allowed residents such as Alexander R. Shepard, a former governor of the District of Columbia and the owner of Batopilas's richest mines, to bring in priceless china, porcelain tubs, pianos, and eventually even electricity to this small town making it the second city in Mexico to have electrical power. The silver is gone and the city that remains is full of faded glory, tropical temperatures, and small town charm.

If you want to beat the heat, take advantage of the high-powered A/C at **Hotel Juanita ❹**, across the main plaza where the bus stops. Rooms cluster around a quiet courtyard and also come with private bath. (☎456 9043. Singles 200 pesos; doubles 300 pesos; 50 pesos for each additional person.) Next door is **Casa Monse ❷**, run by Monse and the English-speaking Fernando. Besides selling Tarahumaran crafts, the pair offer simple rooms with fans and a shared bathroom in a quiet tropical garden filled with mango and kumquat trees. (☎456 9027. Singles and doubles Oct.-Nov. and Jan.-Jun., excluding Easter, 100 pesos; 150 pesos all other times.) If even a fan is too much luxury, **Librado Valderama Contreras ❶** (☎456 9024), will let you camp in his backyard for 30 pesos. From the main plaza, walk past the church and turn left, then right, and then left. Most streets in Batopilas aren't labeled, and with a population smaller than most bars, everyone knows everyone else's name. Comes with a hot shower and a great view. Librado is also a highly experienced muleteer and charges 2000 pesos per day for his services and those of his horses and mules. Excursions go to abandoned mines such as Peñasquito and Las Minas, as well as Satevo, a former 18th-century Jesuit mission that stands 8km south of Batopilas and features a strong Tarahumara influence. Knock on the door of the nearby house to ask to be let in. If hiking or the heat have got you hungry then try **Restaurante Reyna ❸**, which has the usual range of Mexican *antojitos*. (☎456 9057. Tacos 35 pesos. Open daily 8am-3pm and 5-10pm.)

THE TRAIN ROUTE

The Chepe train is one of the best ways to take in the stunning scenery of the Copper Canyon and is a perennial favorite with visitors. Two types of trains make the daily journey between Mochis and Chihuahua. The **second-class train** has spacious reclining seats and clean bathrooms and is well air-conditioned. The **first-class train** is twice as expensive, but for your extra money all you get is tilt-o-matic seats, a dining car, and occasionally an open-air viewing car. In order to see the most spectacular scenery (which lies between Temoris and Creel), grab a seat on the right side of the train if you're on the way to Chihuahua, and the left side if Mochisbound.

Trains go from Los Mochis to Chihuahua (1st-class 13hr., 6am, 1020 pesos; 2nd-class 14hr., 7am, 542 pesos) and from Chihuahua to Mochis (1st-class 6am, 1020 pesos; 2nd-class 7am, 542 pesos). Stops, listed for second-class trains from Mochis, are: **Sufragio, El Fuerte, Loreto, Temoris, Bahuachivo, Cuiteco, San Rafael, Divisadero, Creel, San Juanito, La Junta, Cuauhtémoc,** and **Chihuahua.** At Divisadero the train stops for 15min. allowing passengers the chance to take in the spectacular view and be bombarded by food and arts and crafts vendors.

Though often overlooked, El Fuerte is a far better place to get on/off than Los Mochis, as it is more appealing, cheaper, and safer. Furthermore, whichever way you're going, it allows for an extra two hours in bed.

SINALOA

EL FUERTE ☎ 698

Founded in 1564 by Don Francisco de Ibarra, El Fuerte (pop. 30,000) takes its name from the seeming invulnerability of the last of three forts that stood on this site. A sense of security continues to this day, making El Fuerte an excellent base for seeing Copper Canyon.

🖪🗗 TRANSPORTATION AND PRACTICAL INFORMATION. From the train station, 7km outside of town, you'll have a hard time getting to El Fuerte without a taxi (30 pesos). In town, **Juárez** is the main street and numbers are scattered about on it in a seemingly random fashion. Walk west from Juárez and turn left onto **5 de Mayo,** which puts you in the *zócalo,* in front of the Palacio Municipal. **Trains** leave daily for **Chihuahua** (1st-class 7:30am, 663.5 pesos; 2nd-class 8:40am) and **Los Mochis** (1st-class 1½hr., 6:15pm; 2nd-class 2hr., 8:40pm). **Taxis** gather on Juárez. **Buses** to **Los Mochis** (40 pesos) leave from Juárez and 16 de Septiembre.

The **tourist office** is to the left inside the Fuerte Museo Mirador. (☎893 1501. Open daily 9am-5pm.) **Bancomer,** Constitución 101 at Juárez, has a 24hr. **ATM.** (☎893 1145. Open M-F 8:30am-4pm.) Ask at the register before going upstairs to use the **Internet** at Librería Papelería Hermanos Urias (☎893 0615), Juárez 103 towards the *zócalo.* (Open Su 8am-3pm, M-Sa 8am-8pm. 20 pesos per hr.) The **post office** is in the Palacio Gobierno in the Playuela. (Open M-F 9am-4pm.) **Postal code:** 81820.

🖪🗗 ACCOMMODATIONS AND FOOD. El Fuerte's budget accomodations lie along Juárez. **Hotel San José ❶,** Juárez 108 (☎893 0845), has large rooms and high ceilings. (A wide selection of singles, from plain cots, 30 pesos, to beds with private bath, A/C, and TV, 150 pesos; doubles with fan and bath 100 pesos.) **Hotel Guerrero ❷,** Juárez 210, has rooms with baths, coolers (like weaker A/C), and comfy beds. (☎893 1350. Singles 150 pesos; doubles 200 pesos.) **La Fogata ❸,** Rosales 103, has a semi-outdoor patio connected to Rosa's kitchen. (☎893 9734. Chow 20-40 pesos.) Towards the *zócalo* lies **Restaurante El Mesón General ❹,** Juárez 202. Food is served around an open courtyard, and live music is played occasionally on weekends. (☎893 0206. *Pulpo,* or octopus, 70 pesos; *tacos machaca* 48 pesos. Open daily 8am-10:30pm.) Better values and better views can be found along the river at **El Paseo de Los Aves ❺,** Camino la Galera. Follow 5 de Mayo past Fuerte Museo Mirador as it curves to the right and then to the left; all in all, about a 15-20min. walk. (☎823 0986. Open daily 8am-8pm. *Camarones empanizados* 72 pesos.)

🖪 SIGHTS. Although a **fort** has stood in El Fuerte since 1564, the one that now watches over the town dates to 1610. To reach the fort, take 5 de Mayo past the Palacio del Gobierno and turn left at the sign that reads Fuerte Museo Mirador. On the lower level, rooms are filled with colonial and indigenous artifacts, but the real attraction is the view from the upper level that proved so strategically important to the Spanish. (☎823 1501. Open daily 9am-9pm. 5 pesos.) Continuing along, 5 de Mayo will turn into a gentle stroll along the **Río Fuerte.** Keep your eyes peeled for native birds such as the Crested Caracara, the Mexican Blue-Rumped Parrotelet, and the Plain-Capped Starthroat. Also keep your eyes on the path ahead of you: it's a frequently used cow passage.

LOS MOCHIS ☎ 667

Lying at one end of the CHEPE, the railroad that snakes through Copper Canyon, Los Mochis's major attraction is in leaving it. Founded and developed by US expats, first as a utopian experiment and later as part of a sugar-growing money-making scheme, the US colonial roots are visible in the city's monotonous grid of wide streets and modern buildings. The sugar days are over, but Mochis continues to be an important link between the coast and the interior, funneling goods and backpackers into the mountains efficiently.

⌐ TRANSPORTATION

Municipal buses run throughout the city (4 pesos). The main stop is on Zaragoza at Obregón; ask the driver if he goes to your destination. **Taxis** (☎ 812 0283) wait on the corner of every major intersection.

Buses: Though many bus carriers serve the city, finding the individual stations can be a challenge. The most obvious is the modern station run by **Élite** (☎ 812 1757), at the corner of Juárez and Degollado. The cheaper carrier, **Transportes Norte de Sonora,** goes to: **Guaymas** (5hr., every hr., 113 pesos); **Mazatlán** (5½hr., every hr. 5am-5pm, 118 pesos); **Mexicali** (18hr.; 7, 8:15am; 418 pesos); **Mexico City** (24hr., 6pm, 707 pesos), via **Culiacán** (3hr., 102 pesos); **Tijuana** (22hr.; 4, 7, 8:15pm; 485 pesos), via **Hermosillo** (7hr., 102 pesos). **Transportes del Pacífico** (☎ 812 0347), on Morelos between Leyva and Zaragoza, sends *de paso* buses to similar destinations. Buses to **El Fuerte** and nearby destinations leave from Zaragoza, between Ordóñez and Cuauhté-moc. Buses to **Topolobampo** (every 20min., 10 pesos), leave from a stop on Cuauhté-moc between Prieta and Zaragoza, 1 block north of Obregón. Mochis also has **Pacífico** (coastal destinations to the south) and **Azteca de Oro** stations.

Ferry: The ferry to **La Paz** leaves from the nearby coastal town of **Topolobampo** daily at 10pm. Ticket prices change frequently, and are sold at the **Sematur** office by the ferry until 6pm the day of departure (☎ 862 0141; fax 862 0035). Office open daily 8am-10pm. Tickets are brokered through the travel agency **Viajes Ahome,** Morelos Pte. 392 (☎ 815 6120). Open Su 9am-2pm, M-Sa 9am-2pm and 3-7pm.

Train: The **Chihuahua al Pacífico Train,** or **"Chepe"** (☎ 824 1151), runs between Los Mochis and Chihuahua, with stops throughout the **Copper Canyon.** The posh 1st-class train leaves daily at 6am for **Creel** (557.6 pesos) and **Chihuahua** (1020 pesos). The equally comfortable 2nd-class train leaves at 7am, is about half the price, and only requires sacrificing butt space and dining cars. (296.1 pesos to Creel, 542 pesos to Chihuahua.) Tickets can be purchased in the station or on the train. During peak back-packer season (July-Aug.) you may wish to purchase tickets in advance. **Viajes Fla-mingo,** Hildalgo Pte. 419 (☎ 812 1613), in Hotel Santa Anita, sells tickets.

✸ ⑦ ORIENTATION AND PRACTICAL INFORMATION

The city is laid out in a grid. Downtown, the principal north-south avenues are (east to west) Degollado, Zaragoza, Leyva, Guerrero, and Rosales. Perpendicular to these from north to south are Juan de Dios Bátiz, Cárdenas, Morelos, Indepen-dencia, Obregón, Castro, and Ordóñez. The **tourist office,** on Ordóñez and Allende, is next to the Palacio de Gobierno in the Unidad Administrativa; use the entrance off Ordóñez and turn right. (☎ 815 1090. Open M-F 9am-4pm.) **Bancomer,** on Leyva and Juárez, has 24hr. **ATMs.** (☎ 812 2323. Open M-F 8:30am-4pm and 3:30-7pm, Sa 9am-1:30pm.) **American Express,** on Obregón between Flores and Morelos, cashes traveler's checks. (☎ 612 0590. Open M-F 9am-2pm and 4-6pm, Sa 9am-1pm.) For

emergency services call ☎060 or contact the **police,** Degollado at Cuauhtémoc, in the Presidencia Municipal. (☎812 0033. No English spoken.) The **Red Cross** (☎815 0808 or 812 0292) is located at Tenochtitlán and Prieto, one block off Castro. Other services include: **Hospital Fátima,** Jiquilpán Pte. 639 (☎812 3312; no English spoken); medical assistance at the **Centro de Salud** (☎812 0913); **Internet** at **WebSurf,** in the mall at Obregón and Rosales (15 pesos per hr.; open Su 9am-7pm, M-Sa 9am-9pm); and the **post office,** Ordóñez 226, two blocks off Castro, between Prieta and Zaragoza (☎812 0823; open M-F 9am-3pm). **Postal code:** 81200.

ACCOMMODATIONS AND FOOD

Most decent hotel rooms in Mochis hover around 200 pesos. **Hotel Lorena** ❹ (☎812 6847; fax 812 0239), Obregón 186, comes furnished with everything but a butler: rooms have views, A/C, TV, purified water, and clean baths. (Singles 225 pesos; doubles 305 pesos; triples 345 pesos.) **Hotel Hidalgo** ❸, Hidalgo Pte. 260 between Prieta and Zaragoza, is a step down. Ceiling fans cool off small rooms. (☎818 3453. Singles 160 pesos, with A/C 210 pesos; doubles 240 pesos; triples 260 pesos.) If you must stay at the cheapest place in town, **Hotel Los Arcos** ❷, at Obregón and Allende, is for you. Rooms have limp-looking beds and communal, 24hr. hot showers. (☎812 3253. Singles 100 pesos; doubles 150 pesos; triples 200 pesos.)

The place for excellent late-night grub is **Tacos la Cabaña de Doña Chayo** ❶, Obregón 99, at the corner with Allende. The absurd size of the tacos justifies their relatively high price. (☎818 5498. Tacos 13 pesos, quesadillas 13 pesos. Open daily 8am-1am.) For super-early, pre-train breakfasts, you'll have to resort to **El Taquito** ❸, on Leyva between Hidalgo and Independencia. (Open 24hr. Breakfasts from 25 pesos.) Sanitized, air-conditioned escape from Mochis reality is best found at **Chic's** ❸, located outside the mall at Obregón and Rosales. (Salads 32-35 pesos, fruit platters 18-35 pesos. Open daily 7am-10:30pm.)

SIGHTS AND NIGHTLIFE

If you stick around long enough to see something, a large collection of trees and plants grows in the 16 hectare **Parque Sinaloa,** which used to be the private gardens of Benjamin Johnston, owner of the American-run sugar operation in Los Mochis in the 1920s. Walk to the end of Castro and turn left; the entrance is about half a block down Rosales. Adjoining Plaza Solidaridad is **Santuario del Sagrado Corazón de Jesús,** Mochis's oldest church, built after the founder's Protestant wife donated the land to the people. Nightlife in Mochis tends to be surly and male-dominated. Bars congregate on Obregón near Allende, and most get rowdy and obnoxious by midnight. Fortunately, **Rodeo Bar,** on Obregón at Constitución, has a mechanical horse. (Cover 60 pesos. Open daily 9pm-3am.)

CULIACÁN ☎668

Due to the large amount of traffic to seaside destinations, Culiacán (pop. 600,000) has managed to become the second most important tourist site in Sinaloa. Unfortunately, this isn't the only traffic that passes through Culiacán: the city, nicknamed "little Medellín," is believed to be one of the three centers of Mexico's drug trade. Extra effort has kept the *centro* beautiful, and what little artistic wealth falls to Sinaloa is gathered here, which does make a trip to Culiacán worthwhile.

TRANSPORTATION. The **airport** (☎760 0676) is 10km southeast of downtown. Major carriers include **AeroCalifornia** (☎716 0250), **Aeroméxico** (☎714 0181 or 800 021 4000), and **Aerolíneas Internacionales** (☎712 5443). Culiacán's modern

bus station (☎712 4875) is located 12km from downtown. Buses to the station leave from stops throughout the *centro* and from the **old bus station** on Solano (3 pesos). Taxis cost 50 pesos and are often the only option after dark. **Transportes Norte de Sonora** (☎761 0178) sends buses every hour to: **Guadalajara** (11hr., 424 pesos); **Hermosillo** (325 pesos); **Mexico City** (18hr., 812 pesos); **Monterrey** (17hr.; 5, 7:30pm; 755 pesos); **Tepic** (8hr., 348 pesos); **Tijuana** (996 pesos). **Pacífico** (☎761 4730) goes to: **Ciudad Obregón** (every hr., 124 pesos); **Guaymas** (8hr., every hr., 153 pesos); **Mazatlán** (2½hr., every hr., 134 pesos). **Norte de Sinaloa** heads to: **Los Mochis** (every hr. 7am-9pm, 102 pesos).

🔢🔢 ORIENTATION AND PRACTICAL INFORMATION. The city concentrates on the south side of Río Tamazula. The downtown area is roughly delineated by **Madero, Granados,** the edge of the river along which **Niños Héroes** runs, and **Bravo.** A **tourist office** is located in the Palacio de Gobierno, at Insurgentes and Barraza. (Open M-F 8am-3pm and 5-7pm.) **Banamex** (☎715 0700), Rosales 103, offers **currency exchange** and a 24hr. **ATM.** (Open M-F 8:30am-4:30pm.) Other services include: **emergency** (☎060 or 066); **police,** Federalisimo 2500 (☎761 0152); **Red Cross** (☎752 0207), at Solano and Paleza; 24hr. **Farmacia Red Cross,** 145 Solano; **Hospital Civil de Culiacán** (☎716 4650), Obregón and Romero; **Internet access** at **Net.house,** Juárez 75. (20 pesos per hr.; open Su 9am-2pm, M-Sa 9am-8pm); **post office,** 560 Domingo Rubi (☎712 2170; open M-F 8am-1pm, Sa 9am-1pm). **Postal code:** 80000.

🔢 ACCOMMODATIONS. In 2003, President Fox sent extra federal police to Culiacán as a signal to the city's drug barons. A large contingent ends up standing on the street corners in the *centro puro*, toting rifles with little to do but look imposing. While the area between Bravo and Obregón is very safe, other parts of Culiacán can be pretty dangerous, especially at night. Cheap, relatively safe, but not exactly central **Hotel Louisiana ❷,** Villa Ote. 478, is a high-security hotel with few perks. (☎713 9152. Singles 100 pesos; doubles 120 pesos.) **Hotel Santa Fe ❹,** Hidalgo Pte. 243, greets visitors with an icy A/C blast that makes staying over seem tolerable. Rooms have cable TV, phone, and well-maintained baths. (☎715 1700. Singles 240 pesos; doubles 270 pesos; triples 300 pesos.) **Hotel San Francisco ❺,** Hidalgo Pte. 227, is slightly more expensive and not quite as nice. The un-remodeled section offers A/C, TV, and nice baths with hot water. (☎713 5863. Singles 285 pesos, remodeled 340 pesos; doubles 310/365 pesos.)

🔢 FOOD. For food on the cheap, try **Tacos Ranas ❶,** at the corner of Morelos and Flores, where 3 *tacos al pastor* cost 15 pesos. (Open M-Sa 9am-9pm.) A great view of the Plaza Obregón and good food come together at **Los Antiguos Portales de Culiacán ❺** (☎752 1978), Paliza Nte. 574. (Fajitas 69 pesos. Open daily noon-10pm.) A two-city chain, **Panamá Café ❸** (☎716 8350), Francisco Villa Ote. 51, at Parque de Revolución, and also at Constitución and Lázaro Cárdenas Sur (☎712 9250), serves pastries, coffee, and surprisingly good *comida típica* in a clean, family-style restaurant. (Enchiladas 33 pesos, salads 25-35 pesos. Open daily 7am-10pm.)

🔢 SIGHTS. The city's **shrine to Jesús Malverde,** on Independencia, a 19th-century bandit whose Robin Hood-esque practices led to his execution in 1909, is by far its most titillating attraction. From the *centro,* head west toward Bravo until you reach Madero as it runs along the train tracks. Follow this away from the *centro* until it turns into Independencia. Just off the Plaza Obregón, **Museo de Arte Sinaloa,** Rafael Buelna and Paliza, houses the work of artists such as Diego Rivera, López Saenz, and Frida Kahlo in its wonderfully air-conditioned chambers. (☎715 5541. Open Su 11am-5pm, Tu-Sa 10am-3pm and 5-7pm. 5 pesos, students and children 3 pesos; Su free.)

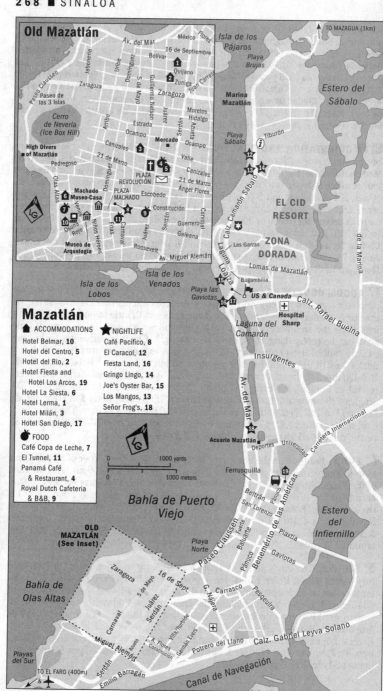

Old Mazatlán

Av. del Mar
México
Flores
16 de Septiembre
Bolívar
Quijano
Zuniga
Juan Carras
Zaragoza
Morelos
Hidalgo
Azteta
Estrada
Ocampo
Mercado
Ocampo
Canizales
Valle
21 de Marzo
Canizales
PLAZA
REVOLUCIÓN
21 de Marzo
Ángel Flores
Machado
Museo-Casa
PLAZA
MACHADO
Escobedo
Constitución
Corrojal
Guerrero
Galeana
Museo de
Arqueología
Roosevelt
Av. Miguel Alemán
Jabonería
Uribe
Domínguez
5 de Mayo
Guillermo Nelson
Juárez
Serdán
Paseo Clausen
Paseo de
las 3 Islas
Zaragoza
Cerro
de Nevería
(Ice Box Hill)
High Divers
■ of Mazatlán
Pedregoso
Domínguez
Ambio
Olas Altas
Venustiano
Osuna
Rojo
Niños Héroes
Carnaval
Frias
Juárez
Serdán

TO MAZAGUA (1km)
Isla de los
Pájaros
Playa
Brujas
Estero del
Sábalo
Marina
Mazatlán
Playa
Sábalo
Tiburón
EL CID
RESORT
Calz. Camarón Sábalo
de la Marina
ZONA
DORADA
Las Garzas
Lomas de Mazatlán
Laguna
Loaiza
Bugambilia
Playa las
Gaviotas
US & Canada
Calz. Rafael Buelna
Hospital
Sharp
Laguna del
Camarón
Insurgentes
Av. del Mar
Acuario Mazatlán
Deportes
Universidad
Carretera Internacional
Ferrusquilla
Beltrán
Pánuco
Estero
del
Infiernillo

Isla de los
Lobos
Isla de los
Venados

Mazatlán

🏠 ACCOMMODATIONS
Hotel Belmar, **10**
Hotel del Centro, **5**
Hotel del Río, **2**
Hotel Fiesta and
   Hotel Los Arcos, **19**
Hotel La Siesta, **6**
Hotel Lerma, **1**
Hotel Milán, **3**
Hotel San Diego, **17**

🍎 FOOD
Café Copa de Leche, **7**
El Tunnel, **11**
Panamá Café
   & Restaurant, **4**
Royal Dutch Cafetería
   & B&B, **9**

⭐ NIGHTLIFE
Café Pacífico, **8**
El Caracol, **12**
Fiesta Land, **16**
Gringo Lingo, **14**
Joe's Oyster Bar, **15**
Los Mangos, **13**
Señor Frog's, **18**

0   1000 yards
0   1000 meters

OLD
MAZATLÁN
(See Inset)

Bahía de Puerto
Viejo

Zaragoza
5 de Mayo
16 de Sept.
Juárez
Serdán
Playa
Norte
Paseo Clausen
G. Carrasco
Pesqueira
Pánuco
Baluarte
Fuerte
Benemérito de las Américas
Plaxtia
Gaviotas
Bahía de
Olas Altas
Carnaval
Aquiles
Miguel Alemán
A. Flores
Constitución
Gaitán Exes
Villa Iturbide
Beltrán
San Lorenzo
Potrero del Llano
Calz. Gabriel Leyva Solano

Playas
del Sur
Serdán
Emilio Barragán
TO EL FARO (400m)
Canal de Navegación

MAZATLÁN ☎ 669

Mazatlán has a history filled with 17th-century Spanish gold shipping and foreign blockades of the port. Not that any of that really matters to the tourists who now blockade her streets in search of golden sands and sunshine. Mazatlán is a forgetful city, making it the perfect place to combine sleepy sun-filled days and debaucherous nights best left unspoken.

◼ TRANSPORTATION

An efficient **bus system** makes navigating the city a breeze. At some point, all municipal buses pass the public market on Juárez, three blocks north of the *zócalo* at Ocampo. The air-conditioned Mercedes "Sábalo-Centro" bus runs from the downtown market, with stops a few blocks from the *malecón* in Olas Altas and at Playa Sábalo in the Zona Dorada (7.5 pesos). "Cerritos-Juárez" continues up to Playa Bruja at Puerta Cerritos. The "Insurgentes" route services bus and train stations, and "Playa Sur" goes to the ferry dock and lighthouse (every 15min. 5am-10pm, 3 pesos). For late-night disco hopping, take a taxi or *pulmonía* (like a large golf cart). Standard fare between Old Mazatlán and the Zona Dorada is 35-40 pesos, depending on time of night (later is more expensive). The walk is more than an hour, giving drivers bargaining leverage, but don't be afraid to haggle with *pulmonía* drivers—there are plenty to choose from.

Airport: Rafael Buelna International Airport (☎982 2399), 18km south of the city. The "Central Camionera" bus goes to the *centro,* but you must return by taxi (150 pesos). Served by **AeroCalifornia** (☎913 2042), El Cid Resort; **Aeroméxico,** Sábalo 310A (☎914 1111 or 800 021 4000); **Alaska Airlines** (☎800 252 7522); **Mexicana,** Pasco Claussen 101-B (☎982 7722 or 800 502 2000).

Buses: The bus station is 3 blocks from the *malecón* and about 2km north of Old Mazatlán, between downtown and the Zona Dorada. To get downtown, catch any of the red buses with "Centro" or "Mercado" on their windshields, 1 block west of the station and about 1 block south, to your right along Benemérito de las Américas (3 pesos, after 9pm 3.5 pesos; buses stop running at 10pm). Avoid the "Sábalo-coco" bus, as it goes downtown only after an enormous loop around the city. Cabs also make the trip (35 pesos and up). **Estrella Blanca Group** (☎981 3811) sends buses to: **Chihuahua** (16hr.; 2, 6pm; 521 pesos); **Ciudad Juárez** (21hr.; 2, 6pm; 754 pesos); **Durango** (7hr., 4 per day, 214 pesos); **Mexico City** (18hr., every hr., 443 pesos); **Monterrey** (17hr., 3 per day, 465 pesos); **Torreón** (12 hr., 3 per day, 241 pesos). **Transportes de Pacífico** (☎981 5156) travels to: **Culiacán** (every hr., 134 pesos); **Los Mochis** (6hr., every hr., 302 pesos); **Puerto Vallarta** (7½hr., 327 pesos); **Tepic** (4½hr., every hr., 140 pesos).

Ferry: Sematur (☎981 7020), at the end of Carnaval, south of Flores and the *centro.* It's a 20min. walk from the *centro* to the ferry docks, or a quick ride on the blue "Playa Sur" bus (3 pesos). Taxis 30-35 pesos. Tickets sold only on the day of departure. Arrive at least 2hr. early to procure a seat. Ticket office open Su-F 8am-3pm, Sa 9am-1pm. Advance ticket purchases are available at a local travel agency. During high season (Dec. and July-Aug.), make reservations at least 2 weeks ahead. 1 ferry every day to **La Paz** leaves around 2:30pm and arrives around 8am (call for fares).

◼ ◼ ORIENTATION AND PRACTICAL INFORMATION

Mazatlán is divided into **Old Mazatlán,** home to the *zócalo* and budget hotels and restaurants, and the **Zona Dorada,** home to the high-rise hotels and big-money entertainment. The boardwalk follows the beach and connects the two sides of the town. Since Mazatlán is spread out, the easiest way to traverse the city is by bus.

TOURIST, FINANCIAL, AND LOCAL SERVICES

Tourist Office: (☎916 5160; fax 916 5166) on Sábalo at Tiburón, on the 4th fl. of the pinkish Banrural building past El Cid resort on the "Sábalo-Centro" bus line. Helpful staff doles out good maps; pick up a copy of *Pacific Pearl*, the monthly English-language newspaper. Open M-F 9am-5pm; reachable by phone Sa 9am-1pm.

Tourist Police: (☎800 903 9200), on Ruíz and Santa Mónica in the Zona Dorada.

Consulates: Canada (☎913 7320), and **US** (☎916 5889), Playa Gaviotas 202 across from the Hotel Playa Mazatlán in the Zona Dorada. US consulate open daily 8am-4pm, Canadian open daily 9am-1pm.

Currency Exchange: *Casas de cambio* are open all day in the northern downtown area, but have poor rates. Stick to banks in the *centro* and the *zócalo*. **Banca Serfín** (☎982 6666), 21 de Marzo and Nelson, across from the *zócalo*, has a 24hr. **ATM.** Open M-F 8:30am-5pm, Sa 10am-2pm.

American Express: (☎913 0600; fax 916 5908), in Centro Comercial Plaza Balboa on Sábalo. Open daily 9am-5pm.

Car Rental: Alamo, Sábalo 410 (☎913 1010), **Budget,** Sábalo 402 (☎913 2000), and **National,** Sábalo 7000 (☎913 6000). Cars with unlimited mileage start at 480 pesos per day.

Laundry: Lavandería Acalá, Azueta 1817 in the *centro*. Wash and dry 12 pesos per kg. Open Su 8:30am-1pm, M-Sa 8:30am-7pm.

EMERGENCY AND COMMUNICATIONS

Emergency: ☎060.

Police: (☎983 4510), on Buelna in Colonia Juárez. Some English spoken.

Red Cross: (☎985 1451), on Zaragoza and Corona. Some English spoken.

Pharmacy: Farmacia Ibael (☎982 6249), on Ángel Flores and Campana. Open daily 8:30am-10:30pm.

Hospital: Sharp Hospital (☎986 5676), on Kumate and Buelna, near Zaragoza park. English spoken. **Hospital General de Zona #3** (☎984 7865; emergency ext. 270 and 271), on Mateos.

Internet Access: Telefona Automática de Pacífico, Flores 810 (☎981 7159), in the *centro*. 15 pesos per hr. Open daily 8:30am-9:30pm. Also **fax** service and **caseta.**

Post Office: (☎981 2121), on Flores at Juárez, across from the *zócalo*. Open M-F 8am-6pm, Sa 9am-1pm. **Postal Code: 82000.**

ACCOMMODATIONS

While it's most fun to stay in the mid-range waterfront hotels of Olas Altas, more budget hotels line Juárez and Serdán in Old Mazatlán and, for the truly self-denying, in the area around the bus station. At any of these, rates may rise substantially during high season (July-Aug. and Dec.-Apr.). The best hotel rates in the Zona Dorada can be found at the **Hotel San Diego** ❺, on Av. del Mar and Buelna right by Fiesta Land. Rooms are clean and feature A/C and TV. (☎983 5703; www.hotel-sandiego.tripod.com. Singles low season 250 pesos, high season 350 pesos; doubles 350/550 pesos.) Alternatively, there are plenty of trailer parks, such as La Posta 1, on Buelna. (☎983 5310. Hook-up 85 pesos.)

OLAS ALTAS

Back in the 1950s, Olas Altas was the focal point of Mazatlán's fledgling resort scene. Although newer restaurants have sprung up, the area remains mostly unchanged since its glory days, perched on the cliffs in a state of rusting glamor. A 10min. walk from the *centro*, Olas Altas connects to the rest of Mazatlán by the "Sábalo-Centro" and other bus lines.

■ **Hotel Belmar,** Olas Altas 166 (☎985 1112), at Osuna. Spacious rooms with baths come with a choice of either a poignant sea view or the more pragmatic TV and A/C combo. Either way, balance the decision with a dip in the pool, or curl up with a book from their library. Singles with A/C and TV 250 pesos, with ocean view 320 pesos. Expect to pay 30 pesos extra Nov.-Apr. ❺

Hotel la Siesta, Olas Altas Sur 11 (☎981 2640 or 800 711 5229), at Escobedo. Tiered wooden walkways connect rooms with A/C, TV, phone, and hot water, set around a verdant courtyard. Singles low season 293 pesos, with ocean view 304 pesos; high season 351/468 pesos. ❺

OLD MAZATLÁN
Downtown offers easy access to most points in the city.

■ **Hotel del Río,** Juárez 2410 Nte. (☎982 4430). Clean white halls and rooms hung with antique cowboy propaganda are a welcome relief from Mazatlán's relentless nautical decor. Pleasant furniture and management, plus a central location. Reserve 2 or 3 days in advance. Singles 100 pesos; doubles 120 pesos. ❷

Hotel Lerma, Bolívar 622 (☎981 2436), at Serdán. Spacious rooms and ceiling fans make the heat bearable. Free parking. Singles 70 pesos, with bath 90 pesos; doubles 100 pesos. Prices rise 10 pesos Jul.-Aug. and Dec.-Apr. ❶

Hotel Milán, Canizales 717 (☎985 3499), across from the Telmex building in the business district. A/C and TV make up for the brown color scheme. Singles 140 pesos; doubles 163 pesos. Prices may rise 30-40% July-Aug. ❷

Hotel del Centro, Canizales 705 (☎981 2673), a step down from Hotel Milán, between Serdán and Juárez. Simple, clean rooms that blend into anonymity. Singles low season 140 pesos, high season 163.8 pesos; doubles 160/210 pesos. ❸

NEAR THE BUS STATION
Hotel los Arcos, Río Panoco 1006 (☎981 3370), around the block to the left from the station's main exit. Recently constructed, with basic rooms. Singles 120 pesos; doubles 140 pesos, with A/C 180 pesos. ❷

Hotel Fiesta, Ferrosquila 306 (☎981 7888), in front of the bus station. Clean rooms have baths and purified water. Enjoy "hot kakes" (20 pesos) or an "homlet" (18 pesos) at the hotel's cafe. Singles and doubles 160 pesos, with A/C and TV 200 pesos. ❸

◗ FOOD

Restaurant prices soar closer to the tourist glam of the Zona Dorada. The *centro*, however, is just the place for quality meals on a budget. The busy **public market,** between Juárez and Serdán, three blocks north of the *zócalo*, serves the best and cheapest food in the area. If you need a headless pig (or a pig's head), look no further. For something more formal, try one of the *centro*'s many inexpensive restaurants or, for the view, an establishment along the *malecón* in Olas Altas. Enjoy your meal with **Pacífico** beer, the pride of Mazatlán.

OLAS ALTAS
Copa de Leche Café, 1220 A Sur (☎982 5753), on the *malecón*. Wake up to eggs and pancakes (28 pesos), with classic *café con leche* (13 pesos), well into the afternoon. Open daily 7:30am-11pm. ❸

NORTHWEST MEXICO

ON THE MENU

SOTOL ME ALL ABOUT IT

Although Tequila's alcoholic goodness has gained a worldwide reputation, few people have heard of its close cousin, sotol.

Sotol, along with tequila and mescal, is made from a plant of the agave family. Unlike tequila, which is made from blue agave, sotol is distilled from the *agavacea dasylirion*, a smaller plant that grows in the mountains and deserts of Chihuahua. *Agavacea* hearts are cooked, shredded, fermented, distilled, and finally aged from six months (*reposado* sotol) to over a year (*añejo* sotol).

Local Indians first discovered sotol's magically intoxicating properties over 800 years ago; it didn't take the Spanish long to realize this as well, and, with the aid of European distillation techniques, they helped to enhance the purification process. Despite having been enjoyed for centuries in the *haciendas* of Chihuahua—indeed, many families brew their own crude version of the drink—sotol has only recently begun to achieve international recognition.

Sotol admirers claim that it has a smoother taste than its better-known relative. But perhaps the sotol's strongest selling point is its price—a bottle of top-notch sotol costs only a fraction of the price of similar-quality tequila.

One of the most prominent sotol distributors is Chihuahua's Vinomex (☎ 614 415 1212; www.vinomex.com.mx).

Mesón Marisquero (☎ 982 8226), on Puerto Viejo at the *malecón*. Marisquero whips up small doses of *ceviche* (10-13 pesos), *tostadas* (28 pesos), and beer (10 pesos). Open Su-Th 11am-11pm, F-Sa 11am-1am. ❸

NEAR THE PLAZUELA MACHADO

🏴 **El Tunnel**, in a tunnel that starts at Carnaval 1207, across from the theater. Great ambience upstaged only by the amazing food. Dedicated to (pre)serving classic Sinaloense cuisine, this place has dished out delicious *gorditas* since 1945. *Gorditas* or *agua de horchata*, 9 pesos. Open daily noon-midnight. ❸

🏴 **Royal Dutch Cafeteria and B&B** (☎ 981 4396; roy-dutch@mzt.megared.net.mx), Constitución and Juárez. Offers only the freshest baked goods and the best coffee in town, (free refills). The couple owning it also runs a **bed and breakfast** ❺ with A/C, cable TV, CD player, movies, and extremely comfortable rooms. They'll even come and pick you up at the airport or bus station. Strudel 22 pesos, sandwich 25 pesos; *café americano* 13 pesos. Rooms 450 pesos. Open M-F 9am-9pm and Sa noon-3pm. Cafeteria closed June-Sept. ❷

Panamá Cafe and Restaurant, Juárez and Canizales, also at Serdán and Morelos. Gusty A/C will whirlwind your appetite for amazing pastries or authentic *sinaloense antojitos* (33 pesos). Salads 25-35 pesos, breakfasts 25 pesos, all served quickly. Open daily 7am-10pm. ❸

👁 🏖 SIGHTS AND BEACHES

BEACHES. Mazatlán's famous beach stretches 16km from Olas Altas, well past the Zona Dorada. North of Old Mazatlán, along del Mar, is **Playa Norte**. Its small waves and general lack of activity make it a decent stretch of sand if you're looking for tranquility. As you approach the Zona Dorada, the beach gets cleaner, the waves larger, and Playa Norte eases into **Playa las Gaviotas.** Past Punta Sábalo, in the lee of the islands, is **Playa Sábalo,** where great waves and golden sand enthrall crowds of sun-worshippers. "Sábalo-Centro" buses pass all these beaches. As Playa Sábalo recedes to the north, crowds thin rapidly and you can frolic alone. In most places, boogie boards (40 pesos) and sailboats (500 pesos per hr.) are available. Take the "Cerritos-Juárez" bus to the last stop and walk left (walking straight ahead brings you to a rocky outcropping with restaurants but little sand) to nearly deserted **Playa Bruja** (Witch Beach), with beautiful sand and 1-2m waves. **Camping** is permitted, but exercise caution after dark and camp in groups whenever possible.

EL FARO. For a 360-degree view of Mazatlán and the sea, climb to the top of El Faro, at the end of the "Playa Sur" bus route: it's the second-tallest lighthouse in the world. The 30min. hike is almost unbearable in the summer; ascend in the early morning or late evening to avoid the heat.

TOWER DIVERS. Mazatlán's tower divers perform acrobatic and dangerous plunges into rocky surf from an 18m high ledge. Dives take place during the day, but be warned that divers will not perform unless they pull in a sufficient amount of money beforehand. The best time to watch is 10-11am and 4:30-6:30pm, when tour buses arrive and tourists fork over their pesos, allowing you—the savvy (unscrupulous) budget traveler—to see dives for free. Great viewing just south of the towers. *(On Claussen, south of Zaragoza and north of La Siesta Hotel.)*

ISLAS VENADOS (DEER ISLAND). For those itching to escape the beaches, the island is a relatively deserted strip of land with fine diving; catamaran boats leave from the Agua Sports Center at El Cid Resort in the Zona Dorada. *(☎ 913 3333, ext. 341. Boats depart daily 10am, noon, 2pm. Round-trip 100 pesos.)*

MAZAGUA. Waterpark mania hit Mazatlán with Mazagua, north of the Zona Dorada near Puerta Cerritos. Go bonkers in the wave pool or shoot down slippery slides. *(Take a "Cerritos-Juárez" bus, 3.5 pesos. ☎ 988 0041. Open Mar.-Oct. daily 10am-6pm. 80 pesos, children under 4 free.)*

ACUARIO MAZATLÁN. One of the largest aquariums in Latin America keeps sharks and other feisty fish (up to 250 breeds in all) in a slew of cloudy tanks, and also hosts performing sea lions and birds. *(Av. de los Deportes 111, off Av. del Mar, 1 block back from the beach; the turn-off is marked with a blue sign. ☎ 981 7815. Open daily 9:30am-6pm. 50 pesos, children ages 5-10 25 pesos.)*

TEATRO ÁNGELA PERALTA. The newly restored and luxurious theater, at Carnaval and Libertad near Plazuela Machado, hosts an impressive variety of cultural programs. *(☎ 982 4447; www.teatroangelaperalta.com. 5 pesos.)*

MUSEO CASA MACHADO. This 19th-century mansion is filled with relics from Mazatlán's glory days as the state capital. The museum's collection of spectacularly gaudy old *Carnaval* costumes makes it worth a visit. *(Constitución 79, just off Plazuela Machado. ☎ 982 1440. Open daily 10am-6pm. 20 pesos, children 10 pesos.)*

MUSEO ARQUEOLÓGICO. This small but interesting museum displays clay figurines, rocks, and dioramas. *(Osuna 72 between the centro and Olas Altas. Open Su 10am-3pm, M-F 10am-6pm. Free.)*

🎵🍸 ENTERTAINMENT AND NIGHTLIFE

Masses of US high schoolers hit Mazatlán each year to drink and break curfew. More than a dozen discos and bars clamor for *gringo* dollars, with only the occasional Mexican rock tune reminding partiers that this is not the US. Prices for transportation and cover are steep and, because most nightclubs cut deals with package-tour companies, the unpackaged tourist is often charged more. Mellower amusements entertain locals in and around the *centro*.

THE CENTRO AND OLAS ATLAS

Altrazor Ars Cafe, Constitutión 517, across from Plazuela Machado. Local Gen-Xers come for the 15-peso beer and live music that kicks off at 8:30pm nightly. Snacks (quesadillas 20 pesos, sandwiches 18 pesos) are also served. Open Su 4pm-1am, M-Sa 9am-2am.

Club Muralla, at the corner of Venus and Osuna, just uphill from the Museo Arqueológico. Look for chairs and tables outside the seemingly anonymous doorway to enjoy a courtyard full of low-stakes gambling and sports TV. Locals sip 10-peso beers, nosh on *ceviche,* and sometimes dance to live bands on weekends until 1am. Don your *guayabera,* channel your cool, and kick it with the best of them. Open daily noon-2am.

Café Pacífico, Constitución 501 (☎981 3972), across from Plazuela Machado. A "classic pub" with an odd assortment of animal skins, rifles, and stained-glass windows. The cool interior and 10-peso beers attract a fun crowd of amiable locals seeking respite from the Mazatlán sun. Marlin burritos 50 pesos. Open daily 10am-2am.

ZONA DORADA

Gringo Lingo, Playa Gaviotas 313 (☎913 7737; www.gringolingo.com.mx), across from the Hotel Sábalo. A young foreign crowd comes to hear music that speaks their language and enjoy some of the least gouged prices the Zona Dorada has to offer. Th live rock music. 10 people get a 15% discount on food and 39-peso 3-for-1 beer deal. Hamburgers 40-58 pesos. Open daily noon-1am.

Mangos, Playa Gaviotas 403 (☎916 0044), set off from the street towards the beach. Filled with a young and trendy crowd who hang out by the beach. Dress code prohibits tennis shoes, flip flops, and shorts; it is enforced at the management's discretion. *Margaritas de mango* are the house specialty (single 32 pesos, double 54 pesos). No cover. Open Su-Th noon-12:30am, F-Sa noon-4am.

Joe's Oyster Bar, Playa Gaviotas 100 (☎983 5353), next to Los Sábalos Hotel. Its beachfront location and relaxed atmosphere make it a good place to put away a few beers before hitting the club scene (2 beers for 30 pesos). Cover 30 pesos, includes one beer. Open daily 11am-3am.

Fiesta Land (☎984 1666), Sábalo towards the southern end of the Zona Dorada. A grouping of several nightspots. Valentino's is a disco with Euro-trash pretensions. Bora-Bora is a beach club by day and more relaxed disco by night. Cantabar is part of Valentino's and features karaoke. Bali Hai is a sport bar and Maui is a snack bar. Despite all being in the same complex, they operate as relatively separate entities—meaning you usually have to pay to get into each one separately, so choose well. Although music varies widely, it is always pre-recorded. Cover varies from free to 150 pesos depending on the crowd. Cocktails 30-35 pesos. Bora-Bora open daily 9pm-4am. Valentino's open daily 9pm-3am.

El Caracol (☎913 3333, ext. 3245), in the El Cid Hotel on Sábalo. A premier 4-level dance club, with insane lights rising from the floor. Beer and mixed drinks 30-40 pesos. No cover. Open daily 9pm-2am.

Señor Frog's (☎985 1110), on Paseo del Mar. The beach resort restaurant whose empire extends from Tijuana to Cancún was born 30 years ago in Mazatlán. A place of pilgrimage for locals and foreigners alike, all of whom check their thrift at the door and enjoy expensive food. Fajitas 65-130 pesos. 110 pesos for a yard-long (868ml) mixed drink. There may be a cover on busy nights. Open daily 11am-2am.

Playa Hotel Bar (☎913 1111), Punta del Sábalo inside the Hotel Playa Real. An older, more sedate crowd comes to hang out in the bar and be serenaded by the romantic strains of live Mexican music every night. Beer 24 pesos, cocktails 40 pesos. Open daily 6pm-midnight.

FESTIVALS

As if the nightly scene weren't garish enough, the city comes out in force each year to celebrate a particularly debaucherous **Carnaval.** More than just a money-making scheme hatched by local hoteliers, Mazatlán's *Carnaval* has a history dating back to the 17th century. Hotel reservations should be made several weeks in advance for this party during the week before Lent.

DAYTRIPS FROM MAZATLÁN

ISLA DE LA PIEDRA

Take a green "Independencia" bus (3 pesos) from the market at Serdán to the Embarcadero de la Isla de la Piedra; it's the small jetty about 250m east of the Sematur ferry station. From there, take a boat to the island (5min., every 10min., 10 pesos roundtrip; last return 7pm). Pulmonías (15 pesos) and taxis (10 pesos) take passengers to the beach from the ferry landing. If walking, go straight from the boat landing and follow the concrete path left, taking the first dirt road that branches to the right across the island for about 10-15min.

A short boat ride from the mainland, Isla de la Piedra boasts 10km of glistening sand, crashing waves, and rustling palm trees. Less crowded and not as shamelessly developed as mainland beaches, the island is a haven of sunshine and ocean popular with Mexican families, and, according to locals, "American Hippies." Take a trip on a banana boat (80 pesos), rent snorkeling equipment (120 pesos per hr.), or borrow a body board (30 pesos per hr.). Aging horses can be hired (85 pesos per hr.) up the beach. If you want to stay longer than a day, **Carmelita's,** a few steps from shore, has clean rooms with A/C, TV, and private baths. (☎987 5050. Doubles 200 pesos, with kitchenette 250 pesos.) **Lety's,** adjacent to Carmelita's, is run by Carmelita's Aunt Lety and her family and serves superb seafood and more. (*Camarones al ajo* 70 pesos. Boogie boards 20 pesos per hr. Showers 3 pesos. Good customers are often invited to camp on her beach or sleep in her rooms, which are some of the cheapest on the island; eat up. Book exchange available. Open daily 7am-midnight or later.) Nothing's nicer than camping on a secluded beach, but be careful, and don't stray too far from the center.

DURANGO

DURANGO

☎618

The scorpion is Durango's celebrated mascot, but this city of half a million undoes its fierce image with its outpouring of museums, church plazas, markets, and bustling *duranguenses*. Colonial mansions pepper the city center, while movie sets for countless American Westerns stand at the periphery. The many factories and textile mills lining the way into town contrast with the historic buildings in the town center that contributed to the government's decision to declare Durango a national monument. Few tourists alight here, despite ample and inexpensive food, lodging, and museums. Film buffs and fans of *el norte* will enjoy a visit, though.

TRANSPORTATION

Durango is most easily accessible by **bus,** and its **Central de Autobuses** is on the eastern outskirts of town.

Intercity Transportation: Ómnibus de México (☎818 3361) runs to: **Aguascalientes** (7hr., 9 per day, 255 pesos); **Chihuahua** (8hr., 4 per day, 368 pesos); **Ciudad Juárez** (18hr., 7 per day, 600 pesos); **Guadalajara** (10hr., 6 per day, 415 pesos); **Mexico**

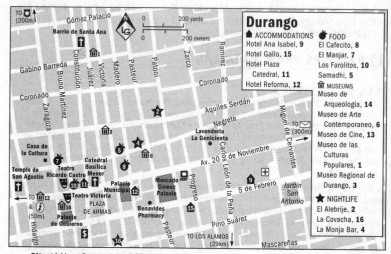

City (11hr., 8 per day, 568 pesos); **Zacatecas** (5hr., every hr., 176 pesos). **Estrella Blanca** (☎818 3061) goes to: **Aguascalientes** (7hr., 3 per day, 255 pesos); **Parral** (6hr., 4 per day, 224 pesos); **Torreón** (3hr., 7 per day, 159 pesos); **Zacatecas** (5hr., 4 per day, 176 pesos). **Transportes de Durango** sends buses to smaller cities in the state.

Local Transportation: To reach the *centro,* exit the station and get on the **Ruta 2 camioneta** which runs from right in front of the station, down 5 de Febrero to the Plaza de Armas (3 pesos). At night, the bus doesn't run; you'll have to take a metered **taxi** (22 pesos).

ORIENTATION AND PRACTICAL INFORMATION

Durango sprawls, but most museums, sights, and hotels cluster within a few blocks of the **Plaza de Armas** and **Catedral.** The main thoroughfares are **5 de Febrero,** which runs east-west past the plaza, and **20 de Noviembre,** parallel to and one block north of 5 de Febrero.

Tourist Office: **Dirección de Turismo y Cinematografía**, Florida 1106 (☎811 1107), next to the Museo de Cine. Fluent in English and French, the staff both dispenses useful information and leads tours to more remote areas. Open M-F 9am-6pm.

ATM and Currency Exchange: Many 24hr. **ATMs** dot the Catedral area. **Banco Serfín,** Constitución 312 Sur (☎812 8033), has great exchange rates and a 24hr. ATM. Open M-F 9am-5pm; exchange M-F 9am-3pm.

Luggage Storage: In the Central de Autobuses. 3 pesos per hr. Open 24hr.

Laundry: Lavandería la Genicienta, Zarco 212 Sur, between 20 de Noviembre and Negrete. Wash and dry 35 pesos per 3kg. Open M-Sa 9am-7:30pm.

Emergency: ☎066.

Police: (☎817 5406), at Felipe Pescador and Independencia. **Tourist Police** ☎800 903 9200.

Red Cross: ☎817 3444 or 817 3535.

Hospital: Hospital General (☎811 9115), at 5 de Febrero and Norman Fuentes.

Pharmacy: Benavides, at Pasteur and 5 de Febrero. Open daily 9am-9pm.

Internet Access: Internet, 20 de Noviembre 119, up the narrow staircase. 6 pesos per 30min. Open daily 10am-11pm.

Post Office: 20 de Noviembre 500 (☎811 4105), at Roncal, 12 blocks from the Plaza de Armas. **Mexpost** and **Telecomm** offices inside. Open M-F 8am-6pm, Sa 9am-1pm. **Postal Code:** 34000.

ACCOMMODATIONS

Durango's hotels are both inexpensive and high-quality. Plus, they're right in the *centro*.

Hotel Gallo, 5 de Febrero 117 (☎811 5290). Chat with the gregarious parrot Francisco and his roost of parakeets, or weep over the *telenovelas* with travelers from all walks of life who gather around the lobby TV. Rooms are clean and spartan, centered around an airy courtyard. All rooms with bath and hot showers. Singles 90 pesos; doubles 110 pesos. Cable TV available in some rooms for an extra 10 pesos. ❶

Hotel Plaza Catedral, Constitución 216 Sur (☎813 2660), off 20 de Noviembre in a convent next to the Cathedral, exudes ambience from its romantic, dimly-lit interior. This historic building couldn't be in a better location, and its rates are a steal. Well-maintained rooms have phones and cable TV. Singles 210 pesos; doubles 240 pesos; triples 270 pesos. ❹

Hotel Ana Isabel, 5 de Febrero 219 Ote. (☎813 4500). The sparkling white walls of this hotel open onto a sunny atrium decked with hanging plants. Nice rooms with clean, tiled bathrooms, all in good repair. Management speaks excellent English and dispenses useful advice. Singles 180 pesos; doubles 250 pesos. ❸

Hotel Reforma, Madero 303 Sur (☎813 1622 or 813 1623). Hard to say if Reforma's decor is at the avant- or rear-g(u)ard(e) of interior design, but it's definitely at an extreme. The halls have enough foliage to be centerfolds for *Potted Plant Digest*. A red refrigerator-looking elevator whisks you up to rooms with color TV, fans, and windows. 3pm check-out allows you to see some more sights before packing. Adjacent cafe is open 8am-8pm. Singles 198-332 pesos; doubles 273-415 pesos. ❸

FOOD

Inexpensive meals aren't hard to rustle up in Durango. While tacos and hot dogs battle for the title of supreme late-night fast food, the day is ruled by the **prickly pear-fruit** plucked from the local cacti. Vendors negotiate the spines and sell them peeled and ready to eat, seeds and all. Look for bags of the green, kiwi-shaped fruit off 5 de Febrero (5 pesos). Those in search of non-instant coffee should try the espresso and cappuccino (10 pesos) at **El Cafecito ❶**, a tiny coffee shop on Madero between 20 de Noviembre and Negrete. (Open M-Sa 9am-6pm.) Other local favorites are *gorditas*, quesadillas with *chicharrón*, and a meaty local stew called *caldillo durangueño*.

Los Farolitos (☎812 7987), on Martínez, 1 block up from the *teatro*. Farolitos focuses on the concept of "taco" with Zen-like clarity, and the result tastes like enlightenment. Though they dabble in quesadillas, take the hint and go for a couple of the big, 7.5 peso tacos (with a variety of *típica* fillings, like *rajas con queso* and *deshebrada con chile verde*). Drinks 7 pesos. Open M-F 8:30am-9pm, Sa-Su 9am-8:30pm. ❶

El Agave, on Negrete between Zaragoza and Hidalgo. Multicolored tablecloths add a festive note to this dimly-lit restaurant. Local couples stare into each other's eyes and dine on upscale local fare, mostly variations on *porle* (50-60 pesos). Open daily 2-10pm. ❹

El Manjar, at Negrete and Zaragoza, a few blocks west of the Catedral. Manjar somehow manages to cram giant feline masks, a blow-up of a tarot magician, a ceramic clown, a wooden Don Quixote, and countless plants into its small space. Breakfast plates with freshly-squeezed orange juice 25 pesos. Open M-Sa 8am-8pm. ❸

Samadhi, Negrete 403 Pte. Healthful, 100% vegetarian fare that pleases a lunchtime crowd of foreigners, students, and the odd non-carnivore *duranguense*. Goldfish paddle around the restaurant's aquarium. Breakfast bargains (30 pesos for granola, eggs, french fries, and beans) and all the usual suspects done vegetarian-style. Open daily 9am-7pm. ❸

👁 SIGHTS

Durango's residents glory in the 1000 historic buildings in their city. The Spanish colonial architecture and silver barons' mansions speckle the *centro* with pink sandstone buildings. The most resplendent of them is the **Catedral Basílica Menor,** on the **Plaza de Armas.** Built between 1691 and 1770, the cathedral glows pink, with interior frescoes, gilding, and massive pillars. The cathedral's bishop once presided over the largest diocese in the world—most of modern Mexico and a large swathe of the American southwest. Be sure to check out the confessional at the back of the cathedral, in the east nave to the right of the altar. Here, in 1738, a devilish dying Spanish don tried to gain salvation; according to legend, a beam of light struck him down. Locals have stayed away from the accursed confessional ever since. Those of questionable moral fiber should do the same.

Durango's huge **Palacio de Gobierno,** on 5 de Febrero between Martínez and Zaragoza, was once the family home of Spanish mining tycoon Juan José Zambrano. After Mexico gained independence, the government seized the mansion for state use. The inside walls and stairwell are decorated with the typical murals depicting the state's history and the golden death mask of Benito Juárez. Just west of the Cathedral, on 20 de Noviembre, stands the pink carved **Teatro Ricardo Castro,** which hosts theatrical productions and film screenings and is considered to be one of the best theaters in northern Mexico. Built around the turn of the century, this elegant, French-style building is named for the Durango musician Ricardo Castro, who contributed to several movie soundtracks. The neighboring **Teatro Victoria** hosts plays, poetry readings, and other events. For a listing of cultural events, check the local newspaper, *Sol de Durango.*

The **Museo de Arte Contemporaneo Ángel Zárraga,** Negrete 301, displays Mexican painting and sculpture from the past 10 years. The highlights include startling abstract paintings from Dulce María Nuñez Rodríguez and sculptures by Juan Soriano. (Open Tu-F 9am-6pm, Sa-Su 11am-6pm. Free.) The **Museo Regional de Durango,** at Serdán and Victoria, behind the Cathedral, houses paintings by Miguel Cabrera and exhibits on art, pottery, and religion among Durango's desert-dwellers before and after the *colonia.* The knowledgeable museum guards love to spin yarns about Durango past and present. (☎812 5605. Open Su 10am-3pm, Tu-Sa 9am-4pm. 10 pesos; Su free.) Designed to make archaeology exciting for the masses, the **Museo de Arqueología Durango,** at Zaragoza 305 Sur, dramatizes Durango's desert cultures with cinematic tricks. (☎813 1047. Open Tu-F 10am-6:30pm, Sa-Su 11am-6pm. 5 pesos, children 3 pesos.)

By far the most-hyped attraction in Durango is its **cinematic history.** Over 200 films, including *The Wild Bunch* (1968), *Blueberry* (2002), and several John Wayne classics have been filmed in the dusty desert outskirts of Durango. The city has recently opened a **Museo del Cine,** Florida 1106 at the corner of Independencia and 20 de Noviembre, to commemorate its golden age of Westerns. The old sound-recording equipment, camera, and Victoria 8 projector give some insight into how cumbersome earlier productions must have been. (Open Tu-Su 9am-6pm. 5 pesos, children 3 pesos.) Some of the original **movie sets** have been left standing and are now popular tourist attractions. One of the most impressive sets is at **Chupaderos,** 10km north of Durango. More Westerns have been filmed in this dusty village than anywhere else in the state. To get there, take a Chihuahuenses bus to "Chupaderos" (30min., every 25min., 13 pesos), and ask the driver to let you off the route near the sets. On the same bus, you may be able to reach **Villa del Oeste,** a movie set now open as an Old West theme park. (Open Sa-Su 11am-7pm.) **Los Alamos,** 29km south of Durango, was the set for *Fat Man and Little Boy* (1989), a film about the development of the atomic bomb in Durango, New Mexico. It may be difficult to get to these sets without a car; ask the tourist office for information about their English-language movie set tours.

🎵 📷 ENTERTAINMENT AND SHOPPING

A variety of courtyard bars featuring live music have sprouted off Negrete behind the Cathedral. **La Monja Bar,** at Negrete and Madero, basks in bright yellow walls. The sheltered patio is open to the warm night air, perfect for relaxing. Live *mariachi* music and ballads sound better with 12-peso tequila and 15-peso *sangría.* (Open F-Su 4pm-midnight.) Come sundown, throw your hands in the air at **La Covacha,** Pino Suárez 500 Pte., at Madero, where locals dance to international and Latin hits. (☎812 3969. Cover 25 pesos. Open Th-Su 9pm-4am.) Slightly more upscale is **El Alebrije** on Serdán 309 Pte. Thursday through Saturday, live romantic music echoes through the brightly-painted courtyard 9pm-midnight. Look for the salamander sign. Alcoholic offerings include wine (15 pesos), beer (15 pesos), and tequila (from 30 pesos).

Though most farmers are kept busy raising cattle (to feed the *campesinos'* endless appetite for beef), a select few have scorpion ranches instead. **Mercado Gómez Palacio** on 20 Noviembre, three blocks east of the Cathedral, is full of the poisonous bugs. Thankfully, most are entombed in transparent plastic bubbles adorning belt buckles, keychains, and fabulously kitschy Durango souvenir clocks. Vendors keep aquariums full of the state arachnid on-site, lending the market a certain edge. You never know what you'll find in your new cowboy boots.

For 10 days during the second week of July, Durango commemorates the city's founding with the **Feria Nacional.** Parades, fireworks, auctions, and carnival rides liven things up, and reservations at hotels are a must. Most of the festivities take place at the **Parque Guardiana,** quite a distance from downtown—you may have to take a taxi (25 pesos).

A history of drugs and Mexico

Whether as a destination for tourists seeking altered states, as a primary producer supplying illicit U.S. demand, or as a nation with its own small but important population of drug users, Mexico has played a crucial role in the development of the markets, policies, and ideologies that shape the drug issue throughout North America. Indeed, while rates of illicit drug use in Mexico have always lagged far behind those of the United States, the two nations' histories with these substances have long been inexorably intertwined.

While today Mexico is mostly recognized as a producer and distributor of drugs for the U.S. market, pre-Hispanic Mexicans famously utilized the many psychotropics indigenous to the region. In the 1950s, this tradition attracted the New York banker and amateur mycologist R. Gordon Wasson and his wife to southern Mexico, where they became the first outsiders to participate in the sacred mushroom rituals of the Mazatec Indians. Wasson's subsequent account of his experiences in *Life* magazine (where he apparently coined the phrase "magic mushrooms") had a powerful impact. Most directly, the article triggered a steady stream of drug tourism from the U.S., with often disrespectful *gringos* invading the tiny hamlet of Huatla in search of magic mushrooms. More generally, however, Wasson's article helped fertilize a growing culture of drug use in the U.S. This latter phenomenon boomed an illicit Mexican drug trade that had been gradually developing since the institution of drug prohibition in the U.S. and Mexico fifty years prior.

As the 60s drew to a close and rates of marijuana use among middle-class American youth continued to skyrocket, the Nixon Administration responded with Operation Intercept, a three-week drug interdiction program that searched nearly every car entering the U.S. from Mexico. Intercept provoked a small-scale diplomatic crisis and proved almost completely ineffective. (The "secret" plan had leaked to the *New York Times* a week early, giving traffickers plenty of time to adjust to the new circumstances.) However, the operation did cause enough economic chaos in the border region to drag Mexico into a greater commitment to U.S. Drug War objectives; it has since been revealed, was this increased involvement was the plan's primary objective from the start.

Of course, this "war" has had few positive results for citizens of either country. Mexico's controversial decision to accede to U.S. demands and begin employing aerial-born herbicides to eradicate opium and marijuana crops in the mid-1970s inspired initial declarations of success. But the sanguine victory speeches were soon tempered by the realization that drug cultivation simply moved elsewhere while Mexican growers adjusted to the new conditions. By increasing its stealth and investment in firepower and bribery, the Mexican industry was by the 1980s, again achieving record production levels. In the meantime, traffickers discovered that many of the marijuana plants sprayed in the eradication efforts could still be sold, thus treating unsuspecting pot smokers on both sides of the border to a product seasoned with the toxic herbicide paraquat.

The 1980s brought more problems for Mexico as increased U.S. efforts against cocaine smuggling through the Caribbean rerouted traffic through Mexico, where the varied terrain, poorly paid—and therefore corruptible—police, and 2000-mile U.S. border have proved nearly impossible to monitor. Thus began an era of unprecedented profits for traffickers, which not only helped to expand drug cartels and resources available to corrupt officials, but also introduced cheap cocaine to the domestic Mexican market. Mexico has since developed its first significant problem with cocaine abuse.

However, the many negative consequences of this "war" have not produced a softening of generally anti-drug attitudes in Mexico. Though many Mexicans still treat their rheumatism by rubbing a tincture of marijuana on their joints, legalization initiatives consistently sink far under the weight of deep societal prejudice against the drug. Excluding alcohol (which is Mexico's biggest substance abuse problem by far), attitudes toward recreational drug use remain overwhelmingly negative, while strong support for prohibition, the sine qua non of the Drug War, endures. Indeed, while Mexico's huge financial commitment to the Drug War can certainly be blamed in part on the need to placate its neighbor to the north, mainstream public attitudes play a crucial role in anchoring what continues to be a costly and failed War on Drugs.

Isaac Campos is a Ph.D. candidate at Harvard University in Latin American history, with a focus on Mexico. He is writing a dissertation on Mexican social and cultural history during the Porfiriato.

NORTHEAST MEXICO

This is desert country: hot, dry, and dotted with cacti. The people of the northeast relish their home. *Norteño* music pumps from every speaker, and residents devour *cabrito* (roasted goat) with their famous beers—Bohemia, Corona, Carta Blanca, and Sol. Silver veins once enriched this desert landscape, leaving fabulous colonial churches and homes for today's traveler to visit. The disparate towns and cities of the Northeast, home to parched white missions and wide streets, exude a sense of calm fostered by small town hospitality and comparatively few tourists.

Vaquero culture still lives on in **Tamaulipas, Nuevo León,** and **Coahuila**. These border states have plenty of American-owned factories and big cities, especially along the Texas border, but the drunken daytrippers detract only slightly from the rich culture of music, food, and small-town friendliness of the borderlands. The capital of *el norte* is Monterrey, Mexico's third-largest city. Its glorious museums—ranging from ancient culture to contemporary art—compete with its blazing nightlife to be the star attraction. The view from Monterrey's central plaza, packed with skyscrapers, colonial churches, and mountains, will thrill any visitor.

If it's beach you crave, the *noreste* offers little more than a taste. Salty Tampico has never drawn flocks of tourists: you can swim, tan on the sand, and munch on fresh seafood, but it's far from picturesque. One of the nation's most gorgeous cities, **Zacatecas** is still adorned with the churches and mansions funded by the silver bonanza. Intricately carved pink sandstone adorns hundreds of buildings throughout this mountaintop city, and its museums will fascinate with religious masks and Joan Miró prints alike. Named for its soothing hot springs, **Aguascalientes** has bustling streets and a festive annual fair.

Many of the riches in *el norte* lie in the state of **San Luis Potosí.** The town of Real de Catorce, a favorite stop for peyote-hungry backpackers, is largely untouched by modernity. *Burros* track through the town, and visitors enjoy mountaintop panoramas. Xilitla offers the eco-warrior caves, waterfalls, rivers, wild parrots, semitropical rainforests, and modernist ruins. The capital city of San Luis Potosí is a jewel—a playground of regional culture, baroque architecture, and colonial appeal. Though comparatively few tourists visit the *noreste*, those who do will discover a unique culture vibrant with history and modern-day verve.

HIGHLIGHTS OF NORTHEAST MEXICO

DELIGHT in the glorious architecture, raging nightlife, and the enormous Gran Plaza of eclectic, fast-paced **Monterrey** (see p. 293).

BATHE in the waterfalls of a kooky Englishman's tropical homage to surrealism at **Las Pozas** (see p. 333); spend the day in nearby of **Xilitla**, the *noreste's* very own Eden.

HONEYMOON in tiny **Real de Catorce** (see p. 330), an ex-mining town high in the Sierra Madres that now specializes in peyote and gorgeous mountain views.

DAYDREAM in lovely **San Luis Potosí** (see p. 322), dubbed "the city of plazas," and enjoy *música en vivo* while soaking up the brilliant northeast sun.

SAVOR traditional *pan de pulque* in **Saltillo** (see p. 302), and wrap yourself in a beautiful handmade *sarape*.

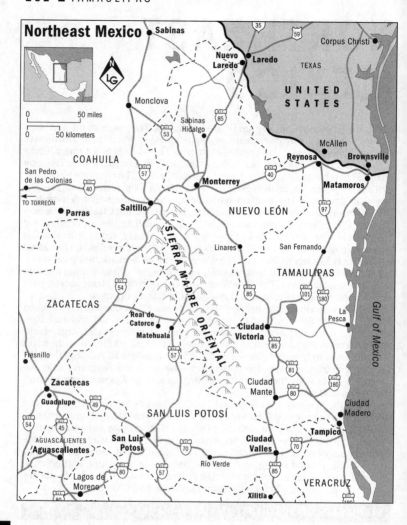

Northeast Mexico

TAMAULIPAS

MATAMOROS
☎ 868

A pedestrian shopping district runs through the center of Matamoros, cutting through to this brash border town's true relaxed soul. Vibrant with Mexican culture, the city houses a new contemporary art museum and stores enough for even the most exuberant shopper. And, like any self-respecting border town, the streets of Matamoros are packed with young people partying to their hearts' content.

CROSSING THE BORDER. To reach Matamoros from Brownsville, Texas, walk or drive across the **International Bridge.** Pedestrians pay US50¢ (or 6 pesos) to cross from either side. Cars pay US$1.50. At this point, the **Río Grande** looks skinny and unimposing—since much of its water has been diverted for irrigation, it's only a 2min. walk over the bridge. If you're traveling farther south than the 22km border zone, pick up your tourist card (US$20) and vehicle permit (US$22). See p. 11 for more information on border crossings.

TRANSPORTATION. From the border crossing, the city extends out in a V-shape following the bend in the Río Bravo. To reach the center of town from the border area, take one of the yellow **minibuses** labeled "Centro" (4.5 pesos). "Central" minibuses go to the bus station, the Central de Autobuses; take care not to

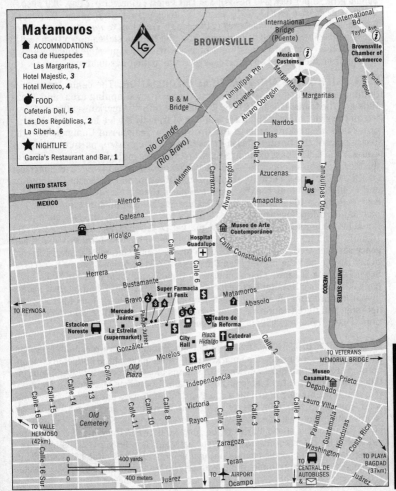

Matamoros

ACCOMMODATIONS
Casa de Huespedes
    Las Margaritas, 7
Hotel Majestic, 3
Hotel Mexico, 4

FOOD
Cafetería Deli, 5
Las Dos Repúblicas, 2
La Siberia, 6

NIGHTLIFE
García's Restaurant and Bar, 1

BROWNSVILLE

International Bridge (Puente)
International Bd.
Taylor Ave.
Mexican Customs
Brownsville Chamber of Commerce
Tamaulipas Pte.
Claveles
Alvaro Obregón
Margaritas
Porter
Ringold
Nardos
Lilas
Calle 2
Calle 1
Azucenas
Tamaulipas Ote.
US
Amapolas
B & M Bridge
Río Grande (Río Bravo)
Aldama
Carranza
UNITED STATES
MEXICO
Allende
Galeana
Hidalgo
Museo de Arte Contemporáneo
Iturbide
Calle 9
Calle 7
Hospital Guadalupe
Calle Constitución
Herrera
Bustamante
Calle 6
Bravo
Super Farmacia El Fenix
Matamoros
Abasolo
Mercado Juárez
Pedro Juárez
Estacion Noreste
La Estrella (supermarket)
Teatro de la Reforma
González
City Hall
Plaza Hidalgo
Catedral
Calle 2
Morelos
TO REYNOSA
Old Plaza
Guerrero
Independencia
Calle 16
Calle 15
Calle 14
Calle 13
Calle 12
Old Cemetery
Calle 11
Calle 10
Calle 8
Victoria
Rayon
Calle 5
Calle 4
Calle 3
Calle 2
Calle 1
Zaragoza
TO VALLE HERMOSO (42km)
Calle 16 Sur
Teran
Juárez
Ocampo
TO AIRPORT
0   400 yards
0   400 meters
TO VETERANS MEMORIAL BRIDGE
Museo Casamata
Degollado
Prieto
Lauro Villar
Panama
Guatemala
Honduras
Costa Rica
Washington
TO CENTRAL DE AUTOBUSES &
Juárez
TO PLAYA BAGDAD (37km)
UNITED STATES
MEXICO

NORTHEAST MEXICO

confuse the two. To return to the border, catch a minibus marked "Puente." These converted school buses (called *peseros*) make continuous stops; wave your hand at them and they'll stop almost anywhere—just yell "¡Baja!" (local transport info ☎817 8882). Don't be shy about asking where your stop is, as the bus name (e.g. "Centro") might not be indicative of the final stop.

Bus traffic to out-of-town destinations flows through the **Central de Autobuses**, on Canales at Guatemala, off Calle 1. (Open 24hr.) **ADO** (☎812 0181) goes to: **Tampico** (7hr., 7 per day 4:15am-11:30pm, 285 pesos); **Tuxpan** (11hr., 4 per day 4:15am-11:30pm, 388 pesos); **Veracruz** (16hr., 4 per day 4-10pm, 541 pesos), with numerous stops in between. **Noreste/Sendor** (☎813 2768) services: **Monterrey** (6hr., 18 per day 1:20-11pm, 198 pesos); **Reynosa** (2hr., 18 per day 6am-10pm, 57 pesos); **San Luis Potosí** (10 hr., 11 per day, 381 pesos). **Transportes del Norte** (☎816 6580) runs to: **Mexico City** (14hr.; *ejecutivo* at 7pm, 840 pesos; 1st-class buses 6 per day, 646 pesos); **Saltillo** (7hr., 6 per day, 249 pesos); **San Luis Potosí** (10hr., 11 per day, 320 pesos). **Ómnibus de México** (☎813 7693) sends 18 buses per day to **Reynosa** (60 pesos), **Saltillo** (249 pesos), and **Monterrey** (218 pesos). Travelers to *noreste* destinations may find it more convenient to depart from the **Noreste station** downtown (☎813 4050), at the corner of Calle 12 and Abasolo, where it's possible to catch buses coming from the Central de Autobuses en route to their destinations.

⊞⊡ ORIENTATION AND PRACTICAL INFORMATION. The center of town is dominated by Abasolo, which hosts a pedestrian shopping area, and Plaza Hidalgo. The **tourist office** (☎812 3630), past the turnstile marking entry into Mexico on the right, offers pamphlets and lots of friendly advice in Spanish. Matamoros maps are also available at the Brownsville Chamber of Commerce on the Texas side of the border. **Casas de cambio** dot the *centro*, particularly along Calles 5 and 6. The best exchange rates are available in the immigration office at the Mexican border checkpoint, in the bus station, or at banks such as **Bancrecer** (☎812 3422), Calle 7 between González and Abasolo, and **Bancomer**, Matamoros and Calle 6, which also exchanges **traveler's checks.** (☎816 3067. Open M-F 8:30am-4pm, Sa 10am-2pm.) 24hr. **ATMs** are available at most major banks. The bus station offers **luggage storage.** (5 pesos for the first hr., 4 pesos each additional hr.) Other services include: the market **La Estrella,** Abasolo between Calle 10 and Calle 11; no **laundromat,** but all hotels listed have laundry services; **emergency** service (☎060); **police** (☎817 0105 or 817 2205) stationed around International Bridge and the border; **Red Cross** (☎812 0044); **Green Cross** (☎817 0287); **Super Farmacia El Fenix,** Abasolo between Calle 7 and Calle 8 (☎812 2909; open daily 8am-10pm); **Hospital Guadalupe** 72 Calle 6 (☎812 1655); and **Internet access** in a little storefront on Abasolo between Calle 6 and Calle 7—look for an "Internet" sign and tinted windows. (10 pesos per hr.) The **post office** is in the bus station. (Open M-Sa 9am-3:30pm.) **Postal code:** 87370.

⊓ ACCOMMODATIONS. Although prices in Matamoros are reasonable, expect little more than the basics. The market area, where most of the budget accommodations are located, quiets down as the shops close—be careful after 10pm. At ▨**Casa de Huespedes Las Margaritas ❸,** on Calle 4 between Abasolo and Matamoros, simple rooms surround a tiled courtyard full of flowers and turtle decorations. A covered patio with couches invites guests to relax outdoors. (☎815 6152. All rooms with private bath and fan. 24hr. bell for late arrivals. Singles 150 pesos; doubles 150-200 pesos.) **Hotel Mexico ❷,** on Abasolo between Calle 8 and Calle 9, provides simple, clean rooms with private bath and fan. (☎812 0856. Singles 140 pesos; doubles 160 pesos; each additional person 40 pesos.) **Hotel Majestic ❷,** in the same block, offers simple rooms with private bath and fan. (☎813 3680. Singles 150 pesos; doubles 220 pesos; each additional person 50 pesos.)

◘ FOOD. Little *taquerías*, fruit stands, and food carts crowd Abasolo and the streets near Plaza Hidalgo. Some focus on perfecting just one dish. For instance, **La Siberia ❸,** on Calle 6 between Bravo and Abasolo, serves only chicken with guacamole and *crema*, whipped up in various delicious combinations. (With tacos or tostadas, 25-40 pesos.) For a wider selection, slip into a booth and sway to the sounds of an old-fashioned jukebox in ▧**Cafetería Deli ❸,** 1307 Calle 7, between Abasolo and Matamoros. Along with the music, the Cafetería serves *huevos rancheros,* a variety of homey tacos, and a range of *antojitos* (☎ 813 9387. Open daily 6am-9pm. Snacks or meals 15-40 pesos.) **Las Dos Repúblicas ❹,** on Calle 9 between Abasolo and Matamoros, the restaurant where the margarita originated, soothes tourists with its harmonious tan leather furnishings, star-shaped light fixtures and relaxed atmosphere. Enjoy drinks from a cushioned chair, next to a fountain and three-story fresco. (☎ 816 6894. Beers US$1.50, mixed drinks US$3, and *antojitos* US$4.)

◙ ♫ SIGHTS AND ENTERTAINMENT. Abasolo, a pedestrian street between Calles 6 and 11, is lined with shops and vendors. Abasolo is known for its shoes, and every other shop seems to be a *zapatería* (shoe store). If you've always wanted cowboy boots, now's the time. For *dulcerías* (candy stores) and a variety of king-sized piñatas, head down Matamoros between Calle 10 and Calle 12. Try **Pasaje Juárez** on Calle 9 between Matamoros and González for everything from colored glasses and silver jewelry to the ubiquitous cowboy belt.

Matamoros's stellar new ▧**Museo de Arte Contemporaneo de Tamaulipas,** on Obregón at Calle 5, first opened its doors in 2002. The museum building is a work of art in itself. Don't miss the sculpture court outside the main building. (Open Tu-Sa 10am-6pm. 15 pesos, students and seniors 10 pesos.)

Discover the history of Matamoros in **Museo Casamata** at the corner of Panamá and Degollado. Casamata itself was constructed in 1830 as a fortress to defend the city against the invading Americans. Converted to a museum in 1970, it is now filled with photos of Revolutionaries and antique guns. The city's history is inscribed in Spanish on the walls of the museum. (Open M-F 8am-8pm, Sa-Su 9am-6pm. Free.) Matamoros's **cathedral** on Calle 5, across from Plaza Hidalgo, is home to a full-size replica of Christ in a glass coffin. The candles are always lit and visitors are always welcome.

For an evening of high culture, stop by the **Teatro de la Reforma** on Calle 6 between González and Aba-

ON THE MENU

MARGARITAVILLE

To be a true margarita connoisseur requires visiting Las Dos Repúblicas, the self-proclaimed birthplace of the famous drink. According to legend, a lovely young lady from Brownsville, Texas, Marguerite Henri, was a restaurant regular back in the 1930s. One day in 1935, she inspired the bartender to mix her that first magical drink. She immediately fell in love with the concoction and, in her honor, the smitten bartender named the drink the "Marguerita." Of course, this is only one of innumerable stories claiming to elucidate the origins of the popular drink. Whether fact or fiction, the tale makes a good excuse to stop in and order a couple of 18oz. margaritas.

The margaritas at Las Dos Repúblicas are available either on the rocks or frozen. If you want to try your hand at the legendary drink, you can try this on-the-rocks version, not unlike the restaurant's secret recipe.

½ cup tequila
¼ cup triple sec or Cointreau
2 tablespoons lime juice
1 cup ice
Salt

Moisten the rims of two margarita glasses or tumblers with water. Press them, upside down, into the salt to coat the rims.

Shake the tequila, triple sec, lime juice, and ice together in a cocktail shaker. Pour and drink. ¡Basta!

solo. Renovated in 1992, the colonial brick building is home to everything from classical drama to *ballet folklórico*—look for event posters throughout town. (☎812 5121. 150 pesos and up, students and seniors ½-price.)

Matamoros's drinking age is 18, so American college students herd across the border from Brownsville to drink. But if you're in the mood to bar-hop, boogie, and booze, think twice. The reasonably priced **bars** and **discos** near the border can be very unsafe at night for drunken kids. For a bar in town, try **Las Dos Repúblicas** (listed above.) Closer to the border, partiers can glug at **Garcia's** (☎812 3929), straight ahead after you cross the International Bridge, on the left side of Obregón. Garcia's has everything a border-hopping tourist could want, day or night. Feast on filet mignon in the classy restaurant (lunch specials US$8, dinner US$11), relax with a Mexican beer at the bar (US$2; mixed drinks US$3-4), or search for bargains in the gift shop and pharmacy. Live music ranges from *mariachi* to rock.

REYNOSA   ☎899

Reynosa specializes in two mutually beneficial businesses: wrecking tourists with earthly delights each night, and piecing them back together each day with dentures, new glasses, and dirt-cheap medical care. This city of almost one million teems with open-air *taquerías*, carts selling *licuados* (sweet fruit drinks), and leather shops. As the day's broiling heat eases, locals head to the Plaza Principal to chat, clowns and musicians competing for their attention. At night, underage Texans mix with Mexicans in the clubs of the Zona Rosa.

⌗ TRANSPORTATION. Reynosa lies across the border from McAllen, Texas, and can be reached by taking 23rd St. 12km south onto Hidalgo and then crossing the **International Bridge.** Routes 2 and 40, from Matamoros and Monterrey, respectively, lead straight into town. The **Central de Autobuses** is on Colón in the southwest corner of town. To reach the *centro* from the bus station, take any "Centro" bus (4.5 pesos) or turn left on Colón, walk eight blocks, and take a right onto Morelos; the plaza is six blocks down. Taking a **taxi** might be a better idea, but drivers are known to overcharge, so try to set a price before getting in. **ADO** (☎922 8713) goes to: **Tampico** (7hr., 6 per day 4:30-11pm, 257 pesos); **Veracruz** (16hr., 6:50 and 8:30pm, 595 pesos); **Villahermosa** (24hr., 6:50 and 11pm, 835 pesos). **Futura** (☎922 1452) offers *ejecutivo* service to: **Monterrey** (3hr., 8pm, 207 pesos); **Mexico City** (15hr., 5:20pm, 846 pesos); **Guadalajara** (15hr., 6 and 8pm, 873 pesos). **Ómnibus de México** (☎922 3307) runs to: **Chihuahua** (15hr., 9am and 10:30pm, 570 pesos); **Monterrey** (3hr., hourly 4am-7pm, 154 pesos); **Saltillo** (5hr., 6 per day 4am-7pm, 189 pesos). **Noreste/Sendor** (☎922 0206) has the most extensive service, including: **Matamoros** (2hr., every 45min., 57 pesos); **Nuevo Laredo** (4hr., every 2hr. 5:15am-9:40pm, 159 pesos); **San Luis Potosí** (11½hr., 8 per day 7am-10:45pm, 359 pesos).

⌗⌗ ORIENTATION AND PRACTICAL INFORMATION. Reynosa is 90km from Matamoros and Brownsville, Texas, and 150km from Monterrey. Central Reynosa is square, with the International Bridge border crossing at the northeast corner. The central plaza, known as **Plaza Principal,** is bounded by Zaragoza on the north, Hidalgo on the west, Morelos on the south, and Juárez on the east. A few blocks east of the Plaza lies the **Zona Rosa,** dotted by bars and the city's budget accommodations. A pedestrian market runs south down Hidalgo, from the Plaza to Colón.

Though there is no tourist office, the **Cámara de Comercio,** on the corner of Chapa and Allende, one block north of Zaragoza and one block east of Juárez, has free maps with listings of restaurants, bars, and hotels. (Open M-F 9am-5pm.) **Casas de cambio** are scattered along Hidalgo and the plaza, but none accept traveler's checks. **Banorte,** on Morelos at Hidalgo (☎922 4690; open M-F 9am-3pm) and

Bancomer, opposite Banorte on Zaragoza (☎922 8101; open M-F 8:30am-4pm, Sa 10am-2pm), offer competitive rates, change traveler's checks, and have 24hr. **ATMs.** Services include: **police** at the border crossing at Aldama and Virreyes in the northeast corner of town (☎922 0008); **Red Cross** (☎922 1314); **Telecomm,** in the building connected to the post office (☎922 0165; open M-F 8am-7:30pm, Sa-Su 9am-12:30pm); **Internet Café,** Matamoros 735 at Chapa, with plenty of computers and A/C (☎922 1981; 20 pesos per hr.); and the **post office** on the corner of Díaz and Colón (☎922 0110; open M-F 8am-4pm, Sa 9am-1pm). **Postal code:** 88500.

⌖ ACCOMMODATIONS. Reynosa's hotels are pricey, with the cheapest located in the Zona Rosa near the border. **Hotel Capri ❹,** at the corner of Allende and Canales, is Reynosa's best deal, but it isn't cheap. At least you'll be in air-conditioned comfort with cable TV. (☎922 2980. Singles 220 pesos; doubles 270 pesos.) **Hotel Avenida ❺,** Zaragoza 885 Ote., sets its sparkling clean, carpeted rooms around a beautiful leafy patio. With proximity to the main plaza and A/C and cable TV, you can't lose. (☎922 0592. Singles 270 pesos; doubles 330 pesos.)

◻ FOOD. Locals will tell you that outdoor stands and open-air cafeterias near the plaza and at the south end of the Hidalgo pedestrian market are the places to enjoy delicious, super-cheap fare. A shining example is **Tacos El Pingüino ❷,** in a food court at the corner of Díaz and Guerrero, one block west of Hidalgo. Plunk yourself down on one of the stools for abundant *tacos de barbacoa* (barbecued beef; 24 pesos) or 12-peso *tortas.* For a splurge, try the local specialty of roasted *cabrito* at **Restaurante El Jardín ❺,** half a block from the plaza on Zaragoza near Hidalgo. Goats roast beyond a glass window as attentive waiters deliver goat tacos. (130 pesos. Open daily 11am-8pm.)

◰ ⏻ SIGHTS AND ENTERTAINMENT. In the evening, locals of all ages crowd the main plaza to enjoy street performers and chill after the day's heat. The **Hidalgo Marketplace,** open to pedestrians from the Plaza to Colón, is a good spot for people-watching. For an abridged history lesson, check out the beautiful storefront **mural** on the corner of Zaragoza, one block east of Canales, and a few blocks south of the border crossing. The mural contains scenes of Mexican life depicting pre-Columbian glory, conquest, revolution and, finally, tourists buying crafts under a Bacardi logo (no mere coincidence—the rum company paid for this particular instance of artistic edification).

Clustered along Ocampo near the border, most nightspots in Reynosa have high and low seasons. During US spring break (Mar.-Apr.), the town turns into a miniature Cancún—all the booze, but (alas!) none of the beaches. The low season is more mellow. Deserted a good chunk of the week, it is only on weekends and Wednesday nights (when there is no cover charge at most bars) that this "Zona Rosa" comes to life with *mariachis* and enthusiastic Texans. Young people head to the **Alaskan Bar and Disco,** on Ocampo between Allende and Zaragosa, a dark, cold *discoteca* with two levels and an enormous dance floor. (Beer US$1, mixed drinks US$1.50. US$10 cover with open bar; W and Sa no cover.) The new **Bar 1040,** at Ocampo and Allende close to the border, offers clubbers a cavernous dance floor; the enormous orange building is hard to miss. (US$10 cover with open bar.) Underage visitors to Reynosa beware: clubs have recently started to enforce the Mexican drinking age of 18. Be sure to bring your ID.

Visitors not interested in shaking it can catch a flick at **Multicinemas,** right on the main plaza. Most are Hollywood movies in English with Spanish subtitles. (38 pesos.) Check out Reynosa's community theater for free at **La Casa de la Cultura,** next door to the Cámara de Comercio on Chapa and Allende just a block from the main plaza. The Casa regularly hosts plays, painting exhibits, concerts and dances;

drop in to see the schedule of upcoming events. (☎922 9989. Open M-F 9am-2pm and 3-7pm; most performances at 7pm.) Reynosa's **Museo de la Ciudad,** at Ortega and Allende, houses a collection of masks, dolls, antique guns, old coins, and other historical artifacts. Most impressive are the historical photos of Reynosa and biography of the man responsible for the museum, Sr. Donato Palacios Saenz. The art exhibit features paintings of bull fighters and ballerinas. (Open Tu-Sa 9am-2pm and 4-8pm, Su 10am-2pm. Free.)

NUEVO LAREDO ☎867

Nuevo Laredo (pop. 500,000) pulses with commerce. From small souvenir shops to enormous trucks bulging with NAFTA-spurred trade, pesos and dollars pour in and out of Nuevo Laredo at a dizzying pace. The city's cheap liquor, abundant crafts, and many plazas attract lots of afternoon tourists, making Nuevo Laredo a good place to visit for a day or evening, though probably not for an extended vacation. After a hard day of buying sombreros, tourists kill time with locals in the town's green plazas before gulping *cerveza* at border bars.

⌸ TRANSPORTATION. From **International Bridge #1,** the most popular tourist crossing, **Guerrero** emerges as the main thoroughfare running south. Three landmarks along Guerrero, **Plaza Juárez, Plaza Hidalgo,** and **Palacio Federal,** define the downtown.

The **airport** (☎714 0705), is southwest of the city, off Mex. 2. **Viajes Furesa,** Guerrero 830 at Canales, offers tickets to **Mexico City** or to **US destinations.** (☎712 9668. Open M-F 9am-7pm.)

The **Central de Autobuses,** Refugio Romo 3800, is far southwest of the city and quite a trek from the *centro.* To get to the border from the bus depot, take any blue-and-white or green-and-white bus marked "Puente." To get to the bus station from the border, take a bus labeled "Central." **Ómnibus de México** (☎714 0617) goes to: **Aguascalientes** (8hr., 3 per day, 508 pesos); **Saltillo** (3½hr., 215 pesos); **Zacatecas** (8hr., 2 per day, 434 pesos). **Noreste/Sendor** (☎714 2100) travels to: **Matamoros** (6hr., 8 per day 7am-midnight, 219 pesos) and **Reynosa** (4hr., 10 per day, 159 pesos). **Turistar, Futura,** and **Transportes del Norte** share an information line (☎714 0670) and a counter, but they maintain separate routes and services. **Transportes del Norte** runs a bus to **Monterrey** (3hr., every 30min., 168 pesos).

⌗⌕ ORIENTATION AND PRACTICAL INFORMATION. Plaza Hidalgo and **Av. Guerrero** make up Nuevo Laredo's center. Four streets surround the plaza: Guerrero on the east, Ocampo on the west, Dr. Mier on the north, and González on the south. The **tourist office,** in the Palacio Federal (a giant stone colonial building just south of Plaza Hidalgo), provides many brochures in Spanish and English. (☎712 7397. Open M-F 8am-8pm.) Major banks line Guerrero near Plaza Hidalgo. **Banorte** (open M-F 9am-4pm) and **Serfín** (open M-F 9am-4pm, Sa 10am-2pm), both on the corner of Canales and Guerrero, both have 24hr. **ATMs. Casas de cambio** line Guerrero near the border. **Luggage storage** is available at the bus station. (Open 24hr. 5 pesos per hr.) **Los Super Frutería Primes,** five blocks south of Plaza Hidalgo on Ocampo and Arteaga, is the closest supermarket to the center of town. (Open M-Sa 7am-9pm, Su 7am-7pm.) Other services include: **Wash Fast,** 3017 Canales (☎722 7906. Wash 16 pesos, dry 20 pesos. Open daily 9am-9pm.); **emergency service** (☎060); **police,** always available at the Palacio Federal or at the border crossing at the north end of Guerrero (☎060); **Farmacia Calderón,** on Guerrero west of Plaza Hidalgo (☎712 5563. Open 24hr.); for medical services, **ISSTE** (☎712 3491), on Victoria and Reynosa east of Plaza Juárez, with a limited English-speaking staff; **Suri Cyber Cafe,** 3112 Canales and Morelos, one block south of Plaza Hidalgo and four blocks east, sporting A/C and cool drinks (☎713 0085. 20 pesos per hr. Open M-F 10am-9pm, Sa 11am-7pm.); **post office,** in the back of the Palacio Federal on the corner of González and Camargo, featuring **fax** and **telegram** service (☎712 2100. Open M-F 8am-6pm, Sa 9am-noon). **Mexpost** is located on the opposite side of the Palacio. (☎713 4717. Open M-F 9am-6pm, Sa 9am-1pm.)

▌ ACCOMMODATIONS. Hotels of all prices are found within a few blocks of the main plazas. There are good bargains if you're willing to look around. **Hotel Alameda ❹,** González 2715, offers clean, comfortable rooms complete with A/C, TV, and phone. The best part: it's right on Plaza Hidalgo. (☎712 5050. Singles 202 pesos; doubles 275 pesos.) **Hotel La Finca ❺,** Reynosa 811, just off González in the southeast corner of Plaza Hidalgo, sits on a quiet street just a few steps from the *centro.* Spacious, clean rooms rise above a red-tile patio and have A/C, cable TV, and phone. (☎712 8883. Singles 270 pesos; doubles 270-340 pesos.) For those who absolutely insist on the cheapest bed in town, **Hotel Asturias ❷,** Hidalgo 2715, at Ocampo close to the border, is rock-bottom. (Rooms 130 pesos.)

▐ FOOD. Pricey tourist border joints aside, most eateries are similar in quality and price, with plenty of tacos, *enchiladas,* and *carne asada* (grilled meat). *Fajitas* and *cabrito* are often sold by the kilogram. Most of the good stuff is right on Guerrero, not far from the plazas. Nuevo Laredo overflows with food carts that serve excellent tacos; many specialize in seafood *(mariscos),* especially shrimp, despite the distance from any body of water. **▨Lonchería El Popo ❶,** on Dr. Mier across from the Palacio Federal, specializes in *lonchos,* very simple sandwiches—either *ternera* (brisket) or hamburger—with amazing savor. Locals relax on the folding-chair patio to talk and enjoy a light meal. (*Lonchos* 12-14 pesos. Open 11am-9pm.) For more meaty local food, try **Restaurante Principal ❹,** on Guerrero just north of Hidalgo Plaza. Order chicken or *cabrito* (115 pesos), then watch through glass windows as they roast and cut it. Ambitious meat-loving groups can even devour the whole animal (800 pesos), while standard entrees (40-60 pesos) are available for the less voracious. (☎712 1310. Open daily 9am-1am.) Those more vegetable-inclined needn't starve in Nuevo Laredo: at the corner of Perú and Reynosa, vegetarian restaurant **El Quinto Sol ❶** awaits to delight the senses. Vitamins, all-natural cookies, and soy hamburgers (20 pesos) are just a few of the healthy treats. For dessert, *nieve* (shaved ice) with granola cereal or sweet sauce (18 pesos) is a must. (☎715 5275. Open M-Sa 7am-10:30pm, Su 10am-10:30pm.) To arrest that sweat, sample the fresh-squeezed juices at **Jugos y Licuados El Centro ❶,** on González at the south end of Plaza Hidalgo. It looks like the other juice stands, but features healthy options like *perejil* (parsley) and alfalfa. (Drinks 10-18 pesos. Open M-Sa 10am-7pm.)

◙▐ SIGHTS AND ENTERTAINMENT. The largest (and most expensive) *mercados* are concentrated around **Guerrero** near the border, many in pedestrian arcades just off the street. Though they offer an ample selection of sturdy wooden furniture, pottery, and *sombreros,* better prices (and higher-quality goods) can be found farther south. Those in search of some notion of culture can head to the **Teatro de la Ciudad** on Guatemala near Aguirre in the southeast corner of town, accessible via the "Viveros" buses; consult the tourist office for listings. For information on the occasional bullfight or wrestling match, look for the posters that blanket Nuevo Laredo's lightposts.

The **Archivo Histórico Municipal,** Calle Herrera 3030, presents rotating shows on the history of the city, displaying photographs from the official archives. (☎712 3485. Open M-F 9am-5pm, Sa 9am-1pm. Free.) Nearby **Casa de la Cultura** (House of

Arts), Herrera 3440, shows a rotating exhibit in its beautiful courtyard. You can also watch the various art, dance, and music classes that start around 4pm.

Strolling up and down Guerrero can be relaxing in the evening, when the three plazas fill with people gaily chatting and passing time; the fountain at Nacatez and Guerrero is a favorite resting spot. But let's face it: the appeal of a border town is often less strolling and more swilling. For drinking fun, duck into any of the local bars close to the border. A more clubby atmosphere can be found at **The New Herradura,** a *centro nocturno* in an orange building at Ocampo and Hidalgo. (No cover. Drinks 30-60 pesos.) To drink and dance under the stars, head to **Pueblo Viejo** at Belden and Galeana. The colonial style and open-air courtyard draw weekend crowds. (Cover ranges from none to US$20; the higher the cover, the more drinks included—up to eight.)

CIUDAD VICTORIA   ☎834

Ciudad Victoria (pop. 230,000) may be the sleepiest state capital in Mexico. At the foot of the Sierra Madre, Victoria can be a relaxing stopover near the US border, as it is primarily a launchpad for ecotourist adventure. Among the sights a short ride from the city are **Cañón del Novillo,** a spot for hiking and camping, and **Boca de San Juan Capitán,** a beautiful stream. Ardent naturalists or those simply looking to escape may enjoy a visit to the **Reserva de la Biósfera el Cielo,** approximately 100km from the city. The city itself is rather prosaic, a quality which lends it a relaxed atmosphere with plenty to explore outside its borders.

▐ **TRANSPORTATION.** From the **Central de Autobuses,** a "Boulevard" minibus can take you to the *centro* (4 pesos). Make sure the driver knows you want to get off near the Plaza Hidalgo. From there, walk two blocks up Calle 8 or 9 to the Plaza, home to most of Ciudad Victoria's attractions. A **taxi** will cost about 30 pesos. From the station, **Transpaís** (☎800 713 1000) runs to: **Ciudad Valles** (4hr., every hr., 127 pesos); **Matamoros** (4½hr., every hr., 172 pesos); **Reynosa** (4½hr., every hr., 176 pesos); **Tampico** (3½hr., every hr. 2:30am-10pm, 131 pesos); **San Luis Potosí** (5-6hr., every hr., 187 pesos). **Senda** (☎675 766 7242) has service to **Monterrey** (4hr., every hr., 177 pesos).

◨ ◪ **ORIENTATION AND PRACTICAL INFORMATION.** Each main street of Ciudad Victoria has both a name and a number (i.e. Calle 8 is also Calle Juan B. Tijerina). To get to the **tourist office,** Calle 9 Hernán Cortés 136, walk seven long blocks along Calle 9 away from the Museum and the Plaza Hidalgo. The staff there will be happy to tell you everything you need to know about Victoria and the state of Tamaulipas. (☎314 0521. Open M-F 9am-9pm.) **Exchange currency** or **traveler's checks** at **Banorte,** on Hidalgo in the main plaza, which also has a 24hr. **ATM. Luggage storage** is available at the bus station. (5 pesos per hr. Open daily 7am-10:30pm.) Other services include: the **market Tienda ISSSTE,** on Calle 13 between Matamoros and Guerrero (open daily 8am-8pm); **Lavandería Virues,** Matamoros 939, between Calles 8 and 9 (wash 12-17 pesos, dry 30-50 pesos, depending on size of load; open M-Sa 9am-8pm); **emergency** service (☎066); **police** (☎312 0195 or 312 4243); **Red Cross,** on Col. López Mateos (☎065 or 316 2077); **Hospital General,** Libramiento Fidel Velázquez Ote. 1845 (☎316 2197); the **pharmacy Benavides,** on the corner of Hidalgo and Calle 9 (open 24hr.); the **Tel.Net Cyber Cafe,** Calle 8 between Hidalgo and Juárez, next to the Hostal de Escandón, provides **Internet access** and **fax** service (☎315 3926; 10 pesos per hr.; open daily 10am-11pm); **post office,** on Calle 8 between Morelos and Matamoros, in the Palacio Federal (open M-F 8am-7pm, Sa 8am-noon). **Western Union** and **Telecomm** are also in the Palacio Federal. (Open M-F 8am-8pm, Sa-Su 9am-2:30pm.) **Postal Code:** 87000.

⚏⚏ ACCOMMODATIONS AND FOOD. While expensive luxury hotels surround Plaza Hidalgo, quality budget lodging can be found a few steps away, hiding in the nearby streets. **Hostal de Escandón ❷**, Calle 8 143, just off the plaza, provides comfortable rooms and pleasant service. The rooms face a small interior courtyard, protected from the brutal sun by a sky-blue dome. (☎312 9004. Singles 148 pesos, with bath, A/C, and TV 189 pesos; doubles 183/230 pesos.)

If you get an urge to dine in a more luxurious setting, try some of the fancy restaurants in the hotels around the *centro*. On the other end of the spectrum, street-side vendors line the shopping area on Hidalgo by Calle 7 until about 6pm. **Los Candiles ❹**, Calle 8 102 across from the Hostal de Escandón, serves up quality Mexican and international dishes (30-80 pesos), as well as an excellent Sunday buffet. (45 pesos. Open Su-M and Sa 7am-midnight, Tu-F 6am-11:30pm. Buffet served Su 1-4pm.) The filling *comida corrida* (38 pesos) at **Café Canton ❸**, Colón 114, just south of the plaza, soothes the palate and helps beat the empty-wallet blues. (Entrees, from breakfast to *antojitos* to hamburgers, 20-55 pesos. Open daily 6am-10:30pm.)

⚏⚏ SIGHTS AND ENTERTAINMENT. The state capital building, Ciudad Victoria's **Palacio de Gobierno**, on the corner of Hidalgo and Calle 17, is relatively grandiose and harbors a few impressive murals, as well as the standard government offices. The **mercados** north of Hidalgo between Calle 6 and 7 offer everything from cartoonish *piñatas* and crafts to goat liver. For those interested in local history and culture, the **Museo de Arqueología, Antropología e Historia,** on the north side of Plaza Hidalgo near the Howard Johnson's, is supposedly open M-F 9am-7pm but often closes unexpectedly. The collection displays a small selection of indigenous art and artifacts, historical photographs, and assorted fossils. The **Centro Cultural Tamaulipas**, on Hidalgo between Calle 16 and 17, hands out cultural calendars and schedules of upcoming concerts and festivals.

Victoria provides relatively easy access to **El Cielo Reserva de la Biósfera,** the state's most impressive nature reserve. Often referred to as simply "La Reserva," it encompasses more than 300,000 acres of lush vegetation, mountains, and wildlife. The area supports hundreds of species of birds, reptiles, and mammals, including bears, armadillos, pumas, and jaguars. To reach the reserve by bus, go to the Transpaís booth at the bus station and ask for a ticket to Gómez Farías. You'll get on a bus to Ciudad Mante, but make sure to have the driver let you off at Gómez Farías, about two hours from Victoria (112km). After disembarking, wait for a blue minibus that takes you downtown (every hr., 5 pesos). There, register at the *caseta de vigilancia* in order to enter the reserve. Further information and accommodations are available in town. Take a 10km hike or rent the services of a 4-wheel-drive taxi (up to 1000 pesos per day).

If you come to Ciudad Victoria in the second week of October, don't miss the **Ciudad Victoria Expo,** featuring music, dancing, and *artesanías* from the area.

TAMPICO ☎833

Though it's a little grimy, pretty crowded, and incredibly hot, Tampico (pop. 295,000) is the northeast's best seaside getaway and a refreshing break for land-locked travelers. At first, the novice backpacker might be overwhelmed by incessantly honking taxis, the overbearing sun, and the general absence of resources for English speakers. Despite the ominous tankers and loads of litter, there's plenty here to reward the intrepid tourist: the pleasant beach is often deserted on weekdays, and Tampico's two main plazas are full of greenery and intriguing architecture. The seafood is wonderfully fresh and beach resorts are a relaxing break from the frenzied pace of the *centro*. Tampico may not be the best place for a week-long getaway, but it's definitely worth a look.

TRANSPORTATION. The **bus station** is on Zapotal, north of the city. Take a taxi (20 pesos), minibus (4 pesos), or *colectivo* (4 pesos) to the *centro*. To return to the bus station, hop on any *colectivo* marked "Perimetral" (4 pesos). **Ómnibus de México** (☎213 4349) goes to: **Ciudad Valles** (2½hr.; 6 per day, mostly in the evening; 96 pesos); **Guadalajara** (12hr., 3 per day 6pm-10:30pm, 420 pesos); **Mexico City** (8½hr., 9 per day, 289 pesos); **Saltillo** (9hr.; 9, 10:40pm; 357 pesos); **Tuxpan** (3½hr., 5 per day 9:30am-5pm, 122 pesos). **Transpaís** heads to: **Matamoros** (7hr., 12 per day, 253 pesos); **Monterrey** (7hr., 16 per day 5am-midnight, 327 pesos); **Reynosa** (7½hr., 12 per day 6:30am-midnight, 257 pesos). **ADO** goes to: **Puebla** (9hr.; 6:15, 9pm; 283 pesos); **Xalapa** (9hr.; 7:30am, 9:45pm; 278 pesos).

ORIENTATION AND PRACTICAL INFORMATION. Tampico centers on two plazas. The **Plaza de la Libertad** is surrounded by Cañonero on the southern waterfront side, with Madero opposite; Aduana and Juárez complete the square. One block past Madero sits the edge of the **Plaza de Armas**, Díaz Mirón. Carranza is on the other side of the plaza, and Olmos and Colón close it up. Mirón is the commercial hub of the *centro*, full of shops, hotels, and markets. Other streets of interest include Altamira (one block from the Plaza de Armas, past Carranza), and López de Lara (one block from Plaza de la Libertad, past Aduana).

The **tourist office**, Colón 102, on the third floor of the Palacio Municipal, has plenty of maps and brochures and a friendly staff. (☎229 2765. Open M-F 9am-7pm). Banks with 24hr. **ATMs** are on and around both plazas. Send money and **exchange currency** or **traveler's checks** at Western Union, on Díaz Mirón in the Plaza de Armas. (Open M-F 9am-7pm). **Luggage storage** is available at the bus station (6 pesos per hr., 40 pesos per day); the **supermarket** Arteli is at 601 Díaz Mirón Ote. (Open daily 8am-10pm.) A **lavandería** is on Díaz Mirón 327. (12.9 pesos for wash and dry. Open M-Sa 9am-7pm.) Other services include: **emergency** service (☎060); **police** (☎224 0304), on Tamaulipas at Sor Juana de la Cruz; **Red Cross**, with ambulance service (☎212 1333; open 24hr.); the 24hr. **pharmacy Fénix**, on the corner of Aduana and Altamira; **Hospital Beneficencia Española**, on Hidalgo and Francita Ejército Nacional (☎217 2400), with English-speaking doctors; **Telecomm**, Madero 311, next to the post office (☎214 1121; open M-F 9am-5pm, Sa 9am-1pm); **LADATELs** around the corners of both plazas; **Internet access**, at Cyber Snack Internet Cafe, 508 Madero Ote. (10 pesos per hr.; open daily 9am-8pm). The **post office**, Madero 309 Ote., in the yellow building on Plaza de la Libertad (☎212 1927; open M-F 9am-5pm, Sa 9am-1pm), has a **Mexpost** office (☎212 3481) inside. **Postal code:** 89000.

ACCOMMODATIONS. Quality budget hotels are rare in Tampico. Four hundred pesos or more nets an excellent room in one of the larger hotels on Madero and Díaz Mirón near the plazas. During the summer, keep an eye out for special "promotions," when hotels slash rates to drum up business. If you're willing to part with a few extra pesos, ⬛**Hotel Posada del Rey ❺**, Madero 218, in the northwest corner of Plaza de la Libertad, gives you comfortable quarters, an excellent view from your room's terrace (100 pesos extra), and a fine restaurant, **La Troya**. (Breakfast 20-30 pesos, entrees 60-100 pesos. Hotel ☎214 1024. Singles 300 pesos; doubles 350 pesos.) The **Hotel Regis ❸**, on Madero Ote. 603, has clean rooms with A/C, bottled water for sale in the lobby, and is probably the best value near the plazas. (☎212 0290. Singles 170 pesos; doubles 240 pesos.). **Hotel Plaza ❹**, Madero Ote. 204, offers a great location, a popular adjoining pizzeria, and comfortable (albeit dark) rooms with A/C. (☎214 1784. Singles 200 pesos; doubles 250 pesos.)

FOOD. Seafood is standard fare in Tampico, where specialties include *jaiba* (blue crab), but the city's best known dish is *carne asada a la tampiqueña* (seasoned grilled steak served with guacamole, refried beans, and red enchiladas). Chow down at a seaside stand or in the covered food court, the **Centro Gastronómico de Tampico,** on the Canonero side of Plaza de la Libertad. Upstairs, you will be accosted by small "restaurant" (countertop) owners pushing their fresh food at low prices. The most crowded counters generally serve the tastiest and cleanest food. ◪**Refresquería el Globito de Tampico ❷,** in the Plaza de Armas on Olmos and Mirón, treats the crowds to an array of delicious sandwiches (15-25 pesos), tacos, and *licuados* (20 pesos). Still hungry? Top it all off with a fantastic banana split (28 pesos. ☎212 8627.) **Naturaleza ❷,** Aduana 107 Nte. One of Tampico's only vegetarian restaurants dispenses a wide variety of soups and *licuados*, without an ounce of meat on the menu. Everything, from *bistec* to hot dog, is made of soy. (Items 20-35 pesos. ☎212 8556. Open daily 9am-9pm.)

◪ ♫ **SIGHTS AND ENTERTAINMENT.** For a seaside getaway, **Playa Miramar** is the northeast's best beach, home to gentle waves and stretches of white sand. The beach is accessible by the "Tampico Playa" bus (30min., 4 pesos), a shared "Tampico Playa" taxi (15min., 4 pesos), or a private taxi (35 pesos). Once there, stake out a spot under a palm frond umbrella on the beach's 10km of sand and expect an endless stream of vendors to disrupt your relaxation.

In the *centro*, nightlife consists of upscale hotel bars or borderline seedy local hangouts. If you really want to party, take a taxi (20 pesos) to ◪**Byblos,** a large black pyramid adorned with Versace images, three fountains, and a black marble bar. Inside, the club hosts the biggest names in Latin music and on Saturdays Byblos pulsates with lasers and video screens. (☎217 0042. Cover 70 pesos. Open W-Sa 10pm-2am.) Bars populated by sailors stationed at the nearby naval base are a stone's throw from Byblos. For some authentic local flavor, head to the intimate **Boys and Girls,** 316 Olmos, for live music, black lights, and beer (10 pesos). Be there on Saturday nights for *música romántica* and a lively *Norteño* show. (Sa cover 20 pesos. Open Th-Su 9pm-2am.) In October, artisans, singers, and folk dancers gather for an annual festival celebrating Tampiqueño culture. Check the tourist office for schedules of events.

NUEVO LEÓN

MONTERREY   ☎81

A neon cross crowns the centuries-old cathedral in Monterrey's central plaza; it's just one example of how *regios* (Monterrey residents) have seized their city's past and refashioned it to serve the present. The city has marvelous museums, but it lives vibrantly in the moment, bursting with hip clubs, restaurants, and art-filled public parks. At three million people and growing, Monterrey is the third-largest city in Mexico, yet it remains overlooked by most foreign tourists. Founded in 1596 by Diego de Monemayor at the foot of Cerro de la Silla (Saddle Mountain), the small trading outpost grew as Monterrey's position between central Mexico and the US made it an important center of business and commerce. Today, the city is home to many of the country's wealthiest businesspeople and known for its shrewd capitalism. It even has a shrine to business, a 30-story modern lighthouse that shoots fluorescent blue laser beams into the mountainous night. Monterrey also has a wealth of cultural life that will reward any visitor; *Norteño* and electronic music, public art, theatre, and dance swell *regios'* hearts with pride and make Monterrey a delight.

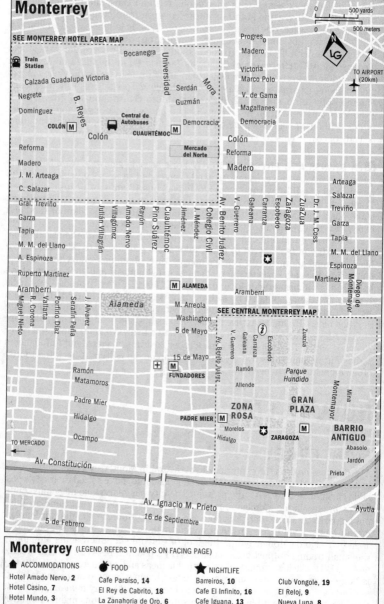

Monterrey

SEE MONTERREY HOTEL AREA MAP

Monterrey (LEGEND REFERS TO MAPS ON FACING PAGE)

🏠 **ACCOMMODATIONS**
Hotel Amado Nervo, **2**
Hotel Casino, **7**
Hotel Mundo, **3**
Hotel Nuevo León, **4**
Hotel Paraíso Reforma, **1**
Hotel Virreyes, **5**

🍴 **FOOD**
Cafe Paraíso, **14**
El Rey de Cabrito, **18**
La Zanahoria de Oro, **6**
Restaurant Mi Tierra, **12**
Taquería Las Monjitas, **11**

⭐ **NIGHTLIFE**
Barreiros, **10**
Cafe El Infinito, **16**
Cafe Iguana, **13**
Casa de Maíz, **15**
Charao's, **20**

Club Vongole, **19**
El Reloj, **9**
Nueva Luna, **8**
Vatikru, **17**

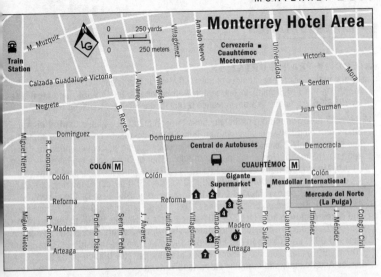

▐ TRANSPORTATION

INTERCITY TRANSPORTATION

Airport: In the far northeast corner of town, off Mex. 54. **Taxis** charge 100-150 pesos for the 20km trip (20-30min.) to the center. **Aeroméxico** (☎8343 5560) and **Mexicana** (☎8356 6611) require 2-3 day advance reservations, more for weekend flights.

Buses: All buses in and out of the city pass through Monterrey's huge **Central de Autobuses** on Colón between Villagrán and Pino Suárez. To reach the city center from the bus station, walk 2 blocks east to the grey subway station at Cuauhtémoc and Colón and take the metro (Line 2, 4.5 pesos) to Padre Mier or Zaragoza. From here, buses go all over Mexico. **Ómnibus de México** (☎8374 0716) departs for: **Aguascalientes** (8hr., 4 per day, 344 pesos); **Chihuahua** (12hr., 3 per day, 500 pesos); **Guadalajara** (12hr., 3 per day, 492 pesos); **Mexico City** (12hr., 3 per day, 584 pesos); **Querétaro** (8hr., 441 pesos); **Zacatecas** (6hr., 5 per day, 268 pesos); and more. **Sendor, Tamaulipas,** and **Noreste** share offices (☎8375 0014) near Sala 5. Noreste heads to **Nuevo Laredo** (3hr., 12 per day, 168 pesos) and **Matehuala** (4hr., every hr., 195 pesos). **Frontera** (☎8375 0987) rolls to **León** (10 hr., 5 per day, 424 pesos) and **Saltillo** (1½hr., every 20min., 50 pesos). Similar service is provided by **Estrella Blanca** (☎8318 3737), **Líneas Americanas,** and luxurious **Futura** and **Turistar.**

LOCAL TRANSPORTATION

Subway: Although buses are useful in providing transportation to points near the city's periphery, Monterrey's amazing **subway** system, the **Metrorrey,** is the best way to get around—it's clean, efficient, and the ride from the bus station to the Gran Plaza takes only 10min. The Metrorrey runs on 2 lines. Line 1 (the yellow line) extends from the western station of **San Barnabe** to **Exposición** in the east. Line 2 (the green line) runs from the north, at **Anaya** station, to Gran Plaza at the **Zaragoza** stop. Line 2 brings passengers to the downtown Zona Rosa and close to the Barrio Antiguo. The lines intersect at **Cuauhtémoc,** which is right next to the bus station and close to many budget hotels. Signs list the train's destination—consult the maps, posted in every station, to figure out which train you should take. Machines sell electronic ride passes in quantities of 1 (4.5 pesos), 2 (8.5 pesos), 4 (16 pesos), 13 (50 pesos), and up. And don't miss the candy-machine-style **book dispensers** at major stations (15-30 pesos per book). The subway runs daily 6:30am-midnight.

Buses: Local buses (5 pesos) usually move in only one direction on any given street, except for on Constitución and Juárez. Popular routes include stops at the Gran Plaza (#18 or 42), points along Padre Mier and Hidalgo (#15), and along the perimeter of the downtown area (#69). To get from the budget hotel area to the city center, take the #1 Central or #17 Pío X bus, both of which run the lengths of Pino Suárez and Cuauhtémoc. Buses run daily 6am-midnight. For more detailed route information, ask locals waiting at the bus stop or the English-speaking staff at the tourist office.

▐ ▐ ORIENTATION AND PRACTICAL INFORMATION

Budget travelers will spend most of their time in two areas. One is the **budget hotel district,** clustered across from the bus station, near the Cuauhtémoc stop of the Metrorrey. The other is Monterrey's *centro*. The **Gran Plaza** (or Macroplaza, as locals affectionately call it) lays a green swath through the downtown area. The *centro* forms a cross shape, with the with Zona Rosa on one side, the Barrio Antiguo on the other, and the Gran Plaza down the center.

TOURIST AND FINANCIAL SERVICES

Tourist Information: Tourist Office, Paez building, 3rd floor (☎8345 6745 or 8345 6805; www.monterrey-mexico.com), on 5 de Mayo between Escobedo and Zaragoza at the north edge of the Gran Plaza. Very helpful English-speaking staff with an abundance of maps and bilingual brochures. Maps are posted all over the *centro*. The useful English-language magazine *What's On Monterrey* is available at the tourist office, the Museo de Arte Contemporáneo, and some hotels. Tourist office open daily 9am-6pm.

Consulates: Canada, Zaragoza 1300 (☎8344 3200; emergency ☎800 706 2900). Open M-F 9am-5:30pm. **UK,** Priv. Tamazunchale 104 (☎8333 7598). Open M-F 8am-5pm. **US,** Constitución Pte. 411 (☎8344 5261; emergency ☎8362 9126), downtown. Open M-F 8am-1pm for passports and citizens' concerns, 9am-5pm for telephone information. 24hr. guard and emergency service.

Currency Exchange: Banks dot Madero near the budget hotels and flood the Zona Rosa, especially along Padre Mier. Many refuse to cash traveler's checks and most of those that do charge high service fees (10%). All have 24hr. **ATMs.** Most open M-F 9am-4pm. Most **Metrorrey** stations also feature ATMs. **Mexdollar Internacional,** 1136 Suárez (☎8374 4311), right by the bus station and the Cuauhtémoc subway stop, offers 24hr. currency and traveler's check exchange at good rates. **Eurodivisas** (☎8340 1683), in Plaza Mexico on Morelos at Galeana, exchanges checks at poorer rates but charges no commission. Open M-F 10:30am-8:30pm, Sa 10am-9pm, Su 11am-8pm. **Western Union:** Ómnibus de México Office at the Central de Autobuses (☎8374 0716), or pick up money transactions from any Bital.

American Express: San Pedro 215 Nte. (☎8318 3304). Catch bus #214 headed for "San Pedro" on Pino Suárez at the stop just past Ocampo. Get off before Calzada de Valle and cross the street. Open M-F 9am-5pm, Sa 9am-1pm.

LOCAL SERVICES

Luggage Storage: At the bus station. 5 pesos per hr., up to 30 days. Open 24 hrs. Remember where you check your bag—there are multiple checks at the station.

Supermarket: Gigante (☎8374 4024), on Colón across from the bus station. Clothes, groceries, baked goods, and an adjoining **pharmacy.** Open daily 8am-10pm.

Laundry: Hotel Royalty (☎8340 2800), on the corner of Hidalgo and Carranza. Open M-Sa. Laundry services available at most *centro* hotels for about 40 pesos per load.

EMERGENCY AND COMMUNICATIONS

Emergency: ☎060.

Police: (☎8345 5419 or 8340 6116), on the corner of Carranza and Espinosa or at the 24hr. stand on Morelos at Paras in the Zona Rosa.

Pharmacy: Farmacia Vida in the bus station. Open daily 9am-11pm. **Benavides** (☎8345 0257), on Morelos past Zaragoza. Open daily 8am-10pm. Pharmacy attached to VIPS restaurant (☎8343 0155), on the corner of Hidalgo and Carranza. Open Su-Th 7am-2am, F-Sa 24hr.

Medical Assistance: Red Cross, Alfonso Reyes 2503 Nte. (☎8375 1616 or 8375 1212), at Henry. **Cruz Verde** (☎8371 5050 or 8311 0033), at Ciudad Madero and Ciudad Victoria. English spoken.

Fax: Telecomm, in the bus station, next to the bus station post office. Open M-F 8am-7pm, Sa-Su 9am-4pm.

Internet Access: Internet cafes flood the Zona Rosa. Standard rates are 20 pesos per 30min., 30 pesos per hr. **Ships 2000,** Escobedo 819 (☎8343 2568), between Padre Mier and Morelos in the Zona Rosa. 14 computers, high-speed fiber-optic connection. 20 pesos per 30min., 35 pesos per hr. Scanning, laser printing, and CD burning also available. Two-story arcade downstairs features the latest video games. Open daily 10am-10pm. For fewer frills but slightly lower prices, try **e-connection** nearby at Escobedo 831. 20 pesos per 30min., 30 pesos per hr. Open daily 9:30am-10pm.

NORTHEAST MEXICO

Post Office: (☎8342 4003) on Zaragoza at Washington, inside the Palacio de Correos. Open M-F 8am-7pm, Sa 9am-1pm. Also on the 2nd floor of the **bus station.** Stairs near Sala 5. Open M-F 8am-4pm, Sa 9am-1pm. There is also **Mexpost** (☎8344 9423), next to the post office inside the Palacio de Correos. Open M-F 9am-5pm, Sa 9am-1pm. **Postal Code:** 64000.

ACCOMMODATIONS

Monterrey can be expensive, but budget hotels do exist. Cheaper accommodations are sprinkled generously in the less glamorous area near the bus station, with easy access to the metro and the city's main points of interest. Be very careful in this area; prostitutes and drug dealers populate seedy neighborhood bars, especially after nightfall. Also, many hotels are full by early afternoon, so act quickly.

Hotels located near the Zona Rosa tend to be of four- or five-star quality, and even three-star accommodations inflate their rates to gouge tourists and business travelers. If you feel like spending 600 pesos, a hotel downtown will reward you with luxury: restaurants, room service, and elegantly decorated rooms.

Hotel Amado Nervo, Nervo 1110 (☎8372 3690), across from the bus station. Somewhat run-down, small rooms come with TV and phone. The balconies on the 3rd and 4th floors provide views of the neighborhood and the mountains that surround the city. Singles 225-310 pesos; doubles 260-350 pesos; triples 530 pesos. ❹

Hotel Casino (☎8372 0219), on Arteaga just off Amado Nervo. Despite its name, staying here is no gamble. Guests are guaranteed clean rooms with bright marble floors. Some rooms are equipped with a *tina de hidromasaje* (jacuzzi). Rooms are 250 pesos, with TV and A/C 300 pesos, with cable TV and jacuzzi 600 pesos. ❺

Hotel Virreyes (☎8374 6610), on Nervo 2 blocks from the bus station. The rooms are basic and sterile, but low prices make this an ideal resting place for wallet-conscious travelers. Singles and doubles 120 pesos, 150 pesos with A/C. ❷

Hotel Nuevo León, Nervo 1007 (☎8374 1900 or 8374 0713), 1½ blocks from the Central de Autobuses. A large statue of Buddha welcomes you to a maze of dark but spacious rooms. Many rooms come with a dresser and a table. Singles with TV and A/C 250 pesos; doubles 350 pesos. ❺

Hotel Mundo, Reforma 736 (☎8374 6850), off Nervo. More luxurious than bus station hotels: A/C works well, TVs are newer, floors shine brighter. Good for a splurge. Singles 280 pesos; doubles 310 pesos. ❺

Hotel Paraíso Reforma (☎8374 6727), on Reforma between Nervo and Villagómez. Not quite paradise, but hardly hell either. Small, dark, colorfully decorated rooms. Singles and doubles 120 pesos, with A/C and TV 180 pesos. ❷

FOOD

Roasted meat is king in Monterrey. Make sure to indulge your carnivorous tooth by eating plenty of *bistecs* (steaks), a regional speciality. Other popular dishes include *frijoles a la charra* (beans cooked with pork skin, coriander, tomato, peppers, and onions) and *machacado con huevos* (scrambled eggs mixed with salsa and dried, shredded beef). For dessert, you'll love *piloncillo con nuez,* a hardened brown sugar candy with pecans, and the heavenly *glorias,* candy balls of nuts and goat's milk. The Zona Rosa, home to some of Monterrey's most expensive shopping, can't be beat for its selection of food. Catering mainly to hungry businesspeople and shoppers, the service is good, the food succulent, and the prices reasonable. For the cheapest food downtown, visit the **taco stands** ❶ that line Coss between 5 de Mayo and Allende. *Buen provecho.*

Restaurant Mi Tierra (☎8340 5611), on Morelos across from Plaza México in the Zona Rosa, offers some of the city's best *taquerías* in an intimate open-air setting. If you can't find a seat, get it to go. Tacos, *enchiladas, tostadas,* and more (25 pesos). Try their specialty *milanesa* (25-40 pesos). Open daily 9am-10pm. ❸

La Zanahoria de Oro, near the Central de Autobuses on Rayón, is a vegetarian oasis in a meat lover's capital. Mexican dishes with mushrooms, *chiles rellenos,* and a few fish dishes (40-50 pesos). All plates served with trimmings. Open daily 8am-6:30pm. ❹

Taquería Las Monjitas (☎8342 8537), on Morelos at Galeana in the Zona Rosa; 2 more on Escobedo and on Galeana. The branch on Escobedo is an imitation cathedral built into a mall. You will be served by waitresses dressed as nuns. Heavenly specialty tacos (40-60 pesos) have names like *El Papa* (the pope) and *La Pecadora* (the sinner). Open daily 8am-11pm. ❹

Cafe Paraíso (☎8344 6616 or 8344 6617), on Morelos at Mina. A great place to take a break from sightseeing in the heart of the *Barrio Antiguo*. The flavored cappuccino will reaffirm your caffeine addiction (30 pesos). This hip spot also serves drinks and good French and Mexican cuisine. Try a sweet crepe for 45 pesos. Live music W-Sa 9pm-midnight. Open Su 4:30am-midnight, M-W 9am-midnight, Th-Sa 9am-2am. ❸

El Rey de Cabrito (☎8345 3352), on Constitución and Cass, behind the Museo de Arte Contemporáneo. El Rey reigns supreme for roasted meat, with plenty of *cabrito* and steak dishes (95-120 pesos). *Regios* take just pride in this regional specialty, which comes straight off the flames, crackling and smoking. Mounted deer and dueling mountain lions add to the elite hunting-lodge atmosphere. Open daily 11:30am-midnight. ❺

◪ SIGHTS

Monterrey's architects were kind to tourists. Not only is the city beautiful and easy to navigate, but most sights are packed into the 40-acre **Gran Plaza** and adjacent **Barrio Antiguo.** A visitor could easily spend the day strolling through the Gran Plaza and admiring the statues, architecture, and greenery, all surrounded by the stunning grey mountains that ring the city. At night, the Barrio Antiguo's streets pump with music and fill with laughing partiers; by day, dancers practice and half-painted canvases line artists' studios in the 18th- and 19th-century buildings. **Art galleries** and **antique stores** line Mina between Padre Mier and Matamoros.

GRAN PLAZA. Bounded by Washington to the north, Constitución to the south, Zaragoza to the west, and Coss to the east, the Grand Plaza displays all elements of Monterrey: government, religion, commerce, romance, and art. It hosts three government palaces: the **Palacio de Gobierno,** the **Palacio de Correos,** and the **Palacio Municipal.** Beyond these immense structures lies the resplendent **Catedral de Monterrey,** its spiritual grandeur rivaling the governmental mammoths. Built between 1603 and 1753, the Catedral features a multicolored dome and a neon cross atop it. Towering above all, however, is the bright orange **Faro del Comercio** (Commerce Lighthouse). Built in 1983 to commemorate the 100th anniversary of Monterrey's Chamber of Commerce, it represents Monterrey's lifeblood—business. Topped with a laser beacon whose light circles the skies at night, the lighthouse begins to pulse with laser light after 10pm on weekend nights, when thousands pack the adjoining Barrio Antiguo in search of some late-night fun. Beneath these towers and spires, the cool garden of the **Parque Hundido** (Sunken Park) draws young lovers and families with boisterous kids. The passion of young couples finds an echo in the nearby **Fuente de La Vida** (Fountain of Life). Built in 1984 by the government of Nuevo León, it contains a gaggle of naked, cavorting demigods who douse the centerpiece, an imposing statue of Neptune.

■**MUSEO DE HISTORIA MEXICANA.** This state-of-the-art museum uses movies, historical artifacts, folk art, comic books, and interactive computer displays to illuminate thousands of years of Mexican history. The enormous climate display room upstairs includes realistic reproductions of forests, deserts, and jungles, complete with plastic animals and chirping bird sounds. Don't miss the walkway and canal beside the museum, perfect for taking a break from the sun. *(Dr. Coss 445 Sur, at the far end of the Plaza 400 Años. ☎8345 9898; www.museohistoriamexicana.org.mx. Open Tu-Su 11am-8pm. 12 pesos, students with ID 6 pesos.)*

■**MUSEO DE ARTE CONTEMPORÁNEO (MARCO).** MARCO's colorful building alone is a work of art—with enormous windows showcasing Monterrey's mountains and a giant geometric fountain inside that spouts like a broken water main. The art is just as spectacular as the building. MARCO exhibits the best of Mexico's innovative modern artists, including Juan Soriano and Enrique Canales. Rotating special exhibits feature international artists and 20th-century movements. *(At the southern end of Dr. Coss, across from the cathedral. ☎8342 4820. Open Tu and Th-Su 10am-6pm, W 10am-8pm. 25 pesos, students and children 15 pesos; W free.)*

TEATRO DE LA CIUDAD. For a calm night away from the city's busy bars and clubs, stop by the Gran Plaza's enormous theater. The Teatro regularly hosts plays, operas, and dance performances. Amateur actors occasionally perform outside. *(On the plaza across from the Fuente de la Vida. ☎8343 8974. Opens 1hr. before evening performances. Information and tickets available at the office facing the Gran Plaza, down the steps near the theater entrance. Open M-F 9am-7pm. Prices vary by show.)*

CERVECERÍA CUAUHTÉMOC MOCTEZUMA. Beer and sports go hand in hand. With this in mind, Monterrey's leading beer manufacturer attached a brewery to the Mexican Baseball Hall of Fame and Museum. Brewery tours take you through the production of Carta Blanca, Tecate, and Dos Equis beers, and conclude in the Beer Garden, where adults can sample a glass or two under the shade of trees and fermentation tanks. Afterward, head to the **Salon de la Fama,** a museum that chronicles the birth of baseball in the mid-1800s and its arrival in Mexico shortly thereafter. Interactive exhibits allow kids of all ages to try their luck at batting, pitching, and catching. *(On Alfonso Reyes, 1½ blocks south of the Anaya metro station on Line 2. ☎8328 5355. Brewery open M-F 9am-5pm, Sa 9am-2pm. Museum open M-F 9:30am-6pm, Sa-Su 10:30am-6pm. Tours given throughout the day in both Spanish and English. Free.)*

PLANETARIO ALFA. This large complex (also called the **Centro Cultural Alfa**) houses interactive science exhibits and shows, as well as gardens and halls honoring Mexico's Pre-Hispanic cultures with sculpture and art. The centerpiece of the Alfa is its IMAX theater, which provides an intense movie experience with its 24m screen. *(Garza Sada 1000, 25min. southwest of the city. Free round-trip transportation available on the ½hr. from the Alfa stop on the Alameda, at the corner of Villagrán and Álvarez. Open M-F 3-7:30pm, Sa 2-7:30pm, Su noon-7:30pm. 30 pesos, with IMAX ticket 65 pesos.)*

▌ NIGHTLIFE

Quiet during the day, at night police cordon off the **Barrio Antiguo** to cars and the streets come alive with party-goers. The action doesn't get started until 10:30pm or so, but early birds get in free at many places. Cafes serve liquor and become more like bars as the night progresses; bars crank the music and turn into clubs. Most people bar-hop, especially on weeknights when fewer bars charge a cover. In addition to the omnipresent *Norteño*, Monterrey also has a hot experimental electronic music scene, with local and visiting DJs presiding over clubs like Vatikru.

BARS AND CAFES

▨ **Cafe El Infinito,** Jardón 904 Ote. (☎8340 3634). This cafe/bar/used-bookstore/art-house movie theater promises radical politics and challenging conversation. Sip international wine (starting at 30 pesos a glass) or exchange a book (free) and read it while sipping coffee (20 pesos). Art films (50 pesos) are shown Th-Sa at 9pm. Open M-Th 8am-1am, F 4pm-2am, Sa 8am-2am, Su 8am-midnight.

Nueva Luna (☎8344 1217), on the corner of Padre Mier and Dr. Coss, boasts the best margaritas in town (available in 5 flavors; 40 pesos) and nightly live music. The 2-for-1 deal on beers (25 pesos) and margaritas (40 pesos) until 9pm makes the relaxed Nueva Luna all the more attractive. Open Su-Th noon-midnight, F-Sa noon-2am.

Barreiros, Padre Mier 1032 (☎8301 2382). The decor of this live-music bar will make you feel like you're relaxing in the *zócalo* of a small Mexican town, surrounded by colonial facades. The loud, live Mexican rock, however, serves as a constant reminder that you're here to party. Beer 25 pesos, mixed drinks 50-70 pesos. F-Sa cover 30 pesos for men. Women get their 1st drink free. Open daily 9pm-2am.

Casa de Maíz, on Abasolo between Mina and Naranjo. The deep red walls and glittering chandeliers add elegance to this *casa*. Dim lights, flowers, and low tables invite romantic whispers. Drinks 50-70 pesos. Open daily 6pm-1am.

CLUBS

Vatikru, Constitución 3050 (☎8335 5508). A crowd of almost 3000 shakes it Sa nights at this extravagant club as an oversized dragon and giant spider preside. Rucos night (Th) eschews the skilled electronica DJ in favor of romantic *boleros* for an older crowd. Pick up a discount voucher at Green Light Records, Morelos 921. Open bar. Cover 120 pesos for women, 190 pesos for men. Open daily 9pm-very late.

Cafe Iguana, Montemayor 927 (☎8343 0822). The young, eclectic crowd fits in with the funky, colorful decor. The night starts punk, and ends electronic. Big, cushy couches line the stone walls and party-goers revel on the open-air patio. Beer 20 pesos, mixed drinks 25 pesos. Cover on nights when live music rocks the Cafe. Open daily 8pm-late.

El Reloj, Padre Mier 860 (☎8343 4232). Reloj always has long lines of youth and reverberating US and Mexican rock. Sa night is the time to see and be seen at this fashionable club. Cover 50-70 pesos. Open daily 9pm until whenever the crowd dwindles.

THE LOCAL STORY

LIKE A RHINESTONE COWBOY

It's impossible to visit Monterrey without hearing *Norteño*, the signature music of northern Mexico. Its name comes simply from *música norteña*, and such music fills the air from all corners: in buses, at markets, in bars, on the street. This *música típica* actually has roots in German and Czech immigrants of the late 1800s, who lived around the Texas border. European folk rhythms—primarily polkas and waltzes—blended with Mexican rural music and *vaquero* (cowboy) culture to produce overlapping types: the story-telling, ballad-oriented *corridos* and the more lively *Norteños*, which come as *cumbios* (upbeat rhythms good for dancing) or *rancheros* (with slightly slower rhythms). Though there are many styles within these forms, the distinguishing characteristic of any *Norteño* is the accordion: without its trademark polka sound, it just wouldn't be *Norteño*.

Groups generally consist of five or six men, sporting matching cowboy hats and garish outfits. The music first exploded in popularity in the 1950s, and in the 1990s popular bands such as Intocable, La Mafia, and Los Tigres del Norte spread the unique music. Love it or hate it, after a few days in Monterrey you'll find yourself humming or singing the hit songs of the moment. If you can't get enough, swing by Monterrey's *barrio antiguo* any night of the week.

GAY AND LESBIAN NIGHTLIFE

After its first-ever Pride March in the summer of 1997, Monterrey has quickly become one of the most gay- and lesbian-friendly cities in Mexico. Young same-sex couples walk the streets of the Zona Rosa and the Barrio Antiguo. Although most nightspots cater primarily to men, women are more than welcome. For more listings, ask for a copy of the free gay and lesbian monthly magazine, *Rola Gay*, at either of these bars.

Charao's (☎8374 1872), at the corner of Garza and Zaragoza, 7 blocks north of the Gran Plaza. An exciting, young crowd of men and women stays late every night. Drinks 15-25 pesos. F-Sa cover 15 pesos for men, no cover for women.

🖼 🎵 SHOPPING AND ENTERTAINMENT

The **Zona Rosa,** particularly along Morelos, is the city's commercial center, with a variety of stores and boutiques ranging from mid-priced to expensive. The new **Plaza Mexico** mall, in the center of the Zona Rosa, exists only for easy spending, with two floors of upscale stores and a food court. Bargain-hunters may prefer the **Mercado del Norte** (also known as **La Pulga**), a seemingly endless maze of vendor stalls covering Reforma, just south of Colón. The clothing vendors, *taquerías*, and music stores stretch from Cuauhtémoc all the way to Juárez. Enter on Cuauhté-moc, directly across from the metro station. (Open daily 9am-7pm.)

Monterrey celebrates **Mexican Independence Day** in style, with partying and parades September 15 and 16. In late November, the **Festival del Barrio Antiguo** shuts down the streets around the Old Neighborhood for a week of cultural events, including open-air theatre, music festivals, dance, and painting exhibitions.

There's also ample opportunity to leave Monterrey for a foray to the nearby hills. **Ecotourism** options include birdwatching, rock climbing, mountaineering, and mountain biking. **Parque Ecológico Chipinque,** a few km south of Monterrey, is ripe for tours, though a guide is recommended. (☎8303 0000; www.chipinque.org.mx.)

COAHUILA

SALTILLO ☎844

Saltillo (pop. 900,000) is an often overlooked retreat from Monterrey. Cosmopoli-tan yet friendly, Saltillo sports cafes, bustling markets, rows of book stores, and sunny, pink-paved plazas. Founded in 1577, the city was named for the small *salto de agua* (spring) that sprung miraculously from the desert. Today, Saltillo is famous for its hand-woven *sarapes*, *pan de pulque*, abundant silver, and the calming oasis of its *centro*, which holds relaxing plazas and a gorgeous cathedral.

▐ TRANSPORTATION

The **Central de Autobuses** is 3km southwest of the *centro* on Echeverría Sur. To get to there, exit the terminal and catch minibus #9 (20min., 6:30am-11pm, 4 pesos); ask if it goes *al centro* before boarding. To return to the station, catch bus #9 at the corner of Aldama and Hidalgo, a block down the street from the cathedral, in front of the furniture store's entrance. A taxi from the bus station to the *centro* costs 35 pesos. From the station, **Frontera** (☎417 0076) runs buses to **Matehuala** (3hr., 7 per day 6:15am-11pm, 163 pesos) and **Monterrey** (1½hr., every 20 min., 50

Saltillo

🏠 ACCOMMODATIONS
Hotel de Avila/
   Hotel Jardín, 2
Hotel Saade, 3
Hotel Urdiñola, 5

🍎 FOOD
Mena Donas, 4
Restaurant Principal, 1
El Vegetariano Feliz, 6

Blvd. Fco. Coss
Presidente Cárdenas
Corona
Muzquiz
Peréz Treviño
Aldama
Guadalupe Victoria
Ramos Arizpe
Escobedo

Emilio Carranza
G. Purcell
Álvaro Obregón
Xicotencatl
Acuña
Allende
Hidalgo
Gral. Cepeda
Matamoros
Carlos Salazar
Acuña
V. Guerrero

Madero
Alameda
Zaragoza

Mercado
PLAZA ACUÑA

Palacio de
Gobierno
& Plaza
de Armas

Catedral de
Santiago

Red Cross

TO 🏛 MUSEO DEL
DESIERTO (2km)

Juárez
De la Fuente

El Serape
de Saltillo

Museo de las
Aves de México 🏛

TO IGLESIA DEL
OJO DE AGUA
& EL MIRADOR
(3 blocks)

TO CENTRAL
DE AUTOBUSES
(1km)

0   300 meters
0   300 yards

pesos). **Omnibus de México** (☎417 0315) serves **Aguascalientes** (7hr., 10 per day 4am-11pm, 294 pesos); **Reynosa** (5hr., every hr. noon-9pm, 189 pesos); **San Luis Potosí** (6hr., 255 pesos); and **Torreón** (3hr., 176 pesos). **Transportes del Norte** (☎417 0902) goes to: **Guadalajara** (10hr., 9 per day, 439 pesos); **Zacatecas** (5hr., 5 per day 3:30am-9pm, 200 pesos); and **Aguascalientes** (5-6hr., 8 per day, 220 pesos). **Futura** (☎417 0902) goes to **Mexico City** (10hr., 8 and 10:30pm, 527 pesos). **Autobuses Saltillo-Parras** (☎417 0063) goes to **Parras de la Fuente** (2½hr., 9 per day 6:30am-7:15pm, 70 pesos).

✦ 🛈 ORIENTATION AND PRACTICAL INFORMATION

Located between the jagged peaks of the Sierra Madre, Saltillo lies 87km southwest of Monterrey along desolate **Mex. 40.** Saltillo's two main streets, **Victoria** (which becomes Benito Juárez in the east) and **Allende** (which becomes Carranza in the north), run perpendicular to each other. Walking east on Victoria, you will find **Plaza de la Nueva Tlaxcala,** the **Palacio de Gobierno,** and **Plaza de Armas,** home to the awe-inspiring Cathedral of Saltillo. Facing the cathedral, walk left until Aldama. Take another left and walk until you reach Allende; here you will find **Plaza Acuña** and the adjoining **Mercado Juárez.** North on Allende (right when facing Plaza Acuña), you will find Saltillo's more upscale hotels, bars, and restaurants.

Tourist Information: A small stand in the bus station offers maps (40 pesos) and answers. For more guidance, try the **tourist office** (☎412 5122) at the corner of Acuña and Coss, 14 long blocks north of Plaza Acuña. English spoken. Open M-F 9am-2pm and 3:30-5pm, Sa 9am-2pm.

Banks: Banamex, Allende at Ocampo, behind the Palacio de Gobierno and right off the Plaza de Armas, has a 24hr. **ATM.** Open M-F 9am-4pm. **Western Union** also available.

Luggage Storage: At the Central de Autobuses. 4 pesos per hr. Open 24hr.

Market: Gumosa, at Mendoza and Acuña near the Plaza Acuña. Open daily 8am-8:30pm. Or you can shop the little stalls of the Mercado Juárez. Open daily 7am-8pm.

Laundry: Juárez 615 (☎412 6305). 30 pesos to wash and dry a load. Open M-F 9am-1pm and 3-8pm, Sa 9am-8pm, Su 10am-2pm.

Police: (☎414 4550 or 414 1037) at Treviño and Echeverría Ote. Also at Acuña and Coss, in the same building as the tourist office.

Emergency: ☎060.

Red Cross: (☎414 3333), at the corner of Cárdenas and Cepeda, east of Hidalgo.

Pharmacy: Madero (☎412 2559), across from Mercado Juárez at the corner of Aldama and Allende. Open daily 8am-midnight.

Fax: Telecomm, Victoria 289 (☎414 2585), next door to the post office. Open M-Sa 9am-4pm, Su 9am-noon.

Internet Access: Ciber Café Conexión, Zaragoza 224 just off the Plaza de Armas. Copies and laser printing also available. 10 pesos per 30min., 15 pesos per hr. Open M-F 9:30am-8:30pm, Sa 9:30am-8pm, Su 11:30am-3pm.

Post Office: Victoria 303 (☎414 9097). Open M-F 9am-5pm, Sa 9am-1pm. **Mexpost** (☎414 1890) inside. Open M-F 9am-5pm, Sa 9am-1pm. **Postal Code:** 25000.

ACCOMMODATIONS

Echeverría, which runs past the bus station at the town's periphery, has several cheap, low-quality places to rest your head. There aren't many lodgings in the *centro*, though there are some luxurious options.

Hotel de Avila/Hotel Jardín (☎412 5916), on Padre Flóres across from the Mercado Juárez. Turquoise walls give this dimly-lit hotel a 1960s feel. The cheapest option in the *centro*. Singles 140 pesos; each additional person 50 pesos. TV 10 pesos. ❷

Hotel Urdiñola, Victoria 211 (☎414 0940), behind the Palacio de Gobierno. Visually exquisite with a marble staircase and stained-glass windows that light up the sunny, tiled courtyard. This retreat is equipped with fans, cable TV, phones, and room service. However, the elegance translates into extravagant prices. Singles 343 pesos; doubles 376 pesos; triples 408 pesos; quads 450 pesos. ❺

Hotel Saade, Aldama Pte. 397 (☎412 9120), 1 block west of Plaza Acuña, has clean, well-furnished, quiet rooms near the heart of the city. Top-floor rooms offer a panorama of Saltillo and the Sierra. Rooms come in 3 styles: *económico,* with twin bed and bath; standard, with more space and TV; and *ejecutivo,* with bed, bath, cable TV, and phone. Singles 265/300/320 pesos; doubles 355/375 pesos. ❺

FOOD

Be sure to sample Saltillo's specialty, *pan de pulque,* bread made with *pulque,* an unrefined cactus drink. Sweet and full of pecans and brown sugar, it's available at ▨**Mena Donas ❶,** Madero 1350, on the extension of Victoria, the absolute best bakery in Saltillo. Half the fun is competing with old women for fresh bread. (☎412

1671. 4 buns for 24 pesos.) The area in and around Mercado Juárez holds a huge number of cheap **taco stands ❶**. Look for *tacos al carbon* for 12 pesos or *al pastor* for 18 pesos. **Cafes ❸** surround the Plaza de Armas and its neighboring streets.

For upscale dining and adventurous dishes, head to the **Restaurant Principal ❺**, Allende Nte. 702, seven blocks north of the Palacio de Gobierno. Their *cabecito* (steamed goat's head; 35 pesos) will leave you with that invigorating post-hunt feel, as will a splurge on grilled ram (100 pesos). Squeamish diners shouldn't worry; traditional *antojitos* are just 40 pesos. Goat and steak dishes (75-100 pesos) are also served. (☎414 3384. Open daily 8am-midnight.) **El Vegetariano Feliz ❸**, on Hidalgo between the cathedral and the Museo de las Aves, serves veggie *comida corrida* (40 pesos), soy "meats," and health foods. (Open 9am-9pm.)

◎ SIGHTS

Saltillo's most stunning sights are its cathedral and open plazas. The **Catedral de Santiago** was built from 1745 to 1800 and towers above the city. Its quirky facade resembles three churches all somehow conjoined. Pilgrims visit the Catedral's Santo Cristo chapel to venerate its 1608 image of Christ. Saltillo's pride and joy is the recently opened **◪Museo del Desierto**, Pérez Treviño 3745, in Parque Las Maravillas. An incredible variety of prickly cacti grow in the Museo's garden, mingling with tortoises and prairie dogs. Inside, exhibits range from dinosaur skeletons unearthed in the Coahuilan desert to a massive ant farm. Getting here is complicated: F-Su, take the tranvía trolley from the cathedral (4 per day, 10:25am-5:25pm, 20 pesos). Otherwise, a taxi costs 45 pesos. (☎410 6633. Open Tu-Su 10am-6pm. 45 pesos, students and children 25 pesos.) Back in town lies **Museo de las Aves de México**, Hidalgo 151 at Bolívar. The museum is home to 80% of Mexico's 1010 bird species, stuffed and displayed in naturalistic settings. (☎414 0168. Open Tu-Sa 10am-6pm, Su 11am-6pm. 10 pesos, students and children 5 pesos.)

To explore Saltillo's history and panoramic view, hike up Miguel Hidalgo and turn left on Espinoza after the Museo de las Aves. The **Iglesia del Ojo de Agua** was built in 1905 on the spot where the "saltillo" was first discovered in 1577. Continue past the church up to the small pink-painted plaza. Known as **Plaza México** or **El Mirador**, this is where Zachary Taylor's army camped before their battle with Santa Anna's troops. The site offers a breathtaking view of Saltillo.

◪ NIGHTLIFE

True clubbers will want to hit **Nitro Bar**, a big club with an open pavilion on one side. It's at the corner of Acuña and Aguirre, 1km from the *centro*. (Beer 10-15 pesos. F cover for men 30 pesos. Open 8pm-late.) Closer to the *centro*, try **Discotec el Companario**, Padre Flores 101, on a pedestrian walkway. Chill at the outdoor tables or shake it under the disco ball inside. (Drinks 15-25 pesos. Open 6pm-late.)

◪◪ SHOPPING AND ENTERTAINMENT

Since the 1600s, Saltillo has enjoyed a long tradition of weaving. Famed throughout Mexico for its colorful wool *sarapes* (shawls), the city has spawned its own style, called the "saltillo." The best place to buy *sarapes* (and watch them made) is **◪El Sarape de Saltillo**, Hidalgo 321 before Museo de las Aves, which is famous for its quality Mexican crafts. (☎412 4889. Open M-Sa 9am-1pm and 3-7pm.) For less expensive *sarapes*, crafts, and silver, visit **Mercado Juárez** behind Plaza Acuña.

To fill your day, the downtown **Centro Cultural (Teatro Garcia Carrillo)**, on Aldama in Plaza Acuña, presents regular sculpture and art exhibitions, films, and concerts, all free of charge. Drop by to check the list of weekly events. (Open Tu-Su 10am-2pm and 4-7pm. Children's theater Sa 11am.)

Saltillo's streets bustle with artistry and cultural pride during the **Feria de Saltillo** in mid-August. This two-week fair, featuring agricultural and art exhibitions, performances, and *sarapes*, dates back to the town's first years in the 16th century.

PARRAS DE LA FUENTE ☎249

True to its nickname, the "Oasis of Coahuila," Parras blooms in the desert. Fields of grapevines *(parras)* and walnut trees surround the little colonial town. Parras's attractions are tranquil: visiting a historic winery, swimming in freshwater *estangues*, relaxing on patios and in plazas, and sampling the local wine.

▐ TRANSPORTATION. Parras's **Central de Autobuses** is right in the *centro* at Ramos Arizpe and Melchor Múzquiz. Only second-class buses serve it. **Autotransportes Saltillo-Parras** (☎422 0870) runs to **Saltillo** (2½hr., 8 per day 6:30am-7pm, 70 pesos). **Autotransportes Parras-Torreón** (☎422 1139) serves **Torreón** (3hr., 5 per day 6:30am-7pm, 94 pesos). The local **camioneta** #12 runs to the vineyards and tourist office via the Central (7 pesos). **Taxis** are available at the Central or by phone (☎422 1111). But the easiest way to get around Parras and environs is by **car.**

◼▐ ORIENTATION AND PRACTICAL INFORMATION. Parras lies between Saltillo (160km away) and Torreón (175km away). The town itself is small. Most hotels and restaurants are close to its main street, **Ramos Arizpe,** which runs west from the Central de Autobuses, past the **Plaza de Reloj,** which stands in front of the town church. **Madero** runs parallel to Ramos Arizpe and just south of it.

The **tourist office** is 3km outside town, on the highway that runs north to Mex. 40. (☎422 0259; www.parras.com. Open daily 10am-1pm and 3:30-7pm.) **Bancomer,** at the corner of Ramos Arizpe and Reforma west of the Plaza de Reloj, has a 24hr. **ATM** (☎422 1044. Open M-F 8:30am-4pm.) The **police** station (☎422 0399) is toward the north of town, on Ingeniero de la O. near C. 16 de Septiembre. The **Red Cross,** Ingeniero de la O. 5 (☎422 0899), is close to the police. **Farmacias Populares,** Ramos Arizpe 139, is a convenient **pharmacy** between the Central de Autobuses and Plaza de Reloj. (☎422 1404. Open Su 9am-3pm, M-Sa 9am-9pm.) **Hospital Guadalupano** (☎422 0017) lies northwest of the *centro* on Viesco, two blocks north of Ramos Arizpe at Lobatón. **Café Internet,** across from Plaza de Reloj on Ramos Arizpe, provides connections for 15 pesos per hr. (Open daily 9am-9pm.) The **post office** also stands across from Plaza de Reloj on Ramos Arizpe. (☎422 0054. Open M-F 9am-3pm.) **Postal code:** 27980.

▐▢ ACCOMMODATIONS AND FOOD. The red-tiled rooms of **Hotel la Siesta ❹**, Acuña 9, combine the elegance of Parras's colonial-style buildings with an affordable price tag. Make a left out of the bus station onto Arizpe, then take the first left onto Acuña. All rooms have TV, phone, and bath. (☎422 0374. Singles 200 pesos; doubles 250 pesos; triples 300 pesos.) **Hotel Parras ❶**, Ramos Arizpe 105, west of Plaza de Reloj, has unabashed concrete walls and few amenities. But the rooms surround a leafy courtyard with apple, walnut *(nuez)*, and fig *(higo)* trees, and a friendly family runs the hotel. (☎422 0644. Rooms, each with two double beds, 100 pesos.) The more deluxe **Hotel Posada Santa Isabel ❺** is at Madero 514, west of the Plaza de Armas and Reforma. Wooden eaves shade the hotel's tile paths and invite guests to relax around the central garden. All rooms have cable TV and A/C. A hotel pool ripples at the side of the main building. (☎422 0572. One bed 380 pesos; two beds 480 pesos; suites with four beds 580 pesos. MC/V.)

Parras has few restaurants. For *"tacos gigantes"* and *comida corrida* (30 pesos), visit **Ricos Burros ❸**, Ramos Arizpe 149, a block west of the Central. From the tables in the garden, you can survey the cacti, the building's crumbling glory, and the stars overhead. (Open daily 12:30-10pm.) The restaurant in the **Hotel Posada Santa Isabel ❹** serves savory *antojitos* in the open-air dining room and patio. (30-50 pesos. Open daily 8am-9pm.) **El Tiburon ❸**, on Reforma south of Ramos Arizpe, serves *comida corrida* like beef soup, fried chicken, and beef milanesa in a simple dining room bedecked with plants. (32 pesos. Open M-Sa 8am-9pm.) While in town, don't miss the local specialty **dulces**, made with walnuts, figs, and lots of sugar. These sticky treats are for sale in the many **dulcerías ❶**.

◩ **SIGHTS AND WINE.** *Parras* is the Spanish word for grapevines, and the surrounding fields live up to the name. The oldest **vineyard** in the New World—established in 1597—still produces wine at **Casa Madero**, 4km outside town. Spanish-language tours begin whenever a group arrives. The dark cellars, period mosaics, and vine-shaded paths are worth seeing even if you can't understand the tour. A taxi from the *centro* costs 40 pesos, or you can take the local bus toward Paila from the bus station for 7 pesos. (Free. Open daily 9am-5pm.)

Good wines and brandies made at the Casa Madero estate are for sale near the winery's entrance (45-130 pesos per bottle). For a larger selection of local wines, visit **Antiguas Bodegas de Perote** in town, close to the bus station on Ramos Arizpe at Galvez. (Wines 40 pesos and up. Open daily 10am-8:30pm.)

For true Bacchic excess, visit Parras from August 3 to 19, during the **Feria de la Uva**. New wines are uncorked, processions snake through town, and everyone celebrates. The wildest days are August 9 and 10.

Non-booze-related sights also grace Parras. Several **estangues**, reservoirs of spring water, invite swimming and waterside relaxation. (Around 30 pesos by taxi.) And the town's tree-lined **plazas** are great for people-watching.

TORREÓN ☎ 871

Torreón began its days as a railroad hub, and for most tourists it remains a waystation in transit. Its inexpensive food and hotels make it a good stopover between Durango, Parras de la Fuente, and Saltillo. And when the blazing sun sets, the dancing in Torreón's Plaza de Armas makes this busy city seem like a small town.

▐ TRANSPORTATION

Bus Station: The **Central de Autobuses de Torreón**, Juárez 4700 (☎ 720 3124), about 4.5km east of downtown. **Estrella Blanca** (☎ 720 0808) provides service to: **Durango** (3hr., 9 per day, 159 pesos); **Guadalajara** (10hr., 4 per day, 470 pesos); **Matamoros** (10hr., 4 per day, 383 pesos); **Mexico City** (13hr., 1 per day, 637 pesos); **Zacatecas** (6hr., every hr., 244 pesos). From the bus station, catch a very slow *pesera* to the *centro* (40min., 3.3 pesos). **Taxis** to the *centro* cost 25 pesos.

▟ ▐ ORIENTATION AND PRACTICAL INFORMATION

All hotels and restaurants and most services listed are located in the area immediately surrounding **Plaza de Armas**, which is bordered on the north by palm-tree-divided **Morelos** and on the south by **Juárez**. **Cepeda** is at the eastern edge of the plaza; **Carrillo** at the western. The expansive **Bosque Venustianao Carranza** is 2km east of the plaza. **Buses** and *carritos* (collective taxis) going to almost any part of Torreón can be caught on Juárez by the plaza.

TOURIST, FINANCIAL, AND LOCAL SERVICES

Tourist Office: While the tourist office, on Pasco de la Rosita 308 (☎732 2244), is a hike from the city center and only mildly helpful, they post wonderful maps in front of the Palacio de Gobierno and Plaza de Armas, and provide a toll-free line (☎800 718 4220) manned by an English-speaking staff.

Banks: Banks with 24hr. **ATMs** cluster near Plaza de Armas. **Banco Santander Serfín** has a **currency exchange** at the corner of Carrillo and Morelos at the Plaza de Armas. (Open M-F 9am-4pm.)

American Express: García 95 Sur (☎718 3620), at Matamoros. Open M-F 9am-2pm.

Luggage Storage: At the bus station. 4 pesos per hr. Open 24hr.

Car Rental: Budget has an office in the *centro* (☎721 9091; budgettr@halcon.laguna.ual.mex). Cars from 730 pesos per day.

Market: Mercado Juárez, on Acuña between Juárez and Hidalgo 2 blocks east of the Plaza de Armas. Sells food, CDs, and cowboy hats.

Laundry: Lavandería los Ángeles, Independencia 37 Ote. (☎713 4459), at Colón. Walk to Independencia and then catch a bus going to Colón (3.3 pesos). Laundry washed and dried (50 pesos). Open M-F 10am-2pm and 4-8pm, Sa 10am-5pm.

EMERGENCY AND COMMUNICATIONS

Emergency: ☎060.

Police: (☎712 1315), at Colón and Revolución.

Red Cross: Cuauhtémoc 462 (☎713 0088 or 713 0192).

Pharmacy: Farmacia Santander (☎712 8738), Morelos and Carillo. Open 24hr.

Hospital: Hospital los Ángeles, Paseo del Tecnológico 909 (☎730 0202). Little English spoken.

Fax: Telecomm/Western Union, Morelos 775 (☎/fax 716 6848), east of the Plaza de Armas. Open M-F 8am-7pm.

Internet Access: Available all over the *centro;* try the stall on Carrillo just south of Juárez and the Plaza de Armas. (15 pesos per hr. Open daily 9am-9pm.)

Post Office: (☎712 0264), Juárez and Galeana, nine blocks east of the Plaza de Armas, on the 1st fl. of the Palacio Federal. Open M-F 9am-5pm, Sa 9am-1pm. **Mexpost** available next door. **Postal Code:** 27000.

▐ ACCOMMODATIONS

Torreón's budget accommodations cluster around **Plaza de Armas** and tend to be large hotels from the 1930s and 1940s. If decaying elegance isn't your style, plenty of functional options can be found along **Morelos** east of the Plaza de Armas for 300-400 pesos.

Hotel Princesa, Morelos 1390 (☎712 1165). This aging hotel stands steps from the Plaza de Armas. The rooms are large and clean with high ceilings and surround two courtyards. The yellow-tiled front section is more cheerful and costs 10 pesos more than the down-at-the-heels back patio. Rooms with bath 80-90 pesos. **❶**

Hotel Galicia, Cepeda 273 Sur (☎716 1111), between Juárez and Morelos. This landmark building from the 1930s has elaborate blue and pink tile, individual balconies, and funky rooms. Pink, flowery stained glass gives the lobby a rosy glow. Forgive the disrepair and live the dream on the Grand Balcony overlooking Plaza de Armas. All rooms with bath. Singles 148 pesos. ❷

Hotel Arriaga, Cepeda 414 (☎716 1055), at the southeast corner of the Plaza de Armas. Arriaga provides A/C, televisions, and phones in all of its rooms. Ask for a room looking over the Plaza de Armas. Singles 180 pesos; doubles 200 pesos. ❸

🍴 FOOD

The many good, affordable restaurants in Torreón guarantee that you won't be washing dishes to pay for your meal. The *centro's* curbs and sidewalks abound with *torta* and *gordita* vendors. Locals crowd **Lonchos Roz y Morelos** ❶, one such cart at Rodríguez and Morelos. (Meaty *loncho* sandwiches 12-16 pesos. Open daily 11am-6pm.) Torreón also specializes in ice cream and frozen yogurt. Look for both on **Morelos** going toward Colón.

🍴 **De Granero,** Morelos 444 Pte. (☎712 7144). Granero is a vegetarian restaurant extraordinaire, popular with Torreón's health-conscious bourgeois. Fruit salads with granola and yogurt 35 pesos. Soy *chorizo* burritos 8 pesos and a wide selection of *licuados* 9-18 pesos. Health food store and bakery attached. Other locations at Estadio and Carranza (☎717 8441) and Constitución 712 (☎718 7661). Open daily 9am-9pm. ❷

Restaurant La Cope de Leche, Valdés Carrillo 359 Sur (☎716 8881). Gets its name from the 50s-style glasses it uses to serve great milkshakes (19.5 pesos). Clean, cozy place to start your day with a large breakfast of eggs, beans, meat, or fruit (37-50 pesos) and juice (9-15 pesos). ❸

🔆 SIGHTS

Parks and museums dot the downtown area, including the centrally-located **Plaza de Armas,** the **Parque de los Fundadores** on Muzquiz and Constitución, the **Alameda Zaragoza Juárez and Donato Guerra,** and the 30-block **Bosque Venustiano Carranza** on Cuauhtémoc between Juárez and Bravo. The museums and parks draw Torreón's squawking kids and doting parents. The optimistically named *bosque* (forest) is home to the **Museo Regional de la Laguna,** Juárez 1300 Ote.; in addition to a display on the Laguna Area's nomadic desert cultures, the museum holds Licio Lago's wonderful collection of Pre-Hispanic art and artifacts, complete with several brilliantly-executed fakes, which have managed to fool even the collector, and still confound some archaeologists. (☎713 9545. Open Tu-Su 10am-6:30pm. 27 pesos, children free.) Not far from the museum, a crew of **break dancers** monopolizes the *bosque's* open-air stage with elaborate pop-locking and headspins. An 80s soundtrack blasts as a group of 30 or so teenage boys meet in the park almost every afternoon to practice the ancient art of "Break." Their acrobatics delight the attentive girls in the bleachers. This is not to be missed. To get to the *bosque,* catch a collective taxi labeled "Ruta Centro" on Juárez at the Plaza de Armas; the taxi drops off (and picks up) two blocks from the park entrance (3.5 pesos).

The **Museo de la Revolución,** Muzquiz and Constitución, has displays on Mexican history and independence. (Open Tu-Su 10am-2pm. Free.) The **Museo del Ferrocarril,** Revolución and Carrillo, displays some of the trains that shaped the city's growth. (☎712 2312. Open Tu-Su 10am-5pm.) Torreón is also home to the third-largest statue of Jesus Christ in the world. **Cristo de las Noas** spreads his arms over the city, fenced in by antennas and satellite dishes. Follow the stairs to the summit for an amazing view of Torreón. A recreated Holy Land—with a calvary and caves of Gethsemane in the works—flanks the Christ statue.

🎵 🎧 ENTERTAINMENT AND NIGHTLIFE

Lounging in the **Plaza de Armas** is by far the most popular type of entertainment in Torreón. On weekends, the whole city comes out to polka, salsa, and tango under the trees as speakers blare *Norteño*. *Caballeros* sport cowboy hats and boots; *damas*, dresses with spangles.

Torreón's bars often feature live music. Across from the plaza, inside Hotel Palacio Real is **El Greco**, Morelos 1280 Pte., a "Ladies' Bar" that has live music. Check the schedule posted outside for a listing of events. (☎716 0000. Happy hour 7-9pm. Open Tu-Sa 6pm-2am.) Locals drink and dance to the nightly live *Norteño* at **El Golfo**, at the corner of Morelos and Blanco. (Beer 15 pesos. Open daily 6pm-1am.)

Torreón has two main festivals: **Feria del Algodón** (the cotton festival, mid-Aug. to mid-Sept.) and **Feria Laguna** (a regional fair, early to mid-Oct.). The **Gran Reguta del Río Nazas,** held in early July, is a boat race on the city's river.

ZACATECAS

ZACATECAS   ☎492

Zacatecas glows with a sunset pink that's easier to recognize than to describe. And, like a sunset, Zacatecas makes people want to see it over and over again. This 2500m high city flourished from a silver boom centuries ago, and today it's a UNESCO world heritage site that still manages to boil over with fun. A stone with a high silver content given to early Spanish colonists by an indigenous Cascane in the mid-1500s triggered the mining frenzy that led to the founding of the town in 1585. Eventually, the Spaniards stripped the surrounding hills of 6000 tons of silver. Although the silver mines have since gone dry, Zacatecas manages to thrive without the mines. Under the patronage of the silver barons, the arts flourished. The rows of grand colonial mansions, parks, and museums testify to an era of lavish consumption in which the great barons swore they would coat the streets with silver. Today, Zacatecas is a busy university town with tremendous churches, museums, parties, and a fun hostel. And, of course, plenty of Corona beer, home-brewed in the state of Zacatecas.

🚍 TRANSPORTATION

Airport: (☎928 0338), accessible by *combis* (☎922 5946) from the Mexicana office (20min., departs 1¼hr. before flight, 50 pesos). **Mexicana,** Hidalgo 406 (☎922 7429). Open M-F 9am-7pm. **Taesa,** Hidalgo 306 (☎922 0050 or 922 0212). Open M-F 9am-7pm, Sa 10am-6pm. **AeroCalifornia,** Juan de Montoro 203 (☎925 2400).

Buses: Central de Autobuses (☎922 1112), Lomas de la Isabélica, at Tránsito Pesado on the outskirts of town. City buses (3 pesos; "Ruta 8" to the *centro*) and taxis (25 pesos to the *centro*) wait outside. After dark, a taxi is the only option. To get to the station from the *centro*, take the "Ruta 8" along Genaro Codino, Hierro, Hidalgo, or González Ortega (all on the bus route). **Ómnibus de México** (☎922 5495) has the broadest range of service, including: **Aguascalientes** (3hr., every hr., 80 pesos); **Ciudad Juárez** (26hr., every hr., 752 pesos); **Durango** (5hr., 15 per day, 176 pesos); **Guadalajara** (5hr., every 45min., 228 pesos); **Matamoros** (11hr., 7 per day, 456 pesos); **Mexico City** (8hr., 10 per day, 400 pesos); **Monterrey** (6hr., 3 per day, 268 pesos); **San Luis Potosí** (3hr., 15 per day, 105 pesos). **Futura** (☎922 0042) and **Estrella Blanca** (☎922 0684) also service the area.

Zacatecas

♠ ACCOMMODATIONS
Hostal Villa Colonial, 6
Hotel del Parque, 10
Hotel María Conchita, 9
Hotel Zamora, 8

🍴 FOOD
Acropolis, 1
El Pueblito, 3
Gorditas Doña Julia, 4
La Única Cabaña, 7
Tacuba Cafe, 5

★ NIGHTLIFE
Café Dalí, 2

🔷🔢 ORIENTATION AND PRACTICAL INFORMATION

Zacatecas is 610 km away from the D.F. on the silver trail; it's 190km from San Luis Potosí. The city streets are not only mercilessly snarled, but their names change frequently, they're sprawled over hills, and many are *callejones* (alleys that often terminate in stairways). **Hidalgo** is the main street, and the **cathedral** is a useful landmark visible from all over town.

Tourist Office: Hidalgo 403 (☎922 3426), on the 2nd fl. Helpful staff answers questions in both Spanish and English and provides a variety of maps and pamphlets. Open M-F 8am-8pm, Sa-Su 10am-6pm. **Coffee addicts** take note: the best coffee in Zacatecas is located downstairs in the same building. Office operates an equally helpful **booth** a block south on Hidalgo, just across from the *teatro*. Open Tu-Su 10am-6pm.

Currency Exchange: Banca Promex, González Ortega 122 (☎922 9369), has good rates and a 24hr. **ATM.** Open M-F 8:30am-5:30pm, Sa 10am-2pm. The 1st blocks of González Ortega and Hidalgo away from Juárez are inundated with banks.

Car Rental: Autos Último Modelo, Alcatraces 147 (☎/fax 924 5509), is among the cheapest in town, with prices starting at 450 pesos per day with the 1st 200km free; **Avis,** López Mateos 615 (☎922 3003, or at the airport at 985 1100). Open M-Sa 8:30am-3pm and 5-7:30pm. **Mazzocco,** Fátima 115 Sierra de Alicia (☎/fax 922

7702), rents everything from cars to buses. **Budget,** López Mateos 104 (☎922 9458; www.budget.com.mx), rents cars from 500 pesos.

Luggage Storage: At the bus station. 3 pesos per hr. 24hr.

Laundry: Lavamatic Plus, Rosadela 18 (☎923 4706), at México. Open M-Sa 9am-5:30pm. 30 pesos per 3kg. The **hostels** also have laundry machines. 25 pesos per load.

Market: A wonderful open-air market follows the twisty Arroyo de la Plata from Independencia to the small bus station at López Mateos, spilling into adjacent streets.

Emergency: ☎066.

Police: Héroes de Chapultepec 1000 (☎922 0507). No English spoken. Or call the 24hr. tourist police hotline at ☎927 2654 or 922 0180.

Red Cross: Calzada de la Cruz Roja 100 (☎922 3005 or 922 3323), off Héroes de Chapultepec, near the exit to Fresnillo. Some English spoken.

Pharmacy: Farmacia Guadalajara, López Mateos 305 (☎922 3862), across the street from the Howard Johnson, is the most visible pharmacy. Open 24hr.

Hospital: Hospital General, García Salinas 707 in neighboring Guadalupe (☎923 3004 or 923 3005). **Dr. José Cruz de la Torre González** (☎924 0703) speaks English.

Fax: Telecomm (☎922 0060; fax 922 1796), on Hidalgo at Juárez. Open M-F 8:30am-7pm, Sa-Su 9am-noon.

Internet Access: The **public library,** at the end of Juárez across from Jardín Independencia, provides free service (30min. limit if someone's waiting). Open daily 9am-9pm. Otherwise the going rate seems to be 15 pesos. **Optimus Prime** at Tacuba 118 (☎922 0423), right across from the fountain, has fast service and competent assistance. Open M-Sa 9am-9pm.

Post Office: Allende 111 (☎922 0196), off Hidalgo. Open M-F 9am-4pm, Sa 9am-1pm. **Mexpost** service next door. Open M-F 9am-6pm, Sa 9am-1pm. **Postal Code:** 98000.

▚ ACCOMMODATIONS

While most budget accommodations have been priced out of the *centro*, they linger at its fringe on **López Mateos,** the main thoroughfare bordering the historic core. Reservations are a good idea at the cheapest hotels. The youth hostel is the best deal, especially for its location.

▨ **Hostal Villa Colonial (HI),** 1 de Mayo (☎922 1980; hostalvillacolonial@hotmail.com), up Callejón Mono Prieto, behind the cathedral. The Lozano clan presides over this island of budget hospitality in the overpriced city center. A crowd of internationals and backpackers revels in the amenities: kitchen, dining room, Internet (15 pesos per hr.), storage, book exchange, and washing machine (25 pesos per 10kg). Ask the owners about outings to nearby towns and to the Corona *cervezería.* Comfortable dorm-style rooms with 4 beds (70 pesos with ISIC or HI card, 80 pesos without). Private rooms (180 pesos) have spectacular views of the cathedral. Pickup service from the bus station from 6-8am and 2-4pm. ❶

Hotel del Parque, González Ortega 302 (☎922 0479), near the aqueduct. The green swathe of the Parque Enrique Estrada provides a pleasant view from the del Parque, though the hotel is an uphill trek away from the major sights. Nice location, clean rooms and bathrooms, and TV. Singles 150 pesos; doubles 160 pesos; triples 200 pesos; quads 230 pesos. ❷

Hotel María Conchita, López Mateos 401 (☎922 1494), just across Mateos from the *zona centro.* Rooms are well-maintained and pleasant and come equipped with phone and TV. Recently remodeled 4th- and 5th-floor rooms aren't worth the price (or stair) hike. Light sleepers should ask for a room away from the noisy highway out front. The late-night restaurant next door offers cheap breakfasts (30 pesos) and other Mexican standards. Singles 150 pesos; doubles 180 pesos; triples 210 pesos; quads 250. ❷

Hotel Zamora, Plazuela de Zamora 303 (☎922 1200), which is the continuation of Independencia just downhill from the Jardín. With a lobby that lingers in the eternal twi-light of *telenovelas*, Hotel Zamora has a good location but a high price tag for its basic rooms. Singles 173 pesos; doubles 200 pesos. ❸

🍴 FOOD

Zacatecas is famous for its sweets. Get that sugar rush with a chunk of *dulce de leche, camote, coco* (coconut), or *batata* (sweet potato)—all 5 pesos, peddled by vendors throughout the *centro*. Zacatecas also hosts a thriving **cafe** culture. One of the best is **Il San Patrizio Café**, Hidalgo 403, in a shady courtyard. (Coffee 12-25 pesos. Open daily 9am-10pm.) For good coffee and an opportunity to meet all of the city's politicians and businessmen, head to **Acropolis** on Hidalgo next door to the cathedral. (Open daily 8am-10pm.) Also try the fashionable new **Tacuba Cafe,** Tacuba 164, across from the mall. (Open daily 4-11pm.)

🍽 **La Única Cabaña,** on Independencia at Juárez. Easily the most popular restaurant in town, this *taquería* does everything right. Fast, hot, and served with excellent salsas. Extraordinarily good quesadillas 7 pesos, tacos 3.6 pesos, ½-roasted chicken meal 37 pesos. Open daily 7am-midnight. ❶

La Leyenda, Segunda de Matamoros 216 (☎922 3853). Masks cover the walls at this homey but date-worthy restaurant. Local specialties like *empanadas de huitlacoche y flor de calabaza* (corn smut and squash flower pastries, 50 pesos) and *birria* (a meaty stew, 50 pesos). Open M-Sa 2-11pm. ❹

El Pueblito, Hidalgo 403 (☎924 3818), downstairs from the tourist office. For a more upscale clientele. Try the Zacatecan *enchiladas* (43 pesos) or the regional sampler (55 pesos). Classy enough to impress your date. Open daily 1-11pm. ❹

Gorditas Doña Julia, Hidalgo 409 (☎923 7955), with additional locations on Tacuba (across from the fountain) on Obregón, and on the freeway out of town. If Doña Julia keeps up the present rate of colonization she'll have to hire a chihuahua to advertise her delicious *gorditas* (6 pesos). Still, locals love these fat little tortilla sandwiches, Zacatecans' favorite takeout—get it *para llevar* to blend in. Open daily 8am-11pm. ❶

📷 SIGHTS

Because of its extraordinary beauty, Zacatecas's entire city center is a UNESCO world heritage site. Strict building codes and prohibitions against gaudy advertise-ment make it hard to tell where the city ends and the museums begin—but it hardly matters since both are spectacular. Not to be missed are the two Coronel museums and the vista of the city from **La Buta.** If you've got a few more days, leave time for the neighboring town of **Guadalupe** and the ruins of **La Quemada.**

🏛 **CATHEDRAL.** The pride of Zacatecas, the pink sandstone cathedral, officially called **Nuestra Señora de Asunción,** was begun in 1729, completed in 1752, and con-secrated as a cathedral 1862. The magnificent building is one of the most beautiful cathedrals in all the Americas. The intricate three-story facade is perhaps the best example of Mexican Baroque and depicts, among a myriad of figures, Christ bless-ing the Apostles and images of the Eucharist. The northern facade bears a repre-sentation of Christ on the cross, and the European Baroque southern facade pays homage to *Nuestra Señora de las Zacatecas.* The interior of the cathedral, in contrast to its lavish exterior, is surprisingly plain, although legend has it that prior to the War of Reform it was as splendid as the outside. *(4 blocks northeast of Juárez, on Hidalgo. Open daily 7am-1pm and 3-9pm.)*

■ **MUSEO DE PEDRO CORONEL.** Housed in the former Colegio de San Luis Gonzaga, a Jesuit college established in 1616 and later a jail, the museum is now home to the tomb, sculptures, unparalleled art collections, and paintings of Zacatecan artist Pedro Coronel. In addition, it has one of the best modern art collections in Latin America, with works by such varied artists as Picasso, Braque, Chagall, Miró, Goya, and Hogarth. *(On Villapando at Serdán. Facing away from the cathedral entrance, cross Hidalgo going right, turn left into the 1st alleyway, turn left as it ends on Dondina, and right at your 1st opportunity, following Villapando to the museum. ☎ 922 8021. Open Su-W, F-Sa 10am-5pm. 15 pesos, students and seniors 10 pesos, children free.)*

■ **MUSEO RAFAEL CORONEL.** Bristle-faced tigers, swarthy Moors, caimans, and gods stare out from the walls of this superb museum that stresses the power of masks. The dramatic **Ex-Convento de San Francisco,** built by Franciscans in the 17th century and then occupied by the Jesuits until the late 18th century, the building seems to be as much a part of the museum as its art objects. The exhibits showcase an enormous collection of masks, figurines, pottery, and puppets donated by Rafael Coronel, brother of Pedro. Thorough labels explain the masks in Spanish, but the masks pull on the imagination, too. Don't miss the rooms with Rafael Coronel's recent photography and surreal paintings. *(To reach the museum from the cathedral, follow Hidalgo, bearing left at the fountain at the 1st fork, and right at the 2nd. Open Tu-Th 10am-5pm. 15 pesos, students and seniors 7.5 pesos, children free.)*

PALACIO DE GOBIERNO. The Palacio de Gobierno was built in 1727 as the residence of Joseph de Rivera Bernández, a count. The building distinguishes itself with the mural that surrounds its interior stairwell. Painted in 1970 by Antonio Rodríguez, the work traces the history of Zacatecas from antiquity to the present. *(Next to the cathedral. Open M-F 9am-8pm.)*

TEMPLO DE SANTO DOMINGO. Built by the Jesuits in 1746, the Temple contains nine Baroque altarpieces covered with enough gilding to make the whole church gleam. There's also a rare 18th-century German pipe organ. *(At the end of Villapando. Open daily 7am-1pm and 5-8pm. Mass held frequently on weekends.)*

MUSEO ZACATECANO. Has a permanent exhibit on the art of the region's native Huichol people as well as a collection of 19th-century *retablos* (icons), which provide something of a crash course in Mexican Catholicism. *(☎ 922 6580. At Dr. Itievro Zol, 2 blocks down from Santo Domingo. Open Su-M, W-Sa 9:30am-5pm. 12 pesos.)*

PARQUE ENRIQUE ESTRADA. Southeast of the downtown area, 39 pink stone arches mark the end of Zacatecas's famous colonial aqueduct, **El Cubo.** Beside the aqueduct is the manicured **Parque Enrique Estrada.** To one side of the park is the former governor's mansion, now the **Museo de Francisco Goitia,** Enrique Estrada 101. The museum displays regional historical artifacts and gives a good account of Mexican history. *(☎ 922 0211. Open Tu-Su 10am-5pm. 20 pesos, students 10 pesos.)*

MUSEO DE ARTE ABSTRACTO MANUEL FELGUÉREZ. This converted prison houses a wide range of Mexican abstract art from the past 40 years. On prison-guard catwalks, you can survey the Manuel Felguérez collection, which takes the former prisoners' position. The museum also sports superb giant canvases from the Osaka 70 exhibit, and temporary exhibits on Mexican and international figures. *(☎ 924 3705. Colón 1. Open Su-M, W-Sa 10am-5pm. 20 pesos, students 10 pesos.)*

CERRO DEL GRILLO. Most people walk up El Grillo to catch the *teleférico* to the much higher Cerro de la Bufa. El Grillo also has a splendid view over Zacatecas, and the Mina el Edén east entrance neighbors the *teleférico* stop here.

MINA EL EDÉN. Discovered in 1583, the Mina el Edén was one of Zacatecas's most productive silver mines until the 1960s, when continual flooding made mineral extraction futile. Now re-opened as a tourist attraction, the interior lacks the beauty of natural caves—its cramped depths make it easy to see why it was sarcastically called "The Mine of Eden" in reference to the miserable conditions suffered by its workers. The tour includes some fairly tame treks across rope bridges and auto-pilot descriptions by Spanish-speaking guides. The mine has two entrances. *(Enter the mine at the east entrance, close to the Grillo teleférico stop. An old mine train will take you to the tour starting point. Open daily 10am-6pm. 20 pesos, children 15 pesos.)*

CERRO DE LA BUFA. Named in Basque for its resemblance to a Spanish wineskin, and surrounded by both myth and history, the Cerro peers down on Zacatecas from the city's highest crag. Museums, a church, and tons of clambering kids stand at the top, but the wide-ranging vista is the real attraction. **Museo de la Toma de Zacatecas,** adjacent to the *cerro*, was built to commemorate Pancho Villa's decisive victory over federal troops in the summer of 1914. The museum displays an array of Revolutionary memorabilia, including photographs, a cannon, and small arms. *(☎ 922 8066. Open daily 10am-4:30pm. 10 pesos.)* On one side of the museum lies the 18th-century **Capilla del Patrocinio**, whose graceful facade and cloistered courtyards are carved from the pink stone that graces many of Zacatecas's monuments. Nearby shops sell arts, crafts, and loads of geodes. A short but steep walk up the hill leads to the Moorish **Mausoleo de los Hombres Ilustres de Zacatecas** (Tomb of the Famous Men of Zacatecas), worth the hike if only for the view of the city. There's yet another vista behind the museum, from the castle where the **Meteorological Observatory** is housed. Climbing around up here is half the fun.

🎵 📷 ENTERTAINMENT & NIGHTLIFE

Zacatecas's nights can be expensive, but the student-fueled nightlife is worth it, alternating between relaxing and raging. The city also has cheap cantinas and pool halls. Night spots listed are in the *centro*, where well-lit, relatively safe streets eliminate the need for cabs. By far the best parties are *callejoneadas*.

NO WORK, ALL PLAY

THE CALLEJONEADA

Zacatecas is a party town, full of bars and clubs, and 30km away from the Corona *cervezería*. But the best parties rove the streets in the noble Zacatecan tradition of the *callejoneada*.

On weekends, crowds of Zacatecans converge on the Alameda, the park at the southeast end of the *centro*. There, they meet up with men guiding *burros* laden with the pleasurable nectar mescal, a generally home-brewed tequila-like drink, also from the maguey cactus. Everyone strings a cup around his or her neck, and a live band leads the *callejoneada* out parading. The mescal, the music, and the festive evening air soon sparks the crowd to begin dancing bacchically through the city's narrow *callejones*. Be prepared for the alcohol's jolt, which the altitude makes stronger: you too, will be kicking up your heels in very little time, which will also make it more difficult to negotiate the stairs that pepper the *callejones*. Luckily, everyone will be equally inebriated, and no one will object if you grab an arm for support.

The *callejoneada* is a long standing tradition in Zacatecas dating back 300 or 400 years. To join this venerable and wild parade, meet at the starting point in the Alameda on weekend nights around sunset. They are very welcoming events, too, so feel free to just join one as it passes by in the street.

El Malacate (☎922 3002), 600m in from the side entrance of the Mina de Edén. Malacate is buried within a mountain—you take a mine train to get to this one-of-a-kind party. You've never experienced a bass beat until you hear it reverberating off the solid stone walls of this former mine shaft. Beer 18 pesos, mixed drinks 25 pesos. Cover 50 pesos. Open Th-Sa 10pm-2:30am.

Rincón de las Troubadores (☎922 6129). Also called Rincón Bohemia. Follow Hidalgo uphill to Callejón de Luis Moya. Romantic ballads and *salsa* play to a roomful of nicely dressed 20- and 30-somethings. Tequila from 32 pesos, beer 18 pesos. Open M-Th 7pm-midnight, Sa-Su 7pm-2:30am.

Café Dalí, Ignacio Hierro 504. This coffee shop/bar fills with students drinking *michelada* (18 pesos) and playing pool. Melting clocks adorn the walls, and the bathrooms are marked by Dalí's portrait (men) and his wife Gaia (women). Beers 15 pesos. Open daily 5pm-midnight, later on weekends.

Malaga, Tacuba 105 (☎044 492 869 1397), across from the fountain. Zacatecas's students cram this club on weekends. Techno/electronica plays on the dance floor. More secluded balcony tables cradle young couples. Cover 100 pesos for men, 40 pesos for women. Open Th-Sa 10pm-3am.

Cultural events—folkloric dance, music of all kinds, and parades—constantly enliven the **cathedral square.** Every Thursday the Zacatecas **state band** stages a free classical concert there at 7pm. The yearly cultural highlight is **Zacatecas en la Cultura,** a festival during *Semana Santa*, in which concerts and artistic activities are held in the elegant Teatro Calderón, on Hidalgo near the cathedral, and throughout the city. Zacatecas is also reputed to have Mexico's best **Morismo,** a mock re-creation of the battle of the Moors and the Spanish enacted with masks and costumes in mid-August. Call the tourist office for specific details. From September 8 to 22, the city celebrates the **Feria Nacional de Zacatecas** with musical and theatrical events, bullfights, agricultural and crafts shows, and sporting events.

▶ DAYTRIPS FROM ZACATECAS

▪ LA QUEMADA

Take a Villanueva bus from the small in-town bus station in Zacatecas on López Mateos to La Quemada (45min., every 30min., 17 pesos). Be sure to specify that you want to get off at the ruins ("las ruinas de la Quemada"). The road to the ruins is on the left of the main route, right after the white, yellow, and blue restaurant with the Corona sign. Walk about 3km along this road to reach the entrance. Site open daily 10am-5pm. 32 pesos, plus 7 pesos for the museum. To get to Jérez from here, walk back to the main route and hop on a bus heading back to Zacatecas. You'll have to get off in Malpaso and change buses to get to Jérez. Ask the bus driver where to get off to wait for the Jérez bus.

About 50km south of Zacatecas lie some very cool ruins that very few people have ever heard of. **La Quemada** (AD 500-800) hasn't yielded any spectacular golden artifacts, nor is it attributable to any major Mesoamerican civilization, and for these reasons the visually stunning ruins have been left more or less untouristed. Hikers will love scrambling over this adobe city. The temples, dwellings, fortresses, and ball court of La Quemada are impressively built into a mountain with a 360-degree view of the surrounding countryside. The site's museum explains the mystery surrounding Quemada's origins. Some postulate that it was the site of the legendary Aztec city Chicomostoc, Tenochtitlán's precursor and capital of the region north of the Río San Antonio. It also offers a scale model of the ruins that is a helpful guide to those interested in the more remote sections.

GUADALUPE

In Zacatecas, catch a Transportes Guadalupe bus from the bus station or the smaller station on López Mateos (30min., 3.5 pesos). Tell the bus driver you want to get off in Guadalupe's centro. From the bus station in Guadalupe, walk a short distance to your left along Mateos and turn right on Constitución at the monument in the center of the street. The cathedral is a couple of blocks in front of you. Catch a return bus to Zacatecas from the same bus station. Cathedral open daily 10am-4:30pm. 20 pesos.

The village, named after the town church, was founded in 1707 as a training site for Franciscan missionaries. The **Ex-Convento de Guadalupe,** located on the main plaza, is known not only for having produced over 3000 missionaries, but for its famous statue of the **Virgin of Guadalupe,** located above the altar. Next to the cathedral is the **Museo de Guadalupe,** which contains paintings depicting scenes from the life of St. Francis, as well as nearly every known incident in the life of Christ. Those yearning for medieval misadventure can walk into the museum courtyard, around the side of the stone block, and down into the dank, dark cistern.

JÉREZ

Zacatecas-Jérez buses run to Jérez (1hr., every 30min. 5:15am-10pm, 26 pesos). To get to the centro from the Jérez bus station, turn right on the street directly ahead. It's a good 25min. walk, so consider taking a cab or a bus (if you can find one).

About an hour's bus ride from Zacatecas lies the quiet colonial town of Jérez (pop. 12,500). If Zacatecas isn't sedate enough, both beautiful colonial buildings and an old-fashioned pace of life calm Jérez. Among the buildings is the **Edificio de la Torre,** built by architect Dámaso Muñetón in 1896. The **Casa-Museo Ramon López Velarde** celebrates the life of the native poet. The **Santuario de Soledad** is a beautiful mid-19th-century church. Also visit the **Iglesia Parroquia.** The impressive **Teatro Hinojosa,** a replica of New York City's Lincoln Center, was built in 1878, and will give you some idea of the town's past mining wealth.

AGUASCALIENTES

AGUASCALIENTES   ☎449

Aguascalientes (pop. 550,000) is famous throughout Mexico for its no-holds-barred Feria de San Marcos, when the whole city goes wild from mid-April to mid-May. For the rest of the year, residents settle down to work, play with their kids in the many plazas, and attend the city's myriad cultural events. Mixed in with modern concrete buildings stand unusual churches, the mural-covered Palacio de Gobierno, and unexpected green spaces. Aguascalientes stood on the old silver trail between Zacatecas and Mexico City, and it still makes a good stopover between the larger cities nearby. When in town, don't miss the Plaza de la Patria or the eerie engravings at the Museo José Guadalupe Posada.

▐ TRANSPORTATION

Buses: The bus station is on Convención Sur and Av. 5, a few blocks west of José Marí Chávez. Green and white city buses with numbers in the 20s or 30s (3.5 pesos) run from outside the bus station to the Mercado Morelos, 2 blocks north of the Plaza de la Patria, the center of town. To get back to the station, take a "Central Camionera" bus or a taxi (20 pesos). **Ómnibus de México** (☎978 2770) goes to: **Ciudad Juárez** (15hr., 6 per day, 830 pesos); **Durango** (7hr., 7 per day, 255 pesos); **Torreón** (6hr., 5 per day, 322 pesos); **Zacatecas** (2½hr., 8 per day, 80 pesos). **Futura** (☎978 2758) goes to:

NORTHEAST MEXICO

Aguascalientes

▲ ACCOMMODATIONS
Hotel Brasil, 3
Hotel Posada de San Miguel, 5
Hotel Rosales, 6
Hotel Señorial, 8

● FOOD
El Zodiaco, 9
Gorditas Victoria, 4
Restaurant Vegtariano Devenad, 2
Rincón Maya, 11

★ NIGHTLIFE
Disco El Cabús, 1
Jubilee, 10
Merendero San Marcos, 7

Museo de Aguascalientes
Templo de San Antonio

Zaragoza

TO ALAMEDA & CENTRO CULTURAL LOS ARQUITOS (700m)

TO BAÑOS TERMALES DE OJO CALIENTE (9.2km)

TO PLAZA KRISTAL (250m)

Madero
Wasco
López Mateos
5 de Febrero

16 de Septiembre
Montoro
Hornedo
Mina

Primo Verdad
Saracho

Hidalgo
Parga

Mercado Morelos

Museo de Arte Contemporaneo

Hospitalidad
Morelos

Díaz de León
Del Sol
Colón
Leona Vicario
Héroes de Chapultepec

TO MUSEO JOSÉ GUADALUPE POSADA (25m)

Farmacia Sánchez
Palmira

Buses to/from Central de Autobuses

Juárez
Centro Parián
San Marcos Plaza (mall)

Colón
Palacio de Gobierno
José María Chávez
Hornedo

Obregón
Riviero Y Gutiérrez

Basílica de la Asunción
PLAZA DE LA PATRIA
Teatro Morelos

5 de Mayo
Moctezuma
Galeana N.

Mercado Jesús Teran
Unión

Guadalupe Victoria

Casa de Cultura

Galeana Sur

TO (3km)

Gorostiza
Allende

Museo Regional de Historia

López Mateos

Liberad
Zapata

Alarcon

Guerrero Norte
Matamoros Norte
Insurgentes

Guerrero Sur
Matamoros Sur

Multicines El Dorado 70
Hospital Hidalgo

Guadalupe

Macias

Correa

Carranza

Nieto
Pocitos
Rayón

Elizondo Norte
F. Elizordo

TO (2km)

TO CENTRAL DE AUTOBUSES

Contreras
Jardín de San Marcos

250 yards
250 meters

LG

SAN MARCOS FAIRGROUND AREA

López Mateos

Área de la Feria

Templo de San Marcos

Pani

Ponce

Expo Plaza

Los Laureles
TO

Acapulco (11hr., 4 per day, 470 pesos); **Cuernavaca** (7hr., 11pm, 320 pesos); **Durango** (6hr., 7 per day, 255 pesos); **Guadalajara** (3hr., every hr. 5am-9pm, 158 pesos); **Mexico City** (6hr., 10 per day, 322 pesos); **Monterrey** (9hr., 8 per day, 344 pesos); **San Luis Potosí** (3hr., 15 per day, 20 pesos). **Primera Plus** (☎978 2671) and **ETN** (☎978 2429) also go to major cities.

✴ 🔃 ORIENTATION AND PRACTICAL INFORMATION

Aguascalientes is 168km west of San Luis Potosí, 128km south of Zacatecas, and 252km northeast of Guadalajara. **Circunvalación** encircles the city, while **López Mateos** cuts through town east to west. From **Plaza de la Patria**, the center of town, most sights are within walking distance. The city takes its *siestas* quite seriously; many sights and businesses close from 2 to 4pm.

Tourist Office: (☎915 9504 or 916 0051), off Plaza de la Patria, in the Palacio de Gobierno. The door opens right onto the plaza. Decent maps and a plethora of brochures, some in English. Open M-F 8am-7:30pm, Sa-Su 9am-6pm.

Currency Exchange: Bancomer, 5 de Mayo 120 (☎915 5115), 1 block from the Plaza, also offers good rates. Open M-F 8:30am-4pm, Sa 10am-1pm.

Emergency: ☎080.

Police: (☎914 2080 or 915 9460), at the corner of Libertad and Gómez Orozco. English spoken.

Pharmacy: Farmacia Sánchez, Madero 213 (☎915 3550), 1 block from the Plaza. Open 24hr.

Hospital: Hospital Hidalgo, Galeana 465 (☎918 4448).

Fax: Telecomm (☎916 1427), Galeana at Nieto. Open Su 9am-noon, M-F 8am-7pm, Sa 9am-1pm. Another office in the bus station. Open M-F 8am-7:30pm, Sa 9am-noon.

Internet Access: Cybercafe 2000, Allende 105 Internal #1 (☎916 9415). 25 pesos per hr., students 20 pesos per hr. Open M-Sa 10am-8pm.

Post Office: Hospitalidad 108 (☎915 2118). Open M-F 8am-6pm, Sa 9am-1pm. **Postal Code:** 20000.

🏠 ACCOMMODATIONS

Budget hotels in **Aguascalientes** are all tucked away on side streets extending from the plaza. As a general rule, the *centro* is much nicer than the area near the bus station; the hotels are better and the prices are about the same. During the **Feria de San Marcos** (mid-April to mid-May), reservations are a must.

Hotel Rosales, Guadalupe Victoria 104 (☎915 2165), off Madero, right across from the Basílica and Plaza Patria. The shady courtyard invites mid-day lounging, and the location is excellent, especially for the price. Simple, clean rooms; a nice courtyard; and TV. Singles 120 pesos; matrimonials 150 pesos; doubles 180 pesos; triples 220 pesos. ❷

Hotel Brasil, Guadalupe Victoria 110 (☎915 1106), 3 blocks up from the Plaza and just around the corner on Guadalupe. Shiny turquoise walls and a waterfall mural cheer up this quiet, clean, friendly hotel. Optical illusions provided by eclectic tiling make every day a trip. Singles 70 pesos; matrimonials 100 pesos; doubles 120 pesos. ❶

Hotel Señorial, Colón 104 (☎915 1630 or 915 1473), at the corner of Montoro, on Plaza de la Patria; the location couldn't be better. Ask for a room with a balcony overlooking the Plaza and cathedral: the view is worth the higher price tag. Nice rooms with cable TV, phone, and a supply of purified water. Singles 200 pesos; doubles 300 pesos; triples 375 pesos; quads 450 pesos. ❹

Hotel Posada de San Miguel, Hidalgo 205 (☎915 7761), at Madero, 3 blocks from the Plaza. Ceiling fans, cable TV, free parking, and complimentary coffee or tea in the morning. Bright orange-and-white walls seem summery. Singles 150 pesos; doubles 190 pesos; triples 210 pesos; quads 260 pesos. ❸

⬛ FOOD

Tons of **street food vendors**—with juice machines, popcorn, tamales, and fruit—fill the *centro*, especially during weekends at the Plaza de la Patria. It would be neglectful to omit the fact that there is a **Tepozuieves** in Aguascalientes, Centro Parián at Juárez and Primo Verdad. If you are uninitiated, go and enjoy this unique and delicious *nieve*.

El Zodiaco, Galeana Sur 113 (☎915 3181). The eye-opening decor combines an open kitchen, orange chairs, formica tables, live canaries, and a painted shrine to the Virgin. Order a sandwich or hamburger (15 pesos) from among the many tasty items in this popular local hangout. Open daily 8:30am-10pm. ❶

Gorditas Victoria, Victoria 108 (☎918 1792), next to the Hotel Rosales. A constant crowd of local families packs this restaurant, devouring every kind of *gordita* (15 pesos) imaginable. Grab your food *para llevar* (to go) and enjoy it in the Plaza. Open daily 8am-8pm. ❶

Rincón Maya, Abasolo 113 (☎916 7574), across the park from Museo Guadalupe Posada. This restaurant celebrates the Yucatán with regional foods like *pollo pibil* (58 pesos) and *tamales yucatecas* (16 pesos each). The *café de olla* is especially spicy and delicious (13 pesos). The food is expensive, but the atmosphere, view, and different flavors are worth it. Open daily 2pm-midnight. ❹

Restaurant Vegetariano Devenad (☎918 2721), at the corner of Zapata and Libertad, just north of Jardín San Marcos, is well worth the walk for those tired of endless meat. Veggies and rice 38 pesos. Quesadillas 15 pesos. Open M-Sa 11am-7:30pm. ❸

👁 SIGHTS

⬛**MUSEO JOSÉ GUADALUPE POSADA.** The museum displays a selection of Aguascalientes-native Posada's grim, delightful, intricate engravings. Cavorting skeletons, nightmare devils, drunks, and lovers populate his images. Posada, an ardent critic of the Porfiriato, set the stage for the scathing social commentary of later Mexican muralists such as Diego Rivera and José Clemente Orozco. The collection includes 220 of his original works and images, the most famous of which is of La Catrina, a society lady-*calavera* (skull) wearing an outlandish hat. Rivera quoted this print in *Sueño de Una Tarde Dominical en la Alameda*, now on display in Mexico City (see **Mexico City: Sights,** p. 114). The museum also has rotating temporary exhibits, like a comparison of Posada's work and the caricatures of Honoré Daumier. *(On León, next to the Templo del Encino, 4 blocks south of López Mateos.* ☎915 4556. *Open Tu-Su 11am-6pm. 10 pesos, students 5 pesos, children free; Su free.)*

PLAZA DE LA PATRIA. The Plaza is shaded by trees and made inviting by numerous benches and burbling fountains. One building at the south of the plaza is a mall. To the north, the Plaza is bordered by the **Palacio de Gobierno,** constructed in the 1660s as a residence for the Marqués de Guadalupe. Fascinating and bitter historical **murals** cover the Palacio's interior. The *conquista* section depicts enslaved Mexicans hauling silver up out of mines, as white-wigged Europeans dance over their heads. Chilean Oswaldo Barra Cunningham—a student of Diego Rivera—

painted the murals in 1961-62 and 1989-92. (Open daily 9am-6pm.) To the south of the plaza is the **Teatro Morelos,** site of the 1914 Convention of Aguascalientes, in which rival factions led by Zapata, Carranza, and Villa grappled over the course of the Mexican Revolution. The posters outside the theater list events information.

BASÍLICA DE LA ASUNCIÓN DE LAS AGUASCALIENTES. The soft grey-and-rose-colored Solomonic Baroque facade of the 18th-century Basílica make it the city's most remarkable structure. The Cathedral's interior, restored in the 18th and 19th centuries, is graced with high ceilings, gold trimmings, and ornate icons, along with 17th- and 18th-century paintings by José de Alcíbar, Andrés López, and Miguel Cabrera. (In the center of Plaza de la Patria. Open daily 7am-2pm and 4-9pm.)

MUSEO DE AGUASCALIENTES. This petite museum—in a not-quite-colonial-style building designed by José Refugio Reyes—exhibits the works of Aguascalientes native Saturnino Herrán. Though Herrán died at 31, he left behind a masterful little collection. His 1917 design for a mural, *Nuestros Dioses,* blends indigenous worship with Catholic in a visually stunning sketch. Rotating exhibits feature Mexican painters, sculptors, and photographers. (On Parga and Zaragoza, across from Templo de San Antonio. Open Tu-Su 11am-6pm. 10 pesos, students and seniors 5 pesos; Su free.)

TEMPLO DE SAN ANTONIO. Take a walk down Zaragoza to get an appreciation of this unusual onion-domed church that rises up at the end of the street. Construction of the church began in 1895 and was completed in 1908 under self-taught architect José Refugio Reyes. The mix of patterns on the interior murals, frescoes, oil paintings, and delicate stained-glass windows matches the eclectic exterior, which blends Baroque, Classical, and Oriental styles. (On Pedro Parga and Zaragoza. From the plaza, walk 3 blocks down Madero, then make a left on Zaragoza and continue for 3 blocks. ☎ 915 2898. Open Su 6:30am-noon and 5:30-9pm; M-Sa 6:30-10am, 11:30am-12:30pm, and 6-9pm.)

JARDÍN DE SAN MARCOS. The area around the Jardín was originally an Indian settlement. Around 1600, *indígenas* erected the **Templo Evangelista San Marcos** on the site. The small church still has services today and is the center of a crowded pedestrian thoroughfare popular with Mexican families in the evenings. The adjacent arcade is lined with bars and vendors, and remains active late into the night. (The Jardín is a 5-10min. walk on Carranza from Plaza de la Patria. Church open daily 7am-2pm and 4-9pm.)

HOT SPRINGS. Aguascalientes does, after all, mean "hot waters," and sure enough, there are several thermal *balnearios* at the edge of town. The most accessible is **Baños Termales de Ojo Caliente.** The turn-of-the-twentieth-century building consists of many private thermal showers and an outdoor swimming pool. The waters are reputed to have cured many cases of rheumatism, as the rheumatic clientele suggests. (Balneario located across the Parque Urbano la Pona at the fork of Revolución and San Luis Potosí. To get there from the city center take an eastbound bus from Maderoz and ask the driver if it is bound for the Balneario. Open daily 7am-7pm. 70-180 pesos per hr.)

OTHER SIGHTS. Clustering around the *centro* are other museums worth a look. The **Museo de Arte Contemporaneo,** at the corner of Morelos and Verdad, displays rotating exhibits, most recently a retrospective on Guatemalan-born abstract painter Carlos Mérida. (☎ 918 6901. Open Tu-Su 11am-6pm. 5 pesos, students and teachers 2.5 pesos.) The **Museo Regional de Historia,** Carranza 118, occupies yet another building designed by Refugio Reyes. The collection explores the area's history, from Pre-Hispanic to Revolutionary. (☎ 916 5228. Open Tu-Su 10am-3pm and 4-7pm. 27 pesos.)

🎵 ENTERTAINMENT

Aguascalientes is not a beacon of wild nightlife except during the Feria de San Marcos. By city ordinance, *discotecas* in Aguascalientes are not allowed in the *centro histórico*, and even on the outskirts they can only open their doors Thursday to Saturday. Bars, on the other hand, are open every night of the week and exist in particular concentration on **Pani,** between Ponce and Nieto, in the area of the San Marcos Fairgrounds just south of the Jardín. Buses stop running around 10pm, making taxis the best way to get around.

Merendero San Marcos, Arturo Pani 144. This bar and grill is one of the most happening places in town. Beer (16 pesos), tequila (30 pesos), and heartfelt live *mariachi* music are served to a mix of tourists and locals. Open daily 1pm-2am.

Disco El Cabús (☎913 0432), Zacatecas at Colosia in the Hotel Las Trojes. Shake your caboose amid the usual flashing lights and bass-heavy dance beats. Don't wear shorts, though—you may be apprehended by the fashion police. Th-F cover 40 pesos, Sa 50 pesos. Open Th-Sa 9pm-3am.

Jubilee, Laureles 602-101 (☎917 0507 or 918 0494). The place to go if you value drinking over dancing. Drinks are about half as much as at other *discotecas,* and the lounging areas are more happening than the dance floor. Live music Th-Sa until 3am. Cover 30 pesos for men, women free. W no cover.

Be part of Mexican *béisbol* by cheering on the hometown **Rieleros** (www.rieleros.com.mx). To get to the stadium, catch a #12, 24, or 25 bus heading east on López Mateos. Snag a bleacher seat in the sun (10 pesos) and compete with local kids in chasing down home run balls. (Season April to September.)

🎉 FESTIVALS

During the ■**Feria de San Marcos** (mid-April to early May), one of Mexico's largest celebrations, everything from cockfights to milking contests takes place in the Jardín de San Marcos. To reach the Expo Plaza, filled with shops and restaurants, walk two blocks to the left down the pedestrian route as you face the Templo in the Jardín. The festival of the patron saint of Aguascalientes, **La Romería de la Asunción** (August 1-15), takes place with dances, processions, and fireworks. The **Festival de las Calaveras** (last week in October and the first week in November) is another occasion for the city to cut loose and celebrate.

SAN LUIS POTOSÍ

SAN LUIS POTOSÍ   ☎444

The "city of plazas," San Luis Potosí (pop. 850,000) lures its happily chatting populace outdoors to lick ice cream and gaze at its many churches. The tranquil city belies a tumultuous history. San Luis was founded in 1592, after Franciscan missionaries began to convert local Guachichil and Tlaxcaltec tribes and prospectors discovered silver and gold. It has twice served as the capital of Mexico. In jail here, Francisco Madero wrote the 1910 *Plan de San Luis Potosí,* which sparked the Revolutionary War. Today, lanterns glow in the cathedrals and fountains at dusk, while bands, magicians, and soap-bubble blowers gather in the town plazas to entertain assembled crowds of young and old. On a warm evening, it's hard to ignore the feeling that San Luis Potosí is the quiet capital of some magical world.

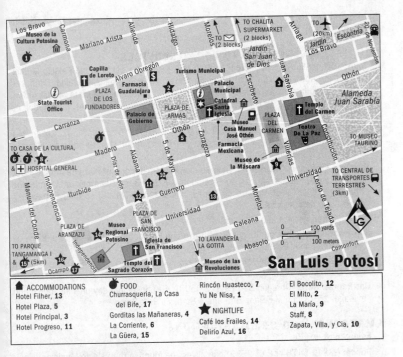

ACCOMMODATIONS
Hotel Filher, **13**
Hotel Plaza, **5**
Hotel Principal, **3**
Hotel Progreso, **11**

FOOD
Churrasqueria, La Casa
del Bife, **17**
Gorditas las Mañaneras, **4**
La Corriente, **6**
La Güera, **15**

Rincón Huasteco, **7**
Yu Ne Nisa, **1**

NIGHTLIFE
Café los Fraíles, **14**
Delirio Azul, **16**

El Bocolito, **12**
El Mito, **2**
La María, **9**
Staff, **8**
Zapata, Villa, y Cia, **10**

TRANSPORTATION

Airport: (☎822 0095), 25min. north of the city. Tickets can be purchased at **2001 Viajes,** Obregón 604 (☎812 2953). Open M-F 9am-2pm and 4-8pm, Sa 9:30am-2pm. **AeroCalifornia** (☎811 8050), **AeroLiteral** (☎818 7371), and **Mexicana** (☎813 3399) fly to various destinations.

Buses: To get downtown from the **Central de Transportes Terrestres,** catch an "Alameda" or "Centro" bus (5:30am-10:30pm, 3 pesos) and hop off at the end of Plaza Alameda at Constitución. Continue down Othón, past Plaza del Carmen, until the city's center, Plaza de Armas (also called Jardín Hidalgo). A **taxi** costs 31 pesos; get your fixed-price taxi ticket at the bus station counter. **Del Norte** and **Futura** (☎816 5543) go to **Chihuahua** (14hr., 10 per day, 630 pesos). **Estrella Blanca** (☎816 5477) sends buses to: **Aguascalientes** (3hr., 7 per day, 120 pesos); **Ciudad Valles** (4hr., 10 per day, 184 pesos); **Guadalajara** (6hr., 5 per day, 224 pesos); **Monterrey** (7hr., every hr., 308 pesos); **Zacatecas** (3hr., every hr., 105 pesos). **Ómnibus de México** (☎816 8161) runs to: **Mexico City** (6hr., 9 per day, 236 pesos); **Reynosa** (9hr.; 2, 8pm; 377 pesos); **Saltillo** (5hr., 2 per day, 255 pesos); **Tampico** (7hr., 3 per day, 272 pesos). **Transportes Tamaulipas** and **Noreste** (☎816 6964) jointly serve **Matehuala** (2hr., 14 per day, 110 pesos) and **Matamoros** (10 hr., 2 per day, 382 pesos).

ORIENTATION AND PRACTICAL INFORMATION

San Luis Potosí is at the center of a triangle formed by Mexico's three largest cities—Monterrey, Guadalajara, and Mexico City. Five main routes (**Rutas 57, 85, 70, 49,** and **80**) snake their way into the city. Once in the city, the streets have a nasty habit of changing names as they pass through the main plazas, so keep that in mind (and a map in hand).

TOURIST, FINANCIAL, AND LOCAL SERVICES

Tourist Office: Turismo Municipal (☎812 2770) is on the 1st fl. of the Palacio Municipal, at the northeast corner of Plaza de Armas. Friendly, English-speaking staff and excellent information. Open M-F 8am-7pm, Sa-Su 10am-2pm. The **state tourist office,** Obregón 520 (☎812 9939) is a block west of Plaza de los Fundadores. Information on attractions in the rest of the state. Open M-F 8am-9pm, Sa-Su 8am-2pm.

Consulate: US, Mariel 103 (☎812 1528). Take a "Morales" bus. Open M-F 8:30am-1:30pm. In case of an emergency, the police and the tourist office have consulate employees' home numbers.

Currency Exchange: Casas de cambio lie along Morelos, north of Plaza de Armas. Many banks lie near Plaza de Armas and are open M-F 9am-3pm. **Banamex,** at Allende and Obregón, 1 block east of Plaza de Armas, has a 24hr. **ATM** and exchanges traveler's checks with no commission.

Luggage Storage: At the bus station. 5 pesos per hr.

Supermarket: Chalita, on the corner of Bravo and Escobedo, 3 blocks north of Plaza de Armas. Open daily 9am-9pm.

Laundry: Lavandería La Gotita, on 5 de Mayo and Comonfort. 25 pesos for a medium load. Open M-Sa 10am-8pm.

Car Rental: Hertz, Obregón 670 (☎812 9500). 400 pesos per day plus insurance and mileage. 25+. Open M-F 9am-2pm and 4-8pm, Sa 9am-2pm.

EMERGENCY AND COMMUNICATIONS

Emergency: ☎066.

Police: (☎812 5476 or 812 2582) can always be found in the Palacio Municipal. Their special female division, "Minerva." aims to help female tourists.

Red Cross: (☎815 3635 or 820 3902), on Juárez at Díaz Gutiérrez.

Pharmacy: Farmacia Mexicana, Othón 180 (☎812 3880), by the Cathedral. Open 24hr.

Hospital: Hospital Central, Carranza 2395 (☎813 0343 or 817 0164), 20 blocks west of the *centro.* Some English spoken.

Fax: Computel, Carranza 360 (☎812 0189; fax 812 0186), opposite Hotel Panorama. Open M-Sa 7:30am-9pm.

Internet Access: Internet, Escobedo 315, on the Plaza del Carmen. 12 pesos per hr. Open daily 9am-9pm.

Post Office: Morelos 235 (☎812 2740), 1 block east and 3 blocks north of Plaza de Armas. Open M-F 8am-5pm, Sa 9am-2pm. Contains a **Mexpost.** Open M-Sa 9am-2pm. **Postal Code:** 78000.

▛ ACCOMMODATIONS

The cheapest hotels are located near the bus station or at Los Bravos and 20 de Noviembre. If you dislike small, dark rooms, head to the *centro,* where old hotels relive their glory days with large rooms and plaza views.

▨ **Hotel Plaza,** Jardín Hidalgo 22 (☎812 4631), on the south side of Plaza de Armas. The city's first hotel looks right onto the plaza—the location couldn't be better. The clean rooms have old-fashioned charm. Ask for a balcony so you can watch and hear the action all night long. Singles 230 pesos; doubles 250 pesos; triples 280 pesos. ❺

Hotel Principal, Juan Sarabía 145 (☎812 0704), near the Templo del Carmen. Bright green sponge-painted walls light up this hotel. A great deal for the location. All rooms with TV. Singles 150 pesos; doubles 200 pesos; triples 250 pesos. ❸

Hotel Progreso, Aldama 415 (☎812 0366), off Guerrero, near Plaza de San Francisco. Tall dark hallways lead to clean dark rooms. Squint your eyes and you can imagine its former beauty. Fans and hot water in all rooms. Singles 230 pesos; doubles 260 pesos; triples 280 pesos; quads 310 pesos. ❹

Hotel Filher, Universidad 335 (☎812 1562), at the corner of Zaragoza, 3 blocks south of Plaza de Armas. Gorgeous rooms, with bright paintings, beautiful wool bedspreads, and wooden furniture that adorn each room. Amenities include bottled water, TV, phone, and A/C. Singles 380 pesos; doubles 428 pesos. ❺

◨ FOOD

San Luis Potosí boasts some of the best food in northeast Mexico. The mango and cantaloupe sold on the street (with chile and lime) is always fresh and ice-cold. *Gorditas* and *sopas*, sold at ridiculously low prices, are made in front of you. *Enchiladas potosinos*, a regional favorite, are stuffed with cheese and then fried. Cactus is used to make such diverse dishes as *melcocha* (molasses candy) and *nopalitos* (cactus slices cooked in a salty mixture of garlic, onion, and tomato sauce). The sheer number and range of restaurants near the *centro* will satisfy everyone, even vegetarians and those looking for international cuisine.

▨ La Corriente, Carranza 700 (☎812 9304 or 812 1965). The decor is a cross between your grandfather's ranch house and the garden of Eden: red tile floors and stucco walls meet a skylight and hanging vines. The traditional Mexican food manages to surpass the relaxing ambience. Try the divine *enchiladas potosinos* (36 pesos) or a juicy steak with guacamole and black beans (75 pesos). Open daily 8pm-midnight. ❺

Rincón Huasteco, Carranza 447. The name says it: Huasteco specializes in Huastecan bread. Crafts in the dining room. *Comida corrida* 42 pesos. Open daily 8am- 11pm. ❹

Yu Ne Nisa, Arista 360 (☎814 3631). Even carnivores will be delighted with this vegetarian restaurant and health food store. The lime-green countertop and chairs are reminiscent of a 1950s diner. Delicious veggie burgers smothered in guacamole and served with carrot salad 30 pesos. *Comida corrida* 45 pesos. A variety of fruit juices and yogurt concoctions are created behind the counter. Open M-Sa 9:30am-8:30pm. ❸

Gorditas las Mañaneras, on Díaz de León between Madero and Carranza. In this speedy joint, division of labor is the name of the game. While one woman pats tortillas into shape, another minds the griddle and adds cactus, eggs, beans, and cheese to your *gordita* (4 pesos). Open daily 6am-6pm. ❶

La Güera, Tata Nacho 799 (☎811 8728), on the left as you approach the Parque Tangamanga, on the block before the entrance. This traditionally decorated treasure offers breakfast (35 pesos; offered 8:30am-noon) and *comida corrida* (45 pesos; offered 1-6pm). From the pickled *nopalito* garnish to the homemade *mole*, everything here is excellent. Open Tu-Su 8:30am-6pm. ❹

Churrasqueria, La Casa del Bife, Ocampo 135 (☎812 3683), behind Plaza de San Francisco. This Argentinean restaurant is the chic choice of upper-class *potosinos*. Start with cheese or meat *empanadas* (25 pesos) and splurge on the house specialty: beef roasted in front of your eyes, thin cut (100 pesos) or thick cut (140 pesos). Open Su 1-6pm, Tu-Th noon-6pm, F-Sa 1pm-midnight. ❺

◎ SIGHTS

As the former center of the state's booming silver and gold trade, prosperous San Luis Potosí had the money and the stature to build some of the country's finest museums, cathedrals, and plazas. The sheer number of beautiful sights can be almost intimidating; fortunately, the majority have historical markers in English and Spanish and are within easy walking distance of one another.

PLAZA DE ARMAS. Called the "city of plazas," San Luis Potosí has four main town squares. The most central of these is Plaza de Armas, filled with trees and lounging *potosinos*. The Cathedral and Palacio de Gobierno border the plaza. At the start of the 17th century, residents watched bullfights from the balconies of the surrounding buildings. Since 1848, a red sandstone gazebo bearing the names of famous Mexican musicians has graced the plaza, which hosts local bands. Today, loudspeakers hooked up to the gazebo blare popular music, political announcements, and soccer games. *(Concerts Th and Sa evenings.)*

CATEDRAL SANTA IGLESIA. The Cathedral is the city's main landmark, with two bell towers that play different melodies every hour. It began as a simple church completed in 1710, and "upgraded" to a cathedral when San Luis Potosí became a diocese in 1855. Miners donated gold and silver to glorify the interior, and marble statues of the apostles (copies of those at San Juan de Letrán in Rome) stand between the Solomonic columns of the Baroque facade. *(Open daily 8am-7pm.)*

PALACIO DE GOBIERNO. The west side of Plaza de Armas is marked by the Neo-classical facade of the Palacio de Gobierno, constructed in 1798. Briefly serving as Mexico's capital in 1863, the structure was renovated in 1950 and is now San Luis Potosí's administrative center. Displays on the second floor feature murals, statues, and plaques. It was in this building that President Benito Juárez signed former emperor Maximilian's death sentence in 1867. *(Open M-F 9am-2:30pm. Free.)*

PLAZA DEL CARMEN. The bright, lively Plaza del Carmen, two blocks east of Plaza de Armas, hosts Sunday festivals, and during the week street performers, vendors, and a crowd of teenagers and college students mill around at night.

TEMPLO DEL CARMEN. This serene church was constructed from 1749 to 1764 and is regarded by many *potosinos* to be the most beautiful religious building in the city. Worshippers pray here all day. It features hanging chandeliers, golden altars, and a huge mural of the Crucifixion. During the Mexican Revolution, the government used the convent to jail local rebels. Once released, the prisoners went on to lead the revolt of San Luis Potosí. *(In the northeast corner of Plaza del Carmen. Open daily 7am-1:30pm and 4-9pm.)*

TEATRO DE LA PAZ. This theater is one of the four most famous and acoustically well-constructed in Mexico—most performers don't even need microphones. The *salón* holds a collection of modern art, the foyer is filled with sculptures and murals, and the theater hosts everything from international dance festivals to "Sesame Street Live." Prices are relatively cheap. *(Behind Templo del Carmen. ☎ 812 9014. Pick up a schedule at the tourist office or look for posters outside the theater. 50 pesos and up.)*

MUSEO CASA MANUEL JOSÉ OTHÓN. This small museum was once the house of one of Mexico's greatest poets, Manuel José Othón (1858-1906). The museum displays some of his manuscripts and photographs and preserves the house's appearance as it was at Othón's death, making it most interesting as a time capsule. *(Othón 225 between Escobedo and Morelos. ☎ 812 7412. Open Tu-F 10am-2pm and 4-6pm. 2 pesos.)*

JARDÍN DE SAN FRANCISCO. San Luis Potosí has at least one garden for each of its seven districts. This one, on Plaza de San Francisco, is distinguished by its bronze fountain, cobblestone streets, and pink sandstone buildings. Recently, the west side of the garden on Universidad has become a nightlife hotspot. Many bars, cafes, and art sellers crowd the street. It's a perfect spot for an evening stroll.

IGLESIA DE SAN FRANCISCO. Construction began on the Iglesia de San Francisco, on the west side of the garden by the same name, in 1686 and continued on and off until 1760. Don't miss the crystal chandelier in the shape of a conquistador's sailing ship. The orange stucco facade displays a Baroque interior beautifully accentuated by flickering votives. *(Open daily 6:30am-1:30pm and 4:30-9pm.)*

MUSEO REGIONAL POTOSINO. The museum occupies the grounds of the former Franciscan convent at Iglesia de San Francisco. The first floor contains artifacts from all over Mexico, including a collection of Pre-Hispanic Huasteca relics. On the second floor, the marvelous Baroque Capilla a la Virgen de Aranzazu sparkles with gilding and pink paint. According to legend, a local 18th-century shepherd found the altar's wooden image of the Virgin Mary in a prickly thicket. The name *aranzazu* means "from within the thorns." *(On Independencia near the corner of Galeana. ☎814 3572. Open Su 10am-5pm, Tu-Sa 10am-7pm. 27 pesos; Su free.)*

MUSEO DE LAS REVOLUCIONES (MUSEO MARIANO JIMÉNEZ). This museum is the birthplace of the 1910 Revolutionary Mariano Jiménez. Guides will gladly explain the significance of the richly painted murals, and a rotating gallery shows some of the best artwork in San Luis Potosí. *(On 5 de Mayo between Abasolo and Comonfort. ☎814 7393. Open Tu-F 10am-2pm and 5-7pm, Sa-Su 10am-2pm. Free.)*

MUSEO TAURINO. By 1895, San Luis Potosí had an active bullring that housed up to 7500 spectators. Today, the abandoned "Plaza de Toros" contains statues of bull fighters. Across the street, the Museo Taurino shows off an impressive collection of posters and suits of famous bullfighters, paying homage to the romance and the violence of the bullfighting culture. *(On Universidad east of Alameda. Walk up the stairs and over the freeway to get there. Open Tu-Sa noon-2:30pm and 5:30-8pm. Free.)*

PARQUE TANGAMANGA. With lakes for boating and fishing, a baseball field, electric cars, and bike paths, this *parque* is an ideal place to picnic and spend the day. The tree- and lawn-filled park is huge, but you can rent a bike to explore it all. Parque Tangamanga houses the **Museo de las Culturas Populares,** focusing on indigenous crafts with rare photo exhibitions of indigenous communities and ceremonies. *(Catch a Route #10 "Perimetral" bus on Constitución across from the Alameda (20min., 2 pesos). Get off at Monumento a la Revolución, a statue of soldiers firing rifles, in the middle of a rotary. Facing the soldiers' backs, take a left and go 3 blocks. Park open Tu-Su 9am-6pm. Bike rental 20 pesos per hr. Museum ☎817 2976. Open Tu-Su 9am-4pm. 2 pesos.)*

◪ NIGHTLIFE

Much of San Luis Potosí's nightlife revolves around upscale bars and live music. The area around Plaza de San Francisco has become very popular with the large student population. Mural portraits of Revolutionaries cover the walls of the patio at **Zapata, Villa, & Cia,** on Iturbide between Aldama and 5 de Mayo. A live band plays for enthusiastic dancers Th-Sa. (Th-Sa cover 50 pesos.) Some restaurants turn into bars at night, like the upstairs of **El Bocolito,** a restaurant on Guerrero in the north corner of the plaza. A rowdy crowd of all ages congregates here for music and food. (☎812 7694. Live music W-Sa 9pm-2am.) You are sure to find students from the university mingling upstairs at **Cafe los Frailes,** Universidad 165. (☎812 5826. Live music F-Sa 9pm-midnight.) For serious dancing, head to Independencia and Ocampo, where patrons of **Delirio Azul** shake their hips (among other things) to the rhythms of *salsa*. (Open Th-Sa.) Closer to *el centro*, **El Mito**, on Plaza de Armas, is *the* place to be on a weekend night. A young crowd packs the dance floor and adjoining balcony as DJs spin the latest Latin dance and pop. (☎814 4157. F-Sa cover 50 pesos. Open W-Sa 9pm-2:30am.) **La María**, at the corner of Escobedo and Guerrero, pumps electronica in a small former home near Plaza del Carmen. Check out the 5m deep well in the middle of the dance floor, a vestige of the city's past. (☎812 3644. F-Sa cover men 25 pesos, women 15 pesos. Open Th-Sa 9pm-2am.) Also close to the *centro* is **Staff**, Carranza 423, where a young, gay-friendly crowd grooves to Latin dance music. (☎814 3074. Cover 25 pesos. Open F-Su.)

▐▀▌ SHOPPING

Shops line Morelos north of Plaza de Armas, and vendors sell silver and crafts on Universidad, east of Plaza de San Francisco. The best shopping is along Hidalgo, called Zaragoza south of the plaza. This street has blocks of small stores, coffee shops, and *heladerías*. **Puros**, Carranza 325, is a gorgeous shop that sells Mexican, Cuban, Jamaican, and Dominican cigars. (☎810 4300. Open daily 10am-9pm.)

▐ FESTIVALS

The last two weeks of August mark the **Fiesta Nacional Potosina**, often called FaNaPo. The fairgrounds are at the southeast edge of town. During FaNaPo, *peseras* come from all over town to see concerts, bullfights, fireworks, and a parade. However, the festival pales in comparison with the city's celebration of *Semana Santa*. The culmination of this festival is the **Procesión del Silencio**. This silent procession involves 25 *cofradías* (local groups), who bear lifelike statues portraying the events leading to Christ's death. The **Festival Internacional de Danza Contemporaneo** invades San Luis Potosí in late July and early August, as dance groups from around the world come to participate in Mexico's most important dance festival. Check the **Teatro de la Paz** for flyers.

MATEHUALA   ☎488

Although Matehuala (pop. 100,000) derives its name from a Náhuatl phrase meaning "don't come," this former mining town is actually quite friendly. The few tourists who do trickle in are mostly adventure-seeking backpackers en route to Real de Catorce, and who are often surprised to find a town so relaxing and pleasant.

▐▀ TRANSPORTATION

Matehuala has two bus stations. The large **Central de Autobuses** is on 5 de Mayo, just south of the city and near the large, red Arco de Bienvenido. The Central sends buses to more destinations than the **small station** in town but is more of a hike. To get downtown from the Central, take a *pesera* labeled "Centro" (10 min., 6:30am-10pm, 3.2 pesos)—ask the driver to let you off near the cathedral, or get off at Hidalgo, next to the Chalita market. **Taxis** charge 25 pesos for the trip.

The Central de Autobuses provides the services of **Transportes del Norte, Frontera, Estrella Blanca**, and **El Águila** to: **Mexico City** (7hr., 9 per day, 380 pesos); **Monterrey** (4hr., every hr., 195 pesos); **Nuevo Laredo** (7hr., 10 per day, 362 pesos); **Querétaro** (6hr., 3 per day, 234 pesos); **Saltillo** (3hr., every hr., 163 pesos); **San Luis Potosí** (2hr., every hr., 110 pesos). **Noreste** (☎882 0997) serves **Monterrey** (4hr., every hr., 195 pesos) and **Reynosa** (7hr., 8 per day, 302 pesos). **Tamaulipas** (☎882 2777) goes to **Real de Catorce** (1½ hr.; 7:45, 9:45, 11:45am, 1:45, 5:40pm; 39 pesos) and **San Luis**

Potosí (2 hr., 18 per day, 110 pesos). Buses to Real de Catorce also stop at the smaller town bus station (☎822 0840), at Guerrero and Mendez. Most buses that stop here continue on to the Central de Autobuses to reach all other destinations.

■ ☆ ☎ ORIENTATION AND PRACTICAL INFORMATION

Matehuala is 261km from Saltillo and 191km from San Luis Potosí. Constantly forking or changing names, the streets of Matehuala are confusing, but so short and close together that you'll never be lost for long. Just look skyward—the cathedral dome will guide you back to the main plaza. **Hidalgo** runs north-south through most of the city; **Juárez** runs parallel to the west. Most points of interest lie somewhere on or not far from the intersection of **Hidalgo** and **Morelos.**

Tourist Information: Cámara de Comercio Morelos 427 (☎882 0110), 1 block east of Hidalgo. **Internet access** (15 pesos per hr.). Open M-F 9am-1:30pm and 4-7:30pm. **Maps** are for sale (10 pesos) at the many pharmacies and *papelerías* around the *centro.* (Tourist help line ☎882 5005).

Currency Exchange: Casas de cambio dot the *centro,* all offering good rates. **Bital,** 111 Reyes (☎882 4818), exchanges cash and traveler's checks and has a 24hr. **ATM.** Open M-Sa 8am-7pm. Many other 24hr. ATMs fill the *centro.*

Markets: Chalita, on Hidalgo 2 blocks from the cathedral, sells groceries and clothing. Open daily 8am-8pm. The **indoor market** next to the Catedral de la Inmaculada Concepción sells crafts and produce. Open daily 9am-6pm.

Laundry: Lavandería Acuario (☎882 7088), Betancourt and Madero, offers self-service wash and dry for 40 pesos per 5kg. Open M-Sa 8:30am-2pm and 4-8pm.

Emergency: ☎060 or 066.

Police: (☎882 0647), next to the bus station.

Pharmacy: Farmacia del Centro, Morelos 623 (☎882 0592). Open daily 9am-midnight. Also, **Farmacia Vida** in the Central de Autobuses. Open daily 7am-11pm.

Hospital: Hospital General (☎882 0445), on Hidalgo a few blocks north of the *centro.* Little English spoken.

Fax: Telecomm, 5 de Febrero at Juárez (☎882 0008), a few blocks east of the *centro.* Also houses a **Western Union** office. Open M-F 9am-7pm.

Post Office: (☎882 0071), at Valle and Negrete. Walk up Constitución, turn right on Independencia 1 block before Iglesia Santo Niño, turn right again on Negrete, and it's on your left at the corner. Open M-F 8am-3pm, Sa 9am-1pm. **Postal Code:** 78700.

☎ ACCOMMODATIONS

Budget accommodations populate the *centro.* Starting at around 80 pesos, the *casas de huéspedes* on Bocanegra are the cheapest options, but spending slightly more will get you considerably nicer rooms.

▧ **Hotel Blanca Estela,** Morelos 406 (☎882 2300). Beautiful wooden furnishings give a classy feel to this narrow hotel. Fans cool small, clean, colorful rooms. All rooms have cable TV and gushing hot showers. Check in early; this may well be the most crowded place in town. Singles 170 pesos; doubles 200 pesos; triples 230 pesos. ❸

Hotel Casino Del Valle, Morelos 621 (☎882 3770), right off Plaza de Armas. The very walls sparkle at this glamorous hotel with reasonable prices. Balconies on each floor, ceiling fans, *agua purificada,* TV, and an attached dance hall. Singles 225 pesos; each additional person 50 pesos. ❹

Hotel Matehuala, Bustamante 134 (☎882 0680), just north of Plaza de Armas. Walkways ring a huge, tiled courtyard in this peaceful colonial-style hotel. Though the rooms are as dark as confessional booths, the soaring ceilings with wooden rafters, white walls, and rust-colored bureaus are decidedly appealing. Ask for a room with a balcony and windows to the outside. Singles 220 pesos; each additional person 40 pesos. ❹

▐ FOOD

The few restaurants in Matehuala are family-owned cafeterias, clustered around Plaza de Armas, with good food at low prices. By 8pm, Matehuala has mostly shut down for the night. For an after-hours meal, visit **Las Tortonas** ❷, next to the Pemex sign on Hidalgo, south of the cathedral. *Tortas* cost a mere 18 pesos, with vegeterian options like egg, cheese, and avocado. (Open daily 8am-10pm.) **Gorditas Panchita** ❶, on Morelos between Cuauhtémoc and Julián de los Reyes and a block from the Catedral, is a local favorite for breakfast and lunch. A circle of laughing women continually pats out fresh *gorditas*, which their male coworker stuffs with *nopal, frijoles, rajas con queso,* and various meats. (*Gorditas* 4 pesos each. Open daily 9am-6pm.) If you're looking for a more formal night out, try **Restaurant Fontella** ❸, Morelos 618, between hotels Casino and Matehuala. Charcoal-roasted specialties, mostly meat, 30-40 pesos. (☎882 0293. Open daily 7:30am-10pm.)

◉ SIGHTS

Matehuala was founded in 1550, but the city's buildings are mostly modern and its main attractions are its placid parks and 20th-century cathedral. Standing solemnly at the center of Matehuala between Juárez and Hidalgo is the recently completed **Catedral de la Inmaculada Concepción,** a copy of Saint Joseph's Cathedral in Lyon, France. Construction began in 1905, but lack of funding slowed progress. In front of the main cathedral is **Plaza Juárez,** now permanently occupied by vendor stalls and makeshift cafes. Sprawling onto adjoining streets, the bazaar is collectively known as **Mercado Arista,** selling leather and ceramic goods and a slew of cheap plastic trinkets. Trees shade the pleasant **Plaza de Armas,** a few blocks north of the Catedral on Hidalgo, and neighboring the stuccoed walls of the **Templo San Salvador.** Relax amidst the limited greenery and street vendors that define **Parque Vicente Guerrero.** For a larger expanse of grass and a pick-up game of basketball, head to **Parque Álvaro Obregón,** just south of Insurgentes.

During the first week of September, Matehuala celebrates the **Festival del Desierto** (Festival of the Desert) with food, music, and art.

REAL DE CATORCE   ☎488

Once a thriving mining town with 30,000 inhabitants, Real de Catorce (pop. 1500) now looms mysteriously on the side of a mountain, a virtual ghost town. At one time one of the largest silver producers in the country, Real de Catorce crumbled as its mines ran dry. The 20th century brought on flooding, destruction, and desertion, leaving behind the empty mine shafts and carts that give Real de Catorce its eerie feel. Today, backpackers and travelers trek to see this town's *burro*-trodden paths and brick ruins and to pay respect to the town's patron saint, St. Francis. With nearby deserts and mountain hikes, Real de Catorce lures adventure lovers from all over Mexico and the world. Huichol Indians make springtime pilgrimages to Real de Catorce to gather peyote, which they consider sacred.

TRANSPORTATION

To get to Real de Catorce, you must go through Matehuala. From Matehuala's cathedral, walk one block up Hidalgo, take a left on Guerrero, and walk down two blocks to Mendez. **Buses** leave from the station at the corner of Guerrero and Mendez. The bus also stops at the Matehuala Central de Autobuses. **Autobuses Tamaulipas** (☎882 0840) will bring you to Real de Catorce (1½hr.; daily 8, 10am, noon, 2, 5pm; 39 pesos). Confirm schedules with the bus driver and arrive early.

The ride to "Real de 14" is guaranteed to whiten the knuckles of the timid traveler; the bus rambles along a winding path chiseled into the mountain. Riders change to a smaller bus for a 2.5km ride through a mountain near path's end. Buses drop off and pick up at the tunnel on the Real de Catorce side.

ORIENTATION AND PRACTICAL INFORMATION

The town's main road is **Lanzagorta,** which runs from the bus stop past the famed cathedral and a few hotels and restaurants. Constitución is uphill from Lanzagorta and parallel to it. Both streets run through **Plaza Principal.**

There are no financial services in Real de Catorce, and hotels do not accept credit cards. Tourist brochures and helpful information can be found at the sporadically-open **tourist office** in the Presidencia Municipal, right on the Plaza Principal. A **town map** is posted outside the office; all the hotels have free maps, too. Services include: **police,** at the **Presidencia Municipal,** next to Plaza Principal (☎888 8751); **LADATEL phone** at the Presidencia Municipal and around town (note that mobile phones have no service in Real de Catorce); **Internet** at El Sótano del Real, Constitución 6A (20 pesos per hr. Open daily noon-midnight.); and the **post office,** on Constitución to the right of the Presidencia Municipal as you are facing it, on the right side of the street. (Open M-F 9am-1pm and 3-6pm.) **Postal Code:** 78550.

ACCOMMODATIONS AND FOOD

Real de Catorce caters to its backpacker crowd with a number of good budget accommodations. Hotel prices vary drastically according to season and day of the week (weekends and festivals are the most expensive). Those traveling to Real de Catorce during *Semana Santa*, December, or in July and August should book in advance and be prepared for steeper prices. The *casas de huéspedes*, on the streets off of Lanzagorta, offer the cheapest lodging. Most hotels are beautiful and richly decorated. For lower prices without lower quality, try **Hotel San Francisco ❶**, on Terán right off Constitución. The family-run hotel has only a few rooms, but it is clean and comfortable. Its upstairs balcony looks out over the whole town and the mountains. (Singles 70-90 pesos, with bathroom 100-120 pesos.) **Hospedaje Familiar ❷**, Constitución 21 just past the Plaza Principal, provides inexpensive and homey lodging within its bright walls. (☎887 5009. Singles 120 pesos; doubles 150 pesos.) Real de Catorce also has some fantastic splurges. **El Mesón de la Abundancia ❺**, Langazorta 11, lies in the former town treasury. It's the oldest building in town, with rooms adorned with private terraces and sitting rooms. The adjoining restaurant/bar serves Mexican and Italian entrees. (50 pesos. ☎887 5044. Singles 550 pesos; matrimonials 650 pesos; triples and quads 750 pesos.) At **Hotel El Real ❺**, the antique furniture, tiled bathrooms, and personal balconies will make you feel like you're on a honeymoon. The hotel's **Restaurant El Real ❺**, with its dim lights and intimate atmosphere, proves that Mexico really can do Italian. (☎887 5058. Singles 300-350 pesos; each additional person 100 pesos; add 50 pesos in high season. Restaurant pizzas and pasta dishes 50-90 pesos.)

Mysteriously, most of Real de Catorce's restaurants serve Italian food. For less expensive Mexican food, try the **taquerías ❶** that line Lanzagorta toward the bus stop. Most of these close by 6pm. At the corner of Zaragoza and Iturbide lies **El Ángel y El Corazon ❹**, a vegetarian restaurant and holistic center. (Changing menu of Mexican, Middle Eastern, and Italian vegetarian specials 50 pesos.)

👁 SIGHTS

Real de Catorce is home to the most beautiful church in northeast Mexico: the **Parroquia de la Purísima Concepción,** in the Plaza Principal. The altar retains its original stucco and painting of the Virgin of Guadalupe and houses a life-size statue of St. Francis, whose miracles have created a devoted following. The squares of wooden flooring are actually doors to subterranean tombs. Side rooms are filled with painted tin sheets testifying to St. Francis's miraculous cures and visa waivers. Across from the cathedral, the **Casa de Moneda,** formerly a mint, houses a small photography exhibit of the town. (Open daily noon-2pm. Free.) At the corner of Morelos and Constitución is **Cine Club.** From Hitchcock to Disney cartoons to recent box office hits, this independent movie house is a gold mine. (Shows F 9pm, Su 11am. Adults 5 pesos, children 2 pesos.)

Norteño and *mariachi* bands occasionally play at the gazebo at **Jardín Hidalgo,** beyond the cathedral between Lanzagorta and Constitución. On Xicotencatl off Zaragoza, the terraced steps of the **Palenque de Gallos** (cock-fight ring) replicate the layout of a classic Athenian theater. At the top of Zaragoza stands the white **Capilla de Guadalupe** (also called the **Panteón**). At the high end of Constitución lies **El Mirador,** an area full of ruined miners' homes that grants a vista of the city. The surrounding cliff, known as **El Voladero,** grants breathtaking views of mountains and valleys, dry riverbeds, and herds of cows on distant hilltops.

For a **horseback tour** of the region, walk from the bus stop down Lanzagorta until you reach Plaza Hidalgo. To the left across Lanzagorta is a stable that rents horses (40 pesos per hr.). Try a 2hr. trip to **Ciudad de las Fantasmas** (Ghost City), an abandoned mining town nearby, or a descent into desert valley. If you're feeling really adventurous, make a two-day trip to a nearby ranch. The guides expect a tip of 50 to 70 pesos; try to arrange a fixed price before the trip. You can also **hike** out to Ciudad de las Fantasmas—just follow the track from the end of Constitución (near the bus stop) uphill and toward the ruins. The hike is about 6km roundtrip.

🎉 FESTIVALS

Semana Santa is the most celebrated festival in Real de Catorce. Nightly parades and glittering candles light up the usually peaceful mountain evenings. October 4 is the feast day of St. Francis of Assisi, Real de Catorce's beloved patron saint. From the end of September through October, the normally quiet town explodes with activity as visitors come from all over Mexico to pray at the cathedral. This **Feria de San Francisco** packs the streets with daily and nightly *fiestas* outside of the cathedral. Local hotels double their rates.

CIUDAD VALLES ☎ 481

Ciudad Valles (pop. 350,000), or Valles, is a crossroads between northeast and central Mexico. It provides easiest access to the Huastecan region, including Xilitla.

The **Central de Autobuses** lies on the outskirts, on Luis Venegas. To get to the municipal bus station in town, take a "Mercado" bus (4 pesos). You can buy tickets for **taxis** from the **ServiBus** stand inside of the station (18 pesos to the *centro*).

From the station, **Oriente** (☎382 3902) serves: **Ciudad Victoria** (4hr., 20 per day, 127 pesos); **Guadalajara** (10hr., 5 per day, 366 pesos); **Matamoros** (8hr., 8 per day, 399 pesos); **Monterrey** (7½hr., 10 per day, 322 pesos). **Vencedor** (☎382 3281) goes to: **San Luis Potosí** (5hr., every hr., 184 pesos); **Tampico** (2½hr., 4 per day 8am-5pm, 91 pesos); **Xilitla** (2hr., every hr. 5am-7pm, 41 pesos).

Banorte, on the corner of Hidalgo and Carranza, has a 24hr. **ATM.** Other services include: **Red Cross** (☎382 0056); **police** (☎382 2185 or 382 2738); **Internet** in the Central at **@Bus** (10 pesos per hr.; open daily 9am-9pm); the **post office,** Juárez 520. (☎382 0104. Open M-F 8am-3pm, Sa 9am-1pm.) **Postal code:** 79000.

If you're stuck in Valles for a night, recently built, inexpensive hotels are around the station. **Hotel San Carlos ❸**, Venegas 140, across from the station, has bright, clean rooms with TV and welcome A/C. (Singles 150 pesos, doubles 200 pesos.) For an easy meal, **Restaurant Don Felix ❷**, also across from the station, serves *comida corrida* for 25 pesos and cheap *antojitos*. (Open daily 7:30am-11:30pm.)

XILITLA   ☎489

Xilitla (he-LEET-la, pop. 10,000) lies at the end of a long, convoluted road like a magnificent reward. The town itself welcomes visitors with friendly locals, fruit fresh from the tree, and low prices. But its true allure is the wilds around it. Coffee plantations intersperse with over 150 caves (including the 450m deep, 6-acre **El Sótano de las Golondrinas**), dozens of waterfalls, wild orchid sanctuaries, rare animals, horseback trails, and rivers ripe for rafting. The most notable attraction, however, is the beautiful and bizarre architectural feat of **Las Pozas** (The Pools). Built by English millionaire Edward James, this tribute to surrealism channels three waterfalls into a fantasy landscape of multicolor concrete and live flowers. Be warned: mist and brief rains roll in frequently.

■ ORIENTATION. Xilitla is a small town with only a few streets, but they're rarely labeled. **Zoragoza,** runs east from just above the bus station and borders the southern edge of **Jardín Hidalgo,** the main square. **Hidalgo** is the Jardín's northern border, **Ocampo** is its western border, and **Bravo** is its eastern border. Two blocks north of the Jardín, **Morelos** runs west to **Las Pozas** 4km away.

■ TRANSPORTATION AND PRACTICAL INFORMATION. The bus station sits on the hillside at the lower edge of town. All buses to Xilitla pass through **Ciudad Valles,** 2hr. to the north. From Valles, frequent buses head to Xilitla. **Vencedor** runs to: **Ciudad Valles** (12hr., 15 per day 5am-7pm, 41 pesos); **San Luis Potosí** (6½hr.; 5am, 12:30, 1:30pm; 190 pesos); **Tampico** (4½hr., 4 per day, 131 pesos). To get to **Plaza Central,** officially **Jardín Hidalgo,** on foot, go up the stairs to the right of the bus station and turn right on Zaragoza. The plaza is a 5min. uphill walk away. **Taxis** to Las Pozas wait up the stairs to the left of the station (60 pesos).

Tourist information about Xilitla can be found at the website of **El Castillo** (www.junglegossip.com), a lovely guest house down the hill from Xilitla's main plaza. Exchange currency or traveler's checks at **Centro de Cambio,** on the right-hand side of Zaragoza as you walk toward the plaza. (☎365 0281. Open daily 8am-8pm.) **Banorte**, on the Zaragoza side of the plaza, also **exchanges currency** and checks and has a 24hr. **ATM.** (☎365 0029. Open M-F 9am-2:30pm.) Other services include: **police,** in the Palacio Municipal (☎365 0085; no English spoken); **Farmacia San Agustín,** on Hidalgo, at the northwest corner of Plaza Principal (☎365 0125; open daily 8:30am-9pm); **LADATEL** phones on Hidalgo, at the north edge of Jardín Hidalgo; the **post office,** in the back of the Palacio on Zaragoza, 2nd fl. (open M-F 9am-3pm). **There is no hospital or Red Cross in Xilitla. Call the police in case of an emergency. Postal code:** 79902.

⚡🏠 ACCOMMODATIONS AND FOOD. In mid-summer and during *Semana Santa*, Xilitla's star hotels—El Castillo and the cabins at Las Pozas—fill up fast and require reservations. The cheapest rooms in town are at little family **hotels ❷** in the market area just east of Jardín Hidalgo. They're basic, similar, and in a bit of a deserted area at night. (Rooms 100-150 pesos.) Down the hill from Jardín Hidalgo is gorgeous ☒**Posada el Castillo ❺**, Ocampo 105. El Castillo was the former home of Plutarco Gastelum, close friend of Edward James and foreman of the Las Pozas project. James himself used to stay here when in Xilitla. Each of the nine rooms has huge windows, and a balcony or verandaOrganic meals available upon request. (☎365 0038; www.junglegossip.com. Rooms 400-950 pesos.) Solitude-seekers can stay in one of the six cabins at **Las Pozas ❺**. The bare rooms come with hot water and sturdy wooden beds. The experience of sleeping surrounded by sur-real sculpture and rushing waterfalls is unforgettable. (☎365 0203. Reception 9am-8pm at the entrance of Las Pozas. Rooms 280 pesos.) For an affordable, clean, and friendly hotel, try **Hotel Ziyaquetzas ❸**, Zaragoza 110, opposite Jardín Hidalgo. The well-lit rooms have cable TV, phone, and bath, and look out over the glorious mountain landscape. (☎365 0081. Singles 180 pesos; doubles 220 pesos.)

Xilitla's streetside vendors sell some of the freshest **fruit** you may ever eat—don't miss the mangos and oranges. Locally grown **coffee**, sold in bulk or brewed, is flavorful and fierce. Little lunchtime **comedores ❷** line the market area just east of Jardín Hidalgo and the church. ☒**La Flor de Cafe ❶**, Hidalgo 215, along-side the church, fills locals with *mole poblano* (10 pesos), fresh *aguas de frutas* (4 pesos), and marvelous *café con leche* (4 pesos). A group of women from sur-rounding communities rotates chef duties. (*Tamales* 2 pesos, enchiladas 3 pesos, chicken with rice and beans 16 pesos. Open daily 9am-9pm.) The open-air **restaurant at Las Pozas ❷** draws tourists from the world over to devour tradi-tional cuisine. The thick corn tortillas and *huevos a la mexicana* (25 pesos) are superb. (*Comida del día* 45 pesos. Open daily 9am-6pm.)

◙ SIGHTS. ☒**Las Pozas** (The Pools), formally called the **Enchanted Garden of Edward James,** are Xilitla's main attraction. The swimmable pools and overgrown greenery do indeed have an enchanted aura, enhanced by the experimental con-crete sculpture growing from the landscape. Edward James himself was an old-fashioned English eccentric. An aspiring artist and friend of Salvador Dalí, James dabbled in poetry and being rich. In the early 1950s, James visited Xilitla and, caught up in its natural beauty, decided to build his home as a living surrealist monument. The result is a universe of concrete, steel, and stone, in wild colors and shapes. Doors open into nothing, winding staircases lead nowhere, the library has no books. To walk to Las Pozas, head downhill on Ocampo, the street parallel to and farthest from the church at Jardín Hidalgo, for two blocks. Make a left onto Morelos. Keep left at the fork and follow the road as it turns into a gravel path. Las Pozas will be on your left. (4km, 40min.) From the top of the stairs near the bus station, a taxi can take you right to the gate for 60 pesos. (Open daily 9am-8pm. 20 pesos.)

Xilitla is famous among **spelunkers** for its varied and deep caves. Many tour guides lead informal explorations: ask at the Las Pozas ticket office about 3hr. tours. (English spoken. 200 pesos per hr.) For a tour with more equipment and caving experience, contact Benito Guzmán Ibargüen at **SierrAventura** a week in advance. He offers guided tours with all equipment provided. (sierraventura@hot-mail.com. Prices vary.) **Mountain biking** and **hiking** tours are available from Felipe Vigiaro, a local who can provide rental bikes. (☎365 0075. Prices vary.)

The **Cueva del Salitre** (Parrot Cave) makes a good early-evening excursion. To reach the cave, head down Ocampo, take a left at Morelos, and follow the road to its end. There, take a left and walk past the PEMEX station. A few hundred meters later, you will come to a mechanic's shop. The cave is a 5min. walk down the hill

behind the shop; you may want to ask the mechanics to help find you a guide (a 10-peso tip is appreciated). Each night at dusk, over 200 green-and-yellow parakeets gather outside the cave, creating an impressive spectacle.

In town, Xilitla's historical draw is the quietly greying **Templo de San Agustín,** on the east side of the plaza. Built between 1550 and 1557, the ex-convent is the oldest colonial building in the state. The stucco exterior has crumbled away, exposing the stone walls beneath, but the interior is beautifully preserved.

Every August 28, the plaza comes alive with fireworks and regional dances for the **Feria de San Agustín.**

CENTRAL MEXICO

The states of **Guanajuato** and **Querétaro** form a vast, bowl-shaped plateau of fertile soil, rolling farms, and verdant hillsides, that shelters some of Mexico's most alluring colonial cities. For more than 500 years, their silver-rich land has brought the region prosperity and shaped its history. In the 18th century, the city of Guanajuato supplied most of Mexico's minting silver, later becoming the commercial and banking center of this thriving region. Today, the area is home to a growing expatriate population in and around San Miguel de Allende, one of the most lively and culturally charged cities in the republic. Nearby, relatively untouristed and mountainous **Hidalgo** attracts tourists to the stunning archaeological site of Tula and numerous hiking opportunities in the Sierra Madre Oriental.

After docking in Veracruz in 1919, Cortés worked his way inland, making his mark on **Puebla** and **Tlaxcala**, where many local tribes joined his entourage. A glimpse into one of the region's 16th-century temples, where images from *indigena* mythology mingle with Catholic icons, illustrates the pervasive strength of these indigenous cultures in the face of attempts at their destruction.

Contrary to popular belief, the **Estado de México** has more to offer than chaotically overpopulated Mexico City. Outside of the giant smog cloud that contains the *Distrito Federal*, wide green plains creep up snowy volcanoes and bustling towns expand against their natural barriers. The state is speckled with impressive archaeological sites, solemn convents, and vestiges of the colonial era.

After Emperor Maximilian built his summer home in Cuernavaca, thousands of Mexicans eagerly followed him and made the state of **Morelos** a prime vacation destination. Mexicans and foreigners alike come to take advantage of Cuernavaca's "eternal spring," Xochicalco's beautifully desolate ruins, and Tepoztlán's striking landscape. Unlike the frenetic capital, parts of surrounding Morelos remain undeveloped, with plentiful tree-covered vistas and unspoiled streams.

HIGHLIGHTS OF CENTRAL MEXICO

DAYDREAM the day away in the perfect colonial town of **Valle de Bravo** (see p. 362).

BURROW underground and wander through the narrow and dimly lit tunnels of the **great pyramid of Cholula** (see p. 395), one of the largest in the world.

DRINK a round or two with your new language-school friends in artsy and intelligent **San Miguel de Allende** (see p. 344).

SHOW OFF your historical knowledge by reciting the *Grito de Dolores*, in little **Dolores Hidalgo** (see p. 350), where Miguel Hidalgo first proclaimed Mexican independence.

FLIRT shamelessly with the brawny and massive statues of warriors at the archaeological site of **Tula** (see p. 360), once the capital of the Toltec Empire.

SALSA through the array of posh nightclubs in sophisticated **Cuernavaca** (see p. 368).

STARE into the wizened, dried-out eye sockets of naturally mummified bodies at **Guanajuato**'s creepy **Museo de las Momias** (see p. 342).

FATTEN UP on the delicious mole dishes and the million and one types of sweets created by centuries of cloistered **Puebla** cooks (see p. 385).

Central Mexico

GUANAJUATO

CENTRAL MEXICO

GUANAJUATO ☎473

The contours of Guanajuato's (pop. 110,000) future—the peaks of economic realization and the pits of repression—were mapped out all the way back in 1558, when massive veins of silver were discovered in the area. Over the next 200 years, the city became one of the wealthiest in all of Mexico, supplying much of the world's silver. Wealth without liberty, however, did not satisfy the *guanajuatenses;* after getting fat under Spanish rule, Guanajuato bit the hand that had fed it. It was during Hidago's stop here in 1810 that the wealthy and poor united, helping to defeat the Spanish at Alhóndiga de Granaditas.

Guanajuato today is livelier than ever, and has effectively reversed its recent reputation as a dirty city. The city's tangle of serpentine streets overflow with monuments to silver barons and Revolutionary luminaries, while its colonial charm is in full effect in the many *callejones* that sneak through Spanish archways and courtyards, leading to myriad museums, cathedrals, and countless other cultural attractions.

▐ TRANSPORTATION

Guanajuato's **bus station** is located about 3km west of town. A local "El Centro" bus from the station will take you to the heart of the city, while "Mercado" buses go to the market. Local buses criss-cross the entire city, running westward above ground and eastward underground (every 5min. 6am-10:30pm, 2.5 pesos). Taxis cost about 15 pesos in town.

Buses: A "Central de Autobuses" bus from Plaza de la Paz will return you to the station. A taxi will do the job for 30 pesos. **Primera Plus/Flecha Amarilla** (☎733 1333) offers 1st-class service to: **Celaya** (2hr., 2:45pm, 72 pesos); **Guadalajara** (4hr., 8 per day 9am-11pm, 214 pesos); **León** (50min., 7 per day 9am-11:30pm, 34 pesos); **Mexico City** (4½hr., 10 per day 5:30am-midnight, 250 pesos); **Salamanca** (1hr.; 5:30, 8am, 12:30, 3:30pm; 45 pesos); **San Miguel de Allende** (1½hr.; 3, 5:15, 7:15pm; 72 pesos). 2nd-class service only reaches **Dolores Hidalgo** (1½hr., every 20min. 5:20am-10:20pm, 37 pesos); **San Luis Potosí** (5hr.; 7:20am, 1, 4:40, 7:40pm; 126 pesos). **Ómnibus de México** (☎733 2607) offers similar service, while **Futura/Estrella Blanca** (☎733 1344) travels to more distant locations.

✳ ▐ ORIENTATION AND PRACTICAL INFORMATION

Guanajuato lies 380km northwest of Mexico City. The city's tangled maze of streets and *callejones* can leave even the best navigator dizzy. **Plaza de la Paz,** the **Basílica,** and **Jardín Unión** mark the center of town. **Juárez** climbs eastward past the *mercado* and Plaza de la Paz, becoming **Obregón** just past the Basílica, then **Sopeña** after Teatro Juárez.

Tourist Office: Coordinadora de Turismo, Plaza de la Paz 14 (☎732 1574), on your right on Juárez. Good, free maps and expensive historical pamphlets. English spoken. Open Su 10am-2pm, M-F 10am-7pm, Sa 10am-3pm.

Currency Exchange: Banks line Juárez and Plaza de la Paz. **BITAL,** Plaza de la Paz 59 (☎732 0018). Open for exchange M-Sa 8am-7pm.

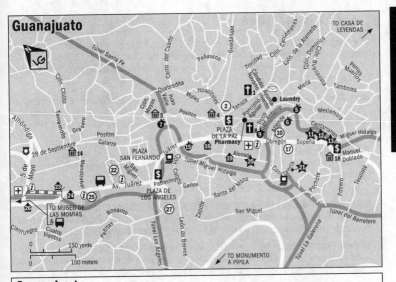

Guanajuato

🏠 ACCOMMODATIONS
Casa Kloster, 19
Hotel la Condesa, 16
Hotel Posada del Carmen, 23
Hotel Posada San Francisco, 24
Posada Hidalgo, 26

🍎 FOOD
Carnitas Sam, 15
La Loca Rana, 7

Pericos Negros, 5
Restaurant Pingüis, 6
Truco No. 7, 9

🚩🏛○ SIGHTS
Basílica de Nuestra Señora
  de Guanajuato, 8
Callejón del Beso, 27
Jardín de la Reforma, 22
Jardín Unión, 10

Mercado Hidalgo, 25
Museo de la Alhóndiga
  de Granaditas, 14
Museo del Pueblo de
  Guanajuato, 4
Museo Iconográfico
  del Quijote, 18
Museo y Casa de
  Diego Rivera, 3
Teatro Juárez, 17

Templo de la Compañía, 1
Universidad de Guanajuato, 2

⭐ NIGHTLIFE
Bar 8, 21
Damas de las Camelias
  es Él, 13
Guanajuato Grill, 20
Puerta del Sol, 12
The Bar, 11

Laundry: Lavandería los Picachos, Ayuntamiento 1. 5kg wash and dry 38 pesos, 10 pesos per additional kg. Open M-F 9:30am-7:30pm, Sa 10am-7pm.

Emergency: ☎060.

Police: Alhóndiga 10 (☎732 0266 or 732 2717). Some English spoken.

Red Cross: Juárez 131 (☎732 0487), 2 blocks from the *mercado.* No English spoken.

Pharmacy: San Francisco de Asís, Aguilar 15 (☎732 8916), just off Plaza de la Paz. Open daily 7am-10:30pm.

Hospital: Clínica Hospital de Especialidades (☎732 2305 or 732 1338), in Plaza de la Paz. No English spoken.

Supermarket: Comercial Mexicana (☎732 9628), 2 blocks from the market on Juárez. Open Su 8am-9pm, M-Sa 8am-10pm.

Fax: Telecomm, Sopeña 1 (☎732 2747), to your left facing Teatro Juárez. Open M-F 8am-7pm, Sa-Su 9am-2pm.

Internet Access: Internet access abounds in the *centro.* **Redes Internet Guanajuato,** Alonso 70 (☎732 0611; root@redes.int.com.mx). Fast connections 10 pesos per hr. Open M-F 9am-8pm, Sa-Su 10am-3pm.

Post Office: Ayuntamiento 25 (☎732 0385), across from the Templo de la Compañía. Open M-F 9am-5pm, Sa 9am-1pm. **Postal Code:** 36000.

CENTRAL MEXICO

▲ ACCOMMODATIONS

A few inexpensive hotels populate the area around the Basílica. More economic lodgings surround the *mercado*. On weekends or during *Festival Cervantino* in October, make reservations well in advance and expect higher prices. The tourist office has a list of families who rent rooms during the festival.

▨ **Casa Kloster,** Alonso 32 (☎ 732 0088). Clean, airy dorms overlook an open courtyard filled with flowers and birds. Sparkling communal bathrooms. Friendly international students swap stories in the upstairs sitting room. Extremely helpful management. Reservations recommended. Dorms 100 pesos. ❷

Hotel la Condesa, Plaza de la Paz 60 (☎ 732 1462). Neon signs and suits of armor enliven the spooky lobby. Rooms with small baths are old but clean; two triples have balconies. Noise from the *discoteca* downstairs is free. Singles 100 pesos; doubles 130-200 pesos; triples 270 pesos. Ask about student discounts. ❷

Hotel Posada San Francisco, Juárez 178 (☎ 732 2467), the big brown hotel next to the market. Bright rooms with tiny, shiny baths, bottled water, and TV. Beware the street noise. Make reservations for weekends. Singles 200 pesos; doubles 250 pesos. ❹

Posada Hidalgo, Juárez 220 (☎ 732 3145). Smallish rooms have faux wood paneling and cramped baths. The restaurant serves breakfast and lunch (all-you-can-eat 40 pesos). Singles 150 pesos. Each additional person 150 pesos. ❸

Hotel Posada del Carmen, Juárez 111-A (☎ 732 9330), near the market. Spiral-carved stone columns decorate the courtyard, and small rooms have TV and fairly spacious tiled baths. Singles 200 pesos; doubles 250 pesos. ❷

▣ FOOD

An abundance of inexpensive restaurants inhabit Guanajuato's plazas. Prices near **Jardín Unión** rise in direct proportion to the number of *gringos* per square inch. You can catch several open-air bargains at Mercado Gavira, by Mercado Hidalgo.

▨ **Truco No. 7,** Truco 7 (☎ 732 8374), the 1st left beyond the Basílica, facing the Jardín. Artsy, spacious, dark, popular with everyone. Fruit salad 18 pesos, sandwiches 13-14 pesos, *carnes* 35-70 pesos, cappuccino 18 pesos. Open daily 8:30am-11:30pm. ❸

Restaurant Pingüis, Allende 3 (☎ 732 1414). Enormous breakfasts and budget-friendly prices attract hordes of locals and travelers. Tacky decorations, egg platters (12-16 pesos), and *pan francés* (15 pesos). Coffee 7 pesos. Open daily 8:30am-9:30pm. ❷

Hostal de Marilú, Calixto 20. This small vegetarian restaurant serves a mountainous *comida corrida* (35 pesos); all-you-can-eat 50 pesos. *Chiles enogada* 30 pesos. Open daily 9am-9pm. ❸

Pericos Negros (☎ 734 0302), Augora del Baratillo Planta Baja, behind the Jardín Unión from Obregón. A great place to chill amongst stone arches and a shaded courtyard; *tortilla española* 25 pesos, *pollo con mole* 40 pesos. Open M-Sa 9am-9pm. ❸

Carnitas Sam, Juárez 6 (☎ 732 0355). If he could make tortillas out of meat, Sam might. Savory *carnitas* (marinated pork) draws meat-lovers late. Good-sized tacos 4 pesos. Open Su 8:30am-6pm, M-Sa 8:30am-3am. ❶

La Loca Rana, Positos 32 (☎ 732 1325), across from Diego Rivera's house. Fill up on the tasty 3-course *menú del día* (30 pesos). Breakfast 20-25 pesos. Good food, big servings, and delicious *agua de jamaica*. Open M-Sa 8am-8pm. ❸

◉ SIGHTS

Guanajuato is loaded with attractions, which range from the historically fascinating to the mind-numbingly grotesque. Most are located in the *centro*.

JARDÍN UNIÓN. One block east of the Basílica, the triangular Jardín is the town's social center. Adjacent shops and cafes are visible through the trees, and musicians add a pleasant air to the vibrant area. In afternoons and evenings, crowds gather on shady benches to hear the state band perform. *(Su noon and 6pm, Th 6pm.)*

TEATRO JUÁREZ. Completed in 1903 for dictator Porfirio Díaz, the theater has an ornate Roman facade—columns, lampposts, statues, bronze lions, and eight staring muses. The posh interior has the feel of an old European opera house. Besides housing government offices, the Teatro hosts plays, operas, ballets, classical music concerts, and the main events of *Festival Cervantino*. *(☎ 732 0183. Faces the corner of Jardín Unión. Open Tu-Su 9am-1:45pm and 5-7:45pm, except performance days. 15 pesos, students 10 pesos. Performances Sa 8pm; tickets 50-80 pesos.)*

▧ MUSEO ICONOGRÁFICO DEL QUIJOTE. This gorgeous example of 18th-century Spanish architecture contains 10 large galleries with over 600 works of art inspired by Cervantes's anti-hero Don Quixote. Most are paintings, but there are sculptures, stained-glass windows, clocks, and chess pieces; Dalí, Picasso, Daumier, Ocampo, and Coronel are all here. *(Manuel Doblado 1, by Sopeña. ☎ 732 3376 or 732 6721. Open Su 9am-2pm, Tu-Sa 9am-6:30pm. Free.)*

BASÍLICA DE NUESTRA SEÑORA DE GUANAJUATO. This elegant 17th-century Baroque structure took 25 years to construct. Dozens of candelabra illuminate the interior, decorated with fine ornamental frescoes and paintings of the Madonna by Miguel Cabrera. A wooden image of the city's protectress, Nuestra Señora de Guanajuato, rests on a pure silver base and is believed to be the oldest piece of Christian art in Mexico. *(On Plaza de la Paz. Open daily 8am-9pm.)*

TEMPLO DE LA COMPAÑÍA. Completed in 1765, this Jesuit temple and college, much larger than the Basílica, was shut down in 1785; just two years later, the Jesuits were expelled from Spanish America altogether. In 1828, the building hosted the Colegio del Estado, which spawned the city's modern university. The ornate stone exterior is striking, with four Churrigueresque facades still intact. The entrance to a small art museum lies to the left of the altar and includes a 17th-century painting of San Ignacio de Loyola and an 18th-century representation of San Francisco de Asís. Ending the exhibit is a spooky *relicario*, a wooden shelf enveloped in gold leaf and holding human bones. *(Next to the university. ☎ 732 1827. Open daily 7:30am-9:30pm. Museum open M-Sa 10am-4pm. 5-peso donation requested.)*

MUSEO DEL PUEBLO DE GUANAJUATO. This 18th-century colonial mansion houses a permanent collection of 18th- and 19th-century works by Mexican artists, including many intricately detailed crafts, and rotating exhibits of contemporary art. An impressive reconstruction of a church facade on the second floor houses a mural with Guanajuato's visual highlights. *(Positos 7. ☎ 732 2990. Open Su 10am-2:30pm, Tu-Sa 10am-6:30pm. 15 pesos, students 5 pesos.)*

▧ MUSEO Y CASA DE DIEGO RIVERA. The museum chronicles the life of Guanajuato's most famous native son, born in 1886 in this house. Visitors can observe old furniture from his childhood home before moving upstairs to chronologically arranged works representing his different artistic periods. Don't miss the watercolor illustrations for the *Popol Vuh* (the sacred book of the Maya), which imitate Maya iconography, nor his preliminary sketch for a section of the mural, later destroyed, commissioned in 1933 by New York's Rockefeller Center. Rotating exhibits fill the top floor. *(Positos 47. ☎ 732 1197. Open Su 10am-2:30pm, Tu-Sa 10am-6:30pm. 15 pesos, students 5 pesos.)*

CALLEJÓN DEL BESO. According to local lore, a Spanish aristocrat living on one side of the "Alley of the Kiss" flew into a rage upon discovering his daughter kissing her impoverished, forbidden lover across the alleyway, and stabbed her to death. Today, local superstition dictates that passing lovers kiss on the third step or face bad luck. Local capitalism dictates that they stop for a 50-peso photo. *(From Juárez, walk south along Plaza de los Ángeles and turn left into the alley.)*

MERCADO HIDALGO. Established in 1910 in honor of the 100th anniversary of the struggle for independence, the *mercado* sells everything from meat to handcrafted woolen dolls. Most of the fun is haggling over the price. The first floor houses some of the best and cheapest meals and candies in town. *(On Juárez by the Jardín de la Reforma. Most stalls open daily 9am-9pm.)*

MUSEO DE LA ALHÓNDIGA DE GRANADITAS. Originally built in 1809 to guard the city's grain supply, this Neoclassical building witnessed the victory of Mexican hero "El Pípila," who massacred over 300 Spaniards holed up here on September 28, 1810. After Hidalgo's rebellion was squelched, the angry Spanish displayed the severed heads of the executed leaders—Hidalgo, Allende, Aldama, and Jiménez—from the corners of the building. Today, the Alhóndiga is an ethnographic, archaeological, and historical museum. Captivating murals covering the ceiling and sides of the stairwells are often mistaken for those of José Clemente Orozco or Diego Rivera; the true painter, José Chávez Morado, was their contemporary. One of the most striking murals features his interpretation of the display of Hidalgo's severed head—lit by unearthly fire and stuck in a bird cage. *(At the west end of Positos. ☎ 732 1112. Open Su 10am-2:30pm, Tu-Sa 10am-1:30pm and 4-5:30pm. 32 pesos, students, seniors, and children under 13 free; Su free.)*

■ **MUSEO DE LAS MOMIAS.** The high mineral content of Guanajuato's soil naturally mummified the 108 corpses now on display in the museum. Cautiously tread through catacombs like the Museo de Culto de la Muerte and view morbid holograms, a mummified fetus, and torture weapons of the colonial era, including a coffin of spikes. Gag at the purplish, inflated body of a drowning victim; a woman buried alive, frozen in her attempt to scratch her way out of the coffin; two fashionable Frenchmen; a man who died by hanging; and another who was stabbed. The museum's oldest mummy has been here for around 135 years, while the most recent acquisition has been here 5 years. The most popular sight in Guanajuato, the mummies draw a larger crowd than less gory museums downtown. At the exit, vendors offer visitors candy figurines of the more memorable mummies, some wearing little *sombreros*. *(Next to the city cemetery west of town. Take a "Las Momias" bus (2 pesos) from in front of the Basílica or the market. Follow signs from the drop-off. Return buses pick up from the same spot. ☎ 732 0639. Open daily 9am-6pm. Museo de las Momias 20 pesos, students and seniors 14 pesos, children 12 pesos. Museo del Culto de la Muerte 8 pesos.)*

MONUMENTO AL PÍPILA. Looking down on the Jardín from a nearby hill, the Monumento al Pípila commemorates the miner who torched the Alhóndiga's front door and opened the way for a riotous massacre of the Spanish. The titanic Pípila looks best at night when spotlights illuminate him. Climb the narrow staircase inside the monument to a small platform at his back, or take the *funicular*. For a magnificent, panoramic view of the city while descending the hill, follow the steeper path down the west side, which ends near the Túnel de los Ángeles. If you're walking up at night, take a friend. *(Follow Sopeña to the east and take the steep but manageable Callejón del Calvario to your right (5min.) before Sopeña starts to curve, or hop on a "Pípila" bus from Plaza de la Paz, 2 pesos. Open daily 8am-8pm.)*

CASA DE LEYENDAS. The museum aims to preserve *guanajuatense* legends, using dioramas and moving figures to retell many of the city's tragic and humorous myths. Cringe as you watch the father of the famous lover from Callejón del Beso violently stab his daughter, then enter an elevator and "descend" into a mine filled with snakes, skeletons, and miners' unrealized dreams. *(Catch a "La Presa" bus (2.5 pesos) down in the tunnels and ask the driver to let you off at Escuela Normal. From the Escuela, walk up the unmarked street to your left for 2 blocks. Veer left at the fork; the museum is at Súbida del Molino and Panorámica. ☎ 731 0192. Displays and guides in Spanish. Open daily 11am-6pm. 40 pesos including brief tour.)*

EX-HACIENDA DE SAN GABRIEL DE BARRERA. The 17 glorious themed gardens, covering about three acres, are perhaps the most beautiful of Guanajuato's many natural attractions. Cobbled paths, labeled and well-groomed flora, and whistling birds create the perfect atmosphere for a stroll. The ex-hacienda itself borders the gardens; its rooms contain 16th-century furniture, silverware, and paintings. *(Catch a "Noria Alta/Marfil" bus across from the mercado (2.5 pesos), and tell the driver you're headed to San Gabriel de la Barrera. ☎ 732 0619. Open daily 9am-6pm. Closed from Christmas to New Year's. 22 pesos, children and students 15 pesos.)*

MONUMENTO A CRISTO REY. The mountain, called the **Cerro del Cubilete**, 2850m above sea level and 20km from Guanajuato, is considered the geographical center of Mexico. This dark, bronze statue of Jesus at the summit, built by local *indígenas*, is 16m tall and weighs more than 80 tons. The blue hills visible from the summit are just as striking. *(From the station, take a "Cristo Rey" bus in the last spot, #24. ☎ 732 8246. Round-trip 3½hr., 9 buses daily 6:15am-4:15pm, 15 pesos.)*

ENTERTAINMENT

Theatre, dance, and musical performances abound. Ask at the tourist office for listings or consult posters around town. On Sunday and Thursday nights in Jardín Unión, the state band performs around 6pm. *Callejonadas* (sing-alongs) happen on Friday and Saturday nights at 8:30pm and depart from Teatro Juárez. Student groups present films almost every day of the week. Check out **Teatro Principal**, Hidalgo 18 (☎ 732 1526; 25 pesos, students and seniors 15 pesos), or **Teatro Cervantes**, on Plaza Cervantes (☎ 732 1169; 17 pesos, students and seniors 15 pesos).

Guanajuato explodes for the last three weeks in October during the **Festival Internacional Cervantino**. The city invites repertory groups from all over the world to make merry with the *estudiantinas* (strolling student minstrels). Festivities take place mostly at local theaters, but also at museums and churches. Tickets are sold by TicketMaster a month in advance and sell rapidly. The **Office of the Festival Internacional Cervantino** (☎ 731 1150) can provide more information. Guanajuato also celebrates the **Feria de San Juan** (June 24), at Presa de la Olla, with dancing, cultural events, fireworks, and sports; and **Día de la Cueva** (July 31), when residents walk to a cave's entrance to honor San Ignacio de Loyola, the patron saint of Guanajuato and founder of the Compañía de Jesús.

NIGHTLIFE

Damas de las Camelias es Él, Sopeña 32 (☎ 732 7587). A sophisticated crowd of professionals and 30-something tourists groove to Latin rhythms. Broad selection of flamenco, jazz, and salsa, and Peruvian and Portuguese music. *Cerveza* 20 pesos and mixed drinks 35 pesos. No cover. Open daily 8pm-5am. Live music F-Sa 11pm-3am.

Guanajuato Grill, Alonso 4 (☎ 732 0287). Fake stars in the covered courtyard, gilt-framed pictures on maroon walls, and pounding Latin and US pop music set the mood. Enjoy beer (20 pesos) or drinks (40 pesos) from tables or booths. Tu no cover; Th cover

40 pesos; F cover 40 pesos after midnight; Sa cover 60 pesos. Beer specials Tu, Th-F. Open Tu, Th-Sa 10pm-4am.

The Bar, Sopeña 10 (☎732 2566). Salsa rhythms fill the room and your body as you enter on the second floor. The crowd doesn't keep Mexicans and foreigners from showing off their moves, while the impressed audience throws back beers (15 pesos) at surrounding tables. Drinks from 35 pesos. Open daily 8pm-4am.

Bar 8 (☎732 7179), at Constancia and Santo del Mono. Thanks to a laid-back atmosphere and cheap drinks, Bar 8 fills its three floors with a student crowd on weeknights. Toast your friends at the bar or play pool. Beer from 15 pesos, drinks from 30 pesos. Tu 2-for-1 beers. No cover. Open Su 1pm-3am, M-Sa noon-3am.

Puerta del Sol, Sopeña 14. Heart-break ballads and candlelight provide a relaxed and romantic setting. Beer 20 pesos, drinks 25-35 pesos, *aguacate relleno de atún* 35 pesos. Live music M-Sa after 8pm; open M-Sa 5pm-3am.

SAN MIGUEL DE ALLENDE   ☎415

In the 18th and 19th centuries San Miguel de Allende (pop. 80,000) was a bustling commercial center and played a pivotal role in the struggle for independence. On September 16, 1810, when Hidalgo, the priest of nearby Dolores, led his rebel army into the city, the town rallied in opposition to Spanish rule under the leadership of Ignacio Allende. In 1826, the infant republic recognized Allende's role in the drive for independence by joining his name to San Miguel's. These days, ex-pats (up to 15% of the population, according to locals) and US visitors, not Revolutionaries, overrun San Miguel, which is somewhat bloated with Reuben sandwiches, Häagen Dazs ice cream, and yuppies looking to painlessly inject their children with some Spanish skills. Still, Mexican life marches on. The lively *mercado* refuses to yield to air-conditioned malls, and the shady plazas, colonial churches, and quiet green gardens retain a quiet appeal.

▐ TRANSPORTATION

Buses: To get from the bus station to the town center, take a "Centro" bus to the corner of Colegio and Mesones, near the statue of Allende on horseback (every 15min. 7am-10pm, 2.5 pesos). Walk 2 blocks west on Mesones, then left 1 block on Reloj to Plaza Allende. Alternatively, take a taxi (20 pesos). **Flecha Amarilla** (☎152 7323) goes to: **Aguascalientes** (4½hr.; 12:30pm, 2:30pm; 110 pesos); **Dolores Hidalgo** (45min.; every 15min. 4:30am-9:15pm, plus 11:45pm; 23 pesos); **Guadalajara** (5hr.; 7:30, 9:45am, 5:30pm; 298 pesos); **Guanajuato** (1½hr.; 7:30, 9:45am, noon, 5:30pm; 70 pesos); **León** (2½hr.; 7:30, 9:45am, noon, 5:30pm; 110 pesos); **Mexico City** (3½hr.; 9:40am, 4pm; 185 pesos); **Querétaro** (1½hr.; 12:30am, 2:30am, and every 40min. 5:20am-8pm; 37 pesos); **San Luis Potosí** (4hr., every 2hr. 7:30am-6:50pm, 110 pesos). **Herradura de Plata/Pegasso Plus** (☎152 0725) and **ETN** (☎152 6407) provide similar service to fewer locations. The **Estrella Blanca** group (☎152 2237) travels to more distant locations.

◢❖ ▐ ORIENTATION AND PRACTICAL INFORMATION

San Miguel is 94km southeast of Guanajuato and 428km northwest of Mexico City. Most attractions are within walking distance of the town center, **Jardín Allende** (or **Plaza Allende**). The streets form a near-grid. **San Francisco, Reloj, Correo,** and **Hidalgo** border the Jardín. East-west streets south of the Jardín change their names every few blocks. The always-visible, towering *basílica* in Jardín Allende can orient even the most frustrated of travelers.

San Miguel de Allende

🏠 ACCOMMODATIONS
Casa de Huéspedes, **8**
Hostal Alcatraz, **1**
Hotel la Huerta, **11**
Hotel Parador San Sebastián, **9**
Hotel Vianey, **10**

🍴 FOOD
El Taco Real, **14**
El Tomato, **12**
La Piñata, **15**
La Villa de Pancho, **2**
Las Musas, **4**
Los Burritos, **7**

⭐ NIGHTLIFE
Agave, **3**
Char Rock, **17**
El Rincón de Alebrije, **6**
El Ring, **13**
La Cucaracha, **19**
Le Petit, **18**
Mama Mía, **16**
Pancho & Lefty's, **5**

TOURIST AND FINANCIAL SERVICES

Tourist Office: Delegación Regional de Turismo (☎/fax 152 6565), on Pl. Allende, to your left as you face the Parroquia. Knowledgeable staff distributes maps. Some English spoken. Open M-F 10am-5pm, Sa 10am-2pm. During high season, groups gather i front of the church in the Jardín for **tours** of the city (1½hr., 40 pesos per person Departure times vary; call for more information.

Consulates: US, Macías 72 Interior 6 (☎152 2357, after-hours emergencies ☎1 0068 or 152 0653), across the street from Bellas Artes. Open M-F 9am-1pm or appointment. For other countries, or to extend visas or visitors' permits, contact the **egación Regional de Servicios Migratorios,** Plaza Real del Conde Shopping Ce 2nd fl. (☎152 2542 or 152 2835). Catch the "Gigante" bus from Colegio and Mes or from Juárez. Documents may be dropped off 9am-12:30pm and picked up 1:30-3pm. Processing takes at least 1 day. Open M-F 8am-8pm.

Currency Exchange: Intercam, Correo 15, San Francisco 4, and Juárez 27 (☎ 154 6660), has great rates. Open M-F 9am-6pm, Sa 9am-2pm. **Banamex** (☎ 152 1040) on the west side of the Jardín, has 24hr. **ATMs.** Open M-F 9am-5pm, Sa 10am-2pm.

American Express: Hidalgo 1 (☎ 152 1856; fax 152 0499). Full financial and travel services. Open M-F 9am-2pm and 4-6:30pm.

LOCAL SERVICES

English Bookstore: El Colibrí, Sollano 30 (☎ 152 0751), near Cuadrante. Paperback fiction, some in French and German. Open M-Sa 10am-2pm and 4-6pm. **Lagundi,** Umarán 17 (☎ 152 0830), at Macías. Large selection of art supplies and magazines in several languages. Open Su 11am-3pm, M-Sa 10am-2pm and 4-8pm.

Library: Insurgentes 25 (☎ 152 0293), between Reloj and Hidalgo. Ex-pats and students gather in the art-filled courtyard. Wide selection of books in English and Spanish. Sells old paperbacks (6-8 pesos) Th 10am-1pm. Library and gift shop open M-F 10am-2pm and 4-7pm, Sa 10am-2pm.

Supermarket: Bonanza, Mesones 43A (☎ 152 1260). Open Su 8am-5pm, M-Sa 8am-3pm and 4-8pm. **Gigante** is even bigger. Take a "Gigante" bus (2.5 pesos).

Laundry: Lavandería el Reloj, Reloj 34 (☎ 152 3843), between Mesones and Insurgentes. Full-service wash and dry 40 pesos per 4kg. Open M-Sa 8am-8pm.

EMERGENCY AND COMMUNICATIONS

Emergency: (☎ 152 0911). Direct contact with Red Cross, fire department, and police. A few dispatchers speak English.

Red Cross: (☎ 152 1616), 1km outside of town on Carretera Celaya. English spoken.

Pharmacy: Botica Agundis, Canal 26 (☎ 152 1198), at Macías. Helpful staff. Open daily 10am-midnight. Call police to find out which pharmacy is open 24hr.

Hospital: Hospital de la Fe San Miguel, Libramiento Mex. 43 (☎ 152 2233 or 152 2320, emergency 152 2545), near the bus station. English spoken. In emergencies, you may also call **Hospital Civil** (☎ 152 0045). English spoken.

Fax: Telecomm, Correo 16-B (☎ 152 3215; fax 152 0081), next to the post office. Open M-F 9am-7pm, Sa-Su 9am-noon.

Internet Access: Internet San Miguel, Mesones 57 (☎ 154 4634; www.Internetsan-miguel.com), with entrance on Reloj. Open Su 10am-6pm, M-Sa 9am-9pm.

Post Office: Correo 16 (☎ 152 0089), 1 block east of the Jardín. **Mexpost** available. Open M-F 9am-5pm, Sa 9am-1pm. **Postal Code:** 37700.

▐ ACCOMMODATIONS

As the "dollar trail" follows waves of tourists, budget accommodations become hard to find in places like San Miguel. In general, prices drop as you mover farther from the Jardín. Rooms fill up fast, particularly during the winter, *Semana Santa*, and September, when the city throws a month-long *fiesta* in honor of Independence Day and the city's founding. Reservations are recommended for these times.

▨ **Hostal Alcatraz,** Reloj 54 (☎ 152 8543; info@hostal-alcatraz.com). This popular hostel has single-sex dorms, but everyone mingles in the TV room and kitchen. Internet access 10 pesos per hr. No curfew. Office open 9am-9pm. 90 pesos, 100 pesos with ISIC or HI card. 20-peso key deposit if arriving after 11pm. ❶

Casa de Huéspedes, Mesones 27 (☎ 152 1378). Good sized-rooms with *talavera* baths branch off of the 2nd-floor plant-filled courtyard. The top-floor terrace has spectacular views of the city's churches; many rooms have balconies with views. Singles 150 pesos; doubles 250 pesos. Monthly rates can be arranged. Reservations are a good idea. ❸

Hotel la Huerta, Callejón de Atascadero 9 (☎ 154 4475). Past where Mesones becomes Aparicio, across the stream. The hotel will be the large blue building on your left. Fountain-filled patios and wood-floored sitting rooms make this place feel like an *hacienda*. Rooms have great city views, *agua purificada*, and large baths; some have hardwood floors. Singles and doubles 250 pesos. Each additional person 50 pesos. Cable TV 50 pesos extra. Off-season discount for language school students: singles 200 pesos, meals included. ❺

Hotel Parador San Sebastián, Mesones 7 (☎ 152 7084). Pleasant rooms have tiled baths, some with kitchenettes. Books and a TV occupy the sitting room off the courtyard. Busy on weekends. Singles and doubles 240 pesos; triples 300 pesos. ❹

Hotel Vianey, Aparicio 18 (☎ 152 4559). Rooms are spacious with hot water bathrooms and a huge courtyard. Singles without bath 150 pesos; doubles with bath 350; quad with kitchenette 350 pesos. ❸

FOOD

The sweet aroma of international cuisine wafts through the cobbled streets of San Miguel, as restaurants and cafes occupy almost every corner. Unfortunately, prices can be as *gringo* as their clientele. For the best value, visit **Calle Insurgentes** and the streets around the *mercado* on **Colegio**.

La Villa de Pancho, Quebrada 12 (☎ 152 1247), at the corner with Insurgentes. Welcome to the kitchen of the very friendly Cristina and Carlos. *Comida corrida* 35-50 pesos, breakfast all day 15-25 pesos, *cerveza* 10 pesos. Open daily 9am-9pm. A **Casa de Huéspedes** is on the 2nd floor with 3 spacious rooms connected by a communal bathroom. 80 pesos. Food and laundry discounts for guests. ❸

La Piñata, Jesús 1 (☎ 152 2060), a block from the Jardín. Join the mellow mix of locals, students, and backpackers feasting on vegetarian-friendly *tostadas* (7 pesos) and sandwiches (12-16 pesos); beware the greasy *queso fundido* (25 pesos). *Comida corrida* 35 pesos, breakfast 20-25 pesos. Open Su-M, W-Th 9am-8pm, F-Sa 9am-11pm. ❸

Los Burritos, Mesones 69-A (☎ 152 3222). Tasty and economical *comida rápida*. *Burritacos* (3 pesos) or *burriquesos* (4.5 pesos) come vegetarian-friendly, too. Ravenous travelers will like the *burrito maxi* (7.5 pesos) and the hot and cheesy *burriqueso maxi* (12 pesos). Open M-Sa 10:30am-6pm. ❶

El Tomato, Mesones 62B. This stylish restaurant deals in organic foods. Fruit juices 20 pesos, tasty salads 48 pesos, and veggie burgers 45 pesos. Meal of the day 60 pesos. Commemorate your visit with an El Tomato mug (40 pesos). Open M-Sa noon-9pm. ❹

Las Musas, Macías 75 (☎ 152 4846), inside Bellas Artes. Italian cuisine in a wonderful, colonial Mexican setting. Feast on sweet pastries created under the supervision of the Italian-born owner. *Strudel de atún* 33 pesos, lasagne 65 pesos, salads 29-39 pesos. Open Su 10am-2pm, M-Sa 9am-8pm. ❹

El Taco Real, Reloj 15 (☎ 152 6677) Serves an affordable and stylish feast. *Pollo con Mole*, *rajas con crema*, and *fajitas de Bisteck* are served in clay pots. Buffet 45 pesos, 5 pesos more for all the *agua fresca* you can drink. ❸

SIGHTS

The cheapest and most effective way to experience San Miguel is on your own two feet—nearly all sites of interest lie within walking distance of the Jardín.

CENTRAL MEXICO

LA PARROQUIA. The neo-Gothic facade and tower of San Miguel's most impressive sight were added to the 17th-century church in 1890 by the *indígena* mason Zeferino Gutiérrez, who supposedly learned the style from postcards of French cathedrals. Pointed arches and flute-like towers enclose chandeliers and gold trim glittering in the sunlight from the tower windows. At the front is a tremendous gold-leaf altar. The basement holds the tomb of former president Anastasio Bustamante. Spotlights illuminate the church at night. *(Next to the Jardín.* ☎ *152 4197. Open daily 5:30am-9:30pm. Mass M-Sa 6, 7, 9am, noon, 8:15pm; all day Su.)*

MUSEO HISTÓRICO DE SAN MIGUEL DE ALLENDE. The birthplace of Ignacio Allende houses a respectable collection of ancient ceramics, Pre-Classical artifacts, historical exhibits of varying interest, and, of course, a tribute to the man himself. *(Cuna de Allende 1, across from La Parroquia.* ☎ *152 2499. Open Tu-Su 10am-4pm. 32 pesos, children and students free. Mini-guide 8 pesos.)*

TEMPLO DEL ORATORIO DE SAN FELIPE NERI. Founded in 1712 and rebuilt many times, the church is an amalgam of styles; its interior is mainly Neoclassical, but the engraved Baroque facade belies *indígena* influences. On the west side, the towers and dome belong to *Santa Casa de Loreto*, a reproduction of the building by the same name in Italy. Enter through the doorway west of San Felipe Neri. The floors and lower wall are covered with glazed tiles from China, Spain, and Puebla. *(At Insurgentes and Loreto.* ☎ *152 0521. Open daily 6:30am-1pm and 6:30-8:30pm. Santa Casa open daily 8am-2pm.)*

IGLESIA DE LA CONCEPCIÓN. Construction on the enormous church began in 1755 and lasted until 1891. A representation of the Immaculate Conception graces the two-story dome, and the ornate gold altar features a likeness of the Virgin in blue metallic robes. *(At the corner of Canal and Macías, near the Jardín.* ☎ *152 0148. Open daily 7:30am-7pm. Mass Su 9:30, 11:30am, and 7pm, M-F 7:30am and 7pm.)*

BELLAS ARTES. Housed in a former convent from the 18th century, this cultural center and art school has a concert hall and galleries with rotating exhibits. The stunning murals around the peaceful, manicured courtyard echo the impressive talent of the students. Look for *campesina* L. R. Santos lassoing a dreaded purple *chupacabra*. The school offers classes in ceramics, dance, art, guitar, and more—a few are even in English. European and US films occasionally show. *(Macías 75, next to Iglesia de la Concepción.* ☎ *152 0289. Open Su 10am-2pm, M-Sa 9am-8pm.)*

OTHER SIGHTS NEAR THE CENTRO. The **Instituto de Allende,** Ancha de San Antonio 20, a hike up Zacateros from Iglesia de la Concepción, houses several galleries with exhibits by local artists and offers art, Spanish, and social studies classes. Every Tuesday, vendors converge upon the **Tianguis del Martes** (Tuesday market) near the municipal stadium to sell their wares. Clothing, groceries, old doorknobs, and assorted odds and ends await the adventurous shopper. Reverberating with the calls of tropical birds, **Parque Juárez** is a large, lush garden just south of the *centro.* *(Instituto:* ☎ *152 0190. Open M-F 8am-5:30pm. Tianguis: To get there, take a 1.8-peso "Gigante" bus from Juárez or a 15-peso taxi ride. Open 7am-4pm. Parque: South of the Jardín on Hermanos Aldama.)*

OTHER SIGHTS AWAY FROM THE CENTRO. The **Jardín Botánico el Charco del Ingenio** is home to colonial-era ruins and a dazzling array of cacti and succulents. About 1,300 species grow along 8km of walking paths in the 100-hectare park. Camping available. Take in a breathtaking view of San Miguel and the surrounding mountains from the **mirador** above the city. Hot springs fans will find their paradise at **La Gruta,** just outside of town. *(Jardín: Mesones 71. Cross the stream on Colegio, turn right on Homobono, and continue up the incline, where it turns into Cuesta de San José and, later,*

Matitlán. Where Matitlán ends, follow the street to the right and continue on the dirt road for about 5min. A taxi from Jardín Allende (12 pesos) is easier. ☎154 4715. Open daily 7am-8:30pm. 20 pesos, students and children 10 pesos. Mirador: From the Jardín, go 2 blocks on Correo to Recreo. Walk right for 10min. One block past Plaza de Toros, take a left and continue uphill 3 blocks until the street ends at the main road, with a sign that says "Salida a Querétaro." The mirador is a few minutes' walk to your right. Or, take a "Gigante" bus (2.5 pesos) from Colegio and Mesones or Juárez—don't stay on all the way to the Gigante. Gruta: Take a "Dolores Hidalgo" bus (10min., 8 pesos) and ask to be let off at the hotel near the billboard. Walk toward the billboard and turn left on the dirt road directly ahead. To reach the springs, veer left. When returning to San Miguel, flag down a bus along the road. Open daily 8am-5pm. 50 pesos.)

🎵📷 ENTERTAINMENT AND NIGHTLIFE

There are as many clubs as churches in San Miguel, and music pumps through the city's veins daily. The magazine *Atención,* available every Monday in the tourist office and at local newsstands, is the best source of information on upcoming concerts, theatrical productions, and lectures. **Bellas Artes** and the **Instituto Allende** post advertisements for art exhibits, openings, and other events. Expect cover charges at clubs to skyrocket during *fiestas,* especially *Semana Santa.*

BARS

Le Petit, Macías 95 (☎152 3229). This restaurant-by-day, bar-by-night is saturated with atmosphere and style—wine racks, watercolor paintings, colonial architecture—which pulls in sophisticates and a young, international student crowd. Drinks aren't bad, either. Beer 15 pesos, mixed drinks from 25 pesos. Open daily 6pm-3am.

Char Rock, Correo 7, 2nd fl. (☎152 7373). This relaxed and casual bar has great live music on the 2nd fl. and a cathedral view from the terrace. Decoration is a bit schizophrenic: candles are on tables and posters of the Beatles and Hendrix dot the walls. Small dance floor. Beer 20 pesos, drinks from 30 pesos. Live music after 8pm. No cover. Open Su-W 6pm-1am, Th-Sa noon-3am.

Agave, Mesones 80 (☎152 5151). By the time evening rolls around, live jazz, reggae, or Latin music will be entertaining an older crowd in this bar/restaurant. Drinks 15 pesos during the pre-music happy hour (5-8pm). Beer 20 pesos. Open 2pm-1am.

La Cucaracha, Zacatecas 22A (☎152 0195). A slow paced place to pound beers (10 pesos) or mixed drinks (20 pesos) with US, British, and Mexican tunes (or the TV) playing in the background. Free bar snacks on Th. Open daily 10am-4pm.

CLUBS

Mama Mía, Umarán 8 (☎152 2063), just off the Jardín, is a favorite destination of foreigners and *gringuita*-friendly locals. Restaurant, bar, and *discoteca* in one, this enormous building is divided into several smaller establishments. **Mama Mía Bar,** to your right as you enter, attracts a 20-something crowd and features live salsa, jazz, reggae, and funk. 50-peso cover F-Sa. Open Th-Sa 9pm-3am. **Leonardo's,** across the entryway, scores points for its big-screen TV. Techno music blares and college-age customers crowd the bar. Open M-W 7pm-2am, Th-Sa 7pm-3am. In front of the entrance is a pricey **restaurant** appealing mostly to tourists and hosting nightly *música folklórica.* Open M-Th 8am-midnight, F-Sa 8am-3am. The **terrace** upstairs pulsates with live music Th-Sa 11pm-2:30am. When there is no live music, a young crowd enjoys the view of the city and chats over beers (21 pesos; drinks 37 pesos). Open F-Sa 9pm-2am.

El Ring, Hidalgo 25 (☎152 1998), features standard *discoteca* and a young crowd. Conversation possible. Drinks 25-80 pesos. Cover W-Th 20 pesos, F 40 pesos, Sa 60 pesos. Open Su 5:30-10:30pm, W 8pm-3am, Th-Sa 10pm-4:30am; nightly in July.

Pancho and Lefty's, Mesones 99 (☎152 1958), provides hours of entertainment for students craving a pounding beat and a big drink. Loud rock and cover bands or DJs spinning techno, disco, and Mexican pop songs thrill a large, fairly touristy crowd every night. W 2-for-1 beers. Sa cover 30-50 pesos. Open daily 8pm-3am.

El Rincón del Alebrije, Mesones 97, features cover bands playing rock hits *en español.* Cover for special events (usually 30 pesos). Open W-Sa 8pm-3am.

FESTIVALS

San Miguel boasts more *fiestas* than any other town in Mexico: a celebration of some sort takes place nearly every weekend. In September, the city celebrates its independence and founding on the third Saturday of the month with **San Miguelada,** a running of the bulls in the Jardín. Bellas Artes hosts the impressive **International Chamber Music Festival** in August; ticket packages start at 1000 pesos and go on sale in February. Other festivals include the **Jazz Festival** in November and **El Día de San Antonio** and **El Festival de Locos** on June 13. San Miguel celebrates the birthday of **Ignacio Allende** (January 21) with parades and fireworks.

DOLORES HIDALGO ☎418

"Mexicanos, viva México!"
——Miguel Hidalgo, Grito de Dolores

Nearly 200 years later, Miguel Hidalgo's rousing words still echo through Mexico's dusty "Cradle of Independence." Dolores Hidalgo (pop. 40,000) has little more to offer than hot, dirty streets, a thriving ceramics industry, and an amazing story. On Sunday, September 16, 1810, Miguel Hidalgo y Costilla, the town's priest, learned that his independence conspiracy had been discovered by the Spanish. Deciding to take immediate action, Hidalgo woke the entire town at 5am by tolling the parish church bell. The town's residents tumbled out of bed and gathered at the church, where Hidalgo delivered an electrifying speech, the *Grito de Dolores*, proclaiming Mexico's independence. Then, calling his flock to arms, Hidalgo rallied an army to march to Mexico City. With this brazen move, Hidalgo not only signed his own death warrant (he was executed a year later), but he single-handedly began the movement that led to Mexican independence.

⬛ TRANSPORTATION. To get downtown from the **Flecha Amarilla bus station,** walk straight out the door and left on Hidalgo. Three blocks down the street are the *jardín*, the tourist office, Plaza Principal, and the Parroquia. Flecha Amarilla (☎182 0639) goes to **Aguascalientes** (3½hr.; 1:30, 3:30pm; 118 pesos); **Guadalajara** (8hr., every hr. 5:20am-12:45pm, 224 pesos); **Guanajuato** (1½hr., every 20min. 5:20am-9pm, 37 pesos) en route to **León** (3hr., 63 pesos); **Mexico City** (5hr., every 40min. 5am-7pm, 163 pesos) via **Querétaro** (2½hr., 58 pesos); **San Luis Potosí** (3hr., every 2hr. 5:30am-8pm, 84 pesos); **San Miguel de Allende** (1hr., every 30min. 5:10am-8:50pm, 23 pesos). To get to Plaza Principal from the **Herradura de Plata bus station,** go out the door on your left as you face Yucatán. Walk down Chiapas, which turns into Tabasco, take a left on Hidalgo, and follow it to the plaza. Herradura de Plata (☎182 2937) goes to many of the same destinations.

⬛ PRACTICAL INFORMATION. Streets change names as they cross the plaza, and the town's points of interest all lie within a few blocks of the center. The **tourist office** is the large yellow building on your right as you exit the Parroquia. Handy maps, but no English spoken. (☎/fax 182 1164. Open M-F 10am-7pm, Sa-Su 10am-3pm.) **Centro Cambiar Paisano,** Plaza Principal 22, has good **exchange** rates. (☎182

4535. Open Su 9am-3pm, M-Sa 9am-5pm.) **Bancomer,** Hidalgo 29, exchanges currency during the week and has 24hr. **ATMs.** (☎182 0590. Open M-F 8:30am-4pm, Sa 10am-2pm.) Other services include: **emergency** service (☎182 0911); **police,** México 2, 11 blocks north of the plaza (☎192 0021; no English spoken); the **pharmacy Botica de San Vicente,** Potosí and Zacatecas (☎182 2417; open daily 9am-10pm); **Hospital General,** Hidalgo 12 (☎182 0013; some English spoken); **Cybercafe.com,** Zacatecas 3 (☎182 0087; 10 pesos per hr.; open Su 10am-4pm, M-Sa 10am-9pm); **post office,** Puebla 22 between Jalisco and Veracruz, one block from Plaza Principal (☎182 0807; open M-F 9am-3pm). **Postal code:** 37800.

▓▒ ACCOMMODATIONS AND FOOD. Quality budget rooms are scarce in Dolores Hidalgo. Prices rise and vacancies fall dramatically during *Semana Santa* and from September 8 to 17, when Independence Day celebrants overrun the town; reservations are advised. **Posada Dolores ❶,** Yucatán 8, one block east of the plaza, has simple, windowless concrete cube rooms—but they're very clean and the family atmosphere is welcoming. Hot water communal bathrooms lack toilet seats. Grab cheap *comida corrida* (22 pesos) in the adjoining restaurant. (☎182 0642. Singles 95 pesos, 150 pesos with bath; doubles 120/180 pesos.) **Hotel Posada Hidalgo ❺,** Hidalgo 15 (☎182 0477) has large spotless rooms with carpeted floors, clean baths, and sauna. (Singles 298 pesos; doubles 348 pesos.) Around the *jardín,* most restaurants are reasonably priced. **Torticlán ❶,** Plaza Principal 28, at the west end, serves tasty food cafeteria-style. Join families and fellow tourists for *tortas* (11 pesos) with juice (7 pesos) or beer (9 pesos). Soyburgers (15.5 pesos) satisfy vegetarians. (☎182 2676. Open daily 9am-5:30pm.) **D'Jardín ❷,** Plaza Principal 30, has substantial meals. Cool off under fans and enjoy Mexican favorites like *chilaquiles* or *flautas* for 25 pesos. (☎182 0252. Open daily 9am-7pm.)

◉ SIGHTS. Most of Dolores's sights lie within four blocks of the bus station, and revolve around the beautiful **Parroquia de Nuestra Señora de los Dolores,** where the *Grito de Dolores* was sounded. Constructed between 1712 and 1778, the church's lavish interior features a main altar surrounded by beautifully ornamented gold leaf columns and two side altars, one Churrigueresque and the other Ultrabaroque. Dress appropriately—no shorts or tight dresses are allowed. The original bell is now positioned atop Mexico City's Palacio de Gobierno. (Open daily 9am-2pm and 4-8pm.) On the west side of the plaza is the **Casa de Visitas,** built in 1786 to house Spanish officials. In the center of the plaza is a huge bronze statue of Hidalgo, the man who made Dolores Hidalgo *la cuna de la independencia nacional* (the cradle of national independence). (Open Su 11am-3pm, M-Sa 10am-6pm.) **Museo de la Independencia,** Zacatecas 6, lies less than one block northwest of the Parroquia. Gory (or inspirational) paintings detail the physical and spiritual costs of Spanish rule and the fight for independence. Relive Hidalgo's *Grito* in an eerie life-size diorama with wooden statues of an inspired Hidalgo and anxious Mexicans. The museum also includes an exhibit on the history of the flag and a shrine to Dolores Hidalgo's favorite musical son, *ranchero* legend José Alfredo Jiménez. (Open daily 9am-5pm. 10 pesos; Su free.) Hidalgo's home from 1804 until 1810, the **Museo Casa Hidalgo,** at Morelos and Hidalgo, one block from Plaza Principal, is somewhat less than thrilling, with his religious and artistic personals and independence artifacts. (☎182 0171. Open Tu-Su 10am-6pm. 32 pesos; Su free.)

Seasonal activities include the **Fiestas de Septiembre** (Sept. 15), Dolores Hidalgo's biggest shindig. Until Zedillo broke tradition, the President himself made an appearance at the Casa de Visitas in election years, re-issuing the *Grito de Dolores.* **Purísima Concepción** (Nov. 30-Dec. 8), is a fair that includes massive *artesanía* sales and pyrotechnic displays.

CENTRAL MEXICO

QUERÉTARO

QUERÉTARO

☎442

Between Mexico City and Guadalajara on the republic's busiest stretch of road, Querétaro (pop. 870,000) has witnessed some of the most decisive moments in Mexican history. The city's many museums recreate, among other important events, Emperor Maximilian's last days. A hike up Cerro de las Campanas (Hill of the Bells) will bring you to the site where the ill-fated ruler spoke his famous last words: "Mexicans, I am going to die for a just cause: the liberty and independence of Mexico." 50 years later, victorious Venustiano Carranza drafted the 1917 constitution in the patriotic city, which established modern Mexico.

Today, Querétaro is a prosperous agricultural and industrial center. Whining grain elevators, monstrous warehouses, and truckloads of squealing pigs assault the senses. Inside the commercial ring, where lantern-like lamps illuminate its many plazas, Querétaro is a colonial wonder; an 18th-century aqueduct of graceful arches still adorns the path to the *centro histórico*. In the city's heart, students and entrepreneurs traverse centuries-old brick streets and narrow *andadores*. Often overlooked by foreigners, the city is a popular destination for Mexicans.

■ TRANSPORTATION

Querétaro lies between Mexico City and Guadalajara on **Mex. 57.** The modern **bus station** (☎229 0061) is on the south side of town, not within walking distance of the *centro*. Take the "Ruta 25" bus on Allende and Zaragoza, "Ruta 8" on Ocampo and Constituyentes, "Ruta 19" at the corner of Madero and Guerrero, or "Ruta 72" on Universidad—all are labeled "Central." (Every 5-10min. 6am-10:30pm, 3.5 pesos.) To catch a bus to the *centro* (4-5 pesos), walk toward the highway, veering to the right and past an eclectic market, toward the sign that says "Paradero de Micros." **Taxis** to most destinations are 22 pesos—tickets are sold inside the station and handed to the driver. Querétaro's bus station is divided into two terminals: Terminal A offers first-class service and Terminal B offers second-class service.

Terminal A: Élite (☎229 0022) drives to: **Acapulco** (9hr.; 11am, 7:45, 10pm; 374 pesos); **Cuernavaca** (5hr.; 11am, 7:45pm; 170 pesos); **Mexico City** (3hr., every hr. 7:30am-8pm, 140 pesos); **Monterrey** (10hr., 8 per day 9am-11pm, 400 pesos); **Tampico** (8½hr., 9:25pm, 287 pesos). **Primera Plus/Servicios Coordinados** (☎211 4001) travels to: **Aguascalientes** (4½hr., 9 per day 6:45am-7:45pm, 205 pesos); **Guadalajara** (5hr., 9 per day, 247 pesos); **Guanajuato** (2½hr., 3 per day 5am-11:15pm, 98 pesos); **León** (2½hr., every hr. 1:39 am-11:45 pm, 110 pesos); **Morelia** (3hr., 15 per day, 115 pesos); **San Luis Potosí** (2½hr., 12 per day, 126 pesos). **Ómnibus de México** (☎229 0029) has similar service. **Autobuses Americanos** (☎229 0003) goes to the US.

Terminal B: Flecha Amarilla (☎211 4001) sends buses to: **Aguascalientes** (6hr., 5 per day 4:50am-3:35pm, 163pesos); **Colima** (12hr., 4 per day, 295 pesos); **Guadalajara** (8hr., every 20min. 5am-4:30pm, 237 pesos); **Guanajuato** (3½hr., 5 per day 11:05am-8:05pm, 80 pesos); **León** (4hr., every hr., 100 pesos); **Manzanillo** (13hr.; 7:05am, 7:30pm; 335 pesos); **Mexico City** (3hr., every 10min., 107 pesos); **Morelia** (4hr., 12 per day 5:05am-11:35pm, 100 pesos); **San Miguel de Allende** (1½hr., every 40min. 6:20am-10:20pm, 32 pesos); **Tula** (6½hr., every hr. 6:40am-9:30pm, 80 pesos); **Uruapan** (7hr., 1:10pm, 160 pesos); **Zamora** (6hr.; 1:45, 3:20am, 7:30pm; 247 pesos). **Flecha Roja/Herradura de Plata** (☎224 0245) provides similar service. The **Estrella Blanca** group (☎229 0245) travels farther north.

Querétaro

▲ ACCOMMODATIONS
Hotel del Marqués, **2**
Hotel Hidalgo, **10**
Hotel R.J., **1**
Posada Colonial, **17**
Posada la Academia, **15**
Villa Juvenil Youth Hostel, **19**

○ 🛈 🏛 SIGHTS
Academia de Bellas Artes, **16**
Casa de la Corregidora, **9**
Convento de la Santa Cruz, **18**
Museo Regional, **11**
Museo de Arte, **12**
Museo de la Ciudad, **6**
Santuario de Nuestra Señora
de Guadalupe, **8**
Teatro de la República, **5**

🍴 FOOD
Café del Fondo, **13**
Cafetería Bisquets
Querétaro, **14**
Ibis Natura
Vegetariana, **7**
La Mariposa, **4**
Restaurante de la Rosa, **3**

🛈 PRACTICAL INFORMATION

Tourist Office: Pasteur Nte. 4 (☎238 5000, ext. 5067; turismo@queretaro.com.mx). Helpful and knowledgeable staff provides maps and event schedules; events and festival information available upstairs. City tours in English, Spanish, and French offered Tu-Su (1hr., 6 per day, 25 pesos). Open daily 9am-8pm.

Currency Exchange: Banks are all over the *centro*. **Banamex** (☎225 3000), on the corner of Juárez and 16 de Septiembre, has a 24hr. **ATM** and changes currency and traveler's checks. Open M-F 9am-5pm, Sa 10am-2pm; exchange window closes by 3pm. **Casa de Cambio,** Corregidora Sur 108 (☎212 8086). Open M-F 9am-5pm, Sa 9am-2pm.

Laundry: Speed Wash, Montes Nte. 42 (☎214 1445). Full-service 10 pesos per kg, 3kg minimum. Dry cleaning available. Open M-F 9am-3pm and 4-8pm, Sa 9am-3pm.

Luggage Storage: In the bus station. 3 pesos per hr.; open daily 6:30am-midnight.

Supermarket: Comercial Mexicana, Zaragoza Pte. 150 (☎216 3357), 7½ blocks west of Corregidora. Take any westbound "Zaragoza" *micro* or walk 20min. Open Su 8am-9pm, M-Sa 8am-10pm.

Mercado: Mercado Hidalgo, on Montes between Hidalgo and Morelos. Small, but full of fresh produce and meat. Inexpensive taco stands (10-15 pesos). Open daily 7am-6pm.

Emergency: ☎066. **LOCATEL** (☎214 3311) finds lost people.

Police: Pie de la Cuesta 112 (☎220 9191), in Colonia Desarrollo San Pablo. No English spoken. The **Ángeles Verdes** (☎213 8424) rescue stranded motorists.

Red Cross: (☎229 0545), at Balaustradas and Circuito Estadio, near the bus station. **Ambulances** (☎229 0505). No English spoken at either.

Pharmacy: Farmacias del Ahorro, Juárez 2 (☎216 1760). Open 7am-11pm.

Hospital: Sanatorio Alcocer Poza, Reforma 23 (☎214 1920), near Corregidora.

Fax: Telecomm, Allende Nte. 4 (☎212 0702; fax 214 3948), west of the *jardín.* Has **telegrams** and **Western Union.** Open M-F 8am-7:30pm, Sa-Su 9am-1pm.

Internet: CNCI, Juárez Sur 68 (☎214 4584). Follow the narrow hallway between the cubicles to get to the *caja* to pay. 20 pesos per hr. Open M-Sa 7am-9pm.

Post Office: Arteaga Pte. 5 (☎212 0112), between Juárez and Allende, 2 blocks south of the *jardín.* Open M-F 8am-5pm, Sa 9am-1pm. **Postal Code:** 76000.

ACCOMMODATIONS

There are several colorful places to lodge near Querétaro's *jardín;* the cheapest are a hike from the *centro.* Call ahead for summer weekends, *Semana Santa* and the end of December: Querétaro is a favorite for Mexico City's weekend warriors.

Hotel del Marqués, Juárez Nte. 104 (☎212 0414 or 212 0554). *Agua purificada* and an enormous stained-glass depiction of Querétaro welcome guests to a sizable reception area. Carpeted, slightly dark rooms have small, clean baths; most with cable TV and phone. Some 2nd fl. rooms have balconies busy Av. Universidad. Parking available. Singles 160 pesos; doubles 200 pesos; triples 220 pesos; quads 240 pesos. ❸

Villa Juvenil Youth Hostel, on Ejército Republicano. Walk east of Juárez on Independencia to Ejército Republicano. On the right is a sports and recreation complex; behind the front offices, the hostel is next to the swimming pool (not open to guests). While a bit remote, it's a bargain and, despite the numerous athletes, space is usually available. No drinking or smoking. Communal bath. Reception 7am-10pm; to stay out later, leave a message at the desk. 20-peso linen deposit. Single sex dorms 30 pesos. ❶

Hotel Hidalgo, Madero Pte. 11 (☎212 8102), just off the *jardín.* A huge courtyard with fountain leads to comfy rooms with small baths and cable TV. Attached restaurant serves tasty, moderately priced food. A large renovation recently encompassed both hotel and restaurant. Singles 240 pesos. Accepts US dollars. ❹

Posada la Academia, Pino Suárez 3 (☎224 2739), close to the *jardín.* Rooms and courtyard are a little run-down, but clean private baths, ceiling fans (which make all the difference on hot summer nights), and cable TV make up for it. Great location for the price. Singles 120 pesos; doubles from 190 pesos; up to 5 people 300 pesos. ❷

Posada Colonial, Juárez 9 (☎212 0239). Rooms sport naked light bulbs and lack windows. Hope for quiet neighbors—some room partitions don't reach the rafters. Bring flip flops for the communal baths. Reception 24hr. Towel deposit 30 pesos. Singles or doubles 100 pesos, with kingsize bed or two beds plus TV 135 pesos, with bathroom 150 pesos. Each additional person 50 pesos. ❶

Hotel R.J., Invierno 21 (☎212 0488), north of Universidad. Not the lap of luxury, but easy on the wallet. Non-smokers may want to sniff their rooms; the suite is airier and well worth the extra 20 pesos. Cheap eats just beyond the hotel. Singles and doubles 100 pesos; suite 120 pesos. 35 pesos for each additional person. ❶

FOOD

Inexpensive restaurants face Jardín Zenea; pricier *loncherías* and outdoor cafes surround nearby Plaza Corregidora. Taco, *torta*, and other fast-food stands line 5 de Mayo and Juárez. Many restaurants stop serving the *menú del día* at 5 or 6pm.

La Mariposa, Peralta 7 (☎212 1166), by the *jardín*. This cafeteria and *pastelería* has been a local favorite for over 60 years. Enjoy various salads (12-32 pesos), *tortas* (18 pesos), or *comida típica* (34-70 pesos) served by impeccable, blue-uniformed, apron-clad waitresses who seem to be from some idealized past. Open daily 8am-9:30pm. ❸

Restaurante de la Rosa, Juárez Nte. 24 (☎212 8784 or 232 9372). Perfectly seasoned Mexican cuisine accompanied by *hacienda*-style decoration. *Enchiladas querétanas* (37 pesos) are a local treat. *Antojitos* 30-44 pesos, *platos fuertes* 22-63 pesos, and a 4-course *menú del día* 30 pesos. Open Su 9am-1pm, M-Sa 9am-7:30pm. ❸

Ibis Natura Vegetariana, Juárez Nte. 47 (☎214 2212), at the *jardín*. Sells vitamins, supplements, and other nutritional products to relieve a meat-wary metabolism. Tasty veggie cheeseburgers (14 pesos), hearty *menú del día* (35 pesos), salads (20-31 pesos) and an enormous selection of flavored yogurt (15 pesos). Open Su-F 8am-9:30pm. ❷

Café del Fondo, Pino Suárez 9 (☎212 0905). This all-ages local hangout boasts an enormous coffee grinder, which produces strong, exotic coffee drinks (10-35 pesos) and the delightful smell of rich coffee done right. Chess games run all day. *Quesadillas* 11 pesos, sandwiches 9 pesos, daily specials 23 pesos. Open daily 7:30am-10pm. ❶

Cafetería Bisquets Querétaro, Pino Suárez 7 (☎214 1481). A huge wooden door welcomes visitors to this popular family restaurant. Plain biscuits 4.5 pesos, with *pollo en mole* 12 pesos. Serves *antojitos* (18-30 pesos), *tortas* (12-30 pesos), salads (23-32 pesos), and a very complete *plato del día* (40-60 pesos). Open daily 7am-11pm. ❸

La Reliquia, Pasteur Nt 10 (☎214 2125). This little restaurant, with wooden tables decorated by grains beneath glass tabletops, caters to young locals. Live music W-F. Breakfast 28-50 pesos; *menú del día* 32 pesos. Open daily 7am-11pm. ❸

SIGHTS

For a break from art exhibits and Churrigueresque churches, Querétaro provides beautiful plazas, parks, and walkways perfect for lazy strolls.

MUSEO REGIONAL. In the **Ex-Convento Franciscano de Santiago** is a beautiful stone courtyard and modern museum. The museum highlights Mexican history with *indígena* artifacts, including a reproduction of a Nanho (a modern indigenous group) chapel: beyond the 4ft. door is an enormous altar. The second floor is dedicated to the Ex-Convent's history; old church music and mammoth audiovisuals wow visitors. (*At Corregidora and Madero, on the east side of the jardín. ☎212 2031. Open Tu-Su 10am-7pm. 32 pesos, students, children under 12, seniors free; Su free.*)

TEATRO DE LA REPÚBLICA. The Teatro recently celebrated its 151st anniversary. In its century and a half, it has borne witness to many decisive events in Mexico's history: the 1867 judgment of Emperor Maximilian, the drafting of the constitution in 1917 in the **Sala de Constituyentes** upstairs, and the 1929 founding of the Partido Nacional de la Revolución (PNR), precursor to today's Partido Revolucionario Institucional (PRI; see p. 69). The theater resembles a European opera house, with four levels of red velvet seating. *Tesoro Turístico*, available in the lobby, lists performances at the theater, including those by the new Philharmonic Orchestra of Querétaro, and other events around town. (*On Peralta, 1 block from the jardín. ☎212 0339. Open Tu-Su 10am-3pm and 5-8pm. Free.*)

CONVENTO DE LA SANTA CRUZ. Built where the Spaniards defeated the Chichimeca Indians, this convent was an integral part of the evangelism movement in Mexico and lower California, and was the first in the Americas to train priests. Nearly everything inside Santa Cruz (built in 1683) is original: the clay pipes and rain-catching system date from the city's aqueduct days, and monks still inhabit the convent. The cell where Maximilian spent his last moments, on the second floor, has been left exactly as it was on the day of his execution. In one courtyard, those so inclined can see bushes with thorns in the shape of crucifixes. A type of mimosa, the bush is known simply as the **Árbol de la Cruz** (Tree of the Cross). According to legend, the thorn bushes grew from a staff planted by a friar. It is said that these are the only trees of this kind in the world; attempts to plant seedlings elsewhere have failed. *(East of Juárez on Independencia. ☎ 212 0235. Open Tu-Sa 9am-2pm and 4-6pm, Su and festival days 9am-4pm. Free, but small donation requested. Courtyard is only accessible during 20 min. tours, in Spanish, English, French, and Italian.)*

SANTUARIO DE NUESTRA SEÑORA DE GUADALUPE. The church's white towers and central dome rise above their surroundings. The stained-glass windows high up let in dim light, and the delicate chandeliers hang against a backdrop of imposing pillars and frescoes that adorn this intricately designed church. The image of *La Guadalupana* is by Miguel Cabrera. *(At Pasteur and 16 de Septiembre. ☎ 212 0732. Open daily 7am-9pm. Mass Su 8, 10am, 2, 7, and 8pm, Tu-Sa 8, 10am, and 8pm.)*

LA ALAMEDA HIDALGO. Built in 1790, the Alameda is a huge park that manages to block out the pressing confusion of the city, making it an ideal spot for a morning jog, romantic rendezvous, or afternoon stroll. *(3 blocks south on Corregidora from the jardín. Entrance on Zaragoza. Open Su-Tu and Th-Sa 8am-7pm.)*

MUSEO DE ARTE DE QUERÉTARO. Housed in an 18th-century Augustinian monastery with a beautiful stone courtyard, the museum's columns are topped with grimacing heads. An exhibit on local architecture sharply contrasts the Baroque paintings. European canvasses, modern Mexican art, and Cristóbal de Villa Pando's 19th-century depictions of the apostles round out the formidable collection. *(Allende Sur 14, between Madero and Pino Suárez, 2 blocks from the jardín. ☎ 212 2357. Open Tu-Su 10am-6pm. 15 pesos, children under 12 and seniors free; Tu free.)*

MUSEO DE LA CIUDAD. This former convent, once the prison of Emperor Maximilian, is now home to religious art and revolving exhibits of contemporary art. *(Guerrero 27, near Hidalgo. ☎ 212 4702 or 224 3756. Open Tu-Su 11am-7pm. 5 pesos, students and children free; Su free.)*

CERRO DE LAS CAMPANAS (HILL OF THE BELLS). Named for the peculiar sound its rocks make as they collide, this hill is where Maximilian surrendered his sword in 1867 before his execution. Directly ahead of the park entrance is the small **chapel** Maximilian's family built and where the emperor and two of his generals were shot. Flowering trees and quiet paths lead the way to an impressive, tree-lined view of Querétaro and a large stone statue of Benito Juárez, who stands proudly over the memorial to his predecessor. Behind the statue is the **Museo del Sitio**, with maps and pictures relating to Maximilian's reign in Mexico. *(Walk north up the jardín on Corregidora and turn left onto Escobedo. Proceed until Escobedo ends at Tecnológico (30min.), take a right and then your 1st left at the park entrance. Or, catch a "Ruta R" bus (5 pesos) on Allende anywhere south of Morelos; enter in front of the statue of Escobedo. Park open daily 7am-6pm. Museum open Tu-F 8am-6pm, Sa-Su 10am-6pm. 1 peso.)*

OTHER SIGHTS. Querétaro's **Acueducto** stretches along de los Arcos, west of the *centro*. This distinctive structure, with 74 arches of pink sandstone and gardens at its base, was constructed in 1735 as a gift to perpetually parched Querétaro from the Marqués de Villas del Águila. A *mirador* overlooks all 1280m of the aqueduct from Republicano, about three blocks past the Convento de la Santa Cruz. Up 5 de Mayo to the east of the *jardín* is the **Plaza de la Independencia (Plaza de Armas),** a monument to the Marqués. Faithful stone dogs surround his statue, drooling respectfully into a fountain. The plaza is bordered by trees, colorful cafes, shaded benches, and beautiful colonial buildings, including the **Casa de la Corregidora,** which housed government officials during colonial times. Today, the Casa is the seat of the state government. **Andador Libertad,** two blocks from the *jardín*, connects Plaza de la Independencia and Corregidora. It is host to a slew of mellow vendors and *artesanía* shops. *(Open Su-M and Th-Sa approximately 10am-9pm.)*

▣ ENTERTAINMENT

The Jardín Zenea is a great place in the *centro* for outdoor activities. Sunday evenings from 6-8pm will find brass band concerts in the gazebo and myriad jugglers, *mariachis,* and magicians perform sporadically. **Jardín de los Platitos,** at Juárez and Universidad, north of the *zócalo,* dances to *mariachi* music. Outdoor theaters are a popular option as well.

NIGHTLIFE

Querétaro has many night clubs popular with locals and visiting 20-somethings from Mexico City. Both the *centro* and the area around Constituyentes and Bernardo Quintana have plenty of options to satisfy late night urges. Remember taxis are more expensive at night. Dress to impress.

La Cantina de los Remedios, Constituyentes 125a (☎248 2350). A Western-style bar door welcomes customers to this wildly decorated *cantina*. Posters of celebrities cover the walls where witty Spanish graffiti has left space; baskets and other crafts hang from the ceiling. The huge bar packs enough liquor to give pause to hardened *charros*. *Botanas* (snacks) 39-105 pesos, *molcajetes* (meat with chiles, tomato, salsa, and beans) 65-105 pesos; beer 27-28 pesos, cocktails 33-43 pesos. Live music 1:30pm-1:30am.

Vazzo, Juárez 30 (☎214 3033), on the west side of the Plaza de la Constitución. The hip place to be for young locals. Huge metal light fixtures and candles the size of cannons light up the covered courtyard sprinkled with black couches and tall tables. Dancing starts late, and people writhe to techno and top-40 anywhere they find space. Beer 18 pesos, drinks from 30 pesos. Cover 50 pesos. Open Th-Sa 9pm-3am.

El Purgatorio, Contituyentes Ote. 127 (☎213 0435). Low ceilings with arched hallways contribute to a dungeon feel, and an energetic crowd seeks redemption in live music from open to closing. This *antro* counts three different themed bars; upstairs flaming letters spell out the name in a more clubby atmosphere. Open W-Sa 8pm-3am.

FESTIVALS

The annual **Feria de Querétaro** usually takes place during the second week of December. The **Feria de Santa Anna,** complete with bulls running through the congested streets, happens on July 26. The whole town dances during the **Celebración de la Santa Cruz de los Milagros** and the **Fiestas Patrias,** which take place during the second or third week of September. Other festivals include the **Feria International del Queso y del Vino** in May or July, a festival commemorating the founding of the city on July 25, and, of course, *Semana Santa* in the week before Easter.

For information about cultural events, stop by the **Casa de la Cultura,** on your right after Carranza splits off from 5 de Mayo. There you can pick up *ACONSE-Jarte,* a comprehensive monthly bulletin including listings on art, dance, theatre, literature, music, and workshops. Alternatively, visit **Querétaro 2000,** a huge stretch of parks and athletic facilities on Quintana. (Take a "Ruta 15" bus from Ocampo or "Ruta B" from Allende. ☎220 6814. Open daily 6am-8pm.)

HIDALGO

PACHUCA   ☎771

Despite its proximity to Mexico City, Hidalgo's capital (pop. 220,000) is not used to tourists; while this does limit its attraction for sight-seers, it also makes it all the more refreshing. The *zócalo*, with it's Reloj Monumental, is absolutely gorgeous, and the heritage of Spanish settlers and English miners has left a unique (and in some cases quite tasty) mark. Nearby small towns and the Chico National Forest provide escape from the bustle of even this city.

⌨ TRANSPORTATION. Pachuca is approximately 90km northeast of Mexico City on **Mex. 85.** The bus station is a fair distance from downtown. Frequent *combis* run from the station to Plaza de la Constitución and the *zócalo* (Plaza de la Independencia; 6am-10pm, 2.5 pesos). From the bus station, **ADO** (☎713 2910) goes to: Mexico City's **Cien Metros** (1¼hr.; every 15min. M-F 4:45am-10:15pm, Sa-Su 5:45am-10:15pm; 44 pesos); **Poza Rica** (4½hr.; 8:20am, noon, 3, 8:45pm; 94 pesos); **Tuxpan** (6hr., 8:20am-8:45pm, 124 pesos). **Flecha Roja** (☎713 2471) goes to: **Mexico City** (1¼hr., every 10min. 4am-10pm, 40 pesos). **Estrella Blanca** (☎713 2747) goes to **Mexico City** (2hr., every 15min. 5:30am-10pm, 40 pesos) and **Querétaro** (4½hr., every hr. 5:15am-6:15pm, 114 pesos).

▟▐ ORIENTATION AND PRACTICAL INFORMATION. Finding one's way can be difficult, as many streets curve and change names. Be prepared to ask for directions. Pachuca's *zócalo* is **Plaza de la Independencia.** Facing the Reloj Monumental, the Plaza is bordered by **Matamoros** on the right and **Allende** on the left. **Guerrero** is parallel to Allende, one block to the left. Matamoros and Allende converge a few blocks away from the Reloj at **Plaza Juárez,** which has two parts: an open cement space with a statue of the man himself and a small park. **Av. Juárez** juts from the statue's base, while **Revolución** extends from the park.

Pachuca's **tourist office** is at the bottom of the clock tower in the *zócalo*. The staff responds to specific queries. (☎715 1411. Open M-F 9am-5pm, Sa-Su 10am-6pm.) The Plaza is filled with banks offering **currency exchange** and **ATMs. Mercado Juárez** lies on the north side of Plaza de la Constitución. Other services include: **emergency** service (☎060); **police** (☎711 1880), in Plaza Juárez; **Red Cross** (☎714 1720); **IMSS** (☎713 7833), off Madero, far from downtown; ubiquitous **Internet access; post office,** Juárez at Iglesias, two blocks south of Plaza Juárez (☎713 2592; open M-F 8am-5pm). **Postal code:** 42070.

▛▐ ACCOMMODATIONS AND FOOD. Hotel de los Baños ❸, Matamoros 205, right on the *zócalo*, is the best deal from M-W, when it offers discounts. (☎713 0700. M-W singles 156 pesos, with king 224 pesos; doubles 188-228 pesos; triples 212 pesos. Th-Su singles 195 pesos, with king 280 pesos; doubles 235-285 pesos; triples 265 pesos.) Fewer than two blocks south of the *zócalo* is **Hotel Noriega ❸,** Matamoros 305. Noriega is a little worn, but has large private baths. (☎715 1555. Singles 150 pesos, with TV 160 pesos; doubles 170 pesos/190 pesos; triples 200 pesos/230 pesos.) A bit farther away, **Hotel América ❷,** 3 de Victoria 203, is standard and cheap. (☎715 0055. Singles 100 pesos, with bath 150 pesos, with king 200 pesos; doubles 200 pesos.)

Although most of the hotels contain restaurants, a better option are the little stores that sell *pastes*. Locals agree that the place to go is mini-chain **Pastes Kikos ❶,** with locations on the *zócalo* and in Plaza Juárez (*pastes* 3.5 pesos). **La Luz Roja**

❶, at the corner of Guerrero, in the *portal* next to Plaza Juárez facing the statue's left shoulder, is a bit cramped due to immense popularity. Try the delicious *pozole* or *morelianos*, both 22 pesos. (Open daily 10am-8:15pm.)

▣ **SIGHTS.** Pachuca's **Reloj Monumental**, 40m high in the Neoclassical style, dominates the *zócalo*. Construction began in 1904 by the same manufacturers who built London's Big Ben, but was stopped a year later due to a shortage of funds. When it was finally completed in 1907, it cost a total of 300,000 pesos, paid in gold. Four female statues on the third level represent the Independence of 1810, the Liberty of 1821, the Constitution of 1857, and the Reform of 1859. To reach **Archivo Histórico y Museo de Minería**, Mina 110, walk one block past the *zócalo* on Matamoros and take the first left onto Mina. Follow it for 1½ blocks. A former mining company office, the museum holds a notable collection of rocks, minerals, mining tools, and heavy machinery. (☎715 0976. Open W-Su 10am-2pm and 3-6pm. 15 pesos, teachers and students 10 pesos, miners and ex-miners free. Video in English and Spanish at 11am, noon, 1, 4, 5pm.)

The **Centro Cultural Hidalgo** is in the **Ex-Convento de San Francisco**. To get there from the *zócalo*, take Matamoros south of the square for one block, turn left on Mina, take it for two blocks, and turn right on Hidalgo (not to be confused with Viaducto Hidalgo). After three blocks you'll be in front of the *centro*. The cultural center contains the **Museo Nacional de la Fotografía**, which surveys the technological history of photography as well as displaying historical Mexican photographs from the end of the 18th century on, including photos by the famous artist Tina Modotti and others. (☎714 3653. Open Tu-Su 10am-6pm. Free.) Across from the museum is the **Museo Regional de Hidalgo**, a small museum which holds temporary exhibits. (Open Tu-Su 10am-6pm. Free.) Adjoining the cultural center is the **Church of San Francisco**. One block past the Ex-Convento is **Parque Hidalgo**, a favorite hangout for local teens. On the way to the Centro Cultural, you will pass by the **Museo Archivo Histórico del Exposición Fotografía**, which puts up temporary exhibits on the history of Pachuca from its huge collection of archives. (☎715 3046. Open M-F 8am-4:30pm. Free.)

NEAR PACHUCA: MINERAL DEL CHICO

Combis run to Mineral del Chico (40min., every 30min. 7:30am-7:30pm, 7.5 pesos). They leave from Galeana; follow Guerrero north of the zócalo and make a left on Galeana, then head uphill about 2 blocks. The stop is unmarked, and so are some of the combis, though drivers desperate for a full car are hard to miss.

Forty minutes of winding mountain roads separate Pachuca from the tiny town of Mineral del Chico (pop. 500). Nestled in **Parque Nacional el Chico**, the town has a few small convenience stores, small restaurants selling either tacos or *pastes*, a small church, and some houses. Numerous hikes and striking views of nearby rock formations make it a great escape from urban congestion. Follow the road that runs uphill to the right from the *combi* stop to reach the spectacular vista point, **Peña del Cuervo** (6km). Turn left at the church and follow the winding road up to the rock formation, dubbed **Tres Monjas** (3km) due to its resemblance to nuns bowed in prayer. On the way there, turn right at the dirt road alongside the **Río del Milagro**, which meanders past old entrances to mines, up past the ruins to the once-glorious **Hacienda de Plan Corande**; 100m from the beginning of the road, cabins are offered for rent (☎5273 3253). Past that you can either go right to the **Unión de Dos Ríos**, or left to the **Trucha Poderosa**, which houses the **Mina del Dios Poderoso**. Tourists will soon be allowed to enter the old mine, which dates back to 1790. The trail goes on for miles and it is easy to just keep walking—remember that you will have to turn around and go back.

CENTRAL MEXICO

NEAR PACHUCA: MINERAL DEL MONTE

Catch a "Mineral del Monte" combi in front of the Iglesia de la Asunción, on the corner of Carranza and Villigran, near the east side of Plaza de la Constitución (5 pesos).

Mineral del Monte (pop. 10,600), 9km north of Pachuca, is a quiet town with brightly painted houses and small stores. **Mina Acosta,** on Guerrero, north of Plaza Principal (20min.), is a relic of Mineral's mining history. This mine passed through the hands of Spanish, English, Mexican, and US owners before finally coming under government control. The building on your left as you enter housed mine managers. The obsidian shards that line the tops of the walls surrounding the mine kept silver robbers out. (Open W-Su 10am-5pm. 20 pesos, students and teachers 12 pesos, miners and ex-miners free.)

Mineral del Monte offers good hiking and climbing opportunities. *Combis* depart from La Madre in front of Deportivo de la Ciudad, a.k.a the Escuela Primaria, for **Peñas Cargadas** (every hr. 6am-5pm; 5 pesos), a massive rock formation up in the hills. At the site, **Cargada Mayor,** on your left, is 100m tall. To its right is **Cargada Menor,** a mere 80m. Next to Menor stands **El Pilón** (70m), and on the far right, **Cerrote** (30m). Many hiking paths weave through the area which, due to its isolation, can be dangerous. **You should not attempt to go alone. Only very experienced rock climbers should attempt to scale the rocks (crosses at the bottom mark spots where several have met their deaths).** Interested climbers should contact **Lucio Ramírez** (Club Alpino, Lerdo de Tejada 4 in Mineral del Monte) or stop by **Club Alpino's** headquarters in Deportivo de la Ciudad. (Climbing excursions Su 7am. Open Su 7am-7:30pm.)

TULA ☎ 778

Tula (pop. 27,500) is a little town with one main attraction: one of the most important archaeological sites in Mesoamerica. Travelers usually come for the day (Mexico City is an 80km jaunt, and Pachuca is only 75km away), but Tula is a quiet, relaxing, and frankly quite pretty town with a unique *zócalo*—brightly painted in orange, blue, and white—and well-kept, economical hotels.

▚ TRANSPORTATION AND PRACTICAL INFORMATION

From Mexico City to Tula, take an **AVM** (☎737 9691) bus from Central de Autobuses del Norte, Sala 8 (1½hr., every 40min. 7am-9pm, 39 pesos). Once in Tula, to reach the *zócalo* from the **bus station** (☎732 0225), head toward the cathedral, visible from most of the city. AVM (☎732 0118) runs to **Mexico City** (2hr., every 20min. 6am-8pm, 30 pesos) and **Pachuca** (2hr., every hr. 4:20am-8:30pm, 35 pesos). **Flecha Amarilla** (☎732 0225) goes to: **Guanajuato** (5hr., 10:15am, 165 pesos); **Morelia** (6hr., 8am, 157 pesos); **Querétaro** (2½hr., 3:45am-7:30pm, 80 pesos).

Banks (with **currency** and **traveler's check exchange** and **ATMs**), **pharmacies,** and **Internet** cafes are easy to find throughout the city. **Police** (☎733 2049) are at 5 de Mayo 408. For **Red Cross,** call ☎732 1250. **LADATELs** are near the bus station and on Zaragoza and Hidalgo.

▚ ACCOMMODATIONS AND FOOD

Despite the dearth of overnight tourists in Tula, the hotels are a pleasant surprise; although spare, they are a good deal and in great shape. **Hotel Catedral ❸,** Zaragoza 106, next to the cathedral, has small, pretty rooms with cable TV. (☎732 0813, fax 732 3632. Singles 160 pesos; doubles 205 pesos; triples 250 pesos; quads 295 pesos.) **Hotel Casa Blanca ❷,** Pasaje Hidalgo 11, has been remodeled recently.

(☎732 1186 or 732 3223; casablancatul@yahoo.com.mx. Singles 140 pesos, with TV 180 pesos; doubles 200 pesos/240 pesos; triples 280/320 pesos.) Budget rooms don't come easy in Tula. The best deal in town is the **Auto Hotel Cuéllar ❸**, 5 de Mayo 23. Rooms come in two varieties: regular and more comfortable. The regular rooms are nice, and all have TVs and private baths. (☎732 0170 or 732 0442; hotel-cuellar@prodigy.net.mx. Regular singles 190 pesos, upgrade 250 pesos; doubles 210 pesos/300 pesos; triples 375 pesos/400 pesos; quads 420 pesos/490 pesos.) Good, cheap food is cooked right in front of your eyes in the **market ❶** behind the cathedral. (*Comida corrida* 20 pesos. Open daily 6am-8pm.) **Restaurante Casa Blanca ❹**, Hidalgo 114, is a nice sit-down restaurant that offers a Gran Buffet (89 pesos, children 63 pesos) or entrees for 29-119 pesos. (☎732 2274. Open Su 8am-7pm, M-Sa 8am-8:45pm.)

🔘 THE ARCHAEOLOGICAL SITE OF TULA

Taxis will take you from the sitio stand on Zaragoza and Hidalgo in town. ☎732 0565. (20 pesos.) Frequent peseros return to the bus station or centro (3 pesos). You can also walk (30min.). From the bus station, turn right on Ocampo and follow signs to the archaeological zone. Open daily 10am-5pm. 32 pesos, children under 13 free; Su free.

Tula's importance in Pre-Hispanic Mexico cannot be overstated. It is the first town in northern Mesoamerica with historical records. Settled and occupied by various small nomadic tribes during the Pre-Classic and Classic Periods, it is thought to have come under the sway of powerful Teotihuacán. In the late Classic Period, however, the area was abandoned and then resettled by a different group—the Toltec-Chichimeca (more commonly, the Toltec). By the early Post-Classic Period (AD 900-1200), the Toltec capital entered a period known as the Tollán phase, marked by construction and expansion. New pyramids arose, the city was carefully realigned, and the population peaked at around 40,000. A close resemblance in architecture between Tula and the Post-Classic Maya center at Chichén Itzá (see p. 641) has led archaeologists to hypothesize on some relationship between the two, perhaps through trade or conquest. The Toltecs, whose name means "builders" in Náhuatl, relied heavily on irrigation and modeled their architecture after the style of Teotihuacán. When crop failures and droughts weakened the capital in 1165, neighboring Chichimecas sacked the city, burning temples and destroying much of what the Toltecs had built. The devastated city went through another ravaging when the Aztecs later occupied and looted it. Today, among the Toltec remains, the Aztecs' temporary stay is evident in bits of scattered Aztec ceramics and pottery. Unfortunately, the ruins as they stand provide little testament to the Toltec's power—not all of the ruins have been excavated, and the ones that have are not in the best shape.

JUEGO DE PELOTA #1 (BALL COURT #1). From the entrance area, a 600m dirt path zigzags past cacti through two sets of vendor stalls before arriving at the main plaza. The first structure to the right as you reach the main plaza is Ball Court #1, just north of the large Edificio de los Atlantes. The court is 67m long and 12.5m wide. Part of a stone decorated with a depiction of a ball player was found here, but now only the feet are visible, on display in the museum. The public sat atop the plaform to watch the game in the I-shaped court below.

EDIFICIO DE LOS ATLANTES (PYRAMID B). To the left lies the monumental Edificio de los Atlantes, Tula's most impressive and best-preserved building. In front of the pyramid stand three rows of 14 columns, which presumably supported some sort of walkway leading to the pyramid. On top of the pyramid are the Atlantes, column-shaped statues of warriors, which originally supported a temple and altar dedicated to Quetzalcóatl. Close inspection of the statues (each a whopping

9.6m tall) at the top of the pyramid reveals traces of red pigment. Standing on the platform you have a great view of the site and also the surrounding courtyside. The sides of the pyramid were decorated with reliefs of jaguars, coyotes, eagles, and feathered serpents, each symbolizing different classes of warriors.

EL COATEPANTLI (THE WALL OF SNAKES). On the side of the Atlantes closest to Ball Court I lies El Coatepantli, the wall of snakes. In Mesoamerican religion, walls generally mark the limits of sacred space and ceremonial enclosures. Reliefs of giant rattlesnakes devouring humans relate to the practice of human sacrifice and the conch shells represent Quetzalcóatl as the planet Venus. These walls are the prototypes of those later built by the Aztecs.

PALACIO QUEMADO (BURNT PALACE). The name of this building (to the left facing the front of Atlantes) is only half truth. It was indeed destroyed by a fire, but it was not a *palacio;* rather an administrative center for government advisors. In the central room, a perfectly preserved *chac mool* was found, and is now exhibited in the museum. In other areas of the building were found offerings of conch shells, turquoise, and what appears to be a storeroom of ceramics and other materials.

TEMPLO PRINCIPAL (PYRAMID C). The Toltecs built their largest building, Templo (or Edificio) Principal, on the eastern boundary of the plaza facing sunrise. Deliberately destructed by the Chichimecas and others following Tula's abandonment at the end of the 12th century, Templo Principal now pales in comparison to Edificio de los Atlantes. Not fully excavated and overgrown with weeds, Templo Principal cannot be scaled from the front—you must scramble up a steep path on the side closest to Atlantes. Tula's main religious building, the temple was likely adorned with a massive sculptural slab found nearby that is covered with images of Quetzalcóatl in his manifestation as Tlahuizcaltec Uhtli, "the morning star."

EL ADORATORIO. In front of Pyramid C lies small El Adoratorio (the shrine), with two distinct stages of construction detected. The original platform of the shrine measured 8.5m on each side. It is thought that the shrine has been looted extensively since the Pre-Hispanic era; on its top, a shattered *chac mool* was found.

EL JUEGO DE PELOTA II. This ball court was discovered in an extreme state of disrepair. Originally the walls were covered with sculpted stone and the court had a decorative ring of rock embedded in each side; only a small fragment of the ring, which rests on a small altar in the northeastern corner of the exterior facade, is preserved. This altar was probably used for ceremonies or sacrifices associated with the game. The Aztecs made a series of modifications to the original plan, making the court smaller and inside the old Toltec ruins. Later, a steam bath was built on top of it.

ESTADO DE MÉXICO

VALLE DE BRAVO   ☎ 726

From the mountain views at the end of every cobblestone street to the luscious fruit sold in the market by traditionally clad *indígenas,* everything about this 16th-century town is perfect. Even the stray dogs look well-fed (well, maybe not). Wealthy Mexico City residents keep vacation homes on the edges of Valle, and though new business has made the town wealthy, it retains a cozy, traditional feel. This is not accidental; in 1972 Valle was declared a "typical town," and among other restrictions, construction on new buildings was strictly curtailed. You don't come to Valle to "do," rather to wander and marvel at the beauty of it all.

■ ⚏ ORIENTATION AND TRANSPORTATION. To get to the *centro* from Valle's bus station, turn right as you exit, walk downhill one block, and make a right on Zaragoza. Continue for two blocks until you see Centro Comercial Isseymym, and turn left. You will see the large church of San Francisco de Asisi at the end of the street. The **market** is one block before the church on the right. To the right of the church, as you face it, is **Plaza Independencia. 5 de Mayo** runs in front of the church, and **Toluca** is the street on the opposite side of the plaza, becoming **Bocanegra** as it continues uphill. Intersecting Toluca and 5 de Mayo is **Pagaza.** Second-class **buses** leave for **Mexico City** (3hr., every 20min. 6am-6pm, 68 pesos) via **Toluca** (2hr., 38 pesos). Tickets are sold in the booth out front; last bus leaves town at 8pm.

⚏ PRACTICAL INFORMATION. Bancomer, across from the church, changes currency or checks and has a 24hr. **ATM.** (☎262 1328. Open M-F 8:30am-4pm.) Other services include: **emergency** service (☎060); **police,** Díaz 200 (☎262 1843); **Red Cross,** on the corner of Jiménez and de la Cuenca (☎262 0391; some English spoken); **tourist office** inside the Palacio Municipal, with booths out front, by the lake, and in the Mercado de Artesanías (all open daily 9am-4pm); **Farmacia Farmapronto,** Arcadio Pagaz 100, in front of the plaza and facing the church (☎262 1441; open daily 8am-10pm); **Computel,** Plaza de la Independencia 6 (☎262 6481; open 7am-9pm); **Café Internet/Videoclub,** Plaza de la Independencia 3, two doors from Computel (☎262 5126; open daily 9am-10pm; 15 pesos per hr.); **post office,** Pagaza 200 (☎262 03 73; open M-F 9am-4pm, Sa 9am-1pm). **Postal code:** 51200.

⚏⚏ ACCOMMODATIONS AND FOOD. Posada Mary ❹, Pl. Independencia 1, has a prime location across from the *jardín,* plus relatively affordable prices and clean, comfortable rooms with sturdy wood furniture. The one single with a balcony facing the plaza is the catch of the lot. (☎262 4261. Singles 230 pesos; doubles 300 pesos; family 400 pesos; cable TV 40 pesos extra, free in singles.) **Posada Familiar ❷,** 16 de Septiembre 417, is about two blocks from the bus station. Look for the "Hotel Interior" sign on the left. Spacious yellow rooms with wood detail, clean blue-tile baths, and TV go for a hefty price, but rooms are not cheap in Valle. The courtyard is pleasantly decorated with fruit trees, which add nicely to a relaxed air. (☎262 1222. Singles 250 pesos; doubles 350 pesos; triples 500 pesos.) The well-kept stone courtyard and fountain at **Posada Doris ❺,** 16 de Septiembre 415, are free, but the rooms are pricey here too. Vibrant colors and comfortable wood furniture go well with the immaculate rooms. (☎262 2182. Singles and doubles 500 pesos; triples 550 pesos.)

Restaurants in this town vary widely by cuisine and price. The nicer places surround the *jardín,* in the shade of *los portales* (the imposing arches). The spaciousness, traditional decoration, and *boleros* in the background of **El Restaurante Portada ❸,** Plaza de la Independencia 101, create a charming atmosphere. Upstairs, a terrace overlooks the plaza. The *sopa de tortilla,* a *plato típico* in Valle, is especially good. (☎262 3383. Entrees 24-85 pesos, *antojitos* 40 pesos. Open daily 8am-11pm.) The attached, second-floor **Paletería La Michoacana ❷** lies through an unassuming door on a great terrace overlooking the plaza. The *paletas* (popsicles; 10 pesos) and ice creams (8, 16, or 24 pesos) come in several flavors, including—try it at your peril—tequila. At **Café Herencia ❷,** Pagoza 100, beaming staff serve fresh, delectable *tortas* (10-18 pesos) and burgers along with several *platos principales* (20-30 pesos). Old black-and-white photos show how little the town has changed in fifty years. (☎262 2790. Coffee 15 pesos, beer 10 pesos. Open Su-Tu and Th-Sa 11am-10pm.) A short walk from the plaza can save you a few pesos: stop at a hole in the wall between the bus station and the *centro* or track down food vendors at the Mercado Municipal, three blocks from the church on Independencia.

◙ SIGHTS. The huge **San Francisco de Asís Church,** which marks the center of town, dwarfs everything around it. A good place to lose yourself for the day or a few hours is the **Mercado de Artesanías,** five blocks down Bocanegra from the *jardín,* left on Durango for two blocks, then right on Juárez. Anything and everything that can be made of wood and clay is available here. Begun in 1985 as a way to preserve native Orcondo artistic traditions, the *mercado* has been a successful attraction ever since. Some traditional works include glazed pottery of every color and finely detailed wood and clay. Prices are somewhat high. (Open daily 10:30am-7pm.)

IXTAPAN DE LA SAL   ☎721

Although being greeted by energetic vendors dying to get you to buy a new *traje de baño* (bathing suit) is kind of disconcerting, just wait for the small town of Ixtapan de la Sal (pop. 17,000) to speak for itself. Past the touristy water park, fancy resorts, and myriad of small hotels, the town is peaceful and charming. It is safe, clean, relaxing, and overall just a wonderful place. In the evening people of every age hang out in the beautiful central plaza, and on the weekends they go off to the themed discos. Ixtapan de la Sal may be forgotten by history books, but pleasant memories will last forever.

⊟ TRANSPORTATION. The **bus station** is actually in Tonatico, a small town just to the south of Ixtapan. Buses usually stop in front of Ixtapan's water park before proceeding to the station. Only a short walk from the center of town, the park is a much more convenient place to disembark (provided you haven't stowed anything under the bus). It also gives you a great chance to see the town. If you get off at the bus station, take an "Ixtapan" *combi* (3.5 pesos). To leave town, you'll have to go to the bus terminal (catch a bus either at the resorts or on Juárez, taxis 20 pesos). **Tres Estrellas de Centro** (☎141 1005) sends buses to: **Mexico City** (express 2hr.; every hr. 6am-6pm, Sa-Su also at 4:30, 5:30, 6:30, and 7pm; 70 pesos. Regular 3hr., every 15min. 3:30-7:40pm, 63 pesos); **Taxco** (1hr., every 40min. 6:10am-7:35pm, 35 pesos); **Toluca** (1hr., every 20min. 5:30am-8pm, 34 pesos); and other locations. **Flecha Roja** (☎141 1005) goes second-class to: **Acapulco** (6hr., 3 per day, 150 pesos); **Taxco** (1¼hr., 30 pesos); **Cuernavaca** (3hr., 6 per day 8am-6pm, 40-45 pesos) and other locations. The buses going to Mexico City will say just "Mexico."

◪⚑ ORIENTATION AND PRACTICAL INFORMATION. Ixtapan's main street is **Juárez,** which ends after 500m at the spa, water park, and resorts. Running parallel to Juárez, to the right while looking toward the resorts, is **Allende.** Some of the main streets perpendicular to Juárez, listed starting from the resorts, are **Constitución, Aldama, 16 de Septiembre, Independencia,** and **20 de Noviembre.** There is no tourist office, but maps of the town are available at the bus station. **Banco Santander** and **Bancomer** both exchange currency and have ATMs; Bancomer also has a **Western Union** (both are on Allende, past the *balneario,* and both are open daily 9am-4pm). Other services include: **luggage storage** in the bus station (3.5 pesos per day; open daily 7am-8pm); **police** on Carretera Federal; **Red Cross,** Carretera Federal next to the police station (☎143 1005; some English spoken); **fax** and **Internet** access easily found throughout the town; **post office,** on 16 de Septiembre, two blocks from the church. (☎143 0223. Open M-F 9am-4pm, Sa 9am-1pm.) **Postal code:** 51900.

⌂▢ ACCOMMODATIONS AND FOOD. If you avoid obscenely priced resorts and spas, Ixtapan has some great deals. **◪Hotel María Isabel ❸,** Kiss 11, is the best bargain. To get there from Juárez, facing the resorts turn right on 20 de Noviembre, take the first right onto Matamoros, and then the first left. The hotel is in the middle of the block on the right and has impeccable rooms, baths, cable TVs with remotes, and a top-floor sun deck. (☎143 0102. 100 pesos per person, 170 pesos with 3 meals.) **Casa de Huéspedes Sofía ❷**, 20 de Noviembre 4, off Juárez, is down one block on 20 de Noviembre. Pink walls, cable TV, fluffy bedspreads, and large baths with purple fixtures reward guests. (☎143 1851. Singles 150 pesos; doubles 300 pesos; triples 400 pesos.) Pleasant **Casa de Huéspedes Francis ❶**, Obregón 6, near the church, has large two-bed rooms, a little worn, but comfortable and clean. (80 pesos per person, 100 pesos with TV.)

Although *taquerías* are easy to find, there are not very many sit-down restaurants around. The snack bar in the bandstand in the *centro* is a great place to grab a *torta* (12 pesos). If you do want a restaurant, **Chimbombo ❷**, on the corner of Juárez and 16 de Septiembre, offers great atmosphere, great food, and great prices. Tacos 8 pesos, *tortas* 12 pesos, *enchiladas* 30 pesos. (☎143 1467. Open Tu-Su 7pm-midnight). **Pepe's Pizza and Pasta ❷**, on the corner of Juárez and Aldama, is a pizzeria with a Mexican flair (in other words, they also serve tacos). Pizzas start at 22 pesos, pastas at 14 pesos. (☎143 1115. Open daily noon-10pm.) **Panificadora Ixtapan ❶**, Obregón 101, near Allende, sells freshly-baked hot bread (1 peso per roll) as well as various *panes dulces*. (☎143 0654. Open daily 7am-9:30pm.)

◎ SIGHTS. Most people visit Ixtapan to enjoy the massive water park/spa/thermal springs complex named **Ixtapan**, at the end of Juárez. (☎143 3000; www.ixtapan.com. Open M-F 7am-7pm, Sa-Su 7am-8pm. Water park open daily 10am-6pm. 140 pesos, children .9-1.3 meters 60 pesos, children under .9 meters free. Lockers 5 pesos, *vestidores* 10 pesos, *cabinas* 15 pesos. Horses are also available for rent in front of the park. 50 pesos per 30min. and 100 pesos per hr.) The park also offers facial massages with mud (75 pesos), facial mud packs (35 pesos), mud shampoos (30 pesos), and hot mud packs (30 pesos). For a less expensive dip in soothing thermal waters, go to the **balneario** in town at the corner of Allende and 20 de Noviembre. Splurge on a massage (130 pesos per 25min.) or mud mask. (Entrance 40 pesos, children under 12 25 pesos. Open daily 7am-6pm.) To reach **Plaza de los Mártires**, facing the water park turn right off Juárez onto Independencia and continue straight three or four blocks. The plaza is a bright, beautiful combination of old and new architecture with a school on one end, a government building on the other, and little shops in between. A picturesque bandstand with a snackbar at its base is in the middle of the plaza. An obelisk-like monument dedicated to the martyrs of the Revolution stands at the side of the **Santuario de la Asunción de Maria**, a striking white church with mauve and rust trim. Inlaid mosaic benches surround the garden, while gold ornamentation, stained-glass windows, and murals adorn the interior. A glass case holds a silver Christ in adjoining **Capilla de la Santísima y del Señor del Perdón**. (Open daily 6am-8pm, office open M-F 10am-2pm and 6-8pm, Sa-Su 10am-2pm.)

TOLUCA ☎722

Toluca ("Those who bow their heads" in Náhuatl) was a thriving Pre-Hispanic center until its conquest by Hernán Cortés. Officially declared a city in 1799, Toluca became the capital of the Estado de México in 1846. Today, old-timers wistfully recall the old Toluca, before industry rapidly expanded, traffic congestion and pollution became serious problems, and the heavy hand of capitalism slapped the town with ungainly billboards. Despite these changes, a lingering small-town atmosphere and incredible cultural attractions still charm visitors.

▐ TRANSPORTATION

The **bus terminal** is tucked between Paseo Tollocan and Berriozabal, southeast of the *centro*. Buses run back and forth from the *centro* to the terminal. To return, board a "Terminal" bus (4 pesos) on Juárez north of Independencia. **Taxis** make the jaunt for 20-30 pesos. **Flecha Roja** serves **Mexico City** (1 hr., every 5min. 4:40am-8:30pm, 30 pesos) and **Querétaro** (3½hr., every 20min. 5am-9pm, 95 pesos). **Naucalpan** goes to Mexico City's Metro stop Torero (1½hr, every 6 min. 5am-9pm, 33 pesos). **Herradura de Plata** (☎217 0024) heads for **Morelia** (4hr., every hr. 6:15am-7:15pm, 160 pesos) and other destinations. **Tres Estrellas** serves: **Cuernavaca** (2½hr., every 30min. 5am-7:45pm, 47 pesos); **Ixtapan** (1hr., every 20min. 6am-8:15pm, 34 pesos); **Taxco** (2½hr., every 40min. 6:20am-6:20pm, 66 pesos); and other destinations.

▟ ▞ ORIENTATION AND PRACTICAL INFORMATION

Paseo Tollocan connects Toluca to Mexico City. The *zócalo*, cathedral, and *portales* constitute the *centro* and are bounded by **Hidalgo** on the south, **Lerdo de Tejada** on the north, **Juárez** on the east, and **Bravo** on the west. **Independencia** parallels Hidalgo one block to the north and forms the south side of the *zócalo*. **Morelos** runs parallel to Hidalgo one block to the south. A word of warning: address numbers on Hidalgo increase in either direction from the center of the *portales*. Most of Toluca's attractions are a short walk from the *portales;* big blue signs marked "M" for museum point the way.

Tourist Office: Urawa 100, Ste. 110 (☎212 6048 or 800 849 1333), at Paseo Tollocan, 6 blocks northeast of the bus station in the large yellow municipal government building behind Wal-Mart. Take any "Wal-Mart" bus. Open M-F 9am-6pm.

Currency Exchange: Bancomer (☎214 3700), on the corner of Juárez and Hidalgo, has a 24hr. **ATM.** Open M-F 8:30am-4pm.

Luggage Storage: In the bus terminal. 5 pesos per hr. Open daily 7am-9pm.

Markets: Mercado 16 de Septiembre, Manuel Gómez Pedraza between Ignacio Rayón and Sor Juana Inés de la Cruz, 2 blocks uphill from the Cosmovitral (see Sights below). Open Su 8am-6:30pm, M-Sa 8am-7:30pm. **Mercado Juárez,** behind the bus station on Fabela. Open daily 8am-6:30pm.

Supermarket: Gigante (☎215 9400), Juárez at Instituto Literario. Open daily 8:30am-10pm.

Emergency: ☎060 or call **LOCATEL** (☎213 3183).

Police: Morelos 1300 (☎214 9352).

Red Cross: (☎217 2540 or 3333), Jesús Carranza, southwest of the *centro,* 1 block south of Paseo Tollocan and 1 block west of Paseo Colón. No English spoken.

Pharmacy: Well-represented throughout town.

Medical Care: IMSS, Paseo Tollocan 620 (☎217 0733), 5 blocks from the bus station. Some English spoken.

Internet Access: Readily available, with good rates.

Fax: Telecomm (☎217 0774), in bus station.

Post office: Hidalgo 300 (☎214 9068), 2 blocks east of Juárez. Open M-F 8am-3pm, Sa 9am-1pm. **Postal code:** 50141.

ACCOMMODATIONS

Inexpensive hotels occupy prime real estate amid the museums and restaurants of the *centro*, but Toluca's budget accommodations have little to offer besides location. With a less than buzzing nightlife, you might spend more time than you want to in a hotel.

Hotel San Nicolás, Bravo 105 (☎214 7196), one block off of Hidalgo. Nice, clean, and cheap. What more could you want? Singles 140 pesos, with TV 170 pesos; doubles with TV 200 pesos. Additional person 10 pesos in singles, 20 pesos in doubles. ❷

Hotel Alpez, Ascencio 200 (☎214 8619), 2 blocks away from Hidalgo. A nice little hotel. Private baths are clean but small. Not overflowing with niceties, but the price is right. Singles 115 pesos, with TV 130 pesos; doubles with TV 235 pesos. ❷

Hotel La Casa del Abuelo, Hidalgo 404 (☎213 3642). Pretty, pink, clean and with a TV in every room. Singles 225 pesos; matrimonials 250 pesos; king size 350 pesos; penthouse 450 pesos. ❹

Hotel Maya, Hidalgo 413 (☎214 4800), a few blocks west of the *centro*. Small and quirky. A small single will leave you in a room with metal walls through which you can hear all your neighbors. A double is much more private and has much better ambience. Communal bathrooms. For safety, the doors are locked at midnight, so plan your night accordingly. Singles 70 pesos; doubles 100 pesos; triples 150 pesos. ❶

FOOD

Restaurants and cheap stalls clutter the storefronts of the *portales*. *Chorizo* (spicy sausage), a local specialty, is served with everything—from *queso fundido* (melted cheese) to *tortas*. Traditional candies include *palanquetas* (peanut brittle), candied fruits, and *dulces de leche* (milk sweets). *Panaderías* on Hidalgo make delicious sweet breads, good for breakfasts or light snacks.

Café Hidalgo, Hidalgo 231A, (☎215 2793). A full menu with great breakfast (30-42 pesos) and filling *comida corrida* (34 pesos) makes this cute cafe a very good place to eat. Open Tu-Sa 6:30-10pm. ❸

Café Dalí, Villada 108A, less than a block south of the *portales*. This cozy cafe is a great place to sip coffee (6-15 pesos) or beer (12 pesos). Pie, *tortas,* donuts, and *cuernitos* (8-18 pesos) are on hand to satisfy any late-night cravings. A neon jukebox plays Latin tunes. Open M-Sa noon-1am. ❷

Café Zodiac, Hidalgo 218. Relax with a sandwich (23-48 pesos) and coffee (15-39 pesos) in this intimate bar-cafe. Around 9pm, live shows entertain an all-ages crowd, including families. Open Tu-Su 6:30pm-11pm. ❸

SIGHTS

Toluca hosts a number of museums which, though small, are excellent and unique. All are organized and maintained by the **Centro Cultural Mexiquense,** which keeps everything smooth and well run.

COMOVITRAL AND JARDÍN BOTÁNICO. For sheer dazzle, few buildings can match this. Built in 1909, this steel Art Nouveau structure housed a market until 1975. In 1980, after a year of design by the artist Leopoldo Flores and four years of work by a team of 60 artisans, the building was re-inaugurated as the **Cosmovitral.** Half a million tiny pieces of colored glass convey the struggle among the forces of the universe. If you can take your eyes off the walls, the building holds a **botanical garden** of plants from all over the world thoroughly labeled in Spanish. (☎214 6785. *Open daily 10am-6pm. 10 pesos, children 5 pesos.*)

CENTRO CULTURAL MEXIQUENSE. This complex outside town houses three separate museums and a library. The **Museo de Culturas Populares** is a beautifully restored *hacienda* with a large collection of Mexican folk art, including an impressive Metepec Tree of Life, a large tree-like object composed of clay figurines. The **Museo de Antropología e Historia** displays all manner of Mexican artifacts, from figurines of Pre-Hispanic cultures to early printing presses and cars. Exhibits at the **Museo de Arte Moderno** include paintings by Diego Rivera and Rufino Tamayo. *(8km out of town. Accessible by "C. Cultural" buses running along Lerdo de Tejada (30min., 4 pesos). All museums open Tu-Su 10am-6pm. 5 pesos each, all 3 museums for 10 pesos; Su and W free.)*

OTHER SIGHTS. Outside of the botanical garden, museums rule. The **Centro Cultural Regional de Toluca,** Ascencio Nte. 103 off Hidalgo, has movie viewings and art exhibits in a building that dates from the beginning of the 20th century. (☎215 1075; culturaentoluca@yahoo.com.mx. Open Su 10am-3pm, Tu-Sa 10am-6pm. Free.) **Museo Felipe S. Gutiérrez,** Bravo Nte. 303 by the Museo José M. Velasco, is a tribute to master painter Gutiérrez (1824-1904), who was praised throughout the world for his skill with portrait paintings. (☎213 2647. Open Su 10am-3pm, Tu-Sa 10am-6pm. 8 pesos, students, teachers, and children 4 pesos; Su and W free.) Striking watercolors by masters like **Vicente Mendiola** and **Ignacio Barrios** fill the **Museo de la Acuarela,** Melchor Ocampo 105, which recently relocated to a new building on the Alameda. (☎214 7304. Open Su 10am-3pm, Tu-Sa 10am-6pm. Free.) A much different place, made for money lovers, is the **Museo Numismática,** Hidalgo 506, a few blocks west of the *portales*. Mexican coins glut the upstairs rooms, while the last two rooms exhibit foreign money. (☎213 1927. Renovations through late 2003. Open Tu-Su 10am-6pm. Free.) The **Museo de Bellas Artes de Toluca,** Santos Degollado 102, near Cosmovitral, was originally a Carmelite convent from 1698. Though it has temporary exhibits of modern art, it has held fast to a primary collection of religious art and relics. (☎215 5329. Open Su 10am-3pm, Tu-Sa 10am-6pm. 10 pesos, students 5 pesos; Su and W free.) A great collection of landscapes, still-lifes, and abstract art by the artistically diverse Japanese-Mexican artist Luis Nishizama is on display at the **Museo Taller Nishizawa,** Bravo Nte. 305, next to the Museo Felipe Gutiérrez. (☎215 7465, Open Su 10am-3pm, Tu-Sa 10am-6pm. 10 pesos, students, teachers, children, and seniors 5 pesos.)

MORELOS

CUERNAVACA   ☎777

Cuernavaca is full of visitors and it seems it has always been that way. First were the Tlahuicans, who founded the city of "Cuauhna'huac" (Place on the Outskirts of the Grove). In 1520, Cortes arrived with an army of Tlaxcaltecans, conquering the city as a stepping stone to Tenochtitlán. Later, generations of *criollos* corrupted the indigenous name to "Cuernavaca." Today, a constant stream of students floods innumerable Spanish-language schools, "living the language" in the company of thousands of other international travelers. Locals aid the learning process by shouting English at anyone who looks vaguely non-Mexican. Restaurants in the *centro* do their part, translating their menus. Meanwhile, *chilangos* rush here en masse on weekends for the relatively clean air. Cuernavaca has also attracted the famous and the infamous, from Gabriel García Márquez to the Shah of Iran. Visitors have helped to spawn an amazing wealth of restaurants, nightlife, museums, and a stylish international scene. Even as Cuernavaca becomes ever bigger and more expensive, the city's history, from its Tlahuican pyramid to its grand 20th-century mansions, continues to entice.

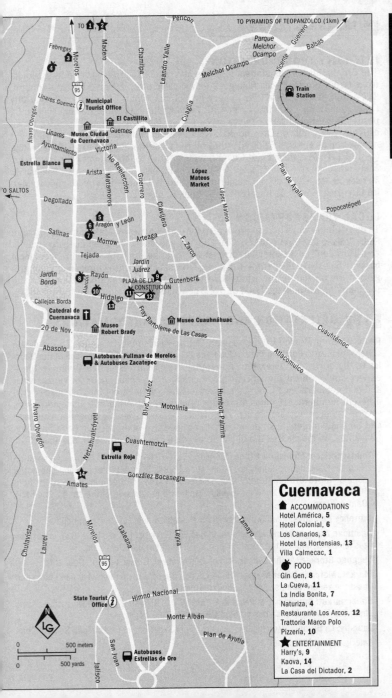

Cuernavaca

♠ ACCOMMODATIONS
Hotel América, 5
Hotel Colonial, 6
Los Canarios, 3
Hotel las Hortensias, 13
Villa Calmecac, 1

🍎 FOOD
Gin Gen, 8
La Cueva, 11
La India Bonita, 7
Naturiza, 4
Restaurante Los Arcos, 12
Trattoria Marco Polo
Pizzería, 10

★ ENTERTAINMENT
Harry's, 9
Kaova, 14
La Casa del Dictador, 2

CENTRAL MEXICO

⌐ TRANSPORTATION

INTERCITY TRANSPORTATION

The **Estrella Blanca bus station**, Morelos 503 (☎312 2626), is several long blocks from Jardín Borda. **Flecha Roja** goes to: **Acapulco** (4hr., every 2hr. 8am-midnight, 207 pesos); **Guadalajara** (9hr., every hr. 6:15am-10pm, 548 pesos); **Mexico City** (1¼hr., every hr. 7am-7pm, 52 pesos); **Taxco** (1¾hr., every hr. 7:05am-9:05pm, 54 pesos). **Tres Estrellas** serves **Toluca** (2½hr., every 30min. 5am-7pm, 47 pesos). Those arriving via Estrella de Oro should cross the street and flag down any northbound minibus on Morelos (3.5 pesos)—they all run past the center of town. **Estrella Roja** (☎318 5934), at Galeana and Cuauhtemotzín, goes to: **Matamoros** (3hr., every hr. 5am-7pm, 55 pesos) and **Puebla** (3½hr., every hr. 5am-7pm, 110 pesos). **Pullman de Morelos** (☎318 9205), on the corner of Abasolo and Netzahualcoyotl, goes to **Mexico City** (1¼hr., every 15 min. 5:15am-9:30pm, 52 pesos).

LOCAL TRANSPORTATION

Taxis go almost anywhere in the *centro* for under 30 pesos. Make sure only to take **Radio Taxis** (☎322 0641 or 317 3766). They are the safest and least likely to swindle you. They don't have meters, so always set prices before hopping in. Frequent **local buses** (3.5 pesos) called *rutas* run along Morelos and Álvaro Obregón and congregate at the *mercado;* the windshield bears the bus's final destination, and the route numbers are on the hood or over the windshield.

✦ 7 ORIENTATION AND PRACTICAL INFORMATION

Route 95 from Mexico City intersects Cuernavaca's main avenues. To reach the *centro*, exit onto **Domingo Díaz** or **Emiliano Zapata**, which splits into **José María Morelos** to the north and **Obregón** to the south. Cuernavaca is not easily navigable—expect random turns and abrupt name changes, especially near the plaza. Even and odd numbers usually stay on different sides of the street but, because of two different numbering systems, buildings opposite each other may have addresses several hundred numbers apart. The official address system changed a while ago and on some streets, it's not uncommon to see two addresses on each building: "400/antes 17" means that the old address was 17 and the official one is 400.

Tourist Offices: Municipal Office, Morelos 278 (☎318 7561), a 10min. walk north on Hidalgo. Open daily 10am-6pm. Information booths in all bus stations and one in the *zócalo*. **State Office,** Morelos Sur 187 (☎314 1412), a 15min. walk south from Hidalgo and Morelos. Look for a yellow wall on the right side of the street. Open M-F 9am-7:30pm.

Currency Exchange: Readily available; some establishments even accept dollars.

American Express: Marín Agencia de Viajes, 13 Gutenberg 3 (☎314 2266), in Las Plazas shopping mall on the *zócalo*. Open M-F 9am-6pm, Sa 10am-2pm.

Luggage Storage: At the Estrella Blanca bus terminal. 3 pesos per hr. Open 24hr.

Market: Mercado López Mateos. Head east on Degollado, up the pedestrian bridge and past the vendor stands. Open daily 9am-8pm.

Supermarket: Superama, Morelos 249 (☎314 0119), half a block towards the *zócalo* from the Estrella Blanca bus station. Open daily 7am-11pm.

Laundry: La Burbuja, Morelos 395. 30 pesos per 3kg. Open M-F 8am-7pm, Sa 8am-2pm.

Emergency: ☎080 or 060.

Police: Members of **Agrupamento Turístico,** a special unit of **Policía Metropolitana** (☎311 2448), wear white polo shirts and black or grey slacks. Open daily 10am-6pm. **Tourist security hotline** ☎800 903 9200.

Red Cross: (☎315 3505), on Ixtaccíhuatl at Río Amatzmac. Open M-F 8am-5pm.

Medical Assistance: IMSS (☎315 5000 or 315 5265), on Plan de Ayala. **Hospital General C.P.R.** (☎311 2210 or 311 2237), on the corner of Díaz and Gómez Ascarrate.

Post Office: Plaza de la Constitución 3 (☎312 4379), on the side of the *zócalo* closest to Hidalgo. Open M-F 8am-6pm, Sa 9am-1pm. **Mexpost** inside. **Postal code:** 62001.

▌ ACCOMMODATIONS

Numerous hotels in every price range are located within walking distance of Cuernavaca's center. Some less glamorous, but cheap, *casas de huéspedes* are on Aragón y León between Matamoros and Morelos. On weekends, you're competing for the small, old rooms with half of Mexico City's middle class; it's best to make a reservation, but ask to see the room before you check in.

Hotel Colonial, Aragón y León 19 (☎318 6414), uphill between Matamoros and Morelos. Rooms are clean and cozy, staff is friendly and helpful, and it's right by the *zócalo.* Front door closes 11pm; ring to be let in. Singles 160-200 pesos; doubles 260-320 pesos. ❸

Hotel América, Aragón y León 14 (☎318 6127), between Morelos and Matamoros. A rose-tiled courtyard pretties up this modest hotel. Great location, well-kept rooms, TV, and private baths. Singles 140 pesos, with TV 175 pesos; doubles 270 pesos. ❷

Los Canarios, Morelos 369 (☎313 0977 or 313 4444), 5 long blocks north of the *zócalo,* but close to Estrella Blanca station. Rooms are worn, but clean and comfortable—also with 2 pools and a tennis court. Singles 130 pesos; doubles 250 pesos; triples 290 pesos. ❷

Villa Calmecac, Zacatecas 114 (☎313 2918; www.villacalmecac.com), at Tanque. From the *centro,* hop on a Ruta 12 bus and head north on Morelos. Get off just past the statue of Zapata and take a left onto Zacatecas. Billing itself as an "ecotourist hostel," it's still pricey for a hostel. Peaceful, far from the *centro.* Clean communal baths. Breakfast included. Dorms 190 pesos; doubles 470 pesos. 10% discount with HI or ISIC. ❸

Hotel las Hortensias, Hidalgo 13 (☎318 5265), across from the plaza. Sweet location. Clean and charming; small rooms are a better deal during the week. Singles 185 pesos during the week, weekend 200 pesos; doubles 230 pesos/270 pesos. ❸

▐ FOOD

If you have any money left over after paying your hotel bill, there's no better place to spend it than in Cuernavaca's restaurants. Plenty of decent, cheap places to eat populate the *centro,* especially around Galeana and Juárez.

▨ **Trattoria Marco Polo Pizzería,** Hidalgo 30, 2nd fl. (☎312 3484). Delicious food made even better by the balconies, attentive service, and neat candlelit tables. Pizzas smothered in thick cheese come in 4 sizes (40 pesos and up). Reservations are a good idea for large parties and for balcony seating. Open Su 1-10pm, M-Th 1:30-10:30pm, F-Sa 1pm-midnight. ❹

Restaurante los Arcos (☎312 1424), on the south side of the *zócalo.* Listen to live music as you sit right on the *zócalo. Comida corrida* 50-80 pesos, breakfast 20-35 pesos, *antojitos* 25-33 pesos. Open daily 10am-midnight. ❸

La India Bonita, Morrow 15 (☎318 6967), less than a block east of Morelos. Originally the home of US Ambassador Dwight Morrow, who named it "Casa Mañana" because, during the building, whenever he asked when something would be complete, workers replied "*mañana.*" Beautiful and peaceful, yet rather touristy. Open Su 9am-6pm, Tu-F 8am-10pm, Sa 9am-11pm. ❹

Naturiza, Álvaro Obregón 327-1 (☎312 4626), one block past Morelos, behind Hotel Canarios. Tasty vegetarian food, far from the throngs of tourists crowding the rest of the *centro. Comida corrida* 40 pesos. Open M-Sa 8:30am-6pm. ❸

La Cueva, Galeana 4 (☎312 4002), across from the *zócalo.* A wide range of food—from seafood to sandwiches to soup—all with tasty, fresh tortillas. Friendly service and the well-stocked bar attract local youth, who pour in around 9pm. *Comida corrida* 28 pesos. Open daily 8am-midnight. ❸

Gin Gen, Rayón 13 (☎318 6046), 2 blocks east of the *zócalo* at Alarcón. Fans, lanterns, and pictures of Chinese pop stars adorn the walls. From 1-5pm, the filling *guisados del día* (soup, rice, 2 entrees, and dessert) go for only 55 pesos. Plenty of meatless dishes (35-70 pesos). Open Su 8am-6pm, M-Th 8am-9pm, F-Sa 8am-midnight. ❹

👁 SIGHTS

Most people do not come to Cuernavaca for the museums, but that doesn't mean they're not worth visiting. There are also some natural havens that you probably wouldn't expect in the middle of a city.

PLAZA DE LA CONSTITUCIÓN AND JARDÍN JUÁREZ. Across from the Palacio de Cortés is the **Plaza de la Constitución,** the heart and soul of the city. Food vendors, *mariachis,* and shoeshiners seek to capitalize on the locals and tourists that always pack the park. Gustave Eiffel designed the bandstand in **Jardín Juárez,** at the northwest corner of the plaza. A local band belts out polka, classical music, and Mexican folk music (Su and Th 6pm).

MUSEO CUAUHNÁHUAC (PALACIO DE CORTÉS). The Palacio de Cortés stands as a reminder of the city's grim history. The *conquistador* Hernán Cortés burned Cuernavaca in 1521 and built this two-story fortress atop the remains of a ruined pyramid. Cortés lived here on and off until his return to Spain in 1540, and his widow remained here until her death. The building served as a prison in the 18th century and became the city's Palacio de Gobierno during the Porfiriato. A grant from the former British ambassador to Mexico (Charles Lindbergh's father-in-law) transformed the Palacio into the Museo Cuauhnáhuac. The museum holds various artifacts from Pre-Hispanic times to the Revolution, including indigenous depictions of the conquest and a Rivera mural at the back, on the second floor. *(The biggest building in the zócalo, off Juárez. ☎312 8171. Open Tu-Su 9am-6pm; tickets sold until 5:30pm. Call ahead for free guided tours. 32 pesos.)*

CATEDRAL DE CUERNAVACA. Begun in 1529 and completed in 1552, and built mainly by indigenous craftsmen, this former Franciscan convent is one of the oldest churches in the Americas. That age hides secrets: about 20 years ago, the removal of aisle altars revealed **Japanese frescoes** depicting the persecution and martyrdom of Christian missionaries in Sokori, Japan. These startling frescoes may have been painted in the early 17th century by a converted Japanese artist. Two smaller chapels flank the main entrance. To the right is the 17th-century **Capilla de la Tercera Orden,** with a beautiful golden altar; to the left is the late 19th-century **Capilla del Carmen,** which has an English mass Sunday at 10:30am. *(3 blocks up Hidalgo from the zócalo, at Morelos. Mass daily 11am. Open daily 7am-2pm and 4-7pm.)*

JARDÍN BORDA. In 1783, Fr. Manuel de la Borda built this garden of magnificent pools and fountains as an annex to the home of his father, wealthy silver tycoon José de la Borda. In 1865, Emperor Maximilian and his wife Carlota established a summer residence here. Today, the garden has a faded splendor. Modern additions include the art collection near the entrance, small theater, cafe, and museum near the emperor's summer home. **Rowboats** are available on the small duck pond. *(Enter through a stone building on Morelos, across from the Cathedral. ☎ 318 1050. Open Tu-Su 10am-5:30pm. 30 pesos; students, teachers, and children 15 pesos; Su free. Rowboats 15 pesos per 30min., 20 pesos per hr.)*

PYRAMIDS OF TEOPANZOLCO. This small site contains the ruins of a pyramid and two temples built by the Tlahuicans, who were conquered by the Aztecs in 1427. Little remains of the temples, located atop the pyramid and dedicated to the God of War, Huitzilopochtli, and the God of Rain, Tlaloc. Another temple honors the wind god Ehe'catl, an incarnation of Quetzalcóatl, with a round base showing Aztec influence. *(Beyond the train station on Balsas. From the marketplace or Morelos, take a 12-peso taxi ride or, for 3.5 pesos, the Ruta #10 at the corner of Degollado and No Reelección. Ask the driver to drop you at the pirámide. Open daily 9am-5:30pm. 28 pesos; Su free.)*

MUSEO ROBERT BRADY. In Robert Brady's Casa de las Torres, there is a bright and beautiful collection of art with pieces by Rufino Tamayo, Frida Kahlo, Diego Rivera, Max Beckman, and others (including Mr. Brady himself). The collection also embraces colonial Mexican furniture, Pre-Hispanic figurines, and indigenous art from many parts of the world. *(Netzahualcoyotl 4, one block off Morelos. ☎ 318 8554 or 314 3529; www.geocities.com/bradymuseum. Open Tu-Su 10am-6pm. Call ahead for a free tour. 30 pesos, students and teachers 15 pesos.)*

OTHER SIGHTS. The scenic little building holding **El Castillito (Museo Fotográfico de la Ciudad de Cuernavaca)** was built in 1900 and has a small, free collection of old photographs of Cuernavaca. *(On Guemes. ☎ 312 7081. Open Tu-Su 10am-5pm.)* Next to the tourist office on Guemes is **La Barranca de Amanalco**, where you can take a peaceful stroll through nature right in the middle of the city; nature's power is evident in all the couples making out. *(Open daily 8am-6pm. Free.)* The most outstanding natural sights, however, are the waterfalls **Salto de San Antón** (41m tall) and **Salto Chico** (20m). Benches at San Antón have great views, but Salto Chico may be prettier. *(To get to Salto de San Antón, follow Degollado across the bridge and down the hill—don't turn. For Salto Chico, beyond the bridge turn right and walk up the hill past the cemetery. Open daily 8am-6pm. Free.)*

🎵 ENTERTAINMENT

Cuernavaca's popularity as a vacation spot fuels glitzy nightlife. **Discos** are typically open from 9 or 10pm to 5am on Friday and Saturday; a few spots also brighten the week. The more popular discos lie beyond walking distance from the *zócalo* in the outlying *colonias* and are best reached by taxi (*rutas* quit about 10:30pm). Only Harry's and Kaova are within walking distance of the *zócalo*. All the spots listed are familiar to cab drivers. An alternative to clubs is the busy **Plazuela del Zacate** on the corner of Hidalgo and Galeana, where restaurants and bars with outdoor seating and live music attract tons of people.

🦐 **La Casa del Dictador,** Jacarandas 4 (☎ 317 3186), a few blocks south of the Zapata statue, on the corner of Zapata in Col. Buenavista. Raging music welcomes a strictly gay clientele (mostly men). Beer 20 pesos. Cover 30 pesos. Open F-Sa 10:30-late.

Barbazul, Prado 10 (☎ 313 1976). A bridge brings you to the main room from the outdoor waterfall. Techno and lights will get you going. Drinks 20 pesos and up. Sa cover men 100 pesos, women free. Open W (low-key) and F-Sa 10pm-late.

Zúmbale, Chapultepec 13 (☎322 5343), next to Ta'izz. Dealing with the trek and the attitude at the door earns you a crowded theme-park air: 4 floors of salsa, *merengue*, and pop, complete with fake waterfall. Beer 35 pesos. Th no cover. F-Sa cover men 100 pesos, women free. Open Th 9pm-4:30am, F-Sa 9:30pm-5am; doors close at 3:30am.

Kaova, Av. Morelos Sur 241 (☎311 5511 or 311 5555; www.kaova.com.mx), 3 blocks south of the cathedral. Best points are the location and lack of cover. Filled with local youth. Beer 25 pesos, domestic drinks 35 pesos. Open W-Sa 9pm-late.

Harry's, Gutenberg 5 (☎312 7669), at Guerrero on the southeast corner of Jardín Juárez. The touristy restaurant isn't worth it, but the bar (which fills up after 10:30pm) is fun at night. F open bar, cover men 120 pesos, women 30 pesos. Open Tu and Th-Sa.

UP Barra Bar, Cuauhtémoc 93-11 (☎312 6305), inside Plaza Vendome. Soft rock stays at lower decibel levels to actually permit conversation. Beer 28 pesos, drinks 30-90 pesos. 2-for-1 on some drinks before 9pm. Open Tu-Sa 7pm-4am.

▶ DAYTRIPS FROM CUERNAVACA

XOCHICALCO

From Cuernavaca, Pullman de Morelos buses go to the Crucero de Xochicalco (30min., every ½hr., 19 pesos). Ask the driver to announce the stop. From there, take a taxi to the site (15 pesos). To return, take a taxi back down to the buses. Site and museum open daily 9am-5pm. Guides give tours in Spanish and English starting in the museum as soon as a group has assembled. 37 pesos; Su free.

Atop a steep plateau amid beautiful rolling hills, Xochicalco (zoh-chee-CAL-co, "house of flowers" in Náhuatl), is one of Mexico's most fascinating—and mysterious—archaeological sites. More a religious and trading center than a city, Xochicalco was first settled during the early Classic Period, around the time neighboring Teotihuacán was reaching its 7th-century zenith. It was not until Teotihuacán's demise around AD 700-900 that Xochicalco truly flourished, becoming an important trading and cultural center, with diplomatic and trading relations linking it with the Maya, Zapotecs, and Toltecs; these varied relationships are evident in the architecture. Among the many construction projects initiated in AD 700 is a ball court almost identical to those of the Classic Maya. Accordingly, some archaeologists speculate that Xochicalco may have been a Maya outpost; others believe that Xochicalco was the mythical **Tamoanchan,** the city where Maya, Zapotec, and Toltec sages met every 52 years to synchronize calendars and renew the cult of Quetzalcóatl. Xochicalco fell around AD 1200, likely due to internal conflict.

Before entering the ruins, visit the **Museo del Sitio de Xochicalco,** to the right of the entrance. Comprehensive exhibits, brochures (8 pesos), and of course the ticket office make the museum a necessary stop. From there, a rocky path leads to the ruins, which are best explored along a circular route. After you enter, walk past the first entrance until the road curves and leaves you in front of some stairs that will take you to the **Plaza de la Estela de los Glifos** (Plaza of the Stela with Glyphs), named for the altar at the center whose stela bears two glyphs related to the god Quetzalcóatl. It is believed that priests plotted the sun's trajectory over the pyramids by tracing the stela's shadow. Behind the altar is the **Gran Pirámide (Structure E),** the biggest structure at the site, topped by a temple. Twin pyramids on the east and west of the plaza, **Structure C** and **Structure D,** were used in the worship of the sun: one is oriented toward sunrise, the other toward sunset.

To the left of the Gran Pirámide there is a good view of the **Juego de Pelota** (ball court) below. Many archaeologists believe that this ball court was one of the earliest in Mesoamerica; ball courts as far south as Honduras show signs of a heavy Xochicalco influence. Also left of the Gran Pirámide is the stairway/portico section, used to protect the city from invasion. Past the portico and up two sets of impressive stairways is the **Plaza Principal,** rebuilt in 1994, which held homes of VIPs, as well as government offices. The top of the Pirámide de la Estela de los Glifos is accessible from here, enclosing a huge central pit that was the burial site for high priests and a place for ritual offerings. In the center of the plaza is the renowned **Pirámide de la Serpiente Emplumada** (Pyramid of the Plumed Serpent). Reconstructed in 1909, it bears reliefs of Quetzalcóatl.

At the rear of the plaza is the tremendous **Acrópolis,** the highest area of the site and supposedly the area where the rulers of Xochicalco lived: the east side was for daily activities, while the west was exclusively ceremonial. Down the slope to the west is the **Hall of the Polichrome Altar,** where a colored altar rests beneath a reconstruction of Toltec roofing. Farther down is a cistern, a sauna used for pre-ball game initiation rites, and **Teotlachtli,** the northern ball court. Two massive rings of rock are attached in the middle—most Mesoamerican ball courts have only one ring. Teams competed for the privilege of being sacrificed atop the Pyramid of Quetzalcóatl, a true honor and a sign of good sportsmanship. Walking through the ball court and turning left will bring you to the entrance to the **Observatorio,** which is in a man-made cave. On the summer solstice, Aztec sages and stargazers adjusted their calendar by peering through a shaft in the ceiling to trace the path of the sun. Tourists may enter every 15min.; wait outside and the guide will get you. If you are in a small group, he might let you stand beneath the light.

TEPOZTLÁN ☎739

Tepoztlán is a village of cobblestone streets hidden among sheer cliffs of mythical beauty, and crowned by a mysterious, ancient pyramid. Many villagers still speak Náhuatl and guard their heritage in part by prohibiting commercial development. The town has remained friendly to small-scale settlement, attracting throngs of resident expatriates as well as tourists, which has helped make prices extraordinarily high. Pack a picnic lunch, spend the night in a town with cheaper hotels, buy your crafts elsewhere, and live the fairy tale, if only for a day.

◪ **TRANSPORTATION.** The *centro*, consisting of the *zócalo*, several government buildings, and the church, is bounded by **5 de Mayo** on the west, **La Conchita** on the east, **Revolución** on the south, and **Zaragoza** on the north. 5 de Mayo turns into **Tepozteco,** which leads straight to the pyramid. "Ometochtli" buses go to and from **Cuernavaca** (40min.; every 15min. 5:45am-8pm; 12 pesos, students 9 pesos). In Tepoztlán they leave from the terminal; in Cuernavaca, from the east side of Mercado López Mateos. To go to or from **Mexico City,** take a Pullman de Morelos or Cristóbal Colón bus (75min., every 40min. 5:15am-7:50pm, 45 pesos). Catch one in Tepoztlán at 5 de Mayo 35, in Mexico City at the Terminal Sur (Tasqueña).

◪ **ACCOMMODATIONS AND FOOD.** Although most of the hotels in town are quite pricey, do not despair. Many little *casas de huéspedes* throughout town will be willing to strike a deal. **Hospedades Karlita ❸,** on Carmelinas, which slopes past the Museo de Arte Prehispánico, has clean and small rooms with communal baths. There are only four rooms, so act quickly. (Rooms for 1-2 people 150 pesos.) For more luxury, try **Posada Ali ❺,** at Netzahuatlcóyotl 2, on the corner with Tepozteco. Rooms are gorgeous, and a rooftop terrace and pool with bar complete the picture. (☎395 1971. Rooms 300-500 pesos.) Most hotels will give you cheaper prices during the week and may even negotiate on the weekend. Dozens of restaurants offering both trendy and traditional Mexican food line 5 de Mayo and Revolución. Prices hover around 40-90 pesos for main dishes; there are some small *taquerías* and *torterías*, especially behind the *zócalo*, but they are few and far between. A gem of a restaurant right in front of the *zócalo* and the intersection of 5 de Mayo and Revolución is **Café Amor ❷**, on 5 de Mayo at Galeana. It serves pizza (30 pesos), crepes (30 pesos), and *tortas gigantes* (13-18 pesos) in an upstairs cafe with a small balcony. (Open daily 3-9pm.)

◐ ◑ SIGHTS AND FESTIVALS. Tepoztlán's crowning attraction is the **Pirámide del Tepozteco;** although only 10m high, its position on top of cliffs still makes it imposing. The area was originally occupied in AD 1200, but was conquered by the Aztecs in 1400. The pyramid itself is a shrine to Tepoztécatl, the patron god of the people; he is related to the maguey plant, pulque, and the moon. The shrine originally held a statue of the god, but a Dominican friar destroyed it in the 16th century. To reach the pyramid, follow 5 de Mayo into town from the bus station (pass the *zócalo* on your right) until the road ends. The 2km hike is a brisk 45min. and the scenery is beautiful, though the trail is steep (and treacherous when wet, frequently the case in summer). Besides appropriate footwear and water, you may want insect repellent. Although some unfortunate souls have died falling from the pyramid, common sense should protect you. (Open daily 9am-5:30pm. 28 pesos.)

The **Museo de Arte Prehispánico** (commonly known as the **Museo Carlos Pellicer**) is at the rear of Capilla Asunción, way behind the *zócalo*. The collection is one large room of beautifully preserved pieces of Tlahuican, Olmec, Maya, Aztec, and *teotihuacano* applied and religious art—unfortunately lacking labels. Spiders keep the pieces company. (☎395 1098. Open Tu-Su 10am-6pm. 10 pesos.)

Celebrations every September 8 jointly honor **Tepoztécatl,** the patron god of Malinalco, who was thought to have been born in this magical valley over 1200 years ago, and the *Virgen. Chinelos*—colorfully attired folk dancers—invite visitors to join in their traditional dance, *el salto*, while musicians play age-old tunes. The night before, participants ascend the mountain to parade down the next day.

TLAXCALA

TLAXCALA

☎246

The colonial city of Tlaxcala (pop. 100,000), where *talavera* architecture fills a small valley just beyond the last remains of Poblano sprawl, cries out for tourists. Despite a growing population and increasing modernization, Tlaxcala retains its small town charm. However, Tlaxcalans were not always so peaceful; unable to withstand the Spanish onslaught during the 16th century, they made a pact with Cortés and sent 6000 warriors to raid and plunder the city of Cholula, ultimately helping Cortés to take Tenochtítlan in 1521. In return, Tlaxcala was granted Spanish protection and recognized as *"muy noble y muy leal"* (very noble and very loyal). Today, few traces of Tlaxcala's mercenary history remain, and its tranquil beauty draws refugees from Mexico City and Puebla on weekends. A great base from which to explore the state's now-deserted convents, untouristed *indígena* communities, and well-preserved ruins, Tlaxcala's museums, art galleries, and cultural center provide an authentic taste of Mexico's heartland.

▐ TRANSPORTATION

Tlaxcala is approximately 85km east of Mexico City and is most easily reached by **Mex. 150.** Don't be fooled by the large number of *colectivos* leaving from the market; Tlaxcala is a very walkable city. Distances are manageable, and it's cheaper and often more direct to chug up the hills yourself than to ride in the VW vans whose 1600cc engines can't handle the steep grades, forcing drivers to take longer routes. Most services are in and around **Plaza de la Constitución** (the *zócalo*) and

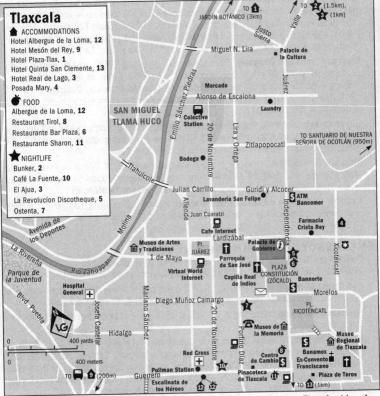

Tlaxcala

🏠 ACCOMMODATIONS
Hotel Albergue de la Loma, **12**
Hotel Mesón del Rey, **9**
Hotel Plaza-Tlax, **1**
Hotel Quinta San Clemente, **13**
Hotel Real de Lago, **3**
Posada Mary, **4**

🍴 FOOD
Albergue de la Loma, **12**
Restaurant Tirol, **8**
Restaurante Bar Plaza, **6**
Restaurante Sharon, **11**

⭐ NIGHTLIFE
Bunker, **2**
Café La Fuente, **10**
El Ajua, **3**
La Revolucíon Discotheque, **5**
Ostenta, **7**

diagonally adjacent **Plaza Xicoténcatl**. To get from the *zócalo* to Revolución, the city's main commercial street, catch a "Santa Ana" *colectivo* by the *mercado* at 20 de Noviembre and Alonso y Escalona, or behind the Parroquía de San José (3.5 pesos). Or take a 40min. walk to save pesos and enjoy the air.

To get to the *centro* from the **bus station**, exit through the glass doors to a swarm of idling *colectivos*. Those facing the right go to the downtown area, the market, and the hotel district along Revolución (3.5 pesos). To return to the bus station, take any combi marked "Central" from the *mercado* or flag one down behind San José at 20 de Noviembre and 1 de Mayo. **Autotransportes Tlaxcala** (☎ 462 0087) runs to **Mexico City** (2hr., every 20min. 5am-9pm, 81 pesos) and **Veracruz** (6hr; 10:30am, 3:30, 5:30, 11:30pm; 130 pesos). **Autotransportes México-Texcoco** (☎ 462 0362) also has service to Mexico City. **Flecha Azul** (☎ 462 3392) serves **Puebla** (55min., every 10min. 5:30am-9:30pm, 12 pesos).

🔼 PRACTICAL INFORMATION

TOURIST, LOCAL, AND FINANCIAL SERVICES

■ **Tourist Office:** Juárez 18 (☎ 465 0960 or 465 0961; www.tlaxcala.gob.mx/turismo), in the lovely turn-of-the-century building at Juárez and Lardizábal. The office sponsors cheap and comprehensive tours of Tlaxcala and its *señoríos* (Pre-Hispanic warrior-cities) every Sa, of Cacaxtla and Xochiténcatl every Su. The tours leave at 10:15am from the Hotel Posada San Francisco on the south side of the *zócalo* (20 pesos). Attentive and friendly staff provide a sea of information, pamphlets (10 pesos), and a fancy computer presentation (also available online). Open M-F 9am-7pm, Sa-Su 10am-6pm.

Currency Exchange: Banamex, Plaza Xicoténcatl 8 (☎462 2055), and **Bannorte,** Portal Hidalgo 10 (☎462 6741), under the *portales,* offer 24hr. **ATMs,** as do several banks on Juárez past the tourist office. The **Centro de Cambio Tlaxcala,** Guerrero 3 (☎462 9085), at the corner of Independencia, exchanges cash and traveler's checks. Open M-F 9am-4pm, Sa 10am-2pm.

Supermarket: Everything from underwear and refrigerators to bottled water and gum can be found at **Gigante,** Valle 66 (☎462 5846), the city's behemoth supermarket, in the shopping center on the corner of Vera. Open daily 8am-9pm.

Markets: Get your fresh produce at the market on the corner of Alonso de Escalona and Lira y Ortega, and along 20 de Noviembre from Zitlapopocatl. Open Su 8am-5pm, M-Sa 8am-8pm. On weekends, vendors sell *artesanías* in **Plaza Xicoténcatl.**

Laundry: Lavandería de Autoservicio Acuario, Alonso de Escalona 13A (☎462 6292). Full-service 11 pesos per kg with a 3kg minimum, 2hr. service is available; self-service 12 pesos per 10min. Open Su 8am-2pm, M-Sa 8am-8pm.

EMERGENCY AND COMMUNICATIONS

Police: (☎462 0735 or 462 1079) at the corner of Lardizábal and Xicoténcatl. Open 24hr. No English spoken. **Tourist police** also available at the same number.

Red Cross: Allende Nte. 48 (☎462 0920), at the corner where Allende dead-ends into Guerrero. 24hr. walk-in emergency service. Staff may speak English—just ask.

Pharmacy: Farmacia Cristo Rey 2, Lardizábal 15, between Xicoténcatl and Independencia. Open 24hr.

Hospital: Hospital General, Jardín de la Corregidora 1 (☎462 0030 or 462 3555), 5 blocks from the *zócalo* at the corner of Camargo and Josefa Castelar. No English spoken. **IMSS** (☎462 3400), on Valle, across the street from the stadium, past the Nestlé factory. Take Juárez from the *zócalo* until it turns into Valle. The clinic is the building on the left once you enter the IMSS compound. No English spoken.

Fax: Telecomm, Díaz 6 (☎462 0047). Also offers Western Union services. Open M-F 8am-6pm, Sa-Su 8am-noon.

Internet Access: Internet cafes abound on the streets surrounding the *zócalo.* A fast connection and open terminal can be found at the 2-story **Internet Cafe,** Independencia 21 (☎466 3597). 15 pesos per hr. Open M-Sa 9am-8:30pm.

Post Office: Plaza de la Constitución 20 (☎462 0004), on the corner of Camargo. Open M-F 9am-4pm, Sa 9am-1pm. **Postal Code:** 90000.

ACCOMMODATIONS

While dirt cheap accommodations aren't exactly plentiful in Tlaxcala, 200 pesos for a single and 250 pesos for a double pays for some very comfortable rooms. Be sure to make reservations on weekends and holidays, as low-cost hotels, especially those near the *zócalo,* tend to fill up quickly.

Hotel Albergue de la Loma, Guerrero 58 (☎462 0424). Although exhausted travelers may find the 62 steps leading to the Albergue's hill-top perch daunting, clean rooms with cable TV, private baths, and large windows that offer an inspiring view of Tlaxcala and the surrounding countryside reward those who make the trek. Spacious, carpeted rooms with 2 to 3 beds each are perfect for family stays. The downstairs restaurant serves inexpensive food daily 8am-10pm. Singles 210 pesos; doubles 266 pesos; triples 310 pesos. MC/V. ❹

Hotel Quinta San Clemente, Independencia 58 (☎462 1989). Follow Independencia south past Plaza Xicoténcatl for about 10min. The peach-colored hotel is on the left 4min. after Independencia starts to curve to the right. Warm pastel rooms, small tiled baths, and a fountain-bedecked courtyard work to compensate for San Clemente's distance from the *zócalo*. All rooms have cable TV and phone. If extra pesos aren't an issue, opt for the suite: a king-sized bed and more space is worth the 30 pesos. Singles 200 pesos; doubles 290 pesos. ❸

Hotel Mesón del Rey, Calle 3 1009 (☎462 9055), across the intersection to the left after exiting the bus station doors. The modern rooms—spacious but gloomy and complete with cable TV, phone, and small bathroom—are the cheapest singles in town. Singles 150 pesos; doubles 200 pesos. 50 pesos for each additional person. ❷

Hotel Plaza-Tlax, Revolución 6 (☎462 7852). From the *zócalo*, head north on Juárez, which changes into Valle; the hotel will be on your left soon after Valle becomes Revolución. Alternately, take a "Santa Ana" or "Gigante" *colectivo* from behind San José, and get off near the large Hotel Jeroc complex. If your priority list ranks discos higher than historic sights, Plaza-Tlax's location–close to the Valle club scene, but far from the *zócalo*–isn't much of a drawback. Clean rooms come with TV and cramped bathrooms. Singles 200 pesos; doubles 250 pesos; triples 320 pesos. ❹

Posada Mary, Xicoténcatl 19 (☎462 9655), is a rare find in Tlaxcala—a cheap hotel near the *zócalo*. What you save in money and transport time you lose in decor. All rooms have private baths with chest-high tile, but peeling paint adorns the remainder; the cement parking lot is none too attractive, either. If the reception is not open, just inquire at any of the open rooms to the left after entering the main gate. Singles 150 pesos; doubles 200 pesos. One room for 6 is a steal at 300 pesos. ❷

Hotel Real de Lago, Av. de los Deportes 15 (☎462 0399). Take Primero de Mayo from Plaza Juárez, cross the foot bridge and follow Av. Joaquín Cisneros Molina to the left. At the 1st intersection, veer right on Col. Aldolfo López Mateos until it turns; the hotel is on the corner. The accommodating staff will be happy to show you to a spacious brown-carpeted room with TV, spotless tiled bath, and fresh towels. A good pick if you don't mind the distance from the *centro*. Singles 250 pesos; doubles 400 pesos. Ask for a discount if you're staying for 3 or more days. ❺

⬛ FOOD

Tlaxcalteca specialties include *pollo en xoma* (chicken stuffed with fruits and other meats), *barbacoa en mixiote* (meat cooked in maguey leaves), and *pulque* (an unrefined alcoholic drink made from the maguey cactus), which is popular both straight and as *pulque verde*, a drink made with honey water, *yerba buena* (spearmint), and lemon juice. With all these yummy treats, it's hard to go wrong when picking a place to eat. For delicious midday meals, duck into one of the small family-run restaurants on **Juárez** between **Zitlalpopocatl** and **Alonso de Escalona,** where *comida corrida* is usually 35 pesos or less. Around the *zócalo*, meal prices rise to 50-80 pesos. For *antojitos*, try the vendors around the *mercado*.

▨ Restaurante Sharon, Guerrero 14 (☎462 2018), between Independencia and Díaz. Big glass windows slide open to the big open kitchen with even larger dining room. Check yourself out in the mirrors that decorate the walls while tasting the 8 *quesos fundidos* (38-42 pesos), or make a meal out of 3 stuffed-to-the-brim tacos (32 pesos). Meat dishes come with salad and beans (42-45 pesos). Open Su-F 1:30-9pm. ❸

Restaurante Bar Plaza, Portal Hidalgo #5 (☎462 4891). Its ideal location and decent prices make Restaurante Plaza a popular place to enjoy a midday meal. Relish a *molca-*

BUGALICIOUS

It has a colorful history, but what really makes Tlaxcala stand out is its resourceful cuisine. Numbered among its most exotic dishes are *maguey* worms, extracted from the bottom of the cactus of the same name, cleaned thoroughly, and then boiled in salt water. They are then fried and served with guacamole or salsa, and are said to be quite tasty; with every serving going for 100 pesos, they are also a bit on the expensive side. If worms don't do it for you, try the crunchy *escamoles*, ant eggs that are collected from nearby hills from depths of up to 2m. The eggs are separated from those larvae with wings (not so good for eating), thoroughly cleaned, and prepared fried with onions, diced green peppers and other spices, and served with guacamole or salsa. The knowledge that you just ate ant eggs runs you only 100 pesos a plate.

For the vegetarians out there, Tlaxcala also offers the somewhat less-wriggly heart of the Maguey cactus. Boiled, cut, and then fried, it too is served with guacamole or salsa and goes for the more affordable price of 60 pesos. To taste every last one of these delicious dishes, head to **Fonda del Museo**, Emiliano Sánchez Piedra (☎462 5708). The restaurant prepares these and other delicious Tlaxcallan dishes using traditional equipment like glazed clay pods and big wooden spoons. Open Tu-Su 9am-7pm.

jete jardín (30 pesos) or the filling *plato del día* (40 pesos) as you watch the cars pass by the city's *zócalo*. A variety of seafood 65-80 pesos, regional dishes 40-70 pesos, sandwiches 25-30 pesos. Open Su 7am-10pm, M-Th 7am-11pm, F-Sa 7am-1am. ❹

Restaurant Tirol, Independencia 7A (☎462 3754), along Plaza Xicoténcatl. Catering to weekday business lunchers and a hip evening crowd, Tirol offers *zócalo*-quality service and food at more reasonable prices. *Sopa tlaxcalteca* 25 pesos, *especialidades regionales* 40 pesos, 4-course *comida corrida* 35 pesos. Open Su 9am-7pm, M-Th 7am-midnight, F-Sa 7am-2am. ❸

Restaurant Albergue de la Loma, Guerrero 58 (☎462 0424). Large helpings complement beautiful views. Patrons peer at Tlaxcala and surrounding hills through floor-to-ceiling windows as they eat hearty breakfasts (20-35 pesos) and *antojitos* (30 pesos), or enjoy local specialties at affordable prices (45-60 pesos). Open daily 8am-10pm. ❸

🔲 SIGHTS

Most of Tlaxcala's attractions center around peaceful streets off **Plaza de la Constitución**, but easy-to-find *colectivos* make the trek to farther sights manageable. Visitors should make sure to see **Cacaxtla** and **Xicoténcatl,** two well-preserved archaeological sites nearby. The tourist office provides cheap, well-structured tours of Tlaxcala City and the archaeological sites.

PLAZA DE LA CONSTITUCIÓN (EL ZÓCALO). The serene Plaza de la Constitución is the heart of Tlaxcala. Look for the octagonal fountain of Santa Cruz in the center by the bandstand. Built in Europe during the 14th century, it was given to the city by King Phillip IV in 1646—no small token considering the distance those stones were hauled—to symbolize Spanish gratitude toward *La Ciudad Leal* (The Loyal City) and its instrumental role in Mexico's colonization. Four other fountains and a gazebo contribute to the draw of this plaza.

PLAZA XICOTÉNCATL. Southeast of the *zócalo* is Plaza Xicoténcatl, dedicated to the young Tlaxcalan warrior **Xicoténcatl Axayacatzin** who fought for the independence of Tlaxcala. Xicoténcatl is a hero today, and his statue commands a center spot in the plaza. Normally a tranquil area, the plaza livens up on weekends as a carousel and small artisan market occupy the grounds.

🔲 **MUSEO DE LA MEMORIA.** A great first stop for anyone on the museum route, El Museo de la Memoria guides visitors through Tlaxcalan history from

1521 to the end of the 18th century, providing essential background information that will make other sites more meaningful. The museum occupies a 16th-century building that once housed the sisterhood of Santa Cruz of Jerusalem; today, interactive computer programs and videos located throughout help explain the various exhibits. Highlights include the enormous diorama of the Ex-Convento Franciscano as it appeared during colonial times (get a good view from the 2nd floor); the room of the Virgen de Ocotlán, where thunderous holy music plays while visitors examine paintings and read about the legend of the Virgin; and a passageway of closely grouped metal shafts that commemorates the diaspora of Tlaxcalans after the alliance with Cortés. *(Independencia 3, across from Plaza Xicoténcatl. ☎ 466 0792. Open Tu-Su 10am-5pm. 10 pesos, students 5 pesos; Tu free. Guided tours 30 pesos; in English or French, US$5.)*

EX-CONVENTO FRANCISCANO DE LA ASUNCIÓN. Built sometime between 1537 and 1540, this was one of the first convents in the Americas. The thick, wooden door of the cathedral opens into a beautiful Romanesque nave and a ceiling of intricate Muslim-influenced *(mudéjar)* woodwork. The main altar contains, among other artifacts, *la conquistadora,* the canvas of the Virgin that Cortés is said to have kept between his armor and his breast. In the first of four chapels is a corn paste sculpture of Christ, *El Cristo de Centi,* which dates back to the 16th century. The side chapel closest to the altar, **La Capilla de la Tercer Orden,** holds the basin used to baptize the four Tlaxcalteca lords at the time of the alliance. *(On the southeast side of Plaza Xicoténcatl a 400-year-old cobblestone way leads about 200m up to the ex-convent. Open M-F 6:30am-2pm and 3:30-8pm, Sa-Su 6am-6:30pm.)*

MUSEO REGIONAL DE TLAXCALA. Meandering through the remains of the once-imposing ex-convent, the museum presents artifacts from nearby archaeological zones, examples of colonial religious-inspired art, and a library with works on Tlaxcalan history. Take a peek through the fence across the cobblestone road at one of Tlaxcala's pride and joys, the **Plaza de Toros.** Named for famed *torero* Jorge "El Ranchero" Aguilar, the plaza has been used since 1788 and comes to life in the last week of October and first week of November, when Tlaxcala celebrates its annual fair. *(Next door to the Ex-convent, on the side closest to the entrance. ☎ 533 4976. Open Tu-Su 10am-5pm. 30 pesos, students free; Su free.)*

PALACIO DE GOBIERNO. The former palace of the viceroys, where Cortés stayed when he was in Tlaxcala, now commemorates the entire history of people in the region. Covering the interior walls of the 16th-century palace are immense murals by Desiderio Hernández Xochitiotzin, depicting everything from early inhabitants of the Valley of Mexico to the Wars of Independence; beneath every section is a reproduction of the 16th century codex that inspired the work. The murals are currently being restored, as the humidity of the walls on which they are painted is causing chipping and discoloration of this amazing piece. *(Next to the zócalo. Open daily 8am-6pm. Free. Guides loiter inside, offering to explain the murals for 70 pesos in Spanish, 150 pesos in English.)*

PARROQUIA DE SAN JOSÉ. With its immense yellow bulk visible from afar, the old parish church, formerly the Cathedral of Tlaxcala, was originally built atop a hermitage dating from 1526 and became an important center of Church administration in the 1640s; it continues to be a religious center. At its entrance stand two stone founts of holy water, where weary pedestrians often pause to relax. The *talavera* tile and brick now covering the exterior of the church were laid over the original mortar facade in the 17th and 18th centuries. Some of the old glory is returned during **La Fiesta de San José,** March 10-19, when the national celebration centers on this landmark. *(Northwest of the zócalo. Open daily 6am-8pm.)*

MUSEO DE ARTES Y TRADICIONES POPULARES DE TLAXCALA. The museum features seven exhibition halls in which artisans demonstrate their crafts. Presentations include a tour of a traditional Otomi steam bath and kitchen, an explanation of textile production, and an exhibition on the making of *pulque*—including a taste of the fiery drink. *(Mariano Sánchez 1, on the corner of Lardizábal. A short walk west on Lardizábal from the Parroquia. ☎462 2337. Open Tu-Su 10am-6pm. 6 pesos, students 4 pesos.)*

SANTUARIO DE NUESTRA SEÑORA DE OCOTLÁN. While San José is Tlaxcala's main place of worship, Ocotlán boasts greater religious, symbolic, and historical significance, and is a prime example of the Churringueresque style, with lavish use of gold throughout the interior, including the altar. Tlaxcala's own Virgin, Nuestra Señora de Ocotlán, appeared in 1541 to an ailing Indian named Juan Diego Bernardino, curing him and ordering him to build the church. The modern-day *santuario* holds the 16th-century wooden image of the Virgin, which is carried through the city streets every year on the first Monday of May. In the interior, a shell motif tops the pilasters and frames the end of the nave. The star of the show is the *camarín*, a small octagonal room located behind the altar where the Virgin is "dressed" for important festivals. *(Head 2 blocks past the tourist office on Juárez, until you reach Zitlapopocatl, then turn right and follow the steep road upwards for about 1km.)*

JARDÍN BOTÁNICO TIZATLÁN. A showcase of Tlaxcala's natural beauty, this garden displays native plants in an otherworldly setting. No bikes, balls, radios, or alcoholic beverages are allowed in the pastoral paradise. Rocky paths meander across a creek to reveal a hidden greenhouse. *(Take a "Camino Real" colectivo from the market and tell the driver where you want to go. On foot, follow Juárez past the tourist office until it turns into Valle and then Revolución. From the hotel district on Revolución, turn left at Camino Real before the brick bridge passes over the road. ☎465 0900. ecologia@tlaxcala.gob.mx. Office open daily 9am-3pm and 4-6 pm; gardens open daily 6am-6pm. Free.)*

THE RUINS OF TIZATLÁN. These tiny ruins, discovered in 1924 a mere 4km outside of Tlaxcala, are all that remains of one of the four *señoríos* (warrior city-states). While the ruins are underwhelming, the view from the site is magnificent. A small *museo del sitio* provides a short history. In front of the site is the golden-domed **Templo de San Estéban;** access to the original, humidity-stricken 16th-century *capilla* of the church is included in admission. *(To reach the ruins, take a 3-peso colectivo from the corner of Sanchez and 1 de Mayo labeled "Tizatlán." Tell your driver where you want to go, and he or she will drop you off in front of a neon green building with a yellow altar out front. Walk left on the stone path, then up several flights of stairs until you reach the ruins at the top behind the Templo de San Estéban. Open daily 10am-5pm. 23 pesos, students free; Su free.)*

🎵 ENTERTAINMENT

On weeknights in Tlaxcala, lights go out early. However, discos on Valle and Revolución and a cluster of bars near the *zócalo* make for raucous weekends. Some of the restaurants and bars under the *portales* feature live music and outdoor seating that attract swarms of hip, coffee-sipping sophisticates.

In Tlaxcala, many of the bars also function as discos on weekends—hence the term "disco-bar." Early in the evening, patrons sit calmly at their tables. Later on, around 11:30pm, a sort of universal twitch sinks in, and the crowd surges to its feet, grinding and undulating in sweaty, drunken bliss.

Ostenta, Plaza de La Constitución 18 (☎468 5373). This low-key *discoteca*, located on the grounds of Tlaxcala's first movie theater, is the newest *antro*. The large screen is still used to display videos as local twenty-somethings dance on the circular main floor or above the crowd in one of the balconies. Beer 22 pesos, mixed drinks 40-60 pesos. Cover 50 pesos. F-Sa 9pm-3am.

El Ajua, Valle 113 (☎462 3544). Pounding rock, pop, and electronica keep the crowd dancing as music videos flash on the enormous front screen and psychedelic images swirl overhead in this black-and-white behemoth. Down a pitcher of beer with your friends at a table (150 pesos) or open up a dance floor of your own, pushing the tables aside. Cover 50 pesos. Open Th 9pm-3am, F-Sa 9:30pm-5am.

Bunker, Valle 63 (☎462 3888). Twenty-something locals get down on the large dance floor to all types of tunes spun by one of Tlaxcala's best. 4 VIP zones pretty much guarantee that you're special. Cover 40 pesos. Open Th-Sa 10pm-late.

La Revolución Discotheque, Portal Hidalgo 9 (☎466 1647), under the *portales*. Dirty dancing a bit closer to home, the bar boasts a crystal tequila bottle worth over 3000 pesos. Young clubbers let the disco's sound system blow their worries aside. Music includes pop, techno, reggae, and *salsa*. Live rock F-Sa. Cover 30 pesos. Open Su-W and F-Sa 1pm-11pm.

Café La Fuente, Guerrero 29 (☎462 9722), at the corner of 20 de Noviembre. If the bar scene along the *zócalo* is too chaotic, this cafe offers the opposite: couples sipping typical coffeehouse fare and sharing tiny semi-private balconies. The dim lights throw the *artesanía*-hung ceiling, on which every decoration is for sale, into shadows as slow jazz plays and the strongly spiked *cafés* work their magic (10-26 pesos). Live music F-Sa from 7pm. Open daily 10am-1am.

FESTIVALS

For information on cultural events in Tlaxcala, head to the **Palacio de la Cultura,** Juárez 62, four blocks from the *zócalo* at the corner of Justo Sierra. To the right as you enter are monthly schedules and announcements of theater productions, dances, and art expositions. The Palacio also stages concerts, exhibits, and performances all over town and in its own courtyard. **Teatro Xicoténcatl** hosts most of the events. The bookstore offers some books in English on Tlaxcalan culture. (☎462 6069. Open M-F 9am-8m, offices open 9am-6pm.)

Tlaxcala's state fair, the **Feria de Tlaxcala,** is held from October 16 to November 15. During the month-long *feria*, exhibitions of crafts and livestock dot the town, while Tlaxcalans from across the state participate in cultural and sporting events. If you have a taste for religious events, stop by Tlaxcala on the first Monday in May to see the sacred pine image of the **Virgen de Ocotlán** paraded through the streets. If that doesn't suit your schedule, visit the Church of Christ the Good Neighbor (to the right of the ex-convent) on July 1 for the celebration of the **Día de la Purísima Sangre de Cristo** (Day of the Purest Blood of Christ).

◪ DAYTRIPS FROM TLAXCALA

▓ CACAXTLA

In Tlaxcala, take a bus marked "Nativitas" or "San Miguel de Milagros" from 20 de Noviembre next to the market or behind San José. Tell the driver where you want to go, and he or she will drop you off at the main entrance (40min., 7 pesos). If you happen to be dropped in San Miguel de Milagros, walk up the windy road, following the signs. If driving, take Mex. 119. ☎416 0000. Open daily 9am-5:30pm. 37 pesos, students free; Su free.

One of the best-preserved and best-presented archaeological sites in the country is the hilltop ruin of Cacaxtla (kah-KASH-tla), 19km southwest of Tlaxcala. The Olmec-Xicalancas, who once dominated the southwest corner of Tlaxcala state and most of the Puebla Valley, built and expanded the city during the Classic Period, between 700 and 900 AD. Cacaxtla was abandoned by 1000, and its inhabitants were driven from the area by Toltec-Chichimec invaders in 1168. Excavation began here in 1975; since then 4000 sq. m of ruins have been unearthed.

The small museum on the right by the entrance contains artifacts and bones collected from the site. From the museum, a paved road leads toward the ruins which, to prevent erosion, are covered by the world's second largest archaeological roof. Once upstairs, visitors move clockwise around ceremonial courtyards, temples, tombs, and palatial remains. Location markers provide historical information in Spanish, English and Náhuatl. The remains of many small rooms within the palace are thought to have been priests' quarters.

Several features distinguish this site from others. One is a latticework window, **La Celosia**, on the west side, opposite the entrance. The free-standing window, made by surrounding a latticework of twigs and branches with mud and stucco, is the only one of its kind in Mesoamerica. Another attraction is the series of murals throughout the site, considered to be among the best-preserved Pre-Hispanic paintings in Mesoamerica. The largest, the **Mural de la Batalla**, depicts a historical-mythological battle of two armies, one dressed in jaguar skins defeating another dressed in eagle feathers along a 26m wall. The still-visible original mineral-based colors show a distinct Maya influence, which may indicate the existence of a trading network linking the Maya and the Olmec-Xicalancas. The walkway ends on one of the pyramid's edges, providing a final touch to the tour: a breathtaking view of the surroundings, limited only by the huge blue hills in the distance.

XOCHITÉNCATL

From Cacaxtla, walk down from the entrance of the archeological site to the highway, Mex. 119, and flag down any colectivo headed right (3.5 pesos). Ask the driver to drop you close to Xochiténcatl site. From there, take a right off the main highway, and another right at the well-marked site entrance. 1km up the hill is the ticket booth. To return to Tlaxcala, walk back down the hill to the town of San Miguel Xochitecatitla and take a "Tlaxcala" colectivo (3.5 pesos). Open Tu-Su 10am-4:30pm. 17 pesos, students free; Su free. Free with Cacaxtla ticket.

The civilization at Xochiténcatl (so-chee-TEN-cahtl) predates Cacaxtla by several hundred years, and its ruins are located on a hill just opposite Cacaxtla. Before they were conquered in AD 300 by the Olmec-Xicalancas, the inhabitants of Xochiténcatl constructed the temple to honor Xochiqueteali, the goddess of fertility. For this reason, archaeologists think, many of the artifacts at the site are figures of women or babies, who were sacrificed with some regularity at the site. There are four pyramids, the largest of which, the **Pyramid of Flowers,** is actually a pyramid on top of a pyramid. The columns on top are thought to have been constructed to bring great fertility to all women who passed through them. To the left of the pyramid is the **Pyramid of the Snake**. The basin on top of the pyramid caught water and served as a mirror in which to observe the stars. Behind the Pyramid of the Snake is a small, flat pyramid, the **Basement of the Volcanoes**. At the far left of the site is the **Spiral Pyramid**. Dedicated to the wind god Ehecatl, it is the only such spiral pyramid known to exist. As no steps were found that lead up the structure, it is believed that priests actually walked the spiral walkway all the way to the top. The pyramid of Ehecatl now has a white cross at its peak, which serves as a ceremonial center to the inhabitants of the area. The site also offers a spectacular view of nearby volcanoes **Popocatépetel, Ixtaccihuatl,** and **La Malinche (Malintzin).** On your way to the site, peek into the small museum near the entrance and view some of the many artifacts found atop the Pyramid of Flowers.

HUAMANTLA

From Tlaxcala, take an ATAH bus from the station to Huamantla (45min., every 10 min., 12 pesos). Ask to be let off near Parque Juárez. To return, continue past Museo Taurino to Absolo and hang a right. Buses marked "Tlaxcala" return to the city from the corner of Absalo and Bravo Nte. By car, take Mex. 119 to Mex. 126.

Though most visitors come to Huamantla, 45km east of Tlaxcala, for its renowned bull-runnings, other sights attract plenty of daytrippers from the capital city. Sights are centered around the *zócalo,* **Parque Juárez.** Northeast of the *zócalo,* the

Museo Taurino, Allende Nte. 205, commemorates Huamantla's famous bullfighting history. Posters, bullfighting attire, and photographs dating from the early 1900s are displayed, including some of renowned female bullfighter Sono Díaz. Before leaving the museum, peek through the fence in the hallway to the left of the courtyard for a glimpse of Huamantla's famous bull ring. (Open M-F 9am-3pm and 5-7pm, Sa-Su 9:30am-2pm. Free.) Among the sights that aren't bull-related is the **Museo de La Ciudad,** a small museum housed in a former grain warehouse for Franciscan monks, located just left of the Palacio Municipal. Its small collection is composed of previews of the town's larger museums, along with pieces that pay homage to the extraordinary citizens of Huamantla. Among the exhibits are huge rugs woven during the annual festival La Noche que Nadie Duerme (The Night No One Sleeps, see below for details), a small replica of the town's gazebo adorned with intruments from the 1926 Humantla city band, and the lenses that were used to take the first picture of the moon, a photo taken by a Humantlan. (Open daily 8am-7 pm.) The **Museo Nacional del Títere,** Parque Juárez 15, is on the west side of the *zócalo,* along de la Reforma. In the year 1835, Huamantla became famous for its *títeres* (puppets) when Rosete Aranda, a *títere* company located in the city, began putting on shows involving more than 5000 puppets. Today, the museum contains the third largest collection of original Rosete Aranda puppets in Mexico. Trace the history of puppets all over the world, examine the elaborate Aranda puppets, and sign your name and comments on the wall of graffiti in the last *sala.* The friendly staff offers guided tours, included in the cost of admission. (☎472 1033. 10 pesos, students 5 pesos. Open Su 10am-3pm, Tu-Sa 10am-2pm and 4-6pm.)

From the museum, walk to the yellow church, the **Parroquia de San Luís,** Parque Juárez 3, located half a block to the left. Constructed in 1641, the parish church's plain exterior belies a respectable collection of artifacts within. The altars are beautiful examples of Baroque artwork and feature a depiction of the Virgin Mary and Christ by the noted artist Miguel Cabrera. (☎472 0310. Open daily 7am-8pm. Free.) On the east of the *zócalo* opposite the museum and *parroquia,* the **Ex-Convento de San Luis Obispo de Tolosa** bears witness to the centuries of tackiness it has endured since it was built by the Franciscians, sometime before 1569. The cloister now functions as a school. (☎472 1000. Open daily 9am-7pm. Free.) On the south side of the *zócalo* is the **Palacio Municipal.** If you enjoyed his murals in Tlaxcala, you can check out Desiderio Hernández Xochitiotzin's work in the entrance of the Palacio, started by the artist but finished by his son. A small **tourist office,** Zaragoza Pte 110 (☎472 2457), has an English-speaking staff and maps of Huamantla. (M-F 9am-7pm, Sa 9am-2pm.)

Huamantla fills with visitors, carpets of flowers and sawdust, and newly-free bulls in a spectacular early August festival. It all begins on ▨**La Noche que Nadie Duerme** (The Night No One Sleeps), August 14, when flower and sawdust designs are displayed over 2km of the city streets and the image of the Virgin is paraded down the carpeted path. On the following Saturday, the streets close for the traditional *huamantlada,* the running of the bulls.

PUEBLA

PUEBLA   ☎222

Puebla (pop. 2 million) was a great social experiment—Renaissance met ruffian, Enlightenment met real world. Conceived by a group of humanist Spaniards, Puebla was to be a crossroads of faith and education, with libraries, schools, and administrative buildings designed to civilize and Christianize. Surprisingly enough,

Puebla

▲ ACCOMMODATIONS
Hotel Catedral, **10**
Hotel Imperial, **2**
Hotel Real del Parián, **7**
Hotel Ritz, **3**
Hotel Teresita, **13**
Hotel Victoria, **11**

🍴 FOOD
Antojitos la Concordia, **17**
Barra Vegetariano
La Zanahoria, **15**
Fonda La Mexicana, **18**
Restaurant El Vegetariano, **12**
Restaurante La Princesa, **9**

★ ENTERTAINMENT
El Alebrije, **14**
La Batalla, **16**
Teorema, **8**

● SERVICES
Farmacias del Ahorro, **6**
Gimnasio Puebla, **5**
Lavandería Roly, **1**
Ultramarinos el Puerto de
Vercruz, **4**

Puebla was completed as planned and to this day is a mix of 17th- and 18th-century European art and ideals and colorful Mexican energy. Built on solid, empty ground, Puebla's streets are said to have been laid by angels who streaked ribbons across the land, forming the grid that makes the city so simple to navigate. Angels notwithstanding, the city has been shaped by pious visitors. Franciscans built hospitals, libraries, and orphanages for illegitimate children, while nuns from a variety of orders set up cloisters and kitchens, where they invented some of Mexico's most famous dishes and the sugar-candy sweets which the city is known for. Today, Puebla is one of the largest and most important cities in the country. Gilded churches elegantly blend with trendy clothing stores, while in the shady *zócalo*, teen hipsters and older locals relax side by side.

TRANSPORTATION

Most sights and accommodations are located within walking distance of the *zócalo*. If traveling farther in an independent **taxi**, set a price before getting in and don't be shy about haggling. Municipal **buses** and **micros** *(combis)*, white VW vans that operate like buses, cost 3 pesos. Anything labeled "Centro" will take you close to the *zócalo*.

Airport: There is an **airport** (☎232 0032) in nearby Huejotzingo, 22km northwest of Puebla on Mex. 150. Regional airline **Aeromar** (☎232 9633) flies to Monterrey and Guadalajara; **AeroCalifornia** (☎230 4855) will take you to Tijuana and Guadalajara.

Bus: CAPU (Central de Autobuses Puebla; ☎249 7211), at Norte and Tlaxcala, is one of the largest bus stations in the country. To get to the *zócalo* from the station, exit to the street, take one of the walking bridges over the nearby highway, and flag down a "Centro" bus. To get back to the bus station, take a northbound bus labeled "CAPU" on Héroes de 5 de Mayo. Official yellow **taxis** labeled *taxis controlados* will make the trip for 35 pesos. From the station, **ADO** (☎230 4000 or 230 4014; www.adogl.com.mx) goes to: **Cancún** (20hr., 11:45am, 824 pesos); **Mexico City** (2½hr., every 40min. 6:20am-10pm, 87 pesos); **Oaxaca** (4½hr., 7 per day, 824 pesos); **Veracruz** (3½hr., 7 per day, 163 pesos). **Estrella Roja** (☎213 8300) offers similiar service to **Mexico City** (69 pesos). **Cristóbal Colón** (☎225 9007) goes to: **Puerto Escondido** (14hr., 7:30pm, 495 pesos) and other resort cities. **Estrella Blanca** (located under the "Futura" sign; ☎249 7561) goes to: **Acapulco** (7hr., 4 per day, 362 pesos); **Cuernavaca** (3½hr., 4 per day, 110 pesos); **Taxco** (5hr., 8am, 122 pesos); and most points north. **Flecha Azul** (under "PTC"; ☎249 7128) goes to **Tlaxcala** (1hr., every 8 min. 5:30am-6pm, 12 pesos). Smaller buses also serve the CAPU station.

ORIENTATION AND PRACTICAL INFORMATION

Puebla, capital of the state of Puebla, is connected through an extensive route network to **Mexico City** (120km northwest along Mex. 150), **Oaxaca** (Mex. 190, 125, or 131), **Tlaxcala** (Mex. 119), **Veracruz** (Mex. 150), and countless other cities. Street names change as they pass the *zócalo*. Numerical addresses follow a rigid pattern: they correspond to the number of the lowest cross-street. For example, Av. 4 Ote. 237 would be bounded by Calle 2 Nte. and Calle 4 Nte. One block farther down, between Calles 4 Nte. and 6 Nte., addresses are in the 400s. Note that there are two major streets in Puebla celebrating the date of Mexico's victory over the French: **Av. 5 de Mayo** and **Blvd. Héroes 5 de Mayo**. Take care not to confuse them.

TOURIST AND FINANCIAL SERVICES

Tourist Office: Av. 5 Ote. 3 (☎246 1285 or 246 2044; www.turismopuebla.com.mx), in the same building as the Casa de la Cultura and the post office. Offers free maps and pamphlets and a very efficient, English-speaking staff. Tours of the city 150 pesos, available in English, Spanish, or French. Open Su 9am-2pm, M-Sa 9am-8:30pm.

Currency Exchange: Banks line Reforma and 16 de Septiembre around the *centro*. Most have 24hr. **ATMs. Bital,** Reforma 316 (☎246 3050), changes money. Open M-Sa 8am-7pm. **Casas de cambio** offer slightly better rates and cluster in the Zona Esmeralda along Juárez, far from the *zócalo*. Try **Casa de Cambio Puebla,** Juárez 1706 (☎248 0199). Open Su 9am-1pm, M-Sa 9am-6pm.

American Express: Calle 10 Sur 3715 2nd fl. (☎243 9783). Cashes and replaces AmEx checks. Open M-F 9am-6pm.

LOCAL SERVICES

Luggage Storage: At the bus station. 3 pesos per bag per hour. Open 24hr.

Markets: Puebla's squawking **Mercado 5 de Mayo,** on Av. 18 Ote. between Calles 3 and 5 Nte., spills into 5 de Mayo and adjoining streets, selling everything from fresh veggies to raw meat. Open daily 8:30am-6pm. For your processed and packaged needs, try **Ultramarinos el Puerto de Veracruz,** Av. 2 Ote. 402 (☎232 9052). Open Su 8am-4pm, M-Sa 8am-9:30pm.

Laundry: Lavandería Roly, Calle 7 Nte. 404 (☎232 9307). 30 pesos for 3kg self-service. Open Su 8am-3pm, M-Sa 8am-9pm.

Car Rental: The many agencies in town include **Avis** (☎/fax 249 6199) and **Budget** (☎230 5008).

EMERGENCY AND COMMUNICATIONS

Emergency: ☎066.

Police: Policía Auxiliar (☎288 1864). No English spoken.

Red Cross: Av. 20 Ote. 1002 at Calle 10 Nte. (☎243 8244, 235 8631, or 234 0000). 24hr. ambulance service. Some English spoken.

Pharmacy: Farmacias del Ahorro, Av. 2 Ote. 15A (☎231 3383). Open daily 7am-11pm.

Hospital: Hospital UPAEP, Av. 5 Pte. 715 at Calle 39 Sur (☎232 3221 or 246 6999). 24hr. service. Some English spoken. **Hospital Universitario** (☎246 6464 or 243 1377), Calle 13 Sur at Av. 25 Pte. 24hr. emergency service. No English spoken.

Fax: Telecomm, 16 de Septiembre 504 (☎246 4188), just south of the post office. Western Union, telegrams, fax. Open M-F 8am-6pm, Sa-Su 9am-noon.

Internet Access: Internet cafes line Calle 2 Sur; shop around for the best price. **Internet Cyber-Byte,** Calle 2 Sur 505B, has lots of computers, fast connections, and free coffee. 15 pesos per hr. Open daily 10am-9pm. **Cyber-Café,** Calle 2 Sur 907C (☎232 4242), 2 blocks farther south. Computer screens embedded in rustic wooden tables. Reasonably quick connections. 20 pesos per hr., 10 pesos with ISIC card. All-you-can-drink coffee 8 pesos. Open Su 11am-5pm, M-Sa 9am-9pm.

Post Office: (☎232 6630) 16 de Septiembre at Av. 5 Ote., 1 block south of the *zócalo*, just around the corner from the state tourist office. Open M-F 8:30am-5pm, Sa 9am-1pm. **Administración 1,** Av. 2 Ote. 411 (☎242 6230). Open M-F 9am-5pm, Sa 9am-1pm. The branches have separate Listas de Correos, for mail pick-up. **Postal Code:** 72000 or 72001.

ACCOMMODATIONS

Puebla is well stocked with budget hotels with most of them within a five or six block radius of the *zócalo*. When walking around the *zócalo*, be on the lookout for large, red "H" signs jutting from tightly-packed buildings. These signs, friends of the weary traveler, indicate that a hotel—most often a cheap one—is near.

▓ **Hotel Imperial,** Av. 4 Ote. 212 (☎/fax 242 4980 or 800 874 4980). On the expensive side, but oh, the amenities! Beautiful bath, phone and cable TV in all rooms, free Internet access, a mini-golf course, a workout area, purified water, laundry service, pool and ping-pong tables, and a Hershey's Kiss on your pillow. Breakfast in the downstairs cafe (7:30-10:30am) and *cena del patrón*—snacks and drinks (8-9:30pm)—included. **30% discount** for proud *Let's Go* readers. Fills up during the weekend. Singles 325 pesos; doubles 467 pesos; triples 507 pesos. ❺

Hotel Teresita, Av. 3 Pte. 309 (☎232 7072). The small rooms are models of modernity, with stuccoed walls, TV, clean and attractively-tiled—though tiny—baths, coordinated bedspreads, and soft lighting. Rooms facing the street are bigger. The staff speaks some English. Check-out 2pm. Singles 180 pesos; doubles 280 pesos. ❸

Hotel Victoria, Av. 3 Pte. 306 (☎232 8992 or 800 849 2793). Convenient location, accommodating staff, and affordable prices—check out the suspended concrete walkways connecting upper-level rooms. Though a little dark, rooms and bathrooms are tidy and spacious. Singles 120 pesos; doubles 170 pesos. ❷

Hotel Ritz, Calle 2 Nte. 207 (☎232 4457). While offering many of the same amenities as Hotel Teresita (TV, tiled private baths, the same new bedspreads), the Ritz has not been as thoroughly renovated, nor is the staff as charming. Still, the location is good, and the free coffee is drinkable. Singles 175 pesos; doubles 250 pesos. ❸

Hotel Real del Parián, Av. 2 Ote. 601 (☎246 1968), across the street from the *mercado* and upstairs from some of Puebla's best bargain restaurants. In a confusing priority of amenities, the Parián offers laundry facilities but messy hallways, private baths without toilet seats, and brightly painted but tiny rooms. Some rooms with balconies available. Singles 130 pesos; doubles 210 pesos; triples 280 pesos. ❷

Hotel Catedral, Av. 3 Pte. 310 (☎232 2368). The decayed glamor will make you sigh and long for the days when the intricate hardwood floors and soaring ceilings were not counterbalanced by dangling bare lightbulbs and less than sparkling communal showers. Extremely spacious rooms. Check-out 1pm. Singles 100 pesos; doubles 120 pesos. A 2nd location, at Av. 3 Pte. 724, has private bathrooms (15 pesos more). ❶

🍴 FOOD

Puebla is most famous for its *mole poblano*, a dark chocolate chile sauce that can be found slathered on chicken, rice, or just about anything. *Mole poblano* just might be the national dish of Mexico, but don't leave Puebla without tasting other regional specialities. Taste *mole pipián*, containing pumpkin seeds and chiles, and *mole adobo*, a spicier blend with cumin powder. Leaving *mole* behind, try *chiles en nogada*, green peppers stuffed with beef and fruit fillings and smothered in white walnut sauce. The patriotic green, red, and white recipe was devised by the nuns of Santa Monica as a birthday present for Mexican Emperor Agustín de Iturbide when he visited the city in 1821 and is now eaten throughout August—Iturbide's birth month. Puebla's famous cooking nuns are perhaps best known for their *dulces* (sweets). Sample their centuries-old recipes and creative genius in the *dulcerías* along **Av. 6 Ote.,** just east of 5 de Mayo, which are filled with delicate, colorful candies, some of which are named after the convents of their origin.

Puebla is also home to a multitude of **taco stands ❶,** many of them on **Calle 5 Nte.** between Avs. 10 and 12 Pte., on **Av. 5 de Mayo** at Av. 14 Ote., and at the **Mercado El Alto,** on the far side of La Iglesia de San Francisco. In addition to the taco-stand staples of *tortas* and tacos, these cheap joints feature *cemitas*, sandwiches made with a special long-lasting bread, which made them popular on ships. While Puebla has a number of fine restaurants, visit these stands for a more authentic (and cheaper) sampling of *poblano* cuisine.

N THE MENU

¡HOLY *MOLE*!

In 17th-century Puebla, nuns of the Santa Rosa order lived lives of devotion through extreme self-denial. They slept without covers on beds of wooden slats, wore crowns of thorns to ward off bad thoughts, and installed 4 ft. doors throughout their convent so that they had to bow their heads in prayer each time they entered a room.

The one area in which the nuns didn't skimp was food. Sor Andrea de la Asunción is said to have concocted the first ever *mole poblano* inside the convent. As the story goes, her sisters gathered around her as she rolled over different types of chiles together, commenting on her skill in grinding the peppers. "*¡Que bien muele!*" ("how well she grinds") became "*¡que bien mole!*" and thus the famed *mole* earned its name. To balance the spicy peppers, the sisters added chocolate, sugar, and 21 other ingredients until they were satisfied with the final product. Today, the Festival del Mole Poblano celebrates the nuns' culinary expertise during the month of June, when chefs submit samples of their own family recipes, hoping to win honors for the best *mole*. The cooking nun phenomenon seems to have been widespread in Puebla; nuns of Santa Rosa, Santa Monica, and other orders are credited with the invention of Puebla's unique *dulces, chiles en nogada,* and other specialties.

▨ Barra Vegetariano la Zanahoria, Av. 5 Ote. 206 (☎232 4813). A high ceiling, a bubbling fountain, and winding cast-iron stair give this veggie hangout the most agreeable ambience around. The real attraction, however, is the trendy but inexpensive food. Order dishes from the menu or go with the plate of the day, which includes 5 different vegetarian dishes and a fruit beverage (39 pesos; Su buffet 59 pesos). Top it all off with a fruit-flavored *licuado* made from yogurt, milk, or soy, served in a tall, old-fashioned milkshake glass (14 pesos). Open daily 7:30am-8:30pm. ❸

Fonda la Mexicana, 16 de Septiembre 706 (☎232 6747), 3 blocks south of the *zócalo*. Strings of *papel picado* line the ceiling and *folklórico* items adorn the walls of this patriotic restaurant. Fonda serves good *mole* and *pipián* dishes—although at prices that may stretch your wallet (*mole* dishes 55-60 pesos). If you're pinching pesos, order the *menu económico* (soup, a main dish, and dessert or coffee, M-F 40 pesos, Sa-Su 45 pesos). Speedy, no-frills service. Open daily 10am-8pm. ❹

Restaurante la Princesa, Portal Juárez 101 (☎232 1195), under the *portales* on the west side of the *zócalo*. Mingle with locals as you enjoy *platillos mexicanos* (6-40 pesos, meat 65-78 pesos). Convenient location, casual, unpretentious atmosphere, and friendly, well-dressed staff add to its appeal. Open daily 8am-10:30pm. V. ❸

Antojitos la Concordia, Calle 2 Sur 509 (☎232 1373). A local favorite for 40 years, Concordia offers good food and good prices. The *plato del día* satisfies at 30 pesos; leave room for the ice cream float or banana split (25 pesos). Surrounded by religious memorabilia and mushy Mexican couples, you'll be charmed by the speedy service and friendly staff, which offset the out-of-touch decor. Open daily 8:30am-9:30pm. ❷

Restaurant el Vegetariano, Av. 3 Pte. 525 (☎246 5462). While the Vege's cafeteria-style 1950s decor may make you think you've come to the wrong place, stay cool—the *chorizo* and *jamón* (sausage and ham) on this menu are made of spiced soy. Fruit drinks 9-15 pesos and gigantic salads 24 pesos. For take-out, bring your own container for a ecologically-minded 5% discount. Their *energética* (28 pesos), tropical fruits topped with yogurt and granola, will make you wish for a franchise in your neighborhood. *Comida corrida* 39 pesos. Open daily 7:30am-9pm. ❸

👁 SIGHTS

Historic Puebla is a sightseer's paradise. Perhaps this is why busloads of Mexican students and North Americans from nearby language schools file into the *zócalo* every weekend, cameras and maps in hand. Most sights are clustered around the *zócalo*, but some are located a few minutes away in the **Centro Cívico 5 de Mayo.**

SIGHTS NEAR THE ZÓCALO

The 1999 Puebla earthquake damaged several of the major sights near the *zócalo*. Most damaged sights were scheduled to reopen in 2002; however, the ruin was more extensive than it seemed, and many sights promise to reopen in 2004.

■ CATEDRAL BASÍLICA DE PUEBLA. Visible from all directions, the massive cathedral is the obvious starting point for any tour of the city. Constructed between 1575 and 1649 by an indigenous labor force working under Spanish direction, the cathedral's dark Baroque facade is enlivened by bright *talavera* domes. No less impressive is its interior, with ornate, inlaid choir stalls behind the freestanding octagonal Altar Mayor, and a statue of the Virgin, known as *la conquistadora* because she arrived with the first Spaniards. *(Guided tours start at 30 pesos, 100 pesos for a group of 10. Open M-Sa 10:30am-12:30pm and 4-6pm.)*

■ MUSEO AMPARO. Three blocks south of the *zócalo*, the Museo Amparo traces the social history of Mesoamerica through art and architecture. An impressive timeline shows artistic and architectural advancement on five continents, and the extensive Pre-Hispanic art collection begins with small artifacts from the far end of time. The *salas of arte virreinal* have been stunningly restored. Skip the 10-peso headphones—the audio presentations offer only the most basic and obvious information. Much more is available in the written guides (in Spanish, English, and French) available for free in each room. *(Calle 2 Sur 708. ☎ 229 3850. Open Su-M and W-Sa 10am-6pm. 25 pesos, students 15 pesos; M free. Guided tour Su at noon, 90 pesos; in English, 175 pesos. Headphones 10 pesos plus 10 peso deposit.)*

CASA DE LAS MUÑECAS. The 1999 earthquake badly damaged the Casa, and it is expected to be only partially reopened in 2004. When it's open, the museum, one of Puebla's most entertaining buildings, is worth a visit. This "House of the Dolls" is decorated on the outside with *talavera* renditions of the labors of Hercules. Some say the sculptures on the outside are the architect's rivals, while others say they are meant to be the city aldermen who protested when the Casa was built higher than the municipal palace was. Inside, the **University Museum** displays exhibits on regional history and portraits of over 200 martyrs. *(Calle 2 Nte. 4 at the zócalo's northeast corner. ☎ 246 2899. Open Tu-Su 10am-5pm. 11 pesos, students 5 pesos; W free.)*

IN RECENT NEWS

LAST OF THE VOCHITOS

Changing market trends finally managed to do what no insecticide could—kill off the original VW beetle. On July 30, 2003 at 9:05am, the last of the classic beetles rolled off the production line of the Volkswagon factory in Puebla (the last to make the car), marking the end of a storied 70-year career that spanned four continents. Beetle number 21,529,464 was born amid bittersweet fanfare, accompanied by a *mariachi* band playing "*El Rey.*" The decision to end production of the car came amid declining sales, stiff competition from newer compact models and, more significantly, a government move to phase out two-door taxis in the capital, where Beetles are ubiquitous, helped spur the downfall.

The 300 classic Beetle assembly-line workers in the massive Puebla plant will be transferred to other departments in the facility, which also produces Jettas and new Beetles.

Still, the original Beetle lives on. While number 21,529,464 is destined for a Nazi museum, over a million of its brethren still crawl the roads of Mexico, where people have adopted the German import as one of their own. One recent survey found that one in every eight passenger vehicles in Mexico is a Beetle, where enthusiastic Mexican drivers bestowed it with the beloved made-up nickname of "vochito" or "vocho."

MUSEO BELLO Y GONZÁLEZ. The Museo Bello, like the Casa de las Muñecas, was badly damaged in the 1999 earthquake. Because the stairs and part of the second floor caved in, the museum is closed indefinitely. The museum displays the art collection of late textile magnate José Luis Bello, including a diverse selection of ivory, iron, porcelain, earthenware, and *talavera* artifacts. Guided tours are offered in Spanish and English, but English tours may be indecipherable. *(Av. 3 Pte. 302 at Calle 3 Sur, 1 block west of the southwest corner of the zócalo. ☎ 232 9475. Open Tu-Su 10am-4:30pm. 10 pesos, students 5 pesos; Tu free.)*

IGLESIA DE SANTO DOMINGO. Puebla's first great religious foundation, this extravagant, gilded church is an important example of Spanish and international Baroque. The building was constructed between 1571 and 1611 by Dominican rural converts. Statues of saints and angels adorn the altar, but the church's real attraction is the **Capilla del Rosario,** a chapel to the left of the altar, laden with enough 22-karat gold to make the King of Spain jealous. Masks depicting an Indian, a *conquistador* in armor, and a *mestizo* hang above three doors on the side of the chapel. On the ceiling, three statues represent Faith, Hope, and Charity. The 12 pillars represent the 12 apostles; the six on the upper level are each made from a single onyx stone. Since there was no room for a real choir, designers painted a chorus of angels with guitars and woodwinds on the wall over the door. *(Between Av. 4 and 6 Pte. on 16 de Septiembre. ☎ 232 3548. Open daily 8am-2pm and 4-8:30pm. No visitors allowed during mass: 8:30am, 6:30, 8pm. Free.)*

CASA DE AQUILES SERDÁN. Originally the home of Aquiles Serdán, printer, patriot, and martyr of the 1910 Revolution, the house is today the **Museo Regional de la Revolución Mexicana.** Hundreds of bullet holes, both inside and out, bear witness to Serdán's assassination. The museum also includes photos of Serdán and other Revolutionary faces and names and newspaper clippings and correspondence that narrate the development of the Revolution. One room is dedicated to Carmen Serdán and other female Revolutionaries. *(Av. 6 Ote. 206. ☎ 242 1076. Open Tu-Su 10am-4:30pm. 10 pesos, children and students 4 pesos; Tu free.)*

EX-CONVENTO DE SANTA MÓNICA. When Benito Juárez's Reform Laws went into effect in 1857, they not only weakened the Church's power, but forced the nuns at the *convento* into hiding. The convent operated in secrecy for 77 years before it was accidentally rediscovered. Today, the Ex-convento serves as a museum of curious and sporadically-labeled religious art, much of which was produced by the nuns themselves. Particularly eerie is a life-sized re-creation of the Last Supper, in which plaster apostles in real robes sit around a colonial dinner table. Even more unnerving is the nun's crypt, where those who died during the period of hiding were quietly plastered into the walls and honored with scrawl that spoke of their lives. Also open to visitors is the beautiful kitchen (doubling as a laboratory) where the nuns first made *chiles en nogada*. *(Av 18 Pte. 103. ☎ 232 0178. Open Tu-Su 9am-6pm. 23 pesos; Su free.)*

EX-CONVENTO DE SANTA ROSA. The birthplace of the original *mole*, from 1683 to 1861 this building housed the nuns of the order of Santa Rosa. Today, the Ex-convent is a museum of *artesanía poblano*, offering examples of arts and crafts from different areas of the state. The kitchen and a nun's cell have been preserved in their original condition and provide a glimpse into the combination of piety and joyous cooking that was cloistered life. On Sunday afternoons, the courtyard doubles as a theater for free concerts. *(Ave. 14 Pte. between Calles 3 and 5 Nte. ☎ 232 9240. Open Tu-Su 10am-5pm. 10 pesos includes a guided tour.)*

IGLESIA DE SAN FRANCISCO. Across Blvd. Héroes de 5 de Mayo from El Parián (see p. 394), Puebla's oldest neighborhood contains the city's oldest church. Built by the Franciscans between 1535 and 1585, it features an incredible *talavera* and orange-red tile facade that contrasts sharply with the ominous bell tower. On your way out, experience the legacy of the city's nuns in the delectable *dulces típicos* being sold in the surrounding plaza. (*Av. 14 Ote. and Blvd. Héroes del 5 de Mayo. Open 24hr.*)

CASA DE LA CULTURA. A base for exploring cultural events in the city, the Casa houses the **Biblioteca Palafoxiana,** an impressive 43,000 volume library that began with Juan de Palafox's 6000-book collection, donated to the city in 1646. His original library includes an illuminated copy of the Nuremberg Chronicle from 1493. Although it, too, sustained extensive damage in the 1999 earthquake, the library has mostly reopened, with a display showing the damage. Ask for a monthly calendar of cultural events at the information desk in the back of the courtyard. (*Av. 5 Ote. 5.* ☎ *246 1301. Open Tu-F 10am-5pm, Sa-Su 10am-4pm. 10 pesos, students 5 pesos; Tu free.*)

CENTRO CÍVICO AND OTHER SIGHTS

With the exception of **Africam Safari,** the following sights are located in the **Centro Cívico 5 de Mayo.** A short trip from the *centro*, the Centro Cívico was the location of the May 5, 1862 **Battle of Puebla,** in which general Ignacio Zaragoza defeated the French in their advance toward Mexico City. The former battleground is now a large, unkempt park, where austere patriotic signs compete for attention with frolicking young lovers. (*To get to the Centro Cívico, Catch a #72 bus or #8 colectivo, both 3 pesos, on Blvd. Héroes de 5 de Mayo, 3 blocks east of the zócalo. Get off when you see a large, multi-armed cement monument to Zaragoza that sits on an empty glorieta. Facing away from the monument, cross the street and walk uphill toward the park.*)

IMAGINE INTERACTIVE MUSEUM. This state-of-the-art interactive museum provides youngsters—and those who are young at heart—hours of fun as they wander through the museum's 150 exhibits. The interactive highlight might be the Venture Simulator, which places the rider in a virtual roller coaster (10 pesos). They also have a bed of nails on which you can lay down, an exhibit on paper recycling, and a chemistry exhibit that teaches you how to make your own hair gel and "rubber bouncy thingy." Though targeted at kids, adults will secretly enjoy the activities and jostle for space at the exhibits. (*Next to the Planetarium.* ☎ *235 3419. Open M-F 9am-1pm and 2-6pm, Sa-Su 10am-2pm and 3-7pm. 35 pesos, children 30 pesos.*)

MUSEO DE LA NO INTERVENCIÓN. This oddly-named museum houses artifacts, paintings, and documents dealing with the Battle of Puebla and General Zaragoza. The museum also features a panoramic recreation of the battlefield as it might have looked in 1862 and exhibits on French rule in Mexico. (*From the Zaragoza monument, follow the road as it curves past a defunct information center. A large concrete Mexican flag marks a fork in the road. To the right is the Fuerte de Loreto, which now houses the museum. Open Tu-Su 10am-4:30pm. 28 pesos; Su free. Guided tours from 30-40 pesos for a group.*)

MUSEO REGIONAL DE ANTROPOLOGÍA. With lots of visual exhibits ingeniously housed in one room, the museum narrates the social history of Puebla state, from man's arrival until today. The huge, armless, life-sized statue of San Cristóbal made entirely out of wood will impress, while other exhibits hold your interest. The model of an indigenous dwelling will make you appreciate your hotel room. (*Once you leave the fort, retrace your steps up the road. The yellow museum is on the right before the intersection.* ☎ *235 8713 or 235 9720. Open Tu-Su 10am-4:30pm. 30 pesos; Su free.*)

PLANETARIUM. Next to the Museo de Historia Natural, the planetarium—in the shape of a giant, glittering, silver pyramid—is currently not active, but plans on reopening its doors in 2004 after renovations are complete. It still offers an **Omnimax** theater, with showings Tu-F at 10am, noon, and 4pm. Across from the museum is the **Recinto Ferial,** an exposition center and fairground. (*Next to the Museo*

Regional de Antropología. ☎235 9720. Open Tu-F 4-6pm, Sa-Su noon-6pm. At 2pm on weekends, there is a free movie (regular format). 25 pesos, students 20 pesos.)

FUERTE DE GUADALUPE. This semi-ruined fort honoring Cinco de Mayo would offer stunning views of Puebla and the surrounding mountains, if it weren't for the many trees that block the view. A new, steep entrance fee makes the long walk to the ruins even less atractive. (Follow the road to the left of the Museo de la No Intervención and take a right at the 2nd intersection. The fort is all the way at the end of the road. 28 pesos; Su free.)

AFRICAM SAFARI. A longer trip takes you to this ecological zoo dedicated to conservation and recreation. The park holds over 3000 free-roaming animals, representing approximately 250 species. The geographically organized theme areas span Asia, the Americas, and Antarctica. Visitors drive through the park, stopping at designated locations to take photos and mingle with the quadrupedal residents. (16km southeast of Puebla, the Safari is best reached by bus. Estrella Roja offers packages that include roundtrip fare from CAPU or the zócalo and park admission. From CAPU: M-F 11am, Sa-Su 10am. From the zócalo: Tu-Su 11am and 2pm. 125 pesos, children 115 pesos. If driving, head to the south of the city and then east, following the signs to Valsequillo. Africam ☎235 8829 or 235 8718. Open daily 10am-5pm. 100 pesos, children 95 pesos. Tip Tours (☎248 5580; www.tiptours.com.mx) organizes tours that depart from the zócalo 11:30am and 2:30pm daily.)

🎵 ENTERTAINMENT

Bars and theaters pile up in the zócalo, while a younger local crowd heads for the bars in **Plazuela de los Sapos,** creating a loud and social weekend scene. Farther from the zócalo, between Calles 21 and 29 Sur on Juárez, is the **Zona Esmeralda,** lined with even more bars and discos. If you're prepared to spring for a cab, however, you may as well continue on to the clubs and bars on the **Recta Cholula,** the highway connecting Puebla and Cholula. The true center of the area's thriving nightlife, the Recta is jam-packed with college and language school students all night, every night. Since buses stop running early, it's best to take a **taxi** (50 pesos). Ask to be let off by the clubs near UDLA (Universidad de las Américas).

Teorema, Reforma 540 (☎242 1014), 3 blocks west of the zócalo. A bookstore/cafe by day, Teorema is a trendy alternative to the bar scene by night. After 9pm, a varied young clientele crowds in to hear nightly live music, chat with friends, and drink café con licor (25 pesos) in this literary lair. Cover Su 15 pesos, M 11 pesos, Tu-W 15 pesos, Th-Sa 20 pesos. Open daily 9:30am-2:30pm and 4:30pm-2am; music starts at 9:30pm.

El Alebrije, Recta Cholula km 2 (☎249 4295). If you're young, beautiful, and rich, El Alebrije welcomes you. Talk to the capitán to get a table, or mingle with friends on one of the zebra-striped dance floors while the pop and electronica thumps and the 42 disco balls twinkle. Drinks from 40 pesos. Cover 50 pesos. Open Th-Sa 10:30pm-4am.

La Batalla, Calle 6 Sur 504A (☎246 3565), in Plazuela de los Sapos. Spiffy young socialites and stout, middle-aged men shake it under low lights to a pounding beat, while Sunday afternoons find bohemians and troblas in the background. 2 for 1 beer special 6-10pm. Beer 20-24 pesos, mixed drinks 30 pesos. Cover Th 15 pesos, F-Sa 25 pesos. Open Su noon-1am, Tu-W 6pm-2am, Th 5pm-2am, F-Sa noon-3am.

🛍 SHOPPING

Home to embroidered textiles, clay ornaments, woven palms, and a 450-year tradition of talavera, Puebla offers numerous and diverse shopping opportunities. At **Mercado el Parián,** with entrances on both Av. 2 Ote. and 4 Ote. at Calle 6 Nte., tourists gather to buy hand-painted talavera ceramics and tiles, as well as leather purses, beads, and other trinkets. For less expensive *talavera* purchases, head to **Av. 18 Pte.**, west of Av. 5 de Mayo. North of El Parián, at Calle 8 Nte. 410, is the **Barrio del Artista**, where *poblano* artists paint and sell their works in the street. Sundays from 10am-6pm, the **Plazuela de los Sapos**, south of the *zócalo* on Calle del Sapo, fills with antique bazaars selling bronze figures, old coins, and *talavera*.

◖ FESTIVALS

The **Casa de la Cultura**, Av. 5 Ote. 5, is the place to go for information about Puebla's cultural events. Pick up a monthly calendar and check the board at the rear of the courtyard for the latest schedules. (☎246 1301. Folk dances Sa and Su. Films Th-Su. Open 24hr.) Also be sure to check the schedule posted inside the **Teatro Principal** (☎232 6085), which lists weekly performances. A new program at **Centro Cultural Santa Rosa** (☎232 9240), located in the **Ex-Convento de Santa Rosa,** includes performances of popular and traditional music and experimental theater. On Sunday afternoons, the courtyard at the Ex-convent hosts free concerts and dance exhibitions.

In addition to June's *mole* cook-off and August's *festival de chiles en nogada*, the city of Puebla celebrates several secular events throughout the year. The end of April kicks off a month-long *fiesta* celebrating May—May 5-25, to be precise. Each day the streets fill with various types of expositions. Special events include *corridas de toros* and cock fights. In the **Festival Palafoxiana,** Juan de Palafox is remembered for his religious influence and the generous donation of his namesake library to the city. The celebration runs from the last Friday in September until November 19, and features dances, concerts, theatre performances, and art.

CHOLULA ☎222

The energy and exuberance of the student population from the Universidad de las Américas, (UDLA for short) unite with small-town hospitality to make Cholula (pop. 95,000) a welcome alternative to the big-city anonymity of nearby Puebla. Olmecs, Zapotecs, Toltecs, and Aztecs all had their moments of glory here, and each left their mark by adding another tier or temple to the city's Great Pyramid. Cholula's ceremonial importance had waned by 1520, when Cortés and his men slaughtered 6000 Cholutecos in what is now known as the Cholula Massacre— punishment for a supposed alliance between the *cholutecas* and the Aztecs. To further punish the city, Cortés vowed to erect 365 churches—one for every day of the year—on top of the city's native temples. While he never completed his goal, the 37 churches in Cholula today have ensured the city's continued role as a place of pilgrimage, both for the faithful and for the curious. An easy daytrip from Puebla or Mexico City, Cholula draws urban escapists with its churches, balmy weather, and lively *portales*. Just don't expect much sleep—bells from the 37 church towers start ringing early on Sunday morning.

▐ TRANSPORTATION

Colectivos to Puebla and destinations within Cholula can be flagged down at a variety of locations in the city center, including the corner of **Av. 4 Pte.** and **Calle 3 Nte.**, as well as at **Morelos** and **Calle 2 Sur** (30min. to Puebla's CAPU, 5 pesos). After the *colectivos* stop running at 10pm, you'll have to negotiate a price with a local **taxi** (40 pesos or more). *Sitios*, available throughout the city, can be found at the southeast corner of the *zócalo*.

To get to the *zócalo* from the Estrella Roja **bus station,** Av. 12 Pte. 108 (☎247 1920), between 5 de Mayo and Calle 3 Nte., walk east to the intersection of Av. 12

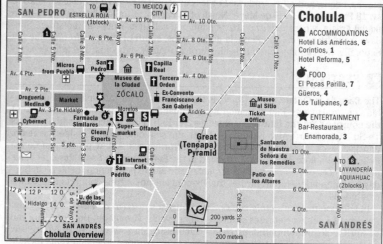

Pte. and 5 de Mayo, turning right on 5 de Mayo. Walk four blocks downhill toward the large yellow church of San Pedro. **Estrella Roja** runs buses to: **Mexico City** via Puebla (2½hr., 2 per hr. 4:25am-8pm, 89 pesos) and **Puebla** (30min., 2 per hr. 4:25am-9pm, 5 pesos). For more destinations, try Puebla's CAPU (see p. 387).

ORIENTATION AND PRACTICAL INFORMATION

Cholula is on Mex. 150, 122km east of Mexico City and 8km west of Puebla. The municipality encompasses two small towns—**San Pedro Cholula** and **San Andrés Cholula.** The *zócalo,* tourist office, and most restaurants are located in San Pedro. San Andrés, on the other hand, is mostly residential and contains everything to the east of the Great Pyramid. The walk between the two can be lonely at night; taxis travel the distance for 20 pesos.

TOURIST AND LOCAL SERVICES

Tourist Office: On the corner of 12 Ote. and 4 Nte. (☎261 2393). A fair walk from the *zócalo,* but the tourist office offers a variety of photocopies that provide helpful information on Cholula. Some English spoken. Open daily 9am-7pm.

Currency Exchange: Casa de Cambio Azteca, Calle 2 Sur 104 (☎247 2190). Open M-F 9am-7pm, Sa 9am-2pm. Banks on Morelos at the *zócalo* have more limited hours but offer comparable rates and have **ATMs. Bital Bank,** Morelos 14 (☎247 6591), cashes **traveler's checks.** Open M-Sa 8am-7pm.

Market: Cosme del Razo, with entrances on Calles 3 and 5 Nte., between Hidalgo and Av. 4 Pte., also in the *zócalo.* Open daily 8am-8pm. On Su and W, the already crowded market swells with even more merchants.

Supermarket: For pre-packaged food and toiletries, try **Tienda Sindical de Consumo Crom,** Alemán 116, a supermarket near the corner of Av. 3 Ote. Open daily 8am-9pm.

Laundry: Lavandería Aquiahuac, on Av. 14 Ote. 2D, 4 blocks east of the pyramid, just after 5 de Mayo. 7 pesos per kg. Open M-Sa 9am-6pm.

EMERGENCY AND COMMUNICATIONS

Emergency: ☎060.

Police: At the Presidencia Municipal, Portal Guerrero 1 (☎247 0562), in the arcade under the arches. Little English spoken.

Red Cross: Calle 7 Sur 301 (☎247 8501), on the corner of Av. 3 Pte., a bit of a hike from the *centro*. Walk-in service. No English spoken.

Pharmacy: Droguería Medina, Hidalgo 502 (☎247 1644), on the corner of Calle 5 Nte. Open 24hr. **Farmacia San Juan Bautista,** Calle 3 Nte. 405 (☎247 3445), on the corner of Av. 6 Pte. Open daily 8am-10:30pm.

Hospital: Clínica de IMSS (☎247 5155), at Calle 4 Nte. and Av. 10 Ote. No English spoken. **Hospital San Gabriel,** Av. 4 Pte. 503 (☎247 0014). No English spoken.

Fax: Telecomm, Portal Guerrero 9 (☎247 0130). Telegrams, fax, Western Union. Open M-F 8am-7:30pm, Sa-Su 9am-noon. **Papelería Toño,** Morelos 8 (☎/fax 247 1149), on the south side of the *zócalo*. Open daily 8am-8pm.

Telephones: LADATELs line Morelos and Hidalgo on the south side of the *zócalo*.

Internet: Internet Cafe, Calle 2 Sur 502B (☎247 8834), at Av. 5 Ote. 15 pesos per hr. Open daily 9am-9pm. **Offanet,** Morelos 212. 13 pesos per hr. Open daily 9am-8pm.

Post Office: Calle 7 Sur 505 (☎247 5917), just past Av. 5 Pte. Open M-F 8am-3pm. **Postal Code:** 72761.

ACCOMMODATIONS

Near the *zócalo* and the pyramid, budget hotels are scarce. While several moderately priced hotels are located north of Cholula on **Carretera Federal México-Puebla,** visitors willing to make the trek should consider staying just 30min. away in Puebla, where they will hit the cheap hotel jackpot.

Hotel Reforma, Calle 4 Sur 101 (☎247 0149), near Morelos. A short stumble from the *portales*. Small private baths paired with street noise and somewhat flimsy doors. Duck into the connected **Bar Reforma** to examine wall murals and photographs of all 128 churches in and around Cholula. Ring to enter after 10:30pm. Singles 180; doubles 240 pesos; triples 320. ❸

Corintios, Calle 5 Nte. 801 (☎247 0495). The trip from the *zócalo* is worth it for the deal. Walk up the winding stairway in the light interior to get to your spacious, bright blue and white room. Private baths have separate compartments for shower, toilet, and sink. Discounts for 3-day and week-long stays. Doors close at 8pm, but extended service allows you to check in all night. Singles 120 pesos; doubles 180 pesos. ❷

Hotel Las Américas, Av. 14 Ote. 6 (☎247 0991). From the *zócalo*, take Morelos and walk past the pyramid approximately 4 blocks. The hotel is on the right after 5 de Mayo. The bright flowers and trimmed grass surround the oasis pool and accent the 70s architecture. Comfortable rooms have TV and phone; curtainless private bathrooms are one giant shower. Visitors should be wary of walking the long, desolate path past the pyramid at night. Singles 170 pesos; doubles 280 pesos; renovated rooms 310. ❸

FOOD

Influenced in part by Puebla's culinary traditions, most of Cholula's restaurants feature several variations of *mole poblano*. For a good variety of cheap local food, wander through the **Cosme del Razo** market and the food stands in the *zócalo*. Cholula's most affordable establishments are located on **Hidalgo,** perpendicular to the *portales*. Toward the bus station, family-owned *torta* shops and market stands offer even better prices, but eating in the *zócalo* can be a great way to meet locals, and the *charla* (chat) is worth the few extra pesos.

■ **Güeros,** Hidalgo 101 (☎247 2188). Select your favorite North American or Mexican tunes from the jukebox as you munch on reasonably-priced regional specialties (20-40 pesos) or *antojitos* (12-18 pesos). Local families and couples populate the modern, spacious eating area, while the bar is an informal meeting place for solo patrons. Tacos start at 9 pesos, sandwiches, *tortas*, and *cemitas* (sub-like sandwiches) 10-22 pesos, and *comida típica* 24-44 pesos. Try one of their inventive pizzas for a very Cholulan twist to a familiar dish. Open daily 9am-midnight. ❸

Los Tulipanes, Portal Guerrero 13 (☎247 1707), on the west side of the *zócalo*. The scenic views of the *zócalo*, piped-in Mexican melodies, and delicious *comida corrida* (40 pesos, Su 45 pesos) draw locals to relax in the shade of *portales*. The moderately priced menu features breakfast (starting at 28 pesos), *antojitos* (18-30 pesos), *comida típica* (45 pesos), and meat and fish entrees (30-55 pesos). Open daily 8am-9pm. ❹

El Pecas Parrilla, Alemán 512A (☎247 1618), at the corner of Av. 7 Pte., offers all the quality service, savory meat dishes, and colorful ambience of tourist restaurants, at lower prices. *Cemitas* and *tortas* 9-18 pesos, tasty *molletes con chorizo* 16 pesos. Open daily 2pm-2am. ❸

👁 SIGHTS

Cholula's chief attractions are also its most visible: the **Great Pyramid** looms over the town's center and the brightly colored towers of Cholula's 37 churches jut above the rest of the city. The June 1999 earthquake that devastated so many of Puebla's sights impacted Cholula as well. Many churches sustained extensive damage. Fortunately, the combined efforts of the government, churches, and community enabled the reconstruction of many churches. Although a few churches, such as the Santuario de Nuestra Señora de los Remedios, are still being repaired, others near the *zócalo* are resplendent in their newly restored beauty.

THE GREAT PYRAMID AND ENVIRONS

TENEAPA PYRAMID. When Cortés destroyed the Toltec temple atop the misshapen hill that dominates Cholula, he was unaware that the hump of earth was actually a giant pyramid. Tunneling into the "hill" in the twentieth century, archaeologists discovered three other pyramids built one on top of the other, indicating successive enlargement of a smaller original pyramid. Archaeologists believe that the original pyramid, dating from roughly 200 BC, was built by the Olmecs or a related group. When the Toltec-Chichimec groups settled in Cholula in the 12th century, they named the pyramid Tlachiaualtepetl, or "man-made hill," and may have practiced human sacrifice atop it. Sophisticated drainage systems kept the structure, by volume the largest pyramid in the world, intact. Today, the tunnels and some excavations on the south and west sides of the pyramid are open to visitors. A joint conservation-excavation program is currently under development, with plans to resume excavation in 2005. (*Entrance is on Morelos, across from the railroad.* ☎247 9081. *Ruins and tunnels open daily 9am-6pm. 32 pesos; Su free.*)

MUSEO AL SITIO. Before entering the Indiana-Jones-style tunnels, visit the museum across the street from the ticket booth. Centered around a helpful diorama of the pyramid (guaranteed to convince skeptics that it is not, in fact, a hill), the museum features area artifacts, tracing Cholula's rise as a ceremonial center. A reproduction of *"Los Bebedores,"* one of the site's famous frescoes and one of the largest murals in Pre-Hispanic Mesoamerica, graces the back room, connected to the main exhibit by a reproduction of a tunnel. Information in both Spanish and English. (☎247 9081. *Open daily 9am-6pm. Free with tickets to the pyramid.*)

TUNNELS AND PATIOS. To reach the open-air excavations on the side of the pyramid opposite the entrance, most visitors walk through the labyrinthine archaeological tunnels that riddle the pyramid's base. Deeper, darker, slightly scary side tunnels can be explored with a guide or by yourself. See if you can find a particularly stunning section of one of the interior pyramids' main staircases, which has been excavated from bottom to top. The underground adventure ends at the south side of the pyramid in the **Patio de los Altares,** a mostly unexcavated grassy area dotted with pyramid chunks in various renovated states. English language pamphlets can be purchased at the bookstore near the end of the outdoor excavations, though the bare essentials can be gleaned from the explanatory markers, written in Spanish and English. Guides help greatly. *(Guides in Spanish or English, 70 pesos.)*

SANTUARIO DE NUESTRA SEÑORA DE LOS REMEDIOS. No ticket is required to reach the Santuario, a church built atop the pyramid in 1594, but the trek is more taxing than a Stairmaster workout. When the Spanish built the sanctuary, they dedicated it to La Virgen de los Remedios to safeguard against the gods from whose ruined temple the walls were constructed. After collapsing in a 1864 earthquake, the structure was rebuilt using much of the original material. Once again Cholulans are repairing the small, flower-filled sanctuary after the 1999 earthquake. Fortunately, the Virgin, set in her fabergé jewelry box, remained unharmed, and celebrations in her honor continue each June and September. On a clear day, the majestic view from the top of church courtyard reaches as far as the snow-capped volcanoes **Popocatépetl** and **Ixtaccíhuatl,** as well as the rest of Cholula and its many churches. *(From the patio, follow the path as it takes you back to the railroad tracks. Make an immediate right where the fence ends and begin climbing. Open daily 8am-6pm. Free.)*

CHURCHES AND THE ZÓCALO

If you don't have the energy to hike to every single one of Cholula's 37 churches, don't despair: four of the most spectacular border the *zócalo* itself.

EX-CONVENTO FRANCISCANO DE SAN GABRIEL. Hoping to use the church for a great conversion, the 16th century Franciscans used Indian labor to construct San Gabriel on top of the Templo de Quetzalcóatl. Despite San Gabriel's imposing size, the Franciscans found it too small for their epic conversion campaign and in 1575 began work on the Capilla Real, two doors down. The altar in today's chapel was built in 1897, utilizing a Neoclassical style designed to emphasize the mass of the already weighty church. *(At the southeast corner of the zócalo. Not open to tourists.)*

CAPILLA REAL. The most visually striking of the city's churches, the 49-domed structure was finished in the early 17th century, filling its role as the long-awaited auditorium for thousands of Indians to hear mass at once. The wall behind the splendid altar is covered with three famous paintings depicting the story of the Virgin of Guadalupe. The Capilla Real lacks the ornate gold filigree of the surrounding churches; its simplicity is defined by the ever-changing panorama of whitewashed arches, soaring domes, and uniquely decorated side-chapels. *(The northernmost church on the east side of the zócalo. Open daily, except 1-3:30pm.)*

CAPILLA DE LA TERCERA ORDEN. Gold ornamentation and seven large 18th- and 19th-century paintings decorate the interior, while the church's small dome balances Capilla Real's vastness. A recent renovation updated the Capilla's somber look, introducing two huge windows on either side of the altar that light up the church. *(Between San Gabriel and Capilla Real.)*

PARROQUIA DE SAN PEDRO. As a 17th-century construction, San Pedro displays an architectural style unique to its age: Baroque meets Renaissance in ornate fashion. The interior has been spectacularly restored and features a *Churringuer-esque* cupola. Eighteenth century paintings adorn the walls, including one of Diego de Borgraf's most powerful depictions of Christ. *(In the northwest corner of the zócalo, entrance on 5 de Mayo. Open daily 6:30am-1:30pm, 4-6pm.)*

CASA DEL CABALLERO ÁGUILAR MUSEO DE LA CIUDAD DE CHOLULA. This small museum traces the continuous habitation of Cholula from about 1000 B.C. Pre-Hispanic pots and artifacts are showcased in the first two exhibits, while the next two contain colonial arts. After an exhibition of modern photography, a visit to the restoration laboratories rounds out the museum. *(4 Ote. 1. Open Su-Tu and Th-Sa 9am-3pm. 20 pesos, students 10 pesos.)*

ON THE OUTSKIRTS OF CHOLULA

SANTA MARÍA TONANTZINTLA. Almost as famous as Cholula itself are several churches in the surrounding villages, particularly Santa María Tonantzintla. Built atop a Pre-Hispanic temple, the church's bright saffron facade hides a startling interior, with over 450 stucco faces staring from the walls and ceiling. Saints, musicians, and chiefs congregate with animals and flowers in an explosion of iconography, the handiwork of the same indigenous artisan who executed the plans of European artists in Puebla's Capilla del Rosario (see p. 392). *(To get to Tonantzintla, take a colectivo marked "Chipilo" at Ave. 6 Ote. and 5 de Mayo. 3-4 pesos. Get off when you see a yellow church on your left; Tonantzintla is a short walk down the pedestrian-only street to your right.)*

SAN FRANCISCO ACATAPEC. A 15min. walk away (or an even shorter 3-peso bus ride) lies the town and church of San Francisco Acatapec. Built in 1588, the facade of the church is almost as ornate as Tonantzintla's walls. The front wall and the dome of the church are entirely covered in brilliant *talavera* tile set into an overgrown graveyard in one of the most exquisite applications of the famous tiles. *(To go directly from Cholula to Acatapec, simply ride a few km farther on the same "Chipilo" bus that you would take for Tonantzintla. Open daily 10:30am-6pm.)*

UNIVERSIDAD DE LAS AMÉRICAS. The elite, private university UDLA (pronounced OOHD-lah), demonstrates the universality of university culture. The verdant, bench-filled campus serves as a respite from the city's dusty mayhem. Students, locals, and visitors find cheap diversion watching UDLA's *béisbol* and *fútbol* teams face neighboring colleges during the fall and spring semesters. **Cafetería Santa Catarina** serves institutionalized Mexican food. Souvenirs are available in the nearby social center kiosk. *(Take an eastbound colectivo anywhere on Av. 14 Ote. 3 pesos. www.udlap.mx. Cafeteria open M-F 7am-9:30pm, Sa-Su 7:30am-8pm.)*

🎵 📷 ENTERTAINMENT AND NIGHTLIFE

Although vibrant and exciting by day, Cholula is even better by night. Most of the cafes and bars on and near the *zócalo* are open daily, and fill up with a lively, yet low-key student crowd from UDLA. For more high-powered and high-cost social activity, venture out of town to the Recta Cholulaon the way to Puebla.

BARS

Bars in Cholula center around the lively *zócalo* and Av. 14 Ote., west of Hotel Las Américas in San Andrés. The bars in San Andrés serve local, slightly older clientele, but those in the *centro* cater to a more diverse, younger crowd. **Bar-Restaurant Enamorada,** Portal Guerrero 1, under the *portales*, feeds and inebriates a social, varied crowd. While patrons visit Enamorada earlier in the day for its affordable *comida típica*, the young crowd flocks to its doors around 10:30pm for the live *trova* music until closing. (Beers 15-19 pesos, mixed drinks 37 pesos, and *café con* *licor* 28 pesos. ☎247 0292 or 247 7022. Open Tu-Su 8am-2am.) **Café Tal**, Porral Guerrero 7, also under the *portales*, provides coffee lovers with a moderately-priced, relaxing place to caffeinate. Start the night right with one of the liquored-up *cafés*. (Coffees start at 8 pesos. Open daily 9am-2am.)

CLUBS

Undoubtedly, the **Recta Cholula** is *the* place to be. Littering the highway between Puebla and Cholula, warehouse-sized *discotecas* are fueled by both cities' youthful energy. Bars and discos in this area frequently reinvent themselves, attempting to get an edge on the market, but you'll find the same student-filled scene regardless of the packaging. Those wanting a wild night of clubbing should dress well and fill their wallets with cash; this is no place for amateurs. To get to the Recta, take a Puebla-bound bus from Av. 14 Ote. past UDLA. Buses stop running around 10pm, so the return trip is best made in a taxi—a pricey finish to a pricey evening. **El Alebrije** (see p. 394) is the top choice of the UDLA crowd. The cheapest drinks around are found at **Deep Lounge**, 14 Pte. 122. Pop, house, and electronica help the night pass quickly, and a good DJ and young, hip crowd close the deal. (☎404 8969. Beer 9 pesos, mixed drinks 12 pesos. Cover 40 pesos. Open Th-Sa 9pm-4am.)

FESTIVALS

A deeply religious town, Cholula celebrates religious festivals with flair. Two different celebrations honor the Virgen de Remedios. Since 1640, Cholula has celebrated the **Bajada de la Virgen** for two weeks in June, when the Virgin descends from her celestial sanctuary to visit the city and surrounding towns. Cholulans carry the figurine through the streets by motorcycle every morning at 7am during the week of the festival. In the evenings, locals revel under the elaborate gateways of flowers, seeds, and glitter decorating the Virgin's route. An even bigger festival takes place from the first day in September to the 8th, the Virgin's **Día Santa. Concierto de las Campanas,** around November 28th, features 130 bell ringers and the continuous playing of 33 church bells from 8-9pm. Celebrations for *Carnaval, Semana Santa,* and Christmas are also big events, when Cholula fills with visitors from Puebla, Mexico City, and surrounding villages.

CENTRAL PACIFIC COAST

Stretching from the quiet fishing hamlets near San Blas to the busy port of Manzanillo, the central Pacific coast boasts kilometer after kilometer of smooth sand massaged by the ebb and flow of the tide. Hot but not overly humid, the region's climate easily pleases, and the sun rarely fails to illuminate the azure skies.

A state of varied terrain, **Nayarit** is marked by volcanic highlands, tropical jungles, and a network of lakes and rivers. The republic's oldest indigenous group, the Huichol, make their home here, brightening village streets with their colorful dress. This verdant region grows the lion's share of the nation's marijuana and served as the setting for *Journey to Ixtlán*, Carlos Castañeda's renowned book describing experiences with hallucinogens in a small town between Tepic and Guadalajara. Hallucinogen use has long been part of Cora and Huichol *indígena* traditions and is still common practice among shamans in their incantations.

South of Nayarit lies **Jalisco,** the most touristed state along the central Pacific coast. Much of the world's perception of Mexican pop culture could be stamped "*Hecho en Jalisco*" (Made in Jalisco). The *jarabe tapatío* (hat dance), *mariachis, charreria* (cowboy culture), and tequila all originated in this state. For much of its history, however, the province remained isolated from the rest of the republic, possessing neither silver nor gold, jewels nor water, fertile land nor agricultural climate. It wasn't until the 1920s, when railroad tracks extended to Guadalajara, that this Sierran town (elevation 1552m) grew into a metropolis; today, it is Mexico's second-largest city. On the coast, Puerta Vallarta—full of discos, English-language bookstores, cafes, and, of course, tourists—further exemplifies Jalisco's boom. Only an hour and a half away, tiny Perula offers a stark contrast with its undeveloped, unspoiled, and almost uninhabited beaches.

Tiny **Colima** is home to spectacular black-sand beaches and pleasant mountain towns where tourists can escape the resort scene and breathe in cool, crisp air. The state is also home to the city of Colima, a sparkling, untouristed gem full of gardens, and Manzanillo, the workhorse of Mexico's Pacific coast. This port has not paused once in 700 years of commerce to wipe its sweaty brow, and only recently has it begun to polish its image for the benefit of visitors.

HIGHLIGHTS OF THE CENTRAL PACIFIC COAST

REVEL in **Guadalajara** (see p. 410), Mexico's 2nd-largest city; home to *jarabe tapatío, la avenida de zapatos,* and many *mariachis.*

GO GAUDY in **Puerto Vallarta** (see p. 426), which is no longer the quiet, secluded paradise of the 1960s. The thriving tourist industry has transformed the city with glitzy nightlife, luxury hotels, shop-stuffed streets, and a very happening **gay scene** (see p. 419). The **best beaches** lie south of the city (see p. 432).

SCORCH your feet on the dazzling black-sand beaches of **Cuyutlán** (see p. 442), which accompany a wondrous lagoon, and quiet solitude.

TRAVEL to **Tequila** (see p. 424), the kitschy and fun birthplace of your favorite liquor.

SNEAK AWAY from it all in **Bahía de Navidad** (see p. 434), where you can swim, surf, and sunbathe on your choice of beautiful beaches. Both **Bahía de Navidad** and **Melaque** (see p. 435) offer budget accomodations and gorgeous beaches on the bay.

CONQUER El Nevado (see p. 449), Colima's own snow-capped volcanic peak.

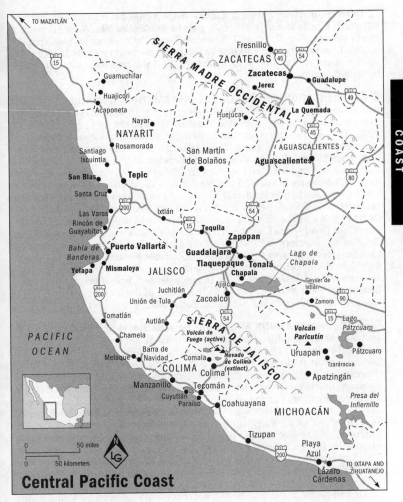

Central Pacific Coast

TO MAZATLÁN

SIERRA MADRE OCCIDENTAL

Fresnillo
ZACATECAS
Guamuchilar
Zacatecas
Jerez
Guadalupe
Huajicori
Acaponeta
La Quemada
Nayar
Huejúcar
NAYARIT
Rosamorada
AGUASCALIENTES
Santiago
Ixcuintla
San Martín
de Bolaños
Aguascalientes
San Blas
Tepic
Santa Cruz
Ixtlán
Las Varas
Rincón de
Guayabitos
Tequila
Zapopan
*Bahía de
Banderas*
Puerto Vallarta
Guadalajara
*Lago de
Chapala*
Tlaquepaque
Tonalá
Yelapa
Mismaloya
Chapala
Geyser de
Ixtlán
JALISCO
Ajijic
Juchitlán
Zacoalco
Zamora
Unión de Tula
Lago
Pátzcuaro
PACIFIC
OCEAN
Tomatlán
Autlán
SIERRA DE JALISCO
Volcán
Paricutín
Chamela
*Volcán de
Fuego (active)*
Uruapan
Pátzcuaro
Tzaráracua
Barra de
Navidad
*Nevado
de Colima
(extinct)*
Melaque
Comala
COLIMA
Apatzingán
Colima
Manzanillo
Tecomán
*Presa del
Infiernillo*
Cuyutlán
Paraíso
Coahuayana
MICHOACÁN
Tizupan
Playa
Azul
0   50 miles
0   50 kilometers
TO IXTAPA AND
ZIHUATANEJO
Lázaro
Cárdenas

NAYARIT

SAN BLAS   ☎ 323

San Blas's corner of the Nayarit Coast is a benevolent Bermuda Triangle. Travelers who run aground here glance at the scruffy *zócalo* and start to wonder why they came, but before they can give the matter much thought, a hot drowsy haze descends, transporting them to a dreamy *siesta* land embedded in the sounds of crashing surf and humming jungle. Some get stranded permanently, drawn by the mythical mile-long wave, the surrounding jungle estuaries, and the Nayarit mountains, full of waterfalls and coffee plantations.

⊟ TRANSPORTATION. The **bus station** is in the *zócalo*, but has limited departure schedules. **Estrella Blanca** (☎285 0043) goes to: **Guadalajara** (5hr., 7am, 214 pesos); **Puerto Vallarta** (3hr.; 7, 10am; 120 pesos); **Tepic** (1¾hr., every hr. 6am-7pm, 40 pesos). **Transporte Noreste y Nayarit** sends its rickety fleet to: **Culiacán** (8hr., 285 pesos); **Mazatlán** (5hr., 180 pesos); **Santiago** (9, 11am, 1pm; 40 pesos); and other local destinations.

⬛🖫 ORIENTATION AND PRACTICAL INFORMATION. San Blas is 69km northeast of Tepic by Mex. 15 and 54. **Juárez**, the town's main street, runs parallel to the bus station on the south side of the *zócalo*. **Batallón** runs perpendicular to Juárez from the *zócalo*'s center and leads to the closest beach, **Playa Borrego.**

The **tourist office** in the Palacio Municipal on the *zócalo* provides maps and information. (☎285 0005. Open daily 9am-6pm.) **Banamex**, on Juárez east of the *zócalo*, changes money and has a 24hr. **ATM.** (☎285 0030. Open M-F 8am-3pm.) Other services include: **police** (☎285 0028), on Sinaloa opposite the bus station, through the last door in the Palacio Municipal as you walk away from the *zócalo;* **Farmacia Económica**, Batallón 49 (☎/fax 285 0111; open daily 8:30am-2pm and 4:30-9pm); **Centro de Salud**, on Batallón and Campeche, five blocks south of the *zócalo*, at the turnoff for Hotel Garza Canela (☎285 0232; no English spoken); **Clínica IMSS**, at Batallón and Guerrero (☎285 0227; open daily 7am-6pm; at other times, enter on Canalizo); **caseta**, Juárez 4, which has **long distance phone** and **fax** service (open daily 8am-10pm); **Internet access** at Mercado 17, just off the *zócalo* (open Su 11am-2pm and 6-11pm, M-Sa 11am-11pm; 15 pesos per hr.); **post office**, at Sonora and Echeverría, one block north and one block east of the northeast corner of the *zócalo* (☎285 0295; open M-F 8am-2pm). **Postal code:** 63740.

🖫🖸 ACCOMMODATIONS AND FOOD. Hotel Morelos ❷ and **Hotel Ranchero ❷** are both immaculate, friendly, and filled with birds and flowers. Hotel Morelos, Batallón 108, three blocks south of the plaza, has a courtyard with washing facilities, a communal kitchen, and the company of a large, tame pelican named "Pinocho." (☎285 0892. Singles and doubles 120-150, with bath 150 pesos.) Across the street, Hotel Ranchero remains orderly despite the chatty parrots and canaries inhabiting its garden. Communal kitchen also available. (Singles and doubles with bath and fan 150 pesos.) Halfway to the beach are **Bungalows la Quinta California ❹.** Keep an eye out for the sign on the left of the road. Bungalows come with kitchen, bathroom, TV, 2 bedrooms and a dining room. English spoken. (www.sanblasmexico.com. Bungalows 200 pesos in the low season.)

Surfers congregate at the **⬛Restaurante Playa Azul ❷**, reached by following Batallón 1km as it winds along the beach past a series of *palapas*, to take in vegetarian food and major carbs at great prices. (Open daily 7am-10pm. Fresh spaghetti and pesto 20 pesos.) Mouth-watering *mariscos* can be found at the seashell-plastered **La Isla ❺**, on Mercado and Paredes. (☎285 0407. Shrimp 70 pesos, fried fish 60 pesos. Open Tu-Su 2-10pm.) **La Familia ❸**, Batallón 18, is, as you might have guessed, a family joint; it has wall-mounted shark's teeth, old drums, sea bottles, and a provocative cow statue. Try the fried fish (47 pesos) and tacos (28 pesos) while wondering how the framed **Mike Tyson boxing glove** got here. (☎285 0258. Open daily 8am-10pm.) Sandwiches (8 pesos) and *tortas* (15 pesos) await customers at **Lonchería Paz ❶** on Canalizo, one block up from the plaza. (Open daily 7am-4pm and 6:30-11pm.)

◪ BEACHES. Known for its symmetrical waves and safe, sandy bottom, San Blas has long been a haven for surfers. Although the Stoner's Cafe, heart and soul of San Blas surf culture, was destroyed in October 2002 by Hurricane Kenna, its spirit and services live on at the ■Restaurante Playa Azul. Here the motto for surf lessons is *"si no te paras no te pagas"* (if you don't stand up, you don't pay) and with instructors like Pompis, the Mexican longboard champion, the confidence is understandable. Besides surfing and food there are showers and camping. (www.stonerssurfcamp.com. Open daily 7am-10pm. Camping 20 pesos. 1hr. with instructor and board 150 pesos; just board 30 pesos per hr. Surf excursions 50 pesos per hr. and the cost of gas.) The president of the San Blas surfing club, Juan García, gives lessons and rents equipment at **La Tumba de Yako**, Batallón 219, about six blocks from the *zócalo*. (☎285 0462. Lessons 150 pesos per hr., surfboard *(tabla)* rental 150 pesos per day.) San Blas's main attraction is the smooth water, packed sand, and long waves of **Playa las Islitas.** During the stormy months of September and October, surfers flock to San Blas in hopes of catching the famous, yearly mile-long wave from Las Islitas all the way to **Playa Matanchén.** To reach Las Islitas, take a bus from the station (every hr. 6am-5pm, 8 pesos; returning 7:30am-4pm) or from the corner of Sinaloa and Paredes in front of the green-trimmed building (15min., 4 per day 8:30am-2:30pm, 6 pesos). The latter bus continues to other beaches, passing Las Islitas on its return to town 1hr. later. A taxi to Las Islitas costs 60 pesos. The first few stretches of sand that greet you are lovely, but more seclusion and prettier coves await farther along. At the southern end of Batallón, **Playa Borrego,** an easily accessible grey sand beach, offers a relaxing view of the coast. Borrego's mosquitos feast on those who dare venture out at sunrise or sunset. Quiet, pretty **Playa del Rey,** off the coast of Borrego, has stronger currents. A *lancha* will take you there from the pier at the west end of Juárez (approx. 7am-4pm, round-trip 20 pesos).

◙ **SIGHTS.** Locals hype San Blas's jungle estuaries—not its beaches—as the town's best attraction. The easiest way to explore the area's ecological wealth is from a *lancha* to the springs of **La Tobara.** The trip is best made in the morning, when the still waters and matted foliage are filled with birds, turtles, iguanas, and, if you look hard, crocodiles. Farther upriver you have the option of swimming or continuing on to the **crocodile farm,** where biologists are attempting (with apparent success) to re-introduce crocodiles to the estuary. Trips can be arranged directly with the boat owners who sit around the small wharf on Juárez's eastern end. (1½-2½hr., daily 7am-4pm, 300-400 pesos.)

For do-it-yourself exploration, stroll to the old 17th-century fort and 18th-century church on top of **La Contaduría** overlooking town. Head east on Juárez as if leaving town, and turn right before the "Cape Victoria 7" sign onto the dirt road behind the restaurants. Veer right off that road onto a stone path that winds uphill. The hill affords a great view of San Blas and the estuaries. Turning west on Juárez will lead to the 19th-century ruins of the **Ex-aduana.** Other hikes in the region include trips to waterfalls, coffee plantations, and the Aztec island of Mexicalitán. Getting to most trailheads requires a taxi or car. For information, ask at the tourist office, which will put you in touch with a guide, or inquire at Restaurante Playa Azul, which offers some of the cheapest tours (La Tobara 260 pesos).

◪ **ENTERTAINMENT.** Except for bands of youths crowded in the *zócalo* on weekends, nights in San Blas are as tranquil as its days. **Mike's CantaBar** rarely gets wild or crazy as dance music rolls and Mike performs vintage rock in what looks like an antique airport lounge. (☎285 0432. Beer 5 pesos, mixed drinks 36 pesos. Live music Th-Su starting around 10pm. No cover. Open daily 8pm-midnight.) For something upbeat and raucous, join the town's teen population at **Disco Voga,** Juárez 75, next to Hotel el Bucanero. (☎285 0101. Beer 12 pesos. Cover up to 30 pesos. Open F-Su 9pm-2am.)

O WORK, ALL PLAY

THE WORLD'S FASTEST GAME, THE WORLD'S STRANGEST NAME

If you think the name *jai alai* (pronounced HIE-lie) doesn't sound like Spanish, you're right. The game and the name are imported from the Basque, a people living in the Pyrenees mountains, linguistically and culturally distinct from both the Spanish and French. Originally played only during Basque holidays—*jai alai* means "merry festival" in Basque—the sport is now being played, and gambled on, all over the world. It was also played as an exhibition sport in the 1992 Barcelona Olympics.

In *jai alai*, two to four players on a three-sided court (spectators sit behind a barrier on the fourth side) use slender straw *cestas* (arm-baskets) to catch and throw an extremely hard ball of rubber and nylon encased in goatskin. The handcrafted balls fly at speeds of up to 300km per hr., earning *jai alai* the Guinness World Record for the "World's Fastest Game." Competitions are similar to squash tournaments, with players rotating on and off the court king-of-the-hill style. Before the introduction of helmets, 30 professional players were killed between 1900 and 1960. Today, *jai alai* is a popular betting sport not only in Mexico, but in many parts of the world, including Spain, France, Italy, Indonesia, and the Philippines.

RINCÓN DE GUAYABITOS ☎327

Named for the "little guavas" that fell in local orchards in days of yore, the only thing falling in Rincón de Guayabitos (pop. 3000) today are 8-year-olds diving into the town's swimming pools. A vacation spot for middle-class Mexican families during July, August, December, and *Semana Santa*, parents kick back in the jungle heat as beaches and pools fill with children. In the off-season, the hotels fill with Canadian and American snowbirds staying for months at a time. Most accommodations cater to people in groups, enticing them into extending their stays with ever-increasing discounts. Anyone with time to kill will find Guayabitos's beautifully verdant hillsides and calm waters a worthy stop on the path to *tranquilidad*.

⌷ TRANSPORTATION. Transportes del Pacífico buses (☎274 0001) in **La Peñita,** at the end of La Avenida on the *carretera,* head to: **Guadalajara** (4hr., every hr. 6am-noon, 200 pesos); **Mexico City** (6, 8pm; 530 pesos); **Tepic** (2hr., every 30min., 55 pesos). If you are going north, take a **Transportes Norte Sonora** bus from the station on the *carretera,* to **San Blas** (3hr.; 8am, 12:15, 3pm; 55 pesos).

▓ ⁊ ORIENTATION & PRACTICAL INFO. Guayabitos snuggles into the southern Nayarit Coast, 100km north of Puerto Vallarta. Rincón's main street, **Sol Nuevo,** runs from the entrance of town at the *carretera* south along the curve of the beach. Many goods and services, including the bus stations, are in the neighboring town of **La Peñita.** To get there, take a white *colectivo* from the church (3.5 pesos) or walk north on the beach, crossing over the rock headland and continuing inland into town.

The **tourist office,** Sol Nuevo 1, at the entrance to town from the highway, has pamphlets and information on less-accessible beaches. (☎274 0693. Open M-F 9am-6pm.) **Banamex,** in La Peñita on La Avenida just before the *carretera,* has a 24hr. **ATM.** (Open for exchange M-F 9am-5pm.) La Peñita has an open-air **market** every Thursday. Other services include: **laundromat,** on Sol Nuevo before the large Los Cocos resort at the south end of the street (open M-Sa 7am-8pm; 10 pesos per kg); **Clínica Rentevía** (☎274 0140), in La Peñita on Acapulco; **police** in La Peñita on the central plaza; **Farmacia CMQ,** on La Avenida in La Peñita at the *carretera* (☎274 1277; open 24hr.); **post office,** at the entrance to town (☎274 0717; open M-F 9am-2:30pm), and **telegram** and **fax** service in the same complex (☎ 274 0354; open M-F 8am-2pm); **Internet Nivel Zero** halfway down Sol Nuevo (☎ 274 1254; 30 pesos per hr.; open M-Th 8am-9pm).

⌨ ACCOMMODATIONS AND FOOD. Accommodations in Guayabitos are "bungalows," which sleep 4-8 people and include a kitchen. Prices are designed for families, so if you aren't traveling with at least four people, you may end up paying for a lot of empty beds. ◼**Villas Buena Vida ❹**, Retorno de los Laureles 2 (☎ 274 0231 or 800 640 3388; www.villas-buenavida.com) delivers the good life that its name promises, with oceanfront terraces, cable TV, A/C, fans, fridges, kitchens, and private baths in all the rooms. Enjoy the private beach or one of three swimming pools. (4-person villa July-Aug. and long weekends 1050 pesos; December and *Semana Santa* 1250 pesos; all other times 900 pesos. 5% discount for cash. 10% discount for a week; 20% discount for two weeks; 35% discount for a month or more. Discounts available for rooms in reduced occupancy.) If you really want to get away, try **Un Rincón del Cielo ❸** (☎ 274 7070), near the town of Monteón. María and Juan check the answering machine once a day so they know when and where to pick up their guests to whisk them to their cliff-top getaway. Terrific views, a secluded beach and mango-filled days await at the Punta Raza. It is out of the reach of phone and power lines; although there's a generator, they'd prefer to leave it off. (2-person rooms 400 pesos, with private bath 500 pesos.) Cheaper hotels line the highway, but the only true budget option lies in neighboring La Peñita, at **Hotel San Juanito ❶** on Valle Punto de Mita 4 just off La Avenida. Simple rooms with private baths and fans. (☎ 274 0036. 100 pesos per person.)

Most families that visit Guayanitos cook their own meals in their bungalow kitchens. Still, lots of informal eateries post their prices outside, allowing you to window-shop for lunch. It's hard to beat the rotisserie chicken places on Sol Nuevo that offer whole chickens for 70 pesos, but the restaurant at **Villas Buena Vida ❸** (☎ 274 0231), may come close with good food and a tremendous seaside view at reasonable prices. (Cheeseburgers 35 pesos. Open daily 8am-8pm.) Eateries also line La Avenida in La Peñita.

⌂ BEACHES. The waters of Guayabitos's main beach are calm enough for floating, but do ask locals about riptides and currents. **Villas Buena Vida** organizes a full range of maritime excursions. A 2hr. snorkeling trip with boat will cost 150 pesos per person; a similar excursion with diving equipment will cost 600 pesos per person. Boats can take you to the inshore volcanic-rock reef around **Isla Islote**.

GIVING BACK

HEROES IN A HALF SHELL

Neither wind nor rain nor, uh, hurricane will keep the dedicated volunteers at **El Campamento Tortuguero el Naranjo** from their appointed rounds. When Hurricane Kenna struck Mexico's Pacific coast in 2002, the *palapas* at Naranjo—one of three organizations dedicated to the conservation of endangered turtles, located just north of Puerto Vallarta—were completely destroyed. Undeterred, the staff continued their task: every night from sundown to sun-up, they scour the beach for nests or eggs of endangered olive ridley, leatherback, and eastern Pacific green turtles, whisking eggs away to a protected hatchery.

Headed by English-speaking Vicente Aldrete, Naranjo focuses on the long-term; the goal is not just protection of the eggs, but understanding of the ecosystems in which the turtles live. The group also works toward education of the locals, who often kill mature turtles while fishing and still consider the eggs a delicacy. The staff is composed largely of dedicated students of biology from Mexican universities, but the UK's **Outreach International** (☎ 01458 274 957; www.outreachinternational.co.uk) sends gap-year students to all three beach locations to participate.

For info directly from the source, contact Vicente care of the Hotel Penamar in Guayabitos (☎ 327 274 1142).

Guayabitos is surrounded by rich mountain jungle. For a pleasant coastal vista, climb the path to the cross that leads up from Sol Nuevo before Los Cocos. Fandor Moreno, at the tourist office, runs 2hr. guided tours (80 pesos per person) to the prehistoric petroglyphs found there. The tours are intended for 3-4 people, though he can always fill extra places at nearby hotels. For a faster-paced view of the countryside, **Tours Lolis** (☎275 0332) organizes 3hr. ATV expeditions along the bird- and crocodile-filled mangroves. (400 pesos per ATV, 500 pesos with kayak trip included; an ATV can fit two people.)

Rincón de Guayabitos is home to **El Campamento Tortuguero el Naranjo.** Although their *palapas* were destroyed by Hurricane Kenna in October 2002, their efforts to conserve turtle populations continue. Volunteers are always welcome and should contact Vicente at the Hotel Penamar (☎274 1142 or 274 1143; fax 274 0225). From about July-Nov. volunteers stay up all night collecting eggs, ensuring the safe return of the mothers to the sea and eventually releasing the young turtles into the ocean. There may be a nominal fee for transportation.

TEPIC   ☎311

Once called *Tepique* (the Place Between the Hills) by Pre-Hispanic inhabitants, Tepic became a center for trade and commerce under the Spanish in the 16th and 17th centuries. Now home to the Nayarit state government, the city is still a cross-roads as well as a haven of slow-paced cafes and shady green parks.

E TRANSPORTATION. Buses leave from the newer station east of the *centro*. To reach the *centro*, cross the street and catch a yellow bus (6am-10pm, 3 pesos), or a **taxi** (15 pesos). To return, take a "Central" or "Mololoa Llanitos" bus from the corner of México Sur and Hidalgo. **Transportes del Pacífico** (☎213 2320) travels to: **Culiacán** (6hr., every hr., 186 pesos); **Guadalajara** (3hr., 10 per day, 124 pesos); **Mexico City** (10hr., every hr. 3pm-7am, 461 pesos); **Puerto Vallarta** (3½hr.; 4, 5pm; 117 pesos); **San Blas** (2hr., every hr. 6am-7pm, 40 pesos).

■ ⁊ ORIENTATION AND PRACTICAL INFORMATION. Situated 170km north of Puerto Vallarta and 280km south of Mazatlán, Tepic links Guadalajara (230km to the southeast) with the Nayarit beaches. The main drag, **México,** runs north-south six blocks west of the bus station. Addresses on this street change from Norte (Nte.) to Sur about four blocks north of **Insurgentes,** the largest east-west street. Yellow minivan *combis* run back and forth daily along México and Insurgentes (6am-midnight, 3 pesos). At its northern terminus, **Plaza Principal** (officially called the *centro histórico*) is dominated by the cathedral on one end and the Palacio Municipal on the other. Most tourist services lie on or near México.

Dirección de Turismo Municipal, Puebla at the corner of Nervo, one block from the bus station, hands out maps and organizes free tours of the city. (☎212 8036 for bus station; 216 5661 for downtown. Open daily 9am-8pm. Tour of historic downtown daily 10am and 5pm; Cerro de la Cruz tour daily 6:30pm; nightlife tour F-Sa 10pm and 11:15pm.) **Casas de cambio** (most open M-Sa 9am-2pm and 4-7pm) clutter México Nte. **Bancomer,** México Nte. 123, a few blocks south of the plaza, has **ATMs.** (Open M-F 8:30am-5:30pm, Sa 10am-2pm.) Other services include: **luggage storage,** in the new bus station (3 pesos per hr.); **police station,** Tecnológica Ote. 3200 (☎211 5851; little English spoken; only accessible by taxi, 10 pesos); **Farmacia CMQ,** Insurgentes at México (open 24hr.); **Hospital General** (☎213 7937), on Paseo de la Loma next to La Loma Park; **Internet** at **Cafetería la Parroquia,** Nervo 18 (15 pesos per hr.; open M-F 8am-9:30pm); **post office,** Durango Nte. 33, between Allende and Morelos (☎212 0130; open M-F 8am-7pm, Sa 8am-noon). **Postal code: 63000.**

▐▌ ACCOMMODATIONS AND FOOD. ▨Hotel Morelia ❶, Morelia 215, has a lush courtyard and clean, simple rooms. (☎216 6085. Singles 70 pesos; doubles 90 pesos; private baths 20 pesos extra.) Next door, **Hotel Pasadena California ❶**, Morelia 215, is slightly cheaper and offers similarly clean, basic rooms. (☎212 9140. Singles 60 pesos, with private baths 80 pesos.) Family-run **Hotel las Americas ❶**, Puebla 317 at Zaragoza, has spotless rooms with TV, fans, and baths. (☎216 3285. Singles 90 pesos; doubles 130 pesos. Each additional person 20 pesos.)

Tepic's tons of fruits, fish, and coffee flow through the capital and into most restaurants. **Restaurant Vegetariano Quetzalcóatl ❹**, on León Nte. at Lerdo, four blocks west of Plaza Principal, hosts a popular buffet (45 pesos, Tu-Sa 1pm) in its leafy courtyard. (☎212 9966. Open Tu-Sa 8:30am-5:30pm.) To sit with the people and shovel in cheap, authentic eats, go to **Restaurant Tirayán ❶**, Zaragoza 20, half a block down from the intersection with Veracruz. (Egg breakfasts 18 pesos, fish filets 31 pesos, *tostadas* 10 pesos. Open daily 8am-9pm.) If you want to get above the thronging masses, then **La Gloria ❺**, upstairs at México and Lerdo Altos next to the cathedral, offers more refined fare and incredible views of the plaza. (☎847 0464. *Filete miñón* 80 pesos. Open daily 8am-11pm.)

◯▐ SIGHTS. The capital of Nayarit, Tepic has gathered to itself the cultural wealth of the region and houses it in a number of fairly sizeable and centrally located museums. Two of these are dedicated to Tepic's most famous artists. The **Museo Amado Nervo**, Zacatecas 284 Nte., celebrates the life, works and exploits of the poet in the house where he was born. (☎212 2652. Open M-F 9am-2pm and Sa-Su 10am-1pm.) The **Museo Emelia Ortiz**, Lerdo 192 Pte., displays the caricatures and *indígena*-inspired art of the Tepic natives as well as local contemporary art. (☎212 2652. Open M-Sa 9am-7pm. Free.) The **Casa Museo de Juan Escutia**, Hidalgo 71 Ote., celebrate the lives of the *niños héroes*, particularly this "Niño Héroe de Chapultepec," one of the group of military cadets who died fighting off US invaders and in the process achieved martyr status. (☎212 3390. Open M-F 9am-2pm and 4-7pm, Sa 10am-2pm). The **Museo Regional de Antropología e Historia de Nayarit**, México Nte. 91 south of the plaza at Zapata, offers an extensive exhibit on Juichol embroidery, accompanied by sparse explanations of the group's other crafts, including their dreamlike, peyote-inspired yarn paintings. (☎215 1900. Open M-F 9am-7pm, Sa-Su 9am-3pm. 32 pesos.) The **Museo de los Cuatro Pueblos**, Hidalgo Ote. 60, also showcases local indigenous groups, with the work of Juichols, Náhuatls, Coras, and Tepehuanos on display. (☎212 1705. Open M-F 9am-2pm and 4-7pm, Sa 10am-2pm.) The **state capital** lies at México and Abasolo, a gracefully domed structure dating from the 1870s.

▶ DAYTRIPS FROM TEPIC

IXTLÁN DEL RÍO

Ixtlán del Río lies between Tepic and Guadalajara on Mex. 15. The 88km journey takes about 1½hr. Most bus services from Tepic to Guadalajara will stop here and cost 40-50 pesos. The town itself stretches along Av. Hidalgo, down which the bus service runs. The tourist office, Hidalgo Pte. 672, offers a series of brochures on the archaeological site and the town itself. (☎243 5639. Open M-F 9am-6pm, Sa-Su 10am-2pm.)

Although there is evidence of human habitation in Nayarit as far back as the third millennium BC, early residents did not reach the highlands until the 4th century BC; Ixtlán, or "place of obsidian," is one of their earliest and perhaps most significant settlements. The early Ixtlán period (300 BC-AD 300) is characterized by a form of subterranean funerary known as Las Tumbas de Tiro. One of these sites has been excavated and demonstrates the familial burial and the ceramics that characterize this period. The culture developed significantly during roughly the next half-millennium, achieving its peak in the Middle Ixtlán period (750-1110AD). During that time, this group, known as the Aztatlán, built the network of stone structures that brought the site the name Los Toriles. The Aztatlan cutlure worshipped the four elements, and it is believed that each of the series of central altars partially delineated by stone colonnades would have been dedicated to gods representing one of these elements. The stepped circular pyramid has a markedly different shape than the others and is the only one with a recognizable dedication: a close examination of the walls will reveal a series of spirals which represent moving air and hence the wind god Ehecatl, who is closely identified with Quetzalcóatl. Although the architecture bears strong Tolteca influences, some features appear to be unique, such as the cruciform windows. The museum, to the left as you enter, sets out other aspects of the culture, as well as the significance of this site in the context of the region's archaeological record. (Open daily 8am-5pm. 23 pesos, adults over 60, teachers, and students free; Su free.)

JALISCO

GUADALAJARA
☎ 33

More Mexican than Mexico itself, Guadalajara (pop. 8 million) is the crossroads of the republic. Here, in the capital of Jalisco state and the country's second-largest city, north meets south, colonial meets modern, and traditional meets cutting-edge. The city has spawned many of Mexico's most marketable icons: bittersweet *mariachi* music, *jarabe tapatío* (Mexican hat dance), and tequila. Founded in 1532 by Nuño de Guzmán, the most brutal of the *conquistadores*, Guadalajara was born in bloodbath; most of the region's *indígenas* were slaughtered, and few Pre-Hispanic traditions survived. In the years following, the city served as the capital of Mexico and a key battleground in the Revolution. Today, Guadalajara entices natives and tourists with parks galore, a bevy of fine museums, four large plazas, and stately colonial architecture. Its markets overflow with local *artesanía*, and painters, thespians, dancers (including the renowned Ballet Folklórico), and street performers continue the city's fine artistic traditions. Meanwhile, the Universidad de Guadalajara, the second-oldest in Mexico, keeps Guadalajara young and colorful it with a measure of intellectual sophistication. Though not built specifically for tourists, Guadalajara nevertheless fulfills their hopes entirely. One can understand why—the city's *tapatío* (as the city's residents call themselves) heritage epitomizes all that was, is, and will be Mexican.

▌ TRANSPORTATION

Airport: Aeropuerto Internacional Miguel Hidalgo (☎3688 5248 or 3818 6100), 17km south of town on the road to Chapala. *Combis* (☎3812 4278 or 3812 4308) run 24hr. and will pick you up from your hotel (40min., 80 pesos). A yellow and white "Aeropuerto" bus passes through the *centro* on Independencia at Los Angeles (every hr. 5:45am-8:45pm, 10 pesos) and makes the trip back from outside "Sala Nacional." Get off at 16 de Septiembre and Constituyentes. Some cabs are metered, and some are not; going to the airport, negotiate a price around 80 pesos. This can be done even if the cab has a meter (on the meter, a trip to the airport runs 120 pesos). Served by: **Aero-California** (☎3616 8284); **Aeroméxico** (☎3669 0202), office on Corona at Madero (open M-Sa 9am-6pm); **Air France** (☎3630 3707); **American** (☎3616 4090); **Continental** (☎3647 4251); **Delta** (☎3688 5397); **United** (☎3616 7993).

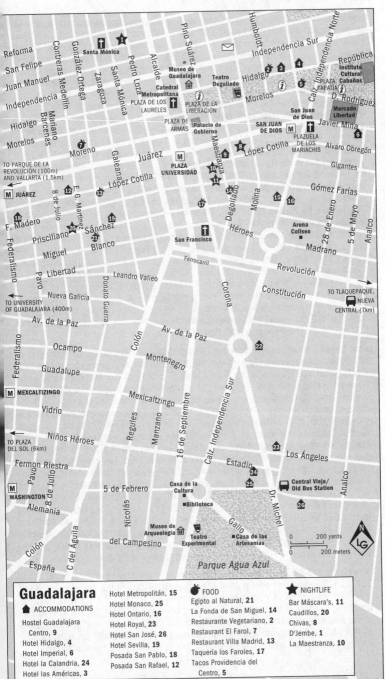

Guadalajara

⌂ ACCOMMODATIONS

Hostel Guadalajara
  Centro, **9**
Hotel Hidalgo, **4**
Hotel Imperial, **6**
Hotel la Calandria, **24**
Hotel las Américas, **3**

Hotel Metropolitán, **15**
Hotel Monaco, **25**
Hotel Ontario, **16**
Hotel Royal, **23**
Hotel San José, **26**
Hotel Sevilla, **19**
Posada San Pablo, **18**
Posada San Rafael, **12**

🍎 FOOD

Egipto al Natural, **21**
La Fonda de San Miguel, **14**
Restaurante Vegetariano, **2**
Restaurant El Farol, **7**
Restaurant Villa Madrid, **13**
Taquería los Faroles, **17**
Tacos Providencia del
  Centro, **5**

★ NIGHTLIFE

Bar Máscara's, **11**
Caudillos, **20**
Chivas, **8**
D'Jembe, **1**
La Maestranza, **10**

Buses: The station, **Nueva Central Camionera,** is in nearby Tlaquepaque. The gargantuan station consists of a failed shopping mall with 7 terminals. Fixed-fare buses and taxis (30-60 pesos, depending on time of day) head downtown frequently, as do "Centro" buses (3 pesos). From downtown, catch a #275, #275A, or "Nueva Central" bus on Revolución or 16 de Septiembre, across from the Cathedral. In a taxi, be sure to specify the *new* bus station. Only partial listings provided; call for more info. **Terminal 1: Primera Plus** and **Flecha Amarilla** (☎3600 0270) go to all major destinations. **Terminal 2:** overflow from Ómnibus de México (Terminal 6) and local carriers. **Terminal 3: Élite** (☎3600 0988). **Terminal 4: Transportes del Pacífico** (☎3600 0979 or 3600 0854) sends 1st- and 2nd-class buses to lots of coastal destinations. Also home to **Transportes Norte de Sonora** (☎3679 0463), with cheap 2nd-class service to distant northern destinations like **Guaymas** (19hr., 784 pesos). **Terminal 5: Línea Azul** (☎3679 0404) goes to many destinations in northeast Mexico. **Terminal 6: Ómnibus de México** (☎3600 0184, 3600 0718, or 3600 0846) provides comprehensive service including: **Aguascalientes** (every hr. 6:30am-midnight, 231 pesos); **Ciudad Juárez** (24hr., 10 per day, 862 pesos) via **Chihuahua** (677 pesos); **Durango** (6 per day, 350 pesos); **La Piedad** (3 per day, 94 pesos); **Matamoros** (7 per day, 605 pesos); **Mexico City** (7hr., every 2hr. 7am-midnight, 387 pesos); **Monterrey** (9 per day, 447 pesos); **Querétaro** (5hr., 3 per day, 229 pesos); **Reynosa** (13hr., 7 per day, 608 pesos); **Tampico** (12hr., 5 per day, 356 pesos); **Tepic** (3hr., every 30min., 168 pesos); **Torreón** (9-10hr., 8 per day, 445 pesos); **Tuxpan** (6 per day, 86 pesos); **Zacatecas** (every hr. 5:30am-12:15am, 196 pesos). **Terminal 7: Estrella Blanca** (☎3679 0404) is the parent company of numerous smaller lines, including Rojo de los Altos and Transportes del Norte. This is the biggest terminal and will take you to almost every major city in the Republic for competitive prices. Many nearby destinations (up to 2-3hr. away) are serviced by the more convenient **Central Vieja** (Old Bus Station), at Dr. Michel across from Parque Agua Azul.

Local Buses: Though usually crowded, always noisy, and sometimes uncomfortable, **minibuses, regular buses** (3 pesos), and big blue **TUR buses** (6 pesos) are an excellent way to get around. Be sure to check the line (A, B, C, or D) of your bus. Generally, A and B run almost the same route along the main drags (with the same numbers), and C and D buses have different routes into the residential neighborhoods. Always check with the driver to confirm the bus's destination. Buses **#60** and **#62** run the length of Calzada Independencia, from the train station past Plaza de Toros. The wired **"Par Vial"** bus runs west on Calzada Independencia, then Hidalgo, before turning onto Vallarta, just short of Mateos. Returning eastward, it cruises Hidalgo 3 blocks north of Juárez. Bus **#258** from San Felipe, 3 blocks north of Hidalgo, runs from near Plaza Tapatía down Mateos to Plaza del Sol, nightclub central. Buses **#52** and **#54** are direct links to downtown along 16 de Septiembre from locations north and south of the city. Bus **#24A** runs the length of Mateos, from Zapopan to beyond Plaza del Sol, in both directions. TUR bus **#707A** circles from the *centro* on Juárez west to Mateos, down to Otero at Plaza del Sol, and north on 16 de Septiembre and Corona to the start of the route. The big red **Cardenal** bus runs west on Madero to Chapultepec along the Zona Rosa, the upscale shopping district west of the *centro*. Bus **#45** returns east on Cotilla. Bus **#51** motors up and down La Paz. Buses run 6:30am-10pm; TUR buses run slightly later.

Subway: (☎3853 7570). The 2 subway lines run smoothly (every 5-10min. 6am-10:30pm, 3 pesos) and offer a great alternative to the bus system for anyone tired of breathing exhaust. A very good map is posted in the stations. **Line 1** runs from the northern boundary of the city, Periférico Nte., more or less along Federalismo to Periférico Sur, with a central stop at Federalismo and Juárez. **Line 2** runs from Juárez and Alcalde/16 de Septiembre, conveniently passing Mina, to Patria in the east. Limited coverage makes the subway more practical than buses for only a few destinations.

▚ **1** ORIENTATION AND PRACTICAL INFORMATION

The heart of the city is the *centro histórico* around **Plaza Tapatía** and **Plaza de la Liberación**. The two major streets **Calzada Independencia** and **Hidalgo/República** (known as República east of Calzada Independencia, and Hidalgo to the west), divide Guadalajara into quadrants. Streets change names at the borders of these quadrants. Note that in addition to Calzada Independencia, Guadalajara has a Calle Independencia, crossing the city east-west just north of the *centro*. The cities of **Tlaquepaque, Zapopan,** and **Tonalá** are all seamlessly joined to the Guadalajara metropolitan area. When taking a bus to the *centro*, make sure you're going to the correct *centro*. The poorer *colonias* (neighborhoods) of Guadalajara can be dangerous any time of day; check with the tourist office before blazing new trails. Throughout Guadalajara, travelers should keep to lighted streets and take taxis after 10pm. Solo women travelers may wish to avoid Calzada Independencia after dark, as the street attracts raucous, drunken men and supports a thriving prostitution trade at all hours. Neighborhoods tend to be significantly worse to the east of Calzada Independencia.

TOURIST AND FINANCIAL SERVICES

Tourist Office: State Office, Morelos 102 (☎3668 1600 or 800 363 2200), in Plaza Tapatía. Friendly staff with helpful maps. Pick up *Guadalajara Weekly* (a free, English-language tourist paper) or *Mexico Living and Travel Update.* Open M-F 9am-8pm, Sa-Su 9am-1pm. Another office in the Palacio de Gobierno. Open daily 9:30am-3pm. Guadalajara, Tlaquepaque, and Zapopan each maintain separate offices. Guadalajara also has two tourist information booths in the Plaza Tapatía, one in the Plaza de la Liberación, one in the Plaza Guadalajara, and one in the Jardín de San Francisco; all are open daily 10am-6pm.

Consulates: Australia, Cotilla 2030 (☎3615 7418; fax 3818 3390), between Vega and Bara. Open M-F 8am-1:30pm and 3-6pm. **Canada,** Local 30 (☎3615 6270 or 800 706 2900 for emergencies; fax 3615 8665), at Hotel Fiesta Americana, on the Minerva traffic circle. Catch a "Par Vial" bus. Open M-F 8:30am-5pm. **UK,** Parra 2539 (☎3616 0629; fax 3615 0197). Open M-F 9am-2pm and 5-8pm. **US,** Progreso 175 (☎3825 2700 and 3825 2998; fax 3826 6549). Open M-F 8am-4:30pm. The **Oficina de la Asociación Consular,** at the UK consulate, can provide listings for other consulates.

Currency Exchange: The block of Cotilla between Corona and Molina is a *mercado* with only one product: money. Rates don't vary much. For banking services, head to **Bancapromex,** on Corona at Juárez. Open M-F 8:30am-5:30pm, Sa 10am-2pm.

LOCAL SERVICES

English Bookstores: Sandi Bookstore, Tepeyac 718 (☎3121 0863), near the corner of Rosas in Colonia Chapalita. Take bus #50 from Garibaldi or the green "Plus" bus from Juárez. New books and newspapers. Open M-F 9:30am-2:30pm and 3:30-7pm, Sa 9:30am-2pm. The **Hyatt,** at Mateos and México, has issues of the *New York Times.*

Cultural Information: Dirección de Educación y Cultura (☎3668 1644), 5 de Febrero and Analco. **Instituto Cultural Cabañas,** Cabañas 8 (☎3617 4322), in Plaza Tapatía. Open M-F 9am-3pm and 6-9pm. Blue and yellow "Ayuntamiento" stands in the major plazas field cultural and tourist queries. Open daily 8am-8pm. Also check out *Pasiones y Sazones,* the Friday supplement of Guadalajara's *Público,* for special events.

Market: Mercado Libertad, Calle Independencia, next to the plaza. An entire wing contains family-run restaurants. Open daily 8am-8pm.

Supermarket: Gigante, Juárez 573 (☎3613 8638), between Martínez and 8 de Julio. Sells just about everything. Open daily 8am-11pm.

Laundry: Lavandería Aldama, Aldama 125 (☎3617 6427), 2½ blocks off Independencía on the left. Open M-Sa 9am-6:30pm. Full service up to 7kg 35 pesos. Self service wash 3 pesos, dry 12 pesos.

Car Rental: Euro Rent-A-Car, Patria 236 (☎3673 5408). Open M-Sa 10am-9pm. **Auto-Rent,** Federalismo Sur 480 (☎3825 1515), at La Paz. Open M-F 9:30am-8pm, Sa 10:30am-6pm. **Vega's,** González 175 (☎3613 1920). Open M-Sa 9am-9pm.

EMERGENCY AND COMMUNICATIONS

Emergency: ☎060 or 080.

Police: Calzada Independencia Nte. 840 (☎3617 6060, ext. 126 or 143), just before the Olympic fountain. For help in English, call ☎3688 0800.

Red Cross: (☎3613 1550 or 3614 2707, emergency ☎085), at Manuel and San Felipe behind Parque Morelos. Some English spoken.

Pharmacy: Farmacia Guadalajara, Mina 221 (☎3617 8555), at Cabañas. Open 24hr.

Hospitals: México Americano (☎3641 3141), at Colones and América. English spoken. **Green Cross Hospital** (☎3614 5252), at Barcenas and Veracruz. English spoken.

Fax: Palacio Federal (☎3614 2664; fax 3613 9915), at Alcalde and Álvarez. Open M-F 8am-6pm, Sa 9am-noon.

Internet Access: Librería de Porrua Hnos., Juárez 16 (☎3521 2830). Distinguished; sports a cafe and Internet services (10 pesos per hr.). Open daily 8am-8pm. **Cafe Internet,** 8 de Julio 73 (☎3614 5736), brews tasty coffee and serves palatable food. Open daily 7am-11pm.

Post Office: (☎3614 7425), on Carranza between Manuel and Calle Independencia. Open M-F 8am-6:30pm, Sa 9am-1pm. **Postal Code:** 44100.

▶ ACCOMMODATIONS

Guadalajara is full of cheap places to stay; budget hotels are most common in the *centro histórico*, and east of downtown along Mina. Unfortunately, some bargain accommodations are plagued by typical big city problems—24hr. traffic, poor room quality, and prostitution. The best values are around the old bus station. A 10-15min. walk from Plaza Tapatía, this area's advantages include proximity to Agua Azul and easy access to buses going to Guadalajara's appealing *alrededores*, Tlaquepaque, Tonalá, Lake Chapala, and Tequila. Regardless of where you stay, call ahead; many places fill up early in the day. Hotels advertising that they cater to families are declaring themselves to be prostitution-free.

AROUND THE OLD BUS STATION

Noise aside, some of the best budget hotels in Guadalajara are found here.

Hotel San José, 5 de Febrero 116 (☎3619 2811; sanjose7@jal1.telmex.net.mx). A cut above the rest. Tiled surfaces and potted palms make the hectic world outside fade away. All rooms with TV, fan, and private bath. Singles 180-210 pesos; doubles 220-250 pesos. ❸

Hotel la Calandria, Estadio 100 (☎3619 6579). The wood paneling and brass detailing is indicative of the care shown here. All rooms very clean and come with private bath and fan. Singles 115 pesos; doubles 150 pesos. TV 20 pesos extra. ❷

Hotel Royal, Los Ángeles 115 (☎3619 8473 or 3650 0914). Clean rooms with TV, private baths, and fans maintain a 50s feel. Singles 110 pesos; doubles 160 pesos. ❷

Hotel Monaco, 5 de Febrero 152 (☎3619 0018). Slightly pricier than some area hotels, but also slightly nicer, Hotel Monaco offers a vacation from the civic grime. Singles 130 pesos; doubles 140 pesos; triples 150 pesos. ❷

ALONG CALZADA INDEPENDENCIA SUR

This area is generally considered safe, but can be extremely noisy at night due to numerous 24hr. diners and *cantinas* in the area.

Hotel Metropolitán, Calz. Independencia Sur 278 (☎3613 2458). A paradise of bland sterility. Rooms with comfortable beds, TV, fan, and neatly tiled bathrooms open to a pleasant, sky-lit courtyard lobby. Beware of windows facing the street, a major bus route. Singles 130 pesos; doubles 150-220 pesos. ❷

Hotel Ontario, Calz. Independencia Sur 137 (☎3617 8099). Across from Hotel Metropolitán, Ontario pleases the traveler who wants to be in the thick of it. Simple rooms with private baths. Singles 90 pesos; doubles 110 pesos. ❶

Hotel León, Calz. Independencia Sur 557 (☎3619 6141), at Dr. Michel. With the promise that there will always be a room for you, it is a good fallback hotel. Fairly clean rooms with private baths. Singles 90 pesos; doubles 110 pesos. ❶

WEST OF CORONA

Prices in this conveniently located area have risen quickly, while improvements in quality of rooms has sometimes resisted such hastiness. The multitudes of surrounding bookstores and vegetarian eateries may justify the extra pesos, though.

Hotel Sevilla, Sánchez 413 (☎3614 9172 or 3614 9354), between Ocampo and Guerra. Sevilla recently underwent extensive remodelling to produce a lobby of gleaming white tile and richly carpeted rooms with TV, private bath, and fan. Singles 200 pesos; doubles 300 pesos. ❹

Posada San Rafael, Cotilla 619 (☎3614 9146). Renovated with an eye to the building's 19th-century charms, this former monastery is a cut above standard Guadalajara fare. Stone walls keep the city at bay. Singles 180 pesos, with TV and remodeled bathroom 250 pesos; doubles 230/280 pesos. ❸

Posada San Pablo, Madero 429 (☎3614 2811; sancarlo007@avantel.net). Large but simple rooms come with private bathrooms. Travelers chat in the kitchen and courtyard. English spoken. Singles 230 pesos; doubles 300 pesos; triples 390 pesos. ❺

AROUND PLAZA TAPATÍA

Swarms of market vendors in need of beds drive up prices and allow hotels to charge more than their rooms are worth. The cheapest hotels may be frequented by prostitutes, while those southeast of Mina should be avoided.

Hostel Guadalajara Centro (HI), Maestranza 147 (☎3562 7520; www.hostelguadalajara.com). Guadalajara's requisite HI hostel offers dorms with private lockers and average communal bathrooms. Private rooms for 1-2 people come with fan and TV. All guests get continental breakfast and 10min. of free Internet. Wash and dry laundry 50 pesos. Check out 10am. Dorms 100 pesos; private rooms 220 pesos. 10-peso discount for HI and ISIC members. ❷

Hotel las Américas, Hidalgo 76 (☎3613 9622 or 3614 1641), at Humboldt, gets high marks for cleanliness and amiable staff. Carpeted rooms with TV, phone, fans, private bath, and purified water. Singles 160 pesos; doubles 210 pesos; triples 240 pesos. ❸

Hotel Hidalgo, Hidalgo 14 (☎3613 5067). Fairly clean with an almost courtyard and prices that can't be beat. No reservations. Bare-bones cubicles 45 pesos; doubles with bath 65 pesos; quads 90 pesos. ❶

Hotel Imperial, Mina 180 (☎3586 5719). Good upkeep and the protected lobby/courtyard arrangement make the Imperial worthwhile. Rooms come with private bath, cable TV, and fan. Singles 180 pesos; doubles 220 pesos. ❸

CENTRAL PACIFIC COAST

◻ FOOD

Guadalajara has plenty of budget eateries, as well as many expensive, upscale restaurants with international cuisine. *Birria* is the hearty local specialty of stewed meat (usually pork) in tomato broth, thickened with cornmeal and spiced with garlic, onions, and chiles. *Tortas ahogadas*, another local specialty, differ from the standard *torta* with a pork rind filling and special sauce slathered on top, soaking what's often slightly stale bread. After your meal, quench your thirst with an Estrella beer, brewed *clara dorada* (golden clear) right in Guadalajara.

THE CENTRO

Ice cream and fast food make the scene everywhere, while *panaderías* (bakeries) crowd southwest of the plaza, primarily on the blocks enclosed by Pavo, Sánchez, Galeana, and Juárez. **Mercado Libertad ❸**, on Calle Independencia, next to the plaza, is a sensory overload. You can find anything here, from *birria* to fried chicken to live animals. (Huge meals average 26 pesos. Open daily 6am-8pm.)

▨ **Restaurant Villa Madrid,** Cotilla 553 (☎3613 4250). One wall consists of a heaping pile of fruit that employees convert into delicious smoothies and huge *licuados* (25 pesos). *Tostadas* (34 pesos), burritos (36 pesos), and everything else served with lots of sides. Open M-F 12:30pm-9pm, Sa 12:30pm-8pm. ❸

La Fonda de San Miguel, Guerra 25 (☎3613 0809 or 3613 0793). Completed in 1694, la Fonda de San Miguel was once Santa Teresa de Jesús, the oldest convent in the city. It has since been flawlessly restored, leaving a gently-arched collonade filled with caged birds. *Enchiladas carmelitas* 37 pesos, *crepas del convento* 37 pesos, *tacos sonorenses* 40 pesos. Open Su-M 8am-6pm, Tu-Sa 8am-midnight. ❸

Egipto al Natural, Sánchez 416 (☎3613 6277). Formerly Restaurant Acuarius, the name may have changed but loyal customers insist that nothing else has, and the traditional budget, vegetarian cuisine will continue. Vegetarian *comida corrida* 35 pesos, juice 10 pesos. Open M-Sa 10am-6pm. ❸

Tacos Providencia del Centro, Morelos 86 (☎3613 9914 or 3613 9925), next to the state tourist office. A full range of tacos and other *botanas* in a beautifully refurbished building. *Tacos al pastor* 4.5 pesos, *sopa de tortilla* 25 pesos. Open Su 10am-6pm, M-Sa 8am-8pm. ❶

Taquería los Faroles, Corona 250 (☎3613 4723), at Sánchez. Los Faroles tempts hordes of locals and visitors with almost every type of taco imaginable. Tacos made from various cow parts 4-7 pesos. Excellent quesadillas with homemade tortillas 10 pesos. The famous *torta ahogada* is a 15-peso meal. Open daily 7am-midnight. ❶

Restaurante Vegetariano, Hidalgo 112 (☎3614 5447), to the left of the black-painted window. A wide array of vegetarian foods, including salads (13-15 pesos). Sandwiches 7-10 pesos, quesadillas 6-8 pesos. Open Su 9am-5pm, M-Sa 9am-7pm. ❶

El Farol, Moreno 466, 2nd fl. (☎3613 6349), at Galeana. The friendly owner makes a mean *chile relleno*. Complimentary *buñuelo*, a fried dough dessert doused with syrup. Entrees 20-40 pesos, tacos 5 pesos, beer 12-16 pesos. Open daily 10am-8pm. ❸

ZONA ROSA

Most of the places listed below are near the Vallarta and Chapultepec intersection, (on the "Par Vial" and #321 buses), where extra pesos buy excellent food and a measure of elegance. Past Chapultepec, Vallarta supports both a 24hr. Sanborn's and a 24hr. VIPs for those seeking late-night refuge from their budget hotels.

Santo Coyote, Lerdo de Tejada 2379 (☎3616 6978 or 3616 8472). Torch-lined paths lead to *palapa*-shaded tables where waiters serve interpretations of the Mexican canon, such as the cactus-and-cilantro-infused *filete "el patrón"* (130 pesos) or the *crema hacienda de cortez* (48 pesos), a soup of pumpkin flowers, grilled chile, and maize. Open daily 1pm-1am. ❺

La Gorda, Niños Héroes 2810 (☎3121 2126). Long a bastion of traditional *tapatío* cuisine, La Gorda has maintained quality and low prices even as it has grown. Another location at Juan Álvarez 1336 (☎3825 2239). Full meals under 50 pesos. Open Su 1-11pm, M-Sa 1:30pm-midnight. ❹

Café Don Luis, Chapultepec 215 (☎3625 6599), at La Paz. The patio area is a reserve of social butterflies sampling a huge coffee selection. *Café americano* 13 pesos with refills, cappuccino 20 pesos. Internet access 15 pesos per hr. Open Su 4pm-midnight, M-Sa 8am-midnight. ❶

🄶 SIGHTS

More a town of monuments than museums, Guadalajara has perfected the concept of "the plaza." The city's many shopping malls spill over into wide public spaces, packed with *mariachis*, tourists, vendors, and street performers. That said, many of the city's finer sights are in its less chaotic *alrededores*—Zapopan's cathedral, Tonalá's market, Tequila's blue agave, and the picturesque towns around Lake Chapala. The tourist office sells a comprehensive pamphlet called *Puntos de Interés* (5 pesos), complete with maps, sites, and suggested walks.

THE CENTRO

PLAZA DE LA LIBERACIÓN. Abuzz with activity, the plaza is the center of historic Guadalajara. Horse-drawn carriages line up near the Museo Regional, waiting to cart you around the city (45min., 120 pesos). The spacious plaza, with its bubbling fountain and large Mexican flag, is surrounded by the cathedral, Museo Regional, Palacio de Gobierno, and Teatro Degollado. Military personnel ceremonially retire the colors daily at 7pm. An enormous sculpture depicts Hidalgo breaking the chains of servitude in commemoration of his 1810 decree abolishing the slave trade, which was signed in the Palacio de Gobierno.

PALACIO DE GOBIERNO. The palace, built in 1751, served as the headquarters of renegade governments under Hildago from 1810-11 and Juárez in 1858. Today, several José Clemente Orozco murals grace the Palacio. Climb to the roof for a great view. *(Open M-F 9am-8pm. Guided tours available in English.)*

CATEDRAL METROPOLITANA. Facing Teatro Degollado across Plaza de la Liberación, the church was begun in 1561 and completed 60 years later. After an 1848 earthquake destroyed its original towers, ambitious architects replaced them with much taller ones. Fernando VII of Spain donated the Cathedral's 11 richly ornamented altars in appreciation of Guadalajara's aid during the Napoleonic Wars. One is dedicated to Our Lady of the Roses and gave Guadalajara its nickname, "City of Roses." Inside the sacristy is the famed *Assumption of the Virgin*, by 17th-century painter Bartolomé Murillo. The towers, known as *cornucopías*, can be climbed with the permission of the administrators, who are holed up in the side of the building facing Teatro Degollado. Descend beneath the altar (take the steps on the right-hand side) where the remains of three cardinals and two bishops keep one another company. The 60m jaunt up the tower affords the best view in town. *(Open daily 7:30am-7:30pm.)*

INSTITUTO CULTURAL CABAÑAS. Once known as the Hospicio Cabañas, this building was constructed in 1801 to house an orphanage. The huge building served as an art school and a military barracks before its present status as an exhibition/

performance/office space. Orozco murals decorate the building's chapel, which was otherwise finished in 1845. The striking *El Hombre de Fuego* (The Man of Fire)—a dramatic reversal of heaven and hell that tops off Orozco's disturbing portrait of Mexican history—peers down from the dome. (*Hospicio and Cabañas, 3 blocks east of Independencia. Open Su 10am-3pm, Tu-Sa 10am-6pm. 8 pesos, students 4 pesos, children under 12 free; Su free. 10 pesos for camera rights—no flash.*)

MUSEO REGIONAL DE GUADALAJARA. In the old San José seminary, this museum chronicles the history of western Mexico—starting with the Big Bang—with art on display as well. Artsy and educational movie screenings, plays, and lectures take place in the museum's auditorium—inquire within or at the tourist office. (*Liceo 60 at Hidalgo, on the north side of Plaza de la Liberación. ☎ 3614 9957. Open Su 9am-5pm, Tu-Sa 9am-5:30pm. 30 pesos, seniors and children under 12 free; Su free.*)

TEATRO DEGOLLADO. Attend the Ballet Folklórico for a good look at breathtaking Teatro Degollado, named for former governor Santos Degollado. Built in 1856, the Neoclassical structure has gold arches, a sculpted allegory of the seven muses, and, on the ceiling, an interpretation by Gerardo Suárez of Dante's *Paradiso*. In addition to ballet, the Theater hosts the Guadalajara Philharmonic and amateur acts. (*On the east end of Plaza de la Liberación. ☎ 3614 4773. Ballet Folklórico performed by the University of Guadalajara Su 10am. Tickets available at the theater box office. Open daily 10am-2pm and 4-7pm. Tickets start at 25 pesos.*)

PLAZUELA DE LOS MARIACHIS. Immediately after you sit down in this crowded plaza, roving *mariachis* will pounce, using every trick in their bag to separate you from your pesos. Prices for songs range from 20 to 35 pesos. *Mariachis* play deep into the night, but beware: late night the Plazuela becomes a stage for roving unsavories, who may employ other methods to acquire your pesos. (*On the south side of San Juan de Dios, the church with the blue neon cross on Independencia at Mina.*)

PARQUE AGUA AZUL. If tired of the congested city streets, take a stroll in this 168,000 sq. m park, which features tropical aviaries, an orchid greenhouse, a butterfly house, and a sports complex. (*South of the centro on Calzada Independencia; take bus #60 or 62 heading south. Open Tu-Su 10am-6:30pm. 6 pesos, children 4 pesos.*)

NORTH OF THE CENTRO
To reach the following sights, take Ruta #60 or 62 north on Calz. Independencia.

ZOOLÓGICO GUADALAJARA. You wouldn't know it from hanging around the Plaza Tapatiá, but ecological wealth surrounds Guadalajara. The zoo boasts over 360 species from around the world. At the far end of the zoo is a spectacular view of the deep Barranca de Huentitán ravine. (*Continue north on Calzada Independencia past Plaza de Toros, and walk 1.5km to the entrance of the zoo from the bus stop on Independencia. ☎ 3674 4488 or 3674 4360. Open W-Su 10am-6pm. 25 pesos, children 15 pesos.*)

CENTRO DE CIENCIA Y TECNOLOGÍA. The center houses a planetarium, exhibits on stars and rocks, and a garden of sculpted plants. (*A 20min. walk from the zoo. Open Tu-Su 9am-7pm. ☎ 3674 4106 or 3674 3978. Museum 4 pesos, planetarium 6 pesos.*)

🎵 📷 ENTERTAINMENT AND NIGHTLIFE

Guadalajara is known for its cultural sophistication and dizzying variety of entertainment options. To keep abreast of all the happenings—from avant-garde film festivals to bullfights—check the listings in *The Guadalajara Weekly, Ocio, Vuelo Libre,* and the kiosks and bulletin boards in places like Instituto Cultural Cabañas. Be prepared to take a taxi after buses stop running (10pm).

BARS AND CAFES

Cheaper, chiller, and closer to the *centro*, Guadalajara's bars are often a much more palatable entertainment option than its pressure-cooker dance halls. The area around Mercado Independencia is packed with *cantinas*, while glitzier options congregate around Chapultepec.

Chai, Vallarta 1509 (☎3615 9426 or 3616 1299). Uber-trendy locals lounge on the terrace or sprawl on huge couches as MTV projects onto the walls. Iced lattes 15 pesos, gourmet sandwiches 35-42 pesos. Open M-Th 9am-midnight and F-Sa 9am-1am.

D'Jembe, Loza 221 (☎3849 8835), between San Felipe and Reforma. Dig the sand floor and the rhythms and decor reminiscent of Africa. Open daily noon-3am.

La Maestranza, Maestranza 179 (☎3613 2085), at Cortilla. Enjoy Italian food and beer (25 pesos). Live trio W 9:30-11:30pm. Open daily 10am-3am.

Bananas Cafe, Chapultepec 330 (☎3615 4191), at Tejada. Images of US pop stars deck the walls. Unique drinks 17-19 pesos. Outdoor seating. Open daily 9am-midnight.

CLUBS

Elegantly dressed partygoers line up outside classy spots along **Vallarta.** An easy daytime bus ride or walk down La Paz from the *centro* becomes a more expensive cab ride (40-50 pesos) after 10:30pm. To save money, arrive early and eat on **Chapultepec** before hitting the clubs. The newly opened shopping mall **Centro Magno** at Vallarta 2455 has become a nightlife mecca. In addition to a very posh disco, the Centro has a multiplex cinema, **Cinepolis** (☎3122 5657), a **Hard Rock Cafe** (☎3616 4560), and its own **Chili's** franchise. The mall is busy with window-shoppers late into the night, offering a surreal vision of the sanitized Mexican Plaza of the Future. More traditional discos with complex track lighting and elevated dance floors surround the older **Plaza Sol,** accessible by cab for about 60 pesos.

La Marcha, Vallarta 2648 (☎3615 8999; www.clublamarcha.com), at Los Arcos. Fancy art, fountains, and pretension galore. Dress to impress and pulse to electronic beats in this converted 2-story 19th-century mansion. Cover men 140 pesos, women 90 pesos.

Bombay Lounge, Hidalgo 2111 (☎3630 6072). A mammoth, multi-tiered disco with raj stylings and a DJ on every floor. Patrons groove to pretty much any kind of dance music they could want to. Open daily 9pm-3am.

Cara o Cruz, Vallarta 2503 (☎3615 7621). Cara o Cruz is much more down-to-earth than one might expect. Patrons hop to *banda*s in a friendly environment. Cover 30-100 pesos. Open W and F-Sa 8pm-3am.

El Mito Disco, on the 2nd fl. of Centro Magno (☎3615 2055). Slightly older crowd, dressed to the nines, grooves to a mix of house, electronic, and *salsa*. W cover men 130 pesos, women free. Th no cover. F-Sa cover 60 pesos. 25+.

GAY AND LESBIAN NIGHTLIFE

There is more gay nightlife in Guadalajara than anywhere in Mexico outside of el D.F. For event listings, check *Amadeus News*, which covers events in both Guadalajara and Puerto Vallarta, or *Odisea*, both of which are at **Chivas.**

Chivas, Cotilla 150 (☎3613 1617), near the corner of Delgollado. With 35 years in the business, Chivas serves as home base for the Guadalajara scene. The bar's many small tables are usually occupied with patrons nursing drinks as they gaze at the TV. Leaf through one of the monthly publications and bring any questions up to the bar. Beer 12 pesos, tequila 30 pesos. Lesbian-friendly. Open daily 5am-3am.

Caudillos, Sánchez 407 (☎3613 5445), near Hotel Cervantes, 3 blocks from the *centro*. This small bar and disco draws regulars who enjoy the 2-for-1 beer (18 pesos), spirited dance floor, and occasional live "sensual performances." Cover 20 pesos. Music starts 8:30pm. Open Th-Su 3pm-3am.

Bar Máscara's, Maestranza 238 (☎3614 8103), at Madero. A popular gay bar with 2-for-1 beers (18 pesos). Don your favorite mask (very optional) and step into the fun. Packed on weekends. Open daily 9am-midnight.

Friends, Moreno 1048 (☎3826 9111), at León. Those willing to go that little bit farther are well rewarded with a disco, bar, and regular shows. Open daily 10am-3am.

ENTERTAINMENT

The ■**Ballet Folklórico** dazzles the world with precise dance, intricate garb, and amusing antics. There are two troupes in Guadalajara. The University of Guadalajara troupe, reputedly better, performs in **Teatro Degollado.** Tickets are available on the day of performance and one day in advance. (☎614 4773. Performances every Su 10am. Box office open daily 10am-1pm and 4-7pm. Tickets 50-150 pesos.) **Ballet Folklórico de Cabañas,** the Jalisco state troupe, performs in Hospicio Cabañas. (Every W 8:30pm. Tickets 60 pesos.) Early arrivals can take a tour of some of the murals inside the Hospicio, which also premiers Mexican films. (Shows daily at noon, 3:50, 6:50, and 9pm. 20 pesos.) The **Instituto Cultural Cabañas** presents live music on an open-air stage in Hospicio Cabañas at least once a week. For schedules, drop by the ticket counter or look for the fliers with the Cabañas insignia (a building with a dome and pillars) for schedules.

University facilities, scattered throughout the city, provide high culture for low budgets. The **Departamento de Bellas Artes,** García 720, coordinates activities at many venues throughout the city. A blackboard in the lobby lists each day's attractions. (Open M-Sa 9am-5pm.)

For both big-budget and art-house films, head to **Cinematógrafo,** Vallarta 1102, just west of the university. A different film shows each week. (☎3825 0514. Screenings at 6, 8, and 10pm. 35 pesos.) Guadalajara has dozens of other cinemas (about 30 pesos); check the newspapers for listings.

SPORTS

Bullfights take place most Sundays (Oct.-Mar.) at either 4 or 5:30pm at **Plaza de Toros,** on Nuevo Progreso at the north end of Independencia. (Take Ruta #60 or 62 buses north. ☎3651 8506. Tickets 70-500 pesos. Open M-Sa 10am-2pm and 4-6pm.)

Fútbol is enormous in Guadalajara, and the **Chivas,** the local professional team, are perennial contenders for the national championship. Matches take place September-May in **Jalisco Stadium** on Calz. Independencia Nte. in front of Plaza de Toros (☎3637 0563; open daily 8am-4pm) and in **Estadio 3 de Marzo,** at the university. Ticket office at Colomos Pte. 2339. (☎3641 5051. Open M-Sa 8am-5pm.)

◖ FESTIVALS

Finding a bench in Plaza de Armas, across from the Palacio de Gobierno, can be a tricky task—several nights a week, the **Jalisco State Band** draws crowds of locals. (Performances Su, Tu, and Th 6:30pm; seat-seekers should arrive before 6pm. Free.) **Plaza de los Fundadores,** behind Teatro Degollado, serves as a stage every afternoon and evening for clown-mimes. Watch and give tips, but unless you like being the butt of jokes, keep out of the mime's view. Every October, Guadalajara explodes with the **Fiestas de Octubre,** a surreal, month-long bacchanal of parades, dancing, bullfights, fireworks, food, and fun. Each day of the month is dedicated to a different one of Mexico's 29 states and two territories.

SHOPPING

The cavernous **Mercado Libertad**, at Mina and Independencia, is touted as the largest covered market in the Americas. Though its size may be exaggerated, there are still oodles of sandals, *sarapes*, jewelry, guitars, dried iguanas, and other witchcraft supplies filling tier after tier of booths. Don't be afraid to bargain. (Open daily 6am-8pm.) The Sunday market **El Baratillo,** on Mina approximately 15 blocks east of Mercado Libertad, is even more tempting. From Mercado Libertad, walk two blocks north to Hidalgo and catch bus #40 heading east or a "Par Vial" bus on Morelos. If you thought Mercado Libertad was huge, check out the real big daddy, which sometimes sprawls over 30 or 40 blocks. Vendors sell everything imaginable, from *tamales* to houses. (Open all day Su.)

DAYTRIPS FROM GUADALAJARA

TLAQUEPAQUE

Take a local #275 or 275A bus or the "Tlaquepaque" TUR bus (10 pesos, 30min.) from 16 de Septiembre on the southbound side. For the main markets, get off at Independencia by the Pollo-Chicken joint on the left; if the driver turns left off Niños Héroes, you've gone too far. To get back to Guadalajara, hop back on a #275 or TUR bus at the corner of Niños Héroes and Constitución, 2 blocks north of Independencia.

While all but the most obvious fragments of Guadalajara's colonial past are obscured by the city's commercial bustle, adjacent Tlaquepaque has learned to preserve and profit from its quaintness. Tlaquepaque's downtown streets are lined with brightly colored 17th- and 18th-century homes; most have been converted into shops selling *artesanías* and home decor. Products tend to be of higher quality and price than similar goods piled high in market trinket shops. **Museo Regional de las Cerámicas y los Artes Populares de Jalisco,** Independencia 237, at Alfareros, set in a beautiful 19th-century residence, sells an interesting collection of regional crafts. (☎3635 5404. Open Tu-Su 10am-6pm.) Another fun, if touristy, spot is **La Rosa de Cristal,** Independencia 232, at Alfareros, where artisans blow glass by hand and sell their work at inflated prices. (☎3639 7180. Glass-blowing M-F 10:30am-1pm, Sa 10:30am-noon. Open Su 10am-2pm, M-Sa 10am-6pm.) Just off Tlaquepaque's main square is the *mercado*, where goods are cheaper and of lower quality than in the shops. A small **tourist information** booth (☎3635 5756) is on Independencia at Parque Hidalgo. Expensive restaurants dot Independencia, offering menus in English, outdoor seating, and delicious food. More affordable meals can be had near the *mercado*. Forget about accommodations: come to Tlaquepaque by day, but spend your nights in far more economical Guadalajara.

ZAPOPAN

Catch a local #275A bus northbound on 16 de Septiembre (40min., 3 pesos). Ask the driver when to get off; most of Zapopan is fairly non-descript. Last bus back 10pm.

Once a small town, Zapopan would now blend easily into the Guadalajara metropolitan area if it weren't for its stunning plaza and giant, famous **Basílica de la Virgen de Zapopan,** erected after a local peasant's vision of the Virgin. The altar holds **Our Lady of Zapopan,** a small cornstalk figure made by *indígenas* in the 16th century. Her healing powers are commemorated by decades worth of *ex votos*, small paintings on sheet metal offering a visual testimony of the cured. During the early fall, the figure of Our Lady of Zapopan frequently moves from church to church throughout Jalisco—each move is occasion for serious partying. One of the most major transfers occurs on **Día de la Raza** (Oct. 12, the day Columbus landed in

America), when the figure makes her way from Guadalajara's Cathedral to Zapopan in a large procession. Pope John Paul II visited the Basílica in 1979, and a statue of the pontiff holding hands with a beaming village boy now stands in the courtyard in front of the church. The **Sala de Arte Huichal,** on one side of the cathedral, displays indigenous art and handicrafts. (Open daily 9am-2pm and 4-7pm.) Both the Basílica and Sala are situated around **Plaza de las Américas,** whose 28 lances represent the nations of the Americas. The market adjacent to the fountain and tree-rich plaza is the best place to grab a cheap taco or roast chicken.

TONALÁ

Local bus #275 and TUR bus #706, which run southbound along 16 de Septiembre, motor to Tonalá (30min., 2 pesos). Get off at the corner of Av. Tonalá and Tonaltecas to greet rows of pottery stores. Bear right on Tonaltecas to reach the plaza.

The town of Tonalá is famous for its delicately painted, earth-toned pottery. Oddly enough, this pottery can be difficult to find in the *grande dame* of Guadalajaran shopping experiences. The huge number of shops surrounding the *plaza principal* multiply into an endless expanse of stands on ▧**market days** (Su and Th), sprawling west down Tonaltecas. Vendors sell local products (glassware, silver dishware, basketry, miniature pottery sets), as well as *artesanías* from throughout Mexico. If it's famed pottery you're after, start at the **tourist office,** Zapata 275A (☎3683 6047 or 3683 1740; open M-F 9am-3pm), one block off the plaza, and ask for information on local pottery factories such as **Concotzín, Erandi Copez Cotilla,** and **Kent Edwards Morelos.** Most factories offer tours, which often include the opportunity to buy slightly imperfect "seconds" at discount prices. Because of its high quality and price of manufacture, Tonalá pottery is made almost exclusively for export, bypassing the local market of bargain hunters and going straight to upscale department stores and boutiques.

NORTH SHORE OF LAKE CHAPALA

Guadalajara straddles the line between Mexico's arid North-Central plain and the lush overgrown hillsides of the Central Pacific Coast. For a taste of the latter, head south from the city to the pretty villages on the north shore of Lake Chapala, Mexico's largest lake. The cooling effect of its waters combined with the mountain barrier conspire to keep the air 22°C/72°F year-round. Such temperate weather has attracted everyone from D. H. Lawrence to Porfirio Díaz to thousands of US and Canadian retirees. Although Guadalajara's vast water consumption and agricultural runoff have diminished the lake's size and made swimming inadvisable, the temperate climate, relaxed atmosphere, and natural beauty are good reasons to pay the north shore a visit.

CHAPALA ☎376

Chapala (pop. 20,000) is the first stop along the road from Guadalajara. Founded by Tecuexe Indian chief Capalac in 1510, it was here that D. H. Lawrence began writing *The Plumed Serpent* during the 1920s. Today Chapala keeps its cool and serves as both the transportation and economic hub of Lake Chapala. Chapala's peaceful streets host the North Shore's most affordable accommodations and are a great place to appreciate the mountains without too much of a tourist veneer.

▣ **TRANSPORTATION.** From the old bus station in Guadalajara, take a "Guadalajara-Chapala" **bus** (45min., every 30min. 6am-9pm, 26 pesos). The new bus station also serves **Chapala** (1¼hr., every hr. 7:45am-5:45pm, 16 pesos). From Ajijic, take any bus—all roads lead through **Chapala** (20min., every 20min., 3.5 pesos). In

Chapala, the entrance of the **bus station** is on Madero at Martínez. Turn left on Madero as you exit the station to reach the lake. "Guadalajara-Chapala" buses back to Guadalajara leave the station on roughly the same schedule as they arrive.

■ ▓ **ORIENTATION AND PRACTICAL INFORMATION.** The lake forms the town's southern and eastern boundaries. **Hidalgo** (called **Morelos** east of Madero) runs west to Ajijic from two blocks north of the lake. **Tourist office,** Madero 407 (☎765 3141), opposite the Palacio Municipal. Open M-F 9am-7pm, Sa-Su 9am-1pm. **Banamex,** Madero 222, has an **ATM.** (☎765 2271. Open M-F 9am-4pm.) The **mercado de artesanías,** on the waterfront, extends four blocks east of Madero's end, on Corona. Services include: **police** (☎765 4444); **Red Cross,** on Fallo across from the seafood restaurants on the *malecón* (☎765 2308; some English spoken); **Farmacia Morelos,** Madero 423 (some English spoken); **post office,** Hidalgo 242b, on the *carretera* to Ajijic (open M-F 8:30am-3pm, Sa 8:30am-1pm). **Postal code:** 45900.

▓ ▓ **ACCOMMODATIONS AND FOOD.** An outstanding choice on the shores of Lake Chapala is ▓**Hotel Cardilejas ❸,** Cotilla 363, something of a *gringo* hideaway run by a cordial elderly gentleman whose well-kept rooms and garden lure the accidental tourist into month—or, in one case, 11-year—long stays. Conveniently located one block off Madero near the bus station (look for the red and white sign), the hotel furnishes a great view of the lake and Chapala's charming rooftops. (☎765 2279. Singles 150 pesos; doubles 180 pesos; triples 250 pesos.)

Although locals seem to survive on a diet of ice cream, Chapala boasts plenty of dining options. The many coffee/pastry shops have relaxed outdoor seating, making diners feel like moneyed retirees regardless of age or financial status. **Che Mary ❶,** at Madero 2, is one of the cheaper places to lounge and eat. (Breakfast specials 30-40 pesos. Open daily 8am-10pm.) Also visit **Restaurant Superior ❸,** Madero 415, at Hidalgo. Steaks 65 pesos, hamburgers 15-25 pesos, breakfast 12-35 pesos. (☎765 2180. Open daily 8am-8pm.)

▓ ▓ **SIGHTS AND ENTERTAINMENT.** While brave weekenders occasionally rev up their jet skis and tear through the calm waters of the lake, pollution and receding shoreline prevent most water sports. Despite the grime, the lake remains beautiful. For a nice view, climb up the stone stairway from Manzanillo four blocks up Madero. Though the trails aren't clear, even the most aimless walking won't get you really lost, and the mist-covered green hillsides are gorgeous from all angles. As a general rule, aim for the crosses west of 1a del Cerrito, which serve as a good landmark. Try asking in town for advice on more ambitious hikes.

Though a number of *artesanía* vendors set up shop along the *malecón,* more enticing wares await in Ajijic. By night, young locals and a peppering of older folks hang at **Los Caballos Locos,** on 5 de Mayo at Corona across from the lakeside park. The jukebox incites foot-stomping *Norteño* romps, and beer and tequila are fairly priced at 13 and 20 pesos, respectively. (Open M-Sa noon-midnight.)

AJIJIC ☎376

With little to do and many expatriates, Ajijic has all the makings of a tourist trap. However, the pretty rows of white, tile-roofed houses, wedged between the azure lake and emerald mountains, attract visitors seeking a glance at "quintessential Mexico" and its stunning vistas. Ajijic's beauty has drawn a bevy of artists and writers whose prolific efforts fill the lakeside galleries. The town's modern amenities and natural charm merit the tourist hype and encourage even the most miserly budget traveler to loosen his purse strings.

TRANSPORTATION. From the old bus station in Guadalajara, take a "Guadalajara-Chapala" **bus** (1hr., every 30min. 6am-9:40pm, 20 pesos), which, after stopping in Chapala, will continue along the lake to Ajijic and points beyond. From Chapala, take a bus to Ajijic via San Antonio from the bus station on Madero and Martínez (20min., every 15min. 6am-8pm, 3.5 pesos). Buses back to Chapala or Guadalajara can be caught along Carretera Chapala, the same route the bus arrived on (1hr., every hr. 6am-8pm, 20 pesos).

▄▐ ORIENTATION AND PRACTICAL INFORMATION. The only paved street in Ajijic is **Carretera Chapala,** which divides the town into north and south. To reach the Plaza, turn left at the only traffic light in town onto Colón. Tourist information can be had at the **Lake Chapala Society's** outpost in a former silkworm nursery at 16 de Septiembre 16a. (Open M-Sa 10am-2pm.) **Bancomer,** Parroquia 2 on the plaza, has a 24hr. **ATM.** Other services include: **Lavandería Real,** just off the plaza (☎766 1044; wash 15 pesos, dry 15 pesos; open M-F 9am-6pm, Sa 9am-3:30pm); **police,** on the plaza at the corner of Colón and Hidalgo, and **Red Cross,** both reachable in an **emergency** by dialing ☎080; English-speaking **Hospital Ajijic,** Carretera Chapala 33 (☎766 0662); **Farmacia Jessica,** Parroquia 18 on the plaza (☎766 1191; open daily 9am-9pm); **Internet service** at Copy-Top, Guadalupe Victoria 2, on the Plaza (☎766 4464; Internet access 20 pesos per hr.; open daily 10am-10pm.); and **post office,** Colón 23, at Constitución (☎766 1888; open M-F 8am-3pm, Sa 9am-1pm). **Postal code:** 75920.

▐ ACCOMMODATIONS. Ajijic has no budget hotels, but don't let that stop you—try asking around, and make it clear that you're prepared to stay in places that choosier expats might turn down. With any luck, someone will offer you a cheap room. **Las Casitas ❹,** Carretera Pte. 20, is one of the best hotel options, with red tile floors, fan, cable TV, private bath, kitchen, and cozy living room with fold-out couch and chimney. (Bungalows for 2 people May-Oct. 350 pesos, Nov.-Apr. 450 pesos.) **Posada las Calandrías ❺,** Carretera Chapala 8, has a flower-filled garden, barbecue space, and a great view of the *laguna* from the terraces. (☎766 1052. Small bungalow with 2 beds 270 pesos; large bungalow with 4 beds 450 pesos.) Both establishments have pools.

▐▐ FOOD AND NIGHTLIFE. Although expensive restaurants dominate the scene, Ajijic will not disappoint the budget traveler. For breakfast, coffee, and *antojitos,* try **Cafe In Acálli ❶,** 16 de Septiembre 6A. (Veggie burgers 13 pesos, quesadillas 16 pesos, coffee 7 pesos. Open Su-Tu and Th-Sa 8am-6pm.) Another cheap local favorite is **Tepalo Restaurant ❸** on Parroquia at the Plaza. Specialties include deep-fried shrimp sandwiches (36 pesos), fish filets (48 pesos), and 28-peso *enchilada* plates. (☎766 0727. Open Su 8am-6pm, M-Sa 8am-8pm.)

At night, people of all ages head to the bar at **Posada Ajijic,** 16 de Septiembre 2, on the *laguna* at Colón, which has live music on weekends—usually *cumbia.* (Beer 15 pesos, tequila 30 pesos. Cover 15 pesos. Open daily 9pm-1:30am.)

TEQUILA
☎374

Surrounded by gentle mountains and prickly, blue-green *agave* plants stretching as far as the eye can see, Tequila has been dedicated solely to the production and sale of its namesake liquor since the 17th century. The town is home to 16 tequila distilleries, and nearly every business in town is linked to alcohol in some way; tourism sustains a slew of t-shirt and souvenir shops, as well as numerous liquor stores in the *centro* and along the route just outside of town. Although it's touristy, Tequila is lots of fun and makes a great daytrip from Guadalajara.

TRANSPORTATION. Rojos de Los Altos buses (☎619 2309) leave for Tequila from Guadalajara's old station (2hr., every 15min. 5:40am-9:15pm, 20 pesos). In Tequila, exit to the left of the station and head down Sixto Gorjón into town. Turn right when the street ends, and then left at the church to get to **Plaza Principal.**

ORIENTATION AND PRACTICAL INFORMATION. All the distilleries are surprisingly close to the town's **Plaza Principal.** The giant José Cuervo and Sauza plants are right next to each other two blocks north of the plaza on a street that starts off as **Corona;** this and several other streets in town tend to change names. Though it's hard to get lost in a town so small, **maps** are available at the **Museo de Tequila,** Corona 34 (☎742 2411), one block off the plaza, which doubles as the tourist office. The tourism board's module is located in a corner of the plaza across from the Palacio Municipal. (Open daily 10am-4pm.) **Banamex,** on Gorjón at Juárez, has a 24hr. **ATM.** (Open M-F 9am-4pm, Sa 9am-1pm). The **police** (☎742 0056) are right next door at Cuervo 33. In a **medical emergency,** call ☎080 for an ambulance. Little English spoken.

ACCOMM., FOOD, & ENTERTAINMENT. Even some hotels are tequila-themed; **Hotel Posada del Agave ❸,** Gorjón 83, on the way to the Plaza, is one of those precious few. Clean rooms decorated in tiles painted with *agave* plants have private baths, cable TV, and fans. (☎742 0774. Singles 180 pesos; doubles 250 pesos.) **Hotel San Francisco ❸,** next to the cathedral, is a clean, comfortable sanctuary. All rooms have private bath and fan. (☎742 1757. Singles 170 pesos; doubles 230 pesos.) Cheap restaurants pack the area around the bus station; roast chicken is a local favorite. Dine at **Avicola ❸,** Gorjón 20, where 30 pesos will buy you half a bird, tortillas, and salsa. (Open daily 7:30am-4pm.) For more ambience, try **Resturant Bar el Sauzal ❷,** Juárez 45, between Gorjón and Cuervo, right by the plaza. (Steak 40 pesos, quesadillas 18 pesos, beer 13 pesos. Open daily 11am-2am.) Taco stands cluster on the right-hand side of the church as you face the entrance.

For the first 12 days of December, Tequila celebrates its **Feria Nacional del Tequila.** Each of the town's factories claims one day, on which it holds rodeos, concerts, cockfights, fireworks, and other festivities. And of course, there are always plenty of drinks to go around.

DRINK. There's not much to do here other than drink or take a **tequila factory tour.** Or maybe you came for the opera? The tourist office runs tours every hour from 11am-3pm from their module on the

THE LOCAL LEGEND

¡TEQUILA TIME!

The best tequila bears a label boasting its content: 100% agave. Around 1600 varieties of this cactus exist in Mexico, but only the blue agave is used for tequila.

Plants take 8 to 12 years to mature, when their huge centers (called *piñas*—pineapples—for their appearance) weigh 35-45kg. Each plant yields around 5L of tequila. The *piñas* are harvested and then cooked for 36hr. in enormous traditional ovens or 12hr. in modern ones. A slightly different process produces the famous Chihuahuan sotol (see Sotol Me All About It, p. 272). *Piñas* are then chopped and mixed with water, and the pulp that's strained off is used for rugs, animal food, and stuffing furniture. The remaining mixture is fermented in tubs, attracting bees, flies, ants, and other bugs. Only 10% of this mixture actually becomes tequila. Be thankful for yeast fermentation—in the past, options included naked, sweaty workers sitting in the vats or throwing in a piece of animal dung wrapped in cloth. The tequila then goes through two distillations to lower the alcohol content. In the factory, you can sip tequila after its first distillation, with an alcohol content as high as 80%. Afterwards it is aged in white oak barrels—the longer the process, the smoother the taste.

All of this can only happen here: it's against the law to produce tequila anywhere but Jalisco and a few surrounding areas.

plaza, for 25 pesos. A better option may be to head straight to the **Sauza** factory tour, rumored to be the best. Join in at the factory or trek to the tour's official start: 50m down the highway past the entrance to Tequila at Rancho Indio, where a demonstration of blue *agave* cultivation precedes a visit to the factory. (☎742 0013. Tours run M-F 11am, 12:30pm, 2:45, and 4pm. 35 pesos.) To see the factory in action, try to arrive early, and avoid *siesta* (2-4pm). One block back toward the plaza is the less impressive **José Cuervo** factory. (Tours daily every hr. M-Sa 10am-2pm. The 10am and noon tours are in English. 30 pesos, students 15 pesos.) For the price of a few shots, you'll learn more than you ever wanted to know about *agave* (the plant from which tequila is distilled), the distillation and aging processes, and the history of the famous liquor. All through the tour the guides will ply you with tequilas and margaritas. The **Museo Nacional de Tequila,** Corona 34, teaches more tequila history with bilingual signs and a gift shop. (☎742 2410. Open Tu-Su 10am-5pm. 15 pesos, children and students 7 pesos.) The **Museo Familia Sauza** in the old Sauza family mansion at Rojas 22 can be visited via guided tour. (Tours approx. every 30min. Open M-F 10am-1:30pm, Sa-Su 10am-4:30pm. Donations suggested.)

PUERTO VALLARTA ☎322

The world fell in love with Puerto Vallarta 40 years ago when Richard Burton came here to film *Night of the Iguana* in 1963. With just 1050 residents, Puerto Vallarta had a long way to go to establish its reputation as a mega-beach resort. However, well in place was Burton's reputation for bedding his leading ladies, as Liz Taylor, having filled that role in *Cleopatra*, knew all too well. Worried that the film's story of three women in one night would become a reality, she followed her paramour to keep an eye on him. Tabloid reporters tagged along, followed by tourists galore, heads filled with ideas of sultry secluded getaways. With the years the passion has faded and, although some of that original charm remains, Puerto Vallarta is covered in the fat of 40 years of resort town growth.

▐▔ TRANSPORTATION

Taxis leave the *centro* for the bus station, Marina Vallarta, or the airport (60 pesos). **Buses** enter the city on México, which becomes Díaz Ordaz. All *combis* and any municipal bus operating south of the Sheraton or labeled "Centro" pass the main plaza, while those labeled "Hoteles" pass the hotel strip. Buses stop at the clearly marked *parada* signs and at the covered benches. Most buses and *combis* travel Insurgentes between Madero and Cárdenas at some point on their route. (Buses and *combis* operate daily 6am-10pm. 3.5 pesos.)

Airport: 8km north of town. To get downtown from the airport, take a "Centro" or "Olas Altas" bus or a taxi. To get back from town, catch a "Novia Alta," "Marfil," or "Aeropuerto" bus on Cárdenas, Insurgentes, or Juárez. Served by **Alaska** (☎221 1350), **American** (☎221 1799 or toll-free ☎800 904 6000), **Continental** (☎221 1025), and **Mexicana** (☎224 8900).

Buses: The modern, mammoth bus station is north of the *centro*, just beyond the airport. To get downtown, take a "Centro" or "Olas Altas" bus or taxi. To get to the bus station from downtown, take an "Ixtapa" bus (3 pesos) northbound at the plaza. **Primera Plus/ Autocamiones Chihuatlán** (☎221 0095) offers service to: **Mexico City** (12hr., 7pm, 642 pesos); **Aquascalientes** (8hr.; 2:30, 3:45pm; 465 pesos); **Guadalajara** (5hr., every hr., 293 pesos); **León** (8hr.; 4:15, 5, 5:30, 10:15pm; 471 pesos); **Manzanillo** (5hr.; 4, 11:30pm; 190 pesos) with stops in **Barra de Navidad** (4½hr, 140 pesos) and **Melaque** (4hr., 120 pesos); **Morelia** (8hr., 11:15pm, 435 pesos); **Querétaro** (12hr.,

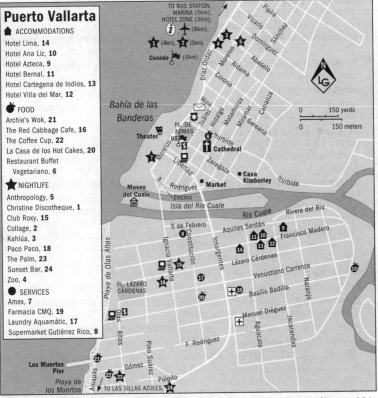

Puerto Vallarta

🛏 ACCOMMODATIONS
Hotel Lima, 14
Hotel Ana Liz, 10
Hotel Azteca, 9
Hotel Bernal, 11
Hotel Cartegena de Indios, 13
Hotel Villa del Mar, 12

🍎 FOOD
Archie's Wok, 21
The Red Cabbage Cafe, 16
The Coffee Cup, 22
La Casa de los Hot Cakes, 20
Restaurant Buffet
Vegetariano, 6

⭐ NIGHTLIFE
Anthropology, 5
Christine Discotheque, 1
Club Roxy, 15
Collage, 2
Kahlúa, 3
Paco Paco, 18
The Palm, 23
Sunset Bar, 24
Zoo, 4

● SERVICES
Amex, 7
Farmacia CMQ, 19
Laundry Aquamátic, 17
Supermarket Gutiérrez Rico, 8

CENTRAL PACIFIC COAST

9am, 505 pesos). **Futura** (☎221 0849), **ETN** (☎221 0450), and **Pacífico** (☎221 0869) offer similar services.

🔆 🛈 ORIENTATION AND PRACTICAL INFORMATION

Running roughly east-west, the not-so-mighty **Río Cuale** bisects Puerto Vallarta before hitting the ocean. **Mex. 200** from Manzanillo runs into town south of the river, becoming **Insurgentes.** The ritzy waterfront between Plaza Mayor and 31 de Octubre, called the **malecón,** is home to pricey restaurants, hotels, clubs, and tacky shirt shops. North of the *malecón,* Morelos becomes Perú before joining the coastal route. North along this route lie the **airport, marina,** and **bus station.** The south end has almost all the cheap hotels, best beaches, and budget restaurants.

Tourist Office: (☎223 2500, ext. 230 or 231), on Juárez in the Presidencia Municipal, and at Ascencio 1712 (☎223 0744; fax 222 0243). Free maps, brochures, and *Passport,* a publication that lists discounts at bars and restaurants. Free local English-language newspapers available. English spoken. Open M-F 8am-4pm.

Consulates: Canada, Blvd. Ascencio 1951 (☎293 0098, emergencies 800 706 2900; fax 293 2894), in the hotel zone. Open M-F 9am-3pm. **US,** Zaragoza 160 (☎222 0069, emergencies 013 826 5553; fax 223 0074), in Vallarta Plaza, on Plaza Mayor. Open M-F 10am-2pm.

Currency Exchange: Banamex (☎226 6110), at Juárez and Zaragoza, in front of the Presidencia Municipal. Open M-F 9am-5pm, Sa 9am-2pm. **Bancrecer,** Olas Altas 246 (☎223 0484), between Carranza and Badillo. Open M-F 9am-5pm, Sa 10am-2pm. Both have 24hr. **ATMs.** *Casas de cambio* are everywhere, especially near the *malecón.* Their rates vary, but are lower than banks. Usually open daily 9am-7pm.

American Express: Morelos 660 (☎223 2955; fax 223 2926), at Abasolo. Open M-F 9am-6pm, Sa 9am-1pm.

Luggage storage: At the bus station. 3 pesos per hr. Open 24hr.

Laundry: Laundry Aguamátic, Constitución 279 (☎222 5978), between Cárdenas and Carranza. 10 pesos per kg. Open M-Sa 9am-8pm.

Bookstore: ▓**Una Página en el Sol,** Olas Altas 339 (☎222 3608) at Diéguez, and Aldama 180 (☎223 0115). Most English-language books 15-45 pesos, book exchanges also welcome. Huge veggie sandwiches 30-40 pesos. Open daily 7:30am-midnight.

Supermarket: Gutiérrez Rico (☎222 0222), at Constitución and Serdán. Open daily 6:30am-11pm.

Car Rental: Almost all rental companies have offices on Ascencio, the hotel strip. **National,** Ascencio km 1.5 (☎221 1226) at the airport. VW with tax, insurance, and 200km US$50 per day. **Thrifty,** Ascencio km 5.5 (☎224 0776 or 224 9280). VWs with tax, insurance, and unlimited km US$60 per day. The cheapest rentals are at **Cafe.com** (☎222 0092); see **Internet Access,** below.

Emergency: ☎060.

Police: Iturbide 1586 (☎222 0106), at Morelos. Some English spoken.

Red Cross: (☎222 1533) on Río de la Plata at Río Balsas. Take a "Cruz Roja" bus from Cárdenas and Insurgentes. English spoken.

Pharmacy: Farmacia CMQ, Badillo 365 (☎222 1330), at Insurgentes. Open 24hr.

Hospital: CMQ Hospital, Badillo 365 (☎223 1919), at Insurgentes. **Hospital Medasist,** Diéguez 2360 (☎223 0444), at Insurgentes. Some English spoken at both.

Internet Access: Cafe.com, Olas Altas 250 (☎/fax 222 0092), at Rodríguez. Offers Internet service (35 pesos per hr.), cafe, small bar, fax and copy service, and cheap car rental. Open daily 8am-2am. **The Net House,** Vallarta 232 (☎/fax 222 6953; www.vallartacafes.com), at Cárdenas. 25 pesos per hr. Open daily 8am-3am.

Post Office: Mina 188 (☎222 1888), left off Juárez past Plaza Mayor. Open M-F 8am-6pm, Sa 9am-1pm. **Postal Code:** 48300.

⚑ ACCOMMODATIONS AND CAMPING

The best budget hotels in Puerto Vallarta are south of Río Cuale, on or near Madero. Prices vary by season: June is the least expensive month, while December is the most. From November to January, reservations should be made two months in advance. Vallarta officially frowns on beach bums, and finding a stretch of beach that isn't directly connected to a hotel requires heading fairly far out of town. Exercise caution when selecting any camping site.

Hotel Azteca, Madero 473 (☎222 2750), between Jacarandas and Naranjo. Friendly staff and a tranquil courtyard generate a relaxed, hassle-free atmosphere. Fans, private bathrooms and *agua purificada* team up with cushy beds and fluffy pillows. Towel deposit 30 pesos. Singles 150 pesos; doubles 200 pesos; kitchen suite for 2 people 350 pesos, for 3 people 400 pesos. Prices rise 50 pesos or less in high season. ❸

Hotel Villa del Mar, Madero 440 (☎222 0785), 2 blocks east of Insurgentes. Brick detailing, wooden doors, and lanterns give the well-scrubbed rooms a rustic feel. Rooftop terrace has a view of the *centro*. Towel deposit 50 pesos. Singles 160 pesos, with balcony 200 pesos; doubles 210/250 pesos; triples 260/300 pesos. In high season all rooms cost what they would with balcony. ❸

Hotel Ana Liz, Madero 429 (☎222 1757). Ana Liz features basic, dim rooms with tiny baths. Tasteful landscape photos and less tasteful 70s disco-style curtains do their best to brighten the place. Singles 180 pesos; doubles 190 pesos; triples 220 pesos. ❸

Hotel Bernal, Madero 423 (☎222 3605). An inviting covered courtyard, clean but old rooms, fans, private baths and purified water. Beds are extremely firm, and pillows may be lumpy. Towel deposit 30 pesos. Singles 150 pesos; doubles 200 pesos. 30 pesos more in high season. ❷

Hotel Lima, Madero 376 (☎222 1661). Lima has brightly painted rooms with private baths and fans. Singles 170 pesos; doubles 200 pesos. Prices may rise 30 pesos in high season. ❸

Hotel Cartegena de Indios, Madero 428 (☎222 6914). The warm *terra cotta* floors give rooms a homey feel; some have good-sized balconies. The small baths may sport a few permanent stains. Singles 160-180 pesos; doubles 190 pesos; triples 260. 20 pesos more in high season. A/C 60 pesos, TV 50 pesos or less. ❸

🟡 FOOD

Puerto Vallarta is full of restaurants; however, finding one that serves more Mexican food than a sizzling fajita platter can be challenging. If you're determined, try the cheaper eateries that cluster along Madero, in the *mercado* (open M-Sa 9am-8pm) to the north side where Insurgentes crosses Río Cuale, or along México, or the all-night taco and quesadilla stands that thrive south of the river. Near the beach on the south side, in an area known as the *zona romántica*, waiters harass passersby to lure them to ambiguously ethnic restaurants while about half of potential patrons duck into boutique coffee shops for sandwiches and solace.

▧ **The Red Cabbage Cafe,** Rivera del Río 204-A (☎223 0411); follow Cárdenas across town and, at the river, turn right. The food here may explain why there are so few Mexican restaurants in Vallarta, as competing with El Repollo Rojo can't be easy. An eclectically decorated but intimate setting by the river. Open M-Sa 5pm-11pm. ❺

▧ **Restaurant Buffet Vegetariano,** Iturbide 270 (☎222 3073), at Hidalgo, a few blocks inland from Plaza Mayor. 100% vegetarian cuisine, with a different theme every night. Join international travelers in the mural-decorated, fan-cooled interior. Buffet includes 5 main dishes (non-dairy options available), soup, salad bar with inventive dressings, *agua fresca*, coffee, tea, and dessert (55 pesos). Dinner buffet daily 11:30am-10pm. 35-peso breakfast buffet M-Sa 8am-11:30am. Open M-Sa 11:30am-10pm. ❹

▧ **La Casa de los Hot Cakes,** Badillo 289 (☎222 6272), at Constitución. Stupendously good breakfasts. Indulge in the specialty pancake or waffle platters (28-43 pesos), or eggs benedict (50 pesos). Open daily 8am-2pm. ❹

The Coffee Cup, Gómez 146-A (☎222 8584), at Olas Altas. The best espresso in Vallarta; high-quality Mexican beans and American styling make for delightful vanilla lattes (31 pesos) and a chocolate sensation of a house special called a black and white (33 pesos). Also on offer is a book loan program and a series of bagels and sandwiches. Wraps 25 pesos. Open Su 8am-2pm, M-Sa 8am-10pm. ❸

Archie's Wok, Francisca Rodríguez 130 (☎222 0411), just before the beach. Specializing in pan-Asian cuisine, Archie used to work his wok as John Huston's personal chef. Archie has since passed on, but his widow maintains the tradition of some of Vallarta's finest food. *Pancit de puerco* 79 pesos. Open M-Sa 2-11pm. MC/V. ❹

THE BIG SPLURGE

COLOR ME AHAB

One of the delights of the Mexican coast has long been whale watching, and it's one of Mexico's most popular tourist activities. There are those, however, who find the blowholes passé, and are more interested in watching in style.

And, to be honest, most boats lack the finesse of the Marigalante, a full-sized galleon with a rowdy crew of the most fearsome pirates ever to go boogie-boarding. After a hearty breakfast and lunch of barbecued meats, passengers will be treated to a whole range of entertainment, including a sword fight, a naval battle, a super pirate torture contest, and the decidedly less Bluebeard-esque banana boat rides, kayaking outings, and boogie boards.

At night, the Marigalante, a replica of Columbus's Santa María, goes out with another purpose in mind: to celebrate Mexican culture and experience the feelings of an outsider stumbling upon Pre-Hispanic Mexico. Dinner is followed by *indígena* dances, *charro* rope tricks, and cockfights, as well as bingo and dancing. Though the Pacific sunset is impressive, the nighttime cruise misses out on the real plus of being on the Marigalante: when you do see a whale you can say "Thar she blows" without feeling like a total idiot.

www.marigalante.com.mx. Pirate Land 630 pesos, Mexico on Board 735 pesos. Book online for a 15% discount.

👁 📷 SIGHTS AND BEACHES

Although the tourist veneer detracts somewhat from Puerto Vallarta's natural beauty, the panorama of the city's 40km coastline and surrounding palm-tree-covered mountains is still enchanting. Water sport enthusiasts have a lot to choose from in Vallarta—aquatic activities are extremely popular, especially during mornings. This is your chance to go **parasailing** (US$20). **Wave runners** (doubles 350 pesos per ½hr.), **banana boat** rides (150 pesos per person), **kayaks** (100 pesos per hr.), and **waterskis** (400 pesos per ½hr.) are also available—ask around at the beach. **Chico's Dive Shop**, 772 Díaz Ordaz, offers scuba diving courses and certification classes. (☎222 1895 or 222 1875; US$18 for 1hr. US$290 for certification classes. English-speaking staff will gladly lower rates for return customers, groups, or payment in cash. Open daily 8am-10pm.) Equestrian fanatics can take to the hills on **horseback;** rentals are available from the stand in the plaza on Olas Altas at Carranza. (☎222 0386. 100 pesos per hr.) Another horse stand (☎222 0376), on the corner of the plaza at Carranza and Suárez, has similar rates.

Some of the least crowded and most gorgeous beaches stretch south of town on the road to Mismaloya (see p. 432) and north into Nayarit (see p. 403). The most popular within Vallarta is **Playa de los Muertos** (Beach of the Dead), a strip in front of the south side's costliest hotels. The south end begins at a rocky cliff and stretches north to the small dock that separates it from **Playa de Olas Altas** (Tall Waves Beach). The clear water at Playa de los Muertos is its primary advantage over its neighbor: Río Cuale empties into the ocean at Playa de Olas Altas, sullying the waters with sediment. To get there, walk west on Cárdenas and then south along Playa de Olas Altas, which continues to Río Cuale before becoming the rocky *malecón*. Near the southern end of Playa de los Muertos is **The Blue Chairs** resort, the world's largest gay and lesbian beachfront resort.

Isla Río Cuale is accessible by short stairways from both bridges spanning the *café con leche*-colored Río Cuale. A tree-shaded pathway runs the length of the verdant island, full of small stores selling postcards, jewelry, and souvenirs. The Museo del Cuale, at the seaward end of the island, houses interesting displays on Mesoamerican culture and regional history. (Open Tu-Sa 12:30pm-7pm. Free.) Stairs, beginning behind the Church of Guadalupe, lead up the mini-mountain amid bougainvillea and hibiscus into the wealthy Zaragoza neighborhood known locally as Gringo Gulch. The prominent bridge spannin the

SHE'S GOT TEQUILA TO RIDE. Tequila has become a place of pilgrimage for college students around the world. Unfortunately, true devotees are often unable to dedicate themselves properly to their worship because of concerns about the return journey. Thankfully, the **Tequila Express** takes care of that. Traveling in restored train cars from the Porfiriato, passengers are taken from Guadalajara to Tequila itself, enjoying the delicious fruits of the town's labor all the way. Upon arrival, visitors are taken on a tour of the Hacienda San José del Refugio, where Casa Herradura tequila is made, and treated to a night of *mariachi* music before being returned, safe and sound, to Guadalajara. ☎333 122 7290 or 333 880 9099. Adults 650 pesos. Children 6-12 400 pesos. A steal for the alcoholic toddler: under 5 free.

apex of the street connects Casa Kimberley, Zaragoza 455, the former love nest of Richard Burton and Liz Taylor, to its rooftop pool in the building across the street. The house has been preserved largely as it was left by Liz when she sold it in 1990. The present owners run it as a bed and breakfast and offer tours of the house. (☎/fax 222 1336; www.casakimberley.com. Tours daily 9am-6pm, 80 pesos. 2-3 person suites 750 pesos, 1100 pesos in high season.)

NIGHTLIFE

After dark, the *malecón* swarms with hundreds of tanned young Mexicans and Americans making eyes at each other. Vallarta has sprouted a thriving **gay scene**, and boasts several clubs catering to gay men and, occasionally, gay women. The action centers on **Díaz Ordaz** along the northern waterfront. All other destinations are reachable by the "Marina Vallarta" bus, which goes to the marina and the hotel strip. After 11pm, you'll be stuck with taxis (60 pesos to the *centro*).

BARS AND CLUBS

Discos pull at those who don't mind dropping at least 50-70 pesos for cover charges and 20-50 pesos for a drink. Most don't get going until 11pm or midnight. Avoid covers and save a small fortune by collecting free passes (which may not be honored during high season) from the condo-hawkers lurking on the *malecón*. You need not buy a condo, just pretend you might.

Zoo, Díaz Ordaz 630 (☎222 4945). The iron-bar dance cages keep up the animal theme. It's the biggest party in town—block-long lines wrap around the building all night. Two-drink minimum on busy nights. Open daily 11:30am-6am.

Christine Discotheque (☎224 0202), Av. Las Garzas, located in the NH Krystal hotel just before the marina. Groups of college kids from the hotel ensure a large and youthful crowd year getting down year round to a wide range of dance tracks. Cover 150 pesos. Th, Su 250 pesos with open bar. Open Su-M and W-Sa 10pm-4am.

Kahlúa, Díaz Ordaz 644 (☎222 2486), on the waterfront. 20-somethings chug 2-for-1 beers (50 pesos) and national drinks (60 pesos). Open daily 11am-3am.

Club Roxy, Ignacio Vallarta 217, between Madero and Carranza. An international, all-ages clientele jams to live reggae, blues, and rock. Beer 25 pesos. No cover. Open daily 8am-4pm. Live music starts at 10:30pm.

Collage (☎220 1505), next to Marina Vallarta, is big enough to house all of Vallarta. The dance floor resembles an ice-skating rink, complete with spectators in the stands. Free pool in back. Almost every night is a special event—foam party, rave with glowsticks, wet t-shirt contest. Beer 25 pesos, national drinks 30-35 pesos. Cover generally 100 pesos. Open daily 10pm-5am.

CENTRAL PACIFIC COAST

GAY NIGHTLIFE

A **gay cruise,** leaving Th 10:30am from the Los Muertos pier, takes partners Noah's-ark-style to a private beach (599 pesos, cash only; includes drinks, snorkeling, and table dancing). Tickets are available from The Blue Chairs resort (see above). The Zona Romántica guide, available in most gay establishments, offers a comprehensive listing of gay and gay-friendly establishments.

▒ **Sunset Bar,** Malecón 4 (☎222 5040), on the rooftop of The Blue Chairs resort on the Playa de los Muertos. Organizes nightly entertainment, often incorporating the talents of Ida Slapter and her Dirty Bitches. A fun and relaxed setting with perhaps the best view, gay or straight, in Vallarta. Beer 25 pesos. Mixed drinks 30 pesos. Happy hour 10am-6pm. Beer 15 pesos. Mixed drinks 20 pesos; big girl cocktails include an extra shot for 10-20 pesos more. Gay bingo Tu 7pm. Open daily 10am-10pm.

▒ **The Palm,** Olas Altas 508 (☎223 4818). The Palm provides a laid-back alternative to the wilder side of the city's gay nightlife with quality entertainment that often attracts a mixed gay/straight crowd. When the diva's passions aren't running high on stage, the fiery red interior sets the stage for a pool game or conversation. Beer 25 pesos, national drinks 30 pesos, 2-for-1 drinks daily 8-10pm. Occasional cover 10 pesos for live music or comedy shows. Open daily 6pm-2am.

Paco Paco, Ignacio Vallarta 278 (☎222 1899), at Cárdenas. Vallarta's hottest gay disco, with great music, lots of floor space, mirrors, strobe lights, and aquariums. Non-dancing options include pool and video games or enjoying the sunset from the rooftop bar. Strip shows midnight and 3am. Beer 25 pesos, national drinks 35 pesos. Cover Th-Su 50 pesos. Open daily 1pm-6am.

Anthropology, Morelos 101 on Plaza Río next to the Vallarta Bridge. Look for the rainbow flag and follow the steps down. Racy fun for everyone. The ground-floor disco hosts strip shows at 8pm. Amateur transvestite, wet t-shirt contest, and female stripper nights; call ahead if you're picky. Men clad only in the slimmest of thongs gyrate all night long on top of the 2nd-fl. bar. Beer 25 pesos, national drinks 35 pesos. Cover M-W 30 pesos, Th-Su 50 pesos. Open daily 9pm-4am.

▶ DAYTRIPS FROM PUERTO VALLARTA

The **Bahía de Banderas** (Bay of Flags) that shelters Puerto Vallarta owes its name to a blunder: when Nuño Beltrán de Guzmán landed here in 1532, he mistook the colorful headdresses of the thousands of natives awaiting him for flags. Today, the Bay offers miles of beautiful and often untouristed beaches. Using Puerto Vallarta as a base, it is possible to reach all points around the Bay.

SOUTHERN COAST

Buses go to Mismaloya from Constitución and Badillo in Vallarta (every 10min. 5:30am-11pm, 4.5 pesos). Taxis cost 80 pesos. "Tuito" buses run to Chico's Paradise from Carranza and Aguacate (every ½hr. 5am-9pm, 10 pesos). Taxis acuáticos are the cheapest way to get to the boats-only beaches. They leave from Muelle de los Muertos and stop at Las Ánimas, Quimixto, and Yelapa (45min., 11am, 90 pesos; return at 4pm). Cruises to points south of Vallarta leave from the marina (9am, US$25 and up; return at 4pm). Information available in the tourist office, at any large hotel, or at the marina.

Vallarta's most popular beaches lie a few kilometers south of the city itself. The first few are monopolized by resorts, and access is usually only through the hotels.

LOS ARCOS. Down the coast lies Los Arcos, a group of pretty rock islands shaped by pounding waves. The coast lacks sand but serves as a platform from which to start the 150m swim to the islands. Bring a mask or goggles or risk missing the tropical fish that flit through the underwater reefscape. Mind your step—the coral is sharp enough to draw blood; use caution and swim with a friend. *(Take the bus to Mismaloya and ask the driver to stop at Hotel de los Arcos.)*

MISMALOYA. The beautiful crescent beach of Mismaloya lies just around the bend to the south. Best known as the site of *Night of the Iguana* and Arnold Schwarzenegger's *cinéma vérité* classic, *Predator*, Mismaloya has recently been taken over by large hotels and is only slightly less crowded than beaches in town. Part of the set from *Night of the Iguana* remains as does one of the crashed helicopters from *Predator*.

BOCA DE TOMATLÁN. Farther down, the road veers away from the coast just beyond Boca de Tomatlán, a narrow cove with a small, relatively untouristed beach. The last place to see on the southern road is **Chico's Paradise,** 5km inland from Boca de Tomatlán. Wash down the view of nearby **Tomatlán Falls** with a beer (20 pesos) at Chico's huge *palapas* or splash in the river and admire the surrounding hills. *(To get to Chico's from Boca de Tomatlán, take a "Tuito" bus from the main highway. 5 pesos. ☎ 222 0747. Open daily 10am-6pm.)*

LAS ÁNIMAS AND QUIMIXTO. Farther south lie the beaches of Las Ánimas and Quimixto, which are only accessible by boat. The twin beaches have long stretches of unoccupied sand backed by small villages and a few *palapas*.

YELAPA. Highly touted by locals, Yelepa is a bit of a fake. Supposedly a secluded peasant fishing village, its "simple" *palapa* huts were designed by a North American architect whose definition of "rustic" included interior plumbing and hot water. Many of these *palapas* are occupied for only part of the year, and short- and long-term rentals can be arranged easily for sometimes surprisingly low prices. The beach fills with vendors and parasailers by day, but the town, a 15min. walk from the beach, remains tranquil, with waterfalls and nude bathing upstream and poetry readings downstream. Don't miss the secluded swimming hole at the top of the stream that runs through town. Follow the path uphill and duck under the water pipes to the right of the trail just before the restaurant. About 15m before it rejoins the stream, a trail leads left to a deep pool overlooking the bay.

NORTHERN COAST

From Puerto Vallarta, flag down a "Punta de Mita" bus on Cárdenas, Insurgentes, Juárez, or Ascencio (every 20min. 9:15am-5pm); to Piedra Blanca (40min., 18 pesos); Destiladeras (1hr., 20 pesos); or Punta de Mita (1¼hr. plus a 4km walk, 25 pesos).

The northern edge of the bay hosts some of the prettiest and least-developed beaches on Mexico's central Pacific coast. **Nuevo Vallarta,** the largest and southernmost of nine small towns on the north bay, is 150km south of Tepic and 20km north of Puerto Vallarta. Protected by a sandy cove, **Playa Piedra Blanca** has wonderfully calm waters. Farther north along the bay is **Playa las Destiladeras,** named for the water that trickles through the rocky cliff. Although the sandy bottom is colored with occasional rocks, rougher waves make the beach perfect for bodysurfers and boogie boarders. **Punta de Mita,** the northernmost point along the bay, is a lagoon sheltered by two rock islets. It is marked by **Corral de Riscos,** a living reef. Freshwater showers in Destiladeras make the bus ride home more comfortable. Bring a bag lunch to avoid inflated prices at the beachside *palapas*.

BAHÍA DE CHAMELA ☎ 315

Tranquil and secluded Bahía de Chamela, 60km northwest of Melaque, marks the northern point of Jalisco's "Ecological Tourism Corridor." A chain of small rocky islands breaks the horizon and 11km of golden-brown sand, dotted with gnarled driftwood and the occasional *palapa*, beckon the beachcomber. The largest village in Chamela is **Perula** (pop. 600), which lacks most services beyond a few hotels and seafood *palapas*, but contents visitors with a charming beach; the starry night is truly inspiring. Though Chamela receives its share of tourism, especially in December and April, the Midas touch has yet to spoil the natural beauty and seclusion of the bay. Although crime is virtually nonexistent in Perula (the nearest police station is 3km away), lone travelers should exercise caution on the deserted beaches and dark roads leading to town.

▐ **TRANSPORTATION.** Second-class **buses** from **Puerto Vallarta** to **Manzanillo** (5hr., 190 pesos) pass through Perula; buses going from **Melaque** or **Barra de Navidad** to **Puerto Vallarta** (4-5hr., 110-130 pesos) also stop in Perula. Always tell the bus driver where you're going in advance so you don't miss the stop. To get to Playa Perula, get off by the big white "Playa Dorada" sign and walk 30min. down a winding dirt road; friendly locals may offer you a ride. To get to Playa Chamela, get off farther south at "El Súper"; a sign points to the beach 1km away. Perula is a 30min. walk along the shore. Hotels in Perula may pick you up. Otherwise, since Perula lacks a formal taxi system, contact Don Migue (☎333 9801), who will take you in his happy pick-up to the beach, your hotel, or back to El Súper for 30 pesos each way. To return, catch a **Primera Plus** bus from the bus stop on the main highway. They head to: **Guadalajara** (3hr.; 8, 10:30am, 4pm; 67 pesos); **Manzanillo** (2½-5hr., every hr. 7:30am-10:30pm, 65 pesos) via **Melaque** (1½hr., 35 pesos); **Puerto Vallarta** (3hr., every hr. 7:30am-10:30pm, 75 pesos).

▐ **PRACTICAL INFORMATION.** The **Centro de Salud** is at the corner of Juárez and Pargo, one block from the Hotel Punta Perula. (☎333 9804. No English spoken. 24hr. emergency service.) There is one **LADATEL** phone outside the Primera Plus Station; your best bet for placing a long-distance call is cajoling one of the hotel or restaurant owners into letting you call collect.

▐▐ **ACCOMMODATIONS AND FOOD.** ▐Hotel Punta Perula ❹, on the corner of Juárez and Tiburón, two blocks from the beach, is the only hotel in town. Comfortable, floral rooms border a massive courtyard filled with trees and overhanging hammocks. Call ahead. (☎333 9782. Low-season singles 200 pesos; doubles 250 pesos. High-season singles 250 pesos; doubles 350 pesos.) Feast on the catch of the day as you relax under palm fronds at **Mariscos la Sirena** ❺, at the northern end of the *palapas* lining the shore. A full kg of fish is 100 pesos, while smaller portions of *pulpo* (squid) are 75 pesos. (☎333 9716. Open daily 8:30am-7pm.)

▐ **BEACHES. Punta de Perula,** the bay's northernmost point, shelters **Playa Perula,** making it perfect for swimming. A 30min. walk down the virgin beach will bring you to the Villa Polinesia Motel and Campsite, marking **Playa Chamela.** Here and farther south, rougher waves invite body surfing and boogie-boarding—but watch out for the frequently powerful undertow. Continuing south brings you to **Playa Rosada** and even more secluded beaches. Occasional *palapas* refresh the parched and weary body-surfer, and *lanchas* from Playa Perula transport wannabe Robinson Crusoes to the nearby islands or on fishing trips (round-trip 300 pesos). Inquire of the fishermen at the point about 1km north of Perula.

BAHÍA DE NAVIDAD

Along with Guadalajara and Puerto Vallarta, Bahía de Navidad forms Jalisco's "Tourist Triangle." However, not all in the triumvirate are equal: with the exception of December and *Semana Santa*, few tourists dot the placid shores of Bahía de Navidad. It's a wonder that more vacationers year-round don't visit the towns of the *bahía*, **Melaque** and **Barra de Navidad**, and their sheltered cove of powdery sand, shimmering water, and scenic, embracing cliffs. During high season the beach between the towns transforms into a river of bronzed bodies and hotels in both towns overflow with tourists. Though restaurants, hotels, and clubs are beginning to invade, the pace of life here is still sleepy: days pass dreamily on the beach, and nights slip by in beachside or thatched-roof pool halls and bars.

Melaque and Barra de Navidad lie 55km northwest of Manzanillo on Mex. 200, and 240km southwest of Guadalajara on Mex. 54. Melaque is the northernmost of the two. They're well-connected by **municipal buses** that shuttle between them (20min., every 15min. 6am-8:30pm, 3.5 pesos). Of course, the 40min. walk along the beach would be the hard-core budget option. **Don't walk after sunset;** some dangerous encounters have been reported. **Taxis** cost 60 pesos.

MELAQUE ☎315

Visitors amble through Melaque's (pop. 7000) placid *zócalo*, splash in the waves, and nibble on fresh fish while watching the sunset from beachside restaurants. There's not much action in Melaque, which suits the place just fine.

⌐ TRANSPORTATION. Melaque's **bus stations** are side-by-side on **Farías**, the main drag parallel to the beach. From the bus station, turn left on Farías and walk two blocks to reach **Mateos**. Another left takes you to the plaza, a few blocks inland. Mateos and **Hidalgo** are the main cross-streets running toward the ocean.

Autocamiones Cihuatlán (☎355 5003) offers second-class service; **Primera Plus/ Flecha Amarilla** (☎355 6110) offers first- and executive-class service. The two are side-by-side at Farías 34. First class service to: **Guadalajara** (5 hr., 7 per day 9:15am-1:15am, 190 pesos); **Manzanillo** (1½hr., 5 per day 3am-8pm, 39 pesos); **Puerto Vallarta** (3½hr.; 3:30, 9:30am; 130 pesos); **Tomatlán** (2hr.; 5, 9pm; 86 pesos). Second-class service to: **Guadalajara** (6½hr., every 2hr. 4am-12:30am, 159 pesos); **Manzanillo** (100min., every hr. 3am-11:30pm, 32 pesos); **Puerto Vallarta** (5hr., every 2hr. 3am-11:30pm, 110 pesos).

⌂ PRACTICAL INFORMATION. Banamex, on Farías, across from the bus station, has a 24hr. **ATM.** (☎355 5277 or 355 5342. Open M-F 9am-3pm.) **Change money** or traveler's checks at **Casa de Cambio,** Farías 27A, inside the commercial center across from the bus station. (☎355 5343. Open M-Sa 9am-5pm.) Other services include: **police,** upstairs at Mateos 52, north of the plaza (☎355 5080; no English spoken); **Red Cross** (☎355 2300), 15km away in Cihuatlán, accessible by "Cruz Roja" bus (every 15min. 6am-8pm, 6 pesos) from the plaza, or by taxi (100 pesos); **Súperfarmacia Plaza,** Mateos 48, on the south side of the plaza (☎355 5167; open daily 7am-8pm); **Clínica de Urgencias,** Carranza 22, two blocks from the bus station (☎355 5608; open M-Sa 8am-2pm, ring the bell outside for 24hr. emergency service); **LADATELs,** on both Farías and Mateos; **casetas,** next to the bus station, Farías 34 (☎355 6310; fax 355 5452; open Su 8:30am-1pm, M-Sa 8:30am-8:30pm); **Internet access** at **Ciber@net,** in the commercial center, Farías 27A (☎355 5519; melaque@ciber.net.mx; 45 pesos per hr.; open M-F 10am-2:30pm and 4-7:30pm, Sa 9:30am-2:30pm); **post office,** Orozco 56, near the corner of Corona, one block from Billiard San Patricio (☎355 5230; open M-F 9am-3pm). **Postal code:** 48980.

⌐⌂ ACCOMMODATIONS AND FOOD. Melaque boasts a crop of snazzy hotels, but few could be termed "budget." Expect rates to rise during high season. Camping is feasible in Melaque if you arrange to stay next to one of the beachside restaurants; expect to pay a small fee. **Hotel Emanuel ❷,** Bugambilias 89, is half a block from the beach. Turn right onto Farías from the bus station and walk five blocks, turning left after the teal mansion. Look for the "Abarrotes Emanuel" sign on your left. Spacious rooms and bungalows have floral decor and clean, white-tile bathrooms; bungalows have very modern kitchens and the huge rooftop bungalow has six double beds in three bedrooms, great for a large group. (☎355 6107. Singles 120 pesos; doubles 160 pesos; triples 200 pesos. Bungalows: 1 person 160 pesos; 2 people 220 pesos; 3 people 280 pesos; rooftop bungalow 900 pesos. No charge for up to 2 children. Discounts available for longer stays.) **Casa de Huéspedes San Juán ❷**, Farías 24, is on the right leaving the bus station, across from the Banamex. Rooms are old and worn, but are one of the best deals. Kitchen units have very basic equipment. (☎355 5270. 1-3 people 100 pesos; bungalows 150 pesos.) You can also try **Bungalows los Arcos ❺**, Farías 2. Take a right at the bus station and walk to the end of the street; it's on the right. If you can ignore the musty smell, you will find clean rooms with powerful ceiling fans. Cramped private baths have hot water. (☎355 5184. 1-3 people 280 pesos; quads 290 pesos.)

During the summer, restaurants ship shrimp in from the north, but come high season, local fishing boats catch everything served in Melaque. Cheaper, more authentic places are located near the central plaza. Cheaper still are the sidewalk food stands that materialize after sunset and the unnamed, dirt-floored eateries in the *mercado*. Locals hail **Restaurant Ayala ❶.** Turn left on the street before Mateos and walk a block; it's on the left. Tasty fish (30 pesos) and burgers with fries (20 pesos) are served in an open-air environment. The *tortas* (15-20 pesos) are delicious and the *comida corrida* (20 pesos) is pretty damn cheap. (☎355 6680. Open daily 7am-5pm.) Caxcan Restaurant overlooks the *zócalo* from its second floor location above the pharmacy as you enter from Mateos. The bar hands out cheap two-for-one drinks to wash down the fishies.

BEACHES AND ENTERTAINMENT. The main attraction in Melaque is its beach. Waves get smaller and the beach more crowded toward the western end. Rent **jet skis** at **Restaurant Moyo,** the last restaurant on the far west end of the beach. (☎355 6104. 2-person 500 pesos per 30min.; 3-person 600 pesos per 30min. **Banana boats** 40 pesos per person for 15min. Available daily 10am-7pm.) Nightlife in Melaque concentrates on the beach until 9:30 or 10pm, as people swim and stroll along the shore enjoying the sunsets. For a mellow, smoky evening with middle-aged men, bring your game to **Billiard San Patricio,** on Orozco and Juárez, up the street from the post office, three blocks from the *zócalo*. Pool tables are in rough shape. Women will likely be uncomfortable here. (Pool and *carambola* 12 pesos per hr., dominoes 4 pesos per hr. Open daily 10am-11pm.) In general, don't get your partying hopes up during the low season; nightlife doesn't awake until the tourists start knocking.

BARRA DE NAVIDAD
☎315

Barra (pop. 6000) is smaller, with less crowded beaches (due to the stronger undertow) than its sister Melaque. However, shaded streets, numerous sidewalk eateries, and popular seaside bars provide a vitality lacking in Melaque. The saltwater *laguna* at the end of town is a great place to swim, play volleyball, or sunbathe. Like Melaque, Barra doesn't offer much in the way of sights, museums, or high-tech entertainment, instead reveling in its own tranquil beauty.

TRANSPORTATION. Veracruz, the main street, runs northwest-southeast, angling off at its end to meet **Legazpi,** which runs north-south, along the beach. The **bus stop** is at Veracruz 226, on the corner of Nayarit. Turn left on Veracruz from the bus station to get to the *centro*. **Primera Plus/Costa Alegre,** Veracruz 269 (☎355 6111), at Filipinas, has first-class service to: **Guadalajara** (5hr.; 7:45am, 3, 5, 6pm;

223 pesos); **León** (10hr., 8:15pm, 440 pesos); **Manzanillo** (1½hr., 4am, 37 pesos); **Mexico City** (13hr., 5pm, 1555 pesos); **Puerto Vallarta** (4hr.; 1:45, 4am; 157 pesos). Second-class buses go to **Guadalajara** (6hr.; 8:15, 11:15am, 2:15, 8:15pm; 160 pesos); **Manzanillo** (1½hr.; 9 per day 7:15am-7:45pm; 32 pesos); **Puerto Vallarta** (5hr.; 7:45, 10:45am, 2:45pm; 130 pesos).

⁊ PRACTICAL INFORMATION. The **tourist office**, at Jalisco 67, offers brochures and semi-usable maps. (☎355 5100. Open M-F 9am-5pm. No English spoken.) Friendly Texans at **Crazy Cactus** (☎355 6099), next to the church on Jalisco, between Legazpi and Veracruz, offer insider advice. The **travel agency**, Veracruz 204A, sells tickets for ETN buses departing from Manzanillo. (☎355 5665 or 335 5666; fax 355 5667. Open M-Sa 10am-2pm and 4-7pm.) Barra has no bank, but a *casa de cambio*, **Cyber@Money**, Veracruz 212C, **changes money** and traveler's checks at high rates without commission. (☎355 6177. Open M-F 9:30am-2:30pm and 4-7pm, Sa 9:30am-2:30pm.) Other service include: **police,** Veracruz 179 (☎355 5399); **Centro de Salud,** on Puerto de la Navidad down Veracruz, just out of town—take a right where a traffic island divides Veracruz, it is the peach building on the right (☎355 6220; 24hr. emergency service; no English spoken); no *casetas*, but **LADATEL** phones line the main streets; speedy **Internet service** at **Cyber@Money**, which also runs a book exchange (30 pesos per hr.; open M-F 9:30am-2:30pm and 4-7pm, Sa 9:30am-2:30pm); **post office,** Mazatlán 11, behind Veracruz. (Open M-F 8am-3pm, Sa 8am-noon.) **Postal code:** 48987.

⌂⌃ ACCOMMODATIONS AND FOOD. You will need a keen eye to spot budget accommodations. Reasonable rooms are occasionally available in private residences—ask around and look for notices in restaurants. All prices are subject to high-season hikes. **Posada Pacífico ❸,** Mazatlán 136, has hot water baths in clean and spacious rooms, most with balconies, over a tree-filled courtyard. Couches and chairs in the open hallways provide a cool place to sit and meet your neighbors. (☎355 5359; fax 355 5349. Singles 150 pesos; doubles 220 pesos. Rentals: coolers 15 pesos, boogie boards 30 pesos, beach chairs 25 pesos, bicycles 55 pesos.) **Hotel Caribe ❸,** Sonora 15, has adequate rooms with clean baths (no toilet seat) and fluorescent-lit desks. Socializing elderly ladies enliven the large lobby. (☎355 59 52. Singles 165 pesos; doubles 260 pesos; TV 40 pesos extra.). It's no longer possible to camp in Barra de Navidad; try Melaque.

For good, inexpensive Mexican food in a pleasant atmosphere, try **Restaurant Paty ❷,** Jalisco 52 at Veracruz. Neon plaid tablecloths are even brighter in the sun. A few vegetarian options. (Quesadillas 20 pesos, *chilaquiles* 25-32 pesos, meat dishes 20-25 pesos. Open daily 8am-11pm.) **Fortinos ❸,** Michoacán 66, has walls decorated with beach paintings and is another pleasant budget option. (☎335 6253. Breakfast 18-28 pesos, *comida corrida* 30 pesos. Open daily 8am-6pm.)

◉⌦ SIGHTS AND ENTERTAINMENT. Crazy Cactus, at the corner of Jalisco and Veracruz, is closed during the summer but rents equipment the rest of the year. (☎355 60 99. Snorkeling gear and boogie boards 50 pesos per ½day, 80 pesos per day; surfboards 70 pesos per ½day, 120 pesos per day; bikes 100 pesos per day.) Bibliophiles should look up **Beer Bob's Book Exchange** at its new location on Tampico.

The short trip across the lagoon to the village of **Colimilla** is pleasant; a *lancha* will deposit up to 10 passengers at the far end of the lagoon or amid Colimilla's palms, pigs, cows, and open-air restaurants (150 pesos). Deserted **Playa de los Cocos,** 1km away, has larger breakers than those in Barra. If you don't want to swim back, remember to set a time to be picked up. Another option is to tour the **lagoon** behind Barra (up to 8 people, 150 pesos) or take a fully-equipped *lancha* (up to 4 people, 250 pesos per hr.) and go tuna or marlin **fishing.** Operators have formed a cooperative, so prices are fixed. Their office and docks lie at the end of Veracruz. (Open daily 7am-7pm.)

Out past midnight? Party at **El Galeón Disco,** Morelos 24, in Hotel Sand's. Sit on cushioned, horseshoe-shaped benches and drink the night away. (☎355 5018. Beer 15 pesos, mixed drinks 35 pesos. Cover 30 pesos. Open daily 9:30pm-3am, low season F-Sa only.) Those who prefer singing can chill at **Terraza Bar Jardín,** Jalisco 70, a **karaoke** bar above Mango Bay. (☎355 6135. Beer 15 pesos. Open daily 6pm-2am.) Another popular rooftop hangout is **La Azotea,** upstairs at Legzapi 152. The thatched roof shelters an animal-themed patio, free pool table, and a great view of the sea. (☎355 5029. Open daily 6pm-2am.) If you want to concentrate your efforts on drinking, make your way to **Piper Lovers,** Legazpi 154A, where the live music is good, drinks are cheap, and pool and ping-pong are free for customers. Piper himself embodies the spirit of the place—shirtless and barefoot, in cut-off camos, he'll drink you under the table, then fall asleep on it. (☎355 6747; www.piperlover.com. Beer 10-15 pesos, mixed drinks 35 pesos. Live music 9pm-2am on weekends, more often in season; open M-Th noon-midnight, F-Sa noon-2am.) Besides Lovers, there are many two-for-one happy hours along Legazpi that make the giddy trip toward inebriation that much cheaper. At **Terrace Capri,** on Legazpi across from the church, hit the dance floor or relax with a drink while watching the waves nuzzle the coast and perhaps catching one of the much-hyped sunsets. (☎355 5217. Beer 15 pesos, drinks 30 pesos. 2-for-1 happy hour 2-10pm. Open daily 2pm-2am.)

COLIMA

MANZANILLO

☎314

With its golden sands, green waters, and bountiful sailfish, Manzanillo (pop. 124,000) has been touted as the emerald of the Pacific. However, eager resort builders have one strike against them—Manzanillo is the workhorse port of Mexico's Pacific coast, attracting ships from as far away as Russia, and conventional wisdom holds that a working port can never become a truly world-class resort.

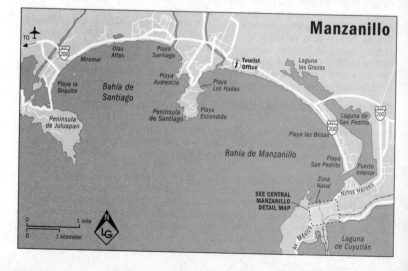

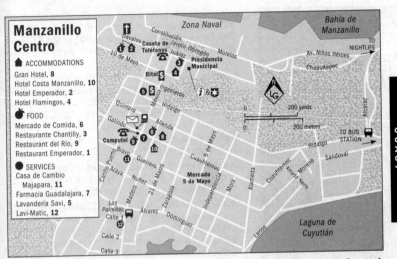

Manzanillo Centro

♦ ACCOMMODATIONS
Gran Hotel, **8**
Hotel Costa Manzanillo, **10**
Hotel Emperador, **2**
Hotel Flamingos, **4**

🍴 FOOD
Mercado de Comida, **6**
Restaurante Chantilly, **3**
Restaurant del Río, **9**
Restaurant Emperador, **1**

● SERVICES
Casa de Cambio
Majapara, **11**
Farmacia Guadalajara, **7**
Lavandería Savi, **5**
Lavi-Matic, **12**

Indeed, Manzanillo's best beaches lie west of the dynamic, sweaty *centro*, beyond a huge stretch of barges and cranes. Those seeking only sand and surf would do better to retreat to a secluded village such as Cuyutlán, but for those excited by lively, crowded beaches—and the nightlife of a real city—Manzanillo delivers.

◧ TRANSPORTATION

White-and-blue "Miramar" and "Centro" **buses** run back and forth between the *centro* and the resort strip at the west of town (30min., every 15min. 5am-11pm, about 4.5 pesos from the *centro* to the beaches).

Airport: (☎333 2525), Playa de Oro, between Barra de Navidad and Manzanillo. Airlines include: **AeroCalifornia** (☎334 1414; open M-F 8am-8pm, Sa-Su 9am-5pm) and **Mexicana** (☎333 2323; open M-F 9am-6:45pm and Sa 9am-6pm). Both airlines have offices in the Comercial Mexicana shopping center, along the "Miramar" bus route. **Taxis** (☎333 1999) from the airport to the *zócalo* 250 pesos.

Buses: Station on Hidalgo, southeast of Jardín Obregón in the *centro*. You can take a taxi (13 pesos) or bus (3 pesos) to the *centro*. From the station, take a "Colomo" bus and get off near the PEMEX gas station. Follow the coastline 6min. to get to the Jardín. **Estrella Blanca** (☎322 4243) goes to: **Acapulco** (12hr., 4pm, 360 pesos); **Lázaro Cárdenas** (6½hr., 4pm, 180 pesos); **Mazatlán** (12hr., 4pm, 430 pesos); **Mexico City** (14hr., 4pm, 476 pesos); **Puerto Vallarta** (6hr., 4pm, 170 pesos); **Tepic** (7hr., 4pm, 258 pesos); **Zijuatenejo** (9hr., 4pm, 235 pesos). **Autobuses del Sur** (☎322 1003), **La Línea/Autobuses de Occidente** (☎322 0123), **Transportes Cihuatlán** (☎322 0515), and **Primera Plus** (☎322 0210) offer similar services. **Autobuses Nuevo Horizonte** (☎322 3900) runs to **Colima** (2½hr., 5 per day 8am-9:40pm, 54 pesos).

⚓🛈 ORIENTATION AND PRACTICAL INFORMATION

Tourist Office: Costera Miguel de la Madrid 1294 (☎333 2277; fax 333 1426; sectur@bay.net.mx), in front of Hotel Karmina Palace. Catch a "Miramar" bus (4.5 pesos) on México or near the Jardín and tell the driver where you're headed. Provides great maps. Open M-F 9am-3pm and 6-8:30pm, Sa 10am-2pm. **Information booths** in front

IN RECENT NEWS

TERRIBLE TREMORS

On January 21, 2003, an earthquake measuring 7.6 on the Richter scale hit the Mexican Pacific Coast. The earthquake was centered near Manzanillo, so the state of Colima was hit the hardest. The 45-second earthquake and its aftershocks severely damaged 16 city blocks in the state capital and killed over 21 people. The earthquake is considered among the strongest in recent history.

However, Colima is definitely no stranger to seismic activity. Since 1973, 11 earthquakes of magnitude 7.3 and above have hit the Central Pacific Coast. An October 9, 1995, earthquake of magnitude 8.0 killed 49 people and virtually leveled Manzanillo. A September 19, 1985, quake, also of magnitude 8.0, killed 9500 people.

The area owes its frequent—and often deadly—earthquakes to the fact that it is perched in a seismically active zone at the junction of three tectonic plates: the North American, the Rivera, and the Cocos.

The destruction from the most recent quake—over 13,000 residential structures were damaged or destroyed, according to the Earthquake Engineering Research Institute—is still being repaired. Although life is slowly returning to normal, cracks in the walls of colonial-era buildings are an uneasy reminder of the region's precarious position.

of the Palacio, around town, and along the beaches offer many of the same maps. Open daily 8am-10pm. Helpful **tourist police** (☎332 1002) in the Palacio Municipal on the *zócalo* distribute maps and brochures.

Currency Exchange: Bital, México 99 (☎332 0950), at 10 de Mayo. Changes traveler's checks before 6pm. Open M-Sa 8am-7pm. 24hr. **ATM. Casa de Cambio Majapara,** México 354 (☎322 6386). Open M-F 9am-2pm and 4:30-7pm, Sa 9am-2pm.

Market: Mercado 5 de Mayo, on 5 de Mayo at Guerrero. Open daily 5am-5pm.

Supermarket: Comercial Mexicana, Costera de la Madrid km 11.5 (☎333 1375). Take a "Miramar" bus from the *zócalo* (4 pesos). Open daily 8am-10pm.

Laundry: Lavi-Matic, Calle 1 1 (☎332 0844). Wash and dry 10 pesos per kg, 3kg min. Open daily 9am-5pm. **Lavandería Savi,** Bocanegra 44, closer to Jardín Obregón than the competition. 10 pesos per kg, 25 pesos min. Open M-Sa 8am-8pm.

Emergency: ☎066.

Police: (☎332 1002 or 332 1004), in the Palacio Municipal. Little English spoken.

Red Cross: (☎336 5770), on Barotes. No English spoken.

Pharmacy: Farmacia Guadalajara, México 301 (☎332 2922), at Galindo, 4 blocks from the *zócalo*. Also sells food and has a small deli. Open 24hr.

Hospital: Centro Médico Quirurgico, Costera 1215 (☎334 0444 or 334 1666). Some English spoken.

Fax: Caseta de Teléfonos Computel, México 302 (☎322 3926). Offers national calls (3.5 pesos per min.) and calls to the US (6.5 pesos per min.). Open daily 7am-10pm.

Internet Access: Movimiento Civil Mexicano, Galindo 30 (☎332 7384), Centro Comercial del Puente. Those willing to make the trek up 3 flights of stairs will be welcomed by A/C and the cheapest access in town (10 pesos per hr.). Open daily 10am-7pm.

Car Rental: Hertz (☎333 3141), on Costera. From 750 pesos a day. Open Su 9am-5pm, M-Sa 9am-1pm and 3-7pm. **Airport office** (☎333 3191).

Post Office: Galindo 30 (☎332 0022). Open M-F 9am-4pm. **Postal Code:** 28200.

ACCOMMODATIONS

Manzanillo's budget accommodations tend to be basic. In general, the area around the *zócalo* is safer than the bus station. **Camping** is permitted on Playa Miramar, but is only recommended during

Semana Santa and in December, when bathroom facilities are available and security is heightened.

Gran Hotel, Cuauhtémoc 81 (☎322 0388). The best deal in town. Clean, spacious rooms with powerful ceiling fan, TV, and tidy private bathroom. A few rooms with terrace. Singles 100 pesos; doubles 200 pesos; triples 300 pesos. ❷

Hotel Flamingos, Madero 72 (☎332 1037), by the *Jardín Obregón*. Carved ceiling beams in lobby, red-tiled hallways, and noisy ceiling fans come at a low price. Spacious, clean rooms and small, tidy baths. Singles 120 pesos; doubles 150 pesos. ❷

Hotel Emperador, Dávalos 69 (☎332 2374), near the *Jardín*. The blank tile walls give this hotel a somewhat institutional feel. Small rooms with rustic wooden furniture are hot, but fans help cool things off. Baths are cramped but neat and have hot water. Singles 115 pesos; doubles 135 pesos; triples 205 pesos. ❷

Hotel Costa Manzanillo, Madero 333 (☎332 2740). Plants and bright bedspreads make the hotel cheery. Medium-sized rooms with baths, wobbly ceiling fan, and TV. Singles 150 pesos; doubles 180 pesos. ❸

🍴 FOOD

Since tourists stake their claims closer to the beach, food at the market and downtown is simple and cheap. During the many festivities enlivening the *zócalo*, food vendors pop up at every corner offering homemade goodies. The obvious local specialty is fresh seafood—whether you prefer it in a spicy *diablo* sauce, sizzled up with lots of garlic, or as a greasy soup, good shrimp and fish dishes are easy to come by and inexpensive near the Jardín.

Mercado de Comida, Cuauhtémoc at Madero. Small, open-air eateries offers a wide variety of seafood and *comida típica* and *corrida* at pretty good prices. Squeeze yourself onto a bench and eat to your heart's content. Most dishes 18-40 pesos. Open daily 7am-10pm; however, most dishes are not ready until 9am and most stores close up shop around 8pm. ❸

Restaurante Chantilly, Madero 60 (☎332 0194), by the massive swordfish statue. Professionals and families feast on good staples in a diner-like setting as waitresses serve tasty enchiladas (32-36 pesos), tuna or chicken salad (38 pesos), and meat (35-70 pesos). Open Su-F 7:30am-10:30pm. ❸

Restaurant Emperador, Dávalos 69 (☎332 2374), below Hotel Emperador. Packed with locals at all hours. Gargantuan *comida corrida* 30 pesos, delicious enchiladas 15 pesos, filling hot cakes 13 pesos. Open daily 8:30am-11pm. ❷

Restaurant del Río, México 330 (☎332 2525). A small, inexpensive place that will fill you up in no time with *comida corrida* (33 pesos) or Mexican specialties (13-28 pesos). Try a barbecue taco (4 pesos) and wash it down with a chilly beer (10 pesos) or *licuado* (10 pesos). Open M-Sa 8am-6pm. ❷

🏖 BEACHES

Manzanillo's beaches stretch along two bays, **Bahía de Manzanillo** and **Bahía de Santiago,** formed by the Santiago and Juluapan peninsulas. Bahía de Manzanillo has more expensive hotels and cleaner, golden sand, but its beach slopes steeply, creating a strong and sometimes dangerous undertow. The beaches at Bahía Santiago are better protected and ideal for swimming, water sports, and sun worshipping.

PLAYA LAS BRISAS. The beach most accessible from the *centro* is Playa Las Brisas, on Bahía de Manzanillo. A few secluded spots remain, but it is for the most part crowded with luxurious hotels and bungalows and decorated with a strange slope formed by the sand that makes rolling down into the waves an easy and enjoyable task. *(Take a taxi for 35 pesos, the "Las Brisas" bus for 4.5 pesos, or a "Miramar" bus and ask to be let off at the* crucero *(crossroads). Go left for more populated beaches or stake out a private spot nearer the junction.)*

OLAS ALTAS. Cleaner water and excellent beaches occupy the rest of the bay, west of Peninsula Santiago. Beyond **Olas Altas** lies **Miramar Beach,** popular with experienced surfers and infamous for its powerful waves and undertow, where you can brave the waves or watch Mexican surfers gracefully glide in the ocean. *(Get off where the footbridge crosses the route. Though crowded, here you'll find top-notch restaurants where you can rent bodyboards and surfboards for 25 pesos per hr.)*

PLAYA LA BOQUITA. The calmer waters of exclusive private beach Playa la Boquita, the westernmost point on the Juluapan Peninsula, make it a popular spot for children and water sport enthusiasts. Be sure to make reservations for snorkeling (2hr., 10am, 200 pesos), scuba diving excursions (2hr., 10am, 500 pesos), or deep-sea fishing (7 or 8am, 350 pesos per hr.). If you're not much of an underwater enthusiast, try taking a horse for a sandy jaunt (available for rent near the last of the *palapa* restaurants; 150 pesos per hr.) or riding in a banana boat (40 pesos.) *(Take a "Miramar" bus to Club Santiago. 40min., 4 pesos. Walk through the white gate along the cobblestone street that becomes a dirt road. 25min. Don't be intimidated by the gate security guards; just ask for Playa Boquita and they will wave you through. Taxis 20 pesos.)*

PLAYA AUDIENCIA. This small but magnificent cove has calm waters, light brown sand, and a gorgeous, rocky vista. *(Take a "Las Hadas" bus for 5 pesos from Niños Héroes or anywhere on Miramar Rte. to the Sierra Radison and follow the path to the beach.)*

▨ NIGHTLIFE

Manzanillo doesn't sleep when the sun sets, and trendy, tourist-oriented clubs along the resort strip play the latest music all night long. "Miramar" buses run along the strip until 9pm. Taxis back to the *centro* cost 30-50 pesos.

▨ **Vog and Bar de Félix,** Costera de la Madrid km 9.2 (☎333 1875), on the beach side. Both discos offer unadulterated, steamy bliss. The 20s and 30s crowd at Bar de Félix greet every new Latin song with roaring applause while the US and Mexican tunes at more upscale Vog inspire dancing in every square inch of space. Vog also offers a game area, with pool tables, foosball, and tall booths. Beer 20 pesos, national drinks from 35 pesos. Vog: cover 50 pesos. Open W-Sa 10:30pm-4am. Bar de Félix: 80-peso drink minimum F-Sa. Open Su 9pm-4am, M-Sa 6pm-6am. Shorter hours during low season.

Colima Bay Cafe, Costera de la Madrid km 6.5 (☎333 1150), on the beach side. Two bars, a sizable dance floor, and a terrace overlooking the Pacific provide plenty of space for dancing. The young, well-dressed crowd knows how to party. Beer 25 pesos, national drinks from 35 pesos. Cover 50 pesos but can vary by event. Open M-F 1pm-2am, Sa 1pm-4am.

CUYUTLÁN
☎313

The lush vegetation, black-sand beach, and mysterious lagoon of quiet Cuyutlán (pop. 1650) offer the traveler a few days of solitary paradise. In low season, darkened buildings and silent streets give it a ghost-town feel, and the huge golden head of Benito Juárez amidst the palm trees of Cuyutlán's *zócalo* is often the only face visible. Summer weekends are slightly busier, but it is only during high season (Dec. and *Semana Santa*) that Cuyutlán truly comes alive.

▐ TRANSPORTATION.

Cuyutlán is an hour's ride down the coast from Manzanillo, off Mex. 200. The only way to get there is through **Armería,** on the highway about 15km inland. From Manzanillo, take a "Colima" bus (45min., every 15min.

5am-10:30pm, 22 pesos) from the station entrance and ask to get off at Armería. To reach the Terminal Sub-Urbana in Armería, exit at the blue "Paraíso" sign and follow the street to the left. If you get dropped off at the other terminal, walk one block left, go right, and walk one more block to reach the Terminal Sub-Urbana. Buses to Cuyutlán leave from here (20min., every 30min. 6:45am-7:30pm, 8 pesos). Buses return to Armería on the same schedule and pick up near the *zócalo*. A **taxi** from Armería to Cuyutlán is about 50 pesos.

ORIENTATION AND PRACTICAL INFORMATION.
The road from Armería parallels the coast and becomes **Yavaros** as it enters town. It intersects **Hidalgo**, which marks the eastern border of the *zócalo*; a left at this intersection takes you to the beach. **Veracruz,** Cuyutlán's other mighty boulevard, parallels Yavaros, one block off the beach. Most of Cuyutlán's municipal services are within one block of the *zócalo*. To get to the beach from the *zócalo*, take a right on Hidalgo. The English-speaking owners of **Hotel Fénix** will change money if they have the cash. **Police** (☎326 4014) are located 2 blocks from the *zócalo* on Hidalgo. The friendly, non-English-speaking officers also provide what little tourist information is available in town. To get to the **Centro de Salud**, take a right onto Yavaros from the *zócalo* and walk 1½ blocks—the center will be on your left.

ACCOMMODATIONS AND FOOD.
Hotels are well maintained, affordable, and comfortable. During high season, rates skyrocket to 200 pesos per person and meals are included to help justify the price; make reservations at least a month in advance. The rooms at **Hotel Fénix ❶**, Hidalgo 201, at Veracruz, may be taller than they are wide, but the second story is encircled by a breezy porch with hammocks, wind chimes, and a great view of the ocean. The friendly owners run a popular bar that serves as the town watering hole. Watch out for the dog that guards the establishment at night. (☎326 4082. Downstairs rooms 90 pesos, upstairs rooms 120 pesos. Make reservations 2 months in advance in high season.) **Hotel Morelos ❷**, Hidalgo 185, at Veracruz, has spacious rooms with clean baths and wooden furniture. Tiled floors, festive colors, a restaurant, a small pool, and all the artificial flowers in Cuyutlán give the place pizazz. (☎326 4013. In high season, 360 pesos per person including 3 meals, no meal-less option. In the low season, 250 pesos per person including 3 meals, 130 pesos without meals.) **Hotel Maria Victoria ❶**, Veracruz 10, is the biggest and most imposing hotel in town. A huge common area lies just through the gates of their posh lobby. Rooms have an unbeatable ocean view but small bathrooms. (☎326 4004. 170 pesos per person.) Almost all of the food in Cuyutlán is served up in **hotel restaurants ❹**; seafood (40-70 pesos) is the obvious specialty. During the day, cheaper fare can be found in *loncherías* around the *zócalo*. Most close early, leaving late-night hunger to **torterías ❶**; one is on Hidalgo and another is on Veracruz across from the Hotel Maria Victoria.

SIGHTS AND ENTERTAINMENT.
Cuyutlán's ▨**black sand beaches** are patrolled by lifeguards who post flags indicating surf conditions. (Lifeguards on duty 8am-6pm in high season, 10am-4:30pm in low season.) Although the shore is packed with families near the Hidalgo entrance, the crowd thins out rapidly at either end, making it easy for you to stake out your own space. Aside from its gorgeous beach, Cuyutlán's biggest claim to fame is the **green wave,** a phenomenon that occurs regularly May and June. Quirky currents and phosphorescent marine life combine to produce 10m swells that glow an unearthly green. The town itself reaches high tide during the **Festival de la Virgen de Guadalupe,** the first 12 days of December during which men, women, and children clad in traditional dress walk 5km twice a day to the town's blue church. The celebrations peak on the twelfth day, when *mariachis* accompany the procession, and the marchers sing tributes to the Virgin. To get your historic-cultural fix, check out the **Museo de Sal,** one block right from the *zócalo* on Juárez. This dirt-floor museum depicts the history of Cuyutlán, and features a huge model of the salt-

making process that aided in the town's development. If you must have a souvenir, 2kg bags of locally-made salt are available at the entrance for 6 pesos. (Open daily 8am-6pm. Voluntary donation.) Cuyutlán's **Tortugario**, 3.5km east of town along Veracruz, is a combination wildlife preserve and zoo. Home to turtles, iguanas, and crocodiles, the Tortugario also has saltwater pools for (human) swimming. Visitors can also take a boat ride in the lagoon (2hr. ride 50 pesos). Taxis will take you to the museum (40 pesos from Armería, 60 pesos from Cuyutlán), or you can ask the bus driver to let you off by the Tortugario sign between Armería and Cuyutlán, then follow the dirt road 3km. (Open daily 8:30am-5:30pm. 20 pesos, children 15 pesos.)

PARAÍSO ☎ 313

Paraíso outclasses nearby **Armería**, but not by much. Pretty black sand beaches make for good swimming, but the lack of amenities and its greater commercialization make it a less desirable getaway than Cuyutlán. Nevertheless, Paraíso is popular among Mexicans for daytrips and weekend vacations.

⊑ TRANSPORTATION. A well-paved road connects Armería and Paraíso, cutting through 7km of banana and coconut plantations before ending at the black sands surrounding Paraíso's few hotels and beachfront restaurants. Follow directions to Cuyutlán, but instead take a "Paraíso" bus (15min., every 30min. 6:45am-7:30pm, 5 pesos) from Armería's Terminal Sub-Urbano. Buses return on the same schedule.

■■ ORIENTATION AND PRACTICAL INFORMATION. Besides the main road from Armería, Paraíso's other street is the dirt **Juventud** (also called **Adán y Eva**), which runs behind the beachfront restaurants. The **police station** is two blocks up from Juventud on the main road. (☎322 0990. No English spoken.) Basic medical attention can be found at the **Centro de Salud**, next to the police station. Long-distance **phone calls** can be made from **Abarrotes Valdovinos**, next to the bus stop. (☎322 0025. Open daily 9am-2pm and 4-9pm.)

■■ ACCOMMODATIONS AND FOOD. At the far left end of the strip you'll find **Hotel Paraíso ❺**, which has spacious rooms with bath and an ocean view. (☎322 4005. Singles and doubles 255 pesos, with hot water 285 pesos, with TV 315 pesos.) The first building to the left of the beach entrance is **Hotel Equipales ❸**, where you'll find no-frills rooms with a view of the shore. (☎332 0990. Singles and doubles 150 pesos, triples and quads 180 pesos.) If you have a group, the new **Hotel Puerta al Paraíso ❺**, by the Centro de Salud, offers accommodations a step above most in town. There is a pool outside and rooms have small, spotless bathrooms. (☎322 0849. 450 pesos for 4 people.) At the far right end of the strip lies **Hotel Valencia ❷**. Somewhat run-down rooms of uneven quality have bath and fake green plants. (☎322 0457. Singles 120 pesos; doubles 200 pesos; triples 250 pesos.) Paraíso's extensive beach makes a soft pillow for **campers,** and Hotel Paraíso provides free access to showers and bathrooms. (Pool access 10 pesos.) Some beachside restaurant owners let you hang hammocks under their thatched roofs. During high season, rooms may be available in **private houses;** ask in stores.

Restaurants run the slim gamut from rustic *enramadas* to cement-floored *comedores*, with seafood-dominated menus. **Restaurant Paraíso ❸**, in Hotel Paraíso at the east end of Juventud, provides snappy service, and string quartets and *mariachis* sometimes appear in the afternoon. (Breakfast 18-28 pesos, tasty shrimp dishes 65 pesos. Open daily 9am-7pm.) The restaurant at **Hotel Valencia ❹** also offers a pleasant atmosphere and seafood dishes. (35-70 pesos. Open daily 8am-6pm.)

COLIMA
☎312

Stately Colima (pop. 130,000) maintains a measure of small-town benevolence and informality. On Sundays, stores close shop as families attend mass, walk in the park, or sit and listen to *mariachi* bands in the gazebo of Plaza Principal. In the shadows of El Volcán de Fuego and El Nevado, Colima has experienced its share of natural disasters—many of its buildings have suffered the wrath of the volcanoes and earthquakes. In January 2003, a earthquake of magnitude 7.6 struck the area, and some parts of the city are still rebuilding. Still, despite the looming giants and recent turbulence, undertouristed Colima is blessed with cool mountain air, a string of museums, beautiful plazas, and the Universidad de Colima. It's a rewarding place to stop en route to the coast.

⌷ TRANSPORTATION

INTERCITY TRANSPORTATION

Airport: Aeropuerto Nacional Miguel de la Madrid (☎314 4160), 2hr. from town. Served by **AeroCalifornia** (☎314 4850) and **Aeroméxico** (☎313 8057). **Taxis** (☎313 0524) from the airport cost 90 pesos.

Bus: Estación Nueva is on the northeast side of town, about 2km from the *centro*. To get there, pick up a "Ruta 5" on Bravo, or "Ruta 4" on Zaragoza (every 5min. 6am-8:30pm, 3.5 pesos), or take a **taxi** (40 pesos). From the station, **Primera Plus** (☎314 8067) sends 1st-class buses to: **Aguascalientes** (6hr., 4pm, 325 pesos); **Guadalajara** (2¾hr., every hr. 5:15am-7:30pm, 146 pesos); **León** (6½hr., 12:30pm, 325 pesos); **Manzanillo** (1hr., every 2hr. 2am-11:40pm, 54 pesos); **Mexico City** (10hr., 9 and 11:30pm, 530 pesos); **Puerto Vallarta** (6½hr., 10:40pm, 230 pesos) via **Melaque** (3hr., 10:40pm, 90 pesos); **Tecomán** (45min., 6:40 and 9pm, 32 pesos). **Autobuses de Occidente/La Línea** (☎314 8781), **Estrella Blanca** (☎312 8499), **Ómnibus de México** (☎312 1630), and **Autotransportes Galeana** (☎313 4785) have similar service. **ETN** (☎312 5899) goes to the **Guadalajara airport, Manzanillo, Mexico City,** and **Morelia. Terminal Suburbana,** known to locals as **Central los Rojos,** is southwest of the *centro;* it offers 2nd-class regional service. The fastest way to get there is to take a "Ruta 2 bus" from Morelos, near Jardín Quintero.

LOCAL TRANSPORTATION

Taxis are one of the most convenient and popular ways to get around Colima. They are fairly cheap (12 pesos gets you to most of the places listed), and it is not unusual for complete strangers to get into the same taxi and split the fare.

⌷ PRACTICAL INFORMATION

Tourist Office: Hidalgo 96 (☎312 4360; turiscol@palmera.colimanet.com). Helpful staff, pamphlets, and maps. English spoken. Open M-F 8:30am-8pm, Sa 10am-2pm.

Currency Exchange: Banamex, Hidalgo 90 (☎312 0285), has a 24hr. **ATM.** Open M-F 9am-5pm, Sa 9am-2pm. **Multicambios de Colima** (☎330 1220), Juárez at Jardín Núñez, changes checks and currency for slightly better rates. Open M-Sa 9am-7:30pm.

Luggage Storage: At the bus station, 3 pesos per bag per hr. Open daily 9am-8pm. Restaurants offer assistance after hours.

Laundry: Lavandería Automática Amana, Domínguez 147 (☎314 4841), behind Hospedajes del Rey. 9 pesos per kg, 3kg min. Open daily 8am-9pm.

Car Rental: SuperAutos (☎312 0752), Av. Rey Colima.

Emergency: ☎066.

Police: (☎312 0967 or 312 2566). Across from the bus station on Carretera Guadalajara. No English spoken.

CENTRAL PACIFIC COAST

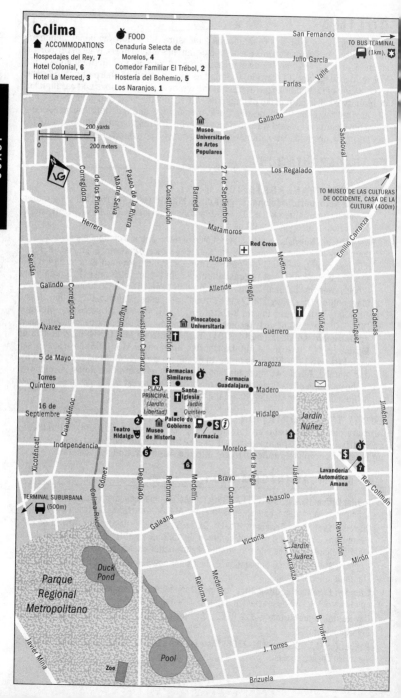

Colima

ACCOMMODATIONS
Hospedajes del Rey, **7**
Hotel Colonial, **6**
Hotel La Merced, **3**

FOOD
Cenaduría Selecta de
Morelos, **4**
Comedor Familiar El Trébol, **2**
Hostería del Bohemio, **5**
Los Naranjos, **1**

Red Cross: (☎313 8787) Aldama at Obregón. No English spoken.

Pharmacy: Farmacia Guadalajara, Madero 16 (☎314 6464), at de la Vega. Also has a **supermarket.** Open 24hr. 2nd location at Hidalgo, on Plaza Principal.

Medical Assistance: Centro de Salud (☎312 3436), Juárez at 20 de Noviembre. Open daily 7am-8pm. **Centro Médico de Colima,** Herrera 140 (☎315 6070).

Fax: Telecomm, Madero 243 (☎312 6064), in the same building as the post office. Open M-F 8am-7:30pm, Sa-Su 9am-noon.

Internet: Colegio Nacional de Capacitación Intensiva, Hidalgo 83 (☎312 0150), off the Jardín Quintero. 20 pesos per hr. Open daily 8am-10pm.

Post Office: Madero 247 (☎315 6070), on the northeast corner of Jardín Núñez. Open M-F 9am-5pm, Sa 9am-1pm. **Postal Code:** 28001.

ACCOMMODATIONS

Cheap lodging may be found near Jardín Núñez, while higher-priced hotels surround the university. Rooms are generally well-kept and come with TV.

Hotel La Merced, Juárez 82 (☎312 6969). Immaculate, fair-sized rooms with TV, fans, cozy furniture, and tall ceilings. White walls, cool green trim, and ceiling beams give La Merced charm. Private parking lot. Singles 160 pesos; doubles 195 pesos. ❸

Hotel Colonial, Medellín 142F (☎313 0877), near Jardín Quintero. Friendly staff. Rooms vary in style and price. Singles 120-160 pesos; doubles 160-200 pesos. ❷

Hospedajes del Rey, Rey Colimán 125 (☎313 3683), under a block from the Jardín Núñez. Huge, plush rooms have fans, cable TV, and wall-to-wall windows. You could eat off the tile bathroom floors (don't). Singles 260 pesos; doubles 360 pesos. ❹

FOOD

Inexpensive meals with traditional favorites like *pozole blanco* and *sopitos*, made Colima-style with thinner tortillas, are easy to come by. Other local treats include the sweet, sometimes chocolatey *enchiladas colimenses*, and *entomatadas*, a spicy *picadillo* (ground beef) dish made with *tomatillos* (little green tomatoes). A jaunt down the side streets of Plaza Principal will lead to budget meals aplenty.

Comedor Familiar el Trébol, 16 de Septiembre 59 (☎312 2900), on the Plaza. Irish flair with a very Mexican taste; a clover complements a large mural of Colima's 2 volcanoes. A popular family spot. Modest *comida corrida* 18-25 pesos. Open Su-F 8am-11pm. ❷

Los Naranjos, Barreda 34 (☎312 0029), north of Jardín Quintero. Classy but affordable. Middle-aged patrons peruse magazines and sip coffee over orange tablecloths. Breakfast 18-40 pesos, *pollo a la mexicana* 41 pesos. Open daily 8am-11:30pm. ❸

Cenaduría Selecta de Morelos, Morelos 292 (☎312 9332), by Jardín Núñez. Delicious and cheap. *Pozole* (pork stew) and *enchiladas dulces* are piled diced onions and fiery sauce (15 pesos). Speedy service. Open Su 1:30-11pm, Tu-F 5-11pm, Sa 1-11pm. ❶

Hostería del Bohemio, Morelos 29 (☎312 0073). Laid-back atmosphere with a relaxing *zócalo* view. Unique omelette with *chorizo* and mushrooms (28 pesos) and tasty *botana* (20-40 pesos). Live music F-Su 6pm-midnight. Open daily 8am-midnight. ❸

SIGHTS

While most visitors come to Colima primarily to explore the natural wonders nearby, the sage traveler will take advantage of Colima's quiet, untouristed Plaza Principal and discover the beauty within the city itself.

PLAZA PRINCIPAL. The gazebo and fountains of the plaza (officially **Jardín Libertad**) are bordered on the north by the **Palacio de Gobierno,** which contains historical murals. The double arcade around the plaza holds the **Museo Regional de Historia de Colima,** the city's newest museum and home to a collection of Pre-Hispanic Coliman ceramics and a glass floor replica of a western Mesoamerican burial site. An eclectic art gallery shares the courtyard. *(Portal Morelos 1 at 16 de Septiembre and Reforma, on the south side of the plaza. Museum ☎312 9228. Open Su 5-8pm, Tu-Sa 9am-6pm. 28 pesos, students free; Su free.)*

SANTA IGLESIA CATHEDRAL. The Spanish first built a church here in 1527; an earthquake destroyed the original wood and palm structure, a fire consumed its replacement. Undeterred, the Spanish built the current church, whose Neoclassical interior sparkles with gilt paint, chandeliers, polished marble, and statues. Unfortunately, another earthquake has damaged it. A statue of San Felipe de Jesús, the city's patron saint, resides in the pulpit designed by Othón Bustos. *(Adjoining the Palacio de Gobierno. ☎312 0200. Open daily 6am-2pm and 4:30-8:30pm.)*

PINACOTECA UNIVERSITARIA. The center displays artwork of students and local painters and hosts performances and poetry readings. Call for a schedule of events. *(Guerrero 35 between Barreda and Constitución. ☎312 2228. Open Su 10am-1pm, Tu-Sa 10am-2pm and 5-8pm. 10 pesos, children and students 5 pesos.)*

MUSEO UNIVERSITARIO DE ARTES POPULARES. The permanent collection includes stunning traditional dresses and masterfully crafted devil masks, figurines recovered from nearby tombs, and descriptions of the pre-Aztec western coast. Twelve-foot puppets called Mojigangas decorate the entrance and central courtyard. A gift shop sells handmade reproductions of local ceramics. *(At Barreda and Gallardo. Catch the "Ruta 7" bus (3.5 pesos) on Barreda between Zaragoza and Guerrero, or walk 15min. northeast of the plaza. ☎312 6869. Open Su 10am-1pm, Tu-Sa 10am-2pm and 5-8pm. 10 pesos, children and students 5 pesos; Su free.)*

MUSEO DE LAS CULTURAS DE OCCIDENTE. The museum features Colima's trademark ceramic figures, rarely seen outside the state, and provides an excellent Spanish narrative of the artifacts' significance to indigenous culture. The **Casa de la Cultura,** at the same site, is the best source of information on cultural events in Colima. *(Galván at Ejército Nacional, an easy ride from the centro. Take the yellow "Ruta #3 Sur" bus (3.5 pesos) on Colimán at Jardín Núñez, or a taxi (10 pesos). ☎313 0608. Museum open Tu-Su 9am-7pm. 15 pesos. Casa de la Cultura open daily 8:30am-9pm.)*

LA CAMPANA. Named for its pre-excavation bell shape, La Campana's currently excavated area comprises only 1% of the estimated 125 acres this ceremonial center once occupied (1500 BC-AD 1500). The discovery of these structures destroyed the myth that the west coast had no organized Pre-Hispanic civilizations or cultural centers. The site has examples of the naturally rounded stone and clay mortar architecture used in AD 900, their advanced drainage system, and clues about burial practices. Site markers in Spanish and English. *(Flag down a "Ruta 7" bus on Constitución, between Jardín Libertad and Jardín Quintero (3.5 pesos), and get off just past the Comercial Mexicana, or take a taxi (13 pesos). Open Tu-Su 9am-5pm. 23 pesos; students free.)*

PARQUE REGIONAL METROPOLITANO. This park offers afternoon strolls or faster-paced buggy rides (17-20 pesos per 30min.) along a man-made duck pond, home to two large, brazen pelicans. Rent a *lancha* (7 pesos per 30min.) for a closer view. A miniature **zoo** houses monkeys, crocodiles, and boars in disturbingly small cages while the pool across the street holds most of Colima's under-14 population. *(On Degollado, 4 blocks south of the plaza. ☎314 1676. Open daily 7am-7pm. 2 pesos. Pool open W-Su 10:30am-4:30pm. Pool admission 10 pesos, children 8 pesos.)*

NIGHTLIFE

Erupting volcanoes aren't the only things shaking in Colima. Hot nightclubs pull in locals and students with cheap beer and fast music. For something more relaxing, try a movie at **Plaza Country** (☎312 0173; open daily 1pm-10pm; 28 pesos) or **Cine Soriana** (☎311 3213; 33 pesos, W 20 pesos), both on Tecnológico/Sevilla del Río. Unfortunately, the recent earthquake wreaked havoc on the bar and club scene.

Argenta, Sevilla del Río 615 (☎313 8012), a 15-peso cab ride from the *centro*. Argenta is the place to be if you know you're cool and know how to dance. It has a huge TV screen, lofty balcony, alternative crowd, and good ambience. Beer 15 pesos, national drinks 40 pesos. Open bar on W and F; cover on those days 90 pesos for men, 40 pesos for women. Cover Th 30 pesos. Open W-Sa 10pm-3am.

Dalí, the Casa de la Cultura's cafe. Melancholy tunes pierce the air and wrench the heart; prints of famous works compete with randomly-shaped and -placed windows to complete the "artistic" scene. Not cheap, but complete with music (9pm-midnight). *Muy romántico.* Beer from 10 pesos, national drinks from 30. Open daily 5:30pm-midnight. Dalí was damaged by earthquake in 2003, but should reopen sometime in 2004.

La Belisaria, Domínguez 479 (☎312 8688), a 10-peso cab ride from the plaza. Without a true dance floor, the young crowd freely dances between tables. With blaring music, don't expect meaningful conversation. Cover W men 100 pesos, 30 pesos women; F 80/30 pesos; Sa 50/25 pesos. Open bar W and Sa. Open W-Sa 10pm-3am.

DAYTRIPS FROM COLIMA

If you want to commune with nature, feel the heat of the nearby volcanoes, or relax by serene lakes and quiet towns, Colima serves as an ideal base.

VOLCÁN DE FUEGO AND LAGUNA MARÍA

Take a "Zapotitlán" bus from the Terminal Suburbana (1½hr.; 7am, 2:40, 5pm; 14 pesos; returns at 8am, 3, 4:30pm) and tell the driver where you're going. From the bus drop-off, it's a 10min. walk up a steep cobblestone road. Since service is infrequent, locals may offer you rides to Comala or Colima if they see you waiting at the intersection.

In Náhuatl, Colima means "place where the old god is dominant." The "old god" is **El Volcán de Fuego** (3960m), 25km from Colima City. Puffs of white smoke continuously billow from the volcano, and lava was visible in 1994, when El Fuego reasserted its status as an active volcano. (Fear not—the tourist office assures visitors that the volcano is not a threat to the city.) Due to the volanco's unpredictable, temperamental, and, er, volcanic nature, access to El Fuego is strictly controlled by an army outpost stationed in Yerbabuena, the last accessible town at the base of the mountain. The **Laguna María** lies right along the path up to the volcano. The still green water of the lagoon acts as a mirror, perfectly reflecting the natural beauty of Colima. The park offers hiking trails (some which lead up to spectacular views of the nearby volcano), fishing (bring your own equipment; 30 pesos per hr. for *lanchas*), and horseback riding. (☎320 8891. 50 pesos per hr.) Horses are permitted to leave the park, so your best bet for tackling El Volcán may be to ride your horse 4km up the cobblestone path to Yerbabuena, and from there determine the mood of the volcano—and of the *militares*. If you can't tear yourself away from the serenity of the lagoon, pitch a tent (80 pesos) or stay in one of the **cabañas ❷**. (☎320 8891, in Colima 330 5445. 300 pesos for 2 people, 550 pesos for up to 6 people, 800 pesos for up to 8 people.)

EL NEVADO DE COLIMA

El Nevado is accessible by car or bus, but the last leg of the trip is only for 4x4 vehicles. Autobuses Sur de Jalisco (☎312 0316) runs to Ciudad Guzmán from the new bus station

(1hr., every hr. 4:30am-8:30pm, 50 pesos) at the base of the volcano. From there, cranky 2nd-class buses (at the far right end of the bus station) limp up to El Fresnito, a village at the base of the mountain home to several guides (8 per day 7am-8pm, 7 pesos, last return at 5:45pm). Guides with vans will transport you to La Joya, the highest point on the mountain accessible by automobile and the starting point for your epic mountain assault.

The nearby and slightly taller **El Nevado de Colima** (4335m) earned its name from the blanket of snow draping it in the winter. Although this volcano offers great opportunities for challenging mountain hiking, the park is open sporadically; if you're planning a trip to the top, call the Seguridad Pública (☎314 5984) and they will check current conditions of the Nevado for you. Agustín Ibarra (☎314 7003) is a reputable guide who leads groups up to the summit. The "El Fresnito" bus drops you off in front of his house, where he'll cart you to La Joya in his 10-person van. The ascent should not be attempted solo or by those without sufficient hiking experience, especially during the rainy season.

LAGUNA CARRIZALILLO

Take an "El Naranjal" bus from the Terminal Suburbana (6 per day 7:35am-6:05pm, 3 pesos, last return at 6:55pm) and tell the driver you want to visit the lagoon. ☎315 5789. Open 24hr. 6 pesos per person.

The waters and banks of **Laguna Carrizalillo** are full of life. Birds maintain a constant twitter in the trees, and lizards and frogs leap underfoot. Camping and horseback riding (30 pesos per 30min.) are available at this peaceful retreat 27km north of Colima, but Carrizalillo's biggest attraction is its incredible view of the volcano.

COMALA

Green buses head to Comala from Colima's Terminal Suburbano (45min., every 10min. 6am-10:30pm, 5 pesos).

South of the lagoons and just 9km north of Colima is the picturesque town of Comala (pop. 19,000), known as *"El Pueblo Blanco de America"* (The White Town of America) for the original white facade of its buildings. The town's lovely *zócalo* is full of white benches, fountains, and orange trees and is bordered by cobblestone streets and lively restaurants serving *ponche* (a punch made from a variety of fruits and liquor), one of the region's traditional drinks. The city's main claim to fame is its colony of indigenous artisans who craft wooden furniture and bamboo baskets. The **Cooperativa Artesenal Pueblo Blanco**, a small *tianguis* (market), stands just outside Comala's *centro*. To get there, follow Carranza from the southeast corner of the *zócalo*, continue across the bridge, and turn right into the compound just past the orange and green "Residential Campestre Comala" sign. Don't go through what appears to be the rusted main gates; instead, keep walking to the door that is by the green modern statue (20min. walk or a shorter bus ride). You can browse through the exhibition gallery or enter the workshops and glimpse the artisans in action as they transform shapeless pieces of wood into stylish furniture. (☎315 5600. Open M-F 9am-3pm, Sa 9am-2pm.) You can also find *artesanía* at the southeast corner of the *zócalo*.

To the east of the *zócalo* lies the **Iglesia San Miguel del Espíritu Santo** with its sky-blue vaulted ceiling and dozens of pigeons. The church is currently under renovation due to earthquake damage. On the other side of the *zócalo* are the city offices, with a four-wall **mural** commemorating Comala's 130-year history and celebrating the "richness of its soil." Unfortunately, the birds who now patrol the church have graciously added their own splotchy art to the mural. For more information, contact the office of Education, Culture, and Tourism in the Casa de la Culture located 5 blocks from the *zócalo* up Hidalgo. (☎315 5547. Open M-F 9am-2:30pm.)

Ask a taxi driver to take you to Comala's famous Zona Mágica—a segment of road where cars can have their engines turned off but still appear to run uphill. Optical illusion or freak of science, it's buckets of fun.

SOUTHERN PACIFIC COAST

The glamorous oceanside resorts of the Southern Pacific Coast attract vacationing families by the thousands. Inland, lovely colonial cities and quiet mountain towns offer Spanish immersion courses, exquisite silver work, dazzling vistas, and a relaxing retreat from the frenzied streets and brilliant sun. Because many of the region's indigenous Purépecha lived by rod and net, the Aztecs called the lands surrounding Lake Pátzcuaro **Michoacán** (Country of Fishermen). The distinctive Purépecha language and terraced agricultural plots have convinced scholars that the Purépecha were not indigenous, but immigrants from what is today Peru. Purépecha rule lasted from around AD 800, when they first settled Michoacán, to 1522, when the Spanish arrived. Michoacán's fertile soil, abundant rain, and mild weather make for bountiful crops, and agriculture swells the state's coffers. The gorgeous beaches and mountains attract wildlife enthusiasts and tourists aplenty.

The state of **Guerrero** has been blessed with good fortune. During the colonial period, the rich mining town of Taxco kept the state and most of New Spain swimming in silver. More recently, the state's riches have been earned along the rugged shores of the Pacific coast. In the 1950s, Acapulco became the darling of the international resort scene, and almost four decades later, neighboring Ixtapa and Zihuatanejo now accommodate their own packs of sun loving vacationers.

Oaxaca has been fractured into a crazy quilt by the rugged heights of the Sierra Madre del Sur. Despite its difficult terrain, the land has inspired a violent possessiveness in the many different peoples—Zapotecs, Mixtecs, Aztecs, and Spaniards—who have fought and died for the region. More than 200 indigenous tribes have occupied the valley over the past two millennia, and over one million *oaxaqueños* still speak *indígena* languages—over 20% of the state's population speaks no Spanish whatsoever. The rich cultural legacies and stunning ruins of Oaxaca's indigenous tribes delight the masses of travelers who come to revel in its diverse beauty. At first intimidating, the confusing network of mountain towns, tiny weaving villages, and pristine Pacific beaches soon begins to enchant.

HIGHLIGHTS OF THE SOUTHERN PACIFIC COAST

HIDE OUT in the gorgeous beaches of the stormy **Michoacán coast** (see p. 475), which boast powerful waves, privacy, and rugged terrain.

SKINNY DIP in a secluded waterfall pool at **Tzararecuita** (see p. 457).

ADORN yourself with silver jewelry in **Taxco** (see p. 477), and enjoy magnificent mountain views from the narrow, hillside streets.

GAZE at your toes through the crystal clear waters of **Barra de Potosí** (see p. 488) and other pristine beaches along the northern **Guerrero coast** (see **Costa Grande**, p. 488), while munching on fresh *pescadillas* (fish tacos) and working on your tan.

BARGAIN for a good price on devil masks, copper vases, woven shawls, guitars, and whatever else tickles your fancy in **Pátzcuaro** (see p. 459).

KICK BACK in **Puerto Escondido** (see p. 527) and nearby **Zipolite** (see p. 524), which draw legions of backpackers ready to sun, surf, and smoke on the beach.

EXPLORE the ruins at **Monte Albán** (see p. 513), the most important Pre-Hispanic historical site in the region and one of the best preserved in Mexico.

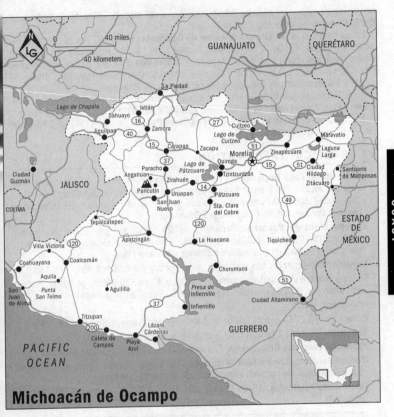

Michoacán de Ocampo

MICHOACÁN DE OCAMPO

URUAPAN   ☎452

Engulfed in red soil, rolling hills, and rows of avocado trees, Uruapan (pop. 300,000) sits on a checkerboard of farmland wrested from the surrounding jungle. Mountain air and plenty of rain keep the city lush and green year-round. Its name means "place where plants always grow and are covered with flowers"; it is also known as Michoacán's Paradise. While it is developing into a commercial center, the surrounding countryside remains a naturalist's dream. Tourists come in droves to explore the nearby waterfall, national park, and **Paricutín Volcano.**

▐ TRANSPORTATION

Uruapan lies 120km west of Morelia and 320km southeast of Guadalajara. To reach the *centro* from the **bus station** on Juárez in the northeast corner of town, hail a **taxi** (25 pesos) or hop on a "Centro" bus. Later in the day, you may have to wait at the bus stop on the street in front of the station (3.5 pesos). Most services are clumped near the *zócalo*, where two separate streets—**Vicente Carranza** and **Emilio Carranza**—honor the Carranza clan.

From the station, **La Línea/Autobuses de Occidente** (☎523 1871) sends first-class buses to **Colima** (9:45pm, 165 pesos); **Guadalajara** (4½hr., 8 per day, 182 pesos); **Lázaro Cárdenas** (8:30, 11:45pm; 180 pesos); **Manzanillo** (9:45pm, 242 pesos); **Mexico City** (7hr.; midnight, 1am, 11pm; 278 pesos); **Morelia** (2hr.; midnight, 1am, 10pm; 84 pesos); **Zamora** (2hr.; 3, 4:45am, 3:15pm; 64 pesos); **Zitácuaro** (3:45, 10:30pm; 131 pesos). Second-class buses serve the same destinations at slightly lower prices. **Primera Plus/Flecha Amarilla** (☎524 3982) and **ETN** (☎523 8608) have similar service at higher prices. **Autotransportes Galeana/Ruta Paraíso** (☎524 4154) and **Parhikini** (☎523 8754) offer regional services.

🛈 PRACTICAL INFORMATION

Tourist Office: Casa Regional del Turista, E. Carranza 20 (☎524 0677), a short walk from the *zócalo*. The friendly folks provide good maps. Some English spoken. Open daily 9am-7:30pm. On weekends, you can get the same maps from the **information booth** in the bus station. Open Sa-Su 9:30am-6pm.

Currency Exchange: Bancomer, Carranza 7 (☎524 1460), has good exchange rates and a 24hr. **ATM.** Open M-F 8:30am-4pm. A block south of the *zócalo* on Cupatitzio are many other banks with competitive exchange rates and ATMs.

Luggage Storage: At the bus station. 5 pesos per bag per hr. Open daily 7am-11pm.

Laundry: Autoservicio de Lavandería, E. Carranza 47 (☎520 9938), at García. Full-service wash and dry 26 pesos per 3kg. Open M-Sa 9am-2pm and 4-8pm.

Emergency: ☎060.

Police: (☎523 2733 or 524 0620), at Eucaliptos and Naranjo. Some English spoken.

Red Cross: Del Lago 1 (☎524 0300), a block from the hospital. No English spoken.

Pharmacy: Farmacia Guadalajara, E. Carranza 3 (☎524 2711). Open 24hr.

Medical Services: Hospital Civil de Uruapan, San Miguel 6 (☎524 8040 or 524 8096), 7 blocks west of the northern edge of the *zócalo*. No English spoken.

Fax: Caseta Telefónica, 15 de Febrero 12A (☎523 6211). Open M-F 7am-9pm, Sa 9am-2pm.

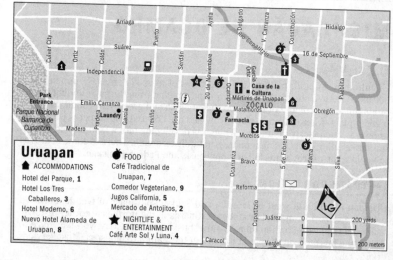

Uruapan

🏠 ACCOMMODATIONS
Hotel del Parque, **1**
Hotel Los Tres Caballeros, **3**
Hotel Moderno, **6**
Nuevo Hotel Alameda de Uruapan, **8**

🍴 FOOD
Café Tradicional de Uruapan, **7**
Comedor Vegeteriano, **9**
Jugos California, **5**
Mercado de Antojitos, **2**

★ NIGHTLIFE & ENTERTAINMENT
Café Arte Sol y Luna, **4**

Internet Access: Júparakua, Independencia 20 (☎519 0434). 12 pesos per hr. Open daily 10am-10pm. **Caseta Telefónica** has Internet access for 15 pesos per hr.

Post Office: Reforma 13 (☎523 5630), 3 blocks south of the *zócalo*. Open M-F 8:30am-3:30pm, Sa 9am-1pm. **Postal Code:** 60000.

▐ ACCOMMODATIONS

The ritzy and affordable coexist on or near the *zócalo* in Uruapan. Stay close to the *zócalo;* other places might be cheaper, but you get what you pay for.

▨ **Hotel Los Tres Caballeros,** Constitución 50 (☎524 7170), north of the *zócalo, but before* 16 de Septiembre. Red tile floors and stone stairways lend subtle charm. Rooms are very clean and in a great spot, making up for tiny baths. Singles 75 pesos; doubles 130 pesos; triples 160 pesos. ❶

Hotel del Parque, Independencia 124 (☎524 3845), west of the *zócalo* and half a block from the Parque Nacional. One of the best. Large rooms circle an airy patio. Backpackers dig the squeaky clean baths. Make reservations for weekends. Singles 155 pesos; doubles 205 pesos; triples 225 pesos. TV 40 pesos. ❸

Hotel Moderno, Degollado 4 (☎524 0212), next to Hotel Oseguera, east of the *zócalo*. Moderno has seen better days, but peach-colored rooms with wood furniture are pleasant, if dark. Get used to the jingle of the electric helicopter ride out front. 70 pesos per person. ❶

Nuevo Hotel Alameda de Uruapan, 5 de Febrero 11 (☎523 4100). Half a block from the *zócalo*. Pricey, but spotless rooms have cable TV, A/C, phone, sizable windows, and clean hot water baths. Singles 280 pesos; doubles 360 pesos; triples 440 pesos. ❺

▐ FOOD

Surrounding farms allow places near the *zócalo* to offer delicious avocado, tomato, and mango dishes for next to nothing. Coffee is another local specialty, and most places serve it strong and hot. For the cheapest meals in town, try the food stands and small restaurants inside the *mercado*.

▨ **Mercado de Antojitos,** between Constitución and V. Carranza, on the north side of the *zócalo*. An outdoor square where dozens of eager restaurateurs vie for your pesos with unique house specialties and standard Mexican favorites (15-30 pesos). Wandering local musicians serenade families. Open daily 8am-midnight. ❷

Comedor Vegetariano, Morelos 14 at Aldama. Vegetariano serves a variety of *licuados*, including concoctions for stomach problems, colds, and even maximum brain functioning (7-10 pesos). Soy *tortas milanesas* (13 pesos), *chilaquiles* (30 pesos). Open Su 1-5pm, M-F 9am-8pm, Sa 9am-5pm. ❷

Jugos California, Independencia 9, just off the *zócalo*. Get your health food kicks under artificial palms. Huge *licuados* served in giant glasses 8-16 pesos, freshly made fruit-flavored yogurt 13 pesos, *tortas* 15-17 pesos, *fresas* 22 pesos. *Nutri-jugos* (16 pesos) specially blended to cure what ails you. Open Su 8am-9pm, M-Sa 7:30am-9pm. ❷

Café Tradicional de Uruapan, E. Carranza 5B (☎523 5680), west of the *zócalo*. Follow your nose here, where locals savor their *café* in a room of richly stained wood. Besides the variety of *cafés* (10-27 pesos), you can enjoy a sandwich (15-27 pesos) or *uruapense* breakfast (46 pesos). Open daily 8am-10:30pm. ❸

🎵 🎭 ENTERTAINMENT AND NIGHTLIFE

Most of Uruapan's dazzling sights are located outside the city. **Parque Nacional Barranca del Cupatitzio,** on San Miguel at the western end of Independencia is a stunning bit of jungle right on the edge of town. The park brims with waterfalls, dense vegetation, shaded cobblestone walkways, and a fishing pond. As tradition has it, a spring formed on the spot the devil tripped while running from a priest who blessed the site. (☎ 524 0197. Open daily 8am-6pm. 12 pesos, children under 10 and adults over 70 10 pesos.) In the city is the **Casa de la Cultura**, Ortiz 1, off the north side of the *zócalo*, with worthwhile art exhibits, occasional movie screenings, and an archaeological and historical museum. (☎ 524 7613. Open daily 10am-8pm.)

Much of the after-hours scene is in cafes. **Café Arte Sol y Luna**, Independencia 15A, close to the *zócalo*, has live music, a relaxed atmosphere, and a daytime restaurant with vegetarian options. (☎ 525 8722. Coffee 10-45 pesos, beer 15 pesos, national drinks 24-35 pesos. Occasional cover 15-25 pesos. Live music Th-Sa night. Open M-Th 11am-9:30pm, F-Su 11am-midnight.) The main *discotecas*, **La Scala** and **Euforias**, both at Puertas de Capitzio 12 in Colonia Huerta del Cupatitzio, are outside of town on the road to Tzaráracua, a 25-peso cab ride from the *centro*. A young, local crowd grooves amidst pulsing lights at La Scala. (☎ 524 2609. Beer 20 pesos, drinks from 25 pesos. Cover 30 pesos Su and Tu-Th; 50 pesos F-Sa. Open Tu-Su 6pm-2am.) Techno, black lights, video screens, a smallish dance floor, and hair gel populate Euforias. (☎ 523 9332. Beer 20 pesos, drinks from 25 pesos. Cover, with open bar, Su and Th men 90 pesos, women free before 11pm and 30 pesos after; F no cover; Sa cover 30 pesos. Open Th-Su 9pm-3am.)

During *Semana Santa*, regional artisans flood the city, parading in alphabetical order according to their home community. Besides walking in the parade, artisans take part in a contest, proffering clay figurines, dresses, and more, seeking to win recognition as the best.

⚡ DAYTRIPS FROM URUAPAN

Uruapan is a convenient place for exploring the interior of Michoacán. The varied landscape encompasses everything from ill-tempered volcanos to picture-perfect waterfalls. If you're saturated with natural beauty, check out the revered image of Christ in **San Juan Nuevo** that was rescued by the village after a volcano eruption. In nearby **Paracho**, a world-famous guitar competition rages in August.

PARICUTÍN VOLCANO

From the station, Autotransportes Galeana/Ruta Paraíso provides service to Angahuán, headed for Los Reyes (☎ 524 4154; 30min., every ½hr. 5am-8pm, 12 pesos). From the stop, walk 3km to the Centro Turístico on the other side of the village. Go straight down the main road, right at the market, and left at the sign for the Centro Turístico. Alternatively, guides may approach you at the bus stop. To return, wait for buses on the other side of the stop (every ½hr., last bus 8:30pm).

A visit to the still-active Paricutín Volcano makes a great daytrip from Uruapan. In 1943 the volcano began erupting, and by the time it quit spewing eight years later, thick porous lava covered the surrounding lands, entire towns had been consumed, and a 700m mountain had sprung up. The lava covered all of San Juan, save part of the village's church, which now sticks out of a field of cold, black stone. Horse rentals are available at Angahuán's **Centro Turístico**. (180 pesos to the volcano, 100 pesos to ruins. Open daily 9am-7pm). Plan for an early start to avoid frequent afternoon thunderstorms, and bring warm clothing. The trip is long but worth the time (4.5km to the church and 13km to the volcano) and money (Purépecha guides charge about 200 pesos). If you tackle the volcano on your own, take care and ask directions first—trails are poorly marked. The Centro Turístico has a small museum that presents indigenous Purépecha life (8 pesos, students 5 pesos) and a restaurant. **Beds ❷** are available from the tourist center. Cabins for 1-6 people 561 pesos; bunks 102 pesos; other options available.

SAN JUAN NUEVO PARANGARICUTIRIMICUARO

From the Uruapan bus station, take an Autotransportes Galeana/Ruta Paraíso bus (☎ 524 4154) to San Juan Nuevo (40min., every 10min. 5am-8pm, 6 pesos). To get back, wait for the same bus on the corner of Cárdenas and Iturbe, 2 blocks from the cathedral.

Ten kilometers west of Uruapan is San Juan Nuevo, founded after the destruction of the old village by the Paricutín Volcano in 1943. Many penitents visit the village to see the **Lord of Miracles,** an image of Christ dating back to the late 16th century. When the volcano erupted, San Juan's 2000 inhabitants abandoned the village and began a three-day, 33km pilgrimage carrying their beloved icon. A beautiful rose brick sanctuary with pastel tiles was eventually built to house the image. Gold leaf, delicate stained-glass windows, and sparkling chandeliers adorn the interior's white walls and vaulted ceilings, and murals visually retell the story. Not quite as refined is the gaudy neon sign above the statue that reads "*Sr. de los Milagros en ti confío*" ("Lord of Miracles, I trust in you"). (Open daily 6am-8pm; mass Su roughly every hr. 6:30am-1:30pm and 5-7pm.) The **museum,** on Av. 20 de Noviembre, a block past the cathedral to the right once you exit the church, has photos of the eruption. (Open M-F 10am-6:30pm, Sa-Su 8am-6:30pm. Free.)

The church and icon are far and away the biggest attractions, but an intense **mercado** in front of the cathedral sells *artesanías* and much more at good prices. Towards the back of the cathedral, you'll stumble on the cheapest and tastiest food in town. Plop down on a bench before *rebozo*-clad women stirring giant vats of *mole* and patting distinctive blue corn tortillas. If you find yourself stranded, the spacious rooms of **Hotel Victoria ❷**, Cárdenas 26, on the left as you exit the cathedral, are a good bet. Some of the clean rooms with hot water (and mint green) baths have cathedral views. (☎ 594 0010. Rooms 140 pesos.)

▧ TZARÁRACUA AND TZARARECUITA

"Zapata-Tzaráracua" buses leave from the south side of the zócalo (25min., every hr. 7am-5pm, 5 pesos). Return bus meets in the parking lot (on the hr. until 6pm). Taxis 40 pesos.

The gorgeous waterfalls 10km from Uruapan cascade 20m into small pools surrounded by lush vegetation. The first, **Tzaráracua** (sah-RA-ra-kwa), is only 1km from the parking lot. Walk down the steps to the right or ride a horse (40-45 pesos round-trip, after bargaining, from the parking lot), down the rocky path to the left. At the main waterfall look but don't swim—there's a dangerous undercurrent. Walk over the water on the bridge or ask a worker to bring you in a suspended boxcar. (Open daily 9am-6pm. 8 pesos, children 4 pesos; parking 10 pesos; cable car 4 pesos.) **Tzararecuita,** 1.5km further, is a waterfall with two smaller pools perfect for swimming. Some people swim naked, but all people should find a guide, since there are many confusing trails. Ask one of the horse handlers or many boys hanging around the bridge; most ask 40 pesos.

PARACHO

From the Uruapan bus station, take an Autotransportes Galeana/Ruta Paraíso bus (☎ 524 4154) bound for Paracho (45min., every 30 min. 4am-8:30pm, 9 pesos).

Tucked away in chilly highlands 30km north of Uruapan, Paracho draws the aspiring and accomplished *guitarrista*. Carefully crafted six-strings pack just about every store, and fantastic bargains are available for all varieties of guitar and some other stringed instruments. (Most stores open 9am-2pm and 4-7pm.) The **Casa de Arte y Cultura,** on the corner of the plaza, has displays on guitars. (Open daily 10am-8pm.) From August 9-13, the town holds an internationally renowned **guitar festival** (info ☎ 525 0077). Musicians and craftspeople partake in a musical dervish of classical concerts, fireworks, dancing, parades, and competitions. A smaller, one-day music fest honors Santa Úrsula on October 22.

ZAMORA
☎ 351

Zamora (pop. 156,000) is affectionately known as *"la cuna de hombres ilustres"* (the cradle of illustrious men). The city has nurtured such greats as Manuel Martínez de Navarrete and Nobel Peace Prize winner Alfonso García Robles. It also supplies the most potatoes in the country, and churns out *fresas* and renowned *dulces*. While not exactly bursting at the seams with tourist offerings, Zamora is a quiet, pleasant place to pass a day and is a convenient stop between Guadalajara and Morelia for exploring Michoacán's natural and colonial beauty.

TRANSPORTATION. The **bus station** is on Juárez, at the edge of town. To get there from the *centro*, take a "Central" bus (3 pesos) from Colón and Hidalgo, or take a taxi (13 pesos). **Autobuses de Occidente/La Línea** (☎515 1119) go to: **Guadalajara** (3hr., every hr. 5:20am-8:10pm, 100 pesos); **Manzanillo** (7hr., 8 per day 3:15am-11:30pm, 195 pesos) via **Colima** (5hr., 140 pesos); **Mexico City** (9hr., every hr. 2:30am-11pm, 228 pesos) via **Morelia** (3hr., 76 pesos) and **Toluca** (7hr., 132 pesos); **Uruapan** (2½hr., every hr. 7:30am-6pm, 56 pesos). **ETN** (☎515 6181), **Estrella Blanca** (☎515 1133), and **Primera Plus** (☎515 1316) provide similar services. **Transportes del Pacífico** (☎515 1125) motors to the north.

ORIENTATION AND PRACTICAL INFORMATION. Most activity is in or around the *centro*, which is bordered by **Nervo** to the north, **Guerrero** to the south, **Morelos** to the west, and **Allende** to the east. **Hidalgo** curves north behind the Cathedral, intersected by **Ocampo**, which runs east-west one block north of the *centro*.

The **tourist office**, Morelos Sur 76, a few blocks from the *centro*, provides good maps. Some English spoken. (☎512 4015. Open Su 10am-2pm, M-F 9am-2pm and 4-7pm, Sa 10am-2pm and 4-6pm.) **Bancomer**, Morelos 250, has a 24hr. **ATM**. (☎512 2600. Open M-F 8:30am-4pm, Sa 10am-2pm; open for **currency exchange** M-F 8:30am-3:30pm.) Other services include: **emergency** service (☎060); **police** (☎512 0022; no English spoken); **Red Cross**, on Calle Mendoza (☎512 0534; no English spoken); **Farmacia Guadalajara**, in the plaza (☎515 7055; open 24hr.); **Hospital Civil**, Serdán 251 (☎512 1202; some English spoken); **Internet access** at **Oficom 2000**, Hidalgo 99, at Colón (☎512 1713; 5 pesos per hr.; open M-Sa 9am-9pm); **post office**, in the Palacio Federal (☎512 0205; open M-F 9am-3pm, Sa 9am-1pm).

ACCOMMODATIONS AND FOOD. The hourly traffic of couples in and out of many of Zamora's cheaper hotels may inspire you to look elsewhere. Try family-oriented **Hotel Nacional ❷**, Corregidora 106, just off the *centro*, which has cramped yet comfy rooms, tidy baths, and a fourth-floor terrace. (☎512 4224. Singles 100-150 pesos; doubles 150 pesos.) Zamora's small restaurants often close by 7pm, but luckily candy shops are open to about 9pm. Try the **Centro Comercial (Mercado) Morelos**, by the *centro* across from the cathedral, for local sweets or cheap eats. **La Pantera Rosa ❸** (The Pink Panther), Hidalgo Sur 234, is a kitschy place for *carnes asadas en su jugo* (grilled beef with beans in a broth, with freshly-made tortillas; 36-40 pesos) and quesadillas (21 pesos). (☎512 1866. Open daily 10am-10pm.)

SIGHTS. Catedral Inconclusa, at Ocampo and 5 de Mayo, 3 blocks from the main *jardín*, is an immense cathedral in the Gothic style that predates the conquest; paradoxically, it is a relatively recent project and currently under construction. Work began in 1898 but halted during the Revolution, in 1914, and wasn't reinitiated until 1988. Even now, the beautiful structure is far from complete—current projections are looking at another 15 years. The building still lacks its towers, but the inside is nearer completion: you can admire the black marble floor, wander the forest of pillars, or perhaps watch the men at work. (Office is to the left as you enter; open daily 9am-5pm. Informational pamphlet 5 pesos.) Nearby are other sights, like the **Géiser de Ixtlan** and its hot springs, served by a 13-peso "Ixtlan" bus.

⚡ DAYTRIPS FROM ZAMORA

▨ LAGO CAMECUARO

Take a "Tangancicuaro" bus from the Sala de Servicios Regionales at the station in Zamora. Autotransportes Zamora-La Luz-Santiago leaves often (15min., every 30min. 6:30am-9pm, 8 pesos). Tell the driver you want to go to the lake, not the village. Follow the sign and walk up a road on the right after you pass a cemetery on the left (1km). ☎553 3453. Open daily 9am-7pm. 10 pesos per vehicle. Water park open Sa-Su 11am-6pm. 30 pesos, children 25 pesos. Alcoholic beverages prohibited.

Peaceful and beautiful Lake Camecuaro is a cheap haven for outdoor recreation. Enormous cypresses surround crystal-clear waters, and swimming is permitted, though the lake is icy. Distractions include rowboats (70 pesos per hr.), *lanchas* with rower (100 pesos per hr.), shady picnic tables, grill pits, volleyball, soccer fields, water park, craft stores, and a few restaurants. Packs of *mariachis* serenade you and hundreds of local families on weekends; weekdays are far emptier. The docile duck population is unfortunately dwarfed by the aggressive mosquito population, so remember insect repellent.

ZARAGOZA ARCHAEOLOGICAL ZONE

From the station in Zamora, take a bus to La Piedad (1hr., every 20min. 5:15am-8:45pm, 22 pesos). From in front of the La Piedad station, catch a "Zaragoza" bus (30min., every hr. 6am-8pm, 6 pesos; last return at 6:30pm); in Zaragoza, follow Calle Flor de Michoacán, the cobblestone road up the hill, and turn left across from the green store. Follow the road as it curves left. Around the spray-painted "Calle Archeológica" sign, local kids will probably be willing to guide you—the ruins are virtually impossible to find without help. Site open M-F 10am-7pm. Free.

The archaeological zone lies along the legendary route of the Aztecs as they migrated from Aztlán to Lake Texcoco. The site was a trading zone for the Purépecha empire that gave Zaragoza its name ("The Place Where Stone Was Worked"). The **Museo Zaragoza** in La Piedad, next to the library, has some historical info and artifacts. Many stones from the ruins are engraved with *caracoles*—spiral shapes mimicking seashells or snails, indicating coastal trade—or with flag shapes. One large, elaborate rock is thought to be a city map. The ruins include a minor **ball court,** an unusual feature in western Mexico. For centuries, locals raided the ruins for construction materials; nowadays it is university-bound archaeologists that carry away the stones, leaving the sight fairly bare. Also in the area are **caves,** high in the cliffs, and a rock depicting the Virgin of Guadalupe, who supposedly appeared here in the 1930s; the rock marks the spot of the miracle.

PÁTZCUARO   ☎434

Michoacán's earthy jewel, Pátzcuaro (pop. 70,000) is set high in the mountains, surrounded by rolling hills and forests, and extending to the shores of expansive (and polluted) Lake Pátzcuaro. The busy center is almost as spectacular as the surrounding landscape: tolling cathedral bells resonate through cobblestone streets and stucco colonial buildings. Pátzcuaro's biggest selling point is its *artesanía*. To increase economic development in the 1530s, Spanish Bishop Vasco de Quiroga encouraged residents of each Purépecha village around the lake to specialize in a different craft. Today Pátzcuaro's plazas overflow with stacks of handmade woolen sweaters, wooden toys, clay of every color, and decorative masks.

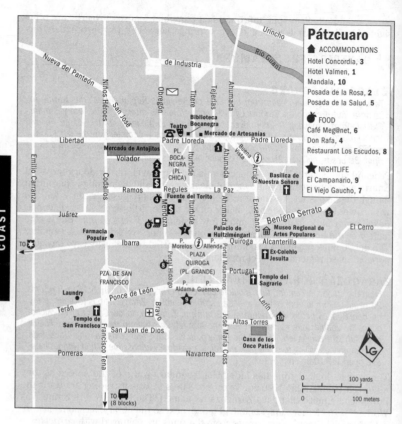

Pátzcuaro

🏨 ACCOMMODATIONS

Hotel Concordia, **3**
Hotel Valmen, **1**
Mandala, **10**
Posada de la Rosa, **2**
Posada de la Salud, **5**

🍎 FOOD

Café Meg@net, **6**
Don Rafa, **4**
Restaurant Los Escudos, **8**

⭐ NIGHTLIFE

El Campanario, **9**
El Viejo Gaucho, **7**

🚌 TRANSPORTATION

Pátzcuaro lies 56km southwest of Morelia and 62km northeast of Uruapan. To reach the *centro* from the **bus station** off Circunvalación, eight blocks south of the *centro*, catch a *combi* (7am-9:30pm, 3.5 pesos) or a city bus (6:30am-10pm, 3.5 pesos) from the lot to the right while leaving the station. **Taxis** cost 15 pesos.

Primera Plus/Flecha Amarilla (☎342 0960) sends 1st-class buses to: **Guadalajara** (4½hr.; 9:25am, 11:30pm; 126 pesos); **Mexico City** (6hr.; 12:15am, 11:45pm; 236 pesos); **Morelia** (1hr.; 6:45, 7:30, 9:30am, 8pm; 26 pesos); **Puerto Vallarta** (8hr., 8:10pm, 513 pesos), and 2nd-class buses to: **Guanajuato** (5hr., 8pm, 140 pesos); **León** (5hr.; 6, 6:15, 9:05, 10:30am, 6:55pm; 158 pesos); **Manzanillo** (9hr., 8am, 220 pesos); **Mexico City** (8hr., 7 per day 7am-midnight, 200 pesos); **Querétaro** (5hr., 11:30pm, 147 pesos); **Zamora** (3hr., 7 per day 6am-10:30am, 54 pesos) via **Morelia** (1hr., 25 pesos). **Herradura de Plata/Pegaso Plus** (☎342 1045) and **Autobuses de Occidente** (☎342 1243) offer more limited service. **Élite** (☎342 4060) travels north, via Morelia. **Autotransportes Galeana/Ruta Paraíso** (☎342 0808) motors to **Uruapan** (1hr., every 10 min. 5:30am-9:30pm, 25 pesos).

ORIENTATION AND PRACTICAL INFORMATION

Pátzcuaro centers around two principal plazas, **Plaza Quiroga** and **Plaza Bocanegra.** Each of these is also, rather confusingly, called by a nickname. Plaza Quiroga is commonly known as **Plaza Grande,** while Plaza Bocanegra often masquerades as **Plaza Chica.** There are not four plazas.

Tourist Office: The **Delegación Municipal de Turismo,** Plaza Quiroga 50A (☎342 1214), is on the northern side of Plaza Grande. Open daily 9am-3pm and 5-7pm. The **Delegación Regional** (☎243 1705), Buenavista 7, has more maps and information about the whole of the state. Open Su 9am-2pm, M-Sa 9am-2pm.

Currency Exchange: Banks with competitive rates are in both plazas. **Banamex,** Portal Juárez 32 (☎342 15 50), on the west side of Pl. Chica, has a 24hr. **ATM** and check and currency exchange. Open M-F 9am-5pm, Sa 10am-2pm.

Luggage Storage: At the bus station. 4-10 pesos per day. Open daily 7am-10pm.

Market: along Lloreda, between Codallos and Obregón. Open daily 8am-6pm.

Supermarket: Merzapack, Mendoza 24 (☎342 5255). Open daily 7am-10pm.

Emergency: Protección Civil (☎342 5656). Some English spoken.

Police: (☎342 0004), on Ibarra, between Espejo and Tangara, inside the Agencia del Ministero Público. Some English spoken.

Pharmacy: Farmacia Popular (☎342 3242), Ibarra at Codallos. Open daily 8am-11pm.

Hospital: Hospital Civil, Romero 10 (☎342 0285), next to San Juan de Dios.

Telephone/Fax: Computel (☎342 2756), on Lloreda next to the Teatro. Offers fax and phone services, plus a *caseta.* Open daily 6am-midnight.

Internet: Meg@Net, Mendoza 8, between Pl. Chica and Pl. Grande, nearer Pl. Grande. 12 pesos per hr., students 10 pesos per hr. Open daily 9am-9pm.

Post Office: Obregón 13 (☎342 0128), ½ block north of Pl. Chica. Open M-F 8am-3pm, Sa 9am-1pm. **Postal Code:** 61600.

ACCOMMODATIONS

Budget hotels are everywhere and those in **Plaza Chica** usually have clean and comfy rooms. If you're lucky, you can score a balcony on the plaza and a private bath. Unfortunately, Pátzcuaro isn't the safest town at night, especially for women. Hotels tend to close their doors around 11pm.

Mandala, Lerín 14 (☎342 4176), near Casa de los Once Patios. Beautiful rooms with attractive wood furniture have sparkling baths. Friendly owners allow use of kitchen facilities, and offer free tea/coffee in the morning. Singles 150 pesos; doubles 250 pesos; triples 300 pesos. Upstairs rooms with private bathrooms are 100 pesos more. Prices vary for *Semana Santa* and *Noche de los Muertos.* ❸

Hotel Concordia, Portal Juárez 31 (☎342 0003), on the west side of Pl. Chica. Rooms are spacious and neat, with soaring wood-beam ceilings and balconies. Communal baths with colored tiles are spotless; this is a great deal. Singles 109 pesos, with bath 220 pesos; doubles 217/365 pesos; triples 313/519 pesos. ❷

Hotel Valmen, Lloreda 34 (☎342 1161), 1 block east of Pl. Chica. Aztec tiles fill green courtyards, and 2nd-floor rooms have balconies. Doors lock at 10pm. Popular with travelers, make reservations for weekends. Singles 100 pesos; doubles 180 pesos. ❷

Posada de la Salud, Serrato 9 (☎342 0058), 3 blocks east of the plazas. Clean rooms along a courtyard. Hot water in mornings and evenings; curfew 10pm. Singles 190 pesos; each additional person 50 pesos. ❸

Posada de la Rosa, Portal Juárez 29, 2nd fl. (☎342 0811), on the west of Pl. Chica. Red-tiled rooms lack light, and sheets for beds. Large, clean communal baths do not come with toilet paper. Curfew 10pm. Singles and doubles 100 pesos, with bath 170 pesos; triples and quads 120/220 pesos. Prices double for *Semana Santa*. ❷

🍴 FOOD

Cheap restaurants surround Plaza Chica and the accompanying market, while fancier joints crowd the hotels on Plaza Grande. *Pescado blanco* (whitefish), *charales* (small fish eaten fried and whole), and *caldo de pescado* (a fish soup) are regional specialties—look near the lake for good prices. In the city you can slurp down *sopa tarasca*, a creamy tortilla soup.

Mercado de Antojitos, in the Pl. Chica. Myriad vendors offer a broad range of food in a vibrant setting, at some of the city's best prices. Sip on *atole de canela* (thick drink with a cinnamon flavor; 5 pesos) on chilly nights or track down standards such as *enchiladas*. *Artesanía* vendors dominate before 7pm. Open daily 8am-10pm. ❷

Restaurant los Escudos, Portal Hidalgo 74 (☎342 0138), inside the Hotel. Stone archways, wood furniture, and beamed ceilings create a traditional air. *Sopa tarasca* 20 pesos, *comida corrida* 40 pesos. The *danza de los viejitos* ridicules the Spanish (Sa 8:30pm). Live organ music daily 1-4pm and 7-10pm. Open daily 8am-10pm. ❹

Café Meg@net, Mendoza 8 (☎342 3655), behind the internet station. The only place to check email and munch on fries simultaneously. Burgers 10-15 pesos, combos 30-35 pesos, *sopa tarasca* 15 pesos. Open daily 10am-10pm. ❶

Don Rafa, Mendoza 30 (☎342 0498). Generous portions are a bit pricey but tasty. Hardwood tables, pottery along the back wall, and old city pictures lend this place a touch of class. *Comida corrida* (48 pesos). Open daily 8am-8pm. ❹

🔎 SIGHTS

The following are a great way to spend an afternoon, but some of the most notable sights are a short trip from downtown (see **Daytrips,** p. 464).

BASÍLICA DE NUESTRA SEÑORA DE LA SALUD. When Bishop Vasco de Quiroga came to Pátzcuaro, he initiated social change and bold architectural projects. Quiroga conceived of the lavender-and-gold Basílica, a colossal structure with five chapels branching off the main nave. Conflicting tales explain their significance: they may represent five major body parts (the head, two arms, and two legs), Christ's five wounds, or Quiroga's ideals for Christian society—wisdom, justice, honesty, work, and love. An enormous glass booth with gilded Corinthian columns protects the potentially edible *Virgen de la Salud*, crafted out of *tatzingue* paste—corn cobs and orchid honey, typical 16th-century statue material—by Tarascan artists in 1546. The interior has a surprisingly open feel. Locals pin pictures of sick relatives in back, hoping for help from the *Virgen*. (*At Lerín and Serrato. Open daily 7am-7:30pm; mass Su every hr. 7am-1pm, also 7 and 8pm.*)

PLAZAS. Statues of Pátzcuaro's two most honored citizens stand in the town's principal plazas. A resplendent, staff-bearing Vasco de Quiroga inhabits **Plaza Quiroga,** a vast, green space, while a massive, bare-chested Gertrudis Bocanegra peers out from the center of smaller **Plaza Bocanegra.** A martyr for Mexican independence, Bocanegra was executed by a Spanish squadron in Plaza Quiroga in October 1817. Locals claim that bullet holes still mark the ash tree where she was tied; the stump is in the southwest corner of Plaza Quiroga.

MUSEO REGIONAL DE ARTES POPULARES. Built in 1540 to house the Colegio de San Nicolás de Obispo, the fort-like walls of the museum enclose a flower-filled courtyard, regional pottery, copperware, textiles, and an arresting collection of *maque* (sumac lacquer). The rear courtyard encloses small Purépecha ruins and the remains of a 16th-century jail cell with a calendar of thousands of tick marks carved in the walls. (☎342 1029. Enseñanza 20, at Alcanterilla, 1 block south of the Basílica. Open Su 9am-3pm, Tu-Sa 9am-7pm. Admission and tour 32 pesos, students free; Su free.)

TEATRO CALTZONTZÍN. Once part of an Augustine convent, this building on Plaza Chica became a theater in 1936. Murals decorate the walls and Greek dramatic masks grace the staircases. The theater no longer screens films, but does host live performances. Other events occur at the **Ex-Colegio Jesuita de Pátzcuaro** (☎342 4477). Ask at the library by the theater for a schedule of events at both locations.

BIBLIOTECA GERTRUDIS BOCANEGRA. Constructed as a church in 1576, the building now houses a library. The former altar displays a giant mural by Juan O'Gorman, narrating a pictoral history of Purépecha civilization up to the Revolution. (Next to the Teatro Caltzontzín. ☎342 5495. Open M-Sa 9am-8pm.)

EL ESTRIBO. Outside of town is a lookout point near the top of a hill. The view of the **Lago de Pátzcuaro** is magnificent, but the trip is only advisable Saturday and Sunday mornings, when other families make the climb—incidents of foul play have been reported. (Approximately 4km from town; the walk takes about 1hr.)

SHOPPING

Plaza Chica's **market** and shops along the passage next to Biblioteca Gertrudis Bocanegra sell Pátzcuaro's unique crafts—hairy Tócuaro masks, elegant Sierra dinnerware, and thick wool textiles. Bargaining is easier in the market or when you buy more than one item, but the stunningly handsome wool articles are bargain-resistant. Thick sweaters, brilliantly colored *saltillos* and *ruanas* (stylized ponchos), vibrant *sarapes*, and dark *rebozos* are Pátzcuaro's specialties; *artesanías* from farther afield are for sale too. (Most shops open daily 8am-8pm.) For many of the same items at cheaper prices, trek out to the surrounding villages.

Higher-quality and more expensive items are at **La Casa de los Once Patios,** named for the 18th-century building's 11 patios, on Lerín near Navarrete. Originally a convent, the complex now houses craft shops and a mural depicting Vasco de Quiroga's accomplishments. The Casa sells cotton textiles, wood and copper crafts, and superb musical instruments such as flutes and student, concert, and classical guitars (250-8000 pesos). Prices may be fixed to discourage haggling. Dance performances occur sporadically in the main courtyard, usually on weekends. (Open daily 10am-8pm; some shops close in the afternoon.)

ENTERTAINMENT

Pátzcuaro's nightlife is confined mainly to restaurants and a few bars. At **El Campanario,** Portales Aldama 12 (☎324 1313), on the south side of Pl. Grande, the masks and *toreador's* costume on the walls are almost as loud as the live music. (Beer 15 pesos, drinks from 35 pesos. Open Su-Th 3-11pm, F-Sa 1pm-3am.) Off-beat **El Viejo Gaucho,** Iturbide 10, a colorful Argentine bar and restaurant with art exhibits, features live music every night, from rock and blues to *cumbia* and salsa. Candlelit tables make this place cozy. (Cover 15 pesos. Music starts at 9pm. Beer 10-18 pesos, drinks from 28 pesos. Open M-Sa 6pm-midnight.)

FESTIVALS

Pátzcuaro parties year-round, but the biggest celebration is the spectacular **Noche de los Muertos** (Oct. 31-Nov. 2). Tourists from around the globe come to watch candle-lit fishing boats proceed to the tiny island of Janitzio. There, families and neighbors keep a two-night vigil in the cemetary, feasting at the graves of loved ones. The first night commemorates lost children; the second remembers deceased adults. Soon after Christmas celebrations end, the town is electrified by **Pastorelas**, religious dances performed on January 6 to commemorate the Adoration of the Magi and on January 17 to honor St. Anthony, patron saint of animals. On both occasions, citizens dress their domestic animals in bizarre costumes, complete with ribbons and floral crowns. A few months later, *Semana Santa* attracts devotees from all over the republic. On Holy Thursday, all the churches in town are visited, and the **Procesión de Imágenes de Cristo** is held on Good Friday, when images of a crucified Christ are carried around town. The faithful also flock here on Saturday for Pátzcuaro's **Procesión del Silencio,** celebrated elsewhere the day before. A crowd marches around town, silently mourning Jesus's death.

◪ DAYTRIPS FROM PÁTZCUARO

JANITZIO

*In Pátzcuaro, hop on a "Lago" combi or bus (3.5 pesos) at the corner of Portal Regules and Portal Juárez. At the docks, buy a ferry ticket at the Muelle General (1hr., ferries leave when full 8am-8pm, 30 pesos round-trip; 35 pesos round-trip to the smaller, less developed islands **Yunuen** and **Pacanda**). Janitzio has no accommodations for the stranded, so make sure you catch the last boat at 8pm.*

The tiny island of Janitzio, inhabited exclusively by *indígenas* who still speak their native Purépecha and Tarasco, subsists on the tourist trade and local fishing. The boat ride to town provides a peek at local fishermen, who use butterfly nets more for show than function—and seek donations. The town's steep main street is lined with stores selling wool goods, hand-carved chess sets, and masks. Among the shops, pricey, restaurants offer fresh whitefish (45-50 pesos) and *charales* (crispy sardine-like fish; 20-25 pesos), as well as *jarros locos* (a concoction of fruit juices, wine, and chile powder; 35-45 pesos). The **statue of Morelos** that towers over the island is the single most memorable sight. Inside the statue, a mural traces Morelos's life and the struggle for independence. Small windows in his back offer nice views, but endless steps lead you to fantastic, if precarious, lookout points at his head and sleeve. Really only two directions exist in Janitzio—up and down; keep walking up and you'll reach the statue. (Open daily 9am-7:30pm. 5 pesos.) For information, go to the **tourist booth**, in front of the shops at the docks. (☎313 6152. Open daily 8am-8:30pm.) One of the best times to visit Janitzio may be on **Noche de los Muertos**, when islanders and tourists alike pour into the tiny mountainside cemetery for an all-night festival commemorating the dearly departed.

TZINTZUNTZÁN

Tzintzuntzán is perched on the northeastern edge of the Lago de Pátzcuaro, 15km from Pátzcuaro, on the road to Quiroga and Morelia. 2nd-class Ruta Paraíso/Galeana buses (☎342 0808) leave the Pátzcuaro bus station for Tzintzuntzán (30min., every 15min. 6am-7:30pm, 7 pesos) en route to Quiroga. Return buses, on the same schedule, stop near the ferry dock to Janitzio. Last bus leaves at 8pm. Taxis returning to either of the main plazas in Pátzcuaro can cost as little as 8 pesos.

The word Tzintzuntzán (seen-soon-SAHN) is believed to be an imitation of the sound of the **hummingbirds** that flit through the sky here in the spring. Tzintzuntzán was the last great city of the Purépecha empire. In the 15th century, the Purépecha lord Tariácuri divided his empire among his two sons and a nephew. When the separated empire was reunited years later, Tzintzuntzán became the capital. Today, its claims to fame are the delicate, multicolored **ceramics** for sale along Principal. Also of interest are the atrium and 16th-century Franciscan **convent,** entered from the gate at the back of the market. Open air chapels, unique to the New World, dot the tree-filled atrium, whose olive shrubs were planted at Vasco de Quiroga's instruction over 450 years ago. (Convent open Su-M and W-Sa 9am-4pm.)

Yácatas, ruined sanctuaries for the gods and tombs for lords, sit on a hill outside the city. Walk up the street in front of the market and convent, and follow the pyramid signs around the hill on the small stretch of *carretera* to the small museum/ticket booth (15min.). The remaining foundations are standard rectangular pyramid bases—what's missing, however, was unique. An elliptical pyramid of shingles and volcanic rock originally crowned each. The Purépecha *yácata* describes this combined circular-rectangular plan. At the edge of the hill overlooking the lake is a sacrificial block from which victims were hurled; the bones of thousands are said to lie at the base. Another structure held a stockpile of enemy heads. The museum has Mesoamerican pottery, jewelry, and an account of Purépecha history. (Open daily 9am-6pm. 28 pesos, children under 13 free.)

SANTA CLARA DEL COBRE

From the Pátzcuaro bus station, Ruta Paraíso/Galeana offers service to and from Santa Clara (20min., every 30min. 6am-8pm, 8 pesos).

Santa Clara shines with *cobre* (copper), 16km south of Pátzcuaro. Long ago rich mines filled the area but, hidden from the Spanish, they remain undiscovered. The townspeople's passion for copper continues undaunted: when electricity came to the town, artisans raided the copper wires for material for pots and pans, causing widespread blackouts. Nearly every store in town sells decorative copper plates, pans, bracelets, bowls, and bells. Prices here are only slightly better than elsewhere in Mexico, but the quality and variety are unbeatable. For a quick look at some imaginative pieces, step into the **Museo del Cobre,** 263 Morelos Ote., one block from the plaza. (Open Tu-Su 10am-3pm and 4-7pm. 2 pesos, children and students 1 peso.) Santa Clara celebrates the **Feria del Cobre,** with a national copper hammering contest, for two weeks in early August.

LAGO DE ZIRAHUÉN

From Pátzcuaro, take an Occidente (☎ 342 1243) bus to Lago de Zirahuén (45min.; 7:15, 9:30, 11:50am, 1, 2, 4, 6:30pm; 8 pesos; last return 4:30pm). Taxis 100 pesos.

The Lago de Zirahuén (Where Smoke Rose) is a fun trip for those who enjoy a crawling pace of life. You could pull a Rip van Winkle and probably not miss a thing here. Smaller than Lago Pátzcuaro and much cleaner, Zirahuén is bordered by farmland, sloping hills, and a few elegant homes. **Camping ❶** here is safe; hike one of the ridges that border the lake and set up on a spot overlooking the water, but be sure to bring a tarp and wet- and cold-weather gear. If the land is privately owned (usually fenced off), you may have to pay a few pesos—ask before pitching your tent. A choice spot is a strip of lakefront about 15m wide on the west end of town (to the left, as you face the lake). Grass grazed short by horses covers the strip. The expensive *cabañas*, to the right along the dirt road bordering the lake (5min.), allow campers to use their bathrooms (1 peso). Heavy rains mid-June to early October can turn your camping soggy.

After roughing it in the great outdoors, head to the *lancha* dock for a smooth ride around the lake (45-60min.; "yacht" 40 pesos, *lancha* 30 pesos; a cooperative office can arrange *lancha* rentals for groups, up to 8 people 300 pesos), then relax at one of the casual lakefront **restaurants ❸** (whitefish 30 pesos). Many restaurants will pack a meal for a picnic; set a price beforehand. Although there is no formal canoe rental, ask around and a local fisherman might rent you his (50-100 pesos), depending on how long you want to use it.

MORELIA
☎ **443**

The state capital Morelia (pop. 575,000) anchors the proud traditions of Michoacán culture and history. Museums, art exhibits, theater, dance productions, and concerts create a vibrant cultural scene, fueled by the city's sizeable student population. Morelia of late has been caught in a whirl of development; sophisticated department stores and fast food joints move in from the outskirts of town, while in the *centro*, vendors sell traditional textiles and wooden crafts alongside bootleg cassettes and spare blender parts. Nearby stand rose-colored stone arcades and grand, white-washed houses, relics of Morelia's colonial magnificence. Its eclectic art and lively downtown make Morelia one of the most vital cities in the country and an important part of Mexico's colonial heritage.

▐ TRANSPORTATION

Morelia lies 230km west of Mexico City on **Mex. 15. Buses** and *combis* traverse the city (6am-10pm, 3.5 pesos). **Taxis** wait at the bus station.

Flights: Aeropuerto Francisco J. Múgica, Carretera Morelia-Cinapécuaro km 27 (☎313 6780), north of the city. Buses no longer serve the airport; a taxi costs 145 pesos. Carriers: **Aeromar** (☎313 6886), **Aeroméxico** (☎313 0140), and **Mexicana** (☎312 47 25).

Buses: The new bus station, the **TAM**, is on the outskirts of town, in front of the stadium that houses the popular Monarcas del Morelia. To get to downtown, take a brown *combi*, which will drop you off in front of La Casa de la Cultura. **Taxis** at the bus station cost 24 pesos to get to the *centro*. Morelia is a transportation hub for Michoacán, and buses head almost everywhere in the country. **Primera Plus/Flecha Amarilla** (☎338 1081) provides 1st-class service to: **Aguascalientes** (5½hr.; 2:30, 8:05am, 12:05, 4:05, 5:05pm; 230 pesos); **Guadalajara** (3½hr., 10 per day 6:15am-11:59pm, 210 pesos); **León** (3hr., 16 per day, 132 pesos); **Mexico City** (5hr., 12 per day, 185 pesos); **Pátzcuaro** (1hr.; 5:40am, 4pm; 26 pesos); **Puerto Vallarta** (9hr., 8:10pm, 513 pesos); **Querétaro** (3hr., 11 per day, 117 pesos); **San Luis Potosí** (6hr., 9 per day, 247 pesos); **Uruapan** (2hr., 7 per day, 84 pesos); **Zamora** (2½hr.; 9am, 1, 3:30pm; 88 pesos). 2nd-class service covers the same destinations. **ETN** (☎334 1059) provides similar, but more expensive, services. **Ruta Paraíso** (☎312 5658) offers 2nd-class local services. **Élite** (☎334 1051) goes to destinations farther north.

▐ PRACTICAL INFORMATION

Tourist Office: Galería de Turismo, Nigromante 79 (☎312 8082), west of the *zócalo* in the castle-like building on the right. Staff distributes maps and a monthly list of cultural events. Some English spoken. Open Su 10am-2pm, M-Sa 9am-7pm.

Currency Exchange: Banks cluster on Madero near the cathedral. **Bancomer,** Madero Ote. 21 (☎312 2990), has a 24hr. **ATM.** Open M-F 8:30am-4pm, Sa 10am-2pm. Try **Banamex,** Madero Ote. 63 (☎322 0338). Open M-F 9am-5pm, Sa 9am-3pm.

Luggage storage: Most bus lines have their own luggage storage. Usually 5 pesos per hr.

Laundry: Lavandería Cuautla, Cuautla 152 (☎312 4806), south of Madero. 26 pesos per 3kg. Open M-F 9am-2pm and 4-8pm, Sa 9:30am-1:30pm.

Emergency: ☎066 or 070.

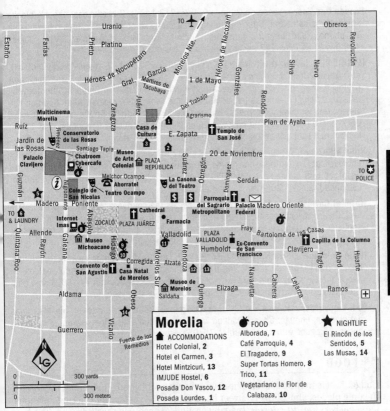

Morelia

ACCOMMODATIONS
Hotel Colonial, 2
Hotel el Carmen, 3
Hotel Mintzicuri, 13
IMJUDE Hostel, 6
Posada Don Vasco, 12
Posada Lourdes, 1

FOOD
Alborada, 7
Café Parroquia, 4
El Tragadero, 9
Super Tortas Homero, 8
Trico, 11
Vegetariano la Flor de Calabaza, 10

NIGHTLIFE
El Rincón de los Sentidos, 5
Las Musas, 14

Police: (☎320 1931), on 20 de Noviembre, 1 block northwest of the Fuente de las Tarascas, at the end of the aqueduct. No English spoken.

Red Cross: Ventura 27 (☎314 5151 or 314 5025), next to Parque Cuauhtémoc. Some English spoken.

Pharmacy: Farmacia Guadalajara, Morelos Sur 117 (☎312 1360), near the cathedral. Also a mini-supermarket.

Hospital: Hospital Civil (☎313 9072), at Ramos and Huarte. Open 24hr.

Fax: Computel, Portal Galeana 157 (☎/fax 313 6256), across from the cathedral. Has a **caseta.** Open daily 7am-10pm. **Telecomm,** Madero Ote. 369 (☎312 0345), in the Palacio Federal next to the post office. Open M-F 8am-7:30pm, Sa-Su 9am-12:30pm.

Post Office: Madero Ote. 369 (☎312 0517), in the Palacio Federal, 5 blocks east of the cathedral. Open M-F 8am-4pm, Sa 9am-1pm. **Postal Code:** 58000.

ACCOMMODATIONS

Unfortunately, budget hotels with weekend vacancies are about as rare as jackrabbits in Morelia. Moderately priced hotels are all over, but for a real bargain (and a better chance at an empty bed), the IMJUDE hostel is worth the walk.

Posada Don Vasco, Vasco de Quiroga 232 (☎312 1484), 2 blocks east and 1½ blocks south of the cathedral. Spacious rooms off a pretty stone-arched courtyard have cable TV, phone, wood furniture, carpeting, purified water, and clean, green baths. Singles 198 pesos; doubles 227 pesos; triples 255 pesos. ❸

IMJUDE Villa Juvenil Youth Hostel, Chiapas 180 (☎313 3177; villaju@prodigi.net.mx), at Oaxaca, 20min. from the *zócalo*. Walk west on Madero Pte., turn left on Cuautla for 6 blocks, then turn right on Oaxaca and continue 4 blocks to Chiapas. Alternatively, take an *amarilla* (yellow stripe) *combi* from the *centro* (3.4 pesos). Neat 4-person single-sex dorms, communal baths, and red-tiled lobby with TV. Sports facilities (except pool) can be used with permission. Linen deposit 50 pesos. Reception 7am-11pm; lockout at 11pm. 20 pesos per meal in the adjoining cafeteria. Dorms 60 pesos. ❶

Hotel Mintzicuri, Vasco de Quiroga 227 (☎312 0664). Railings overflowing with flowers enclose cozy, wood-paneled rooms individually named for *michoacano* towns and equipped with phones and cable TV. Very popular with Mexican tourists—come early or call ahead. Singles 206 pesos; doubles 232 pesos; triples 283 pesos. ❹

Hotel el Carmen, Ruiz 63 (☎312 1725), across the courtyard from La Casa de la Cultura. Clean, stylish accomodations and attractive prices. Rooms are a bit cramped but spotless bathrooms, high beamed ceilings, cable TV, phone, and hardwood furniture come at the right price. Singles 185 pesos; doubles 220 pesos. ❸

Hotel Colonial, 20 de Noviembre 15 (☎312 1897). Most rooms have high ceilings, large windows, private baths, and *agua purificada;* some even have small balconies. Scope them out: all rooms are not equal. Singles 123 pesos, with TV 180 pesos; doubles 156/200 pesos; triples 250 pesos. MC/V on weekdays. ❷

Posada Lourdes, Morelos Nte. 340, at del Trabajo. Unattractive exterior, but the rooms are pleasant enough. *Cheap.* Purified water in the courtyard. 10pm lockout. Singles 45 pesos, 75 pesos with bath; doubles 75/95 pesos. ❶

▮ FOOD

Budget hotels may be scarce, but it's a breeze to find good, cheap food in Morelia. In some places, almost every street has a family-run restaurant offering delicious, inexpensive *comida corrida* (usually around 20 pesos) in the afternoon. The best deals are around the bus station. Restaurants on the *zócalo* are pricier but tend to stay open later. For local specialties, try *sopa tarasca* (a creamy soup made with beans, cheese, and bits of crispy tortilla, flavored by a bitter black chile) or *sopa tlalpeño* (a chicken-based soup with vegetables and *chipotle*), legacies of the Purépecha and Tarasco indigenous groups that once controlled this region.

▨ Trico, Valladolid 8, 2nd fl. (☎313 4232). Elegantly colonial but economical, Trico lures businessmen in suits and families in jeans. Vegetarian options available. Huge breakfasts 30-45 pesos and regional specialties. Open daily 7am-9pm. ❸

Alborada, Lejarza 36 (☎313 0171), right off Madero. A bakery in front and kitchen in back. The *comida corrida* (42 pesos; 37 pesos to go) is mouth-watering; limitless trips to the salad bar. Breakfasts 20-25 pesos, *energéticos* (yogurt, fruit, and honey) 12-18 pesos. Open M-Sa 8am-4:30pm; bakery M-Sa 8am-9pm. ❸

Super Tortas Homero (☎333 0673 for delivery), at Allende and Abasolo. Great *tortas* (17-28 pesos) draw longer lines than a *tortería* has a right to. Open daily 9am-7pm. ❷

El Tragadero, Hidalgo 63 (☎313 0092). Packed with artificial flowers and old images of Morelia. High wood beam ceiling lends a nice feel. Very filling *comida corrida* 37 pesos, large helpings of local specialties like *caldo tlalpeño* or *sopa tarasco* 26 pesos. Open Su 7:30am-8pm, M-Sa 7:30am-11pm. ❸

SOUTHERN PACIFIC COAST

Café Parroquia, Ocampo 360 (☎313 4588). Find tranquility off the beaten path; relax with an *energetico* (15 pesos) and plan your next move. Coffee 10-15 pesos, ice cream 10 pesos. Open daily 10am-7pm. ❷

Vegetariano la Flor de Calabaza, Hidalgo 75 (☎317 1168), south of the *zócalo*. Huge inner courtyard and non-functional fountain. Mammoth *comida corrida* (35 pesos) and *comida típica* at low prices. Savory meatless plates, including delicious yogurt with fruit and cereal (18 pesos). Open M-W 9am-5pm, Th-Su 9am-9pm. ❸

SIGHTS

Packed with museums and cultural centers spanning all aspects of Michoacán's heritage, Morelia is a history buff's dream. Many of its famous buildings are ornamented in a style peculiar to the city—imitation Baroque, frequently identifiable by a flat decorative motif on pilasters and columns. Check out the cathedral for an impressive (and easy to recognize) example.

CASA DE LA CULTURA. A gathering place for artists, musicians, and backpackers, the Casa houses a bookstore, art gallery, theater, palatial inner courtyard, and lovely cafe. Dance, voice, theater, guitar, piano, and sculpture classes are available, and the Casa hosts book signings, art festivals, and literature workshops. Ask for the weekly schedule of cultural events. Unfortunately, the **Museo de la Máscara** has closed indefinitely, taking with it a freaky set of devil masks. *(Morelos Nte. 485, northeast of the zócalo. ☎313 1215 or 313 1320. Open M-F 9am-3pm and 5-8pm, Sa-Su and holidays 10am-2pm and 4-8pm. 3-month classes 150 pesos.)*

CONSERVATORIO DE LAS ROSAS. Built in the 18th century to protect and educate widows and poor or orphaned Spanish girls, the building and its rose-filled courtyard now houses Morelia's premiere music school, the oldest in the Americas. Check with the conservatory's Public Relations office or with the Casa de Cultura for performance schedules. *(Tapía 334, north of the tourist office. ☎312 1469. Open M-F 8am-8pm, Sa 8am-2pm. Public Relations office open M-F 9am-4pm.)*

CATHEDRAL. Overlooking the *zócalo*, the massive cathedral has a stunning interior graced by vaulted ceilings, chandeliers, tapestries, stained-glass windows, a beautiful altar, and a stunning dark wood pipe organ. The oldest treasure is the 16th century *Señor de la Sacristía*, an image of Christ sculpted by *indígenas* out of dry corn cobs and orchid nectar. A gold crown donated by Phillip II of Spain caps it. *(Open daily 5:30am-8:30pm. Masses held Su, ever hr. 6am-noon and 6-8pm.)*

MUSEO MICHOACANO. This museum houses exhibits on the ecology, archaeology, anthropology, history, and art of Michoacán. Learn more about why parts of Michoacán tried to secede from Mexico after the Revolution, during the Cristero Rebellion, and peruse fascinating artifacts, including a surreal crucifix with only the face of Christ, and Franciscan monks' crosses, punctuated with spikes for penitence. *(Allende 305, at the zócalo. ☎312 0407. Open Su 9am-2pm, Tu-Sa 9am-7pm. 30 pesos, seniors and children under 14 free; Su free.)*

MUSEO DE MORELOS. Originally bought by José María Morelos, the parish priest who led the Independence movement after Hidalgo's death, this 19th-century building now houses a museum detailing Morelos's life and martyrdom, including maps of his military campaigns and a rare image of him as priest. It also displays period pieces. *(Morelos Sur 323, southeast of the cathedral. ☎313 8506. Open daily 9am-7pm. 22 pesos, seniors and children under 13 free; Su free.)*

CASA NATAL DE MORELOS. More of a civic building than a museum, the "Birthplace of Morelos" holds glass cases that preserve Morelos's wartime cartography, communiqués, and letters. Also notable are the murals by Alfredo Zalce. An eternal flame commemorates Morelos's birthplace—apparently in the middle of a stone courtyard. (*Corregidora 113.* ☎ *312 2793. Open M-F 9am-8pm, Sa-Su 9am-7pm. Free.*)

CASA DE LAS ARTESANÍAS. This *casa*, occupying part of the **Ex-Convento de San Francisco**, is a huge crafts museum and retail store, selling colorful macramé *huipiles*, straw airplanes, pottery, carved wooden furniture, and guitars. Along the upstairs hallway, crafts stuff rooms labeled with the crafts' town of origin; Paracho carries guitars, Tocuaro contains devil masks, and Santa Clara has copper. For better bargains, visit the towns themselves, or nearby Pátzcuaro. (*Humboldt, east of the zócalo.* ☎ *312 1248. Open Su 10am-4:30pm, M-Sa 10am-3pm and 5-8pm. Free.*)

BOSQUE CUAUHTÉMOC. The *bosque* lets you lose yourself among trees and fountains. A **mini amusement park** with bumper cars (10 pesos) and a train (3 pesos) entertains the young and young at heart. The **Museo de Historia Natural**, in the southeast corner of the *bosque*, is a tiny museum with rotating exhibits on the flora and fauna of Michoacán, past and present, and their uses. On the eastern side of the *bosque* is the **Museo de Arte Contemporaneo Alfredo Zalce**, which displays works in all media by that artist—one of Michoacán's most celebrated—as well as temporary exhibits of contemporary art. Prints sell for 20 pesos. (*To get to the bosque, take a "Ruta Rojo" combi (3.5 pesos) from behind the cathedral on Allende. Amusement park open daily 11:30am-7:30pm. Museo de Historia* ☎ *312 0044. Open daily 10am-6pm. 5 pesos. Museo de Arte* ☎ *312 5404. Open Tu-Su 10am-2pm and 4-8pm. Free.*)

PARQUE ZOOLÓGICO BENITO JUÁREZ. Founded in 1970, this is nonetheless one of the largest (and most pleasant) zoos in Mexico. Thankfully, most animals reside in natural settings rather than tiny cages. Friday night at 8pm a tour (100 pesos) includes dinner. (*Take a maroon combi south on Nigromante or a pink "Santa María" combi from in front of the tourist office (3.5 pesos), or walk south 3km on Nigromante until it becomes Juárez. Entrance on the west side of zoo.* ☎ *314 0488. Open M-F 10am-5pm, Sa-Su 10am-5:30pm. 12 pesos, children 6 pesos.*)

OTHER SIGHTS. At the eastern end of Madero is the city's most recognizable landmark, the statue of **Las Tarascas**, which shows three bare-breasted indigenous women making an offering to the heavens. Nearby is **El Acueducto**, built in the 18th century to meet the city's growing water needs. Though no longer functional, it is a magnificent sight at night. Av. Acueducto runs along it to the university. Across from the cathedral is the **Palacio de Gobierno**, Madero 63, with more historical murals (by Alfredo Zalce). The **Museo de Arte Colonial**, at Juárez 240, proves that colonial artists were solely interested in the crucifixion. (*Palacio de Gobierno open M-F 8am-10pm, Sa-Su 8am-9pm. Museo de Arte* ☎ *313 9260; open M-F 10am-2pm and 5-8pm, Sa-Su 10am-2pm and 4:30-7pm. Free.*)

🎵🎭 ENTERTAINMENT AND NIGHTLIFE

The Casa de Cultura and tourist office carry event listings. Lights, music, and theater draw crowds to **Teatro Morelos** (☎ 314 6202), on Camelina at Ventura Pte., and to **Teatro Ocampo** (☎ 312 3734), on the corner of Ocampo and Prieto (tickets 20-80 pesos). **Corral de la Comedia**, Ocampo 239, at Prieto one block north of Madero, presents comedies written and performed by local artists. (☎ 312 0001. Performances Su 7:30pm, Th-Sa 8:30pm; 60 pesos.) **La Casona del Teatro**, Serdán 35, at Morelos one block north of Madero, hosts comic dramas in Spanish. (☎ 317 3353. Shows generally Su 7:30pm, Th-Sa 8:30pm. 70 pesos.) The **Conservatorio de las Rosas** (see **Sights** above) holds concerts outside of the summer; visit for calendars. The **Casa Natal de Morelos** (see **Sights,** above) shows family movies and holds cultural events. (Events F 8pm; films Tu-W 5 and 7pm, 5 pesos.) **Multicinema Morelia,** on Tapía at Jiménez, next to the conservatory, screens Hollywood's latest. (☎312 1288. Open daily 1:30-10:30pm. 25 pesos before 6pm, 30 pesos after; Spanish subtitles.) The **Planetario** (☎314 2465), on Ventura Pte. at Ticateme, in the Centro de Convenciones, has standard planetarium fare. Take the "Ruta Rojo #3" *combi* from Allende/Valladolid, and watch for the convention center on the right. (Su showings 6:30pm, Tu-Sa 1, 5, 7pm; 20 pesos.)

Young people flock to the colonial charm of ◪**El Rincón de los Sentidos,** Madero Pte. 485. Live music and games such as dominos provide entertainment, while scattered bean bag chairs provide relaxation. High chairs upstairs overlook the band below. (☎312 2903. Beer 18-26 pesos, mixed drinks start at 35 pesos; salads and *antojitos* 38-45 pesos. Open Su-W 8am-midnight, Th-Sa 8am-2am. Live music and cover F-Sa 8pm-midnight.) **Las Musas,** Obeso 290, is appropriate for more a romantic rendezvous as a troubadour pours out his heart through his guitar. In the dimly lit main room, patrons may feel safe to belt out the tune as well. (☎317 4312. Beer 25 pesos. Cover 30 pesos T-Su, live music Th-Sa 10pm-2:30am. Open daily 8pm-3am.) If you prefer scantily clad bodies to merely heavenly ones, writhe with students at Morelia's nightclubs. Most are a 15- to 20-peso cab ride away. Twentysomethings bounce to the latest Spanish and English pop tunes beneath videos at **XO Club,** Ramírez 100. (☎324 0765. Open bar F. Cover men 50 pesos, women 10 pesos. Open W-Sa 10pm-3am.) For a heavier club scene, try one of the newest and most popular clubs, **Knox,** at Periférico Paseo de la República 534. A laser light show complements pop and house anthems, pleasing the young and attractive local crowd. (☎324 7442. Beer 22 pesos, mixed drinks 50 pesos. Open bar W men 120 pesos, women 20 pesos; Th private parties; F 2 for 1 beers; Sa cover 50 pesos. Open W-Sa 10pm-3:30am.) Clubs here have short lives, so ask around for the latest.

SOUTHERN PACIFIC COAST

CIUDAD HIDALGO ☎ 615

Hidalgo (pop. 106,000) is best visited as a base for exploring Michoacán's natural beauty at nearby **Laguna Larga** and the spas of **Los Azufres.**

▗▚ TRANSPORTATION AND PRACTICAL INFORMATION. The city is a 2hr. bus ride from Morelia. From the **bus station, Flecha Amarilla/Servicios Coordinados** motors to: **Mexico City** (6 per day 1:45am-4:30pm, 98 pesos) via **Toluca** (70 pesos) and **Zitácuaro** (20 pesos); **Morelia** (7 per day, 55 pesos); **Pátzcuaro** (12:30am, 6pm; 85 pesos); **Uruapan** (6pm, 110 pesos). **Autobuses México-Toluca** (☎154 0722) and **Autobuses del Occidente/La Línea** (☎154 7073) have more limited service. To get to the *centro,* take a bus headed right on the road in front of the bus station and tell the driver where you want to get off (3.5 pesos). **Micros** operate from a station at Matamoros and Morelos. **Taxis** 15 pesos. The *zócalo* is bordered on the north by **Valle,** on the west by **Cuauhtémoc,** on the south by **Juárez,** and on the west by **Hidalgo. Morelos,** the main commercial drag, is one block south of Juárez.

Services include: **tourist office,** on the second floor of the Altos del Mercado Emiliano Zapata in front of the Plaza Hidalgo (☎154 2111, ext. 220; open M-F 9am-3pm and 5-7pm); **Banamex,** in the northeast corner of the *zócalo,* at Cuauhtémoc and Hidalgo, with 24hr. **ATM** and **currency exchange** (open M-F 9am-5pm, Sa 10am-2pm); **police** (☎154 0029), inside the Palacio Municipal; **Farmacia San Ángel,** Morelos Pte. 5 (☎154 2007, open 9am-11pm); **Centro de Salud,** at the corner of Morelos and Zapata, two blocks left on Morelos from Cuauhtémoc with the *zócalo* at your back (☎154 0263; no English spoken); **Internet access** at **Café Ollin Yolotzin,** León #69, between Matamoros and Morelos (☎154 7265; open daily 9am-8pm).

▗▚ ACCOMMODATIONS AND FOOD. Your best bet and the family choice is the **Hotel Central ❷,** Abasolo 12. From the Palacio Gobierno, walk right for a block, then left on Abasolo for 1½ blocks. Large, clean rooms have TV and phone. (☎ 154 0055. Singles 140 pesos; doubles 300 pesos; triples 340 pesos; quads 450 pesos. Brief city guides are available at the front desk, 20 pesos.) A less attractive option is **Hotel San Carlos ❶**, Cuauhtémoc Sur 22. The peach walls are stained with grime and, with the one bathroom drain beneath the sink, a shower will also bathe any clothes left on the floor. (☎ 154 5647. Singles 70 pesos, with cable TV 100 pesos; each additional person 60 pesos.) Alternatively, the **Hotel Romo ❺**, Abasolo 41, is modern and clean for the desperate or those casual with money. (☎ 154 0650 or 154 6481. Jr. suite 550 pesos; full suite 600 pesos; each additional person 100 pesos.)

Hidalgo is not the place for fine dining. Food vendors abound in the *zócalo* and *mercado;* small joints line Morelos. The **Lonchería Segus ❶**, Morelos Ote. 8, has great *tortas* (5-9 pesos) and other standards (5-25 pesos); pizza and burgers are next door.

▲❶ OUTDOOR ACTIVITIES AND FESTIVALS. Los Azufres, 23km northwest of Morelia, are good for a relaxing bath (as relaxing as growing numbers of tourists and hotels permit; 30 pesos). Head out in a 6:30am *micro* to return at 9am, or take advantage of the lazier afternoon rides from 2:30 to 3:45pm. A more active choice is to spelunk a bit in the **Grutas de Ziranda**. Don't worry about bats—tours end before dusk to avoid the swarms. (Take a 15min. bus ride from Juárez, 3.5 pesos. Short tours daily 9am-5pm. 15 pesos.) Nearby **Laguna Larga** is a series of *presos* (man-made lakes) perfect for hiking, fishing, or camping. Buses leave from the suburban terminal (1hr.; 7am, 2pm; 15 pesos. Return 8:30am, 3:30pm; 15 pesos). To get to the terminal from the *centro*, take Hidalgo south one block, turn right on Morelos and walk three blocks, and find the terminal left on Matamoros. Finally, one of the main festivals is **La Feria de la Conserva;** *conservas* are local fruit treats cooked at high temperatures with sugar; plentiful vendors sell them in traditional pots. Stop by the **tourist office** for more info.

ZITÁCUARO ☎715

Zitácuaro (pop. 200,000) would be a much larger city had it not been destroyed three times during the 19th century—once during the War for Independence (1812), again by Santa Anna's troops (1855), and finally during the French Intervention (1865). The city's long tradition of defiance and survival led Benito Juárez to ordain it *Ciudad de la Independencia* (City of Independence). Today, Zitácuaro has safe streets, large markets, and a population that rises with the sun. A local ordinance has given the city a distinct look: most buildings are red near the ground and white the rest of the way up. Tucked into the eastern edge of the Sierra Madre Occidental, the city seems to have mountains looming at the end of every street. Outdoors enthusiasts will find plenty of opportunities for camping and hiking nearby, but there is little for the more cosmopolitan. Despite its growing population and increasing urbanization, Zitácuaro's cultural traditions have remained as immutable as the mountains.

▐ TRANSPORTATION. Zitácuaro sits 165km west of Mexico City on **Mex. 15**. The **bus station** is at Pueblita Nte. 17 (☎ 153 7265), at the end of Cuauhtémoc Nte., two blocks north of Hidalgo and six blocks east of Revolución Nte. Tickets for **taxis** to the *centro* are sold at a booth inside (15 pesos). "Centro" *combis* are outside the station (6am-9pm, 3.5 pesos). **Flecha Amarilla** (☎ 153 1488) provides second-class service to: **León** (6½hr., 10pm, 182 pesos); **Mexico City** (3hr., 6 per day, 95 pesos) via **Toluca** (1hr., 56 pesos); **Morelia** (3hr., 9 per day 6am-11:45pm, 79 pesos) via **Ciudad Hidalgo** (45min., 20 pesos). **Autobuses de Occidente/La Línea** (☎ 153 0866) offers similar service and goes to: **Lázaro Cárdenas** (12hr., 6:25pm, 404 pesos); **Man-**

zanillo (13½hr., 4 per day, 295 pesos); **Zamora** (6hr., 7 per day 1:45am- 5:30pm, 134 pesos). **Estrella Blanca** (☎153 7173) drives to points north and sends buses to Querétaro (6hr.; 1, 3pm; 163 pesos). **Autobuses México-Toluca** (☎153 7163) has similar, but more limited, local service.

📑🛈 ORIENTATION AND PRACTICAL INFORMATION. Plaza Principal, the city center, consists of Plaza Cívica de Benito Juárez, Plaza Municipal, and Mercado Juárez. Plaza Municipal is bordered by **Tejada** (south), **García** (west), **5 de Mayo** (east), and **Ocampo** (north). **Hidalgo** runs parallel to Ocampo on the other side of the market. The main avenue, **Revolución,** is one block east of 5 de Mayo. Streets end in "Nte." or "Sur," indicating their relation to Hidalgo.

The **tourist office,** Carretera Zitácuaro km 4, is far, but provides helpful maps and brochures. Take an orange *combi* (3.5 pesos) south on Revolución and tell the driver where to let you off. (☎153 0675. Open M-F 9am-3pm and 5-7pm, Sa 9am-2pm.) **Banamex,** Tejada 30, exchanges cash and checks and has a 24hr. **ATM.** (☎153 9020. Open M-F 9am-5pm, Sa 9am-2pm.) The bus station offers **luggage storage.** (8 pesos per bag for 6hr.; open daily 4am-10pm.) Other services include: **emergency service** (☎060) and **"civil protection"** (☎113); **police** (☎153 1137), at the north end of Plaza Municipal; **Red Cross,** Prieto 11 (☎153 1105, 114 on cell phones); **Farmacia Guadalajara,** 5 de Mayo Sur 12A (☎153 8633; open 24hr.); the **Hospital Sanitorio Memorial,** Valle Nte. 10 (☎153 6539)—take a left on Valle from Hidalgo, the hospital is on your left; **Telecomm,** Ocampo 7, with **fax, Western Union,** and **telegraph** services (☎153 1281; open M-F 8:30am-7pm, Sa 9am-2pm); **Armi Internet,** Hidalgo Ote. 17B, near Salazar (☎153 7314; open Su 10am-2pm, M-Sa 9am-9pm; 10 pesos per hour); **post office,** Valle Sur 2—go up Ocampo, cross Revolución and turn left and go half a block on Valle. (☎153 1283. Open M-F 9am-3pm.) **Postal code:** 61500.

🛏🍴 ACCOMMODATIONS AND FOOD. Illuminated signs all over Revolución and the plaza advertise conveniently located (and sometimes inconveniently priced) hotels and *posadas*. Reservations are a good idea in November and December. Put your pesos to good use at the **Hotel América ❷,** Revolución Sur 8. It offers parking, clean rooms with wood floors, spotless baths, and cable TV. The view, however, fails to match the interior. (☎153 1116. Singles 140 pesos; doubles 190 pesos; triples 240 pesos.) Another good, inexpensive option is the recently remodeled **Hotel Lorenz ❷,** Hidalgo Ote. 14. This recently remodeled hotel offers carpeted rooms with cable TV but no phone. Some rooms overlook the peaceful courtyard and its fountain seating. (☎153 0991. Singles 130 pesos; doubles 200 pesos.) **Hotel Conquistador ❺,** Leandro Valle Sur 2, is a great hotel when price is not an issue, boasting a posh reception area, stained glass windows, local miniatures of monarch butterflies, and beautiful marble and tile bathrooms. (☎153 5790; www.conquistadormonarca.com.mx. Singles 295 pesos; doubles 355 pesos; jr. suite 450 pesos.)

The best dining options are on-the-go: stands with fresh fruits and vegetables, quesadillas, or ice cream line 5 de Mayo. A few sit-down restaurants are on Revolución and Hidalgo. Try friendly, inexpensive **Café Chipss ❷** at Hidalgo Ote. 22, east of Revolución. (☎153 1195. Savory *tortas* 7-8 pesos, *licuados* 7-9 pesos, hamburgers 10-15 pesos. Open M-Sa 9:30am-7pm.)

📷 SIGHTS. Afternoons in Zitácuaro slip by quietly beneath the sun in the **Plaza Cívica de Benito Juárez,** where vendors gather, uniformed school children play *fútbol*, and the elderly relax on shaded benches. The **Palacio Municipal,** at the north end of the plaza, holds a stunning mural bringing alive Zitácuaro's history, from settlement by the Mazahuas, through independence, to the present day. The small **Jardín de la Constitución,** on Ojeda Sur three blocks west of the plaza, is filled with flowers, fountains, and shady seats for starry-eyed lovebirds.

THE GREAT OUTDOORS

HOLDING COURT

Eastern Michoacán's beautiful landscape is filled not only with vast coniferous forests and rolling hills peppered with small farming communities, but also, during November and December, over 250 million monarch butterflies. Each October, the diminutive creatures begin their journeys almost simultaneously from their summer homes all over the US and Canada, flying at a regal 20km per hr., and gather on five mountaintops just north of Zitácuaro.

Some scientists say the seemingly inexplicable mass migration is a relic of the ice ages, when southward travel was necessary for reproduction; others insist that even now monarch reproduction is impossible in all but the warmest of climates. Whatever the reason, the sight is stupendous. The butterflies blanket trees, forming orange masses and leaving not a single patch of bark visible.

The best place to be a part of the annual convergence is at the Santuario de Mariposas El Rosario, one of only two butterfly sanctuaries open to the public. Take a green bus labeled "Angangueo" from the station in Zitácuaro, but come ready to hike—the final climb, which must be done on foot, is an exhausting 2km from an already-dizzying 3km. The entrance fee of 15 pesos is well worth it, especially in the morning, when the butterflies are especially fond of stretching their tiny butterly legs.

Zitácuaro's **Cerrito de la Independencia** looks out over not only the city itself, but also miles of lush valleys, forested hills, and spectacular distant blue peaks. To reach the lookout, follow Tejada as it crosses Revolución Sur until it reaches Altamirano, then turn right and follow the paved path climbing through the woods. (Park open daily 6am-7pm.) You can also take an orange *combi* (3.5 pesos) south on Revolución to Cañonaso and walk the four blocks uphill. Ten kilometers south of town on the Huetamo Rte., **Presa del Bosque** also provides spectacular views of the countryside. The dirt road to the right of the main road leads to a lake where adventurous souls swim, camp, fish, and hike. Unfortunately, there is no public transportation, so you'll have to flag down a taxi (70 pesos).

LÁZARO CÁRDENAS ☎753

Named after the famed *michoacano* president who nationalized oil in 1938 and instituted radical land reform, the hot, noisy city of Lázaro Cárdenas (pop. 150,000) is Mexico's most important Pacific port. The city offers all the services that you'll be unable to find in smaller beach towns along Michoacán's rugged and beautiful 260km coast, but the crowded streets and lack of swimmable beaches mean Cárdenas is best as a pit stop or departure point.

▉ TRANSPORTATION. Lázaro Cárdenas lies 382km southwest of Morelia and 122km northwest of Ixtapa. The principal thoroughfare is **Av. Lázaro Cárdenas;** the *zócalo*, **Plaza de la Reforma,** is three blocks east of the *avenida's* intersection with Prieto. *Combis* and buses run along Cárdenas and to nearby beaches.

The **airport** (☎532 1920) hosts carriers **Aerolínea Cuahonte** (☎532 3635 or 532 4900) and **Transporte Aeromar** (☎537 1084). **Buses** run out of independent stations on or near the main drag. **Autotransportes Cuauhtémoc** and **Estrella Blanca,** Villa 65 (☎532 0426), four blocks west of Corregidora, send buses to: **Acapulco** (6hr., every 2hr. 4:15am-midnight, 169 pesos); **Morelia** (6 hr.; 2:30, 10pm; 241 pesos); **Puerto Vallarta** (12hr.; 1:05, 2:02am, 2:30pm; 381 pesos); **Zihuatanejo** (2hr., every 2hr. 4:15am-midnight, 57 pesos). **Estrella Blanca** also provides second-class service to: **Acapulco** (6½hr., every hr. 2:30am-9pm, 108 pesos); **Manzanillo** (6hr.; 2:30, 4:20pm; 220 pesos); **Mexico City** (10hr.; 4:30, 8, 9:45pm; 388 pesos); **Zihuatanejo** (2½ hr., every hr. 2:30am-9pm, 35 pesos). **Autotransportes Galeana,** Cárdenas 1810 (☎532 0262), **Estrella de Oro,** on Jose María Morelos (☎532 1798), and **La Línea,** Cárdenas

171 (☎537 1850), provide similar service. **Parhikuni** (☎532 3006), at the Galeana station, sends buses to **Manzanillo** (6.5 hr., 155 pesos) and **Uruapan** (133 pesos).

⃞ PRACTICAL INFORMATION. Get the maps and info you need to conquer the coast from the **Delegación Regional de Turismo,** Bravo 475, one block east of Cárdenas and two blocks north of Corregidora, in the big white Hotel Casa Blanca. (☎/fax 532 1547. Open Su 9am-2pm, M-Sa 9am-2pm and 5-7pm. No English spoken.) **Banamex,** Cárdenas 1646, **exchanges currency** and has an **ATM.** (☎532 2020. Open M-F 8:30am-4:30pm, Sa 10am-2pm.) So does **BITAL,** Cárdenas 1940. (☎537 2376 or 537 2391. Open M-Sa 8am-7pm.) **Luggage storage** is in the Estrella Blanca bus station. (2-6 pesos per bag per hr.) **Hertz,** Bravo 475, inside Hotel Casa Blanca, offers small VWs for 500 pesos per day (☎532 2570, airport office ☎532 1645; open daily 7am-8pm). Other services include: **police** (☎532 2030), in the Palacio Municipal on Cárdenas at Río Balsas; **Red Cross,** Aldama 327 (☎532 0575); **Farmacia París,** Cárdenas 2002 (☎532 1435; open 24hr.); **Hospital General** (☎532 2842), on Av. 20 de Noviembre 314 and **Centro de Salud,** on Cárdenas (☎535 0004); **Caseta Goretti,** Corregidora 79, with long distance **phone** and **fax** service (☎537 3155; open daily 8am-midnight); **Internet access** at **Sin Límite,** Cárdenas 1745, at the corner of Corregidora (☎532 1480; open daily 9am-9pm); **post office,** Bravo 1307. (☎532 0547. Open M-F 8am-4pm, Sa 9am-1pm.) **Postal code:** 60950.

⃞⃞ ACCOMMODATIONS AND FOOD. The rent-by-the-hour atmosphere of most budget accommodations in town will make you relieved to find **Hotel Reyna Pío ❸,** Corregidora 78, at Cárdenas—even if the toilets lack seats. Settle down on your firm bed as the TV and A/C sing to you. (☎532 0620. Singles 188 pesos; doubles 229 pesos.) The more comfortable **Hotel Delfín ❹,** Cárdenas 1533, has clean rooms, a pool, and a nicely kept courtyard. (☎532 1418. Singles 200 pesos, with A/C 300 pesos; doubles 230/350 pesos.) **El Paraíso ❷,** Cárdenas 1862, by the Galeana bus station, offers traditional fare amid orange, green, and yellow decor straight out of the 70s. The *sopa de tortilla* (18 pesos) and chicken (35 pesos) are both worth a try. *Comida corrida* 20 pesos. At night, people come for the pool tables and bar. (☎532 3233. Beer 15-18 pesos.) For even cheaper eats, the street beside the Galeana bus station is full of **torta** and **taco stands ❶,** most open late.

MICHOACÁN COAST

Michoacán's temperamental, wildly beautiful coastline gives solace and tranquility one moment and ripping, turbulent surf the next. Along the hilly coast, crashing white waves spray into blue skies and deface rocks, while lush tropical vegetation lends a loving touch of green to the state's 260km of virgin beach. Mex. 200, the solitary coastal route, twists up, down, and around the angry terrain. Michoacán's coast is dangerous, and should be treated with caution. The beaches are best suited for surfing and the currents are strong even in designated swimming areas. There are no lifeguards, so use extreme caution. Mex. 200 tends to be deserted and dangerous at night; **Let's Go does not recommend traveling after dark.**

PLAYA AZUL   ☎753

Playa Azul (pop. 5000), a small Pacific town 26km west of Lázaro Cárdenas, is renowned for its soft, golden sands and majestic, rose-colored sunsets that project against the hills. The tempting waves attract surfers and boogie boarders, but the strong undercurrent makes swimming treacherous. Crowded with Mexican tourists during December and *Semana Santa,* the beach is otherwise very quiet. Far from being a polished tourist town, Playa Azul is typically *michoacano:* unmarked dirt roads lined with thatched-roof houses and open-air markets criss-cross the town, while chickens and tanned locals in bathing suits walk the streets. The village is so small that street names are seldom used (or known) by locals.

TRANSPORTATION AND PRACTICAL INFORMATION. The *malecón* runs along the beach; it is called **Serdán** to the west of the plaza and **Zapata** to the east. The other streets bordering the plaza are **Montes de Oca** to the west and **Filomena Mata** to the east. **Lázaro Cárdenas** runs into Playa Azul, then turns perpendicular to the beach, intersecting Carranza, Madero, and Independencia, which parallel the beach. From Lázaro Cárdenas, catch a "Playa Azul" *combi*, in front of Coppel by Corregidora, straight to the beach (45min., every 2min. 5am-9pm, 11.5 pesos). To get to Caleta de Campos from Playa Azul, take a *combi* across from the PEMEX station (5min., every 10 min., 4.5 pesos) and ask the driver to be let off at **Acalpican**, a marked intersection just to the north. From there, hail a bus labeled "Caleta" (1hr., every 30 min. 5:45am-8:30pm, 33 pesos).

Playa Azul has **no bank** or **casa de cambio**, but does offer most other services: the **market Flores Magón**, two blocks east of the plaza (open daily 8am-5pm); **surf board** and boogie board rental from several beach front shops; **police**, across from the PEMEX station (☎532 1855 or 532 0370; no English spoken); **Farmacia Cristo Rey**, on Magón in front of Martita (open daily 9am-9pm); **Centro de Salud**, next door to the post office (no English spoken); **LADATELs**, on the *malecón* or along Independencia; **post office**, on Madero at Montes de Oca, just behind Hotel María Teresa (☎536 0109; open M-F 9am-3pm). **Postal code:** 60986.

ACCOMMODATIONS AND FOOD. Bucolic Playa Azul offers several adequate budget hotels. Call ahead in August, December, and during *Semana Santa*. **Hotel Costa de Oro ❸**, on Madero, three blocks from Lázaro Cárdenas, is the best deal in town. An elegant banister overlooks a dirt courtyard and small pool, and leads to clean, comfortable rooms with tiled floors, mismatched bedspreads, and fans that pack a punch. Bathrooms are clean with hot water. (Singles 150 pesos; doubles 200 pesos.) **Bungalows de la Curva ❸**, on Madero at Lázaro Cárdenas, with kitchenettes and basic furniture but small baths, is a good deal for groups. The lack of screens on windows may cause problems in the morning; the pool is a better way to cool off. (☎536 0377. Singles and doubles 160 pesos; bungalows 300-400 pesos.) **Hotel Andrea ❷**, Zapata 879, offers views of the ocean and crowded *enramadas*. (☎536 0251. Singles 150 pesos; each additional person 50 pesos.)

Palapa restaurants are so close to the shore that the waves will tickle your toes. The bubbly owners of ▧**Coco's Pizza ❹** will make you feel right at home, especially when they look out for those on the lifeguard-less beach. Their *camarones al diablo* (shrimp with chile; 50 pesos) are a spicy taste of heaven. (Open daily 8am-9pm.) Inland, **Restaurante Familiar Martita ❸**, on Magón at Madero, is a cozy family-run restaurant with a variety of dishes at accessible prices. (☎536 0111. *Comida corrida* 25 pesos, breakfast combos 25-35 pesos. Open daily 7am-11pm.) Another cheap, in-town eatery is **Las Palmas ❹**, at Magón across from Martita. This is the place to satisfy a craving for *chimichangas* (35 pesos for 3). A tad pricier than the usual *fonda*, it is also nicer. (Open 7am-11pm.)

PLAYA AZUL TO CALETA DE CAMPOS

Beautiful beaches cover 43km of coastline between Playa Azul and Caleta de Campos. In springtime, around *Semana Santa*, the waters are calmest and most serenely beautiful (most crowded too, of course). **Las Peñas**, 13km west of Playa Azul, is turbulent enough to discourage swimmers, but great for surfing. **El Bejuco**, only 2km west, has a sandy cove with tamer waves and fewer rocks. Go west another 12km and you'll find **Chuquiapan**, a long beach surrounded by tall green palms but littered with stones and driftwood. **La Soledad,** enclosed by cliffs 4km farther west, is cozier. The different layers of color make a nice view, as the waters shift from blue to green before brushing against the dark, volcanic sands. **Mexcal-huacán,** 2km west, offers a fantastic view from a bluff overlooking a desolate, rocky coast. Caleta de Campos comes 7km later. **Nexpa,** a sandy beach with powerful waves, is a surfer haven 5km west of Caleta. *Palapa* restaurants, known as *enramadas,* line most of the beaches.

Caleta de Campos is a tiny fishing village 47km west of Playa Azul, with a pleasant beach. Surrounding hills offer a spectacular view of the coast and, because the water is somewhat sheltered, the surf is calmer than at Playa Azul, and the rolling waves make for good boogie boarding and body surfing. The town, though, is important to the traveler primarily because it is one of few places along this stretch of coast with accommodations and services. The entire town lies along one main street, Melchor Ocampo (known locally as Principal); blink and you'll miss it. The **police station** is by the radio tower on the left as you turn onto Principal from the main highway (☎532 1855 or 532 2030. No English spoken); to reach the **Centro de Salud,** turn right before Principal goes left and walk three blocks up a dirt road. (No English spoken. 24hr. emergency service.) Along this street are also phones, sporadic currency exchange, and a post office. Caleta has two hotels; both are nice and affordable, and fill up during *Semana Santa* and Christmas. The **Hotel los Arcos ❸,** Colegio Militar 5, next to the church as Principal turns left, has clean rooms, some with balconies, and spectacular views of the coast. (☎531 5038. Singles 150 pesos; doubles 200 pesos, with A/C 350 pesos. TV 50 pesos extra.) **Hotel Yuritzi ❹,** off Principal after the church to the left, lacks views but delivers amenities. (☎531 5010; www.hotelyuritzi.com. Singles 240 pesos, with A/C 350 pesos; doubles 300/450 pesos.) From the hotels, walk to the end of Principal, pass the church on the right, and follow the dirt road to the beach (10min.).

Buses (labeled "Michoacanos") running from Lázaro Cárdenas to Caleta de Campos on Mex. 200 leave from Galeana bus station and pass each of the beaches listed above (1½hr., every 20min. 6:20am-8:10pm, 43 pesos). From the highway, you can see signs labeling each beach, usually at a bridge—keep an eye out for them, as bus drivers won't always drop you off accurately. The beaches are a short walk from the highway (5-10min.). To return to Playa Azul or Lázaro Cárdenas, wave down a bus going in the opposite direction (last return at 7:40pm). To get to Nexpa, take a white *combi* from the bus depot at the beginning of Principal in Caleta de Campos (10min., every 40min., 7am-7pm).

GUERRERO

TAXCO
☎762

White buildings capped with red roofs, windy cobblestone streets, and sparkling *platerías* (silver shops) make the old mining town of Taxco (pop. 100,000) an antique gem set in the mountains. Cobblestone alleys coil around colonial churches and streets are so narrow that pedestrians must flatten themselves against walls to let cars pass. Beneath the old-fashioned beauty run the veins of silver that shaped Taxco's history. When silver was discovered in 1524, Taxco became the continent's first mining town, luring craftsmen and treasure-seekers from all over the world. The town's fortune ebbed with the supply of silver, and it was not until the 1930s, when the tourist industry took hold, that Taxco exploded with *platerías.* Today, the streets are aflutter with tourists buzzing through labyrinthine alleys, drawn like flies to the sweet honey of exquisite jewelry.

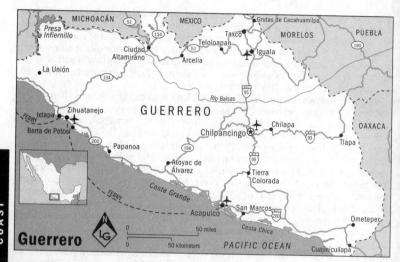

SOUTHERN PACIFIC COAST

TRANSPORTATION

Taxco has two main bus stations. **Estrella de Oro station,** Kennedy 126 (☎ 622 0648), has first-class service to: **Acapulco** (4hr., 5 per day 7:10am-6:10pm, 125 pesos); **Cuernavaca** (1½hr.; 9:15am, 3, 6:30pm; 40 pesos); **Mexico City** (2½hr., 6 per day 6am-7:30pm, 82 pesos); **Iguala** (105min., 5 per day 7:10am-6:10pm, 20 pesos). To get to the *zócalo*, cross the street and walk up the steep hill known as Pilita. When you reach Plazuela de San Juan, which has a small fountain, veer left and you will emerge facing Santa Prisca in the *zócalo*. A "Zócalo" *combi* will make the trip (3.5 pesos), as will a **taxi** (12 pesos almost anywhere in the city).

Flecha Roja station, Plateros 104 (☎ 622 0131), goes to: **Acapulco** (4½hr., 3 per day 12pm-6:30pm, 114 pesos); **Cuernavaca** (1½hr., every hr. 6am-7pm, 41 pesos); and **Toluca** (3hr.; 11:40am, 1:30pm; 65 pesos). To reach the *zócalo*, turn right on to Plateros and left on Alarcón. Turn left on Agostín de Tolsa to get to the *zócalo*.

ORIENTATION AND PRACTICAL INFORMATION

Taxco lies 185km southwest of Mexico City. The town is built into a hillside, making walking a little tiresome but orientation quite simple. The *zócalo*, **Plaza Borda,** is marked by **Catedral de Santa Prisca,** which is visible from most places in town.

Tourist Office: Subsecretaría de Fomento Turístico (☎ 622 2274), at the entrance to town. "Los Arcos" *combis* end in front of the office. Open daily 9am-3pm and 4-6pm. Tourist information is also available at the Flecha Roja station; most hotels have maps.

Currency Exchange: Try any of the very prominent banks. If you are really desperate, some hotels exchange, but the rates generally are not as good.

Market: Mercado Tetitlán, on the street to the right of Santa Prisca or off Hidalgo. Sells everything from meat to jewelry. Open daily 8:30am-8pm.

Police: (☎ 622 0007). Some English spoken.

Emergency: Procuraduría del Turista (☎ 622 2274 or 622 6616). Open M-F 9am-7pm.

Red Cross: (☎ 622 3232), on Plateros, next door to the tourist information *caseta*. No English spoken. Open daily 9am-2pm and 5-7pm.

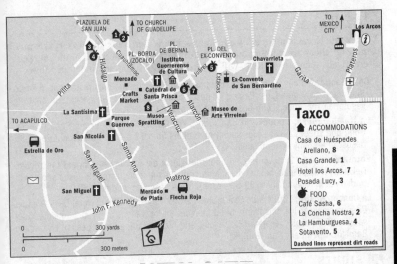

Taxco

ACCOMMODATIONS

Casa de Huéspedes
Arellano, **8**
Casa Grande, **1**
Hotel los Arcos, **7**
Posada Lucy, **3**

FOOD
Café Sasha, **6**
La Concha Nostra, **2**
La Hamburguesa, **4**
Sotavento, **5**

Dashed lines represent dirt roads

Pharmacy: Two are on the Plaza Borda and many others dot the town.

Hospital: IMSS (☎622 3510), on Plateros.

Internet Access and Fax: Available throughout town.

Post Office: Plateros 382 (☎622 0501), near the Estrella de Oro station. Open M-F 8am-3pm. **Postal Code:** 40200.

ACCOMMODATIONS

A good night's sleep does not come cheap in Taxco, but the few budget accommodations are sleaze-free and situated in beautiful old buildings with generally clean rooms. Reservations are recommended.

Casa de Huéspedes Arellano, Pajaritos 23 (☎622 0215). From the *zócalo*, walk down the street to the right of the Cathedral and descend the 1st stairs to the right; the hotel is 3 levels down through the vendor stands. Has 3 charming terraces on which to sunbathe, hang laundry, and relax; communal baths might be the biggest in Taxco. Rooms for 3 or 4 (300/480 pesos) are great for families. Dorms 120 pesos; singles 165 pesos, with bath 210 pesos. ❷

Hotel los Arcos, Alarcón 4 (☎622 1836), follow Agostín de Tolsa from the north end of the *zócalo* and turn right on the 1st street. From the shady courtyard to the expansive rooftop terrace, this hotel offers great places for catching your breath after a day battling the hills. Carved wooden furniture and wrought-iron window bars create a medieval atmosphere. Private bathrooms are clean but small. Singles and doubles 340 pesos; triples 448 pesos. ❺

Posada Lucy, Nibbi 8 (☎622 1780), just past the Plazuela de San Juan. Small rooms have private baths and great views of Taxco. Singles 150 pesos; doubles 200 pesos; triples 500 pesos, with TV 550 pesos. ❸

Casa Grande, Plazuela de San Juan 7 (☎622 0969), on the *zócalo*. You won't fall asleep before 1am, when adjacent bar turns out its lights. Rooms are clean, small, and dark, with adequate communal baths. Singles 120 pesos, with bath 160 pesos; doubles 200/240 pesos. TV 40-50 pesos extra. ❷

SOUTHERN PACIFIC COAST

🍴 FOOD

A quick bite to eat is not readily apparent—where *taquerías* and *torterías* would usually be, there are nothing but silver stores. They are abundant in the markets; alternatively, many restaurants will reward you with balconies and great views.

Café Sasha, Alarcón 3 (cafesasha@hotmail.com). Maybe the only restaurant in Taxco that caters to vegetarians. Pasta (32 pesos and up), burritos (35 pesos), an amazing vegetarian Thai special (65 pesos), and more. Open daily 8am-1am. ❸

La Hamburguesa, Plazuela de San Juan 5 (☎622 0941), down from Casa Grande. Good and speedy service plus satisfying burgers from 12 pesos. Traditional fare 12-35 pesos. Open daily 9am-midnight. ❶

Sotavento, Juárez 2, down the hill from the Iglesia del Ex-Convento toward the *zócalo*. Delicious food at reasonable prices. Menu options run from pasta (38 pesos and up) to traditional Mexican dishes (32-50 pesos). Open daily 1pm-midnight. ❸

La Concha Nostra, Plazuela de San Juan 7 (☎622 7944), 2nd fl. of Hotel Casa Grande. Despite slow service, this is a popular hangout for local teens and young tourists. Quesadillas (21 pesos), lasagna (32 pesos), and pizza (starting at 19 pesos). Live music Sa night. Open daily 8am-1am. ❷

📷 SIGHTS

CATEDRAL DE SANTA PRISCA. Constructed in 1758 with funds donated by silver tycoon José de la Borda, the church's Baroque facade is made of rose stone and decorated with inverted Corinthian columns. Inside are paintings by indigenous artist Miguel Cabrerra, whose racy foci include a pregnant Virgin Mary and the circumcision of baby Jesus. *(Open daily 8am-8pm, mass held every hr. on Su 6am-2pm.)*

CASA HUMBOLDT. Bas-reliefs in Moorish *mudéjar* style decorate this 18th-century colonial home, which continues to get mileage out of being a rest stop for explorer Alexander von Humboldt one night in 1803. The house now holds the collection of the **Museo de Arte Virreinal,** including exhibits on 18th-century Catholic rituals and dress. *(Alarcón 12, past Hotel los Arcos. ☎622 5501. Open Su 10am-3:45pm, Tu-Sa 10am-6:45pm. 15 pesos, students 10 pesos, children 5 pesos.)*

CASA BORDA. Once the 18th-century home of José de la Borda, the Casa now serves as the **Instituto Guerrerense de Cultura.** In addition to a library, a dance studio, and several galleries, the center hosts book readings and concerts. Ask for a schedule. *(Enter on the zócalo. ☎622 6617. Open Su 10am-4pm, M-Sa 10am-8pm.)*

EX-CONVENTO DE SAN BERNARDINO. Built in 1592 as a Franciscan monastery and destroyed in a fire, the Ex-convento was reconstructed in Neoclassical style in 1823. The struggle for independence officially ended when the Plan de Iguala was signed here in 1821. Today a school convenes under the hallowed roof. *(In Plaza del Convento. Follow Juárez past city offices. Open daily 8am-1pm and 2-6:30pm. Free.)*

MUSEO GUILLERMO SPRATLING. Named for American smith William Spratling, who helped jolt the silver industry in the 1930s, this anthropology museum shows his collection of prehistoric indigenous artifacts. *(Delgado 1. Follow the road downhill; the museum is to the left of the Cathedral. Open Su 9am-3pm, M-Sa 10am-5pm. 25 pesos.)*

VIEWS OF TAXCO. The vistas of the city and surrounding hills are best from the **Church of Guadalupe.** From the *zócalo*, take Cayem, to the right of Cuauhtémoc, to Guadalupe, and veer right until you reach the plaza before the church. The walk is very steep, even for Taxco, so you may want to grab a "Guadalupe" *combi*, or take a cab. For a more sweeping view, take a **cable car** to Hotel Monte Taxco. *(Take a "Los Arcos" combi for 3.5 pesos to the white arches at the city's entrance. Before passing through the arches, turn left up a hill, and bear left into the parking lot. ☎622 1468. Cable car runs daily 7:40am-7pm. Round-trip 30 pesos, children 19 pesos, hotel guests free.)*

🎵 🎭 ENTERTAINMENT AND NIGHTLIFE

As shops shut up tight and vendors pack their wares, people head to **Plaza Borda,** in front of the illuminated cathedral. Those with enough energy to dance after hiking Taxco's hills will get their chance at **Windows,** in Hotel Monte Taxco. Accessible only by taxi after 7pm, this bar/dance club offers party atmosphere with an unparalleled view. (☎622 1300. Cover 50 pesos. Open F-Su 10:30pm-late.) For a more relaxed evening, try **La Concha Nostra** for beer (15 pesos) and great conversation.

Taxco's crowded streets somehow manage to accommodate the hordes of tourists that descend on the town during its two major festivals: **Feria Nacional de la Plata,** a national contest during the first week of November that celebrates silver artisanship, and the more popular *Semana Santa* festivities. On Good Friday, hooded *penitentes* process through the streets carrying logs made out of cactus trunks on their shoulders, or subject themselves to flagellation to cleanse their sins. During the annual **Día del Jumil,** on the first Monday of November, Taxco residents make a pilgrimage to the Huizteco hill, where they collect and eat insects known as *jumil.* The brown bugs contain more protein per gram than beef and only appear during this time of year. In December, the **Church of Guadalupe,** from which you can see all of Taxco, comes alive with celebrations of the Virgin.

🖐 SHOPPING

More than 300 *platerías* cater to the steady stream of tourists drawn to Taxco by its silver sheen. If you're dipping uncomfortably deep into your pockets, browse the shops that sell *artesanías* as well as silver, and stop by **Mercado Tetitlán,** behind the Cathedral, (Open daily 8:30am-8pm.) **Mercado de Plata,** just behind the Flecha Roja station, is where locals buy the work of silversmiths from the countryside, who often sell fine goods at cheaper prices. (Open Sa 10am-6pm.)

🞂 DAYTRIPS FROM TAXCO

▓**GRUTAS DE CACAHUAMILPA.** Some of the most beautiful natural wonders in Taxco lie in an extensive network of underground *grutas.* Stalactites, stalagmites, and other formations fill twenty huge *salones* (halls). The columns and ceilings—some as high as 85m—are the work of a subterranean stream that developed into the **Río San Jerónimo.** A guide will point out funny rock shapes and tell fabricated

ALL THAT GLITTERS... Although unscrupulous sellers and cheating craftspeople occasionally pass off *alpaca* (fool's silver) or *plateados* (silver plated metals) to unsuspecting tourists, buying silver in Taxco is usually a sure thing. Many proprietors speak English and accept US currency, but if you stick with Spanish and talk in pesos while bargaining, you lower the risk of being charged tourist prices. While it's fun to ogle glamorous silver in the shops around Plaza Borda, the silver gets less expensive and the employees more amenable to bargaining farther from the *centro.* Bargain at stores with silver workshops by faking out the clerk and heading straight for the artisan. Remember that only the official ".925" stamp on the object's side guarantees that your shiny new charm is indeed silver.

anecdotes, which may not entertain for long. According to lore, the *grutas* were once a hideaway for runaway Indians. *(15-peso "grutas" combis leave every hr. from Taxco's Flecha Roja station, stopping at the parking lot. Taxis cost 80-100 pesos. Flecha Roja buses make the 30min. trip every hr. 6:30am-3:30am for 17 pesos, but will drop you off a bit away. To get to the grutas parking lot, take a right, then another right after the curve. ☎ 734 346 1716. Open daily 10am-5pm. 30 pesos, children 5-12 20 pesos; private guides 150 pesos. Two-hr. tours leave from the visitors center every hr. You can only enter the caves with a tour guide.)*

LAS GRANADAS. Located 26km from Taxco, this ecological reserve is little more than a hike in the woods. This 5km rock trail curls around mountain tops and dips into the valley, bringing hikers to a stunning waterfall. The path is hilly and sunny, so wear comfortable shoes and sunblock. *(Grab a 40min. combi heading to Acuitlapan every 15min. 7am-8pm for 10 pesos. Once there, follow the one road into town. As you enter the main square, look to the far end where the path starts as a dirt road. No set hours. Free.)*

IXCATEOPÁN. 42km from Taxco, the **Templo de Santa María de la Asunción** in Ixcateopán is supposedly the final resting place of Cuauhtémoc, the last Aztec emperor. While a far cry from Tenochtitlán, the marble and stone streets are part of a peaceful setting for the bones, whoever they belonged to. *(1¼hr. "Ixcateopán" combis leave every 30min. 6am-9pm for 19 pesos from in front of Seguro Social on J.F. Kennedy.)*

ZIHUATANEJO AND IXTAPA ☎755

Before resort engineers got their hands on Ixtapa, it was a wild landscape filled with coconut palms, rocky cliffs, and mangrove swamps. Not until the 1970s, when development began on "The Place of the White Sands," did both Ixtapa and its counterpart, Zihuatanejo (see-wah-tah-NEH-ho), find themselves on the tourist circuit. Today, the towns' combined population of about 85,000 thrives almost exclusively on the tourist trade. Ixtapa has been meticulously constructed by Mexican pleasure-engineers catering to moneyed foreigners. Budget accommodations are non-existent amid the sprawling resorts, and cheap food and fun are carefully hidden. Meanwhile, Zihuatanejo, just a 15min. bus ride away, has yet to shake off the net of its fishing town past. Here, budget hotels are steps from the glittering beach. The differences between Ixtapa and Zihuatanejo make a trip here feel like two vacations in one. If you stay in Zihuatanejo and play in Ixtapa, these twins will supply tourist-town glitz with prices and relaxation befitting a fishing village.

▣ TRANSPORTATION

Ixtapa's main road, **Blvd. Ixtapa,** lies past a bundle of waterfront luxury hotels on one side and overpriced stores on the other. **Buses** shuttling between the two cities leave Zihuatanejo from Juárez and Morelos, across from the yellow Elektra store, and Ixtapa from various points on Blvd. Ixtapa (15-25min., daily 6am-10pm, 4 pesos). **Taxis** make the trip between the towns (30 pesos by day, 40 pesos by night) and, in Zihuatanejo, can be found on Juárez, in front of the market.

Airport: (☎554 2070), 15km outside of town. Taxis leave from the airport for Zihuatanejo (150 pesos) and Ixtapa (190 pesos). *Combis* depart from the left side of the airport parking lot to the intersection of Morelos and Juárez in Zihuatanejo (6am-11pm, 4 pesos). You can catch *combis*, marked with a picture of a plane, to the airport from the intersection of González and Juárez in Zihuatanejo (6:30am-10:30pm, 4 pesos). Served by: **America West** (☎554 8634; open Su noon-4pm, M-Sa 9am-5pm); **Continental** (☎554 2549 or 554 4217; open daily 9am-5pm); and **Mexicana**, in Ixtapa (☎554 2227; open daily 8am-8pm) and Zihuatanejo, Guerrero at Bravo (☎554 2208 or 554 2209; open M-Sa 9am-7pm).

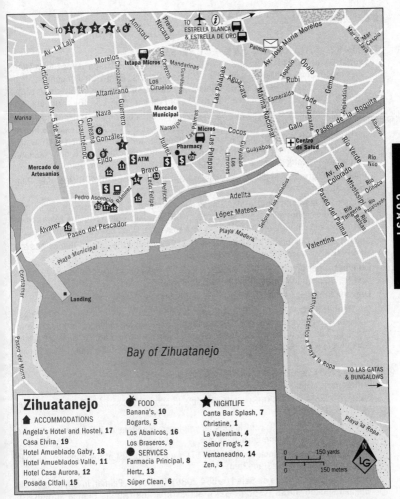

SOUTHERN PACIFIC COAST

Zihuatanejo

♠ ACCOMMODATIONS
Angela's Hotel and Hostel, **17**
Casa Elvira, **19**
Hotel Amueblado Gaby, **18**
Hotel Amueblados Valle, **11**
Hotel Casa Aurora, **12**
Posada Citlali, **15**

♥ FOOD
Banana's, **10**
Bogarts, **5**
Los Abanicos, **16**
Los Braseros, **9**
● SERVICES
Farmacia Principal, **8**
Hertz, **13**
Súper Clean, **6**

★ NIGHTLIFE
Canta Bar Splash, **7**
Christine, **1**
La Valentina, **4**
Señor Frog's, **2**
Ventaneadno, **14**
Zen, **3**

Buses: arrive in Zihuatanejo at the **Estrella Blanca** and **Estrella de Oro** stations, side-by-side on the outskirts of the *centro*. *Combis* (4 pesos), across the street as you leave the station, or taxis (15 pesos) bring you to the center of town. To reach the bus station from the *centro*, hop on a *combi* labeled "Coacoyul" (7am-8:30pm, 4 pesos) across from the market on Juárez. **Estrella de Oro** (☎554 2175) sends buses to: **Acapulco** (5hr., every hr. 5:50am-5pm, 73 pesos); **Cuernavaca** (7hr., 6:40pm, 251 pesos); **Mexico City** (9hr.; 8am, 10pm; 305 pesos); **Papanoa** (1½hr., every hr. 3:45am-7:49pm, 24 pesos). **Estrella Blanca** (☎554 3477) goes to: **Acapulco** (4hr., every hr. 7am-9:35pm, 94 pesos); **Lázaro Cárdenas** (2½hr., every 3hr. 1am-7:30pm, 47 pesos); **Puerto Escondido** (12hr., 7:30pm, 290 pesos).

⓲ PRACTICAL INFORMATION

TOURIST, FINANCIAL, AND LOCAL SERVICES

Tourist Office: SEFOTUR (☎553 1967), on Blvd. Ixtapa, in Ixtapa across from Hotel Presidente. Some English spoken. Open M-F 8am-8pm, Sa 8am-2pm. For complaints or emergencies, call the **Agencia de Ministerio Público en Atención al Turista** in Ixtapa (☎554 5641) or Zihuatanejo (☎354 5641), or **Profeco** (☎554 5236) in Zihuatanejo.

Currency Exchange: Bancomer (☎554 7492), in Zihuatanejo on the corner of Juárez and Bravo. Open M-F 8:30am-4pm, Sa 10am-2pm. Also has a 24hr. **ATM. Money Exchange,** Galeana 6 (☎554 2800), has worse rates but no commission. From the beach, walk a block on Cuauhtémoc, take a right on Ascencio, and make the 1st left onto Galeana. Offers **fax** and **long-distance** service. Open Su 9am-9pm, M-Sa 8am-9pm.

American Express: Heróico Colegio Militar 38, Local 7 (☎554 6242). Open M-F 9am-6pm, Sa 9am-2pm.

Market: The **mercado municipal** in Zihuatanejo on Juárez, 4 blocks from the water, sells fresh produce and has several small eateries. Open daily 6am-7pm. The **Mercado de Artesanías** in Zihuatanejo offers jewelry and souvenirs. Open daily 9am-8:30pm.

Supermarket: Comercial Mexicana (☎483 2184), behind the Estrella Blanca bus station. Take a "Coacoyul" bus. Open daily 8am-10pm.

Laundry: Súper Clean, González 82 (☎554 2347), in Zihuatanejo at Galeana. 12 pesos per kg, 36-peso minimum. Open M-Sa 8am-8pm.

Luggage Storage: Estrella Blanca station in Zihuatanejo. 3 pesos per hr. per bag.

Car Rental: Hertz, Bravo 13 (☎554 2255; fax 554 3050), in Zihuatanejo, rents small VWs for 500 pesos per day including insurance and unlimited mileage. Open daily 8am-6pm. Also has an office in the airport (☎554 2590). **Alamo** (☎553 0206), in the Centro Comercial de los Patios in Ixtapa and at the airport. Open daily 9am-9pm.

EMERGENCY AND COMMUNICATIONS

Emergency: ☎060.

Tourist Police: (☎553 2008), Police Module in Ixtapa, across from Hotel Presidente. Some English spoken.

Red Cross: (☎554 2009), on Huertas as you leave Zihuatanejo. 24hr. emergency and ambulance service. Some English spoken.

Pharmacy: Farmacia Principal (☎554 4217), Cuauhtémoc 29 at the corner of Ejido in Zihuatanejo. Open M-Sa 9am-9pm.

Medical Services: Centro de Salud (☎554 2088), Boquita at Palmar, in Zihuatanejo. No English spoken. **IMSS** (☎554 4824), across from the Estrella Blanca station. No English spoken.

Internet Access: Barnet Zihuatanejo, Ramírez 2. A/C, very fast connections, and plenty of machines. 10 pesos for the first 30min., 20 pesos per hr. In Ixtapa: **Xtapa Connexión** (☎553 2253), Ixtapa Plaza on the walkway to the left of Señor Frog's. 85 pesos per hr., 20 pesos to check email. Open daily 10:30am-10pm.

Fax: Telecomm (☎553 0680; fax 554 3381), beside the Zihuatanejo post office. Fax and **Western Union.** Also next to Señor Frog's in Ixtapa. Open M-F 9am-7pm, Sa-Su 9am-noon.

Post Office: (☎554 2192), off Palmar in Zihuatanejo. From Juárez, turn right on Morelos. At the Pollo Feliz, turn right and walk 2 blocks. Open M-F 8am-3pm, Sa 9am-1pm. **Postal Code:** 40880.

ACCOMMODATIONS

Zihuatanejo has plenty of budget accommodations within a few blocks of the **Playa Municipal**. Prices rise substantially during high season (Dec.-Apr.), as does the number of *gringos* per square foot. If you visit during low season, come with a large group, or plan to stay several days, you will have excellent leverage for negotiating discounts. Many budget places lack hot water, but the cool water that is available is usually refreshing. The tourist office discourages unofficial camping, partly for safety reasons, but if you insist on pitching a tent, **Playa Quieta**, near Club Med in Ixtapa, attracts most campers. All of the following are in Zihuatanejo.

■ **Angela's Hotel and Hostel,** Ascencio 10 (☎554 5084). The sign in front says it all: "Canadian spoken here, poco español, eh." International students and people from all corners are here, relaxing in hammocks, cooking in the well-supplied common kitchen, or making their mark on the courtyard walls. Rooms have private cold-water baths, but a communal hot shower is also available. The owners, Greg and Amanda, welcome guests with open arms. Parking and luggage storage available. Dorms 80 pesos; singles 140 pesos; doubles 175 pesos; suites with kitchen space and bath available for groups of 4-6 80 pesos per person. ❶

Casa Elvira, Álvarez 29 (☎554 2061), 1 block from Playa Municipal. Elvira was the 1st guest house in Zihuatanejo. Rooms are cozy and clean, if a bit small, and have private cold-water baths and strong ceiling fans. The courtyard is full of plants, birds, and gregarious family members; step out back, through the new restaurant (traditional dishes 45-85 pesos, seafood 75-195 pesos), and you're on the beach. Rooms 100-200 pesos, depending on the room and the season; prices often negotiable. ❷

Hotel Amueblados Valle, Guerrero 14 (☎/fax 554 3220 or 554 2084), between Ejido and Bravo. Eight apartments with decently stocked kitchens, couches, ceiling fans, balconies, and daily towel service. Rooms are spacious. 1-3 people May-Nov. 300-350 pesos; Dec.-Apr. 400 pesos. 2-bedroom flat 600 pesos. Prices drop for longer stays. For high season visits, make reservations up to a year in advance. ❺

Hotel Casa Aurora, Bravo 42 (☎554 3046), between Guerrero and Galeana. This tranquil mainstay has a friendly staff and good-sized rooms. Baths are clean and have hot water. Singles 200 pesos; doubles 250 pesos, with A/C 350 pesos; triples 450 pesos. Each additional person 50 pesos. Beachside bungalow with kitchen but no A/C at Playa de la Ropa houses 2; 300 pesos. ❹

Posada Citlali, Guerrero 3 (☎554 2043), near Álvarez. Pricey. Vines droop lazily in the courtyard, and wooden rockers on the terrace encourage you to follow suit. All rooms have overhead fans. Singles 250 pesos; doubles 300 pesos; triples 350 pesos. ❺

Hotel Amueblado Gaby, Ascencio 15 (☎554 2395). The cheapest apartment-style suites. Spacious rooms have A/C or ceiling fans, kitchenettes, and bamboo-styled living room sets. Single/double (1-2 people) 250 pesos; triple/quad (up to 4) 400 pesos. ❹

FOOD

Like the hotels, restaurants in Ixtapa are pricey; however, they serve an array of authentic-tasting international cuisine. Your meal may be more reasonably priced if you eat at a cafe before it switches to the main menu (around 2pm). Restaurants in Zihuatanejo consistently serve fish fresh from the bay at budget prices.

Los Abanicos (☎554 2020), on the corner of Ascencio and Galeana, by Angela's Hotel. This open-air restaurant may look like all the rest in Zihuatanejo, but the food here is cheap and delicious—the *comida corrida* (35 pesos), with a choice of 3 rotating entrees, rice or soup, tortillas, and *agua fresca*, is the best deal on the beach. Great *ceviche* 40 pesos. Open M-Sa 8am-6pm. ❸

Los Braseros, Ejido 26 (☎554 8736), between Galeana and Guerrero. This exuberant open-air eatery specializes in myriad heavenly stir-fried combinations of meat, vegetables, and cheese (usually 52 pesos); everything, down to the purple tortillas, is made to order. Large portions with the refreshing *horchata* make a very satisfying meal. ❹

Banana's, Bravo 4 (☎556 1080 or 556 5103). Locals flock here for the great breakfast combos. Eggs any style with fruit juice or coffee 20 pesos (with meat 25 pesos). The *comida corrida* (30 pesos) has a variety of main course options. Chicken and beef fajitas 50 pesos, seafood 35-70 pesos. Open daily 8am-4pm. ❷

Taquería Chai (☎559 0931), in the Mercado Hacienda, in the corner of Plaza Playa Azul by Andadero de los Hermanos. Good, cheap food. Friendly staff serves hot tacos (4 pesos) and great *agua de jamaica* (5 pesos). Open daily 9:30am-noon. ❶

Bogarts, on Blvd. Ixtapa next to Krystal Hotel (☎553 0333). This is not a cheap gin joint; it is, however, a chance to step into Bogie's most famous movie. Moroccan decorations, a central fountain, and white piano add class, and the fez-wearing waiters are unmistakable. All entrees well over 100 pesos. Open daily 6pm-midnight. ❺

🏖 👁 BEACHES AND SIGHTS

Neither Zihuatanejo's self-conscious charm nor Ixtapa's resorts can eclipse the area's natural beauty. In Zihuatanejo, four patches of sand serve as excellent beaches. They are, clockwise from the municipal pier: **Playa Principal, Playa Madera, Playa la Ropa,** and **Playa las Gatas;** the latter two are easily the best beaches in Zihuatanejo. Ixtapa overlooks the unbroken stretch of **Playa del Palmar** on the Bahía del Palmar, but less heavily touristed beaches lie beyond Laguna de Ixtapa: **Playa Quieta, Playa Linda,** and, at the bay's west edge, **Isla Ixtapa.**

ZIHUATANEJO

PLAYA PRINCIPAL. Playa Principal is downtown Zihuatanejo's beach, in front of the Paseo del Pescador; this beach is more suited to seashell collectors and fishing boats than swimmers, who may have trouble with the many fishing boats. The attractions here are the basketball court, pier, and fish being unloaded at the dock.

PLAYA MADERA. About 200m long, Playa Madera (Wood Beach) was named for being a loading site for local hardwood export. The fine sand and moderate waves show no trace of the beach's lumberyard past, but offer a great place to body surf or play in the waves. Restaurants and bungalows populate the shore, and posh hotels lie off to one side. *(To get there, follow the cement path at the end of Playa Principal.)*

PLAYA LA ROPA. Protected from the rough Pacific by the bay, Playa la Ropa's crescent of sumptuous, white, often-uncrowded sand is the main attraction for tourists from the hotels on the surrounding cliffs. *(Take a "Ropa" bus from along Juárez; 6am-7pm, 4 pesos. You can also make the 4km trip by foot: follow Paseo de la Boquita along the canal over the bridge and turn left, passing Playa Madera. The road curves to the right, past Hotel Casa que Canta; follow the stone road to the left down to the beach. If you're planning on leaving late, you may want to arrange a taxi pick-up beforehand; 20 pesos. Waveriders 350 pesos per 30min., parasailing 200 pesos per 10min.)*

PLAYA LAS GATAS. According to local tales, Purepecha king Calzontzín ordered the construction of the stone wall in Playa las Gatas as protection from the sharks while he bathed. Since then, coral and marine life have overtaken the stone barricade that divides the crystalline waters. Equally colorful, but not nearly as beautiful, lawn chairs and umbrellas from local restaurants (free if you order food;

farther from the dock, some may waive this condition) have invaded the beach. The calm waters welcome snorkelers (equipment rental 40 pesos per day) and kayakers (single-person kayaks 100 pesos per hr., 150 pesos per day). Escape the shops and restaurants by taking the path (2km) behind the last restaurant to the **Garrobo Lighthouse** for a panoramic view. Since it's well hidden, ask any of the waiters for specific directions. *(To reach Las Gatas, take a lancha from the pier in downtown Zihuatanejo (10min., every 15min. 9am-4pm, round-trip 30 pesos; last boat returns 5pm). It is possible to walk over the rocks to Las Gatas from La Ropa, but not easy. Alternatively, you may walk on the road that brought you to La Ropa for another 45min., keeping to the left as it splits.)*

IXTAPA

PLAYA DE PALMAR. Well guarded from Blvd. Ixtapa by a line of posh hotels, Playa de Palmar is an active, spacious, and beautiful beach. Walk a few kilometers on the soft golden sand or join in one of the casual volleyball or soccer games played near the hotel pools. Without the protection of a bay, sizeable waves besiege the beach, attracting parasailers, scuba divers, and jet skiers; the soft sand is good for romantic walks at twilight. *(The beach can be reached by public access paths at either end, near Barcelo's resort or to the right of the Krystal Hotel. Otherwise, clutch your Let's Go confidently, wear your swimsuit proudly, and cut right through the fancy hotel lobbies—this may work best when you're leaving the beach.)*

PLAYA QUIETA AND PLAYA LINDA. About 6km northwest of downtown lie Playas Quieta and Linda. The calm waves of these twin beaches, separated by a large pier, attract both ritzy hotel patrons and pick-up trucks of Mexican families. One or two restaurants near the pier rent horses for around 140 pesos per hr. *(From Ixtapa, follow Blvd. Ixtapa northwest beyond most of the hotels, and turn right at the "Playa Linda" sign. From Zihuatanejo, it is more convenient to use the access road from Mex. 200: take the left, marked Playa Linda, beyond the exit for Ixtapa as you head towards Puerto Vallarta. The road skirts Laguna de Ixtapa and hits the beach farther northwest. Taxis from Ixtapa 40 pesos, from Zihuatanejo 70 pesos. A "Playa Linda" bus from either town visits the two beaches (5 pesos). Buses return to Ixtapa and Zihuatanejo approx. every 15min. until 7pm (4-5 pesos). You can also follow the bicycle path along the road for 4km.)*

ISLA IXTAPA. Some of the most picturesque beaches lie on **Isla Ixtapa**, 2km offshore from Playa Quieta; it is at least a must-visit for snorkeling enthusiasts. Facing the mainland, many restaurants take advantage of the captive audience. The main beach is **Playa Cuachalalate**, frequented by fishermen and waterskiers. **Playa Varadero** is a small beach with calm waters and *palapa* restaurants. On the ocean side of the island, **Playa Coral**, is the least-visited of the three. It has no services and poor swimming, but the coral makes for excellent scuba diving. *(Catch a microbus from Zihuatanejo or Ixtapa to get to the pier at Playa Linda, 4-5 pesos. From there, catch a lancha. Every 15min. 9am-5pm, round-trip 30 pesos.)*

◙ NIGHTLIFE

Although beaches in both towns promise spectacular sun, sand, and waves, the only place to go for crazy nightlife is Ixtapa. **Blvd. Ixtapa,** like most resort strips, is littered with fancy clubs and relaxed bars that rock to the beat of young people; karaoke is the most popular pastime in Zihuatanejo.

IXTAPA

Christine (☎553 0456), Blvd. Ixtapa in front of Hotel Krystal. With stadium-like seats around the dance floor and a light show, Christine is as artificially beautiful as Ixtapa itself. Beer 35 pesos, *bebidas nacionales* 50 pesos. M-Th no cover; F-Sa men 200 pesos, women 100 pesos. Open bar Su 250 pesos, W 300 pesos; women 50 pesos less. Th ladies' night, women free. Open daily from 10pm. No shorts on weekends.

Señor Frog's (☎553 2282), in the Ixtapa Commercial Center, may be a restaurant until midnight, but when the clock strikes twelve, drunk Americans climb on tables to begin the party. Spiral fans whirring at top speed and beers (31 pesos) keep it cool. *Bebidas nacionales* 35 pesos, yard-long drinks 94 pesos. No cover. Open daily 6pm-3am.

La Valentina (☎553 1190 or 552 1250), on Blvd. Ixtapa by the Radisson. The beautiful and scantily clad gather here to pretend they are vacationing in Europe. The villa-style interior looks onto a faux landscape, complete with flashing electric stars and ringed with columns. Open bar. Cover for men 140 pesos, for women 120 pesos; prices rise by 80 pesos during *Semana Santa,* 40 pesos July-Aug. and Dec. Open daily 10pm-5am.

Zen (☎553 0003 or 553 3124), on the Blvd. Ixtapa by the Radisson. Young, rich, and self-consciously urbane hipsters lounge amid couches and modern art. Psychedelic projections swirl as techno pounds in the background. Drinks 30-35 pesos. Cover 130 pesos; no cover July-Aug., men 200 pesos and women 100 pesos in Dec. and *Semana Santa.* Open Tu-Su 10pm-3am.

ZIHUATANEJO

Ventaneando, Bravo 23 (☎554 5390), across from D'Latino. This dark, smoky bar on the third floor is the natural departure point for exploring Zihuatanejo's thriving karaoke scene. Outside of karaoke, hip Spanish music plays; as anywhere, karaoke brings out the cheesy ballads. Things pick up after midnight, when amateur singers strut their stuff. Beer 25 pesos, bucket of 5 beers 90 pesos. No cover. Open daily 9pm-4am.

Canta Bar Splash, Guerrero between Ejido and González. This pint-sized place feels like an aquarium, with painted fish and blue lights washing over the 20-something crowd seated at the bar and in the balconies. Sip a beer (25 pesos) or a mixed drink (35 pesos) as you croon to the Mexican ballad of your choice. Open daily 7pm-3am.

COSTA GRANDE

The Guerrero coast north of Acapulco is often called the Costa Grande, pairing it with a smaller counterpart, Costa Chica, to the south. Though the stretch from Acapulco to Zihuatanejo/Ixtapa has few inviting beaches, ▨**Barra de Potosí,** 20km southeast of Zihuatanejo, and **Papanoa,** 60km farther along Mex. 200, are hidden treasures ideal for wasting the day in the waves.

BARRA DE POTOSÍ   ☎755

For the traveler whose head is spinning from ruins, cathedrals, and kitsch, no better tonic exists than a spell on the seemingly infinite stretch of sand known as **Playa Barra de Potosí.** This small town consists of a shallow lagoon, a forest of palm trees, and waterfront huts; overlooked by developers, it seems caught in perpetual *siesta.* Some of the more exciting activities include taking a dip in the lagoon and wandering over beach; the crashing waves supply some energy to the coast, but it is easy to swim past the break point to water that is peaceful and crystal clear. Eat until you're full, settle into the sand, snooze on a hammock in the shade, and slow down to properly become one with the Mexican earth.

▣ **TRANSPORTATION.** From Zihuatanejo, "Petatlán" or "Peta" buses leave for Potosí from a station on Las Palmas, by Ejido and Juárez (30min., every 15min. 6am-9pm, 6 pesos). Ask to be let off at **Achotes,** a *pueblito* announced by a single black-and-white sign. A pick-up truck will be waiting (or arriving soon) on the side road to collect passengers for the bumpy trip to the *enramadas* by the coast

(30min., 8 pesos). Trucks return to the intersection from the same spot (daily 7am-6pm). The bus to Zihuatanejo leaves from the other side of the route.

ACCOMMODATIONS AND FOOD. Those unskilled in the art of beachside hammock-napping can splurge at **Hotel Barra de Potosí ❺**, a small-scale resort hotel and recent addition to the pristine beach. From the *enramadas* (open-air seaside restaurants), walk away from the lagoon—you can't miss the large white building with blue balconies. Not all rooms have the same amenities, but all have access to the beachside swimming pool and restaurant. (☎556 8434. Singles 250 pesos; doubles 300 pesos; suite 600 pesos.) Next door, **Casa Puesta del Sol ❺** has apartment-style rooms that can be a good deal for groups. (Suites start at 350 pesos.)

There are ten or so **enramadas ❹**, which serve simple seafood dishes at reasonable prices. Enjoy home-cooked food while relaxing in one of the hammocks swinging in the shaded restaurants. In keeping with the casual spirit, some do not have set menus, instead asking you what type of seafood you'd like to eat (expect to spend 50-120 pesos per person). *Enramadas* that face the lagoon offer slightly lower prices, but beware: the lagoon is smelly. (Open daily 7am-6pm.)

SIGHTS AND BEACHES. If you insist on exerting yourself, the only option is to hike up the dirt road to the "lighthouse" atop **Cerro Guamiule** (200m), which guards the southern entrance to the bay. The hill offers a view over the bay and 20km of beaches, but the ascent can be treacherous (particularly when it's wet), and frequently mosquitoes will prevent you from enjoying the view. Worst of all, the *faro* is not so much a lighthouse as a bare bulb on a metal hulk. Your time is much better spent actually on the beaches. To the north of the southernmost beach on the bay, **Playa Potosí,** is the aptly named **Playa Blanca** (White Beach, 3km). Farther up the coast are **Playa Coacoyul** (8km), **Playa Riscaliyo** (19km), and pebbly **Playa Manzanillo** (24km), before a lighthouse (26km) overlooking the northern edge of the bay. All beaches are free of tourists in the summer months but fill with hundreds of domestic visitors during Christmas.

PAPANOA   ☎755

Papanoa is a tiny, delectable town with rolling waves and even less attention than Barra de Potosí. Pigs and roosters scuttle along a road that ends in waterfront *enramadas.* **Cayaquitos,** 2km from town, is the most accessible beach and draws the most people. On the other side of the Hotel Papanoa is the much smaller **Ojo de Agua,** where a ring of hills engenders a feeling of seclusion. Seaside cliffs give **Playa Vicente Guerrero,** 5km away, a more dramatic aspect. Although this beach lacks the crowds (and occasional garbage) of Cayaquitos, it has far more restaurants, all battling to fill your belly with the day's catch. Though there are cheaper places also right on the beach, **Los Arcos ❹** is one of the most attractive options, with a choice of tables and hammocks beneath the palm roof, and even a pool to go along with a variety of *antojitos* (30-55 pesos) and seafood. (60-155 pesos. Open daily 8:30am-8pm.)

TRANSPORTATION. Buses leave from the **Estrella Blanca** station in Zihuatanejo (1½hr., every hr. 3:45am-7:49pm, 28 pesos); frequently, drivers will leave passengers at Cayaquitos at no extra cost. In Papanoa, white trucks pick up passengers under the large tree across the street and to the left of the bus drop-off (6am-7pm, 6 pesos). **Taxis** run to Cayaquitos (15 pesos) and to Vicente Guerrero (30 pesos). If you plan to leave the beach later than 7pm, arrange ahead of time for a taxi to come for you.

ACAPULCO

☎ 744

Once upon a time, Acapulco (pop. 2 million) was a stunningly beautiful playground for the rich and famous. Hollywood legends celebrated their successes here, dancing the nights away in chic clubs, and the privileged few spent their honeymoons lounging on the seductive shores. But times change and fairy tales fade; today, Acapulco is a mere shadow of the luxurious retreat it once was. The city now consists of a crowded beach flanked by tightly packed 14-story hotels, and the slum that starts behind them stretches up the hill. This grimmer Acapulco was born when the flow of vacationers slowed and the hotel job market could no longer keep pace with the waves of immigrants drawn seaward by the prospect of plentiful pesos. Money still controls Acapulco, but now the focus is on pursuit, not spending. Persistent cabbies and peddlers of everything from bubble gum to "free information" run at tourists like eager bulls. Though the high-rise hotels crowding the waterfront have lost their flush of youth, a full roster of festivals and beautification projects promises a revamped Acapulco. Until those projects come to fruition, perhaps it's best to visit the city at night, when darkness shrouds the grime and street lamps evoke a fairy-tale past.

▐ TRANSPORTATION

Airport: Mex. 200, 26km south of the city. Taxis make the run to the airport for 90 pesos; shared cabs (☎462 1095) will do it for 70 pesos. Served by **Aerolíneas Internacionales** (☎486 5630), **Aeroméxico** (☎485 1625), **American** (☎466 9232), **America West** (☎800 235 9292), **Continental** (☎466 9063), and **Mexicana** (☎486 7585).

Buses: Acapulco has 3 bus stations. To get from the **Estrella de Oro station** (☎485 8705), on Cuauhtémoc at Massiu, to the *zócalo* (40min.), cross the street and catch any bus labeled "Zócalo" (3.5 pesos). Taxis charge 30-40 pesos. Estrella de Oro sends buses to: **Cuernavaca** (4hr., every hr. 6am-8pm, 190 pesos); **Mexico City** (5hr., every hr. 6am-2am, 230 pesos); **Taxco** (4hr., every 4hr. 7am-9pm, 120 pesos); **Zihuatanejo** (4hr., every hr. 4:15am-5:30pm, 70 pesos). **Estrella Blanca** has 2 stations: **Centro Papagayo** (☎469 2081), Cuauhtémoc behind Parque Papagayo, and **Centro Ejido** (☎469 2028), on Ejido north of the *zócalo*. The *ejecutivo* class buses leave from Papagayo and travel to: **Cuernavaca** (4hr.; 2:20, 7:30, 11:30am, 5pm; 207 pesos); **Mexico City** (5hr., every hr. on the half hr., 245 pesos); **Puebla** (7hr.; 3, 10pm, midnight; 362 pesos). To get to Centro Papagayo from the *zócalo,* take a "CICI" bus (3.5 pesos) to Parque Papagayo. Cross the park—the bus station is on Cuauhtémoc behind the park. All other buses leave from **Ejido**—just an "Ejido" bus ride (3.5 pesos) away from the *zócalo*. To get to the *zócalo* from either station, take a "Zócalo" bus.

✴ ▐ ORIENTATION AND PRACTICAL INFORMATION

Acapulco Bay lies 400km south of Mexico City and 239km southeast of Ixtapa and Zihuatanejo. Mex. 200 becomes **La Costera** (Costera Miguel Alemán), the main drag that crosses all of Acapulco. **Acapulco Dorado**, or Zona Dorada, is full of restaurants, malls, and hotels; it stretches from **Parque Papagayo** to the naval base. The ultra-chic resorts are on **Acapulco Diamante**, farther east. Budget accommodations and restaurants lie between the *zócalo* and **La Quebrada,** the famous cliff-diving spot. Trying to walk the main drag will suck hours from your beach time, so get familiar with the basics of public transportation. **Buses** run along Costera from Playa "Hornos" or Playa "Caleta" in the west to "CICI" or "Base" in the east and back (3.5 pesos, 4 pesos for an air-conditioned yellow bus). Along Cuauhtémoc, buses run between "Cine Río" in the west and "La Base" in the east (3.5 pesos).

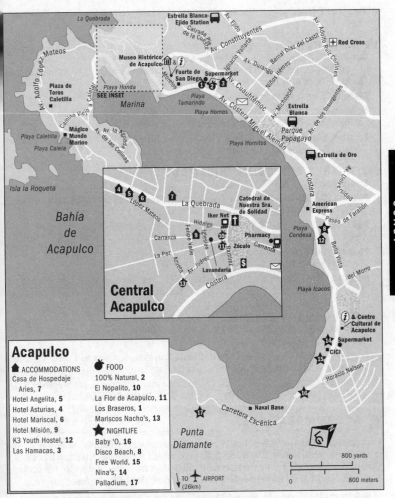

Acapulco

⌂ ACCOMMODATIONS
Casa de Hospedaje
Aries, **7**
Hotel Angelita, **5**
Hotel Asturias, **4**
Hotel Mariscal, **6**
Hotel Misión, **9**
K3 Youth Hostel, **12**
Las Hamacas, **3**

♥ FOOD
100% Natural, **2**
El Nopalito, **10**
La Flor de Acapulco, **11**
Los Braseros, **1**
Mariscos Nacho's, **13**

★ NIGHTLIFE
Baby 'O, **16**
Disco Beach, **8**
Free World, **15**
Nina's, **14**
Palladium, **17**

TOURIST AND FINANCIAL SERVICES

Tourist Offices: SEFOTUR, Costera 4455 (☎484 4583 or 484 4416), in the Centro Cultural de Acapulco, diagonally across from the CICI water park. Helpful staff will overload you with brochures and maps. English spoken. Open daily 9am-11pm. In an emergency, contact the **Procuraduría del Turista** in the same office.

Consulates: Canada (☎484 1305), Centro Comercial Plaza Maravilla, Local 23 at Pologación. Open M-F 9am-5pm. **UK** (☎481 1699), in the Casa Consular-Costera. Open M-F 1-3pm and 4-8pm. **US,** Costera 121, #14 (☎469 0556), in the Continental Hotel. Open M-F 10am-2pm.

Currency Exchange: Banks on Costera have good rates. Open M-F 9am-4pm, most with 24hr. **ATMs. BBVA Bancomer,** at the *zócalo* (☎482 2097). Open M-F 8:30am-4pm, Sa 10am-2pm. **Casas de cambio** line Costera and most stay open until 8pm.

American Express: Miguel Alemán 709 (☎ 483 6968). Open M-F 10am-7pm, Sa 10am-3pm.

LOCAL SERVICES

Car Rental: Hertz, Costera 137 (☎ 485 6889), across from Universidad Americana. Small VW with insurance 575 pesos per day. Open daily 8am-8pm. 2nd location at the airport is open daily 6am-10pm. Others available on Costera.

Market: Constituyentes at Hurtado. Open daily 6am-6pm.

Supermarket: Comercial Mexicana (☎ 484 3373), has 2 locations on Costera, one east of the tourist office and the other 4 blocks east of the *zócalo*. Open daily 8am-11pm.

Laundry: Súper Lavandería, José María Iglesias 9 (☎ 480 0146), between Paz and Hidalgo. 38 pesos per 4kg. Open M-Sa 8:30am-8:30pm.

EMERGENCY AND COMMUNICATIONS

Emergency: ☎ 060 or 066.

Police: LOCATEL (☎ 481 1100) No English spoken. **Tourist Police** (☎ 485 0490) wander the *zócalo*. Some English spoken.

Red Cross: Ruiz Cortines 126 (☎ 445 8178), north of the *zócalo*. Take a "Hospital" bus. Some English spoken.

Pharmacy: Botica de Acapulco, Carranza 3 (☎ 783 8429), a block from the *zócalo*. Open daily 6am-10pm.

Hospital: IMSS, Ruiz Cortines 128 (☎ 445 5377), north of the *zócalo* along Madero. Take a "Hospital" bus. No English spoken. **Sociedad de Asistencia Médica Turística** (☎ 485 5800), in the condominiums across from Plaza Bahía. English spoken.

Internet: Cybercafe IKER NET (ikernet@hotmail.com), upstairs at the corner of Carranza and Escudero, 1 block east of the *zócalo*. Faster connection than most (of the many) in Acapulco. 10 pesos per hr. Open daily 8am-11pm.

Telephones: LADATELs line the Costera. **Caseta Carranza,** Carranza 9, 1 block from the *zócalo*, also has a **fax.** Open M-F 9am-7pm, Sa 9am-3pm.

Post Office: Costera 215 (☎ 482 6321), 2 blocks east of the *zócalo*, in the Palacio Federal. Open M-F 9am-3pm and 4-6pm, Sa 9am-2pm. **Postal Code:** 39300.

♜ ACCOMMODATIONS

Camping on Acapulco's beaches is relatively unsafe. Fortunately, although a far cry from the posh hotels, cheap, no-frills places near the *zócalo* (particularly along Quebrada) provide a haven for international budget travelers. Rates double during *Semana Santa* and late December, and it's a good idea to make reservations.

■ **Hotel Asturias,** Quebrada 45 (☎ 483 6548), up the hill to the left behind the *zócalo*. Powerful ceiling fans, firm queen mattresses, and clean private baths provide an oasis in the frenzied city. Guests drink, relax, and converse in a well-tended courtyard or the pool. Ring the bell after 11pm to return. Singles 140 pesos; doubles 200 pesos; triples 270 pesos. Renovated rooms with A/C and TV cost a little over 100 pesos extra. ❷

Hotel Misión, Felipe Valle 12 (☎ 482 3643), at La Paz, 2 blocks left of the *zócalo* as you face the church. Guests chatting or relaxing in the vine-hung courtyard, traditional decoration, and welcome quiet give Misión a homey feel; the seatless toilets help mitigate that feeling somewhat. Rooms have fans and tiled baths, some have desks and sofas. Singles 150 pesos; doubles 300 pesos. ❸

Hotel Angelita, Quebrada 37 (☎ 483 5734), behind the cathedral, 2 doors from Hotel Asturias. The hallways are packed with tropical plants (live and artificial) and the spotless rooms are packed with perks. Brightly painted blue walls, tiled baths, purified water, top sheets, and a comfy lobby with cable TV make your life easier. Get lucky with multiple room fans. Singles 100 pesos; doubles 150 pesos. ❷

K3 Youth Hostel, Costera 116 (☎481 3111 and 481 3133; www.k3acapulco.com), across from hip Condesa beach. Though the view is obscured, this is the ideal budget answer to the call of La Zona Dorada. Small dorms come with A/C; communal bathrooms are spotless. Internet (20 pesos per hr.), bar, kitchen, and a terrace (to kick back with 30-peso pitchers of beer) over vibrant Costera. 2-bed dorms 150 pesos, plus 100 peso linen deposit; private rooms 525 pesos. Continental breakfast included. ❸

Casa de Hospedaje Aries, Quebrada 30 (☎483 2401). With rooms cheaper than many meals, Casa surprises with queen-size beds, private baths, and strong fans. For a quiet stay, however, head elsewhere—walls that don't reach the ceilings let in all sorts of noise, including rooster cries at dawn. Singles 50 pesos; doubles 100 pesos; triples 150 pesos. ❶

Las Hamacas, Costera 239 (☎483 7006; www.hamacas.com.mx). If powerful fans are not enough for you, Hamacas offers A/C as well as cable TV, phone, and a small terrace looking out towards the restaurant and oddly shaped pool. Singles 600 pesos; doubles 700 pesos; triples 800 pesos. ❻

Hotel Mariscal, Quebrada 35 (☎482 0015), beside Hotel Austurias. Huge balconies off front-facing rooms give you access to whatever welcome breeze there may be, but little in the way of view. Soft mattresses and small TVs with cable will be comfortable for some, but the seat-free toilets and rusting bathrooms may be unpleasant for all. Singles and doubles 120 pesos; triples 180 pesos; six-person suite 350 pesos. ❷

🍴 FOOD

Acapulco's international restaurants cater to tourists' palates, and the chic restaurants between Playa Condesa and the naval base are meant for travelers who don't fret about money. However, interspersed along Costera are many local eateries ready to satisfy any craving, without the high prices. For the cheapest eats, grab a barstool in one of the many *torta* shops on the streets surrounding the *zócalo*.

La Flor de Acapulco, Juárez 1 (☎482 0286), overlooking the *zócalo*. Observe crowds mingling below or look through palms towards the ocean from the terrace of this long-established restaurant (since 1939). Filling *platillos mexicanos* start at 25 pesos, tacos and *quesos* range from 35-40 pesos. For seafood, be prepared to pay upwards of 50 pesos, over 60 pesos for many meat dishes. Open daily 8am-midnight. ❹

Mariscos Nacho's, Azueta 7 (☎482 2891), at Juárez, 1 block west of the *zócalo*. This open-air *marisquería* serves everything from octopus (40 pesos) to baby shark quesadillas (18 pesos), and bustles with sunburned families straggling in from the beach and party-kids dolled up for a night on the town. Open daily 9am-9:30pm. MC/V. ❸

100% Natural, Costera 248 (☎486 2033), at the corner of Vizcaíno. Other branches line the Costera, though the beachside location gives this the greatest allure. A health food restaurant, Natural dishes up versions of Mexican dishes including *molletes* on wheat bread (24 pesos), quesadillas in wheat tortillas (42 pesos), salads (40-48 pesos), soy burgers (42 pesos), and *licuados* (28-35 pesos). Open daily 8am-11pm. MC/V. ❸

El Nopalito, La Paz 230 (☎482 1876), a block off the *zócalo*. This eatery attracts a local crowd with a variety of dishes, only available as part of the *menu del día* (soup of the day, entree, and jello dessert; 28 pesos). Specials of *pozole* (Th) and paella (Su) run 30 pesos. Open daily 8am-7pm. ❷

Los Braseros, Costera 225 (☎483 6516). Traditional decoration welcomes you to traditional meals, including *antojitos* (25-60 pesos), *mariscos* (28-125 pesos), and the mouthwatering specialty of grilled meats, with a dramatic, fiery presentation, served with beans, onions, and guacamole (120 pesos). The Jueves Pozolero show brings green-and-

HE HIDDEN DEAL

ONE PAINFUL CANNONBALL

Hurling oneself half-naked off agged cliffs is not a coming-of-age ritual in Acapulco, but a serious occupation for trained professionals. Not very surprisingly, it's also one of Acapulco's biggest attractions.

At the La Quebrada cliffs around the north side of the bay, *clavadistas*, or cliff divers, perform daily, diving 25-35m off a perilous, jagged stone face and slipping effortlessly into the frothing surf. Although spectators congregate at the bottom level to see the splash, the view of the dive—and what is more beautiful than the arc of the dive itself?—is better from the area to the right of the ticket booth. Besides, those near the bottom are always in danger of seeing a bit more than they paid for: because of the shallowness of the water, the dives must be timed perfectly to hit the cushions of the incoming waves.

As if the dives weren't enough of a show, divers pray rather theatrically (who can blame them?) at a small shrine before the plunge. It's all part of the everyday business of challenging death and impressing the tourists.

To get to La Quebrada, follow López Mateos, the road on your left when facing the Cathedral's entrance. The walk takes about 15min. and ends at the top of a very steep hill. Shows at 7:30, 8:30, 9:30, and 10:30pm (with torches!). 25 pesos.

white *pozole* to your table and look-alikes of Shakira, Thalia, and Pedro Fernández to the stage. Open daily 8am-midnight; shows Th 4:30 and 8:30pm. ❹

El Fogón (☎484 3607), Costera and Yañez, across from the Continental Plaza Hotel. Eat tacos (40 pesos), sandwiches (22-48 pesos), or filling breakfast combos (15-30 pesos) beneath arches and clay pots hanging from the wood beam ceiling. Try the *chilaquiles* (50 pesos), one of many Mexican specialties (48-169 pesos). Open 24hr. ❹

👁 📷 SIGHTS AND BEACHES

If you're in Acapulco, chances are you seek two things: beaches and booze. Have no fear, intrepid traveler—Acapulco delivers. Just keep in mind that you aren't the only one seeking these pleasures. Those in the mood for unadulterated people-watching will be satisfied; just don't be surprised if people watch you back. There are a few chances to get away from sunburn and hangovers: the main museum is the **Museo Histórico de Acapulco**, in the Fuerte de San Diego. The interesting array of exhibits describes daily life, the city's role in national history with the Morelos rebellion, and the port's international prominence, connecting Mexico and Asia through trade and evangelization. (☎482 3828. Open Tu-Su 9:30am-6:30pm. 32 pesos, students free; Su and festival days free.)

PENÍNSULA DE LAS PLAYAS. At the westernmost tip of Acapulco Bay, on the seaward side of the peninsula, lie **Playas Caleta** and **Caletilla**. If you don't mind sharing the sea with small fishing boats, swimming is good in the calm water, though the hundreds of frolicking families make it hard to find empty beachside turf and the water is dirty closer to the restaurants. A narrow road separating the two beaches leads to **Mágico Mundo Marino**, a water park with slides, pools, and a small zoo. You can also take boats to the island **La Roqueta**, with its own zoo, across the bay. *(Boats from Mágico Mundo daily 9am-6pm. 40 pesos. Zoo open M and W-Su 10am-5pm. 5 pesos. Mágico Mundo ☎483 1215. Open daily 9am-6pm. 30 pesos, children 15 pesos.)*

FROM HOTEL LAS HAMACAS TO PARQUE PAPAGAYO. This stretch of sand along the **Costera**, away from Old Acapulco, is blessed with fewer highrises and smaller crowds than other beaches. **Playas Tamarindo, Hornos,** and **Hornitos,** between Las Hamacas Hotel and the Radisson, are called the "afternoon beaches" because fishermen haul in their midday catches here. The waves are moderate and the sand is ideal for beach sports. Nevertheless, urban Acapulco and the Costera do intrude through the thin line of palm trees backing the beach.

Those needing a break from the relentless sun should head to **Parque Papagayo,** sprawling from Costera to Cuauhtémoc. Entering on Costera by the Gigante supermarket, you'll find a roller skating rink, shaded paths for bikers and walkers, and an artificial lake in the center surrounding an aviary. Children will enjoy the wading pool, exotic birds, and zillion spots for hide-and-seek. An amusement park with an assortment of kiddie rides occupies the southeast corner. *(☎ 485 2490. Park open daily 7am-8pm; rink open daily 4-10:30pm. 13 pesos, with skate rental 25 pesos. Amusement park ☎ 485 9623. Open daily 4-11pm. Rides 8 pesos.)*

FROM LA DIANA TO THE NAVAL BASE. A trip to **Playa Condesa,** at the center of the bay, brings you to the sandy center of Acapulco. Strong waves and a rapidly dropping sea floor discourage swimmers but open the waters to windsurfers and jet skiers. Ashore, throngs of sun worshippers lounge under their blue umbrellas (20-30 pesos), while hordes of vendors offer everything from mangos-on-a-stick to bathing suits; by night, the area transforms into a hip nightspot. Farther down, between the golf course and naval base, is **Playa Icacos.** As you move toward the base, the waves become gentler, attracting families and miniature jellyfish.

The **CICI,** a fun water park, lets you hurl yourself head-first down winding water slides or watch trained dolphins perform. For big-spending dolphin-lovers, the CICI now offers the chance to swim with flippered friends; above water you can experience the thrill of the sky coaster. *(Costera at Colón. Follow Costera until you see the orange walls painted with large green waves; otherwise take a "CICI" or "Base" bus. ☎ 484 1970. Open daily 10am-6pm. 60 pesos. Dolphin shows M-F 2pm, Sa-Su 2pm and 4pm. Swimming with dolphins 590 pesos for 30min., 960 pesos for an hr.)*

PUERTO MARQUÉS. Lacking the pre-packaged polish of the strip, the beach town of **Puerto Marqués** encompasses a ribbon of sand lined with restaurants. The bus ride is the real attraction; views from the top of the hill are magnificent. As the bus rambles along, the Bahía de Puerto Marqués and the pounding surf of **Playa Revolcadero** come into view. Both offer a variety of water sports, including surfing and scuba diving. Catch a *colectivo* from Puerto Marqués (6 pesos) to get to quieter and less crowded **Playa Bonville.** *(From the bus station across from Comercial Mexicana at Playa Hornitos, on the beach side of the street, take a "Glorieta" bus to La Glorieta. From there, catch a "Puerto Marques" bus.)*

🎵 🎭 ENTERTAINMENT AND NIGHTLIFE

In Acapulco, every night is Saturday night. Luring young party-seekers from the capital, the town transforms at night into one continuous strip of partying along the Costera, with the best clubs beach side near the CICI. Unlike Cancún, Acapulco also has several gay nightlife options. Most clubs thump from 11pm to dawn and charge over 100 pesos for cover, which usually includes open bar. It's always easier and cheaper for women to get in, and many clubs offer deals to women on weeknights. For further discounts (albeit small ones), grab the cards the solicitors hand out as you walk down Costera—he gets a commission, you get 20 pesos off the cover price, and everybody goes home a little happier.

CLUBS AND BARS

▨ **Palladium** (☎ 446 5486), on the Carretera Escénica las Brisas. This space-age structure is on a cliff with a fabulous view of the harbor and downtown. Plan on taking a taxi (45 pesos). The club reverberates with pop music and dancing begins at midnight, when lights descend from the ceiling. Cover for men 280 pesos, women 210 pesos; Tu and Th women 50 pesos until 12:30am. Open bar. Open Tu and Th-Su 10:30pm-5am.

▓ **Free World,** Costera 25 (☎484 3591). The newest club on the Costera is still in the throes of its grand opening celebration. Grab a drink from the oh-so-neon bar as you plan your attack for one of three themed areas or head straight for the indoor pool (Th weekly pool party). You will have to shell out for Acapulco's best, though. Cover for men 310 pesos, women 250 pesos. Open bar all night. Open Th-Sa 10:30pm-5am.

Salón Club Premier, Costera 3117 (☎481 0114). Premier pulls in a more distinguished clientele looking to dance to *cumbia, merengue*, or salsa, or to lounge at chairs scattered about. This old style nightclub relives the glory days of the Acapulco golden age, when places like this were the norm, not the exception. Beer 40 pesos, mixed drinks 45 pesos; cover 100 pesos. Open Tu-Su 10pm-6am.

Disco Beach, Costera 1111 (☎484 8230; www.discobeach.com). One of the most famous and happening clubs on Costera. Cavern-like decoration downstairs contrast with an open-air bar that looks on Playa Condesa, letting you choose sweaty club or refreshing chill beach vibe. If you are young, cool, and missing a lot of money, you may well be here. Cover for men 320 pesos, women 250 pesos; W ladies' night. Beer 20 pesos. Live music upstairs Tu and Th-Sa. Open daily 11pm-6am.

Baby'O, Costera 22 (☎484 7474). The *Fraggle Rock*-style cave interior houses a slightly less frenetic and more sophisticated atmosphere than its rambunctious neighbors. M-Th cover 140 pesos for men; M-W 70 pesos for women, Th no cover and 2 free drinks for women. F-Su cover 250/150 pesos. Drinks 40 pesos. Open daily 10:30pm-4am.

Nina's, Costera 2909 (☎484 2400), on the beach side near CICI. A mature clientele grooves to live tropical music, peppered with impersonations of famous Latin dancers and singers. Black lights bring alive the already brightly colored walls. Open bar. Cover 220 pesos; Th women 50 pesos. Open daily 10pm-5am.

GAY AND LESBIAN NIGHTLIFE

Savage Disco, Av. de los Deportes 10B (☎484 1800). Leopard-print chairs and zebra-striped bar are stand-out features of this club. Dance amid strobes and booming music or check out the spicy transvestite shows at 1 and 3am. Mixed crowd for shows. Beer 30 pesos. 50 peso cover is good for Demás as well (see below). Open daily from 11pm.

Relax, Lomas del Mar 4 (☎484 0421), 1 block east of Carlos 'n' Charlie's. Mostly male customers frequent this above-average bar with fine service, which is more "relaxed" than most. Lounge area pumps in Cher (and more) on several TVs on the first floor; groove armadas head upstairs. Su-Th no cover; F-Sa 50 pesos, 1 drink included. Open daily from 10pm. Transvestite shows F-Sa 3am.

Demás, Av. de los Deportes 10A (☎484 1800), next to Savage. The heavy darkness cannot disguise the pervasive construction worker theme, reinforced by suspender-clad waiters in hard hats and a steel rod dance floor. Of course there are rowdy Chippendale shows (from 11:30pm) on weekends! Beer 25 pesos, *bebidas nacionales* 40-45 pesos. Cover 50 pesos, includes one drink; no cover Su-Th. Open daily 10pm-5am.

Picante, Privada Piedra Picuda 16 (☎484 2342), behind Carlos 'n' Charlie's. Young, lithe, and predominantly male clientele enjoy late-night racy entertainment under black lights. Dress code prohibits cross-dressing to avoid possible harassment. No cover. 2-drink min. Beer 25 pesos, *bebidas nacionales* 40 pesos. Strip show and table dances from midnight on. Open daily 10pm-4am.

SPORTS AND FESTIVALS

Corridas take place at **Plaza de Toros Caletilla,** 200m west of Playa Caleta near the abandoned yellow *jai alai* auditoriums. (☎483 9561. Dec.-Apr. Su 5pm.) Tickets are sold at the plaza at 4:30pm on fight days.

The Acapulco tourist office organizes a variety of festivals to lighten tourists' wallets. **Festival Acapulco** in May is a celebration of music, and the **Black Film Festi-**

val takes places during the first week of June. On December 9, men and women from around the globe journey to Acapulco to test their cliff-diving skills (or watch others) during the **Torneo Internacional de Clavados en La Quebrada.**

OTHER ENTERTAINMENT

Those too tired for yet more draining beach and club life will find milder entertainment at **Plaza Bahía,** a large shopping mall on Costera, 4 blocks east of La Gran Plaza, on the beach side. Speed around a tiny **Go-Karts** race course on the third floor. (☎440 5204. 25 pesos for 1 or 30 pesos for 2 per 5min. Open daily 10am-midnight.) Bowl away at **Bol Bahía** on the fourth floor. (☎485 0970. 30 pesos per person per game or 180 pesos per hr. for a group; shoes 10 pesos. Open Su noon-midnight, M-Sa noon-1am.) Catch a first-run US movie at **Cinema 5** on the third floor. (☎486 4255 or 485 9892. Tickets 38 pesos. Movies shown daily 3-10pm.)

◪ DAYTRIPS FROM ACAPULCO

PIE DE LA CUESTA

Buses leave from Costera, across the street from Sanborn's. Buses marked "Pie de la Cuesta Playa" stop on the road along the beach; those labeled "Pie de la Cuesta Centro" stop on a parallel street in town (40min., 3.5 pesos). From there, turn left down a dirt road; you should see the ocean. At the end of the road, turn right toward the base. Buses shuttle between the base and the centro (3.5 pesos). A blue and white combi will take you as far as La Barra, where the lagoon water flows into the ocean (5 pesos). A popular water park, El Castillo de Los Moyis, lies along the same road (☎482 2040. 50 pesos, kids 30 pesos.) To return to Acapulco, hail a bus in town headed back to the city.

A single-lane runs through Acapulco's hills to Pie de la Cuesta—a small town known for its absolutely regal sunsets—ending at the narrow road that separates the rough-and-tumble Pacific from the placid waters of **Laguna de Coyuca.** Despite its proximity to Acapulco, Pie avoids the crowds. Swimming is not the best option here: the pounding surf and strong currents make the ocean a dangerous choice, while the still, green water of the lagoon suggests pollution (the floating garbage confirms it); still, the lagoon does have the area's best waterskiing. Many restaurants and clubs near the air base offer **ski rental** at similar prices. Try the friendly staff at **Chuy ❸** (☎460 1104; 450 pesos per hr.) or **Tres Marías ❸** (☎460 0178). Both offer food: breakfasts and *antojitos* start at 20 pesos and seafood at 35 pesos. Unfortunately, aggressive *lancha* agents often interrupt rest and relaxation, pitching tours of the lagoon (3hr.; about 50 pesos per person). For those staying over, ◪**Villa Roxana ❸,** a blue-and-white building a few blocks from the bus stop, creates a little utopia with hammocks, a swimming pool, and immaculate rooms with fans and private baths. A beachside hammock may well be the best vantage point for one of the famed sunsets. Some rooms have kitchens and TVs. (☎460 3252. 100-150 pesos per person.) Beyond the pharmacy toward the base is **Acapulco Trailer Park ❶,** Av. Fuerza Aeria 381, with campgrounds, trailer hook-ups, bathrooms, and a pet raccoon named Charlie. (100-150 pesos, prices negotiable.)

OAXACA

OAXACA   ☎951

Perched on a giant plateau that gracefully interrupts the Sierra Madre del Sur's descent into the Oaxaca valley, the city of Oaxaca de Juárez (pop. 400,000) shines with funky grace. The city's surname honors native son Benito Juárez, a Oaxacan

Oaxaca State

Zapotec and Mexico's only *indígena* president. Oaxaca was also the birthplace of the much less loved dictator Porfirio Díaz, who got nothing but a lone street name to commemorate his iron reign. Although selective in its presidential honors, there is not much order to Oaxaca. It is a collision of tombs, temples, churches, rugs, jars, chocolate, diesel fumes, tiny storefront shops, language schools, foreigners, students, *indígenas*, hostels, hotels, apartments, and houses. History feels present in this modern city with an evident colonial past, where hand-made crafts are produced in machine-made quantities. Most of the sights—and blights—scattered about Mexico are here in some form. As visitors become smitten with Oaxaca's superb food, culture, highland setting, and delicious contradictions, days spill into weeks, months, and, on occasion, years.

◨ TRANSPORTATION

Most parts of the city are easily accessible by foot. Local buses *(urbanos)* cost 3.5 pesos; ask around for the correct line. Taxis run anywhere in the city for 30-40 pesos. Walk along a major street or find a *sitio* sign for an unoccupied cab.

    Airport: Aeropuerto Juárez (☎511 5040 for the tourist info booth), on Mex. 175, 8km south of the city. You can hire a private **taxi** from the airport (93 pesos), but it is much

Oaxaca

➤ ACCOMMODATIONS
Casa Arnel, 2
Hostal Guadalupe, 10
Hostal Misión San Pedro, 17
Hotel Mina, 28
Hotel Chocolate Posada, 32
Hotel Pasaje, 29
Hotel Reforma, 19
Hotel Santa Clara, 15
Magic Hostel, 24
Plata/Gelatina Hostel, 20

● FOOD
Antojos Regionales
Los Olmos, 13
Chocolate la Soledad, 31
Chocolate Mayordomo, 30
Cafe Gecko, 8
Comedor Guelaguetza, 3
El Chinito, 23
Flor de Loto, 14
Fonda Mexicana, 27
La Casa de la Abuela, 22
La Rana Feliz, 26
Las Quince Letras, 11
Pizza Nostrana, 7
Restaurant Morelos, 18
Restorán Cafe Alex, 21

★ NIGHTLIFE
502, 6
Cafe-Bar La Resistencia, 5
La Candela, 16
La Casa del Mezcal, 25
La Costumbre, 4
La Divina, 9
La Tentación, 12

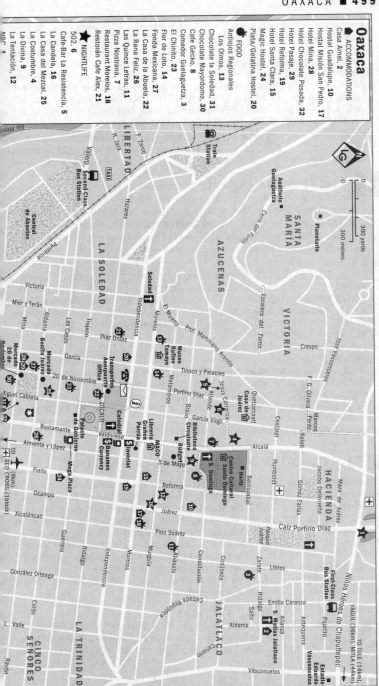

SOUTHERN PACIFIC COAST

cheaper and just as easy to share one of the **Transportes Aeropuerto** vans with other travelers—buy a ticket at the airport exit (22 pesos to the *centro*). Vans will take you from your hotel to the airport, with prices varying depending on the hotel. Arrangements should be made a day in advance by phone or at the office several doors down from the post office on Plaza Alameda. (☎514 4350. Open M-Sa 9am-2pm and 5-8pm.) Airlines served by the airport include: **AeroCaribe,** Fiallo 102 (☎516 0229 or 511 5247); **Aeroméxico,** Hidalgo 513 (☎516 3229 or 516 3765); **Mexicana,** Independencia 102 (☎516 8414 or 516 7352), at Fiallo; **AeroCalifornia,** Morelos 1207 (☎241 8570); and **Aviacsa** (☎518 4555, airport office ☎511 5039).

Buses: Two bus stations serve Oaxaca. The **first-class bus station,** Niños Héroes de Chapultepec 1036 (☎513 3350), is 11 blocks north of the *centro*. To get to the *centro*, cross the street and take a westbound "Centro" *urbano* (3.5 pesos) or a taxi (30-40

> **! EXCEPTIONS TO THE RULE.** Under most circumstances it's better (not to mention safer) to take 1st-class buses rather than 2nd-class buses. An exception to the rule is the ride from **Oaxaca** to **Puerto Escondido.** First-class buses tend to take a route through Salina Cruz that is about 5hr. longer than the 2nd-class bus route, which goes directly. Measure the increased efficiency and lower costs against the increased discomfort and danger.

pesos). **ADO** (☎515 1703) heads to: **Mexico City** (6½hr., 16-17 per day, 271 pesos); **Puebla** (4½hr., 7-8 per day, 202 pesos); **Tuxtepec** (6½hr.; 9:30, 11:30pm; 186 pesos); **Veracruz** (7hr.; 8:30am, 10:15pm, midnight; 267 pesos). **Cristóbal Colón** goes to: **Bahías de Huatulco** (8hr.; 9:30am, 9:30, 11pm; 178 pesos); **San Cristóbal de las Casas** (12hr.; 7:30, 9pm; 242 pesos); **Tehuantepec** (4½hr., 14-16 per day, 113 pesos); **Tuxtla Gutiérrez** (10hr.; 7, 9, 10:15pm; 241 pesos); **Puerto Escondido** (10hr.; 9:30am, 10:30, 11:30pm; 188 pesos). Tickets for ADO and Cristóbal Colón available at 20 de Noviembre #204 as well as at the numerous travel agencies around the *zócalo*. The **second-class bus station** houses regional bus lines and is 7 blocks southwest of the *zócalo*, just north of the Central de Abastos market. It's a good idea to buy tickets early. On their market days, buses to surrounding towns leave every 10 min. To get to the *centro*, take a "Centro" *urbano* in front of the main terminal. If walking, exit left out of the terminal, cross busy Periférico, and follow the street as it turns into Trujano. After 7 blocks, Trujano reaches the *zócalo*. A taxi will cost 20 pesos.

✳🛈 ORIENTATION AND PRACTICAL INFORMATION

Oaxaca, between the towering Sierra Madre del Sur and the Puebla-Oaxaca range, sits in the Oaxaca Valley 523km southeast of Mexico City. Principal access to Oaxaca from the north and east is via **Mex. 190** as well as the brand-new *"super-carretera,"* **Mex. 135** from Puebla. The city's ground zero is the *zócalo*, comprised of the square and the block-long Plaza Alameda de León, just north of the square. The five-block stretch of Alcalá between the *zócalo* and the Iglesia de Santo Domingo to the north features a high concentration of museums, restaurants, craft shops, and tourists. Many of Oaxaca's streets change names as they pass the *zócalo*. It is also common for two or more streets to share the same name, so it helps to specify neighborhood as well as street when directing cabbies.

TOURIST AND FINANCIAL SERVICES

Tourist Offices: SEDETUR, Murguia 206 (☎516 0123; http://oaxaca.gob.mx/sedetur). Maps, brochures, and an English-speaking staff. Open daily 8am-8pm. **CEPROTUR,** also at Murguia 206 (☎514 2155; fax 516 0984), handles all matters of tourist safety.

Open daily 8am-8pm. **Info Booth** (☎511 0740) at the airport. Also check the *Oaxaca Times* (www.oaxacatimes.com), a free English newspaper available at SEDETUR.

Consulates: In an emergency, CEPROTUR (see above) will obtain consular assistance. **Canada,** Suárez 700 (☎513 3777). Open M-F 11am-2pm. **US,** Alcalá 407 #20 (☎514 3054 or 516 2853), at Morelos, beneath an arched doorway. Open M-F 9am-3pm.

Currency Exchange: Banamex, Valdivieso 116, east of the cathedral, changes currency and has 24hr. **ATMs.** Open Su 10am-2pm, M-F 11am-7pm. **Inverlat,** at the corner of Independencia and Alcalá, offers similar rates and 24hr. **ATMs.** Open M-F 9am-5pm, Sa 10am-3pm. Numerous smaller currency exchanges surround the *zócalo.*

American Express: Valdivieso 2 (☎516 2700), at Hidalgo across from the *zócalo.* A **travel agency** inside sells plane tickets and bus tickets. Financial services open M-F 9am-2pm and 4-6pm, Sa 9am-1pm; travel agency open M-F 9am-8pm, Sa 9am-7pm.

LOCAL SERVICES

Luggage Storage: At the 1st-class bus station. 5 pesos per day.

Bookstores: Librería Grañen Porrúa, Alcalá 104 (☎516 9901), is known for its collection of art and architecture books and offers a small number of books in English. The cafe in back serves *comida corrida* (35 pesos). Open daily 10am-9pm. **Librería Universitaria,** on Guerrero between Armenta y López and Valdivieso, buys and sells English paperbacks. Open M-Sa 9am-2pm and 4-9:30pm. **Amate Books,** Alcalá 307 (☎516 6960), in Plaza Alcalá. Sells North American magazines and books about Mexico in several languages.

Libraries: Biblioteca Circulante, Alcalá 305. Everything from the *New Yorker* to *Sports Illustrated* for 1 peso. Open M-F 10am-1pm and 4-7pm, Sa 10am-1pm. The **Instituto de Artes Gráficos de Oaxaca,** Alcalá 507 (☎516 6980), across from Santo Domingo, has a library with works in various languages, as well as a museum of changing art exhibits. Open daily 9:30am-9pm; museum open Su-M, W-Sa 9:30am-8pm. Free.

Cultural Centers: Centro Cultural Ricardo Flores Magon, Alcalá 302 (☎514 0395), at Independencia. Hosts free plays, dance performances, concerts, and gallery openings (daily during high season). Monthly listings can be found on the *Programación Cultural* at the front desk. **Casa de la Cultura,** Ortega 403 (☎516 2483), at Colón. Hosts theater productions, concerts, summer music and art classes, and art exhibits. Open M-F 9am-6pm, Sa 9am-3pm and 4-6:30pm. **Instituto Oaxaqueño de las Culturas** (☎516 3434), at the corner of Madera and Tecnológica, has a similar program. To get there, take a westbound "Sta. Rosa" *urbano* from the corner of Independencia and Tinoco y Palacios (2.5 pesos). Listings in the monthly *Guía Cultura* (free at SEDETUR).

Markets: Oaxaca's enormous **Central de Abastos** is the ultimate shopping experience. Walk 8 blocks west of the *zócalo* on Trujano. Open daily 8am-8pm. **Mercado Benito Juárez,** at the corner of 20 de Noviembre and Aldama, 2 blocks from the *zócalo,* sells crafts, produce, flowers, and clothing. Its annex, **Mercado 20 de Noviembre,** on the next block, has a variety of cheap food stalls. Both open daily 6am-9pm. **Mercado de Artesanías,** at the corner of García and Zaragoza, offers artisan wares. Prices and quality are often better in nearby villages where the crafts originate. Open daily 8am-8pm.

Laundry: Lavandería, 20 de Noviembre 605B (☎516 2342). Open M-Sa 9am-8pm. 45 pesos per 3.5kg of clothes.

Car Rental: Budget, 5 de Mayo 315 (☎516 4445). Also at the airport (☎511 5252). VWs 600 pesos per day, less during off-season. Open daily 8am-1pm and 4-7pm. **Hertz,** Labastida 115 (☎516 2434), between 5 de Mayo and Alcalá, charges 550 pesos for a VW sedan. Open M-Sa 8am-7pm. **Alamo,** 5 de Mayo 205 (☎514 8534), offers Chevy sedans without A/C *(sin aire)* for 650 pesos per day. Open daily 8am-8pm.

SOUTHERN PACIFIC COAST

EMERGENCY AND COMMUNICATIONS

Emergency: ☎066.

Police: Aldama 108 (☎516 2726), south of the *zócalo*, between Cabrera and Busta-mante. Little English spoken. Open 24hr. Between 8am-8pm, go first to Ceprotur at Murguia 206.

Red Cross: Armenta y López 700 (☎516 4803), between Pardo and Burgoa. Some English spoken. 24hr. ambulance service.

Pharmacy: Farmacias del Ahorro, Niños Héroes de Chapultepec 1102, next to ADO. Many other locations in the city. Open 24hr. Also Hidalgo 603, at 20 de Noviembre. Open daily 7am-11pm.

Hospitals: Hospital Civil, Díaz 400 (☎515 1300), 1.5km north of town. No English spo-ken. **Hospital Reforma,** Reforma 603 (☎516 6100), at Humboldt. English spoken.

Fax: Telecomm (☎516 4902), Independencia at 20 de Noviembre, around the corner from the post office. Open M-F 8am-6pm, Sa 9am-4pm.

Telephones: LADATELs are everywhere, with an especially large concentration in front of the post office in the *zócalo*. *Casetas* available at **Computel,** Independencia 601 (☎514 8084), across from the Telecomm office. Open daily 7am-10pm.

Internet Access: Mega Plaza, Guerrero 100, on the south side of the *zócalo*. Lots of computers, speedy connection. 10 pesos per hr. Open Su 8am-9:30pm, M-Sa 7:30am-9:30pm. Internet access is absolutely everywhere in Oaxaca, usually for 10 pesos or less per hour.

Post Office: (☎516 2661), on the west side of Plaza Alameda de León. Open M-F 8am-7pm, Sa 9am-1pm. **Postal Code:** 68000.

ACCOMMODATIONS AND CAMPING

Cheap beds are everywhere in Oaxaca. Hotels south of the *zócalo* stick to the same formula: singles for around 100 pesos (more for a private bathroom) with rooms stacked around bland concrete courtyards. Accommodations farther north are better deals: they're just as cheap but, friendlier and with aesthetic appeal, they are escapes from the streets' frenzied capitalism rather than extensions of it. Reservations are advised on *fiesta* weekends: especially during the *Guelaguetza* in July, *Semana Santa* before Easter, and the *Día de los Muertos* in early November. For longer stays in the city, reasonably priced rooms are available for rent. Check the tourist office and *Oaxaca Times* for listings. **Departmentos del Cuento,** Quintana Roo 107, off Berriozabal past La Iglesia Santo Domingo, rents six one- or two-person rooms with kitchen and bath. (☎514 2288. 2000-2500 pesos per month, utilities included.)

NORTHEAST OF THE CENTRO: JALATLACO

Jalatlaco is about a 10-block walk northeast of the *zócalo*. Unlike other hotel areas, it is not located near Oaxaca's numerous Calles de "Huge Trucks Without Mufflers or Catalytic Convertors," ensuring you the rarity of peace and quiet.

Casa Arnel, Aldama 404 (☎515 2856; casa.arnel@spersaoaxaca.com.mx), at Hidalgo, across from the Iglesia San Matias Jalatlaco. Airy and attractive, Casa Arnel's main draws are a courtyard jungle full of talking parrots and a rooftop terrace with a spectac-ular view of the Oaxacan skyline. This hotel offers a bar, Internet service (15 pesos per hr.), a travel agency, a library, laundry service, and breakfast (7:30-9:45am, not included). Rooms are clean, colorful, and blessedly quiet. Prices rise in high season. Singles 150/180 pesos, 250/350 pesos with bathroom. Doubles 250/280 pesos, 300/350 pesos with bathroom. ❷

Hostal Guadalupe (HI), Juárez 409 (☎516 6365), between Abasolo and Constitución. Ideally situated between the buzz of the *zócalo* and the peace of Jalatlaco, Guadalupe is also home to some of Oaxaca's finest, cleanest bathrooms. Amenities include TV, courtyard seating, kitchen access, and new laundry facilities. 60 pesos, 55 pesos with HI card; private bedroom 130 pesos. ❶

NORTH OF THE ZÓCALO: THE CENTRO

For the aesthetically discerning traveler, this part of town not only offers the best architecture (many of the hotels are in old colonial buildings), but also the best location for those looking to stay close to Oaxaca's artifacts and galleries.

Hotel Reforma, Reforma 102 (☎516 0939), between Independencia and Morelos, 3 blocks past the left side of the cathedral. Features hand-carved wood furniture and a nice view of the city. Singles 150 pesos; doubles 250 pesos; triples 350 pesos; quads 450 pesos. ❷

Hostal Misión San Pedro, Juárez 200 (☎516 4626), on the corner of Morelos. Though San Pedro lacks the ambience and services of many of the other hostels in town, bathrooms and dorm-style bedrooms are clean, silent, and some of the cheapest in town. 50 pesos; singles 140 pesos; doubles 180 pesos. ❶

Hotel Sta. Clara, Morelos 1004 (☎516 1138). Clean rooms and a bright, quiet red-tiled courtyard. Singles 150 pesos; doubles 250 pesos; triples 350 pesos, includes private bath. ❷

SOUTH OF THE ZÓCALO

Filled with budget hotels—four or five on the same block, particularly along **Díaz Ordaz** and **Mina**—discriminating tastes can be obliged on a budget here. Many hotels face noisy streets—ask for a room in the back or on an upper floor.

Magic Hostel, Fiallo 305 (☎516 7667), between Guerrero and Colón. This terrific hostel is friendly, colorful, and lively without being overcrowded or intrusively loud, and it has plenty of nooks and crannies as well as comfy social space. Amenities include a courtyard and second floor terrace/bar/communal kitchen, video/DVD rental (20/30 pesos), laundry service, cheap refreshments, paperback exchange, and rapid Internet access (10 pesos per hr.). Basic co-ed dorms 50 pesos; singles 150 pesos. ❶

Hotel Mina, Mina 304 (☎516 4966), at 20 Noviembre, is one of the cheapest options for those who prefer a private room. Plain rooms have sturdy beds. Communal baths are tidy and convenient. Singles 100 pesos; doubles 160 pesos; triples 200 pesos. ❷

Plata/Gelatina Youth Hostel, Independencia 504 (☎514 9391), 1 block west of the *zócalo*. Outfitted with typical hostel decorations such as flags and eclectic art as well as foosball and ping-pong tables, a cafe/bar, and Internet access. Beds 50 pesos. ❶

Hotel Pasaje, Mina 302 (☎510 4213), 3 blocks south of the *zócalo*. Well-scrubbed, tiled rooms offer cable TV and open onto a plant-filled courtyard. Bathrooms are large and clean—top notch. Location provides convenient access to markets, restaurants, and chocolate shops, but also car horns and diesel exhaust. Singles 160 pesos; doubles 190 pesos; triples 260 pesos. ❷

Hotel Chocolate Posada, Mina 212 (☎516 5760). A treat for die-hard dessert fans, the courtyard of this hotel houses the elegant cafe of the attached chocolate shop, Chocolate la Soledad (see p. 505). Rooms are clean and comfortable. Singles 150 pesos; doubles 200 pesos. ❷

 FOOD

Considered by many to be the culinary capital of Mexico, Oaxaca offers preposterously large amounts of food for preposterously low prices. Locals turn to watch as uninitiated tourists are served *hayadas* (enormous tortillas piled high with top-pings) and giggle in disbelief. Oaxacan cooking features seven kinds of the heavy chile-and-chocolate sauce, *mole*, served in a variety of ways. Other staples include *quesillo* (boiled string cheese), *chorizo* (spicy sausage), *tasajo* (thinly cut steak), and *chapulines* (tiny cooked grasshoppers doused in chile—truly yummy). Another specialty now found in all parts of the republic, *tamales* are made of ground corn stuffed with beans, chicken, or beef and wrapped in banana leaves before baking or boiling. Oaxaca's trademark drink, sold everywhere, is cactus-based tequila cousin *mezcal*.

The *zócalo* itself is besieged by middle-priced, middling-quality restaurant/bars; cheaper and more authentic *fondas* and *comedores* can be found southwest of the centro. Alcalá features pricier and more international food. The fastest and cheap-est regional meals are at the markets and taco stands on Trujano Las Casas, south-east of the *zócalo*.

La Casa de la Abuela, Hidalgo 616, 2nd floor (☎516 3544), at the corner of the *zócalo* and Plaza Alameda. A large menu of Oaxacan cuisine. Savor delicious renditions of Oax-aca's famous *sopa de guias* (squash soup; 31 pesos) and *chapulines* (58 pesos) while marveling at the restaurant's postcard-perfect views of the cathedral and *zócalo*. Finish with a cup of *té de poelo* (a regional herbal brew; 13 pesos) or *cafe de olla* (spiced cof-fee; 13 pesos). Entrees 80-110 pesos. Open daily 1-10pm. ❹

Pizza Nostrana (☎514 0778), at the corner of Alcalá and Allende. Looks more expen-sive than it is: wood furniture, real tablecloths, sophisticatedly dim lighting, sharply-dressed waiters. Still, a meal can be had for less than 60 pesos. Pizza starts at 47 pesos, large portions of spaghetti start at 45 pesos. Open daily 1-11pm. ❹

El Chinito, 20 de Noviembre 209. For the low price of 60 pesos, the fowl will be pulled dripping from the oven and dropped into a pile of rice and tortilla on your plate. A whole chicken serves 2-3. Halves and quarters are also available (30 and 20 pesos, respec-tively). Open daily 8am-9pm. ❸

Restorán Cafe Alex, Díaz Ordaz 218 (☎514 0715). Amazing menu runs the gamut of Mexican cuisine. Garden seating available. Breakfast 27 pesos, *comida corrida* 36 pesos, special vegetarian menu 26-38 pesos. Open Su 7am-noon, M-Sa 7am-9pm. ❸

Fonda Mexicana, 20 de Noviembre 408 (☎514 3121). One of the most popular lunch spots south of the *zócalo*. Always packed with non-*gringos* seeking gigantic *hayudas*, which start at 15 pesos. *Comida corrida* includes purified fruit water and a dessert (35 pesos). Cheap beer 8 pesos. Open M-Sa 8am-5pm. ❷

Comedor Guelaguetza, Zarate 100 (☎515 7234). Cheap and fresh food for those in the Jalatco neighborhood. *Comida corrida* is 30 pesos; try the savory *chicken pozole*. Breakfast 30 pesos, 3 burritos 20 pesos. Open daily 7am-9pm. ❶

Restaurant Morelos, Morelos 1003 (☎516 0558). Try this homey, pink- and green-walled eatery for a friendly, local-filled eating experience. Breakfast 20-30 pesos; *comida corrida*, 30 pesos, with huge baskets of homemade nachos and a dangerous salsa picante. Open daily 7am-6pm. ❶

La Rana Feliz, Aldama 217 (☎516 0713). The *pollo en mole* (30 pesos) at this happy frog more than makes up for the complete lack of atmosphere. Great for a quick, super-casual sit-down meal. Entrees 20-30 pesos. Open daily 8:30am-9:30pm. ❸

Antojitos Regionales Los Olmos, Morelos 403, at Crespo. For those still unaccustomed to Oaxaca's big breakfast and diminutive dinner lifestyle, Antojitos is the right place. Perfect for filling the stomach before a night of dancing, they whip up cheap eats: the *patitas en vinagre* is the most expensive item on the menu (12 pesos). *Tomate de mole*, quesadillas, and *tortas* 12 pesos. Open daily 7pm-midnight. ❶

Las Quince Letras, Abasolo 300 (☎514 3769). Offers a large menu of regional special-ties. Breakfast starts at 26 pesos. For dinner try the *sopa oaxaqueña* (28 pesos), a powerful Oaxacan super-stew. Entrees 50-80 pesos. Open daily 8am-9pm. ❹

Flor de Loto, Morelos 509 (☎514 3944). This simple, dimly lit cafe offers a haven for vegetarians in this typically blood-thirsty town. Regional (i.e. meaty) food also served. Veggie soups 15 pesos, *enchiladas de soya* 30 pesos, mushroom tacos 30 pesos, spa-ghetti 30 pesos. Open daily 8am-10pm. ❸

▐ CAFES AND CHOCOLATE

Chocolate shops produce Oaxaca's favorite confection at the corner of **Mina** and **20 de Noviembre.** Follow your nose to see the chocolate-making process and grab lots of free samples. If you don't make it to the area, don't worry—nearly every restaurant in the city serves *chocolate caliente* (hot chocolate). Also keep an eye out for *café de olla*, a sweet, spicy coffee, and *tejate*, a cold, corn-based drink. Many cafes sit on Alcalá and Abasolo between 5 de Mayo and Reforma.

▨ Chocolate Mayordomo (☎516 1619), at the corner of Mina and 20 de Noviembre, with a second shop across the street. King of Oaxaca's sweets market, Mayordomo churns out the chocolate and assaults onlookers with free samples. Buy some solid chocolate for the road (25-30 pesos per 500g) or sit with a cup of the city's cheapest hot choco-late (small 8 pesos). Open daily 7am-9pm.

Chocolate la Soledad, Mina 221 (☎526 3807), across the street from Mayordomo. This chocolate and spice shop fronts the Hotel Chocolate Posada (see p. 503) and sells the sweet stuff in all shapes, sizes, and flavors. Indulge yourself with a double hot choco-late (15 pesos) in the vine-covered courtyard cafe. Open Su 8am-2pm, M-Sa 8am-6pm.

Cafe Gecko, 5 de Mayo 412-3 (☎516 2285), half a block south of Iglesia de Santo Domingo. Civilized breakfasts (20 pesos) and sandwiches served in the quiet, leafy courtyard. Convenient Internet access (10 pesos per hr.) and *chocolate caliente* (15 pesos) draws a crowd of museum-hoppers. Open M-Sa 8:30am-8pm.

◎ SIGHTS

Oaxaca's attractions tend towards the highbrow. From museums full of Zapotec artifacts to baroquely gilded cathedrals, the city offers visitors a view of the varied, and often conflicting, cultures that have called Oaxaca home. Many of the sites of interest are crowded between the *zócalo* and Santo Domingo, including the many studios and galleries that give Oaxaca its reputation as an art mecca.

▨ IGLESIA DE SANTO DOMINGO. Higher, mightier, and in better shape than the *catedral*, Santo Domingo is the city's tallest building. One of the best examples of Mexican Baroque, the church was begun in 1575 but was not consecrated until 1611. Since then, Santo Domingo has functioned as a place of worship, a museum, and even a military barracks for both sides of the Reform Wars and the Revolution. Swaths of gilded stucco cover the imposing interior. Local artists completed the altar in 1959. It is one of the most elaborate (and expensive) of its kind and a treat for even the most jaded, seen-every-church tourists. The **Capilla de la Virgen del Rosario,** to the right as you walk in, is from 1731. Though much older, it, too, holds relatively new altar works, some of them inaugurated as late as the 1960s. (*3 blocks past MACO, on the Andador Turístico. Open Su 7-11am and 1-7:30pm, M-Sa 8am-7:30pm. Capilla open daily until 7pm.*)

▨ CENTRO CULTURAL SANTO DOMINGO. The ex-convent next door to the Igle-sia de Santo Domingo was converted into the prestigious **Museo de las Culturas de**

Oaxaca. The stellar museum houses rooms and rooms of Mixtec, Zapotec, Spanish conquest-era, and more recent Mexican artifacts, but the prime attraction is the treasure extracted from Tomb 7 in Monte Albán; the gold, silver, turquoise, bone, and obsidian jewelry and artifacts are some of the grandest Zapotec material ever found. The Centro also houses the new **Jardín Etnobotánico**, a fairyland of giant cacti and flowering trees and the 17th-century **Fray Francisco de Burgoa** library collection. (☎ 516 2991. Open Tu-Su 10am-8pm. The only way to view the garden is through a free guided tour. English tours Tu and Th 11am, Sa 11am and 4pm. 37 pesos.)

CATEDRAL DE OAXACA. Originally constructed in 1553 and reconstructed after earthquake damage between 1702 and 1733, the cathedral dates from a time when the Mexican Church and State were unified. The building is governmental and imposing, if somewhat rundown, with the structural focus provided by the ornate bishop's seat. The facade is Baroque-style bas-relief, and the interior contains 14 side chapels. The exterior is alive with dawdlers, children playing with strange balloons, and young girls waiting to ambush the unsuspecting with their wares. (In the northeast corner of the zócalo. Open daily 7am-9pm.)

PALACIO DE GOBIERNO. Oaxaca's Palacio de Gobierno was constructed in the mid-19th century. Contemporary art expositions decorate the pleasant open-roofed *palacio*. At the top of the stairs, a mural by Arturo García Bustos, which acts as a pictorial cheatsheet on state history, culminates with Benito Juárez's oft-repeated phrase *"El respeto al derecho ajeno es la paz"* ("Respect for the rights of others is peace"). (On the south side of the zócalo. Open 24hr.)

BASÍLICA LA SOLEDAD. A minor but absorbing attraction is the funky museum of religious art located next to the 17th-century church. The museum houses an astonishing array of objects—such as model ships, shell-and-pasta figurines, homemade cassette tapes, and a stuffed cat—sent from around the world as gifts to the Virgin, who is said to have appeared here in 1620. (Independencia 107, 4 blocks behind the post office. ☎ 516 5076. Open daily 8am-2pm and 4-7pm. 2 pesos.)

CASA DE BENITO JUÁREZ. Mexico's most beloved president lived here for 10 years as a child (1818-28). With living room, bedrooms, kitchen, and a "bookbinding/weaving shop," the house has been reconstructed in 19th-century, upper-class *oaxaqueña* style and features informational displays on Mexican culture and politics during Juárez's time. (García Vigil 609, 1 block west of Alcalá. ☎ 516 1860. Open Su 10am-5pm, Tu-Sa 10am-7pm. 27 pesos.)

MUSEO DE ARTE CONTEMPORÁNEO DE OAXACA (MACO). This colonial building is known as the Casa de Cortés, although historians insist that it was not, in fact, Cortés's estate. Nevertheless, the 18th-century upper-class home is an example of vice-regal architecture, a style used by *conquistadores* and their heirs. The 15-room museum features three-month rotating exhibitions of mostly abstract art and in the past has showcased *oaxaqueños* Rufino Tamayo, Francisco Toledo, and Rodolfo Morales. (Alcalá 202, a block down Andador Turístico on the right. ☎ 514 1055. Open Su-M and W-Sa 10:30am-8pm. 10 pesos; Su free.)

MUSEO DE ARTE PREHISPÁNICO DE MÉXICO RUFINO TAMAYO. This museum features the artist's personal collection of Pre-Hispanic objects. The figurines, ceramics, and masks that Tamayo collected are meant to be appreciated as works of art rather than artifacts, resulting in a hybrid art gallery and archaeological museum. (Morelos 503, between Díaz Ordaz and Tinoco y Palacios. ☎ 516 4750. Open Su 10am-3pm, M and W-Sa 10am-2pm and 4-7pm. 20 pesos, students 14 pesos.)

TEATRO MACEDONIO ALCALÁ. An Oaxacan beauty, this theater, constructed at the turn of the 20th century, exemplifies the style fostered by dictator Porfirio

Díaz, who had a taste for French art and intellectual formulas. (*5 de Mayo at Indepen-dencia, 2 blocks behind the cathedral.* ☎ *516 3387. Weekly shows 6 and 8pm. 20 pesos.*)

OTHER SIGHTS. If you're looking for a beautiful view of the city and surrounding hills, head to the **Cerro de Fortín** (The Hill with the Beautiful View). The Escalera de Fortín begins on Crespo, leading past the Guelaguetza amphitheater to the **Plane-tarium Nundehui.** Balance the splendor of the vista against the cardiological trauma inflicted by the grueling climb. (*Planetarium* ☎ *514 7500. Open Th-Su 10am-1pm and 5-8pm. 30 pesos.*) Also worth a visit is the **Centro Fotográfico Álvarez Bravo,** Murguía 302, between Reforma and Juárez, which displays rotating photography exhibits. (☎ *516 2880. Open M and W-Su 9:30am-6pm. Free.*)

🎵🎭 ENTERTAINMENT AND NIGHTLIFE

Nightlife in Oaxaca ranges from quiet and ultra-civilized to ear-splitting and near-frenzied. At night, the *zócalo* itself is open until 9 or 10pm, as both tourists and locals drink beer and calmly take in the green trees, fountains, and playing chil-dren. A walk up the Alcalá past the closed museums and craft shops will guarantee encounters with roving and loitering bands of youth. There's usually something happening inside the city's bars and discos, and sometimes also outside, where borderline sacrilegious activities take place on the steps of the Iglesia de Santo Domingo. Some bars are closed on Sunday, but Monday is by far the quietest day of the week. Those debilitated by the previous night's activity can catch a recent flick in English with Spanish subtitles at **Ariel 2000** (☎ 516 5241), at the corner of Juárez and Berriozabal. The Guerreros, Oaxaca's professional baseball team, play just northwest of the complex at the **Estadio Eduardo Vasconcelos,** on the corner of Vásconcelos and Niños Héroes de Chapultepec (tickets 10-50 pesos). **Sala Ver-sailles,** Ocampo 105 (☎ 516 2335), three blocks east of the *zócalo,* hosts live shows. Most nightlife can be reached by foot, and taxis (35 pesos) go everywhere.

BARS

Centered in the **Alcalá** and two blocks west, near **Díaz** and **Allende,** most bars are within safe walking distance of the *zócalo.*

   La Costumbre, Alcalá 501, opposite the entrance to Santo Domingo. A little too tight for dancing. Beer 15 pesos, cocktails 27 pesos. Open M-Sa 8pm-2:30am.

   La Divina, Gurion 104, across from the south side of Santo Domingo. Popular among the city's younger student bourgeoisie. Trippy ceramic artwork and nooks for close conver-sation. Live music many nights. Beer 18 pesos. No cover. Open Tu-Su 9pm-1am.

   Cafe-Bar La Resistencia, Díaz 503 (☎ 514 9584), at Allende. The name and interior design (posters of figures like Che Guevara and Malcolm X) clash with the slacker clien-tele. The only revolution here is against sobriety. Beer 18 pesos. No cover. Open Tu-Sa 8pm-2am.

   La Tentación, Matamoros 101 (☎ 514 9521). A favorite bar of locals and travelers alike, good for both dancing and chilling out. Sip a Sol for only 10 pesos, and wait for a good song so that *oaxaqueños* can put you to shame with their rhythm. Salsa W nights.

   La Casa del Mezcal, Flores Magón 209. This classy-but-casual, stucco-walled establish-ment is the premiere place to try Oaxaca's favorite beverage. Plain *mezcal* 10 pesos, specially aged/flavored types 15-20 pesos. Open daily noon-1am.

CLUBS

Several hard-core discos lie near the first-class bus station on **Díaz Ordaz** at **Niños Héroes de Chapultepec,** 11 blocks north of the *zócalo.* A taxi is the best way to reach these clubs (35 pesos).

■ **La Candela,** Murguía 413 (☎514 2010) at Pino Suárez. The dance floor, situated in an elegant, well-lit courtyard, surrounded by tables, and rocked by a tight *salsa* band, draws a crowd diverse in age, skill, and nationality. Cover 25 pesos M-Th, 40 pesos F-Sa. Live music Tu-Sa from 10pm. Open daily 2pm-1:30am.

NRG, Díaz 102-B (☎515 0477), 1 block from Héroes de Chapultepec. NRG is simply a great place to dance. Spanish music W, pop mix other nights. Beer 20 pesos. No cover W; cover Th 30 pesos men, women free; cover F-Sa 40 pesos. Open W-Sa 9pm-3am.

GAY AND LESBIAN NIGHTLIFE

In typical *machista* fashion, Oaxaca's gay and lesbian nightlife is a well-kept secret. The city's one gay club is, however, popular, well-managed, and safe.

502, at Díaz 502, across from La Resistencia. As the city's only gay and lesbian night-club, 502 can afford to be selective. The club is private; ring the bell outside the door and wait for the bouncer to unlock it. No drugs, heavy drinking, or transvestism allowed. Cover 50 pesos. Open F-Sa 11pm-5am.

FESTIVALS

On the two Mondays following July 16, known as **Los Lunes del Cerro** (Hill Mondays), representatives from all seven regions of Oaxaca state converge on the Cerro del Fortín for the festival of ■**Guelaguetza.** Guelaguetza recalls the Zapotec custom of reciprocal gift-giving. At the end of the day's traditional dances, performers throw goods typical from their regions into the outstretched arms of the crowd gathered in the 12,000-seat stadium. In between the gatherings are festive food and handicraft exhibits, art shows, and concerts. (Front-section seats 300 pesos, back-section seats free, but you must come very early to get a seat. Call tourist office for reservations.)

As the *mezcal* capital of the world, Oaxaca is justifiably proud of itself. During the **Fiesta Nacional del Mezcal,** held July 17-24, Oaxacans and foreigners alike gather themselves in Parque Juárez to drink themselves numb. Vendors crowd the park, and everyone stumbles from booth to booth, giddy from the unlimited free shots. If you've exceeded your taste-test tolerance, take a seat and enjoy the festival's live music, traditional dances, and fireworks.

Oaxaca's exquisitely beautiful **Día de los Muertos** celebrations (Nov. 1-2) have become a huge tourist draw in recent years. Most travel agencies offer expeditions to the candlelit, marigold-filled village graveyards. Shops fill with molded sugar *calaveras* (skulls), while altars to memorialize the deceased are erected throughout the city. Because these celebrations occur for very personal reasons, locals might not appreciate being photographed as they remember their deceased.

On December 23, Oaxacans celebrate the unique **Noche de los Rábanos** (Night of the Radishes). The small tuber is honored for its frequent use in Oaxacan cuisine and its extremely carve-able form. Masterpieces of historic or biblical themes made entirely in radish fill the *zócalo*, where they are judged. Hundreds of people admire the creations and eat sweet *buñuelos*, tortillas with honey. Upon finishing the treat, make a wish and throw the ceramic plate on the ground; if the plate smashes into pieces, your wish will come true.

■ DAYTRIPS FROM OAXACA

The villages surrounding Oaxaca attract travelers by taking once-functional items, be they rugs, jars, or decaying temples, and displaying them as authentic representations of beauty in ways of life vanished or vanishing. Villages often specialize in particular products: **Arrazola** and **San Martín Tilcajate** make wooden animals; **San Bartolo Coyotepec,** black clay pottery; **Atzompa,** green clay pottery; **Ocotlán,** natural

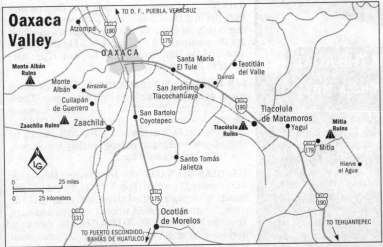

Oaxaca Valley

clay pottery; **Teotitlán del Valle,** wool *sarapes;* and **Villa Díaz Ordaz** and **Santo Tomás Jalietza,** textiles and weavings. Likewise, many villages hold *mercados* on specific days to attract visitors: Miahuatlán (Monday), Atzompa (Tuesday), San Pablo Etla (Wednesday), Zaachila (Thursday), Ocotlán (Friday), and Tlacolula (Sunday).

The **"Tourist Yu'u" program ❶** operated by SEDETUR rents out guest houses in Abasolo, Papalutla, Teotitlán del Valle, Benito Juárez, Tlacolula, Quialana, Tlapazola, and Santa Ana del Valle. Accommodations include five beds, a kitchen, and clean bedding; proceeds benefit the community. (☎ 516 0123. Open daily 9am-2pm. 70 pesos per person, 25-peso discount for students in some villages; camping in the garden 25-30 pesos.) Additionally, you can try one of the *paseos culturales*, which introduce visitors to the traditional medicinal, agricultural, and artistic practices of the 13 villages in the area.

All the villages can be reached by the *taxis colectivos* that leave the Central de Abastos (3-10 pesos depending on distance). At the intersection of Periférico and Las Casas is an Inverlat bank. Destinations are labeled on taxi windows and on signs along the road. Buses are easy to find on the Mitla route (Mex. 190), but may be more difficult to locate on other routes. Some companies offer bike tours to outlying towns; contact the tourist office for more information.

FROM OAXACA TO MITLA (MEX. 190)

All the following destinations are accessible via a Mitla-bound bus, leaving from the 2nd-class station in Oaxaca (1hr., every 10min. 8am-8pm, 10 pesos). Most people visit these sites as daytrips, but the tourist office in Oaxaca can arrange for overnight stays in Teotitlán del Valle and Tlacolula.

SANTA MARÍA EL TULE. This friendly little town (pop. 7000), just 14km outside Oaxaca, houses one of Mexico's great roadside attractions: the **Tule Tree.** The 2000-year-old, 42m sabino tree has an astounding circumference of 58m—the largest girth of any tree on earth. Don't be deceived into thinking the first tree you see is the big one—it's just the 1000-year-old baby. There is a fee (2 pesos) to approach the fence closest to the tree, but the glory of this botanical behemoth can be appreciated within a 100m radius. In fact, farther may be better, as pictures taken too close will look like nothing more than a big piece of bark. *Ask the bus driver to drop you off at El Tule; then ask for el árbol (the tree).*

FROM THE ROAD

BUS A MOVE

Riding the bus in Mexico is more exciting than in parts of the world with uniformly enforced traffic laws; here it is often more terrifying and dangerous. Signalling or lane-changing is a once-a-week kind of community service and *cinturones de seguridad* (seatbelts) generally lie idle. *Colectivo* drivers often squeeze five adult passengers into a sedan, which leaves one person, the *gringo* if one is available, splayed awkwardly on the emergency brake. If you are this passenger, you will regularly have a hand running up and down your thigh—don't be uncomfortable, just do your part to allow the driver to shift while he passes a semi-truck on a blind uphill curve.

If you are riding a local bus, know that drivers are generally more concerned with maintaining forward motion than with your safety. If you are getting off, move to the front as your stop approaches. As the bus slows, descend the steps; when the door opens, leap clear, and expect to hit the ground running. If you are boarding, make sure that the driver is aware of you and prepared to stop. Then, gather your backpack/luggage/children, and when the door opens, leap aboard and assume a crouching position, ready to grab whatever railings, passengers, sacks of fruit, or loose livestock will stabilize you as the bus accelerates and you make your way to your seat.

DAINZÚ. The Dainzú ruins, 22km from Oaxaca, date from the first Pre-Classic phase at Monte Albán. This site is only for the avid ruin-goer: Dainzú's pyramids are the smallest and least excavated in the Oaxaca area and lie 1km from the main road. *(Open daily 8am-6pm. 22 pesos.)*

SAN JERÓNIMO TLACOCHAHUAYA. The walls of the **Iglesia de San Jerónimo** in nearby San Jerónimo Tlacochahuaya (pop. 4700), 23km from Oaxaca, illustrate Zapotec decorative techniques applied to Catholic motifs. It was built at the end of the 16th century by Dominicans seeking to escape worldly temptation. *(Open daily 7am-2pm and 4-6pm.)*

TEOTITLÁN DEL VALLE. Twenty-eight kilometers from Oaxaca, Teotitlán (pop. 7000) is the oldest community in the state, settled about 2000 years ago. The source of many beautiful woolen *sarapes* and rugs, Teotitlán is home to 200-300 families who earn their livelihood by spinning and weaving. Doormat-sized rugs are around 200 pesos; larger, more elaborate ones can go for upwards of 5000 pesos. Many allow tourists to visit their workshops. Teotitlán is not as accessible as many of the other stops on the road; it's 4km from where the bus drops you off, but *taxis colectivos* (3 pesos) pass every five minutes from the main road to town, and a few workshops are scattered within walking distance of the main road. Many vendors accept credit cards and some will deliver large *sarapes* to hotels in Oaxaca.

TLACOLULA DE MATAMOROS. Tlacolula (pop. 13,500), 33km from Oaxaca, is one of the largest towns in the area. It hosts a lively market (Su early morning-late afternoon), which features *mezcal*. A better draw than the town itself is **Lambityeco**, a small collection of Zapotec ruins several kilometers before the town. Occupied from AD 600 to 1000, after the Zapotecs abandoned Monte Albán, the village peaked from 700 to 775. The ruins consist of one main pyramid and several houses, with some visible murals. The site also features the only known portraits in the Oaxaca ruins area, unsettling carvings of Zapotecs buried in the site's tombs. *(Open daily 8am-6pm. 17 pesos, Su free.)*

YAGUL. Thirty-six kilometers from Oaxaca, Yagul—meaning "tree" or "old stick"—was a Zapotec city inhabited primarily from 700 BC to AD 1521, though there is evidence of human presence as early as 3000 BC. Less archaeologically impressive than Mitla, Yagul's isolation and disarray—the ruins are scattered about a small mountain whose rocky paths lead to outcroppings with spectacular 360-degree views—make it a more adventurous and aesthetically striking site. A gorgeous 1.5km jaunt through cornfields and up a hill preps the visitor for the wide green view of a mountain-ringed valley that awaits at the top. If you go on a weekday, you'll be able to act out your long-held fantasies of Zapotec kingship with lizards as your only audience. The more famous buildings and tombs are in the **Acrópolis,** the area closest to the parking lot, 2km north of the road. If you bring some friends you can start a pick-up game in the restored ball court, the largest of its kind in the Oaxaca Valley, though archaeologists have only a vague idea about how the game was played. The **Court of the Triple Tomb** is to the left of the ball court. Carved with an image that resembles a jaguar, the tomb is divided in three sections, with stone faces covering the largest section. Beyond the ball court rises the **Council Hall;** behind that is the **Palace of the Six Patios,** believed to have been home to the city's ruler. Heading back to the parking lot, take the left-hand trail that climbs uphill to the rocky outcropping to catch a great view of the cactus-covered hills. Continue on by heading back to the fork in the path and taking the other trail. It leads to a Zapotec fortress built as a fallback in case the town was attacked. Even farther up is the mountaintop. Turn right and walk through brush for a while to find the unmarked basins carved out of the mountaintop, which, it is speculated, were Zapotec bathtubs. *(Site open daily 8am-5pm. 27 pesos, Su free.)*

MITLA

After arriving in Mitla, find the huge highway welcome sign. Walk under the sign; this is the town's main road. Following the green signs, continue on the road for 15min. until you reach the church in front of the ruins. Site open daily 8am-5pm. 27 pesos; Su free.

Mitla: City of death! Bring your camera. Enveloped by a Zapotec-speaking village, this archaeological site, 44km east of Oaxaca, has a bloody history: until the 16th century, it was a place of worship for the gods of the underworld and witnessed both animal and human sacrifice. Although Mitla began as a small village around 1000 BC, the Zapotecs came to occupy it when the Mixtecs forced them out of Monte Albán. It was later appropriated by the Mixtecs and became the largest and most important of the late Mixtec cities. When the Spaniards arrived in the valley, Mitla was the only ceremonial center of the Mesoamerican Classic Period still in use, and they put a stop to the pagan nonsense by subjugating the Mixtecs, destroying their buildings, and erecting a church on top of the ruins. Interestingly, the Catholic archbishop of Oaxaca built his home to echo the horizontal lines of the Zapotec priest's residence in Mitla, in what was either an architectural tribute or an expression of dominance.

Walking to the ruins from the town's main road, you will first come upon the **Grupo del Arroyo,** possibly the least interesting archaelogical site in Mexico: a flat stone patio from AD 1100. Continuing on the main road, the ticket booth is in the yellow building on the far side of the red-domed church; it contains a few artifacts and several dioramas of the site. To the left, and symbolically in the shadow of the church are the three patios known as the **North Group** or **Catholic Establishment.** One of them has been almost completely buried by the church. The central patio is on the other side; here, and in the surrounding rooms, you can see pieces of Mixtec paintings, supposedly telling Mixtec history, done in red on stone. The more impressive ruins are across the road in the **Grupo de las Columnas (Group of the Columns),** decorated inside and out with intricate geometric designs. Beyond the entrance are two patios joined at one corner. In the first, which features the **Hall of the Columns,** the five chambers form a cross; for years, Spaniards thought this proved that the Mixtecs somehow knew the story of Jesus. On the second patio behind and to the right of the first, two tombs are open to visitors. Tomb Two has large stones covered with mosaic patterns. The roof of Tomb One rests on a single huge column known as the **Column of Life.** Pilgrims travel here each year to embrace the column. In exchange for the hug, the column supposedly tells them how much longer they have to live. The two other groups, **Grupo del Sur (South Group)** and **Grupo de Adobe,** are farther from the site, southeast and across the river from the main ruins. Use the diagrams at the site to find these two ruins if you wish to see them, though neither is well preserved.

ARRAZOLA, CUILÁPAM, ZAACHILA, AND ATZOMPA (MEX. 131)

Arrazola, Cuilápam, and Zaachila can all be reached by taking a Zaachila-bound bus (4 pesos) from the second-class bus station. It's easy to hop from one town to the next; go back to Mex. 131 and flag down another colectivo. To get to Arrazola from Mex. 131, ask the driver to drop you off at Arrazola and take another colectivo up the hill. To get back to Mex. 131 from Arrazola, take a Oaxaca-bound colectivo; otherwise, it's a long walk to the highway. Though close to the other three, Atzompa does not lie on Mex. 131. From Oaxaca, it can be reached via a separate colectivo (40min., 8 pesos).

ARRAZOLA. This small, hilly village is the hometown of Manuel Jiménez, one of Mexico's most famous artisans. Jiménez is the creator of **alebrijes,** brightly colored figurines of demons and zoo animals. While success has made his pieces unaffordable to most (small pieces go for US$170), his workshop is worth visiting. To get there, walk up Arrazola's main road, passing the plaza and turning left at the first intersection onto Obregón. Continue past the end of the pavement, following as it curves right. The home is on the right-hand side, opposite a corn field. Ring the buzzer on the green gate. A glimpse of the Jiménez family's kinetic cedar wood sculptures and the possibility of a conversation with the man himself make the substantial trek from Mex. 131 worth the effort. Nearly all the households in town make figurines to supplement their incomes. A medium-sized iguana *alebrije* will cost about 120 pesos. *(20min. from Oaxaca on Mex. 131.)*

CUILÁPAM DE GUERRERO. Cuilápam (pop. 12,800) has a hauntingly lovely 17th-century **Dominican monastery.** The highlight of the site—aside from the breathtaking vistas—is the cell that was once occupied by the Revolutionary hero Vicente Guerrero in 1831 before his death by firing squad on the patio outside. Today, all that remains is a portrait of him in his cell and a monument on the spot where he fell. Built as a retreat for Spanish monks wishing to remove themselves as far as possible from civilization, the upper floor now cloisters archaeologists laboring to reconstruct the region's history in the monk's old stone cells. *(25min. from Oaxaca on Mex. 131. Open daily 10am-6pm. 23 pesos. Video 30 pesos.)*

ZAACHILA. Zaachila (pop. 25,700), the stronghold of the Zapotecs before they fell to the Spanish in 1521, hosts a fascinating market each Thursday. Spend your pesos on preserved bananas and squealing pigs. A yellow and orange cathedral dominates the center of town. To the right and behind the church, a street heads uphill to a partially uncovered archaeological site. Until 1962, locals prohibited excavations to prevent the intrusion of outsiders. Exploration since has been limited, but two Mixtec tombs with well-preserved jewelry have been uncovered. The town's gold, turquoise, jade, and bone artifacts (as well as the tourist dollars they would have attracted) have been moved to the national museum in Mexico City (see p. 116). The eerie tombs—the only decorated ones in Oaxaca—are worth a visit. Wide-eyed owls (messengers of the Zapotec underworld) stare from the damp stone walls, while portrayals of the Gods of Death lurk in the dimmer recesses. *(40min. from Oaxaca on Mex. 131. Open daily 9am-6pm. 23 pesos. Video 30 pesos.)*

ATZOMPA. Atzompa (pop. 11,000), where that magnificent blend of clay and sprouts, the **Chia Pet**®, was born. Natural, green-glazed pottery can be found here at better prices than in Oaxaca. The **Mercado de Artesanías** is a publicly funded forum that brings together the work of the town's artisans. While the selection is good, no bargaining is allowed. Ask around for Delores, an artisan who will demonstrate the Atzompa method for a price. *(Though close to the other villages, Atzompa does not lie on Mex. 131. Take a taxi colectivo marked "Aztompa" from the street north of the bus station. 40 min., 8 pesos.)*

SAN BARTOLO COYOTEPEC AND THE ROAD SOUTH (MEX. 175)

For all three towns, take an Ocotlán-bound bus from the second class bus station or from Transporte Oaxaca Pacífico (☎514 1867) at Armento y Lopez 721, across the street from the Red Cross building (10 pesos).

SAN BARTOLO COYOTEPEC. San Bartolo, 12km south of Oaxaca, is the only place in Mexico that creates the ink-black pottery that populates souvenir shops throughout the state. The dark color comes from the local mud. Though the town had been making the pottery for centuries, it wasn't until 1950, when the diminutive Doña Rosa accidentally discovered that it could be polished, that it became an art form. Doña Rosa kept the polishing technique a family secret for 12 years, then gave it to the town, which has been supported by the craft ever since. In the market, on the east side of Mex. 175, villagers sell jet-black vases, luminaires, figurines, you name it. Many substantial pieces go for under 30 pesos. The polished pottery will only hold water for 20min. or so before soaking it up—only the less-attractive grey pieces are waterproof. Doña Rosa's son carries on the family tradition and gives free demonstrations to groups in the Nieto workshop, several blocks up the town's main street, Juárez, on the west side of Mex. 175. *(Market open daily 9am-8pm. Nieto workshop open daily 9am-2pm, and, if it doesn't rain, 4-6pm.)*

SANTO TOMÁS JALIETZA. Four kilometers farther south and slightly left of the main road, Santo Tomás's artisans specialize in weaving "cotton garments" on back-strap looms by sitting on the ground and tying the looms to a tree. The items produced here are more practically useful than most Oaxacan crafts—purses, shirts, vests, and dresses.

OCOTLÁN DE MORELOS. Above the valley in the foothills of the Sierra Madre del Sur, 33km south of Oaxaca, Ocotlán (pop. 22,000) offers a fairy-tale powder blue **church** and what is undoubtedly Oaxaca's finest shoe-flower-bread-taco-rug-shirt-fruit-chili-backpack-knife-hat-belt-spoon-bucket-tupperware-china-birdcage-pliers-extension cord-bra-saddle-Japanese handheld game-80s picture of Demi Moore **market**. *(Market open F 10am-8pm.)*

NEAR OAXACA:

▨ MONTE ALBÁN

Autobuses Turísticos buses to Monte Albán leave the Hotel Rivera del Ángel, Mina 518 (☎516 5327), between Mier y Terán and Díaz Ordaz, several blocks southwest of the zócalo (30min, every 30min. 8:30am-4pm). Tickets must be purchased exactly 10 min. before bus leaves; round-trips with fixed-return are 24 pesos, but leave little time at the site. Tickets to return later can be bought in the Monte Albán parking lot for 12 pesos. Site open daily 8am-6pm. 37 pesos, 67 pesos with video camera. Though many travel agencies can set you up with hassle-free transportation and excellent guides, it is usually cheaper to transport yourself and, if you want one, find a guide once you reach the mountain. English-language guides charge 150-300 pesos for a 1½hr. tour, depending on the size and negotiating skills of your group (☎516 1215).

High above Oaxaca, Monte Albán, the ancient mecca of the Zapotec "cloud people," now watches over the surrounding mountains in utter stillness. Visitors to Oaxaca should not leave without seeing the ruins, some of the most important and spectacular in Mexico. Mysteriously abandoned by both the Zapotecs and Mixtecs over 1000 years ago, the sacred capital of Monte Albán *feels* ancient. Unless you're an expert on Pre-Hispanic civilizations (or the type that likes her ruins unexplained) a good guide (or the guidebook, sold for 55 pesos in the museum store) to Monte Albán can really make the visit.

HISTORY. The monolithic, geometric stone structures are all that remain of the vast Zapotec capital that once sprawled 20km over three mountaintops. First constructed circa 700 BC, Monte Albán flourished during the Classic Period (AD 250-900), when it shared the spotlight with Teotihuacán and Tikal as the major cultural and ceremonial centers of Mesoamerica. This was the greatest Zapotec capital—the people cultivated maize, built complex drainage systems for water, and engaged in extensive trade networks, especially with Teotihuacán (see p. 138). As Monte Albán grew, daily life was carefully constructed to harmonize with supernatural elements: architecture adhered to the orientation of the four cardinal points and the proportions of the 260-day sacred calendar, and residences were organized in families of five to ten people in four-sided houses with open central courtyards. To emphasize the congruence between household and cosmos, families buried their ancestors beneath their houses to symbolize their transmigration to the underworld below. Excavations of burials in Monte Albán have yielded not only dazzling artifacts, but also valuable information on social stratification.

The history of Monte Albán can be divided into five parts, spanning the years from 500 BC until the Spanish conquest in the 16th century. During **periods I** and **II**, Monte Albán rose as the Maya and Zapotec cultures intermingled. The Zapotecs adopted the Maya *juego de pelota* (ball game) and steep pyramid structure, while the Maya appropriated the Zapotec calendar and writing system. Almost all of the extant buildings and tombs, as well as several urns and murals of *colanijes* (richly adorned priests), come from **Period III** (AD 350-700). Burial arrangements of varying size and richness show the social divisions of the period: priests, clerks, and laborers lived and died apart. For reasons that remain unknown, Monte Albán began to fade around 750. Construction ceased, and control of the Zapotec empire shifted to other cities such as Zaachila, Yagul, and, later, Mitla. Possible explanations for the abandonment include drought, over-exploitation of resources, and unrest. As with other Zapotec strongholds during the subsequent **periods IV** and **V**, the Mixtecs took over. The Mixtecs used Monte Albán as a fortress and a sacred metropolis, reclaiming the tombs left by the Zapotecs. Dr. Alfonso Caso discovered **Tomb 7** in 1932; the treasure found within more than quadrupled the number of previously identified gold Mixtec objects. The treasures from Tomb 7 are now on display at the Museo de las Culturas de Oaxaca (see p. 506).

A small, free on-site museum displays some stone carvings, but the most interesting exhibit by far is a case full of human skulls, some deformed through disease, some through deliberate manipulation of infants' skulls, presumably for ritual beautification.

BALL COURT. After passing through the ticketing station just beyond the museum, walk left up the inclined path leading diagonally toward the ruins. Before reaching the Main Plaza, you will see the remains of several small buildings on your left and the ball court in front of you. The sides of the court, which now look like bleachers, were once covered in stucco and plaster, and served as bouncing boards for the ball toward the goal. In contrast to the Aztecs' gorier use of the game to determine sacrificial victims, the Zapotecs used it to solve all kinds of conflicts and as a means of predicting future events.

MAIN PLAZA. Passing the ball court on your left, you will enter the huge Main Plaza, with the mountain-like **North Platform** on the right, and smaller structures lined up on your left. The Main Plaza is flat, remarkable when one considers that the mountain from which it was cut was originally peaked. On your left, look for

The Palace (Building II). Like other Pre-Hispanic ruins, the structures at Monte Albán were civic and residential as well as religious; this pyramid served as the home of one of Monte Albán's important dignitaries.

MOUND Q. Past the palace sits Mound Q, the ugly red-headed stepchild of Monte Albán, notable for its banality. Even the archaeologists normally willing to claim "great religious and administrative importance" for any pile of rocks suggest only half-heartedly that Mound Q "may be a temple."

SOUTH PLATFORM. Kitty-corner with the palace and forming the plaza's south end is the South Platform, one of the site's highest structures. Another contains a message roughly translated as "North Platform Sux, South Platform Rulz!" believed to be North America's first recorded Zapotec graffiti. The top affords a commanding view of the ruins, valley, and mountains beyond. On both sides of the staircase on the plaza level are stelae carved with priests and tigers. One stela is believed to depict a former Monte Albán king.

BUILDING OF DANCERS. Walking left of the platform to the plaza's west side, you will first come across **System M** and then the Building of Dancers. The reliefs on the center building are known as "dancers," though they more likely depict chieftains conquered by Monte Albán. The over 400 figures date from the 5th century BC and are nearly identical to contemporary Olmec sculptures on the Gulf Coast. Many of the figures show evidence of genital mutilation.

BUILDINGS G, H, I, AND J. Crossing back to the center of the platform, the first structure you hit is Building J, formed in the shape of an arrowhead. Unlike any other ancient edifice in Mexico, it is asymmetrical and built at a 45-degree angle to nearby structures. Its broad, carved slabs suggest that the building is one of the oldest on the site, dating from 100 BC to AD 200. Many of the glyphs depict an upside-down head below a stylized hill. Archeologists speculate that these images represent conquests, the head indicating the tribe defeated and the glyph identifying the region conquered. The next group of buildings moving north, dominating the center of the plaza, are buildings G, H, and I—likely comprising the principal altar of Monte Albán.

NORTH PLATFORM. Finish off the Main Plaza by visiting the North Platform near the entrance, a structure almost as large as the plaza itself. The platform contains the **Sunken Patio** as well as the site's highest altar, the best place to view the entire site and lose yourself in passing clouds.

TOMBS AND MUSEUM. Continue straight on the path, exiting the site to **Tomb 104.** Duck underground, look above the entrance, and gaze at the urn, which is covered with interwoven images of the maize and rain gods. On your way out of the site, be sure to stop by the museum, which gives a chronological survey of Monte Albán's history and displays sculpted stones from the site's earlier periods. Although the collection is still impressive, some of the more spectacular artifacts have unfortunately been hauled off to museums in Oaxaca and Mexico City. Near the parking lot is the entrance to **Tomb 7,** where the spectacular cache of Mixtec ornaments mentioned above was found.

BAHÍAS DE HUATULCO ☎958

Huatulco's promotional literature proclaims it "Paradise Found," as if a band of hardy adventurers hacked their way through the jungle and came upon a vast series of huge beach resorts connected by a freshly paved network of highways. A better name might be "Prefabricated Paradise." This constructedness is not neces-

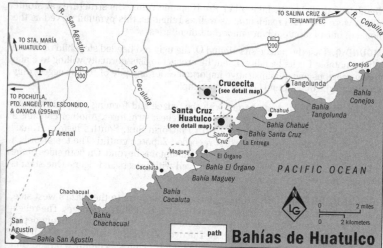

Bahías de Huatulco

sarily a bad thing; authenticity never cleaned anyone's bathroom. Huatulco is well-designed, very clean, and devoid of the slummy neighborhoods that surround most Mexican tourist areas. It is useful as a sort of decompression chamber for those coming from places like Zipolite back to civilization. Huatulco is still a low-key beach town, but clearly in touch with the most current methods of attracting people with money and taking that money from them. Transportation is expensive, as are all hotels inside La Crucecita (which, of course, is a good ways from the beach). The high costs mean that the clientele is almost exclusively middle- and upper-class families, with few backpackers. Watch for neighborhoods with charming names like "Sector F."

▐ TRANSPORTATION

Airport: The airport (☎ 581 9007), 19km from the town of Santa Cruz, is served by **Aerocaribe** (☎ 587 1220) and **Mexicana** (☎ 587 0243). To get to the airport, take a taxi (25min., 100 pesos) or a "Sta. Maria" *micro* from the corner of Guamuchil and Carrizal in Santa Cruz (8 pesos). Ask to be let off at the airport, and walk approximately 500m to the right of where the driver drops you.

Buses: The **Cristóbal Colón station** (☎ 587 0261) is at the corner of Gardenia and Ocotillo in La Crucecita. To get to the *zócalo*, exit left and walk 4 blocks down Gardenia. Cristóbal Colón goes to: **Mexico City** (14-15hr.; 4:30, 8:20pm; 441 pesos); **Oaxaca** (8hr.; 4:45, 11pm; 178 pesos); **Puerto Escondido** (2hr.; 6 per day 3-9:30am, 52 pesos); **San Cristóbal** (11hr.; 8:45, 11:45pm; 241 pesos); **Tuxtla Gutiérrez** (8hr.; 8:45, 11:45pm; 203 pesos). **Estrella Blanca** (☎ 587 0103), farther down Gardenia at Palma Real, travels to: **Acapulco** (10hr.; 5, 9am, 9pm; 217 pesos). The best way to get to **Pochutla,** gateway to Mazunte, Puerto Ángel, Puerto Escondido, and Zipolite, is a **Transportes Rápidos de Pochutla** *micro;* they leave from Carrizal after it curves into an east-west road on the north end of town (1hr., every 15min. 5:30am-9pm, 12 pesos).

✳ ▐ ORIENTATION AND PRACTICAL INFORMATION

Huatulco and its *bahías* (bays) consist of 35km of beach and cove on the southern Oaxacan coast between the Coyula and Copalita rivers, about 295km south of

Oaxaca de Juárez. The most practical place to stay is **La Crucecita,** in the middle of a string of nine bays, which are, from east to west: Conejos, Tangolunda, Chahué, Santa Cruz, El Órgano, Maguey, Cacaluta, Chachacual, and San Agustín. La Crucecita houses the bus stations and the few existing budget accommodations. **Santa Cruz,** the bay closest to La Crucecita, offers the best access to the airport.

TOURIST, FINANCIAL, AND LOCAL INFORMATION

Tourist Office: SEDETUR (☎581 0176 or 0177), inconveniently across from the commercial center in Tangolunda on Juárez; cross to the left side of Juárez at the Argentina Restaurant. Open M-F 8am-3pm, Sa 9am-1pm. Information is more accessible at the **Módulo de Información,** in the *zócalo* toward the east side. Helpful maps and advice. Be sure to check the **official taxi tariffs,** posted on the side of the Módulo; many tourists pay more than they should. Open M-F 9am-2pm and 4-7pm during high seasons.

Currency Exchange: Bital, on the corner of Sabali and Bugambilias, has a **currency exchange** and **ATM.** Open M-Sa 8am-7pm. Half a block from the park on Guamuchil is a 24hr. ATM. **Bancrecer,** Bugambilias 1104, before Macuil and Ocotillo in La Crucecita, exchanges currency and has a 24hr. ATM. Open M-F 9am-5pm, Sa 10am-2pm. Large hotels exchange money at slightly less favorable rates.

Market: 3 de Mayo, on Guamuchil off the *zócalo,* sells trinkets, produce, and meat. Open daily 7am-8pm.

Laundry: Lavandería Estrella, on Flamboyan at the corner of Carrizal, offers same-day service. 35 pesos per 3kg. Open M-Sa 8am-9pm.

Car Rental: Budget, Ocotillo 404 (☎587 0010), 1 block from the 1st-class bus station. VW sedans 480 pesos per day. Also at the airport (☎581 9000). Open daily 8am-8pm.

EMERGENCY AND COMMUNICATIONS

Police: Blvd. Chahué 100 (☎587 0210), in back of the peach government building, 200m south of the intersection of Guamuchil and Chahué. No English spoken.

Emergency: ☎060.

Red Cross: Blvd. Chahué 110 (☎587 1188), next door to the post office and police. No English spoken.

Pharmacy: Farmacia La Clínica (☎587 0591), at Gardenia and Sabali, 4 blocks to the right when exiting the bus station. Closer to the *zócalo* is **Farmacia del Carmen** (☎587 2012), on Guamuchil at Carrizal. Open daily 8am-10pm.

Hospital: Centro de Salud, Carrizal 202 (☎587 1421) at the corner of Guamuchil. No English spoken. Also **Central Médica Huatulco,** Flamboyan 204 (☎587 0104), on the *zócalo.* Emergency services. English spoken.

Fax: Telecomm (☎587 0894; fax 0885), next to the post office. Open M-F 8am-7:30pm, Sa-Su 9am-12:30pm.

Internet Access: El Telefonito (☎587 1794), at Buganbilias and Chacah. 15 pesos per hr. Open daily 8am-10:30pm.

Post Office: Blvd. Chahué 100 (☎587 0551), in the peach government building. Open M-F 8am-3pm, Sa 9am-1pm. **Postal Code:** 70989.

▗ ACCOMMODATIONS AND CAMPING

Camping is a way to escape Huatulco's high-priced hotel scene, but it is allowed only on Chahué, Cacaluta, and Conejos bays. Even in these locations, camping is a risky affair; there is little security, and Cacaluta and Conejos have in the past been sites of confrontation between police and illegal Central American immigrants. **Under no circumstances should you attempt to camp on Santa Cruz or Tangolunda;** hotel security will not be kind. If camping isn't your thing, prepare yourself for slim pickings. All affordable hotels are in La Crucecita, and even those tend be over-priced. Some families rent out rooms, and those willing to search around and negotiate will be rewarded for the effort. Rates rise 20-50% during high season (July-Aug.); listings below are low/high season ranges.

Hotel Posada San Agustín (☎587 0368), on Macuil at Carrizal. Spotlessly clean, bright, and run by a young family, the posada has fans, balconies, and a somewhat noisy atmosphere. Singles 120/180 pesos; doubles 220/350 pesos. ❷

Posada Lido, Flamboyan 209 (☎587 0810), ½ block east of the *zócalo*. 10 very clean rooms, with double beds, fans, and TV. A family shares the building, so it's just like living at home, if you grew up in a Mexican resort town. Communal baths. Singles 150 pesos; doubles with private bath 300 pesos. ❸

Hotel Benimar, Bugambilias 1404 (☎587 0447), at Pochote. Dusky interior harbors fans and full baths. Folks congregate in the lobby to watch TV. Singles and doubles 200/250 pesos; triples 250/300 pesos; quads 350/400 pesos. ❹

Posada del Carmen, Palo Verde 307 (☎587 0593), 2 blocks north of the Cristóbal Colón station. This small hotel has new, clean rooms with tile floors that, unlike in most Mexican budget hotels, look like they were designed by someone who was not color blind. Singles 200/250 pesos; doubles 250/350 pesos. ❹

▐ FOOD

In Huatulco, pricey tourist restaurants experiment in Italian pastas and poorly rendered sushi, while restaurants near the *zócalo* charge handsomely for Mexican dishes. A few cheap options are available on most menus. The best bargains are tacos and barbecued chicken found on **Bugambilias** and **Carrizal.**

El Pollo Imperial (☎587 0498), on Carrizal, just north of Macuil. El Pollo's popular and tasty barbecued chicken comes with beans and pasta salad (¼ chicken 26 pesos, entire chicken 75 pesos). Open daily 9am-8pm. ❸

La Crucecita (☎587 0906), 1 block past the *zócalo* at Bugambilias and Chacah. Upgrade from the plastic tables of taco shops to the plant-rich courtyard of La Crucecita, which manages pleasant dining without exorbitant prices. *Tlayuda*s 40 pesos, *torta*s and sandwiches 22 pesos. Open M and W-Su 7am-10pm. ❷

Restaurant-Bar La Tropicana (☎587 0661), Guanacastle at Gardenia, across from Hotel Flamboyant. So-so food comes 2nd to location, popularity, and hours. Fish filet 50 pesos. *Antojitos* (30-35 pesos) or the wild variety of *torta*s (30 pesos) are the best bet. Open 24hr. ❸

Oasis Café (☎587 0045), at Bugambilias and Flamboyan. Crowded at all hours, with entrees at all prices (from 35 pesos). Open daily 7am-midnight. ❸

◀ BEACHES

As might be expected in a town meticulously designed to rake in tourist dollars, Huatulco's nine bays and 36 beaches, spread over 35km, pose a transportation challenge. It's hard to get off the beaten track without handing over pesos for a taxi or *lancha*. Fortunately, three of the bays are accessible by *colectivos* that leave from the intersection of Guamuchil and Carrizal (4 pesos to Tangolunda, 3 pesos to Santa Cruz). If you plan to take a tour, the tourist bureau recommends going through an official agency in town rather than one of the "guides" vending their services in the street; many tourists have been ripped off in the past. Storefronts such as the **Módulo de Información** next to the Cristóbal Colón station are not official; only the *módulo* in the *zócalo* offers solid advice. If you plan on indulging in water sports, consider going through the company itself to save pesos, rather than dealing with a travel agency. **Hurricane Divers,** at Bahía Chahué, has reliable diving expertise. (☎587 1107. Open daily 9am-7pm.) **Piraguas** (☎587 1333), in La Crucecita, guides white water rafting trips down nearby Río Capolita.

BAHÍA CHAHUÉ. Closest to La Crucecita is Bahía Chahué, which remains relatively unpopulated save for the **beachside camp ❶** of Hotel Castillo, whose facilities are available for a 20-peso charge. Due to economic recession, Chahué is a resort ghost town. Hotels stand half-finished and finely landscaped brick paths lead nowhere. Though the weedy construction zone before the beach is ugly, the beach itself offers a fine stretch of sand perfect for quiet sunbathing. The water is generally safe for swimming, but sometimes rough. (*Take a "Tangolunda" or "Santa Cruz" colectivo. Ask to be let off at Chahué. Alternatively, walk 2 blocks east on Guamuchil to Blvd. Chahué and take a right, then walk 10min. until you come to a T-intersection. The left branch leads to Tangolunda, the right to Santa Cruz. Go straight; Chahué is 5min. down the road.*)

BAHÍA SANTA CRUZ. Bahía Santa Cruz harbors *lanchas*, a profusion of *palapa* restaurants, and a huge, overpriced commercial district. Of its two beaches, **Playa Santa Cruz** and **Playa la Entrega,** Entrega is the better, enticing with good snorkeling, swimming, and a lesser chance of colliding with a banana boat, but it is a 36-peso taxi ride away. Equipment can be rented at Entrega toward the left end of the beach facing the water. Playa Santa Cruz, just past the *lanchas* at the entrance to town, is easier to reach, but smaller and more crowded. Equipment can be rented past the *lanchas*. **Restaurant Ve el Mar,** on the side of the beach nearest the *lanchas*, reputedly has the best seafood in the area. Fish and shrimp cocktails start at 45 pesos. At high tide, waiters carrying towering plates of *mariscos* are forced to leap onto chairs to avoid drenching their white patent shoes. (*Taxis, 40 pesos, or lanchas, 150 pesos per 10 people, will take you from Santa Cruz to Playa Entrega. Equipment 40 pesos per day. To get to Santa Cruz, continue down the right branch of Blvd. Chahué, a 10min. walk or 5min. ride past Bahía Chahué. Restaurant ☎587 0364. Open daily 8am-10pm.*)

BAHÍA MAGUEY. Also 2km from Playa Santa Cruz and less crowded than Entrega, Bahía Maguey is another hot spot for snorkeling and swimming. (*Taxis 45 pesos and lanchas up to 500 pesos per 10 people.*)

BAHÍA TANGOLUNDA. Another affordable, accessible beach, Tangolunda, in the town of the same name, is home to the Zona Hotelera and the Bahía's swankest resorts. The beach is steep and the surf occasionally rough, but it's worth the trip just to look at the huge, opulent hotels. (*Take a 5-peso colectivo; alternately, walk to the right from the hotels when facing the sea.*)

OTHER BAHÍAS. If you don't mind splurging on transportation, **La India, San Agustín,** and **Cacaluta** are best for snorkeling and diving. Cacaluta is also known for its lush plant life and breezes. San Agustín is the most crowded, while Cacaluta, La India, Conejos, and El Órgano are the best shots at solitude. The only other beaches accessible by land are **La Bocana, Bahía Cacaluta** (4WD only), and **Bahía San Agustín;** taxis charge hefty rates to travel this far. Another option is renting a bike or car for the day (see **Practical Information,** p. 516). *Lanchas* from the **Cooperativa Tangolunda** in Santa Cruz travel to other beaches (prices vary by beach and size of boat, but are guaranteed to be high—over 400 pesos). If you go in the morning you may find people to share the ride, and during the low season you can bargain for lower rates. The *cooperativa* offers the most economical all-day tour of the bays, stopping at Maguey and San Agustín, where you can snorkel with an English-speaking guide and eat lunch. (*☎587 0081. Open daily 8am-6pm. Tours 10 and 11am in high season; 11am in low season. 250 pesos. Call 1 day in advance.*)

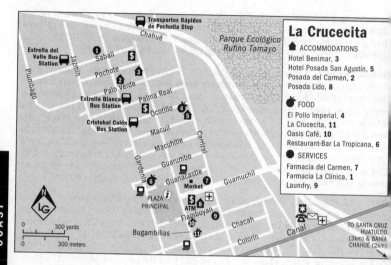

La Crucecita

▲ ACCOMMODATIONS

Hotel Benimar, 3
Hotel Posada San Agustín, 5
Posada del Carmen, 2
Posada Lido, 8

● FOOD

El Pollo Imperial, 4
La Crucecita, 11
Oasis Café, 10
Restaurant-Bar La Tropicana, 6

● SERVICES

Farmacia del Carmen, 7
Farmacia La Clínica, 1
Laundry, 9

🎵 ENTERTAINMENT

The abundance of family vacationers in Huatulco means nightlife isn't quite as wild as in other beach towns. The *zócalo*, though, tends to be fairly crowded and there are a few rockin' joints in Santa Cruz, a 13-peso taxi ride from La Crucecita.

LA CRUCECITA

Restaurant Bar La Crema (☎587 0702), at Gardenia between Flamboyan and Chacah, on the 2nd fl. overlooking the *zócalo*. Wicker chairs, a pool table, a large, mixed crowd, loud Mexican and American music, and kitsch. Beer 15 pesos. Open daily 8pm-4am.

Cafe Internet Choco Latte (☎587 0165), across from La Crema, on the bottom floor of Hotel Misión Los Arcos. Outdoorsy European ambience and relatively cheap access make the concept of traveling thousands of miles to a beautiful country and then sitting in front of a computer screen slightly less ridiculous. Astoundingly clean bathrooms. *Café americano* 10 pesos. Internet 30 pesos per hr. Open daily 8am-11:30pm.

Iguana Bar, at the northwest corner of the *zócalo*, features a live iguana and sports on TV. Next to the Portales restaurant. Tacos 44 pesos, beer 15 pesos. Open daily 8am-2am.

SANTA CRUZ

El Dexkite (☎587 0971), past the *lancha* docks on the left. Torches light a strip of private beach, while partiers dance in the sand and consume economical drinks. 40 pesos for .5L of beer, 50 pesos for 1L. The action starts at midnight. Cover 60 pesos. Open daily 10pm-5am in high season; closed in low season.

La Aqua (☎587 0017), past the public beach entrance, down Mitla to where it curves, is a standard disco experience. Cover 60 pesos. Open daily 10pm-late in high season, Th-Sa 10pm-late in low season.

Santa Cruz Huatulco

TO LA
CRUCECITA
(3km)

Boulevard Benito Juárez

Huajutla
Miahuatlán
Mixtepec
Nochixtlan

Calle E-1a
Calle E-4

Tlacolula
Zoquiapan

*Ecological
Reserve*

Boulevard Santa Cruz

PLAZA
S. MIGUEL

Calle Mitla

Monte Albán

Ocotlán

Pochutla

■ **Cooperativa
Tangolunda**

Calle Mitla

*Ecological
Reserve*

*Bahía de
Santa Cruz*

Calle Acatlán

0 — 150 yards
0 — 150 meters

N

SOUTHERN PACIFIC COAST

POCHUTLA

☎ **958**

Though you may be disoriented after the long and terrifying bus trip through the mountains and think that Pochutla's thick, hot air hints at the proximity of the ocean, do not disembark. You will find yourself not in a beachside paradise but rather a transportation hub filled with buses, taxis, and dust. Come here only to stock up on money and other necessities.

Taxis colectivos headed to **Puerto Escondido** (50 pesos), **Puerto Ángel** (5 pesos), **Zipolite** (15 pesos), and beyond leave from the downhill part of town, across from the Estrella del Valle bus station. The most efficient way to travel between coast towns is by *camioneta* (every 20min. 6am-8pm; 5 pesos to Puerto Ángel, 7 pesos to Zipolite or Mazunte). The second-class **bus station,** on the right side of Cárdenas as you enter the city, sends buses to: **Oaxaca** (7hr.; daily 5, 6:15, 7:30am; 70 pesos); **Mexico City** (12hr.; 6, 7pm); **Puerto Escondido** (1hr., 7 per day). **Tránsitos Rápidos de Pochutla,** just past the second-class station, goes to **Bahías de Huatulco** (1hr., daily every 15 min. 5:15am-8:20pm, 12 pesos) and **Oaxaca** (7hr.; 9:45am, 2:15, 11pm; 90 pesos).

Most banks, services, and shops, as well as the town's two bus stations are on **Cárdenas,** the main street. Bus stations and cheaper hotels are downhill, closer to the freeway entrance, while banks and supermarkets are farther uphill, where the road curves right. To reach the *zócalo,* church, and main outdoor market, follow Cárdenas uphill and turn right on Juárez a block after the area where the *colectivos* drop-off. **Inverlat,** just after Juárez branches off Cárdenas to the right, uphill from the bus stations, has a 24hr. **ATM** (open for exchange M-F 9am-5pm), as does **Bital,** north of the *zócalo* on Cárdenas. (Open for exchange M-F 8am-7pm, Sa 8am-3pm.) **Mercado 15 de Octubre,** 25m uphill from the Cristóbal Colón station on the right, sells mainly food. (Open daily 6am-9pm.) Other services include: **police,** in the Palacio Municipal to the left of the church (☎584 0159; no English spoken); **Farmacias de Más Ahorro,** just before Juárez on Cárdenas, open 24hr.; **Hospital General,** also known as **SSA,** between Pochutla and Puerto Ángel (☎584 0219; no English spoken); **Internet access** at **Componet,** on the left on Cárdenas as the hill begins to climb (10 pesos per hr.; open M-Sa 9am-9pm); **post office,** right on Juárez toward the *zócalo* and to the left of the church, behind the Palacio Municipal. (Open M-F 8am-3pm.) **Postal code:** 70900.

Hotel Santa Cruz ❶, just up the street from the Cristóbal Colón station, has clean rooms for crashing in the event of a long layover. (Singles 70 pesos; doubles 120 pesos.) **Hotel Izalo ❶**, on Cárdenas just past Juárez, is quieter and a bit fancier. (Singles 130 pesos; doubles 300 pesos.) **Cafe Cafe ❸**, off Cárdenas on the far side of the *zócalo*, serves a small selection of baguettes, starting at 30 pesos. (*Café americano* 8 pesos. Open daily 8am-11pm.)

PUERTO ÁNGEL ☎958

Between the more developed resorts of Huatulco and Puerto Escondido are Puerto Ángel, Zipolite, and Mazunte, none of which are directly accessible by bus. Unfortunately, the area bore the brunt of Hurricane Pauline in 1997. Since then, the towns have struggled to rebuild; construction continues on many streets, trash lines once picturesque pathways, and the dog population seems on the verge of conquest. In comparison to Huatulco's contrived opulence and Puerto Escondido's slightly affected hipness, Puerto Ángel is just a beach. Yet it is scenic, swimmable, and secluded—enough for most.

⌸ TRANSPORTATION. Puerto Ángel is 240km south of Oaxaca and 68km east of Puerto Escondido. All transportation in or out of Puerto Ángel passes the **sitio stand** on Uribe. Puerto Ángel is second in the great **camioneta** loop linking Pochutla, Zipolite, and Mazunte (every 20min. 6am-7pm, 3-8 pesos depending on which way you're going). **Taxis** link Puerto Ángel to: **Pochutla** (15min.; 50 pesos, 5 pesos shared), **Zipolite** (10min.; 30 pesos/5 pesos), and **Mazunte** (20min.; 30 pesos/5 pesos). They can be flagged down anywhere along Uribe or Principal.

▰▱ ORIENTATION AND PRACTICAL INFORMATION. The *carretera* that connects Pochutla to Zipolite becomes Puerto Ángel's main drag as it runs through town and later **Principal** as it descends the hillside from Pochutla; finally called **Uribe,** it curves 90 degrees to the right and hits downtown. The *sitio* stand and all the town's hotels lie directly on or close to this main road. After Uribe curves right, **Playa Principal** skirts the road on the left. The only significant side street, **Vasconcelos,** branches to the right off Uribe soon after the turn.

Services in Puerto Ángel are minimal; most must be begged, borrowed, or imported from nearby Pochutla. The **tourist office** is at Uribe and Vasconcelos. (Open daily 9am-2pm and 4-8pm.) There is **no bank** in Puerto Ángel; several upscale hotels change money at exorbitant rates. A **market** 25m to the right on the street after Vasconcelos offers little more than produce. (Open daily 7am-8pm.) Other services include: the **supermarket Cedemar,** on the right at Pallo Bello; **police,** reachable via the **Agencia Municipal; Farmacia Villa Florencia,** attached to the hotel of the same name, on Uribe shortly past the turn-off for Vasconcelos (☎584 3044; open daily 8:30am-9pm); **Hospital General (SSA),** between Puerto Ángel and Pochutla (no English spoken); **Centro de Salud,** at the top of Vasconcelos to the left on a dirt path (open daily); **Telecomm,** next to the post office (open M-F 9am-3pm); **Gel@net,** at Vasconcelos 3, just after Hotel Soraya, with a long distance **caseta.** (Internet 20 pesos per hr. Open daily 8am-10pm.) The town lacks working **LADATELs;** several other *casetas* are farther up Uribe. The **post office** is at the 90-degree turn. (**No Mexpost**. Open M-F 9am-3pm.) **Postal code:** 70902.

⌂ ACCOMMODATIONS. Though prices rise during July and August, the city is filled with options year-round. Most hotels are on or right off Uribe. Reservations recommended during July, August, December, and *Semana Santa.*

Hotel Capy (☎584 3002), on the left 5min. up the hill, at the street leading to Playa Panteón. Well-maintained rooms, and private baths. Its impressive view of the cove is best appreciated while enjoying a moderately priced meal in the quality balcony restaurant. Fish filet 45 pesos. Singles 100 pesos; doubles 150-170 pesos; triples 190 pesos; quads 200 pesos. ❷

El Peñasquito, on the left on the side street leading to Playa Panteón. A clean, safe bungalow with hammocks. 50 pesos per night. ❶

La Buena Vista (☎584 3104; www.labuenavista.com), off Uribe before it starts climbing—watch for the sign. Elegant rooms and bungalows situated on the leafy hillside overlooking the bay. Amenities include private hammocks, a terrace-top swimming pool, and a patio restaurant (vegetarian *tamales* 60 pesos). Doubles 330-480 pesos. ❺

Gundi y Tomas (☎584 3068; gundtoma@hotmail.com), conveniently situated on a hill by the taxi stand. Clean, artsy rooms feature terraces with scenic vistas and hammocks. Kitchen, laundry, restaurant, and shuttle service to neighboring beaches and the airport. Doubles 160 pesos, with bath 180 pesos. Also rents rooms in the nearby **Hotel Almendro.** Doubles with bath 200 pesos. ❸

Puesta del Sol Hotel (☎584 3096; puesta_del_sol@puertoangel.net). Look for the sign after Uribe starts to climb. In an elegant old-school Mexican house; doesn't look like it would offer some of the cheapest rooms in the city. Cheap meals, interior courtyard, Internet available. Singles 100 pesos, with bath 180 pesos; doubles 130 pesos. ❷

Casa Arnel Puerto Ángel (☎584 3051), off Uribe on the right before the hill. Clean rooms with baths, second floor patio with hammocks. Laundry, Internet available (15 pesos per hr.). Singles 150 pesos; doubles 170-180 pesos. ❸

🍴 **FOOD.** Much of the fish that fries in Zipolite first saw land in Puerto Ángel. Recently deceased, yet-to-be-prepared fish pile up alongside many restaurants. By the basketball court between Playa Principal and Uribe, the tasty seafood at **Restaurant Maca** ❹ compensates for the concrete atmosphere. Prices are moderate to high, but the fish are fresh to barely-dead and the serving sizes are big to enormous. An upstairs bar has 274 cocktails on the menu. (Fish filet 45-60 pesos. Seafood soup 70 pesos. Restaurant open daily 8am-11pm. Bar open daily 4pm-3am.) **Beto's Restaurant Bar** ❸, on Uribe across from Hotel Capy. (Fish filets 27 pesos. Open daily 4pm-midnight.) **Restaurant Villa Florencia** ❸, at the Villa Florencia hotel on Uribe, has a reasonably priced international menu that features breakfast, tacos, seafood, spaghetti, and hamburgers. (Octopus 48 pesos. Open daily in high season 7am-midnight, in low season 2-11pm.)

🏖 **BEACHES.** Though Puerto Ángel's cove is small and slightly crowded, its beaches still have sparkling water and white sand. **Playa Principal,** off Uribe, is closest to the docks and fishing boats. Though slightly grimier, it offers a tad more breathing room than **Playa Panteón.** Refreshment stands envelop both beaches. The two beaches, connected by a stone walkway, encircle a harbor with superb snorkeling. Panteón is also accesible via a footpath near the footbridge on Uribe, or by the paved side street branching left farther up Uribe. On Panteón, **Azul Profundo** rents snorkeling gear and leads tours. (☎584 3109. Snorkeling tours 100 pesos per hr., scuba tours 450-600 pesos per hr., fishing tours 300 pesos per hr.)

For better sand and more space, head east to **Playa Estacahuite** (a-stack-o-wheatie). Over the headland from Puerto Ángel's bay, Estacahuite's three little beaches (the 3rd is to the right of the path) are pristine. Although they can be reached by *lancha* from Puerto Ángel (100-150 pesos) or taxi (starting at 25 pesos round-trip), the walk is pleasant and easy (30min.). From Playa Principal, turn right on Uribe and walk uphill toward Pochutla. The dirt road to Estacahuite branches to the right as the road curves uphill, just past the telephone pole numbered E0034. Follow the road as it climbs and curves left around a hill and finally plunges steeply to the beach. Snorkeling is good and the beach is a beauty, but be careful—emergency services are far away. Farther down the coast is **Playa Boquilla,** the only other beach accessible by land. The sand is smooth and the waves small. The beach is difficult to reach without taxi or *lancha.* It's 4km on the road to Pochutla, then another 3km along a dirt road to the right (marked by a "Playa Boquilla" sign). Take a *camioneta* (3 pesos) or *taxi colectivo* (5 pesos) to the sign and walk, or take a snorkeling trip and remain at the beach, arranging to be picked up when the tour returns (100 pesos). Keep in mind that, like in Playa Estacahuite, services are nonexistent in Playa Boquilla. The walk back can be grueling, though many of the houses along the trail sell refreshments.

ZIPOLITE ☎958

Zipolite's reputation precedes it. The town is widely regarded as a European hedonist's paradise; nudity is the rule on the west end of the beach, and joints are as common as coffee. During high season, visitors flock to Zipolite; as with most beach towns, however, the town becomes nearly deserted during low season. For those interested less in fleshy delights and more in the surf, Zipolite's beach is unfortunately plagued by dangerous currents. Nowadays, it seems that many beach-seeking tourists head to Mazunte (see p.526), which has a nicer beach. Zipolite also has had problems with crime, so visitors should exercise caution.

TRANSPORTATION. Just 4km west of Puerto Ángel, Zipolite is easily accessible by any vehicle rumbling down the poorly paved coastal road. *Camionetas* (3 pesos), *taxis colectivos* (5 pesos), and *taxis especiales* (30 pesos) pass more frequently. From Pochutla, *taxis colectivos* are 7 pesos during the day. At night, take a private taxi. (25min., 70 pesos.)

ORIENTATION AND PRACTICAL INFORMATION. Zipolite consists of one 2km stretch of beach and the roads that run behind it. Look for the sign pointing toward the waves; to get to the major hotels, go down the dirt road at the west end of the beach. While there is **no currency exchange** in Zipolite, most hotels and *cabañas* accept dollars, and some of the bigger ones accept traveler's checks. The nearest hospital, **General Hospital,** is between Puerto Ángel and Pochutla. (☎584 0219. No English spoken.) **Farmacia Fraya,** on the road across from the police station at the east edge of town, has limited medical supplies and houses a small general store. (Open daily 8am-10pm.) Supplies are cheaper in Pochutla. **Zipolnet Communications,** on a dirt road running perpendicular to the west end of the beach, has *casetas,* fax, and Internet. (Internet 15 pesos per hr. Open M-Sa 8am-10pm.)

ACCOMMODATIONS. Almost every *palapa* on the beach has huts out back, most with relatively clean shared baths. Whichever you choose, be sure to put valuables in a safe box. Nicer, more secure **cabañas ❶** and rooms are on the west side of the beach. (Hammocks 30 pesos; *cabañas* 80 pesos.) Alongside the beach is **Hotel Brisa Marina ❶,** a multi-story hotel with clean rooms from the simple to near-luxurious. Owned by an American expat, the hotel is also home to two pet *tejones,* a raccoon-like creature native to Mexico. (☎584 3193; brisamarina@prodigy.net.mx. Singles 60 pesos, with bath 100 pesos; doubles 150 pesos, with balcony and bath 200 pesos. Because *tejones* have been known to bite, the hotel does not accept families with small children.) Almost to the west end of the beach, **Posada San Cristóbal ❶,** a tree- and hammock-filled courtyard opening onto the beach, projects powerful rays of lethargy. Communal bathrooms are clean, and each bed comes with its own mosquito net. (☎584 3191. Singles 70 pesos, with bath 100 pesos; doubles 120 pesos. Discounts for longer stays.) For a more private experience, try **Lo Cósmico ❸**, at the far west end of the beach, with rustic cabins perched on a hill overlooking the sea and communal baths. (Rooms 150-200 pesos.) **La Choza ❶**, a short walk east of Paraiso, rents budget rooms. (☎584 3190. Rooms 80 pesos, with bath 100 pesos.) On the east side of the beach, **Lyoban ❶** rents cheap *cabañas* and hammocks and features a lobby with restaurants, bar, a safe, and lockers. (Hammocks 50 pesos; singles 100 pesos; doubles 150 pesos.)

█ **FOOD.** Seafood and pasta restaurants abound, and the hordes of health-conscious environmentalists ensure that vegetarian dishes are easy to find. Most of the best restaurants are at the west end of the beach. **San Cristóbal ❸** is a seafood-based breakfast (starting at 20 pesos) and lunch hot spot. (☎584 3191. Fish filets 40-45 pesos. Open daily 7am-11pm.) Your best bet for Italian is **El Alquimista Restaurant and Pub ❸**, just past San Cristóbal. (Huge bowls of delicious spaghetti 40 pesos, pizza 45 pesos. Open daily 5pm-1am.) **2 de Diciembre ❸**, about two blocks north of El Paraiso at the corner of two dirt roads, serves stellar vegetarian meals (35 pesos). Also popular is their extensive *pay* (pie) menu, ranging from all-natural fruit pies to the decadent *pay de chocolate*. (Open Tu-Sa 6:30am-12:30am.)

█ **BEACHES AND WARNINGS.** Besides the sea, the only sights in Zipolite are sunbathers or brutal waves coming in from two directions, creating a series of channels that suck unsuspecting, naked swimmers out to sea. Although ferocious, these channels are not very wide. If you find yourself being pulled from shore, do not panic and do not attempt to swim directly toward the beach; rather, swim parallel to the beach until clear of the seaward current. Also watch for red and yellow warning flags on the beach that mark especially dangerous areas. Many people have drowned at Zipolite, and warnings should be taken seriously. If you do swim, keep close to the shore in areas that are highly populated. Zipolite is plagued by theft, so keep an eye on your valuables when you step in for a dip. Better yet, leave them locked somewhere. A final warning: **scorpions** are common in Zipolite. Give your boots a good shake before plunging your feet in.

WEST FROM ZIPOLITE

The following sites, listed from east to west, are all accessible via a "Mazunte" *camioneta* from Zipolite (every 20min. 6am-7pm, 3 pesos), or any Zipolite-bound *camioneta* from Pochutla.

EL MARIPOSARIO. An easy walk or short *camioneta* ride on the road to Mazunte leads to the Mariposario, the closest of three conservation-education centers. The netted sanctuary pays a much overdue tribute to the butterflies that flutter through Mexican forests like confetti. Frogs and iguanas are also on display. The preserve covers three hectares of land, and the butterflies get special attention from the guides, one of whom speaks English. The tour (20min.) includes a visit to the sanctuary. (Open Tu-Sa 9am-4pm. 20 pesos.)

SAN AGUSTINILLO. Four kilometers from Zipolite, the small town of San Agustinillo perches on a beach of the same name, where an European beach scene awaits under the *palapas*. Although developing, San Agustinillo remains less colonized and less hyped than Zipolite, although it is also less lively and accommodations are a bit shabbier. The two coves that form the harbor have fairly manageable surf (stay away from the rocks), which can be harnessed with body boards, fins, or surfboards rented from **Mexico Lindo** (30 pesos per hr.). Many beginners start here before braving the bigger waves at Zipolite. Mexico Lindo also rents some of the best **rooms ❷** on the beach: new and clean with fans, private baths, and double beds. (Singles and doubles 100 pesos.) The **restaurant ❹** serves a mean 60-peso fish filet. (Open daily 8am-10pm.) Other accommodations in town are basically the same: slightly dingy cabañas 50 pesos, hammocks 20 pesos.

MAZUNTE

☎958

Dreadlocks are the new tie-dye, and Mazunte is the new Zipolite. This 1km stretch of beach is one of the most beautiful on the Southern Pacific coast and attracts backpackers from all over the world to happily laze on its white sand. At night, enjoy fresh seafood at one of the beachfront *palapas* while watching hippies twirl fire batons to the beat of a dozen bongos.

TRANSPORTATION. Mazunte can be accessed by taking a "Mazunte" *camioneta* from Zipolite (every 20min. 6am-7pm, 3 pesos). *Camionetas* also run to and from Pochutla (approx. 7 pesos).

ORIENTATION AND PRACTICAL INFORMATION. Mazunte is a 1km stretch of beach with a secluded cove on the far west end. Parallel to the beach is the main road, which runs between Mazunte and nearby towns. A dirt road running between the main road and the beach is full of signs for rooms to rent. The **Internet** cafe, **Caseta Telefónica Omar** (20 pesos per hr.), is also on this road. There are **no LADATELs,** and other than a few poorly-stocked convenience stores and some houses that take in **laundry,** there are no amenities in town. **La Casa de Chelita,** down the dirt road from Telefónica, will wash your clothes (30 pesos per 12 pieces), but better values are to be found by asking around the *palapas*. A small **tourist information** stand on the east end of the main road is open sporadically.

ACCOMMODATIONS. La Luna Nueva ❶, off a dirt path midway down the main road, offers one of the best deals in town. The bed and breakfast has three rooms with mosquito nets, fans, hammocks, and a clean common bathroom. (Doubles 70 pesos.) If La Luna Nueva is full, **Posada del Arquitecturo ❶,** up a hill on the left side of the western dirt road, just before the cove, is a good alternative. It sports clean, pretty *cabañas*, hammocks, some bamboo beds, and a clearing for camping. (Hammocks 30 pesos; suspended double beds 45 pesos; *cabañas* 150-280 pesos.) You can also try **Cabanas la Ziga ❷,** on the far east end of the beach, which has large clean rooms and a few hammocks. (Singles 120 pesos; doubles 150 pesos.) For a bit of a splurge, down the western-most dirt road and up a hill is **La Alta Mira ❺,** which has 10 elegant private bungalows nested along the rocky hillside overlooking the cove. Although lacking electricity, these are the most luxurious rooms in town. (☎584 3104. Bungalows 350-450 pesos.) In addition to the hotels, many houses between the main road and the beach rent rooms; the *palapa* restaurants on the beach rent hammocks and hammock spaces. (15 pesos if you have your own hammock, 20 pesos to rent one of theirs.)

SIGHTS. Besides the excellent and popular **beach,** the town's main attraction is the **Museo de la Tortuga** (National Mexican Turtle Center), the first thing you see coming into town. Though the number of people looking out for the health of the Oaxacan coast is still dangerously small, interest is growing. An anchor in the movement, the museum draws tour buses to Mazunte to observe turtles large and small in outdoor tanks; the specialized aquarium containing six sea turtle species, five river species, and three land species; and the obligatory gift shop. The museum also serves as a research center, seeking new ways to protect the species—presumably the goal of a recent project documented with photographs and charts, that involved gluing large transmitters to the backs of sea turtles. (Open Su 10am-2:30pm, W-Sa 10am-4:30pm. 20 pesos. Tours approx. every 10min.) A short 1.5km *camioneta* ride east of Mazunte is **Playa Ventanilla,** which has vicious, swimmer-hostile waves and dirty sand. The reason to make the trip is the **Cooperativa Ventanilla.** The Cooperativa is a 700m walk down the dirt path marked by the "La Ventanilla" sign and houses a small colony of families who work to preserve the wetland wildlife system at the mouth of the Tonameca River. The group runs amazing *lancha* tours (1hr.; 35 pesos, children 6-12 15 pesos) that pass through the mangrove swamps. Guides paddle through the lagoon in small boats, pointing out enormous crocodiles lurking only feet away. The tour includes a stop on an island in the middle of the lagoon which houses a mangrove farm, baby croc pens, and a refreshment stand. (Open daily 6am-7pm.)

⬛⬛ FOOD AND NIGHTLIFE. All the restaurants at the beach have varied menus and uniformly fresh and delicious seafood at reasonable prices. Most are open late and double as bars until even later. Restaurants offer a range of foods including a whole red snapper with french fries, rice, and avocado (approx. 50 pesos), garlic shrimp (70 pesos), quesadillas and *tortas* (10-20 pesos), and breakfasts (20-25 pesos). On the west end of the main road, **Palapa Tania ❷** has huge platters of food at slightly lower prices. (Fish 30-50 pesos, *ceviche* 30 pesos, *pollo a la mexicana* 35 pesos.)

For nightlife and great dancing, **La Barrata ❷** is the place to go. On a path off the westernmost dirt road, an international crowd salsas the night away, drinking cheap beer and great *caipirhinas* (25 pesos).

PUERTO ESCONDIDO ☎954

The narrow highway that runs into Puerto Escondido winds out of the mountains and parallels the coast. Lined on both sides by jungle, it rarely reveals the blue water to the south until the forest parts for the city, revealing a thousand lights crawling out of the Pacific Ocean into the hills. This first impression may be the best thing about Puerto Escondido, but waves also await the surf-loving traveler. Playa Zicatela is considered one of the world's best surfing beaches. The rest of the city is tourist-generated sprawl—not particularly noteworthy, but not destructively gaudy or trashy either.

▐ TRANSPORTATION

Airport: (☎582 0492) is best reached by taxi (35 pesos). **AeroCaribe** (☎582 2023) flies to Mexico City, Oaxaca, and Bahías de Huatulco.

Buses: All of the bus stations are scattered uptown, just past the *crucero*. To get to the beaches and hotels, simply walk downhill. The parking lot of **Estrella Blanca** (☎582 0086) can be seen across the freeway at the curve of Oaxaca. Buses go to: **Acapulco** (8hr. semi-direct; 4, 10, 11:30am. 9½hr. regular, 7 per day 5am-2pm. Both 196 pesos); **Bahías de Huatulco** via **Pochutla** (2½hr., 6 per day 7am-7pm, 35-53 pesos); and **Mexico City** (12hr.; 6:30,7:30, 8:30pm; 399 pesos). On Hidalgo 2 blocks to the right of Oaxaca is **Estrella de Valle** (☎582 0050), with the best service to **Oaxaca** (6½hr., 11 per day, 85-92 pesos). **Cristóbal Colón,** 1 Nte. 207 (☎582 1073) sends buses to: **Bahías de Huatulco** (2hr., 8 per day 8:45am-9:30pm, 52 pesos); **San Cris-**

tóbal de las Casas (14hr.; 6:30, 9:30pm; 292 pesos); **Tuxtla Gutiérrez** (12hr.; 6:30, 9:30pm; 255 pesos). Cristóbal Colón also travels 1st-class to Oaxaca, but by a route that takes 5hr. longer than 2nd-class service. Micros to **Pochutla** leave from the *crucero* (1hr., every 30-60min., 15 pesos).

✦ 🛈 ORIENTATION AND PRACTICAL INFORMATION

Built on a hillside 294km south of Oaxaca on **Mex. 175,** Puerto Escondido is bisected by **Mex. 200,** also known as **Carretera Costera,** which divides uphill from downhill. The main tourist corridor, known as the **Adoquín, Las Cadenas,** and **Gasga** at different sections, loops down from Mex. 200, scoops the main beach, and reconnects again at the **crucero.** Going east from the *crucero* will take you to **Zicatela.** Locals may insist that Puerto Escondido is safe, but recent assaults on tourists have prompted the tourist office to recommend that travelers stay in groups and avoid isolated beaches, even during daylight hours. **Taxis** can be found by the tourist information booth and along Carretera Costera and Calle de Morro in Zicatela; they are the safest way of getting around after nightfall (15 pesos).

Tourist Office: Módulo de Información Turística (☎582 0175), the booth at the beginning of the pedestrian walkway, down Gasga from the *crucero.* Advice in your language or something close to it. Open M-F 9am-2pm and 4-6pm, Sa 10am-1pm. If the office is unavailable, try the IFOPE library.

Currency Exchange: Banamex (☎582 0626), on Gasga as it curves up from the tourist corridor, exchanges traveler's checks and has an **ATM.** Open 24hr. **Money Exchange** (☎582 2800), on the Adoquín halfway up the hill, has bad rates but convenient hours. Open daily 8am-9pm. Good rates and **ATMs** are available at **Bancrecer,** on Hidalgo between Oaxaca and 1 Pte. Open M-F 9am-5pm, Sa 10am-2pm. **Bital** (☎582 1824), 1 Nte. at 3 Pte., also has **ATMs.** Open M-F 8am-7pm.

Markets: Mercado Benito Juárez, 8 Nte. at 3 Pte. Typical goods in an organized setting. Open daily 5am-8pm, but busiest W and Sa, when the fresh produce comes in.

Supermarket: Ahorrara (☎582 1128), at 3 Pte. and 4 Nte. Open Su 8am-4pm, M-Sa 8am-9pm.

Laundry: Lavamática del Centro, Gasga 405, uphill from the pedestrian walkway on the right, next to Banamex. 15 pesos per kg. Open Su 8am-5pm, M-Sa 8am-8pm.

Library: IFOPE Library (ifope@yahoo.com), in Rinconada by Monte de Piedad. 900 books in English, French, German, and Spanish. Open W and Sa 10am-2pm.

Luggage Storage: None at the bus stations, but nearby Hotel Mayflower will guard your belongings. 10 pesos per day.

Car Rental: Alamo (☎582 3003), on Perez Gasga across from the tourist info booth.

Emergency: In an extreme emergency, contact Sheila Clarke (☎582 0276) or go to the Hotel Mayflower and find owner Minne Dahlberg (☎582 0367); the two head **Friends of Puerto Escondido International (IFOPE),** a neighborhood watchdog group of area expatriates. They will get you in contact with your embassy, the police, or medical help.

Police: (☎582 0498), on the bottom floor of the Agencia Municipal, on 3 Pte. at the corner of Hidalgo. No English spoken.

Red Cross: (☎582 0550), 7 Nte. between Oaxaca and 1 Pte. No English spoken. 24hr. ambulance service.

Pharmacy: Farmacia La Moderna 1, Gasga 203 (☎582 0698 or 582 2780) as it curves down from the *crucero.* Open 24hr.

SOUTHERN PACIFIC COAST

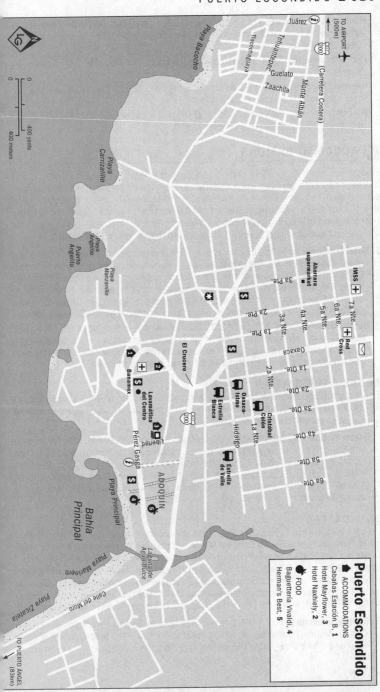

TO AIRPORT
(500m)

Juárez

200
(Carretera Costera)

Tlacochauaya
Tehuantepec
Guelato
Zaachila
Monte Albán

Playa Bacocho

Playa Carrizalillo

Playa Angelito
Puerto Angelito

Playa Manzanillo

IMSS

7a. Nte.
6a. Nte.
5a. Nte.
4a. Nte.
3a. Nte.
2a. Nte.
1a. Nte.

Red Cross

Ahorrara supermarket

3a. Pte.
2a. Pte.
3a. Pte.
1a. Pte.

Oaxaca

1a. Ote.
2a. Ote.
3a. Ote.
4a. Ote.
5a. Ote.
6a. Ote.

Oaxaca-Istmo

Cristóbal Colón

Hidalgo

El Crucero

Banamex

Lavamática del Centro

Liberad

200

Pérez Gasga

Estrella Blanca

Estrella de Valle

ADOQUIN

Playa Principal

Bahía Principal

Playa Marinero

Laguna de Agua Dulce

Playa Zicatela
Calle del Moro
Playa del Moro

TO PUERTO ÁNGEL
(83km)

Puerto Escondido

ACCOMMODATIONS
Cabañas Estación B, 1
Hotel Mayflower, 3
Hotel Naxhiely, 2

FOOD
Baguetería Vivaldi, 4
Herman's Best, 5

0   400 yards
0   400 meters

Medical Assistance: IMSS (☎582 0142), Av. 2 Pte. and 7 Nte. **Centro de Salud,** Gasga 409 (☎582 0016), is a small, minimal-expense medical clinic. No English spoken. Open 24hr. for emergencies.

Fax: Telecomm (☎582 0957), next door to the post office. Open M-F 8am-7:30pm, Sa 9am-noon.

Internet: Tigre@zul, on the Adoquín near the tourist office, is also a bar and cafe. 25 pesos per hour. Open daily 8:30am-11pm.

Post Office: 7 Nte. 701 (☎582 0959), at Oaxaca, a 15min. walk uphill from the *crucero.* Open M-F 8am-3pm. **Postal Code:** 71980.

ACCOMMODATIONS

Budget accommodations in Puerto Escondido are bested in terms of location and ambience by comparably priced *cabañas* and hotels on Zicatela, which offer better access to beaches. Prices fluctuate in Puerto Escondido, rising during the busy months of March, April, July, August, and December. During high season, many hotels have no officially posted rates. Rates listed are for low season. Reservations are recommended during *Semana Santa,* Christmas, July, and August.

Hotel Mayflower (☎582 0367), on Libertad. From the bus station, cross the *crucero* and go left down a steep hill. The road ends, but stairs descend on the right to the entrance. Bright and funky, Mayflower is more like a deluxe youth hostel than a hotel. Clean, tiled rooms with private baths and balconies surround a common area with hammocks and shelves of books. Communal kitchen, pool tables, and a rooftop bar. Dorms 65 pesos; singles 150 pesos; doubles 180-200 pesos; each additional person 50 pesos. ❶

Hotel Naxhiely, Gasga 301 (☎582 3065). Not as nice to look at as the Mayflower, Naxhiely is still a reasonably priced option for those who prefer the institutional comforts of a hotel over *cabañas.* Clean but somewhat run-down rooms include private bath and fan. Singles 150 pesos; doubles 200 pesos. Discounts in low season. ❸

ABOVE CARRIZALILLO

The area around the new Boulevard Benito Juárez above Playa Carrizalillo is newly developed, with several cafes, shops, and restaurants, including a branch of the Cafecito restaurant from Zicatela.

Hostel Shalom, a 7-minute walk west on Calle Hidalgo, between Manzanillo/Angelito and Carrizalillo. A homely jumble of dorms, cabanas, tents, hammocks, and private rooms, this hostel is laid-back and all the more social for its relative isolation. Amenities include a communal kitchen and a 24hr. bar. Bathrooms leave something to be desired. Dorm bed with mosquito net 55 pesos; 6-person bungalows 60 pesos; private rooms 60 pesos; hammock 30 pesos; tents 40 pesos. ❶

ON ZICATELA

Despite its location (15min. by foot from the tourist corridor), the many restaurants, bars, and *cabañas* on **Calle del Morro,** which runs in front of the beach, make Zicatela a self-sufficient neighborhood. The cheapest *cabañas* (around 50 pesos) might not be secure; lock your valuables if possible. Most safe *cabañas* have taken advantage of the tourist horde, and their rates are now higher than those at many budget hotels. During high season, make reservations several weeks in advance. Other than the first two, the *cabañas* below are listed east to west.

Hotel Buena Vista (☎582 1474; buenavista101@hotmail.com). Perched on a hill above Calle de Morros, Buena Vista is, with its spectacular view of the beach, good for people who have a hard time pulling themselves away from the surf. Some of the rooms come with kitchen and balconies, and all have clean private baths. Be sure to call several weeks in advance. Singles and doubles 150-350 pesos depending on size and season; 50 pesos per additional person. Monthly rates available. ❷

Hotel Ines (☎582 2792), in the middle of the Zicatela. This large, stylish hotel offers a wide variety of rooms situated around a beautiful courtyard with a pool and an outdoor restaurant/bar. A great value for all the amenities. Outdoor *cabañas* 70 pesos in low season, 90 pesos in high season. Clean, spacious doubles range from 120 pesos (with sink and shower but no toilet) to 350 pesos (huge, with bath and A/C). Laundry service 13 pesos per kg. ❷

Cabo Blanco (☎582 0337). Cabo Blanco has some of the cheapest *cabañas* on the strip. Clean, pleasant rooms with fans. Its motto is: "where legends are born." Owners Gary and Roxana run a restaurant during high season, and their year-round M night fish fry/dance parties are famous. Singles 80 pesos; doubles 125 pesos. ❶

Las Olas (☎582 0919). Olas is a bargain for all its amenities. Rooms have small kitchens, fans, personal security boxes, and private baths. All rooms 200 pesos. ❸

Bungalows Zicatela (☎582 0798). A laid-back atmosphere, pool, and rustic bungalows. Rooms are simple and attractive. Singles 150 pesos; doubles 250 pesos, with kitchen 350 pesos. ❷

Hotel Acuario (☎582 0357). Though on the expensive side, Acuario is a perennial favorite with surfers. Spend the extra pesos to frolic in the pool and support the hotel's conservation efforts—they've installed a special water purifier that cleans and reuses all hotel wastewater. Doubles 250 pesos, with A/C or view 350 pesos. Bungalows with kitchen, 400 pesos. ❹

Cabañas Estación B (☎582 2251), at the far end of Zicatela beach. Moved to its new location in late summer 2003, Estación remains true to the original *cabaña* spirit. Each comes with mosquito netting, a hammock, and use of the clean communal baths. Complimentary breakfasts are popular with everyone. *Cabañas* 70 pesos; hammock 40 pesos; camping 30 pesos. ❶

Buena Onda, on the far end of Zicatela, a 30min. walk down the beach or an easy 3 peso truck ride. Remote and unspoiled. New *cabañas* sit right on the water. A great place for beginning surfers to practice, but swimmers should beware the choppy waters. Streetside restaurant El Salvador serves all varieties of seafood. *Cabañas* 70 pesos. ❶

FOOD

Though not so fish-crazy as cities like Veracruz, where vendors often wander the streets selling questionable sacks of recently-deceased shrimp, Puerto Escondido's proximity to the ocean means most restaurants add seafood to their otherwise standard Mexican menus. Most seafood entrees are slightly pricier than other options, but good deals can be found. The large expatriate community has brought a variety of international cuisine to Puerto Escondido, and Italian restaurants take up a good portion of Gasga. Baring your belly on the beach makes for a health-conscious crowd, so vegetarian fare is also abundant, especially along Zicatela.

El Cafecito y Panadería Carmen's Bakery (☎582 0516). Frequented by European backpackers, beach babes, studly surfers, and hammock vendors. The slightly expensive menu makes everyone happy with garlic grilled shrimp (69 pesos; includes rice, vegetables, and bread), a variety of homemade breads, vegetarian-friendly Mexican cuisine (30 pesos), and huge surfer breakfasts (20-25 pesos). New location on Benito Juárez up from Carrizalillo is slightly smaller. Open daily 6am-10pm. ❹

Baguettería Vivaldi, at the east end of the Adoquín. Tasty food for the homesick or anyone tired of the Mexican/Italian axis of grease. Vivaldi offers a number of interesting baguette sandwiches starting at 28 pesos. Crepes start at 25 pesos. Menu in Spanish, English, and German. Open daily 7am-midnight; longer hours during high season. ❷

Herman's Best, just past the east end of the tourist corridor. Herman may not know how to cook too many things, but if you crave grilled fish, this is the place. Chat with the Big Man himself about his fish-flipping prowess and impressive collection of family photos. Slightly out of place in a line of Italian restaurants, Herman's serves savory, garlic-encrusted whole fish with rice, salad, and tortillas (25 pesos). Open daily 2-10pm. ❸

Restaurante Vitamina T, on the east end of the Adoquín. Open just about all the time, with cheap food served hot and fast. Breakfast 20 pesos. Fruit salad 10-15 pesos. The *tortas* are among the best in town (15 pesos). Open daily 7am-1am. ❷

◢ BEACHES

Snorkelers may rent equipment from **Puerto Angelito** (30 pesos per hr.) or **Aventura Submarina,** on the Adoquín across from the tourist booth. (☎582 2353. 70 pesos per day.) Aventura Submarina also leads diving trips (550 pesos). **Noyola Surf Company** (☎582 2569), midway down Calle de Morlos on Zicatela, offers surfing lessons. (8 and 11am, 250 pesos per hr. Includes equipment.) At most beaches, restaurants rent out umbrellas (35 pesos per day); it probably makes more sense to buy a few drinks and use them for free. The following beaches are all established and relatively safe. Still, you should stay in a group and not visit at night unless headed to a restaurant. Adventurers exploring secluded beaches must exercise caution.

PLAYA PRINCIPAL. The main beach of Puerto Escondido, Playa Principal lies just beyond the stores and restaurants that line the Adoquín and is often crowded with *lanchas*, *palapas*, and cavorting families.

PLAYA MARINERO. Continuing east along the shore, you'll pass a small *laguna* on your left. Immediately after is Marinero, less crowded than Principal and good for swimming and sunbathing. Waves get more violent the farther along you go.

PLAYA ZICATELA. Stepping over the rocks will take you to Zicatela, reputedly the third-best surfing beach in the world. The talented surfer dudes bobbing up and down in the water, waiting to ride the next killer wave all have many years of experience. Unless you are very well practiced, please don't try to partake of their fun—you will risk a fate worse than wiping out. The best times for surf-watching are around 7:30am and 6:30pm—times vary with the tide.

PLAYAS MANZANILLO AND ANGELITO. On the other side of Playa Principal, the clear, calm waters of Playas Manzanillo and Angelito attract snorkelers and swimmers alike. Both tend to be quite crowded in the early afternoon, with Manzanillo the quieter of the two. *Lanchas* from Playa Principal (15 pesos) or taxis (15 pesos) will bring you here. If you prefer to walk (20min.), go west on Gasga to Banamex and take a left; continue left toward the ocean when the road turns to dirt. You will come to a fork in the dirt path; the left path leads to Manzanillo, the right leads to Angelito. The two beaches are separated by an easily-crossed rock barrier.

▨ PLAYA CARRIZALILLO. Farther west is Playa Carrizalillo, the best of Puerto Escondido's established beaches. Scenically secluded in a cove at the base of a steep hill, Carrizalillo's waters are calm enough for swimming or snorkeling, while offshore waves are substantial enough for surfing or body boarding. To get here, take a taxi (15 pesos). Because waters between Angelito and Carrizalillo are very rough, traveling by *lancha* may be a bad idea. To walk, continue straight on the dirt road instead of turning left for Angelito and Manzanillo, and continue until you come to the Rotary Club basketball courts. Make a left and keep walking downhill.

New stairs lead down from Benito Juárez. Past Carrizalillo, the waves again turn wild and dangerous—do not attempt to swim here.

PLAYA BACOCHO. Less scenic (and slightly dirtier) than other beaches, Playa Batocho is noteworthy because it provides the best sunset view around and features two beach clubs, **Coco's** and **Club de Playa Villasol,** which allow use of their bars and pools for 35 pesos per day. Bacocho is best reached by taxi (35 pesos).

■ NIGHTLIFE

The Adoquín is the center of Puerto Escondido's nightlife, though even it can be a bit sparse in the off-season. All the best places are right on the strip, eliminating the need for a taxi, or making for an easy ride from Zicatela (15 pesos).

BARS

In the early evening, every restaurant and bar has a happy hour, which usually lasts three or four hours and features cheap beers and two-for-one cocktails. Head to the tourist corridor for the ideal bar-hopping setting. The most popular, **Barfly,** in the middle of the strip, spins pounding techno music and features an open-air second level. (Beer 20 pesos, cocktails 35 pesos. Open daily 8pm-2am.) **Wipeout Bar,** just past Barfly on the right, plays techno, blastingly loud techno. (Open M-Sa 9pm-2am.) **Los 3 Diablos** hosts a well-tanned crowd of youngsters who play pool and strain to converse over loud rap and rock. (Open Tu-Su 9pm-2am.) Just past the strip and on Zicatela, **Banana's** feels like a sports bar with its TV and pool table. (☎582 0005. Pool 30 pesos per hr. Open daily 8am-2am.)

CLUBS

After a day of surfing and sun, most are too tired to dance, leaving the disco scene a little weaker than one might expect. **El Tubo,** behind Wipeout Bar on Playa Principal, plays reggae, salsa, and rock. The crowd at this popular after-bar destination spills onto the beach by the end of the night. (Open daily 10pm-4am.) **Discoteque Bacocho,** in the Bacocho residential district, is the only full-fledged dance club. You'll have to shower and throw something nice over that thong bikini. Taxis whisk you there for 35 pesos. (☎582 2137. Cover 30 pesos. Open daily in high season, F-Su 10pm-5am in low season.) Many clubs close during low season.

ISTHMUS OF TEHUANTEPEC

East of Oaxaca, the North American continent narrows to a slender strip of land 215km wide, known as the Isthmus of Tehuantepec or *el istmo*. The region is home to patches of Zapotec culture, and many residents speak only a few Spanish words. In *el istmo*, the traditional way of life is not an act for tourists.

TEHUANTEPEC ☎971

Tehuantepec (pop. 60,000) is the oldest and most historically significant of *el istmo*'s three principal cities. Founded by Zapotec emperor Cosijoeza, it contains some of the first churches built by *indígenas*, a few from the 16th century. Come here to see modern-day Zapotec life in full swing.

■ TRANSPORTATION. To get to town from the Cristóbal Colón/ADO bus station, 1.5km north of the *centro*, make an immediate left as you exit the station. This street becomes Héroes, veers to the right, and eventually dead-ends. Turn right and walk a few more blocks; make a left on Hidalgo and follow it to the *zócalo.* **Taxis** are 15 pesos. **Cristóbal Colón** (☎ 715 0108) travels to: **Huatulco** (3hr.; 12:10, 2, 7am; 74 pesos); **Mexico City** (12hr.; 5:40, 7:40, 9:10pm; 386 pesos); **Oaxaca** (5hr., 11 per day 12:30am-7:55pm, 113 pesos); **Tuxtla Gutiérrez** (6hr.; 2:30am, 10pm; 132 pesos). Buses also go to **Juchitán** (30min., 5 per day 10:40am-9:40pm, 14 pesos) and **Salina Cruz** (30min., 12 per day 5:30am-midnight, 9 pesos). The fastest, cheapest way to travel to neighboring Juchitán and Salina Cruz is to walk two blocks on 5 de Mayo to the *carretera.* Southbound buses to Salina Cruz (8 pesos) stop frequently, as do northbound buses to Juchitán (9 pesos).

⊞🔢 ORIENTATION AND PRACTICAL INFORMATION. Most of the action centers around the *zócalo,* which is bounded on the north by **22 de Mayo,** the east by **Juárez,** the south by **5 de Mayo,** and the west by **Romero.** Hidalgo runs north-south and begins on the north side of the plaza between the parallel streets of Romero and Juárez. The Palacio Municipal is on the south side of the *zócalo.* **Tourist information** is available at the Casa de la Cultura, 50m off the street two blocks north of the *zócalo.* The *zócalo* is besieged by **banks;** one is **Serfín,** on the north side of the *zócalo,* with a 24hr. **ATM. Farmacia El Pastillero** is south of the *zócalo* at Juárez 13. (Open daily 8am-9pm.) **LADATELs** are in the *zócalo.* Other services include: **police** (☎ 715 0001), at the back of the Palacio Municipal; **Centro de Salud** (☎ 571 0180), two blocks north of *zócalo;* **Telecomm,** next to the post office (open M-F 8am-6pm, Sa 9am-noon); **Internet access,** on 5 de Mayo at the *zócalo* (10 pesos per hr.; open daily 8am-10pm); the **post office,** on the north side of the *zócalo* (open M-F 8am-3pm). **Postal code:** 70760.

🔢🔲 ACCOMMODATIONS AND FOOD. Travelers to Tehuantepec should head straight to **Hotel Oasis ❷,** a block south of the *zócalo* on Romero. Rooms are clean, sunny, and breezy, with fans, large beds, and firm mattresses. The real reason to go is the knowledgeable staff, who can tell you all about the history of the area. (☎ 715 0008. Singles 130 pesos; doubles 170 pesos.) The hotel also contains the **Restaurant El Almendro ❸,** one of the nicer establishments (breakfasts 30 pesos) with an airy, wood-furnished bar that draws a crowd in the evenings with cheap beers and satellite TV. **Hotel Posada Donaji ❷,** Juárez 10, two blocks south of the *zócalo,* offers good rooms with TV and fans. (☎ 715 0064. Singles 140 pesos, with A/C 170 pesos; doubles 190 pesos/220 pesos.) For budget meals, try the **Mercado de Jesús Carranza ❶,** on the plaza's west side. (Open daily 8am-8pm.) A quieter, pricier option is the colorful **Café Colonial ❹,** two blocks south of the *zócalo* at Romero 66. (☎ 715 0115. Open daily 8am-10pm.)

🔲 SIGHTS. Tehuantepec's most notable sight is also the best place to find tourist information; the morning library staff at the **Casa de la Cultura** will be happy to fill you in. (☎ 715 0114. Open M-F 9am-2pm and 5-8pm, Sa 9am-2pm.) The Casa is housed in the **Ex-convento Rey Cosijopi,** a 16th-century Dominican building named after the Zapotec leader who ordered its construction, and now holds a small wax museum (featuring such greats as Porfirio Díaz), a library, and diverse workshops and exhibits. A 15min. walk south of the *zócalo* will bring you to **San Blas** where, as in Juchitán's *mercado,* traditional dress and customs are abundantly evident.

🔳 ENTERTAINMENT. Between May and September, each of Tehuantepec's 14 communities holds its own week-long 🔳**festival,** beginning with a *baile velorio* at night followed by a special mass the next morning and several days of parades, live music, dancing, and extensive consumption of *cerveza* by all. Tourists are welcome, though a local chaperone is usually necessary to get into some of the social events. Admission to the **Vela Sandunga,** in the last week of May, and the **Vela Tehuantepec** (Dec. 26), requires traditional dress for women and *guayaberas* for men: part of the purpose of these *velas* is to preserve the culture of the town. At the Vela Sandunga, each *barrio* picks a representative to compete for the title of *Reina de la Vela*. The Vela Tehuantepec is a party, held in the main square, to which native *"tehunos"* return each year from all over Mexico and beyond.

JUCHITÁN ☎971

If grandmothers ruled the world, it would probably look like Juchitán. One begins to suspect that there is some sort of government-sponsored flower subsidy, since the open market would not seem capable of supporting the vast number of vendors that crowd the *zócalo*. There is also an unusually high incidence of ribbon-selling. Throughout, women wear traditional dress—loose fitting, embroidered shirts and long, full floral skirts. Juchitán's traditional crafts are meant to be worn, and the aesthetic is an overwhelmingly important part of town life.

⧠ TRANSPORTATION. To get to town from the first-class bus station, follow **Prolongación 16 de Septiembre** to the right. It soon splits into **5 de Septiembre** and **16 de Septiembre**, which run parallel and eventually form the west and east sides of the *zócalo*, respectively. **Gómez** is the street to the north of the *zócalo*, **Juárez** is to the south. The *palacio municipal* and the market are to the east of the *zócalo* on 16 de Septiembre. *Taxis colectivos* run to the *centro* (3 pesos) from the left side of the bus station exit. **Local buses** connect Juchitán with the isthmus towns of **Tehuantepec** (30min., 10 pesos) and **Salina Cruz** (1hr., 20 pesos). **Cristóbal Colón** (☎711 2565) sends buses to **Mexico City** (11½hr.; 12:05am, 8:15, 8:30, 8:45, 9:30pm; 419 pesos) and **Oaxaca** (4½hr., 11 per day 12:05am-4pm, 124 pesos).

⧠ PRACTICAL INFORMATION. The **tourist office** is on the first floor of the building to the north of the *zócalo*, toward the west side. (☎710 1971 or 715 5413. Open M-F 9am-2pm and 5-8pm.) **Banamex**, 5 de Septiembre 12 on the *zócalo*, exchanges currency and has several 24hr. **ATMs.** (Open M-Sa 9am-5pm.) Other services include: **Farmacia 24 Horas**, 2 de Abril at Gómez, one block east of the *zócalo* (open 24hr.); **police**, in the Palacio Municipal (☎711 1235; no English spoken); **Telecomm:** across from post office, (open M-F 8am-7:30pm, Sa-Su 9am-noon); **post office**, Gómez and 16 de Septiembre (open M-F 8am-7pm). **Postal code:** 70000.

⧠⧠ ACCOMMODATIONS AND FOOD. At **Hotel Modelo ❷**, 2 de Abril 21, half a block from the market, large rooms are spare with cold showers. (☎711 2451. Singles 120 pesos; doubles 150 pesos.) **Hotel Don Alex ❸**, 16 de Septiembre 48, offers more luxurious digs, with large rooms and clean private baths. (Singles 170 pesos, with A/C and TV 250 pesos; doubles with A/C and TV 320 pesos.)

Juchitán is perhaps the best of the three principal *istmo* towns in which to sample regional cuisine. Unusual food prevails: iguana, deer, armadillo, and rabbit are plentiful and often turn up stuffed into various tortillas, *tamales*, and tacos. The tame of heart can stick to *topotes*, an interesting variant on the *tostada*, with a circular corn patty as a base. The town's **market** is a must-eat. **Los Chapulines ❹**, 5 de Septiembre at Morelos, five blocks north of the *zócalo*, also offers regional food. Think before ordering the house specialty, which is, not surprisingly, *chapulines* (grasshoppers; 70 pesos). Traditional *carne* dishes (50-60 pesos) come with salad, rice, beans, bread, and tortillas. (☎712 0196. Open daily 7am-11:30pm.)

⧠ SIGHTS. The **Mercado 5 de Septiembre** consumes an entire block east of the *zócalo*. Support the flower market and, if you are an old Mexican woman, join in the latest gossip. Try on festival clothing on the second floor; the skirts and blouses are made of velvet and ornately embroidered with flowers to represent woman's connection with nature. Keep in mind that the vendors are interested in investigating the relationship between Zapotec clothing and your money—haggling is advised. (Open daily 6am-8pm.)

At the corner of Domínguez and Colón, Juchitán's **Casa de Cultura** is filled with art and music workshops and home to a collection of regional archaeological artifacts. To get there, walk south on 5 de Septiembre from the *zócalo* toward the Banco Serfín sign. Turn right at Serfín and pass Parque Chariz on the left; the *casa* is on the right. (Open M-F 10am-3pm and 5-8pm, Sa 10am-2pm.) Before the *casa*, the church of **San Vincente Ferraro** is worth a peek. Constructed in 1528, the church has been remodeled many times but retains an ancient air. Most of the simple, whitewashed architecture dates from the 17th century.

NEAR JUCHITÁN: EL OJO DE AGUA

Across the highway from the 1st-class station in Juchitán, 2nd-class buses leave often for Ixtepec (30min., 10 pesos). In Ixtepec find the buses that go to Tlacotepec, which are right around the corner from the return buses to Juchitán. Tlacotepec buses sometimes drop off and pick up at the balneario (25min., every hr., 6 pesos). If not, get off at the "balneario" sign and take a 25min. walk. Balneario open 24hr. 12 pesos.

Approximately 1hr. northwest of Juchitán by bus, El Ojo de Agua, a bubbling *balneario* (natural spring), is the best way to beat the oppressive *istmo* heat without reaching for a refreshing grain-based beverage. Cement walls have been erected at the source, directing the spring's flow through several large pools connected by small waterfalls. In contrast to most crusted-tile Mexican spas, small fish swim near the sand and rock bottom of the pools, and tree trunks jut from the sides. Beware assault by tadpoles. Though trash detracts from the scene, the water itself remains clean, clear, and cool, constantly replenished by the spring.

SALINA CRUZ   ☎ 971

Salina Cruz offers little but oil refineries to tourists, but its central location makes it a convenient stop for buses. **Cristóbal Colón** (☎714 1441) runs to: **Huatulco** (3hr.; 4:30, 6:15, 8am; 76 pesos); **Mexico City** (11½hr.; 7:15, 7:30, 9:15, 11pm; 439 pesos); **Oaxaca** (5hr., 5 per day 1am-11:50pm, 121 pesos). The Cristóbal Colón **station** is a 30min. hike from the *zócalo*. Spare yourself the trouble: turn right and walk until you hit the main street, then catch a blue *microbus* (3 pesos); taxis cost 10 pesos. **Estrella Blanca** (☎714 5437) sends second-class buses to **Acapulco** and all stops in between, including **Bahías de Huatulco** and **Puerto Escondido** (4 per day 6:15am-11pm). From Cristóbal Colón, walk right on the main street three blocks, then take another right. The Estrella Blanca station is half a block down on the right. To get from the second-class *"istmo"* stop to Cristóbal Colón, walk left past the buses to the first cross street and take a left. Walk approximately five blocks and hang a right; the station is near the corner on the left.

GULF COAST AND CHIAPAS

Tropical beauty, indigenous traditions, Caribbean music, and sweeping poverty unite the states of the southern Gulf Coast, which welcome travelers to beaches, natural reserves, and small towns aplenty.

Stretching 300km along the Gulf of Mexico, steamy **Veracruz** encompasses breathtaking beaches, burgeoning cities, and vast spaces filled only by roaming cattle and lush vegetation. The ancestral home of the Huastec, Totonac, and Olmec civilizations, Veracruz witnessed Cortés's first steps on American soil, and has since endured foreign intervention and invasion by the Spanish (1825), the French (1839), and the United States (1847 and 1914). Today, many residents continue to live off the land, cultivating tobacco and coffee, and running small-scale cattle ranches, but Veracruz's main income comes from oil and fishing. *Veracruzanos*, also known as *jarochos*, are renowned for their delightful sense of humor, wonderful seafood and coffee, and Afro-Caribbean inspired music. *Marimba* rhythms and Caribbean colors flow through the steamy port city of Veracruz day and night, and beautiful mountainous Xalapa overflows with art and culture.

Tabasco lies southeast of Veracruz along the Gulf of Mexico, dotted with lakes and swamps, criss-crossed by rivers, and swathed in dense jungle. Untouristed beaches line the northern coast, and the southern and eastern borders overflow with nature sanctuaries. Once the center of Olmec territory, Tabasco gives a glimpse into its mother culture with the ruins at La Venta. Villahermosa, the capital, rises from the center of the jungle, its colonial identity battling modern growth.

Chiapas sits south of Tabasco and for centuries has been known for environmental diversity—its cloud-enveloped heights contrast with dense, lowland rainforest. One of Mexico's most beautiful cities, San Cristóbal de las Casas, renowned for its cobblestone streets and surrounding *indígena* villages, rests high amid these peaks. The state forms part of the Maya heartland; the Lacandón Rainforest shields the remote ruins of Bonampak and Yaxchilán as well as fiercely traditional groups of Lacandón Maya. Chiapas's *indígenas* remain true to their roots—in many communities, schools teach in the local dialect as well as Spanish. The EZLN rebellion of 1994 drew the world's attention to Chiapas and the highland region's increasing land conflicts, which pit small-scale Maya farmers against wealthy ranchers and the national government.

HIGHLIGHTS OF THE GULF COAST

INHALE the rich vanilla aromas of **Papantla** (see p. 547), "the city that perfumes the world," and carry the scent with you to the awesome ruins at **El Tajín** (see p. 550).

STRIKE a pose at the stunning **Cascada de Texolo** (see p. 543), where movie stars galore have filmed famous scenes in the glistening falls.

GULP the thin air of **San Cristóbal de las Casas** (see p. 583), set atop lush green mountains in the Chiapan cloud forest.

TREK through the jungle to the archaeological sites of **Yaxchilán** (see p. 599) and **Bonampak** (see p. 601), home to some of Mexico's most well-preserved Maya ruins.

DROOL in amazement at the Olmec artifacts situated in a spectacular, outdoor jungle-setting in **Villahermosa's Parque-Museo La Venta** (see p. 572).

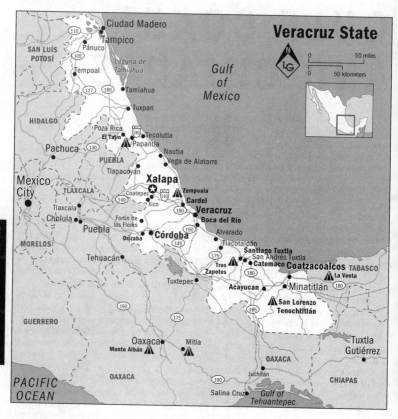

VERACRUZ

XALAPA (JALAPA)   ☎228

The first thing you notice upon entering Xalapa (pop. 500,000) is the weather; the cool, temperate climate provides a welcome oasis in the muggy state of Veracruz. A self-proclaimed cultural center, Xalapa boasts a burgeoning university, an excellent orchestra, and one of the top archaeological museums in the Americas. Conquered by the Aztecs in 1460, this Totonac city was part of the empire until Cortés claimed the land for Spain. Xalapa is the birthplace of the *xalapeño* (jalapeño) pepper, and the city's fertile soil nourishes Mexico's rich, mellow coffee. Visitors today find a plethora of artistic performances and showcases, a vibrant nightlife, and a number of beautiful parks. Though the center bursts with commerce and boisterous students, there's always time to sit, take in the glorious breeze, and relax over a cup of coffee. Xalapa can be what you make of it: a whirlwind tour of art, archaeology, and culture, or just a place to take a nice, long break.

TRANSPORTATION

The **train station** is at the extreme northeast edge of the city, a 40min. walk or 22-peso taxi ride from the *centro*. There are two bus stations. **CAXA,** 20 de Noviembre 571, east of the city center, services distant cities and has long-distance phones, telegraph and luggage service, shopping, and restaurants. **Terminal Excelsior,** west of the *centro* on Allende, is a roundabout where you can catch buses to neighboring towns. To get from the **bus station** to the *centro*, catch a bus marked "Centro" or "Terminal" (4.5 pesos); taxis cost 22 pesos. Make sure to specify which station.

From CAXA, **ADO** (☎812 2525) travels first-class to: **Catemaco** (5hr., 9 per day 7am-7:45pm, 138 pesos); **Mexico City** (5hr., 18 per day, 162 pesos); **Papantla** (4hr., 10 per day, 126 pesos); **Puebla** (3hr., 10 per day, 93 pesos); **San Andrés Tuxtla** (3hr., 11 per day, 127 pesos); **Santiago Tuxtla** (3hr., 5 per day, 120 pesos); **Tuxtepec** (5hr.; 6am, 3:35pm; 134 pesos); **Veracruz** (every 30min. 5am-11pm, 55 pesos). Slower, cheaper second-class service to similar destinations is provided by **Autobuses Unidos (AU).**

ORIENTATION AND PRACTICAL INFORMATION

Located in the center of the state, Xalapa is 104km northwest of Veracruz on **Mex. 140** and 302km east of Mexico City. Downtown centers around the **cathedral** and

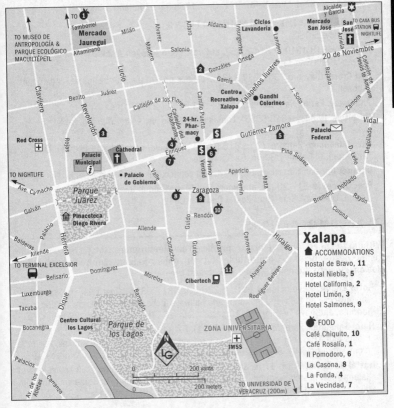

Xalapa

▲ ACCOMMODATIONS
Hostal de Bravo, **11**
Hostal Niebla, **5**
Hotel California, **2**
Hotel Limón, **3**
Hotel Salmones, **9**

🍴 FOOD
Café Chiquito, **10**
Café Rosalía, **1**
Il Pomodoro, **6**
La Casona, **8**
La Fonda, **4**
La Vecindad, **7**

GULF COAST & CHIAPAS

the **Palacio de Gobierno. Enríquez,** which runs along **Parque Juárez,** separates the two. Streets that branch from Enríquez toward the park and the Palacio de Gobierno run downhill, while those on the cathedral side travel uphill to the markets.

TOURIST, FINANCIAL, AND LOCAL SERVICES

Tourist Office: (☎842 1214). On Enríquez, in the Palacio Municipal, 3rd floor. English-speaking staff doles out maps and helpful information. Open M-F 9am-3pm.

Currency Exchange: Banks with **ATMs** line Enríquez and the surrounding streets. Most will **change money** and **traveler's checks.**

Markets: Mercado Jauregui, 2 blocks behind the cathedral, serves as an open-air supermarket, selling meats, fresh produce and a variety of other goods. Open Su 7am-5pm, M-Sa 7am-9pm. **Mercado San José,** just northwest of La Iglesia de San José, sells bushel upon bushel of fruits and vegetables. Open daily 7am-8pm.

Laundry: Ciclos Lavandería, on Landero. Wash and dry 18.5 pesos per 3kg. Open M-F 9am-7:30pm, Sa 9am-4pm.

Luggage Storage: At the bus stations. 4 pesos per hr., 30 pesos per day. Open 24hr.

Bookstores: Several bookstores are at Xalapeños Ilustres and Mata just past the Centro Recreativo. **Gandhi Colorines** sells a few English-language books for the travel-weary.

Car Rental: Alamo, 20 de Noviembre Ote. 522 (☎817 4313). Exit to the right from the bus station, walk downstairs and through the small shopping center. On the opposite side of the street. Must be over 21. Open M-Sa 9am-2pm and 4-8pm.

EMERGENCY AND COMMUNICATIONS

Emergency: ☎060.

Police: (☎818 1810 or 814 3327), at Cuartel San José, on Alcalde y García, just north of the Iglesia San José.

Red Cross: Clavijero 13 (☎817 3431), 1 block uphill from Parque Juárez. Little English spoken.

Pharmacy: Farmacia Reforma, Enríquez 41 (☎817 2220). Open 24hr.

Hospitals: IMSS, (☎818 5555), Lomas del Estadio just south of Bravo. No English spoken.

Fax: Telecomm, Zamora 70 (☎816 2167), just before the Palacio Federal. Open Su 9am-1pm, M-F 8am-7:30pm, Sa 9am-5pm.

Internet Access: Cibertech, Bravo 10. Fast connections only 7 pesos per hr. Open 24hr.

Post Office: (☎817 2021), at Zamora and Diego Leño in the Palacio Federal. **Mexpost** inside. Open M-F 8am-4pm. **Postal Code:** 91001.

⌂ ACCOMMODATIONS

Without the need for travelers to splurge on air-conditioning, Xalapa is a gold mine for the peso-pinching. Comfortable and convenient lodging can be found on **Revolución,** close to the *centro*, the market, and the parks.

Hotel Limón, Revolución 8 (☎817 2204; fax 817 9316), just past the cathedral. Brightly-covered tiles lend the lobby and hallways a cheerful glow. Rooms are tidy, comfortable, and have TV. Singles 110 pesos; doubles 170 pesos; triples 220 pesos. ❷

Hotel Salmones, Zaragoza 24 (☎817 5431). For a few extra pesos, enjoy large carpeted rooms with A/C, phone, and TV. A good, reasonably priced restaurant adjoins. Ask for a room with a balcony. Singles 260 pesos; doubles 290 pesos; triples 320 pesos. ❺

Hostal de Bravo, Bravo 11 (☎818 9038), below Zaragoza. Friendly staff serves one of Xalapa's few hostels, with tidy rooms, large windows, fans, and TV. Gorgeous patio with tables. Singles 175 pesos; doubles 205 pesos; each additional person 20 pesos. ❸

Hotel California, Gonzáles Ortega 1, on the north side of a small park, where Juárez intersects with Carrillo Puerto. Not exactly lovely, but it compensates with low prices. Rooms are spartan and come with fans. Singles and doubles with one bed 85 pesos; much larger rooms with two beds 160 pesos. ❶

Hostal Niebla, Zamora 24 (☎817 2174). Students seeking cheap rooms and a true hostel experience often find themselves at this "alternative" establishment, with sparkling 6-bed dormitory-style rooms. Beds 110 pesos. ❷

🍴 FOOD

Xalapeño food is cheap, plentiful, and often accompanied by *lechero (café con leche)*. Along with Xalapa's specialty *cafés*, visitors should be sure to sample regional foods: pickled chiles, jalapeño peppers, *picaditas* (flat corn cakes with mashed beans and cheese), and *garnachas* (bean-filled fried corn cakes). Don't miss the *pambaza*, a food served on round bread and stuffed with beans, tomato, lettuce, and other goodies. Tortillas are handmade in almost every restaurant.

▨ La Fonda, Callejón del Diamante 1 (☎818 7282). Quite simply the best food around. Eat upstairs for better ambience, and don't leave without trying the cactus and egg soup and the cactus salad (26 pesos). Chicken *mole* and steak prepared *al gusto* run 54 pesos, but delicious *pambazas* go for only 10 pesos. Open M-Sa 8am-5:30pm. ❸

Café Chiquito, Bravo 3 (☎812 1122), 2 blocks south of Enríquez. Open-air restaurant with gurgling fountain. Enjoy one of many chicken and steak offerings (20-40 pesos) amidst *xalapeño* students. Open daily 8am-11pm. Live music M-Sa after 9pm. ❸

Il Pomodoro, Primo 11 (☎841 2000). Excellent pizzas (30-50 pesos), pastas, and tiramisu (18 pesos) in this restaurant decorated with giant wooden wine racks and Roman wall murals. Open Su 1-10:30pm, M-Th 1pm-midnight, F-Sa 1pm-1am. ❸

Café Rosalía, Abasolo 2 (☎817 5638), 1 block past the north end of the Mercado Jauregui. Walk up Revolución and look to the right for the sign. Wooden booths and great food attract vendors to this 50-year-old market-side institution. There's no menu here; come prepared to order. 4 *super enchiladas* 15 pesos. Open daily 10am-7pm. ❶

La Vecindad, Enríquez 12 (☎818 3265). Cheerful, central, and very quick. The meat goes straight from the skillet to some decent tacos, enchiladas, and quesadillas (31 pesos). Open daily 8:30am-midnight. ❸

La Casona, Zaragoza 20 (☎818 2119). For those with a little extra money, La Casona has a quality menu packed with standard Mexican entrees and more creative dishes (60-100 pesos). The walls are filled with photos of old Xalapa, and the plantlife strewn around the bar fosters a relaxed, comfortable atmosphere. Open daily 8am-midnight. ❺

👁 SIGHTS

▨ MUSEO DE ANTROPOLOGÍA. The finest museum in the country after Mexico City's Museo Nacional de Antropología (see p. 116), Xalapa's museum focuses exclusively on the state of Veracruz. The museum is designed to be viewed in chronological order, showcasing the various indigenous tribes as each came to power. On your journey, you'll be treated to ten huge Olmec heads, each weighing 20 tons, in addition to countless artifacts, fossils, and skeletal remains. A picturesque garden sits just outside the museum at all points; if you're tired, you can step out for a moment and relax in the shade. The museum is best viewed with one of the knowledgeable University of Veracruz students who lead tours. *(Catch a yellow "Tesorería" bus on Enríquez for 4.5 pesos, take a taxi for 18 pesos, or walk on Enríquez/Camacho away from the cathedral. Make a left on Av. Xalapa and continue for several blocks until you see the museum on your left (45min.). ☎815 0920. Open daily 9am-5pm. 40 pesos, students 20 pesos, children under 12 free; video camera 40 pesos. Free 1½hr. tours in Spanish given daily at 11:30am.)*

GULF COAST & CHIAPAS

PARQUE ECOLÓGICO MACUILTÉPETL. Xalapa's biggest, most beautiful park is Parque Ecológico Macuiltépetl, where, with a little trekking, you can enjoy the flora and fauna native to the hills around the city. A brick path meanders past lip-locked lovers to the summit of an extinct volcano 186m above Xalapa, where a spiral tower looks out over city and mountains. If you don't feel like walking the 4km path to the top, you can cheat and take the stairways. *(Take a "Mercado-Corona" colectivo (3 pesos) from Revolución and Altamirano, or hail a taxi (20 pesos). Open daily spring and summer 7am-5pm, fall and winter 6am-6pm.)*

UNIVERSITY OF VERACRUZ. The large man-made "lakes" of **Paseo de los Lagos** lap against the university's hillsides below Enríquez. Not exactly an architectural gem, UV's institutional box-style buildings are painted in comely shades of blue and green. Still, pine trees and a lakeside path make it worth a visit. Pop into one of the art galleries for information on workshops and exhibitions.

PARQUE JUÁREZ. This park serves as Xalapa's surrogate *zócalo*. Relax, catch the breeze, and take in the superb vista. Two staircases in the park's platform lead down to the **Agora de la Ciudad.** The center harbors a small cafe, several galleries, and a screening room where film festivals take place. *(Open Tu-Su 8am-9:15pm.)*

PINACOTECA DIEGO RIVERA. Xalapa's artistic gem is the Pinacoteca, a small museum that houses many of Rivera's more experimental canvases—Impressionism, collage, Cubism, travel sketches, and a charming dose of horse-human bestiality. *(Herrera 5, just below Parque Juárez. ☎818 1819. Open Tu-Su 10am-6pm. Free.)*

CALLEJONES. Xalapa takes pride in its old cobblestone alleys, many of which are associated with gory love stories. **Callejón del Diamante,** off Enríquez, honors a diamond that could detect an unfaithful lover. Legend has it that a Spaniard gave the diamond to his Mexican wife, who then played hanky-panky with a local while he was away. The darkened diamond alerted the Spaniard who, enraged, slaughtered his wife. Appropriately, cafes and eager street vendors now line the callejón. In the southwest corner of the city, off Rebsamen, is **Callejón de la Calavera,** named for a wife who decapitated her cheating, drunken husband. The lovers of **Callejón de Jesús te Ampare** were killed by a widower who went mad with jealousy upon seeing the happy couple. *"Jesús te ampare"* (Jesus protect you) was the last thing the girl managed to say to her lover.

🎵 ENTERTAINMENT

Xalapa, in typical college-town fashion, has two varieties of nightlife: the cultural (theatre, classical music, *ballet folklórico*) and the bawdy (drinking, dancing, and what follows). After attending a high-culture performance, bicker about the symbolic use of color in one of the city's cafes, most of which are full until about 11:30pm. Later on, disco fever rages on **Camacho** and near the bus station on **20 de Noviembre.** Figure out what follows on your own. Late night jaunts require a taxi (20 pesos), but it's a small price to pay for wild, sweaty fun.

CLUBS AND BARS

Esfinge (☎818 3818), at 20 de Noviembre and Maestros Veracruzanos, just before the bus station. A new addition to the late-night scene, Esfinge adopts an Egyptian air: the upper levels of the club are inside a blacklight pyramid and a sphinx stands guard with the bouncers. On the upper floors, dancers can revel in the fantastic scenery and the mysterious lighting. Tired? Head downstairs to the restaurant of the same name for a hamburger or two (35-40 pesos). No cover. Open F-Sa 9pm-3am, restaurant open daily 1pm-3am. Show your copy of Let's Go for a free beer with your meal.

La Séptima Estación, 20 Noviembre 571 (☎817 3155), just below the 1st-class bus station. There are a few clubs at La Estación, reached by a dark, private road running through the chirping, whirring *xalapeño* jungle. A mostly local crowd fills the cavernous spaces to capacity. Beer 15 pesos. Cover F-Sa 35 pesos. Open Th-Sa 9:30pm-3am.

La Casona, Calzada del Tajar 2 (☎841 5254), right across 20 de Noviembre from the bus station. Not to be confused with the restaurant of the same name, La Casona invites a 20-something crowd to drink, sing, and dance along to live salsa, pop, and rock. Live music starts at midnight. Cover F-Sa 50 pesos. Open W-Sa 10pm-3am.

Zonic, Camacho 8 (☎817 0268). One of the few gay nightlife options in Xalapa, Zonic hosts a mature, bar-like scene with packed corridors more conducive to pressing than dancing. Beer 25 pesos, mixed drinks from 22 pesos. No cover. Open W-Sa 7pm-4am.

XCAPE, 20 de Noviembre 641 (☎812 5075), 4 blocks down 20 de Noviembre to the right of the station. This two-tiered bar/club soothes with a more sedate scene: patrons dance to salsa bands on the lower level and live rock/pop on the top floor. Cover 30 pesos. Open Th-Su 9pm-4am. Live music starts at 11pm.

For information on cultural events, visitors should check listings in the local newspapers or head to the **Centro Recreativo Xalapa,** Xalapeños Ilustres 31 (☎817 3110). In addition to offering brief classes and lectures on almost anything you would want to know about the city and local culture of Xalapa, the Centro posts information on all the upcoming concerts and ballets in the city. (Open daily 9am-2pm and 4-7pm.) The **Agora de la Ciudad,** in Parque Juárez, offers similar services, keeping Xalapa's students up-to-date. Events include weekly performances by the **Orquesta Sinfónica de Xalapa,** university expositions, recitals, and art exhibits. Staff at both the Centro and Agora can tell you where to find what you're looking for.

During the **Festival de Junio Musical** (late May-June), the symphony hosts concerts, and performers stage theater productions and recitals throughout the city. Xalapa also celebrates the month-long **Feria Internacional de Xalapa,** which features a variety of cultural, artisan, and sporting events (April or May).

⬛ DAYTRIPS FROM XALAPA

⬛ XICO'S CASCADA DE TEXOLO

To get to Xico from Xalapa, walk west on Allende until you reach Galeana and a large park. You will see a roundabout: this is Terminal Excelsior. From there, take any "Xico" bus (30min., 11 pesos). You will drive through a few towns on the way. When you see signs saying "Xico" and "Entrada de la Ciudad," alert the driver and exit the bus. The bus will deposit you on Calle Hidalgo. From there, turn left and walk one block uphill to Calle Zaragoza. Turn left onto Zaragoza, the road that eventually turns into the path to the falls. The road forks at 2 points along the way—take the right fork both times. Taxis sometimes make the trip to the falls, but the ride is neither smooth nor quick.

In the town of Xico, 19km outside of Xalapa, mules and horses share the road with automobiles. Besides pastoral bliss, Xico has one huge selling point—the dramatic waterfall of **Texolo,** just 3km from town. If it looks like it's out of a movie, that's because it is. Several US movies were filmed here, including *Romancing the Stone* and *Clear and Present Danger.* Somewhat less glamorously, car and deodorant commercials have also been shot at the falls. In any case, Hollywood has left no trace of its presence, and few tourists frequent the site. The only sign of civilization is the conveniently placed **Restaurant el Mirador ❷.** (Excellent *empanadas* 20 pesos. Open daily 9am-7pm.) To get to the base of the falls, head left before the footbridge crossing the gorge and go down the cement steps with the blue railings. Take a right at the fork. The vista at the bottom of the pass is like something out of a fantasy book. The rocks are often slippery and deserted, so exercise extreme caution and wear appropriate footwear. Also note that the walk to the falls is a long and lonely one: try not to go by yourself and don't hike to the falls at night. The insects are silent but ferocious—bring bug repellent.

TUXPAN (TUXPAM) ☎ 783

With a beautiful river, a welcoming atmosphere, and palm trees at every corner, Tuxpan (pop. 120,000) draws tourists from all over Mexico. Perhaps due to the heat, foreigners have yet to join in the fun. Just beyond the seafood markets, couples amble along the Río Tuxpan, while the humidity of the mellow plaza encourages lethargic lounging. Tranquil and beautiful, Tuxpan makes a great getaway.

⊡ TRANSPORTATION. Tuxpan, 347km northwest of Veracruz, spreads along the northern bank of Río Tuxpan. Each bus line has its own station; to get to the town center from any one, walk to the river and turn right. **ADO,** Rodríguez 1 (☎834 0102), close to the bridge and three blocks east of Parque Cano down Reyes Heróles, heads to: **Papantla** (1½hr., 8 per day, 36 pesos); **Veracruz** (5½hr., 15 per day, 156 pesos); **Xalapa** (5hr., 5 per day, 161 pesos); **Matamoros** (11hr., 3 per day, 388 pesos). **Ómnibus de México,** Independencia 30 (☎834 1147), under the bridge, sends first-class buses to: **Mexico City** (6hr., 6 per day, 168 pesos); **Monterrey** (10hr., 4 per day, 440 pesos); **Guadalajara** (10hr.; 5, 9pm; 507 pesos); **Querétaro** (10hr.; 8:15, 9pm; 260 pesos), and second-class buses to most nearby destinations.

▦▨ ORIENTATION AND PRACTICAL INFORMATION. Reyes Heróles (or simply, *"el bulevar,"* the boulevard) is Tuxpan's main thoroughfare, running along the river. One block north lies Juárez, followed by Morelos. Activity centers around two plazas: **Parque Rodríguez Cano** on the waterfront, just south of the busiest part of town, and **Parque Reforma,** the town's *centro,* between Juárez and Morelos, a few blocks west of Parque Rodríguez Cano. The bridge marks the eastern edge of town and streets parallel to the water run roughly east-west.

The **tourist office,** Juárez 20, in the Palacio Municipal in Parque Rodríguez Cano, has lots of maps and brochures. Enter on the Juárez side across from Hotel Florida. (☎834 0177; www.tuxpam.com.mx. Open M-F 9am-3pm and 5-8pm. Some English spoken.) **Bancomer,** on Juárez between the two parks, **exchanges money** and has one of the town's numerous 24hr. **ATMs.** (Open M-F 9am-3pm.) Other services include: the **supermarket Super Alan,** on Juárez between the two parks (open daily 8am-9pm); **Lavandería México,** Reyes Heróles 57, three blocks west of the centro (☎834 2708; 12 pesos per kg., 2hr. service; open M-Sa 8am-8pm); **emergency service** (☎060); **police,** Libramiento López Mateos 520 (☎834 0252); **Red Cross,** next to the police (☎834 0158; English spoken); the **Hospital Civil** (☎834 0199); **Farmacia D'Tuxpan,** on Morelos, between the two parks (☎834 2569; open 24hr.); **Telecomm,** Ortega 20, two blocks off of Morelos (☎834 0167; open Su 9am-noon, M-F 8am-7:30pm, Sa 9am-5pm); **LADATELs** scattered around the two main plazas; **CyberSpace Snack and Net,** at the corner of Benito Juárez and Veracruz, west of the plazas (10 pesos per hr.; open M-F 9am-10pm, Sa 10am-10pm); **post office,** Mina 16, with **Mexpost** inside. From Parque Reforma, follow Morelos toward the bridge, and take the first left onto Mina (☎834 0088; open M-F 9am-4pm). **Postal code:** 92801.

▛ ACCOMMODATIONS. Budget accommodations in Tuxpan cluster around the two central parks. **Hotel Riviera ❺,** Reyes Heróles 17, across from the river, boasts clean, bright rooms with A/C, phone, and TV. Make sure you get a room facing the river. (☎834 5349. Singles 310 pesos; doubles 370 pesos.) The **Hotel España ❸,** Clavijero 11, near the bus stations, may not have the prettiest rooms, but the bed is soft and the price is right. (☎834 8527. Singles and doubles 150 pesos.) **Hotel Parro-**

quia ❺, Escuela Militar 4, left of the cathedral on Parque Rodríguez Cano, has rooms with fans, TV, and phone, at reasonable prices. Ask for a room with a balcony. (☎834 1630. Singles 253 pesos; doubles 300 pesos.) **Hotel El Huasteco** ❹, Morelos 41, is a block left of Parque Reforma when facing the river. Most of the rooms are small and windowless, but low prices and a good location make it comfortable enough. (☎834 1859. Singles with A/C 200 pesos; doubles 250 pesos.)

🗋 **FOOD.** Along *el bulevar*, especially near the bridge, food vendors grill cheap seafood tacos and *gorditas*, and downtown itself has no shortage of small restaurants and *taquerías*. On a hot, humid evening in Parque Reforma, nothing is more refreshing than a *licuado* of fresh seasonal fruits (10-12 pesos). A great place to dine, 🗇**Los Girasoles** ❹ (The Sunflowers) is a dancer's paradise on weekends. This waterfront restaurant and bar, on Reyes Heróles at Hernandez, is decorated with phones, license plates, instruments, and bikes nailed to the wall. Everything, from the steak entrees (60-90 pesos) to fried plantains (35 pesos), is delicious, and the friendly, energetic waitstaff will make you feel right at home. (☎834 0392. Open Su-F 12:30pm-midnight, Sa 12:30pm-6am—kitchen closes soon after midnight.) **El Mejicano** ❸, Morelos 49, opposite Parque Reforma, seats you among bright colors, lots of wooden paneling, and imitation Riveras. The regional menu includes quesadillas (26 pesos) and *enfrijoladas* (warm tortillas rolled in a black bean sauce and stuffed with cheese or chicken, 32 pesos) and vegetarian options. (☎834 8904. Open daily 6am-midnight.) To save some money, head to **Restaurant el Rey** ❷, on 5 de Febrero 19. Starting on Morelos, walk away from the river at the Banca Azteca; turn left at the Pollo Feliz on to 5 de Febrero. The atmosphere may not be great, but the large portions and tiny prices (*comida corrida* 16 pesos) are unbeatable.

🗇🗇 **SIGHTS AND BEACHES.** *Tuxpeños* are justifiably proud of their beautiful river and scenic shores. Palm trees line the boardwalk and piles of well-priced pineapples, bananas, shrimp, and fish await at the market under the bridge.

Those interested in Mexico's intimate relationship with Castro should visit 🗇**La Casa de la Amistad Mexico-Cuba**, across the river via a blue ferry (2 pesos). Exhibits include photos of Castro taken during his stay in Tuxpan while exiled from Cuba in the late 1950s, and pictures celebrating Cuban accomplishments in art, music, and sports. From the ferry, walk two blocks from the river, then turn right on

NO WORK, ALL PLAY

WHAT WOULD JESUS DO?

An oft-forgotten Bible story tells the tale of a 12 year-old Jesus taking a little trip to the synagogue with Mary and Joseph. At the end of prayers, the parents turned to head home. The problem? Jesus was nowhere to be found. Terrified, the holy couple searched high and low for their son with no success. Fortunately for the entire Christian world, Jesus, good temple-going boy that he was, was only a few steps away, discussing scripture with the temple elders.

Understandably, *tuxpeños* feel that nearly losing the Messiah is a big deal. Every December 7th they celebrate El Día del Niño Perdido (The Day of the Lost Child) to commemorate the near miss. townspeople lay out candles on their porches, their front lawns and along most of the streets. The scene is especially striking outside of town, where electricity is scarce and the small flames illuminate the unpaved roads. Children armed with lanterns motor along in tiny cardboard "cars," looking for the savior. As it happens, they usually find treats instead, in a winter version of Easter egg hunts.

The city of Tuxpan is proud of its holiday, feeling that its vigilance symbolizes a measure of devotion to their faith. Happily for all involved, Jesus is invariably "found" that evening, the celebration ends, and giddy children run home to share stories and enjoy the evening's haul.

Obregón and follow it to its end; the museum is on your left. (Open daily 8am-7pm. Free.) The most interesting site in the *centro* is **El Museo de Arqueología,** Juárez 45, in the Parque Reforma. The museum has artifacts from the pre-colonial settlements of the Olmec, Huastec, and Toltec. (Open M-F 9am-8pm, Sa 10am-1pm.)

Twelve kilometers from the city center, Tuxpan's **Playa Azul** can be crowded with families and slightly dirty, but the fine sand stretches far enough for you to stake a claim somewhere under the wild coconut palms. Accessible by the "Playa" bus (catch it on Reyes Heróles, last bus returns from beach at 8pm; 5 pesos).

■ **NIGHTLIFE.** If you want to sample the local scene, there are a number of bars in Tuxpan's *centro*. More exotic nightlife can be found after the crowds in the Parque Reforma thin out, a few blocks down the river at Los Girasoles. Saturday nights, live rock draws the biggest crowds. (Cover Sa 40 pesos. See Accommodations, below.) **Mantarraya,** Reyes Heróles, one block past the bridge, is the perfect place to break it down to not-quite-current pop and techno hits with a mixed-age crowd. Some Saturdays, the club features enormously popular "dance shows." (☎834 0051. Cover 20-40 pesos, including 2 drinks. Open F-Sa 8:30pm-3am.)

■ **FESTIVALS.** Every Sunday night, locals crowd the parks for **Domingos Familiares** (Family Sundays). In Parque Rodríguez Cano, little kids jump on trampolines and drive bumper cars while parents chat. In Parque Reforma, older couples dance to Latin classics and prove romance never dies. All the while, adolescents march in single-sex packs, eyeing each other from afar. On a grander scale, August 15 marks the beginning of the **Feria Exposición,** a week-long display of town spirit. Traditional dance and song, cockfights, and open-air theatre productions abound. On December 7, Tuxpan celebrates **El Día del Niño Perdido** (see p. 545).

POZA RICA

☎783

Known more for its industry than its history or culture, Poza Rica is one of the busiest oil centers in the country. The lush, green city serves as a transportation hub for the northern part of the state, providing easy access to nearby Papantla and the ruins of **El Tajín.**

■ **TRANSPORTATION.** From the two adjoining bus stations in the northwest corner of town, the *centro* is accessible by "Centro" or "Juárez" minibuses (10-15min., 4 pesos). The station on the left is served exclusively by ADO, while the one on the right has several lines with less extensive service. **ADO** goes to: **Brownsville** (6 per day, 467 pesos); **Mexico City** (5hr., every hr., 140 pesos); **Papantla** (30min., every hr., 11 pesos); **Tampico** (5hr., every 30min., 150 pesos); **Tuxpan** (45min., every 30min., 28 pesos); **Veracruz** (4½hr., every hr., 126 pesos); **Villahermosa** (12hr., 12 per day, 377 pesos); **Xalapa** (5hr., 12 per day, 137 pesos). From the other station, **Ómnibus de México** goes to **Guadalajara** (10hr., 4 per day, 480 pesos). **Transportes Papantla** motors to smaller, regional destinations.

■ **PRACTICAL INFORMATION.** Poza Rica provides most services, but there is no tourist office; **Bital,** in Soriana Plaza next to the bus stations, **exchanges currency** and **traveler's checks** and has a 24hr. **ATM** (☎822 1877; open M-Sa 8am-7pm); the **supermarket Soriana** is to the right as you exit the stations (open daily 8am-10:30pm); **luggage storage** is in the bus station next to ADO, across from Turistar (3 pesos per hr.; open 24hr.); **emergency** services (☎060); **Red Cross** (☎822 0101); **police** (☎822 0407); **pharmacy** in the non-ADO station (open 24hr.); **Telecomm,** next to the post office (open M-F 8am-7:30pm, Sa 9am-5pm, Su 9am-noon); **post office,** Calle 16 Ote., facing Parque Juárez, accessible by minibus from the *centro*, has **Mexpost** inside (☎823 0102; open M-F 8am-4pm, Sa 9am-1pm). **Postal code:** 93261.

▐▜ ACCOMMODATIONS AND FOOD. Should you decide to spend a night in town, several mid-priced to expensive hotels are available in the *centro*, along **Cortines**. Near the stations resides the dirt-cheap **Hotel Farolito ❶**, to the left as you exit either station. Your penance for saving pesos? Rooms with peeling paint and a musty smell. All rooms have fans. (☎824 3466. Singles 90 pesos; doubles 120 pesos.) Nicer, clean rooms with A/C and TV await guests at **Auto Hotel Los Arcos ❹** down the road. (☎822 1600. Singles 250 pesos; doubles 300 pesos.) The restaurant and bar **Palma Sola ❶** next door is an excellent place to relax and grab a bite. *Antojitos* 15 pesos, mixed drinks 30 pesos, entrees 40-80 pesos. (☎823 5373. Open daily 8am-10pm.) For a quick meal between buses, a number of countertop restaurants dot the **Soriana Plaza ❶** just a few steps away from the station. *Gorditas* and enchiladas 7-20 pesos. (Most open daily 8am-10pm.)

◖ SIGHTS. The archaeological site of **▨El Tajín** (see p.550) is just 20min. from Poza Rica, halfway to Papantla. To get there from the bus station, take the minibus to the *centro* and ask the driver to let you off at **Monumento a la Madre,** on the corner of Cortines and Cárdenas. From there, hop on any bus that says "Papantla" or "Chote" (7.5 pesos), which will drop you right at the entrance. Also, if you find yourself on an exceptionally long layover between buses, the **MMCinema** on the Soriana Plaza shows the latest American movies for low prices (30-50 pesos).

PAPANTLA
☎784

Papantla (pop. 81,000) has many elements of a perfect, out-of-the way stop. Nestled in the green foothills of the Sierra Madre Oriental, this small town has more than its share of amazing vistas. One of the few remaining centers of Totonac culture, Papantla sits 12km north of the **El Tajín ruins,** once an important Totonac city during the Classic Period. Conquered by the Aztecs in 1450, the Totonacs soon took revenge upon their enemies by joining Cortés in his march to Tenochtitlán. After the conquest, the Spanish discovered the city's delicious, long-cultivated vanilla and introduced it worldwide, titling Papantla "city that perfumes the world." Papantla now straddles traditional Catholicism and *indígena* pride, with its hallowed cathedral showcasing a Totonac mural and Totonac dances on display every weekend. The ruins and surrounding landscape are both beautiful and impressive, but vanilla is now widely available, and the oppressive heat and unattractive, predominantly cement architecture detract from the experience.

▐ TRANSPORTATION. Papantla lies 250km northwest of Veracruz and 21km southeast of Poza Rica on **Mex. 180.** From the **ADO bus station,** Juárez 207 (☎842 0218), to the *centro*, turn left on Juárez and veer left at the fork. The walk is steep but short. If you've got too many bags, or you just can't stand the hill, taxis (10 pesos) pass frequently along Juárez. If arriving at the **second-class bus station,** 20 de Noviembre 200, commonly called **Transportes Papantla,** turn left outside the station and ascend 20 de Noviembre three blocks, to the northwest corner of the plaza. **ADO** goes to: **Mexico City** (5hr., 7 per day, 152 pesos); **Tuxpan** (1½hr., 4 per day, 36 pesos); **Veracruz** (4hr., 8 per day, 116 pesos); **Xalapa** (4hr., 10 per day, 126 pesos); **Poza Rica** (45min., 20 per day, 11 pesos). Call ahead—buses are often booked before they arrive in Papantla.

▰▐ ORIENTATION AND PRACTICAL INFORMATION. The central plaza, **Parque Téllez,** is bordered on the south by a whitewashed **cathedral,** on Nuñez y Domínguez, and on the north by **Enríquez.** The **tourist office** is in the Palacio Municipal, at the western side of the main plaza; enter on the right side as you face the Palacio. A helpful staff doles out information packets and cultural recommendations. (☎842 0026, ext. 714. Open M-F 9am-3pm and 6-9pm.) Banks on

HE LOCAL LEGEND

FLY GUYS

They are regarded as heroes, and you can see them daily for only 10 pesos. They are the renowned *voladores* of Papantla and El Tajín, caretakers of an ancient Totonac tradition and darlings of the entire community.

The performance begins with five elaborately costumed men climbing a stationary pole to a platform at least 28m above the ground. The *voladores* (fliers) first salute the four cardinal points in a dance around the pole. Four of the five then wind ropes around the pole, tie them to their feet, and start to "fly"—hanging upside-down from the ropes, spinning downwards, and assuming different ritual positions in request for specific weather conditions. Each flier corresponds to the sun, wind, moon, or earth. The fifth man plays a flute and dances on the pole's peak—which is little broader than his foot.

Spanish missionaries belittled the tradition, calling it a game or demonic practice. Like many indigenous ceremonies, the flights of the *voladores* gradually died out. But half a millennium later, the *voladores* are going strong once again, performing in Papantla every Sunday and at El Tajín whenever a crowd gathers, where they ask only for a small donation to cover their expenses. They are a living exhibit in Mexico City's Museo Nacional de Antropología too, where performers replay the traditional dance.

the northern side of the plaza, including **Bital,** have 24hr. **ATMs** and **exchange currency.** (☎842 0001. Open M-Sa 8am-7pm.) Services include: the **supermarket General de Muebles de Papantla,** Azueta 200, one block from the main plaza (☎842 0023; open Su 10am-2pm and 4-8pm, M-Sa 8:30am-8:30pm); **emergency** service (☎060); **police** (☎842 0075), in the Palacio Municipal; **Red Cross,** on Escobedo off Juárez (☎842 0126); the **pharmacy El Fénix,** Enríquez 103E, at the north end of the plaza (☎842 0636; open daily 8am-11pm); **IMSS** (☎842 0194), 20 de Noviembre at Lázaro Cárdenas—from the ADO station, take a right and walk two blocks to Cárdenas, then turn left and IMSS is half a block up on the right; **Clínica del Centro Médico,** on 16 de Septiembre near the tourist office (☎842 0082; little English spoken); **Telecomm,** on Olivo, off 20 de Noviembre near Hotel Totanacapán (open Su 9am-noon, M-F 8am-7pm, Sa 9am-5pm); **LADATELs,** along Enríquez in the main plaza; **Internet access** at Ciber-Tropic Internet, Nuñez y Domínguez 102, just half a block away from the Cathedral (10 pesos per hr.; open daily 8:30am-9:30pm); **post office,** on Miguel Negrete--walk two blocks west of the plaza on Enríquez, then take Negrete at the fork in the road (☎842 0073; open M-F 9am-4pm). **Postal code:** 93400.

⚑ ACCOMMODATIONS. The lovely **Hotel Totanacapán ❺** is on 20 de Noviembre at Olivo, four blocks from the plaza. The hallway murals, spacious rooms, large windows, and complimentary bottled water place it a cut above the rest. Rooms have TV, phone, and A/C. (☎842 1224. Singles 255 pesos; doubles 280 pesos.) **Hotel Pulido ❷,** Enríquez 205, two blocks to the left of the main plaza, facing the cathedral. With a tiled courtyard and powerful fans, Pulido is a haven for budget travelers. (☎842 0036. Singles and doubles 160 pesos.) A step up in ritz, **Hotel Tajín ❺,** Núñez y Domínguez 104, half a block to the left from the plaza as you face the cathedral, has a miniature stone-carved replica of a pyramid at El Tajín in the lobby. Shared balconies open to panoramic views. Perks include bottled water, cable TV, and phones. Guided horseback tours are available with one-week advance notice. (☎842 0121. Singles 265 pesos, 357 pesos with A/C; doubles 366/478 pesos. Each additional person 60 pesos. Horse tours US$30 per hr.) If these rates make you uneasy, head to **Hotel México ❶,** Nuñez y Domínguez 110. Although the rooms can't compare to the other hotels in town, you won't find cheaper accommodations in all of Papantla. (☎842 0086. Singles 100 pesos; doubles 150 pesos.)

FOOD. Papantla's best and most popular restaurants are around the *zócalo*. These touristed restaurants serve regional goodies, usually beef and pork. Specialties include *molotes*, Mexican dumplings of spiced meat wrapped in a boiled corn shell, and *bocoles*, stout fried tortillas filled with egg, cheese, sausage, or chicken. **La Hacienda ❸**, Reforma 100, on the western end of the central square, treats diners to excellent service, a terrace-top view of the plaza, and delicious *bocoles* (25 pesos). (☎842 0633. Entrees 20-45 pesos. Open daily 7:30am-11pm.) Just steps away from the plaza on 20 de Noviembre, the tiny **Taquería el Vaquero ❶** has only one thing on the menu: tacos. But at 2 pesos, with your choice of meat filling, these are the best deal (with the spiciest salsa) in town. (Open daily 8am-4:30pm.) The **Restaurant Por Si Acaso Me Recuerdas ❷**, Juan Enríquez 102, sits to the left of the main plaza when facing the cathedral. Bring a friend or two and enjoy the quiet of this small local hideaway. The food comes fast, hot, and cheap. (☎842 1112. Four *bocoles* 12-16 pesos, chicken *mole* with rice 25 pesos. Open Su-W 7am-1am, Th-Sa 24hr.) **Restaurante Sorrento ❸**, Enríquez 105, caters to locals with lots of regional specialties (25-60 pesos). (☎842 0067. Open daily 7am-midnight.)

SIGHTS. Papantla's biggest attractions are relics of its Totonac heritage. Even the Catholic **Catedral Señora de la Asunción,** overlooking the Parque, has a remarkable 50m long, 5m high stone mural, called *Homenaje a la Cultura Totonaca*, on its outer wall. The mural—based on a relief from El Tajín—depicts eager Totonac ballplayers vying for the honor of ritualistic death and deification. On Sunday afternoons, in the cathedral's spacious courtyard, **Plaza de los Voladores,** *voladores* (see p. p. 548) acrobatically entreat the rain god Tlaloc to water local crops. **Monumento al Volador,** Papantla's latest effort to enshrine its famous *voladores*, is a gigantic, flute-wielding *indígena* statue erected atop a hill in 1988 and visible all over town. To reach the monument, from which all of Papantla is visible, walk up Reforma, the road that passes the entrance to the cathedral (5-10min.). Both the view of the city and of couples making out at the statue's base are memorable. **Museo de la Ciudad,** at Pino Suárez and Madero, displays murals on Totonac history, traditional clothing, and an impressive photographic time line of local history. (☎842 0221. Open Tu-Su 10am-2pm and 4-8pm. 10 pesos.)

SHOPPING. Activities besides Totonac-based sightseeing are few. The town's two markets are situated next to the *zócalo*. **Mercado Juárez,** at Reforma and 16 de Septiembre off the southwest corner of the *zócalo*, specializes in fruits, vegetables, and freshly butchered meat. **Mercado Hidalgo,** on 20 de Noviembre off the northwest corner, is packed with *artesanía*, clothing, meat, and souvenirs. This is the best place to buy Papantla's world-renowned **vanilla**—a few stands sell high-quality extract (20-100 pesos) and wonderfully sweet liqueur (120-200 pesos per bottle); others have figurines made with vanilla sticks. If you're counting pesos, shopkeepers are usually happy to give out small samples of the good stuff.

FESTIVALS. In early June, the 10-day Festival of Corpus Christi celebrates both the indigenous and Christian traditions of Papantla. Most of the action occurs at a fair just outside town, with artistic expositions, fireworks, traditional dances, and cockfights. To get to the festival from the *centro*, flag down a taxi (15 pesos) or take any *pesero* (3 pesos) from 16 de Septiembre behind the cathedral and ask for the *feria*. In town, the *voladores* perform as often as three times a day, morning, afternoon, and evening. Once every 52 years, the Totonac equivalent of a century, the festival takes on larger proportions.

GULF COAST & CHIAPAS

NEAR PAPANTLA: ▨ EL TAJÍN

El Tajín is accessible from Papantla via the white-and-blue peseros that stop at the corner of 16 de Septiembre and Reforma, next to the cathedral's courtyard (30min., every 15min. 5am-8pm, 9.5 pesos). Hop on a "Poza Rica" bus (it may also say "Chote" and "Tajín") and check with the driver to make sure it stops at El Tajín. The bus will pass through the town of El Chote, then stop at the entrance to El Tajín. To return to Papantla, catch a "Papantla" bus outside the museum (last bus at 5pm, 9.5 pesos). Ruins open daily 8am-7pm. 30 pesos, under 13 and over 60, free; Su free.

The sight of the ruins at El Tajín gives a grand impression of the thriving Totonac civilization that spread across modern-day northern Veracruz during the Classic Period. Though the ruins were "discovered" by the Spanish in 1785, restoration work did not begin until 1939. El Tajín now sits as a maze of stone-carved temples and pyramids, each laden with religious meaning. The area was probably settled around AD 100 by Huastec peoples before the Totonacs razed their structures and began developing the area early in the Classic Period (AD 300-400). The Totonac name is a Spanish derivative of the Náhuatl *Tutu Nacu*, which means "three hearts" and refers to the three major city centers of Totonac culture, including El Tajín. In Totonac, "Tajín" means "thunder," "lightning," or "hurricane"; it is believed that the Totonacs dedicated this city to the god of rain. In the mid-Classic Period (AD 600-900), El Tajín was a Totonac capital, perhaps subservient only to Teotihuacán in the Valley of Mexico. The area declined in importance early in the post-Classic Period, around AD 1200; it is unclear whether the inhabitants died out or simply left. Most archaeologists now believe the city was conquered and burned by invading nomadic tribes such as the Chichimeca. The Totonacs who remained in the area were brought under the control of the Aztecs in the late 15th century.

MUSEUM AND ENTRANCE AREA. Next to the entrance stands the *voladores'* large pole (performances June-Aug. daily every hr., Sept.-May weekends only). The daring acrobats typically request a 10-peso donation. Books (50 pesos) on El Tajín are sold at the store adjoining the **information desk.** A small **restaurant ❸** at the entrance makes seafood *comida corrida* (35 pesos). Entering the ruins, you pass **Museo de Sitio,** a museum featuring original mural fragments and a morbidly fascinating display of ancient skeletons, some with cracked skulls and visible bone injuries. From the museum, a straight path leads to the ruins, which are unlabeled. The best sources of information are guidebooks or a guided tour (15 pesos).

PLAZA DE ARROYO. The Plaza, the central rectangle formed by four tiered pyramids, lies just to the left of the gravel road. Each pyramid points toward the northeast at a 20-degree angle, a common feature among the site's early buildings.

JUEGO DE PELOTA SUR (SOUTH BALL COURT). Past the pyramids, two low-lying, slanted constructions to the left of the main path frame a central grass ball court, where the Totonac's famous one-on-one ball game was played. Every 52 years, a contest was held between the most valiant ballplayers; if you've picked up on the pattern, you'll probably realize the winner earned the honor of being decapitated (and deified). Approximately 17 such courts grace the ruins of Tajín, and this one is famous for its carved stone walls depicting the ball games in action.

THE CENTRAL ZONE. Across from the plaza stands an elevated central altar surrounded by two climbable temples. Left of the altar is a split-level temple with a statue of Tajín. This area is the Central Zone, notable for the diverse styles and functions of its buildings.

LA PIRÁMIDE DE LOS NICHOS. To the northwest stands the Pyramid of Niches, El Tajín's most recognizable structure, with seven levels and a total of 365 niches corresponding to the days of the year. Each niche was once painted crimson and blue. The Totonacs kept time in 52-year epochs, during which a single flame was kept continuously burning. At the end of each epoch, the carefully nurtured flame was used to ritually torch many of the settlement's buildings; each new epoch of rebuilding and regeneration was inaugurated by the lighting of a new flame. Ritual ceremonies are now held annually at the pyramid. During the vernal equinox, farmers place seeds in the pyramid's niches and later retrieve them for planting.

TAJÍN CHICO. Atop a hill to the north a series of large stepping stones and a staircase lead to **Tajín Chico.** While Tajín was a public religious and social center, archaeologists hypothesize that Tajín Chico provided shelter to the ruling class and political elite. Less excavated areas, it is rimmed with "no access" signs.

VERACRUZ ☎229

The oldest port city in the Americas, Veracruz (pop. 420,000) is an assault on the senses. Intense humidity and often unbearable heat envelop the city, while a powerful scent of salt water and fish pervades the air. A curse by day but a blessing by night, the city's tropical climate makes for gorgeous nighttime strolls along the beach and through the *zócalo*. Small *marimba* bands and lone guitarists pop in and out of restaurants and bars, providing a constant soundtrack, while nocturnal vendors raise their voices against the music, trying to make their sales pitches heard. The city has a storied military past, and is immensely proud of its seafaring and military histories; many of the local sights are devoted to naval warfare and the heroic encounters of bygone times. The city has survived a two-year assault by the Spanish, a French occupation, and two American occupations. Though the fortresses have long since been knocked down, Veracruz today stands tall, proud of its heritage and ready to welcome anyone willing to experience it.

▗ TRANSPORTATION

Airport: (☎934 3774), 8km south of downtown Veracruz on Mex. 150. Taxis will take you there for 120 pesos. **Aeroméxico** (☎935 0142) and **Mexicana** (☎932 2242).

Buses: From Parque Zamora, Mirón connects the *centro* to the **Central de Autobuses Veracruz (CAVE),** Mirón 1698, which houses all the city's major bus lines. To get to the *centro* from the bus station, get on a "Díaz Mirón" bus headed north to Parque Zamora (4.5 pesos). Some buses run all the way to the *zócalo;* others stop at the park. To return to the bus station, take a southbound "Díaz Mirón" bus from anywhere along 5 de Mayo. **ADO** (☎937 5788) goes to: **Cancún** (21hr., 9pm, 653 pesos); **Catemaco** (3hr., 8 per day, 78 pesos); **Córdoba** (1½hr., 29 per day 6am-11:30pm, 65 pesos); **Fortín de las Flores** (2hr.; 1, 6pm; 69 pesos); **Mexico City** (5½hr., 16 per day, 232 pesos); **Oaxaca** (6½hr.; 8:20am, 3:25, 10:30pm; 267 pesos); **Orizaba** (2½hr., 29 per day 6am-11:30pm, 76 pesos); **Tuxtla Gutiérrez** (12hr., 4pm, 330 pesos); **Tuxtepec** (3hr., 6 per day, 78 pesos); **Puebla** (4½hr., 9 per day, 163 pesos); **Xalapa** (1¾hr., every 30min. 6am-11:30pm, 55 pesos). **AU** (☎937 5732), 1 block behind the ADO station on the right side, offers 2nd-class service to similar destinations for about 10-15 pesos less.

✦⚡ ORIENTATION AND PRACTICAL INFORMATION

Veracruz sprawls along the coast in the southwest corner of the Gulf of Mexico, 104km south of Xalapa and 424km east of Mexico City. Along the south coast, Veracruz merges with the glam suburb **Boca del Río.** Home to luxury hotels, shopping malls, and sparkling shorelines, it is easily reached by the "Boca del Rio" buses which leave from **Zaragoza,** one block toward the bay from the *zócalo* (4.5 pesos). Buses are less frequent at night; taxis are a safer choice.

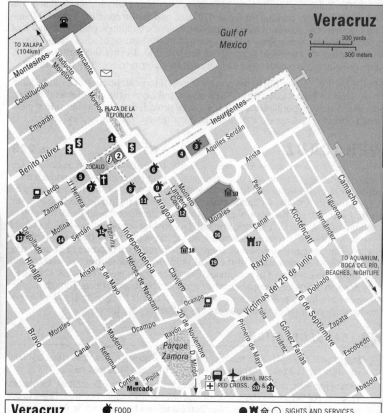

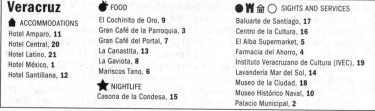

Veracruz

ACCOMMODATIONS
Hotel Amparo, **11**
Hotel Central, **20**
Hotel Latino, **21**
Hotel México, **1**
Hotel Santillana, **12**

🍴 **FOOD**
El Cochinito de Oro, **9**
Gran Café de la Parroquia, **3**
Gran Café del Portal, **7**
La Canastita, **13**
La Gaviota, **8**
Mariscos Tano, **6**

⭐ **NIGHTLIFE**
Casona de la Condesa, **15**

● 🏠 🏛 ○ SIGHTS AND SERVICES
Baluarte de Santiago, **17**
Centro de la Cultura, **16**
El Alba Supermarket, **5**
Farmacia del Ahorro, **4**
Instituto Veracruzano de Cultura (IVEC), **19**
Lavandería Mar del Sol, **14**
Museo de la Ciudad, **18**
Museo Histórico Naval, **10**
Palacio Municipal, **2**

Tourist Office: (☎939 8800, ext. 158), facing the *zócalo*. Tons of brochures and friendly, English-speaking staff. Open Su 10am-6pm, M-Sa 8am-8pm.

Currency Exchange: A slew of banks and *casas de cambio* pack the corner of Juárez and Independencia, 1 block north of the *zócalo*. **Banamex,** open M-F 8:30am–5pm, Sa 9am-2pm; and **Bital,** open M-Sa 8am-3pm; both have 24hr. **ATMs.**

American Express: Serdán 704 (☎931 0838). English-language travel advice and services. Open M-F 9am-7:30pm, Sa 9am-1:30pm.

Markets: Mercado Hidalgo, Cortés at Madero, 1 block from Parque Zamora, sells fruit, vegetables, *piñatas,* and more. Open daily 8am-8pm.

Supermarket: El Alba, Lerdo 270 (☎932 2424), between Independencia and 5 de Mayo. Open M-Sa 9am-2:30pm and 5-9pm.

Laundry: Lavandería Mar del Sol, 610 Madero. 20 pesos per load, with a max. of 3kg. Open M-Sa 7:30am-10pm.

Luggage Storage: At the bus station. 5 pesos per hr., 30 pesos per day. Open daily 7am-11pm.

Bicycle Rental: on Camacho at Bolívar, along Villa del Mar beach. 25-30 pesos per hr.

Emergency: ☎060 or 066.

Police: (☎938 0664) at Colonial Palieno.

Red Cross: (☎937 5411), on Mirón between Orizaba and Abascal, 1 block south of the Central de Autobuses, has **ambulance** service. No English spoken.

Pharmacy: Farmacia del Ahorro, Gómez Farías 2 (☎937 3525). Open 24hr.

Hospital: IMSS, Mirón 61 (☎932 1920), or **Sanitario Español,** 16 de Septiembre 955 (☎932 0021). No English spoken at either.

Fax: Telecomm (☎932 2508), on Plaza de la República. Open Su 9am-noon, M-F 8am-7pm, Sa 9am-5pm.

Internet Access: Netchatboys, Lerdo 369, between Madero and 5 de Mayo. 10 pesos per hr. Open M-F 9am-8:30pm, Sa-Su noon-8pm. **Webcafe,** Rayon 579A, near Parque Zamora. 15 pesos per hr., students 12 pesos per hr. Open M-Sa 10am-10pm.

Post Office: Marina Mercante 213 (☎932 2038), at Plaza de la República. **Mexpost** inside. Open M-F 8am-4pm, Sa 9am-1pm. **Postal Code:** 91700.

ACCOMMODATIONS

Accommodations in Veracruz generally boil down to the expensive, luxurious beachside hotels and cheaper, less glamorous abodes closer to the *centro*. Veracruz has three high seasons: *Carnaval* (the week before Ash Wednesday), *Semana Santa*, and midsummer. Many of the hotels fill up well in advance during these times; be prepared to pay extra too. The added necessity of a room with A/C in this steamy city ups the price even more. Rooms near the *centro* are relatively safe; those at the bus stations, convenient but pricey.

NEAR THE CENTRO

Hotel Amparo, Serdán 482 (☎932 2738). If there are backpackers in Veracruz, they're probably here. Very comfortable rooms with fans and hot water are neat and inexpensive. Singles 130 pesos; doubles 210 pesos. Cable TV 30 or 40 pesos extra. ❷

Hotel México, Morelos 343 (☎931 5744). Big rooms with charming wooden paneling. Fans, phone, and TV. Singles 150 pesos; doubles 200 pesos. ❸

Hotel Santillana, Landero y Coss 209 (☎932 3116). A few steps away from the waterfront, Santillana offers reasonably sized rooms with all the amenities (except A/C). The purple-green courtyard, interesting wallpapering schemes, and caged parrots emanate a garish charm. Singles 150 pesos; doubles 300 pesos. ❸

NEAR THE BUS STATION

Hotel Latino, La Fragua 1180 (☎937 6599). Exit left from the ADO station and walk 1½ blocks. The best bet for a stay near the station. Incredibly soft beds, bright colors, and large bathrooms amply compensate for the sparsely furnished rooms. Singles 180 pesos, with A/C 220 pesos; doubles 280/320 pesos. ❸

Hotel Central, Díaz Mirón 1612 (☎937 2350), to the right of the ADO station. Modern-looking hotel with a faux-marble lobby and dim hallways. Big rooms have TV, phone, and bath. Singles 230 pesos, with A/C 270 pesos; doubles 280/340 pesos. Inquire about budget singles on the roof, which, despite the unusual setting, aren't much worse than the standard rooms. ❹

❖ FOOD

Small restaurants surround the fish markets on **Landero y Coss.** Eccentrically decorated, these are the places to dig into the mountains of fish, shrimp, octopus, and crab hauled out of the gulf on a daily basis. For a cheaper, slightly more frantic experience, try **Mercado Hidalgo ❸,** where seafood stands sell fish and shrimp dishes for around 30 pesos. Restaurants under the *portales* in the *zócalo* offer yummy dishes and a *marimba* beat—for a price. Wherever you choose to dine, don't miss out on the distinctive *veracruzano* fare—just keep in mind the rule to always steer clear of raw fish. Regional specialties include *huachinango* (red snapper), *filete relleno* (fish fillet stuffed with *mariscos*), *arroz a la tumbada* (rice in a sauce that includes—of course—shellfish), and *jaiba* (large local crab).

Gran Café de la Parroquia, Gómez Farías 34 (☎932 2584), on the *malecón.* A Veracruz tradition. The entire town seems to gather here, often filling the enormous space. Entrees run about 90 pesos, but the real draw is the *lechero* (13 pesos). Your meal will be accompanied by the sound of spoons clinking against tall glasses of the famous coffee. Open daily 6am-1am. ❺

La Canastita, on the corner of Hidalgo and Zamora. A few blocks away from the hustle and bustle of the *centro,* Canastita serves up delicious *tortas* (8-15 pesos), tacos (4 pesos), and other *antojitos.* Open M-Sa 9am-6pm. ❶

Gran Café del Portal (☎932 9339), on Independencia and Zamora, at the southwest corner of the *zócalo.* Another one of Veracruz's favorite hangouts. Diners here sip coffee, eat delicious food (entrees 70-100 pesos) and watch the nighttime scene unfold before their eyes. Open M-F 9am-10pm, Sa-Su 9am-11pm. ❺

Mariscos Tano, Molina 20 (☎931 5050), 1 block south of the *zócalo.* Veracruz's seafaring pride is on full display here, with a model ship at the counter and stuffed sea-creatures filling the rafters. The owner proudly displays pictures of his reign as king of *Carnaval. Mariscos* and popular regional entrees (translated into English on the menu) go for 40-70 pesos. Open daily 9am-10pm. ❸

El Cochinito de Oro, Zaragoza 190 (☎932 3677), at Serdán. Cheap, quality seafood (55-70 pesos) and friendly service explain El Cochinito's 50-year popularity with locals. The ever-changing *menú del día* goes for 50 pesos. Open daily 7am-5pm. ❸

La Gaviota, Callejón de Trigueros 21 (☎932 3950), ½ block from the intersection of Zaragoza and Serdán. The quiet, simple ambience and regional specialties are reminiscent of *zócalo* quality at more affordable prices. *Filete a la veracruzano* 48 pesos, *antojitos* 12-22 pesos. Open 24hr. ❸

❻ SIGHTS

Veracruz's importance to Mexico has not been lost on foreign invaders, who have often targeted the port as their first point of attack. This history has left its mark on the sights, imbuing remnants of the military past with deep, nationalist meaning. Students from the Naval Academy amble about the streets even today, bearing testament to Veracruz's perpetual military readiness.

CASTILLO DE SAN JUAN DE ULÚA. The fortress, Veracruz's most important historic site, rests on a fingertip of land jutting into the harbor. Using coral chunks as bricks, construction began sometime after Cortés's arrival under the order of Charles V. It was intended as part of the system of fortifications built to protect

Spanish treasure from Caribbean pirates. After 1825, political figures were seen as the more pressing danger, and it became a high-security jail for the likes of presidents Benito Juárez and Porfirio Díaz. Famous *políticos* aside, San Juan's best-known prisoner was the folk hero **Chucho el Roto**, who is believed to have escaped from San Juan three times. *(Take a "San Juan de Ulúa" bus (4.5 pesos) in front of the Aduana building in Plaza de la República. Unfortunately, buses come very infrequently and stop running at 5pm. The only other option, taxis charge around 60-70 pesos. ☎938 5151. Open Tu-Su 9am-5pm. 20 pesos; Su free. Guided tours in Spanish, 10 pesos, will help you to understand all that you see.)*

▧ MUSEO HISTÓRICO NAVAL. The museum, located on the grounds of Veracruz's Naval School, is a sailor's air-conditioned dream. Gallery after gallery of model ships, entertaining dioramas on seafaring history, and displays on Veracruz's naval successes and shortcomings make for an enjoyable navigation of Mexico's rich maritime history. *(The Naval School occupies the entire block bordered by 16 de Septiembre, Arista, Montero, and Morales; the entrance is on 16 de Septiembre. ☎931 4078. Open Tu-Su 9am-5pm. Free.)*

BALUARTE DE SANTIAGO. Built in 1526, the Baluarte is today the sole remnant of the stone wall that once encircled a good part of the city, protecting the inhabitants from pirates. The wall, along with the eight other *baluartes* (small forts), was torn down in the late 19th century. The museum inside displays a collection of Pre-Hispanic gold ornaments called *Las Joyas del Pescador*, named for their rescue from the ocean by a lucky octopus fisherman. Around the back of the fort, a spiral staircase leads to a pretty tower view. *(On Canal between 16 de Septiembre and Farías, 1 block from the Naval School. ☎931 1059. Open Tu-Su 10am-4:30pm. 30 pesos; Su free.)*

MUSEO DE LA CIUDAD. Completely renovated in summer 2000, this museum features paintings and dioramas depicting the history of the city from Pre-Hispanic times to the present. Indigenous artifacts, colonial accounts, and DVD documentaries on military encounters will bring you up to speed on everything you ever wanted to know about Veracruz. *(Zaragoza 397. Down Canal away from the water, and right on Zaragoza. ☎931 8410. Open Su-M and W-Sa 10am-6pm. 25 pesos, students 10 pesos.)*

ACUARIO DE VERACRUZ. A popular family beachside attraction, the aquarium features fish, sharks, and turtles native to the gulf. *(In the Centro Comercial Plaza Acuario, a shopping mall on the left when facing the ocean at*

THE LOCAL LEGEND

CHUCHO AND HIS MERRY MEN

Robin Hood, prince of thieves: friend to the poor, scourge to the rich, gallant leader of a brave group of virtuous vagabonds. Pity he's not real. Even if he were, he'd have a tough time topping Veracruz legend Jesús Arriaga. Fed up with the income inequality in early 20th century Mexico (and perhaps inspired by Sherwood Forest fantasies) Arriaga organized a band of "social bandits," took the slick-sounding nickname "Chucho el Roto," and set about robbing the rich and giving to the poor.

Eventually, the authorities caught up with Chucho and sent him to San Juan de Ulúa, Veracruz's version of Alcatraz. Unfazed, the social bandits arranged a daring escape by boat. Chucho soon found himself back in the hands of the authorities, though, and back at San Juan de Ulúa. After another escape and capture, the powers that be were unwilling to suffer more humiliating defiance. Chucho was tortured and eventually killed in a cell at San Juan. Chucho's body was sent to Mexico City on a train for burial.

And that should have been that. As the story goes, the trip was uneventful—until the coffin was opened in el D.F., only to reveal...absolutely nothing. The hero had the last laugh. Chucho el Roto's legend spread through the state of Veracruz, proving the incontrovertible fact: you can't keep a good man down.

THE BIG SPLURGE

UN POQUITO DE CUBA

You've seen them everywhere. You recognize the design: four pockets and vertical stripes. And you know that without one, you can't possibly hope to blend into the background in Veracruz (as if clothing could hide your accent and sunburn). What are these stylish shirts, and where can you hope to get your hands on one?

Look no further. These shirts are the famed *guayaberas*, hot-weather shirts that have defined style in Veracruz and beyond for years. The story begins with Cuban guava pickers, who were tired of shimmying up and down trees countless times to harvest individual fruits. The four-pocket *guayabera* expedited the task and the fashion spread quickly. It found its way to Panama, then to Mexico, where Carlos Cab Arrazate added the thin pleats connecting the pockets. His grandson continues the family business: **Guayaberas Finas,** Zaragoza 233, in Veracruz city. (☎ 931 8427. Open Su 10am-4pm, M-F 9:30am-8pm, Sa 9:30am-7pm.)

Originally *guayaberas* were all white, but time brought new colors and patterns; they now exist for both sexes and cost 350 to 1000 pesos and up. If you need more validation than local popularity, check out US President Eishenhower's note of appreciation on the store wall. A bit of fashion advice, preppy: these shirts are not meant to be tucked in.

Villa del Mar. Catch a "Villa del Mar" bus on Zaragoza (4.5 pesos). ☎ 931 1020. Open M-Th 10am-7pm, F-Su 10am-7:30pm. 50 pesos, children 25 pesos.)

INSTITUTO VERACRUZANO DE LA CULTURA (IVEC) AND THE CENTRO DE LA CULTURA. Just a few paces away from each other, the Instituto (on the corner of Canal and Zaragoza) and Centro (just above IVEC on Landero y Coss) hand out all the information you need for a cultural outing. Schedules keep tourists and college students posted on the latest concerts, art exhibitions, and performances in the city. (IVEC ☎ 931 4396. Open M-F 9am-8pm, Sa-Su 9am-6pm. Centro open daily 8am-8pm.)

⚫ BEACHES

The general rule for beaches in Veracruz is that the farther from the city, the nicer the beach; still, it's practically impossible to escape the distant oil barges and tugboats. **Playa Villa del Mar** is a pleasant hour-long walk from the *zócalo* along the waterfront. It is also accessible via one of the frequent "Villa del Mar" or "Boca del Río" buses (4.5 pesos) that stop on Zaragoza and along Camacho. Few people swim at Villa del Mar—thatch-roofed restaurants have set up camp along the boardwalk, and their beachside presence makes frolicking in the sand almost impossible. Still, the restaurant huts and bars create a lively atmosphere at night.

The best beach in the Veracruz area (although that's not saying much) is **Playa Mocambo,** in the neighboring city of **Boca del Río.** Take a "Boca del Río" bus and get off at the mall, Plaza de las Americas (30min.). The beach is on the other side of Hotel Torremar. Veer left for the beach or go straight into **Balneario Mocambo,** which has a clean, Olympic-sized public pool surrounded by artificial palm trees, changing rooms, and a pool side bar-restaurant. (☎ 931 0288. Open daily 10am-6pm. 25 pesos, children 20 pesos.) Those who define their beach experiences by attitude rather than turquoise water will find plenty of laid-back lounging in the residential area down the coast from the hotel.

🎵 📷 ENTERTAINMENT & NIGHTLIFE

In the evening, the hymns of the cathedral spilling out into the *zócalo* yield to the sexy rhythms of *marimbas*. Vendors spread their wares on the paths, and bars and restaurants fill with merry drinkers and *mariachi* bands. Apart from this spontaneous merrymaking in the *zócalo*, most action takes place along **Camacho,** the seaside road connecting Veracruz and

Boca del Río. Just before the purple high-rise landmark Hotel Lois, **Ruiz Cortines** branches off Camacho, marking a great place to get off the "Boca del Río" bus.

BARS AND CLUBS

Big Fish (Aquarius), Camacho 10 (☎959 5506). Tiny tables, giant couches, and a beautiful view of the beach make Aquarius a popular choice for nightlife. The bar turns into a hot dance club on weekend nights. No cover. Open daily 2pm-1am.

Salsoteca (☎921 7935), on Camacho, four blocks down the beach from Ruiz Cortines. This giant stone mountain beckons with pounding salsa, rock, and pop music. Cover 50 pesos. Open F-Sa 10:30pm-5am.

Roka/Loft, on the corner of Camacho and Ruiz Cortines. Offering special promotions, an occasional open bar, and thunderous dance beats, these adjacent clubs are at the center of beach nightlife. Open Th-Sa 10pm-late.

Casona de la Condesa, Callejón de Lagunilla 19 (☎931 4158). A young, well-dressed crowd descends on one of the few downtown clubs for live bands, dancing, and beer. Reservations and/or a working knowledge of Spanish might help you get past picky bouncers. No cover. Open Tu-Su 10pm-3am.

FESTIVALS

Every December 31, from midnight until dawn, *veracruzano* families dress in their Sunday best and fill Camacho, looking east to the Gulf of Mexico to witness the first sunrise of the year. With that auspicious start, a year of celebrations begins. The climax comes early, in the days ahead of Ash Wednesday, when **Carnaval** invades the *zócalo* with nine days of festivities. The **Festival Internacional Afrocaribeño** spans ten wild days in mid-July. Enjoy music and dancing in the *zócalo* and elsewhere around the clock.

▶ DAYTRIPS FROM VERACRUZ

ZEMPOALA

*From the 2nd-class bus station on La Fragua behind the ADO station, Autobuses TRV sends buses to **Cardel** (45min., 17 pesos). Exit out the right side of the station on to Azueta, and walk 2 blocks to the right; the Zempoala bus pick-up is on the cross street at the T-intersection. From there, take a bus to **Zempoala** (25min., 7 pesos). Ask the driver to let you out at the ruins, at the intersection of Ruíz and Troncoso Norte. When returning, Veracruz buses from Cardel run every 10min. from midnight to 8pm, every 15min. until 10pm. Site open daily 9am-4:30pm. 32 pesos; Su free.*

The impressive ruins at **Zempoala**, or **Cempoala**, lie 40km north of Veracruz off Mex. 180. Zempoala was one of the largest southern Totonac cities and part of a federation that covered much of Veracruz. During its peak in the 14th and 15th centuries, the city may have had as many as 120,000 inhabitants, and many believe it to be the Totonac Post-Classic successor to El Tajín (see p. 550). In 1458, however, the Aztecs conquered Zempoala and forced the Totonac to join the Aztec federation. When Cortés arrived in 1519, the humbled city had only about 30,000 residents and was eager to assist an enemy of the Aztecs, lending Cortés soldiers and supplies.

The site now consists of stone structures surrounding a grassy field next to present-day Zempoala. The palm trees and peaceful setting of the ruins seem incongruous with their bloody history. The structure closest to the entrance is the **Temple of Death**. To the left of the main path are three **pyramids**. The pyramid on the left is dedicated to Tlaloc (god of rain), the one on the right to the moon, and the one in the center, decorated with circular stone receptacles for the hearts of people sacrificed in religious offerings, to the sun. To the right of the main path is the **Templo Mayor**, the largest building on the site. When Cortés arrived, the Spaniards erected an altar to the Virgin on top of the temple, forcing Catholicism on the Totonacs. In front of the Templo Mayor is the **throne** where the king observed sacrifices. The throne faces the temple known as **Las Chimeneas.** This area played a central role in the Totonac "New Five Ceremony," a five-day fast that took place every 52 years when a cycle of the ritual calendar ended. Every spring equinox, people still come to the circle to expel negative energy and absorb positive energy.

LA ANTIGUA

Take a 2nd-class TRV bus from the Central, behind the ADO station (30min., 12 pesos). Tell the driver you want to get off at La Antigua—on the way to Cardel and Zempoala—and keep an eye out for the stop, marked by the tollbooth and a small sign pointing to the left. Cross the street and follow the main road for 15min. until you reach the town's main drag. To return, go back down the road; buses to Veracruz pass frequently from dawn to 9pm.

When Cortés landed on the coast of Mexico in 1519, he and his army moved north, settling here, the first Spanish town in Mexico. Cortés named the town Villa Rica de la Vera Cruz, but when the city was reestablished in 1599 in its present location 28km away, the old town came to be known as just that—La Antigua. The modern-day reality is an interesting juxtaposition of 16th- and 21st-century architecture in the middle of the town.

Unlabeled streets and the jungle's tendency to interrupt all things orderly make finding the town's older buildings something of a scavenger hunt. Crossing the street and taking the perpendicular road branching left of the main road, you'll come to the **Parroquia de Cristo del Buen Viaje,** which dates from the mid-17th century; the interior contains two 16th-century baptismal fonts carved by early indigenous converts. Passing the *zócalo* and continuing down the street, the famous **Casa de Cortés,** where the *conquistador* supposedly lived for a time, is back from the road on the left. The cannon was brought over from Spain by the man himself. Farther down the street, the tree that divides the road holds legendary status as the site where Cortés first armed himself for the fateful 1519 expedition. Built in 1523, the **Edificio del Cabildo** was the first office of the Spanish government in Mexico. The most beautiful of the buildings is the **Emerito del Rosario.** Finished in 1524, the building features stations of the cross rendered in Talvera tile. To find these buildings, all relatively close to one another, it's best to ask locals to point the way.

CÓRDOBA
☎ 271

Friendly, bustling Córdoba (pop. 175,000) feels like a rare Gulf breeze in comparison to the sweltering state capital nearby. The Spanish founded Córdoba in 1618, intending for it to serve as a defensive post against anticipated slave rebellions at nearby sugarcane plantations. Later, the city would establish itself as a place of freedom and compromise—the Treaty of Córdoba was signed here, bringing Mexico independence from Spain.

▛ TRANSPORTATION. All buses arrive at **Cordinados Córdoba** (☎ 727 0468), 3km from the *zócalo* along Av. 4. To get to the *zócalo*, also called the Plaza de Armas, from the bus station, exit to the right and take a "Centro" bus (4.5 pesos). **ADO** has first-class service to: **Mexico City** (4½hr., 24 per day, 173 pesos); **Oaxaca** (6hr.; 12:10, 2, 10am, 5pm; 203 pesos); **Orizaba** (40 min., 18 per day, 12 pesos); **Palenque** (8½hr., 8:35pm, 406 pesos); **Puebla** (3hr., 12 per day, 108 pesos); **Tulum** (17½hr., 5:30pm, 670 pesos); **Tuxtepec** (3hr., 4:10pm, 76 pesos); **Tuxtla Gutiérrez** (11hr.; 9:50, 10:25pm; 363 pesos); **Veracruz** (1½hr., 25 per day, 65 pesos); **Villahermosa** (5½hr., 6 per day, 299 pesos); **Xalapa** (3hr., 17 per day, 90 pesos). Other lines offer second-class service to some destinations. To reach Orizaba (9 pesos) or Fortín de las Flores (5 pesos) from Córdoba, hop on a westbound bus from anywhere on Calle 13.

🔳🔳 ORIENTATION AND PRACTICAL INFORMATION. Córdoba is 125km southwest of Veracruz, along Mex. 150. The city is easy to navigate; numbered *avenidas* run northwest to southeast, with numbered *calles* crossing them at right angles. The odd-numbered *avenidas* and *calles* are all on one side of Calle 1 and Av. 1, with the even numbers on the other side. The *zócalo* is at the center, bounded by Calles 1 and 5 and Av. 1 and 3.

The **tourist office** (☎712 2581) is under the *portales* on the right side of the Palacio Municipal, on the northwest side of the *zócalo*. (Open M-F 8:30am-7pm, Sa 9am-1pm.) **Casa de Cambio Puebla,** 117 Calle 2, between Av. 1 and 3, **changes currency,** as do many banks around the *zócalo*. **Inverlat,** on the corner of Av. 1 and Calle 3, and **Bital,** at Av. 1 and Calle 4, have 24hr. **ATMs.** The **market** is bounded by Calles 7 and 9 and Av. 8 and 10. (Open daily 7am-9pm.) Services include: **luggage storage** at the bus station (5 pesos per hr.); **emergency** service (☎060); **police** (☎712 6720 or 712 1027), in the Palacio Municipal; **Red Cross** Calle 9 710 (☎712 0300 or 712 0090), between Av. 7 and 9; **Farmacias de Dios,** at Av. 1 510, between Calles 5 and 7 (☎712 0064; open 24hr.); **IMSS** (☎714 3800), on Av. 11 between Calles 1 and 2; **Internet access** at **Liz Internet Cafe,** on the corner of Calle 3 and Av. 2 (open daily 9am-9pm; 8 pesos per hr.); **post office,** Av. 3 303, one block southwest of the *zócalo* (☎712 0069; open M-F 8am-4pm, Sa 9am-1pm). **Postal code:** 94500.

🔳🔳 ACCOMMODATIONS AND FOOD. Córdoba's affordable establishments, concentrated on Av. 2 between Calles 9 and 11, make it ideal for a one-night stand. **🔳Iberia ❷,** Av. 2 919, is the best bargain. Luxurious rooms feature TV, phone, fans, dark wood furnishings, and extremely powerful showers. (☎712 1301. Singles 150 pesos; doubles with one bed 180 pesos, with two beds 250 pesos; triples 330 pesos. Each additional person 30 pesos.) For a cheap, no-frills stay, **Hotel Tress Cado ❶** offers tiny, passable rooms. Walls are cracked, but not crumbling. (☎712 2374. Singles and doubles 60 pesos, TV 10 pesos extra.) Indulge yourself at **Hotel Virreynal ❺,** Av. 1 309, across from the church in the *zócalo*. Spacious rooms include A/C, phone, and TV. The adjoining restaurant provides room service. (☎712 2377. Singles 265 pesos; doubles 290 pesos. Each additional person 20 pesos.)

Casa de la Abuela ❶ (☎712 0606), on Calle 1 between Av. 2 and 4, has cooked quality, affordable meals for two generations. The photos all over the walls enhance the family feel, and quality *tortas* (10 pesos) and *antojitos* (6-22 pesos) certainly don't hurt. **Restaurant Vegetariano ❸,** at Calle 1 and Av. 5, serves, predictably enough, no meat products. A vegetarian *comida corrida* goes for 32 pesos. (☎712 6934. Open M-Sa 8am-8pm.) For masticators on a budget, try **Las Delicias ❶,** on Av. 2 between Calles 5 and 7, where *antojitos* start at a low 3 pesos. (☎714 8651. Open daily 7:30am-11:30pm; a slightly fancier restaurant of the same name keeps the same hours just down the street toward the *zócalo*.) **Restaurant Virreynal ❹,** in Hotel Virreynal, offers a classier experience. Families and guests of the hotel come for meat and vegetarian entrees (40-70 pesos) right in the middle of downtown. (☎712 2377. Open daily 9am-11pm.)

🔳 SIGHTS. Dominating the *zócalo's* southeast side is the **Parroquia de la Inmaculada Concepción.** Constructed in 1621, the church combines both Baroque and Neoclassical styles. Now the city's primary place of worship, the Parroquia is distinctive not only for the mango-colored exterior, but also for its infamous bells, which can be heard for miles around. Located under the *portales* on the *zócalo's* northeast side is **Casa Zevallos.** Now a hotel, Zevallos has a plaque in the inner courtyard, commemorating the site where Juan O'Donojú, acting Spanish viceroy, and Agustín de Iturbide, conservative rebel leader, agreed on the terms of Mexico's independence on August 24, 1821. Across the *zócalo*, half a block away at Calle 3 303, lies the **Museo de la Ciudad de Córdoba,** home to archaeological finds, interesting murals, and a small art gallery. (Open daily 9am-2pm and 4-7pm. Free.)

At night, the *zócalo* comes alive, with music from the local bars drifting into the center square. Although the city's nightlife options are fairly limited, you can try your hand at any of the *zócalo's* bars or at the nearby **Utopia**, on Av. 7 between Calles 4 and 6. A mixed crowd comes and listens to live bands playing *trova*, filling the blacklit bar shortly after midnight. Open W-Sa 10:30pm-3am.

■ **FESTIVALS.** Calm and tranquil, neighboring **Fortín de las Flores** comes alive during the last week of April through the first two weeks of May, when the **Expo Feria de la Flor Fortín** takes center stage. Florists, merchants, and horticulturalists descend on the city to enjoy the best that the area has to offer, conveniently assembled throughout the downtown area. If you're itching to see some plantlife the rest of the year, you can head 7.5km north to **Tropical World,** in nearby Santa Elena, which specializes in orchids and tropical flowers from Hawaii and Brazil. Unfortunately, no buses go up to Santa Elena, and taxis are expensive (90 pesos).

ORIZABA ☎272

Near the base of Mexico's highest peak sits Orizaba (pop. 175,000). Formerly a center for sugarcane distillation, modern Orizaba has turned to production, churning out barrels of beer and cement. The city itself may not be fascinating, but its extensive parks, mountain views, and excellent climate make for a welcoming and relaxed atmosphere.

⌐ TRANSPORTATION. Orizaba's two main bus lines maintain separate stations. To get to the *zócalo* from the **ADO station** (☎724 2723), at Av. 6 Ote. 577, between Calles 11 and 13 Sur, exit to the left and walk to Calle 3 Sur; cross the road and continue 3 blocks to the *zócalo*. ADO has first-class service to: **Cancún** (19hr., 8:10pm, 736 pesos); **Córdoba** (40min., 26 per day, 12 pesos); **Mexico City** (4hr., 16 per day, 165 pesos); **Oaxaca** (6hr.; 1, 11:10am, 6:15pm; 184 pesos); **Veracruz** (2hr., 25 per day, 76 pesos); **Villahermosa** (7hr., 5 per day, 310 pesos). From the second-class **AU station** (☎725 1979), at Calle 8 Pte. 425 between Calles 5 and 7 Nte., exit left and cross the bridge; take the first right and walk toward the church towers.

■⚡ ORIENTATION AND PRACTICAL INFORMATION. Orizaba lies 16km west of Córdoba and 25km northwest of Mexico's tallest mountain, **Pico de Orizaba.** Most points of interest are near **Parque Castillo,** bounded by Madero on the west, Colón on the south, Calle 3 Sur on the east, and Av. 3 Ote. on the north. **Av. 6 Ote.,** three blocks south of the *zócalo*, is the main thoroughfare.

The **tourist office,** upstairs in the Palacio de Hierro at Madero and Av. 2, displays photos of Orizaba, hands out maps, and arranges adventure tours. (☎726 5861. Open M-F 10am-8pm.) Several banks south of the *zócalo* provide **currency exchange** and 24hr. **ATMs,** including **Banamex,** on the corner of Av. 2 Ote. and Madero, and **Serfín,** directly across the street. Other services include: **luggage storage,** at the ADO station (5 pesos per 3hr.); **Mercado Melchor Ocampo,** bounded by Av. 5 and 7 Ote. and Madero and Calle 2 Nte.; **Super Lavandería Orizaba,** Calle 11 Sur and Av. 4 Ote. (wash and dry 33 pesos for 3kg; open M-F 9am-3pm); **emergency** service (☎060); **police** (☎724 6400), at the corner of Circunvalación Nte. and Av. 5 Ote.; **Red Cross,** Colón Ote. 253 (☎725 2250), between Calles 5 and 7 Sur; **Farmacias Cova-donga,** Calle 5 Sur and Av. 4 Ote. (☎725 7433; open 24hr.); **IMSS,** at Gardenias (☎724 1480); **LADATELs,** on the northwest side of the *zócalo*, just past the *parro-quia;* **Benja's Internet,** Av. 7 Ote., between Calles 4 and 6 Nte. (10 pesos per hr.; open M-Sa 9am-9pm); **post office,** Av. 2 Ote. 282, at Calle 7 Sur, with **Mexpost** inside. (☎725 0330. Open M-F 8am-4pm, Sa 9am-1pm.) **Postal code:** 94300.

⚏ ACCOMMODATIONS AND FOOD. The small rooms at **Hotel Arenas ❷**, Calle 2 Nte. 169, between Av. 3 and 5 Ote., are clean and come with TV, fans, and access to a jungle-like courtyard. (☎725 2361. Singles 120 pesos; doubles 170 pesos.) **Hotel San Cristóbal ❷**, Calle 4 Nte. 243, between Av. 5 and 7 Ote., has spartan rooms with fans and hot water. (Singles 100 pesos; doubles 160 pesos.) More luxurious accommodations are available at **Grand Hotel de France ❺**, Av. 6 Ote. 186. The giant stone courtyard leads you into large, plush rooms with A/C, cable TV, and phone. (☎725 2311. Singles 250 pesos; doubles 320 pesos.)

Always-crowded **La Hogaza ❷**, Calle 4 Nte. between Av. 3 Ote. and Colón, serves good food quickly and cheaply. The extensive *menú del día* (30 pesos) is one of the best deals in town. (☎726 0529. Open daily 8am-5:30pm.) Visit **Antojitos Mexicanos ❶**, Calle 2 Nte. 174, for some quick *tortas* (8 pesos) and *taquitos* (3 pesos). (☎723 4724. Open daily 8am-11pm.)

◎ SIGHTS. The **Museo de Arte del Estado**, Av. 4 Ote. between Calles 25 and 27, is a bit of a trek, but holds unforgettable works. If you prefer riding to walking, take an eastbound bus from Av. 6 Ote. The museum hosts fabulous rotating exhibits, featuring some of Mexico's best modern art, a collection of works by Diego Rivera, and paintings by artists from the state of Veracruz. (Open Tu-Su 10am-5pm. 10 pesos, students and seniors 5 pesos; Su free.) If you want to get closer to nature, the **Cascada de la Trompa del Elefante** (Waterfall of the Elephant's Trunk) awaits just outside the city limits. Part waterfall, part hiking trail, the *cascada* and its famous **500 Escalones** attract *orizabeños* who want to jog, picnic, or stop by the falls themselves. Although it's a pretty sight, make sure that you're willing to pay the price of climbing up the stairs once you're done. To get to the falls, catch the red-and-yellow Estrella Roja buses on the corner of Av. 3 Ote. and Calle 2 Nte. Ask the driver to let you off at Calle Isabel la Católica (5 pesos). Walk down Isabel as it curves left around a small blue church, continue over the bridge, and follow signs for the Hotel Fiesta Cascada. Buses return to the *centro* on Calle Isabel, picking up from one block beyond the drop-off point. At night, much of Orizaba gathers in **Parque Alameda**, where you can run, watch kids play on the giant trampolines, take in the breeze, and snack on fried plantains and *papas fritas*. To get there, simply follow Colón Pte. away from the *zócalo* and over the bridge.

LOS TUXTLAS

Calm and relaxing, Los Tuxtlas nestle in the moist foothills of southern Veracruz. The region's three main towns—San Andrés Tuxtla, Santiago Tuxtla, and Catemaco—have distinct personalities. With quality cheap accommodations and transportation options, the fairly large town of **San Andrés Tuxtla** makes a good base for exploring the foothills. More touristed **Catemaco** is known for its *brujería* (witchcraft) and beautiful lagoon. Only 30min. from the Olmec site of Tres Zapotes, the small **Santiago Tuxtla** is primarily an archaeological stop.

SAN ANDRÉS TUXTLA   ☎294

Lodged between the lush lakeside resorts of Catemaco and the Olmec artifacts of Santiago, San Andrés (pop. 140,000) binds together Los Tuxtlas. The tobacco and cattle-raising town offers a cache of budget hotels, an entertaining *zócalo*, and nearby natural attractions.

⚏ TRANSPORTATION. Both the first- and second-class **bus stations** are on Juárez, which branches off of Mex. 180. To get to the center from either station, exit left and follow Juárez as it descends a steep hill, crosses a small stream, and gradually ascends to meet the cathedral in the northern corner of the *zócalo*. **Taxis**

travel the same 15min. route for 13 pesos. **Autotransportes los Tuxtlas** (☎942 1462), based in the 2nd-class station, sends buses to: **Catemaco** (20min., every 10min. 4:30am-6pm, 5 pesos); **Santiago Tuxtla** (20min., every 10min. 2:45am-6pm, 5 pesos); **Veracruz** (3½hr., every 15min. 4:30am-6pm, 65 pesos). **ADO** (☎942 0871), at the first-class station, serves: **Mexico City** (7½hr.; 9:45, 10:30, 11:10pm; 304 pesos); **Puebla** (6hr.; 9:45, 10:30, 11:10pm; 235 pesos); **Veracruz** (2½hr., 19 per day 12:20am-9:25pm, 72 pesos); **Villahermosa** (5hr., 8 per day, 155 pesos). **AU** (☎942 0984) goes to **Xalapa** (4hr.; 5:30, 9:35pm; 112 pesos). *Taxis colectivos* also drive to Catemaco and Santiago Tuxtla (12.5 pesos).

■ ■ **ORIENTATION AND PRACTICAL INFORMATION.** San Andrés is located midway between Catemaco and Santiago. Before the cathedral, **Juárez** intersects **Constitución** to the left and **Madero** to the right, in front of the Palacio Municipal.

Bancomer, half a block south of the *zócalo* on Madero, **exchanges money** and has a 24hr. **ATM.** (Open M-F 9am-5pm, Sa 9am-1pm.) **Mercado 5 de Febrero** lies near the *zócalo.* To get there, walk on Madero, turn right on Carranza, and continue to the market. (Open daily 8am-8pm.) Other services include: **laundry** at **Lava Maac,** Hernández 75, at Revolución (☎942 0926; 8 pesos per kg; open M-Sa 8am-8pm); **police,** in the Palacio Municipal (☎942 0235; no English spoken); **Red Cross,** Boca Negra 25, north of the *zócalo* (☎942 0500; no English spoken); **Farmacia Garysa,** Madero 3, on the *zócalo* in the Canada building (☎/fax ☎942 4434; open 24hr.); **Hospital Civil** (☎942 0447), the orange-and-blue building on Barrera at the edge of town; **ISAT Internet,** at the corner of Suárez and Argudín (☎942 3805; 12 pesos per hr.; open daily 9:30am-10:30pm); **post office,** at La Fragua and 20 de Noviembre, one block from the *zócalo* (☎942 0189; open M-F 8am-3pm). **Postal code:** 95701.

■ ■ **ACCOMMODATIONS AND FOOD.** San Andrés has great budget accommodations. Two of the best bargains are within spitting distance of each other on Suárez. To get there, walk left from the cathedral and turn right at the orange supermarket, continuing uphill past the movie theater. **Hotel Colonial ❶,** Suárez 7, has small clean rooms, ceiling fans, a comfortable lobby, and a charming upstairs *sala.* (☎942 0552. Singles 50 pesos; doubles 90 pesos.) **Hotel Figueroa ❷,** Suárez 10, across the street, has bigger, more comfortable rooms, and higher prices. (☎942 0257. Singles 100 pesos; doubles 120 pesos. Cable TV 20 pesos extra.) Those living in the A/C fast lane may spurn the great bargains and upgrade to **Hotel Isabel ❸,** Madero 13, to the left of Hotel Parque. (☎942 1617. Singles 165 pesos, with A/C 220; doubles 215/295 pesos.)

Several sidewalk cafes on the *zócalo* serve breakfast and coffee, accompanied by a pleasant view of small-town life. With good, cheap *antojitos* (14-30 pesos) and great pastries, **Winni's Restaurant ❷,** south of the *zócalo*, across from Hotel Isabel on Madero, draws chatting locals to its outdoor tables. (☎942 0110. Open daily 8am-midnight.) A block farther away from the *zócalo*, **La Surianita ❷** cooks cheap, filling meals. (☎942 4442. *Antojitos* and egg dishes 10 pesos, meat entrees 25 pesos. Open daily 8am-10:30pm.) The older and more affluent **Restaurant del Parque ❹,** on the ground floor of Hotel Parque in the *zócalo*, has a classier atmosphere and good coffee. (☎942 0198. *Antojitos* 20 pesos, entrees 50-90 pesos. Open daily 7:30am-midnight.)

■ ■ **SIGHTS AND ENTERTAINMENT.** Even non-smokers will be impressed by the **Fábrica Tabacos San Andrés** (☎942 1200), the birthplace of Santa Clara cigars. From the *zócalo*, walk up Juárez to the ADO terminal. Take a right around the corner, and continue about 200m down the street past the entrance to the bus parking lot. The management welcomes visitors, and, if you're polite, a staff member will walk you through the entire process. The store near the entrance sells the final product. Bottom-of-the-line cigars are affordable (105 pesos and up), but a box of 25 of the finest *puros* goes for much more (around 800 pesos). If you can overcome the vivid Freudian imagery, pick up the Magnum, Guinness record holder as the world's longest marketed cigar. Note that customs regulations may limit the number of cigars you can take back into your country.

Although there isn't exactly a happening club scene in San Andrés, plenty of bars on the *zócalo* provide locals with beer and something to do at night. **Nuestro Bar,** on Independencia just off the *zócalo*, is one of the more popular establishments, with live music on Wednesdays, dancing, and *fútbol* on TV. Beer 12 pesos. Open daily 2pm-3am. Cover Sa 30 pesos.

NEAR SAN ANDRÉS: SANTIAGO AND TRES ZAPOTES ☎294

To get to Santiago, take a bus (5 pesos) from the Autotransportes los Tuxtlas station in San Andrés. To get to Tres Zapotes from Santiago, walk downhill from the bus station to the zócalo. Turn left onto Zaragoza, at the front edge of the zócalo, and walk until you get to a T intersection. Turn to the right and make a quick left over the footbridge, which will carry you to Morelos, from which a taxi colectivo will whisk you to Tres Zapotes (30min., 15 pesos). Tell the driver that you want to go to the museo. Buses marked "Tres Zapotes" also pass through this stop, but are cheaper (10 pesos) and slower. Tres Zapotes open daily 8am-6pm. 23 pesos; Su free.

Of Tuxtla's three cities, the smallest, Santiago (pop. 50,000), has the least to offer visitors. In the town itself, the most impressive sight is the **massive Olmec head** at the far end of the *zócalo*. At 45 heavy tons, it's the largest such head ever discovered. Small-town charm and enormous noggins aside, Santiago's main draw is the nearby archaeological site of Tres Zapotes, more remarkable for its age than its appearance. Half an hour's ride through small tobacco-growing towns, Tres Zapotes was a chief Olmec ceremonial center that peaked between 300 BC and AD 300, though evidence indicates that the area may have been occupied as early as 1200 BC. The site itself remains largely unexcavated, but the small **museum** has a few (well-preserved) artifacts on display. The casual observer will likely be disappointed—Tres Zapotes is better suited to those with an academic interest.

The centerpiece of the site is a large Olmec stone head. The first of the dozen or so Olmec heads ever found, it was discovered in 1862 by a *campesino* who at first thought it was an overturned cooking pot. To the left of the head is **Estela C,** which, together with its more famous upper half, bears the oldest written date in the Americas—31 BC—inscribed in late Olmec, or Spi-Olmec, glyphs similar to those later used by the Maya. The date is depicted as a bar (representing the number 5) and two dots, totaling seven on the Olmec calendar. **Estela A** lies in the transept to the left. Decorations on the stela include an Olmec face, a man holding an axe, and a serpent coiling in upon itself. **Estela D,** to the right of the head, depicts four people whose relative heights symbolize their power and importance.

To cool off after a day as Tres Zapotes, visit the nearby **Cascada del Salto de Eyipantla;** at 50m high, it's worth huffing down the 245 requisite steps and 5-peso fee. To reach the waterfall, take a *micro* labeled "El Salto" from the middle of the market below Calle 5 de Mayo (30min., 5 pesos). It makes drop-offs and pick-ups at the entrance to the falls; last return bus at 8:15pm.

CATEMACO ☎294

The most touristed town in Las Tuxtlas, Catemaco (pop. 51,000), is surrounded by a gorgeous lagoon. Don't be surprised when you are approached by men anxious for you to "see the monkeys." They simply want you to take a *lancha* tour of the Laguna Catemaco, which passes by La Isla de los Monos. Fairly quiet in the off-season, Catemaco picks up during *Semana Santa* and during the summer cele-

THE BIG SPLURGE

ECOPLEASURE

Tired of spending your nights in boiling hotel rooms? Looking for a way to get back to nature? The Catemaco-to-Coyame *pirata* route may have just what you need, albeit for a price. Whether you want pampering or a little bit of roughing it, you can easily find the escape you need.

5km away from Catemaco is the **Parque Ecológico Educativo de Nanciyaga** (☎943 0199). Hidden deep within the forest off the main road, the "ecological educational park" bills itself as the northernmost tropical rainforest in the world. In reality, Nanciyaga is more of a fancy spa: guests are treated to boat tours, mud baths, massages, the occasional open-air concert, and saunas in the traditional Olmec-style *temascal* sweat lodge (300 pesos). 500 pesos buys a two-person bungalow for the night, while four-person *familiares* go for 600 pesos.

Sound too soft? A little farther is Tebanca, where the Rancho el Freno (☎942 0105) serves as a base for camping, kayaking, and nature treks. 2 days of camping, guided hikes, access to the Poza Reyna nature reserve, and meals 399 pesos.

To get to Nanciyaga, take the *pirata* from Catemaco until you see the Nanciyaga sign. Walk up the dirt path on the right through the forest for 10min. To get to Rancho el Freno, ask the *pirata* driver to take you to Tebanca, along the Coyame route.

bration of the town's patron saint, Saint Carmen, when *gringos* and *chilangos* come to enjoy regional cuisine and Catemaco's much-hyped *brujería*.

⎑ TRANSPORTATION. Catemaco lies on **Mex. 180** and is a popular bus stop. From the **Autotransportes los Tuxtlas** second-class stop, turn right and follow the curve of road past the "Bienvenidos a Catemaco" arches. Take a straight path for 10-15min. to the spires of the *basílica*. Autotransportes los Tuxtlas travels to **San Andrés** (20min., every 20min. 2am-7pm, 5 pesos) and other regional destinations. The **ADO** station is along the waterfront on the *malecón*. To get there from the church, walk down to the *malecón* and take a left. The station is several blocks down the street. ADO (☎943 0842) heads to: **Mexico City** (9hr., 10pm, 301 pesos); **Puebla** (6hr., 10pm, 232 pesos); **Veracruz** (3hr., 7 per day 5:30am-5pm, 76 pesos); **Xalapa** (3hr., 4 per day 6:15am-5pm, 131 pesos). **AU** (☎943 0777) goes to **Mexico City** (9hr.; 11:30am, 9pm; 262 pesos).

⦿⦿ ORIENTATION AND PRACTICAL INFORMATION. Streets are poorly marked, but the *basílica* in the *zócalo* is almost always visible. Standing with your back to the front door of the *basílica*, **Carranza** is the street to the right that runs past the Palacio Municipal. To the left is **Aldama**, and one block downhill from that is **Playa**, followed by the *malecón*. Perpendicular to these streets, across the *zócalo* is **Boettinger; Ocampo** is the street behind the church.

The **tourist office,** in the Palacio Municipal on the *zócalo*, offers maps of *pirata* (public transportation pick-ups) routes, brochures, and helpful, though limited, advice. (☎943 0016. Open M-F 9am-3pm.) Other services include: **Bital,** across Carranza from the *basílica*, with 24hr. **ATMs;** the **supermarket Super de Todo,** right next to the *basílica* (open Su 8am-3pm, M-Sa 8:30am-9pm); **police,** in the Palacio Municipal (☎943 0055; no English spoken); the **pharmacy Garysa,** on the *malecón* (open daily 7am-midnight); **Centro de Salud,** on Carranza, in a white building with a blue roof, three blocks away from the *zócalo* on the left (☎943 0247; some English spoken); **Internet access** at the aptly-named **Internet,** on Carranza and Ocampo (open daily 8am-1am); **post office,** on Cuauhtémoc, which branches off Carranza some blocks from the *zócalo*, away from the *basílica*. **Postal code:** 95870.

⌂⌂ ACCOMMODATIONS AND FOOD. Most hotels lie around the *zócalo* and the waterfront. During Christmas, *Semana Santa*, and most of July, hotels fill up quickly, and prices generally rise 20-30 pesos. The **Hotel Julita ❷,** Playa 10, one block downhill from the *zócalo*, is blessed with an unbeatable location and large, clean rooms with fans. (☎943 0008. Singles 110 pesos; doubles 140 pesos.) **Hotel Acuario ❷**, at Boettinger and Carranza, has smaller, slightly older rooms right on the *zócalo*. (☎943 0418. Singles 100 pesos; doubles 180 pesos.)

Lake views differ more than menu choices in Catemaco's waterfront restaurants. *Mojarra* and *topote* fish are endemic to the lagoon, as are *tegogolos*, the famous Catemaco sea snails. *Mojarra* is prepared in a variety of ways, while bite-sized *topote* is fried whole and often heaped on *tamales*. If you can fight the temptation to eat on the waterfront, the best food is at **La Casona ❹**, on the *zócalo* on Aldama. Your view will be of a peaceful wooded garden rather than the lake; the seafood and steak entrees (40-70 pesos) are all delicious. (☎943 0813. Open daily 7am-8pm.) You can find classic *mojarra* (70 pesos) at **Los Sauces ❶**, on the *malecón* at Rayón, to the left if coming downhill from the *basílica*. (☎943 0548. Open daily 9am-9pm.) Nearby, **El Pescador ❹**, on the *malecón* at Bravo, offers similar flavors, fares, and views. (☎943 0705. Open daily 10am-8pm.)

◙ **SIGHTS.** The rocky beaches of **Laguna Catemaco** are a refreshing break from the hot Veracruz sun. The water immediately in front of town is not safe for swimming, but a hiking path runs along the edge of the lake (walk down from the *zócalo* to the waterfront and turn left). The trail will guide you 1.5km to **Playa Expagoya** and then another ½km to the more secluded and sandier **Playa Hermosa**, the first swimmable beach. The path can be extremely dark at night; please employ all due caution. It's also possible to swim off a *lancha* in the deeper and sometimes clearer waters in the middle of the lake.

The best way to see Catemaco is on a ▓**lancha tour** that departs from the shore of the lagoon downhill from the *zócalo* (50 pesos on a *lancha colectiva* or 250 pesos for the whole boat). The tour lasts 1½hr. and takes you past several small islands and various attractions. Strange birds and water lilies aside, by far the most popular sight is **Isla de los Changos**. A group of wild, red-cheeked *changos* (mandrills, a type of baboon) was brought from Thailand for a scientific experiment at the University of Veracruz in 1979—scientists wanted to see if the animals could survive in a new environment. Lo and behold, 25 years later the *changos* are alive, well-fed, and posing for snapshots. En route to the island, you'll pass a cave-shrine that stands on the spot where the town's namesake, local fisherman Juan Catemaco, had a vision of the Virgin Mary over a century ago. His statue, poised elegantly at the tip of the lagoon, overlooks the calm waters. Negotiate with the *lanchistas* for longer trips, including an exploration of the rivers that feed the lake or a trip past the nearby tropical forests.

▓▓ **NIGHTLIFE AND ENTERTAINMENT.** Catemaco's bars and discos are the best in the Tuxtlas, although nightlife only really heats up during high seasons. Many bars and clubs shut down or operate irregularly in low season. Most (if not all) of the best bars are right on the beachfront. Your best bet is likely to walk along the street until you find a place that catches your fancy. Street lamps and blacklights aside, the *malecón* can get very dark at night, and all travelers are advised to be cautious. To experience the witching hour, head to **La Séptima Bruja**, on the *malecón* right near Playa and Hotel Julita. Open all year, with live music on Fridays and Saturdays, the bar is one of most popular nightspots in the city. (☎943 0042. Open Tu-Su 7pm-3am. No cover.) If you want to get away from the city, take a cab (25 pesos) to **Chanequa's** (☎943 0042 or 943 0001), a video bar in Hotel Playa Azul, catering to the chic hotel crowd. Catemaco's major secular celebration, **Day of the Fisherman,** occurs on May 30, when a procession of manually-powered *lanchas* parade across the lagoon and locals compete in a fishing tournament. The town also celebrates the day of its patron saint, **Saint Carmen,** on July 16.

NEAR CATEMACO: THE GULF COAST

Public transportation is limited to Transportes Rurales pick-up trucks, called piratas *by locals. Piratas depart from the eastern edge of town. To get there from the zócalo, cross Carranza starting from the basílica, keeping the Palacio Municipal on your left, walk 6 blocks, and turn right onto Lerdo. From there, walk 5 more blocks until you pass the sign on the left, indicating the distance to all* pirata *destinations. Fares 5-20 pesos, depending on the destination. Just outside town the road forks into 2 main routes. One heads north to Montepío on the Gulf Coast and the other goes east to Coyame on the opposite side of Lake Catemaco. Piratas depart for both (every 30min. 6am-7pm), but only when enough passengers have boarded.*

Catemaco, near the Gulf Coast's secluded beaches, lures sun-worshippers looking for hiking, fishing, posh spas, rare wildlife, and miles of gorgeous beach.

CATEMACO TO MONTEPÍO. On the way to Montepío is **Sontecomapán** (18km from Catemaco), a small town beside a saltwater lake that empties into the Gulf. *Lanchas* are available for excursions on the lake and down the coast (60 pesos per person on a *colectivo;* 250 pesos for a private boat). If you want to go to **Playa Jicacal** and **Playa Escondida,** you will have to ask the *pirata* driver in advance to let you off, then walk 30min. to stony, empty Playa Jicacal. The pink *cabañas* of **Hotel Icacos ❹**, near the entrance to the beach, contain two large beds, a fan, and little else. (☎942 0556. *Cabaña* singles 200 pesos; doubles 300 pesos.) Instead of turning right to Playa Jicacal, you can walk uphill 10min. to the left to Playa Escondida and the simple, white **Hotel Playa Escondida ❹**. (☎942 3061 in San Andrés. Singles and doubles 250 pesos.) This beach offers the safest **camping ❶** (25 pesos) in the area; inquire at the hotel. Beach access for non-guests costs 10 pesos. Visitors who want a secluded beach without the walk through the jungle can have the *pirata* drop them off at the second-to-last stop, **Balzapote.**

The *pirata* route ends on a bluff overlooking the beach at **Montepío** (2hr. from Catemaco), also home to a small fishing town. **Lonchería Susi ❶** offers rooms with private bath. (Singles 50 pesos; doubles 100 pesos.) The new **Hotel Posada San José ❺**, on the bank of the small river leading to the beach, is more expensive and luxurious. (☎942 1010 or 942 2020 in San Andrés. Singles 290 pesos; doubles 330 pesos.) Montepío's biggest attractions are the *cascadas* up from the beach. The best way to reach the falls is with a guide; you can find one at the driveway to Posada San José. Most people go by horse, taking the guided trip to **Cascadas de Revolución,** inland and midway down the beach (80 pesos). Excursions to the other *cascadas* can be arranged, or you can rent a horse and try to find them by yourself (30 pesos per hr., 40 pesos with guide).

ACAYUCAN ☎924

At the junction of Hwy. 180, which runs between Veracruz and Villahermosa, and Hwy. 185, which crosses the Isthmus of Tehuantepec, lies Acayucan (pop. 100,000), a transportation hub for southern Veracruz. The city lacks major sites, but its location makes it a frequent stopover point.

▛ TRANSPORTATION. Acayucan's **bus station** (☎245 1142), on Acuña in Barrio Tamarindo, is on the eastern edge of the city. Many buses are *de paso* and tickets go fast, so get to the station early. To get to the *zócalo*, exit right and walk straight to the town's main street, Hidalgo. Either turn left and walk straight for 10min. to reach the *centro*, or catch a westbound "Centro" *colectivo* (5 pesos). **ADO** goes to: **Mexico City** (7hr., 10 per day, 353 pesos); **Oaxaca** (8hr.; 12:20am, 10:15, 10:45pm; 227 pesos); **San Andrés Tuxtla** (2hr., 5 per day, 42 pesos); **Veracruz** (3½hr., 16 per day, 133 pesos); **Villahermosa** (4hr., 13 per day, 114 pesos); **Xalapa** (6hr., 9 per day, 185 pesos). *Urbanos* line the street outside and travel to nearby destinations.

⁊ PRACTICAL INFORMATION. Bital and **Serfín,** side by side at Victoria and Zaragoza on the plaza's south side, provide **currency exchange** and 24hr. **ATMs.** (Open M-Sa 8am-5pm.) Services include: **emergency** service (☎060); **police** (☎245 1078); **Red Cross,** Ocampo Sur 4, between Victoria and Negrete (☎245 0028; some English spoken); **Internet Acayucan,** a block north of the *zócalo,* on Pipila off Guerrero (open daily 9am-9pm); **post office,** a block north on Moctezuma and left on Guerrero. (☎245 0088. Open M-Sa 8am-4pm.) **Postal code:** 96001.

⌐⌐ ACCOMMODATIONS AND FOOD. Hotels and restaurants surround the *zócalo.* **Hotel Jesymar ❸,** Moctezuma 206, one block north of the *zócalo,* is the best budget lodging in Acayucan. (☎245 0261. Rooms with phone, TV, and balconies. Singles and doubles with fans 153 pesos, with A/C 193.5 pesos.) **Hotel Plaza ❷,** Victoria 37, opposite 3 Hermanos, has large, tidy rooms overlooking the *centro.* (☎245 1344. Singles and doubles with fan 117 pesos, with A/C and TV 234 pesos.)

After exiting the bus station and walking to the *zócalo,* you will encounter hordes of taco stands and *torta* shops. **Obélix ❶,** in the *zócalo* on Victoria, is known for quick and inexpensive *tortas* (13 pesos) and tacos (2.5 pesos). **Soyamar ❶,** Guerrero 601, is a vegetarian oasis: there's not a single piece of meat on the menu. (☎245 1744. Open M-F 7am-8pm.)

NEAR ACAYUCAN: SAN LORENZO TENOCHTITLÁN

From the mercado in Acayucan, go to the line of regional buses and ask for one going to "Texistepec" (sometimes labeled just "Texi"), which will bring you to the town's bus depot (30min., 7.5 pesos). From Texistepec, catch a blue "Villa Alta" urbano, which stops in San Lorenzo (45min., 12 pesos) and Zona Azuzul (1¼hr., 20 pesos). Buses leave at 8, 10am, 2, 3, and 5pm; the last bus from Zona Azuzul back to Texistepec leaves at approximately 5:15pm. Taxis go to the 2 sites (70 pesos and 120 pesos, respectively); if enough can be rounded up to go colectivo, fares are 15 and 20 pesos.

A pilgrimage best reserved for archaeology buffs, reaching the Olmec remains of San Lorenzo is a labor of love. The sites aren't the best in Mexico by any means, but if you're simply trying to see every significant point of archaeological interest in the country, you'd have to include this one. San Lorenzo Tenochtitlán is the collective name given to the three Olmec sites of San Lorenzo, Tenochtitlán, and Zona Azuzul. Of these three centers, San Lorenzo is believed to have been the largest and oldest, flourishing between 1200 and 900 BC. Among the Olmec artifacts unearthed here are the earliest known ball player figurines, as well as serpentine and jadite statues. Though many of the artifacts found in the initial 1947 excavations have been relocated to museums elsewhere, finds from excavations in 1994 remain in the area and anchor local collections. Today, the largest is in **Tenochtitlán,** where an assortment of artifacts are displayed under a protective shelter near the town's main dirt road. The exhibit includes a giant Olmec stone head, the only one of the 10 heads found at the three sites to remain in the area.

About 5km farther down the main dirt road lies the microscopic town of San Lorenzo. Several kilometers from the town are the actual ruins of San Lorenzo, but little remains to be seen. Approximately 3km past San Lorenzo is the third original Olmec ceremonial center, Zona Azuzul. Two small shelters atop the hill house the modest but remarkably well-preserved collection. The first hut holds four stone statues, two depicting kneeling human forms and two depicting jaguar forms. The second hut has larger jaguar figures. (Site open daily 8am-6pm. Free, except for a good tip to the site's caretaker.)

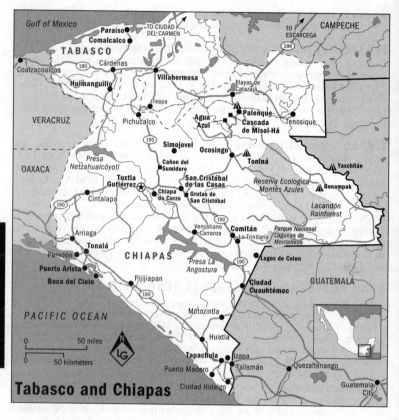

Tabasco and Chiapas

TABASCO

VILLAHERMOSA ☎ 993

Villahermosa (pop. 1.6 million) is neither a *villa* (small village), nor is it *hermosa* (beautiful). The capital of Tabasco state is a metropolis that has capitalized on oil discoveries and its strategic location along the Río Grijalva, one of few navigable rivers in the republic. Founded by Cortés in 1519 as Santa María de la Victoria, it was an agricultural center of minor importance, accessible only by river. In the past 50 years, oil-spurred growth has created a dense and rather inelegant forest of satellite dishes, luxury hotels, apartment complexes, and fast food places. Still, Villahermosa's proximity to the Palenque ruins and its strategic position between Chiapas and the Yucatán make it a common stopover for travelers. Happy (and dry) is the well-prepared tourist: the weather behaves like clockwork—be prepared for showers every afternoon during the rainy season (June-September).

TRANSPORTATION

Airport: (☎356 0156), on the Villahermosa-Macupana Highway, 14km from downtown. Taxis shuttle between the airport and the *centro* (40 pesos *especial*, 15 pesos *colectivo*). Major airlines have offices in Tabasco 2000, including: **Aeroméxico,** Cámara 511 Locale 2 (☎800 021 4000); **Aviacsa,** Via 3 120 Locale 10 (☎316 5733); **Aerocaribe,** Via 3 120 Locale 9 (☎316 5047); **Mexicana,** Via 3 120 Locale 5-6D (☎316 3132).

Buses: The **1st-class terminal** is on Mina at Merino. **ADO** runs to: **Acayucan** (4hr., 12 per day 3:15am-7:55pm, 114 pesos); **Cancún** (11hr., 8 per day 12:25am-10:10pm, 427 pesos); **Campeche** (5hr., 12 per day 1:35am-11:50pm, 207 pesos); **Mexico City** (11hr., 16 per day 12:30am-10:30pm, 467 pesos); **Oaxaca** (11hr.; 6, 7:55, 9:25pm; 380 pesos); **Palenque** (2hr., 10 per day 3am-9:15pm, 68 pesos); **Puebla** (8hr., 5 per day 6am-11:15pm, 398 pesos); **San Andrés Tuxtla** (4hr., 8 per day 3:30am-11pm, 155 pesos); **San Cristóbal de Las Casas** (6hr., 7:30am, 141 pesos); **Tuxtla Gutiérrez** (7hr.; 7:15am, 1:30, 2:30, 10:25pm; 138 pesos); **Xalapa** (9hr., 5 per day 3:30am-10:30pm, 298 pesos). Also serving the station are **Cristóbal Colón, TRS,** and **Altos.** To reach downtown from the 1st-class station, walk 2½ blocks to your right on Mina to Méndez. From there, take a *combi* labeled "Pqe. Juárez" a few minutes to Parque

Villahermosa

🏠 ACCOMMODATIONS
Hotel del Centro, 2
Hotel Madero, 10
Hotel Palma de Mallorca, 4

🍴 FOOD
Café La Cabaña, 9
Cockteleria Rock and
   Roll, 7
Restaurant-Bar Impala, 8
Restaurant Los Tulipanes, 11
Tacolandia, 5

● SERVICES
Farmacias del Ahorro, 6
Supermarkets, 1 & 3

Juárez. Most hotels are south of the park on Madero or the parallel Constitución. Walking the same route takes 15-20min. Upon exiting the terminal, head right down Mina for 11 blocks, then turn left onto 27 de Febrero. 8 more blocks take you to the Madero intersection. To get downtown from the **2nd-class terminal,** on Ruiz Cortines, 2 blocks left of Mina, cross Grijalva on the pedestrian bridge left of the station exit and hop on an "Indeco Centro" bus (4.5 pesos); disembark at Parque Juárez on Madero. To continue on foot (25min.), cross the bridge and continue south on Mina for 3 blocks until you reach the ADO station (see above). A cab ride to the center of town costs 15 pesos. 2nd-class service reaches many regional destinations.

Radio Taxi: (☎314 3456 in the *centro*, ☎316 6421 in Tabasco 2000). On call 24hr.

■ ? ORIENTATION AND PRACTICAL INFORMATION

Villahermosa is 20km from the Chiapas border. The spine of the downtown area is **27 de Febrero. Zona Luz,** the pedestrian-only downtown area, is enclosed by **5 de Mayo, Zaragoza, Madero,** and **27 de Febrero. Paseo Tabasco** runs north-south and connects the **Tabasco 2000** complex to the *centro*, intersecting 27 de Febrero in front of the cathedral. *Saetas* (public buses) and *combis* (4.5 pesos) run 6am-10pm.

TOURIST AND FINANCIAL SERVICES

Tourist Office: de los Ríos 113 (☎316 3633 or 316 2889), in Tabasco 2000, diagonally behind the Palacio Municipal. Open M-F 8am-4pm. Booths are at the entrances of **Parque Museo la Venta** (open daily 8am-4pm), the **Museo de Historia** (open daily 4-8pm), and the **ADO Station** (open daily 8am-8pm).

Currency Exchange: Banks abound in Zona Luz and on Po. Tabasco. **Banamex,** on Madero at Reforma, and **Bancomer,** on Madero next to VIPS by Reforma, have 24hr. **ATMs.** Banamex open for exchange M-F 8am-1:30pm, Bancomer open M-F 8am-4:30pm.

American Express: Po. Zabarco 715 (☎315 3999), in the office of Turismo Creativo. Open M-F 9am-6pm, Sa 9am-1pm.

Car Rental: Dollar, Po. Tabasco 600 (☎315 4830). Open daily 8am-9pm. Chevrolets 551 pesos per day. **Alamo,** Po. Tabasco 302-L. Open Su 9am-2pm, M-Sa 8am-8pm. Chevrolets 447 pesos per day.

LOCAL SERVICES

Luggage Storage: At the bus station. 5 pesos per hr. Open daily 7am-10pm.

Market: Mercado Pino Suárez, bordered by Pino Suárez, Constitución, Hermanos Zozaya, and Grijalva, in the northeast corner of town. Open daily 5am-8pm.

Supermarket: Maz, on Madero at Zaragoza. Open daily 7am-9:30pm.

Laundry: Lavandería Top Klean, Madero 303, next door to Hotel Madero. 15 pesos per kg. Open M-Sa 8am-8pm.

EMERGENCY AND COMMUNICATIONS

Emergency: ☎066.

Police: Aldama 101 (☎315 2633 or 315 2630), in Zona Luz. The main office is at 16 de Septiembre at Periférico (☎315 2517). No English spoken.

Red Cross: (☎315 5600 or 315 5555), on Sandino in Col. 1 de Mayo. Take a taxi. Some English spoken. 24hr. ambulance service.

Pharmacy: Farmacias del Ahorro, Méndez 1405 (☎314 0603 or 315 6606 for delivery). Open 24hr. Also in the Zona Luz near the corner of Reforma and Aldama, across from the Howard Johnson.

Hospital: IMSS, Carretera Villahermosa (Av. Universidad) km 205 (☎357 2567). **ISSTE,** 27 de Febrero 1803 (☎315 0619, 315 0648, or 315 9231).

Fax: Telecomm, Lerdo 601 (☎314 2494), at Sáenz around the corner from the post office. Open Su 9am-1pm, M-F 8am-7:30pm, Sa 9am-5pm.

Internet Access: Several cluster near Zaragoza and Aldama. **Multiservicios Computacional,** Aldama 621 (☎312 2166). 10 pesos per hr. Open daily 8:30am-9pm.

Post Office: Sáenz 131, at Lerdo. Open M-F 8am-3pm, Sa 9am-1pm. **Postal Code:** 86000.

▛ ACCOMMODATIONS

In Villahermosa, any hotel wealthy enough to purchase more than a door-width space on the ground floor is probably out of the "budget" price range. The most inexpensive hotels are found in Zona Luz but may be crowded, so call ahead.

Hotel del Centro, Suárez 209 (☎312 5961), between Sánchez and Méndez. Neat rooms have TVs, fans, and memento graffiti from past tenants. Lobby has plants and couches. Singles 170 pesos, with A/C 220 pesos; doubles 220/270 pesos. ❸

Hotel Palma de Mallorca, Madero 510 (☎312 0144 or 312 0145), near the intersection of Zaragoza and Madero. Another hotel with tacky interior and cheap rooms. Singles 133 pesos; doubles 153 pesos, with A/C 184 pesos. ❷

Hotel Madero, Madero 301 (☎312 0516), near 27 de Febrero. Central location; try to get a room away from the street. All rooms have A/C and TV, but are otherwise plain, even unattractive. Singles 300 pesos; doubles 400 pesos; triples 500 pesos. ❺

▐ FOOD

Villahermosa, like the rest of Tabasco, specializes in *mariscos* (seafood) and various swamp creatures. A typical *tabasqueño* dish—not for the faint of heart—is tortoise sautéed in green sauce and blood and then mixed with pickled armadillo. Another favorite is *pejelagarto* (lizardfish), with a lizard-like head, and *mojarra* (a local fish), flavored with ingredients like *chipilín*, *chaya* leaves, and *amashito* chile. To drink, try traditional *pozol*, made from ground cornmeal, cocoa, and water. If someone offers you *venado* (venison) be aware that wetland deer are rare and the hunting process is often destructive. Although *taquerías* litter the downtown area, most restaurants specializing in seafood are either far or expensive. The best places for regional foods are roadside restaurants and *palapas* along tourist routes like the Teapa Comalcalco. For lovers of American junk food, there are McDonald's, Burger King, KFC, and Domino's Pizza in the Zona Luz.

▨ Restaurant Los Tulipanes (☎312 9217 or 312 9209), in the CICOM complex, specializes in *comida tabasqueña*. Enjoy fresh seafood on the banks of the Río Grijalva in this local favorite. It's expensive—seafood dishes start at 100 pesos—but the high cost means high quality, not tourist-inspired extortion. Open Su 1-7pm, M-Sa 8am-11pm. ❺

Tacolandia, Aldama in Zona Luz. Casual and extremely popular taco shop emits mouth watering smells all day long. Tacos start at 3.5 pesos. Open M-Sa 7am-10pm. ❶

Café la Cabaña, Juárez 303 near 27 de Febrero. Drink coffee with the old folks of Villahermosa. Frappuccino or cappuccino 15 pesos. Coffee beans 80 pesos per kg. Open Su 9am-9pm, M-Sa 7am-10pm. ❷

Restaurant Bar Impala, Madero 421 (☎312 0493). A cluttered hole-in-the-wall taco shop that should look familiar, wherever you've been in Mexico. Tasty *tamalitos de chipilín*, *panuchos* (fried tortilla shells stuffed with meat and beans), and tacos for 4 pesos. Open M-Sa 9:30am-8pm. ❶

Cocktelería Rock and Roll, Reforma 307 (☎ 312 0593), across from Hotel Miraflores. This joint specializes in seafood cocktails and old men swilling Corona. Cocktails 60-85 pesos. Open daily 10am-midnight. ❺

🔘 SIGHTS

For a city unconcerned with tourism, Villahermosa has a surprising number of museums within walking distance of Zona Luz. Downtown is home to a series of pedestrian streets lined with cafes, ice cream shops, and more hair salons and shoe shops than should be legal.

▦ **PARQUE-MUSEO LA VENTA.** Located south of Tabasco 2000, the park features 33 Olmec sculptures, lifted from their original locations in La Venta, Tabasco, and western Veracruz and re-planted in Villahermosa by Carlos Pellicer Cámara. From the small museum at the entrance, enter the outdoor jungle-setting that reveals the impressive Olmec artifacts on a well-marked, 1km path. Wild animals in the park's **zoo** complete the tropical setting. The **Parque Tomás Garrido Canabal** surrounds the museum; the sprawling park has a large lagoon, landscaped alcoves, hidden benches and fountains, and several sculptures—which lure plenty of teenagers making out. Beware: the *mirador* claims to offer a panoramic view of the city, but the 40m climb yields an aerial view of trees and the lagoon. *(Take a "Petrolera" bus (4 pesos) from Parque Juárez to the Pagés Llergo and Ruiz Cortines intersection. Walk northeast on Ruiz Cortines for 10min. to the entrance. Alternatively, take a "Tabasco 2000," "Carrisal," or "Palacio" bus to the Tabasco and Ruiz Cortines intersection and cut through Parque Canabal to the entrance. Entrance to the Parque Tomás is on Tabasco and Grijalva. Taxis 14-15 pesos. From Tabasco 2000, follow Po. Tabasco to Ruiz Cortines, a 10-15min. walk. ☎ 314 1652. Ticket office open daily 8am-4pm. Museum open Tu-Sa 9am-4:30pm. 30 pesos.)*

MUSEO DE HISTORIA DE TABASCO. The small museum displays artifacts and pictures on state history, but the building itself is the most interesting exhibit. A wealthy merchant had the famous blue edifice, known as the **Casa de los Azulejos** (House of the Tiles), built between 1889 and 1915 and decorated with Italian and Spanish baroque tiles, plus Egyptian ones along the ledge of the outside walls; a different style adorns each room. Today's occupants are old sewing machines and historical documents. Eleven classical sculptures decorate the roof; the seated female figures are said to be the merchant's family members. *(At the corner of Juárez and 27 de Febrero in Zona Luz. ☎ 314 2172. Open Su 10am-6pm, Tu-Sa 10am-8pm. 5 pesos.)*

CICOM. The **Museo Regional de Antropología Carlos Pellicer Cámara** is the main draw at Villahermosa's Center for the Investigation of Olmec and Maya Cultures (CICOM). The museum displays Olmec and Maya artifacts from nearby archaeological sites La Venta and Comalcalco. The center houses a public library, art school, and theater. *(From Zona Luz, the museum is a 15min. walk south along Río Grijalva. The #1 and "CICOM" buses pass often. ☎ 312 6344. Open Tu-Su 9am-6pm. 10 pesos.)*

TABASCO 2000. Northwest on Paseo Tabasco, away from the city center and Río Grijalva, the complex features futuristically bland buildings and pedestrian-unfriendly streets light years away from the car-free walkways of Zona Luz. The long strip of stucco and concrete buildings includes the city's **Palacio Municipal,** a convention center, several fountains, an upscale shopping mall, and a **planetarium** with **Omni Max** flicks dubbed in Spanish. *(Take a "Tabasco 2000" or "Palacio" bus from Parque Juárez and get off at the square across from the mall with the Tabasco 2000 sign. ☎ 316 3641. Mall shops open daily 9am-9pm; planetarium shows 4 and 6pm. 25 pesos.)*

YUMKÁ. Just 16km from the bustle of Villahermosa, animals run freely throughout the 101-hectare park, which reproduces the four *tabasqueño* ecosystems: jungle, savannah, wetlands, and gift shop. Visitors travel about in trolleys, boats, and on foot, seeing animals in their natural habitats. *(To get there, take a combi marked "Rancheria Dos Montes" from the market on Suárez (4.5 pesos). Tell the driver where you want to get off. Combis are relatively infrequent; a taxi especial (70-80 pesos) is quickest. Open daily 9am-4pm. 40 pesos, children 20 pesos; 10 pesos extra for a lancha lagoon tour.)*

CASA MUSEO CARLOS PELLICER. This small museum has the answers to your questions about the man whose name plasters every wall in town. Personal info, family belongings, and most importantly, his pants, are all here. *(Sáenz 203. ☎312 0157. Open M-Sa 10am-7pm.)*

🎵 🎙 ENTERTAINMENT AND NIGHTLIFE

The Zona Hotelera in and around Tabasco 2000 is home to a number of discos and clubs. Here, Villahermosa's young and wealthy dress up and get down to a mix of salsa and tropical music. Taxi drivers are well acquainted with hot club spots and are the only safe means of reaching the distant locales at night.

Ku Rock House, Sandino 548 (☎315 9431 or 315 9433), in Col. 1 de Mayo. Rocking, sweaty, pounding, and with manageable prices. Cover W-Th 50 pesos, F-Sa 60 pesos. Open W-Sa 9pm-late.

Liquid o Solid Sports Bar, in the Zona Hotelera, next to the Hyatt. Food served in the "solid" portion of the bar, drinks in the "liquid" video-bar. Blue lighting and "sports bloopers" videos. Solid bar open Tu-Su 6pm-2am; liquid bar open Th-Sa 9pm-2am.

Flambouyant (☎315 1234), an elegant bar and club in the lobby of a swank Hyatt. Frequently has live bands. Beers 30 pesos. Open Su-Th 7pm-1 or 2am, F-Sa 7pm-3am.

Factory Video Bar, Av. Méndez 1602. Cheap bar/club features electronica and 20-peso beers. Sa cover men 50 pesos. Open W-Sa 9pm-3am.

CULTURAL EVENTS

Villahermosa presents a few "cultural" options. The **Centro Cultural Villahermosa** on Madero at the corner of Zaragoza, across from Parque Juárez, posts a weekly program of events around the city and at the Centro itself, including recitals and screenings. The cafe in the back of **Galería el Jaguar Despertado,** Sáenz 117, near Reforma in the Zona Luz, features live classical and jazz performances. A weekly program of cultural events is often outside the door; performances are usually at 8pm. There is also a gallery upstairs. (☎314 1244. Open Su 9am-3pm, M-Sa 9am-9pm.) Across the street, **Colegio de Arte Tabasco,** Sáenz 122, features contemporary *tabasqueño* artwork, much of it for sale. (Open Su 9am-3pm, M-Sa 9am-9pm.)

🏛 DAYTRIPS FROM VILLAHERMOSA

As the largest city in the mostly rural state of Tabasco, Villahermosa serves as a base for dozens of daytrips into the state's northern coast and southern jungle.

THE RUINS OF COMALCALCO

The ruins of Comalcalco are 3km outside the city of the same name, 52km northwest of Villahermosa. Though Comalcalco has a historic church and several budget hotels, it's better to skip the city and visit directly from Villahermosa. Taxis colectivos to Comalcalco leave frequently from Alberto Reyes at Mina on the other side of the supermarket Chedraui's from the 1st-class bus station (45 min., 35 pesos) and stop at the ADO station. From there, take a Paraíso-bound bus (4 pesos) and ask to be let off at "las ruinas." You will be at an access road—walk or wait for a minibus (3 pesos). Getting back is easiest near closing time, when the bus stops at the main gate. Site open daily 10am-5pm. Tours in Spanish, English, French, and Italian. Admission 32 pesos; 1½hr. tour 250 pesos.

Unpublicized and generally ignored by backpackers, the Maya ruins of Comalcalco are surprisingly extensive, though the mosquitoes may be enough to discourage many. Named somewhat mundanely after the *comal* (an iron pan for making tortillas), the city was built during the Classic Period (100 BC-AD 800) at the western frontier of Maya territory. Because the Tabasco Maya, known as Chontals, lacked stone for their temples, they used baked clay, making Comalcalco the oldest brick city in all the Americas.

The main road, left from the museum entrance, will take you into the main plaza. The 10-level, 25m **pyramid** left of the site entrance is Comalcalco's landmark. Under an awning on the building's north face, the remains of a carving of a giant winged toad and several humans are all that's left of decorations that once covered the structure's surface. Past temples II and III, a path leads to the **Gran Acrópolis,** an 80m complex of temples and private residences. Look closely at the dilapidated walls and you can see the insides of Comalcalco's brickwork and oyster-shell mortar. Among the ruins is the precarious-looking **Palacio,** with half a vault somehow still intact, and what is thought to have been a bathtub and cooling system. From the top of the acropolis, it's possible to look out and see what the jungle looked like before deforestation and radio towers. Walk back down and keep an eye out for the sculptural remnants preserved in protected corners. Especially interesting reliefs are on the east side in the **Tomb of the Nine Men of Night;** the figures are believed to represent the nine night gods of the Maya pantheon.

PARAÍSO

Though both 1st- and 2nd-class buses run from Villahermosa to Paraíso (44 and 25 pesos, respectively), it is better to go by a taxi colectivo, which leaves from the lot on the far side of Chedraui's (1¼hr., 35 pesos). Colectivos stop on 2 de Abril near the Paraíso zócalo. To reach the 2nd-class bus station from the zócalo, walk 2½ blocks away from Juárez, the main street, to Buenos Aires. The station is 9 blocks farther to the left.

Only 71km from Villahermosa, Paraíso and its beaches are a reasonable option for beating the heat. The sweltering town has several budget hotels, but your best option may be to sleep in a hammock or to camp under a *palapa:* many beaches have free facilities. Though not gorgeous, beaches are clear, uncrowded, and safe.

Public beaches lie east and west of the city. Those northwest, including **Varadero, El Paraíso, Pal Mar,** and **Paraíso y Mar,** are reachable by the "Playa" *combi* that leaves from the 2nd-class bus station (20min., every hr., 5 pesos). All are about 500m from the main road and have **palapas ❶** where you can hang a hammock for free. Varadero and El Paraíso are the nicest by far; both have restaurants and the latter has hotels and a pool (20 pesos).

Alternatively, an eastbound bus to Chiltepec leaves every 30min. from the 2nd-class bus station. The first stop is **Puerto Ceiba** (15min., 4.5 pesos), a small fishing village on the edge of Laguna Mecoacán, a 51,000-hectare oyster breeding ground. Local fishermen give *lancha* tours of the lagoon; ask at any of the docks along the way. Across the bridge from Puerto Ceiba is **El Bellote,** another small fishing town located between the lagoon and the Río Seco, with several good, affordable restaurants. Near the end of the bus route, 27km east of El Paraíso, is the town of **Playa Bruja;** just east is the beach itself, with *palapas* and a restaurant.

TEAPA AND ▧ LAS GRUTAS COCONÁ

To get to Teapa, take a taxi colectivo from the corner of Madero and Sánchez, past Parque Juárez (1hr., 35 pesos); buses make the trip more often (every 30min.; 2nd-class 30 pesos, 1st-class 35 pesos), but take much longer. To return to Villahermosa, take a red taxi colectivo from Teapa's main drag. Combis for the grutas leave from Bastar on the right-hand side of the church in Teapa (every 30min., 3 pesos). Taxis charge 15 pesos. Caves open daily 9am-4pm. 20 pesos, children 10 pesos. Guides cost about 40 pesos.

Amid countless farms and ranches 52km south of Villahermosa, Teapa is a pleasant base for exploring nearby attractions. In the town itself are several worthwhile 18th-century churches, including the Franciscan **Temple of Santiago Apostol** and Jesuit **Temple of Tecomájica**. The real reason for traveling to Teapa, however, are **Las Grutas Coconá**, just 2km outside of the city. Discovered in the late 1800s by two adventurous brothers hunting in the woods, the caves are like a visit to another planet. They wind 500m into the hillside as eerie, piped-in flute music and dramatic lighting do their thing (quite well) to enhance the enormous caverns, underground lagoons, and bizarre formations. Guides offer their services; as with other *grutas*, they are most adept at pointing out formations that resemble other objects (the Virgin Mary, the head of a moose, etc.). The explanations are interesting but, since the caves are lit, your time may be better spent exploring on your own.

EL AZUFRE

Take a combi from Teapa's market and tell the driver where you want to go (7 pesos). Taxis cost 40 pesos. Returning is more difficult: climb the hill from the spa to the main road, and flag down a taxi or bus. Open daily 6am-7pm. 30 pesos, children 15 pesos.

Another 15min. *combi* ride from Teapa is El Azufre, a little oasis of a spa with two large sulfur *albercas*, which supposedly have therapeutic qualities. Also available at the site are bathroom facilities, *palapas*, and an upscale **hotel ❺**. (Rooms 305-550 pesos, camping free with entrance fee.)

TAPIJULAPA AND PARQUE NATURAL DE LA VILLA LUZ

Two buses serve the town, leaving every hour from Tacotalpa. To get to Tacotalpa, catch a taxi colectivo (1hr., 35 pesos) next to the ADO station. 2nd-class buses leave for Tacotalpa (1½hr., every 30min. 5:30am-9pm, 28 pesos). Colectivos stop on Tacotalpa's main drag. Half a block farther down on the same street, red and white buses leave for Tapijulapa plaza (40min., every hr. 5am-6pm, 5 pesos); buses also leave from Teapa. To reach the Tapijulapa lancha dock, from which you can access the Parque, go 2 blocks past the plaza to the end of the street, turn right and head 1 block downhill. Return buses to Tacotalpa leave from the station, 2 blocks north of the plaza (every hr., last one at 7pm). Buses and colectivos returning to Villahermosa from Tacotalpa stop running around 8pm.

While traveling to Tapijulapa, 90km south of Villahermosa, the bus crosses into the state's highest mountains, where the humidity lets up and the distinction between slumber and consciousness becomes blurred.

Getting to the **Parque Natural de la Villa Luz**, 3km from Tapijulapa, requires a *lancha* (20 pesos round-trip). Climb the stairs in front of you after you arrive to enter the park. Go through the gates on the other side of a field; guides are at the house just past the fence. Farther on, take the left fork to the abandoned home of former governor Tomás Garrido Canabal, whose name you should recognize from Villahermosa. The house has been outfitted with some token artifacts (an old sewing machine) and declared a museum. 10min. farther up the path is the top of the *cascadas*. It is safe to bathe in the waist-high, sulfur-rich water, but you may want to wait until you reach the spas at the end, where you'll have surer footing.

The right fork beyond the field leads to another fork in the road. Stay right to reach **La Cueva de las Sardinas Ciegas**. The cave's odd name comes from the native sardines that, having adapted to their dark environment, are all blind. Every year on the Sunday before Easter, residents of Tapijulapa gather at the cave for the **Pesca de la Sardina**. While dancing to the music of the *tamborileros*, celebrants toss powdered narcotic plants into the water, which stun the fish and cause them to float to the top of the water for easy harvesting. The left fork leads to the spas—an area with several pools, all filled with therapeutic sulfur water. Returning to the *lancha* dock will take about 25min. The entire trek takes approximately 2hr. Tip your guide at least 20-25 pesos.

GULF COAST & CHIAPAS

OXOLOTÁN

From Tapijulapa, walk straight through the building opposite the plaza and climb the stairs on the opposite side of the street. Check out the view from the small courtyard at the top; the 17th-century Santiago Apostol church on the right side of the courtyard is also worth a visit. Walk through the first courtyard and downhill 1 block to the main road. The green and white Oxolotán bus picks up here (40min., every hr., 5 pesos). After exiting the bus, with your back to the station, turn right and walk 2 blocks; the church is to your left on the cross street and the museum entrance is on the opposite side. Return buses to Tacotalpa leave every 1-1½hr. 5:30am-5pm. Museum open daily 9am-5pm. Free.

Farther down the road from Tapijulapa is Oxolotán (pop. 2000), a tiny, sleepy town in the middle of nowhere, albeit an exquisitely beautiful nowhere. The town's **Ex-convento de Santo Domingo** is a good excuse to visit, but the real reasons for going are the bus ride into the mountains and the amenity-free restfulness of the town. In 1550, when the Dominicans got around to evangelizing Tabasco, Oxolotán was an important trade center because it was the last navigable point on the Río Grijalva. When the ex-convento was finally finished in 1578, the town's importance had flagged and the Dominicans relocated to Tacotalpa, leaving Oxolotán with a grand, empty parish church. The church has been in use for the last 400 years, and recent renovations turned the cloister into a polished museum. The undecorated stone walls and quiet courtyards exude a tranquility that permeates the town, whose *zócalo* is the ex-convento's former patio.

RESERVA DE LA BIOSFERA PATANOS DE CENTLA

Though Tabasco's eco-tourism industry has been slow in its attempts to take flight, the state's predominant feature (after its oil reserves) is its natural beauty. If you're willing to negotiate, it's possible to see the amazing jungle on a very limited budget. One of the best places to do this is the **Reserva de la Biosfera,** a preserve encompassing 302,000 hectares of the wetlands. Set aside by the government in 1992, the land is home to 50,000 people, most of whom live in small fishing villages along the river systems deep inside the preserve. In addition to Centla's waterfalls, swamps, rivers, and the incredible variety of animals that inhabit them, the preserve represents a point of conflict between ecologists and the economic interests of the indigenous peoples who live here. Small turtles sell for 100 pesos in the open market, and venison goes for even more, giving residents incentive to hunt protected animals. This hunting is the bane of the people who work at the preserve's station at **Tres Brazos.** For information on visiting, contact the director of the program, Juan Carlos Romero, Paseo de la Sierra 613 (☎310 1431), in the Colonial Reforma. Exploring the reserve will take initiative, but *lanchistas* and locals will help you out, and the *crocodilos* will ensure an exciting time.

AGUA SELVA ECOTOURISM PROJECT

Reaching the project is a challenge. Buses to Herradura leave from the 2nd-class terminal in Villahermosa (11 per day, 43 pesos). If you are interested in an intensive hiking tour or an overnight jungle adventure, stop on the way in Huimanguillo. Jorge Pagole (☎375 0002) of the Hotel del Carmen, Morelos 39 (take a cab, 15 pesos) offers a variety of trips (1-day trips start at 300-400 pesos). Others can do shorter trips more cheaply. From Herradura, pasajeras (pick-up trucks) leave for Malpasito roughly every half-hour and return regularly. Pasajeras leave for Francisco J. Mújica from Herradura between 2 and 3pm daily (20 pesos); ask around to make sure one's coming, the next transportation between the two is at 5am. There is no transportation between Malpasito and Francisco J. Mújica.

Agua Selva encompasses 15,000 hectares of land bordering Chiapas and Veracruz. Located 142km southwest of Villahermosa, the project offers two main attractions: water and the jungle. With over 100 waterfalls, small mountains ranging up to 1000m, thick vegetation, and abundant wildlife (including armadillos, jaguars, and a wide variety of birds), the natural attractions necessary for the project's success are certainly there. Though the infrastructure is sorely underdeveloped, Agua Selva's natural beauty makes a strong argument for braving the hassle.

MALPASITO. The tiny village of Malpasito is home to a few attractions. Upon arriving, ask to be dropped at the home of **Catalina Martínez,** who manages the tourist flow into Agua Selva and is available for questions at any time. She can provide you with information about Malpasito and also arrange for a **guide** (60 pesos per day)—perhaps her grandkids. **Guillermo Pérez Cajija ❶** rents out a two-room *palapa* in his backyard. The *señora* of the house prepares meals for a low price. Malpasito is a rural village with no services—rooms are very basic. Do not expect blankets. Expect cockroaches.

A short, 1km hike on a path just uphill from the *pasajera* dropoff point leads to the Post-Classic Maya **Zoque Ruins of Malpasito** (admission 23 pesos). Little is known about the Zoque Maya, other than that they offered little resistance to the Spanish. Before entering the site, check out the **petroglyphs,** over 60 ancient sketches of animals, birds, humans, and geometric shapes in rock. To your left after the short walk from the entrance to the clearing is the obligatory **ball court,** complete with what appears to have been a locker room. On the plaza past the ball court, stairs lead to a second, smaller plaza, which offers a breathtaking view of the surrounding mountains. Ask your guide to lead you to the small waterfall beyond the ruins, which you can climb and which has a pool at its base that is safe for swimming. From here, several trails lead further into the mountains, where you can check out the *La Pava* and *La Copa* rock formations. Another waterfall is down the hill from the site and left at the road. Follow this road into the hills until it ends at a dilapidated shack; follow the path inside of the fence away from the shack, cross the wooden footbridge, and continue down the slope until the path splits. The right branch winds down to the base of a fall, the left branch leads to the top. The walk takes about 30min.

FRANCISCO J. MÚJICA. The other village with accommodations and tourist resources near Agua Selva is Francisco J. Mújica, approximately 20km west of Herradura. **Antonio Domínguez** manages an **albergue ❶** (35 pesos per person). Sr. Domínguez can help you find a trustworthy guide with whom to view the surrounding area. **Cascada Velo de Novia** (Bridal Veil Falls) is just an hour's hike from the village; beyond it is a steep canyon that you can descend (carefully and with the aid of the guide's rope) to a ledge that leads beneath the falls. The caves in the surrounding area contain petroglyphs as well, which guides can point out to you. Sr. Domínguez can also arrange for transport and a guide to the village **Carlos A. Madrazo,** 4km beyond Francisco J. Mújica, where there are other noteworthy sights. **Cascada de Aguaima,** another 4km from Madrazo, is a thundering *cascada* where two rivers converge to form the Río Pedregal.

CHIAPAS

TONALÁ ☎966

The beach towns in Oaxaca manage to be prettier, livelier, more secluded, and better serviced, but the Chiapan town of Tonalá (pop. 75,000) provides easy access to **Puerto Arista** and **Boca del Cielo,** lesser beaches that share a lazy vibe. Aside from *Semana Santa* and weekends in July and August, they are practically abandoned, with lights out by 8pm. Tonalá proper is a giant sauna, unbelievably hot and humid, and offers little besides food and lodging for tourists.

▐ TRANSPORTATION

Autotransportes Tuxtla Gutiérrez, Hidalgo 56, five blocks south of the *zócalo*, has first-class bus service to: **Mexico City** (13hr., 5pm, 335 pesos) via **Puebla** (11hr., 285 pesos). First-class buses, including **Maya de Oro** (☎663 0540), leave from the Cristóbal Colón station, six blocks north of the zócalo, for: **Mexico City** (13hr., 8pm, 444 pesos); **Oaxaca** (6½hr., 9:30pm, 180 pesos); **Puebla** (10hr., 8pm, 387 pesos); **Tapachula** (3hr., 20 per day 1am-7:40pm, 180 pesos); **Tuxtla Gutiérrez** (3hr., every hr. 3am-7:30pm, 65 pesos). **Taxis** (☎663 0620) cruise up and down Hidalgo and hang out in the *zócalo* (40 pesos to Puerto Arista). If you're getting up early, the 24hr. **radio-taxis** (☎663 2299) located on Hidalgo in the *zócalo*, will get you at your hotel. **Luggage storage** is 5 pesos per day, in the bus station.

▐▐ ▐ ORIENTATION AND PRACTICAL INFORMATION

Tonalá lies 223km northwest of Tapachula and 172km southwest of Tuxtla Gutiérrez. All **bus stations** are on **Hidalgo,** Tonalá's main street. To get to the *zócalo* from the Cristóbal Colón bus station, take a left and head six blocks south. Both the Autotransportes Tuxtla Gutiérrez and Fletes y Pasajes bus stations are south of the *centro*. As the coastal highway, Hidalgo runs roughly north-south through town. To the east, **Rayón** parallels Hidalgo, while to the west run **Matamoros, Juárez,** and **Allende.** Listed from north to south, **Madero, 16 de Septiembre, 5 de Febrero, Independencia,** and **5 de Mayo** run east-west, completing the grid.

The **tourist office** is at Hidalgo and 5 de Mayo, two blocks south of the bus station, on the second floor of the Esmeralda building. (☎663 2787. Open M-F 8am-4pm.) **Banamex,** Hidalgo 137 at 5 de Febrero, near the *zócalo*, exchanges currency and has a 24hr. **ATM.** (☎663 0037. Open M-F 9am-3pm.) Other services include: **police** (☎663 0103), on Calle Libertad, two blocks north of Cristóbal Colón and to the right; **Farmacia el Pastillaero,** 16 de Septiembre, half a block west of Hidalgo (☎663 3198; open 24hr.); **Hospital General** (☎663 0687), 27 de Septiembre at Mina; **Red Cross** (☎663 2121), on Joaquín Miguel Guttiérez; **Internet access** at **Ciber Club Cafe** on Hidalgo, three blocks south of Cristóbal Colón and three blocks north of the *zócalo* (10 pesos per hr.; open daily 9am-11pm); **post office,** 10min. walk west of Hidalgo on 16 de Septiembre (open M-F 9am-4pm). **Postal code:** 30500.

▐ ACCOMMODATIONS AND FOOD

Maintaining health and sanity in sweltering Tonalá may require spending extra money for A/C. Cheaper rooms of comparable cleanliness and atmosphere are available in Puerto Arista. The **Hotel Tonalá ❸,** a few blocks south of the Cristóbal Colón station, has high rates for little space in its plain rooms. (☎663 0480. Singles 160 pesos; doubles with TV and fan 200 pesos; triples with TV and A/C 280 pesos.) **Restaurant Sambors ❶** at Madero and Hidalgo, on the *zócalo*, has good food and a wide-angle view of the *zócalo*. (☎663 0680. *Tortas* 12 pesos, *licuados* 9 pesos. Open daily 9am-1am.) **Restaurante Nora ❹,** Independencia 10, less than a block east of Hidalgo and a block from the *zócalo*, is a refuge from the heat. (☎663 0243. 3-course *comida corrida* 45 pesos. Open M-Sa 8am-6pm.) For even cheaper meals, several small **comida típica** restaurants ❶ sell *pollo rostizado* for under 20 pesos.

TUXTLA GUTIÉRREZ ☎961

Energetic young Tuxtla Gutiérrez (pop. 568,000) is the capital of Chiapas and the focal point of commerce and transportation for most of southern Mexico. "Tuxtla"

Tuxtla Gutiérrez

🏠 ACCOMMODATIONS
Hotel Avenida, **4**
Hotel Del Pasaje, **8**
Villas Deportivas Juvenil, **6**

🍎 FOOD
La Antigua Fonda, **5**
Las Pichanchas, **7**
Restaurante Imperial, **1**
Restaurante Vegetariano Nah-Yaxal, **3**
Restaurante Virginia, **9**
Restaurante Tuxtla, **2**

Parque Madero/Botanical Gardens

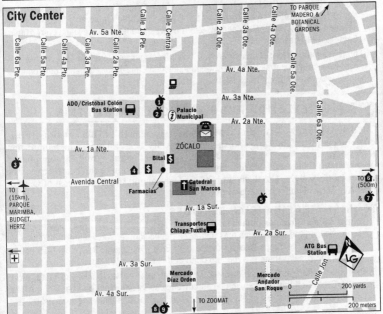

City Center

comes from the Náhuatl *tuchtlan*, meaning "place where rabbits abound," while "Gutiérrez" originates from Miguel Gutiérrez, a progressive *chiapaneco* governor who, rather than succumb to imperialist right-wing forces, wrapped himself in the Mexican flag and dramatically leapt to his death from a church spire. Tuxtla today is a modern city—crowded, bustling, and noisy.

▤ TRANSPORTATION

Airport: Aeropuerto Francisco Sarabia (☎ 615 0537) is 15km southwest of town. Taxis to town 20 pesos. **Aerocaribe,** Av. Central Pte. 206 (☎612 0020 or at the airport 612 1772). **Aviacsa,** Av. Central Pte. 1144 (☎612 8081 or at the airport 612 3355).

Buses: The **ADO/Cristóbal Colón bus station,** 2 Nte. Pte. 268, is 2 blocks from the *zócalo.* Cristóbal Colón (☎612 5122) goes to: **Cancún** (18hr., 12:30pm, 510 pesos); **Mexico City** (15hr.; 1:30, 5:25pm; 555 pesos); **Oaxaca** (10hr.; 11:30am, 7:15pm, midnight; 241 pesos); **Palenque** (6hr.; 5am, 12:30pm, midnight; 120 pesos); **Puebla** (13hr., 7pm, 485 pesos); **Puerto Escondido** (11hr.; 8:15, 11pm; 225 pesos); **San Cristóbal de las Casas** (2hr., 6 per day 5am-midnight, 25 pesos); **Tehuantepec** (6½hr.; 11:30am, 8:45, 10:45pm, midnight; 132 pesos); **Tapachula** (6hr., 12 per day 6am-midnight, 179 pesos); **Veracruz** (12hr., 9:50pm, 371 pesos); **Villahermosa** (7hr.; 6, 11:15am, 3, 11:30pm; 138 pesos). **Altos** goes to similar destinations for slightly cheaper. The **Autotransportes Tuxtla Gutiérrez (ATG) bus station** (☎612 0322), Av. 3 Sur 712, sits in a cul-de-sac at Av. 3 Sur and Calle 7 Ote. ATG has less frequent, slower buses at cheaper fares to similar destinations. Travelers from **Chiapa de Corzo** disembark at the small station at the corner of Calle 2 Ote. and Av. 2 Sur. To reach **Chiapa de Corzo,** hop on a **Transportes Chiapa-Tuxtla** *microbús* at the station (25min., every 10min., 6 pesos) or grab one leaving town on Blvd. Corzo. One of the cheapest ways to get to **San Cristóbal** is via **Transporte Colosio,** which sends *combis* from Av. 3 Sur between Calles 2 and 3 Ote., and Av. 2 Sur between Calles 3 and 4 Ote. (every 10min. 5am-9pm, 30 pesos).

Local Transportation: Combis (VW van *colectivos*) run frequently throughout the city, east-west on Av. Central, north on C. Central, east on Calle 1 Sur Pte., and south on Calle 1 Sur Ote. (6am-10pm, 4.5 pesos).

✦🔢 ORIENTATION AND PRACTICAL INFORMATION

Tuxtla lies 85km west of San Cristóbal and 293km south of Villahermosa. *Avenidas* run east-west and *calles* north-south. The city's central axis, which intersects the *zócalo*, is formed by **Avenida Central** and **Calle Central.** Streets are numbered according to their distance from and geographical relation to the central axis. For example, Calle 2 Sur Ote. lies south of Av. Central and two blocks east of C. Central. Av. Central changes to **Corzo** in the east.

TOURIST AND FINANCIAL SERVICES

Tourist Office: Dirección Municipal de Turismo (☎612 5511, ext. 214), 2 Nte. Ote. at C. Central, on the street which runs under the public square. Very helpful staff. Open M-Sa 8am-8pm. The **State Tourism Office** is at Blvd. Domínguez 950, about 15 blocks west of the *zócalo.* There is a *módulo* open at this location M-F 9am-9pm.

Currency Exchange: Tuxtla's *zócalo* and Av. Central are filled with banks and **ATMs. Bital,** on C. Central off the *zócalo,* **exchanges currency** M-Sa 8am-7pm and has 24hr. **ATMs. Bancrecer,** on the corner of Av. Central and Calle 1 Pte., has the same services.

LOCAL SERVICES

Luggage Storage: Free at the tourism office in the *zócalo.*

Markets: Tuxtla's crazy **Mercado Díaz Orden,** on C. Central between Av. 3 and 4 Sur, has food and trinket stands. Open daily 6am-8pm. **Mercado Andador San Roque,** Calle 4 Ote. between Av. 3 and 4 Sur, has the best straw hats in town, oodles of wicker, and several cheap eateries. Open daily 7am-4pm.

Supermarket: Chedraui's, Blvd. Corzo, on the left just past the military base. Take an eastbound "Ruta 1" *combi* from a block west of the *zócalo* on Av. Central. **Fyrsa,** Av. Central Ote., about 50m west of INDEJECH. Open daily 8am-9:30pm. **Super-Wal-Mart,** C. Central and 6a Calle Ote. Everything and more. Open daily 9am-5pm.

Car Rental: Hertz, Blvd. Domínguez 1195 (☎615 5348), in Hotel Camino Real. Sedan 605 pesos per day. Open Su 9am-5pm, M-Sa 8am-8pm. **Budget Rent-A-Car,** Blvd. Domínguez 2510 (☎615 1382). Sedans 605 pesos per day. Open daily 8am-7pm.

EMERGENCY AND COMMUNICATIONS

Emergency: ☎060 or **Policía de Seguridad Pública** (☎614 4024). No English spoken.

Police: Tourist assistance: ☎800 903 9200.

Pharmacy: Farmacia del Ahorro, Av. Central and C. Central. Open 6am-midnight.

Red Cross: 5 Nte. Pte. 1480 (☎612 0096 or 614 2831). Little English spoken.

Hospital: Sanatorio Rojas, 2 Av. Sur Pte. 1487 (☎612 5414). Some English spoken.

Fax: Telecomm (☎613 6547; fax 612 4296), Av. 1 Nte. at 2 Ote., next to the post office. Open Su 9am-1pm, M-F 8am-6pm, Sa 9am-5pm.

Internet Access: Internet cafes cluster on C. Central past Av. 4 Nte. and on Av. Central east of the *zócalo*. **Ciber Café,** at C. Central Nte. 402 (☎614 6336), has fast connections and lots of computers. 8 pesos per hr. Open M-Sa 9am-9pm.

Post Office: (☎612 0416), on Av. 1 Nte. at 2 Ote., on the northeast corner of the *zócalo* in the corridor to the right of the Palacio Municipal. Open M-F 9am-5pm, Sa 9am-1pm. **Mexpost** available. **Postal Code:** 29000.

ACCOMMODATIONS

There are not enough backpackers in Tuxtla to support hostels or even hotels with hostel-like communal leanings, but cheap rooms abound, especially near the *mercado* around Av. 5 Sur. To avoid the mayhem of the market, head north to Av. Central Pte., where rooms are only slightly more expensive. Be aware that bathing in these places may be a lukewarm experience at best.

Hotel del Pasaje, Av. 5 Sur Pte. 140 (☎612 1550 or 612 1552), ½ block west of C. Central. This large hotel has quiet rooms with plenty of amenities—free purified water, fans, private baths with actual shower curtains. Singles 90 pesos, with A/C 140 pesos; doubles with A/C and TV 170 pesos. ❶

Hotel Avenida, Av. Central 244 (☎612 0807), between 1 and 2 Pte., has a nice central location and big rooms. Singles 150 pesos; doubles with cable TV 200 pesos. ❸

Villas Deportivas Juvenil, Blvd. Corzo 1800 (☎612 1201), next to the footbridge over the road. From 1 block west of the plaza on Av. Central, catch an eastbound *combi* and ask the driver to let you off at INDEJECH (een-day-hesh). A huge community sports center with 2 floors of dorm-style rooms on the east side. Institutional and perhaps deserted except in high season, but clean and cheap. Cafeteria open M-F 7am-9pm, Sa 7am-3pm. Breakfast 13 pesos, lunch and dinner 18 pesos each. Dorms 40 pesos. ❶

FOOD

Culinary miracles are rare in Tuxtla, but cheap eateries abound. *Carnes*, Chiapas-style, come prepared in *pepitas de calabaza* (squash seeds) or *hierba santa*. Other favorites include *pozol* and *tazcalate*, beverages with corn and cocoa bases. *Tamales* in Tuxtla come with every filling imaginable and can be had for 5 pesos. For the adventurous, *nucús*, edible ants, are plentiful at the start of the rainy season. Several new restaurants boldly proclaim their vegetarian leanings.

■ **Las Pichanchas,** Av. Central 837 (☎612 5351), between Calles 8 and 9 Ote. Sharp waiters, traditional decorations, an upscale courtyard, *marimba* music, and nightly *ballet folklórico* performances (9pm) accompany reasonable prices for *carne salada con pepita de calabaza* (50 pesos), *tamales* (2 for 26 pesos), and *tazcalate* (12 pesos). Open daily noon-midnight. ❸

Restaurante Vegetariano Nah-Yaxal, Calle 6 Pte. 124 (☎613 9648), ½ block north of Av. Central. A leader in Tuxtla's vegetarian movement, Nah has colonized several storefronts around the *centro*. Full vegetarian *comida corrida* 46 pesos. Delicious *licuados* of all kinds 10-25 pesos. Open daily 7am-10pm. ❹

Restaurante Imperial, C. Central Nte. 263 (☎612 06 48), 1 block north of the *zócalo*. Excellent *comida corrida* (32 pesos), *antojitos* (8-26 pesos), and breakfasts (10-22 pesos). Open daily 8am-6:30pm. ❸

La Antigua Fonda, Calle 1a Sur Ote. 346. Cheap, solid Mexican classics. Tacos 4 pesos, *carne* dishes 25-35 pesos. Open daily 8am-11pm. ❸

Restaurante Tuxtla, Av. 2 Nte. and C. Central. Big lunches with the fixings for 30 pesos. Lots of meaty choices. Open daily 7:30am-6:30pm. ❸

Restaurante Virginia, across the corridor from Hotel del Pasaje. Cheap food and friendly service makes up for the cafeteria atmosphere. Breakfast 22 pesos, hamburgers as big as your head 15 pesos. Open daily 7am-10pm. ❷

◎ SIGHTS

MIGUEL ÁLVAREZ DEL TORO (ZOOMAT). Here, more than 1200 animals are featured in a natural Chiapan jungle. The quetzal and tapir are not in any other zoo and some endangered species, like the acrobatic spider monkeys, are in hardly any others. Some animals roam freely, as do numerous children and refreshment stands. *(Closed for renovations but will reopen by summer 2004. From Calle 1 Ote. between Av. 6 and 7 Sur, take the "Cerro Hueco" or "Zoológico" bus (every 30min., 3.5 pesos). Open Tu-Su 8:30am-4:30pm. Free.)*

PARQUE MADERO. Many of Tuxtla's attractions reside in Parque Madero. In the middle of the park is **Teatro de la Ciudad Emilio Rabasa.** Films by Latin American directors and performances of *ballet folklórico* dominate the schedule (hours vary; performances begin around 6pm on weekends and cost 20 pesos). To the north of the theater is a children's amusement park, **Conviviencia Infantil.** (Open Tu-Su 10am-10pm.) The far end of the amusement park holds the open-air **Teatro Bonampak,** which has free folk dance performances (Su 5pm). South of the *teatro* lies a broad concourse, lined with fountains and busts of famous Mexicans. Down the walkway on the right is **Museo Regional de Chiapas,** which displays regional archaeological finds along with Olmec and Maya artifacts. (Open Tu-Su 9am-4pm. 32 pesos.) To the left is the new **Museo de Paleontología,** which has a small collection of regional fossils and a display of unique Chiapan amber. (Open Tu-F 10am-5pm, Sa-Su 11am-5pm. 30 pesos.) Down the concourse on the left, you'll find **Jardín Botánico Dr. Faustino Miranda,** a mini-Chiapan jungle. (Open Tu-Su 9am-6pm.) Across the garden is **Museo Botánico.** (Open M-F 9am-4pm, Sa 9am-1pm.) *(Parque Madero begins in the northeast part of town at the intersection of 11 Ote. and 5 Nte. Walk, or take a "Km. 4-Granjas-5 de Mayo" combi from Calle 4 Ote. between Av. 4 and 5 Sur. 3 pesos.)*

PARQUE DE MARIMBA. West of the *zócalo* at Av. Central and Calle 8 Pte., this lovely park fills with people for the daily *marimba* concerts (6pm).

▶ DAYTRIPS FROM TUXTLA GUTIÉRREZ

▨ CAÑÓN DEL SUMIDERO

Next to the ADO bus station, vans marked "Tuxtla" can take you to "El Cañón" (30 pesos). From where you are dropped off, cross the yellow footbridge over the highway and turn left on the road. The lancha docks are on the left. Boats leave when they are full (2hr.; 8am-5pm; 85 pesos). To get back to Tuxtla, go back to the highway and wait for a "San Cristóbal" bus at the bus stop on the near side of the road (20 pesos).

Proper description of **Cañón del Sumidero,** whose image adorns the Chiapas state seal, would require the invention of new, compound adjectives such as "super-huge-large" and "giganto-normous." A *lancha* journey through the canyon begins with views of cornfields, but shortly after the Belisario Domínguez bridge, the hills leap to form near-vertical cliffs, rising over 1.2km above the water. Protected as a natural park, the steep walls are home to troupes of monkeys, hummingbirds, and falcons, while the murky waters harbor crocodiles and turtles. Along the river lie several caves and waterfalls—the park's most famous waterfall is **Árbol de Navidad,** which dashes over a series of moss-covered rock formations in the shape of a pine tree before disintegrating into the fine mist that envelops passing boats. The 200m hydroelectric dam **Netzahualcóyotl** marks El Sumidero's northernmost extremity; along with three other dams on Río Grijalva, it provides 25% of Mexico's electricity. When the Spanish defeated the Chiapa Indians in 1528, the Chiapa threw themselves from these cliffs rather than be captured. These days, people who are finished with sodas and snacks heroically throw their detritus in the water.

The *lanchas* leave from the quaint, untouristed town **Chiapa de Corzo.** Sights in town include the red-and-white, 16th-century **Catedral de Santo Domingo,** one block south of the *zócalo* (open daily 6am-2pm and 4-6:30pm), and the *zócalo's* **fountain,** shaped like the crown of Queen Isabella of Spain. Often called **La Pila,** the famous fountain taps underground waterways 5km long and provided the town with fresh drinking water during a 1562 epidemic. Inside, tile plaques tell the story of the colonial history of Chiapa. If a daytrip blends into night, one place to stay is the somewhat expensive **Hotel Los Ángeles ❸.** Rooms surround a parking lot. (☎686 0048. Singles 175 pesos; doubles 195 pesos; triples 220 pesos; quads 250 pesos.)

SIMOJOVEL

From Tuxtla Gutiérrez, buses to Simojovel leave from Transporte. It is also possible to get there by taking a combi *from in front of the transportation station to Bochil, a town of Tzotzil Maya, then a* camioneta *or* combi *to Simojovel. Catch return buses at the station (daily 9:45, 11:45am, 1, 5:45 pm). To return to Tuxtla, it may be easier to take a* combi *or* pasajera *from 20 de Noviembre and Allende to Bochil;* buses, combis, *and* colectivos *leave from there to Tuxtla frequently.*

Simojovel is so high in the mountains, even *gringos* won't sweat. It also sits atop some fine amber mines, which are the small town's tourist draw; amber in Mexico only comes from Chiapas. Like many other Mexican craft towns, Simojovel lacks clear boundaries between residence, workshop, and store: people sell amber out of homes and odd locations such as pharmacies. There are also official stores, such as the **Bazar Choj-choji** on 26 de Abril just past the far side of *zócalo* from the taxi/*camioneta* drop-off. The town has an informal air: even at the Bazar prices are not marked. Be wary of *gringo* rates and, as in every Mexican business transaction, don't reveal your cash before the price is finalized.

SAN CRISTÓBAL DE LAS CASAS ☎967

Most Mexican cities pack their charm into a pedestrian walkway or two lined with museums and cafes, surrounded by diesel-burning trucks with loud horns threatening the cobblestone peace. But San Cristóbal is an entire city of charm dropped into a ring of green mountains. Founded in 1528, the city, named for its now de-sanctified patron saint St. Christopher and Bartolomé de las Casas, a crusader for indigenous rights, sits in the midst of several indigenous villages on the edge of the politically unstable Lacandón rainforest. San Cristóbal's lovely buildings, Maya markets, diverse eateries, and happening nightlife offer something for everyone.

INSURRECTION On January 1, 1994, *indígena* Zapatista insurgents caught Mexico by surprise by overtaking parts of San Cristóbal. The situation is currently stable; tourists to the city and neighboring villages should not encounter problems as long as they carry their visas and passports. Those who come with political or human rights agendas, however, are unwelcome and could face deportation.

▐ TRANSPORTATION

First- and 2nd-class bus stations are scattered along the Pan-American Highway near Insurgentes. To get downtown from the **Cristóbal Colón station,** take a right (north) on Insurgentes and walk seven blocks to the *zócalo*. Cristóbal Colón (☎678 0291) sends buses to: **Cancún** (17hr., 2:30pm, 473 pesos); **Comitán** (1½hr., 10am, 39 pesos); **Mexico City** (3:30, 6pm; 580 pesos); **Palenque** (5hr.; 2, 8:25am, 2:30pm; 96 pesos); **Playa del Carmen** (2:30pm, 452 pesos); **Tuxtla Gutiérrez** (2hr., 9 per day 11:30am-10pm, 38 pesos). **Altos** goes to: **Mérida** (4:35, 7pm; 327 pesos); **Ocosingo** (12:15am, 10:35, 11:35am; 35 pesos); **Tapachula** (6 per day 7:30am-midnight, 137 pesos); **Villahermosa** (11:25am, 142 pesos). From the other bus stations, walk east on any cross-street and turn left onto Insurgentes. For a **taxi,** call ☎678 9340.

▐ PRACTICAL INFORMATION

TOURIST AND FINANCIAL SERVICES

Tourist Office: SECTUR (☎678 6570 or 678 1467), ½ block south of the *zócalo*. Open Su 9am-2pm, M-Sa 8am-8pm. **City office** (☎678 0665) at the northwest end of the Palacio Municipal. Open M-F 8am-8pm, Sa 9am-8pm.

Currency Exchange: Bancomer, Plaza 31 de Marzo 10 (☎678 1351), on the south side of the *zócalo*, has a 24hr. **ATM.** Open M-F 8:30am-4pm, Sa 10am-2pm.

Car Rental: Budget, Mazariegos 39 (☎678 3100), 3 blocks west of the *zócalo*. VW sedans 605 pesos per day. Open M-Sa 9:30am-2pm and 4:30-7pm.

Bike Rental: ▦Los Pingüinos, 5 de Mayo 10-B (☎678 0202). Also at Ecuador 4-B. 65 pesos for 3hr., 100 pesos per day. Also offers small group tours to some of the less touristed Indian villages for 200 pesos. Tours leave at 8:15am and must be booked a day in advance. Open M-Sa 10am-2:30pm and 3:30-7pm.

LOCAL SERVICES

English Bookstore: La Pared, Hidalgo 2 (☎678 6367), ½ block south of the *zócalo*. Buys and sells new and used books. Open M-Sa 10am-2pm and 4-8pm.

Markets: Between Utrilla and Domínguez, 7 blocks north of the *zócalo*. Best selection Sa. Open daily 6am-4pm. Huge **artisan's market** forms around the Santo Domingo Church, 5 blocks north of the *zócalo* on Utrilla. Open daily 8am-5pm.

Supermarket: Super Mas, on Real de Guadalupe, two blocks east of the *zócalo*. Open daily 8am-8pm.

Laundry: Tintorena y Lavanderia, Guadalupe Victoria, 2 blocks west of the *zócalo*. 14 pesos per kg. **Cuca's Wash,** Guadalupe Victoria, 6 blocks west of the *zócalo*. 30 pesos per 3kg. Fast service.

EMERGENCY AND COMMUNICATIONS

Emergency: ☎066.

Police: (☎678 0554), in the Palacio Municipal. No English spoken.

San Cristóbal de las Casas

✈ ACCOMMODATIONS
La Casa of Gladys, 2
Hotel la Noria, 28
Hotel los Robles, 18
Magic Hostel, 10
Posada Jovel, 3
Posada la Media Luna, 26
Rancho San Nicolás, 25
Youth Hostel, 23

● FOOD
Cafetería del Centro, 13
Centro Cultural el Puente, 14
El Gato Gordo, 17
La Salsa Verde, 5
Restaurante Madre Tierra, 29
Ristorante Italiano, 9
Restaurante París México, 16

★ NIGHTLIFE
El Circo, 6
Las Velas, 15
Latino's, 24
La Doña, 8
La Revolución, 4

● SERVICES
Blue Bar, 22
Budget, 20
Cuca's Wash, 11
Farmacia del Ahorro, 21
La Pared Bookstore, 19
Pingüinos Bike Rental, 1
Su Super, 27
Super Mas, 7
Tintoria y Lavandería, 12

GULF COAST & CHIAPAS

GIVING BACK

SEEKING SUNNIER SKIES

Mexico's indigenous peoples have long suffered from illiteracy, disease, and other social ills associated with poverty. As much as 90% of the indigenous population lives below the poverty line. Nowhere is the problem more pronounced than in Chiapas, where a large population of Maya live.

In an effort to improve the lives of the Maya communities of Chiapas, a small group of people founded the non-profit organization Cloudforest Initiatives. For over 15 years, Cloudforest Initiatives has organized travel seminars for people who wish to learn more about the Mayan people and their culture. Programs include language study, housing with a Mexican family, and a chance to explore and reflect on the movement for democratic transformation and civil rights in southern Mexico. Travelers also have the chance to live in a Tzotzil Maya community in the highlands of Chiapas, to share daily life, and work with the community in construction or other labor.

In addition, Cloudforest Initiatives is a major advocate of fair trade products. It distributes crafts from Maya artisans internationally. It also sells Cloudforest Coffee, organically grown by Maya farmers in the Chiapan highlands. Buying the coffee helps support both the Maya economy and sustainable farming practices.

For more information, visit www.cloudforest-mexico.org.

Red Cross: Allende 57 (☎678 0772), 3 blocks south of the Pan-American Highway. No English spoken.

Pharmacy: Farmacia del Ahorro (☎674 5310), Mazariegos at Rosas. Open daily 7am-11pm.

Hospital: Hospital General, Insurgentes 24 (☎678 0770), 4 blocks south of the *zócalo* in Parque Fray Bartolomé.

Internet: Cyber Cafe, just south of the *zócalo* on Hidalgo. 5 pesos per hr. Open M-Sa 11am-10pm. **El Puente,** Real de Guadalupe 55 (☎678 4157), 2½ blocks east of the *zócalo*. 6 pesos per hr. Open daily 8am-11pm.

Post Office: (☎678 0765), on Cuauhtémoc at Rosas, 1 block southwest of the *zócalo*. **Mexpost.** Open M-F 9am-7pm, Sa 9am-2pm. **Postal Code:** 29200.

■ ACCOMMODATIONS

An influx of backpackers has created a demand for cheap hotels and hostels, and San Cristóbal has responded with a plentiful supply, conveniently near the *centro*. Camping is only available outside town (see below). Due to the altitude, the temperature often drops below 10°C (50°F), making blankets indispensable.

✷ Magic Hostel, Guadalupe Victoria 47 (☎674 7034). Unbeatable for its atmosphere—travelers congregate at all hours in the central courtyard and cozy kitchen. 24hr. hot water. Internet 8 pesos per hr., book exchange, video rental, cheap beer. Dorms 40 pesos; private rooms 50 pesos per person. ❶

✷ La Casa di Gladys, Cintelapa 6 (☎678 5775), in El Barrio del Cerrillo, 7 blocks northeast of the *zócalo*. This "black hole hostel" sucks guests in. Halls are lined with hammocks and cozy alcoves perfect for doing nothing. Free Internet. Breakfast 18 pesos. Beds 40 pesos; rooms with two double beds 120 pesos. ❶

Youth Hostel, Juárez 2 (☎678 7655), between Madero and Flores. The name says it all. Very cheap clean rooms with spotless communal bathrooms and a TV in the common area. Dorms 35-40 pesos. ❶

Hotel la Noria, Insurgentes 18-A (☎678 6878). One of the cheaper high-end hotels around the *zócalo*. Rooms surround a funky, sky-lit courtyard and have cable TV and carpeted floors. Singles 250 pesos in high season, 200 pesos in low season; doubles 450 pesos/280 pesos. ❺

Posada Jovel, Paniagua 28 (☎678 1734), northeast of the *zócalo*. Small rooms with colorful *serape* bedspreads, terraces with city views, and cozy reading areas. Singles 150 pesos; doubles 200 pesos; triples

250 pesos. The annex across the street has beautiful foliage on the terraces and features cable TV. Singles 250 pesos; doubles 350 pesos; triples 400 pesos. ❸

Hotel los Robles, Madero 30 (☎678 0054), 2 blocks from the *zócalo*. Rooms come with private bath. Singles 150 pesos; doubles 180 pesos; triples 200 pesos. Discounts may be available for larger groups. ❸

Posada la Media Luna, Dr. José Flores 1 (☎678 8814). Media Luna has a lovely courtyard, pastel rooms with private baths, and a 600-movie video library. Breakfast included. Singles 100 pesos; doubles 120 pesos, with private bath 170 pesos. ❷

Rancho San Nicolás, Dobilla 47 (☎678 0057), 1km east of town. Take a taxi (15 pesos). If no one is around, ring the bell of the *hacienda* across the road. Call in advance July-Aug. and Dec.-Feb. Parking 10 pesos. Bike rental 15 pesos per hr. Camping 40 pesos; rooms 50 pesos per person. ❶

▐▌ FOOD AND CAFES

RESTAURANTS

San Cristóbal caters to international tourists, with several Italian restaurants, a few Chinese places, and a French bistro or two. Somehow prices have stayed low, and the *menú del día* usually costs 35 pesos or less.

▨ **Centro Cultural el Puente,** Real de Guadalupe 55 (☎678 3723), 2½ blocks from the *zócalo*. A cafe/language school/cinema/restaurant/dance hall/Internet cafe. Breakfast 30 pesos. *Menú del día* 25 pesos. Be aware that the 3-for-1 beer happy-hour deal features half-sized Coronitas. Open daily 11am-11pm. ❸

▨ **Ristorante Italiano,** Real de Guadalupe 40L. Super-fine pasta prepared with several sauces (30 pesos). Amazing brick-oven pizza. Open Tu-Su 1-10:30pm. ❸

El Gato Gordo, Madero 28 (☎678 0499), between Domínguez and Colón. Ideal for budget-style face-stuffing. Vegetarian *menú del día* 20 pesos, gut-busting sandwiches on homemade bread 15 pesos. Open M, W-Su 9am-10:30pm. ❷

Restaurante Madre Tierra, Insurgentes 19 (☎678 4297), opposite the Iglesia de San Francisco, 2½ blocks south of the *zócalo*. Choose a corner and dig into the *menú viajero* (40 pesos). Also has a bakery. Quiche 12 pesos. Open daily 8am-10pm. ❸

La Salsa Verde, 20 de Noviembre 7 (☎678 7280), 1 block north of the *zócalo*. It's hard to miss this taco diner with its red and green sign, red lamps, and green tablecloths. Tacos 4 pesos. Open daily 8am-midnight. ❶

Restaurante París México, Madero 20 (☎678 0695), 1½ blocks east of the *zócalo*. French *menú del día* 38 pesos, Mexican *menú del día* 32 pesos. Unholy "Francomex" *menú del día* 45 pesos. Open daily 7am-11pm. ❸

Cafetería del Centro, Real de Guadalupe 15B (☎678 6368), 1 block east of the *zócalo*. Cafeteria-like atmosphere. Killer breakfasts 28 pesos. *Comida corrida* 35 pesos. Open daily 7am-9:30pm. ❸

CAFES

Proceeds from both of the following help indigenous coffee producers.

Cafe Museo, María Flores 10 (☎678 7876), between Utrilla and Domínguez. A combination coffee museum, garden, and pastry shop. Organic coffee 8-15 pesos. Live music almost every night 8-10pm. Open Su 4-10pm, M-Sa 9am-10pm. ❶

La Selva Cafe, Rosas 9 (☎678 7243), at Cuauhtémoc. A jungle patio and coffee production diagrams entice sippers and pastry enthusiasts. Organic coffee and tea 8-26 pesos; beans 26 pesos per ¼kg. Open daily 9am-11pm. ❷

◎ SIGHTS

■**NA-BOLOM.** San Cristóbal's most famous attraction is the "House of the Jaguar," a private home that turns into a museum twice daily. Guided tours explore the estate of Frans and Trudy Blum, whose name was misinterpreted as Bolom (jaguar). The Blums worked among the dwindling *indígena* communities of the **Lacandón Rainforest** on the Guatemalan border from 1943 until Trudy's death in 1993. Today, international volunteers continue the Blum's work by conducting tours of their Neoclassical *hacienda* and library. The library's manuscripts focus on Maya culture, rainforest ecology, and the plight of indigenous refugees. The small **chapel** (originally intended to be a Catholic seminary) serves as a gallery of religious art. Other rooms are devoted to archaeological finds from the nearby site of **Moxviquil** (mosh-UEE-queel), religious artifacts from the Lacandón Rainforest, and a selection of the 50,000 pictures Trudy took of the jungle and its inhabitants during her life. Na-Bolom also **rents rooms ❺** furnished by Frans and decorated by Trudy, complete with fireplace, mini-library, antique bath, and original black-and-white photos. *(Guerrero 33, in the northeast section of the city at the end of Chiapa de Corzo. ☎678 1418; nabolom@sclc.ecosur.mx. Guided tours 11:30am and 4:30pm, followed by a 15min. film. Shop open daily 9am-1pm and 4-8pm; library open M-Sa 11am-2pm. Communal dinners served daily in the old dining room at 7pm; 110 pesos. Make reservations 2hr. ahead. Singles 350 pesos; doubles 470 pesos. Those interested in volunteering in the house or garden should contact the main office at least 2 months prior to arrival. 50 pesos.)*

MUSEUM OF MAYA MEDICINE. Also called the **Centro de Desarrollo de la Medicina Maya (CEDEMM),** this museum features life-sized models recreating Maya healing rituals, strong-smelling herbs, hypnotic shaman prayers, and a display that explains the use of black spider's teeth to treat inflammation of the testicles. Those with an iron stomach can view a graphic video on Maya midwifery. Medicine men are on hand to advise you on any problems you may have. *(Blanco 10, 1km north of the market. ☎/fax 678 5438. Open M-F 9am-6pm, Sa-Su 10am-4pm. 20 pesos.)*

ZÓCALO. Since its construction by the Spanish in the 16th century, San Cristóbal's *zócalo*, **Plaza 31 de Marzo,** has been the physical and spiritual center of town. The **Palacio Municipal** stands on the west side of the plaza and the yellow **Catedral de San Cristóbal** dominates the north side of the plaza. Inside, the Cathedral features a splendid wooden pulpit and chirping birds in the rafters. *(Open daily 7am-7pm.)*

EL MUSEO DE AMBER. This old monastery houses an exquisite collection of Chiapan amber, from Pre-Hispanic jewelry to modern sculptures. An exhibit downstairs shows you how to identify genuine amber, an important skill in the markets of San Cristóbal. *(Plaza de la Merced, in the Ex-Convento de la Merced. ☎678 9716. Open Tu-Su 10am-2pm and 4-7pm.)*

IGLESIA Y EX-CONVENTO DE SANTO DOMINGO. The most beautiful church in San Cristóbal, Santo Domingo was built by the Dominicans from 1547-1560 and enlarged to its present size in the 17th century. The elaborate if poorly maintained stone facade houses an inner sanctuary, delicately covered in gold leaf and dozens of portraits, most anonymously painted in the 18th century. Inside, the **Centro Cultural de los Altos de Chiapas** houses an excellent multimedia exhibit on the history of San Cristóbal and Chiapas, with colonial artifacts, photos, and *chiapaneo* textiles. The Ex-Convento's grounds make up the artisan market. *(On Utrilla beyond the Iglesia de la Caridad. Open daily 10am-5pm. Tours in Spanish. 32 pesos; Su free.)*

VISTA. Two hilltop churches overlook San Cristóbal. **El Templo del Cerrito San Cristóbal,** on the west side of town, is accessible by a set of stairs at the intersection of

Allende and Domínguez. **El Templo de Guadalupe,** to the east, can be reached by walking west on Real de Guadalupe. Both areas can be almost deserted at night, except for lurking Mexican teenagers. It's best to go during the day or with friends.

NIGHTLIFE AND ENTERTAINMENT

Both discoers and those with mellow tastes will enjoy a night on this town. For those with aching feet or technophobia, **Cinemas Santa Clara** (☎678 2345), on 16 de Septiembre between Escuadrón and 28 de Agosto, shows US movies (20 pesos). **Cinema el Puente,** Real de Guadalupe 55 (☎678 3723), three blocks from the *zócalo*, inside Centro Cultural el Puente, screens US and Mexican films and documentaries (15 pesos), and gives **salsa lessons** (Tu and Th 7-8pm; 40 pesos).

BARS

Las Palomas, Hidalgo 3. Trendy furniture, high ceilings, and an upscale crowd. Beer 15 pesos, cocktails 28 pesos—try a Mayan Sacrifice. Live music 9:30-10:30pm. Open daily 9am-midnight.

Cafe Bar la Revolución, on 20 de Noviembre, 2 blocks from the *zócalo*. This hopping spot has political-themed decor and live music. Beer 15 pesos. Open daily 10am-3am.

La Doña, Real de Guadalupe 20, one block from the *zócalo*. This Cuban-themed bar and restaurant is always packed with enthusiastic salsa dancers. Live music from 9pm. 2-for-1 cocktails 6-8pm. All-you-can-eat Mexican buffet is a hit with hungry travelers. Breakfast 35 pesos, dinner 50 pesos.

Latino's, Madero 23. Calls itself a restaurant-bar-club, offering food, pool tables, 19-peso beers, and live music after 10pm. Open M-Sa 8pm-3am.

CLUBS

Blue Bar, Rosas 2 (☎678 2200), one block west and ½ block south of the *zócalo*. Guards pat down all men before letting them into this den of flashing lights and thumping dance beats. Live reggae until midnight. Open M-Sa 9pm-6am.

Las Velas, Madero 14 (☎678 0417), ½ block east of the *zócalo*. Candles light the way to the bar and the stage, where the band jams after 11pm. 2-for-1 beers 9-11pm. F-Sa cover 10 pesos. Open daily 9pm-3am.

El Circo, on 20 de Noviembre, 1 block from the *zócalo*. A spirited crowd dances to all kinds of beats, from live salsa to 80s classics. Open M-Sa 8pm-3am.

SPORTS

San Cristóbal's most prized recreation is horseback riding. Guided rides to San Juan Chamula leave **La Casa de Gladys** (☎678 5775; daily at 9:30am). **Rancho San Nicolás** rents horses, as do **Ranch Nuevo** and **Magic Hostel** (see **Accommodations**). **Marcos,** a popular English-speaking guide, gathers groups at Cafetería del Centro at 9am every day for 4hr. trips to Chamula (80-100 pesos.)

FESTIVALS

A schedule of events is posted at the Centro Cultural el Carmen, three blocks south of the *zócalo* on Hidalgo. August brings the month-long **Feria de Ambar** to the Centro Cultural, and artisans from all over Chiapas come to sell their amber. An annual **film festival** is held in Teatro Zebadúa (☎678 3637), two blocks north of the *zócalo* on 20 de Noviembre. In San Cristóbal and nearby villages, hardly a week goes by without some kind of religious festival. On Easter Sunday, *Semana Santa* gives way to week-long **Feria de la Primavera y de la Paz.** Before riotous revelry begins, a local beauty is selected to preside over the festivities, which include concerts, dances, bullfights, cockfights, and baseball games. Hotel rooms must be reserved several months in advance. During the **Fiesta de San Cristóbal,** July 18-25, the city's desanctified saint is vigorously celebrated with religious ceremonies, concerts, and a staggering number of fireworks. In one of the more interesting traditions of the *fiesta*, a procession of cars, trucks, and *combis* from all over Chiapas crawl up the road to Cerro San Cristóbal. At the top, the driver opens the hood and door on the driver's side so that the engine and controls can be blessed with holy water by a Catholic priest, in the hope of avoiding accidents on the perilous mountain roads for another year.

SHOPPING

San Cristóbal is a financial crossroads for the indigenous peoples of the Chiapan highlands. The daily **market** overflows with fruit, veggies, and assorted cheap goods. For souvenirs and jewelry, look to the market around **Iglesia y Ex-Convento de Santo Domingo** (open daily 8am-5pm). Try going Sunday, when *indígenas* from nearby villages turn out in droves, or visit the villages themselves (see **Daytrips from San Cristóbal de las Casas,** below). **Utrilla** and **Real de Guadalupe,** the two streets radiating from the northeastern corner of the *zócalo*, are dotted with colorful shops that sell *típico* attire and amber. Tucked into the Ex-Convento is **San Jolobil,** "House of Weaving," a cooperative of 800 weavers from Tzotzil and Tzeltal villages in the *chiapaneco* highlands whose objective is to preserve and revitalize ancestral weaving techniques. While many top-quality *huipiles* cost more than your flight home, San Jolobil is a good place to admire the area's traditional garments. (☎/fax 678 2646. Open M-Sa 9am-2pm and 4-6pm. AmEx/MC/V.)

DAYTRIPS FROM SAN CRISTÓBAL DE LAS CASAS

A host of indigenous villages lie within easy reach of San Cristóbal. Sunday morning is the best time to visit the markets of nearby villages, but because all buses originate in San Cristóbal, visiting more than one village in a single morning is difficult. *Combis* leave various stands in the vicinity of the market. Destination signs are rarely accurate; always ask drivers where they're going.

Visiting on your own may give you more freedom, but guides will let you in on secrets you'd miss otherwise. Highly regarded and knowledgeable **Mercedes Hernández Gómez** leads 5hr. tours. Look for her huge golf umbrella at the *zócalo*. (Tours daily 9am. 100 pesos for Chamula and Zinacantán tours.) **Raul and Alex** have a wealth of information on everything from regional customs to the Zapatista uprising. Look for their blue *combis* daily at 9:30am on the Cathedral side of the *zócalo*. (☎678 3741; 100 pesos for Chamula and Zinacantán tours.)

> **! NO PICTURES, PLEASE.** The local Maya practice a unique fusion of Catholicism and native religion. In this system of faith, it is commonly believed that cameras capture a piece of the spirit. While visiting these villages, avoid taking pictures in churches, and always ask before taking pictures of individuals; some may request a few pesos in return for a photo.

SAN JUAN CHAMULA

Combis to Chamula stop on Cárdenas, 1 block west and 1 block north of the market (15min., every 15min. 5am-6pm, 7 pesos). To reach Chamula by car, drive west from the zócalo on Victoria and bear right after crossing the small bridge on Diagonal Ramón Larraínzar. Go right at the fork; Chamula is at the end of the 4km road.

The community of San Juan Chamula (pop. 80,000), "the place of adobe houses" in Tzotzil, is the largest and most touristed village near San Cristóbal. The town, comprised of 110 *parajes* (clusters of 15-20 families), is known for its colors (black and blue), its Carnaval, and its shamanic-Catholic church. Chamulans expelled their last Catholic priest in 1867 and are legendary for their resistance to the government's religious and secular authority. Villagers have far greater faith in the powers of local shamans than in those of the regional Catholic church—the bishop is allowed into the church only once a month to perform baptisms. Similarly, the government medical clinic is only used after shamanic methods have failed. Before entering the chaotic **church**, which also functions as a hospital, you must obtain a permit (10 pesos) from the tourist office in the *zócalo*. At the front of the church is a sculpture of St. John the Baptist, who, after the Sun, is the second most powerful figure in the Chamulan religion. Jesus Christ, who is believed never to have risen, resides in a coffin. Chamulans take their religion seriously, and unholy residents are promptly expelled from the village. Separate shrines honor each saint, which occupy the residence of the current cargo holder (or *mayordomo*), responsible for that saint—look for the leaf arches outside signaling the house's holy function. Homes and chapels are generally not open to the public—you'll have to join an organized tour for a peek into private Chamulan life.

The best time to visit Chamula is one week before Ash Wednesday, during **Carnaval**, which draws approximately 70,000 *indígenas* and 500 tourists daily. The festivities originate in an ancient Maya ritual concerning the five "lost" days, or *wayeb*, at the end of a 360-day *tun* cycle. In addition to Chamula's Carnaval and the charging of the *autoridades* (cargo holders; Dec. 30-31), the city celebrates the *fiesta* of **San Juan Bautista** (June 22-24), **San Sebastián** (Jan. 19-21), **San Mateo** (Sept. 21-22), and the **Virgen de Fátima** (Aug. 28).

SAN LORENZO ZINACANTÁN

Combis *to Zinacantán (10 pesos) leave from the lot near the market (daily 6am-8pm). If driving, follow Victoria west from the zócalo and turn right after crossing the bridge on Diagonal Ramón Larraínzar. Turn left at the fork.*

Eight kilometers from Chamula lies the colorful community of Zinacantán (pop. 38,000), comprised of a ceremonial center and outlying hamlets. Village women wear ribbons on each braid, and men flaunt dazzlingly red *chuj*. The village's flower industry has flourished of late, and Zinacantán has begun international exportation of its flowers. The many plastic-roofed structures that dot the hillsides are, in fact, greenhouses. Somewhat exceptional for a *chiapaneco* village is Zinacantán's acceptance of Catholic clergy. The village's handsome, whitewashed **church** dates to the 16th century and, along with the small white convent, is used for both Catholic and pre-conquest forms of worship (admission 5 pesos). Animal sculptures lining the interior attest to the pervasive presence of *indígena* religion. The Catholic priest, independent of the village church, merely busies himself with confirmations, baptisms, and weddings. Zinacantán's festivals include **Fiesta de San Lorenzo** (Aug. 7-11), **Fiesta de San Sebastián** (Jan. 19-22), and **Semana Santa**.

SAN ANDRÉS LARRAÍNZAR

Combis *leave from the lot on the right side of the road after you cross the bridge north of the market on Utrilla (50min., 5am-4pm, 15 pesos). It's best to return before 2pm—the market shuts down and combis stop running soon after. By car, take the road northwest to Chamula and pass the village. On a curve 10km later, a sign reading "S.A. Larraínzar" points left to a steep road up the side of the valley; the village lies 6km beyond the fork.*

The site of the Zapatista negotiations in 1995 and 1996, San Andrés Larraínzar lies 26km northwest of San Cristóbal. Because there are no commercial tours to the village, its 5000 citizens are more disposed toward visitors. The village colors of red, black, and white appear on most clothing and market items. Mexicans refer to the village as Larraínzar, but local Tzotziles prefer San Andrés. Since many villagers are loathe to carry their produce all the way to San Cristóbal, San Andrés's **market** (open F-Su until 1pm) is better stocked than the ones at Chamula or Zinacantán. For a panoramic view of the surrounding valleys and patches of cornfields, walk up the hill from the main church to La Iglesia de Guadalupe.

CHENALHÓ

Taxis colectivos for Chenalhó leave from an alley off the right side of Utrilla, 1 block before the bridge as you walk north from the market (1¼hr., 6am-4pm, 20 pesos). If driving, continue on the road past Chamula for about 20km.

Foreigners are rarely spotted at Chenalhó (pop. 10,000), which seems more remote from San Cristóbal than 32km would suggest. Typical dress for men varies from white or black ponchos worn over pants and bound with heavy belts to short, white tunics. Women who have not adopted more current fashions dress uniformly in dark blue skirts and white *tocas* (shawls) embroidered with bright orange flowers. The **market** spreads into the plaza in front of the church on Sunday and sells mostly foodstuffs, including *chiche*, a potent drink made from fermented cane. Villagers enthusiastically wave visitors into **San Pedro,** the church in the town's center, which serves as both secular and religious meeting place. Chenalhó residents celebrate **Carnaval** and **La Fiesta de San Pedro** (late June). For a nice view of the town and mountains, follow the road on the far side of the *zócalo* up the hill to the blue-and-white church past the graveyard. For some do-it-yourself ecotourism, follow the highway back toward San Cristóbal. Just past the elementary school is a tiny path that winds along a fence and through a corn field, eventually reaching a scenic, climbable waterfall.

HUÍTEPEC ECOLOGICAL RESERVE

The reserve lies just off the road to Chamula, 3.5km from San Cristóbal, and can be reached by any combi headed in that direction; ask the driver to let you off at the "Reserva Huítepec" (10min., every 15min., 6 pesos). Birdwatching tour daily 7am-10am. Su special plant-specific tour. To return, go 500m downhill toward San Cristóbal to a combi stop (2.5 pesos). Open Tu-Su 9am-4pm. 20 pesos. Guided tours for 2-8 people 200 pesos.

The Huítepec Ecological Reserve, on the east face of the **Huítepec Volcano,** provides a chance to explore an evergreen cloud forest ecosystem. Two trails wind around the park, which is home to over 100 species of birds and more than 300 species of plants. Those known for medicinal properties or religious importance are marked by small signs. The shorter of the two trails makes for an invigorating, self-led 2km hike, rising up 2390m. The longer 8km hike is led by a guide.

ROMERILLO AND TENEJAPA

Combis and taxis to Romerillo and Tenejapa leave from Utrilla 1 block west and 1 block north of the market (15-20 pesos).

Marked by 32 blue and green wooden crosses, **el Cementerio de Romerillo,** on the way to Tenejapa (pop. 5000), sits atop the Chiapan highlands. This local cemetery comes alive during **Día de los Muertos** (Nov. 2). The planks on each mound of dirt are pieces of a relative's bed or door, and old shoes are scattered around for the spirits' use. The town of Tenejapa, 28km from San Cristóbal, is surrounded by mountains, canyons, and corn fields. Crosses representing the tree of life stand at crossroads, near adobe homes, and in front of **La Iglesia de San Ildefonso.** The women's *huipiles* are replete with traditional symbols such as the sun, earth, frogs, flowers, and butterflies. Men wear black ponchos tied at the waist with a belt, red and white trousers, dark boots, and a purse diagonally across the chest. Religious and community leaders carry a staff of power and wear a long rosary necklace. Tenejapa's *mercados* (Su and Th mornings), the **Fiesta de San Alonzo** (Jan. 21), and the **Fiesta de Santiago** (July 23) attract crowds from near and far.

AMATENANGO DEL VALLE

Walk 2 blocks east of the bus station on the Pan-American Highway, and a small bus terminal will be on the right. Take a bus to Teopisca (10 pesos) and transfer to a bus headed for Amatenango del Valle (5 pesos).

Amatenango del Valle, known for its fine pottery, sits 37km southeast of San Cristóbal toward Comitán. Female artisans create the hand-molded pitchers, vases, pots, and jars that are traditionally baked with firewood. **La Casa de Juliana** is the most visited cooperative pottery house, with an original *temascal* (steam bath).

GRUTAS DE SAN CRISTÓBAL

Take the bus to Teopisca and ask to be let off at the grutas (6 pesos). To return, hop on any westbound combi. From the highway, a 5min. walk through the park brings you to the entrance. Open daily 9am-5pm. 10 pesos. Vehicle entrance 10 pesos.

From the small entrance at the base of a steep wooded hillside, a tall, narrow fissure, incorporating a chain of countless caves, leads almost 3km into the heart of the rock. A modern concrete walkway, up to 10m above the cave floor at points, penetrates some 750m into the caverns. The dimly-lit caves harbor a spectacular array of stalactites, columns, and formations said to resemble objects such as Santa Claus. For a little post-cave recreation, the fellows from Rancho Nuevo, across from the entrance, offer horseback riding.

OCOSINGO ☎ 919

The strategic importance of Ocosingo, the nearest large settlement to the Lacandón rainforest—the fringes of which harbor the majority of Zapatista rebels—is as obvious as the many military personnel who walk its streets. Ocosingo's residents still bear painful memories of the January 1994 uprising, when a shootout in the market between the army and Zapatista-friendly locals claimed dozens of lives. Despite the military backdrop, dusty streets, and ramshackle buildings, Ocosingo is a safe and quiet base from which to explore the nearby ruins of **Toniná**. Perhaps more importantly, the city is also the home of *quesillo*, huge balls of cheese that are sold from windows and doorways city-wide.

▐ TRANSPORTATION

Ocosingo lies 72km northeast of San Cristóbal and 119km south of Palenque. To get to the *zócalo* from the **Cristóbal Colón bus station** or the **Autotransportes Tuxtla station,** walk uphill three blocks and go left at the "Centro" sign. **Autotransportes Tuxtla Gutiérrez** (☎ 673 0139), on the highway, motors to: **Campeche** (9pm, 170 pesos); **Cancún** (3pm, 300 pesos); **Mérida** (9pm, 225 pesos); **Palenque** (7 per day, 45 pesos); **Playa del Carmen** (3pm, 245 pesos); **San Cristóbal** (10 per day, 28 pesos); **Tulum** (3pm, 235 pesos); **Tuxtla Gutiérrez** (10 per day, 50 pesos); **Villahermosa** (7 per day, 85 pesos). **Cristóbal Colón** (☎ 673 0431), right next door, goes to **México City** (7pm, 448 pesos); **Palenque** (12 per day, 49 pesos); **Puebla** (7pm, 359 pesos); **San Cristóbal** (10 per day, 82 pesos) via **Tuxtla Gutierrez** (41 pesos).

✈ ▐ ORIENTATION AND PRACTICAL INFORMATION

Ocosingo is laid out in a compass grid, with *avenidas* running east-west and *calles* running north-south. Street numbers increase from the intersection of **Av. Central** and **Calle Central.** From the *zócalo*, Hotel Central lies to the north, the Iglesia de San Jacinto to the east, and the Palacio Municipal to the west. **Banamex,** on the northwest corner of the *zócalo*, does not change currency, but will give cash advances on major credit cards and has a 24hr. **ATM.** (☎ 673 0034. Open M-F

9am-5pm.) Other services include: **market,** four blocks downhill east on Av. 2 Sur.; **luggage storage,** at the Colón station (10 pesos per day); **police** (☎ 673 0507 or 673 0015), in the Palacio Municipal on the west side of the *zócalo;* the **pharmacy Cruz Blanc,** Av. 2 Sur and Calle 1 Ote., one block south of the church (☎ 673 0233; open daily 7am-10pm); **Centro de Salud,** Av. Central 16, just west of the *zócalo;* **Telecomm,** on Av. Central, two blocks west of the *zócalo* (open M-F 9am-3pm, Sa 9am-1pm); **post office,** Av. 2 Sur 12, between C. Central and Calle 1 Ote. 12, one block south of the *zócalo* (open M-F 9am-3pm, Sa 9am-1pm). **Postal code:** 29950.

ACCOMMODATIONS AND FOOD

Ocosingo has a broad range of rooms; a few offer luxurious amenities at decent prices. **Hotel Central ❷,** C. Central 5, on the north side of the *zócalo,* is an oasis of clean, well-ventilated rooms with comfortable beds, spacious baths, bottled water, and cable TV. (☎ 673 0024. Singles 140 pesos; doubles 180 pesos; triples 200 pesos.) **Hotel Bodas de Plata ❶,** Av. 1 Sur at Calle 1 Pte., off the southwest corner of the *zócalo,* is a true budget hotel, with fans, private baths, and little else. (☎ 673 0016. Singles 80 pesos; doubles 80 pesos; triples 100 pesos; quads 120 pesos.)

Restaurant la Montura ❹, in Hotel Central, is overpriced, but the outdoor tables are the most pleasant in town. (Entrees 45-50 pesos. ☎ 673 0550. Open daily 7am-11pm.) **El Buen Taquito ❶,** on C. Central on the north side of the *zócalo,* is everything a budget taco joint should be, replete with blaring TV and plastic tables. (Tacos 2.5 pesos. Open daily 6:30pm-midnight.) **El Desvan ❹,** on the south side of the *zócalo,* overlooks the park. (Pizza 40-45 pesos. Open daily 9:30am-11pm.)

DAYTRIPS FROM OCOSINGO

TONINÁ RUINS

15km east of Ocosingo, the ruins are easily accessible by "Toniná" combis, which leave from the market (20min., every 30min., 10 pesos) and drop you at the newly-dedicated museum. The ruins are 500m farther down the road. Open daily 9am-4pm. 30 pesos; Su free. The lack of explanatory signs means a guide can be very helpful (about 150 pesos).

Encompassing 6 hectares, Toniná was a huge fortress-like religious and administrative center that flourished during the Classic Period. The city was mysteriously abandoned in the 13th century. At the turn of the century, the governor of Ocosingo removed stones from the site to build roads; the pyramids can never be fully restored. The site features a museum showcasing disturbing decapitated statues and re-creations of the complex's appearance before it was abandoned.

The entrance path leads east of the ruins across the river up a small gully, emerging at the stone rings and five ground markers of the main **ball court.** Next to the ball court is the sacrificial altar, the **Temple of War.** Across the field, ruins of a smaller ball court lie near the steps of the giant **acropolis.** The first tier contains the **Palace of the Underworld,** with representations of Ik (god of wind) decorating its facade and inner walls. It was believed that those who made it through the labyrinth without man-made light would gain power from the gods of the underworld.

The fourth tier housed governors' bedrooms. On the far right of the fifth tier is the **Mural de las Cuatro Eras.** At the center is a royal grave where archaeologists discovered a stone sarcophagus holding a king's body and two unidentified corpses. **The Altar de Monstruo de la Tierra** is on the right side of the sixth level. The seventh level of the pyramid, Toniná's religious focal point, supports four large pyramids. **The Temple of Agriculture,** right of the terrace, is decorated with roof combs. To the left is the **Temple of the Prisoners.** Despite the name, which comes from the reliefs of prisoners at the base, archaeologists believe that this mound once housed the king and royal family. Behind it are the **Pyramid of Finances** and the higher **Pyramid of War,** which served as an observatory and still offers a great view.

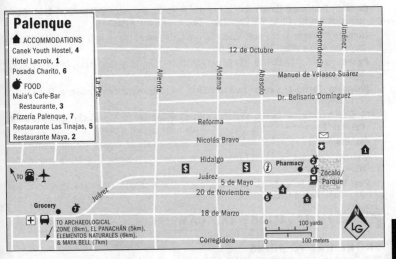

Palenque

🏠 ACCOMMODATIONS
Canek Youth Hostel, **4**
Hotel Lacroix, **1**
Posada Charito, **6**

🍴 FOOD
Maia's Cafe-Bar
 Restaurante, **3**
Pizzería Palenque, **7**
Restaurante Las Tinajas, **5**
Restaurante Maya, **2**

PALENQUE ☎ 916

In all of Mesoamerica, three sites are world-renowned for their expression of the beauty, power, and glory of the Maya Classic period. Honduras has Copán, Guatemala has Tikal, and Mexico has Palenque. These impressive ruins straddle a magnificent 300m high natural *palenque* (palisade) in the foothills of the Chiapan highlands. Dense jungle meets the bases of Palenque's breathtaking pyramids, and the sounds of birds, monkeys, and crashing waterfalls echo off the walls. The town of Palenque (pop. 63,000) is not nearly as picturesque, but it serves as an important crossroads for travelers who come to visit the ruins, sample the waters of the famous *cascadas* of Agua Azul and Misol-Ha, make forays into the heart of the Lacandón jungle, and begin excursions to Maya sites in Guatemala.

⬛ TRANSPORTATION

The **ADO bus station,** plus several local transportation hubs, are all five to eight blocks west of the *parque* on Juárez. To get to the *parque* from the stations, walk uphill (east) and follow Juárez as it goes to the left. **ADO** (☎345 1344) runs 1st-class buses to **Campeche** (6hr.; 8am, 9pm; 168 pesos); **Cancun** (12hr., 8pm, 389 pesos); **Chetumal** (7½hr., 8pm, 221 pesos); **Mexico City** (12hr.; 6, 8, 9pm; 534 pesos); **Oaxaca** (13hr., 5:30pm, 393 pesos); **Playa del Carmen** (11hr., 8pm, 378 pesos); **Puebla** (10½hr., 7pm, 465 pesos); **San Cristóbal** (4hr., 9:45am, 87 pesos); **Villahermosa** (2hr., 11 per day 7am-10pm, 68 pesos). **Altos** runs to **Ocosingo** (50 pesos) and **Tuxtla Gutiérrez** (110 pesos) at 3, 3:30, 11:30am, 2, and 8pm. **Taxis** (☎345 0112) are 40 pesos to the ruins and to El Panchán and Maya Bell, and 15 pesos in town.

⬛ 🛈 ORIENTATION AND PRACTICAL INFORMATION

Palenque occupies the northeast corner of Chiapas, 274km from Tuxtla Gutiérrez. *Avenidas* run east-west, perpendicular to the north-south *calles*.

 Tourist Office: In the **Casa de las Artesanías,** at the corner of Juárez and Abasolo. Helpful staff speaks some English. Open Su 9am-1pm, M-Sa 9am-9pm.

Currency Exchange: Bancomer, Juárez 40. Open for exchange M-F 8:30am-4pm. **Banamex,** Juárez 62. Open M-F 9am-2pm. Both have 24hr. **ATMs.**

Luggage Storage: At the Autobuses de Tuxtla Gutiérrez station, a ½ block toward town from the ADO station. 2 pesos per hr.

Police: (☎345 0141, 345 0148, or 345 0239), on Independencia, in the Palacio Municipal.

Pharmacy: Farmacia Central (☎345 0393), on Juárez near Independencia. Open daily 7:30am-10:30pm.

Medical Assistance: Centro de Salud y Hospital General (☎345 0733), on Juárez near the main bus station, at the west end of town. No English spoken.

Fax: Buho's (☎345 0195), near the tourist office on Juárez. Open daily 8am-9pm.

Internet: Cibernet (☎345 1710), on Independencia between 5 de Mayo and 20 de Noviembre. 10 pesos per hr. Open daily 8am-11pm.

Post Office: Independencia at Bravo, north of the *parque*. Open M-F 9am-4pm, Sa 9am-1pm. **Postal Code:** 29960.

ACCOMMODATIONS AND CAMPING

ON THE WAY TO RUINS

El Panchán, 1.5 km from the entrance. This backpacker's oasis, set away from the road in the lush jungle, is legendary among travelers. Three sections each have their own style: **Beto's** ❶ has cheap *cabañas* with shared bath (singles 50 pesos; doubles 70 pesos); **Jungle Palace** ❶ has hammocks (20 pesos); **Margarita and Ed's** ❸ offers well-appointed rooms and *cabañas* and private baths (doubles 150-250 pesos). **Cafe Don Mucho's** ❸ has huge entrees (40 pesos) and nightly live music and fire-dancing.

Maya Bell Trailer Park and Camping (☎348 4271), 500m from the ruins. Pitch a tent (30 pesos), string up a hammock (15 pesos), or put down a sleeping bag (30 pesos). Trailer and car space (15 pesos), and rooms with fans and private baths. Singles 200 pesos; doubles 250 pesos; triples 280 pesos. 150 peso deposit. Camping ❶/rooms ❸

IN TOWN

Canek Youth Hostel, 20 de Noviembre 43 (☎345 0150). An average, institutional-looking hostel with fans, decent baths, and mountain views, but no lounge space. Dorm beds 50 pesos; rooms 50 pesos per person. ❶

Posada Charito, 20 de Noviembre 15 (☎345 0121), between Independencia and Abasolo, ½ block west of the *parque*. Budget hotel has large, clean rooms in painfully bright colors. Private baths. Prices change with the season. Singles 50-100 pesos; doubles 100-200 pesos; triples 150-300 pesos. Each additional person 50-100 pesos. ❶

Hotel Lacroix, Hidalgo 10 (☎345 0014), just off the *parque*. A large, gaudy Maya mural leads to cozy, cool, blue rooms with blue baths. No hot water. Singles 160 pesos; doubles 190 pesos; triples 220 pesos. In low season, prices drop 40 pesos. ❸

FOOD

Travelers have about as much chance of finding a cheap restaurant in Palenque as they do of discovering why the Maya abandoned the city. For produce, try the **market** on Juárez seven blocks northwest of the city, or head to the **grocery store** on Juárez just east of the bus station. If you're staying on the road to the ruins, stock up beforehand if you don't want to be limited to restaurants.

Restaurante las Tinajas, 20 de Noviembre at the corner of Abasolo. This cozy spot serves heaping platters of classic Mexican food to crowds of locals and tourists alike. Breakfast specials 26-36 pesos. Open daily 7am-11pm. ❸

Restaurante Maya (☎345 0042), off the *parque*. Known as the "most ancient restaurant in Palenque", it's only 2050 years younger than the ruins. Breakfasts 32-50 pesos, *antojitos* 29-47 pesos, *carnes* 49-80 pesos. Open daily 7am-11pm. ❹

Maia's Cafe-Bar Restaurante, at Juárez and Independencia. Popular due to its prime location, and with good food, too. *Pollo* tacos (37 pesos) dodge the grease. *Comida corrida* with a wide variety of choices 28-38 pesos. Open daily 7am-11pm. ❸

Pizzeria Palenque, on Juárez about 2 blocks east of the bus station. Individual pies with a range of funky toppings are 40-60 pesos at this backpacker-heavy pizza parlor. ❹

👁 SIGHTS

▨ THE ARCHAEOLOGICAL SITE OF PALENQUE

The ruins, 8km west of town, are most accessible by combis (6am-6pm, 10 pesos) that depart from Hidalgo on Allende. There are 2 entrances: the 1st is 50m from the site museum; the other is 2km farther. Take the first entrance walking from Maya Bell or Pánchan, and buy a ticket at the museum. **Visiting the ruins at night is prohibited and extremely unsafe.** *Do not take shortcuts to the back entrance from the campgrounds or the road—the dense jungle will isolate you from any other nearby tourists. Site open daily 8am-4:45pm. Museum open Tu-Su 10am-8pm. 37 pesos. Guided tours available at main entrance, 350 pesos for up to 7 people, 500 pesos for more.*

Palenque began as a small farming village in 100 BC, and grew steadily throughout the Pre-Classic Period. By around AD 600, Palenque had begun to flourish, reaching its zenith over the next 200 years. Palenque owes much of its success to the club-footed king **Pacal** ("sun shield" or "white macaw"), who inherited the throne from his mother **Zac-Kuk** in AD 615 at the age of 12. Pacal lived into his fifth *katun* (20-year period) and was succeeded in AD 683 by his elderly son **Chan-Bahlum** ("jaguar-serpent"), who celebrated his ascension by building a great pyramid-crypt, the **Temple of the Inscriptions,** for his father. It was during the rule of these kings that most construction at Palenque took place. Soon after Chan-Bahlum's death in AD 702, Palenque slipped into oblivion, perhaps due to siege at the hands of the rival Totonacs or another Maya city. The site museum suggests an intriguing possibility: that Palenque was abandoned intentionally because elders felt its time

GULF COAST & CHIAPAS

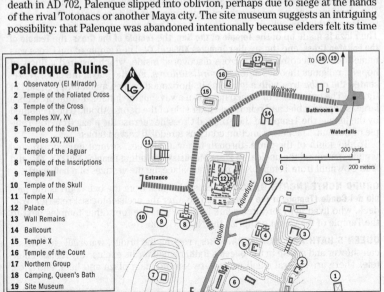

Palenque Ruins

1 Observatory (El Mirador)
2 Temple of the Foliated Cross
3 Temple of the Cross
4 Temples XIV, XV
5 Temple of the Sun
6 Temples XXI, XXII
7 Temple of the Jaguar
8 Temple of the Inscriptions
9 Temple XIII
10 Temple of the Skull
11 Temple XI
12 Palace
13 Wall Remains
14 Ballcourt
15 Temple X
16 Temple of the Count
17 Northern Group
18 Camping, Queen's Bath
19 Site Museum

TO ⑱ ⑲

Walkway

Bathrooms ■

Waterfalls

0 — 200 yards
0 — 200 meters

Entrance

Otolum

Aqueduct

was over. The city was abandoned around AD 800, and when Cortés arrived in the 16th century, he marched right through without noting its existence. Today, though impressive, the ruins of Palenque merely hint at the city's former majesty.

TEMPLO DE LAS INSCRIPCIONES (TEMPLE OF THE INSCRIPTIONS). Right of the entrance is the tomb of **Alberto Ruz,** one of Mexico's most famous archaeologists, who insisted on being buried there. Past that tomb lies the Temple of the Inscriptions; its 69 steps represent King Pacal's 69 years of reign. Named for its tablets, the temple was the tomb of King Pacal and the first substantial burial place unearthed in the Americas. After finding six skeletons, Ruz dug into the interior crypt, removing over 400 tons of rubble by hand. There he discovered the king's perfectly preserved, elaborately carved sarcophagus. The figure in the lower center of the tablet is Pacal himself, shown descending into the underworld with the *ceiba* tree directly over him. Visitors can view the royal crypt and sarcophagus. A hollow duct, designed to allow Pacal's spirit to exit the underworld and communicate with Palenque's priests, is on the right after the staircase.

TEMPLO DEL JAGUAR. A trail leads up the mountainside to the east of the Temple of the Inscriptions. About 100m along this trail, on the right, is the Temple of the Jaguar. Dare to descend the pitch-black stairwell inside the structure, and you'll be rewarded with an old, slimy well.

EL PALACIO (THE PALACE). In the center, across from the Temple of the Inscriptions, is the trapezoidal, postcard-perfect palace complex, a labyrinth of patios, rooms, and Palenque's signature three-story tower. The palace was most likely used for residential purposes, with royalty occupying the spacious quarters on the north side, and maids and guards in the cramped quarters on the south side. The tower, unusual for the Maya, may have been for astronomical observation. T-shaped ducts throughout cooled the air and doubled as representations of Ik, the god of the breezes. Visitors can climb down the staircase from the top of the platform to explore the dimly-lit network of underground passageways.

PLAZA DEL SOL (PLAZA OF THE SUN). The path between the palace and the Temple of Inscriptions crosses the recently reconstructed aqueduct before leading to Plaza of the Sun, which is usually crowded with tourists seeking good views. The Plaza is made up of the **Temple of the Sun,** the **Temple of the Cross,** the **Temple of the Foliated Cross,** and the smaller **Temples XIV** and **XV.** The Temple of the Cross was named for a stucco relief of a cross discovered inside, which inspired a flurry of hopeful religious theories among *conquistadores.* For the Maya, the cross represented the *ceiba* tree with a snake as its horizontal branch and a bird perched at the top. The outer layer of stucco has worn away, but the inner sanctum protects a large, sculpted tablet and reliefs on either side of the doors. About to be reclaimed by the jungle, the Temple of the Foliated Cross lies across the plaza from the Temple of the Sun. The inner sanctum contains a reddish carved tablet.

To the south of the plaza, through the wall of trees, several unreconstructed temples surround the uncleared **Plaza Maudslay,** including **Temples XVII, XX, XXI,** and **XXII.** Downhill from Temple XIV, past the palace, lie the vestiges of a **ball court.**

GRUPO NORTE (NORTH GROUP). Across the path from the ball court is the **Templo del Conde (Temple of the Count),** named after the archaeologist Frederick Waldeck, who lived here for three years in the 1830s. The four other temples next to the Temple of the Count comprise the North Group.

QUEEN'S BATH AND MONTIEPA. After crossing the bridge, waterfall enthusiasts can shower and splash in the **Queen's Bath,** named for its exclusively female clientele. There are several small ruins between the main plaza and back entrance, where the jungle has not been cleared. Overgrown banks and shallow water make swimming impractical. Palenque is full of paths leading to unrestored ruins and cascades; bring bug spray and a buddy if you want to explore.

⚡ DAYTRIPS FROM PALENQUE

CASCADAS DE AGUA AZUL AND MISOL-HA

Tours leave from all of the hostels and hotels in town around 9am—you'll be picked up in a combi. 100 pesos gets you transportation: 30min. to Misol-Ha, 30min. to another nearby cascada, and 3hr. to Agua Azul. Combis from the bus station in Palenque leave for Misol-Ha (25 pesos) and Agua Azul (35 pesos) frequently. Agua Azul open daily 8am-5pm. Misol-Ha open 24hr. Each 5 pesos, cars 20 pesos.

These two large *cascadas* (waterfalls) have seduced many a tourist. **Agua Azul,** 58km south of Palenque, is a breathtaking spectacle. The Río Yax-Há jumps down 500 individual falls, slipping in and out of rapids, whirlpools, and calm spots. **Currents are extremely dangerous,** however, so swimming is only advisable in a few places. *Comedores* and gift shops cluster within a 20min. walk of the entrance, and camping ❶ is available 10min. upstream from the entrance. (Tents 15 pesos; hammocks 20 pesos; beds 50 pesos.) Rather than numerous small falls, **Misol-Ha,** 20km south of Palenque, has one giant one. At its base is a pool for swimming. Bring a flashlight if you want to explore the cave behind the falls. Be aware that if there is a hard rain, Agua Azul becomes Agua Café.

YAXCHILÁN

Rising from the banks of the Usumacinta River deep within the Lacandón jungle are the archaeological treasures of Yaxchilán and, 8km away, **Bonampak.** Covering 8 sq. km and extending across the river into Guatemala, only one-fourth of Yaxchilán has been fully excavated. Already the vast number of stelae and hieroglyphics have revealed a rich history. The EZLN uprisings of the mid-90s postponed development of the site, so a journey still resembles the archaeological expeditions of old. This ancient city is so remote and the enveloping jungle is so wild that giant caterpillars, butterflies, and howler monkeys far outnumber human visitors.

⚡ PRACTICAL INFORMATION

The nearest town to Yaxchilán, **Frontera Corozal,** is 197km southeast of Palenque. The road between Palenque and Corozal is smooth, and constant patrolling by Mexican security forces ensures relative safety. Yaxchilán is a *lancha* cruise (40min.) down the Río Usumacinta; currents make it a longer trip back (1hr.). The safest and cheapest way to reach the site, however, is through an insured travel agency that is familiar with the idiosyncrasies of Mexican security forces. Palenque agencies charge from 500 pesos for one-day trips (6am-8pm), which include 2 meals, transport, and a visit to Bonampak and Yaxchilán, to 800 pesos for two-day trips (6am-8pm the next evening), which include 5 meals, a stay at the *albergue* near Bonampak, and a 3hr. guided jungle tour. If you want to go on your own, **Transportes Chancalan** runs *combis* to Frontera Corozal (2½hr., every 2hr. 6am-4pm during high season, 80 pesos). Note that you will most likely face the military, pay tolls, and have to shell out a hefty sum for a *lancha.* No matter how you get to the site, bring your passport and visa to deal with army roadblocks. Also, bring all you need with you—the nearest services of any kind are in Palenque.

⌐ ACCOMMODATIONS

The handful of residents near the site entrance have recently begun to offer **camping** space for constantly changing prices. The new **Centro Ecoturístico Escudo Jaguar ❶** in Frontera Corozal offers colorful *cabañas* with firm beds and fans. It also offers camping and a *palapa* with 15 hammock spaces and a common bathroom. The Escudo runs *lancha* trips to the site; make arrangements at the hotel. (☎201 6440. Singles and doubles 250 pesos; triples and quads 350 pesos; hammock and tent space 40 pesos. Tours 950 pesos for 1-6 people, 1200 pesos for 7-10 people.)

◉ SIGHTS

THE ARCHAEOLOGICAL SITE OF YAXCHILÁN
Tourist office ☎ 345 0356. Open daily 8am-5pm. 40 pesos; Su free.

Yaxchilán ("Green Rocks") is famous for its thousands of glyphs, which almost completely narrate its history. The city began humbly around 350 BC as a fishing and farming village along the Usumacinta. Yaxchilán's emblem glyph began to appear at other places such as El Cayo, Piedras Negras, and Bonampak after AD 526, suggesting that it may have influenced those sites and perhaps been a regional capital. Years of bloody conquest and expansion during the reign of **Shield-Jaguar** (AD 726-742) made Yaxchilán one of the most important cities of the late Classic Maya. Shield-Jaguar's son, **Bird-Jaguar**, took the throne in AD 752 and reinforced his rule through royal intermarriages and alliances with neighboring regions. This was Yaxchilán's greatest period of construction, as it rose to the peak of its power. Evidence exists of trade with cities as far as Teotihuacán in this period. By AD 900, lesser nobles were flouting whatever ruling authority was left and began constructing their houses in old royal ceremonial centers. Along with many other Maya cities of this time, Yaxchilán weakened and was eventually abandoned.

Visitors enter Yaxchilán through the **Labyrinth,** a system of underground passageways, symbolizing the underworld, that have not yet been fully explored. Bring a flashlight to view the original stucco work. The end of the labyrinth opens into the vast **Grand Plaza.** Running west to east, the 500m long and 60m wide plaza was the monumental heart of the city, lined by temples and palaces on both sides. The first significant structure on the north side of the plaza is **Building 16,** across from the Labyrinth; three doorways, each with carved lintels, are all that remain. The middle one depicts a scene with Bird-Jaguar holding a ceremonial bar dated AD 743. Farther down the Grand Plaza is the **ball court,** built for two players during Shield-Jaguar's rule. Between Building 16 and the ball court on the south side of the plaza stands a 350-year-old *ceiba* tree of life.

East of the ball court is **Stela 1,** dating from AD 782, depicting the king and his wife undergoing a ritual self-sacrifice. North of the plaza, past Stela 1, stands **Building 6,** also called the **Temple of Chac,** with original stucco still retaining some of its colors. A few meters past the Temple on the left lie remains of the hieroglyphic steps leading to the ancient bridge connecting Yaxchilán to sites in Guatemala. Yaxchilán's most elaborate and important carving—**Stela 11,** to the east of Building 6—is engraved on four of its six sides and depicts the transfer of power from Shield-Jaguar to Bird-Jaguar. The monolith was originally found towering in front of Building 40 and eventually left here after numerous failed efforts to send it to Mexico City. Across from Stela 11, on the south side of the plaza, past some circular altars and another stela dedicated to Bird-Jaguar, is **Building 20.** Next door, to the west, is **Building 21,** with original stucco on its superior facade and an engraved lintel depicting the birth of Bird-Jaguar. Inside the building is a stela dating from AD 743, showing one of Shield-Jaguar's wives, **Lady Ik-Skul**, sacrificing her tongue.

Some minor buildings round out the rest of the south side. Before them is a long, steep slope with lintels describing the rise of power of Shield-Jaguar and his first wife, **Lady Fist-Fish**, that climbs past **Buildings 25** and **26** on the left, reaching the immense **Building 33** at the top. Ordered by Bird-Jaguar IV, this is the best-preserved of Yaxchilán's buildings and is called the **House of Music**. Supposedly, as storms blow in from the north over Guatemala, the wind creates music as it passes over the building's openings. Inside sits a decapitated statue of Bird-Jaguar himself. No one knows how, when, or why his head came to rest in the next room, but when archaeologists attempted to replace it, they were stopped by the Lacandón Maya, who believe that at the moment the head is rejoined the end of the world will begin. The trail behind Building 33 leads to the opposite side of the grand acropolis, composed of **Buildings 39, 40,** and **41**. To reach Building 41, cut through the small plaza. The unimpeded panoramic view of the Mexican jungle and Guatemalan highlands merits the 10min. hike. If you've got some energy left, take the detour up the mountain to the left to the **small acropolis,** which is composed of 13 buildings perched 75m above the grand plaza. The ruins themselves are not particularly striking, but a glimpse of the river below can be caught through the trees.

BONAMPAK

Transportes Chancalan runs combis from Palenque at 5 de Mayo between Allende and Juárez (50 pesos). They stop in San Javier, a 5km walk from Lacunjá, where you can catch a cab for the remaining 3km. Colectivos are not protected by Mexican security, making assaults easier and more frequent. Open daily 8am-5pm. 32 pesos; Su free.

Since their discovery in 1946, the murals of Bonampak (Painted Walls), 8km from Yaxchilán, have single-handedly changed scholars' conceptions of the Maya. The violence in many murals dispelled the idea that the Maya were a peaceful people. The city was probably subordinate to Yaxchilán and reached its peak late in the Classic Period, around AD 600-800. Despite 12 centuries and an ill-advised kerosene dousing by a restoration team, its one-of-a-kind *al fresco* paintings still leave visitors gaping.

Much of what is known about Bonampak pertains to a ruler known as **Chaan Muan II,** who is depicted on the 6m-high **Stela 1,** the first major sight in the **Great Plaza.** Aligned with the central floor of the House of Paintings, the uppermost portion is in total disrepair. Enough remains to present the figure of the king holding a spear and shield (dated AD 787). Two other important stelae are situated close to the plaza on the wide steps: **Stela 2,** on the left, depicts Chaan Muan II with two women performing a ritual self-sacrifice. **Stela 3,** on the right, features a richly attired Chaan Muan II standing over a prisoner. The prisoner's beard is a rarity in Maya art, which seldom portrayed facial hair. Stela 2 depicts Chaan Muan II and his mother initiating an alliance with his wife from Yaxchilán.

THE REAL PEOPLE. The Lacandón Maya, or Winik (Real People), as they call themselves, have succeeded for centuries longer than any other Maya people in maintaining their traditional religious practices and beliefs. While other groups fused indigenous religion with Christianity during the first two centuries of colonial rule, the Lacandón refused to accept any facets of Christianity until the 1950s. At that time, the town of Lacanha Chan Sayab converted to Protestantism; in the 1970s, their neighbors in Mansabak adopted Seventh Day Adventism. However, the Lacandón of Nahá continue to live entirely outside Christianity to this day. Only a few hundred people still identify themselves as Lacandón (largely defined by speaking Lacandón Maya), and a good number live in San Javier, near Crucero Bonampak.

The **Temple of Paintings,** or **Building 1,** is a three-room building just above and to the right of the Great Plaza. Over the three doorways, from left to right, are lintels of Knotted-Eye Jaguar (an ancestor of Chaan Muan II), Shield-Jaguar II of Yaxchilán, and Chaan Muan II, all about to execute a prisoner. The two-headed serpent bar is a staff of rulership. Inside, the murals of the three rooms combine to form a narrative that reads from left to right. In Chamber 1, the murals depict a procession and the ascendancy of an heir to the throne on the right side of the room. Chamber 2 shows a fierce battle in a forest—over the doorway is a display of tortured prisoners pleading for mercy from the jaguar-skin-robed royalty of Bonampak. Chamber 3 is a portrait of a victory celebration with dancers and musicians; it also depicts the royal family undergoing self-sacrificial rituals. Behind and above the Temple of Paintings are a set of buildings numbered 4-8 from right to left. Climb behind Building 4 to get a look at roofless Building 10.

COMITÁN ☎963

The last city on the Pan-America Highway before the Guatemalan border, Comitán (pop. 110,000) is close to many ecotourism attractions. The town itself is beautiful and well manicured, with an idyllic hilltop *zócalo*, great cafes, and few tourists.

▐ TRANSPORTATION

The **bus station** (☎632 0980), is at Domínguez 43. To reach the *zócalo*, cross the highway and turn left. After 200m, take the first right onto Calle 4 Pte. Sur. Walk five blocks to Central Benito Juárez, turn left, and then walk three blocks north past the post office to the *zócalo*. **Taxis** (☎632 5630) cost 15 pesos. **Altos** goes to: **Cancún** (1:30pm, 491 pesos); **Ciudad Cuauhtémoc** (3:40, 9:25, 10:55am, 2, 6:55pm; 36 pesos); **Mexico City** (1:10, 3:30, 4:45pm; 574 pesos); **Ocosingo** (1:30, 3:30pm; 68 pesos); **Palenque** (1:30, 3:30pm; 121 pesos); **Puebla** (1:10, 3:30, 4:45pm; 511 pesos); **Tapachula** (7 per day 1:50am-11:25pm, 101 pesos); **Tuxtla** (7 per day 3:40am-11:45pm, 67 pesos); **San Cristóbal** (1:10, 3:30, 4:45pm; 36 pesos).

▟ ▐ ORIENTATION AND PRACTICAL INFORMATION

Boulevard Domínguez (the Pan-American Highway) runs north-south, passing the town to the west. Street numbers increase in all four directions away from the *zócalo*, and are named according to the quadrant in which they fall. **Avenidas** run north-south and **calles** east-west. If an address reads Av. 5 Pte. Sur between Calles 2 and 3 Sur Pte., it is 5 blocks west and 2½ blocks south of the *zócalo's* northwest corner, which is the intersection of **Calle Central** (called Juárez) and **Avenida Central** (called Domínguez, not to be confused with Blvd. Domínguez).

The municipal **tourist office** is at Central 6, next to the Palacio Municipal. (☎632 4047. Open M-F 8am-4pm.) Guatemalan **visas** can be obtained from the **Guatemalan Consulate,** Av. 1 Sur Pte. 26, at Av. 2 Pte. Sur, marked by a blue and white flag. Obtaining a visa will take 10-30 days (US$25), but they aren't required for citizens of the US, UK, Australia, or EU. (☎632 0491. Open M-F 9am-5pm.) **Bancomer,** on the southeast corner of the *zócalo*, has a 24hr. **ATM.** (Open M-F 8:30am-4pm, Sa 10am-2pm.) Other services include: **market,** on C. Central, just before Av. 2 Ote., one block east of the *zócalo* (open daily 6:30am-5pm); **Supermás,** on Calle 2 Sur Pte. between Domínguez Sur and Av. 1 Pte. Sur. (☎632 1727; open daily 8am-9pm); **police,** in the Palacio Municipal (☎632 0025; no English spoken); **Red Cross** (☎632 1889), on Calle 5 Nte. Pte., 3½ blocks west of the highway; **Farmacia Esquivar,** on the south side of the *zócalo* (☎632 4350; open daily 7am-10:30pm); **Centro Médico de Comitán,** on Av. 1 Pte. Sur between Calles 2 and 3 Sur Pte. (☎632 0067; some

English spoken); **Telecomm,** Domínguez Sur 47, 1½ blocks south of the *zócalo* (open Su 9am-1pm, M-F 8am-6pm, Sa 9am-5pm); **Internet access** at **Dante's Pizza,** a block north of the *zócalo* on the east (15 pesos per hr.; open daily 10am-10:30pm); **post office,** Domínguez 45 (open M-F 9am-3pm, Sa 9am-1pm). **Postal code:** 30000.

ACCOMMODATIONS AND FOOD

Accommodations near the *zócalo* will go easy on your wallet. **Hospedaje San Francisco ❶,** Av. 1 Ote. Nte. 13, one block from the *zócalo* on the corner of Calle 1 Ote. Nte., has a plant-filled, *hacienda*-style courtyard and rooms with comfortable beds and private baths. (☎632 0194. Singles 50 pesos; doubles 100 pesos; triples 150 pesos.) **Hospedaje Primavera ❶,** C. Central 2, has basic rooms with shared baths. (☎632 2041. Singles 60 pesos; doubles 80 pesos; triples 100 pesos.) **Hospedaje Las Margaritas** 1, Av. 1 Pte., 4 blocks east of the small church of San Sebastián, has clean, small rooms and communal baths. (50 pesos per person.)

For meals on the go, taco stands line the road in front of the market. Home-cooked *chiapaneco* cuisine, such as *butifara* (pork served cold), is available at restaurants. For elegant dining at bargain prices, try **Alis ❸,** C. Central 21 between Av. 1 Pte. Nte. and Av. 2 Pte. Nte. (☎632 1262. *Huevos chiapanecos* 35 pesos, *oax-queños* 50 pesos. Open daily 8am-6pm.) **Taco-Miteco ❶,** C. Central Nte. 5, near Palacio Municipal, serves tacos. (3 for 14.5 pesos. Open daily 8am-11pm.) **Café Quiptic ❶,** housed in the Casa de Cultura on the east side of the *zócalo*, is always crowded with Comitecos of all ages enjoying wonderful coffee and light meals on the stone patio. Cappuccino is 15 pesos, traditional Mexican dishes 30-50 pesos, and coffee 100 pesos per kg. Proceeds aid **La Sociedad Campesina Magesterial de la Selva,** a grassroots organization for farm workers. (Open daily 8:30am-11pm.)

SIGHTS

The **Casa Museo Dr. Belisario Domínguez,** Domínguez Sur 35, features 19th-century medical instruments and a re-creation of Dr. Belisario's pharmacy, including such products as Dr. Bell's Pine Tar Honey. (Open Su 9am-12:45pm, Tu-Sa 10am-6:45pm. 5 pesos.) The **Museo de Arte Hermila Domínguez de Castellanos,** Domínguez Sur 51, 1½ blocks south of the *zócalo*, is set behind a colonial facade and houses paintings, sculptures, and photography. (Open Su 9am-1pm, Tu-Sa 10am-6pm. 2 pesos.) The **Museo Arqueológico de Comitán,** Calle 1 Sur Ote. and Av. 2 Ote. Sur, in the **Centro Cultural Rosario Castellanos,** houses prehistoric artifacts, information on Chinkultic, and flattened Maya skulls. (Open Tu-Su 10am-5pm.)

DAYTRIPS FROM COMITÁN

PARQUE NACIONAL LAGUNAS DE MONTEBELLO

In Comitán, blue combis leave Av. 2 Pte. Sur 23 between Calles 2 and 3 Sur Pte. for either Bosque Azul or Tziscao (1hr., 5:30am-4:30pm, 15 pesos). Combis swing by the Cristóbal Colón bus station, for those who want to head straight to the lakes.

Here visitors will find lakes and lagoons in all shades of blue and green. The main destination is the **Lago Bosque Azul ❶,** which has a few facilities, a restaurant (open daily 7am-10pm), and free camping. A crowd of children will offer to lead you to **Las Grutas,** a cave with an underground lake. Horses and paddle boats are available for rent behind the restaurant. As the *parque* is huge and some places are quite isolated, women should exercise caution and consider taking *combis*.

Similar services are available on the shores of **Lago Tziscao.** The *combi* will drop you off at the road into town; follow this road. Take a right over the hill, just before the road becomes dirt, where it will curve left, and continue along the shore for 500m to the **Hotel Tziscao ❶,** with rooms and *cabañas* for 70 pesos per person and communal cold-water baths. A large lobby has a TV and communal dining tables. (☎ 633 1303. Delicious fish filets 40 pesos. Restaurant open daily 6am-10pm. Camping also available for 15 pesos per person.) A few kilometers west of the park entrance at the access road to **Chinkultic, Doña María's ❶** and **El Pino Feliz ❶** rent *cabañas* for 30 pesos per person. Anyone with a raft will row you across the Guatemalan border for about 70 pesos per person, where you can buy cheap Guatemalan beer and have your picture taken at the Guatemala/Mexico border monument.

LA CASCADA EL CHIFLÓN

Take a combi to El Puente de San Vincente en La Mesilla (not La Mesilla in Guatemala) from the La Angostura bus station on the highway between Calles 1 and 2 Sur Pte. (45min., every 20min. 5am-5pm, 16 pesos). From the bridge, follow the dirt road 500m before coming to a barbed-wire fence. Cross it (carefully) and continue along the road that becomes a narrow trail, skirting the banks of the river upstream to the falls (40min.). The trail is not marked but is fairly well-trod; if lost, follow the river downstream.

Named for their whistling sound, this series of waterfalls 45km west of Comitán on the Tzimol-Tuxtla road are an impressive 120m high. Hiking efforts will be rewarded when you set foot on the highest and nearest mount to the waterfall. **El Restaurante ❷** serves fresh fish from the lake and meat from the ranch (20 pesos). Beer and *botanas* (appetizers) cost 10 pesos. (Open daily 8am-9pm.)

LAGOS DE COLÓN

Catch a lake-bound combi from the Transportes Mariscal station between Calles 1 and 2 Sur Pte. on the highway (every 20min. 6am-4pm, 20 pesos).

The warm, crystal-clear waters of the Lagos de Colón lie in a valley 70km southeast of Comitán and are connected by streams and waterfalls. To reach the mouth of the waterfalls, follow the path from 100m before the lakes into the woods (15-20min.). The Lagos also house a turtle pond near the entrance; unfortunately, the turtles now swim amidst litter. A Maya ruin, **Lagartero,** stands 2km away.

CHINKULTIC

"Montebello" combis drop you off at the access road; from there, it's a 2km walk or bike ride uphill to the entrance. Local restaurant owners rent bikes for 20 pesos. Site open daily 9am-4pm. 23 pesos. Large groups free.

The ruins of Chinkultic lie 32km from the Pan-American Highway, on the way to Lagunas Montebello. The ruins date from the late Classic Period, and the city probably reached its peak in the 1st or 2nd century AD, making it one of the last western Maya settlements. Follow the *sacbé*, traverse the jungle, cross the stone bridge, and climb the wooden steps to reach Chinkultic's 7th-century pyramid. Birds, lily pads, a cool breeze, and **Lago Tepancuapan** are among Chikultic's many virtues. Toward the entrance, on the left, is a quadrangle for religious sacrifices. Near the exit, stelae of victorious warriors and ball players guard the ball court.

TENAM PUENTE

Combis leave the station at Av. 1 Pte. Sur between Calles 2 and 3 Sur Pte. and drop you at the ruins (every hr. 6am-6pm, 15 pesos). Site open daily 9am-4pm. Free.

This white stone city, whose name means "fortification" in Náhuatl, commands two sq. km encompassing a T-shaped ball court, burial palaces, *cruz de la madera* (wooden cross), and a tiered pyramid.

TAPACHULA ☎962

Tapachula (pop. 300,000) bustles with sidewalk swapmeets, cheap diners, and *marimba* music echoing through into the night. Hot, noisy, and dirty, Tapachula, as far as tourists are concerned, is just a point of entry into Guatemala.

▛ TRANSPORTATION. The **airport** is on the road to Puerto Madero, about 17km south of town. It's served by **Aeroméxico**, Av. 2 Nte. 6 (☎626 2050), and **Aviacsa** (☎626 0372). Tapachula's **1st-class bus station** (☎626 2891) is northwest of the *zócalo* at Calle 17 Ote. and Av. 3 Nte. To get to the *zócalo*, take a left upon exiting onto Calle. 17 Ote., walk 1½ blocks, take a left on Av. Central, and continue south six blocks. Take a right on Calle 5 Pte. and go three blocks west to the northeast corner of the plaza. A *centro*-bound *combi* can be caught across the street from the bus station (3.5 pesos). **Altos de Chiapas** goes to **Comitán** (5hr., 6 per day, 100 pesos) and **San Cristóbal de las Casas** (6 per day, 124 pesos). **Cristóbal Colón** heads to **Mexico City** (18hr., 5 per day 2:15-9:20pm, 606 pesos); **Oaxaca** (11hr., 8pm, 355 pesos); **Puerto Escondido** (12hr., 10:45pm, 324 pesos); **Tuxtla Gutiérrez** (6hr., 12 per day, 179 pesos). **Tica** runs buses to **Guatemala City** (150 pesos).

◪ ▟ ORIENTATION AND PRACTICAL INFORMATION. Tapachula is 18km from Talismán along the Guatemalan border and 303km west of Guatemala City. *Avenidas* run north-south, and *calles* run east-west. *Calles* north of **Calle Central** are odd-numbered; those south are even-numbered. Similarly, *avenidas* east of **Av. Central** are odd-numbered, while those west of it have even numbers. Tapachula's *zócalo* is at **Calle 3 Pte.** between **Avenidas 6** and **8 Nte.**, northwest of the intersection of Av. and C. Central. Each street is divided into Norte and Sur or Oriente and Poniente by the axes centered at this intersection.

The **tourist office** is in the old Palacio Municipal, south of the Iglesia de San Agustín, on the west side of the *zócalo*. (☎626 1485, ext. 140. Open M-F 8am-9pm.) **Inverlat**, on the east side of the *zócalo* at Calle 5, has a 24hr. **ATM**. (Open M-F 9am-5pm.) **Mercado Sebastián Escobar**, 10 Av. Nte. between Calles 3 and 5 Pte., sells produce and baked goods. Other services include: the **supermarket San Agustín**, in the southwest corner of *zócalo* (open 24hr.); **police, Base de Seguridad Publica**, km 2.5 on Carretera Antiguo Aeropuerto (☎625 2851); **Red Cross** (☎626 1949), across from post office; **Farmacia 24 Horas**, Av. 8 Nte. 25, at 7 Calle Pte. (☎628 6448; free delivery 7am-11pm); **Hospital General** (☎628 1070), on the airport highway; **Internet** at **Cyber City**, Av. 2 Nte. between C. Central 1 Pte. (10 pesos per hr.; open M-Sa 9am-9pm), and at **Café Tata**, facing the bus station (10 pesos per hr.; open daily 8am-10pm); **Telecomm**, next to post office (fax 626 1097; open M-F 8am-7:30pm, Sa 9am-5pm); **post office**, at Calle 1 Ote. 32, between Av. 7 and 9 Nte. (☎626 2492; open M-F 8:30am-2:30pm, Sa 9am-1pm). **Postal code:** 30700.

▛▛ ACCOMMODATIONS AND FOOD. Due to border traffic, budget rooms are a dime a dozen in Tapachula, especially near the market. Unfortunately, many rooms are as noisy and dirty as the rest of the city. **Hostal del Ángel ❷**, Av. 8a Nte. 16, about half a block from the *zócalo*, is a pleasant hotel with clean, simple rooms surrounding a small courtyard. (☎625 0142. Singles with fan 120 pesos, with TV and A/C 260 pesos; doubles 150/320 pesos.) **Hotel Algarcas ❸**, Av. 6 Nte. 12A, has rooms with fans, phone, cable TV, and very low ceilings. (Singles 150 pesos; doubles 210 pesos; triples 270 pesos.) **Hotel Esperanza ❺**, Av. 17 Ote. 8, across from the bus station, is a clean but somewhat pricey hotel that may be just the ticket if you are stuck overnight waiting for a bus. (Singles 250 pesos; doubles 300 pesos.)

GULF COAST & CHIAPAS

Taco and pastry **stands ❶** crowd the *zócalo* area, selling 4- to 8- peso tacos and *tortas.* Grab a meal at the **San Juan market** on Calle 17 Pte., north of the *centro* (open daily 6am-5pm). Typical Mexican restaurants line the southern edge of the *zócalo* and Chinese restaurants are on Calle 1 Pte., east of the *zócalo.*

CROSSING THE BORDER. The Maya may have known no borders, but tourists are not so lucky. Citizens of the US, Canada, and European Union countries do not need a visa to enter Guatemala for stays up to five months. Citizens from other countries need to get a visa from the Guatemalan consulate in Comitán. If you plan on staying more than five months, check with an immigration office in Guatemala; otherwise, you might have to pay a fee when you leave. By far, the easiest and safest way to cross into Guatemala is to take a direct bus from Tapachula or Talismán to Guatemala City. If you choose to brave the crossing on foot, Unión y Progreso buses leave Calle 5 Pte., half a block west of Av. 12 Nte., for Talismán (30min., every 15min., 8 pesos). Tapachula buses drop passengers at the entrance to the Mexican emigration office. Present your passport and visa at the office and follow the crowd across the bridge, where you'll need to pay a toll (approx. 65 pesos). Get your passport stamped at a small building on the left. A taxi from Tapachula's *zócalo* to Talismán costs 80 pesos.

CIUDAD CUAUHTÉMOC ☎963

A popular border crossing to Guatemala, Ciudad Cuauhtémoc lies only 4km from the border. Travelers will find only a few services in town. **Altos** (☎631 4242) goes to: **Mexico City** (11:30am, 585 pesos) via **Puebla** (522 pesos); **Tapachula** (10:50am, 12:30, 6:30, 9:30pm; 69 pesos); **Tuxtla Gutiérrez** (5 per day 11:30am-9:30pm, 101 pesos) via **Comitán** (36 pesos) and **San Cristóbal** (68 pesos). The bus station is in the same building as the town's only hotel, **Hotel Camino Real ❷**, which charges 100 pesos for a bed in spartan yet airy rooms. There is a restaurant on the ground floor. *Especial* and *colectivo* taxis and *camionetas* leave from the front of the bus station for nearby **Comalapa** (7 pesos), **Comitán** (25 pesos), and **Guatemala** (*colectivo* 5 pesos). About 25m down the road to Guatemala, a doctor's office adjoins **Farmacia San Ángel.** (Open Su 8am-noon, M-Sa 8am-2pm and 4-8pm.) There is a small **grocery** to the left of the bus station. (Open daily 7am-8pm.)

YUCATÁN PENINSULA

On the Yucatán Peninsula, at the extreme southeastern edge of Mexico, between the Gulf of Mexico and the Caribbean, imagination meets reality. Vestiges of complex Maya civilizations, legends of pirates and Spanish *conquistadores*, images of steamy mosquito-infested jungles, and modern centers of trade and sultry pleasures come together in the ultimate travel experience.

Facing the Gulf of Mexico to the west, quiet **Campeche** inspires romantic images of history and legend. Over two millennia of ruins enshrine savage pirate raids, brutal Spanish conquest, and ancient wars between Maya dynasties. Ruling the northern coast, **Yucatán** overflows with cross-cultural treasures. Gorgeous colonial cathedrals and buildings in the Mérida metropolis, and the stunning Maya ruins at Chichén Itzá and Uxmal embody the cultural roots of the *mestizo* nation. Finally, the Maya Riviera on the Caribbean coast of sublime **Quintana Roo,** on the peninsula's eastern side, exudes an unbridled hedonistic appeal. History takes a backseat to the allure of careless pleasures amid natural treasures, including luscious jungles and crystalline waters along barrier reefs. Here, that ornate riot of US taste, Cancún—joining the Garden of Eden and a beachside Vegas—is king.

In the peninsula's small towns, besides the weekly visit from the Coca-Cola truck and the emerging Internet cafes, the culture remains very fixed in once dueling traditions. Maya is still the primary language of many locals, and indigenous religious practices persist within the boundaries of Spanish-instilled Catholicism. Yucatecan women still carry bowls of corn flour on their heads and wear embroidered *huipiles*, while modern Maya men fish and farm for subsistence. Increasingly, however, a new culture is leaving its mark on traditional Mexico as workers, lured by the shine of pesos, are moving to the cities to work in *gringo*-friendly restaurants, weave hammocks for tourists, or act as archaeological guides. The engineering of pristine pleasure-playgrounds in new places around the peninsula has brought tourists in droves while transforming some of the indigenous culture into a gimmick for dollars, especially as more and more tourists pour in to experience "authentic" Maya culture. The result is a modern-day twist on the age-old tension between native and foreign, real and imaginary.

HIGHLIGHTS OF THE YUCATÁN PENINSULA

EXPLORE renowned Maya ruins at **Chichén Itzá** (see p. 641).

GET DOWN with the young, the beautiful, and the very drunk in wild **Cancún** (see p. 655), Mexico's biggest resort, and the ruling king of US spring break.

BEHOLD thousands of brilliant orange-red flamingos at **Río Lagartos** (see p. 653).

CRUISE through the **Ruta Puuc** (see p. 630), an eclectic assembly of ruins embraced by the jungle.

SOAK up the sun in the laid-back island of **Isla Mujeres** (see p. 664), which draws a hip, international crew of backpackers.

CLIMB the largest Maya structure ever built at the sweaty jungle-shrouded ruins of **Calakmul** (see p. 616).

Yucatán Peninsula

YUCATÁN

CARIBBEAN SEA

Gulf of Mexico

TABASCO

CAMPECHE

QUINTANA ROO

BELIZE

GUATEMALA

Calakmul Biosphere Reserve

Sian Ka'an Biosphere Reserve

Banco Chinchorro

Villahermosa

Ciudad del Carmen

Isla Holbox

Cabo Catoche

Isla Contoy

Isla Mujeres

Cozumel

Isla Cozumel

San Miguel

Puerto Morelos

Playa del Carmen

Cancún

Chiquilá

El Cuyo

Río Lagartos

San Felipe

Dzilám de Bravo

Progreso

Sisal

Celestún

Mérida

Izamal

Valladolid

Chichén Itzá

Ek' Balam

Piste

Tizimín

Kantunil Kin

Ideal

Xcaret

Xcán

Akumal

Kel-Ha

Tulum

Cobá

Punta Allen

Majahual

Xcalak

Chetumal

Oxtankah

Calderón

Kohunlich

Xpujil

Becán

Chicanná

Xpujil

Escárcega

Champotón

Seybaplaya

San Lorenzo

Campeche

Tenabo

Calkiní

Becal

Hopelchén

Tabasqueño

Hochob

Balamku

Chicanná

Calakmul

Edzná

Grutas de Xtacumbilxunaan

Grutas de Loltún

Sayil

Kabah

Labná

Xlapak

Uxmal

Oxkintok

Umán

Muna

Ticul

Kantunil

Mayapán

Okutzcab

Yaxuná

Grutas de Balankanché

Dzibilchaltún

Santa Rosa

Polyuc

Felipe Carrillo Puerto

Laguna Bacalar

Calakmul Biosphere Reserve

180

261

176

295

307

184

186

24

180

180

261

186

180

295

50 miles

50 kilometers

Campeche

⌂ ACCOMMODATIONS

Hostal del Pirata, 25
Hotel Colonial, 24
Hotel Reforma, 11
Hotel Regis, 20
Monkey Hostel, 12

🍴 FOOD

Marganzo, 10
Nutrivida, 22
Restaurant Campeche, 13
Restaurant la Parroquia, 21
Restaurante del Parque, 9

○ 🍴 🛈 🏛 SIGHTS

Baluarte de la Soledad, 8
Baluarte de San Carlos &
    Museo de la Ciudad, 5
Baluarte de San Francisco, 28
Baluarte de San Juan, 26
Baluarte de San Pedro, 29
Baluarte Santiago, 3
Baluarte de Santa Rosa, 23
Iglesia de Guadalupe, 16
Iglesia de San Francisco, 17
Templo de Nuestra Señora de la
    Purísima, 14

Iglesia de San Román, 19
Jardín Botánico, 2
Mansión Carvajal, 15
Puerta de Tierra, 27
Puerta del Mar, 7
Torres de Cristal, 4

★ NIGHTLIFE

Captain Lafitte's, 1
KY8, 6

CAMPECHE

CAMPECHE   ☎ 981

At the western edge of the Yucatán, Campeche (pop. 200,000) long existed only on the fringes. For the Maya, it was "Ah Kin Pech"—loosely translated as a mythical "Place of the Serpents and Ticks." For colonial Spaniards, it was the gateway into the untamed south; after 1540, it was a chief port in the New World, which led it to become a prize for pirates, given the shallow waters and lack of mangroves that line the rest of the coast. Pirates infamously raided the city until the late 17th century, when the Spanish finally built a fortress of bulwarks, walls, cannons, and forts for protection. Today, at the edge of the peninsula's tourist boom, Campeche draws quite a crowd to see the remains of the defensive constructions and the stunning colonial churches, and to walk the streets of the colorful, historic *centro*.

▐ TRANSPORTATION

A confusing network of **buses** (3 pesos) links Campeche's distant sectors to the old city. The market, where **Gobernadores** becomes the **Circuito**, is the hub for local routes. Buses can be flagged down, but do not regularly stop in the city center. **Taxis** (☎816 1113) operate out of three stands: Calle 8 at 55, left of the cathedral; Calle 55 at Circuito, near the market; and Gobernadores at Chile, near the bus terminal. Intra-city travel is 15-20 pesos, more after dark.

Airport: (☎816 3109), on Porfirio, 13km from the city center, served by **Aeroméxico** (☎816 6656). Taxis from the airport to the *centro* cost 35 pesos.

Buses: 1st- and 2nd-class terminals stand at Gobernadores and Chile, 500m from the old city. To reach the Parque Principal from the bus terminals, catch a "Gobernadores" bus (3 pesos) across from the station and ask the driver to let you off at the Baluarte de San Francisco. Turn right into the old city and walk 4 blocks on Calle 57 to the park. Taxis run from the bus station to the *zócalo* (20 pesos). If walking (15min.), head left on Gobernadores and turn right at the Circuito. 3 blocks later, turn right on Calle 57 through the stone arch and walk 4 blocks to the park. **ADO** goes to: **Cancún** (7hr.; 11, 11:30pm; 256 pesos); **Chetumal** (7hr., noon, 195 pesos); **Ciudad del Carmen** (11 per day, 105 pesos); **Mérida** (2½hr., 10 per day, 87 pesos); **Mexico City** (16hr., 4 per day, 673 pesos); **Oaxaca** (9:55pm, 530 pesos); **Palenque** (12:30am, 2, 11am; 168 pesos); **San Cristóbal de las Casas** (9:45pm, 244 pesos); **Veracruz** (12hr.; 1, 9pm; 433 pesos); **Villahermosa** (7hr., 7 per day, 207 pesos); **Xpujil** (5hr., noon, 139 pesos). 2nd-class buses such as **ATS, TRP, TRT,** and **Sur** leave from the terminal behind ADO (☎816 2402, ext. 2405) for many of the same destinations. Prices are slightly cheaper (**Mérida** every 30min., 72 pesos; **Ciudad del Carmen** 93 pesos), but buses stop in every town on the way. The **Unión de Transportistas de Camino Real** station, on Gobernadores near Balderas across from the gas station, offers even lower prices to limited destinations within Campeche; buses leave every 30min.

![i] PRACTICAL INFORMATION

Tourist Office: Calle 55 3 (☎811 3989), between Calles 8 and 10, right next to the cathedral. Some English spoken. Open M-F 9am-3pm and 6-9pm. You can also visit **Casa Seis** at the Casa Cultural, Calle 57 6 (☎816 1782), across the *zócalo*. Open daily 9am-9pm. English spoken at both offices.

Currency Exchange: Banamex (☎816 5252), at the corner of Calles 53 and 10. Open M-F 9am-5pm, Sa 9:30am-2pm. 24hr. **ATM.**

American Express: (☎811 1010), Calle 59 between 16 de Septiembre and the shore. Open M-F 10am-2pm and 5-7pm, Sa 9am-1pm.

Luggage Storage: At the ADO bus station. 3 pesos per hr. Open 6am-10pm.

Car Rental: Maya Rent-a-Car (☎816 2233; viasetur@yahoo.com.mx), Av. Ruiz Cortines 51, in the Hotel del Mar lobby. Open M-F 7am-6pm and 7-9pm.

Market: On Circuito Baluartes, between Calles 53 and 55. Open Su sunrise-3pm, M-Sa sunrise-sunset.

Supermarket: San Francisco de Asís (☎816 7977), in Plaza Comercial Ah Kin Pech, behind the post office. Open daily 7am-10pm.

Laundry: Lavandería y Tintorería Campeche, Calle 57 (☎816 5142), between Calles 12 and 14. Same-day service. 14 pesos per kg. Open M-Sa 8am-4pm.

Police: Av. Lázaro Cárdenas 16 (☎816 2309), at López Portillo. No English.

Red Cross: (☎815 2411), Av. Las Palmas at Ah Kin Pech, 1km up the coast from the old city. No English spoken.

Pharmacy: Farmacia Canto, Av. López Mateos 365 (☎816 6204), at Lazareto. 24hr.

Medical Assistance: IMSS (☎816 5202), López Mateos at Talamantes y Quintana Roo. No English spoken. **Hospital General** (☎816 0920), Central at Circuito Baluartes.

Fax: Telecomm (☎816 5210), in the Palacio Federal, opposite Mexpost. Open M-F 8am-7:30pm, Sa-Su 9am-12:30pm.

Internet Access: The Password, Calle 12 138B (☎811 1984), between Calles 53 and 55. 10 pesos per hr. Open daily 10am-10pm.

Post Office: (☎816 2134), 16 de Septiembre at Calle 53 in the Palacio Federal. Open M-F 9am-3pm. **Mexpost** (☎811 1730) next door. Open M-F 9am-3pm, Sa 9am-1pm.

Postal Code: 24000.

ACCOMMODATIONS

Campeche has so far avoided the price boom that has swept most of the Yucatán Peninsula. Budget accommodations abound in the old buildings of the historic center, and inexpensive hostels are popping up. In July and August, Campeche swells with Mexican and European tourists. Call ahead for reservations.

Hostal del Pirata, Calle 59 47 (☎811 1757; ericagui40@hotmail.com), between Calles 14 and 16. Quieter and slightly more spacious than the Monkey Hostel, El Pirata offers shuttles to the bus stop, 2 complete kitchens, lamps and fans in spacious sleeping areas, breakfast, and bike rentals (30 pesos per half-day, 50 pesos per day). Dorms 65 pesos; semi-private rooms for two 75 pesos each; private rooms 190 pesos. ❶

Monkey Hostel (☎800 226 7324; www.hostalcampeche.com), between Calles 57 and Calle 10 on the corner of the *zócalo*. Monkey Hostel is in the heart of the action and provides a rooftop terrace so that you won't miss a beat. Breakfast, Internet (5 pesos per 20 min.), bike rental (20 pesos for 2 hours, 5 pesos every hour after), kitchen, and washing machines. Dorms 70-75 pesos; private room 160 pesos. ❶

Hotel Colonial, Calle 14 122 (☎816 2222), between Calles 55 and 57. Tall rooms with clean baths have a mint green, retro look. Singles 146 pesos; doubles 175-199 pesos; triples 234 pesos. Each additional person 29 pesos. A/C 76 pesos extra. ❷

Hotel Reforma, Calle 8 257 (☎816 4464). Clean rooms with fully tiled walls that match the floors. TV but no hot water. Singles and doubles 130 pesos, with A/C 230 pesos. ❷

Hotel Regis (☎816 3175), on Calle 12 between Calles 55 and 57. Large, white rooms with checkered floors, comfy beds, TV, fan, and A/C. Ask for a balcony. Singles 264.5 pesos; doubles 315 pesos; triples 366 pesos; each additional person 40 pesos. ❺

Villa Deportiva Universitaria (☎816 1802), on Mélgar, 1½ blocks from the coastal highway. From outside the north walls of the city (Calle 49C), catch a bus marked "Lerma," "Playa Bonita," or "ISSTE" heading toward the water. Clean, single-sex dorm rooms with 4 bunks and communal baths straight out of high school await. Often full July-Aug. and Dec.; call to reserve. Bunks 25 pesos; 25 peso deposit. ❶

FOOD

Campechan cuisine is known for combining Yucatec specialties with European style and the flavors of the sea. Sample *pan de cazón* (stacked tortillas filled with baby shark and refried beans, covered with an onion, tomato, and *chile* sauce). Other local specialties include *pámpano en escabeche* (pompano broiled in olive oil and flavored with onion, garlic, *chile*, and orange juice), Campechan caviar, and *chicozapote*, a regional fruit. Numerous stalls and *loncherías* at the market carry the city's cheapest food.

Marganzo (☎811 3898), on Calle 8 between Calles 57 and 59, is as fresh and colorful as its food. Something for everyone's budget (*tamales* 21 pesos, fish parmesan 64 pesos) and suave *mariachis* (Tu-Th 6:30-10pm) combine to make this one of the best dining experiences in town. Open daily 7am-11pm. ❹

IN RECENT NEWS

HOLY WATER

You may have noticed an absence of bridges on the lush Yucatán Peninsula, which lacks even a trickle of surface water. The whole peninsula rests on a porous limestone shelf, and rain water seeps right into the ground. The absorbed water finds itself in a complex network of underground rivers, all eventually flowing to the ocean. Along the way, cracks break the surface of the earth, revealing the water beneath in what are known as *cenotes*. Experts have estimated that approximately 4000 *cenotes* exist in the Yucatán. Many caves with *cenotes* have elaborate stalactite and stalagmite formations that likely formed during the Ice Age.

The ancient Maya, who relied heavily on the rains that fell from May to October, worshipped some *cenotes*, believing them to be the residences of the rain god Chac. *Cenotes* were a necessity for survival (and pleasure), and some Maya cities were built around *cenotes*. Most notably, the great city of Chichén Itzá has several *cenotes*, including the "Cenote of Sacrifice," where archeologists have found sacrificial remains.

Today, these cool, fresh water openings are great places for swimming and diving and the region's only source of fresh water. However, cave diving should only be done under the supervision of a trained guide, as many people have died in the act.

Restaurant la Parroquia, Calle 55 8 (☎816 2530), between Calles 10 and 12. Low prices, heaping portions. A cavernous and popular all-night local eatery with TV around the clock. Fat, steaming stacks of pancakes with honey 33 pesos, the same price as the extensive *comida del día*. Open 24hr. ❷

Nutrivida, Calle 12 167 (☎816 1221), between Calles 57 and 59. Vegetarians rejoice! All-natural food such as apple yogurt (6.5 pesos) and meatless burgers (12.5 pesos) served fast. Meat eaters can keep veggie friends company, with chicken sandwiches (8 pesos) and tuna salad. Open M-F 8am-2pm and 5:30-8:30pm, Sa 8am-2pm. ❷

Casa Vieja, on Calle 10 (☎811 8106), between Calles 55 and 57. Slightly pricey menu, but the balcony overlooking the *zócalo* is an excellent place to dine. Baguette sandwiches 45-60 pesos, chicken fajitas 62 pesos. Open M 5:30pm-2am, Tu-Su 8:30pm-2am. ❹

Restaurante Campeche, Calle 57 (☎816 2128), between Calles 8 and 10. A/C cools the blue-and-yellow decor while diners browse a long menu of local and international offerings, from 35-peso breakfasts to 40-peso chicken dishes and seafood starting at 68 pesos; ice cream dessert 16 pesos. Open daily 6:30am-midnight. ❹

Restaurante del Parque, Calle 8 251 (☎816 0240), at Calle 57. Tablecloths and cushioned chairs make this the height of budget elegance. *Tortas al pastor* 24 pesos and *pan de cazón* 45 pesos. Open daily 6:30am-11pm. ❷

◐ SIGHTS

With ancient stone beautifully illuminated by the moonlight and myriad street lamps, Campeche's historical treasures are best viewed by night. The city has eight *baluartes* (bulwarks), visible along Circuito Baluartes or from the "Circuito Baluartes" bus that circles the historic center. The only remaining walls of the fortress are at **Puerta de Tierra** and **Baluarte de la Soledad,** both of which house small museums and allow you to walk along their terraces. The convenient red "Tranvía" trolley tours major sights and historic neighborhoods, and the green "El Guapo" or "Super Guapo" trolleys give a guided tour on the way to Fuerte de San Miguel or Fuerte de San José el Alto; catch them all in the Parque Principal on Calle 10 at the green kiosk (☎811 1138; 45min. each; 70 pesos). Most other sights are within walking distance of the historic center.

FUERTE DE SAN MIGUEL. Completed in 1801, this fort now houses the impressive **Museo Arqueológico de Campeche,** which has intriguing exhibits on the ruins in the state, ancient Maya city life, religion, war, power, trade, and views of death and afterlife. On the top level, where the city and sea stretch expansively before the viewer, 20 cannons still stand guard. *(Take a 3-peso "Lerma" or "Playa Bonita" bus from Circuito Baluartes, ½ block toward the sea from the market. Ask the driver to drop you off at the Castillo stop, then walk up the steep hill on the left until the road forks; the left turn leads to the fort. Open Tu-Su 8:30am-7:30pm. 23 pesos.)*

FUERTE DE SAN JOSÉ EL ALTO. Built in 1792, San Miguel's smaller fort stands guard on the opposite side of the city. The path leading to the drawbridge winds deliberately to prevent attacking pirates from using battering rams on the gate. Today, ships and armaments, weapons and models of pirate ships from the 14th-19th centuries, are exhibited inside. *(The "Bellavista" or "San José el Alto" bus, caught at the same place as the bus for San Miguel, will drop you halfway up the hill, a 3min. walk from the fort. Open Tu-Su 8am-8pm. 23 pesos.)*

IGLESIA DE SAN ROMÁN. The church houses the image of **El Cristo Negro** (The Black Christ), carved in ebony and venerated by *campechanos* in Mexico. The church was built for future protection and good luck after a locust plague struck the city. *(A few blocks southwest of the centro on Calle 10. Open daily 6am-noon and 4-8pm.)*

MUSEO DE LAS ESTELAS MAYA. Inside the **Baluarte de la Soledad,** is a small collection of Maya stelae and reliefs from around the state, plus other archaeological exhibits. *(Off Calle 8 near Calle 57 behind Parque Principal. Open daily 8am-8pm. 23 pesos.)*

JARDÍN BOTÁNICO XMUCH'HALTUN. Enclosed by the walls of the **Baluarte de Santiago,** over 250 plant species thrive in the tiny open-air courtyard, shaded by trees and filled with benches, fountains, and frogs. *(Calles 8 and 51. Open Su 9am-1pm, M-F 9am-8pm, Sa 9am-1pm and 5-8pm.)*

IGLESIA DE SAN FRANCISCO Y ANTIGUO CONVENTO. This church, built in 1546 on an ancient Maya foundation, marks the site of the first Catholic Mesoamerican mass in 1517 and the baptismal site of the grandson of Hernán Cortés. The three bells atop the Renaissance-style architecture toll for humility, obedience, and chastity. Ask the caretaker to open the gate to the roof for a view. *(About 1km from the center of town on Alemán. Open daily 8am-noon and 5-8pm.)*

TEMPLO DE NUESTRA SEÑORA DE LA PURÍSIMA CONCEPCIÓN. Francisco de Montejo initially ordered the construction of Campeche's cathedral in 1540, but the massive structure was not completed until 1705. The marble altar, stained-glass windows around the chapel, Renaissance paintings, and fresh flowers are worth stopping for. *(Open daily 6am-9pm. Free.)*

MUSEO DE LA CIUDAD. This small museum within the Baluarte de San Carlos recounts the history of the city from the 16th to the 18th centuries, displaying various relics created by cultures from the Maya through to the pirates and the Spanish, including a discussion of the *muralla* and the *baluartes* that surround the center. *(At the corner of Calles 8 and 65. Open Tu-Su 8am-7pm. Free.)*

PARQUE ECOLÓGICO. An under-utilized city park that offers a small aquarium, walking paths, amusement park games, and tours through the plant world. Convenient for those visiting Fuerte de San Miguel; turn right at the top of the hill instead of left. *(Open Tu-F 9am-1pm and Sa-Su 10am-4pm. Tours Tu-F at 9:30, 10:30, 11:30am; Sa-Su at 10:30, 11:30am, 2, 3pm. 1 peso.)*

BEACHES. By any conceivable definition, downtown Campeche lacks a "beach." For something prettier, catch a **"Playa Bonita"** bus to the beach of the same name 30min. away. The sand and shells that fill up with families during summer afternoons are maintained by a wall with stairs leading to the water. For a more beautiful beach, but without *palapas* and other services, try **Playa Ceyba**. Take the bus to Alameda (25 pesos) and from there, the 3-peso *camión* to the beach.

ENTERTAINMENT

Traditional music and dance infuse Campeche's evening air and nourish its cultural roots nearly every night. The city sponsors various outdoor events, such as the **sound and light show** at Puerta de Tierra, Calles 59 and 18, which tells the story of the *campechanos* staving off foolhardy pirates. Weather permitting, 8 actors and documentary film clips fill the 80min. show with action. (Tu and F-Sa 8:30pm, 20 pesos; M-Sa from July to mid-Aug.) The state band, local trios, and dance groups strike up *campechano* music and moves in Parque Principal. (Th-Su 7:30pm.) The Casa de Cultura Seis, off the *zócalo*, holds **bingo**. (Sa 6:30pm. 1 peso per board.) More events are scheduled during high season (July-Aug. and Dec.); ask for a program at the tourist information center. Families, couples, and kids ride bikes along the *malecón* or admire the musical fountain, next to the *zócalo* on Calle 8 by Calle 53, on quieter nights. *Campechanos* celebrate the feast of **San Román** (Sept. 14-30), the city's patron saint, in the fall.

On weekends, two clubs draw university students and a lively bar keeps the night active until early morning. Enormous crowds are jammed on two floors in **KY8**, at Calles 8 and 59; the first floor tries to imitate Cancún clubs, while the second features live rock bands. (Cover 40 pesos. Open F-Sa 10pm-3am.) **Jaxx**, on Av. Resurgimiento, offers a similar atmosphere, hours, and prices, with more varied music, but is farther from the *centro*. For a full night and mixed crowd, try **Captain Lafitte's**, complete with pirate waiters, indoor *motes*, and hard-wood boat decor. Opens for "fast food" dinners at 7pm; the music and dancing kick in later. Live music W-Th, *discoteca*-style DJ F-Sa. Inside Hotel del Mar at Calle 59 and the shore. (☎816 2233. Burgers 43 pesos, pasta with pesto 40 pesos, salads 35-56 pesos, beers 25 pesos; 80-peso minimum. Open daily 7pm-2am, F-Sa after 10pm.)

DAYTRIPS FROM CAMPECHE

EDZNÁ

Catch a bus in the lot across the park from the market on República. The building at the entrance is marked "SUR" and buses run from Campeche to Pich (7am and every hr. 10am-4pm, 40min., 18 pesos). Be sure to ask the driver when he will return. Site open daily 8am-5pm. 32 pesos. Bring bug repellent and water. Allow a minimum of 1½-2hr. to visit the site. No on-site food vendors.

Edzná, "House of the Itzáes," was named for its ruling family during its zenith in the late Classic Period (AD 600-900), when it was the most important city in western Campeche. The site covers 25 sq. km and had a unique rainwater distribution system composed of an elaborate network of 29 canals, 27 reservoirs, and more than 70 *chultunes* (man-made water cisterns). The centerpiece of the ruins is the **Edificio de Cinco Pisos** (Building of the Five Floors), which, at 31m high, towers over the surrounding valley from atop the magnificent **Gran Acrópolis,** a large base that supports several structures. Sixty-five stairs, some adorned with hieroglyphics over 1300 years old, lead to tiers of columns crowned by a five-room temple, which once housed a stela with an engraving of the god of corn. The sun illuminated the stela twice yearly, signaling planting and harvesting times. Next to the Edificio is the architecturally intriguing **Templo del Norte,** remodeled at least four times over 1100 years. The alterations and superstitions of this stylistically varied temple are believed to correspond to the political circumstances in Edzná. The east side of Gran Acrópolis faces the 135m wide stairway of **Nohoch-Ná** (Large House), which functioned as a stadium for events in the principal plaza as well as an administrative center; it is in the Peten monumental style. Be sure to see the remains of the **ball court,** whose loops are now missing, but whose small size and sloped sides allow one to fully picture the game in action. The **Temple of Masks** has three-dimensional stucco masks of the sun god in two stages, representing sunrise and sunset. The crossed or squinted eyes on the incredibly well preserved masks are typical of the Maya and considered a sign of beauty. The **Small Acropolis** is the oldest building at the site, but the **Patio de los Embajadores** near its entrance is a modern addition in name: it took its name in honor of the many ambassadors who have visited the site since it began employing Guatemalan refugees to help with the reconstruction in 1986. The path that leads to the right by the site entrance provides a nice walk but ends with only a small group of ruins that look minuscule by comparison.

RÍO BEC AND XPUJIL   ☎983

The Río Bec archaeological sites include several of varying size and importance strewn over 50 sq. km along **Mex. 186,** the Escárcega-Chetumal highway. From AD 400-800, before the rise of Uxmal and Chichén Itzá to the north, these former Maya cities formed the heart of human civilization in the Yucatán. Situated between Central America and the rest of Mexico, these sites were a crucial crossroads; among the ruins is the largest Maya structure ever built, and the region shows great promise for untangling enigmas of Mesoamerican civilization. Organized tours of Río Bec are arranged in Campeche or Chetumal, but peso-pinchers should use **Xpujil** (ISH-poo-heel) as a base. The village straddles Mex. 186, a few kilometers west of the Campeche-Quintana Roo border, offering easy access to the sites.

⌐? TRANSPORTATION AND PRACTICAL INFORMATION

Xpujil is organized around the junction of Mex. 186 and the road to Dzibalchén. Driving is the best way to avoid wasting time, but buses run between all the major sites. The **ADO bus station** (☎871 6027) is on the north side of the highway, just east of the junction. *De paso* buses go to **Chetumal** (7, 11:30am, 3:30, 4:30pm; 56 pesos); **Escárcega** (7 per day, 68 pesos). Both are on the way to further, more luxurious destinations. Buses leaving at 6, 10:30am, and noon will drop you at **Becán** (5 pesos) and **Chicanná** (7 pesos), and can pick you up to return to Xpujil at 1:30 or 4pm. **Taxis** at the junction go to the ruins for hefty sums. Blue taxis will take groups from the junction to and from **Calakmul** (450-500 pesos, with wait time) or **Hormiguero** (120 pesos), or to Becán (20 pesos one-way). The small *combis* on all sides of the intersection leave for Escárcega at 6, 7:30am, and 4pm (50 pesos); toward Hormiguero at 11am, noon, 1, and 2pm (8 pesos); and Chetumal at 6, 8am, and 4pm—but schedules are "flexible" and return trips not dependable.

A **pharmacy** (which also offers **medical services**) is at the southeast corner of the junction. (Open Su 8am-1pm, M-Sa 8am-1pm and 3-8pm.) Cheap **Internet service** and many small grocers border the intersection; the **post office** is at the southwest corner. There is **no bank** and no ATM. **Postal code:** 24640.

⌐⌐ ACCOMMODATIONS AND FOOD

Three options exist west of town, each with decent restaurants and plenty of ants. **Hotel Calakmul ❹,** in the pink building 600m from the junction, has rustic *cabañas* with mosquito nets and shared baths. (☎/fax 871 6029. Singles and doubles 200 pesos, with bath 450 pesos; each additional person 100 pesos.) Atop a small hill 400m further west, **Bungalows El Mirador Maya ❺** has much nicer *cabañas* with private baths. (☎871 6005. Singles and doubles 250 pesos, with A/C 350 pesos; each additional person 50 pesos.) **Templo Maya ❺,** at the archaeological zone of Xpujil, has new rooms and the most economical dining. (☎871 6053. Quads 250 pesos.)

◪ THE RÍO BEC RUINS

Río Bec was settled late in the Pre-Classic period, around 300 BC, and reached its zenith some time later, in the middle of the Classic Period. Small and virtually ignored by tourists, the ruins are significant for the "Río Bec" architectural style, a mixture of Petén from the south and Chenes from the north, resulting in distinctively rounded corners and false front stairways on flanking towers. The stones were once covered by a layer of stucco, which is still visible in many places. Cross-shaped designs, representative of the four cardinal directions, and masks of Itzimna (Earth Monster) are also characteristic features of Río Bec.

XPUJIL. Christened for the local cattail plant, Xpujil, across the street from El Mirador Maya, is the closest of the sites, just 1km from the junction. Composed of 17 building groups, Xpujil most likely reached its peak around AD 500-750. The first ruin you will see is **Structure IV.** Note the holes in the interior walls, niches for placing offerings. Continue farther to **Structure I,** the centerpiece. It deviates from typical Río Bec architecture, with three towers instead of two. Enter the passage on the southeast side of the southern tower to climb the treacherous steps for a bird's-eye view of the site. *(Open daily 8am-5pm. 28 pesos.)*

BECÁN. Seven kilometers west of town, Becán ("Trench"), named for the 16m wide, 5m deep defensive moat around it, was the region's political, economic, and religious capital from AD 600-800. As you enter the site, bear right after crossing the bridge and enter the 66m passageway. You will emerge near majestic **Structure VIII,** one of the largest examples of Río Bec architecture and one that features a tall stela on top, likely a historical record. Scramble around to the northern tower and try to find the secret staircase (unfortunately blocked off at the top). **Structure IX** is the tallest pyramid at 32m high, once the religious center of the city. Continue on to **Structure X,** whose upper temple has representations of the god Itzamná and whose south side harbors an incredible frieze of a king emerging from a serpent's mouth. The **ball court** lacks the normal glyphs and detailed engravings, but does have elaborate, maze-like courtyards behind it. Before crossing the bridge on the way out, take a detour to the right to **Structures I-IV.** Here you'll find steam baths built over a simple palace, examples of the Río Bec checkerboard motif in **Structure II,** and a circular altar, erected AD 1100-1200 and dedicated to the wind god by the infiltrating cult of Kukulcán. *(Open daily 8am-5pm. 32 pesos.)*

CHICANNÁ. Named for the striking facade of its **Structure II,** Chicanná ("House of the Serpent's Mouth") was a small elite center—a rich suburb of Becán, 2km east, with roots in the late Classic Period (300 BC-AD 250); it was discovered in 1966. The first building you will stumble upon is two-story **Structure XX,** the tallest at the site. The masks at all four corners (lined up with the cardinal directions) are typical of Chenes style, as are the rosettes framing human faces under the benches on the lower level. Passing the decrepit **Structure XI** will bring you to the main plaza. **Structure I** is a fantastic example of Río Bec architecture, and **Structure II** awaits on the eastern side of the plaza, sacred because of its relationship to the rising sun. The main entrance depicts a serpent's mouth, with large eyes overhead and teeth framing the opening. The northern side of the building still shows original color: red, yellow, and green squares stand out on the frieze. *(Open daily 8am-5pm. 28 pesos.)*

◪CALAKMUL. Deep within the rain forests of the Calakmul Biosphere Reserve, only 30km from the Guatemalan border, lies the enormous archaeological site of

Calakmul. Covering 25 sq. km, the site is still being excavated. It is already evident that Calakmul was a city of profound importance in the Maya world, most likely a regional capital with anywhere between 60,000 and 200,000 people at its peak (AD 400-800). The jungle-shrouded ruins are eerily littered with 120 stelae, guarded by a wide variety of colorful, giant web-spiders. Calakmul's greatest claim to fame is its giant pyramid, the largest Maya structure ever built, a man-made mountain of stone towering 53m above the jungle floor and covering an area of five acres. The first plaza on the path was a center for astronomical observation. Bordering it are three structures used for recording the movements of the sun, moon, and stars. A path from the northwest corner of the plaza leads to the **grand acropolis, ball court,** and, farther on, **wall remains.** Southeast of the giant pyramid is another pyramid, still being extracted from the surrounding jungle. *(The road to Calakmul branches off Mex. 186, 60km west of Xpujil. From there, it's a 65km ride on a paved road through the jungle. Leave as early as 4am to see wildlife. Open daily 8am-5pm. 32 pesos. Toll 60 pesos.)*

BALAMKÚ. Sixty kilometers from Xpujil and 1.5km down the road to Calakmul lies a newly discovered site that boasts a remarkably detailed **frieze,** documenting the king's cycle of birth and death. The king emerges from the mouth of a crocodile, which, in turn, comes out of an earth-monster, linking the underworld to the earth. To see the frieze, follow the arrows to **Casa de los Mascarones** and enter through the metal structure on its left side. *(Open daily 8am-5pm. Take the 6, 10am, or noon bus from Xpujil to Conhuas—30 pesos—and return at noon or 3pm. 28 pesos.)*

YUCATÁN

MÉRIDA ☎999

Hub of the Yucatán Peninsula, Mérida (pop. 950,000) is a rich blend of proud indigenous history, powerful colonial presence, and modern international flavor. The city was founded in 1542, by **Francisco de Montejo,** atop what was once the Maya metropolis of **T'ho.** The Maya called the city "Place of the Fifth Point" to indicate that it was the center of the universe, the spot between the four points of north, south, east, and west. Modern Mérida continues to serve as an important center in the new Mexican cosmology of capitalism. The city's commercial centers burst with *jipis* (Panama hats) shipped from Campeche, *hamacas* from Tixcocob, and *henequén* (hemp) from all over the Yucatán Peninsula. The city attracts people as well, drawing visitors and immigrants from all over the world, but not yet succumbing to big-city indifference. While street cleaners struggle to maintain Mérida's reputation as "The White City," intimate conversations swirl about the ever-crowded *zócalo* and numerous city parks, the government sponsors nightly cultural performances, and every Sunday families come out to enjoy Mérida at its best and spend a day dedicated to art, food, and culture.

▐ TRANSPORTATION

Mérida's **municipal buses** run daily (6am-midnight, 4 pesos), and a bus headed in the right direction will usually drop you within a few blocks of your destination. **Taxis** do not roam the streets soliciting riders; call **Radio Taxi** (☎923 4046) for a ride, or go to one of the stands along Paseo de Montejo, at the airport, or in the *zócalo*. Expect to pay at least 20-25 pesos for a trip within the *centro*. **Taxis colectivos** (more commonly known as *combis*) charge 3.5 pesos for any destination in the city; drop-offs are on a first-come, first-serve basis.

Yucatán State

Mérida

▲ ACCOMMODATIONS
Casa Bowen, **20**
Hotel Montejo, **9**
Hotel Mucuy, **12**
Hotel San José, **19**
Hotel Trinidad, **7**
Hotel Trinidad Galería, **3**
Nómadas Youth Hostel, **2**

🍎 FOOD
Café La Habana, **15**
Cafetería Pop, **10**
El Rincón, **18**
El Tucho, **4**
Los Gran Almendros, **14**
Restaurante Amaro, **16**
Restaurant "Café"
  Express, **17**

★ NIGHTLIFE
Ay Caray!, **5**
Azul Picante Salsa Bar, **6**
El Establo, **8**
La Trova, **11**
Pancho's, **13**
Vatzya, **1**

YUCATÁN

Airport: 7km southwest on Mex. 180. Taxis to the *centro* cost 85-135 pesos depending on the number of people and bags. **Aerocalifornia** (☎920 9355 or 946 1682). **Aerocaribe,** Paseo Montejo 500B x 45 y 47 (☎928 6790). **Aeroméxico,** Paseo Montejo 460 x 35 y 37 (☎920 1293, toll-free 800 021 4000). **American Airlines** (☎925 5967, toll-free 800 904 6000). **Aviacsa,** Paseo de Montejo 475 x 37 y 39 (☎925 6890, toll-free 800 006 2200). **Continental** (☎926 3100, toll-free 800 706 800). **Mexicana,** Paseo de Montejo 493 x 43 y 45 (☎924 6633, toll-free 800 502 2000).

Buses: Mérida's 2 main terminals are southwest of the *centro*. To reach the *zócalo* from either, walk north to Calle 63 3 blocks away, turn right, and walk another 3 or 4 blocks.

1st-class terminal, Calle 70 555 x 71 (☎924 8391). Serves: **Campeche** (every 15-45min., 87 pesos); **Ticul** (7:30am, 42 pesos); **Cancún** (20 per day, 165 pesos); **Chetumal** (7:30am, 1, 6, 11pm; 185 pesos); **Chichén Itzá** (6:30, 9:15am, 1pm; 62 pesos); **Mexico City** (2, 5:30pm, 779 pesos; 10am, 420 pesos; 6:15, 9:15pm, 714 pesos); **Palenque** (8:30am, 10, 11:30pm; 255

pesos); **Playa del Carmen** (12 per day, 196 pesos); **San Cristóbal de las Casas** (9pm, 409 pesos); **Tulum** (6:30, 11am, 1pm; 126 pesos); **Valladolid** (10 per day, 83 pesos); **Veracruz** (10:30am, 9pm; 540 pesos); **Villahermosa** (14 per day, 293 pesos).

2nd-class terminal, Calle 69 544 x 68 y 70 (☎923 3387). Goes to most of the same places for less: **Campeche** (5 per day, 72 pesos); **Cancún** (18 per day, 120 pesos); **Chichén Itzá** (hourly 6am-midnight, 45 pesos); **Playa del Carmen** (5am, 123 pesos); **Tulum** (5 per day, 171 pesos; 5am, 98 pesos); **Valladolid** (6 per day, 60 pesos).

To go to **Progreso,** head to the Autoprogreso station at Calle 62 x 65 y 67 (every 15min., 12 pesos). The **Noreste** station (Calle 67 x 50 y 52) covers: **Tizimín** (every 2 hours, 73 pesos), **Izamal** (every hr. 6:15am-9pm, 27 pesos), **Celestún** (17 per day 5:15am-8:30pm, 37 pesos) and other smaller towns.

✴🛈 ORIENTATION AND PRACTICAL INFORMATION

Mérida sits on the west side of Yucatán state, 30km south of the Gulf Coast. Even-numbered streets run north-south, with numbers increasing to the west; odd-numbered streets run east-west, increasing to the south. Addresses in Mérida are given using an "x" to separate the main street from the cross streets and "y" ("and" in Spanish) to separate the two cross streets if the address falls in the middle of the block. Thus "54 509 x 61 y 63" reads "Calle 54 509, between Calles 61 and 63."

TOURIST, FINANCIAL, AND LOCAL SERVICES

Tourist Information: (☎924 9290), in the Teatro Peón Contreras. Distributes *Yucatán Today.* Open daily 8am-9pm. Also at the **Palacio del Gobierno** (☎928 2258; open Su 8am-2pm, M-Sa 8am-8pm), at the first class bus station (open 8am-2pm), and near the US consulate (open M-Sa 8am-8pm). Tourist info at ☎942 0000, ext. 133.

Travel Agencies: Yucatán Trails, Calle 62 482 x 57 y 59 (☎928 2582 or 928 5913; yucatantrails@hotmail.com). Canadian owner Denis Lafoy is a good source of information and hosts a party for travelers the first F of every month. Check in at the store or *Yucatan Today* for details. Open M-F 8am-7pm, Sa 8am-1pm.

US Consulate: Paseo de Montejo 453 (☎925 5011; fax 925 6219), at Colón. Open M-F 8am-1pm.

Currency Exchange: Banamex (☎924 1011), in Casa de Montejo on the *zócalo*, has a 24hr. **ATM.** Walk through the courtyard. Open M-F 9am-5pm, Sa 9am-2pm. Other banks cluster on the Paseo de Montejo and Calle 65.

American Express: Paseo de Montejo 492 x 41 y 43 (☎942 8200 or 942 8210). Open M-F 9am-2pm and 4-6pm, Sa 9am-1pm. **Money exchange** closes 1hr. earlier.

Luggage Storage: At the 2nd-class terminal, 3 pesos per hr. from 7am-11pm. At the first-class terminal, 5 pesos per day.

Car Rental: Mexico Rent-a-Car, Calle 57A 491 (El Callejón del Congreso), Dept. 12 x 58 y 60, or Calle 62 483A x 57 y 59 (☎927 4916 or 923 3637). English, French, and Italian spoken. VW Beetles with unlimited kilometrage, 380 pesos per day in high season, 280 pesos per day in low season. Open Su (at Congreso location only) 8-10am, M-Sa 8am-12:30pm and 6-8pm. **World Rent-a-Car,** Calle 60 486A x 55 y 57 (☎924 0587; worldrentacar@hotmail.com). English spoken. As low as 270 pesos per day; cars with automatic transmission and A/C available. Open daily 7am-10pm. **Tourist Car Rental,** Calle 60 421 x 45 y 47 (☎924 9471 or 924 6255), also offers low rates.

English-Language Bookstore: Librería Dante, Calle 59 x 60 y 62 (☎928 3674), and on the northwest corner of the *zócalo* (☎923 9060). Books related to the region. Open Su 10am-6pm, M-Sa 8am-9:30pm. Several other locations around town.

Laundry: La Fe, Calle 61 518 x 62 y 64 (☎924 4531), 1 block west of the *zócalo*. 40 pesos per 3kg. Open M-F 8am-7pm, Sa 8am-4pm.

Market: 4 sq. blocks south of Calle 65 and east of Calle 58. Open dawn to dusk.

Supermarket: San Francisco de Asís, (☎924 3011), Calles 65 x 50 y 52, across from the market in a huge grey building. Open Su 7am-3pm, M-Sa 7am-9pm.

EMERGENCY AND COMMUNICATIONS

Emergency: ☎060.

Police: (☎925 2034; tourist police 925 2555, ext. 260), on Reforma (Calle 72) x 39 y 41, accessible by the "Reforma" bus. English spoken by tourist police.

Red Cross: Calle 68 533 x 65 y 67 (☎924 9813 or 983 0211). Some English spoken.

Pharmacy: Farmacia Canto, Calle 60 513 x 63 y 65 (☎924 1490). Open 24hr.

Hospital: Centro Médico de las Américas, Calle 54 365 (☎926 2111), at Calle 33A. **Clínica de Mérida,** Calle 32 242 x 27 y 25 (☎920 0411). English spoken at both.

Internet Access: Cybernet, Calle 57-A 491 (El Callejón de Congreso). 20 pesos per hr. Open M-Sa 9am-9pm. **Cibercafe Sta. Luci@** (☎924 8947), on the northwest corner of Calles 62 and 55. 20 pesos per hr. Open daily 8am-11pm.

Fax: (☎928 5997), in the same building as the post office. Enter on Calle 56. Telegrams and Internet access. Open Su 9am-noon, M-F 8am-7pm, Sa 9am-4pm.

Post Office: (☎928 5404) on Calle 65 x 56 y 56A, in the Palacio Federal. Open M-F 8am-3pm. **Mexpost** next door. Open M-F 9am-5pm, Sa 9am-1pm. **Postal Code:** 97000.

◤ ACCOMMODATIONS

Choosing budget accommodations in Mérida is like deciding in which bygone era to stay. Many once elaborate, turn-of-the-century private mansions are now affordable hotels, clustering near the main bus station and the *zócalo*. The hotels right outside the 2nd-class bus station or along the street 4 or 5 blocks south of the *zócalo* near the other stations have tempting offers, but the neighborhood is not recommended for nighttime wanderers.

Nómadas Youth Hostel, Calle 62 433 x 51 (☎924 5223; nomadas1@prodigy.net.mx). A comfortable haven for backpackers, with mosquito netting and clean facilities including full kitchen, outdoor patios, and free make-it-yourself breakfast. Several options for sleeping: tent space (43 pesos), covered hammocks (48 pesos), bunks (78 pesos), private rooms with bath (195 pesos for a double). Ask for a spot towards the back, away from street noise. ISIC and HI discounts. ❶

Hotel Trinidad, Calle 62 464 x 55 y 57 (www.hoteltrinidad.com). A hidden refuge behind a grungy, yellow stucco facade. Two well-maintained, spacious rooms with four dorm-room style beds and lockers nestle amidst the 290-peso deluxe rooms, winding vines and patios. Common baths are clean, with hot water. Breakfast included. 75 pesos per bed. 20% student discount on beds and rooms. ❶

Casa Bowen, Calle 66 521B x 65 y 67 (☎928 6109), between the main bus station and the *zócalo*. Large rooms in this beautiful colonial mansion have fans, firm beds, and clean bathrooms. Rooms in the adjoining building not as attractive, but still comfortable. Reservations recommended in Aug. and Dec. Singles 150 pesos; doubles 200 pesos, with A/C 300 pesos; each additional person 50 pesos. ❸

Hotel Mucuy, Calle 57 507 x 56 y 58 (☎928 5193). Comfy rooms with fans, spotless walls, and clean baths line a sunny courtyard that masks the hotel's location. Laundry service 20 pesos per kg. Tours and refrigerator available. Reading room and tuned piano in the lobby. Singles 160 pesos; doubles 180 pesos; triples 210 pesos. ❸

Hotel Trinidad Galería, Calle 60 456 x 51 (☎923 2463; www.hoteltrinidadgaleria.com). Artists and eccentrics will feel at home in this quirky colonial mansion, where all types of artwork, from international folk to modern, adorn the halls. Couches and fountain in the lobby, outdoor pool, plus clean and decorated old rooms. Singles and doubles 225 pesos; triples 250 pesos. A/C 150-225 pesos extra. ❹

Hotel Montejo, Calle 57 507 x 62 y 64 (☎928 0390; www.hotelmontejo.com), 2 blocks north of the *zócalo*. Large wooden doors protect maroon arches and a lush garden. Fairly clean rooms have wooden ceiling beams, window porticos, TV, and baths. Singles 230 pesos; doubles 275 pesos. Each additional person 50 pesos. A/C 65 pesos extra. 10% discount with *Let's Go* in low season. ❹

Hotel San José, Calle 63 503C x 62 y 64 (☎928 6657). A spacious, old but clean building with tiled floors and simple rooms in a prime location off the *zócalo*. Singles with sink 85 pesos, with bath 110 pesos; doubles 95/130 pesos. ❶

◘ FOOD

Mérida's specialties make use of the fruits and grains that flourish in the Yucatán's hot, humid climate. Try *sopa de lima* (freshly squeezed lime soup with chicken and tortilla bits), *pollo pibil* (chicken with herbs baked in banana leaves), *poc-chuc* (pork steak with onions doused in sour orange juice), *papadzules* (chopped hard-boiled eggs wrapped in corn tortillas served with pumpkin sauce), *huevos motuleños* (refried beans, fried egg, chopped ham, and cheese on a crispy tortilla, garnished with tomato sauce, peas, and fried banana), and always satisfying *horchata* (rice and almond milk). Great meals can be found in the casual joints along the *zócalo*. The cheapest food in town is at the **market ❶**, particularly on the second floor of the restaurant complex on Calle 56 at Calle 67 (Yucatec dishes 10-15 pesos; most stalls open Su 8am-5pm, M-Sa 8am-8pm). The Mercado de Santa Ana at Calle 60 y 47 is smaller, with booths that may be a little cleaner.

▩ **Restaurante Amaro,** Calle 59 507 x 60 y 62 (☎928 2451). Exquisitely prepared traditional dishes, plus delicious vegetarian options such as eggplant curry (52 pesos), *chaya* crepes (52 pesos), and fruit salads (44 pesos). Attentive service and incredibly intimate candle-lit tables set in a quiet courtyard make for some of the finest dining on the peninsula. Open daily 11am-2am, with live *trova* music after 9pm. ❹

Restaurante "Cafe" Express (☎928 1691), Calle 60 x 59 y 61, across from Parque Hidalgo. One of the oldest places in town, the service lives up to the name. Paintings of Old Mérida decorate the walls, and the view of Parque Hidalgo makes for a very visual dining experience. All-inclusive breakfasts 23-35 pesos, sandwiches 18-40 pesos, entrees 50-75 pesos, meal of the day 52 pesos. Open daily 7am-midnight. ❸

Cafetería Pop, Calle 57 501 x 60 y 62 (☎928 6163). This clean, air-conditioned cafeteria serves up cheap, simple food. Breakfast specials (20-35 pesos) served 7am-noon; other entrees (30-50 pesos) served noon-11pm. Open daily 7am-11pm. ❸

El Rincón (☎924 9022), Calle 60 x 59 y 61, off Parque Hidalgo. Set in a pleasant outdoor courtyard with serenades daily noon-3pm by a *trova* trio. *Sopa de lima* 33 pesos, fruit or veggie salads 30 pesos, *pollo pibil* 60 pesos. Open daily 7am-10:30pm. ❸

Los Almendros and **Los Gran Almendros,** Calle 50 493 x 57 y 59 (☎928 5459) on Parque Mejorada, and at Calle 57 468 x 50 y 52 (☎923 7091), respectively. Upscale, world-famous Yucatec food with pictures on the menu draws tourists and locals. *Poc-chuc* or *pavo* 76 pesos. Los Almendros, with live *trova*, open daily 10am-11pm. Less touristy Gran Almendros, with instrumental music, open daily 1-5pm. ❺

 El Tucho, Calle 60 482 x 55 y 57 (☎924 2323). Entertains customers with comedy troupes and live music as waiters ferry trays of free hors d'œuvres for those just ordering drinks (beers 22.5 pesos, 27 for cocktails). Live music 12:30pm-2:30pm and 8-9:30pm; shows 3-8pm. Meals 59 pesos. Open daily 11:30am-9:30pm. ❹

Café la Habana, Calle 59 511 x 62 (☎928 6502). This air-conditioned cafe looks upscale, has great service, and is among the most popular. A great place for great coffee. Breakfast specials start at 28 pesos, coffee starts at 9 pesos. Open 24hr. ❸

◉ SIGHTS

Mérida stands as a testament to the fascinating history of the Yucatán. Surrounded by historic palaces and a towering cathedral, the busy *zócalo* is the capital's social center. On Sundays, the streets are closed to traffic and vendors cram in dozens of stalls. Yucatec folk dancers perform in front of Palacio Municipal as crowds of people enjoy *Mérida en Domingo*. If you can't make the Sunday festivities, take a step inside the bustling maze of markets off Calle 65, go to one of many theaters or museums, or just wander the streets. Free 1½hr. walking tours of the city begin at 9:30am in the information office of the Palacio Municipal on Calle 62.

▩ PALACIO DE GOBIERNO. Built from 1879 to 1892, the Palacio fuses two architectural styles—Tuscan (main floor) and Dorian (upper floor). Inside, giant murals painted by Mérida native Fernando Castro Pacheco in the 1970s dramatically chronicle the tumultuous history and lasting pride, or *indigenismo*, of the peninsula. Together with the eerily poetic paintings inside the Versailles-like *salon de historia*, the Palacio offers one of the finest and most inspiring aesthetic experiences in the Yucatán. *(On the north side of the zócalo. Open daily 8am-10pm.)*

CATEDRAL DE SAN ILDELFONSO. Begun in 1563 and finished in 1598, the immense Catedral is the oldest on the continent and holds a 20m wooden crucified Christ, the world's largest indoor crucifix. The cathedral's stone blocks were stolen from the Maya temples of T'hó; the unusually barren interior was looted during the Mexican Revolution in 1915. *(On the east side of the zócalo. Open daily 6am-7pm.)*

CASA DE MONTEJO. Probably begun by Francisco de Montejo, then governor of Yucatán, in 1549, this house was occupied by his descendents until 1980, whereupon it was sold to Banamex. Built with stones from the Maya temple T'hó, the carved facade follows the Toltec tradition of portraying warriors standing on the heads of their conquered. *(On the south side of the zócalo. Open M-F 9am-5pm.)*

MUSEO DE ARTE CONTEMPORÁNEO (MACAY). The collection of modern Yucatec art is displayed around a central courtyard. *(On the east side of the zócalo, just south of the church. Open Su-M and W-Sa 10am-5pm. 20 pesos; Su free.)*

TEATRO PEÓN CONTRERAS. Named for the Mérida poet, José Peón Contreras, the beautiful building was built around the turn of the century and is notable for its marble Rococo interior. Frequent concerts and shows visit *el teatro;* see the box office for more information. *(On the corner of Calles 60 and 57. ☎923 7354.)*

UNIVERSIDAD AUTÓNOMA DE YUCATÁN. The headquarters of the state's national university is housed in a Hispano-Moorish complex from 1938. The ground floor has a gallery with works by local artists and a screening room for a variety of films. *(On Calle 57 x 60. Galería open Su 10am-2pm, M-F 9am-1pm and 5-9pm, Sa 10am-1pm. Movies Su 10:30am, F 5pm. Free.)*

CULTURE. CULTUR, the government agency that promotes tourism in Yucatán, runs everything from ruins to Celestún tours and gives student discounts. Students with ID can pay as little as 20 pesos for the 150-peso flamingo tour by getting a waiver at the main office in Mérida. Calle 60 299. ☎942 1900; cultur@finred.com.mx.

■**MUSEO REGIONAL DE ANTROPOLOGÍA E HISTORIA.** Mérida's most impressive museum is housed in a magnificent Italian Renaissance-style building, the **Palacio Cantón.** The collection includes Maya head-flattening devices, jade tooth inserts, sacrificial offerings recovered from the *cenote sagrado* of Chichén Itzá, and a Chichén Itzá *chac-mool*, in addition to intriguing exhibits on Mayan sciences and language, and the distinctive notions of beauty. A trip will increase your appreciation of the ruins. Most exhibits are in only Spanish. *(On the corner of Paseo Montejo and Calle 43. ☎923 0557. Open Su 8am-2pm, Tu-Sa 8am-8pm. 20 pesos; Su free.)*

PASEO DE MONTEJO. Aging French-style mansions and boutiques line the Paseo's brick sidewalks, culminating in the **Monumento a la Patria.** In faux-Maya style, the stone monument, built from 1945 to 1956, depicts major figures of Mexican history holding rifles and constitutions. On the other side of the monument, the *ceiba* (the Maya tree of life) stretches above a pool of water, enclosed by states' coats of arms. For an interesting detour from the Paseo, veer left (southwest) onto **Colón,** a street flanked by historic mansions in varying stages of decay.

CENTRO CULTURAL DE MÉRDIA OLIMPIA. A recently renovated exhibition hall with four galleries, the Centro hosts well-known artists and art from all over the world, as well as many locals. Multiple exhibits show at once and change every 3-4 months. The theater in the complex also has free performances Friday nights at 8pm. *(Calle 62 y 61, just north of the municipal building. Open Tu-Su 10am-10pm. Free.)*

MUSEO DE ARTE POPULAR. The small museum has exhibits on modern-day Maya customs and handicrafts. It shares the building with a school of design and a relaxing student lounge. *(5 blocks east of the zócalo on Calle 59 on the west side of Parque de Mejorada. Open Su 9am-2pm, Tu-Sa 8am-6pm. 10 pesos; Su free.)*

MUSEO DE LA CANCIÓN YUCATECA. A small museum that's home to song sheets, instruments, trophies, and, best of all, hall-of-fame-style portraits of the area's best singers and music makers (CDs available). The center also hosts free concerts the last two Wednesdays of every month at 9pm. The first is typical music and the second is a collage of poetry, *trova*, and Yucatec music. *(Calle 57 y 48. ☎923 7224. Open daily 9am-5pm. 15 pesos; Su free.)*

PARQUE ZOOLÓGICO DEL CENTENARIO. Inside a large park complete with rides for kids, walking paths, and food stands are captive tigers, bears, and hippos. The zoo features a large aviary with all sorts of birds and fountains that visitors can walk through, too. These and other international creatures make for a good show while wandering or while riding the miniature train that makes circuits of the park. *(On Calle 84 x 61 y 59, or at the corner of Calle 59 and Calle 86, Itzáces. Snag a bus (4 pesos) at Calle 65 x 56 and ask to be let off at "El Centenario." Park open Tu-Su 6am-6pm; zoo open Tu-Su 9am-5pm. Both free. Mini train 1 peso.)*

OTHER SIGHTS. The many churches, statues, and parks scattered throughout Mérida's *centro* invite exploration. The old **Arco,** Calle 50 x 61, is one of the three remaining arches in Mérida, built at the end of the 17th century to mark the extent of the *centro*. **Iglesia Santiago,** on Calles 59 x 72, one of the oldest churches in Mexico, is worth a visit, as is **Iglesia de San Juan de Dios,** on Calle 64 x 67 y 71, and the Franciscan **Convento de la Mejorada,** at Calle 59 x 48 y 50, which has now been turned into the department of architecture for MACAY University.

♫ ♨ ENTERTAINMENT AND NIGHTLIFE

BARS AND CLUBS

For a relaxing evening, try one of Mérida's many excellent local beers, like the distinctive **Montejo León** and the darker **Negra León,** both tough to find beyond the peninsula. Local establishments give free snacks, *bocaditas*, after the purchase of a few beers, especially if you ask. Live music and dance abound at **Pancho's,** Calle 59 509 x 60 y 62, an open-air joint frequented by European tourists, where *sombrero*-wearing hosts serve you free popcorn. (☎923 0942. Happy hour M-F 6-8pm. Live music W-Sa 9pm-1:30am. Open M-Sa 6pm-3am.) Three night spots crowd each other on Calle 60 between Calles 55 and 57: try the **Ay Caray!** disco (cover 50 pesos); salsa at the **Azul Picante Salsa Bar** (☎924 2323); or drop by **El Establo,** Calle 60 482A x 55 y 57, where young *merideños* and tourists shoot pool and dance under *sombrero* lamp shades. (☎924 2289. Cover men 40 pesos, women 30 pesos. Live music from 10:30pm.) For more traditional music, head to dark and intimate **La Trova,** on the corner of Calles 57 and 60. (☎924 9442. Live music M-Sa 9:30pm-1:15am.) Multi-colored dance clubs with A/C, such as **Mambo Café,** which plays live salsa, and the pop-heavy **Tequila Bongo** in Plaza Américas and Plaza Dorada, respectively, are far from the center and have higher cover charges; Wednesday is usually ladies' night. Taxis run 50 pesos. **Vatzya** in Hotel Fiesta Americana, Colón x Calle 60, is where the young and trendy dance. (Cover 40-50 pesos. Open W-Sa 10pm-2am.) Two bars, **Greco's** and **La Luna,** side-by-side on Avenida Canek, cater to gays and lesbians, respectively.

FESTIVALS

When in Mérida, do as *merideños* do—keep your eyes peeled for announcements of upcoming events posted around the *zócalo*, get the day-by-day monthly cultural guides from the tourism offices and check in *Yucatán Today* magazine, free in the tourist office. The Mérida municipal government provides a series of music and dance events, something to do each night for free:

Monday: Outdoor concerts with *yucateco* dancing in the Palacio Municipal (9pm).

Tuesday: 1940s-style big-band concerts in Santiago Park, Calles 59 x 72 (9pm).

Wednesday: *Miércoles de Espectáculo,* a show in the Centro Cultural on Calle 59 near Parque Centenario (9pm). Regional plays also go up in the Jardín de los Compositores near the Palacio Municipal (9pm).

Thursday: The Serenade, the most historical event in Mérida, with music, poetry, and folklore in Santa Lucía Park, Calles 60 x 55 (9pm). *Recordar es Vivir* in Parque Zoológico del Centenario (4pm).

Friday: University Serenade, in the main university building, Calles 60 x 57 (9pm). Theatrical performance at the Centro Cultural (8pm).

Saturday: *Noche Mexicana,* a night of national dance performances and arts and crafts, on Paseo Montejo between Calles 47 and 49 (7-11pm). Also "En el Corazón de Mérida," in which restaurants in the historical center move their tables into the streets under the stars. Live music, 8pm-1am.

Sunday: *Mérida en Domingo,* when art vendors, strollers, food stalls, and live music vie for space in the *zócalo* and surrounding streets (9am-9pm).

🔲 SHOPPING

Mérida offers the best shopping in the Yucatán, which is both a blessing and a curse—nagging vendors and high-pressure salespeople accompany the quality goods. The main **mercado** occupies the block southeast of the Palacio Federal, spreading outward from the corner of Calles 65 and 58. The second-floor **artisans' market,** part of the modern building behind and to the right of the Palacio Federal, sells *artesanías*, regional clothing, and the omnipresent hammock. The best hammocks are those made out of the traditional hemp-like fiber, as they last the longest and are the lightest to carry. Peruse white *huipiles* (250-350 pesos), *rebozos* (220 pesos), and *guayaberas* (150-250 pesos). Cheaper goods such as *huaraches* are sold on the first floor. Although jewelry stores line the streets, the best prices are at the smaller *prestas*, in the market, or at the *zócalo* every Sunday. All genuine silver has .925 stamped on it to verify it.

DAYTRIPS FROM MÉRIDA

DZIBILCHALTÚN

Buses leave from the Autoprogreso station (7:20, 9:20, 11:20am, 3:20pm; 7 pesos). They will drop you off at the access road to the ruins, a 5min. walk from the entrance, en route to Progreso. Return bus schedule is 1hr. later than the departure in the same place. To get back at other times, walk 5 km to the Conkal road and wait for a combi that runs between Mérida and the further villages. Autoprogreso buses and Mérida-bound combis abound on Mex. 261, passing by in both directions every 15min. They are often full, and it can take a while to get back to Mérida. Taxis charge 350 pesos for a round-trip ride and 2hr. waiting time. Site open daily 8am-5pm; museum open Tu-Su 8am-4pm. 55 pesos, children under 13 free; Su free. Parking 7 pesos.

Saying the name correctly only makes getting there that much harder. Situated 20km north of Mérida en route to the Gulf coast, Dzibilchaltún (dzi-beel-shahl-TOON; Place Where There Is Writing on Stones) sprawls over 19 sq. km of jungle brush. The site flourished as a ceremonial and administrative center, with a peak of 40,000 inhabitants at one point, from approximately 500 BC until after the arrival of the Spanish in the 1540s, making it one of the longest continuously inhabited Maya settlements. The excavated site now houses a 300m "ecological path," with nearly 100 different species of birds and labeled plants, and **El Museo del Pueblo Maya,** which displays carved columns from Dzibilchaltún and Maya ceramics. The museum is the first building to the left of the entrance. The path leading to the museum is lined with an all-star gallery of Maya stelae with original sculptures from Chichén Itzá and Uxmal.

From the museum, follow the path to *sacbé* No. 1, the central axis of the site, and turn left. At the end of this road lies Dzibilchaltún's showpiece that covers 24,300 square meters, the fully restored **Templo de las Siete Muñecas (Temple of the Seven Dolls),** from the 5th century. The seven clay "dolls" discovered in this temple are on display in the museum. Shortly after sunrise, a huge shadow mask of the rain god Chac appears when the sun's rays pierce the temple during the spring and autumn equinox. The other end of *sacbé*, No. 1 leads to a Maya temple converted into a chapel by Franciscan missionaries. Just beyond the eastern edge of the quadrangle is **Cenote Xlacah** (Old People Cenote), which served as a sacrificial well and source of water, and now also as a lily pad garden. Divers have recovered ceremonial artifacts and human bones from the depths of the 44m deep *cenote*. While the *cenote* is not the most striking, the water invites a non-sacrificial dip. A path to the south leads past several smaller structures and the site's exit.

CELESTÚN   ☎ 998

Celestún (pop. 5500) is an ideal destination with seafood restaurants by the beach, inexpensive waterfront hotels, and pervasive *tranquilidad*. Many come for the warm shallow waters and refreshing breeze, or on daytrips from Mérida to visit the town's main attraction, **Río Celestún Biosphere Reserve,** home to over 200 species of birds, including pelicans, cormorants, flamingos, and the occasional stork.

🖃 🔁 TRANSPORTATION AND PRACTICAL INFORMATION. Celestún lies 96km southwest of Mérida on the Gulf Coast. To get there by bus, go to the Noreste bus station in Mérida on Calle 67 between Calles 50 and 52. If you're driving, follow Mex. 281 into town; it becomes Calle 11, the main east-west street. Calle 11 passes the *zócalo* and hits the shore two blocks later. Odd numbers increase to the south, while even numbers increase to the west, towards the beach. The *zócalo* is bounded by Calles 11, 13, 10, and 8. **Autobuses del Occidente** sends buses from a small booth at the corner of Calles 8 and 11, at the *zócalo*, to **Mérida** (2hr., 17 per day 5am-8pm, 37 pesos).

Services include: **police,** on the Calle 13 side of the *zócalo* (☎916 2050; operator speaks English); **Farmacia Don San Luis,** Calle 10 108, between Calles 13 and 15 (☎916 2002; open daily 8am-11pm); a **health center** on Calle 5 between Calles 8 and 10 (☎916 2046; open M-Tu 8am-3:30pm, W-Su open 24hr.; no English spoken); **Telecomm,** on Calle 11 at the *zócalo* (☎916 2053; open M-F 9am-3pm); **Internet** at Hostel Ría Celestún (15 pesos per hr.) or Hotel María del Carmen. There is **no bank, no ATM,** nor any way to exchange traveler's checks, so come prepared.

ACCOMMODATIONS AND FOOD. Mexican tourists and biologists flock here in July and August; call ahead to make sure there's room. Most accommodations are on Calle 12. **Hotel San Julio ❷,** Calle 12 93A between Calles 9 and 11, faces a sand patio that opens onto the beach. The blue rooms and baths are sparse but clean. (☎916 2062. Singles 100 pesos; doubles 120 pesos, with TV 150 pesos; each additional person 20 pesos.) **Hostel Ría Celestún ❶,** Calle 12 104a x 13, has new, clean, and simple facilities with hot water, towels, kitchen, TV/VCR, hammocks, snorkel gear, and an owner who can guide you to some of the hidden beauties of the area. (☎916 2170. Dorms 60 pesos; 3-person private rooms 150 pesos.). Vacationing *merideños* love the spotless rooms with TV and fans of **Hotel Sol y Mar ❸,** on Calle 12 between Calles 11 and 13, one block from the beach. (☎916 2166. Singles and doubles 150 pesos, with A/C 250 pesos; large suites with kitchen, fridge, and A/C 350 pesos. Prices rise 20-30 percent in July and Aug.) **Hotel María del Carmen ❺,** Calle 12 111 at Calle 15, is right on the beach and has small, golden rooms with sea views, balconies, and immaculate baths. (☎916 2061. Singles and doubles 250 pesos. Each additional person 50 pesos.)

Restaurants line Calle 12 and the beach, and *loncherías* cluster in the *zócalo*. At **Restaurant la Playita ❹,** Calle 12 99, between Calles 9 and 11, flavorful plates of *jaiba frita* (fried blue crab) are 50 pesos. (☎916 2052. Open daily 9am-9pm.) **El Lobo ❸,** on the southwest corner of the *zócalo*, Calle 13 y 10, serves hot waffles (30 pesos), pancakes (25 pesos), pizza (45 pesos), and assorted *cafés*. (11 pesos. Open daily 8am-noon and 7pm-midnight.) **Pelicano's ❸,** Calle 12 90 at Calle 9, has cheap fried fish (35 pesos) and crab claws (70 pesos), but, sadly, no pelicans. (☎916 2193. Open Su-Tu and Th-Sa 11am-7pm.)

SIGHTS. Celestún's estuary is a major wintering site on the central migratory bird flyway, and boat tours allow you to explore the exotic **Ría** the birds inhabit. The best tour takes you from the beach south along the coast until you enter La Ría, where you'll wind through a river tunnel of intertwined tree branches, pass the petrified forests of **Tampetén,** and observe the abandoned village of **Real de Salinas,** with a breathtaking view of the salt fields. Heading north through La Ría, you'll reach **Isla de Pájaros** (Island of Birds), an avian playground with, depending on your luck, hundreds to thousands of flamingos. The tour ends with a visit to a cold, freshwater *cenote* where you can take a refreshing dip. If you want to see more ruins, ask your boat captain to enter the inlet at **Punta Ninum.** Riding down the inlet and walking into the jungle, you will come to **Can Balam,** an almost undiscovered site. Three main tour operators offer different packages. The co-op of fishermen on the beach at the end of Calle 11 is convenient, leaving right from the beach, and their tour allows you to travel along the shoreline before entering Ría. (3hr., 150 pesos per person with a min. of 6 people; make sure to request any of the

YUCATÁN

above sites you want to see before paying, as prices may rise.) Tours operate daily 8am-4pm. Tours given by CULTUR (the state government's tourist agency) leaves from their center on Mex. 281, 2km before the town of Celestún. They have two options: the 80min. tour costs 400 pesos for boat rental and 40 pesos per person with a max. of 6 people; the 2½hr. tour costs 800 pesos for boat plus 40 pesos per person. Tours operate daily 8am-5pm. **Celestún Expeditions,** on Calle 10 between 9 and 11, offers "Eco-tours with a difference," as well as birding, shelling, jungle walks, and anything else you could possibly dream of doing in Celestún. (☎916 2049. Open M-Sa 7am-5pm.)

If boating isn't your thing, the bike ride through the key is almost as stunning, minus flamingos. Late afternoon sun and silence makes the scenery that much better. Follow Av. al Puerto Abrigo south until you hit the entrance to the Charcas del Sal. 4km down the dirt road is Real de Salinas, an abandoned town that survived on the salt industry until the Revolution. Through the ruins and 2.8km farther down the road at Punta Lastre is a freshwater spring. On the way back, follow the trails on the west to find a private beach perfect for cooling off. A bike ride in the opposite direction, north along the shore, will take you to the tallest lighthouse on the peninsula, **Palmar Faro** (20km from the Celestún center), and to the peaceful Maya Playa. Bike rental (15 pesos per hr.) is available at Hostal Celestún, where owner Marcos will be able to guide you in the right direction if he's around. Beaches to the north are more scenic and serene than those closer to the port.

PROGRESO ☎969

Only 30km north of Mérida on the northwestern Yucatec coast, Progreso (pop. 45,000) entices weary *merideños* seeking a convenient weekend retreat. For decades the seaside city, with its 6km pier stretching indefinitely to the horizon, acted as land-locked Mérida's port, exporting Yucatec *hequén* (hemp) to the world. Today, a different kind of cargo passes through the harbor—the city plays host to a never-ending stream of cruising tourists, courting docked foreigners with fresh seafood and soothing beaches. Progreso's cool evenings, colorful vistas of sea and sky, and pervasive tranquility are a welcome break from big-city Mérida.

▐ TRANSPORTATION. Autoprogreso buses travel to Mérida's Autoprogreso station (40min., every 15min. 5:20am-10pm, 12.5 pesos). To get to the *zócalo* from the Progreso station (☎955 3024), on Calle 29 between Calles 80 and 82, walk east on Calle 29 to the end of the block, turn right and walk one block on Calle 80. To reach the beach, follow Calle 80 in the opposite direction. *Colectivos* also leave from the northern side of the *zócalo* for Merida (11 pesos) whenever they're full.

▐▐ ORIENTATION AND PRACTICAL INFORMATION. Calle 19, Progreso's brick *malecón* runs east-west along the beach. Odd-numbered roads run parallel to the *malecón*, increasing to the south. Even-numbered streets travel north-south and increase to the west. Progreso's *zócalo* is bounded by Calles 31 and 33 on the north and south, and bisected by Calle 80, the main street where banks, Internet access, and other services are located.

The helpful **tourist office** sits in the northeast corner of Progreso's pinkish **Casa de la Cultura,** north of the lighthouse on Calle 80 between Calles 25 and 27. (☎935 0104. Open M-F 8am-2pm and 4-8pm, Sa 8am-1pm.) **Banamex,** Calle 80 126, between Calles 27 and 29, has a 24hr. **ATM.** (☎935 0899. Open M-F 9am-5pm, Sa 9am-2pm.) Other services include: **laundry,** Calle 29 132, between Calles 76 and 78, with next-day service (☎935 0856; 7 pesos per kg; 3kg min.; open M-Sa 8am-6pm); the **supermarket San Francisco de Asís,** at Calle 80 144 between Calles 29 and 31 (☎955 3760; open daily 7am-9pm); **police** (☎935 0026), in the Palacio Municipal on the west side of the *zócalo;* **Farmacia Canto,** at the southwest corner of Calles 29 and 80 (☎935 1103; open daily 7am-10pm); **Centro Médico Americano,** at Calles 33 and 82 (☎935 0951; some English spoken); **Internet access** at **Inter Coffee del Sureste,** on Calle 80 between Calles 29 and 31 (☎935 0746; 12 pesos per hr.; open daily 8am-midnight); **Telecomm,** next door to the post office (open M-F 8am-6pm, Sa-Su 9am-noon); **post office,** Calle 31 150, west of Calle 78, just off the *zócalo* (☎935 0565; open M-F 8:30am-3pm). **Postal code:** 97320.

⌂⌂ ACCOMMODATIONS AND FOOD. Hotel prices in July and August tend to soar—doubling on weekends—and rooms may be hard to come by; plan ahead during the spring rush as well. All hotels listed have hot and cold water and fans. Camping on the beach, with several pay bath houses along the *malecón,* is also permitted and generally safe; think about giving the drunks who hang out under the pier a little space. Find great indoor value at **Hotel Miramar ❷,** Calle 27 124, between Calles 74 and 76, and sleep the night away in spacious, classy rooms with neat baths and skylights or four well-ventilated, fiberglass space-age rooms with escape-pod-like baths. (☎955 0542. Singles and doubles 150 pesos; doubles 200 pesos, with A/C 260 pesos. Each additional person 50 pesos.) Nearer to the beach is **Hotel Vialmar ❸,** Calle 70 121, with clean, comfortable rooms that surround a sparkling pool and upstairs rooms with balconies. (☎935 5879; hotelvialmar@yahoo.com.mx. Doubles 175, with TV 40 pesos.) **San Miguel ❸,** on Calle 78 148, before Calle 28 in a central location, offers spacious, beachy rooms with A/C. (☎935 1357. Singles 180 pesos; doubles 220 pesos. TV 20 pesos.)

The *pescado frito* signs on nearly every corner attest to Progreso's obsession with cheap seafood, from the markets on the northeast corner of Calles 29 and 80 to small *loncherías* behind the main drag. The CoMex shopping center, Calle 76 at Calle 29, hides an air-conditioned food court with affordable options from pizza to, ahem, "French" cuisine. For seafood, take a stroll down the *malecón* to **Restaurant los Cocos ❹,** between Calles 76 and 78. Fresh fish are fried to a golden brown (40 pesos); have it served to you on the beach for 5 pesos more. (Open daily 9am-7pm.) You can't see the ocean from **El Cordobés ❸,** Calle 80 150 at Calle 31, but a view of the *zócalo* accompanies solid *comida típica* (30-60 pesos). (12 pesos. ☎955 2621. Open daily 6am-midnight.) **Flamingos ❸,** on the *malecón* near Calle 72, is known for having some of the coldest beers on the beach, in addition to seafood specialties, Chinese food (45-60 pesos), cilantro or Yucatec pastas (30-40 pesos), chicken (45-60 pesos), and salads. (☎935 2122. Open daily 8am-1am.)

◐◖ SIGHTS AND BEACHES. Progreso's shallow waters, beach boardwalks, and *palapas* attract hordes of visitors in August, but remain somewhat calm the rest of the year. **Puerto de Altura** *muelle* (pier), Mexico's longest, appears to extend infinitely from the beach west of the *malecón.* Because the peninsula's limestone shelf descends so gradually into the sea, the pier had to stretch 6km to reach deep water. The beach east of the pier along the *malecón* is where the action is—prime territory for food and art vendors. To get a glimpse of the scene from above, climb the 120 steps of **El Faro,** the 19th-century lighthouse, at Calle 80 near Calle 25, between 8am and 2pm. For a more placid but perhaps less picturesque experience, try the beach at **Chelém,** 9km west of town, or the wind-sheltered beach at **Yucalpetén,** just before Chelém near the naval dock. *Combis* leave for Chelém across from the parking lot of Supermarket San Francisco on Calle 80 (every 15min. or when full, 4.5 pesos). The wider, cleaner beaches to the east of town in **Chicxulub** are lined with summer homes of Mérida's well-to-do and provide for nice walks. Near the border of Chicxulub and Telchac Puerto is a large rock formation where snorkelers can see tropical fish. Before heading to this beach, however, you owe yourself a stop at **Uaymitun Reserve,** where a three-story observation tower allows you to look out at blue-and-green marshes that are home to thousands of pink flamingos. Mornings are the best time to see the birds, but a pink line is visible across the water at any time in the day. The reserve will lend you binoculars between 8am and 6pm. To get there, take a *combi* from the northwest corner of Calles 82 and 29 to Chicxulub (3 pesos). At the *zócalo*, cross the street to continue to the observatory in another *combi* (4 pesos) and let the driver know your stop.

If sunbathing and fishing have you bored, the largely unexplored Maya city and salt distribution center of **X'cambó** lies 15km east of Uaymitun and 25km east of Progreso, at the end of a 2km access road that intersects the road to Telchac Puerto. The easiest way to get there from Progreso is by taxi (200-250 pesos round-trip); bus service only officially leaves from Mérida. The small, recently restored site consists of several structures and two pyramids—one of which supports two large, unidentified stucco masks and offers a panoramic view of the coast. A peculiar, still functioning church was built into the side of one of the pyramids 50 years ago in honor of the Virgin of X'cambó. Small paths branch from the site to unexcavated ruins and tiny villages. (Open daily 9am-5pm. 37 pesos.)

▨ LA RUTA PUUC

Dozens of exciting Maya ruins, collectively known as La Ruta Puuc, lie across the Puuc Hills between Mérida and Campeche. Between 300 BC and AD 1500, these sites, ranging from tall castles honoring the rain gods to deep caves believed to be passages to the underworld, were home to over 25,000 people. "Puuc" refers to the 7500 sq. km region as well as the earliest epoch of the Maya, and it is associated with a particular architectural style.

There are no metropolitan or resort areas in Puuc, but a few towns make good rest stops for multi-day trips. **Muna, Ticul, Oxkutzcab,** and (usually most conveniently) **Santa Elena** offer roofs and food to travelers; the most fitting place will depend on what area you are traveling to and what type of accommodations you desire. For most, 2-3 days should provide ample time for exploration. Visitors from Mérida or Campeche will take Mex. 180 to Mex. 184, which runs east and forms the northern border of much of Puuc; together with Mex. 261, it frames most of the ruins. The sites **Oxkintok** and **Las Grutas de Calcehtok,** not properly part of the Ruta, are 20km northwest of Muna and the ruins of **Mayapán** 30km northeast of Muna. **Uxmal** lies 80km south of Mérida on Mex. 261 and 16km south of Muna. Santa Elena sits 16km east of Uxmal and 8km north of **Kabah.** The Sayil-Oxkutzcab road branches to the east 5km south of Kabah, heading to **Sayil, Xlapak, Labná, Hacienda Tabi, Las Grutas de Loltún,** and ends up in Oxkutzcab, 19km east of Ticul. The four towns make a semi-square about the region: Muna is farthest northwest and closest to Oxkintok and Calcehtok; Ticul is the largest town and fairly central; Santa Elena is south-central and nearest Kabah and ruins to the south; and Oxkutzcab is in the southeast, at the end of the Ruta as you drive east from Mérida/Campeche.

Because of the number of sites (and the relatively small size of some) scattered in the area, renting a car in Mérida is the easiest and most flexible way to see what you came for. The roads are generally good and will bring you through jungle and indigenous villages on your way between sights. Travel agencies in both Mérida and Campeche offer organized tours, which are frequently whirlwind affairs. **Autotransportes del Sur** sends a "Ruta Puuc" bus from Mérida at 8am that will whisk you through Kabah, Sayil, Xlapac, Labná, and Uxmal—with enough time left over to return by 4pm. The bus spends 30min. at the sites and 2hr. at Uxmal (87 pesos; admission to sites not included). No other buses travel the Sayil-Oxkutzkub road. Unorganized public transportation is definitely the most difficult and will undoubtedly lead to frustrating waits. Buses are most frequent in mornings, but return trips are never guaranteed. 2nd-class buses do travel Mex. 261 frequently and will stop when requested. *Combis* run frequently between Oxkutzcab, Ticul, Santa Elena, and Muna—and will make almost any trip if paid enough. To pursue this option, it is best, though not easy, to catch *combis* from the *zócalo* in Muna.

THE SIGHTS

OXKINTOK

By car, follow the signs for Oxkintok as you approach Maxcanú from the east. Bits of the road are unpaved. Open daily in summer 9am-6pm, in winter 8am-5pm. 28 pesos.

Oxkintok lies 42km northwest of Uxmal, on the west end of the rolling Puuc hills. The three large sets of restored ruins date approximately from the Classic Period (AD 300-1050) and show the rounded Puuc architectural style. By car, Oxkintok merits a visit: it is well maintained and the faded orange structures, standing out against a lonely green backdrop and rolling hills (some are as-yet-unrestored pyramids), create a beautiful and still untouristed setting. Views are best atop the **Ah-May Pyramid,** the tallest structure at 25m, and the **Ah-Canul Palace;** for a very different experience, take a flashlight to explore the three-story **Laberinto** (Labyrinth), in which a tomb was found. Workers can take you through the narrow corridors and 16 subterranean rows, perhaps once a prison or training camp for *sacerdotes*.

LAS GRUTAS DE CALCEHTOK

Follow the signs marked "Grutas" on approach to Oxkintok; the caves are 2km southwest of the ruins. One family from the ejido mans the entrance and will take you on a 2-3 hr. tour through the caves for 15-20 pesos per person. There's no fee without the tour, but you should be careful about going in alone. Bring bug repellent and a flashlight.

From above, the cavern looks like it opens into a jungle, with a tropical ecosystem maintained by honeybees, parrots, and leafy plants that fill the oasis. Once you descend the ladder, however, it soon becomes clear that you have entered an underground mystery, as light and life peter out together. The extremely knowledgeable guide will take you deep inside the 2km long pitch-black caverns, his lamps illuminating thousands of stalactites, stalagmites, and comically-shaped rock formations—the head of Frankenstein, a crocodile, etc.—on the way to Maya ritual and sacrificial grounds used 2000 years ago. During the Caste War 150 years ago, a group of 60 Maya survived for months in the permanent darkness of the *grutas* while the Spanish Army lay in wait outside.

■ UXMAL

Uxmal sits just off Mex. 261. Autotransportes del Sur runs the 1½hr. route from Mérida for 43 pesos; the "Ruta Puuc" bus also stops here. From Campeche, take a Camioneros de Campeche bus to Mérida (3hr., 5 per day, 55 pesos) and ask to be dropped at the ruins' access road. Return buses dry up after 8pm. Site open daily 8am-5pm; light and sound show 7pm in winter, 8pm in summer. 87 pesos including show; show alone 30 pesos; Su 37 pesos. Parking 10 pesos. Guides 350 pesos for 1-20 people. Free luggage storage.

Uxmal will impress, if not astonish, with enormous palaces, numerous legends, and breathtaking architecture. Meaning either "thrice built" or "region of fruitful harvests," Uxmal had two major developmental periods over a tumultuous 2000-year history (800 BC to AD 1200). Construction of hydraulic projects, such as cisterns and mini-reservoirs, during the village stage permitted urbanization, as the city peaked at 25,000 inhabitants and dominated southwestern Yucatán, from AD 700-1000. Although it was subordinate to Mayapán and Chichén Itzá in the Mayapán League, Uxmal was the largest of the Puuc sites and exercised control over nearby Kabah, Sayil, and Labná. Neighboring Xius brought the cult of Quetzcóatl in the 10th century and merchants became the city's new rulers. In the 12th century, many inhabitants fled conflict with Mayapán, moving to nearby Maní. Two principal documents record this history: the sacred Chilam Balam, a chronicle from after the Spanish Conquest, confirms the account of the Spanish Friar Alonso Ponce, who based his *"Relación"* on an encounter with a local Maya in 1586. Despite painstaking restoration, the immense totality that once dominated the hills has yet to be fully realized. Travelers can venture into the surrounding jungle to see many as-yet-unexcavated structures.

CHULTUNE. This cistern, used to collect water for the city, immediately greets the visitor. Many Maya sites depended on *cenotes* for collecting water, but the normally dry plan around Uxmal (and other Puuc sites) forced residents to use such *aguadas*, limestone-lined depressions in the earth that serve as reservoirs.

PYRAMID OF THE MAGICIAN. According to legend, the 35m pyramid was built overnight by a dwarf who hatched from a witch's egg and grew to maturity in a year. The king challenged the dwarf to build the structure overnight, angry that the dwarf had defeated him in other feats. The dwarf completed the task and was deemed magician of the land. The pyramid was really probably built in five stages from AD 600-1000. Multiple stages of construction are apparent in the mix of stonework used and the differences among successive levels. The pyramid's round shape is unique both at Uxmal and among other sites. Two long-nosed masks on either side of the western staircase represent Chac, the rain god.

QUADRANGLE OF THE BIRDS. Immediately west of the pyramid lies the Quadrangle, named for the bird sculptures adorning the structures on its western side and the palm leaves, or feathers, that skirt the roof. Buildings enclose the north and south sides as well; all center on an altar or patio whose use is not known.

QUADRANGLE OF THE NUNS. Continuing to the west is a large quadrangle—Uxmal's famed nunnery, which dates from AD 900-1000 and was misnamed by the Spanish who thought its many rooms resembled a convent. The four buildings were built on different levels, and each has a distinctive decor. Masks of the trunk-nosed rain god Chac adorn the northern building; the eastern building has intricate lattice work and Venus symbols, with snake heads at each end; the southern building contains a series of hut sculptures, thought to represent temples as they were created at the dawn of the civilization; and the western building shows kings and bound prisoners in high relief plus serpents perhaps related to the Toltec deity Quetzalcóatl. To the south lies the 34m-long **ball court.** Only the western glyph-engraved stone ring remains. Well-padded players once played *pelota* with a hardened rubber ball. The game was part of a ritual for fertility and cosmic stability, which sometimes involved human sacrifice. The court runs from north to south. The eastern side represents good and light; the western side, evil and darkness.

CEMETERY GROUP. Emerging from the ball court, a narrow path leads to the Cemetery Group, a small, leafy plaza bounded by a pyramid to the north and a temple to the west. Stones that were once platforms at the foot of the pyramid bear haunting reliefs of skulls. To the west, the **Pigeon House,** typical of older constructions with a plain facade and cornice, has three doors leading to the central patio.

PALACIO DEL GOBERNADOR (GOVERNOR'S PALACE). From the ball court, head south up the escarpment to this enormous palace. Replete with strikingly well preserved engravings and arches, it was one of the last buildings constructed, probably around AD 1000; the attention to detail has led many to consider it Uxmal's finest example of architecture. Intertwined serpents cover much of the frieze, which lies between diagonally-placed Chac masks that create their own serpintine illusions. The center features a sovereign, perhaps a former resident of this prominent Puuc building, majestically seated in a throne.

CASA DE LAS TORTUGAS (HOUSE OF THE TURTLES). The outwardly simple two-story house is on the northwest corner of the escarpment. Realistic, sculpted turtles adorn the upper frieze; they may have symbolized rain.

GREAT PYRAMID. Also known as "The Dwarf's House," this reconstructed pyramid consists of nine square levels (standard shapes, in contrast to the dwarf's pyramid), stretching 80m long and 30m high. In the legend, the spiteful ruler tried to undermine the taller but less traditional dwarf-magician's pyramid by complaining that its base was neither square nor rectangular but oval. The only solution was clearly that he and the dwarf settle their quarrel by seeing who could break a *cocoyol* (a small, hard-shelled fruit) on his own head. The dwarf-magician handily slipped a turtle shell into his skull and easily cracked the *cocoyol*, while the unfortunate governor crushed his own unaltered skull. Atop the pyramid sits the **Macaw Temple**, with many engravings of the bird on its facade. Inside is a Chac-motif throne. The masks and artwork of this building represent the 8th-century Codz-Poop ("rolled-up mat") style, with a more rounded look than other art in Uxmal.

THE DOVE COTS. Built with a design similar to the nunnery, the northern and southern temples are the only ones now standing. The name derives from a series of roof-combs, which look like nesting sites, in the northern building. The protruding stones once supported stucco and stone figures now guarded in museums.

CASA DE LA VIEJA. From the entrance, follow the trail south to five buildings surrounding a patio. Among these is the Casa, one of the oldest constructions in Uxmal, dating from AD 670-770. It supposedly belonged to the witch who birthed the famed dwarf. 500m further south is **El Templo de los Falos** (the Temple of the Phalli), where phallic structures symbolizing earthly and human fertility once adorned the top of the small structure. Phallic imagery is uncommon to other Maya art and its frequent presence in Uxmal suggests outside influence.

KABAH

23km southeast of Uxmal, Kabah is bisected by Mex. 261 and is easily reachable by any 2nd-class bus running between Mérida and Campeche. Buses only stop if you approach the driver beforehand, or if he sees a person wildly gesticulating on the side of the highway. Travel is easier with the "Ruta Puuc" bus. Open daily 8am-5pm. 28 pesos; Su free.

Once the second-largest city in the northern Yucatán, **Kabah** (Sir of the Mighty Hand) was built with the blood and sweat of many slaves. The site's highlight is the visual feast of the ▧**Codz Poop Temple** (Wall of Masks), the single most psychedelic piece of architecture on the Yucatán Peninsula. Close to 300 three-eyed faces (in varying conditions) of the rain god, Chac, protrude from the facade of the temple, staring, laughing, screaming, or grinning, depending on your state of mind. Unlike structures of pure Puuc style, characterized by plain columns and a superior decorative frieze, Codz Poop is covered with ornamental stone carvings of Chac from top to bottom, resembling more the Chenes style; Chac's prominence relates to the importance of rain for the inhabitants of Kabah, where no rain falls for half the year. Behind the temple are two impressive statues, still tall and proud, if overshadowed. Continue east and you will come across the two-story **Palacio;** 200m along a path to the left will take you to **Las Columnas.** The site is thought to have served as a court where justices settled disputes and gods comprised the jury. Across the street by the parking lot, a short dirt road leads to rubble (right), more rubble (left), and the famous **Kabah Arch** (straight). The arch marks the beginning of the ancient *sacbé* that ended with a twin arch in Uxmal. The archway's perfect alignment with the north-south line testifies to the Maya's astronomical skill.

SAYIL

Sayil lies 5km off Mex. 261 on the Sayil-Oxkutzcab road, a stop on the "Ruta Puuc" bus. Buses between Mérida and Campeche pass by the crucero 5km from the site hourly. Site open daily 8am-5pm. 28 pesos.

The **Palace of Sayil** stands out among the region's ruins as one of the only asymmetrical buildings. The unique, three-story structure was constructed from AD 800 to 1000. It harbors 90 rooms, which served as storage, administrative space, and housing for 350 people; in the foundation are eight underground cisterns. The *sacbé* across from the Palace leads to **El Mirador**, a lofty pyramidal temple topped by a peculiar roof-comb, typical of early Puuc architecture, but now lacking decorative elements once present. To the left a 100m path leads through the jungle to the **Estela del Falo** (Stela of the Phallus), a tribute to Yum Keep, a Maya god of fertility. The peaceful feminine figure with the large manhood is worth a look. Among the buildings lying in pieces is **El Templo de las Cabezas** (The Temple of Heads/Masks), across the street and up a dirt path. The masks may be scarce, but the steep, difficult hike leads to a splendid view of Sayil's palace.

XLAPAC

The "Ruta Puuc" bus stops here for 20min at 10:30am. To stay longer, hire a combi in nearby Oxkutzcab. Site open daily 8am-5pm. 23 pesos.

Xlapac ("Old Wall") lies between Labná and Sayil. The classic Puuc **El Palacio,** with plain walls and doorways below an ornate frieze of stone mosaics, pays homage to Chac with its impressive triple-decker masks of the rain god. Little else is put together, so there's not much to command attention.

LABNÁ

Labná lies 17km east of Mex. 261. No buses make the trip past Labná. The "Ruta Puuc" bus that stops 10am-10:30am or a private car is the best way to get here. Open daily 8am-5pm. 28 pesos.

Labná was constructed toward the end of the Late Classic period (AD 700-1000), when the Puuc cities were connected by *sacbé* (paved, elevated roads). A short, reconstructed section of the *sacbé* runs between Labná's two most impressive sights: the palace and the stone arch. On the northern side, to the left as you enter the site, stretches the not-fully-restored **palace,** built in 12 stages; its 67 rooms, seven patios, and two levels lack architectural unity. What Labná is famous for, though, is the picturesque **Arch of Labná,** 3m wide and 5m high. Archaeologists believe that the arch could have served as a ceremonial entry point for victorious returning warriors, as a vaulted passageway linking two ceremonial patios, or as an entrance for the upper class into the ceremonial area and common ground. The lattice designs and detail are in the late Puuc style. Beyond the arch, atop a rocky pyramid, stands the observatory, **El Mirador.** The roof-comb of El Mirador was once magnificently decorated with stucco-modeled figurines, typical of early Puuc. Back toward the palace, **El Templo de las Columnas** is off the *sacbé* to the right. The smooth, tiny columns on the upper face, the middle layer, and the molding are great examples of the Puuc Junquillo style from AD 800-1000.

HACIENDA TABI

The Hacienda is accessible only with a reliable car. On the Sayil-Oxkutzcab road, take the road that branches off south of the Grutas de Loltún. Follow the signs. The dirt access road to the Hacienda goes straight (4km to the site) when the main road veers right. Open daily 9am-5pm. 15 pesos. If you want more than sightseeing, the Hacienda functions as a bed and breakfast and has camping space as well, by reservation. (☎923 9454 or 996

8283; gabiort@hotmail.com. 540 pesos for 2 people includes room, breakfast and dinner; inquire for camping prices.)

The Hacienda stands as a monument to another part of Mexico's history, giving a glimpse of early Spanish architecture and, through the museum, the colonial social system; the museum addresses the theme of the area with a look at the Maya in colonial Mexico. Spanish families lived on the land as early as 1569, but Maya ruins go back much further. By 1900 the *hacienda* was a sugar-producing facility; a fire and turnover in ownership changed the make-up of the Hacienda, but visitors today can still see machinery, remnants of a church, and the most impressive sight, the beautiful **Casa Principal,** which greets you inside the gates. Large fields make for a nice place to picnic.

GRUTAS DE LOLTÚN

Snag a combi to Oxkutzcab from Calle 25A between Calles 24 and 26 in Ticul (every 10min., 7 pesos); you'll be let off at the intersection of Calles 23 and 26. Combis and colectivos leave for Loltún across from Oxkutzcab's market, 20 de Noviembre. Ask to be dropped at the caves (10min., 5 pesos). Entrance with tours only. Tours daily 9:30, 11am, 12:30, 2, 3, 4pm; available in both Spanish and English. 48 pesos does not include guides, who will ask for tips. Parking 10 pesos.

Winding through the rock, the Grutas de Loltún comprise what is believed to be the largest cave system in Yucatán state, though it has yet to be fully explored. "*Loltún*" means "stone flower" in Maya, and the fascinating, natural formations in the caves warrant the name. Additionally, the enormous caverns hold the earliest evidence of humans in the entire Yucatán, as well as fossils of extinct mastodons and saber-toothed tigers from the Ice Ages. Around 2000 BC, the ancient Maya settled here to take advantage of the caves' water and clay. Thousands of years later, Maya *campesinos* returned seeking refuge from the Caste War (1847-48). Important caverns include the **Galería de las Manos Negras** (alternatively "Room of Inscriptions"), full of handprint murals; the **Na Cab** (House of the Bees), named for the many niches in the cavern wall that host beehives; the **Gallery of Fallen Rocks,** created by ancient meteorites; and the Maya Gallery with an Olmec-sculpture known as "La Cabeza de Loltún," most likely acquired through trade. Several caves contain hollow stalactites and columns—strike each one with the heel of your hand and listen as a soft booming sound *("loltún...loltún...")* reverberates throughout the caves. Archaeologists speculate that the Maya used these formations as a means of underground communication.

MAYAPÁN

Mayapán is 39km southeast of Mérida on Mex. 18 and 6km northwest of Tekit on the same road. It's the only site north of Mex. 184 and is not officially part of the Ruta Puuc; Ticul is the nearest base, a 1hr. drive away. Combis make the trip between Mérida and Tekit. Colectivos leave from Mérida every 30 min. (15 pesos); 13-peso buses leave from the station regularly too. Open daily 8am-5pm. 23 pesos.

The ruins of Mayapán do not fully capture its impressive history, but the paintings make it worth the trip. From AD 1000 to 1200, the city was dominated by Chichén Itzá, which controlled the Mayapán League. After AD 1200, the 12,000 people of Mayapán overthrew Chichén Itzá and came to control the league. Destruction came to the 4 sq. km city in 1441, when Ah Xupan of Uxmal rebelled against the Cocom dynasty in a fight to retrieve his daughter, a princess the prince of Chichén Itzá had captured; many, like those at Uxmal before, fled to nearby Maní. Restoration began in 1948 and, particularly since 1995, has produced several impressive structures, reminiscent of Chichén Itzá. The principal pyramid is the **Pyramid of Kukulcán,** a smaller version of Chichén Itzá's Pyramid, with square lines and little

YUCATÁN

detail. The peak affords a view of the rest of the compact site. To the west are the 3 stucco models with painted warriors; the round shape of the **Templo Redondo** stands out. **El Templo de Pescadores** has nicely preserved murals and within the site are 32 *cenotes*, one of which is near the **Caracol.**

THE TOWNS

Uxmal is the only site with accommodations and food readily available—and those rooms that are convenient all belong to luxurious, multi-star hotels. However, 5km north of the ruins on Mex. 261 are the pink rooms and clean bathrooms of **Rancho Uxmal ❸** (singles and doubles 250 pesos, each additional person 50 pesos) and the attached, *palapa*-covered **restaurant/bar ❹**, serving breakfast (30-50 pesos) and Yucatec favorites. (40-65 pesos. ☎977 6254 or 977 5621. Open daily 7:30am-8pm.) Across from the ranch is **Cha Ka Nah Restaurant ❹**, with generally the same menu and a sparkling pool. At the ruins, **Restaurant Yax-beh ❹**, with A/C, makes sandwiches (35-45 pesos) and *comida típica*. (48-65 pesos. Open daily 8am-8pm.) Nearby Santa Elena, Muna, Ticul, and Oxkutzcab offer cheaper digs and are better bases for exploring other sites.

MUNA   ☎997

A mere 15km northeast of Uxmal, Muna (pop. 3500) is the best place for getting an early start at the ruins. It is a new stop for tourists, with **Internet access**, a *zócalo* with *loncherías* and many **combis** (6 pesos to Uxmal), a **Copercaja currency exchange** booth, and basic services. Only 25km from Ticul and close to the Mérida highway, Muna is a convenient spot for most sights within the Puuc boundaries. It even has a 17th-century church and ex-convent for those who haven't gotten their sightseeing fix at the ruins. The one and only **Hotel GL ❷**, Calle 26 200, is right before the *zócalo*, just off the highway as you approach from Uxmal. This brand new, simple inn allows you to park outside your room, take a hot shower, sleep under a fan, and be on your way. (☎991 0097. 120 pesos for a double bed, 240 for two double beds and hammock space.)

TICUL   ☎997

Ticul (pop. 35,000) is a convenient and inexpensive base for exploring the Puuc sites of Uxmal, Kabah, Sayil, Xlapak, and Labná, as well as the Grutas de Loltún and the ruins of Mayapán. For those with wheels, a number of *cenotes* and colonial buildings await exploration in the nearby towns of **Teabo**, 30km southeast, and **Holcá**, 105km to the northeast. **Maní**, 15km east of Ticul, features a colonial monastery; **Tekax**, 35km to the southeast, a hermitage; and **Tipikal**, an impressive colonial church. Ticul is home to the 17th-century **Templo de San Antonio** (open daily 8am-6pm) and hosts a **Tobacco Fair** starting in early April. Celebrations commemorating the town's founding run July 17-27.

🖪 TRANSPORTATION. Ticul's **bus station** (☎972 0162) is on Calle 27 x 22 y 24, behind the church. Buses go to **Mérida** (every hr., 35 pesos). *Combis* leave from in front of Hotel San Miguel for **Muna** (9 pesos); **Santa Elena, Uxmal,** and **Kabah** (11 pesos) from Calle 30, between Calles 25 and 25A; and for **Oxkutzcab** from Calle 25A, between Calles 24 and 26 (every 15min., 8 pesos).

🖪🔋 ORIENTATION AND PRACTICAL INFORMATION. The main road, **Calle 23,** runs east-west with all odd-numbered streets, increasing to the south. Even-numbered streets run north-south, increasing to the west. The *zócalo* is east of **Calle 26;** most activity is between the *zócalo* and Calle 30, three blocks west.

Nearby, on **Calle 25,** a strip of Maya statuettes pay tribute to ancient gods. **Currency exchange** is available at **Bital,** Calle 23 195, on the northeast corner of the *zócalo,* as is a 24hr. **ATM.** (☎972 0006. Open M-Sa 8am-7pm.) Other services include: **police,** on Calle 23, at the northeast corner of the *zócalo* (☎972 0210; no English spoken); **Farmacia Canto,** Calle 23 202, at Calle 26 (☎972 0581; open Su 8am-1pm and 5-9pm, M-Sa 8am-10pm); **Centro de Salud,** Calle 27 226, between Calles 30 and 32 (☎972 0086; no English spoken); **Telecomm,** Calle 24A between Calles 21 and 23, northeast of the *zócalo* (☎972 0146; open M-F 9am-3pm, Sa 9am-1pm); **Internet Cafe Flashnet** on the east end of the *zócalo* (☎972 1508; 10 pesos per hr.; open 8am-2am); a **market,** off Calle 23, between Calles 28 and 30, with food stands, produce, and more (open daily 6am-2pm); **Super Solomon,** across from the market, for groceries (open daily 8am-2:30pm and 6pm-10pm); **post office,** in Palacio Municipal, on the northeast side of the *zócalo.* (☎972 0040. Open M-F 8am-2pm.) **Postal code:** 97860.

▎◖ ACCOMMODATIONS AND FOOD. Hotel Sierra Sosa ❷, on Calle 26, near the northwest corner of the *zócalo,* has firm beds, clean baths, strong fans, and TV. (☎972 0008. 1-2 people 120 pesos; doubles with two beds 150 pesos. Each additional person 25 pesos. A/C 45 pesos.) **Hotel San Miguel ❷,** on Calle 28 half a block north of Calle 23, is inexpensive and it shows. The rooms are not dirty, just worn. (☎972 0382. Singles 100 pesos; doubles 150 pesos, 180 pesos for 2 beds.) **Hotel San Antonio ❸,** Calle 25A 220 x 26 y 26A, is surprisingly affordable for all that it offers: phone, TV, and A/C in clean rooms and a great location off the park. (☎927 1893 or 927 1894. Singles 175 pesos; doubles 234; up to 4 people 292.5 pesos.) After a hot day on the Ruta Puuc, Ticul is the place to refuel and rehydrate. **Loncherías ❶,** along Calles 23 between Calles 26 and 30, serve the town's cheapest food; the old train station on Calle 25 x 22 is also always open for cheap eats. **Los Almendros ❹,** right off the Ticul-Chetumal highway, now offers a refreshing pool in addition to its famous food, such as *poc-chuc* (pork cooked with onions, beans, tomatoes, and dangerous habañero peppers; 46 pesos) and *pollo pibil* for 43 pesos. (☎972 0021. Open daily 9am-9pm.) **Restaurant Los Delfines ❹,** Calle 27 x 28 y 30, serves shrimp dishes, *chiles rellenos* (48 pesos), and welcome jars of lemonade. (☎972 0401. Open daily 11am-7pm.) **Pizzeria la Gondola ❸** is a taste of Italy in the heart of the Yucatán. Spaghetti is 28 pesos, pizza 50 pesos. (☎972 0112. Free delivery. Open daily 8am-1pm and 5:30pm-midnight.)

OXKUTZCAB   ☎997

Oxkutzcab (pop. 30,000) lies farthest east along the Ruta. It is closest to the Grutas de Loltún and, because tourists have not yet discovered it, you may get more for your money. Known as the "orchard of the state," the central market overflows with fruits and vegetables; climb the hill on Calle 54 to the Santa Isabel Church for a look at the entire city, called the second most beautiful in the state; or stop by the old railroad station, now a *casa de cultura.* The sights and activities are a nice complement to the basic services a traveler would want in a stopover town.

▐ TRANSPORTATION. The **Mayab bus station** is on Calle 51, 2 blocks from the center x Calle 54 y 56. Buses go to **Chetumal** (8 per day, 117 pesos); **Cancún, Playa del Carmen, Tulum** (8 per day; 160, 134, 112 pesos respectively); **Campeche** (6pm, 75 pesos); **Mérida, Muna,** and **Ticul** (19 per day 6:45am-7:35pm; 38, 15, 6 pesos). *Combis* leave across from the market for the **Grutas de Loltún** (8 pesos).

▊ PRACTICAL INFORMATION. Farmacia María del Carmen, Calle 51 106 x 52 (☎975 0165), is open 7am-11pm; **Hospital IMSS,** Calle 64 x 49 y 51, has 24hr. emergency service. **Police** (☎975 0615). **Internet access** is available at **Interc@fe,** Calle 52

YUCATÁN

101 x 53. (Open 8:30am-10:30pm; 15 pesos per hr.) **Telecomm** offers **fax** from the municipal building. (Open M-F 9am-3pm, Sa 9am-noon.) **Banamex,** Calle 50 x 51 y 53, has 24hr. **ATM.** The **post office** is on Calle 48 x 53 y 55.

⌐ ACCOMMODATIONS. Easy parking at the places listed below relieves the primary burden of traveling with a car. All are within walking distance of public transportation. **Hotel Puuc ❹,** Calle 55 80 x 44 (☎975 0103), 5 blocks from the center on the *combi* route to Loltún, offers everything a luxury hotel would, including A/C and shampoo packets, for a humble price of 200 pesos per room; triples 300 pesos. **Hotel Rosalía ❶,** Calle 54 101 x 51 y 53, is the favorite among traveling vendors because of its comfort and value. Well-kept rooms with TV, fan, and private baths are 50m from the bus station and 100m from the *centro*. (☎975 0167. 90 pesos for one bed; 120 pesos for 2 beds. Each additional person 10 pesos. 180 pesos with A/C.) **Hospedaje Dorán ❶,** is marginally cheaper and far less appealing. (☎977 7714. Singles and doubles 80 pesos; 90 pesos for 2 beds. 10 pesos for TV.)

SANTA ELENA   ☎999

This tiny town of 4000 Maya residents has the basics and then some, with a park, an 18th-century church (once the site of a Maya pyramid) that affords magnificent views from its roof (ask the sacristan the way up; open Su-F 3-6pm), and, next to the church, a small museum that showcases mummies, recently unearthed from beneath the church. (Open daily 8am-6pm.) Its late-era ruins at the site of **Mulchic,** however, have not been reconstructed; the 2km trail from Mex. 261, 700m toward Mérida, is more worthwhile than neglected ruins amidst such splendor. Basics include **police** (☎992 1015), at the north end of the *zócalo*, and the **Farmacia Mirna** (☎991 7920), one block west of the *zócalo* on Calle 20 (open daily 8am-10pm); find Dr. Luis Sansores Mian next door at **Consultorio Médico** (☎991 7920).

E TRANSPORTATION. Buses bound for Campeche from Mérida pass town on Mex. 261 (7:30, 10:30am, 1:30, 6:30pm), as do buses headed the opposite way (7 per day 6am-8pm). The "Ruta Puuc" bus stops at 9:30am along the highway. It proceeds to Uxmal, but you'll need a lift or a *combi* to return to Santa Elena. To reach **Grutas de Loltún,** hop on the 7:30am bus bound for Oxkutzcab, then take a *colectivo* or 8-peso *combi* to Ticul, and another from there to Loltún.

⌐◻ ACCOMMODATIONS AND FOOD. Three accommodations lie along Mex. 261 sufficiently far from the small *centro* to feel secluded in any of them. ◪**Sacbé Camping-Bungalows ❶,** km 127, offers weary travelers several options for the night. The cheapest is to stay on the pristine campgrounds with solar-heated showers and toilet facilities, outdoor grills, and a mosquito-netted thatched hut where the owners serve good meals. The new hostel is complete with a kitchen and screened-in rooms; for more privacy, stay in the small, furnished bungalows with hot water, fans, and clean baths that vary in size and price. (☎985 858 1281; sacbebungalow@hotmail.com. Breakfast 26 pesos; dinner 40 pesos, 32 for vegetarians. Campsite and hammock space 30 pesos per person; hostel 60 pesos; bungalows 160-190 pesos for 2 people, each additional person 30 pesos.) ◪**The Flycatcher Bed and Breakfast ❺** is perfect for escape and relaxation, 100m off Mex. 261. Four spacious rooms, adorned with local crafts and cast-iron work and with 2 double beds each, are set in a beautiful orchard and come with fresh homemade breakfasts. (www.mexonline.com/flycatcherinn.htm. 300 pesos per room.) Across the road and only 150m farther from Uxmal lies **Hotel/Restaurant El Chac-Mool ❶,** with available hammock space in private *cabañas* (50 pesos) and four single rooms with clean, private baths and fans. (Rooms 150 pesos, 200 pesos in high season.) The adjacent **restaurant ❸** is the best (and one of the only) in town. It serves up large helpings of eggs, tacos, chicken, sandwiches, and veggies options for 35-45 pesos.

(☎996 2025. Open daily 10am-9pm.) **La Central,** off the *zócalo*, is a newer option (run by a family that used to cook for luxury hotels), with traditional Yuctec food at affordable prices. (☎996 8511. Open until 8pm.)

IZAMAL ☎988

Izamal ("dew that falls from heaven" in Maya) has given itself nicknames for every one of its characteristics, perhaps to test which attracts the most tourists. The name "City of the Hills" refers to the town's many Maya pyramids, remnants of the time Izamal (pop. 23,000) was the principal religious center of the Yucatec Maya. It is also known as *"La Ciudad Amarilla"*: Izamal's main buildings and world-famous convent are now all painted a rich egg-yolky yellow with white trim. And, as the name *"La Ciudad de las Tres Culturas"* suggests, Izamal harmoniously blends Maya pyramids, Spanish architecture, and *mestizo* character. The city's tranquility is broken only by the occasional school-produced *ballet folklórico*, the clattering of *calesas victorianas* or *calandrias* (horse-drawn carriages), and the whoops of children playing in the street. *Domingos Culturales* (Cultural Sundays) are a good time to meander through the central park to listen to traditional music, enjoy Yucatecan foods, and see the unique local *artesanías*.

▐ TRANSPORTATION. The **bus station** (☎954 0107) is between Calles 31 and 33 on Calle 32, behind the municipal palace. **Oriente** and **Autocentro** buses leave from the terminal for: **Cancún** (5½hr., 13 per day, 91 pesos); **Valladolid** (2hr., 13 per day, 33 pesos); **Mérida** (1½hr., every 30min. 5:30am-2am, 27 pesos). There are no car taxis—going by horse-drawn carriage is the only option.

▐▐ ORIENTATION AND PRACTICAL INFORMATION. The road from Hoctún, 24km to the southwest, becomes Calle 31, which runs east-west as all good odd-numbered streets do, increasing to the south. Calle 31 runs past the Convent (on the right going east), passing north-south streets with decreasing even numbers. Calles 28, 31, 32, and 33 frame the town's *zócalo*, municipal palace, and market.

For **tourist information,** head to the main office of the Palacio Municipal, just west of the *zócalo*. (☎954 0241, ext 14. Open daily 8am-3pm and 5-8pm.) Or direct your questions to any of the **Policía Turística** in brown-and-cream-colored uniforms patrolling the *zócalo* (8am-6pm). **BanNorte,** on the corner of Calles 31 and 28, just north of the Convent, exchanges currency and has a 24hr. **ATM.** (☎954 0425. Open M-F 9am-3pm.) Other services include: **police** (☎954 0009), across from the bus station in the Palacio Municipal; **market,** on the corner of Calles 30 and 33; **Farmacia Itzalana,** on the corner of Calles 31 and 32 (☎954 0032; open 24hr., knock if closed); **IMSS** (☎954 0241), two blocks south and three blocks east of the *zócalo* at the corner of Calles 37 and 24; **Telecomm,** on the corner of Calles 31A and 32, behind the Palacio Municipal, with **Internet** access (☎954 0263; Internet 15 pesos per hr.; open M-F 9am-3pm); **LADATEL,** in the **post office,** on the corner of Calles 31 and 30A (☎954 0390; open M-F 8am-3pm). **Postal code:** 97540.

▐▐ ACCOMMODATIONS AND FOOD. For a chance to stay inside one of the colonial homes, walk north on Calle 30. Right before the corner at Calle 27 is **Posada Flory ❸,** where the warm *señora* will welcome you into one of the 10 rooms she has uniquely decorated. All rooms have TV, private bath with hot water, fans, and optional A/C. Guests are welcome to use her kitchen and purified water or hang out in the living room under the 6m high ceiling. (☎954 0562. 150-250 pesos per room.) The most relaxing accommodations in the city are at beautiful **Macan Ché Bed and Breakfast ❺,** Calle 22 305, between Calles 33 and 35, southeast of the *zócalo*. To get there, take one of the carriages waiting on the north side of the Convent (5-10 min., 10 pesos). Twelve suites with outdoor porch, fans, and *agua puri-*

ficada nestle within a wonderful garden in front of a pool. Sleep well and wake up to a large and delicious freshly-made breakfast on a *palapa*-covered patio. (☎954 0287; www.macanche.com. Suite with breakfast 250-300 pesos.) For cheaper and far inferior rooms, look to **Hotel Canto ❷**, Calle 31 303, on the northern edge of the *zócalo*. The hotel has somewhat run-down rooms, with baths and bugs. (Singles and doubles 100 pesos; up to 3 people 120 pesos.)

Don't plan on late-night wining and dining in the Yellow City; most restaurants close by early evening. Locally lauded **Restaurant Kinich-Kakmó ❹**, Calle 27 299, between Calles 28 and 30, makes regional dishes such as *pierna asada a la yucateca, escaseche oriental,* and *poc-chuc kinich kalemó* (60 pesos each) under a plant-heavy *palapa* as well as the vegetarian *papadul* (squash salsa inside rolled tortillas with a hard-boiled egg and tomato sauce on top. (35 pesos. ☎954 0489. Open daily 11:30am-5:30pm.) The tranquil **El Toro ❸**, on Calle 33 between Calles 30 and 32, overlooks the Convent and cooks up delicious beef filet *a la tampiqueña* (60 pesos) with freshly-made corn tortillas and big glasses of *agua de horchata* or lemonade (8 pesos). Also available are breakfast (20-pesos), sandwiches (28 pesos), and burritos (28 pesos. ☎967 0549. Open daily 9am-11pm.) **Los Portales ❷**, on the corner of Calles 30 and 31A next to the market, has the best view of the *zócalo* and cheap, filling meals. They will put together any of the traditional ingredients on site if you don't see what you want. (☎954 0302. Full breakfasts 26 pesos and lunch special 35 pesos. Open daily 7am-8:30pm.)

◙ **SIGHTS.** The huge—and incredibly yellow—**Convento de San Antonio de Padua** consists of three main parts: the **church**, built in 1554; the **convent**, built in 1561; and the **atrium**, built in 1618 with 75 arches and second in size only to the Vatican. After the church entrance at the atrium and a statue of the Pope, several original 16th-century frescoes hang on the facade. Inside the Baroque church is an ornate altar with a doorway at the top, through which Izamal's statue of the Immaculate Conception is wheeled out for Mass daily at 7pm. The room behind the altar is a small museum (2 pesos; open Tu-Su 9am-1pm and 3-6pm) that exhibits pictures and mementos of the Pope's visit to Izamal in August of 1993. Continue up the stairs to arrive at Mexico's oldest *camarín*, where the statue of the Immaculate Conception rests when not in use. (Open 8am-1pm.) Fray Diego de Landa commissioned this statue in 1558 in Guatemala. There were originally two statues, called *Las Dos Hermanas;* one was sent to Mérida and the other to Izamal. In 1829, Izamal's statue was destroyed in a fire, and Mérida's copy was brought here. It is said, however, that the Izamal original was saved and taken to the nearby pyramid of Kinich-Kakmó. Every December 8, at the beginning of the town's 15-day *fiesta,* the two are said to switch places in *El Paso de las Dos Hermanas.* More legends are told at Izamal's small community **museum**, on the north side of the Convent, on Calle 31, which details Izamal's three historical phases and has a model of the city in 500 BC. (Open Tu-W and F-Su 10am-1pm and 4:30-8:30pm. Free.)

Only five of the pyramids in Izamal are open to visitors and all are within walking distance. After ascending the 34m-high pyramid of **Kinich-Kakmó** (dedicated to the fire and sun god, whose name means Fire Parrot or Sun Face) visitors can truly appreciate Izamal's most dominating structure, which looks out over the city. This massive pyramid, measuring 200m by 180m, is the fifth-largest in the country and the second-largest in the Yucatán Peninsula. Kinich-Kakmó was built during the Early Classic period (AD 400-600) and formed the northern border of the ancient city's central plaza. (Enter on Calle 27 between Calles 28 and 28A.) It was once outclassed by **Pap-Hol-Chac** (House Full of Lightning), the largest pyramid in ancient Izamal before its ruin, on which was built the convent that served as home to Maya priests. Other pyramids dot Izamal, blending with the modern cityscape. **Itzamatul** looms to the east and is accessible on Calle 26, between Calles 29 and 31.

The 22m-tall structure was dedicated to the god Zamná and now has picked up a small garden at its base as well. **Habuc** (Dress of Water) is the most removed, on Calle 26, between Calles 35 and 37. **Chal Tun Ha** (Eye of Water in Stone), behind the Green River hotel on Calle 41, was recently restored. **El Conejo,** on Calle 22 between Calles 31 and 33, is also open to the public; through the shop Hecho a Mano on 31A, one can catch a glimpse of **Hum Pic Tok.** The most centrally located pyramid, **Kabul** (Creative Hand), is just north of the *zócalo* and is the place where the mask of Zamná was found. Unfortunately, surrounding homes and businesses make it almost impossible to reach. (All pyramids open daily 8am-5pm. Free.)

CHICHÉN ITZÁ ☎985

Gracing hundreds of glossy brochure covers and suffering the footfalls of thousands of tourists, the Post-Classic Maya ruins at Chichén Itzá seem almost an archaeological cliché. Once here, however, the hype is understandable. The swarms of tourists surprisingly do not interfere with appreciation of the history behind the magnificent, well-preserved site, and their presence evokes days a thousand years past when Chichén Itzá embodied all the political and cultural grandeur of ancient Maya civilization. The awesome stone structures' faultless architecture and mystic decor, together with the sheer size of this former Maya

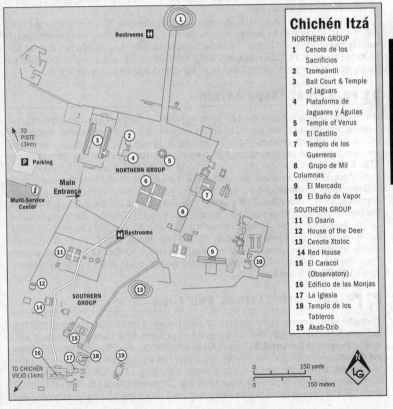

Chichén Itzá

NORTHERN GROUP
1 Cenote de los Sacrificios
2 Tzompantli
3 Ball Court & Temple of Jaguars
4 Plataforma de Jaguares y Águilas
5 Temple of Venus
6 El Castillo
7 Templo de los Guerreros
8 Grupo de Mil Columnas
9 El Mercado
10 El Baño de Vapor

SOUTHERN GROUP
11 El Osario
12 House of the Deer
13 Cenote Xtoloc
14 Red House
15 El Caracol (Observatory)
16 Edificio de las Monjas
17 La Iglesia
18 Templo de los Tableros
19 Akab-Dzib

Restrooms

TO PISTE (3km)

P Parking

Main Entrance

Multi-Service Center

NORTHERN GROUP

Restrooms

SOUTHERN GROUP

TO CHICHÉN VIEJO (1km)

0 — 150 yards
0 — 150 meters

N

YUCATÁN

capital, inspire awe at the skill and creativity of Maya builders. Yet more enigmatic is why this amazing ingenuity was devoted to horrific rites of human sacrifice. Whatever doubts you may have about Chichén Itzá living up to its reputation, lay them aside: the ruins merit a long, loving visit from all who cross the Yucatán. Only 2.5km away, the town of **Piste** (pop. 3100) offers a range of services. The main reason for a night's stay would be to get a good sleep after the light-and-sound show at Chichén Itzá and enter the ruins again at 8am in relative peace. Avoid visiting around noon, when the sun scorches and the tourist wave peaks.

▣ TRANSPORTATION

The ruins of Chichén Itzá lie 1.5km from **Mex. 180,** the highway running from Mérida (119km west) through Valladolid (42km east) to Cancún (200km east). The two access roads are the main road from the west and another from the east. Mex. 180 becomes **Calle 15** in Piste, the town's main drag. Piste has two functionally equivalent bus stations, both on Calle 15. There is also a bus station at the ruins. The main Piste **bus station** (☎851 0052) is between the Pirámide Inn and Posada Novelo on the eastern edge of town. **ADO** treks to **Cancún** (2½hr., 4:30pm, 110 pesos); **Mérida** (1½hr.; 2:30, 5pm; 62 pesos); **Playa del Carmen** (8am; 2:45, 4:30pm; 141 pesos); **Valladolid** (1hr.; 11am, 3, 4:30pm; 24 pesos). Second-class **Oriente** buses run to Cancún (77 pesos) and Mérida (44 pesos) almost every hr. from 6am-9:30pm, stopping at all the towns in between.

Reaching the ruins is easy. If you would rather skip the 20min. walk from Piste, catch a **taxi** (25 pesos) or wait in the bus station for an eastbound bus (every 30min. until 5:30pm, 5 pesos). To get to Chichén Itzá from other towns, see bus listings for Mérida (see p. 617), Cancún (see p. 655), and Valladolid (see p. 647). To return to Piste, wait in the bus parking lot until a taxi or bus swings by (every 45min.).

▣ PRACTICAL INFORMATION

Services in Chichén Itzá are at the site's western entrance. (Open 8am-9pm, shops close at 5:30pm.) Across from the ticket counter is a small **information booth** that offers free **luggage storage.** (Open daily 8am-5:30pm.) The bus station also offers free luggage storage. (Open daily 6am-6pm.) Restrooms, currency exchange, an **ATM,** a restaurant, an ice cream parlor, a gift shop (which accepts US dollars), a bookstore, a small museum, and **parking** (10 pesos) are available at the site.

Beyond art markets and over-priced food, you will have to visit Piste for most services. There is a 24hr. **ATM** outside the Restaurant Fiesta in Piste, 2 blocks before the *zócalo.* Other services include: **police** (☎851 0097), at the Camandancia on the east side of the *zócalo;* **Farmacia Isis,** Calle 15, west of the *zócalo* (☎851 0216; open 24 hr.); **Clínica Promesa,** Calle 14 50 (☎851 0005), in the blue-green building west of the *zócalo* and 100m north of Mex. 180; **Caseta Telefónica,** across from the bus station, which also **exchanges money** (☎851 0088; open daily 10am-6pm); **LADATELs,** along Mex. 180.

▣ ACCOMMODATIONS AND FOOD

Though luxury hotels have begun to invade, plenty of economical lodging remains in Piste. Extreme budget travelers can camp or sleep in a hammock under a *palapa* at **Posada el Carrousel ❶,** Calle 15 41 (☎851 0078), for 25 pesos, or at **Pirámide Inn ❶,** which is a little closer to the ruins and has a pool, for 40 pesos. Both offer bathrooms, electricity, and gardens. For those seeking a bed, the accommodations below are either on or just off Mex. 180/Calle 15. **Posada Olalde ❷,** left off Calle 15 onto Calle 6 across from Restaurant Carrousel down the dirt road, is a pleasant stay and a great value with large, spotless rooms in the main house and well-kept bungalows off the intimate courtyard. (☎851 0086. Singles 135 pesos; doubles 180 pesos; 2-person bungalows 160 pesos. Discounts for students and in low season.) Another option is **Posada el Paso ❷**, Calle 15 48. Simple rooms off the mustard-yellow tiled hall have windows and a fan, and hot water can be turned on. (Singles 135 pesos; doubles 150 pesos.) The rooms are basic at **Posada Novelo ❸**, but the pool and the location next to the main bus station (and closest to the ruins) beckon exhausted explorers. (☎851 0275. Singles and doubles 180 pesos.)

Those too engrossed with the ruins to think about eating should consider themselves lucky—pickings are slim in Chichén Itzá. The on-site **restaurant ❹** specializes in *comida non-típica:* high prices and small servings. (Smoothies 35-45 pesos, entrees 50-65 pesos.) Picnickers save a few pesos by packing a lunch from one of the **small grocers** lining Calle 15 in Piste, near the *zócalo*. **Las Mestizas ❹**, across from Hotel Chichén Itzá, has good *comida regional* like *pollo* or *cochinita pibel* (baked chicken or pork wrapped in banana leaves, with tomatoes, onions, and salt; 48 pesos) and breakfasts in an airy restaurant. (☎851 0069. Open Tu-Su 7am-11pm.) Tasty and inexpensive food abounds at *palapa*-covered **Restaurant Carrousel ❷**. *Chilaquiles con pollo* (fried tortillas with cheese, onions, and chicken) are 20 pesos, as are *enchiladas*. (☎851 0078. Open daily 7:30am-11pm.) **Los Pájaros ❸**, a tad west of Restaurant Carrousel, is equally good and cheap. (☎858 1287. Dishes 25-35 pesos. Open daily 8am-10pm.)

◉ ▓ THE ARCHAEOLOGICAL SITE OF CHICHÉN ITZÁ

Open daily 8am-6pm. 87 pesos; Su half-price. Site museum open daily 8am-6pm. Free. Light-and-sound show (in Spanish) daily 8pm in summer, 7pm in winter. Show lasts 45min. 30 pesos, free with admission. Headphones with English translation 25 pesos. 2hr. guided tours begin at the entrance and cost upwards of 480 pesos for groups of up to 20.

The settlement of Chichén Itzá took place over three periods; the first two are grouped together and called the **Maya Phase** (or **Chichén Viejo**), when the area was occupied by Puuc and Maya, and the third is the **Toltec-Maya Phase** (or **Chichén Nuevo**), when the Toltecs and Maya were predominant. The name Chichén Itzá means "by the mouth of Itzá's well," implying that the area's earliest inhabitants were drawn here by two nearby freshwater *cenotes*. Settlers arrived in the first period around AD 700, the Maya Classic Era, during which Maya strength centered in Chiapas and Guatemala. These early settlers may have built the structures found today at Chichén Viejo, though scholars disagree. The second period, in the late Classic or early Post-Classic Era around AD 900, saw more central construction, including the inner pyramid of El Castillo and the original Temple of Chacmool (beneath Templo de los Guerreros). The last period began in the 11th century with the arrival of Itzá, a Maya group from Tabasco. A dwindling group of experts adheres to the traditional view that sometime before 1000, Toltec tribes of Tula infiltrated the Yucatán and overcame peaceful Maya settlements, bringing with them the cult of plumed serpent Quetzalcóatl (Kukulcán in Maya). The more widely accepted view, however, is that Chichén Itzá, a crossroads of trade and ideas, eventually incorporated Toltec practices into its own culture. Toltec influence is evident in the distinctive reclining *chac-mools*, statues of the rain god Chac with their heads turned sideways, holding forth plates to receive an offering or sacrifice. Gran Plaza, El Castillo, Templo de Guerreros, Observatory, and Juego de Pelota were all constructed during this period. In the 12th century, Chichén Itzá formed the powerful **Mayapán League**, through which it dominated the remaining Maya city-states in the Yucatán. In 1461, Chichén Itzá was abandoned due to war with rival city-state Mayapán, though religious pilgrimages to the site continued well after Spanish conquest.

YUCATÁN

For a more comprehensive (and air-conditioned!) understanding of Chichén and its people, visit **Centro Cultural Cecijema,** Calle 15 45, just west of the bus station in Piste. The grey building houses a small selection of Maya ceramic replicas, a modest library, and rotating exhibits. (☎851 0004. Open M-Sa 8am-5pm. Free.) The **information center** and a few services can be found at the main entrance to Chichén Itzá, on the western side of the ruins. A small **museum** presents the site's history, the first writings about the ruins by Bishop Diego de Landa in 1565, photos of its earlier conditions, and sculptures and objects removed from the Sacred Cenote.

The green panels throughout the ruins, though they might confuse you all day, pop open for the evening **light-and-sound show,** which is a spectacle not to miss. If you trust your bug repellent, the 25min. nighttime stroll from Piste is quiet and well-lit; otherwise, take a taxi (25 pesos).

EL CASTILLO (THE CASTLE). Chichén's trademark edifice El Castillo (also known as Pyramid of Kukulcán) stands as tangible evidence of the astronomical mastery of the ancient Maya—and offers spectacular views of the site. The 91 steps on each of the four faces, plus the upper platform, total 365; 52 panels on nine terraced levels equal the years in a Maya calendar cycle. A staircase divides each face of the nine terraces, yielding 18 sections representing the 18 Maya *uinal* in each *tun* of the Long Count dating system. Easily the most impressive feature is the precise alignment of El Castillo's axes, which produce a bi-annual optical illusion. At sunrise during the spring and fall equinoxes, the rounded terraces cast a serpentine shadow down the side of the northern staircase. A light-and-shadow lunar serpent-god, identical to that of the equinoxes, creeps down the pyramid at the dawn of the full moon following each equinox.

El Castillo sits atop an older Classic-era temple, which can be entered at the western side of the north staircase's base. At the bottom, if you position yourself correctly and clap, you will hear a quick echo that incredibly augments the sound and makes it sound like a snap. After climbing the steps you'll be grimacing like the *chac-mool* in the ceremonial chamber. Check out the fanged jaguar throne with jade eyes behind the chamber. *(Inner temple open daily 11am-3pm and 4-5pm. Free.)*

JUEGO DE PELOTA (BALL COURT). Northwest of El Castillo sits a playing field, bounded by high parallel walls, with temples at the north and south ends that were most likely added after its initial construction. Measuring 146m by 37m, Chichén boasts the largest ball court in Mesoamerica and amazing side-to-side echoes. The height of the walls suggests that the game wasn't always played according to the rules on this court because it is unlikely that anyone would be able to get the ball high enough to score without using their hands or feet. The elaborate game played here fascinated Cortés so much that he took two teams back to Europe in 1528 to perform before the royal court.

TZOMPANTLI (PLATFORM OF THE SKULLS). A short distance from the ball court in the direction of the open grassy area is a platform typical of Toltec-Maya architecture that once exhibited the bare skulls of prisoners and enemies. The eerie columns of bas-relief skulls on the lower platform walls, lined up like gravestones, conjure horrific images of bloody skulls strung together to strike fear in the hearts of enemies. Nine skeletons were found beneath the mound that was used to perform ceremonies.

PLATAFORMA DE JAGUARES Y ÁGUILAS (PLATFORM OF THE JAGUARS AND EAGLES). Next to Tzompantli, this platform supports animals representing the warrior castes, who were ordered to kidnap members of other tribes for sacrifices to their gods. On either side of the feathered serpent heads on the balustrades, reliefs of jaguars and eagles clutch human hearts in their claws.

TUMBA DEL CHACMOOL (TEMPLE OF VENUS). Directly north of El Castillo is the Temple of Venus, a square platform decorated with a feathered serpent holding a human head in its mouth. The temple's reliefs symbolize the planet Venus, other stars and planets, and give information on their motions. The platform was most likely used for ceremonies.

CENOTE DE LOS SACRIFICIOS (SACRED CENOTE). Three hundred meters north of El Castillo and connected via a *sacbé*, this 60m-wide subterranean pool was Chichén Itzá's most important religious symbol. The rain god Chac, believed to dwell beneath the surface, requested frequent gifts in exchange for good rains. Elaborate rituals, beginning atop El Castillo and culminating in the unfortunate victim's 25m plunge to death, appeased the god. Since 1907, over 30,000 sacrificial remains—including skulls, teeth, and jewelry—have been dredged from the 14m of water, beginning with the work of anthropologist Edward Thompson. In the 1960s, scuba divers discovered more remains, suggesting that children and young men were the sacrifices of choice. The mystical feel is still present at the *cenote*, where birds and bats shoot across the cavern.

TEMPLO DE LOS GUERREROS (TEMPLE OF THE WARRIORS). On the left as you return from the *cenote*, and northeast of El Castillo, this temple presents an array of carved columns that supported a roof, but now stand like a great army. On the temple itself, before two great feathered serpents and several sculpted animal gods, is one of Chichén's best-preserved *chac-mools* and a table where human hearts were ritually extracted. This building's ornamentation shows heavy Toltec influence: a nearly identical structure stands in Tula, the former Toltec capital to the west. The temple was built over the former Temple of Chacmool. *(Closed to the public.)*

GRUPO DE MIL COLUMNAS (GROUP OF A THOUSAND COLUMNS). Extending to the south and east of the Templo de los Guerreros, the group of columns contains an elaborate drainage system that channeled rainfall away from what is believed to have been a civic or religious center.

EL BAÑO DE VAPOR (THE STEAMBATH). The structure is divided into 3 sections. In the interior, water was poured over hot rocks, creating steam to purify those in religious ceremonies or with poor health. Visitors can crawl through a small opening and imagine the process taking place. The steambath ritual is one of the oldest known traditions of the people in the region.

EL MERCADO (THE MARKET). The final ruin before entering the older, central zone has taller columns and wider vaults that show the advances in architecture made over time.

TUMBA DEL GRAN SACERDOTE/EL OSARIO (THE HIGH PRIEST'S GRAVE). This is the first structure to the right of the path leading to the southern, or central zone. The distinctive serpent heads mimic El Castillo, and a natural cave extends from within the pyramid 15m into the earth. The human bones and votive offerings of gold, silver, and jewels found in this cave are thought to have belonged to the ancient high priests of Chichén Itzá.

EL CARACOL (THE OBSERVATORY). One of few circular structures built by the Maya, this ancient planetarium consists of two rectangular platforms with large, west-facing staircases and two circular towers. The tower's spiral staircase earned it the name El Caracol (The Snail). The slits in the dome can be aligned with the major celestial bodies and cardinal directions, and the red handprints on the walls were supposedly made by the hands of sun god Kinich Ahau.

YUCATÁN

TEMPLO DE LOS TABLEROS (TEMPLE OF THE PANELS). Just south of the Observatory, this small ruin has carved panels and rows of columns. Though difficult to decipher, the panels on exterior walls contain emblems of warriors—jaguars, eagles, and serpents—in three rows. The upper part of the structure is believed to have been a site for fire-related ceremonies.

EDIFICIO DE LAS MONJAS (THE NUNNERY). At the end of the South Group, these buildings, built over six phases, were probably the imposing residence of a high priest. To the Spanish, however, the stone rooms looked suspiciously like a convent—hence the ruins' name. Above the entrance on the east side of the building, Maya glyphs are still visible. Also on the east side is the **annex,** which predates the rest of the Nunnery. Above the doorway facing the small courtyard is a spectacularly preserved bas-relief of a seated royal-divine figure. Many rooms in the nunnery have doorways that lead to dark corridors, home to bats and frogs.

LA IGLESIA (THE CHURCH). For similar reasons, the elaborate building diagonal to the Nunnery was misnamed the Church. One of the oldest buildings at the site, its top-heavy walls are encrusted with intricate masks of hook-nosed Chac. The "church" fuses a variety of cultural styles: over the doorway are Maya stone lintels, while the use of wood and inclined edges indicate a Toltec influence. Above the door, the four *bacabs* that hold up the sky at four cardinal points are represented by a crab, a turtle, an armadillo, and a snail.

AKAB-DZIB. Sixty meters east of the nunnery, this complex earned its name for the "dark writing" found in its 17 rooms. The oldest parts of this structure are believed to be Chichén's most ancient constructions—the two central rooms date to the 2nd or 3rd century, while the annexes on either side and to the east were added later. Inside, the small, red handprints of Kinich Ahau dot the ceiling.

CENOTE XTOLOC. To the east of the Southern Group, either off a small trail from near the Market or on the first left off the main trail, is the *cenote,* in the hollow beyond the ruined temple of Xtoloc and dedicated to that lizard god. No path goes down the slope through undergrowth, and swimming is prohibited due to dangerous currents. The secular counterpart to the holy waters of the Sacred Cenote, this pool at one time provided all of Chichén with drinking water. Follow *sacbé* No. 5, which becomes a narrow, winding trail, to get behind the observatory.

⚡ DAYTRIPS FROM CHICHÉN ITZÁ

GRUTAS DE BALANKANCHÉ

6km east of Chichén Itzá and 2km past the Dolores Alba Hotel, the caves are easily reached from Chichén or Piste by any eastbound bus on Mex. 180 (4 pesos). When boarding, be sure to tell the driver where you are headed. You can also take a taxi (30 pesos, 60 pesos round-trip, including wait). To get back, catch any westbound vehicle, but be prepared to wait a while. Entrance permitted only with tours, daily in Spanish at noon, 2, and 4pm; in English at 9, 11am, 1, and 3pm; in French at 10am. 30-45min., 48 pesos. 2-person minimum. Free small museum and luggage storage.

Descend into the ultra-humid corridors of the Maya underworld at the inner caves of Balankanché, which were only rediscovered in 1959 when a local tour guide noticed the passageway blocked with stones. Archaeologists believe the cave was a center for Maya-Toltec worship of the rain god Chac (Tlaloc) and the serpent god Kukulcán (Quetzalcóatl) during the 10th and 11th centuries. For unknown reasons, subterranean worship in Balankanché stopped at the end of this period, and the offerings of pottery and sculpture rested undisturbed for nine centuries.

Explorations have opened 450m of caves 25m deep in which one could easily get lost if not for the light show that entertains and guides visitors. Pass by stalactites carved to resemble leaves, a huge column representing the sacred *ceiba* tree (the tree of life) and three groups of ancient ceramic vessels and stone sculptures as hidden speakers with slightly garbled sound tell the story of the cave's past. The impressive stalactites and ceramics merit a visit, even if you have only a few extra hours on hand.

YAXUNÁ

The only "public transportation" to Yaxuná is a delivery truck you can flag down; it leaves Piste at 6am and returns at 1pm on M and F. Your best options are either to rent a car or hire a taxi in Piste. There are two routes to Yaxuná. The better takes you west on Mex. 180 to Libre Unión and then through Yaxcaba, a small town (300 pesos round-trip). The poorer road cuts through jungle, and taxistas charge more to cover possible damage to the car (450 pesos).

Thirty kilometers south of Chichén Itzá, Yaxuná is home to the ruins of yet another ancient Maya city. The temple was built by the Maya of Cobá, who were planning to declare war on the people of Chichén Itzá late in the Classic Period. To keep a close eye on their enemy, the Maya of Cobá aligned their temple with El Castillo. The most interesting feature of the site is the 100km *sacbé*, which connected Yaxuná to Cobá, making it the longest in the peninsula.

VALLADOLID ☎985

In the middle of the Mérida-Cancún route and only 30min. from Chichén Itzá, Valladolid (pop. 70,000) ought to be jammed with tourists. Strangely enough, most bypass it and the beautiful colonial churches and natural *cenotes* it offers. In 1543, Spaniard Francisco de Montejo attacked the city, then the Maya city of Zací, which held out for several years before succumbing. Despite the imposing churches and grid-like streets (which continue to make the city easy to navigate) that were reminders of Spanish dominion, the Maya were not so easily defeated. In 1848 they rose up and took the city hostage for several months in what is now known as the Caste War. The Maya hold on to their past today: the language is still heard among Indian women weaving *huipiles*, between vendors on street corners, and among many around the city's archaeological sites and cenotes. A broader, regional identity exists as well, as most restaurants are proud to serve local food and drink, especially Montejo beer.

█ TRANSPORTATION

Traversed by Mex. 180, Valladolid lies in the heart of Yucatán state, between Mérida and Cancún. The **Oriente station** is on the northwest corner of Calles 54 and 37. (☎856 3449. Open 6am-10pm.) Later buses board at the **ADO station** in the *centro*, at Calles 39 and 46; most buses stop at both stations. To get to the *zócalo* from the Oriente Station, walk south one block on Calle 54 to Calle 39. Turn left and go for six blocks. Better yet, if you have no luggage stowed underneath, you can get off your bus before the bus station at the *zócalo* (look for a big twin-towered cathedral). ADO buses travel to: **Cancún** (2hr., more than 20 per day, 60 or 83 pesos); **Chichén Itzá** (1hr., every hr. from 12:15am, 15 or 26 pesos); **Mérida** (2½hr., every hr. from 12:15am, 60 or 83 pesos); **Playa del Carmen** (2½hr., 8 per day from 7:30am, 63-102 pesos); **Tizimín** (1hr., every hr. from 5:30am, 20 pesos); **Izamal** (1½hr., 12 per day, 33 pesos); **Chiquilá** (2½hr., 2:30am, 57 pesos).

■ ❼ ORIENTATION AND PRACTICAL INFORMATION

Even-numbered streets in Valladolid run north-south, increasing to the west. Odd-numbered streets run east-west, increasing to the south. Except for Cenote X'keken, in the nearby village of **Dzitnup,** and the Ek' Balam ruins, everything lies within walking distance of the *zócalo* (circumscribed by Calles 39, 40, 41, and 42); blocks are spaced out, so what appears a short jaunt might really be a long haul.

Tourist Information: The city hall (☎856 2063), on the corner of Calles 40 and 41, provides information and pamphlets. Some English spoken. Open daily 9am-8pm.

Currency Exchange: Bancomer (☎856 2150), on the Calle 40 side of the *zócalo.* 24hr. **ATM** next door. Open M-F 8:30am-4pm, Sa 10am-2pm. **Banamex** and **Bital,** on Calle 41 between Calles 42 and 44, offer the same. Open M-Sa 8am-7pm.

Bike Rental: Refaccionaria de Bicicletas Silva and the sports store of **Antonio Negro Aguilar** (☎856 2125), both on Calle 44 between Calles 39 and 41. 5 pesos per hr. Open daily 8:30am-4pm.

Market: 5 blocks northeast of the *zócalo,* bordered by Calles 30, 32, 35, and 37. Fresh and cheap fruit, meat, and vegetables. Open daily 6am-3pm.

Supermarket: Super Maz (☎856 3774), 3½ blocks west of the *zócalo* on Calle 39. Open daily 7am-10pm. **Super Willy's** and more on Calle 39 between Calles 42 and 46.

Laundry: Lavandería Tintorería Progreso (☎856 2756), across from Super Maz. 2hr. full service, 8 pesos per kg, 3kg minimum. Open M-Sa 8am-2pm and 5-8pm. **Lavandería Tintoría el Gaucho,** Calle 42 165, between Calles 27 and 29. 2hr. wash and dry service 7 pesos per kg. Open M-Sa 8am-8pm.

Emergency: Red Cross ☎856 2413.

Police: (☎856 2100) on Calle 41, 10 blocks east of the *zócalo.* Some English spoken.

Pharmacy: El Descuento (☎856 2615), Calle 42 at Calle 39, on the *zócalo.* Open daily 8am-9pm. Several more are on the western side of the *zócalo.*

Hospital: (☎856 2883), on the corner of Calles 51 and 52.

Fax: Telecomm, on Calle 41, west of Museo San Roque, between Calles 38 and 40.

Internet Access: Xenyx Cybercafé, between Calles 37 and 39. 10 pesos per hr. Open Su 9am-3pm, M-Sa 9am-10pm.

Post Office: (☎856 2623), on the Calle 40 side of the *zócalo.* Open M-F 8:30am-3pm. **Postal Code:** 97780.

▛ ACCOMMODATIONS

Penny-pinchers will want to stay away from the pricey hotels bordering the *zócalo.* Better bargains can be found one block west, especially on Calle 44.

▨ **Albergue/Hostal La Candelaria (HI)** (☎856 2267), in peaceful Parque La Candelaria on the corner of Calles 35 and 44. A spacious new hostel with a laid-back atmosphere. Features hand-wash laundry areas, full kitchen, peaceful lunch patio, breakfast, TV room, bike rental (5 pesos per hr.), free lockers, and strong fans. Bunks 65 pesos. ❶

Hotel Zací, Calle 44 191 (☎856 2167), between Calles 37 and 39. A relaxing vacation from your vacation. Complete with phone, cable TV, and a glittering pool. Colonial rooms have carved dressers and surround a grassy courtyard. Singles 200 pesos; doubles 281 pesos; triples 328 pesos. A/C 60-70 pesos extra. ❹

Hotel María Guadalupe, Calle 44 198 (☎856 2068), between Calles 39 and 41. Rooms with clean baths, ceiling fans, and dark wood furniture. Singles 130 pesos; doubles 150 pesos; triples 180 pesos. ❷

Hotel Lily, Calle 44 192 (☎856 2163), between Calles 37 and 39, across from Hotel Zací. 2 options available, both fine values. Hostel-like accommodations with shared bathrooms and hammock holes: singles 90 pesos; doubles 120 pesos. Nice rooms with private bathrooms: singles 110 pesos; doubles 140 pesos. TV 20 pesos extra. ❶

🍴 FOOD

Comida yucateca, which blends European and Mexican flavors, tops every menu. Try *poc-chuc* (tender slices of pork marinated in a Yucatec sauce, covered with pickled onions), *panuchos* (tortillas filled with beans and topped with either chicken or pork, lettuce, tomato, and hot sauce), or *escabeche oriental de pavo* (a hearty turkey soup with pasta). *Xtabentún* is a delectable liquor of anise and honey.

Bazar Municipal, Calle 39 at Calle 40, right off the *zócalo.* A narrow courtyard crowded with cafes serving *comida típica,* pizzerias, and juice bars. Prepare to be bombarded. Breakfast 15-20 pesos. *Comida corrida* options usually include meat, beans, rice, tortillas, and a drink for 20-25 pesos. Hours vary by restaurant, but most are open daily 6am-midnight. ❷

Restaurante Cenote Zací (☎856 2107), on Calle 36 between Calles 37 and 39. Underneath a giant *palapa,* surrounded by jungle trees and atop a *cenote,* this restaurant has enough space and tables to feed truckloads. The best of Valladolid in one: traditionally dressed waiters, great *cenote* view, and excellent *comida yucateca* (entrees 40-50 pesos) and liquor selection, including *xtabentún* (12 pesos). Sandwiches 25-30 pesos. Open daily 8am-6pm. ❹

Restaurante María de la Luz (☎856 2071), on the west side of the *zócalo,* in the Hotel María de la Luz. Eat c*omida corrida* (35 pesos) in unusually open and light surroundings and watch the life of the *zócalo* through breezy French bay doors. Vegetarian and some US dishes available, as is the hotel pool; listen to mom and wait 30min. after you eat. Open daily 6am-10pm. ❸

Las Campanas, Calle 42 199 (☎856 2365), on the southwest corner of the *zócalo.* Situate yourself right and get an eyeful of the Franciscan Cathedral while listening to live music (daily 9pm-midnight). *Comida yucateca,* including *queso relleno* (wedge of cheese stuffed with meat, egg, and salsa), and sprinklings of US grub start at 25 pesos. Open daily 7am-midnight. ❸

📷 SIGHTS

While most visitors take the next bus to Mérida or Chichén Itzá, those seeking a heavy dose of history, *cenotes,* and cathedrals have come to the right place. The natural Yucatec jungle makes a steamy backdrop that complements the colonial city in a mix of natural and man-made beauty.

CATEDRAL DE SAN SERVASIO. According to legend, two criminals were pulled from the church and murdered by an angry mob. When the bishop learned of the mob action, he had the church destroyed. It was rebuilt in 1720-1730 and is the only one on the peninsula to face north instead of east. The massive colonial twin towers make this an unmistakable physical landmark, while the many altars within reflect equal Spanish determination to control the religious landscape. *(Over the zócalo on Calle 41. Open Su 6:30am-2pm and 4-10pm, M-Sa 7am-1pm and 4-8:30pm. Free.)*

MUSEO DE SAN ROQUE. This museum, with just over a decade under its belt, greatly enhances the city's cultural value. It links the area's present to its roots, reaching back through the conquest to the Pre-Hispanic Maya. Even those more interested in shopping may value their purchases more after learning about the crafts. The courtyard makes for a good place to relax and admire sculptures. *(On the northwest corner of Calles 41 and 38. All exhibits in Spanish. Open daily 9am-9pm.)*

YUCATÁN

CENOTE ZACÍ. In the middle of the city, Cenote Zací (pronounced sah-KEY) is a cavernous hollow full of protruding stalagmites, tropical gardens, and daredevil divers, with serene green-blue water in the midst of it all. The sight of sun's rays illuminating fish below is beautiful, but the park and zoo above need attention. *(3 blocks east of the zócalo, on Calle 36 between Calles 37 and 39. Open daily 8am-7:30pm. 10 pesos, children 5 pesos. Free view from the palapa restaurant on the edge.)*

EL PASEO DE LOS FRAILES (THE STREET OF THE FRIARS). This picturesque, colonial street with colorful, flat front houses, provides the perfect setting for a stroll. Many residents leave their doors open—just don't be too nosy peeking in at courtyards. *(Calle 41A between Las Cinco Calles and San Bernardino.)*

SAN BERNARDINO DE SIENA. Affiliated with the **Ex-Convento de Sisal,** the church was built over a *cenote* (visible from inside) in 1552 with stones from the main Maya temple. It is the oldest ecclesiastical building in the Yucatán and bears a unique, square pattern. A large image of the Virgin of Guadalupe hangs on the altar in back. *(On Calle 41A, at the end of Paseo de los Frailes. Open Su-M, W-Sa 9am-1pm and 4-6pm. Free, but donations accepted.)*

CASA DE LA CULTURA. The building housing the city's cultural center was originally a convent and later a home to diplomats. Art exhibits are on display inside (free) and the caretaker, don Jorge, can fill you in on upcoming traditional dance performances. If there is no show, you may be able to join a class (10 pesos). The region's traditional dance, *jarana*, involves braiding ribbons about a pole; classes also cover traditions from Jalisco and Veracruz. *(Next to the municipal building on the eastern side of the zócalo. ☎856 2063 ext. 1216. Dance classes mostly in late afternoons and evenings.)*

🎵🎭 ENTERTAINMENT AND NIGHTLIFE

Valladolid is a small, quiet city that offers a small, quiet night scene. As with most small towns, look to the *zócalo*, beautifully illuminated at night, for strolling families, Maya vendors, friendly beggars, lively political oratory, and guitar-strumming teens. For later in the night, **Vaía Ral,** a recent Cancún-style disco (the biggest in Yucatán state), is only a few blocks northwest of the ADO bus station (near the fairgrounds). The youthful crowd, eager for some big city action, parties hard, dancing and romancing deep into the night. (Open F-Su 10pm-late. 80 pesos.) Valladolid hosts many cultural celebrations and parties in addition to the standard weekend activities. The *Fiestas de la Noche*, celebrating San Servasio with masses, bands, food, and dancing in the *centro* at night, occurs October 3-30. From January 24 to February 3, the Celebration for the *Virgen de la Candelaria* brings bull fights and traditional music and dance to the fairgrounds.

🔁 DAYTRIPS FROM VALLADOLID

🏞 CENOTE DZITNUP (X'KEKÉN)
6km west of town. To get there by car or bike, take Calle 39 to the highway toward Mérida. Make a left at the sign for Dzitnup and continue to the entrance plaza on your left (20min.). Without wheels, catch a morning colectivo (5 pesos) in front of the Hotel María Guadalupe. Open daily 7am-6pm. 12 pesos, children free.

The gorgeous *cenote*, ironically bearing a Maya name that means dirty, has refreshingly cold water and allows you to escape underground in its pool. Visit before midday to catch a beam of light slicing through a circular hole in the roof, bathing the cavern in blue. Bring a towel, some warm clothes, and a swimsuit. **Cenote Sambula** (10 pesos) is only 200m away and offers beauty on a smaller scale.

EK' BALAM

The ruins are 25km northeast of Valladolid and accessible only by car, taxi, or organized tour buses. Taxis run about 200-225 pesos round-trip; the driver will generally wait up to 2hr. Taxis colectivos, if they are running, are a far better deal at 20 pesos. Site open daily 8am-5pm. 22 pesos; holidays and Su free.

Ek' Balam ("Black Jaguar") was a Maya city that flourished in the late Classical period, around AD 700-1000. The site was discovered little more than 30 years ago, so excavation is still very much in progress. It contains several temples, a rare circular observatory, a ball court, a stone sacrificial table upon which the victorious ball team was beheaded, and a magnificent pyramid; all is organized around a main plaza. The pyramid itself is one of the most massive in the Yucatan; it's not quite as tall as other Maya pyramids (30m), but its base is an astonishing 160m long. Note the two giant unexcavated mounds flanking the pyramid—among structures archaeologists expect to find are more pyramids reaching 20-25m in height. The ruins are generally uncrowded and, as reconstruction continues apace, definitely merit a visit—if you can handle the hefty taxi fare.

TIZIMÍN   ☎986

Tourists from around the world take advantage of Tizimín's prime location to explore the eastern part of Yucatán state. Both colonial Valladolid and the nature reserves of San Felipe and Río Lagartos lie within an hour's drive on Mex. 295. The archaeological sites of Ek' Balam and Kulubá are also not far away. Others flock to Tizimín (pop. 80,000) to take part in the many religious processions that culminate at the town's ambitiously restored colonial church and convent, and to witness the area's Maya congregate in the nearby village of Kikil to practice ancient religious ceremonies. While Tizimín's mornings are big-city busy, meaning you can probably find anything you are looking for from banks to boutiques, things quiet down to small-town proportion in the sultry afternoons, and you can enjoy evenings in which a cacophonous chorus of birdsongs around the carefully manicured Parque Principal seems to be the only thing stirring the warm air.

E TRANSPORTATION. Tizimín is located in the heart of eastern Yucatán, 55km north of Valladolid and 65km south of the Gulf Coast. Its **bus station** is on the northwest corner of Calles 46 and 47. Buses run to: **Cancún** (3hr., 5 per day, 77 pesos); **Izamal** (2½hr.; 11am, 4pm; 41 pesos); **Mérida** (3hr., 11 per day, 60-77 pesos); **Playa del Carmen** (8:30am, 89 pesos); **Río Lagartos** (45min.; midnight, 10am, 7:30pm; 20 pesos).

ORIENTATION AND PRACTICAL INFORMATION. Tizimín's even-numbered streets run north-south, increasing to the west. Odd-numbered streets run east-west, increasing to the south. The city centers on the Parque Principal, which is framed by Calles 50, 51, 52, and 53. To get to the Parque Principal from the bus station, walk two blocks west and two blocks south. **Bancomer,** on the corner of Calles 48 and 51, exchanges currency and has a 24hr. **ATM** (☎863 2381; open M-F 8:30am-4pm.), as do **Bital** (open M-Sa 8am-7pm) and **Banamex** (open M-F 9am-4pm), both on the *parque*. **Lavandería de los Tres Reyes** is three blocks south of the Parque Principal on Calle 57, between Calles 52 and 54. (☎863 3883. 7 pesos per kg. Open daily 8am-1:30pm and 5-7:30pm.) Other services include: **police** (☎863 2013), in the Palacio Municipal on the corner of Calles 51 and 52; **Farmacia YZA,** on the corner of Calles 51 and 52 (☎863 4462; open 24hr.); **Hospital General San Carlos,** Calle 46 461 (☎863 2157); **Internet access** at **Instituto de Computación,** on Calles 50 and 52 (10 pesos per hr.; open daily 8am-10pm); the **post office,** Calle 53, south of the church (☎863 3210; open M-F 8:30am-3pm). **Postal code:** 97700.

🎢🏠 ACCOMMODATIONS AND FOOD. In Tizimín, going budget might be your only option, but watch out for big price increases in July and August. The rooms at **Posada Marian ❷**, on Calle 51 between Calles 48 and 50, are large and slightly run-down, but most have remodeled bathrooms and cable TVs. (☎ 863 3066. Singles and doubles 120 pesos, with A/C 130 pesos; each additional person 15 pesos.) **Hotel 49 ❹**, Calle 49 373, has amazingly clean rooms with color and style, plus TV. (☎ 863 2136. Rooms from 200 pesos for 2 people, 373 pesos for 4 people. Ask for a discount and get 20% off; there are hammock hooks in some rooms to accommodate more people.) **Posada María Antonia ❸**, Calle 50 408, sits directly behind the statue of a woman on the south side of the church. The small, clean rooms all have two beds, TV, and A/C. (☎ 863 2384. Singles and doubles 160 pesos.) **Hotel San Carlos ❸**, Calle 54 407, between Calles 51 and 53, is the farthest from the *zócalo*, but the most comfortable, with spotless rooms, private baths, and an inviting garden. (☎ 863 2094. Singles 150 pesos; doubles 160 pesos; A/C 25 pesos extra.) Find nice, big, pricey rooms at **Hotel San Jorge ❺**, Calle 53 412, on the southwest corner of the Parque Principal, with a small pool in back. (☎ 863 2037. Singles 250 pesos; doubles 280 pesos; A/C 30 pesos extra. Prices double in high season.)

Dining options in Tizimín are limited, no matter what your budget. However, meat-lovers can rejoice—due to Tizimín's ranching community, with over 1000 ranches in the city limits, meat is fresh and abundant. Booths selling tacos and *tortas* at the *mercado*, on the southwest corner of Calles 47 and 48, and scattered *loncherías* serve the city's cheapest food. The town's favorite family diner is **Restaurant Tres Reyes ❹**, on the southwest corner of the Parque Principal, which advertises "La Mejor Comida del Mundo," and is owned by the lively and friendly Willy Canto. Live *ranchero* music, Sundays from 3 to 7pm, accompanies the traditional meals (55-75 pesos). (☎ 863 2106. Open daily 7:30am-midnight.) **César's ❸**, Calle 53 400, near the post office, is also well-established and loved. It recently opened an upstairs addition, **El Mirador**, to accommodate the masses. Diners can sit downstairs in a cheerful stone and stucco Italian-style pizzeria or upstairs on delicate, hand-painted chairs that look out over the park. Dine on fine meats (from 48 pesos), salads (19-30 pesos), pizza (26-45 pesos), burgers (24 pesos), pasta (20-25 pesos), and more. (☎ 863 2152. César's open daily 5pm-1am. El Mirador open daily 9am-2am.)

🏛🎉 SIGHTS AND FESTIVALS. Much work has recently been done to renovate the colonial structures that dominate Tizimín's center. On the east side of the Parque Principal stands the majestic **Iglesia de los Tres Reyes**, still the city's main church, built in 1666. (Open to the public daily 6am-2pm and 4-8pm.) On the corner of Calles 48 and 51, the massive, fortress-like **Ex-Convento de Franciscanos** was completed two years before the church and recalls the city's great age.

Tizimín's main attractions are two relatively underrated historical sights outside the town proper, **Ek' Balam** (see p. 651) and **Kulubá**. The ruins at Kulubá, 33km east of town, have been under reconstruction since 1998 and will not officially open to the public until around 2005. For now, you can talk to the ranchers who own the surrounding property to get access. Julio César (see below) can also help you find your way. Dating from the late Classic period (AD 800-1000), Kulubá represents the easternmost point of Puuc architectural influence. The Edificio de las Ues, a structure 40m long, 8m high, and 7m wide, is carved with "U"s all along its facade. The original red stucco paint is still visible on the carved portions of the stone. The second partially restored building features two surprisingly well-preserved pairs of masks of the rain god Chac and other carved ornamentation.

The tiny town of **Kikil** (pop. 5000), 5km north of Tizimín, is home to the remains of the first colonial church in the area, and the fresh waters of Nohock Dzonot de Kikil, a crystal clear *cenote*. To get there, take a taxi (100-150 pesos round-trip including wait) or, to save pesos, get dropped off by a Río Lagartos-bound bus or a *combi* (10 pesos). Known to locals as **La Iglesia Kikil,** the church, which burned in the mid-19th century during the Caste War, is just to the right of the highway as you enter Kikil from Tizimín. Legend has it that years ago, residents threw a stone at a passing Catholic priest, who then predicted that the church would be laid to ruin. Just inside the gate of the small courtyard, to the left as you face the church, stands a carved stone baptismal font that rings like a bell when struck. The church and the ex-convent are slowly being rebuilt as art centers. Many Maya live in Kikil; you will not only come across their language, but also many of their customs and rituals, which continue alive and well. To return to Tizimín, catch one of the south-bound buses, which pass only about every two hours, or a more frequent *combi*, between 8am and 5pm.

The most important of the town's religious processions is **La Feria de los Tres Reyes,** (Dec. 30-Jan. 13), when pilgrims pour into Tizimín from the surrounding towns and countryside, almost doubling the population of the town. While the parades, dancing, bullfights, and banquets last for two weeks, the most important day of the festival is January 6, El Día de los Reyes, when the pilgrims file through the church to touch the patrons with palm branches. In May and June, visitors to Kikil can enjoy traditional Maya ceremonies such as the **Kaash Paach Bi,** a spiritual cleansing for the land, and the **Chaa-Chac,** a rain prayer. During January and June, Kikil participates in a **pig head dance ritual,** praising and giving thanks to Tsimin, a Maya deity.

Those curious about Tizimín can find out anything they want to from one man, **Julio César,** a fountain of information about the region's Maya ruins. Initially a photographer, he became increasingly interested in the Maya culture he was documenting and now has a small museum upstairs that features his photos as well as artifacts from Maya sites. He himself wrote the first extensive documentation of the site of Kulubá and is eager to point tourists in its direction and to show travelers around other significant sites or ceremonies. (☎863 4944. Look for him at his photography studio on Calle 50 39A near Calle 49. 300 pesos for a trip to Kulubá. Prices negotiable. Studio open daily 8am-9pm.)

RÍO LAGARTOS   ☎986

In naming Río Lagartos (pop. 3500), the Spanish made two mistakes. What they thought was a purely fresh-water river was actually a 53km inlet of ocean water, and what they thought were *lagartos* (alligators) were really crocodiles. Today, this small fishing town is rebuilding from a September 2002 hurricane at the same time as it steadily adapts to its role as an ecotourist hotspot. One of four villages within the 60,000-hectare Ria Lagartos National Park, Río Lagartos is at the head of the inlet, the most convenient place from which to launch into the park. From the small tour boats, you will see the rare mangrove forest, many of the 357 different bird species, crocodiles, and, most spectacularly, some of the 30,000 long-legged orange-red flamingos. The quaint town is a nice place to spend the night and there are plenty of tour variations for those wanting to spend more time in the area or to explore some of the islands and beaches in the reserve.

🖪🔀 TRANSPORTATION AND PRACTICAL INFORMATION. Río Lagartos lies on the northern shore of the eastern Yucatán on a tiny peninsula, 65km north of Tizimín. Streets are numbered but change names frequently and point in every possible direction. **Calle 10** is the town's main street and runs all the way to the waterfront past the main square. A good reference point is the flamingo fountain at the southern edge of the main park. One block east of the fountain is the **bus station. Noreste** offers service to **Tizimín** (45min., 10 per day 5:30am-5:30pm, 20 pesos) and **Mérida** (4 per day, 85 pesos). Other services include: the **Ria Lagartos Visitor's Center,** the orange building on the left of Mex. 180 before arriving in the town (open 7am-6pm); the **police station** (☎862 0002), in the pink municipal building just south of the basketball court in the main square, two blocks north of the fountain; **Centro de Salud**, on Calle 17 off Calle 10 (☎862 0033; open M-Sa 8am-noon and 3-7pm); **Internet access** at **Tocho.com** on Calle 9 near Calle 14, on the waterfront (15 pesos per hr.; open 9am-11pm). Río Lagartos lacks most other services, so you may want to stock up before arriving.

ACCOMMODATIONS AND FOOD. The clean rooms inside the **Posada Leyli** ❷ on Calle 14 at Calle 11 offer the island's best values (☎862 0106. Singles 120 pesos; doubles with bath 200 pesos. Prices rise in July and Aug.) **Posada Lucy ❹**, on the northern waterfront, has five clean rooms with private bath. (☎862 0130; martin_rio2000@hotmail.com. Singles and doubles 250 pesos in high season, 200 pesos in low season.) **Posada Anette ❹** (☎862 0035), offers similar prices for rooms with cable TV for up to 3 people, and gives discounts for smaller parties. The **Cabañas Escondidas ❸** behind Restaurante Isla Contoy provide simple, rustic lodgings with one bed, two hammock hooks, a fan, and private bath. They are as close to the water as you can get. (☎862 0000. *Cabañas* 150 pesos for 2 people, 200 pesos for more. Prices rise 50 pesos in July and Aug.) **Restaurante Isla Contoy ❹**, Calle 19 134, west of the fountain (follow the signs), cooks seafood on the shore (tasty *filet relleno con camarones* 60 pesos) and provides tourist information and boat tours. (☎862 0000. Open daily 7am-10pm.) Relatively cheap seafood is served in a festive ambience at **Los Negritos ❸**, on Calle 10 133, a little south of the flamingo fountain. Most dishes cost 35-45 pesos. (☎862 0022. Open 8am-8pm.) To reach **Las Gaviotas ❹**, walk north from the fountain until you reach the water at Calle 9, then turn left; the restaurant is near Calle 14. Relax on the waterfront while enjoying *ceviche* and *sopa de mariscos*. Main dishes are 40-55 pesos. (☎862 0130. Open daily 10am-7pm.)

SIGHTS AND ENTERTAINMENT. The town's main attraction is the multitude of flamingos, one of the largest concentrations in the Western Hemisphere, that live in **Río Lagartos National Park**. To see them, you must hire a boat captain. On the fascinating 2½hr. boat tour through mangrove forests, you will encounter jumping fish, a crocodile or two, a host of extremely rare birds, and an amazing vista of hundreds, or perhaps thousands, of orange-red flamingos. The best time to see the flamingos is around 6:30am or near sunset. Don't miss the beach that hosts one of the world's oldest salt processing operations. In front of the mountains of salt lies *agua rosada*, a pink river that forms naturally as the water evaporates. The river and the mud along the shoreline are believed to have healing effects; visitors are invited to bathe in the river and apply mud face masks. The tour usually ends with a visit to the freshwater **Chiquilá cenote**, where you can take a refreshing dip. The *cenote* is also accessible by land.

To ensure a safe and ecologically responsible trip through the fragile wildlife reserve, choose a tour guide who is certified by the national park. **Río Lagartos Expeditions**, Calle 19 134, located in the Isla Contoy restaurant, is a little hard to find but worth the trip, especially for bird enthusiasts. The people there speak English, provide binoculars and bird identification books, have insurance, and are incredibly knowledgeable. (☎862 0000; riolagartosecotours.nstemp.com.) **Unión de Lancheros**, a group of fishermen who offer tours and trips in the low season, are at the first kiosk you come to on Calle 9. **Flamingo Tours** is just beyond the Unión kiosks. Most places charge 400-600 pesos per tour boat (up to 6 people), depending on the length of time you are out, and almost all are willing to make a deal, especially in the low season. Fishing prices are 85-100 pesos per hour, and shops open at 6:30am. There is a 20 peso park entrance fee as well. For more time in the reserve, you can hire a boat to take you to **Tatzulen**, a 10km hiking path, or to the private beach on the island of **Holchit**. On the mainland you can hop on a bus (every hr.) and be let off at **Pentucha**. The park has recently built a 200m wooden boardwalk that leads to a *cenote* full of turtles, crocodiles, and amazing plant life. The neighboring town of **San Felipe** is another port where many are happy to spend a few hours strolling along the waterfront.

With most people busy flamingo-watching and fishing during the day, the streets of Río Lagartos are perpetually quiet and empty. The one exception is the town Fiesta, which runs from the second Saturday in July to the end of the month, in honor of Santiago Apostal, the younger brother of Spain's patron saint.

QUINTANA ROO

CANCÚN   ☎998

Perfectly situated on the sparkling Caribbean coast, the once modest city of Cancún (pop. 500,000) has erupted into a metropolis whose alcohol-soaked, disco-shaken, sex-stirred, high season insanity (late December, spring break, and July 15-August 15) surpasses any other in the Western Hemisphere. Ask university students who have "done" Spring Break Cancún and their eyes will inevitably glass over while their heads shake in lingering disbelief as they recall night after night of drunken debauchery. However, taking flaming shots upside-down while onstage in a bikini contest is not the only way to see this fishing-village-gone-party-town. Budget travelers who seek culture and relaxation do have to work a little harder and trek a little farther, but within the city, downtown is calm and local-dominated in comparison to the Americanized Zona Hotelera. Cancún's location and cheaper airfares also makes it a great jump-off point for many budget-friendly excursions up and down the Turquoise Coast, to spots such as the nature preserves at Río Lagartos and Xel-Ha and the Maya ruins at Chichén Itzá and Tulum, which are part of what is known as the Maya Riviera.

▐▌ TRANSPORTATION

INTERCITY TRANSPORTATION

Airport: (☎886 0028), south of the city on Mex. 307. To reach either the downtown area or the Zona Hotelera, buy a ticket for the shuttle van **Green Line** (US$9), which will take you directly to your hotel. Alternately, take your wallet for a spin with the pricey taxis. Airlines include: **AeroCaribe** (☎884 2000); **Aeroméxico** (☎886 0003); **American** (☎886 0086 or 800 904 6000); **Continental** (☎886 0006); **Delta** (☎800 902 2100); **Lan Chile** (☎887 2406); **LACSA** (☎887 3101); **Martinair** (☎886 0486); **Mexicana** (☎886 0068); and **US Airways** (☎800 003 0777).

Buses: (☎884 1378, 800 702 8000 for reservations). The station is downtown on the corner of Uxmal and Tulum, facing Plaza Caribe. The three major bus companies are **ADO, Riviera**, and **Mayab**. Some destinations are: **Campeche** (6hr.; 7:45, 11:30am, 7:30, 10:30pm; 256 pesos); **Valladolid** (2hr.; 5, 6, 9, 11am, 2:30, 3:15, 4:30, 5:30pm; 83 pesos); **Palenque** (14hr., 7:30pm, 389 pesos); **Chichén Itzá** (2½hr.; several daily; 75-115 pesos, depending on company); **Playa del Carmen** (1hr., every 10min., 32 pesos; buses directly from the airport US$8); **Chiquilá** (3hr., 6 per day, 45 pesos). Several buses are also available for **Mérida, Tulum** (44 pesos), and **Chetumal** (142-170 pesos).

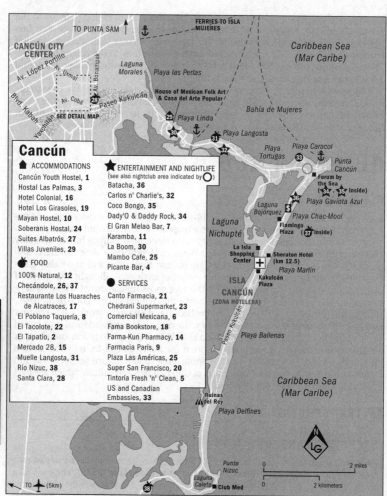

Cancún

🏠 ACCOMMODATIONS

Cancún Youth Hostel, **1**
Hostal Las Palmas, **3**
Hotel Colonial, **16**
Hotel Los Girasoles, **19**
Mayan Hostel, **10**
Soberanis Hostal, **24**
Suites Albatrós, **27**
Villas Juveniles, **29**

🍗 FOOD

100% Natural, **12**
Checándole, **26, 37**
Restaurante Los Huaraches
  de Alcatraces, **17**
El Poblano Taquería, **8**
El Tacolote, **22**
El Tapatio, **2**
Mercado 28, **15**
Muelle Langosta, **31**
Río Nizuc, **38**
Santa Clara, **28**

⭐ ENTERTAINMENT AND NIGHTLIFE
(see also nightclub area indicated by ○)

Batacha, **36**
Carlos n' Charlie's, **32**
Coco Bongo, **35**
Dady'O & Daddy Rock, **34**
El Gran Melao Bar, **7**
Karamba, **11**
La Boom, **30**
Mambo Cafe, **25**
Picante Bar, **4**

● SERVICES

Canto Farmacia, **21**
Chedrani Supermarket, **23**
Comercial Mexicana, **6**
Fama Bookstore, **18**
Farma-Kun Pharmacy, **14**
Farmacia París, **9**
Plaza Las Américas, **25**
Super San Francisco, **20**
Tintoria Fresh 'n' Clean, **5**
US and Canadian
  Embassies, **33**

Ferries: To get to **Isla Mujeres,** take a bus marked "Pto. Juárez" to the 2 ferry depots north of town (Punta Sam for car ferries, Puerto Juárez for passenger ferries; 15min). Express service (20min., every 30min 6am-9pm, 35 pesos) and regular service (45min., every 2hr. 8am-6pm, 18 pesos). At the **Embarcadero,** Kukulcán km 4, Blue Water offers transport (ferries leave at 9:30, 10:30, 11:15am, 12:45, 1:30pm; US$15). Many tour companies in the Zona Hotelera also provide ferry service from 150 pesos.

LOCAL TRANSPORTATION

Getting around Cancún is a snap, as the city's public buses shuttle sunburned beachcombers to and fro with ease. **Taxis** operate within the Zona Hotelera (up to 45 pesos), within downtown (up to 13 pesos), and between the two (up to US$45). Be sure to set a price or rate first. **Buses** marked "Hoteles" run between the bus station downtown and the Zona's tip at Punta Nizuc (6 pesos). They stop at any blue sign along Tulum and Kukulcán, but are also very willing to make unscheduled

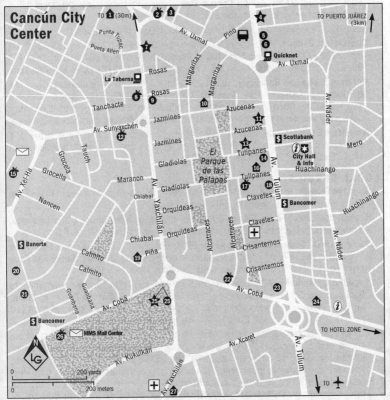

Cancún City Center

stops for new fares. To get off the bus in the Zona Hotelera, push one of the little square red buttons on the ceiling when in sight of your stop—if you don't know where you need to get off, mention the name to the bus driver, with a *por favor*. While many places rent **mopeds** and **bicycles** (useful for exploring the 18km of beaches and action along Kukulcán), buses are much cheaper and nearly as convenient if you have a specific destination.

◆ 🛈 ORIENTATION AND PRACTICAL INFORMATION

Perched on the northeastern tip of the Yucatán Peninsula, Cancún lies 285km east of Mérida via Mex. 180 and 382km north of Chetumal and the Belize border via Mex. 307. Cancún is divided into two areas: **downtown** Cancún, the *centro*, where you'll find more bargains but no beaches, and Isla Cancún, or the **Zona Hotelera**, with fewer bargains but oh-so-much beach and glam. The Zona is a slender "7"-shaped strip of land, and addresses along its one main road are given by kilometer number. Kilometer numbers increase from 1 to 20, roughly north to south.

TOURIST AND FINANCIAL SERVICES

Tourist Offices: Tulum 5 (☎887 4329, ext. 114; relacionespublicas@cancun.gob.mx), inside the Ayuntamiento Benito Juárez. Open M-F 9am-8pm. The **Visitor's Bureau,** at the corner of Náder and Cobá (☎884 6531), offers similar items and help. Open daily

9am-2pm and 4-7pm. Ask for **Cancún Tips,** a free English-language magazine full of useful information and maps. Also available at the airport and at Plaza Caracol.

SECTUR Office: Pecari 23, S.M. 20 (☎881 9000). Open M-F 9am-5pm.

Consulates: Canada, Plaza Caracol, 3rd fl. at km 8.5 (☎883 3360 or 883 3361; fax 883 3232). Open M-F 9am-5pm. **UK**, in Royal Sands Hotel (☎881 0100). Open M-F 9am-3:30pm. **US**, Plaza Caracol, 3rd fl. at km 8.5 (☎883 0272). Open M-F 9am-1pm.

Currency Exchange: Bancomer, Tulum 20 (☎884 4400), at Calle Claveles. Open M-F 8:30am-4pm, Sa 10am-2pm. **Banamex,** Tulum 19 (☎881 6402) gives cash advances and has **ATMs**. Open M-F 9am-5pm, Sa 9:30am-2pm. Small, independent exchange booths are plentiful in the city center and give better rates than vendors accepting dollars.

American Express: Tulum 208 (☎881 4020), 3 blocks south of Cobá. Open M-F 9am-6pm, Sa 9am-1pm. Also in the Zona Hotelera on the 1st fl. of Plaza Kukulcán at km 13 (☎885 3905). Open daily 10am-5pm.

LOCAL SERVICES

Luggage Storage: At the bus station. 5 pesos per hr. Also across the street at Clase Élite; 15 pesos per 6hr., 50 pesos for 24hr. Open 24hr.

English Bookstore: Fama, Tulum 105 (☎884 6541), between Claveles and Tulipanes. Newspapers, magazines, guidebooks, and more. Open Su-Th 9am-9pm, F 9am-5pm.

Supermarket: Comercial Mexicana (☎880 9164), across from the bus station on Tulum. Open daily 7am-midnight. Smaller but more centrally located is **Super San Francisco** (☎884 1155), on Tulum. Open Su 7am-9pm, M-Sa 7am-10pm.

Laundry: Lavandería "Alborada," Náder 5 (☎884 1584), behind the Ayuntamiento Benito Juárez. Self service 10 pesos. Open M-Sa 9am-8pm. **Tintoría Fresh 'n' Clean,** on Tulum next to Comercial Mexicana. Self service (10 pesos per 3kg), drop off (10 pesos per kg), or dry clean. Open M-Sa 9am-9pm.

Car Rental: Rental options are everywhere in Cancún: along the Zona Hotelera, in the *centro,* and at the airport (look for the booths on your left as you exit customs). Prices range from US$35-55 for a car without A/C and US$50-80 per day with A/C. However, special promotions can push rental prices down to as low as US$25 per day. Most rental options offer free pick-up at your hotel. **Alamo,** at km 9.5 (☎886 0168), has prices starting at US$43 per day. **Avicar,** Tulum 3 (☎887 2389 or 884 9635; www.avicar.com.mx), has many locations with air-conditioned cars including insurance starting at US$35 per day with the coupon in *Cancún Tips*. Open 8am-7pm daily.

Moped Rental: Look for vendors between km 3 and 5. 100 pesos per hr., 500 pesos per day. **Bicycles** and **in-line skates** also for rent, 70 pesos per hr., 160 pesos per day.

EMERGENCY AND COMMUNICATIONS

Emergency: ☎066.

Police: ☎884 1913.

Red Cross: Yaxchilán 2 (☎884 1616). English spoken.

Pharmacies: Several along Tulum and Yaxchilán. **Farmacia París,** Yaxchilán 32 (☎884 3005), at the intersection with Rosas. Open 24hr.

Medical Assistance: Hospital Americano, Viento 15 (☎884 6133, after hours 884 6319), 5 blocks south on Tulum after its intersection with Cobá. For an **ambulance,** call **Total Assist** (☎884 8082), at Claveles 5 near Tulum. English spoken.

Fax: (☎884 1529), next to the post office. Open M-F 8am-6pm, Sa 9am-1pm. Telegram service and Internet also available.

Internet Access: Internet cafes are not hard to find, especially near the bus station on Tulum and Uxmal. **La Taberna,** Yaxchilán 23 (☎887 7300) is also a sports bar and cafe. Open daily 10am-5am. **Quicknet** (☎892 3132), Uxmal 2 on the corner of Tulum, features Windows XP for downloading photos. Open daily 10am-1am. Both charge 5 pesos per 15min. and 15 pesos per hr.

Post Office: (☎884 1418), Xel-Ha at Sunyaxchén. Open M-F 8am-6pm, Sa-Su 9am-12:30pm. **Postal Code:** 77500.

ACCOMMODATIONS AND CAMPING

Trying to find cheap accommodations in Cancún is not for the faint of heart. The closest budget travelers will stay to the Zona Hotelera is the Villas Juveniles, located at the far end of the Paseo Kukulcán: all other budget options are located downtown. Bring ear plugs to ensure a good night's rest at any hostel. Hotels are scattered throughout the *centro*, but at 250 pesos per person during the off season (spring and fall), they cater to a very different group. Finally, any tourist agency can set you up at one of the behemoths in the Zona. Keep in mind that prices generally rise during the summer and winter by 25%, and reservations are a good idea any time of the year.

Mayan Hostel, Margaritas 17 (☎892 0103; www.cancunhostel.com), a block from the bus station. A warm, multi-lingual family runs the hostel, and they do whatever they can to make you feel comfortable and safe while showing you their country. Mexican ceramics and tropical plants adorn the spacious rooftop patios that overlook a park. The location is central but quiet, and the *palapas* and fans keep you cool at night. Lockers and sheets provided; TV, kitchen, and Internet available. US$9 per night. ❶

Hotel Los Girasoles, Piña 20 (☎887 3990; www.los-girasoles-cancun.web.com). Hidden on a small side street but convenient to the main streets and shopping centers, this newer, well-lit hotel offers A/C, cable TV, kitchenettes, and clean, cheerful rooms that are cleaned daily. Rooms 300 pesos, a steal at 280 pesos with mention of *Let's Go*. ❺

Cancún Youth Hostel (HI), Palmera 30 (☎887 0191; www.mexicohostels.com), 4 blocks west of the bus station, off of Uxmal. This multilevel hostel is friendly and well-equipped, with a full kitchen, private lockers, hot showers, laundry (30 pesos), bike rental, and Internet (9 pesos per hr.). One room has A/C, and powerful fans keep the other 50 bunk beds well cooled. Rooms 100 pesos per night. ❶

Suites Albatrós, Yaxchilán 154 (☎884 2242), 2 blocks south of Cobá. It's easy to forgive the extra effort to get here after walking through the shady courtyard into one of the apartment-like rooms. Full kitchens, A/C, plus large beds and closets. Rooms upstairs have balconies with laundry lines and sinks. Make reservations at least 3 days in advance. One of the best values in Cancún. Doubles 300 pesos. ❺

Soberanis Hostal, Cobá 5 and 7 (☎884 4564; www.soberanis.com.mx). This new, centrally located hostel has 4 rooms with 2 bunks each, equipped with lockers and refreshing A/C. A TV room and kitchen facilities are in the works, but for now the cleanliness and class make this place worthwhile. Rooms US$12, mention *Let's Go* for 20% off. ❷

Hotel Colonial, Tulipanes 22 (☎884 1535), off of Tulum. 50 well-kept rooms with TV and hot water face a courtyard. Though somewhat pricey for the area, the Colonial's great location in the *centro* makes it a favorite among vacationing Mexicans. Doubles 300 pesos, with A/C 350 pesos. ❺

Hostal Las Palmas, Palmera 43 (☎884 2513; hotelpalmascancun@hotmail.com), 3 blocks from the bus station. Divided into 2 large rooms and has relatively little decoration and socializing space; still, with A/C and free continental breakfast, it offers the conveniences of others and is a good deal. Rooms US$10. ❷

Hotel María Isabel, Palmera 59 (☎884 9015), 3 blocks west of the bus station. Although sparse, the 12 blue and yellow rooms are clean and peaceful. A/C, TV, and hot water. Dorms 120 pesos; singles 250 pesos; doubles 270 pesos. ❷

Villas Juveniles, Kukulcán at km 3 (☎849 4360). Catch any "Hotelera" bus. For those who plan to beach or club it, this is the cheapest place near the Zona Hotelera. 25 single-sex dorm rooms with 8 bunk beds apiece and lockers (bring your own lock). Sheets and pillows provided. 2 communal baths with no hot water. Dorms 100 pesos; pitch a tent on the back lawn for 50 pesos per person. ❶

🍴 FOOD

Although hard to find, a surprising number of affordable places in the resort-heavy Zona Hotelera serve tasty, authentic cuisine. Still, prices tend to be lower and quality higher in the *centro*. The uninitiated should avoid the many street vendors, who follow few (if any) health codes. For some of the cheapest meals around, head to **Mercado 28 ❶**, behind the post office and circumscribed by Xel-Ha—but still beware of less sanitary stands. Alternatively, many restaurants between Tulum and Yaxchilán and in the center of **El Parque de las Palapas ❸** serve authentic and affordable meals priced from 25 to 65 pesos.

🍴 **El Tapatio** (☎887 8317), at the corner of Uxmal and Palmera. This open-air restaurant/bar offers a variety of *comida típica*. Always busy, but customers are less inclined to be irresponsible with alcohol than elsewhere on this Pleasure Island. Satiate your appetite with the *muy rico*, Jalisco-style *pozole* (44-74 pesos) and a fruit smoothie (17-32 pesos). Open Su 9am-11:30pm, M-Sa 8am-1:30am. ❹

100% Natural, near the corner of Yaxchilán and Sunyaxchén in the *centro* (☎884 3617; www.100natural.com.mx). Another location at km 13. Featuring big servings with the freshest ingredients (vegetarian and carnivorous), a soothing garden atmosphere, and a vast menu—42 different combinations of juice (26 pesos), oatmeal with nuts and fruit (30 pesos), eggs or pancakes for breakfast, burgers (soy or beef), salads, and Mexican entrees (35-62 pesos) for later—this Mexican-owned chain is perfect for eating well and feeling good. Live music F-Su 9am-noon. ❹

El Tacolote, Cobá 19 (☎887 3045), Look for the sombrero-sporting yellow chicken out front. A wide menu of seafood available, plus delicious tacos (14-44 pesos) and quesadillas (16-21 pesos) are great deals. Mariachis daily 9-11pm, longer on weekends. Mention *Let's Go* for a complimentary drink with dinner. Open daily 1pm-1am. ❸

Río Nizuc, Paseo Kukulcán at km 22. Take the "Hoteles" bus (4 pesos) to be rewarded with shady *palapas* and a view of the river. Dip your feet while the cook prepares sizable servings of *tikin xic* (fresh barbecued fish; 60 pesos). Seafood entrees 60-70 pesos. A perfect place to escape Cancún chaos while still enjoying the tropical splendor. Open daily 11am-6pm. ❺

Vegetarianos, Cobá 81 near Tankah (☎887 1755). Started 10 years ago by a chef who has since been invited to share her secrets on Cancún's cooking channel, this intimate restaurant will give vegetarians a chance to try the true flavors of Mexican cuisine in an all-you-can-eat buffet (59 pesos). Open 8am-8pm. ❹

Muelle Langosta, at km 5 (☎849 4727). Good food near Playa Langosta. Fried fish and *tikin xic* are yummy at 55 pesos each. All-you-can-eat breakfast served 7:30am-noon (35 pesos). Open daily 7am-11pm. ❸

Checándole, at km 11.5 in the Flamingo Plaza food court (☎885 1302) and Xpu-Hill 6 (☎884 7147). Dishes out authentic Mexican and Yucatec food; the *tampiqueña* (a huge strip of steak with beans and guacamole; 72 pesos) is a favorite. Tacos (26-52 pesos) and burritos (30 pesos) are tasty and inexpensive. Open daily noon-10pm. ❸

Santa Clara, (☎889 9548), a chain at various locations around town. Cool down with some of the best ice cream in Cancún. Single scoop 22 pesos; double scoop 42 pesos. Open daily 10am-10:30pm. ❶

El Poblano Taquería (☎883 9037), on Yaxchilán near Punta Nicchehabi, recently moved to larger digs and expanded its menu. Shrimp tacos (18 pesos), fine cuts of meat (65 pesos), and *gringas* (17 pesos) cooked late. Open daily 5pm-4am. ❷

Restaurante Los Huaraches de Alcatraces, Tulipanes 23 (☎884 2528), near El Parque de las Palapas. Serves up salads, sandwiches (15-22 pesos), milkshakes, breakfasts (25-55 pesos), and dinners (30-70 pesos) cafeteria style. Open daily 7am-11pm. ❷

🔵 SIGHTS

Cancún does not obsess about museums, history, or culture. One bright spot is **El Embarcadero** at km 4 (www.elembarcadero.com), home to both the **Teatro de Cancún** and **La Casa del Arte Mexicana.** The theater features varied performances, mostly in Spanish. (culturaytradicion@prodigy.net.mx. Tickets US$20-25.) La Casa del Arte was recently set up by two people working to promote Mexican culture, and focuses primarily on folk art. Headsets play a 20min. walking tour of the museum. This is a great break from the sun, and a chance to appreciate more than Mexico's natural wonders. The small details of the crowded displays make it worth the trip. (☎849 4332. Open daily 9am-9pm. US$5.) The small archaeological site of **El Rey,** on the lagoon at km 18, provides a different glimpse into local history. The ruins were once part of a Maya fishing community that inhabited what is now the Zona Hotelera from AD 150-1200. When the Spanish arrived, bringing their lethal illnesses, the Maya buried their dead in the foundations of their houses and moved on. The centerpiece of the site is the king's pyramid, though it will only impress those who have yet to see any of the other, spectacular ruins in Mexico. (Open daily 8am-5pm. 30 pesos. Tours in English or Spanish US$10.)

🔵 BEACHES

The world famous beaches of Cancún are rightly renowned: multi-hued turquoise waters gently caress the endless, sparkling Caribbean coastline, home to much tanned and burned skin. Although you'll usually have plenty of company on the sands, Cancún's beaches are long enough (22 km!) and wide enough to accommodate swimming, napping, volleyball games, reading, meditating—you name it. And don't fret about the wall of luxury hotels standing between you and the glorious surf. All beaches in Mexico are public property, and there are regular public access points to the beaches along Kukulcán.

Stealing the show on the north side of the Zona Hotelera are **Playa Langosta** (at km 5.5) and **Playa Tortugas** (at km 6.5). Less spectacular and also less crowded are **Playa las Perlas** (at km 2.5) and **Playa Linda** (at km 3.5) to the west. On the east side of the Zona Hotelera, **Playa Chac-Mool** starts just south of Punta Cancún; the 1m high waves are as thrilling as Cancún's surf gets. Heading south, you'll come across pleasant **Playa Marlín** (at km 12) and quiet **Playa Delfines** (at km 17.8), the closest you will come to serenity without consumerism.

Water sports enthusiasts are in luck: Cancún offers opportunities to participate in nearly every aquatic sport known to mankind. As in most resort areas, prices in Cancún are much higher than those in lower profile neighboring communities. Many organized recreational activities can be arranged through the luxury hotels lining the beaches, or through private companies and tour guides. You might want to have a sense of how much you want to spend or what you want to do before starting to bargain with the vendors who have their own plans for your money. Other activities less directly related to the water, such as bungee jumping (around US$20), are available too.

YUCATÁN

La Crea Escuela de Tabla Vela, at km 3. Windsurfing and sailing instruction (1000 pesos for 8 classes) or equipment rental (250-300 pesos per hr.) from a less commercial venue. Open 10am-5pm daily.

Aqua World, at km 15.2 (☎848 8300). A popular choice for exploring Cancún's water paradise. Jungle tours (US$45) and waterskiing (US$38-50 per 30min.) are offered in the oft-forgotten Laguna Nichuplé. Open daily 7am-10pm.

Scuba Cancún, at km 5 (☎849 7508, or 849 4736; www.scubacancun.com.mx). Well-established dive and watersport center offers 2hr. scuba diving lessons, using both training pool and ocean (US$84); snorkeling (US$27), deep-sea fishing (from US$77), and much more. Open daily 8:30am-8pm.

Blue Water Adventures, at km 5 (☎849 4444; www.bluewateradventures.com.mx), across from Playa Tortugas. Offers a range of aquatic adventures along with jungle tours (US$38.50), snorkeling tours (US$38.50), big game fishing (US$77-99), and waterskiing (US$1 per min.). Open daily 8am-8pm.

🎵🎬 ENTERTAINMENT AND NIGHTLIFE

Movie theaters have many of the same movies you would find in the US; the Plaza Kukulcán is one place to check. However, as night descends, Cancún morphs from a beachgoer's playground into a hotspot primarily for bars and clubs. Out in the Zona, expect to see tipsy tourists parading down Kukulcán, drinks in hands and smiles on faces. If you have the money, these are some of the biggest and hottest clubs in the Western Hemisphere. Crowds in the Zona differ according to time and season. April hosts US college students, June welcomes high school and college graduates, and late night year-round belongs to the stream of wealthy international tourists. The more authentic Mexican sounds and crowds center on, well, the *centro*. Locals favor bars and discos at the south end of Tulum near Cobá and at the north end of Yaxchilán near Sunyaxchén. Most establishments in Cancún open at 9pm, get going after midnight, and close when the crowds tire, around 5 or 6am. Don't worry if you're the only one at 11pm. The masses are on their way.

BARS

Most bars in the *centro* are along Yaxchilán, near Uxmal, and Tulipanes, off Tulum. In the Zona Hotelera, don't bother seeking out local bars—the party is at clubs and chains like Carlos 'n Charlie's, T.G.I. Friday's, and Señor Frog's.

🎸 **Roots,** Tulipanes 26 (☎884 2437; fax 884 5547), off Tulum. Caribbean-colored walls and eclectic artwork with a music motif set the stage in this superior jazz 'n' blues joint that opens to the pedestrian walkway. Live regional musicians Tu-Sa; shows Tu-Th 9pm to midnight, F-Sa 10pm-2am. No cover. Open Tu-Th 5pm-1am, F-Sa 5pm-2am. Serves food until midnight Tu-Th, until 1am F-Sa.

El Gran Melao Bar, Yaxchilán 22 at Calle Punta Allen. A slightly older crowd dances and relaxes to live Caribbean (usually Cuban) music. Open M-Sa 9pm-3am.

Carlos n' Charlie's, at km 5.25 (☎849 4052). Alcohol flows from early in the morning into infinity. Even at midday drunken Americans crowd in, getting downright dirty by the lagoon. Live bands play the evenings; the hot night air turns the makeshift dance floor into a sea of beer, sweat, and hormones. Open bar US$13. Open daily 10am-3am.

La Yaxch, at Uxmal and Yachtitlán (☎898 0486), is a local hang-out where you can challenge friends in pool (tournaments every 2 weeks), darts, or foosball, listen to live rock W-Sa after 10pm, or just sit back and take in the scene over drinks (20-40 pesos). Open daily 5:30pm-4am.

CLUBS

Most of the glitziest clubs and discos are near the Zona's Punta Cancún, near **Playa Caracol** and **Forum by the Sea**. Older travelers beware: Cancún's glam clubs attract US youth eager for sinful pleasures. Dress code for the discos is simple; less is more, tight is just right. Bikini tops often get women in for free; use your judgment in more laid-back clubs. US dollars rule in the Zona.

Coco Bongo, at km 9 in Forum by the Sea (☎883 0592). Steamy, exhilarating, unstoppable. Rock, pop, and hip-hop pound at one of the hottest clubs. The stage, bar, tables, and even dance floor are full of dancing partiers. Cover US$20, includes open bar.

Mambo Cafe, in Plaza las Americas (☎887 7891), is the best place for true *salsa* nightlife. Frequented by locals and curious visitors, those eager for a non-Spring Break night will delight in the relatively cheap cover: 50 pesos for men, 30 pesos for women. Open Th-Su late.

Dady'O, at km 9.5 in Forum by the Sea (☎883 3333). The cave-like entrance lets you know you're headed into a disco inferno. The cave opens onto a stage and dance floor streaked with lasers and pulsating with strobes, with tables and chairs looking down from crevices above. Bikini contests held regularly. Snacks available (30-60 pesos). Staff outside will fill you in on the nightly special. Cover US$20. Open daily 10pm-late.

Batacha, at km 10 in the Hotel Miramar Misión (☎883 1755). Dance under refreshing *palapas* to live *salsa* and *merengue* at this colorful local favorite. Cover 45 pesos. Open daily 10pm-late.

Dady Rock (☎883 3333). Provides the headbanging alternative to Dady'O next door. Hosts 2 live bands every night and offers open bar deals (US$15) several nights per week. Cover US$20. Open daily 6pm-late.

La Boom, at km 3.5 (☎849 7591). 2 nightclubs, a bar, and a pizzeria under the same roof. Serious dancers groove with lasers and...phone booths. Ladies night and open bar vary week to week. Cover US$20.

GAY AND LESBIAN NIGHTLIFE

Cancún doesn't live outside all rules of Mexican propriety—there is little gay and lesbian nightlife, with, surprisingly, none at all in the Zona.

Karamba, Tulum 9 (☎884 0032), on the corner of Azucenas. Pretty much the only happening gay disco in town. A spacious, multilevel gay bar and disco with pop-art murals and a wide variety of dance music beneath wild blue and purple lights. Nightly theme shows or contests start at 1am, cover US$5-6. Open Tu-Su 10pm-5am.

THE BIG SPLURGE

XCARET: XCELLENT BUT XPENSIVE

Legend has it that the Maya bathed themselves in the clea sacred water of the *cenote* o Xcaret ("inlet" in Mayan) during their pilgrimage to Cozumel. The settlement peaked in importance in the 15th century. Fifty kilometers south of Cancún and jus south of Playa del Carmen, Xcaret is now the site of a privately owned and operated theme park dedicated to Maya culture, the natural splendor of the Maya Riviera, and ecological preservation. To be admitted to the massive seaside complex, you'll have to pay a hefty $49 entrance fee, but it is money well spent.

The sprawling site is complete with an abundance of attractions including underground rivers reconstructed Maya villages ruins, an aviary, a museum, a beach, a lagoon, wading pools dolphins, snorkeling and scuba diving tours, stables, botanica gardens, jungle cats, monkeys bats, and a mushroom farm. And it doesn't stop there. At night Xcaret puts on a variety of shows from folkloric dances to ancien Maya rituals.

Buses to Xcaret leave from the Xcaret information center opposite Plaza Caracol in Cancún (daily 9, 10, 11am) or from Tulun (daily 8:15am). ☎883 3143 o 883 3144; www.xcaretcan cun.com. Open daily 8:30am 10pm. US$49, ages 5-12 US$24.50.

Picante Bar, Tulum 20 (www.picantebar.com). A quieter "men's bar." Transvestite and strip shows Th-Sa. Like Karamba, Picante is open to all and "straight-friendly."

SPORTS

Death comes every Wednesday at 3:30pm to the **Plaza de Toros** (☎884 8372 or 882 8248), on Bonampak at Sayil. Tickets for the 2hr. bullfights—which always end with the bull's slaughter—are available at travel agencies on Tulum (300 pesos per person, children under 12 free; group discounts available) or at the bullring on a fight day. Alternatively, catch your favorite sports teams from the US at the sports bar **Caliente,** km 3, where the red velvet seats and huge screens give it a serious boost in class. Drinks, snacks, and coverage of every imaginable sporting event from the college level up are all here. (Open M-F 11am-midnight, Sa-Su 10am-midnight. Horse racing bets, minimum bet US$2.)

SHOPPING

Cancún is best enjoyed if you don't have a fixed budget. Recognizable international brands on sale in the plazas Terramar, Caracol, Flamingo, and Kukulcán, between km 9 and 13, will swallow your dollars whole in the Zona. In the *centro*, artisan markets line Tulum, north of Cobá; be ready to bargain.

FESTIVALS

El Parque de las Palapas, between Tulum and Yaxchilán in the very center of town, hosts free regional music and dance performances during the weekends. The **Folkloric Ballet of Cancún** (☎881 0400 ext. 193), located in the convention center on the Zona Hotelera, puts on some excellent shows, occasionally in the Plaza de Toros. Admirable foresight or lucky timing could mean enjoying Cancún's celebrated **Jazz Festival** (mid- to late-May) or the refreshing **Caribbean Festival** (November). Check with the tourist office for more information and exact dates.

ISLA MUJERES   ☎998

In 1517, Francisco Hernández de Córdoba happened upon this tiny island, looking for slaves to work in Cuban mines. He found instead hundreds of small female statuettes scattered on the beaches and named it Isla Mujeres (Island of Women). Hernández had stumbled upon a sanctuary for Ixchel, the Maya goddess of fertility and the moon. For years Isla Mujeres (pop. 14,500) was a small fishing village with few other visitors. It wasn't until the 1950s that vacationing Mexicans discovered the pristine island and Australians, Europeans, and North Americans followed, transforming it into a hot spot for hippies and backpackers. While some locals still fish, most now cater to daytrippers, fresh from Cancún every morning, or those using the island as a base for exploring **Isla Contoy,** a bird sanctuary 24km away. Although the *centro* has become a full-fledged tourist haven, buildings do not crowd the beaches as in Cancún, and one can certainly still find tropical serenity on **Playa Norte** or get a glimpse of local life, complete with daily *siestas* and late-night dancing.

■ TRANSPORTATION

INTERCITY TRANSPORTATION

Ferries are the only way to reach Isla Mujeres. They leave from **Puerto Juárez,** 3km north of downtown Cancún and are accessible by a "Puerto Juárez" bus (15min., 4 pesos) or by taxi (from 16 pesos). **Express service boats** (20 min., every 30 min. 6am-9pm, 35 pesos) are more expensive than **normal service** boats, which take much longer (45min.; 7:30, 10:30am, 1:30, and 5pm; 20 pesos). Other companies offer

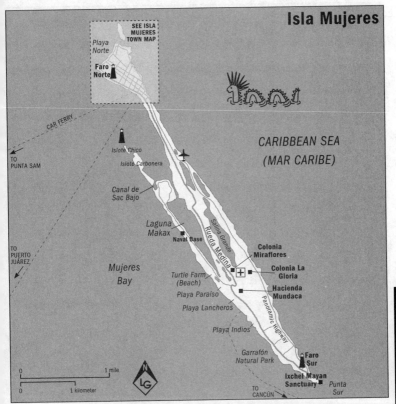

Isla Mujeres

SEE ISLA
MUJERES
TOWN MAP

Playa
Norte

Faro
Norte

CAR FERRY

Islote Chico

Islote Carbonera

TO
PUNTA SAM

CARIBBEAN SEA
(MAR CARIBE)

Canal de
Sac Bajo

Laguna
Makax

Salina Grande

Rueda Medina

Naval Base

Colonia
Miraflores

TO
PUERTO
JUÁREZ

Mujeres
Bay

Turtle Farm
(Beach)

Colonia La
Gloria

Panoramic Highway

Hacienda
Mundaca

Playa Paraíso

Playa Lancheros

Playa Indios

Garrafón
Natural Park

Faro
Sur

Ixchel Mayan
Sanctuary

Punta
Sur

TO
CANCÚN

0   1 mile
0   1 kilometer

YUCATÁN

deluxe service for 75-120 pesos. Arrive early—ferries are notorious for leaving ahead of schedule when full. A **car ferry** runs to Mujeres from Punta Sam, 5km north of Puerto Juárez (5 per day; 12.5 pesos per person, from 50 pesos per car, depending on size). Come at least 30min. ahead of time for the car ferry.

LOCAL TRANSPORTATION

Walking is the best way to navigate the island's lovely *centro*. The best way to explore the ends of the island is to rent a moped, bike, or golf cart, all more common than cars. Red **taxis** (☎877 0066) line up at the stand directly to the right as you come off the passenger dock and zip to **Playa Paraíso** (33 pesos), **Playa Lancheros** (22 pesos), **Garrafón** (44 pesos), and the **Maya sanctuary** (44 pesos). You should have no problem catching one elsewhere. Public **buses**, on the other hand, go only as far as **Playa Lancheros** (4 pesos).

⚡ ⚹ ORIENTATION AND PRACTICAL INFORMATION

Isla Mujeres is a narrow landmass (7.5km by 1km) 11km northeast of Cancún, and the town—the *centro*—is laid out in a rough grid at the northwest corner of the island. Perpendicular to the dock is **Rueda Medina**, which runs the length of the island along the coastline, past the lagoon, Playa Paraíso, Playa Lancheros, and the Garrafón Reef.

Isla Mujeres Town

🏠 **ACCOMMODATIONS**
Hotel Carmelina, **12**
Hotel Marcianito, **14**
Hotel Xul-Ha, **4**
Poc-Na Youth Hostel, **3**
Roca Hotel, **15**

🍴 **FOOD**
Bamboo, **6**
Café Cito, **10**
El Poc-Chuc Lonchería, **16**
French Bistro Francais, **13**

🔴 **SERVICES**
Coral Scuba Diving Center, **9**
Farmacia La Mejor, **18**
Lavandería Ángel, **7**
Lavandería Tim Phó, **17**
Pepe's Rentals, **11**
Tarzan Watersports, **1**

⭐ **NIGHTLIFE**
Kokonuts, **8**
La Junglia, **5**
La Palapa, **2**

Islote El Yunque

CARIBBEAN SEA

Playa del Secreto

Playa Panchalo

Clínica del ISSSTE

Mercado

Moto Kan Kin

Faro Norte

Rueda Medina

ZÓCALO

Mujeres Bay

0 — 200 yards
0 — 200 meters

Bahía

FERRY TO PUERO JUÁREZ (CANCÚN)

TO GARRAFÓN,
BAHÍA DE MUJERES (CAR FERRY)
IXCHEL, PLAYA PARAÍSO,
PLAYA LANCHEROS ✚ RED CROSS

TOURIST, FINANCIAL, AND LOCAL SERVICES

Tourist Office: (☎877 0307), on Rueda Medina. On the right-hand side after the first left beyond the port. Open M-F 9am-8pm, Sa-Su 9am-2pm. **Isla Travel,** Hidalgo 15 (☎877 0025 or 877 0845) can also help with plans and bus tickets. Open M-Sa 9am-6pm.

Currency Exchange: Bital (☎877 0005), on Rueda Medina to the right after exiting the port. Has a 24hr. **ATM.** Open Tu-Sa 8am-7pm. Another ATM is across Morelos at **Banamex.**

Books: Cosmic Cosas, Matamoros 82 (☎860 3495). Buy, sell, and exchange books in many languages, or rent games. Open daily 10:30am-9pm.

Laundry Service: Lavandería Tim Phó, Juárez 94 (☎877 0529), at Abasolo. 45 pesos per 4kg. 2hr. turnaround. Open Su 8am-2pm, M-Sa 7am-9pm. **Lavandería Ángel,** Hidalgo local A-3 near the beach. 30 pesos per 4 kg. minimum. Open M-Sa 7am-9pm.

Rentals: Pepe's Rentals, Hidalgo 19 (☎/fax 877 0019), between Matamoros and Abasolo. Golf carts 120 pesos per hr., 300 pesos per day. Open daily 9am-6pm. **Moto Kan Kin,** Abasolo 15 (☎877 0071), between Hidalgo and Guerrero. Mopeds 80 pesos per hr., 280 pesos per day. Open 8:30am-5pm daily.

Police: Hidalgo at Morelos (☎877 0098, 877 0458 for emergencies), in the Palacio Municipal. Open 24hr. No English spoken.

Red Cross: (☎877 0280), at the Colonia La Gloria, toward the south end of the island.

Pharmacy: La Mejor, Madero 17 (☎877 0116), between Hidalgo and Juárez. Open daily 9am-10pm.

Supermarket: Súper San Francisco, Morelos 5 (☎887 1094 or 887 1092). Open M-Sa 7am-10pm, Su 7am-9pm.

Medical Assistance: Centro de Salud, Guerrero 5 (☎877 0117), at Morelos. The white building at the northwest corner of the *zócalo*. Open 24hr. **Dr. Antonio E. Salas** (☎877 0477), at the **Clínica del ISSTE** (Open M-F 8am-3pm) on the corner of López Mateos and Carlos Lazo, speaks English and will make house calls.

Fax: Telecomm, Guerrero 13 (☎877 0113), next to the post office. Open M-F 9am-3pm, Sa 9am-12:30pm.

Internet Access: Compucentro, Madero 14 (☎887 0744). 25 pesos per hr. Open daily 10am-1am. **Ciberceso,** in Plaza de las Mujeres on Hidalgo, burns CDs and has a color printer. Internet 15 pesos per hr. Open 9am-midnight.

Post Office: (☎877 0085) Guerrero and López Mateos, at the northwest corner of town, 1 block from the Playa Norte. Open M-F 9am-4pm. **Postal Code:** 77400.

■ ACCOMMODATIONS AND CAMPING

Prices increase by about 100 pesos during the high season (July-August and December-April). During those times, inquire ahead and consider making reservations. Many visitors stay in Cancún, where hotels are more plentiful and have A/C. For those disdainful of A/C, camping facilities with electricity and restrooms for a max. of 18 people are available at Punta Sur (☎ 888 0375).

■ **Poc-Na Youth Hostel,** Matamoros 15 (☎877 0090; www.hostelworld.com), on the northeast coast near Playa Panchalo. An international assortment of backpackers, guitar-strumming Americans, and vacationing Mexicans converge in the shady courtyard, clusters around pool tables, and kick backs in hammocks while looking out at crashing waves. Spacious and clean; bring your own lock. Restaurant open daily 7am-11pm. Tent space 65 pesos; bunk beds 90-100 pesos; private rooms 200 pesos. ❶

Hotel Xul-Ha, Hidalgo 23 (☎877 0075), between Matamoros and López Mateos. Large rooms have ceiling fans and mirrors; refrigerator and books in the lobby. Singles and doubles with fan 180 pesos, with A/C and TV 250 pesos. ❸

Hotel Carmelina, Guerrero 4 (☎877 0006), between Abasolo and Madero. Bright colors liven up the well-kept rooms. Reservations recommended Dec.-Jan. Singles with fans 180 pesos; doubles with A/C 280 pesos; triples 300 pesos. ❸

Hotel Marcianito, Abasolo 10 (☎877 0111). Recently remodeled, this hotel manages to avoid the faded blues, greens, and yellows of other Mexican budget hotels and offers peaceful, well-kept rooms. Singles 200 pesos; doubles 250 pesos. ❹

Roca Hotel, Hidalgo 93 (☎877 0407). In a central location behind a pretty gift shop on a pedestrian-only street, the 10-room inn offers a great deal with TV and fans in every room. 155 pesos for one double bed, 300 pesos for two. ❸

◘ FOOD

Seafood abounds in Isla Mujeres. Try *pulpo* (octopus) or *ceviche* (seafood marinated in lime juice, cilantro, and other herbs). Be wary of the restaurants near the plaza and along the Rueda Marina as they are a bit pricier. Also, plan ahead—many restaurant owners close between lunch and dinner for *siesta*.

French Bistro Francais, Matamoros 29, at Hidalgo. Flavors from all over the world come together in a healthful menu. Yogurt (32 pesos) and crepe specials (31 pesos) are popular morning picks, and yummy grilled seafood, cooked with a French flavor, satisfies all. Open daily 8am-noon and 6-10pm. ❸

YUCATÁN

Bamboo (☎877 1355), Hidalgo between Matamoros and López Mateos. This newly opened restaurant already has a loyal clientele who followed Chef Ziggy from Café Cito. Open the day with a fresh, hearty breakfast menu including crepes (27.50 pesos) and fruit with granola and yogurt (40 pesos, big enough for 2), using island-grown ingredients. The restaurant also reels people in with a happy hour (2-4pm; 2 drinks for 25 pesos) and a dinner menu, including vegetarian quesadillas. Open until 11pm. ❹

Café Cito, Matamoros 42 (☎877 0438), at Juárez. Sand and shells under the see-through tabletops let patrons pretend they never left the beach. Replenish body and soul with freshly made crepes, sandwiches, and orange juice. Open high season 8am-2pm and 5-10:30pm; low season 8am-2pm. ❸

El Poc-Chuc Lonchería, Juárez 5, on the corner with Abasolo. Colorful murals of sharks and Maya temples soothe the senses as you dine relatively cheaply on traditional fare from Quintana Roo, such as *salbute* (18-65 pesos). Open M-Sa 8am-10pm. ❸

👁 📷 SIGHTS AND BEACHES

Beaches in Isla Mujeres are peaceful and tranquil. Hotels are far off the shore behind trees, leaving a lot of space for playing or resting. The most popular and accessible beach is **Playa Norte**, on the north shore, where gentle winds and waves lull sunbathers to sleep. The water is shallow and you can wade fairly far out, or recline under the palapas in the hammocks of La Barra de Kin in the north. On the southwest side of the island, **Playa Lancheros** and **Playa Paraíso** open onto Mujeres Bay, forming a smaller beachfront broken up by numerous boat docks. On the south end of the island, the **Faro Sur**, a lighthouse powered by an assortment of old car batteries, overlooks rocky bluffs, providing excellent views. Paths and stairways carved into the rock allow you to descend the cliffs to meet the crashing surf.

A throng of vendors meets each ferry, offering bicycles (60 pesos per day) and mopeds for rent (80 pesos per hr.), as well as fishing and snorkeling trips to nearby **Isla Contoy**, a wildlife sanctuary reef with over 100 bird species. Captain **Ricardo Gaitan**, Madero 16 (☎877 1363 or 877 0798; riccontoy@hotmail.com), and many others can take you on a wonderful trip. (Open daily 9am-4:30pm. Equipment, breakfast, and lunch, 300 pesos.) The **Coral Scuba Diving Center**, Matamoros 13-A and Hidalgo (☎877 0763), has some of the cheapest scuba diving packages (US$29) and lessons (US$59) and snorkel trips (US$15). **Tarzan Watersports**, on Playa Norte near Guerrero, offers an aquatic adventures and rents beach gear. (☎877 0679. Open daily 9am-5pm. Waterskiing US$50 per 30 min., kayaks US$25 per hr., 1hr. windsurfing lesson US$50.) **Bahía**, to the right of the dock on Rueda Medina (☎877 0340), sells fishing supplies. (Open 9am-9pm daily.)

To see endangered sea turtles, head over to the **Turtle Farm**, across the *laguna* from the northern half of the island and northwest of **Playa Paraíso**. This biological research station breeds three species of sea turtles. Female turtles, captured by **Eco Caribe** in May, lay their eggs in the safety of the station's beach throughout the summer and are returned to the wild in October. The young are reared for a year before they, too, are released. (Open daily 9am-5pm. Guide 20 pesos.) Visitors can enjoy exciting cable rides, snorkeling, and an oceanside swimming pool at the **Garrafón Natural Park** (US$10), located to the southeast of **Playa Lancheros.**

The Maya ruins of **Ixchel**—a pilgrimage destination for women who sought help from the goddess of fertility—are on the southern tip of the island, accessible by taxi (40 pesos). Most of the site was reduced to rubble by Hurricane Gilbert in 1988, but a partially reconstructed one-room building and an awesome panorama of the Yucatán and the Caribbean await those who make the journey.

NIGHTLIFE

Isla Mujeres offers relaxing nightlife for those wanting to escape the mega-resorts and throngs of drunken American teens in Cancún. Most of the best nighttime activity is concentrated at the north end of Hidalgo. Around sunset, tourists and locals bounce from one bar to the next toasting with half-price Happy Hour bargains. The two-story **Kokonuts,** Hidalgo 65, has a slightly older feel. Patrons refresh themselves with tequilas and ice-cold beers and dance under a *palapa* to every strain of *música latina.* (☎877 0797. Open daily 7pm-late.) **La Junglia,** across from Kokonuts, is the favorite of local youth. (Open daily 8pm-3am.) For something closer to the beach, **La Palapa,** on Playa Norte to the right of Hidalgo, hosts a temporary dance floor on the sand adorned with lights and glow-in-the-dark artwork. (Open daily 11am-6am.) **Nitro Club** is a true *discoteca* suitable for all who like to dance. (Open late F-Su.)

ISLA HOLBOX   ☎984

Isla Holbox (ohl-BOSH) was settled in 1873 by descendants of pirates who came to the isolated 40km by 2km finger-shaped island to start a new, more tranquil life of fishing. Almost 130 years later, the island remains a peaceful refuge. Nearby travelers in Cancún and vacationing Mexicans needing to get away escape to Holbox's boat-lined shores, desolate sands, and quiet village (pop. 3000), where all the people and all the dogs have known each other all their lives. Though this island is small and unbelievably slow-paced, that doesn't stop the *holboxeños* from enjoying themselves, nor should it stop you; it's not so small that you will feel trapped among other vacationers. *Semana Santa* and July and August may be the only times when you will feel you have to share the island. There are few mosquitoes, but bring baby oil to prevent the *chaquistes* (tiny, vicious bugs) from biting you.

TRANSPORTATION AND PRACTICAL INFORMATION

Isla Holbox lies just off the northern coast of Quintana Roo, in the Gulf of Mexico. Getting there requires planning. The easiest way is to take a **bus** from **Cancún** (8am, 12:30, 1:30pm; 50 pesos) to **Chiquilá,** then hop on a "Los 9 Hermanos" *lancha* (approx. every 2hr. 6am-6pm, returning 5am-5pm; 30 pesos). You can also get to the **ferry** at Chiquilá via second-class bus from several cities, including: **Mérida** (6hr., 11:30pm); **Tizimín** (3hr.; 12:30, 4, 11am, 2pm); **Valladolid** (2:30am, 57 pesos). Return buses to Valladolid, Cancún, Mérida, or Tizimín meet the ferry (all at 5:30am). The Cancún and Tizimín buses leave Chiquilá at 7:30am and 1:30pm as well, and the Tizimín buses also have a 4:30pm departure. If you miss the last ferry, Chiquilá's **Puerta del Sol ❷** will welcome you. (☎875 0121. 100 pesos per night.) The ferry dock is on the southwestern edge of the island, 150m from the bus stop.

In Holbox, **police** (☎875 2166 or 875 2165) may be found at all hours sitting on the benches of **La Alcaldia Municipal** (☎875 2110), the greyish-pink building on the corner of Juárez and Díaz. The **Centro de Salud** (☎875 2163 or 875 2164), a blue and white building 200m from the dock on the right side of Juárez, houses a 24hr. doctor. There is **no bank** on the island, so **bring all the cash you will need.** **Fax** and telegram service are on the corner of Juárez and Díaz at Telecomm. (☎875 2053. Open M-F 9am-3pm.) **TELMEX** phones are scattered throughout the village and park. **Internet el Parque** offers **money exchange, fax,** phone, and **Internet** service (20 pesos per hr.) at the northwest corner of the park. (Open daily 9am-midnight.)

♦ ACCOMMODATIONS AND CAMPING

Finding places to stay on Isla Holbox isn't a problem, especially in the low season, but you get what you pay for. The *cabañas* on the beach offer incredible views and amenities, often with on-site pools or restaurants, but they cost about four times as much as places without the view. Many family-run *posadas* cluster around the *zócalo* or Parque Juárez, which is about 500m north of the dock. Prices can easily double during high season. Free camping is available on the beach, but make sure your things are well-secured, as it may not be all that safe.

Posada D'Ingrid (☎875 2070), 1 block northwest of the *zócalo*, at Morelos and Joaquín. Gleaming rooms with sparkling baths and fans open up to a *palapa*-roofed patio with speakers and card tables. A/C available. Singles 150 pesos; doubles 200 pesos, with A/C and TV 250 pesos. ❸

Posada la Raza (☎875 2072), on the west side of Parque Juárez. Owners take pride in making their *posada* feel like home. Clean white rooms with new fixtures. Singles and doubles 150 pesos, with A/C 350 pesos. Discounts for longer and off-season stays. ❸

Posada los Arcos (☎875 2043; saul9542@hotmail.com), next door to Posada La Raza. Clean, well-kept rooms have 2 beds and fans. Boasts a large, fake flamingo- and flower-filled courtyard. The only place in town to rent bikes (15 pesos per hr., 60 pesos per day). Singles 100 pesos, with A/C and TV 200 pesos. Each additional person 50 pesos. Prices increase 50% in the high season. ❷

Posada Playa Bonita (☎875 2102), near the beach off the NW corner of Juarez, combined with the Buena Vista Restaurant/Grill. Rooms with fridge, fan, 2 beds, bath, and style. 250 pesos in the high season, 150 pesos for up to 3 people. 70 pesos for two full meals at the restaurant with stay. ❸

Posada Don Joaquín (☎875 2088), on Igualadad just east of Parque Juárez, the 3rd house on the left, with a Coca-Cola sign on the doorway. Large, makeshift rooms with cement floors, fans, and private bath are the cheapest on *La Isla*. Ask in Abarrotes Addy if you are interested in staying (and saving money!). Look at the rooms first; quality is somewhat uneven. Rooms 60 pesos for 2 people, 80 pesos for 3. ❶

◗ FOOD

Given that Isla Holbox's economy is based on fishing, it should be no surprise that most restaurants serve seafood. The *loncherías* that open in the park for breakfast and late night snacks are the cheapest option and probably the most reliable, since some restaurants only open in the tourist season and others open when they feel up to it. **Restaurant Edelyn ❹**, Palomino, on the southeast corner of the park, grills large fish or steak (40 pesos) and flips pizza (from 35 pesos) in its two-story *palapa*. (☎875 2024. Open daily 10am-12pm.) **Pelicano's ❸**, near Edelyn on Palomino, serves generous portions of international dishes and has live music at peak times. Their specialty, *papas rellenas* (stuffed potatoes, 30-35 pesos), is always made fresh and filled with anything from seafood to veggies. (Open 9am-4pm and 7pm-midnight.) One block south of Parque Juárez on Palomino, the *palapa*-covered **Zarabanda**, named after a Caribbean rhythm, prepares excellent seafood dishes. (☎875 2094. Open daily 9am-9pm.) **Cariocas Restaurant ❹**, 1½ blocks east of the *zócalo* on the northern shores, carefully flavors the zesty fish filet *a la veracruzana* (grilled fish with tomatoes, onion, green peppers, bananas, and olives; 53 pesos) and the steak *a la tampiqueña* (46 pesos) with beans and guacamole. (☎875 2210. Open daily 9am-10pm.) For natural juices, a wide assortment of healthful and therapeutic shakes (13-20 pesos), and tropical fruit salads (25 pesos with either yogurt or granola), head to **La Isla del Colibri ❷**, at the southwest corner of the *zócalo*. (☎875 2000. Closed W.)

🏖 🎵 BEACHES AND ENTERTAINMENT

New hotels release their guests onto the picturesque north shore of the island each morning, but you can still soak up Isla's tranquility on some of its gorgeous sun-saturated beaches. The **Playas de Recreo,** just north of town, are fairly crowded with fishing boats, but less than 1km east of town lie fairly desolate, seashell-sprinkled sands and emerald-colored waters caressed by gentle winds. Tourists can also take a 2km trek on the inland road to **Punta Mosquito,** where a 25km stretch of virgin beach begins and many locals go to pull up conches. Rent a bike from Posada los Arcos (see p. 670) if you want to trek beyond walking distance.

Several tiny islands and an inlet on the mainland, only accessible by boat, will thrill admirers of nature, especially birdwatchers. **Isla Pájaros,** home to nearly 40 species of birds including flamingos and pelicans, lies 30min. southeast of the dock. Walkways and viewing terraces await visitors. On the mainland west of Isla Holbox, also accessible by boat, is **Ojo de Agua Yalahau,** an inlet fed by a subterranean freshwater spring. Finally, across the lagoon that separates Isla Holbox from the mainland is **Isla Pasión,** named for the amorous pairs of both birds and humans that "relax" there off-season; it is now also home to a lookout tower that offers a true bird's-eye view. Fishermen, who have established a cooperative, offer **tours of the islands** (6hr. tour from 800 pesos). Find the fishermen near the ferry dock or ask for Peter Pan (seriously). Fisherman-led tours offer the most direct interaction with nature. The **Delfín Artículos de Pesca** house (☎875 2018), one block from the northern shores on Juárez, also offers tours. Prices from both are similar. (Generally, 4hr. tours go from 600 pesos for up to 6 people.) There are also 2hr. tours that leave from Playa Recreo and circle the island for 50 pesos per person. Contact the Tarpoon Club (☎875 2144 or 875 2155) on the northern shore for **fly fishing.** At **Isla Contoy,** where you can snorkel and visit the biology center and the crocodile farm, set up to help save two endangered breeds found on the island (10 min. by boat).

The small size and relative isolation of Isla Holbox would seem to forecast a sleepy evening, but the locals are a rowdy bunch. To see *holboxeños* at their liveliest, cruise the brightly lit Parque Juárez at dusk, when friends and families gather to socialize, enjoy the playground, play the local *lotería,* and watch the basketball and volleyball games. During high season, Isla Holbox's restaurant/bar scene caters to tourists and a disco opens at **Cariocas Restaurant** (see Food, above). (Margaritas and piña coladas 25 pesos.) Pelicano's also holds residents' attention throughout the night with drinks, tunes, and live music in season. For more natural entertainment, head to the north shore at night. If conditions are right, you can witness *ardentía,* a rare and completely natural **phosphorescence.** Microorganisms respond to movement in the water by turning bright green; just kick the water or stir it with your hands to see the glow. For a guide, take an **ecotour** with the Tortugas Marinas conservation group, northeast of the *zócalo* on Igualdad. (☎875 2153. Tours Apr.-Sept., when several endangered species come to shore to nest.)

PLAYA DEL CARMEN ☎ 987

It is understandable that this town of 25,000, smack in the middle of Quintana Roo's legendary Maya Riviera, is growing faster than perhaps any other city in Latin America. Playa tempts travelers with its proximity to the dive sights of Cozumel, the shameless hedonism of Cancún, and the inland Maya ruins, while the true seduction may occur on the long stretch of silky white beach married to spectacular turquoise surf. In the past decade, travelers heading to the reefs of Cozumel have "discovered" Playa and decided to stay, bringing with them the flavors, architecture, and spirit of their homes. The awesome beach, excellent food, sunset happy hours, burgeoning nightlife, and perfect location for exploring the Yucatán make Playa a tourist's paradise.

Playa del Carmen

ACCOMMODATIONS
Cabañas Las Ruinas/Popul-Vu, **14**
Hostel Playa, **5**
Posada Freud, **1**
Posada Lily, **16**
Posada Papagayo, **8**
Urban Hostel, **7**

Estas Son Las
 Mañanitas, **12**
Media Luna, **1**
R. La Tarraya, **15**
Todo a las Brasas, **9**

FOOD
Amigo's Restaurant, **13**
Café Tropical, **4**

NIGHTLIFE
Blue Parrot, **2**
Capitán Tutix, **10**
Karen's Grill, **11**
Mambo, **6**

TRANSPORTATION

Buses: From the station (☎873 0109 or 878 0309) at the corner of Quinta and Juárez, **ADO** goes 1st-class to: **Chetumal** (4½hr., 12 per day, 139 pesos); **Mexico City** (25hr.; 12:15, 7:17pm; 864 pesos); **Orizaba** (14hr., 7:15pm, 707 pesos); **Puebla** (23hr., 6:15pm, 795 pesos); **San Andrés** (9½hr.; 3:45, 10:15pm; 476 pesos); **Veracruz** (12hr.; 3:45, 10:15pm, 624 pesos); **Villahermosa** (12hr., 8 per day noon-10:15pm, 395 pesos). **Cristóbal Colón** goes to: **Palenque** (11hr., 4 per day, 337 pesos); **San Cristóbal** (15hr., 4 per day, 428 pesos); **Tuxtla Gutiérrez** (16hr., 3 per day, 463 pesos). **Premier** goes to **Mérida** (5hr., several daily, 181-196 pesos), via **Ticul** (3½hr., 147 pesos). Many lines offer service to **Tulum** (1hr., 10 per day, 28 pesos).

Taxis: Standard rates to: sights **around Playa** (40 pesos), **Xcaret** (80 pesos), **Akumal** (195 pesos), **Cancún** (355 pesos). All prices may be negotiable.

Ferries: Playa del Carmen is also accessible via ferry from **Cozumel** (see p. 677).

ORIENTATION AND PRACTICAL INFORMATION

Playa is located on the Maya Riviera, 34km south of Cancún and 90km north of Tulum. The ferry to Cozumel docks two blocks south and one block east of the bus station, where Calle 3 hits the beach. **Juárez** runs northwest from the beach to the Cancún-Chetumal road, **Highway 307**, 1.5km away. **Quinta** (Avenida 5) is a pedestrian walkway lined by popular shops and restaurants running parallel to the beach. East-west *calles* increase by two in either direction from Juárez; north-south *avenidas* increase by five from the beach.

Tourist Office: (☎873 2804), on the corner of Juárez and Av. 15. English, French, Italian, and German spoken. Open M-F 9am-9pm, Sa-Su 9am-5pm.

Currency Exchange: Bital (☎873 0404), on Juárez, 1 block west of the *zócalo*. Exchanges currency and traveler's checks. 24hr. **ATM.** Open M-Sa 8am-7pm.

Bookstore: Fama (☎873 0939), on Juárez between Av. 10 and 15. Open daily 9am-10pm.

Laundry: Lavandería Tintoría, on Calle 6 between Av. 5 and 10. Same day wash and dry service 16 pesos per kg. Self-serve wash 13 pesos per 3kg, driers 13 pesos per 15min. Open daily 7:30am-7:30pm.

Emergency: ☎066.

Police: (☎873 0191), on Juárez, 2 blocks west of the plaza between Av. 15 and 20. English spoken.

Pharmacy: Farmacia del Carmen (☎873 2330), on Juárez, opposite the bus station. Open 24hr. **Playa Mart** (☎803 1779), on the northwest corner of the *zócalo* off Juárez, is an all-in-one store with fairly complete groceries in back. Open 8am-10pm.

Medical Assistance: Red Cross (☎873 1233), Av. 25 at Juárez. **Centro de Salud** (☎873 0314), on the corner of Juárez, across from the post office. Some English spoken.

Internet Services: La Taberna Internet Cafe (☎803 0447 or 803 0448), on the corner of Calle 4 and Av. 10. 18 pesos per hr. Open daily 10am-3am. **Maya Systems** (☎803 2281), Calle 6 and Av. 10; 15 pesos per hr. Also has **fax.** Open daily 11am-1am.

Post Office: (☎873 0300), on Juárez, 3 blocks from the plaza. Open M-F 9am-5pm, Sa 9am-1pm. **Mexpost** in the same building. Open M-F 9am-3pm. **Postal Code:** 77710.

ACCOMMODATIONS AND CAMPING

With Playa's stunning recent growth, luxury accommodations are proliferating and budget accommodations are relatively scarce. Hostels are probably the way to go if you are looking to spend less than 200-250 pesos per night, the going rate for the cheapest hotels. During high season (Dec. 21-Apr. 15 and July 15-Sept. 15), prices are especially high and reservations are necessary. Most establishments lie along Quinta or Juárez, near the beach—but the farther away, the cheaper.

Posada Freud (☎873 0601; www.posadafreud.com), on Quinta, between Calles 8 and 10. Palm trees and colorful hammocks draw passersby to Freud's 11 unique abodes with clean, hip decoration. Coffee makers, refrigerators, and wit and charm from manager Carlos come with rooms. Call ahead for reservations. Rooms from US$25. ❺

Hostel Playa (☎879 3928; www.hostelplaya.com), on the corner of Calle 8 and Av. 25. The three men's and three women's bedrooms circle a spacious living area complete with games, books, hammocks, a full kitchen, and TV/VCR. The owners provide everything from the morning's coffee and bathroom scales to snorkel rentals. If the prices survive growing demand, this deal will only get better as Playa expands. 90 pesos per person, 80 pesos with ISIC card; private doubles 220 pesos. ❶

Posada Papagayo (☎873 2497), Av. 15 between Calles 4 and 6. Spacious, nicely furnished rooms await the traveler who goes the extra mile to find Papagayo. Singles and doubles 150 pesos; triples 200 pesos. Prices rise 100 pesos in high season. ❸

Posada Lily, the flaming pink building on Juárez, 1 block west of the plaza. This noisy but convenient location near the bus stop houses small, cushy beds in clean rooms. Singles 120 pesos; doubles 150 pesos; triples 200 pesos. ❷

Urban Hostel (☎879 9342 or 803 3378), on Av. 10 between Calles 4 and 6. This conveniently located hostel with a bohemian feel, 2 blocks from the beach, offers single-sex bunk beds under a giant *palapa,* ceiling fans, lockers, and a kitchen for an almost unbeatable price. 95 pesos per person. ❶

Cabañas Las Ruinas/Popul-Vu (☎873 2749). This eclectic place is almost perfectly located. Hostel-style *cabañas rústicas* have ceiling fans and tiny, stiff military beds, plus communal bath and cooking facilities. 200m north of the ferry dock, they are a hop, skip, and jump from Juárez and Quinta. Hammock-space and camping 100 pesos per person, available only in high season. Singles and doubles 160 pesos, 180 pesos with private bath. Each additional person 60 pesos. Prices rise in high season. ❷

◖ FOOD

It can be hard to find a bargain amongst Quinta's flashy restaurants with distinctly French and Italian flavors, which cater to a growing European expatriate population. While Playa is the place to splurge on a meal, if you decide not to, the host of *loncherías* west of Av. 10 and near Calle 6 that serve inexpensive *tortas* and regional cuisine will take care of you. Breakfast vendors flood the *zócalo* early.

Todo a las Brasas, next to Urban Hostel on Av. 10. This new restaurant presents an original take on an old favorite: the barbequed chicken comes with grilled vegetables alongside 5 creative versions of salsa, inlcuding chile-nut and cilantro. Get a complete meal with chicken, roasted veggies, beans, rice, a drink, and more for 20 pesos. Eat in or take out. Open 11am-8pm. ❷

Estas Son las Mañanitas, on Quinta between Calles 2 and 4. Even picky locals recommend this interesting blend of Mexican and Italian food. Pizza starts at 45 pesos and traditional Mexican dishes at 54 pesos. ❹

Media Luna (☎873 0520), on Quinta between Calles 12 and 14. This eatery has found its niche experimenting with fusion foods, bringing together international ingredients into well-prepared and -presented dishes. Vegetarians will be in heaven, and chicken offerings will satisfy all but the most serious meat-and-potatoes diners. The spacious seating makes lingering comfy. Tasty tropical fruit crepes 55 pesos, luscious fruit platters with granola 50 pesos, creative salads 50-70 pesos. Open daily 8am-11:30pm. ❹

Restaurant La Tarraya (☎873 2040), at the end of Calle 2, on the beach. This budget-friendly restaurant/bar is perfect if you don't want to leave the beach, even for a second. Fish filet *tikin xic* (barbequed fresh fish) 85 pesos per kg. Open daily noon-9pm. ❸

Café Tropical (☎873 2111), on Quinta, between Calles 8 and 10. Enjoy the generous portions of falafel, hummus, chicken, and seafood while seated beneath a gigantic shady *palapa.* Smoothies 27 pesos, big sandwiches 41 pesos, omelettes with a rich variety of fillings 39 pesos, other entrees 55-138 pesos. Open daily 7am-1am. ❹

Amigo's Restaurant (☎803 1125), on Calle 2 between Av. 10 and 15. This Mexican restaurant with jukebox serves omelettes (20 pesos), and later in the day, tacos (6 pesos) and other typical *lonchería* food at fairly low prices: even seafood is under 60 pesos. Open daily 7am-10pm. ❸

◖ BEACHES AND WATERSPORTS

Lined with palm trees and skirting the turquoise waters of the Caribbean, Playa's beaches are sandy, white, and oh-so-relaxing. They are relatively free of seaweed and coral, strewn instead with scantily (if at all) clad tourists. In search of an aquatic escape? Vendors near the *zócalo* have a "special offer, just for you"—which may involve snorkeling, scuba diving, or fishing. Depending on your bargaining ability, 120-160 pesos will buy you an hour's worth of windsurfing. Some of the fancier hotels just south of the pier rent varied equipment, as do shacks a few hundred meters north. Several dive shops also await on the western side of the *zócalo*. The **Abyss Dive Shop,** on the beach at Calle 12, in the Blue Parrot, will fulfill all your diving and snorkeling desires. It services 13 different dive sites and caters to all skill levels. (☎873 2164; www.abyssdiveshop.com. "Discover" scuba trips US$69. Open water courses US$350. 2-tank dive US$59. 2½hr. snorkeling trips 250 pesos. Snorkeling equipment 60 pesos. Open Su 8:15am-6pm, M-Sa 8:15am-9pm.)

◨ ♪ NIGHTLIFE AND ENTERTAINMENT

Come nightfall, the shops on Quinta close and the street transforms from a busy thoroughfare of vendors into a glitzy nightspot. Sun-lovers recuperate from the day's rays by swaying in hammocks and jiving to guitar-strumming, flute-playing locals. At **Karen's Grill,** on Quinta, 1½ blocks north of the plaza, waiters start the party by escorting women to the dance floor and pouring *café flambé* waterfall-style, all to the rhythms of *salsa* and *merengue*. (☎879 4064. Live South American music daily 6pm-midnight. Happy Hour 10am-1am.) Swings replace the conventional bar stools at the **Blue Parrot Inn Palapa,** on the beach at Calle 12. It was once on a list of the 10 best bars in the world—and it hasn't lost its touch. Kick back to live music, starting up at 10pm Th-Sa, play pool, dance, or watch the waves crash as you cherish your beer. (☎872 0083. Open 24hr. Ladies drink free M 8pm-midnight.) **Capitán Tutix,** a restaurant by day and bar by night, is also on the beach, at Calle 4. Live music, mostly rock, from 10pm-2am daily. (☎873 1748. Open 9am-4am.) **Mambo** is Playa's newest addition, reeling in crowds with a tropical atmosphere of color and salsa music. Dancers begin arriving at 11:30pm and the band goes on at midnight. For preparation, go for a 70 peso salsa lesson before the club opens at 11pm; details at the club. Alternatively, indulge your hankering for Hollywood at **Cinema Playa del Carmen,** four blocks west of the *zócalo* and one block north of Juárez. (Tickets 10-15 pesos.)

AKUMAL ☎984

Akumal, "Place of the Turtles" in Maya, is a high-class, luxury resort catering to an older, wealthier crowd who are drawn to its older, wealthier activities. Once a coconut plantation, monied entrepreneurs put their money elsewhere to make this the first resort on the Maya Riviera. The town is a string of upscale hotels lining the bay, plus 200 indigenous families living a few kilometers away across the highway. Don't let this deter you, oh fearless budget traveler: you can find some deals, and world-class diving and snorkeling at the biggest living reef in the Western hemisphere is worth a few extra bucks. Besides the tourism possibilities, an international assortment of scientists and students at CEA, the **Centro Ecológico Akumal,** will teach you the latest about Caribbean hurricanes, endangered sea turtles, environmentally beneficial toilets, and coral ecosystems.

◨ ⁊ TRANSPORTATION AND PRACTICAL INFORMATION. Akumal is located

on the Maya Riviera, 37km south of Playa del Carmen and 30km north of Tulum. The Akumal resort area is a short 1-2km toward the ocean from the small *pueblo* by Mex. 307. **Taxis** are available at the highway and can take you to the resort area for 10-15 pesos. To get to either Tulum or Playa del Carmen, you can flag a **bus** down on Mex. 307, but it's probably easier to take the white vans going north or south that generally pass each hour (10 pesos).

Travel Services of Akumal, right outside CEA, has it all: car and bike rental, telephone, fax and email, **money exchange,** airport transportation, and tours to nearly every sight. (☎875 9030; www.akumaltravel.com. Open M-F 9am-1pm and 3-5pm, Sa 9am-1pm. **Exchange booth** open M-Sa 8am-1pm and 2pm-6pm.) The **supermarket Super Chomak,** on the right as you approach the main gates, has an **ATM** and stocks all the essentials, but prices can be outrageous. (☎875 9016. Open daily 7am-9pm.) For better prices but lesser selection try the mini-super across the street, **Las Palmas.** Market stands with fruits and veggies open M, W, and Sa 8am-5pm. Other services include: **Lavandería,** next to Las Palmas. (18 pesos per kg, 2kg min.; open M-Sa 7am-1pm and 5-7pm); **emergency** service (☎060; for medical service try to get to Playa del Carmen to avoid outrageous costs); **police** (☎875 9345); **Internet, fax,** and phone at **Cyber Paradise,** across from the Dive Shop. (US$6 per hr. Open M-F 9am-8pm, Sa 9am-6pm.) **Postal Code:** 77760.

⌂🏠 ACCOMMODATIONS AND FOOD. The Centro Ecológico Akumal, or **CEA ❷,** is the only budget option in Akumal. The center hosts university students from Mexico and abroad who are volunteering or studying. As long as there is space, CEA is happy to have others at the ecologically conscious compound. The large, well-lit rooms (four beds in each) have private baths and some come with welcome A/C. The center has a communal kitchen and hot showers. During university breaks, the Ecocenter gets busy and fills up fast. Email or call ahead to make reservations. (☎875 9095; cea94@cancun.com.mx. Rooms 100 pesos per person.) **Posada Que Onda ❺,** beyond the lagoon at the end of the signs, is the next cheapest place. Still, the beautifully furnished rooms, pool, and nearby restaurant are pricey for a lone traveler. (☎875 9101. Rooms sleep up to 4 for 450 pesos.)

Like the hotels, most restaurants in Akumal go straight for the wallet. Yet a couple of places do serve food at budget-friendly prices. **Ecocina ❸,** just outside the CEA, is economical and eco-conscious, and about the only place belonging to locals. It offers new, tasty dishes daily. (Breakfast 30 pesos, lunch specials 45 pesos, milkshakes 15 pesos. Open daily 8am-3pm.) **Lonchería Alenmalito ❹,** right next to Super Chomate, also offers decent food at decent prices. (Breakfast 15 pesos. Lunch and dinner 35-65 pesos. Open daily 6am-9pm.) Another *lonchería,* behind Las Palmas, is a lunch-only spot popular with locals. For a more expensive treat, try **La Cueva del Pescador ❺,** near CEA. Sit outside at a table cut from a giant tree trunk or eat indoors and dig your toes into the sand. Seafood is the favorite, and entrees average a hefty 75-150 pesos. (☎875 9205. Open M-Sa 11am-9pm.)

⌂🏖 BEACHES AND SIGHTS. The beach of Akumal Bay is famed for its white sands and the clarity of its tranquil waters, protected by the offshore reef. Shallow waters close to shore contain a remarkable variety of animal life in the sea grass and just beyond. Coral, inch-long lettuce slugs, sleeping fish, and large sea turtles are just a few of the creatures you may come across. Although snorkelers, divers, and sunbathers litter the beach and bay, there still seems to be room for all. The **Akumal Dive Shop** rents snorkeling equipment (US$5 per day); be aware that fins are disruptive to habitats. The dive shop also organizes snorkeling and scuba trips. Certification courses available. (☎875 9032; www.akumal.com. US$45 for 1-tank dive, US$60 for 2. Fishing trips US$100 for 2½ hrs., up to 4 people. Sailing trips US$30-60. Open daily 8am-5pm.) If you want to expand your environmental horizons, CEA (see p.48) hosts lectures on a variety of topics, from sea turtles to the modern Maya to theories of dinosaur extinction. (☎875 9005; www.ceakumal.org. Lectures M-F 4:30pm. Free, but donations accepted.) CEA also offers night walks to the nesting beach where sea turtles lay their eggs. Bring water, a flashlight, and a camera. (Walks Apr.-Nov. daily 9pm, starting with a brief lecture at the Dive Shop. Make reservations at the CEA office. 100 peso donation requested.)

Laguna Yul-Ku, past the house of a Grateful Dead band member, is the other hidden secret among the homes of the rich and famous. Be glad the lagoon is public property, with several points of entry. Some charge, so ask someone if you can't find a free entry point (try across the street from the beachfront hotels). Getting in is certainly worth it. The expansive lagoon, set amongst mangrove trees and crazy-wild rock formations, is all fresh water, which bubbles up from a cenote and is home to many fish. The color of the lagoon's water is as astonishing as the size. (Official entry 8am-5:30pm daily. 10 pesos for a locker, 100 pesos for snorkel gear.)

COZUMEL ☎987

The calm, tropical diving mecca of Cozumel—"land of the swallows" in Maya—has seen its share of history. French diver Jacques Cousteau called attention to the amazing coral formations and colorful marine life of **Palancar Reef,** the world's second-largest barrier reef, and inspired divers from all over. Today the island's turbulent history of vanquished Maya, conquering Spaniards, pirate bases, and tragic mass desertions has reversed under recent tourist build-up: it is popular among those wishing to explore Mexico's natural beauty without foregoing luxury and service. Much of the island remains undeveloped and ripe for exploration: miles of empty white beach, Maya ruins, and crocodile-filled lagoons encourage travelers to look beyond the island's city, San Miguel de Cozumel (pop. 80,000).

Isla Cozumel
▲ CAMPING
Punta Morena, **1**
Punta Chiqueros, **3**

TRANSPORTATION

Most people reach the island via **ferry** from Playa del Carmen to the west, or **Puerto Morelos** to the north (☎871 0355, for Puerto Morelos. 2½hr.; Su-M, W-Th, and Sa 5am and 5pm; 55 pesos, with car 735 pesos.) The car ferry is nevertheless inconvenient and unpredictable. Ferries between **Playa del Carmen** and Cozumel run hourly 7am-10pm; tickets are available at the dock in Cozumel or from the booth on Playa's plaza (45min., round-trip 146 pesos). An airport (☎872 0485), 2km north of town, provides an alternative to the bus-ferry ordeal. **Aerocaribe** (☎872 3456) offers a 20min. **air shuttle** from Cancún; **Continental** (☎872 0487), and **Mexicana** (☎872 2945) serve Cozumel as well.

ORIENTATION AND PRACTICAL INFORMATION

The island of Cozumel is 18km east of the Quintana Roo coast and 85km south of Isla Mujeres. At 53km long and 14km wide, Cozumel is Mexico's largest Caribbean island. The main town, **San Miguel de Cozumel** (home to the island's ferry docks), is

YUCATÁN

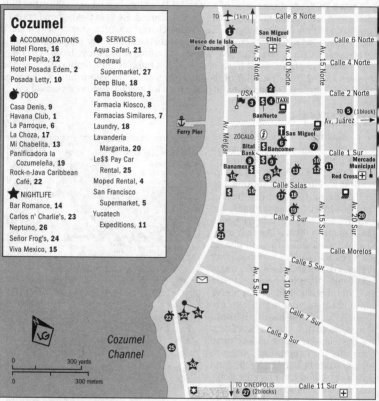

Cozumel

🏠 ACCOMMODATIONS
Hotel Flores, **16**
Hotel Pepita, **12**
Hotel Posada Edem, **2**
Posada Letty, **10**

🍴 FOOD
Casa Denis, **9**
Havana Club, **1**
La Parroque, **6**
La Choza, **17**
Mi Chabelita, **13**
Panificadora la
  Cozumeleña, **19**
Rock-n-Java Caribbean
  Café, **22**

★ NIGHTLIFE
Bar Romance, **14**
Carlos n' Charlie's, **23**
Neptuno, **26**
Señor Frog's, **24**
Viva Mexico, **15**

● SERVICES
Aqua Safari, **21**
Chedraui
  Supermarket, **27**
Deep Blue, **18**
Fama Bookstore, **3**
Farmacia Kiosco, **8**
Farmacias Similares, **7**
Laundry, **18**
Lavandería
  Margarita, **20**
Le$$ Pay Car
  Rental, **25**
Moped Rental, **4**
San Francisco
  Supermarket, **5**
Yucatech
  Expeditions, **11**

located in the middle of the west coast. Downtown streets are clearly labeled and numbered with stubborn logic. Beaches lie to the east and west of the southern half which, though undeveloped, can be easily explored by moped or car. The perimeter road makes a 75km loop along the sea, with several view and swim points. Catch a **taxi** (☎872 0236 or 872 0041) easily as you come off the dock to the airport (32 pesos) or to Punta Moreno (115 pesos)—agree on a price first.

TOURIST, FINANCIAL, AND LOCAL SERVICES

Tourist Office: (☎872 7563), on the 2nd fl. of Plaza del Sol, in the *zócalo*. English spoken. Open M-F 9am-5pm.

US Consulate: (☎872 4574, emergencies 872 6152), on the 2nd fl. of Plaza Viamar, in the *zócalo*. Open M-F noon-2pm.

Currency Exchange: BanNorte (☎872 0718), Av. 5 Norte, between Juárez and Calle 2, exchanges traveler's checks. Open M-F 9am-4pm. **BITAL** (☎872 0182), on the plaza, has a 24hr. **ATM.** Open M-Sa 8am-7pm.

Car Rental: LE$$ Pay (☎872 4744 or 872 1947; lesspay@prodigy.net), on Melgar 628, about 1km south of town. VW Safaris (US$35 per day), Jeeps (US$60 per day), and mopeds (300 pesos per day) available. Discounts for multi-day and weekend rentals. Open daily 8am-8pm. **Budget** (☎878 0903), on Av. 5 between Calle 2 and 4. US$33 per day, with A/C US$38-50 per day. Open daily 7:30am-2pm and 4-7pm.

Moped Rental: Rentadora Sol y Mar (☎ 869 0545), across from Hotel Posada Edem on Calle 2. 100 pesos per hr., 250 pesos per day. Open daily 9am-6pm.

Bike Rental: Rentadora Cozumel (☎ 872 1120 or 872 1503), on Av. 10 between Calle 1 and Salas. 50 pesos per day. 7pm return. Open daily 8am-8pm.

Bookstore: Fama (☎ 872 5020), on Av. 5, between Juaréz and Calle 2 Norte. CDs, books, magazines, and maps in English. Open daily 9am-10pm.

Supermarket: Chedraui (☎ 872 5404), Melgar 1001. Open 8am-10pm.

Laundry: Lavandería Margarita (☎ 872 2865), on 20 Sur. Wash 15 pesos, dry 11 pesos per 10min., more for full service. Open Su 8am-5pm, M-Sa 7am-9pm.

EMERGENCY AND COMMUNICATIONS

Emergency: ☎ 066. Some English spoken.

Police: (☎ 872 0409) on Calle 11 Sur, in the Palacio Municipal. Some English spoken.

Red Cross: (☎ 872 1058), on Av. 20 Sur at Salas. Open 24hr.

Pharmacy: Farmacia Kiosco (☎ 872 2485), on the *zócalo* near Hotel López. Everything for the sun-happy or sun-sick tourist. Open Su 9am-10pm, M-Sa 8am-10pm.

Medical Assistance: Centro Médico de Cozumel, 1 Sur 101 (☎ 872 3545), at Av. 50.

Fax: (☎ 872 0056), by the post office. Open M-F 8am-7:30pm, Sa-Su 9am-12:30pm.

Internet Access: Modutel Communicaciones (☎ 869 3029; fax 869 3030), on Av. 10 between Calle 2 and Juárez. 20 pesos per hr. Open daily 8am-2am.

Post Office: (☎ 872 0106), off Melgar, just south of Calle 7 Sur along the sea. Open M-F 9am-4pm, Sa 9am-1pm. **Postal Code:** 77600.

▐ ACCOMMODATIONS AND CAMPING

Since they cater primarily to foreign divers with cash to burn, hotels are generally more expensive in Cozumel than on the mainland, but the extra pesos do not guarantee higher-quality. Consider asking to see the room before paying—quality may vary considerably within a hotel. Try to grab a room before noon during high season. Camping, particularly on secluded spots at **Punta Morena** ❶ and **Punta Chiqueros** ❶ on the east side, may be the cheapest option—certainly the most peaceful. Punta Morena also delivers simple *cabañas* with double beds and private baths for 200 pesos.

Posada Letty, Calle 1 272 (☎ 872 0257). Well-kept green and blue rooms have big windows and big beds, and feel more like a house than a hotel. Singles 198 pesos; doubles 220 pesos. Each additional person 50 pesos. Prices drop 10% in low season. ❹

Hotel Posada Edem, Calle 2 12 (☎ 872 1166), between Av. 5 and 10. Small, slightly run-down but functional pink rooms with fans; *agua purificada* in lobby. One of the cheapest places in town; fish, turtles, and parrots will greet you. Singles 150 pesos; doubles 180 pesos. Each additional person 50 pesos. ❸

Hotel Flores, Salas 72 (☎ 872 1429; fax 872 2745), on Av. 5, 50m from the sea. Clean white rooms, some with ocean view. Singles and doubles 248 pesos, with A/C 308 pesos. Prices drop 10% in low season. ❹

Hotel Pepita, Av. 15 120 (☎ 872 0098), just south of Calle 1 Sur. It costs a little extra, but the private bath, refrigerator, A/C, free coffee, and pretty courtyard make this a nice place to stay. Singles and doubles 300 pesos. Each additional person 50 pesos. ❺

Palma Dorada Inn, Salas 44 (☎ 872 0330, pdinn@prodigy.net). A 3-star inn with a homey feeling, starting at 235 pesos. Rooms with A/C and balcony for 290 pesos; coffee and pastries included. Prices rise in the high season. ❹

◖ FOOD

Like any Caribbean island, Cozumel serves up plenty of seafood—but high prices target the resort-vacationer, not the budget traveler. Moderately priced restaurants lie a few blocks from the *centro*, and small cafes hide away on side streets. The **market** at Salas between Av. 20 and 25 Sur has fresh meat, fish, and fruit; **loncherías ❶** next door are the most authentic and cheapest places. For a sweet treat, stroll into **Panificadora la Cozumeleña ❶**, Av. 3 Sur 34; for pocket change you can get pastries that melt in your mouth. (☎872 0189. Open daily 7am-10pm.) *Paleterías* and *neverías* (ice cream shops) have what you need to cool off.

Casa Denis (☎872 0067), on Calle 1, across from the flea market on the *zócalo*. Enjoy home-cooked recipes and the attentive staff beneath photos of Che Guevara fishing with Fidel Castro. Breakfast 23-37 pesos, Maya pork tacos 35 pesos, other *comida regional* 82-120 pesos. Open Su 5-10:30pm, M-Sa 7am-10:30pm. ❺

La Choza, at Rosado and Av. 10, is known for having the best shrimp *fajitas* on the island, complete with delicious fresh guacamole. It has authentic vegetarian options, too (60 pesos). All meals at this open-air, relaxed restaurant come with soup. ❺

Mi Chabelita (☎872 0896), on Av. 10 between Calle 1 and Salas. A variety of regional favorites at favorable prices (33-43 pesos): this *cocina económica* is the best deal in town. Don't miss the refreshing milkshakes (13 pesos). Open M-Sa 8am-9pm. ❸

Rock-n-Java Caribbean Café, Melgar 602 (☎872 4405), near LE$$ Pay. Fruit-topped, multi-grain French toast (44 pesos), coffee (20-32), fresh salads (33-55 pesos), and healthy entrees (36-85 pesos) come with a view of the Caribbean. Great vegetarian options. Open Su-F 7am-11pm, Sa 7am-2pm. ❸

La Parroque, Av. 10 40, between Calle 1 and Juárez. Chill with the locals on this 2nd-floor restaurant and bar overlooking Av. 10, and enjoy 3 *tacos con carne* (36 pesos), quesadillas (28 pesos), or the seafood soup (45 pesos). Open daily 11am-2am. ❸

Havana Club (☎872 2098), Melgar 21, on the 2nd fl. of Diamonds International. This upscale waterfront cafe/bar features live bands playing the finest in Cuban salsa and jazz (daily 1:30-3pm), plus Cuban delicacies (40-80 pesos) and drinks (mojito 70 pesos). Cuban cigars available. Open M-Sa 9am-11pm. ❹

◖◗ BEACHES AND SIGHTS

DIVING

Many visitors make the trek to Cozumel with one plan: diving and snorkeling in the island's beautiful coral reefs. If you arrive *sans* equipment, have no fear: dive shops proliferate like bunnies in Cozumel, concentrated on the waterfront and along Calle 3 Sur between Melgar and Av. 10. The standard rate for snorkeling equipment is US$4-8 per day. Scuba gear is, of course, more expensive (US$30-60 per day). Always consider safety before price; look for shops affiliated with **ANOAAT** (Asociación Nacional de Operadores de Actividades Aquaticas Turístico) or **IANTD** (International Association of Nitrox and Technical Divers).

Once you have your equipment ready, mopeds or bikes are the best way of getting to the ideal spot, but taxis make carrying gear easier. Snorkelers will want to head south toward **Playa la Ceiba** and **Chankanaab National Park;** divers should go toward one of the reefs hugging the southeast side of the island. Note that some reefs (like the Colombia and Maracaibo reefs) have strong currents that only more experienced divers should venture. Be sure to ask before diving. (US$350 for 4-day full certification courses, US$180 for referral certification dives.)

DON'T TOUCH THE CORAL! We repeat: don't touch the coral! You will kill the coral. Then you'd feel pretty bad about yourself, wouldn't you?

Del Mar Aquatics (☎872 1900), 200m north of La Ceiba Hotel, 7km south of town. Rents snorkeling (US$6 per day) and scuba equipment (US$34 per day), and offers deep-sea fishing, night and day dives, and snorkeling trips. Open daily 7am-7:30pm.

Aqua Safari (☎872 0101; www.aquasafari.com), Melgar at Calle 5 Sur. Single-tank dive US$35; 2hr. snorkeling boat trip US$20, equipment US$5. Night dives and training courses available. Open daily 7am-2:30pm and 4-6:30pm.

Yucatech Expeditions (☎872 5659) Av. 15 between Calle 1 and Salas. Specializes in cave diving and tours; extensive classes available. Open M-Sa 11am-1pm and 6-9pm.

Deep Blue, Salas 200 (☎872 5653, US 214-343-3034), near Av. 10. Extended range divers offering rental gear, courses, computerized diving, various day and night dive trips, snorkleing trips (US$40, including refreshments and equipment), and deep sea fishing from US$300 for 4 people.

BEACHES

Beachcombers should not be disheartened by the beaches near San Miguel: the island's true treasures lie outside of town. While those looking to frolick in the waves may be disappointed by the sharp coral hidden below, sunbathers and snorkelers will find paradise. From San Miguel, traveling 7km south on Melgar will bring you to the small **Playa la Ceiba,** the beachfront of the Hotel la Ceiba. The clear waters off the beach have excellent snorkeling—and less than 100m offshore lurks the underwater grave of the plane wreck from the James Bond film "Survive." Several kilometers farther south, past the Chankanaab National Park, the uncrowded **Playas Francisco** and **Palancar** are considered the best beaches on the island and are as jumping-off points for exploring the famous Palancar Reef. Beautiful and less touristed beaches line the east coast of the island; their magnificent turquoise waters and large waves tempt surfers (boards US$ 12 near Punta Morena). Given the strong undertow, swimmers, especially, should exercise caution.

 WE WEREN'T KIDDING. The Palancar Reef of Cozumel, part of the second-largest reef system in the world, draws legions of scuba fanatics to its colorful depths. However, few visitors realize the biological importance of the majestic coral pillars: if they are destroyed, the entire ecosystem disintegrates. International law prohibits harvesting coral, but does not forbid the purchase or exportation of coral-derived crafts. Many shops in Cozumel sell goods made from coral; tourists who buy them contribute to the destruction of the splendid reefs they came to see. Lesson: no matter how cute the trinket, **don't buy coral.**

SIGHTS

Chankanaab National Park, 9km south of downtown off Melgar, protects a beautiful bay circled by a well-kept botanical garden, museum, dolphin pen (visitors can pay to swim), and restaurants. The clear, oval lagoon used to be open to swimmers, but is closed because excessive traffic was damaging to the coral; now visitors ogle the array of tropical fish from shore. The abundant fish and stunning coral formations in the bay, open to snorkelers and scuba divers, are the real attractions now. Equipment rental facilities lie in the park. (☎872 2940. Open daily 7am-7pm. Admission US$10.) At the southern tip of the island, 27km from downtown, the recently opened **Punta Sur Ecological Reserve** wows visitors with boat rides through crocodile-infested lagoons, snorkeling (equipment rental included in admission), and the small ruins of a Maya tomb. The lighthouse at Punta Celerain within the reserve presents a thrilling view of the sand dunes on Cozumel's southern shores. (Open daily 8am-4pm. 150 pesos.)

A former Maya trading center, Cozumel is littered with dozens of ruins. None of them, unfortunately, are well preserved. The very small **El Cedral,** the oldest ruins on the island, are on a road off Melgar, a few kilometers south of Playa San Francisco. (Open daily 8am-5pm. Free.) The only excavated and reconstructed ruins are at **San Gervasio,** which include the remains of an observatory and several houses, temples, and arches that once made up the most prominent community in Cozumel. (Take Juárez out of town; after 8km, a "San Gervasio" sign marks a gravel road branching to the left. Follow the road another 6km. ☎800 2215. Open daily 9am-6pm. 50 pesos.) The air-conditioned **Museo de la Isla de Cozumel,** on the waterfront between Calles 4 and 6, is small but worth a visit. Its four themed rooms are full of photos, poetry, coral, marine and jungle trivia, and artifacts. The Coral and Reefs room, with its colorful exhibits and wealth of information on Cozumel's marine treasures, may especially enrich the underwater experiences of prospective snorkelers and scuba divers. (☎872 1475 or 872 1434. Open daily 9am-5pm. US$3.) For some free entertainment near town, stop by **Viva Mexico,** where dancers perform 15min. regional pieces every hour from 10am-3:30pm M-Sa and guests sample free tequila nightly (8pm-10pm).

■ NIGHTLIFE

Like almost everything else on the island, the nightlife in Cozumel is both relaxing and tourist-heavy. Around the *zócalo* in downtown San Miguel, divers kick back after a day at the reefs and docked tourists unload their cash at places like Hard Rock Cafe. If you're looking for a party, Carlos n' Charlie's, Viva Mexico, and Neptuno are typically where it's at. Drink prices are about the same everywhere: 30-40 pesos for beer or tequila shots, more for famous Mexican margaritas. Look for 2-for-1 drink coupons in local shops.

Neptuno, Calle 11, has a classy, multi-level dance floor, blasting lasers, and music that draws both locals and visitors after about midnight. Foam parties F-Su after 2am. Cover 30 pesos. Open Tu-Su 9pm-6am.

Carlos n' Charlie's (☎872 1505), on Melgar. Always happening, this restaurant/bar entertains *gringos* with drinks, slammer contests, and ridiculous Rules of the House, finishing with "there are no rules." Open Su 5pm-1:30am, M-F 10am-1:30am, Sa 11am-1:30am.

Viva Mexico, Melgar 199 (☎872 0799), near the main plaza. Open-air restaurant by day and *discoteca* by night. Music and ocean view will please all. Open daily 10am-5am.

Señor Frog's, above its older brother, Carlos n' Charlie's, on Melgar. Made for a slightly younger crowd and families, with constant interaction from friendly waiters and the nightly bilingual MC. Black lights and neon signs make the place seem alive even when the crowd wanes.

Bar Romance, on Calle 1 between Av. 5 and 10 inside Plaza California. A sleepy karaoke bar and dance floor with a local clientele. Open daily 7pm-2am.

PUERTO MORELOS ☎998

Even the gods would be content with the unspoiled coral reef and pristine white sand beach of Puerto Morelos (pop. 4500). The serene beauty and sleepy peace inspire pride in the townspeople, and locals do everything they can to preserve this calm while trying to share it with a growing number of visitors. Waterskiing is forbidden here, as are resort hotels and other Cancún-style hedonism. Friendly Puerto Morelos has become a popular vacation destination for Mexicans in need of relaxation and tourists tired of frenetic city life. Stop for a day here to enjoy meditating on the beach, exploring the reef, or kicking back in a bar, and you may decide to never leave.

⌷ TRANSPORTATION. Catch **buses** at Mex. 307, 2km west of town, to **Playa del Carmen** and **Cancún** (every 15 min, 16 pesos). To get to the *centro*, take a taxi (16 pesos) from the highway. A car ferry leaves for Cozumel from the port 500m south of the *zócalo*. (☎871 0355. 1.5hr.; Tu, W, and Sa 5am; less than US$10, with car 735 pesos.) Those with cars should arrive in advance to secure a place in line.

◪⌷ ORIENTATION AND PRACTICAL INFORMATION. Puerto Morelos is located on the east coast of Quintana Roo, 30km south of Cancún and 30km north of Playa del Carmen. **Mex. 307** runs north-south, and passes 2km west of the town center. The town itself is laid out in a simple grid, organized around a central *zócalo*, which borders the beach. Juan Loya has a **tourist information stand** (☎830 1420; jjloya64@hotmail.com; open 9am-5pm) on the north of the *zócalo* outside the **Casa Martín Supermarket,** and can help with **car rentals** (400 pesos per day), tours, and more. **Marant Travel,** Tulum 1 (☎871 0332), on the southwest corner of the *zócalo*, offers **tourist information** and **Internet** access (15 pesos per hr.). **Mor Ex,** at the southwest corner of the *zócalo*, provides currency exchange; an **ATM** is located on the north side, under Restaurant El Pescador. In case of **emergency,** call ☎060. **Farmacia San José Obrero,** Rojo Gómez 2, is on the west side of the *zócalo*. (☎871 0053. Open 8am-2pm and 4-10pm.) For medical assistance, visit the **Centro de Salud,** southeast of the *zócalo*. (Open M-Sa 8am-2pm; also M, Tu, F 6-8pm.) The **police** are at the northwest corner of the *zócalo*. (☎871 0117. Some English spoken.) The **post office** is on the western side of Mex. 307. **Postal Code:** 77580.

⌷⌷ ACCOMMODATIONS AND FOOD. Though there may be more places to stay than things to do, budget accommodations are scarce in Puerto Morelos; the best option may be camping on the beach. Ask the police for permission. If traveling in a group, try sharing a suite—many have room for up to six. Rates vary by as much as US$25 between the high and low seasons. **Arrecifes ❹,** right on the beach, is well kept and a steal in the high season. (☎887 0488. Large suites 500-600 pesos for up to 6 people.) **Amar Inn ❺,** between Mexicano and Cárdenas, a walk north of the *zócalo*, perches three private cabins and three rooms around a courtyard on the beach. (☎871 0026. Cabins come with fridges and fans. US$30-55.) Budget-friendly restaurants are rare. The 12-year-old **El Tío ❸,** just north of the zócalo on Melgar, is a favorite for breakfast, lunch, and snacks. It serves *caldo de pescado* (fish soup; 40 pesos), *tamales* and *empanadas*. (Open daily 6am-11pm.) **Tortería el Pirata ❹,** on the northwestern corner of the *zócalo*, offers good seafood and chicken plates (55-85 pesos) and sandwiches (25-40 pesos). (☎871 04 89. Open daily 7:30am-10:30 pm.) Restaurant and bar **Don Pepe ❹,** Rojo Gómez 4, northwest of the *zócalo*, also serves fresh seafood (45-65 pesos) in addition to 18-peso coconut creams, and also features late night activity. (☎871 0602. Open daily 1pm-1am. Karaoke starts 6pm.) Several coffee shops border the *zócalo* to the southeast.

◪⌷⌷ SIGHTS, BEACHES, AND NIGHTLIFE. Snorkeling and scuba diving are the best ways to explore the coral reef, which was designated a national park in 2000. Several dive shops along the *zócalo* rent equipment. **SubAqua Explorers** (☎871 0012; open daily 9am-4pm and 6-9pm) and the beachside **Mystic Diving** (☎871 0634; www.mysticdiving.com) will gladly indulge many aquatic interests. (2hr. snorkeling trips with equipment 200-250 pesos, 4hr. fishing trips US$250 for up to

6 people.) The shorebound can visit **Goyo** and his **Custom Jungle Adventures** (☎871 0189; www.mayajungle.com), on Rojo Gómez just north of the *zócalo*. Goyo will lead you inland and show you Maya villages, medicinal trees, or refreshing *cenotes*. Tours leave from his *palapa* (US$40). Bike rental is available next door for the independent.

You can also enjoy yourself for free. While waves crash into the popular coral reef 600m off shore, the ocean waters gently massage the uncrowded beach. White sands, emerald waters, and Mexican children improvising watery playgrounds around the docks make a day at the beach here virtually unforgettable.

Nightlife in Puerto Morelos is refreshingly different than elsewhere on the Maya Riviera. Rather than multitudes of bars packed with drunken tourists and clubs that pulsate late into the night, people have a more laid back approach. Many people choose to spend evenings on the beach, sipping tequila and watching the clear sky. On Friday and Saturday nights, either the main square or a park across the highway frequently host dancing. Don Pepe and upstairs at **El Viejo Pescador** host nighttime activities in the square.

TULUM ☎984

On the edge of the *Etaib* (Black Bees) jungle, atop a rocky seaside cliff, stands the walled Maya "City of the Dawn." While the scale of the ruins does not rival that of Uxmal or Chichén Itzá, many of the buildings are still intact; most of all, the backdrop of white sands and breaking Caribbean waves makes the site unforgettable. First settled in the 6th century AD, Tulum was the oldest continuously inhabited city in the New World when the Spanish arrived; today, sun worshippers of a different kind tramp to the ancient port. With an unparalleled natural setting, counting both inland and coastal wonders, Tulum's temples attract an increasing number of daytrippers from Cancún. Unfortunately, Tulum is not much of a walking city, and getting from place to place on a short trip can eat into valuable time. For those with longer plans, the two bases for exploring the ruins, beaches, and numerous *cenotes* are the village of Tulum and the many *cabañas* that line the beach for 9km south of the ruins.

▐ TRANSPORTATION

Getting around the Tulum area can be time-consuming and expensive. Although numerous taxis are readily available at the crossing point—the *crucero*—in Pueblo Tulum, along Mex. 307, and at various *cabañas*, the relatively pricey fares add up fast. Thirty pesos will take you from town to the closest *cabañas*, but fares rise quickly as you travel farther south. The best budget option for those with ambitious plans is to rent a bicycle and give your legs an old-fashioned workout. To get to any of the sites near Tulum off the highway, wave down one of the many white *colectivo* vans (10 pesos) that pass nearly every 10min. from 8am to 9pm, going all the way to Playa del Carmen.

There are two **bus stations.** The main station (☎871 2122) is on the east side of Mex. 307, right in the middle of the Pueblo. The waiting room of the main terminal is sandwiched between two currency exchange booths. Buses head to: **Cancún** (2hr., every hr., 55 pesos); **Chetumal** (3hr., 11 per day, 94-111 pesos); **Chichén Itzá** (3hr., 2:30pm, 70 pesos); **Cobá** (1hr., 5 per day, 23 pesos); **Mexico City** (24hr., 1:10pm, 838 pesos); **Palenque** (12hr.; 4:15, 5:45pm; 309-323 pesos); **Playa del Carmen** (1hr., every hr., 29 pesos); **Mérida** (4hr., 2:30am, 114 pesos); **San Cristóbal de las Casas** (14hr.; 4:15, 5:45pm; 401-420 pesos); **Veracruz** (21hr., 4:30pm, 598 pesos). The other bus station serves those leaving the Tulum ruins near the entrance to the park at the *crucero*, next to the Hotel Copal. Buses going to Playa del Carmen and some leaving the main terminal stop here.

ORIENTATION & PRACTICAL INFO

Located 42km southeast of Cobá and 127km south of Cancún, Tulum is the southernmost tourist attraction on the Caribbean coast of Quintana Roo, known as the **Maya Riviera,** and the easternmost of the major Maya archaeological sites. Tulum sprawls over three separate areas: the **crucero** (crossroads), which is near the ruins, the **beach cabañas,** which line the one coastal road, Carretera Boca Paila, and **Pueblo Tulum,** off Mex. 307 (Av. Tulum). Coming from the north, you will come first to the *crucero,* about 3km before town, where several restaurants, hotels, overpriced minimarts, and a gas station take advantage of traffic to the ruins. One kilometer south of the *crucero* is a turn-off leading to food and lodging at the beachside *cabañas,* about 2-3km from Mex. 307. Pueblo Tulum also offers a handful of roadside restaurants, hotels, and services. Addresses for places along the beach are often in terms of their distance from the ruins.

Tourist Office: There is no official tourist office, but the **Weary Traveler Backpacker's Center** (☎871 2389 or 871 2390; www.intulum.com), across the street from the bus station, offers maps and information about lodging and sights. Open 24hr.

Currency Exchange: Bital (☎871 9201 or 871 2079), 2 blocks north of the bus station on Av. Tulum. No commission on traveler's checks. 24hr. **ATM.** Open M-Sa 8am-7pm. Many exchange booths line Tulum and are at the *crucero* in the Hotel Acuario and next to the bus office in Pueblo Tulum.

Police: (☎871 2055), in the Delegación Municipal near Bital.

Pharmacy: Canto Farmacia (☎871 2319), on the west side of Mex. 307, across the street from the bus station. Open daily 8am-11pm.

Supermarket: Super Marcaribe (☎871 2226), 4 blocks north of the bus station. Open daily 7am-10:30pm. **Mini-Super El Pipazo** (☎871 2271), south of Cabañas Copal, next to the Nohock Tunich Cabañas. Open daily 7:30am-9pm.

Laundry: Lavandería Burbujas (☎871 2465), 2 blocks east of the bus station. Wash and dry 13 pesos per kg. Express service additional 20 pesos per kg. Open M-F 8am-7pm, Sa 8am-2pm. **Aquamatic,** on Tulum near Centauro Nte. Self-service and drop-off.

Bike Rental: Many beach hotels rent bikes, but rentals are hard to find in the center. **Punta Piedra,** 5km from the ruins. 60 pesos per day, 50 pesos for guests.

Car Rental: Ana y José, km 7 (☎871 2477; www.tulumresorts.com) has another location on Tulum, near Osiris and Beta. From US$35 in the low season and US$55 at high season. Open daily 8:30am-8:30pm.

THE BIG SPLURGE

QUICK, ROBIN — TO THE BATCAVE

If you could see it in an IMAX theater for US$13 or see it in real life for US$40, which would you choose? In the Yucatan, you have the choice. Underground *cenotes* or fresh water rivers, between Tulum and Akumal provide an experience not to be missed.

Riding 2.5km into the jungle on the back of a buggy, you arrive at a small hole with a ladder. It's the **Tak Be Ha** (Place of Hidden Waters) *cenote,* your first entrance point on this three-cavern tour into the waters below. Your wet suit keeps you warm and the flashlight helps guide you through limestone formations and stalactite gardens as you snorkel along down winding paths. Because there are few entrance points for light, there are no plants, and visibility is a low 300 ft. Bats flutter overhead at many points, and lights placed by the company help make the experience one that will tickle all of your senses. The **Caverna de Mar cielogos** (Bat Cavern) and **Cenote Dos Ojos** (Two Eyes) will continue to seem otherworldly and impress and baffle you with their natural offerings throughout the 2½hr. tour of the longest *cenote* system in the world.

Tours at 9, 11am, and 1pm daily. US$40, shorter trips US$25; 1-tank dive US$50, 2-tanks US$90. Hidden World Cenote Park, 2km south of Xel Ha on the Tulum-Playa del Carmen Hwy. ☎877 8535.

Medical Assistance: At the **Centro de Salud**. Take the 1st left heading south from the bus station, and then another quick left. Open 24hr. for emergencies.

Internet Access: The Weary Traveler Backpacker's Center (☎871 2461), across the street from the bus station. 20 pesos per hr. Open 24hr. **Bohemio's**, near the post office. 15 pesos per hr.

Post Office: A few hundred meters into town on Mex. 307. Open M-F 9am-4pm. **Postal Code:** 77780.

■ ■ ACCOMMODATIONS AND CAMPING

The *cabañas* of Tulum offer a unique experience that shouldn't be missed. Cheap, right on the white beaches, without electricity (bring a flashlight and some candles) or phones, the *cabañas* offer a chance to live fruitfully without modern civilization—at least for a few days. There's nothing like waking to crashing waves and the ocean breeze that passes through an open window or the cracks between the sticks and palm fronds that enclose you. Chill on the pristine beaches in hammocks, revel at late-night beachside fires, and perfect your tan. Bring mosquito netting and repellent; the bugs can be nasty. During the high season (mid-Dec. to Apr. and July-Aug.), arrive early in the morning or make reservations.

Don Armando Cabañas (armandoscabanas@yahoo.com.mx), on the access road less than 500m south of the ruins. A humble paradise with a basketball court, dive shop, restaurant, and the most happening nightclub in town: it's like an all-inclusive resort for those without big bucks. The bar brings in locals and internationals. *Cabañas* are solid and secure; ask to be away from the bar if you're not a night owl. Camping 30 pesos. *Cabañas* 160-220 pesos, with private bath 350 pesos. ❶

Cabañas Copal (www.cabanascopal.com), 5km south of the ruins on the beachfront road. Copal is a freeing experience, with cliff-top views of crashing waves, little electricity (though hot water, phones, and wireless Internet are all available), and a mostly "clothing optional" environment. *Cabañas* with common bath and shower 300 pesos, with private bath 600 pesos. Prices rise 200-300 pesos in the high season. ❺

Hotel Cabañas Diamante K, km 2.5 on Boca Paila (www.diamantek.com). This classy place caters to a range of needs and budgets. At night, garden torches light the area and paths connect the *cabañas*, restaurant, bar, and shops to help you keep sand from permanently attaching itself to you. Beachside hammocks may convince you to stay longer. Electricity available 10am-2pm and 7pm-midnight. Singles 150 pesos; doubles 250 pesos; suites up to 2000 pesos. ❸

The Weary Traveler Hostel (☎871 2389 or 871 2390; tourdesk@intulum.com), across from the bus station. A backpacker opened this hostel in 2001 to create the hostel he yearned for while on the road. Daily rides to the beach and other sites, free breakfast, and ▨ **barbeques** make it like summer camp—especially if you had to do your cleaning; no one else will. BBQ runs Su 6pm-midnight, culminating in fire shows, live music, and dancers. Outdoor communal kitchen, sheets, and lockers (without locks) included. Internet and restaurant on-site. Single beds 75 pesos; double beds 135 pesos. ❶

■ FOOD

Although points of interest in Tulum tend to be rather spread out, hearty, inexpensive food is never far away. The *pueblo* has many cheap *loncherías* and minisupers not far from the bus station, while the *crucero* and the beachside *cabañas* offer satisfying budget-friendly restaurants with international cuisine. These listings cover more adventurous places for more padded wallets.

▨ **¡Qué Fresco!** (US ☎ 1-415-387-9806; www.zamas.com) at Zamas, 5km south of Tulum ruins. The beautiful location, on a point with blue-green waves rushing by on both sides, and tasty food make the prices well worth it. Healthy, fresh Mexican options, including vegetarian dishes (from 60 pesos), as well as pizzas (from 40 pesos). Unique salsas made from mango, pineapple, and other inventions accompany each meal. Hearty breakfasts start at 38 pesos. Open daily 7am-10pm. ❺

El Tacontento, on Mex. 307, north of Bital. The unassuming appearance hides a reputation for amazing seafood and Italian-style dishes. Pastas start at 45 pesos, fish at 75 pesos and *ceviche* at 60 pesos. Not a place for strict vegetarians. ❹

La Nave Pizzería, Av. Tulum 570 (☎ 871 2592). Handpainted tables, thin crust brick-oven pizzas with fresh ingredients and toppings (from 38 pesos), and the special spinach or seafood raviolis (50-70 pesos)—made daily by the Italian owners—are a great treat, even if they are out of place. Open daily 7:30am-11pm. ❹

Azul Tapas Bar, Av. Tulum between Osiris and Bite. A one-of-a-kind in Tulum, the lounge music, sleek, silver bar stools, and floor seating with throw pillows draw an international audience. *Tapas* include hummus (from 20 pesos), bagels, croissants, eggs (25-30 pesos). Open daily 8am-11pm high season, from 6pm low season. ❸

◉ SIGHTS

THE BEACH. Swimming, splashing, and tanning on the beach are popular ways to end a hot day in Tulum, and nude bathing is no longer a rare phenomenon. All beaches are public, and **Playa Paraíso** offers a bar. Off-shore, waves crash over the **barrier reef,** the largest in the Americas: it runs the full length of the Yucatán Peninsula and Belize. Although the water is not as clear as at Xel-Ha or Akumal, the fish are just as plentiful. To mingle with them, rent scuba and snorkeling equipment from **Aquatic Tulum** at Don Armando Cabañas, which also offers trips to the reef and a nearby *cenote*. (☎ 871 2096. Snorkeling US$5 per day, trips US$12; 1-tank dive US$30, 2-tank dive US$50. Open daily 8am-5:30pm.) Another option is **Punta Piedra,** 5km south of the ruins, a bit past Cabañas Copal. Snorkeling equipment (50 pesos per day), all-inclusive 3hr. trips from their beach (200 pesos), and various dive trips (US$40 for 1, US$70 for 2) are all available. (Open daily 7:30am-7pm.) **Tankah Dive Shop,** near the *crucero*, has trips to what it claims is the best snorkeling/diving location, Tankah Bay. Other packages include diving courses and small group tours to Sian Ka'an Biosphere. (☎ 807 2149. tankahdivinn@lycos.com.)

CENOTES. The hidden treasures of Tulum are its numerous *cenotes*, sunken in the jungle throughout the area. **Cenote Escondido** and **Cenote Cristal** are both 3km south of the intersection of Mex. 307 and the road to Cobá (admission 30 pesos, divers about 15-20 pesos more at all cenotes). Here you will find freshwater tropical fish, green underwater vegetation, and cool, crystal clear waters. Following the road to Cobá west out of town, after 1.6km you will come across the **Cenote Calaveras,** named for its squash-like shape—but also called the **Temple of Doom.** Look for a path behind a newly constructed house on your right (admission 30 pesos). Continue on the main road 1.5km farther to the clearly marked, mini-paradise **El Gran Cenote,** regarded as the best *cenote* in the area for snorkeling (admission 50 pesos, divers 65 pesos). Its unforgettable beauty is like something out of a fairy-tale—bats, birds, and butterflies alike flutter over the cold, clear blue waters filled with friendly fish and green lily pads. Discovered more recently than its more famous (and crowded) neighbor is **Cenote Dos Ojos.** *Cenotes* are generally open from 8am to 4pm. You must be an experienced open water diver to dive alone, but the calm and clear waters are great places to learn. Other free *cenotes* are hidden

YUCATÁN

across the street from the ranches and hotels at the southern end of Boca Paila right before Sian Ka'an; an especially large one lies behind a wood gate opposite Rancho San Erik. Ask at Punta Piedra for a map of them.

THE ARCHAEOLOGICAL SITE OF TULUM

The ruins lie a brisk 10min. walk east of Mex. 307 from the crucero; the amusement park-style train (15 pesos) covers the distance in slightly less time. Tickets are sold at a booth to the left of the parking lot and at the entrance to the ruins. Open daily 8am-6pm. 37 pesos. Guided tours available in several languages (45min. tour for 5 people 250 pesos); inquire at the crucero.

Perched on a cliff overlooking the calm, blue Caribbean, the ruins at the beautiful site Tulum ("Wall" or "Fortification" in Maya) are what remains of one of the last pre-Columbian Maya cities to be inhabited. The city was first constructed around AD 500, in the middle of the Maya Classic Period, but its strategic position on a seaside cliff, where it was easily defended, kept it inhabited for over a millennium. Not until well into the Post-Classic Period, in the 15th and 16th centuries, did Tulum reach its zenith as a fortification and religious center. Most of the 50 or so structures at the site are temples dedicated to religious ceremonies and living quarters for nobles and priests. In 1544, the city fell to Spanish conquerors, but it continued to serve for defense from which the Spanish fended off English, Dutch, and French pirates. As late as 1847, Tulum provided refuge for Maya fleeing government forces during the Caste War. Today the ruins are infested with mosquitoes and tourists—many of whom cool off at the small beach located within the site. Most buildings at the sight have plaques with brief descriptions.

THE WALL. The impressive wall protecting the city's landward sides is the first structure greeting visitors to Tulum. The wall, made of small rocks wedged together, was originally 3.6m thick and 3m high. It shielded the city from aggressive neighbors from other Maya city-states and prevented all but the 150 or so priests and governors of Tulum from entering the city for most of the year. Every evening, the rays of the setting sun illuminate representations of the Maya "Descending God" that covers the western walls. From the southernmost wall, once a lookout point, admire a view that can make your trip.

HOUSE OF THE HALACH UINIK AND THE PALACIO. To the left of the entrance lie a grave and the remains of platforms that once supported huts. Behind these are the House of the Halach Uinik (House of the Ruler), characterized by a traditional four-column entrance, and the Palacio, Tulum's largest residential building. One step closer to the ocean is the **Casa del Cenote** which, with jungle reaching from its base to embrace it, has a positively mystical look to it.

TEMPLO DE LOS FRESCOS (TEMPLE OF THE PAINTINGS). The temple is a great example of Post-classic Maya architecture. Layering suggests it was built in three separate stages. Inside, 600-year-old murals, with some original colors still visible, show deities intertwined with serpents, fruits, and flowers. Masks of Itzamná, the Maya Creator, are in the northwest and southwest corners of the building.

EL CASTILLO (THE CASTLE). The most prominent structure in Tulum, El Castillo looms to the east over the rocky seaside cliff, commanding a view of the entire walled city. Walk on the cliff side for a view of the natural beauty. The pyramid, built in three separate stages, was probably not meant to be a pyramid at all: the current structure was probably only built around the 12th or 13th centuries AD. A double-headed, feathered serpent sprawls across the facade, with a diving god in the center; elsewhere, bee-like imagery may allude to the importance of honey in

Caribbean trade. More recently, El Castillo served as a lighthouse, aiding returning fishermen seeking the gap in the barrier reef. In front of the temple is the **sacrificial stone** where the Maya held battle ceremonies and sacrificed prisoners of war.

TEMPLO DE LA SERIE INICIAL (TEMPLE OF THE INITIAL SERIES). On a plaza to the southwest of El Castillo is the Temple of the Initial Series. Named after a stela found here, the temple bears a date that corresponds to the beginning of the Maya religious calendar in the year AD 761.

TEMPLO DEL DIOS DECENDIENTE. The Temple of the Descending God, with a fading relief of a feathered, armed divinity diving from the sky, stands on the opposite side of the plaza. Archaeologists believe that this figure, seen at various buildings in Tulum, symbolized the setting sun.

TEMPLO DE VIENTOS (TEMPLE OF THE WINDS). Perched on its own precipice on the northeast side of the beach, the Temple of the Winds was ingeniously designed to act as a storm-warning system. Sure enough, before Hurricane Gilbert struck the site in 1988, the temple's airways dutifully whistled their alarm.

⚑ DAYTRIPS FROM TULUM

SIAN KA'AN BIOSPHERE RESERVE

*Follow the coast road just 7km south of Tulum to the "Maya Arch," at the entrance. The **Amigos de Sian Ka'an**, who work to maintain the reserve, lead the best tours (US$68), departing from Tulum. Call their offices in Cancún (☎880 6024; open M-F 10am-6pm), Felipe Carrillo Puerto (☎834 0813), Chetumal (☎837 1637), or at Cabañas Ana y José in Tulum (☎880 6022) for more information and to reserve a place. The main office for the reserve is in Cancún at Kukulcán km 4.5 (☎849 7554). **Centro Ecológico Sian Ka'an** (☎984 871 2499; www.cesiak.org) has more info. Park entrance 20 pesos.*

Sian Ka'an ("Where the Sky is Born") comprises roughly 10% of the state of Quintana Roo (1.6 million acres) and is Mexico's largest coastal wetland reserve. Protected by federal decree on January 20, 1986, the immense reserve was Mexico's first UNESCO Natural World Heritage site and encompasses tropical forests, *cenotes*, savannas, mangroves, lagoons, and 112km of coral reef. It is home to 1200 species of flora, 345 species of birds, 103 species of mammals, and 27 Maya archaeological sites. The best way to see Sian Ka'an is by boat. You can drive a car or ride a bike along the poorly maintained coastal road for 57km, which has several turn-offs to the beach, before arriving in Punta Allen, home to manatees and dolphins. Most of what you will see, as iguanas and crabs scurry in front of you, is a wall of dense jungle on either side. There are 3 short hiking trails within the reserve, plus a great *cenote* for swimming, right at the entrance. If you get to Punta Allen, a small fishing town established before the reserve was created, you may be able to find a fisherman on his day off willing to take you on a tour.

XEL-HA

Xel-Ha lies 15km north of Tulum; ask any northbound bus to drop you at Xel-Ha (10 pesos). Taxis charge 50-60 pesos. To get back at the end of the day, vigorously wave down a bus on its way to Tulum or Cancún. Locals will usually be able to tell you when the next one is due to pass. (☎875 4070; www.xelha.com.mx. Open daily 8am-6pm. US$25, Sa-Su US$19; all-inclusive—snorkel gear, lockers, towels, and all-you-can-eat at restaurants—US$52.)

Xel-Ha (SHELL-ha; Where the Water is Born) is like an interactive aquarium set in the Yucatec jungle. Nestled amidst 184 hectares of jungles, caves, and coves, Xel-Ha allows visitors to take in the beauty of the area with convenience. Float in an inner tube or snorkel down the nearly 4m deep central river as it flows from a *cen-*

ote, and admire parrot fish and meter-long jackfish. Stop to swing on a rope-walk or climb a cliff wall with the aid of drilled holes. It is no wonder that an average of 1600 people or more enter the park daily. With dolphin swims ($90US extra, watching is free), dishes of fish food that lure huge schools of fish, paths amidst rock formations, *cenotes*, and comfy beach chairs and hammocks overlooking the river, it's easy to spend a whole day here—and share it with many others. For relative peace during busy times, cross the inlet and explore the underwater caves, or stay dry and visit the sea turtle nesting camp on the beach (May-Oct). Try to arrive before noon, when tourists arrive by the busload. If you don't get the all-inclusive admission, you can rent towels (US$3) and snorkel gear (US$10), available at the shower area. Bring your own insect repellent: the mosquitoes may be lethal.

Besides the water activities, there is a small archaeological site on the highway, 100m south of the park entrance. **El Templo de Los Pájaros** and **El Palacio,** small Classic and Post-Classic ruins, were only recently opened to the public. The former (the farthest into the jungle) overlooks a peaceful, shady *cenote* where swimming and rope swinging are allowed; so-so upkeep may send you right back to Xel-Ha.

▧ HIDDEN WORLDS

3 trips daily from Hidden Worlds Dive Center, several hundred meters south of the park entrance. Getting there requires the same patience as getting to Xel-Ha: hop on a colectivo from Tulum (roughly every 10min., 10 pesos) at the side of the road, or flag one going to Tulum from Playa del Carmen. Tours include 3 snorkel stops in caves, with all equipment included. (☎ 877 8535; www.hiddenworlds.com.mx. 9, 11am, 1pm. US$40.)

Cenote Dos Ojos ("Two Eyes"), 1km south of Xel-Ha, is the longest and most extensive set of underwater caverns in the world, stretching 33,855m—with more still being discovered. Originally a dry cave system with limestone formations in shades of amber, as well as calcic stalactites, stalagmites, and natural wind-etchings, the caverns flooded long ago. Snorkelers and divers lower themselves into the caves and find haven with tetras, mollies, and swordfish. You must be a certified open water diver to dive in the sometimes crowded Dos Ojos (1-tank US$50, 2-tank US$90), but there are 1500ft. of cavern to see with just snorkel gear and a flashlight. (The dive center has also installed lights to illuminate the beautiful sights that made it to IMAX in 1999.) **Tak Be Ha** ("Place of Hidden Waters") is like an underwater and underground mystical garden.

COBÁ

The Maya ruins of Cobá are less than 50km northwest of Tulum. To get to the ruins from the Cobá bus station, walk south on the main street in town as far as the T-junction at the lake. Take a left on Voz Suave; the ruins are a 5min. walk down this road. Remember to bring a water bottle, hat, and plenty of mosquito repellent. Ruins open daily 7am-6pm. 37 pesos. Parking 10 pesos; bike rental inside 25 pesos. Tour guides can be found at the entrance. A 45min. tour for 1-6 people starts at 250 pesos, but bargaining is certainly an option. Allow at least 2hr. to see most of the site. Buses do not return to Tulum until 4, 5, or 6pm, but taxis (200 pesos) wait hungrily outside; share the ride.

Stretching over 70 sq. km deep within the jungle, the ruins of Cobá recall what was perhaps the largest of all Maya cities. Inhabited at various intervals for over a millennium, the population reached 55,000 at Cobá's peak, from AD 800 to 1100. The city flourished in the Classic Period as a crossroads for the entire Yucatán Peninsula, connecting distant Maya cities through its vast network of *sacbé,* ancient Maya roadways. By the Post-Classic Period, Cobá had mysteriously lost its power to nearby cities such as Tulum and Xcaret. Today, the tranquil, shaded ruins, surrounded by several shallow lakes, receive far less attention than those at Chichén Itzá and Tulum. The government has poured less money into the site, leaving an estimated 6,500 buildings unexcavated. Nevertheless, work slowly continues at Cobá, each year bringing to light new structures.

Through the gate, the site's main attractions lie in a Y-shaped formation. The **Grupo Cobá** dates from the Early Classic Period (AD 300-600) and is near the entrance, at the base of the "Y." **Templo de la Lluvia** (Temple of the Rain) looms an impressive 28m high. Different levels are evident for each of seven 52-year periods, each under a new chief priest. Only the front face of the temple has been excavated, revealing a corbel-vaulted passageway that you can explore. In front of the structure is a stone **sacrificial table**, for animal offerings to Chac, the rain god. A second passageway leads farther south and has red plant dye from the 5th century still visible on the walls; it leads visitors to **Plaza del Templo,** where assemblies were once held. Return to the main path for a look at the **ball court** with its intact stone arches. The ball game was part of a sacred ceremony in which the movement of the round rubber ball (as with Mexico's current sacred game, *fútbol*, players could not touch the ball with their hands) symbolized the sun and moon. Various sources say that the winners were sacrificed as an honor and that the Maya believed the game maintained cosmic order.

One kilometer further up the "trunk" of the "Y" and another kilometer up the right branch brings you to the you to the **Grupo Macanxoc** and its eight stelae. On the way, a section of the well-engineered Maya *sacbé* awaits. This particular road is 20m wide and 4m above the jungle floor, made to weather otherwise crippling tropical rainstorms. The ornately carved stone slabs of the Grupo Macanxoc were memorials above the tombs of Maya royals, but unfortunately, their pictorial secrets are now barely discernible. The one exception is the first, the impressive and well-preserved **Retrato del Rey,** which portrays a king, with *quetzal*-feather headdress and bow and arrow, on top of the heads of two slaves.

Along the left-hand branch of the "Y" is the **Templo de las Pinturas** (Temple of the Paintings), named for the richly colored frescoes that once adorned the building. Follow an unmarked trail northwest of the temple to the three stelae of **Chumuc Múl.** The first depicts a kneeling Maya ballplayer, forever preserved with his ball— it is the tomb of a victorious captain. The second stela shows a princess, while the third portrays a priest. His seal is stamped on top of the slab with a jaguar's head, a common Maya symbol of worship. Two hundred meters past lies **sacbé No. 1,** a road that reached all the way to Chichén Itzá, 101km west. Runners were posted every 5km to deliver messages via a series of quick dashes. Images of the honeybee god around the site are a reminder of Cobá's past as an economic hub, as the Maya used honey (along with salt, coconuts, and jade) as a medium of exchange.

Several hundred meters farther, toward the pyramid **Nohoch Múl,** you'll come upon another ball court, Temple 10, and the well-preserved Stela 20. Finally, you will see towering Nohoch Múl, the tallest Maya structure in all the Yucatán, jutting out of the jungle. A climb up this breathtaking, 42m high stone pyramid will make the entire visit to Cobá worth your while. The pyramid's nine levels and 127 steps, where Maya priests once led processions, display carvings of the "diving god" similar to the ones in Tulum. Spectacular views of Lake Cobá, Lake Macanxoc, and the surrounding area awaits. **When descending, it is especially important to be careful not to lose your footing—several people have slipped and died during the descent.**

On your way out, the large lake just outside the ruins has a few crocodiles; local entrepreneurs have discovered tourists are willing to pay 5 pesos to watch them being fed. Crocodiles are never very domesticated, though—the better place for a swim after a hot day at the ruins is the *cenote* on the far side, which feeds the lake.

CHETUMAL ☎ 983

Residents of Quintana Roo are proud of Chetumal (pop. 200,000), the relatively new capital of Mexico's youngest state, which hugs the Belizean border and has yet to feel the rush of big city life. Founded in 1898 to intercept arms shipments to Maya insurgents and prevent illegal timber harvesting, Chetumal was leveled by a hurricane in 1955. The reconstruction produced wide avenues, modern architecture, and a waterfront boulevard. The city is home to an extensive shopping district and a world-class Maya museum, and serves as a great entrance point into the wild jungles and emerald lagoons of the surrounding areas.

TRANSPORTATION

Airport: (☎832 0465), 5km southwest of the city on Aguilar. **Aerocaribe** and **Mexicana,** (☎832 6675). **Aviacsa** (☎832 7676), Cárdenas at 5 de Mayo.

Buses: (☎832 5110), Insurgentes at Belice. To reach the *centro* from the station, your best bet is a taxi (10 pesos). Buses go to: **Belize City, Belize** (3hr.; 11:45am, 3, 6pm; 70 pesos); **Campeche** (7hr., noon, 196 pesos); **Cancún** (5½hr., 170 pesos); **Mérida**

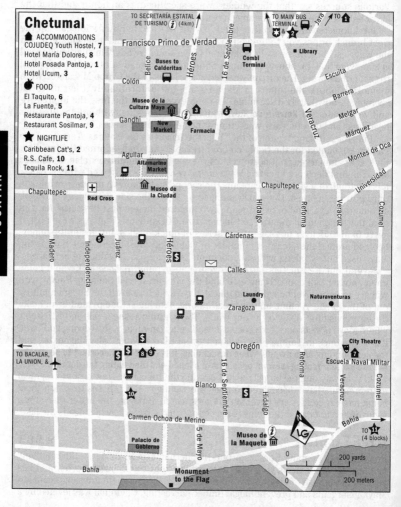

Chetumal

🏠 ACCOMMODATIONS
COJUDEQ Youth Hostel, 7
Hotel María Dolores, 8
Hotel Posada Pantoja, 1
Hotel Ucum, 3

🍴 FOOD
El Taquito, 6
La Fuente, 5
Restaurante Pantoja, 4
Restaurant Sosilmar, 9

⭐ NIGHTLIFE
Caribbean Cat's, 2
R.S. Cafe, 10
Tequila Rock, 11

(7:30am, 1:30, 5, 11:30pm; 185 pesos); **Mexico City** (22hr.; 4:30, 9pm; 725 pesos); **Playa del Carmen** (4½hr., 10 per day, 140 pesos); **Tikal** (6:30am, 2pm; 225 pesos); **Tulum** (3½hr., 6 per day, 111 pesos); **Villahermosa** (9hr., 9 per day, 256 pesos); **Xcalac** (4hr.; 4, 6am, 3:15pm; 50 pesos); **Xpujil** (2hr., 5 per day, 51 pesos). At 1:30am and 7:45pm, buses leave for **Ocosingo** (253 pesos); **Palenque** (198 pesos); **San Cristóbal de las Casas** (285 pesos); **Tuxtla Gutiérrez** (318 pesos). Buses to **Belize** leave from behind the Mercado Lázaro Cárdenas.

Combis: On Francisco Primo de Verdad, 2 blocks east of Héroes. *Combis* leave for **Bacalar** (45min., every 40min. 6am-8pm, 13 pesos); **La Unión** (2½hr., every hr. 6am-6pm, 30 pesos); **Santa Elena** (every hr., 8 pesos).

✈🔃 ORIENTATION AND PRACTICAL INFORMATION

Tucked into the Yucatán's southeastern corner, Chetumal is just north of the Río Hondo, the natural border between Mexico and Belize. The thriving shopping district lines **Héroes,** starting at **Mercado Viejo** and extending 1km south to the bay. At the southern terminus of Héroes lies **Bahía,** a wide avenue flanked by statues, small plazas, and playgrounds that follows the bay for several kilometers. From here you can see part of Belize, the long, distant spit of land to the right as you face the sea. **Taxis** will take you anywhere in town (9-13 pesos).

Tourist Offices: Módulos de información are in the *centro* on Gandhi, between Héroes and Belice, and on Bahía between Reforma and Hidalgo, near Marqueta de Payo Obisbo. Open daily 9am-6pm. **Secretaría Estatal de Turismo** (☎835 0860), north on Héroes, 4km from the *centro*. English spoken. Open M-F 8am-5pm.

Currency Exchange: Bancomer (☎832 5300), on Juárez at Obregón, has good rates and a 24hr. **ATM.** Open M-F 8:30am-4pm, Sa 10am-2pm.

Consulates: Belize, Carranza 562 (☎044 983 877 28). To enter Belize for 30 days, US, Canadian, and EU citizens need only a valid passport and a bus ticket. Open M-F 9am-2pm and 5-8pm, Sa 9am-2pm. **Guatemala,** Chapultepec 354 (☎832 3045), at Cecilio Chi. US, Canadian, and EU citizens don't need a visa. For those who do (US$15), the process is quick. Open M-F 10am-2pm.

Market: Altamarino (or **El Mercado Viejo**), on Aguilar at Héroes. Open daily 6am-6pm. **Super San Francisco de Asís,** next to the bus station. Open daily 7am-10pm. **Mercado Lázaro Cárdenas,** north of the *centro* between Héroes and Veracruz, and Cabrera and Segundo Circuito Periférico. Open daily 6am-3pm; additional stalls on Tu and F.

Laundry: Lavandería "Rot Yeg", Zaragoza 141 (☎832 0378), at Hidalgo. 13 pesos per kg, 3kg minimum. 3hr. service. Open M-Sa 8am-8pm.

Emergency: ☎066.

Police: (☎832 1500), on Insurgentes at Belice, next to the bus station. English spoken.

Red Cross: (☎832 0571), on Chapultepec at Independencia. No English spoken.

Pharmacy: Farmacia Canto, Héroes 99 (☎832 0483). Open Su 7am-3pm, M-Sa 7am-11pm.

Hospital: Hospital General, Quintana Roo 399 (☎832 1932), at Sordio.

Fax: Telecomm (☎832 0651), by the post office. Open M-F 8am-6pm, Sa-Su 9am-12:30pm.

Internet: Compucentro (☎832 8038), on Zaragoza at 5 de Mayo. 10 pesos per hr. Open daily 9am-10pm. **Webcenter Internet,** between Aguilar and Chapultepec, off the pedestrian area. 8 pesos per hr. Open Su 9am-9pm, M-Sa 8am-2am.

Post Office: Calles 2 (☎832 2578), 1 block east of Héroes. Open M-F 9am-4pm, Sa 9am-1pm. **Postal Code:** 77000.

ACCOMMODATIONS

Chetumal's budget accommodations are far from fancy, but they score points for location. A stroll down Héroes, south of the market, will open up many options. Reservations are necessary from mid-July through August. Those wanting a unique experience can look into the lagoon-side ranches.

Hotel María Dolores, Obregón 206 (☎832 0508), ½-block west of Héroes. Donald Duck image points the way to clean aqua rooms with strong fans and private baths. Restaurant inside. Singles 150 pesos; doubles 165-190 pesos; triples 220 pesos. ❸

Hotel Ucum, Gandhi 167 (☎832 0711: fax 832 6186). Spotless rooms have tile floors and modern bathrooms. Singles and doubles 180 pesos; with cable TV 200 pesos, with A/C 250 pesos; triples 200 pesos. ❸

COJUDEQ Youth Hostel (☎832 0525), Escuela Naval. From Héroes, walk east on Obregón. Small but neat single-sex dorms with 2 bunks each and institutional bathrooms. Bed with sheets, pillow, and locker 30 pesos. ❶

Hotel Posada Pantoja, Lucio Blanco 81 (☎832 1781), 4 blocks from Veracruz. What you lose in location, you gain in comfort and service. Spacious, cheerful rooms with cable TV, A/C, and free coffee. Singles 200 pesos; each additional person 50 pesos. ❹

FOOD

Chetumal serves a spicy blend of Mexican and Belizean cuisine as well as some Chinese buffets and Arabian options for vegetarians. **Loncherías ❶,** at the market on Héroes and Aguilar, and on Obregón, west of Héroes, are the best deals.

Restaurante Pantoja, Gandhi 181 (☎832 3957). A very popular family restaurant. Delicious *comida casera del día* (complete homemade meals that rotate daily; 30 pesos) and great breakfasts beat market prices (10-25 pesos). Open M-Sa 7am-6:30pm. ❸

Restaurant Sosilmar (☎832 6380), on Obregón, in the Hotel María Dolores. Tasty fish filets (58 pesos), *milanesa de puerco* (50 pesos), or *comida del día* (40 pesos) served amidst plenty of pink. Breakfasts 25-40 pesos. Open daily 8am-10:30pm. ❹

El Taquito, Calles 220 (☎833 1602). Snack on tacos and *antojitos* under a huge, fan-cooled *palapa*. Beef tacos 7 pesos, quesadillas 11 pesos, *brocheta vegetariana* 30 pesos. Open M-Sa noon-5pm and 7pm-1am. ❷

Machachado Pinocho, at the corner of Morelos and Camelias. This local favorite will reward your 7-peso taxi ride with cheap *antojitos*, ice-cold *machachados* (ice cream shakes; 18 pesos), and plenty of company. Open daily 6am-midnight. ❶

La Fuente, Cárdenas 222 (☎832 5373). A small dining area at the front of a health food store offering fresh juices and vegetarian *antojitos*. 3 tacos 15 pesos, burgers 20 pesos, sandwiches 18 pesos. Open M-Sa 8am-4pm, store open until 6pm. ❷

SIGHTS AND ENTERTAINMENT

At the northern end of the market is the **Museo de la Cultura Maya,** on Héroes between Gandhi and Colón. The very cool interactive museum explores the Maya's three-leveled cosmos—the earth, underworld, and heavens—with glyphic text, sculptures, stelae, and models of famous Maya temples. (Maya storytelling Sa 6pm. Open Tu-Su 9am-7pm. 50 pesos.) Stop in at the free art galleries next door, which showcase the work of regional artists. The informative **Museo de la Ciudad,** in the **Centro Cultural de las Bellas Artes,** Héroes 68, south of the market, details the history of Chetumal and has art exhibits next door as well. Check with the office about other cultural events or shows. (Open Tu-Su 9am-7pm. 10 pesos.) See the more recent architectural history of the city at the **Museo de la Maqueta,** which features a model of Payo Obispo (the city's name until 1936) in a small period house.

(On the corner of Hidalgo and Bahía. Open Su 10am-3pm, Tu-Sa 9am-8pm. Free.)
The nearest beach is the *balneario* at **Calderitas.** Buses leave from Colón, between
Héroes and Belice. (15min., every 30min. 7am-9pm, 4 pesos.) Although the water is
turbid and the shores rocky, the beach draws crowds during summer and school
holidays. Going left at the fork on Héroes (instead of right, towards Calderitas)
and following the signs for 12km will bring you to **Oxtankah,** a set of ruins that was
constructed over many centuries, beginning in AD 200. In 1531, the Spaniards
arrived and constructed a church before being forced to flee two years later. The
few remains today showcase an intriguing mix of Maya and Spanish architecture
and history. For **jungle adventures** or other eco-tour excursions, contact **Naturaventuras,** Zaragoza 103. (☎832 0340; www.naturaventuras.com.)

Chetumal's young nightlife scene is growing along with the rest of the city. A 20-
something crowd gets down Cancún-style at **Rock Shots Cafe,** on Juárez between
Blanco and Merino. (☎832 9712. Cover 30 pesos, Sa ladies free before midnight, Su
no cover for anyone. Open Th-Su 11pm-4am.) **Caribbeans Cat's,** Veracruz 451, at
Gonzales, a short taxi ride from the *centro*, is the newest disco in town, attracting
a wider range of partiers with popular tunes. (☎832 9145. Cover 40 pesos.) **Tequila
Rock,** on Bahía, brings in the clubbers with its waterfront location.

▶ DAYTRIPS FROM CHETUMAL

BACALAR

*Buses leave from inside the station at the corner of Hidalgo and Verdad. (45min., every
40min. 6am-9pm, 13 pesos.) Return buses run until 8pm. The route passes Laguna Milagros in Huaypix, Cenote Azul, and Xul-Ha before reaching Bacalar. There are accommodations in Bacalar for those who don't want to leave. Entrance to Bacalar 5 pesos.*

The road to the town of Bacalar (36km from Chetumal) provides several freshwater options for swimming, all of which are nicer than Calderitas. All have waterside restaurants or nearby vendors, *palapas* for picnicking, and parking space.
Twenty-five minutes from Chetumal is beautiful **Laguna Milagros,** where visitors
can swim, rent kayaks, and sunbathe. The bus route passes the serene, 90m deep
Cenote Azul, a favorite of divers, where those who like adventure will enjoy plunging from the 5m platform overhead. Tourists should exercise caution, however;
two divers recently died after getting trapped in an underwater cave. The first
entrance to one of the largest and most picturesque lakes in all of Mexico, **Laguna
de Siete Colores** (or **Laguna Bacalar**), so named for the seven hues reflected in its
depths, is in the town of Xul-Ha, which offers snorkels and other equipment rentals. Past the **Fuerte de San Felipe** in the town of Bacalar, 45min. from Chetumal, is
the best and most popular area for swimming, wading, and taking in the scene. The
fresh water is warm, clear, and carpeted by powdery limestone, with shallow
areas for those fearing the depths of other attractions. Nearby are bathrooms,
dressing rooms, fruit vendors, expensive dockside restaurants, and a campground.

EL SENDERO DEL ADVENTURERO

*Contact Arturo Can Moo in Chetumal (☎836 5918; ecoturismocalderon@hotmail.com).
Naturaventuras (see p. 695) can arrange a day complete with rappelling and other adventures. "La Unión" combis leave from Chetumal (every hr. from 4am, 25 pesos to Calderón).*

Ninety minutes south of Chetumal lies the small *ejido* of Calderón (pop. 300), as
well as unexplored jungle. The *ejido* had sustained itself through hunting and
slash-and-burn farming until a biologist stepped in in 2001. He began to work with
a group to preserve the lands and help them make a living in a new way—ecotourism. After two years of work building facilities, the group is beginning to welcome
travelers looking for something new. They can take you on a 2hr. walk through the
Sendero Adventurero and point out medicinal plants, orchids, lion footprints,
snake skins, and other unexpected jungle treasures—and also offer you a deli-

cious lunch of Belizean, Oaxacan, or Yucatec cuisine. Though the trail does take you past two lagoons and a small *cenote*, to really see some beautiful bodies of water, try a second, more rigorous trail nearby that passes four different *cenotes*.

CENOTE COCODRILO DORADO

Take a "La Unión" combi from Chetumal (over 2hr, every hr. from 4am, 30 pesos) to the end of its route, and continue to walk straight on the road until the houses end and the road splits. Turn right onto the dirt road and continue past a farm. Cross the creek and, from the top of the hill, you will see the cenote and the Río Hondo. This route takes 30-45min. from where the road splits—other trails (best done with guides) take longer. To rappel the cenote cliff wall or arrange a camping trip, contact Naturaventuras (see p. 695).

Named for a golden crocodile that supposedly looms below, this *cenote* provides an unforgettable sight with its brilliant blue waters set against a 75m cliff wall. There are plenty of trails that wind around the *cenote* and along the **Río Hondo,** which separates Mexico from Belize. Monkeys and tropical birds are common here, especially for those who choose to camp and observe in the early morning.

MAHAHUAL AND XCALAC

From Chetumal, buses go to Mahahual, 154km away (3hr., 6am and 3:15pm, 40 pesos). Buses leave Mahahual for Chetumal at 6am, 2:30, and 3:30pm, and an occasional combi leaves at around 11am. To go farther up the coast, instead of returning to Chetumal, go to Limones (20 pesos), a small crossroads town where many buses stop. Xcalac is accessible from Chetumal and Mahahual via bus or combi.

La Costa Maya, the stretch of idyllic coast running from Mahahual to Xcalac, provides a picture of what Cancún looked like 40 years ago. The quietest of the seaside fishing villages, Mahahual, with its new pier for Caribbean cruise ships, and Xcalac, the southernmost community on the peninsula extending south from the Sian Ka'an Biosphere Reserve, are considered "the next big thing" in Quintana Roo. Of the two, Mahahual stands out. Luxury resorts are a few years in the making, but travelers can still savor affordable deep-sea fishing and palm-lined beaches with turquoise waters perfect for sunning, swimming, and snorkeling. The beaches near town are clean, raked of seaweed daily, and those looking to go offshore will not have to go far. **Blue Ha** diving center, km 4, is certified by the Professional Association of Diving Instructors. (Dives 300 pesos, 2 tanks 600 pesos; equipment 150 pesos.) **U Yumil C'eh,** about 10km from Mahahual, is the southernmost area of the Sian Ka'an Biosphere Reserve (see p. 689), and offers camping and educational facilities in addition to its natural wonders. Tours can be arranged through Alfredo Escamilla (☎ 044 983 753 7517; http://uyumilceh.tripod.com).

Visitors to Mahahual should know that services are limited. Electricity is in short supply and there is **no bank. La Cabaña del Tío Phil ❺,** 2km from town, is an ecological resort that sells *tranquilidad* at a fair price. *Cabañas* have solar panels that provide 24hr. power for fans and hot water in private baths. Mosquito nets, murals, and snorkel gear for guests complete the package. (☎ 835 7166. 300 pesos for up to 4.) A pair of clean and comfortable rooms are behind the pizzeria **La Luna de Plata ❸.** The restaurant has good food, too. (Pizza 20 pesos, pasta 45-90 pesos.)

Nearby off the coast is enticing **Banco Chinchorro,** Mexico's largest atoll, a dream-come-true for snorkelers and experienced divers. Sharks, sea turtles, fish, and a multitude of corals coexist with the second-largest shipwreck site in the world, and visitors can see several fishermen's dwellings built on stilts over the water.

KOHUNLICH

67km west of Chetumal on Mex. 186. Ride any combi from the terminal at Hidalgo and Verdad heading toward Villa or Bravo (1hr., every hr., 30 pesos). Ask to be let off at the crucero of Kohunlich, and travel 9km down a dirt road to the entrance, preferably by car.

Kohunlich, a Maya ceremonial center of the early Classic Period famed for its stucco masks, is a garden of palm trees and wild flowers. Its name originates from the English "Cohune Ridge," a tropical palm with copious foliage. More than 200 Petén- and Río Bec-style structures from three periods of development await in the depths of the jungle. The **Pirámide de los Mascarones** (Pyramid of the Masks) is lined with several impressive 5th-century masks portraying the sun god Kinich Ahau, whose thick eyebrows and lips recall Olmec sculptures. To the west is **Plaza de las Estelas** (Plaza of the Stelae), a huge ceremonial center. To the east of the plaza stands the **acropolis,** the largest building at the site, with 8m vaults, and the half-demolished rooms of the **residential complex** and **palace.** To the south of the plaza lies a **ball court,** stripped of stone arcs and markers. The farthest excavated structure is the **Building of the 27 Steps,** a residence for the Maya elite from AD 600 to 1200. Niches once used to store incense canisters and furnishings line the walls.

DZIBANCHÉ

Several km west of the crucero of Kohunlich on Mex. 186 is the Morocoy turn-off (km 58). The turn-off for Dzibanché is 3km beyond Morocoy.

Dzibanché was once a powerful city, flourishing from AD 300 to 1200. Thomas Gann discovered the site in 1927 and gave it its name, meaning "carved in wood," because of the lintels in Temple V. The highlight of the site is the Early Classic pyramid, **Temple I,** or "Temple of the Owl," where a large tomb with valuable offerings including a sculpted owl was found. **Kinichná,** or "House of the Sun," is 2km north of Dzibanché, and though its structures are small, they were once part of a bigger site and still bear some evidence of their grand past.

APPENDIX

MEASUREMENT CONVERSIONS

1 inch (in.) = 25.4 millimeters (mm)	1 millimeter (mm) = 0.039 in.
1 foot (ft.) = 0.30 m	1 meter (m) = 3.28 ft.
1 yard (yd.) = 0.914m	1 meter (m) = 1.09 yd.
1 mile = 1.61km	1 kilometer (km) = 0.62 mi.
1 ounce (oz.) = 28.35g	1 gram (g) = 0.035 oz.
1 pound (lb.) = 0.454kg	1 kilogram (kg) = 2.202 lb.
1 fluid ounce (fl. oz.) = 29.57ml	1 milliliter (ml) = 0.034 fl. oz.
1 gallon (gal.) = 3.785L	1 liter (L) = 0.264 gal.
1 acre (ac.) = 0.405ha	1 hectare (ha) = 2.47 ac.
1 square mile (sq. mi.) = 2.59 sq. km	1 square kilometer (sq. km) = 0.386 sq. mi.

SPANISH QUICK REFERENCE

PRONUNCIATION

Each **vowel** has only one pronunciation: *A* ("ah" in father); *E* ("eh" in pet); *I* ("ee" in eat); *O* ("oh" in oat); *U* ("oo" in boot); *Y*, by itself, is pronounced the same as Spanish *I*. Most **consonants** are pronounced the same as in English. Important exceptions are: *J*, pronounced like the English "h" in "hello"; *LL*, pronounced like the English "y" in "yes"; *Ñ*, pronounced like the "gn" in "cognac." *R* at the beginning of a word or *RR* anywhere in a word is trilled. *H* is always silent. *G* before *E* or *I* is pronounced like the "ch" in "chutzpah"; elsewhere it is pronounced like the "g" in "gate." Because it became used as a placeholder by Spaniards transcribing native languages, *X* has a variety of pronunciations: depending on dialect and word position it can sound like English "h," "s," "sh," or "x." *Tl*, another placeholder, is pronounced with the tongue at the teeth, as if to make the "t" in toy; the air is expelled out the sides of the mouth, without releasing the tongue. Spanish words receive **stress** on the syllable marked with an **accent** (´). In the absence of an accent mark, words that end in vowels, "n," or "s" receive stress on the second to last syllable. For words ending in all other consonants, stress falls on the last syllable. The Spanish language has masculine and feminine nouns, and gives a **gender** to all adjectives. Masculine words generally end with an "o": *él es un tonto* (he is a fool). Feminine words generally end with an "a": *ella es bella* (she is beautiful). Pay close attention—slight changes in word ending can have drastic changes in meaning. For instance, when receiving directions, mind the distinction between *derecho* (straight) and *derecha* (right).

PHRASEBOOK

ENGLISH	SPANISH	ENGLISH	SPANISH
		Essential Phrases	
Yes/No	Sí/No	Hello/Goodbye	Hola/Adíos
Go on!/Come on!/ Hurry up!	¡Ándale!	Until later	Hasta luego/Nos vemos
Please	Por favor	I'm sick/fine	Estoy enfermo(a)/bien
Thank you	Gracias	Could you speak more slowly?	¿Podría hablar más despacio?
You're welcome	De nada	I don't speak Spanish	No hablo español
Excuse me	Perdón/Disculpe	Sorry	Lo siento
How do you say it in Spanish?	¿Cómo se dice en español?	It doesn't matter	No importa
We'll see	Vamos a ver	Perhaps	Tal vez/Puede ser
Who knows?	¿Quién sabe?	Of course	Claro que sí
I forgot	Se me olvidó.	That's the way it is	Así es
Do you speak English?	¿Habla inglés?	How are you?	¿Cómo está?/¿Qué pasa?
Can you repeat that? Again?	¿Lo puede repetir?/ ¿Otra vez?/Mande.	Where are (the mummies)?	¿Dónde están (las momias)?
What?	¿Cómo?/¿Qué?/ ¿Mande?	Where is (the center of town)?	¿Dónde está (el centro)?
I don't understand	No entiendo	Good morning (Good afternoon/night)	Buenos días (Buenas tardes/noches)
What is your name?	¿Cómo se llama?	My name is Selma Hayek	Me llamo Selma Hayek
How do you say (ice cream) in Spanish?	¿Cómo se dice (ice cream) en español?	Why (are you staring at me)?	¿Por qué (me mira)?
Look!/Listen...	¡Mira!	Whoa! Geez!	¡Híjole!
I am hot/cold	Tengo calor/frio	I want/would like...	Quiero/Me gustaría...
How much does it cost?	¿Cuánto cuesta?	That is cheap/expensive	Es barato/caro
Closed/Open	Cerrado(a)/Abierto(a)	Let's Go is the best	Let's Go es el mejor
		Your Arrival	
I am from the US/ Europe.	Soy de los Estados Unidos/de Europa	What's the problem, sir?	¿Cuál es el problema, señor?
Here is my passport	Aquí está mi pasaporte	I lost my passport	Se me perdió mi pasaporte
I will be here for less than 6 months	Estaré aquí por menos de seis meses	I don't know where the drugs came from	No sé de donde vinieron las drogas
I have nothing to declare	No tengo nada que declarar	Please do not detain me	Por favor no me detenga
		Getting Around	
How do you get to (the bus station?	¿Cómo se puede llegar a (la terminal de autobuses)?	Is there anything cheaper?	¿Hay algo más barato/ económico?
Does this bus go to (Guanajuato)?	¿Este autobús va a (Guanajuato)?	On foot	A pie
Can I buy a ticket?	¿Puedo comprar un boleto?	How do you get there?	¿Cómo se puede llegar?

ENGLISH	SPANISH	ENGLISH	SPANISH
How long does the trip take?	¿Cuánto tiempo dura el viaje?	Is it near/far?	¿Está cerca/lejos de aquí?
I am in a hurry	Estoy de prisa	I'm coming	Voy
I am going to the airport	Voy al aeropuerto	The flight is delayed/cancelled	El vuelo está retrasado/cancelado
I lost my baggage	Se me perdió mi equipaje	Is it safe to hitchhike?	¿Es seguro pedir aventón?
Freeway (no toll)	Autopista/vía libre	Toll road	Carretera de cuota
Turn right/left	Doble a la derecha/izquierda	Continue straight	Siga derecho
I would like to rent (a car)	Quisiera rentar (un coche)	Please let me off at...	Por favor, déjeme en...

Accommodations			
How much does it cost per day/week?	¿Cuánto cuesta por día/semana?	Does it have air-conditioning?	¿Tiene aire acondicionado?
Is there a cheap hotel around here?	¿Hay un hotel económico por aqui?	Are there rooms with windows?	¿Hay habitaciones con ventanas?
Do you have rooms available?	¿Tiene habitaciones libres?	I am going to stay for (four) days	Me voy a quedar (cuatro) días
I would like to reserve a room	Quisiera reservar una habitación	Are there cheaper rooms?	¿Hay habitaciones más baratas?
Can I see a room?	¿Puedo ver una habitación?	Do they come with private bath?	¿Vienen con baño privado?
Do you have any singles/doubles?	¿Tiene habitaciones sencillas/dobles?	I'll take it	Lo acepto
The bathroom is broken	El baño está roto	Can I borrow a plunger?	¿Me puede prestar un émbolo?
Who's there?	¿Quién es?	I'm coming!	¡Voy!
There are cockroaches in my room	Hay cucarachas en mi habitación	Dance, cockroaches, dance!	¡Bailen, cucarachas, bailen!

Eating Out			
I am hungry/thirsty	Tengo hambre/sed	Do you have hot sauce?	¿Tiene salsa picante?
Where is a good restaurant?	¿Dónde hay un restaurante bueno?	Table for (one), please	Mesa para (uno), por favor
Can I see the menu?	¿Puedo ver la carta?	Disgusting!	¡Que asco!
Enjoy the meal!	íBuen provecho!	How horrible! What a shame!	¡Qué barbaridad!
This is too spicy	Pica demasiado	I am going to be sick	Voy a vomitar
I would like...	Quisiera...	Delicious!	¡Qué rico!/¡Delicioso!
Where is the bathroom?	¿Dónde está el baño?	Check, please!	¡La cuenta, por favor!
Do you have anything vegetarian/without meat?	¿Hay algún plato vegetariano/sin carne?	Do you take credit cards?	¿Aceptan tarjetas de crédito?

Emergency			
Help!	¡Auxilio!/¡Ayúdame!	Call the police!	Llame a la policía!
I am hurt	Estoy herido(a)	Leave me alone!	¡Déjame en paz!
It's an emergency!	¡Es una emergencia!	I have been robbed!	¡Me han robado!
Fire!	¡Fuego!/¡Incendio!	They went that-a-way!	¡Se fueron por allá!
Call a clinic/ambulance/doctor/priest!	¡Llame a una clínica/una ambulancia/un médico/un padre!	How can we solve this problem?	¿Cómo podemos resolverlo?

ENGLISH	SPANISH	ENGLISH	SPANISH
I need to contact my embassy	Necesito comunicar con mi embajada	I will only speak in the presence of a lawyer	Sólo hablaré en presencia de un(a) abogado(a)

Medical			
I feel bad/better/worse	Me siento mal/mejor/peor	I have a cold/a fever/diahrrea/nausea	Tengo gripe/un fiebre/diarrea/náusea
I have a headache	Tengo dolor de cabeza	I have a stomach ache	Tengo dolor de estómago
I'm sick/ill	Estoy enfermo(a)	It hurts here	Me duele aquí
I'm allergic to (cows)	Soy alérgico(a) a (las vacas)	Here is my prescription	Aquí está mi receta médica
What is this medicine for?	¿Para qué es esta medicina?	I think i'm going to vomit	Pienso que voy a vomitar
Where is the nearest hospital/doctor?	¿Donde está el hospital/doctor más cercano?	I haven't been able to go to the bathroom in (four) days	No he podido ir al baño en (cuatro) días

(Informal) Personal Relationships			
What is your name?	¿Cómo te llamas?	Pleased to meet you	Encantado(a)/Mucho gusto
What's up?/What's shakin'?	¿Qué tal?/¿Qué hay?/¿Cómo te va?	He/she/it seems cool	Me cae bien
Where are you from?	¿De dónde eres?	I'm (twenty) years old	Tengo (veinte) años
It's my first time in Mexico/with a goat	Es mi primera vez en México/con una cabra	I have a boyfriend/girlfriend/goat	Tengo novio/novia/cabra
What's your sign?	¿Cuál es tu signo?	I'm a communist	Soy comunista
I am gay/straight	Soy gay/No soy gay	Would you like to go out with me?	¿Quieres salir conmigo?
Do you have a light?	¿Tienes fuego?	It's true. Politicians can never be trusted.	Es verdad. No se puede confiar en los políticos.
I had the very same dream!	¡Tenía el mismo sueño!	No thanks, I have many diseases.	No gracias, tengo muchas enfermedades.
Please stop kissing me	No me beses más, por favor	I love you	Te quiero
What happened to you?/What's wrong?	¿Qué te pasó?	Why not?	¿Cómo no?
No more weed for me, thanks	No más mota para mi, gracias	What a shame: you bought Lonely Planet!	¡Qué lástima: compraste Lonely Planet!

Numbers and Days			
0	cero	12	doce
1	uno	13	trece
2	dos	14	catorce
3	tres	15	quince
4	cuatro	16	dieciseis
5	cinco	17	diecisiete
6	seis	18	dieciocho
7	siete	19	diecinueve
8	ocho	20	veinte
9	nueve	21	veintiuno
10	diez	22	veintidos
11	once	30	treinta
31	treinta y uno	80	ochenta
40	cuarenta	90	noventa

APPENDIX

ENGLISH	SPANISH	ENGLISH	SPANISH
41	cuarenta y uno	100	cien
50	cincuenta	150	ciento cincuenta
60	sesenta	1000	mil
70	setenta	1 million	un millón

ENGLISH	SPANISH	ENGLISH	SPANISH
Sunday	domingo	today	hoy
Monday	lunes	tomorrow	mañana
Tuesday	martes	day after tomorrow	pasado mañana
Wednesday	miércoles	yesterday	ayer
Thursday	jueves	day before yesterday	antes de ayer/anteayer
Friday	viernes	weekend	fin de semana
Saturday	sábado	the other day	el otro día

GLOSSARY OF TERMS

aduana: customs
agua (purificada): water (purified)
agua fresca: water flavored with flower petals and/or fruit
ahora: now
al gusto: as you wish
albergue: accommodation
almuerzo: lunch
amigo/a: friend
andador: pedestrian walkway
andén: platform
antojito: appetizer
arroz: rice
artesanía: artisanry, crafts
autopista: freeway
avenida: avenue
azulejo: glazed tile
baboso/a: drooling fool
bahía: bay
balneario: public pool; spa
baño: bathroom
barato: cheap
barranca: canyon
barrio: neighborhood
basílica: basilica, church
batido: milkshake
béisbol: baseball
biblioteca: library
bistec/bistek: beefsteak
bobo/a: fool, idiot
bonito/a: pretty
borracho/a: drunk
bosque: forest; park
brujería: witchcraft
bruto: rough, coarse
buen provecho: bon appetit
buena suerte: good luck
buey (slang): man, buddy
burro: donkey
caballero: gentleman
cabaña: cabin
cabrito: (little) goat
café: coffee; cafe
cajero automático: ATM
caldo: soup, broth, or stew
calle: street

callejón: little street; alley
camarero: waiter
camarón: shrimp
cambio: change
camión: bus; commercial truck
camioneta: pick-up truck
campo: countryside; field
cantina: saloon, bar (mostly-male clientele)
capilla: chapel
cara de cholita: slutface
carne (asada): (roast) meat
carnitas: pork
caro: expensive
carretera (de cuota): highway (toll-road)
casa: house
casa de cambio: currency exchange booth
cascada: waterfall
caseta: phone stall
castellano: Spanish, Castilian
catedral: cathedral
cena: supper
cenote: freshwater sinkhole
centro: center (of town)
cerro: hill
cerveza: beer
ceviche: (raw) fish stew
cochinada: obscenity
colectivo: shared taxi
colonia: neighborhood
combi: small local bus
comedor: small diner
comida: food; afternoon main meal
comida corrida: fixed menu
conquistador: (Spanish) conqueror
consulado: consulate
convento: convent
correo (registrado): mail service/registered mail
corrida: bullfight; race
criollo: Creole, colonial Spaniard born in the New World

crucero: crossroads
cruz: cross (Christian)
cuadra: street block
cuarto: room
cuenta: bill/check
cucaracha: cockroach
cueva: cave
cuota: toll
charro: cowboy
chavo/a: guy, kiddo
chico/a: child; small
chicle: chewing gum
chicharrón: bite-sized pieces of fried pork rind
chilaquiles: fried tortilla casserole
chimichanga: fried, filled tortilla
chuleta de chancho: pork chop
chupacabra: demon that sucks goat blood
dama: lady
de paso: bus originating at another station
deporte: sport
desayuno: breakfast
dinero: money
discoteca: dance club (popular music)
disputa: argument
dulce: sweet
embarcadero: wharf
enchilada: baked filled tortilla with red or green sauce
entrada: entrance
entrañas: guts, intestines
este: east; this
extranjero: foreigner
farmacia: pharmacy
faro: lighthouse
federales: federal law enforcement
feria: festival; holiday
fiesta: party; holiday
flauta: large fried taco; flute

fresa: strawberry; (slang) arrogant, yuppie
frijoles: beans
frito: fried
frontera: border
fuente: fountain
fumar: to smoke
fútbol: soccer
gabacho: white American
géiser: geyser
glorieta: traffic circle
gobierno: government
gordo: fat
gracias: thank you
grande: big
grasa: fat (from food)
gratis: free (no charge)
gringo: person from the US
grosero: uncouth
grueso: thick, heavy
gruta: cave
guapo/a: handsome/foxy
guayabera: loose-fitting shirt
güebón (slang): lazy ass
güero: blond, fair
hacienda: ranch
hamaca: hammock
harina: flour
helado: ice cream
higo: fig
hombre: man
huarache: traditional sandal
huevos (revueltos, fritos): eggs (scrambled, fried)
huipil: traditional blouse
iglesia: church
indígena: indigenous; native
isla: island
jamón: ham
jardín: garden
jarra: pitcher
jefe: boss
jugo: juice
ladrón: thief
lago: lake
lancha: boat
langostina: lobster
lavandería: laundromat
leche: milk
libre: free, independent
licuado: smoothie
loma: hill
lonchería: lunch place
llamada (por cobrar): call (collect)
machaca: dried, shredded beef
madera: wood
maíz: corn
malecón: promenade
'mano (slang): bro
manteca: lard
mantequilla: butter
mar: ocean; sea
maricón (vulgar): homosexual

mariscos: seafood
matrimonial: double bed
menso: dumbass
mentira: lie, falsehood
menú del día: pre-set meal
mercado: (outdoor) market
merienda: afternoon snack
mesa: table
mestizo: mixed race (European and *indígena*)
metro: subway
microbús: minibus
mochila: backpack
migra (slang): US immigration
mirador: viewpoint
mole: chocolate and chile sauce for chicken
mollete: french bread with refried beans and cheese
mona (slang): cute
mono: monkey
mordida: bribe
mota: weed, pot
muchacho/a: child
muelle: wharf
mujer: woman
museo: museum
nieve: snow
niño/a: child
nopal: broad cactus leaf
norte (Nte.): north
noticia: news
novio/a: boyfriend/girlfriend; fiancé/fiancée
nuez: walnut
oeste: west
oriente (Ote.): east
palacio: palace
palapa: palm-thatched beach bungalow
palenque: palisade
panadería: bread shop
parada: a stop (bus or train)
parque (de remolque): park (trailer park)
parroquia: parish (church)
paseo: promenade
pelota: ball; Pre-Hispanic ritual game
pequeño: small
pescado: fish
pesero: small local bus
peligro: danger
picante: spicy
pirámide: pyramid
plata: silver
playa: beach
pollo: chicken
pollero (slang): person who transports illegal immigrants
poniente (Pte.): west
posada: inn
postre: dessert
pozo: well
primera clase: first class

pueblo: town; community
puerta: door
puerto: port
pulpo: octopus
queso: cheese
rebozo: shawl
refresco: soft drink
ropa: clothes
ruinas: ruins
ruta: route; local bus
sábana: sheet
sabor: flavor; taste
sacbé (Maya): raised road
sacerdote: priest
salida: exit
salud: health
segunda clase: second class
selva: jungle
semana: week
SIDA: AIDS
sierra: mountain range
siesta: afternoon nap
simpático/a: friendly/nice
sitio: place, site
stela: upright stone monument
supermercado: supermarket
sur: south
taberna: tavern, bar
tacos al pastor: tacos with pork soaked in adobo chiles
taquería: taco stand
taquilla: ticket booth
talavera: white, glazed earthenware from Puebla
tarifa: fee
tejano/a: Texan
telenovela: soap opera
templo: church; temple
tianguis: *(indígena)* markets
tienda: store
típico: typical; traditional
tipo de cambio: exchange rate
toalla: towel
tocino: bacon
tomar: take; drink
tonto/a: dumb
toro: bull
torre: tower
torta: sandwich
tortería: *torta* shop
trago: drink, swig
trolebús: electric bus or "trackless trolley"
turismo: tourism
turista: tourist; diarrhea
tranquilo: peaceful
vaquero: cowboy
valle: valley
vía libre: freeway (no toll)
yanqui: yankee
zócalo: central square
zona: zone; region

APPENDIX

DISTANCES (KM) AND TRAVEL TIMES (BY BUS)

	Acapulco	Chihuahua	Cancún	El Paso	Guadalajara	La Paz	Mazatlán	Mérida	Mexico City	Monterrey	Oaxaca	Puebla	San Cristóbal	San Luis Potosí	Tijuana	Veracruz
Acapulco		2440km	1938km	2815km	1028km	4917km	1429km	1779km	415km	1402km	700km	544km	1036km	828km	3228km	847km
Chihuahua	24hr.		3262km	375km	1552km	3237km	1031km	2945km	1496km	834km	2154km	1625km	2785km	1195km	1548km	1841km
Cancún	33hr.	47hr.		3637km	2442km	6499km	2963km	319km	1766km	2506km	1693km	1895km	902km	2267km	4810km	1421km
El Paso	29hr.	5hr.	54hr.		1549km	3009km	1406km	3320km	1871km	1209km	2529km	2000km	3127km	1569km	1320km	2216km
Guadalajara	15hr.	17hr.	45hr.	25hr.		4159km	521km	2125km	676km	885km	1222km	805km	1853km	348km	2340km	1021km
La Paz	60hr.	46hr.	96hr.	41hr.	60hr.		3508km	6180km	4733km	4071km	5279km	4862km	5883km	4283km	1689km	5050km
Mazatlán	21hr.	15½hr.	53hr.	25hr.	8hr.	50hr.		2646km	1197km	940km	1743km	1326km	2374km	799km	1819km	1542km
Mérida	29hr.	42hr.	4hr.	47hr.	40½hr.	92hr.	40hr.		1449km	2189km	1374km	1791km	743km	799km	4491km	1104km
Mexico City	6hr.	20hr.	26hr.	25hr.	10hr.	68hr.	18hr.	22hr.		950km	546km	129km	1177km	413km	3044km	345km
Monterrey	18hr.	12hr.	38hr.	17hr.	11hr.	60hr.	17hr.	32hr.	12hr.		1533km	1116km	1918km	537km	2382km	1085km
Oaxaca	9hr.	29hr.	29hr.	34hr.	17hr.	77hr.	27hr.	24½hr.	9hr.	21hr.		417km	631km	959km	3590km	450km
Puebla	7hr.	22hr.	24hr.	27hr.	12hr.	71hr.	20hr.	20hr.	2hr.	14hr.	4hr.		1048km	542km	3285km	303km
San Cristóbal	16hr.	39hr.	17hr.	44hr.	28hr.	88hr.	19hr.	12½hr.	18hr.	30hr.	12hr.	16hr.		1590km	4193km	833km
San Luis Potosí	10hr.	14hr.	31hr.	18hr.	6hr.	60hr.	12hr.	27hr.	5hr.	7hr.	20hr.	16hr.	23hr.		2743km	846km
Tijuana	46hr.	22hr.	72hr.	36hr.	36hr.	24hr.	26hr.	66hr.	44hr.	36hr.	53hr.	46hr.	62hr.	36hr.		3361km
Veracruz	13hr.	28hr.	21hr.	33hr.	17hr.	76hr.	26hr.	13hr.	8hr.	17hr.	8hr.	4½hr.	13hr.	13hr.	52hr.	

INDEX

A

Acapulco 490–497
accommodations
  cabañas 26
  camping 25
  hostels 23
  hotels 24
  reservations 25
  trailer parks 25
Agua Azul. See Cascadas de Agua Azul
Agua Selva 576
Aguascalientes
  city 317–322
  state 317–322
Aguilar, Jerónimo de 61
AIDS 21
Ajijic 423–424
Akumal 675–677
Alamo, The 65
Alamos 238–240
alcohol
  beer 74
  Kahlúa 74
  mezcal 510
  Pacífico 271
  piña colada 74
  ponche 450
  pulque 74, 379
  Tecate 156
  tequila 74
alebrijes 512
Alemán, Miguel 69
Allende, Ignacio 63, 344, 348, 350
altitude 20
Álvarez Bravo, Manuel 76
Álvarez, Juan 65
amber 583
Amecameca 142
American Express 13
Amtatenango del Valle 593
Ángeles Verdes 34
La Antigua 558
aquariums
  Mazatlán 273
  Museo de la Tortuga 527
  Veracruz 555
Árbol de la Cruz (Tree of the Cross) 356

Árbol de Navidad 583
architecture 75
Armería 443, 444
Arrazola 508, 512
art 74–76
Arturo, the dancing monkey 563
Asociación Nacional Automovilística (ANA) 34, 95
ATM cards 14
Atzompa 508, 512
Axayácatl 121
Axayacatzin, Xicoténcatl 380
Aztec ruins
  Malinalco 143
  Templo Mayor 110
  Tula 361–362
Aztec Stone of the Sun 75
Aztecs 2, 61–62, 75, 84, 109, 118, 121, 122, 361, 459, 547
El Azufre 575

B

Bacalar 695
Bahía de Banderas 432
Bahía de Chamela 433–434
Bahía de la Concepción 188–190
Bahía de los Ángeles 177–178
Bahía de Manzanillo 441
Bahía de Navidad 434–438
  Barra de Navidad 436–438
  Colimilla 437
  Melaque 435–436
Bahía de Santiago 441
Bahía Kino 232–233
Bahía Todos Santos 164
Bahías de Huatulco 515–520
  La Crucecita 517
  Santa Cruz 517
Baja California Sur 179–214
Baja California, Norte 149–178
Balamkú 617
Balbuena, Bernardo de 77
Balzapote 566
Barra de Navidad 436
Barra de Potosí 488

Barrancas del Cobre 260–263
  Creel 256–258
  El Fuerte 264
  Los Mochis 265–266
  Sierra Tarahumara 260
  train through the canyons 263
Batopilas 262–263
Battle of Celaya 67
beaches
  Acapulco 494
  Akumal 676
  Bacalar 695
  Bahía de Banderas 432
  Bahía de Chamela 434
  Bahía de la Concepción 189
  Bahía de los Ángeles 178
  Bahía de Manzanillo 441
  Bahía de Santiago 441
  Bahía de Todos Santos 164
  Bahía Kino 233
  Bahías de Huatulco 518
  Barra de Navidad 436
  Barra de Potosí 488
  Cabo San Lucas 208
  Caleta de Campos 477
  Cancún 661
  Catemaco 565
  Chetumal 695
  Cozumel 681
  Cuyutlán 443
  Guaymas 236
  Isla de la Piedra 275
  Isla Holbox 671
  Isla Mujeres 668
  Ixtapa 487
  La Paz 200
  Mahahual 696
  Manzanillo 438
  Mazatlán 272
  Melaque 435
  Michoacán Coast 475
  Montepío 566
  nude 433, 525, 687
  Papanoa 489
  Paraíso (Colima) 444
  Paraíso (Tabasco) 577
  Pie de la Cuesta 497
  Playa Azul 475

INDEX